Wissenschaftliche Untersuchungen
zum Neuen Testament

Herausgeber / Editor
Jörg Frey (München)

Mitherausgeber / Associate Editors
Friedrich Avemarie (Marburg)
Markus Bockmuehl (Oxford)
Hans-Josef Klauck (Chicago, IL)

246

Pseudepigraphie und Verfasserfiktion in frühchristlichen Briefen

Pseudepigraphy and Author Fiction
in Early Christian Letters

Herausgegeben von

Jörg Frey, Jens Herzer, Martina Janßen
und Clare K. Rothschild

Unter Mitarbeit von
Michaela Engelmann

Mohr Siebeck

Jörg Frey ist Ordinarius für Neues Testament an der Ludwig-Maximilians-Universität München.

Jens Herzer ist Ordinarius für Neues Testament an der Universität Leipzig.

Martina Janssen ist Pastorin und Lehrbeauftragte an der TU Braunschweig.

Clare K. Rothschild ist Assistant Professor for Scripture Studies an der Lewis University, Romeoville, Illinois.

Michaela Engelmann ist wissenschaftliche Mitarbeiterin am Institut für Neutestamentliche Wissenschaft der Theologischen Fakultät der Universität Leipzig.

ISBN 978-3-16-150042-8
ISSN 0512-1604 (Wissenschaftliche Untersuchungen zum Neuen Testament)

Die Deutsche Nationalbibliothek verzeichnet diese Publikation in der Deutschen Nationalbibliographie; detaillierte bibliographische Daten sind im Internet über *http://dnb.d-nb.de* abrufbar.

© 2009 Mohr Siebeck Tübingen.

Das Werk einschließlich aller seiner Teile ist urheberrechtlich geschützt. Jede Verwertung außerhalb der engen Grenzen des Urheberrechtsgesetzes ist ohne Zustimmung des Verlags unzulässig und strafbar. Das gilt insbesondere für Vervielfältigungen, Übersetzungen, Mikroverfilmungen und die Einspeicherung und Verarbeitung in elektronischen Systemen.

Das Buch wurde von Gulde-Druck in Tübingen auf alterungsbeständiges Werkdruckpapier gedruckt und von der Großbuchbinderei Spinner in Ottersweier gebunden.

Vorwort

Der vorliegende Band geht auf ein zweitägiges Symposium zum Thema „Pseudepigraphie und Verfasserfiktion in frühchristlichen Briefen" zurück, das am 15./16. Juni 2007 im Rahmen der Veranstaltungsreihe Münchener Bibelwissenschaftliche Symposien an der Evangelisch-theologischen Fakultät der Ludwig-Maximilians-Universität in München veranstaltet wurde. Anlass war der durch ein Forschungsstipendium der Alexander von Humboldt-Stiftung ermöglichte Forschungsaufenthalt von Clare K. Rothschild in München am Lehrstuhl von Jörg Frey im akademischen Jahr 2006/2007, in dessen Rahmen ein Buchprojekt zum pseudo-paulinischen Charakter des Hebräerbriefs durchgeführt und zum Abschluss gebracht werden konnte.[1]

Die Diskussion des Phänomens Pseudepigraphie und der spezifischen Fragen um den Hebräerbrief ließ eine präzisere Erörterung der Vielfalt pseudonymer Konstruktionen und des Facettenreichtums der im Hintergrund stehenden Motive notwendig erscheinen – in Anbetracht einer nach wie vor oft zu undifferenzierten und festgefahrenen Diskussion in der Bibelwissenschaft. Es reicht nicht mehr aus, im Blick auf eine Schrift lediglich die Frage nach ihrer Authentizität oder Pseudonymität aufzuwerfen, vielmehr ist zu diskutieren, wann bzw. unter welchen Voraussetzungen von Pseudepigraphie gesprochen werden kann, welche Typen und Spielarten von pseudonymer Autorschaft es gibt, wodurch die Anwendung einer solchen Darstellungsweise motiviert und wann bzw. unter welchen Umständen sie als ‚legitim' oder ‚illegitim' zu bezeichnen ist. Ist Pseudepigraphie tatsächlich, wie oft behauptet, ein gebräuchliches und allgemein akzeptiertes Darstellungsmittel in einer bestimmten Epoche, Gruppe oder Bildungsschicht? Die oft allzu schematischen Antworten auf solche Fragen erscheinen angesichts der Vielfalt der pseudonymen Konstruktionen von Autoren, Adressaten, Situationen, Gegnern usw. zu undifferenziert. Es ist daher notwendig, im Kontext eines weiten Spektrums von Möglichkeiten pseudonymer Darstellungsformen zu einer differenzierten Beschreibung der jeweils vorliegenden Konstruktionen zu gelangen, die ein präzises Urteil über den Typus, die Intention und die Implikationen einer jeweiligen literarischen Gestaltung erlaubt.

---

[1] C. K. ROTHSCHILD, Hebrews as Pseudepigraphon. The History and Significance of the Pauline Attribution of Hebrews, WUNT 235, Tübingen 2009.

Diese Diskussion wurde im Rahmen des Münchener Symposiums von neun Referenten aus sieben Ländern aufgenommen. Die Mehrzahl der in diesem Rahmen gehaltenen Vorträge wird in dem vorliegenden Band in einer erweiterten Form abgedruckt und durch eine größere Zahl weiterer Beiträge ergänzt, durch die wesentliche antike Horizonte pseudonymer Autorschaft sowie der ganze Bestand der als pseudonym geltenden neutestamentlichen Briefe in der Unterschiedlichkeit der in ihnen begegnenden Verfasser-, Adressaten- und Situationskonstruktionen berücksichtigt werden. Wir danken den Referentinnen und Referenten sowie den zusätzlich angefragten Autorinnen und Autoren für ihre substantielle Mitarbeit an dem Projekt, die es möglich gemacht hat, dass dieser Band zu einer Bestandsaufnahme wesentlicher Aspekte der gegenwärtigen Pseudepigraphieforschung werden konnte. Insbesondere danken wir David E. Aune, der als einer der ‚Altmeister' der literaturgeschichtlichen Forschung zum Neuen Testament die Mühe auf sich genommen hat, alle Beiträge zu lesen und ein Nachwort zu den hier gebotenen Forschungsarbeiten zu verfassen.

Das Symposium wurde am Lehrstuhl von Jörg Frey geplant und durch die von der Humboldt-Stiftung gewährten Betreuungsgelder finanziert, wobei insbesondere der damaligen Sekretärin Brigitte Becker für ihre umsichtige Organisation zu danken ist. Bereits in der inhaltlichen Konzeption des Symposiums hat sich Martina Janßen mit großem Ideenreichtum eingebracht. Die Sammlung und Redaktion der Beiträge erfolgte am Lehrstuhl von Jens Herzer in Leipzig, was ohne die souveräne Projektleitung und inhaltlich wie technisch außerordentlich gründliche Mitarbeit von Michaela Engelmann nicht möglich gewesen wäre. Sie hat die Druckvorlage erstellt und zusammen mit Clare K. Rothschild und Martina Janßen sowie den studentischen Hilfskräften Claudia K. Tost (Leipzig), Ann-Sophie Wich und Miriam Guggenmos (beide München) Korrektur gelesen. Die Register wurden schließlich von Sebastian Ziera und Paulus Enke (beide Leipzig) sowie Kathrin Hager und Miriam Guggenmos (beide München) erstellt. In Bezug auf die formale Gestaltung der Beiträge ist darauf hinzuweisen, dass für die deutschsprachigen Aufsätze die Abkürzungsverzeichnisse der RGG[4] sowie der TRE zugrunde gelegt sind; die englischsprachigen Beiträge folgen den Regeln des SBL-Handbook of Style.

Der Erstherausgeber dankt der Alfried Krupp von Bohlen und Halbach-Stiftung für die Arbeitsmöglichkeiten im Rahmen eines Forschungsjahres als Senior Fellow am Alfried-Krupp-Wissenschaftskolleg Greifswald, während dessen der Abschluss des Bandes erfolgte. Ein besonderer Dank gilt der Alexander von Humboldt-Stiftung, durch deren Engagement die hier dokumentierte internationale Zusammenarbeit ermöglicht wurde und mit deren großzügigen Betreuungsmitteln auch die weiteren Kosten der Erstellung des Bandes bestritten werden konnten. Schließlich danken wir dem Verlag Mohr Siebeck und seinem Team für die Übernahme des Bandes und die bewährte und wie immer erfreuliche Zusammenarbeit bei der Drucklegung.

München / Leipzig / Estebrügge / Chicago, im Juli 2009
                                                  Jörg Frey
                                                  Jens Herzer
                                                  Martina Janßen
                                                 Clare K. Rothschild

Inhaltsverzeichnis

Einführung

MARTINA JANSSEN / JÖRG FREY
Einführung 3

I. Frühjüdische Kontexte

LEO G. PERDUE
Pseudonymity and Graeco-Roman Rhetoric.
Mimesis and the Wisdom of Solomon 27

KARINA MARTIN HOGAN
Pseudepigraphy and the Periodization of History
in Jewish Apocalypses 61

EIBERT TIGCHELAAR
Forms of Pseudepigraphy in the Dead Sea Scrolls 85

II. Griechisch-römische Kontexte

WOLFGANG SPEYER
Göttliche und menschliche Verfasserschaft im Altertum 105

MARTINA JANSSEN
Antike (Selbst-)Aussagen über Beweggründe zur Pseudepigraphie 125

MARCO FRENSCHKOWSKI
Erkannte Pseudepigraphie?
Ein Essay über Fiktionalität, Antike und Christentum 181

KATHARINA LUCHNER
Pseudepigraphie und antike Briefromane 233

TIMO GLASER
Erzählung im Fragment.
Ein narratologischer Ansatz zur Auslegung
pseudepigrapher Briefbücher 267

ROBERT MATTHEW CALHOUN
The *Letter* of Mithridates.
A Neglected Item of Ancient Epistolary Theory 295

III. Frühchristliche Kontexte

HARRY Y. GAMBLE
Pseudonymity and the New Testament Canon 333

EVE-MARIE BECKER
Von Paulus zu „Paulus".
Paulinische Pseudepigraphie-Forschung als
literaturgeschichtliche Aufgabe 363

MARTIN HÜNEBURG
Paulus versus Paulus.
Der Epheserbrief als Korrektur des Kolosserbriefes 387

NICOLE FRANK
Der Kolosserbrief und die „Philosophia".
Pseudepigraphie als Spiegel frühchristlicher Auseinandersetzungen
um die Auslegung des paulinischen Erbes 411

TREVOR THOMPSON
A Stone that *Still* Won't Fit.
An Introductory and Editorial Note for Edgar Krentz's
"A Stone that Will Not Fit" 433

EDGAR KRENTZ
A Stone that Will Not Fit.
The Non-Pauline Autorship of Second Thessalonians 439

TREVOR THOMPSON
As If Genuine.
Interpreting the Pseudepigraphic Second Thessalonians 471

JENS HERZER
Fiktion oder Täuschung?
Zur Diskussion über die Pseudepigraphie der Pastoralbriefe 489

CLARE K. ROTHSCHILD
Hebrews as a Guide to Reading Romans 537

MATTHIAS KONRADT
„Jakobus, der Gerechte".
Erwägungen zur Verfasserfiktion des Jakobusbriefes 575

MATT JACKSON-MCCABE
The Politics of Pseudepigraphy and the Letter of James 599

KARL MATTHIAS SCHMIDT
Die Stimme des Apostels erheben.
Pragmatische Leistungen der Autorenfiktion in den Petrusbriefen 625

LUTZ DOERING
Apostle, Co-Elder, and Witness of Suffering.
Author Construction and Peter Image in First Peter 645

JÖRG FREY
Autorfiktion und Gegnerbild im Judasbrief
und im Zweiten Petrusbrief 683

JUTTA LEONHARDT-BALZER
Pseudepigraphie und Gemeinde in den Johannesbriefen 733

STEFAN KRAUTER
Was ist „schlechte" Pseudepigraphie?
Mittel, Wirkung und Intention von Pseudepigraphie in den
Epistolae Senecae ad Paulum et Pauli ad Senecam 765

Nachwort

DAVID E. AUNE
Reconceptualizing the Phenomenon of Ancient Pseudepigraphy.
An Epilogue 789

Autorenverzeichnis 825

Stellenregister 829
Autorenregister 878
Sach- und Personenregister 894
Register griechischer Begriffe 902

Einführung

Einführung

von

MARTINA JANSSEN / JÖRG FREY[*]

1. Zum Thema: Perspektiven der Pseudepigraphieforschung

Der vorliegende Band „Pseudepigraphie und Verfasserfiktion in frühchristlichen Briefen" geht auf ein internationales und interdisziplinäres Symposium zurück, das vom 15.–16. Juni 2007 im Rahmen der „Münchener Bibelwissenschaftlichen Symposien" stattgefunden hat. Genau 200 Jahre zuvor – im Jahr 1807 – bestritt Friedrich Daniel Ernst Schleiermacher die Echtheit des Ersten Timotheusbriefes, was einem „Donnerschlag für viele Theologen"[1] gleichkam und gewissermaßen den Beginn der neutestamentlichen Pseudepigraphiediskussion markierte. Deren letzte umfassende Dokumentation erschien 1977 mit dem von Norbert Brox herausgegebenen Sammelband „Pseudepigraphie in der heidnischen und jüdisch-christlichen Antike".[2] Seitdem sind über 30 Jahre vergangen und die Diskussion gestaltet sich nach wie vor lebendig und kontrovers, nicht zuletzt deswegen, weil der Annahme von „Fälschungen" in der Bibel in den Augen vieler Forscher eine gewisse theologische Brisanz nicht abzusprechen ist. Nicht selten war deswegen das erkenntnisleitende Interesse in der Pseudepigraphieforschung ein dogmatisches, das die historisch-kritischen Ergebnisse mitunter präjudizierte.

Fragen der Echtheitskritik an antiken Schriften und die sich daran anschließenden Überlegungen über mögliche Gründe, warum ein Autor unter falschem Namen schreibt und wie dieses Verfahren heute zu bewerten ist, haben eine lange Geschichte hinter sich. Die Anfänge der Echtheitskritik

---

[*] Die Einführung wird von beiden Autoren gemeinsam verantwortet, doch war für den ersten, thematischen Teil Martina Janßen verantwortlich, während Jörg Frey den zweiten, auf die Konzeption des Bandes bezogenen Teil verfasst hat.

[1] So formuliert in einer zeitgenössischen Rezension; vgl. H. PATSCH, Die Angst vor dem Deuteropaulinismus. Die Rezeption des ‚kritischen Sendschreibens' Friedrich Schleiermachers über den 1. Timotheusbrief im ersten Jahrfünft, ZThK 88 (1991), 451–477 (471).

[2] N. Brox (Hg.), Pseudepigraphie in der heidnischen und jüdisch-christlichen Antike, WdF 484, Darmstadt 1977.

gehen bis in die Antike selbst zurück.³ Im Humanismus erfährt die Unterscheidung von echten und unechten Schriften eine Renaissance und erreicht im 17. Jh. mit Richard Bentleys bahnbrechender Untersuchung zur pseudepigraphischen Briefliteratur griechisch-hellenistischer Provenienz einen Höhepunkt.⁴ Im Bereich der Bibelwissenschaften brachte die Bestreitung der Echtheit des Ersten Timotheusbriefes durch Schleiermacher (1807) die Diskussion in Gang, die sich in der Folgezeit äußerst komplex gestaltete.⁵ Zwischen den beiden Extrempolen, der Verteidigung der Echtheit aller neutestamentlichen Schriften auf der einen und der holländischen Radikalkritik auf der anderen Seite, etablierte sich mit der Zeit der auch heute im deutschsprachigen Raum weitgehend anerkannte Forschungskonsens: Von den 27 Schriften des Neuen Testament tragen lediglich die sieben echten Paulusbriefe den Namen ihres realen Verfassers, alle anderen Schriften sind anonym oder pseudonym. Allein dieser Befund führt die Relevanz des Themas klar vor Augen, das die theologische Forschung seit über 200 Jahren bewegt. Drei Fragestellungen greifen dabei ineinander: 1) die Frage nach Echtheit oder Unechtheit einer Schrift (Echtheitskritik); 2) die Frage nach Motivation, Intention und Rezeptionsbedingungen einer pseudepigraphischen Schrift (Pseudepigraphieforschung); 3) die Frage, wie biblische Pseudepigraphie heute zu verstehen und bewerten ist (Schrifthermeneutik).

Nahm am Anfang der bibelwissenschaftlichen Echtheitsdiskussion die mögliche Unechtheit biblischer Schriften mitunter die Dimension eines kanontheologischen Skandals an und erzeugte heftige Gegenwehr, so konnte apostolische Pseudonymität auch schon zu Beginn der Forschungsgeschichte als Ausdruck des Kanonbewusstseins gedeutet werden. Im Sinne idealistisch-dialektischer Denkmodelle interpretierte z.B. K. R. Köstlin

---

[3] Vgl. dazu M. JANSSEN, Unter falschem Namen. Eine kritische Forschungsbilanz frühchristlicher Pseudepigraphie, ARGU 14, Frankfurt a.M./New York 2003.

[4] R. BENTLEY, A Dissertation upon the Epistles of Phalaris, Themistocles, Sokrates, Euripides, and Others. And the Fables of Aesopus..., London 1697 (ins Deutsche übertragen: Leipzig 1857).

[5] F. D. E. SCHLEIERMACHER, Ueber den sogenannten ersten Brief des Paulos an Timotheos. Ein kritisches Sendschreiben an J. C. Gass, Berlin 1807. Zu den Reaktionen siehe PATSCH, Angst (s. Anm. 1), 451–477. Eine ähnliche Wirkung im englischsprachigen Raum hatten die Forschungen von Edward Evanson (E. EVANSON, The Dissonance of the Four Generally Received Evangelists, and the Evidence of Their Respective Authenticity Examined, Ipswich 1792); siehe dazu A. STRACHOTTA, Edward Evanson (1731–1805). Der Theologe und Bibelkritiker. Ein Beitrag zur anglikanischen Kirchengeschichte des achtzehnten Jahrhunderts, TABG 12, Halle 1940.

(1851)[6] Pseudonymität als eine Synthese von einander gegenläufigen Prinzipien, nämlich der „fortwährenden Änderung und Bewegung" und „dem Bewusstsein sich immer gleich bleibender Wahrheit". Pseudonyme apostolische Schriften erscheinen somit als ein „aus dem Apostolischen heraus sich entwickelnder Fortschritt des Geistes." Solche hermeneutischen Zugänge blieben zunächst vereinzelt. Oft führten die Ergebnisse der historisch-kritischen Exegese in die bibelhermeneutische Aporie, die gewissermaßen zum „Warten auf ein volleres Licht" (J. S. Candlish [1891])[7] verdammte.

In den 30er Jahren des 20. Jh. folgte eine Fokussierung auf die psychologisch-moralischen Implikationen pseudonymer Literaturproduktion.[8] Man versuchte, den Widerspruch zwischen religiösem Anspruch, sittlichem Ernst und der Tatsache der Fälschung aus der psychischen Verfassung der Autoren zu erklären. Der unter falschem Namen schreibende Autor sei „überwältigt von den religiösen Gedanken" (A. Meyer [1932]) bzw. von „Wogen religiöser Erregung" (R. F. Merkel [1936]), so dass „im Halbdunkel des Unterbewusstseins das Gewissen zum Schweigen gebracht wird" (F. Torm [1932]). Solcherlei psychologische Zugänge verfolgten unterschiedliche Zielrichtungen. Für Frederik Torm stellte das psychologische Gutachten über den Verfasser einer unter dem Verdacht der Pseudonymität stehenden Schrift gewissermaßen einen Echtheitsbeweis dar: Bietet die Psyche ein integeres Bild, so muss die Schrift echt sein. A. Meyer hingegen versuchte, Pseudepigraphie als „heilige Poesie" psychologisch zu erklären und so zu rechtfertigen.

In den 60er/70er Jahren kam neue Bewegung in die Pseudepigraphieforschung. Sowohl die umfassende Dokumentation und Aufarbeitung des relevanten Materials als auch unterschiedliche methodische Ansätze verhalfen zu einer differenzierteren Betrachtung von pagan-antiker, jüdischer, biblischer und altkirchlicher Pseudepigraphie. Mit der Arbeit von Josef Sint (1960)[9] und den zahlreichen Untersuchungen von Wolfgang Speyer,

---

[6] K. R. KÖSTLIN, Die pseudonyme Litteratur der ältesten Kirche. Ein Beitrag zur Geschichte der Bildung des Kanons, ThJb(T) 10 (1851), 149–221. Eine ähnliche Denkstruktur findet sich in jüngerer Zeit bei D. G. Meade; s. Anm. 16.

[7] J. S. CANDLISH, On the Moral Character of Pseudonymous Books, Exp. 4 (1891), 91–107.262–279 (= ders., Über den moralischen Charakter pseudonymer Bücher, in: Brox, Pseudepigraphie [s. Anm. 2], 7–42).

[8] F. TORM, Die Psychologie der Pseudonymität im Hinblick auf die Literatur des Urchristentums, SLA 2, Gütersloh 1932; A. MEYER, Besprechung von Torm, Pseudonymität, ThLZ 58 (1933), 354–357 (= Brox, Pseudepigraphie [s. Anm. 2], 149–153); ders., Religiöse Pseudepigraphie als ethisch-psychologisches Problem, ZNW 35 (1936), 262–279; R. F. MERKEL, Kirchen- und religionsgeschichtliche Fälschungen, Süddeutsche Monatshefte 33 (1935/36), 693–699.

[9] J. A. SINT, Pseudonymität im Altertum. Ihre Formen und ihre Gründe, Commentatio-

allen voran seiner 1971 erschienenen Monographie „Die literarische Fälschung im heidnischen und christlichen Altertum"[10], erschienen reichhaltige Materialsammlungen[11] zur antiken Pseudepigraphie, die auch heute noch wertvolle Differenzierungsansätze enthalten, biblische Pseudepigraphie aber weitgehend aussparen. Was Wolfgang Speyer mit seinen umfassenden Arbeiten im Bereich der Altphilologie geleistet hat, dem entsprechen dann im Bereich der frühchristlichen Pseudepigraphie die Forschungen von Norbert Brox. Abgesehen von seinen zahlreichen Arbeiten zur Forschungsgeschichte, zu einzelnen pseudepigraphischen Schreiben des Neuen Testaments und der Alten Kirche und zu den mentalitätsgeschichtlichen Rahmenbedingungen[12] war es das Verdienst von Brox, die

---

nes Aenipontanae 15, Innsbruck 1960. Sint unterscheidet zwischen „psn Schrifttum aus mythischen und religiösen Triebkräften" und „psn Schriften aus literarischen Gestaltungskräften".

[10] W. SPEYER, Die literarische Fälschung im heidnischen und christlichen Altertum. Ein Versuch ihrer Deutung, HAW I/2, München 1971. Speyer hat darüber hinaus zu etlichen Einzelaspekten wie z.B. Echtheitsbeglaubigungen (ders., Bücherfunde in der Glaubenswerbung der Antike. Mit einem Ausblick auf Mittelalter und Neuzeit, Hyp. 24, Göttingen 1970) gearbeitet, wobei forschungsgeschichtliche (z.B. ders., Italienische Humanisten als Kritiker der Echtheit antiker und christlicher Literatur, Stuttgart 1993) und wirkungsgeschichtliche (z.B. ders., Das entdeckte heilige Buch in Novalis' Gedicht „An Tieck", Arcadia 9 [1974], 39–47) Arbeiten das Forschungsprofil abrunden; besonders einflussreich indes wurde seine These von der ‚echten religiösen Pseudepigraphie'; vgl. Anm. 24. Vgl. insgesamt zu den Arbeiten Speyers JANSSEN, Namen (s. Anm. 3), 75–102. Zweifelsohne haben Speyers Untersuchungen die Pseudepigraphieforschung auf eine neue Basis gestellt, wobei die Übertragung seiner Ergebnisse auf die neutestamentliche Pseudepigraphie auch noch nach fast 40 Jahren in einigen Bereichen ein Forschungsdesiderat darstellt.

[11] Im Bereich der jüdisch-hellenistischen Literatur zu nennen sind zudem vor allem die Arbeiten von Martin Hengel (M. HENGEL, Anonymität, Pseudepigraphie und „Literarische Fälschung" in der jüdisch-hellenistischen Literatur, in: K. von Fritz [Hg.], Pseudepigrapha I. Pseudopythagorica – Lettres de Platon – Littérature pseudépigraphique juive, EnAC 18, Vandœuvres/Genève 1972, 231–308 [Diskussion: 309–329]; zur erweiterten Form vgl. ders., Judaica et Hellenistica. Kleine Schriften I. Unter Mitarbeit von R. Deines, J. Frey, C. Markschies, A. M. Schwemer mit einem Anhang von H. Bloedhorn, WUNT 90, Tübingen 1996, 196–251) und Nikolaus Walter (N. WALTER, Der Thoraausleger Aristobulos. Untersuchungen zu seinen Fragmenten und zu pseudepigraphischen Resten der jüdisch-hellenistischen Literatur, TU 86, Leipzig 1964; ders., Jüdisch-hellenistische Pseudepigraphie als Index interkulturellen Austauschwillens, in: J. Irmscher [Hg.], Die Literatur der Spätantike – polyethnisch und polyglottisch betrachtet, Amsterdam 1997, 13–22).

[12] Im Bereich der neutestamentlichen Literatur widmete sich Brox vor allem den Pastoralbriefen (vgl. z.B. N. BROX, Die Pastoralbriefe übersetzt und erklärt, RNT, Regensburg [4]1969; ders., Zu den persönlichen Notizen der Pastoralbriefe, BZ.NF 13 [1969], 76–94) und dem Ersten Petrusbrief (vgl. z.B. ders., Der erste Petrusbrief, EKK XXI, Zürich u.a. 1979; ders., Zur pseudepigraphischen Rahmung des ersten Petrusbriefes,

Einführung

Erforschung neutestamentlicher Pseudepigraphie von dogmatischen Tabus zu befreien und dadurch den Weg zu einer objektiven Sichtweise zu ebnen. Brox scheute nicht davor zurück, den Begriff „Täuschung" mit biblischen Schriften zu verbinden. Auch für die neutestamentliche Literatur gilt: „Die Täuschung stellt als Manipulation (häufig nicht hinsichtlich ihrer Kunstfertigkeit) eine Trivialform der Literatur dar und ist in den Augen der Antike noch dazu nicht unbedenklich. Die heutigen Überlegungen ... dürfen das beides nicht kaschieren wollen."[13]

Das Spektrum der Fragen und Forschungsinteressen seit den 60er/70er Jahren war breit und die Methodenvielfalt beachtlich. Komparatistisch-literaturwissenschaftliche, religionswissenschaftliche, bibeltheologische und ideengeschichtliche Herangehensweisen stehen nebeneinander, ergänzen und befruchten sich; zentrale Fragestellungen bilden sich heraus. Stets war Pseudepigraphieforschung dabei mit der Erforschung der mentalitätsgeschichtlichen Rahmenbedingungen verbunden, die erst einen angemessenen Verstehenshorizont ermöglichen. Ein – häufig apologetisch überfrachteter – Diskussionspunkt war hier die Frage nach dem Echtheitsbewusstsein und dem Begriff des geistigen Eigentums in der Antike. Wenn es ein solches Bewusstsein geistiger Urheberschaft nicht gab, war pseudonyme Literaturproduktion automatisch von dem Verdacht literarischer Anrüchigkeit befreit. Kritik an solchen weit verbreiteten pauschalen Urteilen zwingt zu genauerem historischen Hinsehen, wie es etwa Wolfgang Speyer und Norbert Brox wiederholt eingefordert haben: Die antike Vorstellung von „geistigem Eigentum" kann zwar mit modernen urheberrechtlichen Bedingungen nicht verglichen werden, ist aber in der Antike durch-

---

BZ.NF 19 [1975], 78–96). Brox bezog in seinen Forschungen stets den Bereich der altkirchlichen Literatur mit ein (vgl. z.B. ders., Pseudo-Paulus und Pseudo-Ignatius. Einige Topoi altchristlicher Pseudepigraphik, VigChr 30 [1976], 181–188; ders., Quis ille auctor? Pseudonymität und Anonymität bei Salvian, VigChr 40 [1986], 55–65). Einflussreich wurden vor allem seine Monographie „Falsche Verfasserangaben. Zur Erklärung der frühchristlichen Pseudepigraphie", SBS 79, Stuttgart 1975, und seine Arbeiten zur Methodik der Pseudepigraphieforschung (s. Anm. 13 und 17).

[13] Ders., Zum Problemstand in der Erforschung der altchristlichen Pseudepigraphie, Kairos 15 (1973), 10–23 (23). Ein Blick auf die Erforschung pseudepigraphischer Literatur altkirchlicher oder apokrypher Provenienz zeigt, dass man hier weitaus unbefangener war; vgl. z.B. G. BARDY, Faux et fraudes littéraires dans l'antiquité chrétienne, RHE 32 (1936), 5–23.275–302 (= ders., Betrug und Fälschungen in der Literatur der christlichen Antike, in: Brox, Pseudepigraphie [s. Anm. 2], 163–184 [Auszüge]); aktuell jetzt P. F. BEATRICE, Forgery, Propaganda and Power in Christian Antiquity. Some Methodological Remarks, in: W. Blümer u.a. (Hg.), Alvarium (FS Gnilka), JAC.E 33, Münster 2002, 39–51. Im altkirchlichen und apokryphen Bereich wurde Pseudepigraphie oft als Fälschung zur Durchsetzung von kirchenpolitischen Interessen und als Mittel der Autoritätssicherung gedeutet. In der Spannung zwischen Orthodoxie und Häresie sah man geradezu ein Movens für pseudepigraphische Literaturproduktion.

aus vorhanden und erfährt ganz unterschiedliche Begründungen.[14] Jedoch muss zwischen den jeweiligen literatursoziologischen Orten und geographischen Räumen unterschieden werden. Vor allem die von Martin Hengel (1972) angestoßene Diskussion um einen spezifisch jüdischen Begriff von geistigem Eigentum sei genannt.

Insgesamt wurde mit der Zeit die Auffassung, Pseudonyme seien ein bewusster Rekurs auf historische Persönlichkeiten im Sinne einer literarhistorischen Zuordnung mit dem Ziel der fiktiven Vervollständigung ihrer Werke, in Frage gestellt und durch eine Interpretation der Pseudonyme ersetzt, die in den Namensangaben personale Chiffren, literarische Gestalten, paradigmatische Repräsentanten, Traditionsgaranten oder Identifikationsfiguren sieht.[15] Bedeutung erlangte auch hier die Position von Martin Hengel: Es geht bei der Namensangabe weniger um eine Autorenzuweisung als um die Einordnung in eine bestimmte transsubjektive Tradition bzw. in einen religiösen Traditionsstrom (M. Hengel [1972]) – ein Gedanke, den David G. Meade (1986) in seiner Dissertation weiterentwickelt hat.[16]

Gegenstand der äußerst vielschichtigen Diskussion war weiter die Frage, ob *neutestamentliche* Pseudepigraphie Sonderbedingungen unterliegt oder nicht. Die exemplarische Diskussion zwischen Kurt Aland, der für eine exklusive Betrachtung plädiert, und Norbert Brox, der in seinen Arbeiten neutestamentliche Pseudepigraphie stets in den Kontext gemeinantiker Literatur stellt, führt dies eindrucksvoll vor Augen.[17] Komparatis-

---

[14] Vgl. jetzt auch aktuell K. SCHICKERT, Der Schutz literarischer Urheberschaft im Rom der klassischen Antike, Tübingen 2005.

[15] Vgl. z.B. mit unterschiedlichen Akzentuierungen W. STENGER, Timotheus und Titus als literarische Gestalten. Beobachtungen zur Form und Funktion der Pastoralbriefe, Kairos 16 (1974), 252–267; BROX, Problemstand (s. Anm. 13); HENGEL, Anonymität (s. Anm. 11).

[16] D. G. MEADE, Pseudonymity and Canon. An Investigation into the Relationship of Authorship and Authority in Jewish and Earliest Christian Tradition, WUNT 39, Tübingen 1986. Es geht nicht um eine erstarrte Überlieferung eines *traditum*, sondern um einen lebendigen Überlieferungsprozess (*traditio*), der ein dialektisches Zusammenspiel von Kanonbewusstsein und Vergegenwärtigung ist. Die paradigmatische Bedeutung der Vergangenheit führt zur Vergegenwärtigung der Tradition in Form von Interpolation und Pseudepigraphie. Diese sei insofern „a claim to authoritative tradition, not primarily a statement of literary origins" (ebd. passim). Vgl. ähnlich H. NAJMAN, Seconding Sinai. The Development of Mosaic Discourse in the Second Temple Judaism, JSJ.S 77, Leiden/Boston 2003.

[17] Vgl. N. BROX, Methodenfragen der Pseudepigraphieforschung, ThRv 75 (1979), 275–278, und K. ALAND, Falsche Verfasserangaben? Zur Pseudonymität im frühchristlichen Schrifttum, ThRv 75 (1979), 1–10. Beiden Zugängen ist je eine eigene Gefahr inhärent; die inklusive Betrachtung kann in phänomenologische Beliebigkeit münden, wäh-

tisch orientierte und interdisziplinär angelegte Arbeiten bemühen sich bis heute, neutestamentliche Pseudepigraphie in einen größeren allgemein-antiken Zusammenhang zu stellen und daraus zu erklären, wobei besonders die Pseudepigraphie in antiken Schulzusammenhängen nach wie vor eine große Rolle spielt.[18] Dennoch sind neutestamentliche Pseudepigraphen nicht nur Zeugnisse antiker Literatur, sondern *auch* Bestandteile der Heiligen Schrift. Diese theologische Dimension neutestamentlicher Pseudepigraphie zieht sich wie ein roter Faden durch die Forschungsgeschichte. Haftet pseudepigraphischer Literaturproduktion bereits prinzipiell ein Beigeschmack im Sinne von falsch, epigonal und moralisch anrüchig an, so verschärft sich dieser Eindruck im Fall religiöser Literatur: Wie vertragen sich sittlich-religiöser Ernst, Anspruch auf Wahrhaftigkeit oder gar Inspiriertheit mit dem Abfassen von Schriften unter falschem Namen? Echtheitskritik an biblischen Schriften und die daraus resultierende Pseudepigraphiefrage beschränkte sich nicht auf die philologische und historisch-kritische Fragestellung, sondern erweiterte diese oft um eine bibelhermeneutische und sachlich-theologische Dimension.[19] Neben den genannten allgemein religionsethischen und dogmatischen Aspekten ist die theologische Frage von neutestamentlicher Pseudepigraphie immer auch eine *kanon*theologische. Hier wiederum bietet sich eine komplexe Sachlage, die historische und bibeltheologisch-hermeneutische Fragen gleichermaßen umfasst: Welche Rolle spielen Kanonisierungsprozesse im Hinblick auf die Produktion pseudepigraphischer Schriften? Welche Bedeutung hatte die Kanonisierung für die Rezeption pseudapostolischer Schriften? Wie ist heute mit pseudepigraphischen Schriften innerhalb des Kanons umzugehen, wobei differierende Kanonverständnisse möglicher-

---

rend exklusive Zugänge möglicherweise einer ideologisch motivierten Engführung Tür und Tor öffnen können.

[18] Vgl. dazu M. FRENSCHKOWSKI, Pseudepigraphie und Paulusschule. Gedanken zur Verfasserschaft der Deuteropaulinen, insbesondere der Pastoralbriefe, in: F. W. Horn (Hg.), Das Ende des Paulus. Historische, theologische und literaturgeschichtliche Aspekte, BZNW 106, Berlin/New York 2001, 239–272.

[19] Die theologische Dimension biblischer Pseudepigraphie führte nicht zuletzt dazu, dass das Vorhandensein pseudepigraphischer Schriften im Neuen Testament nur schwer akzeptiert wurde. Auch wenn nach katholischem Kanonverständnis Echtheit und Kanonizität einander nicht automatisch bedingen, kam es forschungsgeschichtlich betrachtet im protestantischen Bereich eher zu einer Akzeptanz von pseudepigraphischen Schriften innerhalb des Kanons als im katholischen. Allerdings stellt neutestamentliche Pseudepigraphie unter bestimmten dogmatischen Prämissen auch noch heute vor allem im Bereich evangelikaler Bibelwissenschaft ein Problem dar. Dieser Aspekt scheint gegenwärtig an Relevanz zu gewinnen, da evangelikale Schriftauffassungen zunehmend die exegetische Diskussion beeinflussen.

weise auch zu konfessionellen und innerkonfessionellen Differenzierungen zwingen?[20]

Angesichts der Brisanz dieser Fragen verwundert es nicht, dass durch die Jahrzehnte hindurch immer wieder theologische Erklärungen unterschiedlichster Art für frühchristliche Pseudepigraphie erschienen sind, die aufgrund ihrer apologetischen Zielrichtung oft den Charakter von Rechtfertigungen haben.[21] Wie im Bereich der Apokalyptikforschung[22] griff man in der Bibelwissenschaft auf verschiedenartige inspirationstheologisch motivierte Deutungsversuche zurück. Kurt Alands These von der „Zeit der echten Pseudonymität" (1961ff.),[23] in der der Autor einer „Feder" gleicht, „die vom Geist bewegt wird", wurde ebenso einflussreich und zum Gegenstand kontroverser Diskussionen wie Wolfgang Speyers Kategorie der „echten religiösen Pseudepigraphie" (1965/1966; 1971),[24] bei der der Au-

---

[20] Eng hiermit verbunden ist die Frage nach dem angemessenen Verständnis der Kanonkriterien. Hier stehen sich die Sichtweise von Armin Daniel Baum, der Echtheit im Sinne literarischer Authentizität versteht, und die u.a. von Karl-Heinz Ohlig geprägte Auffassung, es handle sich bei den pseudepigraphischen Autorenangaben um einen Verweis auf *sachliche* Kontinuität, unvereinbar gegenüber; vgl. A. D. BAUM, Literarische Echtheit als Kanonkriterium in der alten Kirche, ZNW 88 (1997), 97–110; ders., Pseudepigraphie und literarische Fälschung im frühen Christentum. Mit ausgewählten Quellentexten samt deutscher Übersetzung, WUNT II/138, Tübingen 2001; K.-H. OHLIG, Die theologische Begründung des neutestamentlichen Kanons in der alten Kirche, Düsseldorf 1972.

[21] Dies zeigt sich nicht zuletzt an terminologischen Entschärfungen (z.B. ‚Heteronymität', ‚Allonymität', ‚Deuteronymität'); vgl. z.B. H. JORDAN, Geschichte der altchristlichen Literatur, Leipzig 1911, 140; P. MÜLLER, Anfänge der Paulusschule. Dargestellt am zweiten Thessalonicherbrief und am Kolosserbrief, AThANT 74, Zürich 1988, 305–320; I. H. MARSHALL, The Pastoral Epistles, ICC, Edinburgh 1999, 84. Dies entspricht dem Bemühen der allgemeinen Pseudepigraphieforschung, eine differenzierte Terminologie zu entwickeln, die eine Unterscheidung zwischen ‚guten' und ‚schlechten', d.h. legitimen und illegitimen Formen von Pseudepigraphie verfolgt; vgl. z.B. R. SYME, Fraud and Imposture, in: von Fritz, Pseudepigrapha (s. Anm. 11), 1–17 (= SYME, Fälschung und Betrug, in: Brox, Pseudepigraphie [s. Anm. 2], 295–310); A. GRAFTON, Forgers and Critics. Creativity and Duplicity in Western Scholarship, Princeton 1990, 6.

[22] Vgl. z.B. D. S. RUSSELL, The Method and Message of Jewish Apocalyptic, 200 BC – AD 100, London 1964, 127–139.

[23] K. ALAND, Das Problem der Anonymität und Pseudonymität in der christlichen Literatur der ersten beiden Jahrhunderte, in: ders., Studien zur Überlieferung des Neuen Testaments und seines Textes, ANTT 2, Berlin 1967, 24–34; ders., Noch einmal: Das Problem der Anonymität und Pseudonymität in der christlichen Literatur der ersten beiden Jahrhunderte, in: E. Dassmann / K. S. Frank (Hg.), Pietas (FS Kötting), JAC.E 8, Münster 1980, 121–139.

[24] W. SPEYER, Religiöse Pseudepigraphie und literarische Fälschung im Altertum, JAC 8/9 (1965/66), 88–125 (= Brox, Pseudepigraphie [s. Anm. 2], 195–263); ders., Fälschung (s. Anm. 10), 37ff. u.ö.; ders., Fälschung, pseudepigraphische freie Erfindung und „echte religiöse Pseudepigraphie", in: von Fritz, Pseudepigrapha (s. Anm. 11), 331–366

tor „unter einem Zwang aus transzendentem Bereich" steht. Daneben findet sich in der katholischen Bibelwissenschaft der Rückgriff auf eine anamnetisch orientierte Inspirationslehre: So deutet Josef Zmijewski (1979) Pseudepigraphie als „objektiven Tatbestand der apostolischen Sukzession" und sieht in dem unter einem Pseudonym schreibenden Verfasser das „Werkzeug, durch das der eigentliche Verfasser redet".[25]

Abgesehen von solchen Inspirationstheorien erscheinen weitere, ganz unterschiedliche Versuche, biblische Pseudepigraphie zu erklären und theologisch zu rechtfertigen. Vor allem in der katholischen Exegese finden sich kondeszendenztheologische Erklärungen von Pseudepigraphie als *logos embiblos* (K. H. Schelkle [1961]),[26] die im weiten Kontext von Akkomodationstheorien zu verorten sind und sich auf die „Befreiungsenzyklika" *Divino afflante spiritu* (1943) von Pius XII stützen. Petr Pokorný (1984)[27] hingegen betont aus protestantischer Perspektive „Gottes Bekenntnis zu zweifelhaften Praktiken" und fordert *sola gratia* auch für Fälschungen. Eine hervorgehobene Rolle nimmt indes der in breiten Teilen der Bibelwissenschaft bezeugte Verweis auf „mildernde Tatumstände" ein, wobei oft auf gemeinantike Konventionen, mangelndes Bewusstsein von geistigem Eigentum oder die Medizinerlüge (*pia fraus*) verwiesen wird. Die Legitimierung von Pseudepigraphie als unvermeidlichem kirchenleitenden Instrument, das letztlich der „ökumenischen Verantwortung" (K. M. Fischer [1977])[28] entspringt, erlangte nicht zuletzt durch Udo Schnelles „Einleitung in das Neue Testament"[29] eine beachtliche Breitenwirkung, die bis heute anhält. Wieder andere Erklärungsmodelle, die vor allem die Pseudepigraphie des Zweiten Petrusbriefes und der Pastoralbriefe im Blick

---

(Diskussion 367–372). Die Kategorie der „echten religiösen Pseudepigraphie" ist bereits bei Josef Sint angedacht („psn Schrifttum aus mythischen und religiösen Triebkräften"); vgl. Anm. 9.

[25] J. ZMIJEWSKI, Apostolische Paradosis und Pseudepigraphie im Neuen Testament. „Durch Erinnerung wachhalten" (2 Petr 1,13; 3,1), BZ 23 (1979), 161–171. Diesen Interpretationsansatz übernimmt und modifiziert H. J. RIEDL, Anamnese und Apostolizität. Der Zweite Petrusbrief und das theologische Problem neutestamentlicher Pseudepigraphie, RST 64, Frankfurt a.M. u.a. 2005. Riedels Schlüssel für die Lösung des Problems der neutestamentlichen Pseudepigraphie liegt in der Deutung von Pseudepigraphie als „Ausdruck *anamnetischer Apostolizität*" (a.a.O. 241). Siehe dazu die Rezension von M. Janßen (ThLZ 132 [2007], 1315–1317).

[26] K. H. SCHELKLE, Die Petrusbriefe. Der Judasbrief, HThK.NT XIII, Freiburg i. Brsg. ²1963, 245–258 (247 Anm. 3).

[27] P. POKORNÝ, Das theologische Problem der neutestamentlichen Pseudepigraphie, EvTh 44 (1984), 486–496, vgl. ders., Art. Pseudepigraphie I. Altes und Neues Testament, TRE 27 (1997), 645–655.

[28] K. M. FISCHER, Anmerkungen zur Pseudepigraphie im Neuen Testament, NTS 23 (1977), 76–81.

[29] U. SCHNELLE, Einleitung in das Neue Testament, Göttingen ⁴2002, 325–329.

haben, beziehen sich auf die literarische und pragmatische Ebene: Hinter den falschen Autorenangaben stünden keine Täuschungsabsichten, sondern die „Autorfiktion" sei ein „anerkanntes Prinzip" (H. Hegermann [1970]) und die Verfasserfiktion sei somit durchschaubar.[30]

Der nicht selten apologetisch anmutenden Zielrichtung der Pseudepigraphiehermeneutik in all ihren unterschiedlichen Facetten liegt ein ganz bestimmtes Verständnis von Literaturproduktion unter falschem Namen zugrunde, das die neutestamentliche Bibelwissenschaft lange mit der altphilologischen Wissenschaft („*spuria*"!) und mit der alttestamentlichen Forschung teilte, die mittels Literarkritik „echte" Worte z.B. des Jesaja von sekundären Erweiterungen zu trennen suchte: Nur das Originale ist das Wahre; Phänomenen wie Pseudepigraphie und Interpolation haftet hingegen als Verfallserscheinungen etwas moralisch (und theologisch) Anrüchiges an, das nicht zuletzt aus „Flucht vor personaler Verantwortung" (H. Balz [1969])[31] resultiert. Damit ist Pseudepigraphie als epigonenhaft qualifiziert.

Erst in jüngster Zeit verfestigt sich die Tendenz, pseudepigraphische Schriften als eigene theologische Entwürfe wahrzunehmen und zu würdigen.[32] Damit zusammen hängt das Bewusstsein, dass es *die* neutestamentliche Pseudepigraphie nicht gibt. Vielmehr gerät die Eigenständigkeit und Unterschiedlichkeit der einzelnen neutestamentlichen Schreiben verstärkt in den Blick. Dies verändert die Wahrnehmung entscheidend. Die pseudepigraphische Abfassung einer Schrift wird nicht mehr auf eine apologetische Standardsituation im Rahmen einleitungswissenschaftlicher Topik

---

[30] Vgl. dazu beispielsweise die Beiträge von H. HEGERMANN, Der geschichtliche Ort der Pastoralbriefe, ThV II (1970), 47–64; A. VÖGTLE, Der Judasbrief. Der 2. Petrusbrief, EKK XXII, Solothurn u.a. 1994, 127ff.; R. J. BAUCKHAM, Jude. 2 Peter, WBC 50, Waco 1983, 134 u.ö. Aktuell auch H.-J. KLAUCK, Die antike Briefliteratur und das Neue Testament. Ein Lehr- und Arbeitsbuch, UTB 2022, Paderborn u.a. 1998, 304f. u.ö.

[31] H. R. BALZ, Anonymität und Pseudepigraphie im Urchristentum. Überlegungen zum literarischen und theologischen Problem der urchristlichen und gemeinantiken Pseudepigraphie, ZThK 66 (1969), 403–436.

[32] Ähnliche Entwicklungen finden sich im Hinblick auf die alttestamentliche Redaktionskritik, die auch jüngere literarische Schichten als eigene theologische Entwürfe würdigt und ins Zentrum der Forschung stellt. Gleiches gilt für die Neubewertung pseudepigraphischer Briefe in der altphilologischen Forschung. Pseudonyme Briefliteratur und Kleinliteratur werden in ihrer Eigenständigkeit wahrgenommen und zum Gegenstand altphilologischer Forschung; vgl. z.B. N. Holzberg (Hg.), Der griechische Briefroman. Gattungstypologie und Textanalyse, Classica Monacensia 8, Tübingen 1994; P. A. ROSENMEYER, Ancient Epistolary Fictions. The Letter in Greek Literature, Cambridge 2001. Hinzuweisen ist an dieser Stelle auch auf die zunehmende Erforschung und Würdigung apokrypher Literatur, die größtenteils pseudonym oder anonym ist. Die daraus resultierenden Erkenntnisse tragen nicht zuletzt etwas für das Verständnis auch der neutestamentlichen Pseudepigraphie aus.

reduziert, sondern fungiert zunehmend als Schlüssel zum Verständnis der jeweiligen Schrift. Entsprechende Untersuchungen z.B. zu den Pastoralbriefen (M. Wolter [1988];[33] A. Merz [2004][34]), dem Kolosserbrief (A. Standhartinger [1999]),[35] dem Zweiten Thessalonicherbrief (R. Börschel [2001]),[36] den Petrusbriefen (K. M. Schmidt [2003])[37] und dem Jakobusbrief (2003)[38] führen dies vor Augen.

In jüngster Zeit finden sich unterschiedliche Zugänge zum Phänomen der neutestamentlichen Pseudepigraphie, die zum Teil an alte Ansätze anknüpfen, diese differenzieren und neu akzentuieren, zum Teil aber auch neue Wege zum Verständnis der Pseudepigraphie eröffnen. So nimmt der Rückgriff auf wissenssoziologisch orientierte Zugänge zu, die die Aufmerksamkeit auf die jeweilige *Funktion* des Pseudonyms im Rahmen der Identitätskonstruktion und -sicherung lenken (z.B. M. Wolter [1988]; R. Börschel [2001]).[39] Weiter vorangetrieben wurde auch die Differenzierung der unterschiedlichen Formen von Pseudepigraphie (M. Wolter [1997]; R. Zimmermann [2003/2004]),[40] wobei sich die leitenden Faktoren

---

[33] M. WOLTER, Die Pastoralbriefe als Paulustradition, FRLANT 146, Göttingen 1988.

[34] A. MERZ, Die fiktive Selbstauslegung des Paulus. Intertextuelle Studien zur Intention und Rezeption der Pastoralbriefe, NTOA 52, Göttingen/Freiburg (CH) 2004.

[35] A. STANDHARTINGER, Studien zur Entstehungsgeschichte und Intention des Kolosserbriefes, NT.S 94, Leiden u.a. 1999.

[36] R. BÖRSCHEL, Die Konstruktion einer christlichen Identität. Paulus und die Gemeinde von Thessalonich in ihrer hellenistisch-römischen Umwelt, BBB 128, Berlin u.a. 2001.

[37] K. M. SCHMIDT, Mahnung und Erinnerung im Maskenspiel. Epistolographie, Rhetorik und Narrativik der pseudepigraphischen Petrusbriefe, HBS 38, Freiburg i. Brsg. 2003.

[38] P. von Gemünden / M. Konradt / G. Theißen (Hg.), Der Jakobusbrief. Beiträge zur Rehabilitierung der ‚strohernen Epistel', Beiträge zum Verstehen der Bibel 3, Münster 2003.

[39] So Regina Börschel in Bezug auf den Zweiten Thessalonicherbrief (vgl. Anm. 36). Im Rahmen der Konstruktion der christlichen Identität in Thessalonich fungiert der Zweite Thessalonicherbrief als „die Fortsetzung des signifikanten Gesprächs zur Sicherung der Identität nach dem Tod des Sinnvermittlers" (dies., Konstruktion [s. Anm. 36], 366ff. u.ö.). Die identitätsstiftende Funktion von Pseudonymität im Fall der Pastoralbriefe betont auch Michael Wolter in seiner Habilitationsschrift (s. Anm. 33). Vgl. allgemein zu diesem Aspekt z.B. B. Aland / J. Hahn / C. Ronning (Hg.), Literarische Konstituierung von Identifikationsfiguren in der Antike, Studien und Texte zu Antike und Christentum 16, Tübingen 2003.

[40] M. WOLTER, Art. Pseudonymität II. Kirchengeschichtlich, TRE 27 (1997), 662–670 (anonyme, pseudepigraphische und symbolische Pseudonymität); R. ZIMMERMANN, Unecht – und doch wahr? Pseudepigraphie im Neuen Testament als theologisches Problem, ZNT 12 (2003), 27–38; vgl. ders., Anonymität, Pseudonymität und Pseudepigraphie, in: K. Erlemann / K. L. Noethlichs (Hg.), Neues Testament und Antike Kultur. Bd. 1: Prolegomena – Quellen – Geschichte, Neukirchen-Vluyn 2004, 65–68; ders. Art. Pseudepigraphie/Pseudonymität, RGG[4] 6 (2003), 1786–1788. Zimmermann unterscheidet zwi-

der Klassifizierung nun an den Entstehungsursachen von Pseudepigraphie und weniger an der moralischen Wertigkeit orientieren.

Vor allem aber profitiert die Pseudepigraphieforschung von dem Einfluss literaturwissenschaftlicher Methoden auf das Neue Testament. Durch eine kommunikationstheoretisch-hermeneutische Herangehensweise gelangt man zu einem differenzierten Autorbegriff (E. Reinmuth [1998]: „der fiktive Autor in der Rolle des abstrakten Autors").[41] Die Frage danach, wie Autorfiktion ‚funktioniert' und mit welchen Mitteln sie erzeugt wird, lenkt den Blick weiter auf die technische Seite von Pseudepigraphie: Was sind die einzelnen Elemente der Autorfiktion, wie werden sie eingesetzt und wie wird die Autorfiktion zementiert („Echtheitsbeglaubigungen")? Welches Bild entsteht beim Leser und wie wirkt es? Pseudepigraphieforschung erschöpft sich nicht in dem Phänomen der Autorfiktion, sondern nimmt ebenso die Konstruktion des fiktiven Adressaten und der fiktiven Situation in den Blick. Gerade in Bezug auf letztgenannten Bereich wird gegenwärtig ein Desiderat deutlich, da zu oft die aus den Briefen rekonstruierte Situation als ‚real' rezipiert wird und als Basis für historische Schlussfolgerungen dient. Die konsequente Deutung pseudepigraphischer Texte als fiktionale Literatur führt zu einer vertieften, interdisziplinär angelegten Auseinandersetzung mit antiken Fiktionalitätstheorien und zur Rezeption der entsprechenden altphilologischen Diskussion (z.B. K. M. Schmidt [2003]).[42] Man nimmt pseudepigraphische Texte als fiktionale Literatur wahr und überträgt Elemente der Erzähltheorie auf fiktionale Briefe. Nicht zuletzt steht die textpragmatische Leistung des Stilmittels der Prosopopoiie auf dem Prüfstand: Ist Täuschung Voraussetzung zur Wirkung? An dieser Stelle bricht die Frage nach der ‚Durchschaubarkeit' der Verfasserfiktion wieder auf („offene Pseudepigraphie"), wobei das vormals apologetisch motivierte erkenntnisleitende Interesse durch ein literaturwissenschaftliches ersetzt wird.

---

schen überlieferungsgeschichtlich motivierter Pseudepigraphie, gattungsbedingter, imitativer, zufällig oder technisch bedingter und religiöser Pseudepigraphie. Die neutestamentlichen Schriften ordnet er jeweils in diese Kategorien ein.

[41] E. REINMUTH, Hermeneutik des Neuen Testaments, Göttingen 2002, 104–107; ders., Zur neutestamentlichen Paulus-Pseudepigraphie, in: N. Walter / E. Reinmuth / P. Lampe (Hg.), Die Briefe an die Philipper, Thessalonicher und an Philemon, NTD 8/2, Göttingen u.a. 1998, 190–200.

[42] S.o. Anm. 37. Eine solche Tendenz ist auch in weiteren Bereichen der Bibelwissenschaft auszumachen; vgl. z.B. R. LUX, „Ich, Kohelet, bin König...". Die Fiktion als Schlüssel zur Wirklichkeit in Kohelet 1,12–16, EvTh 50 (1990), 331–342; U. LUZ, Fiktivität und Traditionstreue im Matthäusevangelium im Lichte griechischer Literatur, ZNW 94 (1993), 153–177; K. Backhaus / G. Häfner (Hg.), Historiographie und fiktionales Erzählen. Zur Konstruktivität in Geschichtstheorie und Exegese, BThSt 86, Neukirchen-Vluyn 2007.

Aber auch theologische Zugänge zur Pseudepigraphie (z.B. R. Zimmermann),[43] bibeltheologische Untersuchungen (H. J. Riedel [2004])[44] und dezidiert kanontheologische Forschungen (A. D. Baum [2001]) verschaffen sich in jüngster Zeit Gehör. Neutestamentliche Pseudepigraphie als Bestandteil des Kanons ist indes nicht nur in theologischer Hinsicht relevant, sondern auch in literarischer. Dass die einzelnen neutestamentlichen Pseudepigraphen keine isolierten Schriften, sondern auf andere Schriften innerhalb des Kanons bezogen und möglicherweise durch sie motiviert sind, zeigt allein das Verhältnis zwischen Judasbrief und Zweitem Petrusbrief. Auch in Bezug auf das *Corpus Paulinum* wurde dieser Aspekt immer wieder stark gemacht, wie die Deutung des Epheserbriefes als mögliche Einleitung zu einer Paulusbriefsammlung oder die These, die Pastoralbriefe seien als Abschluss des *Corpus Paulinum* konzipiert, zeigen. Die Wechselbeziehung zwischen Pseudepigraphie und Kanon rückt in das Zentrum des Forschungsinteresses. Neben komparatistisch angelegten Untersuchungen zu antiken Editions- und Kanonisierungsprozessen bringen vor allem Forschungen zur Intertextualität Licht in diese Funktion von Pseudepigraphie. Die Dissertation von Annette Merz (2004)[45] über das Pseudepigraphiekonzept der Pastoralbriefe zeigt nicht nur, wie Pseudepigraphie als „fiktive Selbstauslegung" funktioniert, sondern liefert auch Kriterien für die Frage nach der sachlichen Angemessenheit der Inanspruchnahme eines Pseudonyms.

Ein letzter Punkt sei angemerkt: Schon Schleiermachers Bestreitung der Echtheit des Ersten Timotheusbriefes führte zu einer Apologie der Echtheit mit immer ausgewogeneren Argumenten. Auch heute brechen Echtheitsfragen neu auf, wodurch der zumindest in breiten Teilen der deutschsprachigen Forschung etablierte Forschungskonsens in Frage gestellt wird. Dabei kehrt sich die apologetische Richtung gewissermaßen um: Die Annahme von Pseudepigraphie muss verteidigt und in ihren einzelnen Elementen erklärt werden, was wiederum zu einem vertieften Verständnis der jeweiligen pseudepigraphischen Konzeption führen kann. Abgesehen von der Diskussion über den Zweiten Thessalonicherbrief geraten gegenwärtig vor allem die Pastoralbriefe verstärkt in das Zentrum des Forschungsinteresses: Lässt sich die Eigenart der drei Schreiben des Paulus an seine Schüler besser unter der Voraussetzung ihrer Echtheit oder unter der Vor-

---

[43] S. Anm. 40 und R. ZIMMERMANN, Lügen für die Wahrheit? Das Phänomen urchristlicher Pseudepigrafie am Beispiel des Kolosserbriefs, in: O. Hochadel / U. Kocher (Hg.), Lügen und Betrügen. Das Falsche in der Geschichte von der Antike bis zur Moderne, Köln u.a. 2000, 257–272.

[44] Vgl. z.B. die Arbeit von Hermann Josef Riedl zum Zweiten Petrusbrief (s. Anm. 25).

[45] Vgl. Anm. 34.

aussetzung ihrer Unechtheit verstehen? Die aktuellen Erklärungsmodelle schwanken von der Interpretation der Pastoralbriefe als antikem Briefroman bis zur Infragestellung der Corpushypothese bei gleichzeitiger Annahme der Echtheit zumindest einzelner Briefe. Das einstige „Kabinettstück"[46] neutestamentlicher Pseudepigraphie ist damit zum Testfall und zur „Herausforderung an die neutestamentliche Wissenschaft"[47] geworden.

2. Zum vorliegenden Band

In Anbetracht dieser Situation will der vorliegende Band die Problematik und Vielfalt der gegenwärtigen Diskussion dokumentieren, die neueren Ansätze zusammenfassen und eine differenziertere Diskussion voranbringen. Die darin versammelten Aufsätze sollen die Vielfalt antiker Briefpseudepigraphie und die damit verbundenen Probleme vor Augen führen sowie einen repräsentativen Querschnitt der aktuellen Forschung zur Pseudepigraphie in Antike und Neuem Testament geben. Da die neutestamentlichen Briefe stets im Zentrum der Diskussion standen, liegt der Schwerpunkt auf der neutestamentlichen Briefliteratur. Dabei wird eine repräsentative Breite angestrebt, die nicht nur alle im Neuen Testament als pseudonym beurteilten Briefe (einschließlich des Hebräerbriefs und der Johannesbriefe) berücksichtigt, sondern diese Untersuchungen auch in einen breiteren Kontext relevanter Bereiche frühjüdischer und griechisch-römischer Pseudepigraphie stellt. Daher werden aus den Bereichen außerhalb des Neuen Testaments jene herangezogen, die für das Verständnis der Entstehung der neutestamentlichen Briefe und der pseudonymen Texte inhaltlich von Bedeutung sind. Dazu gehören u.a. die Literatur der frühjüdischen Apokalyptik, die Weisheits- und Testamentenliteratur, aber auch der antike Briefroman und – zumindest mit einem knappen Blick – die nachneutestamentliche apokryphe Briefliteratur. Dass die Erklärung und Bewertung des Phänomens der Pseudepigraphie kontrovers ist und bleibt, zeigt sich auch an den in diesem Band zusammengestellten Beiträgen.

Der Band ist nach den unterschiedlichen religionsgeschichtlichen Kontexten gegliedert, so dass den beiden Teilen zu frühjüdischen (I.) und griechisch-römischen Kontexten (II.) ein sehr viel breiterer Teil zu frühchristlichen Kontexten (III.) folgt, in dem die einzelnen neutestamentlichen Briefe behandelt und übergreifende Probleme thematisiert werden. Auf

---

[46] BROX, Verfasserangaben (s. Anm. 12), 24. Ähnlich auch P. TRUMMER, Die Pastoralbriefe als Paulustradition, BET 8, Frankfurt a.M. 1978, 74, der von „totaler Pseudepigraphie" spricht.

[47] J. HERZER, Abschied vom Konsens? Die Pseudepigraphie der Pastoralbriefe als Herausforderung an die neutestamentliche Wissenschaft, ThLZ 129 (2004), 1267–1282.

eine weitere Untergliederung konnte in Teil III. verzichtet werden. Das Arrangement folgt hier der Reihenfolge im neutestamentlichen Kanon.

2.1 Frühjüdische Kontexte

Der erste Teil zu *frühjüdischen Kontexten* enthält drei gewichtige Beiträge zu frühjüdischen Schriftenkreisen, in denen wesentliche Hintergründe der urchristlichen Pseudepigraphie studiert werden können. *Leo G. Perdue* spannt dabei den weitesten Horizont auf, beginnend mit der altorientalischen Literatur Mesopotamiens und Ägyptens. Perdue verfolgt die Frage nach den Anfängen der Zuschreibung von Werken an ‚individuelle' Autoren, vor allem im Kontext der Weisheitsliteratur des Alten Orients und dann auch des Alten Testaments und nachbiblischen Judentums bis hin zur Sapientia Salomonis. Dabei erweist sich die rhetorische Technik der *mimesis*, der Nachahmung älterer Autoren, als ein wesentlicher Faktor der literarischen Gestaltung, was z.B. im Blick auf die Sapientia wahrscheinlich macht, dass deren literarische Technik von den intendierten Lesern des Werks erkannt werden konnte.

Mit der frühjüdischen Apokalyptik betritt *Karina Martin Hogan* in ihrem Beitrag ein zweites Feld der biblisch-frühjüdischen Tradition, das für den Hintergrund der frühchristlichen Pseudepigraphie von großer Bedeutung ist. Ausgehend von der Periodisierung der Geschichte in frühjüdischen Apokalypsen untersucht sie die geschichtliche Stellung der jeweils als pseudonyme Autoren gewählten Figuren und deren Funktion hinsichtlich der Übermittlung von Traditionen. Die pseudonymen Autoren apokalyptischer Texte wie Henoch, Noah, Mose, Baruch, Daniel und Esra erscheinen in dieser Perspektive als ‚Brückenfiguren', die angesichts der Erfahrung von Diskontinuität in der Geschichte die Kontinuität der Überlieferung repräsentieren und somit gefährdete Identität wieder herstellen und sichern.

Ein interessantes Untersuchungsfeld, das besondere Beachtung verdient, sind die Textfunde vom Toten Meer, weil hier in einzigartiger Weise anhand erhaltener Manuskripte Einblicke in die literarischen Prozesse von Fortschreibung, Interpretation und Kanonisierung möglich sind. Nicht zuletzt haben die Qumran-Funde unser Wissen über zahlreiche bisher bekannte ‚Pseudepigraphen' wie z.B. der Henoch-Tradition, das Jubiläenbuch oder die Patriarchentestamente auf eine neue Grundlage gestellt und eine Vielzahl ‚neuer' pseudepigraphischer Texte ans Licht gebracht. *Eibert Tigchelaar* gibt in seinem Beitrag einen Überblick über die hier zu gewinnenden Einsichten und diskutiert die unterschiedlichen Formen ‚parabiblischer' Texte sowie die Frage nach dem Zusammenhang zwischen bestimmten Texten und Textgattungen, den für sie gewählten Pseudonymen und evtl. im Hintergrund stehenden religiösen Gruppen. Ein kleiner Anhang benennt zumindest einige Texte, die – nach der fragmentarisch erhaltenen Evidenz – als Briefe gelten können.

2.2 Griechisch-römische Kontexte

In einem zweiten, umfangreicheren Teil (II.) werden wesentliche Textbereiche der griechisch-römischen Literatur untersucht und zugleich weitere übergreifende Sachfragen pseudonymer Autorschaft beleuchtet.

Zunächst erörtert *Wolfgang Speyer*, einer der ‚Altmeister' der Pseudepigraphie-Diskussion,[48] in einem weiten Rahmen die Frage von göttlicher und menschlicher Verfasserschaft in der Antike. Als ein Ursprung pseudonymen Sprechens und Schreibens erscheint dabei die erfahrene und oral oder literarisch weitergegebene Gottesrede. Speyer weist so erneut auf die religiöse Dimension im Hintergrund pseudepigraphischer Verfasserkonstruktionen hin.

Martina Janßen erörtert in ihrem materialreichen Beitrag die ausgesprochen vielfältigen antiken (Selbst-)Aussagen zur Pseudepigraphie. Dabei zeigt sich eine differenzierte Palette von Möglichkeiten, wie es zu unrichtigen Verfasserangaben kommen kann: Diese reichen von einer unabsichtlich, aus Irrtum oder Verwechslung zustande gekommenen falschen Zuschreibung über die ästhetisch-literarische Form der Prosopopoiie, die Abfassung eines Werks im Auftrag eines anderen oder auch im Kontext einer Schule, die pseudonyme Abfassung im Interesse, einen anderen zu diskreditieren oder ihm zu schaden, bis hin zur Pseudonymität im Interesse, dem eigenen Werk größere Wirkung und Autorität zu verschaffen. Alle diese Kategorien sind differenziert zu betrachten und in ihrer Übertragbarkeit auf Phänomene des frühen Christentums zu reflektieren, wenn die frühchristlichen Schriften angemessen und nicht anachronistisch verstanden werden sollen.

Die Diskussion, inwiefern Pseudepigraphie erkennbar war oder gar erkannt werden wollte, nimmt *Marco Frenschkowski* mit Blick auf die pagane Antike und – im Vergleich damit – das frühe Christentum auf, wobei die Pastoralbriefe, Judasbrief und Zweiter Petrusbrief als Paradigmen dienen. Frenschkowski beleuchtet das erstaunliche Phänomen, dass frühchristliche Autoren ihren paganen oder häretischen Gegnern den Vorwurf der Fälschung entgegenhalten konnten, während sie mit der Möglichkeit falscher Zuschreibungen im eigenen Kreis und beim eigenen Schrifttum nur selten rechneten, was sich für Frenschkowski durch das ‚subkulturelle' Milieu des frühen Christentums erklärt. Insgesamt ergibt sich aus diesen Beobachtungen eine größere Skepsis gegenüber der beliebten, da apologetisch brauchbaren These, dass die frühchristliche Pseudepigraphie, etwa in

---

[48] S. dazu o. Anm. 10.

den Pastoralbriefen oder im Zweiten Petrusbrief, für die jeweiligen Leser ‚durchschaubar' gewesen sein sollte.[49]

Die beiden folgenden Beiträge beleuchten ein im exegetischen Horizont häufig vernachlässigtes Feld der antiken Literatur und eine relativ neue Diskussion: das Phänomen pseudepigraphischer Briefsammlungen oder der sogenannten antiken ‚Briefromane'. Dabei rekurriert *Katharina Luchner* auf die Forschung zu diesen Sammlungen mit spezieller Berücksichtigung der Platon- und Chion-Briefe und plädiert am Ende eher für eine kritische Position zur These, dass in diesen Sammlungen ‚Briefromane' zu sehen seien. Die Interpretation der Briefsammlungen als ‚Briefromane' erscheint auch in der klassischen Philologie als ein ‚apologetischer' Versuch, die Sammlungen vom Geruch der ‚Fälschung' zu befreien und in den Horizont literarischer Fiktionalität zu stellen. Doch lassen nur wenige dieser Sammlungen das für Romane auch in der Antike vorauszusetzende narrative Kontinuum sowie das konsistente *ēthos* ihres Helden erkennen. Demgegenüber nimmt *Timo Glaser* die narratologische Lektüre von Briefsammlungen als eine mögliche Lektüre positiv auf, wobei er neben den Chion-Briefen die ‚Briefromane' des Aischines und des Euripides diskutiert und am Ende die Übertragung des Paradigmas auf die Pastoralbriefe vorschlägt, deren Lektüre als ‚Paulusbriefroman' die Konstitution eines neuen Paulusbildes unter Aufnahme der älteren Tradition verständlich machen könnte.

Der letzte Beitrag dieses Teils – und ein besonderes Glanzstück des vorliegenden Bandes – bringt ein instruktives Beispiel für die Diskussion um pseudepigraphische Briefe und Briefsammlungen in der griechisch-römischen Antike. *Robert Matthew Calhoun* übersetzt und kommentiert den als ‚Einleitungsbrief' mit dem Corpus der Briefe des Marcus Iunius Brutus verbundenen Brief eines gewissen Mithridates zusammen mit weiteren Testimonia für das Corpus dieser Briefe. Das Schreiben ist deshalb besonders interessant, weil sich der Autor offen über seine eigene Tätigkeit in der Herausgabe und vermutlich Erweiterung des Corpus der Brutusbriefe äußert. Am Ende seines Beitrags deutet Calhoun einige Aspekte an, in denen der Mithridates-Brief die Produktion und Kanonisierung neutestamentlicher Briefe und insbesondere Pseudepigrapha illustrieren könnte.

2.3 Frühchristliche Kontexte

Der umfangreichste Teil (III.) des vorliegenden Bandes erfasst ‚frühchristliche Kontexte'. Dabei werden – grob in der Reihenfolge des neutestamentlichen Kanons – alle in der Forschung als pseudonym angesehenen

---

[49] S. zu dieser Diskussion o. Anm. 30.

bzw. als solche diskutierten Briefe mit ihrer jeweiligen Verfasserkonstruktion behandelt, z.T. unter übergreifenden Gesichtspunkten.

Zur Eröffnung der Diskussion thematisiert *Harry Y. Gamble* die kanongeschichtlichen und kanontheologischen Aspekte des Themas. Sein Beitrag über „Pseudonymity and the New Testament Canon" erörtert die Bedeutung des Phänomens der Pseudepigraphie für das Verständnis der Herausbildung des Kanons. Gamble skizziert zunächst historisch die Sammlung der einzelnen neutestamentlichen Teilkorpora und zeigt dabei, dass die Bedeutung der Autorschaft bzw. der ‚Authentizität' der jeweiligen Schriften im Prozess der Kanonbildung nicht einheitlich hoch veranschlagt werden kann. Er erörtert sodann den Umgang mit pseudonymen Schriften in den Kanonisierungsdiskursen der frühen Kirche und beleuchtet abschließend das theologische Problem der kanonischen Pseudepigrapha und die – unterschiedlich wirksamen – Strategien der Interpreten, die Präsenz pseudonymer Schriften im Kanon zu erklären und zu legitimieren.

Eve-Marie Becker bietet in ihrem Beitrag zur paulinischen Pseudepigraphie-Forschung als literaturgeschichtlicher Aufgabe einen knappen Forschungsüberblick zur Echtheitskritik der paulinischen Briefe, um auf diesem Hintergrund einerseits die Bedeutung der Orthonymität in der paulinischen Epistolographie und andererseits die Problematik und Funktion der paulinischen Pseudepigraphie im Ganzen zu skizzieren.

Die detaillierte Besprechung der einzelnen pseudepigraphischen Paulusbriefe leitet *Martin Hüneburg* mit seiner Analyse des Epheserbriefes ein, die dieses Schreiben als eine korrigierende Bearbeitung und Weiterführung des Kolosserbriefes ausweist. Dabei zeigt sich schon anhand dieser beiden literarisch eng miteinander zusammenhängenden pseudopaulinischen Schreiben die Differenziertheit des Phänomens der paulinischen Pseudepigraphie. Diese Beobachtung wird gestützt durch den Beitrag von *Nicole Frank*, die den Kolosserbrief als Paradigma zur Rekonstruktion der Entstehung paulinischer und allgemeiner der frühchristlichen Pseudepigraphie aus der Nötigung zur Auseinandersetzung um das Erbe des Paulus deutet.

Die Diskussion um den Zweiten Thessalonicherbrief ist besonders heftig, zumal angesichts der Tatsache, dass der Zweite Thessalonicherbrief selbst auf die Möglichkeit pseudonymer Briefe verweist und damit evtl. sogar den Ersten Thessalonicherbrief als gefälscht hinstellen könnte. Während in der deutschsprachigen Forschung die große Mehrheit der kritischen Exegeten den Zweiten Thessalonicherbrief als Pseudepigraphon ansieht, ist die Diskussion v.a. im nordamerikanischen Raum nach wie vor kontrovers. Als Beitrag zur Diskussion wird hier das bislang unveröffentlichte ‚Seminar Paper' von *Edgar Krentz* aus dem Jahr 1983 dokumentiert, das die deutschen Impulse v.a. aus dem Kommentar von Wolfgang Trilling in den amerikanischen Kontext transportierte und dort eine langsame Wende hin zur Pseudepigraphie-These veranlasste. Die kurze editorische Notiz von *Trevor Thompson* führt in die forschungsgeschichtliche Bedeutung dieses Textes ein und stellt ihn in den Rahmen des gegenwärtigen Diskussionsstandes. Die aktuelle Diskussion um den Zweiten Thessalonicherbrief führt Thompson dann in seinem eigenen Beitrag weiter, der die schwierige Suche nach einem historischen Ort des Zweiten Thessalonicherbriefes seit Ferdinand Christian Baur diskutiert und nach dem Durchgang durch die wichtigsten Textdaten die Forderung nach einer Methode der Interpretation unterstreicht, die die Komplexität der pseudonymen Konstruktion und die ‚doppelte Persönlichkeit' des Autors eines pseudonymen Briefes hinreichend berücksichtigen kann.

Das ‚Sturmzentrum' der paulinischen Pseudepigraphie sind jedoch seit den Anfängen der kritischen Forschung die Pastoralbriefe.[50] Die Diskussion über dieses ‚Corpus' nimmt *Jens Herzer* in seinem ausführlichen Beitrag auf. Dabei zeichnet er zunächst in einem forschungsgeschichtlichen Überblick die Entstehung des gegenwärtig dominierenden Forschungsparadigmas nach und weist auf bislang unerledigte Probleme hin. Die bloße Frage nach ‚echt' oder ‚unecht' erscheint auch hier zu sehr simplifizierend, weil sie den Charakter der einzelnen Schreiben und ihr gegenseitiges Verhältnis nicht hinreichend berücksichtigt. Herzer plädiert zugleich gegen die in der Exegese wohlfeile apologetische ‚Erklärung' der Phänomene: Im Falle der Pastoralbriefe ist durchaus mit der Möglichkeit der ‚Fälschung' zu rechnen, andererseits ist die Anwendung der Kategorie der ‚Fiktion' geschichtstheoretisch besser abzusichern. Am Ende steht die provokante These, dass innerhalb des ‚Corpus' zwischen unterschiedlichen Autoren und Abfassungssituationen zu differenzieren ist. Nur der Erste Timotheusbrief kann als (relativ spät zu datierende) ‚Schulpseudepigraphie' verstanden werden, hingegen können Zweiter Timotheusbrief und Titusbrief als eigenständiger Teil der vom Ersten Timotheusbrief rezipierten Paulustradition gelten, so dass für diese beiden Schreiben die Frage der paulinischen Verfasserschaft noch einmal eigens und unabhängig vom Ersten Timotheusbrief zu prüfen ist. Der Beitrag zeigt mithin, wie durch differenziertere Beschreibungskategorien die oft schon als abgeschlossen betrachtete Diskussion um einzelne neutestamentliche Pseudepigrapha wieder neu belebt werden kann.

Als Teil des Corpus Paulinum und damit unter der irrigen Annahme paulinischer Verfasserschaft ist auch der Hebräerbrief lange überliefert worden, und es ist eine offene Frage, ob er nicht auch als vermeintliches Pseudepigraphon Eingang in den neutestamentlichen Kanon gefunden hat.

---

[50] S. dazu o. Anm. 1.

Clare K. Rothschild, deren Projekt zur Pseudonymität des Hebräerbriefes den Anlass für das dieser Sammlung zugrunde liegende Münchener Symposium und damit auch für die Zusammenstellung des vorliegenden Bandes bot, erörtert in Ergänzung zu den Überlegungen in ihrer eben erschienenen Monographie[51] die spezifischen Allusionen des Hebräerbriefes auf den Römerbrief und die Parallelen zwischen beiden in der Schriftrezeption und stellt die These auf, dass der Hebräerbrief (zumindest auch) als Anleitung zu einer im Sinne des Autors ‚besseren' Lektüre des Römerbriefes und somit als subtile Umdeutung dieses Paulusbriefs fungieren konnte.

Die Diskussion zum Corpus der ‚Katholischen Briefe' beginnt mit zwei Beiträgen zum Jakobusbrief, dessen Zuschreibung in der internationalen Forschung nach wie vor umstritten ist. *Matthias Konradt* begründet in seinem Beitrag erneut die These der Pseudonymität des Jakobusbriefes, auch im Vergleich mit dem, was aus anderen neutestamentlichen Texten als Position des historischen Jakobus zu erkennen ist. Konradt analysiert die Verfasserfiktion des Jakobusbriefes und fragt nach den Gründen, die den tatsächlichen Autor veranlasst haben können, zu dieser Konstruktion zu greifen. *Matt Jackson-McCabe* beleuchtet angesichts der nach wie vor verhärteten Fronten in der Pseudepigraphiedebatte die Frage, welche Loyalitäten und welche ‚Politik' die Vertreter der unterschiedlichen Positionen leiten. Dabei verfolgt er in instruktiver Weise die Geschichte der christlich-theologischen Bewertung des Jakobusbriefes von Euseb bis Luther und problematisiert die literaturgeschichtliche Diskussion um das in beiden Diskursen bestehende Ineinander von innertheologischen und externen literarischen Argumenten und Leitmotiven. So wendet sich letztlich die Frage, was die ‚beste Lektüre' und die angemessenste Interpretation sei, in die viel kontextuellere Frage, für wen bzw. in welchem Kontext diese Lektüre als die ‚beste' gelten kann und zu bevorzugen ist.

Die folgenden drei Beiträge wenden sich den beiden Petrusbriefen und dem mit dem Zweiten Petrusbrief literarisch eng verbundenen Judasbrief zu. *Karl Matthias Schmidt* vergleicht in seinem Beitrag die in den beiden Petrusbriefen vorliegende Autorfiktion, wobei insbesondere die pragmatische Funktion der beiden Schreiben im Kontext der jeweiligen Gemeinde in den Blick genommen wird. *Lutz Doering* wendet sich eingehender dem Petrusbild des Ersten Petrusbriefes zu, das nach dieser Analyse darauf abzielt, das Heidenchristentum in seiner ‚Diaspora'-Situation zu erreichen und – in der Tradition der jüdischen Diasporabriefe – an die grundlegende Autorität des Urchristentums zurückzubinden. *Jörg Frey* beleuchtet in seinem Beitrag vergleichend die Relation von Autorfiktion und Gegnerbild

---

[51] C. K. ROTHSCHILD, Hebrews as Pseudepigraphon. The History and Significance of the Pauline Attribution of Hebrews, WUNT 235, Tübingen 2009.

im Judasbrief und im Zweiten Petrusbrief, wobei sich trotz der stofflichen Nähe und literarischen Abhängigkeit eine tief greifende Differenz sowohl in der Wahl der pseudonymen Legitimationsstruktur als auch in der Durchführung der Autorfiktion zeigt. Dabei wird deutlich, dass die Interpretation pseudepigraphischer Briefe mehr als bisher damit rechnen muss, dass nicht nur das Bild des Autors, sondern auch die literarisch repräsentierte Situation der Adressatengemeinde sowie insbesondere das Bild der jeweiligen Gegner Bestandteil der literarischen Fiktion sind und keineswegs eine sichere Basis zur Interpretation bieten können. Die beispiellose Gegnerpolemik des Zweiten Petrusbriefes wirft dabei insbesondere die Frage auf, inwieweit sie zu großen Teilen auf Entlehnungen aus dem Jud und anderen polemischen Stereotypen beruht und damit zumindest partiell ebenso wie die Autorfiktion als ‚Fälschung' gelten muss, was für die ethische Bewertung des Schreibens wie auch der thematisierten Sachverhalte von Belang wäre.

Die Diskussion der Katholischen Briefe wird durch einen Beitrag von *Jutta Leonhardt-Balzer* zu den Johannesbriefen abgeschlossen. Diese drei Briefe werden nur selten unter dem Aspekt der Pseudepigraphie diskutiert, doch verdienen die komplexen Abfassungs- und Zuschreibungsverhältnisse, die Anonymität der Texte, die auffällige Nennung des *presbyteros* als Autor des Zweiten und Dritten Johannesbriefes und die in den Überschriften erfolgende Zuschreibung an einen im Text der Briefe (wie auch des Vierten Evangeliums) nicht erwähnten Johannes hier Beachtung, weil sie die Variabilität der Prozesse und Hintergründe im Umfeld der Beanspruchung und Zuschreibung von Autorschaft im frühen Christentum noch einmal in einem breiteren Horizont verdeutlichen.

Im letzten Beitrag dieses Teils geht der Blick über das Neue Testament hinaus, jedoch nicht etwa auf die Probleme des Corpus Ignatianum, sondern auf eine eher schlichte, aber interessante ‚apokryphe' Schrift, den pseudonymen Briefwechsel zwischen Paulus und Seneca. *Stefan Krauter* fragt hier dezidiert nach den Kennzeichen ‚schlechter' Pseudepigraphie und deutet den Briefwechsel sowohl anhand stilistischer Kriterien als auch aufgrund der inhaltlichen Dürftigkeit des Briefwechsels als ein solches Beispiel einer simplen, eben literarisch und theologisch ‚schlechten' Verfasserfiktion.

Als einer der ‚Altmeister' der literaturgeschichtlichen Erforschung des Neuen Testaments kommentiert *David E. Aune* in seinem Nachwort die in diesem Band gebotene Diskussion. Dabei geht er nicht auf alle Beiträge gleichermaßen ein, sondern stellt die einen ausführlicher, die anderen knapper in den Horizont der Forschung und benennt am Ende einige Aspekte für den Fortgang der Diskussion. Es ist zu hoffen, dass die hier gebotenen Überlegungen im Ganzen zu einer differenzierteren Wahrnehmung der in den einzelnen Texten vorliegenden Autor-, Situations- und Gegnerkonstruktionen führen, die denn erst ein präzisiertes Urteil über den Typus, die Intention und die Implikationen der jeweiligen literarischen Ausgestaltung ermöglicht.

I. Frühjüdische Kontexte

Pseudonymity and Graeco-Roman Rhetoric

Mimesis and the Wisdom of Solomon

by

Leo G. Perdue

1. Definition: Pseudonymity and Pseudepigraphy

In contrast to anonymity (ἀνωνυμία) in which a work does not disclose its author, pseudonymity (ψευδώνυμος) or "false name" refers to a text wrongly claiming to be written by an author in the title, the subscription, or the text itself. A related term, pseudepigraphy (ψευδεπίγραφα) literally means "false writing."[1] According to William Adler, in the early church the term "pseudepigrapha referred to religious compositions falsely attributed to a revered figure of the past."[2] Pseudepigraphic texts at times were identified as apocryphal, although the two terms, pseudepigraphy and apocrypha, were not viewed to be identical in meaning. The term apocrypha, beginning in early third and the late second centuries BCE, was used in two general senses: first, hidden or mysterious books, and second, spurious ones (i.e., literary forgeries). Eventually in Protestantism, the apocrypha came to be seen as the core of the pseudepigrapha, since there were numerous other texts that existed in addition to this small collection. The fourteen or fifteen books bore this name, not because they were inauthentic, but rather because they raised the matter of canon. The question whether they are canonical receives different answers given by Judaism (no), Catholicism (yes), and Protestantism (no).

---

[1] D. A. Carter, "Pseudonymity and Pseudepigraphy," in *The New Testament Dictionary Background* (eds. C. A. Evans and S. E. Porter; Grand Rapids, Mich.: Intervarsity, 2000), 857–58, and W. Speyer, *Die literarische Fälschung im heidnischen und christlichen Altertum: Ein Versuch ihrer Deutung* (Handbuch der Altertumswissenschaft I/2; München: Beck, 1971).

[2] W. Adler, "The Pseudepigrapha in the Early Church," in *The Canon Debate* (eds. L. Martin McDonald and J. A. Sanders; Peabody, Mass.: Hendrickson Publishers, 2002), 211–228 (211). Also see A. D. Baum, *Pseudepigraphie und literarische Fälschung im frühen Christentum: Mit ausgewählten Quellentexten samt deutscher Übersetzung* (WUNT II/138; Tübingen: Mohr Siebeck, 2001).

Since not all pseudepigraphic books are literary forgeries, the distinction between literary forgery, a pseudonymous writing, and a pseudepigraphic work is important to maintain.[3] The first has the calculated intention to deceive for a variety of reasons, including harboring the desire to achieve notoriety by associating a text with a famous person, the association of writing with a famous figure to add credence to the argument, economic profit (i.e., financial payment), malice and vitriolic criticisms (e.g., to sully someone's name or a particular idea), honor or respect shown to a particular person by attributing a text to him/her, and the identification with the teachings and thought of a earlier person or group.[4] The second has normally been understood as deception either in order to claim authority for the text or to contain the avowal of a writer to stand within the tradition of the author. The third, pseudepigraphic writings, resulted from either intentional deception or honest mistakes.[5]

It is clear from the numerous references to forgeries and their condemnation that Graeco-Roman writers were aware of this practice. They also used their own knowledge of literary criticism, in particular their familiarity with the vocabulary and style of famous authors, to assist in verifying works falsely attributed to an author.[6] The issue of pseudonymity and pseudepigraphy has been debated frequently by Biblical scholars. Much of the church's scholarship has focused on the issue of authority, arising in part from the fact that the New Testament quotes or alludes to texts not included in the early Jewish canon.

2. Authorship in Antiquity[7]

2.1 Introduction

In the West, interest in determining the authorship of a text in antiquity was not pursued prior to the fifth century BCE, when it was a question of interest in Classical Greece. As we shall see, pseudonymity and pseudepi-

---

[3] See B. M. Metzger, "Literary Forgeries and Canonical Pseudepigrapha," *JBL* 92 (1972): 3–24 (4).

[4] Carter, "Pseudonymity and Pseudepigraphy" (see n. 1), 859, and Metzger, ibid., 5–12.

[5] Baum, *Pseudepigraphie und literarische Fälschung im frühen Christentum* (see n. 2), 9.

[6] Metzger, "Literary Forgeries and Pseudepigrapha" (see n. 3), 13–4.

[7] For a brief introduction, see K. van der Toorn, "Authorship in Antiquity," ch. 2 in *Scribal Culture and the Making of the Hebrew Bible* (Cambridge, Mass.: Harvard University Press, 2007), 27–49.

graphy were frequently practiced in the ancient Near East.[8] While in the ANE authorship may at times have been viewed as collective, i.e., texts were produced by the scribal communities, attribution to individuals was a significant practice especially among the composers of the wisdom corpora. However, it was not until the Renaissance that efforts to ascertain who actually composed a writing was seriously undertaken in order to separate what appear to be accurate claims from those that were false.[9] The notion of literary property developed in Greece in the fifth century BCE, although forgeries continued to appear. In Latin literature, forgeries appeared as early as the late second century BCE.[10] Thus authorship was a matter of concern in both the eastern cultures and those of the west.

2.2 Cuneiform Literature[11]

Colophons and epilogues were commonly written in the scribal cultures of the ancient Near East. In Mesopotamia the name of the scribal copyist, the owner of the text, or its patron may be mentioned, but only rarely the name of the original author. Although as we shall see, the sapiential texts did forth the presumed or falsely claimed composer. On occasion a god (or gods) is described as the one who "speaks" in the text or is the composer (e.g., "Dumuzi and Enkidu: the Dispute between the Shepherd-God and the Farmer-God," *ANET*^{3}, 41–42). Cases in which the patron/author is listed include the "Law Code of Lipit-Ishtar" (*ANET*^{3}, 159–161) and the "Law

---

[8] This opposes the view of P. R. Davies, "Spurious Attribution in the Hebrew Bible," in *The Invention of Sacred Tradition* (eds. J. R. Lewis and O. Hammer; Cambridge: Cambridge University Press, 2007), 258–275 (259), who considered the matter of authorship to be unimportant in the literary tradition until the Hellenistic age.

[9] Of course, under the impress of postmodernism, the "death of the author" has led to the recognition that the author, even if identified, is not the primary interpreter of his/her text. More importantly the author is not some isolated individual with "special" insight, but rather the social location and communities surrounding the writer and audiences shape both the text and its variety of meanings. The writer and meaning are not related, for writing destroys every "voice," i.e., no single meaning can be attributed to a text for there is none. Instead, the writer is but a "scriptor" who creates the text but is not its authoritative interpreter, see R. Barthes, "The Death of the Author," in *Image-Music-Text* (ed. idem; London: Fantana, 1977), 142–48.

[10] "Forgeries, Literary," *OCD*: 604–5.

[11] The standard work on cuneiform colophons is H. Hunger, *Babylonische und assyrische Kolophone* (AOAT 2; Kevaelaer: Verlag Butzon & Bercker, 1968). Other studies on authorship include W. G. Lambert, "Ancestors, Authors, and Canonicity," *JCS* 11 (1957): 1–14; idem, "Additions and Corrections," *JCS* 11 (1957): 112; idem, "A Catalogue of Texts and Authors," *JCS* 16 (1962): 59–77 (59–62); B. R. Foster, "Self Reference of an Akkadian Poet," *JAOS* 103 (1983): 123–30; idem, *Before the Muses* 1 (3d ed.; Baltimore: CDL Press, 2005), 21, and J. Wyrick, *The Ascension of Authorship* (Cambridge, Mass.: Harvard University Press, 2004), 95–7.

Code of Hammurabi" (*ANET*³, 163–180), both of whom are implied to be the "authors" of these laws in both the prologue and the epilogue.[12] In a more indirect indication of authorship, Assurbanipal claims to have learned "the craft of Adapa the sage, the hidden esoteric knowledge of the whole of the scribal art."[13]

While anonymity proved to be the general rule, there were important exceptions. The few texts to which authors are ascribed were customarily important in the literary cultures of their civilizations, and their editors sought either to honor or to ascribe them to famous heroes, especially men who were kings and sages. The "Epic of Gilgamesh" begins with a legendary account of Gilgamesh, the King of Uruk (*ANET*³, 72–99, 503–507). In positioning a legend about a famous man at the beginning, the scribal editor transforms him into the text's author. Through this means the "Legend of Naram-Sin"[14] and the "Legend of the Birth of Sargon" (*ANET*³, 119) become pseudepigraphic works. The authority of texts appears as the primary reason for assigned authorship by imputing them to famous heroes and creators of civilizations in the distant past. In Mesopotamia there were also texts where particular authors are identified, although the correctness of this claim is not verifiable. One important culture myth, an Assyrian text, is the Song of Era in which Kabti-ilāni-Marduk is identified as the author.[15]

2.3 Egyptian Literature

Egyptian scribes, who produced copies of Egyptian literary texts, beginning as early as the Twelfth Dynasty (1985–1773 BCE), created a brief form of the colophon: *jw=f pw* "it has come (to the end)" (P. Prisse II,9). A slightly extended form, found in Sinuhe (P. Berlin 3022, col. 311), "The Dialogue of a Man with his Son" (P. Berlin 3024, col. 154–155), and the "Instruction of Ptah-hotep" (P. Prisse XIX,9), reads: "it has come from its beginning unto the end even as it has been found in writing." The addition of the name of the copyist is also attested, "it has come from its beginning unto the end even as it has been found in writing when it was written by

---

[12] Cf. the Mesha Stele of Moab (*ANET*³, 320–21).

[13] M. Streck, ed., *Assurbanipal und die letzten Assyrischen Könige* II (Leipzig: J. C. Hinrichs, 1916), 256 n. 18. Also see his statement: "I understand the script of stone inscriptions from before the flood, which are difficult, obscure and confused" (see T. Bauer, *Das Inschriftenwerk Assurbanipals* Bd. II [Leipzig: Zentralantiquariat der Deutschen Demokratischen Republik, 1972], 85).

[14] B. R. Foster, "The Legend of Naram Sin," in *From Distant Days. Myths, Tales, and Poetry of Ancient Mesopotamia* (ed. idem; Bethesda, Md.: CDL Press, 1995), 171–77.

[15] *COS* 1.404–16.

the scribe N" (*Naufragé*, P. Ermitage, "Amenâa, sons of Ameny, Life, Power, Health").[16]

In addition to colophons, scribes sometimes introduced the text by the adding of a prologue in which the name and title(s) of the presumed author are given. Thus the introduction to "The Instruction of Ptah-hotep" (*ANET*[3], 413) reads:

> The Instruction of the Mayor and Vizier Ptah-hotep, under the majesty of the King of Upper and Lower Egypt: Izezi, living forever and ever. The Mayor and Vizier Ptah-hotep says: ...

Egyptian instructions usually consist of two major parts: a prologue that identifies the teacher and the occasion of its utterance (written after the instruction) and a list of teachings (earlier than the prologue) of a general nature. It is not likely that the prologue to this instruction (or any other one for that matter) and the teachings that followed were actually written by the author identified. This particular instruction (*sb3yt*) identifies the teacher as a vizier to King Izezi who reigned in the Fifth Dynasty (2494–2345 BCE), although this was likely fabricated by the unknown author, a sage, either in the late Sixth Dynasty (2345–2181 BCE) or perhaps as late as the Twelfth Dynasty.[17] The purpose of the list and its prologue was to pass down important teachings of behavior and virtue as seen at the time of their composition, which would guide young students in the necessary attributes for serving the divine king in some administrative capacity. In this instruction, the prologue contains the story of the vizier receiving the permission of his Lord to select his son as his successor and to educate him in the "ideas of the ancestors." There is, in addition, a second earlier introduction which reads:

> The Beginning of the Expression of Good Speech, spoken by the Hereditary Prince and Count, God's Father and God's Beloved, eldest son of the king, of his body, the mayor and Vizier, Ptah-hotep, in instructing the ignorant about wisdom and about the rules for good speech, as of advantage to him who will hearken and of disadvantage to him who may neglect them (*ANET*[3], 413).

It is likely that the first, more general introduction is added by a later editor and that the earlier is the second added, for it provides more precise information and reflects a greater interest in the identification of the role of the sage. While it is impossible to determine the precise authorship of the instruction, it is likely a text that was attributed to the authorship of a fa-

---

[16] See G. Lenzo Marchese, "Les colophons dans la literature égyptienne," *BIFAO* 104 (2004): 359–76.

[17] See W. Kelly Simpson, ed., *The Literature of Ancient Egypt* (New Haven, Conn.: Yale University Press, 2003), 129–48.

mous sage of the Old Kingdom to provide it authority and greater influence.

A much briefer prologue introduces the list of teachings in the "Instruction for King Meri-ka-Re." The text (Papyrus Leningrad 116A from the Eighteenth Dynasty, 1550–1295 BCE) has been reconstructed to read:

[The beginning of the instruction which the King of Upper and Lower Egypt: ... made] for his son, King Meri-ka-Re (*ANET*³, 414–415).

This text, placed in the period of the First Intermediate Period (2160–2055 BCE), an era of turmoil in Egyptian history, does reflect the difficult political and economic disasters of the time. Attributed to the last king of the Herakleopolitan Dynasty that ended by 2125 BCE, King Khety, who is presented as deceased when he instructs his son, does appear likely to have been composed during this time. Lichtheim considers the text to be pseudepigraphic, in that it was not written by this ruler, but it does appear to have been genuine in the sense of its composition during the time of his reign.[18] A piece of political propaganda, the instruction provides counsel to the new king at the time of his coronation on how to rule the kingdom wisely and well in order to bring about cosmic harmony and political order.[19] Thus, the authority of the instruction is increased by attributing it to a dead king, who now is transformed into Osiris, the ruler of the underworld, and it justifies the actions of the king to secure stability by indicating they are the will not just of the earthly, divine ruler, but also of the ruler of the land of the dead.[20]

A similar royal testament is "The Instruction of King Amen-em-het," the first ruler of the Twelfth Dynasty (1985–1956 BCE).[21] The best copy is preserved in Papyrus Millingen of the Eighteenth Dynasty, although this manuscript, while copied, was eventually lost. This royal "author" or teacher is also presented as deceased. The recipient of the instruction is Senusert I (1971–1928 BCE) at the time he "appeared as a God," likely his coronation. In this text, the dead king relates the events that led to his as-

---

[18] M. Lichtheim, "Royal Instructions," *COS* 1.61.

[19] See A. Schaff, *Der historische Abschnitt der Lehre für König Merikarê* (SBAW 8; München: Beck, 1936).

[20] For the political nature of the text, see A. Volten, *Zwei altägyptische Schriften* (AAeg 4; Copenhagen: Einar Munksgaard, 1945), and S. Herrmann, *Untersuchungen zur Überlieferungsgestalt Mittelägyptischer Literaturwerke* (Deutsche Akademie der Wissenschaften zu Berlin Institut für Orientforschung 33; Berlin: Akademie, 1957).

[21] The authority of this text also is enhanced by its coming from the dead father, now reigning as Osiris, king of the underworld, and it too legitimates the decisions made by the new ruler to re-establish order in the kingdom of Maat. See especially W. Helck, *Der Text der Lehre Amenemhets I. für seinen Sohn* (2d ed.; Kleine Ägyptische Texte 1; Wiesbaden: Harrassowitz, 1988).

sassination, thus leading to the warning to the successor that he not trust any court official and that he eliminate any who oppose his rule. This theme of regicide is unique in Egyptian literature. The period to which the text is attributed, the early Twelfth Dynasty, follows the end of the disastrous First Intermediate Period. The content of this instruction well fits this period, which causes Lichtheim to argue that the new ruler commissioned the writing of this text to a court scribe for reasons of authorizing and legitimating his rule and the various decisions he made to secure political and social order.[22]

Also from the Middle Kingdom, the stele of Sehetepibre from the Twelfth Dynasty has an instruction with a very brief prologue that introduces a pseudonymous instruction, since its engraving on the stele of this sage suggests he is the author. This sage had been a high official under two kings: Sesostris III and Amenemhet III. Two manuscripts, which are longer, are also known that date from the Eighteenth Dynasty of the Ramesside period. The instruction is written to extol the divine king as Horus who sits on the throne of Egypt and hence is usually regarded as one of the "loyalist instructions."[23]

The beginning of the teaching which he made for his children: I have something important to say; I shall have you hear it, and I shall let you know it: the design for eternity, a way / of life as it should be and of passing a lifetime at peace.[24]

According to Loprieno, the Loyalist Instructions point to the "complicity between author and reader which characterizes fictionality." These include three semantic neutralizations of spheres which could be conflictual: anonymity, loyalty to either god or king (or understood as both), and the contrast between a successful life and surviving death. The first is illustrated by the fact that the "author" of this particular instruction composing an *encomion* of loyalty to the king makes use at times of materials borrowed from the vizier Mentuhotep who lived a century earlier. This problem disappears in the New Kingdom copies which make no mention of any author. The second is expressive of the beginning of the desire for a more personal relationship with the god (*ntr*) who is not named. The third is the effort to remove the tension between success in life with the hope for an afterlife. Moral and virtuous behavior is now required for the transition to the West and not simply mortuary preparations and religion.[25]

---

[22] M. Lichtheim, "Amenemhet," *COS* 1.66.

[23] See Simpson, *The Literature of Ancient Egypt* (see n. 17), 172–77, and A. Loprieno, "Loyalistic Instructions," in *Ancient Egyptian Literature: History and Forms* (ed. idem; Leiden: Brill, 1996), 403–14.

[24] Simpson, ibid., 173.

[25] Loprieno, "Loyalistic Instructions" (see n. 23), 405–12.

In the New Kingdom (1550–1295 BCE), "The Instruction of Any"[26] has a brief Prologue that is preserved on a tablet in the Berlin Museum (No. 8934):

> Beginning of the educational instruction made by the Scribe Any of the Palace of Queen Nefertari.[27]

The content of this text, attributed to a minor scribe in the kingdom, suggests this date offers two innovations, according to Lichtheim: it is directed, not to the aristocracy, but to the "middle class," and the debate between the father and son in which the latter complains the former's teaching is too complex to understand. Even so, the father is presented as prevailing in the argument. The text is given to instruct students who hope to enter the royal bureaucracy.

The "Instruction of Amenemope," composed sometime during the Ramesside period (1295–1069 BCE), is also a text that speaks to students anticipating becoming minor officials in the royal administration. The ideal person, "the silent man," is content with being a person of humble circumstances, having a modest position and few possessions.[28] Well known among biblical scholars due to the editor of the collection in 22.17–24.22, "The Sayings of the Wise," who knows and uses this text, this instruction contains lines that at times exhibit parallelism and are placed into lines of bicola, tricola, and quintrains. In addition, the instructions are grouped into thirty chapters. The Prologue is rather lengthy, for it includes not only the names and offices of the teacher and his student, but also their duties and the nature of the content of the instruction that follows.

> Beginning of the teaching for life,
> The instructions for well-being,
> Every rule for relations with elders,
> For conduct toward magistrates;
> Knowing how to answer one who speaks,
> To reply to one who sends a message.
> So as to direct him on the paths of life,
> To make him prosper upon earth;
> To let his heart enter its shrine,
> Steering clear of evil;
> To save him from the mouth of strangers,
> To let (him) be praised in the mouth of people.
> Made by the overseer of fields, experienced in his office,
> The offspring of a scribe of Egypt,

---

[26] See Lichtheim, *COS* 1.110–15. The single manuscript preserving this instruction is Papyrus Boulaq 4 of the Cairo Museum.

[27] Queen Ahmes-Nefertari was the wife of King Ahmose.

[28] See M. Lichtheim, "The Instruction of Amenemope," *COS* 1.115–22. This text is preserved in its entirety in the British Museum Papyrus 10474.

The overseer of grains who controls the measure,
Who sets the harvest-dues for his lord,
Who registers the islands of new land,
In the great name of his majesty,
Who records the markers on the borders of fields,
Who acts for the king in his listing of taxes,
Who makes the land-register of Egypt;
The scribe who determines the offerings for all the gods.
Who gives land-leases to the people,
The overseer of grains, [provider of] foods,
Who supplies the granary with grains;
The truly silent in this of Ta-wer,
The justified in Ipu,
Who owns a tomb on the west of Senu,
Who has a chapel at Abydos,
Amenemope, the son of Kanakht,
The justified in Ta-wer.
[For] his son, the youngest of his children,
The smallest of his family,
The devotee of Min-Kamutef,
The water-pourer of Wennofer,
Who places Horus on his father's throne,
Who guards him in his noble shrine,
Who ...
The guardian of the mother of god,
Inspector of the black cattle of the terrace of Min,
Who protects Min in his shrine,
Hor-em-maakher is his true name,
The child of a nobleman of Ipu,
The son of the sistrum-player of Shu and Tefnut,
And chief songstress of Horus, Tawosre.[29]

While it is possible this instruction is pseudonymous, the details of this prologue are such that it is also feasible that the identities of its author and editor, Amenemope, as well as the scribe, his son, who receives the teaching, are historical.

Finally, the prologue to "The Instruction of 'Ankhsheshonqi" (fifth to the third century BCE),[30] composed in Demotic, has a narrative prologue and conclusion, which is reminiscent of the West Semitic text, "The Instruction of Ahiqar." The author is identified as a priest of the sun god Re in his temple at Heliopolis. According to the prologue, 'Ankhsheshonqi was imprisoned because of his failure to report a plot to assassinate the king. The question of the veracity of this ascription or its pseudonymity

---

[29] Lichtheim, *COS* 1.116.

[30] Eadem, *Ancient Egyptian Literature III: The Late Period* (Berkeley, Calif.: University of California Press, 1980), 159–84. The manuscript is British Museum Papyrus 10508. The state of this instruction is rather fragmentary in many places.

cannot be answered. However, the narrative, probably added later, suggests it is a pseudonymous instruction.

While not every instruction in ancient Egypt is clearly pseudonymous, many obviously are. The prologues range from very brief introductions to more extended ones, concluding with the narrative of 'Ankhsheshonqi. One may conclude that pseudonymity is a frequent characteristic of Egyptian wisdom instructions in order to provide additional authority and legitimacy to the teachings.

2.4 Pseudonymity and Wisdom Texts in Ancient Egypt

Composers of texts in the ancient Near East, which are anonymous, generally have been understood not to be important as individuals with unique insights and understandings that differentiated them from others. However, some of the revered sages of the past are known and remembered through the centuries as those who are said to have offered understandings of virtue, politics, life and death, and the cosmos that were insightful and even authoritative. These sages, to some of whom classical instructions were attributed, were famous for their wisdom in the cultural periods in which they lived and taught. Thus pseudepigraphic wisdom writings were attributed to them. The text, "In Praise of Learned Scribes" ($ANET^3$, 431–432), written ca. 1300 BCE, glorifies prominent sages of the past whose writings provided them immortality. Eight are mentioned in this text, five and perhaps six of whom have wisdom instructions, which are attributed to them. Four of these are depicted on the wall of the chapel of a Ramesside tomb at Saqqara. These scribes were honored through the collective memory of their social class who carried on their work largely under the veil of anonymity. The ones listed are:

1. Hor-dedef
2. Ii-em-hotep
3. Neferti
4. Khety
5. Ptah-em-Djedhuti (= Djed-Djehuti?)
6. Kha-kheper-(Re)-seneb
7. Ptah-hotep
8. Kairis

The best case for the identification of an historical figure who delivers an instruction is Amenemope. The others are anonymous, pseudonymous, and pseudepigraphic instructions from the Early Bronze Age to the Hellenistic period. In addition to those already mentioned, these include the following instructions: "The Instruction of Prince Hordjedef" (Fifth Dynasty, BCE), "The Instruction for Kagemni" (late Old Kingdom), "The Instruction of a Man for His Son" (1985–1773 BCE), "The Instruction of Kheti, the Son of

Duauf" (between 2150 and 1750 BCE), the "Discourses of Sisobek" (Middle Kingdom), the "Instruction of Amennakhte" (New Kingdom), and the "Teaching of Pordjel" (the Ptolemaic period). Other genres that include names of pseudonymous or pseudepigraphic composers are the disputation/dialogue and the lament: "The Admonitions of an Egyptian Sage" (or "Ipuwer"; ca. 2000 BCE) and the "Lament of Khakheperre-sonbe" (ca. 1950 BCE).[31] Imhotep was a legendary sage, physician, priest, architect, and eventually worshipped as a god who is said to have composed several wisdom texts (e.g., see $ANET^3$, 432), although no text survives bearing his name.

2.5 *Authorship in the Cuneiform Wisdom Tradition*

The cuneiform tradition also has important examples of sapiential texts, which name the authors/recipients. However, others are anonymous. Generations of scribes and storytellers participated in the shaping of a final form of a text. Thus, it is senseless in most cases to speak of an original author who is not mentioned.[32] Even so, it is clear that the famous ancestors of scribes are well known in tradition and are said to have produced texts, which their scribal "descendants" have passed down. These ancestral names, much like modern surnames, are the attempts to link scribes with the famous sages of the past. Thus, they are much like family names. This concern with authorship begins as early as the Cassite period and continues into Parthian times. The naming of authors was the attempt to add authority and legitimacy to the text and its teaching. The Cassite period was the epoch in which the major cultural works of Akkadian literature obtained the form housed and later discovered in the great libraries. The use of ancestral names pointed to scribes who held positions at court and functioned in the temple, thus indicating that scribes lived with the families whose educated elders taught them their trades. Thus, one may speak of tribal families living in the major cities. There are also colophons that point to the belief that divine knowledge revealed to the antediluvian sages led to

---

[31] For translations, see J. B. Pritchard, *Ancient Near Eastern Texts* (3d ed.; Princeton, N.J.: Princeton University Press, 1969 = $ANET^3$); G. Burkard et al., eds., *Texte aus der Umwelt des Alten Testaments* 3. *Weisheitstexte* 2 (Gütersloh: Gerd Mohn, 1991) = *TUAT*; M. Lichtheim, *Ancient Egyptian Literature* (3 vols.; Berkeley, Calif.: University of California Press, 1973.1976.1980), and eadem, *Egyptian Wisdom Literature in the International Context* (OBO 52; Göttingen: Vandenhoeck & Ruprecht, 1983); H. Brunner, *Die Weisheitsbücher der Ägypter: Lehren für das Leben* (Zürich: Artimus & Winkler, 1998); Simpson, *The Literature of Ancient Egypt* (see n. 17), and *COS* 1.110–24; 483–97; 561–93.

[32] Lambert, "Ancestors, Authors, and Canonicity" (see n. 11), 1.

the canonical texts of Babylonian culture, a point that supports this civilization's understanding of canonicity (cf. Berossus).[33]

The Assyrian "Catalogue of Texts and Authors" (1000–650 BCE) from the library of Assurbanipal mentions authors by using the phrase *ša pî* ("from the mouth of") or "from the mouth of Ea" (the Babylonian god of wisdom) or "from the mouth" of a particular editor. Four categories of authors are identified in this list:

1. Ea,
2. legendary heroes, particularly primeval sages: (Oannes-)Adapa, Enmerkar, a king and sage, Kabti-ilāni-Marduk, Enmedugga, and Lu-Nanna,
3. scholars (*ummânu*) whose family origin (ancestry) is not indicated: Pappatum, Taqīša-Gula, Bullutsa-rabi, Sin-liqi-unninni, Enlil-ibni, and Ur-Nanna. They usually bear the titles of either lamentation-priest or magician.
4. and men who are the "son" of an ancestor and bear the titles of magician, or lamentation-priest, or haruspex. Those with legible names are Andullu, Enlil-bān-kudurri, Gimil-Gula, Ekurdumununna, Ibni-Marduk, and Gimil-Nanai. Rīmūt-Gula was either the author or the ancestor of the one said to have produced the text. The city in which they were active, if legible, is mentioned: Babylon and Eridu. In this final category, it is clear that the human scribe is identified as the author of a text. There is no reason to doubt the authenticity of the authorship of the fourth group.

The third category of men who are authors is difficult to assess critically. According to Lambert, it is unlikely that the information concerning this group is historical, although there could be some degree of factuality in this list. The references to the authorship of the famous prediluvian sages in the second category who passed down their revealed wisdom is the stuff of legendary invention similar to the presentation of Ea as an author coming from a mythological world view.[34] Thus pseudepigraphy and pseudonymity, especially in regard to sages, do occur on occasion in this literature and possibly some texts even carry the names of sages who wrote them. However, the factuality of authors mentioned actually composing preserved texts is rare.

Sapiential texts are found in a variety of genres. They include the Sumerian text, "The Instructions of Shuruppak" (earliest version ca. 2500 BCE), the disputation: "The Babylonian Theodicy" (Cassite period; an acrostic that contains the name of the author: "I, Saggil-kīnam-ubbib, the incantation priest, am adorant of the god and the king"); the psalm/poem: "The Šamaš Hymn" (perhaps Middle Babylonian, this text has an Assurbanipal colophon published in Streck, VAB VI.358; *BWL*, 121–138), and "The Poem of the Righteous Sufferer" (*Ludlul bēl nēmeqi*, Cassite period; written by Šubši-mešrê-Šakkan, who refers to himself in a dream in the

---

[33] Ibid., 1–14.
[34] See idem, "A Catalogue of Texts and Authors" (see n. 11), 59–77.

third person; *BWL*, 20–62).³⁵ In the Sumerian King List, Enmeduranki, a king who reigned "before the Flood," was said to have received divine secrets before his ascension (thus mantic wisdom) and was described as the recipient of the gift of divination and the tablet of the gods in a text published by Lambert.³⁶ Ahiqar's sayings are attached to a legend about a famous sage who was said to hail from Assyria, although Aram is the place of origins for both parts of the text, the prose narrative and the instructions (*ANET*³, 427–430; see Tob 1:21–22; 2:10, 11, 19; 14:10).³⁷ A Neo-Babylonian list of Assyrian kings and their chief counselors add the reference to Aba-enlil-dari, wrongly called the *umânnu* of Esarhaddon, who the Aramaeans call Aḫuqar. The legend, which proceeds the sayings, indicates the well known sage served at the courts of Sennacherib and Esarhaddon. The sayings (8th century BCE, written in a general Aramaic script of southern Syria) do not mention Ahiqar, indicating that the tradition of his authorship of the sayings derives only from the later narrative (6th century BCE, imperial Aramaic). Kottsieper contends the narrative consists of two different stories eventually brought together. The court story refers to him as a "wise scribe" who was father and counselor either to all Assyria or to its army, while the original introduction presents him as a counselor of the king. The combined introductions tell of the sage's betrayal by his nephew, Nadin, who falsely accuses him of participation in a royal assassination plot. Eventually he was restored to the king's good graces, while the evil nephew received what he deserved.

---

³⁵ See Foster, "Self-Reference of an Akkadian Poet" (see n. 11), 123–30. He indicates there are four means of self-reference that may be distinguished in this text: "the poet either refers to himself by name or selects words or particles that linguistically refer to the speaker"; 'distancing' in which the poet uses "second and third person to refer to the first person speaker"; "the speaker's choice of verb forms, the temporality or activity of which are intended to point to him"; and "poetic devices invigorated by the author so that they extend and refine his self-reference beyond sing worlds to include whole passages." A possible fifth means is "the relationship between the form of the text and the author's self-reference," in this case the hymn (123).

³⁶ T. Jacobsen, *The Sumerian Kinglist* (Chicago: University of Chicago Press, 1966). For the full text of Enmeduranki, see W. G. Lambert, "Enmeduranki and Related Matters," *JCS* 21 (1967): 126–38. For a discussion of mantic sages in Mesopotamia and Israel, see my essay, "The Mantic Sage," in *The Contribution of the Dead Sea Scrolls towards Understanding Prophecy in the Hebrew Bible* (from the proceedings of the Edinburgh DSS and HB seminar; eds. A. Lange and K. De Troyer; Peeters, forthcoming, 2009).

³⁷ See now the essay by I. Kottsieper, "The Aramaic Tradition: Ahikar," in *Scribes, Sages, and Seers. The Sage in the Eastern Mediterranean World* (ed. L. G. Perdue; FRLANT 219; Göttingen: Vandenhoeck & Ruprecht, 2008), 109–24.

3. Pseudonymity and Pseudepigraphy in the Old Testament

The identification of authors of some canonical texts of the Old Testament was not perceived to be important, while it is in others. The actual composers, editors, and copyists were usually hidden in the social class of scribes and sages who carried out their work largely under the veil of anonymity. In the Bible, Ben Sira is the first to identify himself as its author (Sir 50:27; cf. the Prologue of his grandson). His is the one book whose authorship can be attested historically.

In Israel and Judah Solomon and David are associated especially with a particular genre or set of genres: apocalyptic, proverbs, lists, songs, and psalms. The prophetic texts include sections that may be considered to be in most cases brief speeches uttered by an historical figure, the additions of later prophetic sayings by unidentified spokesmen, and the insertions of edited materials. The Book of Isaiah for example may include some texts from a figure of this name, as well as oracles and texts by unnamed prophets, including those found in Second- and Trito-Isaiah. In addition, scribes also inserted edited information and viewpoints.

In the Old Testament, more than half of the books lack any mention or attribution of authorship. Spurious attributions include Deuteronomy ascribed to Moses, who by implication became the author of the entire Pentateuch. The discovery of the "Book of the Torah" in 2 Kgs 22–23 is a likely explanation given by the Deuteronomistic History for the origin of the Book of Deuteronomy, thus providing it a secondary form of legitimacy.[38]

Comparable to the cuneiform colophons are the superscriptions of many of the psalms. David (73), Solomon (2), and Moses (1) are attributed spuriously authorship of various psalms, while Asaph (12), Heman the Ezrahite (1), and Ethan the Ezrahite (1), perhaps singers or choir directors, are also mentioned.[39] More than half of the psalms have the *superscription* לדויד ("for/to David"), possibly an attribution of authorship (*lamed auctoris*) or an expression of dedication. Fourteen even have the appearance of biographical allusions.[40] In 11QPs[a], col. XXVII,2–11 David is presented as the writer of 3600 psalms, 364 songs to sing before the altar, 52 songs for the Sabbath offering, 30 for the offering of the New Moons for the solemn assemblies and the Day of Atonement, 446 he spoke, and 4 for making music over the stricken. Altogether there were 4050 songs associated with David, they were spoken "through prophecy," thus enhancing the authority

---

[38] See, for example, van der Toorn, *Scribal Culture and the Making of the Hebrew Bible* (see n. 7), 27–36.

[39] Wyrick, *The Ascension of Authorship* (see n. 11), 93–102.

[40] Davies, "Spurious Attribution in the Hebrew Bible" (see n. 8), 269.

of this already famous ruler. This text mentioning "David's Compositions" describes his psalm-composing as an act of sapiential/scribal prophecy. In the Septuagint psalms, more biographical psalm headings are provided and some compositions (Pss 145–148) are attributed to Haggai and Zechariah, while Psalm 64 has the names Jeremiah and Ezekiel. In the Tanakh Solomon is represented as the author of Proverbs, Canticles, Qoheleth, and Wisdom. In Proverbs he is mentioned in 1:1, 10:2, 25:1, and in the Song of Songs, Solomon is the author (1:1) and sometimes mentioned in the text. The Prologue in Qoheleth indirectly refers to Solomon ("The words of Qoheleth, the son of David, king in Jerusalem") and 2:7–9 alludes to him. Daniel, a famous sage of antiquity (Ezek 14:14), is written some time following the victory of the Maccabean revolt (164 BCE) and attributed to this ancient hero of antiquity (Hebrew Daniel = Ezek 14:14, Dan'el in Ugarit). Only chs. 7–12 are attributed specifically to Daniel, thus comprising a pseudonymous text of apocalyptic visions belonging to the Hellenistic era.

Among the prophets nine have superscriptions bearing their dates and names: Isaiah, Jeremiah, Ezekiel, Hosea, Amos, Micah, Zephaniah, Haggai, and Zechariah. Six others have simply a name, although Malachi may be a title ("my messenger"). These are presented as the revealed words of Yahweh to the prophets. Many have been edited by scribes in order to provide information and to insert their own literary, theological, and political agenda. Prophetic books were attributed to prophets by the Chronistic writings (2 Chron 26:22, 35:25), while prophecies uttered by unknown prophets were often placed within existing prophetic books (e.g., II and III Isaiah). 2 Chron 35:25 attributes the authorship of Lamentations to Jeremiah.

Thus, in Israel and Judah anonymity is the most common feature of written texts. With the exception of Moses, the mentioned authors of specific texts are Yahweh (through prophecies), kings (David and Solomon), and sages. These factors parallel the common tradition of authorship in the ancient Near East.

3.1 Attribution of Authorship in Early Jewish Tradition

Authorship becomes a common element of Jewish literary culture in the Hellenistic and early Roman periods, when anonymity is replaced almost entirely by pseudonymity and pseudepigraphy. Texts bearing the names of well known culture heroes and seers begin to appear. A Talmudic tractate that refers to the authorship (canonical order) of the books of the Old Testament is *Baba Batra* (14b–15a), while other early examples include Josephus (*Ag. Ap.* 1.8), Ben Sirah (Prologue, 44:5, and 44–49), and Philo (*Contempl.* 3.25). The canonical categories of the writers of the (oral) Torah were followed in succession in Tractate Avot (1.1): "Moses received the law from Sinai and committed it to Joshua, and Joshua to the elders, and the elders to the prophets; and the prophets committed it to the men of the Great Assembly." Legends appearing in various early Jewish texts that speak of authorship or preservation of biblical books includes 2 Macc 2:13–15, which narrates that Judas Maccabeus collected the scrolls, lost due to the war, even as Nehemiah had done in the library that included "books about kings and prophets, writings of David and letters of kings about votive offerings." *4 Ezra* 14, following the revolt against Rome, tells of Ezra being instructed to take five men and many tablets and to depart for 40 days. A supernatural drink increases his wisdom and memory, whereupon he dictates to the five scribes the entire contents of 94 books. The 24 books of Scripture are restored along with 70 hidden ones, which are presumably those later known as the Jewish Pseudepigrapha. The Letter of Aristeas also contains the legend of 72 translators from Jerusalem who come to Alexandria by order of King Ptolemy II to translate the Books of Moses into Greek. This gives the LXX, at least the Torah, the authoritative status of the Greek translation.

4. Schools and Rhetoric[41]

4.1 Introduction

While authority and legitimacy appeared to be the two primary reasons for the false claims and attributions of authorship, there seems to be another important consideration in Graeco-Roman literature: μίμησις (*imitatio*), an important feature of rhetoric.

4.2 Paideia

Greek παιδεία infiltrated Hellenistic and Roman schools of the empires and became the primary means of influencing the cultures of the colonies brought within Alexander's and the Roman Empires. *Paideia* involves two related features: the process of education that culminates in a young man's eventually taking his place in society, and the character of the educated

---

[41] W. V. Harris, *Ancient Literacy* (Cambridge, Mass.: Harvard University Press, 1989); N. M. Kennel, *The Gymnasium of Virtue* (Chapel Hill, N.C.: University of North Carolina Press, 1995); R. Cribiore, *Writing, Teachers, and Students in Graeco-Roman Egypt* (ASP 26; Atlanta: Scholars Press, 1996); eadem, *Gymnastics of the Mind* (Princeton, N.J.: Princeton University Press, 2001), and D. Kah and P. Scholz, *Das hellenistische Gymnasion* (Wissenskultur und gesellschaftlicher Wandel 8; Oldenburg: Akademie Verlag, 2004).

person.[42] In western civilization, the "cultivated mind" was thought to enable a person to become virtuous and civilized. Schools were of three types: the gymnasium, the school of rhetoric, and the tutoring of sophists.

4.3 Gymnasia[43]

During the Hellenistic period, γυμνασία had become both schools of study and physical activity. The three stages in Greek education[44] included, first of all, teaching young boys the basic skills of reading and writing. Entrance into a secondary school was the next stage. Now students engaged in advanced language study that comprised learning to compose complicated texts and to master grammar. In addition the study of the classics began. The third stage had as its purpose the formation of the ideal person who was learned, physically fit, and virtuous. Graduates were suited for a number of different social and professional roles. Superior students in the gymnasia would often later attend *ephebeia*, which were professional schools for the education of military officers, teachers, and high ranking officials, posts that required specialized education.

The literature[45] studied in the educational curriculum of both gymnasia and schools of rhetoric, included model speeches that were to be imitated. These came from the poems of Homer, the plays of poets like Euripides, the works of Greek historians, and the declamations of especially famous orators. In addition, there were rhetorical handbooks (τέχναι or τέχναι λόγων or προγυμνάσματα) that provided students different *dicta* for learning to speak, debate, engage in dialogue, and present speeches noted for delivery, elocution, and persuasiveness.[46]

---

[42] A. Mendelson, *Secular Education in Philo of Alexandria* (Cincinnati: Hebrew Union College, 1982), 1.

[43] R. Doran, "The High Cost of a Good Education," in *Hellenism in the Land of Israel* (eds. J. J. Collins and G. E. Sterling; Christianity and Judaism in Antiquity 13; Notre Dame, Ind.: University of Notre Dame Press, 2001), 94–115. Also see M. P. Nilsson, *Die hellenistische Schule* (München: C. H. Beck, 1955); H. I. Marrou, *A History of Education in Antiquity* (New York: Sheed & Ward, 1956); C. Pélékidis, *Histoire de l'Éphebie Attique dès Origines à 31 avant Jésus Christ* (Paris: Boccard, 1962), and S. G. Miller, ed., *Arete: Ancient Writers, Papyri, and Inscriptions on the History and Ideals of Greek Athletics and Games* (3d ed.; Berkeley, Calif.: University of California Press, 2004).

[44] See R. F. Hock, "Paul and Graeco-Roman Education," *Paul in the Graeco-Roman World: A Handbook* (ed. J. P. Sampley; Harrisburg, Pa.: Trinity International, 2003).

[45] I. Worthington, ed., *A Companion to Greek Rhetoric* (Blackwells Companions to the Ancient World; Oxford: Blackwell Publishing, 2007), and R. A. Lanham, *A Handlist of Rhetorical Terms* (2d ed.; Berkeley, Calif.: University of California Press, 1991).

[46] See *Rhetorica ad Herennium* (1st century BCE; author unknown) as the earliest complete and detailed treatment of rhetoric.

4.4 Schools of Rhetoric[47]

One may trace the origins schools of rhetoric to the Classical Age in Greece. When Hellenization spread into the ancient Near East, due to the conquests of Alexander the Great, these schools began to appear with varied curricula. Unlike attendance in the gymnasia where rhetoric was also an important subject, Greek citizenship was not a requirement for participation in these schools. The best schools were located in cities, especially Rome, Athens, Antioch, Pergamum, or Alexandria, and thus required a lengthy residence.[48] Handbooks (ἑρμηνεύματα or *colloquia*) were written and shaped to set forth rules for oratory and composition.[49] Students entered rhetorical schools to study theory, speeches of great orators, the writings of famous authors, and the declamation of their teachers.[50] One way to study these texts was practice through imitation (μίμησις) of various types of declamation and their composition. Declamation was considered by the teachers in these schools to be the most important art that was to be achieved by the learned man.

4.5 Jewish Schools in Graeco-Hellenistic Alexandria

From the third century BCE, Alexandria became the primary center of Hellenistic education until its incorporation in the latter part of the first century BCE into the expanding Roman Empire. Some Jews of privilege who were citizens of the *poleis*, attended Greek gymnasia, at least until the reign of Claudius when the recognition of new citizenship for Jews became unlawful.[51] Attendance in these schools, along with participation in other aspects of Greek and Roman cultural life, including the games[52] and the theater, opened highly educated Jews, who would have had to hold the status of citizen, to a new world that was not seen as inhibiting the liberal practice of their religion. Many Jewish writings were written in Greek dur-

---

[47] G. A. Kennedy, "Historical Survey of Rhetoric," in *Handbook of Classical Rhetoric in the Hellenistic Period (330 B.C. – A.D. 400)* (ed. S. E. Porter; Leiden: Brill Academic Publishers, 2001), 18–9.

[48] T. Habinek, *Ancient Rhetoric and Oratory* (Blackwell Introductions to the Classical World; Oxford: Blackwell, 2005), 60.

[49] Cribiore, *Gymnastics of the Mind* (see n. 41), 15.

[50] Kennedy, "Historical Survey of Rhetoric" (see n. 47), 18–9.

[51] L. Robert, "Un Corpus des Inscriptions Juives," *REJ* 101 (1937): 73–86.

[52] H. A. Harris, *Greek Athletics and the Jews* (Cardiff: University of Wales Press, 1976). He notes that there is no evidence that even orthodox Jews refused to attend the games, once they presumably were established in Jerusalem in association with Jason's gymnasium. However, this is an argument from silence, since we cannot be certain this school was actually built and used by Jews. And there is no textual basis supporting his argument.

ing the Hellenistic period, and even the Torah was translated. The merging of Jewish religious ideals with the Greek world, including religion, occurred in the writings of many Hellenistic Jews.[53]

In Philo's essay, *On the Preliminary Studies*, he describes in detail Greek παιδεία and refers to its curriculum of philosophy, grammar, geometry, and music. However, philosophy ranked about all other disciplines, receiving the honorific title of the "lawful wife" (*Prelim. Studies*, 74–76). The other disciplines were her "handmaidens." The areas of philosophy which were studied included ethics and physics (especially cosmology).[54] Philo also refers to the ἐγκύκλιος παιδεία ("rounded education") in *Spec.* 2,230, *Prov.* 2,44–46, and *Congr.* 74–76, which included education of the elite Jewish students in both the humanities and the sciences.[55] Philo also speaks of "Sabbath schools" where the general population was taught a variety of virtues: good sense, temperance, courage, justice, and so on (*Spec.* 2,62). He notes, in addition, that Sabbath schools are in the thousands in every city (*Mos.* 2,216). These were likely attached to synagogues. Indeed, the people devoted their Sabbaths to study to improve their character and to examine their consciences (*Opif.* 128). He notes in *Spec.* 2,63–64 that the faithful on the Sabbath study both duty to God and duty to others. Thus, it may be that the population who was literate studied on the Sabbath, examining ethics in particular.[56]

5. Rhetoric[57]

5.1 Introduction

Rhetoric was a key component of Graeco-Roman education. The teachers of rhetoric were normally sophists, philosophers, and school instructors. The art of rhetoric was a much desired skill in many arenas of life, especially among the wealthy (see the treatise on public speaking by Dio Chrysostom, *Dic. exercit.* [= *Or.* 18]).[58] The sophists especially placed rhetoric

---

[53] See V. Tcherikover, *Hellenistic Civilization and the Jews* (New York: Athenaeum, 1970), 352.

[54] Kah and Scholz, *Das hellenistische Gymnasion* (see n. 41).

[55] J. M. G. Barclay, *Jews in the Mediterranean Diaspora from Alexander to Trajan (323 BCE – 117 CE)* (Edinburgh: T&T Clark, 1996), 161.

[56] Josephus claims he studied the major Jewish schools (Pharisees, Sadducees, and Essenes) and was instructed by the desert hermit, Bannus.

[57] See Kennedy, "Historical Survey of Rhetoric" (see n. 47), 3–41.

[58] Important works on rhetoric include D. L. Clark, *Rhetoric in Graeco-Roman Education* (New York: Columbia University Press, 1957); G. A. Kennedy, *The Art of Persuasion in Greece* (Princeton, N.J.: Princeton University Press, 1963), and T. Cole,

at the center of *paideia*. Indeed, it was viewed as the culmination of the *enkyklios paideia*.[59] Rhetoric became a necessary skill of teachers and philosophers in their arguments about a variety of issues in trying to convince their audiences of the truthfulness of their position.

5.2 Rhetoric and Mimesis: Imitation of Literary Models[60]

In Greek gymnasia and schools of rhetoric, one technique of learning declamation is by imitating the style, literary techniques, and treatment of subjects in the great poets, historians, and philosophers. Even more importantly, students were especially encouraged to imitate the literary style of their teachers.[61] These impersonations provided not only proper literary and ethical models, but also the opportunity to develop a figure's arguments presented in his speech. While plagiarism was roundly condemned in Graeco-Roman literature, the imitation of earlier writers was a normal and acceptable practice.[62]

Exercises of impersonation (μίμησις, ἠθοποιία, and *imitatio*) and praise (ἐγκώμιον) were common, then, in the teaching and learning of rhetoric.[63] The first, impersonation, involved the practice of studying and memorizing declamations that prepared students to assume the roles of mythological, heroic, or literary figures. These exercises encouraged students to use their imaginations and skills to develop the arguments of the figures within a new context. The second, ἐγκώμιον, is a panegyric that praises a significant person, thing, or idea (see Aristotle, *Rhet.* 2.20, 1393a23–1394a18).[64] This was occasionally combined with the historical recounting of the past through the celebration of ancestors, gods, and cities.

The Origins of Rhetoric in Ancient Greece (Ancient Society and History; Baltimore, Md.: Johns Hopkins University Press, 1991). For rhetoric in the Wisdom of Solomon, see C. Larcher, *Études sur le Livre de la Sagesse* (EBib; Paris: J. Gabalda et Cie, 1969), 185–87.

[59] T. Morgan, *Literate Education in the Hellenistic and Roman Worlds* (Cambridge Classical Studies; Cambridge: Cambridge University Press, 1998), 190–239.

[60] According to *Rhetorica ad Herennium*, imitation is one of three methods, along with theory and practice, which enables the student to acquire the faculties of invention, arrangement, style, memory, and delivery. "Imitation stimulates us to attain, in accordance with a studied method, the effectiveness of certain models in speaking." See *Creative Imitation and Latin Literature* (eds. D. West and T. Woodman; Cambridge: Cambridge University Press, 2007), 1–16.

[61] Cribiore, *Gymnastics of the Mind* (see n. 41), 228.

[62] This distinction between imitation and plagiarism is seen, for example, in Seneca's statement that Ovid imitates Virgil "not as pilferer but as open appropriator" (*Suas* 3.7).

[63] Cribiore, *Gymnastics of the Mind* (see n. 41), 228.

[64] J. H. Freese, *Aristotle: Art of Rhetoric, Vol. XXII* (LCL 193; Cambridge, Mass.: Harvard University Press, 1926).

Among the great rhetoricians is Isocrates who lived in the first half of the fourth century BCE. His outline of the features (ἰδέαι) of rhetoric is found in 13.6–7: proper selection of the elements of rhetoric (invention), joining and ordering together "striking thoughts" (arrangement), and the clothing of these thoughts in elegant phrase (style). What is especially required of the student is the knowledge of different kinds of discourse and an imaginative mind. Rhetoric for him required the ability to expound upon "the principles of the art" of speech. An important method of instruction was the use of his own written declamations and himself as an example that his students are to imitate.[65]

One of the best treatments of Latin rhetoric is provided by Quintilian.[66] In his discussion, he emphasized *imitatio* as an important way that students learned to read and write, for learning is understood according to a prescribed standard (*Inst.* 10.2). He stresses that the imitation of literary models should lead to literary creativity.[67] While he stresses the study of the classics, he also speaks of the possibility of even making improvements. Thus, the student is to move beyond imitation to write even more creative literary works. Subsequently, artistry does not simply reside in the past, but is ever open to development in the present and the future. Creativity may be inspired by works that have preceded, but it may move toward greater artistry in new works that possess their own vitality and force. In addition, Quintilian indicates that not one model, but several should be used in a student's speeches. In his view, imitation accounts for the countless allusions found in literary works.

5.3 Rhetoric and Mimesis: Imitation of Human Models

Related to the common emphasis on the moral character of the rhetorician is the fact that *mimesis* also involves ethics. Democritus, *frg.* 39 (2.155.5), stresses that "one must either be good or imitate a good man" (ἀγαθὸν ἢ εἶναι χρεὼν ἢ μιμεῖσθαι, cf. *frg.* 79 [2.160.5f.]), "it is bad to imitate the wicked and not even to wish to imitate the good" (χαλεπὸν μιμεῖσθαι μὲν τοὺς κακούς, μηδὲ ἐθέλειν δὲ τοὺς ἀγαθούς). For Aristotle in *Ars Poetica*,[68] *mimesis* is a path to knowledge by which poets come to an under-

---

[65] See Isocrates, *Soph.* 16–18. Y. L. Too, *The Rhetoric of Identity in Isocrates: Text, Power, Pedagogy* (Cambridge: Cambridge University Press, 1995).

[66] See G. A. Kennedy, *Quintilian* (TWAS 59; New York: Twayne Publishers, 1969), 113.

[67] Compare Dionysius of Halicarnassus, *On Imitation*. See M. Heath, *Dionysius of Halicarnassus, On Imitation* (Wiesbaden: Franz Steiner Verlag, 1989).

[68] G. A. Kennedy, *Aristotle On Rhetoric: A Theory of Civic Discourse* (Oxford: Oxford University Press, 1991).

standing of the character and emotion of the human model, if they are to produce writing that is worthwhile. Horace wished to be considered among the great lyricists of ancient Greece, but to be so he had to imitate not only their poetry, but also their character. They are the models whose creative minds and moral actions are to be emulated. Thus, the writing of elegant poetry is related to virtuous living. The relation between parents and children (Euripides, *Hel.* 940f.) and between teachers and students (Xenophon, *Mem.* 1.2.3; 6.3) is also expressed in terms of the imitation of character.[69] In the *Institutio oratoria*, Quintilian rarely makes a concession to expediency, but rather emphasizes the morality of the speaker. The orator must be a good and virtuous man, thus connecting his understanding to the Stoics Cleanthes and Chrysippus who regard rhetoric as "the science of speaking rightly." Some say that "bad men also can be orators, and others, with whose view I agree, confine this name ... to the good" (*Inst.* 2.15.2).

Dionysius of Halicarnassus, a Greek teacher of rhetoric in the second half of the first century BCE, composed three volumes on imitation. He wrote in his first, partially preserved treatise, *On Imitation*, that μίμησις was the chief rule in the teaching or rhetoric, although it was necessary to chose one's models (*On Imitation* 5.36.4). In his arguments, he makes an important distinction to keep in mind. Imitation involves the inspection and study of the best models. Emulation (ζῆλος), however, is "an activity of the soul moved toward admiration of what seems fine" (*On Imitation* 5.35.6). For Dionysius imitation involves more than a literary process, for it has to do with moving beyond merely mimicking declamations to craft a more creative, literary, and evocative piece. Among the ancient writers whose literary value and virtues are worthy of imitating, he examines historians and their compositions. In writing of Thucydides, he describes the historian's notable characteristics as "recording the truth," disallowing "literary license," and "blamelessly and single-mindedly maintaining the principle of avoiding all malice and flattery." He goes on to write that these aspects "are admirable and worthy of imitation. [The most important thing of all is never to lie willingly or to defile one's own conscience]" (*Thuc.* 1.8). Elsewhere, in his *Letter to Gnapus Pompeius*, he writes that the greatest quality of an historian is "the ability ... to examine even the hidden reasons for actions and the motives of their agents, and the feelings in their hearts ..., and to reveal all the mysteries of apparent virtue and undetected vice" (*Pomp.* 6). Finally, Horace portrays the different qualities of Lucilius, which are considered to be taken as exemplary. Indeed these are considered to embody features of Horace's own life and work (*Ars*

---

[69] W. Michaelis, "μιμέομαι κτλ.," *TDNT* 4:659–70.

1.26.10–12; 3.30.13–14; *ep.* 1.19.32f.; also see Horace's portrayal of Alcaeus, *Ars* 1.32).[70]

Especially in the Greek literature of early Judaism, emphasis is placed on imitating exemplary men and God: *T. Benj.* 4.1, *T. Jos.* 3.1, and *T. Ab.* 4.3, 4.5. In 4 Macc 9:23 the eldest brother cries out to his brothers "take me as an example" (μιμήσασθέ με, ἀδελφοί), meaning it is better to die a martyr rather than transgress the law (cf. 13:9 and Dan 3:17ff.). In the *Letter of Aristeas* the good king should imitate God in dealing with his subjects 188, 210, 280, 281. In Philo, *Sacr.* 123 one is to imitate worthy physicians who do what is humanly possible even in hopeless cases or *Mos.* 1,158 where Moses set himself and his life as a model for imitation: παράδειγμα τοῖς ἐθέλουσι μιμεῖσθαι. Children do good, if they imitate their fathers (*Sacr.* 68). In *Migr.* 149 Lot refuses to imitate the better (take Abraham's advice) in order to become better. The Logos imitated the Father (*Conf.* 63), while men should imitate God: *Decal.* 111; *Leg.* 1,48, *Virt.* 168; *Spec. Laws* 4,73. Josephus writes of the imitation of the good and the wicked and their qualities in *Ant.* 5.98, 8.315, 12.203, and 17.97.

In the New Testament, Heb 11:4ff., 12:1f. point to examples of faith, although not specifically mentioning the duty of imitating them (however, see 12:2f.). For Hebrews it is not human virtue that is mentioned, but rather what is stressed is that the willingness to take up the same way of faith as the saints who have gone before is necessary to attain the promised inheritance. Finally Paul presents himself as a model: 2 Thess 3:7, 9; Phil 3:17; 1 Cor 11:1 = 4:16, and 1 Thess 1:6, while in Eph 5:1 Paul is an imitator of God.

6. The Wisdom of Solomon: Features of Greek Rhetoric

6.1 Introduction

My argument that mimesis is a major factor in the pseudonymity of Wisdom is based in part on the recognition that this writer was well familiar with Graeco-Roman rhetoric. Another factor to consider is the realization that, counting Wisdom, the wisdom corpus has four of its five books written by pseudonymous authors. The composers and editors of four of the five books of the wisdom corpus (Job, Proverbs, Qoheleth, and Wisdom) wished to identify their authors with Solomon (Proverbs, Qoheleth, and Wisdom) and, in one case, a legendary paragon of righteousness, Job (cf. Ezek 14:14). These four books were pseudonymous (Prov 1:1, Qoh 1:1),

---

[70] C. W. Macleod, "Horatian Imitatio and Odes 2.5," in *Creative Imitation and Latin Literature* (see n. 60), 89–102.

although the term Qoheleth, likely a title for "one who assembles" (teacher?), is frequently mentioned in the text itself (1:2; also see 12:9–14). Ben Sirah is the one sapiential composer who historically is known as the real author of his sapiential book (50:27; verified by his grandson in the Prologue).

6.2 Pseudonymity

While the social location of the author is not identified in Wisdom, it is possible he taught in a Jewish school of rhetoric or synagogue school.[71] His command of Hellenistic Greek, especially with a Hebraic tinge (e.g., *parallelismus membrorum* and a variety of Hebraisms), his knowledge of Greek rhetoric, and his awareness of certain philosophical teachings, including in particular those of Stoicism, suggest a well educated rhetor or teacher providing instruction in a Hellenistic Jewish school or to youth of Jewish families of privilege (cf. Philo, *Spec.* 2,62; and *Mos.* 2,16).[72] The question of where the rhetor who composed Wisdom would have received his education in Hellenistic culture and Jewish religion may be answered by the suggestion that he likely attended both a Greek school of rhetoric and a Jewish "house of study," which would have been attached to an Alexandrian synagogue.[73]

While the author of the Wisdom of Solomon pseudonymously identifies himself as King Solomon in 9:8 (cf. 7–9), he does not do so to attempt to deceive his audience. His own name, historical context, and social class are not known. The book is generally attributed to an anonymous Jewish sage, living in Alexandria of Egypt,[74] who wrote his text in Greek[75] sometime between the first century BCE and 40 CE, that is, from the end of the Ptolemaic period to the early period of the Roman rule of Egypt.[76] His

---

[71] For this date, see M. Kolarcik, *The Book of Wisdom* (NIB 5; Nashville: Abingdon Press, 1997), 438–40.

[72] See D. Winston, *The Wisdom of Solomon* (AB 43; Garden City, N.Y.: Doubleday, 1979), 14–63.

[73] See J. J. Collins, *Jewish Wisdom in the Hellenistic Age* (OTL; Louisville, Ky.: Westminster John Knox, 1997), 150–57. Otherwise, he would at least have listened to lectures by a sophist who instructed him in a variety of subjects, including popular renditions of current philosophies.

[74] The lengthy narrative on the exodus and the polemic against idolatry and animal worship strongly suggest an Egyptian origin.

[75] The best critical Greek text is that of J. Ziegler, *Sapientia Salomonis* (Göttingen Septuagint 12/1; Göttingen: Vandenhoeck & Ruprecht, 1962).

[76] The earliest references to the Wisdom of Solomon are those of Irenaeus (140–202 CE; *Haer.* 3.4, 7.5), Clement of Alexandria (175–230 CE), and the Muratorian Fragment (180–190 CE) that includes it within the New Testament canon. In addition, the similarities of Wisdom to Philo (20–50 CE) also suggest a common date. Winston points to the

mastery of rhetoric indicates that he merges traditional Jewish salvation history and creation theology with Hellenistic literary forms to create a text that suggests what Solomon in this new historical and social setting would say to his fellow Jews. The historical setting of his speech of exhortation (λόγος προτρεπτικός)[77] may have been the pogrom of Flaccus in 38 CE, due to the indications of persecution and opposition throughout the writing.[78] By adopting the name of Solomon, the writer allows the dead king to address an audience of Jews in a new context. Assuming the role of the wise and noble King Solomon, the rhetor gives reign to his imagination in order to encounter the life and thought of one of the most revered figures in Jewish tradition. He even enters into the mind, voice, and life of Solomon at a time when the famous ruler of the hoary past has excelled in his education that has prepared him to rule justly and well (chs. 7–9).

The author, who also served as an apologist of Judaism, drew from Greek philosophy, popularly understood, to compose his text: the Stoic understanding of the Logos and the four cardinal virtues as well as the Platonic teaching of the immortality of the soul and the corruptibility of the flesh that impeded the practice of the moral life. He also admired Greek philosophical religion in rejecting idols, although he chastises philosophers for having failed to recognize the creator in the beauty and order of the world. Thus, in his composition the pseudonymous author suggests an appropriate accommodation to Hellenistic culture, but not complete acculturation.[79] The use of the name Solomon adds legitimacy to his views.

---

early first century CE as the period of composition on the basis of the occurrence of numerous Greek words and phrases that do not appear before this period (*The Wisdom of Solomon* [see n. 72], 12–25).

[77] Winston, ibid., 18–20, and J. M. Reese, *Hellenistic Influence on the Book of Wisdom and its Consequences* (AnBib 41; Rome: Pontifical Biblical Institute, 1970), 117–18.

[78] See my essay, "Rhetoric and the Art of Persuasion in the Wisdom of Solomon," in *The New Testament in its Hellenistic Context* (eds. S. E. Porter and A. W. Pitts; Leiden: Brill, forthcoming).

[79] Hengel uses acculturation to explain Hellenization and the Jews, and not syncretism or assimilation (M. Hengel, *Judaism and Hellenism: Studies in their Encounter in Palestine During the Early Hellenistic Period* [2d ed.; trans. J. Bowden; 2 vols.; Philadelphia: Fortress Press, 1974], 1:114).

7. Rhetoric and the Wisdom of Solomon

7.1 The Anonymous Author as Rhetor

As the formulation of rhetoric took on more precise shape, different types of rhetoric were developed: epideictic that shaped the elegant character of the literary artistry, forensic speech delivered in the courtroom, political and deliberative oratory spoken before the assembly and occasionally even larger crowds, and protreptic or persuasive speech articulated by teachers, polemicists, and sophists seeking to prove the authenticity of their teaching, to attract students and other adherents, and to prevail in an argument.

During the Roman period, rhetoric took on a greater emphasis and was highly valued as an art and skill.[80] Prior to the Caesars and even during their reigns, some rhetoric was used to oppose tyrants especially when the Principate's assumption of autocratic power led to restrictions placed on free and open debate among the Roman elite.[81] This anti-tyrannical rhetoric provided an increase in the social status of plebeians and less powerful patricians. Wisdom's criticism of pagan kings who, unlike the Jewish Solomon, disregarded justice and ruled by means of repressive power (6:1f.) fits well pro-republican criticism of despotic behavior of rulers and prefects of the empire and its kingdoms (e.g., see Cicero). However, the Jewish rhetor's tone, less than reproachful, may be a means of attempting to encourage his community to seek to persuade the prefect and other Roman officials in Alexandria and possibly elsewhere to allow Jews to assume an increased social status that might even lead to the attainment of citizenship and other privileges given to the powerful in the *polis* and the larger empire. This was an important effort undertaken by Philo in leading two Jewish embassies to Rome, first to speak with Caligula and then with Claudius. These efforts led finally to the decision of Claudius that, while the Jews were not allowed to have Alexandrian citizenship, their ancestral religious customs should be permitted as they had been during the reign of Augustus. While the Jews could enjoy the rights not to have their synagogues desecrated and not to be forced to participate in pagan customs

---

[80] Tacitus contended that the health of the Roman state was directly related to the wisdom and the persuasive abilities of highly intelligent speakers (*Dial.*). This is not a call to *libertas*, but rather an exhortation to reject the decisions being made by "an ignorant multitude" and to establish a hierarchy of one or more gifted orators who maintain the social structure that culminates in the elitism of the wealthy and highly educated (cf. Habinek, *Ancient Rhetoric and Oratory* [see n. 48], 12–3).

[81] Ibid., 11–2. This is especially noticed in the orations of Cicero, a defender of the Republic, who attacked the despotism of some of the Roman elite, including Marc Anthony whom he accused of being despotic and "un-Roman."

that violated their religious sensibilities, they also were not allowed to participate in the *gymnasia*, which was open only to Greek citizens.

Speaking imaginatively as the long dead Solomon (cf. chs. 7–9), the rhetor addresses the "judges of the earth" and kings (1:1, 6:1), likely only a rhetorical device, and yet it was possible for rhetors who represented constituencies to address public assemblies, either gathered for open lectures, or to make a presentation in the prefect's court.[82] Pretence as a feature of his oration would have allowed him, as Solomon, to address orally an audience in a Jewish assembly by feigning a public of judges and prefects.

7.2 Rhetoric and Rhetorical Forms in the Wisdom of Solomon[83]

The author of Wisdom knows numerous rhetorical features, which he uses throughout his *protreptic*. This is especially clear when he enters into the mind of the young Solomon who aspires to obtain from Wisdom eloquence beyond mere ornamentation (8:8c, 12). While the rhetor places emphasis on a popular understanding of classical philosophy and Hebrew texts, he also allows for improvements to the literary artistry of traditional Solomonic texts, something that Hellenistic Greek offered as a possibility. Thus, those who listen to and study his text would be encouraged to move beyond imitation to write even more creative literary works. Artistry does not reside in the past, in this case the presumed writings of a long dead Solomon, but is ever open to development in the present and the future.

Examples of his ability to compose clearly, to proceed logically, to make transitions smoothly from one topic to the next, to return to his main subject after a series of digressions, to provide appropriate answers to his questions, to balance gracefully words and phrases, and to make use of engaging images are found in such texts as 4:3–5; 5:9–12, 13; 7:9–10, and 17:18–19.[84]

Perhaps the most noticeable feature of the Greek literary influence on the book is its overarching structure that combines προτρεπτικός ("hortatory"), ἐπιδεικτικτός ("declamation, exhibition, display"), and ἐγκώμιον ("praise, eulogy, panegyric").[85] The term πανηγυρικός ("for an

---

[82] See J. G. Gammie, "The Sage in Hellenistic Royal Courts," in *The Sage in Israel and the Ancient Near East* (eds. idem and L. G. Perdue; Winona Lake, Ind.: Eisenbrauns, 1990), 147–53.

[83] While the rhetor of Wisdom uses numerous Greek forms common especially to rhetorical speeches and texts, he also at times gives his own distinctive meanings to Greek vocabulary words (Larcher, *Études sur Le Livre de la Sagesse* [see n. 58], 182).

[84] Ibid., 185–87.

[85] M. Gilbert, "Wisdom Literature," in *Jewish Writings of the Second Temple. Apocrypha, Pseudepigrapha, Qumran Sectarian Writings, Philo, Josephus* (ed. M. E. Stone; CRIBT 2; Philadelphia: Fortress Press, 1984), 283–324.

assembly"; cf. LXX Ezek 46:11, Hos 2:13, 9:5, Amos 5:21)[86] refers to a formal oration, verse, or narrative of praise regarding a person, virtue, event, city, state, or deity. Thus the praise is intended to be laudatory and not critical. One occasion of this type of panegyric was the public oration given at the games in Athens in which the assembly of athletes and spectators were exhorted to emulate the examples of their esteemed "ancestors." While this exact term does not occur in Wisdom, it is suggested in both the behavior of Solomon (chs. 7–9) and the righteous (2:1–3:9). A related expression is ἐγκώμιον (see Aristotle, *Rhet.* 2.20, 1393a23–1394a18).[87] This was occasionally combined with the historical recounting of the past through the praise of ancestors, gods, and cities. The rhetor of Wisdom engages in the praise of Wisdom (6:12–16, 7:22b–8:1), including her acts of salvation of the ancestors from Adam to Moses (10:1–11:1). When he assumes and plays the role of Solomon (ἠθοποιία), he presents Solomon as engaging in a royal περιαυτολογία (self-praise, 7:1–22)[88] and as offering panegyric praise of and love for Wisdom (8:2–9:18). While self-praise is to be avoided, it is legitimate when uttered by others. It is also acceptable in one's defense of his good name or when pleading for justice to those who have defamed him. Plutarch justifies legitimate boasting to enhance one's reputation in order to achieve a greater good.[89] This would be the case with Solomon who presents himself in the text as the paragon of royal virtue and righteous rule in contrast to that of pagan kings and as a model of virtue for youth in Jewish schools to emulate.

In addition, other common forms and elements of Greek rhetoric present in this book include the δίπτυχος (diptych, "doubled, folding"; e.g., the pairing of the "skilled woodcutter" and the metal worker in gold and silver, both of whom make idols), σύγκρισις ("comparison: a comparison of opposite or contrary things"; see the contrastive pairing of the wicked and the righteous in 2:1–3:19 and the wicked enemies of Israel and the righteous Israelites in 12:19–27),[90] ἀποστροφή ("when one turns away from all oth-

---

[86] See D. A. Russell and N. G. Wilson, eds., *Menander Rhetor* (Oxford: Clarendon Press, 1981). Menander made frequent use of panegyrics in his treatises.

[87] See T. R. Lee, *Studies in the Form of Sirach 44–50* (SBLDS 75; Atlanta: Scholars Press, 1986), and B. Mack, *Wisdom and the Hebrew Epic: Ben Sira's Praise of the Fathers* (CSJH; Chicago: University of Chicago Press, 1985). Cf. Wis 10:1–11:1.

[88] Plutarch, "On Praising Oneself Inoffensively," *Mor.* 7; Dio Chrysostom, *Fifty-seventh Discourse* and Quintilian, *Inst.* 11.1.15–28. See H. D. Betz, "De Laude kipsies (*Moralia* 539A–547F)," in *Plutarch's Ethical Writings and Early Christian Literature* (ed. idem; SCHNT 4; Leiden: Brill, 1978), 367–93.

[89] See D. F. Watson, "Paul and Boasting," in *Paul in the Graeco-Roman World* (ed. J. P. Sampley; Harrisburg: Trinity International, 2003), 77–100.

[90] The *synkrisis* is a literary technique of contrasts, which in Wisdom places in opposition the features of creation that brought salvation to Israel with those that effectu-

ers to address one," in Wisdom's case the prayer uttered to God, chs. 16–18), προσωποποιία ("the putting of imaginary speeches into one's own or another's mouth," e.g., the speech of the wicked in 2:1–20),[91] εὐλογία ("praise," e.g., the praise of wisdom in 7:22–8:1),[92] συνεκδοχή ("a figure of speech in which a more comprehensive term is used for a less comprehensive one, or vice versa"), and διαίρεσις ("separation").[93] As noted earlier, the literary form of the text is the λόγος προτρεπτικός ("speech of persuasion")[94] that seeks to persuade an audience to pursue a particular course of life (e.g., Wis 6:12).[95]

Perhaps the most noticeable feature of the Greek rhetoric on the book is its overarching form that combines προτρεπτικός ("protreptic"), ἐπιδεικτικτός ("declamation, exhibition, display"), and ἐγκώμιον ("praise, eulogy, panegyric").[96] While a πανηγυρικός ("panegyric, praise at a festival") is suggested in Wisdom (e.g., 19:22), the rhetor also makes use of additional types of oratory, including the κατηγορία ("accusation"; cf., e.g., Wis 2:21–24), the ἀπολογία ("apology"; cf. the apology for the conquest of Canaan in Wis 12:3–18, and the punishment of the Egyptians in Wis 11:15–12:2), the ἐγκώμιον ("praise"; cf. Wis 7:22–8:1), and the ἐπιτάφιος (funeral oration; cf. Wis 3:1–9).[97] The identity of the wicked has been debated, but they are likely prominent Egyptians who had a Greek education, although not in a gymnasium, and appropriated a popularized, vulgar, and not altogether correct understanding of Epicureanism.[98]

---

ated disaster for the Egyptians (16:1–4, 5–14, 15–29; 17:1–18:4; 18:5–25, and 19:1–12). An earlier one occurs in 11:1–14.

[91] LSJ 1533. See the speech of the wicked in Wis 2.

[92] See the praise of Wisdom in 7:22b–8:1 and the hymn to the Lord as the cosmic warrior (5:17–23, cf. Isa 59:17).

[93] *Diaeresis* is the classification of the world of phenomena according to the dialectical principle of the separation of things that are similar and yet different. The rhetor makes use of this principle in arguing that what punishes one group benefits another (thus the plagues). See Wis 15:18–16:1.

[94] Winston, *The Wisdom of Solomon* (see n. 72), 18–20.

[95] T. C. Burgess, *Epideictic Literature* (New York: Garland Publishers, 1987), 229–30, and S. K. Stowers, *Letter Writing in Graeco-Roman Antiquity* (LEC 5; Philadelphia: Westminster, 1986), 92.

[96] Gilbert, "Wisdom Literature," in *Jewish Writings of the Second Temple* (see n. 85), 283–324.

[97] The last two mentioned are examples of epideictic oratory.

[98] Winston provides numerous citations that are similar to the pessimism of the opponents of the teacher (*The Wisdom of Solomon* [see n. 72], 115).

7.3 Solomon as a Model of Virtue

Rejecting the divine kingship of Ptolemaic kings and Roman rulers, the rhetor plays the role of Solomon (προσωποποιία). The ruler cult in Ptolemaic and Roman Alexandria serves as the background of the rhetor's speech and prayer in 7:1–9:18. In contrast to Hellenistic and Roman rulers,[99] Solomon is a mere mortal who serves as the paragon of the ideal ruler who they should imitate in their governance and behavior: "I also am a mortal (θηντός) like other humans" (7:1a). In 9:5 he confesses that he is but a "man, weak and of short duration." These texts clearly oppose the ruler cult of Ptolemaic and Roman rulers who were believed to be divine immortals, either at birth or in their *apotheosis* at death. By contrast, the human Solomon asserts, "No king has had a different beginning of existence, for there is one entrance into life and one way out" (7:5–6, cf. Philo, *QE* 2,673). His virtue and election became the means by which the legitimation of his reign occurs (9:7). His immortality, like that of the righteous man, derives from the same Wisdom's dwelling within him due to his righteousness.

The rhetor describes Solomon's praise of Wisdom (chs. 7–9) by indicating his preference for her over scepters and thrones, while claiming that her value exceeds that of gold, silver, and gems (cf. 1 Kgs 3:1–15, Prov 3:14f., 8:10f., 16:16). Wisdom is the source of wealth and all good things, grants him friendship with and knowledge of God, enables him to speak correctly and in a refined manner, provides him with unerring knowledge of all things, and teaches him both the virtues of self-control, prudence, justice, and courage, and the knowledge of divine works and commandments. Further, as his teacher and the one who dwells within him, Wisdom grants to him knowledge of the past and foreknowledge of things yet to come. This "artificer" of all things dwells within Solomon's "undefiled body," a view based on the Platonic dualism of body and soul (8:20).[100] Finally, God has chosen Solomon to be king and to judge the people, to build a temple on the holy mountain, and to construct an altar in the city of God's habitation (see Alexander's building of the temple of Isis and Ptolemies' construction of the temples of Serapis and Harpocrates). Thus, the ideal ruler is the one who is dedicated to the worship of God and hon-

---

[99] L. Cerfaux and J. Tondriau, *Un concurrent du christianisme: le culte des souverains dans la civilization gréco-romaine* (Bibliothèque de théologie 3/5; Tournai: Desclée & Cie, 1957); A. Wlosok, ed., *Römischer Kaiserkult* (Wege der Forschung 372; Darmstadt: Wissenschaftliche Buchgesellschaft, 1978); S. R. F. Price, *Rituals and Power: The Roman Imperial Cult in Asia Minor* (Cambridge: Cambridge University Press, 1984), and H.-J. Klauck, *The Religious Context of Early Christianity* (Minneapolis/St. Paul: Fortress Press, 2003), 250–330.

[100] Winston, *The Wisdom of Solomon* (see n. 72), 199.

ors his presence and temple through gifts. Finally, God has chosen Solomon (cf. 2 Sam 7 and Ps 89) to be the paragon of human virtue and to engage in righteous rule.

7.4 The Imitation of Solomon's Virtue

The trustworthiness and ethical character of the rhetor is to be revealed through the rhetor's speech, in this case represented pseudonymously as that of Solomon. Through Solomon the rhetor becomes, by means of the awakening of the imagination, both his and his audience, the virtuous model for people to imitate. In Graeco-Roman rhetoric, as noted above, impersonation was an important way to study and learn the literary and virtuous characters of declamations by allowing students to play the roles of mythological, heroic, or literary figures. These exercises encouraged students to use their imaginations and skills to develop the arguments of the figures within a particular context. The rhetor himself assumes the role of Solomon (chs. 7–9), the paragon of wisdom and the builder of the temple in Jewish history, who says his love for wisdom exceeds all else (cf. 1 Kgs 3:1–15), leading him to pray to acquire her. The virtues and benefits which Solomon enjoys are those he shares with the faithful Jews: righteousness (1:1, 15), truth (1:4), justice (3:10–13, 5:18–23), the punishment of the wicked (1:7–11, 11:15–12:2), the goodness and protection of God (1:13–14), the anticipation of divine salvation of those who persevere in righteousness and loyalty to God (4:7–19, 19:22), and immortality (1:15, 3:4, 5:15–23). Thus, the audience who hears this declamation is encouraged also to enter into the mind and life of Solomon to learn the elegance of speech and the virtues of the moral life.

8. Conclusion

8.1 Anonymity, Pseudonymity, and Pseudepigraphy in Early Judaism

Beginning in the Hellenistic period, individual authorship became customary in the Eastern Mediterranean world. Now the individual claimed his/her own recognition, often serving under wealthy people in a patronage system or in teaching in Graeco-Roman schools. At the same time a significant number of pseudepigraphic and pseudonymous writings began to appear during the third century BCE in the West. This tradition had already made its debut for two millennia in the ancient Near East. In Hellenistic Judaism a large number of pseudepigraphic texts were attributed to figures of hoary antiquity, including Enoch, Noah, Moses, Solomon, and Baruch, among others. One corpus of texts in Israel and the ancient Near East in which anonymity, pseudonymity, and pseudepigraphy played an important role was wisdom. This may have resulted from the fact that scribes were copyists and editors who developed traditions, found especially in colophons, and often attached legends, superscriptions, and epilogues.

8.2 The Wisdom of Solomon and Rhetoric

The literary character of this λόγος προτρεπτικός points to an anonymous Jewish writer who was extremely knowledgeable of Graeco-Roman rhetoric and well skilled in its application. This suggests that the author was a rhetor who had studied in a rhetorical school and who undertook to compose a declamation to the Alexandrian Jewish *gerousia*, present in an assembly in a synagogue, or to a group of students. The rhetor merged Greek rhetorical forms and moral philosophy with Jewish traditions of creation and redemptive history, in particular the plagues and the exodus, elements of Philonic mysticism, and Jewish ethics.[101] While he considers Judaism superior to the pagan religions of the Hellenists, he still uses Greek rhetoric and moral philosophy to aid in the integration of these two different cultures.[102] The primary intention of the rhetor's use of προτρεπτικός is to exhort Jews to remain steadfast in their loyalty to their traditions, ethnicity, and religious identity, especially under the duress of ridicule and abuse at the hands of their Greek and Egyptian opponents. The occasion for the address suggests it is a time of violence, in which the Jewish *politeuma* is enduring victimization for its religious and cultural difference. This xenophobic harassment that broke into intense oppression may have taken place in pogrom that received the support of the civil authorities. If so, the most likely pogram would have been the one initiated and pursued by Flaccus in 38 CE. The rhetor's hope for the future is based on his faith in the immortality of the souls of the righteous and the anticipated salvific acts of God (Wis 19:22).

8.3 Mimesis (μίμησις) as Literary Process and Moral Virtue

Imitation is an important feature of Greek and Latin rhetoric, mentioned often by Greek and Latin teachers of rhetoric. Wisdom's author is well versed in the elegance and techniques of imitation and provides his audience with a text for emulation in the enhancement of their own rhetorical skills and creative, literary writing and speaking. This text would have served well the students and social roles of Jews (teachers, jurists, politi-

---

[101] Idem, "The Sage as Mystic in the Wisdom of Solomon" in *The Sage in Israel and the Ancient Near East* (see n. 82), 383–97.

[102] For example, see J. M. Modrzejewski, *The Jews of Egypt: From Rameses II to Emperor Hadrian* (Princeton, N.J.: Princeton University Press, 1995), 67.

cians, members of the *gerousia*, and so on) who were engaged in improving their own artistic skills and rhetorical knowledge. In addition, the topic of the moral character of the rhetor was a common one in Graeco-Roman teachings on rhetoric. This combined with the use of *mimesis* in which the audience was to emulate the ethical qualities of the speaker/writer as revealed in the text. Selecting the wise Solomon of Jewish tradition as his pseudonym, the rhetor entered into the mind and life of this legendary figure of the past in order to set forth teachings in moral philosophy that should address the contemporary audience in Alexandria. These included the preference for wisdom over wealth, health, beauty, insight, the rejection of guile and resentment, worthy thoughts, knowledge and skill in crafts, love of righteousness, self-control, prudence, justice, and courage. Because of Solomon's receiving of wisdom, he shall have honor, glory, admiration, keen judgment, and wise, just, and courageous rule. Those who heard, read, and studied this text had as their model of virtue the legendary Solomon now, at least in the imagination, addressing them.

While there may be a variety of explanations for the rhetor's selection of the pseudonym of Solomon, *mimesis* is perhaps the best explanation for its occurrence in this text, not deception, the desire for wealth, placement in a school tradition, and claims of authority. Thus, the audience is to emulate the literary quality and the moral virtues of this protreptic, which is attributed by the rhetor to Solomon. This case is not an example of deceit. Rather, entering the mind and thought of the famous, wise king of the past was a literary model for people to imitate. No one would have thought Solomon was actually speaking the words in this text.

Pseudepigraphy and the Periodization of History in Jewish Apocalypses

by

KARINA MARTIN HOGAN

1. Introduction

The discussion of pseudepigraphy in the literature of Second Temple Judaism, and in particular in apocalyptic literature, has very different contours from the debate on New Testament pseudepigraphy. In large part this is because, with the exception of Daniel, the Jewish apocalypses are not canonical, so a major component of the New Testament debate (the tension between pseudonymity and canonicity) is missing from the discussion. The lower stakes may account for the relative lack of interest in the ethical dimension of apocalyptic pseudepigraphy, or at least less direct engagement with the question of whether or not the apocalypses are "forgeries" intended to deceive their audiences.[1] Thus, most recent scholarship on Jewish apocalyptic literature accepts pseudepigraphy as an "authority-conferring strategy," which may have deceived some members of its original audience, but which is so nearly ubiquitous in the apocalyptic literature that it must have been recognized as conventional within the circles that produced it.[2]

---

[1] Examples of this concern in the New Testament debate include K. D. Clarke, "The Problem of Pseudonymity in Biblical Literature and its Implications for Canon Formation," in *The Canon Debate* (eds. L. Martin McDonald and J. A. Sanders; Peabody, Mass.: Hendrickson, 2002), 440–68; E. Verhoef, "Pseudepigraphy and Canon," *BN* 106 (2001): 90–8; D. G. Meade, *Pseudonymity and Canon: An Investigation into the Relationship of Authorship and Authority in Jewish and Earliest Christian Tradition* (Grand Rapids, Mich.: Eerdmans, 1987); B. M. Metzger, "Literary Forgeries and Canonical Pseudepigrapha," *JBL* 91 (1972): 3–24. Lewis Donelson's brief but instructive summary of the "current discussion on pseudepigraphy" suggests that much of it has been pure speculation; his own work focuses on the literary techniques of pseudepigraphy. See L. R. Donelson, *Pseudepigraphy and Ethical Argument in the Pastoral Epistles* (HUT 22; Tübingen: Mohr Siebeck, 1986), 9–23.

[2] See, most recently, M. E. Stone, "Pseudepigraphy Reconsidered," *Review of Rabbinic Judaism* 9 (2006): 1–15 (9–12). This is essentially the conclusion about pseudepigraphy reached by John J. Collins in his dissertation, *The Apocalyptic Vision of the Book*

On the other hand, some influential scholars have argued that the pseudepigraphy of the Jewish apocalypses is essentially different, specifically with respect to psychological motivation, from that of early Christian and other pseudepigraphic writings. W. Speyer classified a number of Jewish apocalypses as "echte religiöse Pseudepigraphie," meaning that the actual authors experienced a type of inspiration that caused them to identify fully with figures from the past.[3] D. S. Russell similarly posited a psychological process whereby the apocalypticists identified with their pseudonyms, claiming that it involved three Hebraic tendencies that are alien to modern thought: "the idea of corporate personality, the peculiar time-consciousness of the Hebrews and the significance of the proper name in Hebrew thought."[4] While these psychological approaches to explaining apocalyptic pseudepigraphy have rightly been called into question by more recent scholars, it is worth considering in what sense the authors of apocalypses did identify with their pseudonyms. Christopher Rowland suggests that

---

of Daniel (HSM 16; Missoula, Mont.: Scholars Press, 1977), 73–4, and maintained in his more recent works; e.g., idem, *The Apocalyptic Imagination: An Introduction to Jewish Apocalyptic Literature* (2d ed.; Grand Rapids, Mich.: Eerdmans, 1998), 39–40; idem, "Pseudepigraphy and Group Formation in Second Temple Judaism," in *Pseudepigraphic Perspectives: The Apocrypha and Pseudepigrapha in Light of the Dead Sea Scrolls* (eds. E. G. Chazon and M. E. Stone; STDJ 31; Leiden: Brill, 1999), 43–58. The term "authority-conferring strategy" comes from the title of an article on Mosaic pseudepigraphy by H. Najman, "Interpretation as Primordial Writing: *Jubilees* and its Authority Conferring Strategies," *JSJ* 30 (1999): 379–410; see also eadem, *Seconding Sinai: The Development of Mosaic Discourse in Second Temple Judaism* (JSJSup 77; Leiden: Brill, 2003), 1–16, 41–69.

[3] W. Speyer, *Die literarische Fälschung im heidnischen und christlichen Altertum: Ein Versuch ihrer Deutung* (Handbuch der Altertumswissenschaft I/2; München: C. H. Beck, 1971), 150–60; idem, "Echte religiöse Pseudepigraphie," in *Pseudepigrapha I: Pseudopythagorica – Lettres de Platon – Littérature pseudépigraphique juive* (K. von Fritz, ed., Entretiens sur l'antiquité classique 18; Vandœuvres-Genève: Fondation Hardt, 1972), 333–66; idem, "Religiöse Pseudepigraphie und literarische Fälschung," in *Pseudepigraphie in der heidnischen und jüdisch-christlichen Antike* (ed. N. Brox; Wege der Forschung 484; Darmstadt: Wissenschaftliche Buchgesellschaft, 1977), 195–263.

[4] D. S. Russell, *The Method and Message of Jewish Apocalyptic, 200 BC – AD 100* (Philadelphia: Westminster, 1964), 132–39. The psychological notion of "corporate personality," developed by H. W. Robinson in *Corporate Personality in Ancient Israel* (Philadelphia: Fortress Press, 1964) has been refuted by, among others, J. W. Rogerson, "The Hebrew Conception of Corporate Personality: A Re-examination," *JTS* 21 (1970): 1–16. Similarly, the notion of "contemporaneity" developed by T. Boman in *Hebrew Thought Compared with Greek* (London: SCM, 1960), on which Russell depends, had already been called into question by James Barr in *Biblical Words for Time* (London: SCM, 1962). The third idea that Russell proposes, that by appropriating the name of someone from the past, an apocalypticist saw himself as an "extension" of that person, is purely speculative. See Meade, *Pseudonymity and Canon* (see n. 1), 6–7.

apocalyptic seers experienced their visions in the context of reflection on Scripture.[5] Presumably, they chose the pseudonyms they did because they perceived a significant similarity between their own historical situations and experiences, and those of particular biblical figures.[6]

Von Rad long ago pointed out that apocalypses tend to be attributed to wise men or scribes (e.g., Enoch, Daniel, Ezra, Baruch) and suggested that this indicates that the apocalyptic literature has its origins in wisdom circles.[7] While virtually no scholar accepts von Rad's thesis in its original form, it gave rise to an ongoing debate about the relationship of wisdom and apocalyptic literature.[8] That debate has tended to focus on the social context and function of Jewish apocalyptic literature in recent years,[9] while in the same period comparatively little attention has been paid to apocalyptic historiography.[10] Significantly, the question of the historical con-

---

[5] C. Rowland, *The Open Heaven: A Study of Apocalyptic in Judaism and Christianity* (New York: Crossroad, 1982), 214–40.

[6] While acknowledging that in many cases pseudepigraphy was a deliberate strategy to gain authority for visions, Rowland suggests that "a case can be made for some visions at least being linked with a pseudonymous author precisely because the character of the experience itself drove the visionary to the conclusion that narrating in the name of some other person was the only way in which he could do justice to the nature of the experience" (Rowland, ibid., 245). Cf. Collins, *Apocalyptic Vision* (see n. 2), 72.

[7] G. von Rad, *Old Testament Theology* (trans. D. M. G. Stalker; 2 vols.; New York: Harper & Row, 1962–1965), 2:301–15. He was arguing against the prevailing view at the time, that apocalyptic literature was a development of prophecy. Besides the identity of the pseudonymous authors as wise men or scribes rather than prophets, his main argument was that the deterministic and universal view of history in the apocalypses has more in common with the wisdom literature than with the prophetic understanding of salvation history. Von Rad expanded his treatment of the problem in the fourth edition of his *Theologie des Alten Testaments* (München: Kaiser, 1965), 2:316–38, and argued further that the apocalyptic view of "the divine determination of times" is shared by the wisdom literature, in *Wisdom in Israel* (trans. J. D. Martin; Nashville: Abingdon Press, 1978), 263–83.

[8] A classic articulation of the problem is J. J. Collins, "Wisdom, Apocalyptic and Generic Compatibility," in *In Search of Wisdom: Essays in Memory of John G. Gammie* (eds. L. Perdue et al.; Louisville: Westminster John Knox, 1993), 165–85. The most up-to-date review of the debate is in L. DiTommaso, "Apocalypses and Apocalypticism in Antiquity (Part II)," *Currents in Biblical Research* 5.3 (2007): 367–432 (374–84).

[9] See, for example, the essays collected in *Conflicted Boundaries in Wisdom and Apocalypticism* (eds. B. G. Wright III and L. M. Wills; SBLSym 35; Atlanta: Society of Biblical Literature, 2005). For a review of recent scholarship on this topic, see L. DiTommaso, "Apocalypses and Apocalypticism in Antiquity (Part I)," *Currents in Biblical Research* 5.2 (2007): 235–86 (250–65).

[10] See DiTommaso, "Apocalypses and Apocalypticism in Antiquity (Part II)" (see n. 8), 384–90. He defines "apocalyptic historiography" as "the intellectual construct characteristic to historical apocalyptica [sic] by which data about the past, present and future

sciousness of the Jewish apocalypticists has not been considered in relation to the problem of pseudonymity.[11] Rather than attempting a full discussion of apocalyptic historiography and its relationship to pseudepigraphy, this essay examines the relationship between the periodization of history in several Jewish historical apocalypses and the particular figures who were chosen to be the pseudonymous authors of those apocalypses. It argues that the scribal identity, or at least scribal activity, of these pseudonymous authors is intimately related to their historical location and their role of providing continuity and transmitting traditions between historical periods that were perceived to be discontinuous.

2. The Periodization of History in Jewish Historical Apocalypses

The periodization of history is by no means an innovation of apocalyptic literature; the biblical historians used periodization to make sense of the past (and in fact it is hard to imagine writing a history without some form of periodization).[12] The most obvious difference between biblical and apocalyptic historiography is that in the apocalyptic literature, history is presented (at least partly) prospectively, in the form of *ex eventu* prophecy. Another common element that sets the historical apocalypses apart from most biblical historiography is determinism: the belief that the course of human history, and especially the time of the end, has been set from the beginning. In a deterministic historiography, individual human figures are not so much agents whose actions influence events, as symbols that define

---

are selected and arranged" ("History and Apocalyptic Eschatology: A Reply to J. Y. Jindo," *VT* 56 [2006]: 413–18 [414]).

[11] A recent treatment of the historical consciousness of Jewish apocalyptic writers is G. W. E. Nickelsburg, "History-Writing in, and on the Basis of, Jewish Apocalyptic Literature," in *Historical Knowledge in Biblical Antiquity* (eds. J. Neusner, B. D. Chilton and W. S. Green; Blandford Forum: Deo Publishing, 2007), 79–104. Although he raises the issue of pseudepigraphy at the outset (80), Nickelsburg does not address the question I am asking: how is the choice of apocalyptic pseudonyms influenced by the apocalypticists' view of history?

[12] The periodization employed by the biblical historians is sometimes at odds with that used by modern historians of ancient Israel, however. See S. Japhet, "Periodization Between History and Ideology: The Neo-Babylonian Period in Biblical Historiography," in *Judah and the Judeans in the Neo-Babylonian Period* (eds. O. Lipschitz and J. Blenkinsopp; Winona Lake, Ind.: Eisenbrauns, 2003), 75–89; eadem, "Periodization Between History and Ideology II: Chronology and Ideology in Ezra-Nehemiah," in *Judah and the Judeans in the Persian Period* (eds. O. Lipschitz and M. Oeming; Winona Lake, Ind.: Eisenbrauns, 2006), 491–508.

the period in which they live, often by opposition to it. The particular figures with which this essay is concerned—Enoch (and Noah), Moses, Baruch, Daniel and Ezra—are exceptions to this rule, in that they bridge historical periods that are presented as discontinuous, or even opposite to one another. Before examining the various ways in which these figures fulfill a "bridging" function, it will be necessary to describe the way in which the Jewish apocalypses that are attributed to them periodize history. For this purpose, I will treat the selected apocalyptic reviews of history in the probable order of their composition: The Animal Vision and Apocalypse of Weeks in *1 Enoch*, Dan 7–12, the *Testament of Moses*, *4 Ezra*, and *2 Baruch*.

2.1 The Animal Vision and the Apocalypse of Weeks

1 Enoch contains two historical apocalypses, both reviews of history from creation to the eschaton. In the first, the Animal Vision (*1 En.* 85–90), the periodization of history is not explicit but can be inferred from repeated patterns and motifs. This allegory of biblical history can be divided into three eras: (1) from Adam and Eve to the Flood (85.3–89.8); (2) from the renewal of creation to the final judgment (89.9–90.27); and (3) a second renewal of creation and return to the primordial state (90.28–38).[13] The long middle era can be subdivided into three periods on the basis of three acts of divine judgment that recall the Flood, the paradigmatic act of divine judgment: the Exodus, the Babylonian destruction of Jerusalem, and the eschatological judgment. The Flood is presented as the result of the sins of the Watchers, represented as stars that fall from heaven (86.1; 88.1, 3).[14] The human beings and giants who perish in the flood are represented by different types of animals, while Noah is a white bull who became a man, and his three sons are bulls of different colors (89.1, 9).

Besides Noah and his sons, the first period of the post-Flood era highlights two more white bulls (Abraham and Isaac, 89.10–11), a white ram who begets twelve sheep (Jacob, 89.12), and then two more sheep (Moses and Aaron, 89.16–18). It ends with an act of divine judgment upon Israel's first Gentile enemy, the Egyptians (represented by wolves), which is described in terms reminiscent of the Flood: "And the water swelled up and rose until it covered those wolves" (89.26).[15] Moses, who carries over from the first period to the second just as Noah carried over from the first era to

---

[13] G. W. E. Nickelsburg, *1 Enoch 1: A Commentary on the Book of 1 Enoch Chapters 1–36, 81–108* (Hermeneia; Minneapolis: Fortress Press, 2001), 354–55.

[14] Nickelsburg points out that for the author of the Animal Vision, *1 En.* 6–11 represents "the definitive way to read Genesis 6–8" (ibid., 359).

[15] Nickelsburg's translation ibid., 366; cf. his comment, ibid., 379.

the second, is also said, like Noah, to become a man, when he constructs the Tabernacle (89.36).[16] In the second period (89.28–58), the sheep (Israelites) and rams (their kings) alternately prevail over and are oppressed by various kinds of wild animals (Gentiles), until in a third act of divine judgment, this time upon Israel, the "Lord of the sheep" abandons them into the hands of the wild beasts (89.55–58). In the third period (89.59–90.27), which lasts until the final judgment, the focus shifts from individual Israelite heroes, represented by animals, to the rule of seventy angelic "shepherds" to whom the "Lord of the sheep" hands over his flock.[17] The sub-division of this period into four periods of 12, 23, 23, and 12 shepherds, respectively, may be influenced by a four kingdoms schema like that found in Dan 2 and 7, and the number 70 recalls the "seventy weeks of years" in Dan 9 (see below), but it is likely the case that the Animal Vision and Dan 7–12 drew on common traditions, rather than one directly influencing the other.[18]

Each of the previous three judgments (the Flood, the Exodus and the Babylonian conquest of Jerusalem) can be seen as a precursor to the final judgment, which comes at the end of the period of the angelic "shepherds." At that time, the fallen stars, the seventy shepherds and the blinded sheep will be judged and burned (90.20–27). The era that follows the final judgment (90.28–38) represents a gradual return to the pristine state before the fall of the Watchers and the Flood, in that initially the other animals are merely subservient to the sheep, but after the advent of a white bull (a messianic figure), the sheep and all other species are transformed into cattle.

The Apocalypse of Weeks (*1 En.* 93.1–10 + 91.11–17), which is embedded in the Epistle of Enoch (*1 En.* 92–105), is much briefer than the

---

[16] Some commentators have explained "becoming a man" as necessary to the activity of building, which is ascribed to Noah and Moses, but since the author of the Animal Vision is not otherwise very concerned with realism, it is more likely that it represents elevation to an "angel-like status," as Nickelsburg tentatively suggests (ibid., 375, 381).

[17] According to Nickelsburg, the author of the vision transforms the prophetic symbol of negligent shepherds, normally applied to human rulers (cf. especially Ezek 34 and Zech 11), by combining it with the notion of heavenly rulers of the nations (Deut 32:8 LXX, *Jub.* 15.32, Ps 82). See ibid., 391.

[18] Ibid., 391–93. The first period of 12 shepherds, which may begin during Manasseh's reign, includes the Babylonian destruction of the Temple and the Exile; the second period of 23 shepherds must represent the Persian period; the third period of 23 shepherds covers the Hellenistic period from Alexander into the second century; and the final period, the years leading up to the eschaton, including (in the present form of the Animal Vision, at least) the Maccabean revolt.

Animal Vision but it shares a similar view of history.[19] The periods are more clearly delineated: there are seven "weeks" until the beginning of the eschaton and then three "weeks" of eschatological events. The first week is a time of righteousness, ending in the days of Enoch (93.3). The Flood, called "the first end," falls in the second week, which ends with the covenant with Noah, called "a law ... for sinners" (93.4). The election of Abraham marks the conclusion of the third week (93.5), and the Sinai covenant (and building of the Tabernacle) falls at the end of the fourth week (93.6). The building of the Temple comes at the end of the fifth week (93.7), and its destruction at the end of the sixth week (93.8). The seventh week is characterized by perversity, but at its conclusion, "the chosen will be chosen" (93.10), and they will be given wisdom, and a role in executing judgment on the wicked, in the eighth week (91.11–12). The Temple will be restored at the conclusion of the eighth week (91.13), righteousness will spread over the whole earth in the ninth (91.14), and "everlasting judgment" will be executed upon the Watchers in tenth (91.15). After that, "a new heaven will appear" (91.16)—to complement the newly righteous earth—and "there will be weeks without number forever" of piety and righteousness (91.17).[20]

While none of the biblical heroes is mentioned by name in either the Animal Vision or the Apocalypse of Weeks, there can be little doubt about their identification, based on their descriptions and the order in which they appear. Whereas the emphasis is on the biblical heroes themselves in much of the Animal Vision, in the Apocalypse of Weeks it is more on the events associated with them, which fall at the conclusions of "weeks." The following events and characters are emphasized in both Enochic reviews of history: Enoch and the fall of the Watchers; the Flood and covenant with Noah; Moses, the Sinai covenant and building of the Tabernacle; the building of Solomon's Temple; the ascension of Elijah; and the destruction of the Temple and Babylonian Exile. Both take a dim view of the entire Second Temple period and deny the legitimacy of the Second Temple itself, and both envision a long eschatological period, with the redemption of Israel, and subsequently of the whole world, happening in stages.

2.2 Daniel 7–12

In contrast to the universal scope (creation to eschaton) of the two historical apocalypses in *1 Enoch*, the periodization of history in Dan 7–12 spans

---

[19] Nickelsburg ("History-Writing" [see n. 11], 83) says it is "either a prototype for the Animal Vision or a stylized summary of it."

[20] See Nickelsburg's commentary on the Apocalypse of Weeks in *1 Enoch 1* (see n. 13), 438–50.

only the period between the pseudepigraphical setting (the Babylonian Exile) and the actual time of the author. Two systems of periodization coexist in Dan 7–12. The four kingdoms schema in ch. 7 (which is introduced in ch. 2) is world-historical in outlook,[21] while the "seventy weeks of years" introduced in ch. 9 represent the duration of Jerusalem's desolation, from its destruction by the Babylonians through its desecration by Antiochus IV Epiphanes.[22] The chronological framework of the book of Daniel as a whole is based on the four kingdoms schema, assuming the sequence Babylonians, Medes, Persians and Greeks (i.e., the Hellenistic kingdoms of the Ptolemies and Seleucids), and is therefore impossible to reconcile with actual historical events and persons. The main inaccuracies are making Belshazzar the son of Nebuchadnezzar (5:2; he was the son of King Nabonidus, who was unrelated to Nebuchadnezzar, and was a regent for his father, never a king) and inventing a king "Darius the Mede" (6:1) who took over the kingdom of Babylon after the death of Belshazzar.[23] The apocalypse in Dan 7–12 fits within the chronological framework established by the tales in chs. 1–6, setting the first two visions (chs. 7 and 8) in the reign of Belshazzar, ch. 9 in the reign of Darius the Mede, and the long final revelation (chs. 10–12) in the third year of King Cyrus the Persian (10:1, cf. 6:29).

The first three kingdoms are passed over lightly in chs. 7, 8 and 11. Although ch. 11 goes into some detail on earlier events in the Hellenistic period, the focus is on the demise of the fourth (Hellenistic) kingdom. Likewise, only the final week of the seventy is described in any detail, in Dan 9:26–27. Both historical schemata presuppose an eschatological reversal, and in fact the historical focus throughout chs. 7–12 is on the events leading up to that expected reversal; namely, the crisis under Antiochus Epiphanes, culminating in the desecration of the Temple. The duration of the period from the desecration to the end is described in several different ways in these chapters: "a time, times and half a time" (7:25, 12:7); "twenty-three hundred evenings and mornings" (8:14); "half a week [of years]"

---

[21] On the historical background of the four kingdoms schema found in Dan 2 and 7, see Collins, *The Apocalyptic Imagination* (see n. 2), 92–8; idem, *Daniel: A Commentary on the Book of Daniel* (Hermeneia; Minneapolis: Fortress Press, 1993), 166–70. See also A. Momigliano, "The Origins of Universal History," in *The Poet and the Historian: Essays in Literary and Historical Biblical Criticism* (ed. R. E. Friedman; Chico, Calif.: Scholars Press, 1983), 133–55 (144–48).

[22] That is, it covers the same period from the point of view of Jerusalem. In contrast to the seventy shepherds of the Animal Vision, the seventy weeks of years are not subdivided into four periods, but rather into three very uneven periods of 7 weeks, 62 weeks and 1 week (Dan 11:25–27). Thus the author of Dan 7–12 clearly has not made any attempt to harmonize the two systems of periodization.

[23] See Collins, *Daniel* (see n. 21), 29–33.

(9:27), "one thousand two hundred and ninety days" (12:11), revised to "one thousand three hundred and thirty-five days."[24] This redundancy reveals a strong sense of determinism about the current crisis, or one might say a conviction that the turning point of history is at hand.

Despite the relative lack of interest in the first three kingdoms *per se* in Dan 7–12, Daniel's periodization of history according to four kingdoms was extremely influential on later Judaism. The fourth kingdom was naturally identified as Rome during the Roman period; this reinterpretation of the four kingdoms schema (and of the fourth beast in Dan 7) can be seen in later apocalypses (*4 Ezra* 12.11, Rev 13:1–8, cf. *2 Bar.* 39.5–8), in Josephus (*Ant.* 10.276), and frequently in rabbinic literature.[25]

2.3 The Testament of Moses

Although the *Testament of Moses* (also known as the *Assumption of Moses*) is not technically an apocalypse because it is a revelation to Joshua by Moses, not by an otherworldly being, it mainly consists of an *ex eventu* prophecy of the history of Israel from the time of Joshua through the end times, with apocalyptic eschatology.[26] Its historical review does not go back to the beginning of human history, partly because of its pseudepigraphic setting and testamentary form, but also because its focus is more narrowly on Israel than is the case in *1 Enoch*. In fact, this book contains the earliest attestation of the idea that the world was created for the sake of Israel (1.12).[27]

---

[24] See ibid., 322, 400–1.

[25] On the reinterpretation of Daniel in later apocalypses, see G. K. Beale, *The Use of Daniel in Jewish Apocalyptic Literature and the Revelation of St. John* (Lanham, Md.: University Press of America, 1984); on Josephus' "Daniel segment," see G. Vermès, "Josephus' Treatment of the Book of Daniel," *JJS* 42 (1991): 149–66; on the use of the four kingdoms schema and the identification of the fourth kingdom with Rome in rabbinic midrash, see J. Neusner, *Judaism and its Social Metaphors: Israel in the History of Jewish Thought* (Cambridge; Cambridge University Press, 1989), 153–63, 169–70.

[26] Nickelsburg includes the *Testament of Moses* in "History-Writing" (see n. 11). Its final form can be dated with some certainty between 4 BCE and 30 CE, but Nickelsburg believes it is a reworking of a document written just prior to the Maccabean Revolt, so slightly earlier than the Animal Vision of *1 Enoch* and Dan 7–12 (ibid., 84). On the apocalyptic features of the *T. Mos.*, see Nickelsburg's introduction to *Studies on the Testament of Moses: Seminar Papers* (ed. idem; SBLSCS 4; Cambridge, Mass.: Society of Biblical Literature, 1973), 11–4. Collins (*Apocalyptic Imagination* [see n. 2], 132) notes, however, that the *T. Mos.* is less deterministic than most apocalypses, in that the course of history can be influenced by human intercession (in chs. 4 and 9).

[27] J. J. Collins, "The Date and Provenance of the Testament of Moses," in *Studies on the Testament of Moses* (see n. 26), 15–32 (27).

The periodization of history in the *T. Mos.* follows the Deuteronomic schema of sin-punishment-repentance-salvation, in two cycles.[28] In the first cycle, the main example of sin is the division between Israel and Judah, which is presented, in typical Deuteronomic fashion, as apostasy from the Temple on the part of the ten northern tribes (ch. 2).[29] The first punishment is the destruction of Jerusalem and the Babylonian Exile; in exile, significantly, the twelve tribes of Israel reunite in mourning and repentance (ch. 3). An intercessor arises, who is identified only as "one who is over them," and in answer to his prayer the two (southern) tribes are returned to their land (ch. 4).[30] The sin in the second cycle is once again division within the chosen people, this time "as to the truth" (5.2)—evidently concerning the Second Temple (5.3–6). The remainder of the second cycle is somewhat garbled because ch. 6, which alludes to events in the time of King Herod and his sons, is probably a later addition to a historical review that originally culminated with the persecution under Antiochus Epiphanes (described in ch. 8).[31] The eschatological redemption of Israel is apparently brought about by the intercession of one Taxo, who advocates martyrdom and leaving vengeance to God (9.6–7).[32] Whether the original composition

---

[28] Nickelsburg, "History-Writing" (see n. 11), 88.

[29] Collins, *Apocalyptic Imagination* (see n. 2), 130.

[30] Translation by J. Priest in *OTP* 1:929. The identity of this intercessor has been the source of much speculation. R. H. Charles identifies him as Daniel on the basis of a general similarity between his prayer and that in Dan 9 (*The Assumption of Moses* [London: Black, 1897], 14). Goldstein thinks it is more likely to be Isaiah than Daniel if it is a human intercessor, but he thinks it is most probably an angel, assuming that the title "one who is over them" is taken from Job 33:23. See J. Goldstein, "The Testament of Moses: Its Content, its Origin and its Attestation in Josephus," in *Studies on the Testament of Moses* (see n. 26), 51. Tromp identifies him as Ezra, on the grounds that Ezra is a fitting counterpart to Moses. See J. Tromp, *The Assumption of Moses: A Critical Edition with Commentary* (SVTP 10; Leiden: Brill, 1992), 174–76. None of these identifications takes into account that the real counterpart of this figure in the *T. Mos.* itself is Taxo, who is otherwise unknown. Therefore the identity of the intercessor in ch. 4 may not matter; what matters is his function.

[31] This theory of the book's redaction history was first suggested by Jacob Licht in "Taxo, or the Apocalyptic Doctrine of Vengeance," *JJS* 12 (1961): 95–103, and developed by Nickelsburg in his dissertation, *Resurrection, Immortality and Eternal Life in Intertestamental Judaism* (HTS 26; Cambridge, Mass.: Harvard University Press, 1972), 28–31, 43–5, 97. Collins considers this redaction history probable (*Apocalyptic Imagination* [see n. 2], 129), but Tromp maintains that the book is an original composition of the first century CE (ibid. 120–23).

[32] Scholars are divided on whether there is a causal relation between Taxo's (and his sons') promised martyrdom (9.6–7) and the divine visitation described in the poem in the following chapter. Licht, ibid., first proposed such a causal relation, and he is followed by a number of scholars, including Collins (ibid., 131), and G. W. E. Nickelsburg (*Jewish Literature Between the Bible and the Mishnah: A Historical and Literary Introduction*

dates to the second century BCE or the early first century CE, the important point about the periodization of history in the *T. Mos.* is that the author saw his own historical situation as parallel to the Babylonian Exile, and looked for an intercessory figure to bring about the transition from divine punishment to redemption.

2.4 Fourth Ezra

Fourth Ezra adopts Daniel's four kingdoms schema and with it, an even more extreme focus on the recent past, in the Vision of the Eagle (chs. 11–12). The vision alludes only obliquely to the first three kingdoms (11.39–40), while the angelic interpreter (Uriel) simply identifies the eagle as the "fourth kingdom that appeared in a vision to your brother Daniel," and acknowledges that "it was not explained to him as I now explain it to you" (12.11). The vision and interpretation make veiled references to Roman rulers from Caesar (treated here as the first emperor) through Domitian, according to most scholars.[33] It is on the basis of the Vision of the Eagle that the book is commonly dated to the last years of the reign of Domitian, or shortly after his death.[34]

Although the Vision of the Eagle reveals more about the author's view of the recent past than about his perspective on Israel's history, there are reflections elsewhere in the book of an eschatologically-oriented Deuteronomic periodization of history similar to that of the *T. Mos.* and *2 Baruch* (see below). First, the setting of the book thirty years after the destruction of Zion by Babylon (3.1) implies that the Babylonian conquest is the paradigmatic event, and Israel's current crisis is merely a recapitulation of it, as is also the case in *2 Baruch* and the *T. Mos.* Ezra's opening monologue in ch. 3 contains a brief summary of Israel's history, although it functions differently from the other examples considered here in that it does not extend beyond the fictive date of the book and serves as an argument or

---

[2d ed.; Minneapolis: Fortress Press, 2005], 76, 247). J. Priest disagrees; see his introduction to the *T. Mos.* in *OTP* 1:923.

[33] See, for example, M. E. Stone, *Fourth Ezra: A Commentary on the Book of Fourth Ezra* (Hermeneia; Minneapolis: Fortress Press, 1990), 363–65; E. Schürer, *The History of the Jewish People in the Age of Jesus Christ (175 B.C.–A.D. 135)* (rev. and ed. G. Vermès, F. Millar and M. Goodman; 3 vols.; Edinburgh: T&T Clark, 1986), 3/1:298–300; R. J. Coggins and M. Knibb, *The First and Second Books of Esdras* (CBC; Cambridge: Cambridge University Press, 1979), 240–44.

[34] An alternative view, that the vision and its interpretation were significantly revised around 218 CE, is proposed by L. DiTommaso, "Dating the Eagle Vision of 4 Ezra: A New Look at an Old Theory," *JSP* 20 (1999): 3–38. For a critique of his proposal and an alternative theory about the "updating" of the vision after the death of Domitian, see K. Martin Hogan, *Theologies in Conflict in 4 Ezra: Wisdom Debate and Apocalyptic Solution* (JSJSup 130; Leiden: Brill, 2008), 182–85.

complaint against God. Ezra treats the transgression and punishment of Adam as the paradigmatic event setting the course of human history (it is recapitulated in the Flood, 3.10) and especially Israel's history (just as Adam transgressed the one commandment due to the presence of the "evil heart," Israel has consistently transgressed the Sinai covenant for the same reason [3.20–22], leading ultimately to the fall of Jerusalem to Babylon).[35]

The final chapter of *4 Ezra* contains a reckoning of the time remaining to the end which divides "the age" into ten or twelve periods (the versions disagree), but without connecting these periods to any historical events (14.11–12).[36] And then the final verse of the book, which is missing from the Latin version, records Ezra's translation to heaven "in the seventh year of the sixth week, five thousand years and three months and twelve [or twenty-two] days after creation" (14.49). Even though both of these forms of periodization can be reconciled with a world-age of 6000 years, which is found in some rabbinic sources and is compatible with the idea that the Temple was built in the 3000th year after creation (10.45), they cannot be reconciled with one another.[37] Thus it appears that the author of *4 Ezra* was less concerned with calculating the exact amount of time between the pseudepigraphic setting and his own time (in contrast to Dan 7–12) than with understanding the events of his own time as conforming to the pattern of biblical history.

2.5 Second Baruch

Like *4 Ezra*, *2 (Syriac Apocalypse of) Baruch* is set at the time of the Babylonian destruction of Jerusalem, and was written sometime between 70 and 132 CE.[38] It contains two symbolic visions, the interpretations of

---

[35] Although Ezra's brief historical review does not make any reference to the divided monarchy or the fall of Samaria (in contrast to *T. Mos.* and *2 Baruch*), the northern tribes are the subject of a long digression (13.39–50) in the sixth episode, which envisions a restoration of the twelve tribes in the messianic age.

[36] For the textual variants, see Stone, *Fourth Ezra* (see n. 33), 414, and 421 for a discussion of parallels. The fact that two apocalypses of the same period, *2 Baruch* and the *Apocalypse of Abraham*, divide history into twelve periods makes that the more likely figure.

[37] Stone assumes that a "week" in 14.49 means a millennium (*Fourth Ezra* [see n. 33], 442), so Ezra's translation takes place approximately 1000 years before the end of the age, whereas 14.11–12 places Ezra either 1250 years before the end (if 9 ½ out of 12 periods have passed) or 300 years before (if it is 9 ½ out of 10), assuming a 6000-year world age. For a more detailed treatment of the problem, see Hogan, *Theologies in Conflict* (see n. 34), 209 n. 12.

[38] Since there is only one, very obscure piece of internal evidence pointing to a more exact date (*2 Bar.* 28.2), the discussion of the dating of *2 Baruch* has tended to focus on its date relative to *4 Ezra*, with which it clearly has some sort of literary relationship.

which employ two different types of periodization: a brief four kingdoms schema in chs. 39–40, and a much more detailed recounting of biblical history from creation to the eschaton, in chs. 55–74. The reference to four kingdoms comes in the interpretation of the vision of the forest and the vine (*2 Bar.* 36–37), in which the "tall cedar" of the vision is identified as a "fourth kingdom ... whose power is harsher and more evil than those which were before it."[39] Although there is nothing in either vision or interpretation to identify this kingdom definitively with Rome, it could hardly be identified otherwise, given the generally accepted dating of the book and the fact that the fall of the fourth kingdom coincides with the revelation of the Messiah.

More interesting for present purposes is the interpretation (in *2 Bar.* 56–74) of the vision of the clouds in ch. 53; this is a detailed account of human history schematized as twelve alternating periods of dark and bright waters (i.e., periods of wickedness alternating with briefer periods of righteousness), followed by a period of more intense darkness (representing the author's own time) and a final bright period (representing the messianic age). Unlike the Animal Vision and the Apocalypse of Weeks in *1 Enoch*, this retelling of biblical history includes the names of individuals and unambiguously identifies the key events that mark the beginnings and ends of periods. The following chart outlines the dark and bright periods according to *2 Bar.* 56–74:

Dark:
1. Sin of Adam through Flood (56.5–16)
3. Wickedness of the land of Egypt (58)
5. Days of the Judges (60)
7. Jeroboam through fall of Samaria (62)
9. Days of Manasseh (64–65)
11. Fall of Zion to Babylon (67)
[13]. Eschatological woes (70–71)

Bright:
2. Abraham, his son and grandson (57)
4. Moses and his generation (59)
6. David, Solomon, building of Zion (61)
8. Hezekiah and deliverance of Zion (63)
10. Josiah's reform (66)
12. Restoration of Zion, Second Temple (68)
[14]. Messianic age (72–74)

The emphasis on Zion in this review of history is notable, but not surprising, given that the destruction of Jerusalem is a central theme of this apocalypse. The evaluation of periods and figures is entirely consistent with the Deuteronomistic history, but as in the other historical apocalypses, the whole pattern of biblical history was pre-determined from the beginning, according to ch. 69. There is something of a gap, however, between the

---

Although there are good arguments on both sides of this question, the balance of the evidence points to *2 Baruch's* dependence on *4 Ezra*. See Nickelsburg, *Jewish Literature* (see n. 32), 283–85. For a summary of the possible interpretations of 28.2 and their implications for the dating of the book, see M. F. Whitters, *The Epistle of Second Baruch: A Study in Form and Message* (JSPSup 42; Sheffield: Academic Press, 2003), 149–55.

[39] Translation by A. F. J. Klijn in *OTP* 1:633.

restoration of the Temple and the beginning of the eschatological events, which are described in extremely general, conventional terms in ch. 70. The entire Second Temple period is summed up in one sentence: "But it will happen after these things [i.e., after the restoration of the Temple cult] that there will be a fall of many nations" (68.7). Perhaps the author felt no need to go over that period again, since it is covered by the four kingdoms schema in ch. 39. But that does not explain why neither vision contains any specific reference to events in the author's own time, which presumably corresponds to the period of the eschatological woes. The contrast with Daniel and *4 Ezra* is striking: there is none of the *ex eventu* prophecy of events in the author's present to make more credible the predictions of an eschatological reversal. The author clearly looks forward to the messianic age as the end of Israel's suffering (chs. 40 and 72–74), but it does not appear to be the purpose of either vision to suggest that the advent of the Messiah is imminent.

3. The Pseudonymous Authors as Bridge Figures

The reviews of history in the apocalyptic texts considered here, to the extent that they encompass the whole of biblical history, consistently identify three moments as watershed events or breaking-points in the historical narrative: the Flood, the Exodus, and the Babylonian destruction of Jerusalem and subsequent Exile. Since these apocalyptic works tend to view the present situation in which they were written as another breaking-point, parallel to one or all of those events of the past, those events could be described as paradigmatic, in the sense that they provide a model for understanding the present. Deutero-Isaiah may have been the first author to present the Flood (or its aftermath; 54:9) and the Exodus (e.g., 43:16–21) as paradigmatic events, analogous to the present situation—in his case the end of the Babylonian exile. The authors of the apocalypses under consideration are able to use the Babylonian Exile and Return, which is analogous to the Flood in its destructive aspect and to the Exodus in its redemptive aspect, as a paradigm for the events that they are living through. Hence it is no surprise that these historical apocalypses are set around those three paradigmatic events. What is interesting is the way in which the apocalyptic seers who are their pseudonymous authors function to counteract the tendency to perceive history as broken into discrete periods by these watershed events. Primarily through scribal activity, and secondarily through oral teaching, they provide continuity of tradition across the perceived breaks between historical periods. In this section, I will look at the pseudonymous authors in the order in which they appear in the biblical narrative.

3.1 Enoch and Noah

The Flood represents the most complete break imaginable between historical periods, from the biblical perspective, according to which Noah and his family are the sole survivors. Yet the pseudepigraphic premise of all of the apocalypses contained in *1 Enoch*, and *2 (Slavonic) Enoch* as well, is that they were written by Enoch before the Flood. The advantages to an apocalyptic author of choosing Enoch as a pseudonym are obvious, since he is able to "predict" all of Israel's history, but the choice presents one large problem: how to explain the transmission of texts written before the Flood. The Enoch literature is exceptional among the apocalypses considered here in that Noah is the actual bridge-figure, in the sense that he lives on earth both before and after the Flood, but it is Enoch's apocalyptic writings that he transmits.[40] Enoch is addressed as "righteous scribe" in the Book of the Watchers (*1 En.* 12.4) and the motif of his scribal activity runs through all of the apocalypses in *1 Enoch* and is also prominent in *2 Enoch*.[41]

First Enoch in its final form is quite concerned to establish a relationship between Enoch and his great-grandson, Noah, in order to account for the survival of Enoch's writings. Noah figures prominently in the Animal Vision: he is one of only two figures transformed from an animal into a man (89.1), the other being Moses (89.36). He is also singled out in the Apocalypse of Weeks (93.4), but in neither of those short apocalypses is the question of textual transmission addressed. There is a segment in the Book of Parables, the latest portion of *1 Enoch*, in which Noah comes to his great-grandfather in distress, and Enoch explains to him what is about to happen to the earth (chs. 65–67), and then gives him the Book of Parables (68.1). A narrative in 81.1–82.4, which is interpolated into the Book of Luminaries (72–82) but which may belong to the same strand of tradition as the Book of the Watchers, records the giving of books written by Enoch to Methuselah, "so that [he] may give (them) to the generations of

---

[40] There are some references to a book or books by Noah himself (in *Jubilees* 10.13–14, 21.10, *Genesis Apocryphon* 5.29 and *Aramaic Levi Document* 10.10), but if any book attributed to Noah ever existed, it did not survive. See M. E. Stone, "The Book(s) Attributed to Noah," *DSD* 13 (2006): 4–23. Stone believes that such a book probably was known to the authors who mention it. For the contrary view, see C. Werman, "Qumran and the Book of Noah," in *Pseudepigraphic Perspectives* (see n. 2), 171–81.

[41] E.g., *1 En.* 68.1 (Parables), 81.6 (Luminaries), 83.10 (Dream Visions), 92.1, 104.11–12 (Epistle), *2 En.* 23.6, 33.8–9, 35.2, 40.2–13, 47.1–2, 48.6–7, 64.5, 66.8, 68.2. References are to the longer rescension (J) of *2 Enoch*, translated by F. I. Andersen, in *OTP*. On the scribal consciousness of *1 Enoch*, see A. Y. Reed, "Heavenly Ascent, Angelic Descent and the Transmission of Knowledge in 1 Enoch 6–16," in *Heavenly Realms and Earthly Realities in Late Antique Religions* (eds. R. Boustan and eadem; Cambridge: Cambridge University Press, 2004), 47–66 (48–9).

eternity"—presumably by passing it on to Noah.[42] The theme of the transmission of Enoch's books down to the end of days is picked up in the conclusion of the Epistle (104.9–105.2), and the presumption that Noah is the means of transmission is confirmed in the appendix on the birth of Noah that immediately follows in chs. 106–7, which affirms the transmission of revelation from Enoch to Noah through Methuselah and Lamech (107.3).[43]

Similarly, *2 Enoch* ends with a notice of Noah's survival of the flood (ch. 73), and a good bit of the book (chs. 36–68) is taken up with Enoch's instruction of his son and grandsons during the thirty days that he is allowed to return to earth after receiving revelations for sixty days in heaven. Moreover, it says that the 366 books that Enoch wrote while in heaven (ch. 23) were handed over to his sons (68.2; cf. 47.2). More explicitly, in ch. 33 God appoints angels to preserve Enoch's writings and those of his ancestors until the end of the age, when God will raise up a righteous man to reveal those writings (ch. 35).[44]

3.2 Moses

The book of *Jubilees* is technically an apocalypse, in that it is a revelation to Moses mediated by an angel, but it is generally considered an example of the "rewritten Bible" genre, since it is a retelling of Gen 1–Exod 12 with a strong halakhic emphasis.[45] Nevertheless, its pseudepigraphical premise, that Moses received other revelations on Mt. Sinai in addition to the Torah, and wrote them down, is alluded to in *2 Baruch* and *4 Ezra* (*2 Bar.* 4.5, 59.3–11, *4 Ezra* 14.5–6). Moses is presented as a paradigmatic apocalyptic seer in those works, in the sense that Baruch and Ezra are modeled on him. Moses is the quintessential bridge figure, in that he lived during the period of Israel's enslavement in Egypt (albeit without direct experience of being a slave), led Israel through the Exodus and Sinai events and the forty years in the wilderness, during which all of the other members of his generation died, except for Joshua and Caleb, who were much younger than Moses but old enough to remember the Exodus (Num 14:30, Josh 14:6–10, 24:29). Moses led the children of the Exodus generation right up to the

---

[42] Nickelsburg thinks this passage originally fell at the end of the Book of the Watchers and functioned as a narrative bridge to the Epistle. See Nickelsburg, *1 Enoch 1* (see n. 13), 334–37.

[43] Compare *Jub.* 7.38–39, which records the same chain of transmission.

[44] Incidentally, in *2 Enoch* there is another survivor of the flood, Noah's nephew Melchizedek, who is preserved in the Garden of Eden, but this subplot (in chs. 69–72) does not have any connection to the transmission of Enoch's writings.

[45] On *Jubilees* and 11QTemple as Mosaic pseudepigrapha, see Najman, *Seconding Sinai* (see n. 2), 41–69.

point of entry into the Promised Land, at which point he passed on the leadership of Israel to Joshua and died (Deut 31–34).

The *Testament of Moses* is an account of that transition of Moses' leadership, and hence can be considered a rewriting of Deut 31–34.[46] Joshua's acceptance of leadership is overshadowed in the *T. Mos.*, however, by his reception of the text itself, designated a "prophecy" (1.5), which is a revelation of Israel's future.[47] There is a striking emphasis on the means of preservation of the written prophecy down to the author's present: Moses tells Joshua to "arrange [the scrolls], anoint them with cedar, and deposit them in earthenware jars in the place which (God) has chosen from the beginning of the creation of the world ..." (1.17). The scrolls to be preserved in this way clearly include the text of the *T. Mos.* itself. Later, Moses admonishes Joshua to "keep these words and this book" (10.11), and the words spoken by Moses to Joshua are themselves the text of the testament, "And when Joshua heard the words of Moses, so written in his testament, all the things which he had said, he tore his garments and fell at Moses' feet" (11.1). The testament is again self-referential in 3.11–13, when at the time of the Babylonian destruction of Jerusalem the people exclaim, "Is this not that which was made known to us in prophecies by Moses ...? These things which have come upon us since that time are according to his admonition declared to us at that time." Since the scrolls themselves are sealed until the time of the end, it may be that Moses' "prophecies" concerning Israel's future are believed to have been transmitted orally down to the time of the Babylonian Exile, as well as being preserved in writing "until the day of recompense" (1.18).

It is worth noting that Moses is described near the end of the *T. Mos.* as "the great messenger," who was continuously occupied with interceding on behalf of his people and reminding God of the covenant (11.17). Earlier in the book he is called "the mediator of the covenant" (1.14, cf. 3.12), a role for which he was "prepared from the beginning of the world" (1.14). This role is significant because it ties Moses to the other two focal figures in the book: the "one who is over them" (4.1) during the Babylonian Exile, whose intercession leads to the restoration of Jerusalem (4.7), and Taxo, whose martyrdom apparently brings about the divine visitation in the end time.

---

[46] D. J. Harrington, "Interpreting Israel's History: The *Testament of Moses* as a Rewriting of Deut 31–34," in *Studies on the Testament of Moses* (see n. 26), 59–70, citing Nickelsburg, *Resurrection, Immortality and Eternal Life* (see n. 31), 29.

[47] For Moses' foreknowledge of Israel's future transgression and punishment, based on an interpretation of Deut 32 as a prediction, cf. *2 Bar.* 84.4–5, *L.A.B.* 19.2–7 and Josephus, *Ant.* 4.303, 313–14.

3.3 Baruch

In *2 Baruch*, in contrast to the book of Jeremiah (43:6–7, in which he is taken to Egypt with Jeremiah) or the book of Baruch in the Apocrypha (which is supposedly written in Babylon, according to 1:1), Baruch remains in and around Jerusalem after its destruction by the Babylonians.[48] The destruction of Jerusalem (rather than the Exile) is very much the focus of the book; it begins in the days leading up to the destruction and the rest takes place in the weeks immediately following it. The book begins with Baruch protesting the imminent destruction of "Zion" (3.1–9, 5.1) and being reassured by God that the city that is about to be destroyed is not the true Zion, which is preserved with God (4.1–6).[49] Although God commands Baruch to leave the city before it is destroyed, he also commands him to "stay here in the desolation of Zion" while Jeremiah goes to the exiles in Babylon (10.2–3). Baruch remains in the valley of Kidron with the people who were not taken into exile, but returns several times to Mount Zion to pray in the ruins of the Temple (10.5, 35.1) and receives some of his revelations there.

Baruch's close ties with Zion enable him to console the survivors of the destruction who remain in the land, assuring them that Zion will be "renewed in glory" and "perfected into eternity" (32.4).[50] This message is part of his role as a bridge between the present desolation and future redemption of Israel. To this end, Baruch is told that he will be "preserved until the end of times to be for a testimony" (13.3, cf. 25.1), which turns out to mean that he will shortly be taken up to heaven alive and kept there until the last days, when he will be required to testify concerning the retribution that came in his own days (13.5–11).[51] The motif of testimony, combined

---

[48] On the historical Baruch ben Neriah and the development of his persona in the various texts attributed to him, see J. E. Wright, *Baruch ben Neriah: From Biblical Scribe to Apocalyptic Seer* (Studies on Personalities of the Old Testament; Columbia, S.C.: University of South Carolina Press, 2003).

[49] "Zion" carries several different meanings in *2 Baruch*, as in other texts of the period: the Temple, Jerusalem, or the inhabitants thereof. Moreover, the author refers to the Land as "the region of Zion." See L. I. Lied, *The Other Lands of Israel: Imaginations of the Land in* 2 Baruch (JSJSup 129; Leiden: Brill, 2008), 31–58.

[50] Whitters suggests that the cumulative message of Baruch's three speeches to the people left in the Land (31–4, 44–6, 77), which he sees as precursors to the Epistle of Baruch in 78–87, is "Things are bad now and will get worse, but eventually (eschatologically), Zion will be restored" (Whitters, *Epistle of Second Baruch* [see n. 38], 42–8 [46]).

[51] *Pace* Klijn (*2 Baruch* in *OTP* 1:625 n. 13a), there is no conflict between the theme of Baruch's imminent "departure" from this world (mentioned in 43.2, 44.2, 46.7, 48.30, 76.2, 78.5, 84.1) and that of his being "preserved" until the end, as 76.2 makes clear. It is only when addressing the people that Baruch suggests that he is about to die (e.g., 44.2), but that is because he is hiding from them that he is going to be "taken up" (46.7).

with the testamentary character of Baruch's speeches to the people, recall the closing chapters of Deuteronomy, to which *2 Baruch* alludes several times, sometimes explicitly likening Baruch to Moses.[52] Baruch is unique among the bridge figures under consideration here, however, in that he is expected to return to earth to testify in person in the last days.[53]

At the same time, Baruch also participates in the more typical apocalyptic manner of bridging from the pseudepigraphic setting to the present, through writing. The book ends with a lengthy letter (78–87) from Baruch to the "nine and a half tribes which were across the river" (78.1), that is, the Northern tribes who were taken into captivity by the Assyrians. In fact Baruch was asked by his people to write to their brothers in Babylon to strengthen them as he had strengthened those remaining in the Land (77.12). This he agreed to do, adding that he would also write to the nine and a half tribes (77.17), but while he did write two letters (77.19, 85.6), only the letter to the "lost tribes" is included in the book. Assuming that the author chose to include only one letter to avoid redundancy, it is significant that he chose the one with the broader audience, perhaps to indicate that the message of the book (which the letter summarizes) is intended for all Jews everywhere.[54] Moreover, the letter is specifically intended to be handed down to future generations (84.9). Since Baruch is the putative author not just of the letter, but of the book as a whole, the letter functions to underscore his role as a bridge both between Jews of the Land of Israel and Jews of the Diaspora, and between Jews of the Babylonian period and Jews of the (author's) present.

3.4 Daniel

Although the book of Daniel begins with a reference to the siege and destruction of Jerusalem, the book is set entirely in Babylon, although not entirely during the period of the Exile. The effect of adding the kingdom of the Medes between the Babylonians and Persians (see the discussion of the chronology of Daniel above) is to make Daniel a part of the royal administration of three different empires in his lifetime—three of the four kingdoms in his vision in ch. 7, in fact. Since he was taken into exile from Jerusalem to Babylon in his youth, and is referred to repeatedly as one of the "exiles of Judah" (2:25, 5:13, 6:14), Daniel's lifetime extends beyond the Babylonian Exile both temporally and spatially. Simply by outliving the Babylonian and Median kingdoms, Daniel sends a message about the

---

[52] See *2 Bar.* 19.1–3, 59.4, 76.3–5, and especially 84.1–7.

[53] Although Ezra is likewise "taken up" to heaven at the end of *4 Ezra*, there is only a hint that he will return in the last days; see below.

[54] Whitters, *Epistle of Second Baruch* (see n. 38), 49.

power of patient endurance. Moreover, Daniel serves as an example of maintaining Judean traditions while in exile, such as keeping the dietary laws (1:8), persisting, against a royal prohibition, in thrice-daily prayer (6:11) and consulting the writings of Jeremiah (9:2).

Besides straddling Judah and Babylon, and the pre-exilic, exilic and post-exilic periods, Daniel acts as a bridge between the Babylonian Exile and the Maccabean period, when Dan 7–12 was written. As Gabriel explains to Daniel, he must keep the content of his visions secret, because they are "for the distant future" (8:26; literally, "for many days").[55] Daniel's prayer in ch. 9, which refers to the Babylonian destruction of Jerusalem, can easily be read as describing the persecution under Antiochus IV Epiphanes as well, especially the desolation of the sanctuary (9:17; cf. 9:27). Although the visions also allude to events closer to Daniel's lifetime, the focus of Daniel's interest (not surprisingly) is the events of 167–163 BCE. For example, in ch. 11, the remainder of the Persian period, in which Daniel is receiving the revelation, is summarized in one verse (11:2); the Hellenistic period from Alexander to Seleucus IV Philopator (d. 175 BCE) is given the most detailed treatment in the book in 11:3–20; while the remainder of the chapter (11:21–45) is dedicated to the reign of Antiochus Epiphanes, with a shift from *ex eventu* prophecy to true prediction in 11:40.[56]

In the final chapter of Daniel, the concern for the textual preservation of the revelations to Daniel and their transmission down to the author's own time comes to the fore: "You, Daniel, keep the words secret and seal the book until the time of the end" (12:4; cf. 12:9). Although Daniel is not portrayed as a scribe to the same extent as Enoch, Moses, and Baruch in the works discussed above, his concern with the interpretation of Jeremiah's "seventy years" (9:2) is certainly a scribal one, and his wisdom is associated with writing in 1:17. Still, the type of wisdom that Daniel is chiefly known for, on the basis of the tales, is mantic wisdom, not scribal wisdom. In some way, presumably, the Daniel of the tales was a model for the author(s) of the apocalyptic chapters, who probably belonged to the *maskilim*, whose activities included teaching (11:33).[57] Thus, while Daniel himself is not portrayed as a teaching sage, he is responsible for preserving in writing the wisdom that was revealed to him, so that it can be dissemi-

---

[55] Translation by Collins, *Daniel* (see n. 21), 328.

[56] Ibid., 377–90.

[57] Collins suggests that the wisdom of the *maskilim* was in some way a development of the "mantic wisdom" of Daniel in the tales (*Daniel* [see n. 21], 69–70), and that they instruct "the many" (11:33) in the "apocalyptic wisdom" contained in the revelations to Daniel (ibid., 385).

nated to a broader audience at the "time of the end" by his "followers," the *maskilim*.

3.5 Ezra

Although the biblical Ezra is to some extent a bridge figure, in that he is called a "scribe skilled in the Torah of Moses" (Ezra 7:6) and he brings that supposedly ancient document with him from Babylonia to Jerusalem to promulgate it there (Neh 8), in *4 Ezra* he becomes even more markedly a bridge figure, a kind of second Moses. Ezra the apocalyptic seer is placed anachronistically among the exiles in Babylonia, in the thirtieth year after the destruction of Jerusalem (3.1), which he apparently witnessed (3.29). Thus the direction of his biblical migration (Babylonia to Jerusalem) is reversed, and he becomes a link to the pre-exilic past. Although *4 Ezra* again defies the biblical record by having Ezra "taken up" to heaven alive like Baruch (14.9, and 14.50 in Stone's translation), rather than returning to Jerusalem, he retains his biblical association with the restoration of the Torah. According to *4 Ezra*, the Torah (here meaning all of the Jewish Scriptures, as becomes clear from the figure 24 books, mentioned in 14.45) was destroyed along with Jerusalem (4.23, 14.21), breaking the chain of tradition stretching back to Moses. In the final episode of the book (ch. 14), after being implicitly but unmistakably compared to Moses (14.1–8), Ezra prays to be inspired to restore the lost Scriptures: "If then I have found favor before thee, send the holy spirit into me, and I will write everything that has happened in the world from the beginning, the things that were written in your law ..." (14.22).[58]

Ezra's petition is granted, and then some, as he is inspired to dictate ninety-four books to five scribes over forty days: in addition to the twenty-four books of Scripture, seventy books "in [which] are the springs of understanding, the fountains of wisdom and the river of knowledge" (14.47). These books, which are reserved for "the wise among [the] people," are generally identified as apocalyptic texts, probably including *4 Ezra* itself, since in 12.37–38, Ezra is instructed to write down everything he has seen, and to teach it to "the wise among [the] people."[59] This self-referential tendency is typical of the apocalyptic works examined here, and is a concomitant of the phenomenon of pseudepigraphy.[60] Thus, by teaching the

---

[58] Ezra's forty days of fasting during the restoration of the Scriptures (14.42–44) may be meant to recall Moses' forty-day fast during the re-inscription of the tablets of the covenant (Exod 34:28), while Moses earlier forty days on Mt. Sinai (Exod 24:18) are paralleled by the forty-day time frame of the first six episodes of *4 Ezra*. See M. P. Knowles, "Moses, the Law and the Unity of 4 Ezra," *NovT* 31 (1989): 257–74 (261–65).

[59] Stone, *Fourth Ezra* (see n. 33), 441.

[60] Compare, e.g., *1 En.* 82.1, 104.11, Dan 12:4, *T. Mos.* 1.17, 3.11–13, *2 Bar.* 84.9.

wise and then by writing the ninety-four books, Ezra's scribal legacy extends all the way to the time of the end.

It appears that the author of *4 Ezra* expected Ezra to appear on earth again in the messianic age, because the last verse (in all versions but the Latin, to which two Christian apocalypses were appended) says that he was "caught up, and taken to the place of those who are like him" (14.50), while earlier in the book it says that those righteous people who survive to see the messianic age will "see the men who were taken up, who from their birth have not tasted death" (6.26, cf. 7.28). Nevertheless, Ezra's role in the eschatological age, if any, is not made explicit, in contrast to Baruch's, which is to be a witness to the divine judgment in his own days (*2 Bar.* 13). Instead, there is a far greater emphasis on Ezra's scribal activity, without which, *4 Ezra* suggests, there would be no surviving Scriptures (or other written revelations) that originated before the Babylonian Exile. More than in any of the other apocalypses considered here, in *4 Ezra* the Babylonian destruction of Jerusalem and the Exile entails a complete rupture in the transmission of the traditions of Israel, which has the effect of elevating the importance of its bridge figure and pseudonymous author, Ezra.

4. Conclusion

The periodization of history in the Jewish apocalyptic texts examined here is clearly influenced by earlier biblical views of the history of Israel, particularly that of the Deuteronomistic History, with its cycles of sin, punishment, repentance and salvation. Moreover, there is plenty of biblical precedent for viewing the Flood, the Exodus and the Babylonian Exile as paradigmatic events. All of these apocalyptic texts are to a certain extent exegetical, in that they are responding to, or interpreting, biblical claims about Israel's past. Yet, by casting Israel's history in the form of *ex eventu* prophecy, they bring a new perspective of determinism as well as an explicit claim to divine revelation, both of which set them apart from the biblical narratives and histories. Another obvious difference is the extent to which the apocalyptic view of history is shaped by eschatological expectations. While observing these tendencies, the feature of apocalyptic historiography with which this essay has been primarily concerned is its schematization of history into periods and its emphasis on the radical breaks, or dualistic contrasts, between the periods.

Paradoxically, this emphasis on the discontinuity of history in Jewish apocalypses goes hand in hand with a reverence for continuity of tradition, particularly written tradition.[61] Hence, figures that span two or more periods of history, and especially those that bridge major watershed events, become the focal points of apocalyptic historiography.[62] Given that pseudepigraphy is a necessary concomitant of *ex eventu* prophecy, it is not hard to see why the apocalypticists would have chosen such bridge figures, and especially those that were associated with scribal activity in Scripture or tradition, as their pseudonyms. The responsibility for carrying knowledge, or tradition, forward across the breaks in history rested on a few individuals, including Enoch and Noah; Moses; and Baruch, Daniel and Ezra. If an apocalypticist had new revelation to add to the tradition, its authority would be greatly increased by attributing it to one of these great bridge figures from the past. Without denying that the authors of apocalyptic literature may have identified psychologically with the figures they adopted as pseudonyms, I am suggesting that their schematic view of history, combined with their reverence for written tradition, influenced their choice of pseudonyms.

---

[61] On the roots of the high regard for writing seen in many of these apocalyptic texts, see H. Najman, "The Symbolic Significance of Writing in Ancient Judaism," in *The Idea of Biblical Interpretation: Essays in Honor of James L. Kugel* (eds. eadem and J. H. Newman; JSJSup 83; Leiden: Brill, 2004), 139–73.

[62] Abraham is another individual who is a focus of several of the reviews of history considered here: the Animal Vision and Apocalypse of Weeks in *1 Enoch*, the opening monologue of *4 Ezra*, and the vision of the dark and bright waters in *2 Baruch*. Although Abraham does not entirely fit the profile of a bridge figure, it is worth noting that both *Jubilees* and the *Apocalypse of Abraham* invent a past for Abraham, involving the repudiation of idolatry prior to his call by God to leave his home and go to the Promised Land. Hence, these apocalyptic works arguably transform Abraham into a bridge between the post-Flood primeval period and the period of the ancestors, by focusing on his life before his call.

Forms of Pseudepigraphy in the Dead Sea Scrolls

by

EIBERT TIGCHELAAR

1. Introduction

At the end of the 1950s, little more than a decade after the discovery of the first scrolls in Qumran cave 1 in 1947, the corpus of Dead Sea Scrolls was roughly, and largely for practical reasons, divided into three categories: (1) biblical or canonical manuscripts; (2) apocryphal and/or pseudepigraphic texts; and (3) sectarian or Essene works.[1] Although this categorization was first and foremost practical, we may reflect on it to describe the problems related to the issue of pseudepigraphy in the Dead Sea Scrolls and in Scrolls scholarship. First, we observe that the categories are of different natures, as issues of canonization, literary genre, and provenance, all play a role in the categories. Second, each of the categories is problematic.

We may call those manuscripts "biblical" or "canonical"[2] which contain the text (or part of the text) of one or more books or compositions that would later be included in Tanakh. It is clear from quotations and commentaries within the corpus that most of those "biblical" texts had a special position for those who composed other texts that are found in the corpus. However, many of the characteristics of the later canon of biblical books should not anachronistically be assumed for this corpus of Dead Sea Scrolls from the period around the turn of the era.[3] Thus, the "Bible" or collection of authoritative scriptures of those who copied and deposited the

---

[1] Cf., e.g., F. Moore Cross, *The Ancient Library of Qumran* (Garden City, N.Y.: Doubleday, 1958), 34 [3d ed.; Minneapolis: Fortress Press, 1995, 44]; J. T. Milik, *Dix ans de découvertes dans le Désert de Juda* (Paris: Cerf, 1957), 23–39; idem, *Ten Years of Discovery in the Wilderness of Judaea* (trans. J. Strugnell; London: SCM, 1959), 20–43.

[2] In most cases the term used is "biblical"; in DJD I:46–7, the distinction is between "ouvrages canoniques" and "ouvrages non-canoniques," the latter being distinguished in three categories: "commentaires," "apocryphes," and "ouvrages nouveaux de la 'bibliothèque Essénienne.'"

[3] The corpus contains manuscripts that have been dated on paleographic grounds from the mid-third century BCE to the late first century CE. However, the hands of the vast majority of manuscripts have been dated to the first century BCE and the early first century CE.

corpus probably was not entirely identical to the later Tanakh. It has been suggested it included *Jubilees*, the *Enochic* writings, Sirach and Tobit,[4] and one may question whether "biblical" books like Ruth, Ecclesiastes, Canticles, Chronicles, or Ezra, belonged to "the Dead Sea Scrolls Bible."[5] A second aspect is even more pertinent, and puts into a different perspective the observation just made: whereas the notion of a canon draws a sharp distinction between a fixed collection of texts and other ones, the corpus does not show evidence of clear boundaries between scriptures and non-scriptures. From that perspective, there is no such thing as a "Dead Sea Scrolls Bible," but only of an open-ended collection of more and less authoritative scriptures. Also, the later canonical idea of the fixation of the text of the canonical books, does not yet hold true for the Dead Sea Scrolls, where both the textual and the literary form of the "biblical" books has not yet been fixed.

The second category, of the apocryphal and/or pseudepigraphic texts, is problematic for various reasons. Within Christianity, these terms express the deutero-canonical and non-canonical status of those Early Jewish writings that had been preserved in Christianity.[6] However, the diverging views on the canonicity of some books and the different use of the labels among Roman Catholics and Protestants have also complicated the use of the terminology in scholarship. More or less, the Catholic deutero-canonical books are not regarded as canonical among Protestants who call them apocrypha; and, whereas Catholics designated non-canonical Early Jewish writings as apocrypha (of the Old Testament), Protestant scholars referred

---

[4] Cf. M. Abegg Jr., P. Flint and E. Ulrich, *The Dead Sea Scrolls Bible: The Oldest Known Bible Translated for the First Time into English* (San Francisco: HarperSanFrancisco, 1999).

[5] The literature is extensive. Cf., e.g., E. Ulrich, "The Notion and Definition of Canon," in *The Canon Debate* (eds. L. Martin McDonald and J. A. Sanders; Peabody, Mass.: Hendrickson, 2002), 21–35; P. W. Flint, "Scriptures in the Dead Sea Scrolls: The Evidence from Qumran," in *Emanuel: Studies in Hebrew Bible, Septuagint, and Dead Sea Scrolls in Honor of Emanuel Tov* (eds. S. M. Paul et al.; VTSup 94; Leiden: Brill, 2003), 269–304, and E. Tigchelaar, "Wie haben die Qumrantexte unsere Sicht des kanonischen Prozesses verändert?" in *Qumran und der biblische Kanon* (eds. J. Frey and M. Becker; Neukirchen-Vluyn: Neukirchener Verlag, 2009).

[6] For a good overview of the different uses of the terms, cf. L. T. Stuckenbruck, "Apocrypha and Pseudepigrapha," in *Dictionary of Early Judaism* (eds. J. J. Collins and D. C. Harlow; Grand Rapids, Mich.: Eerdmans, forthcoming). Cf. also M. de Jonge, *Pseudepigrapha of the Old Testament as Part of Christian Literature* (Leiden: Brill, 2003), 9–17. Note that R. H. Charles, *The Apocrypha and Pseudepigrapha of the Old Testament* (Oxford: Clarendon Press, 1913) also included three texts that had not been preserved through Christianity (*Pirke Aboth*; the *Story of Ahikar*; the *Fragments of a Zadokite Work*).

to those as pseudepigrapha (of the Old Testament).[7] In modern scholarship, scholars have chosen between different options: they more or less adopt the traditional labels, or suggest to redefine the terms more strictly according to the forms of literature,[8] or use these terms broadly (and more or less as synonyms),[9] or avoid them altogether.[10] A second problem is how we should actually define pseudepigraphy; which texts should one call pseudepigraphic, and to what extent has it a heuristic value to place these texts into one category? Against a traditional description of pseudepigraphy as "texts falsely ascribed to an author (usually of great antiquity) in order to enhance their authority and validity," Bernstein tried to depart from a more neutral description "the phenomenon of composing texts or portions of texts which are placed in the mouth of ancient figures." He subsequently introduced a series of categories of pseudepigraphy (authoritative, convenient, decorative; internal or external; strong or weak) as found amongst the Dead Sea Scrolls, based primarily on a description of the authorial voice in the work, but also on his own estimation of the authorial intent.[11] However, even though Bernstein makes many important

---

[7] The different terminology is also reflected in the French and English editions of Milik's introduction. His *Dix ans* (see n. 1), 29, refers to "deutérocanoniques," and "apocryphes de l'Ancien Testament," whereas *Ten Years* (see n. 1), 31–2, renders these by the "Deutero-canonical books of Apocrypha," resp. "Pseudepigrapha of the Old Testament."

[8] D. Dimant, "Old Testament Pseudepigrapha at Qumran," in *The Bible and the Dead Sea Scrolls. Vol. 2: The Dead Sea Scrolls and the Qumran Community* (ed. J. H. Charlesworth; Waco, Tex.: Baylor University Press, 2006), 447–67 (448–49, 462), who states that the "century-old literary concept and definitions applied to this literary are ill-adapted to deal with the complexity of the phenomena emerging from Qumran" (448–49).

[9] Cf., e.g., E. G. Chazon and M. E. Stone, eds., *Pseudepigraphic Perspectives: The Apocrypha and Pseudepigrapha in Light of the Dead Sea Scrolls* (Leiden: Brill, 1999), and E. G. Chazon, D. Dimant, and R. A. Clements, eds., *Reworking the Bible: Apocryphal and Related Texts at Qumran* (Leiden: Brill, 2005), which do not clearly distinguish between apocrypha and pseudepigrapha.

[10] Thus, e.g., F. García Martínez, *The Dead Sea Scrolls Translated* (Leiden: Brill, 1994), xlix, when he distinguishes between three categories: "biblical works, associated religious literature, sectarian works." This also holds true for the *Discovery in the Judaean Desert* series which adopted the term parabiblical as an umbrella term for texts like *Jubilees*, Tobit, as well as new Qumran texts many of which were called apocrypha or by names starting with "Pseudo-." Cf. E. Tov, "Foreword," in DJD XIII:ix–x (ix). On the history of the term "parabiblical," cf. D. K. Falk, *The Parabiblical Texts: Strategies for Extending the Scriptures among the Dead Sea Scrolls* (London: T&T Clark, 2007), 3–5.

[11] M. J. Bernstein, "Pseudepigraphy in the Qumran Scrolls: Categories and Functions," in *Pseudepigraphic Perspectives* (see n. 9), 1–26 (3). Cf. throughout his article the references to the intentions of the authors.

and interesting observations, his distinctions between different kinds of pseudepigraphy (especially the strong and the weak one) tend to be artificial and subjective.

Here, the third category of "sectarian" or "Essene" texts need not concern us in detail. Whereas in the 1950s the sectarian character of virtually all new texts from Qumran was assumed, this changed with the study of the *Temple Scroll* in the early 1980s, and even more with the publication of the Cave 4 materials in the 1990s: a majority of texts does not exhibit the supposedly sectarian characteristics of the Cave 1 texts (and the association of the Scrolls and the site of Qumran with the Essenes is more problematic than was assumed in the past).[12]

Though disputes about the categories of "biblical" and "sectarian" texts at first sight have little to do with the phenomenon of pseudepigraphy of some Scrolls, they reveal the schemata that reflected and influenced scholarship. Thus, the three categories reflected a historical model according to which (with the exception of Daniel) canonical books preceded chronologically apocryphal and pseudepigraphal ones, which in turn were older than sectarian texts. At the same time, these three categories were thought to reflect the literature of respectively Judaism at large, specific Jewish movement, and only the Dead Sea Scrolls sect. But, most importantly, the traditional supposition of the primacy of biblical texts, and the 19th-century Graetzian assumption of the canonization of Torah at the time of Ezra and of the prophets before Sirach, provided an explanation for both pseudepigraphy and sectarian literature. Pseudepigraphy would have been necessitated by the closure of the first two parts of the canon, which suggested that prophecy and revelation had ended in the time of Ezra: new ideas would only have been accepted if ascribed to figures before Ezra. In contrast, the Qumran-sect would have had no need for pseudepigraphy, since it accepted the idea of God's revelation of his mysteries to the Teacher of Righteousness (1QpHab 7.3–5).[13] Such assumptions would explain why there are no patently sectarian pseudepigrapha: pseudepigraphy would have been a pre-sectarian phenomenon, not needed by the sect. Recent studies of scripture, the processes of canonization, and the phenomenon of reworking of scripture amongst the Dead Sea Scrolls, therefore also have a direct impact on our views on pseudepigraphy, as indicated by

---

[12] Cf., e.g., F. García Martínez, "¿Sectario, no-sectario, o qué? Problemas de una taxonomía correcta de los textos qumránicos," *RevQ* 23/91 (2008): 383–94, with references to earlier work.

[13] The absence of pseudepigraphy among the so-called "sectarian scrolls" has long been noted. Cf., e.g., J. J. Collins, "Pseudepigraphy and Group Formation in Second Temple Judaism," in *Pseudepigraphic Perspectives* (see n. 9), 43–58 (55–8).

Brooke, who stated: "The whole topic of pseudonymity and canon needs to be revisited in light of all the evidence that now exists in the Qumran library."[14]

2. Discussing Pseudepigraphy in the Dead Sea Scrolls

The publication of all the Dead Sea Scrolls materials has made it possible to classify the texts in more detail, specifically with regard to content and literary genre.[15] However, in many of the present classifications, the categories "pseudepigrapha" and "pseudepigraphic" have been eliminated. For example, Lange rejects the use of the label "pseudepigraphic" for "parabiblical texts" (apparently also for traditional pseudepigrapha like *1 Enoch*),[16] and only uses the term for "pseudepigraphic ascriptions of already existing texts by a later editor," as in the ascriptions of psalms to David, Manasseh, and Obadiah.[17]

In their textbook, VanderKam and Flint very briefly discuss the phenomenon of pseudepigraphy, and give a list of "pseudepigrapha as a group of writings falsely attributed to an ancient figure," found among the scrolls. Their list contains previously known texts, such as Daniel, Tobit, and the following traditional Pseudepigrapha: *Psalms 151A, 151B, 154* and *155*; parts of *1 Enoch, Jubilees,* and compositions related to the *Testaments of the Twelve Patriarchs*.[18] But they also enumerate a much larger number of "New Pseudepigrapha" found among the scrolls, which they group around the biblical figures that feature in them, namely Noah, Jacob, Judah or Benjamin, Levi, Rachel, Joseph, Qahat, Amram, Moses, Joshua, Samuel, David, Jonathan (?), Solomon (?), Elijah, Elisha, Jeremiah and Eze-

---

[14] G. J. Brooke, "Between Authority and Canon: The Significance of Reworking the Bible for Understanding the Canonical Process," in *Reworking the Bible* (see n. 9), 85–104 (94).

[15] Cf. especially A. Lange (with U. Mittmann-Richert), "Annotated List of the Texts from the Judaean Desert Classified by Content and Genre," in *The Texts from the Judaean Desert. Indices and an Introduction to the DJD Series* (ed. E. Tov; Oxford: Clarendon Press, 2002), 115–64; for an overview of different classifications of "parabiblical" literature, cf. Falk, *Parabiblical Texts* (see n. 10), 5–14.

[16] Lange, ibid., 117: "parabiblical literature should not be understood as a pseudepigraphic phenomenon, i.e., the ascription of a literary work to a biblical author, but as a form of scriptural revelation, comparable to the phenomenon of literary prophecy."

[17] Ibid., 122 n. 1.

[18] J. VanderKam and P. Flint, *The Meaning of the Dead Sea Scrolls: Their Significance for Understanding the Bible, Judaism, Jesus, and Christianity* (London: T&T Clark, 2002), 189–204 (202–3).

kiel, Malachi, Esther (?), Daniel, Suzanna (?).[19] However, later in their book they discuss the same list under the caption "Other Rewritten Scriptures" and summarize that "there are many texts that deal with biblical characters and use the stories and other kinds of texts in new settings."[20] But that alone, of course, does not warrant the label "pseudepigrapha."

Another list is offered by Dimant, who distinguishes between apocrypha and pseudepigrapha, those previously known and previously unknown, but also other works related to the Hebrew Bible. Dimant proceeds from a more narrow definition of pseudepigraphy, accepting only those works that were conceived by the author to fit a pseudepigraphic figure,[21] and hence only lists as "previously known pseudepigrapha" found among the scrolls *1 Enoch, Jubilees*, the *Aramaic Levi Document*, and *Text about Naphtali*[22]; and as previously unknown pseudepigrapha only the *Temple Scroll*. For some reason the headings of the Aramaic "Compositions related to the Bible," as well as "Nonbiblical Pieces,"[23] do not use the title pseudepigrapha, even though she does regard two categories of them as pseudepigrapha, namely the "pseudepigraphic words of prediluvian figures and of biblical Patriarchs," and "pseudepigraphic apocalypses and visions attributed to seers in Babylon."[24]

It makes little sense to describe all so-called "parabiblical" literature as pseudepigraphic, but Dimant's narrow definition would exclude texts that traditionally would be called pseudepigraphic. Rather than presenting a new definition and resulting list, I will first chart the different kinds of texts that, from one perspective or another, might qualify for the label "pseudepigraphic." We may start with the observation that the types of texts described by Lange as "Parabiblical texts," or by Flint and VanderKam as "Rewritten Scriptures," can be categorized in two main groups, to wit (1) interpretative rewritings of earlier scriptures, in the form of "Rewritten Scripture," paraphrase, or retelling, of either entire books, or sections of books, or even as a pastiche of different passages, sometimes with expansions based on older traditions or coming from the author's in-

---

[19] Ibid., 203–4. They also mention the *Genesis Apocryphon*, in which several different patriarchs feature.

[20] Ibid., 227–32 (232).

[21] Dimant, "Old Testament Pseudepigrapha at Qumran" (see n. 8), 448 n. 6.

[22] The text was published as 4Q215 *Testament of Naphtali*, but in choosing a different name Dimant wants to avoid the impression that the text was identical to the known Greek *Testament of Naphtali* or the Medieval Hebrew one.

[23] Dimant, "Old Testament Pseudepigrapha at Qumran" (see n. 8), 457–58.

[24] Ibid., 463–64.

terpretation; and (2) new compositions that are not based on earlier scripture, but are attributed, or closely related to scriptural figures.[25]

3. Two Types of "Parabiblical" Texts

3.1 Extending Scriptures by Interpretative Rewritings

The first group can be described as extending scripture by interpretative rewriting.[26] Examples are *Jubilees* and the *Temple Scroll*, which contain extensive interpretative rewritings of parts of the Torah, but also have parts that do not have their origin in the Torah. Many other less well-preserved texts also are interpretative. The *Genesis Apocryphon*, as well as some so-called Moses Apocrypha, notably *Words of Moses* (1Q22), and *Apocryphal Pentateuch A* (4Q368) and *B* (4Q377) describe events from the Torah. The *Apocryphon of Joshua* is concerned with exegetical questions arising from the "biblical" book of Joshua, and reworks the text according to the author's agenda. The *Pseudo-Ezekiel* manuscripts are closely related to the prophetic book of Ezekiel, but there are also rewritings of some of the *ketuvim* or "Writings." Thus, *Apocryphal Lamentation A* (4Q179) rewrites parts of Lamentations, and *Wiles of the Wicked Woman* (4Q184) and *Beatitudes* (4Q525, 5Q16) are closely related to the text of Prov 1–9.

Much of the discussion about the nature of such texts has focused on *Jubilees* and the *Temple Scroll*. *Jubilees* is written in such a way that it presents itself as Moses' writing down of an angel's dictation of the contents of the heavenly tablets, whereas the *Temple Scroll* is composed as direct divine speech by God to Moses. Generally, these books are referred to as pseudepigrapha, even though both compositions do not claim to have been written by Moses. Schiffman therefore suggested that both texts are actually divine pseudepigrapha,[27] while Najman emphasized that *Jubilees* presents itself explicitly and throughout as a written record, whereas the *Temple Scroll* lacks *Jubilees*' emphasis on the written character.[28] Here we

---

[25] Cf., in more detail, as part of an overall categorization of the corpus of Dead Sea Scrolls, E. Tigchelaar, "Dead Sea Scrolls," in *Dictionary of Early Judaism* (see n. 6).

[26] I adopted the terminology of extending scriptures from Falk, *Parabiblical Texts* (see n. 10), 21.

[27] L. H. Schiffman, "The Temple Scroll and the Halakhic Pseudepigrapha of the Second Temple Period," in *Pseudepigraphic Perspectives* (see n. 9), 121–31; repr. in idem, *The Courtyards of the House of the Lord: Studies on the Temple Scroll* (ed. F. García Martínez; STDJ 75; Leiden: Brill, 2008), 163–74.

[28] Cf. the discussion of *Jubilees* and the *Temple Scroll* by H. Najman, *Seconding Sinai: The Development of Mosaic Discourse in Second Temple Judaism* (JSJSup 77; Leiden: Brill, 2003), 41–69 (59, 68–9).

do not have the type of pseudepigraphic text where an author attempts to authorize his own writing under the name of another, ancient author. Rather, the strategies of authorization of the compositions are different, and in *Jubilees* rather complex. We do not exactly know how the authors and editors of the *Temple Scroll* intended to authorize the text, apart from the fact that Pentateuchal sections have been rephrased into a first person divine voice (as generally in the Priestly source, but contrary to the style of Deuteronomy where Moses refers with third person references to God), and the figure of Moses is largely missing from the composition (also contrary to the Priestly source, where divine speech to the people is embedded in divine speech to Moses where he commands him to speak).[29] In *Jubilees* the text is authorized both as angelic revelation and as the faithful record of Moses' scribal activity,[30] and ultimately as reflecting the texts of the heavenly tablets. In these compositions, authorization is not accomplished through attribution of authorship to Moses, but by describing the revelation in authorized forms.

Both texts are based on a text very similar to the Torah, and may be characterized as rewritings of sections of the Pentateuch; but what was the intended relation of those new texts (*Jubilees*; *Temple Scroll*) to this Torah? Scholarly explanations wavered between the rewriting as commentary on or as replacement of an authoritative Torah.[31] Partly due to the publication and study of the so-called *Reworked Pentateuch* manuscripts,[32] many scholars have taken a more fluid look at the notion of authoritative scripture: in rewriting existing texts (scriptures) new texts acknowledge the authority of those texts, but also provide a new interpretive context for those older scriptures.[33] As such, *Jubilees*, and probably also the *Temple Scroll*, were meant to supplement and explain the earlier texts, not to supplant them.[34] References to the first Torah in *Jubilees* (*Jub.* 6.22), or the omission in the *Temple Scroll* of laws with which the author was not concerned, support the hypothesis that the authors/editors intended to supple-

---

[29] Cf. discussion in Schiffman, "The Temple Scroll and the Halakhic Pseudepigrapha" (see n. 27), 121–25.

[30] Najman, *Seconding Sinai* (see n. 28), 63–6.

[31] For overviews of the discussion cf. Bernstein, "Pseudepigraphy" (see n. 11), 13–5 (on the *Temple Scroll*); Schiffman, "The Temple Scroll and the Halakhic Pseudepigrapha" (see n. 27), 121–24, 127.

[32] There is an ongoing discussion about the "scriptural" status and interpretive techniques of those manuscripts. Cf. most recently, with ample reference to different positions in the discussion, M. M. Zahn, "The Problem of Characterizing the 4QReworked Pentateuch Manuscripts: Bible, Rewritten Bible, or None of the Above?" *DSD* 15 (2008): 315–39.

[33] Najman, *Seconding Sinai* (see n. 28), 45–6.

[34] Ibid., 46, esp. n. 2.

ment. The manuscript evidence of the Dead Sea Scrolls confirms, at least for *Jubilees*, that this also was what actually happened.

A clue for understanding the corpus of interpretative rewriting is that many rewritten texts adopt the literary forms of their models, including the choice of narrative voice. One might distinguish between the third person narrative descriptions of the *Apocryphon of Joshua*, which reworks the literary composition of the earlier book of Joshua, or the first person voice of Ezekiel in the *Pseudo-Ezekiel* texts, but the difference may largely be due to the voice of the earlier texts. Likewise, as in the scriptural examples, the first person voice in sapiential literature is largely anonymous, even though the titles of the books might have expressed the fictional authorship. Thus, in view of the reworking of Prov 1–9 in *Beatitudes*, one may expect that this text was at its beginning attributed to Solomon, and if a few more words had been preserved in 4Q525 1 1, we might have called this text a pseudepigraphon, perhaps with the title *Pseudo-Solomon*.[35]

3.2 Expanding Scriptures by Ascribing Traditions to Scriptural Figures

The second group consists of writings that expand scriptures by ascribing traditions, or new texts, to "biblical" figures. It is typical of this group that the texts, which are implicitly or explicitly attributed to biblical figures, do not primarily interpret or rewrite scripture, but present new compositions. Many of those texts are written in Aramaic, and use first person narratives. Those also are the texts that are most commonly described as pseudepigrapha. Apart from Aramaic texts, this group also consists of Hebrew texts that generally do not use the first person, but the third person voice.

Some of the oldest manuscripts among the Dead Sea Scrolls contain texts attributed to the prediluvian patriarch Enoch, which use the first-person voice for Enoch, and hence present a typical case of pseudepigraphy. In the case of Enoch (as well as Daniel), this pseudepigraphy is sometimes referred to as apocalyptic pseudepigraphy (in contrast, for example, to the pseudepigraphy of testamentary literature), where the strategy of pseudepigraphy would be used for authorization of apocalyptic prophecy by placing it in the mount of an ancient figure, and to enable the device of *ex eventu* prophecy. This only partially explains the pseudepigraphy of the Enochic writings. Whereas the *Apocalypse of Weeks* and the *Animal*

---

[35] In his edition of 4Q525 in DJD XXV, Émile Puech concluded that the text was attributed to either David or Solomon. On the basis of the relation with Prov 1–9, E. Qimron, "Improving the Editions of the Dead Sea Scrolls," *Meghillot* 1 (2003): 135–45 (138–41), and E. Tigchelaar, "Lady Folly and Her House in Three Qumran Manuscripts: On the Relation Between 4Q525 15, 5Q16, and 4Q184," *RevQ* 23/91 (2008): 371–81, suggest the title *Divre Shlomo or Words of Solomon*.

Apocalypse contain *ex eventu* prophecy, the earliest Enochic writings, such as the *Book of Watchers* and the *Astronomical Book* do not use that device. Rather, the oldest attributions to Enoch describe his heavenly journeys and emphasize his status as a scribe. In the case of Enoch, we do not know to what extent the terse biblical descriptions found in Genesis, especially that "he walked with God/divine beings" (Gen 5:22, 24), which would have enabled him to transcend the worldly sphere, triggered the growth of such traditions around the figure of Enoch, or whether Genesis already reflects the existence of such traditions. In the latter case, the attribution to Enoch of writings that describe the other worlds is primarily a scripturalization of earlier traditions.

The use of the first person voice in the writings attributed to Enoch may have different reasons. Enoch's journey reports share form-critical elements with earlier prophetic vision reports, and therefore may be based on the pattern already established in Ezek 40–48 and Zech 1–6, where the vision reports use the first person voice. Or, alternatively, Nickelsburg has argued that the first collection of Enochic writings was organized according to the literary form of the testament genre, which also generally employs first person speech.[36] Whereas the use of the first person therefore may be attributed to the literary form or genre, one should also note its relative preponderance in Aramaic narrative compositions. Apart from the apocalyptic, visionary, and testamentary first person reports found among the Dead Sea Scrolls, virtually all of which are written in Aramaic, we also have the Tobit romance, the first part of which is a first person report, the different first person sections (of Lamech, Noah, and Abram) of the narratives of the *Genesis Apocryphon*, and, outside the Dead Sea Scrolls, the narrative framework of Ahiqar.

The corpus contains a series of other Aramaic texts that use first person voice and are attributed to biblical figures, even if the fragmentary nature sometimes makes it difficult to know the identity of the fictional first person. Thus, from the predeluvian patriarchs, there are texts attributed to Enoch, and (as part of the *Genesis Apocryphon*) to Lamech and Noah. The *Genesis Apocryphon* also contains a section with Abram as first person narrator (19.1–21.22), before the text turns to third person narrative in 21.23–22.34. Other manuscripts contain testaments or other texts attributed to Jacob, his sons, as well as to the son and grandson of Levi:[37] the frag-

---

[36] G. W. E. Nickelsburg, *1 Enoch 1: A Commentary on the Book of 1 Enoch Chapters 1–36, 81–108* (Hermeneia; Philadelphia: Fortress Press, 2001), 22–6.

[37] Most of the these texts were preliminarily discussed by J. T. Milik, "Écrits préésséniens de Qumrân: d'Hénoch à Amram," in *Qumrân: Sa piété, sa théologie et son milieu* (ed. M. Delcor; BETL 46; Leuven: University Press, 1978), 91–106, and published by

ments of 4Q537 may be remnants of a *Testament of Jacob*; those of 4Q538 of a *Testament of Benjamin* or a *Testament of Judah*;[38] and 4Q539 of a *Testament of Joseph*. The sigla 1Q21, and 4Q213–214[39] preserve fragments of the *Aramaic Levi Document*, related to the Greek *Testament of Levi* of the *Testaments of the Twelve Patriarchs*, whereas the first person of 4Q540–541 has tentatively been identified as Levi (hence the name $apocrLevi^{a-b}$). 4Q542 preserves a *Testament of Kohat*, and 4Q543–548 (and perhaps also 4Q549) the so-called *Visions of Amram*. Perhaps one should add to this group the *Aramaic New Jerusalem*, whose first person voice may have been Jacob's.[40] Many of those texts have elements of the genre "testament," which by definition claims to be the report of a patriarch's or leader's farewell speech, and is not written by the first person speaker himself.[41]

Those Aramaic texts present different topics and styles, ranging from autobiographical overviews by the patriarchs of their own lives, via recounting of dreams or visions, general admonitions to sons, and sapiential instructions, to teachings on sacrifice and the priesthood. It is consistent with the pre-Mosaic lineage of the protagonists that these texts do not refer to the Mosaic scriptures, but in contrast describe ancestral instructions and revelation through visions and dreams. The interest of most of those texts in priesthood and sacrifice, suggests a priestly-Levitical provenance, and one gets the impression that those Aramaic texts were more concerned with the ancestral "scriptural" priestly figures, the seven "men of his favor" (4Q545 4 18), than with the text of the Torah.

É. Puech in DJD XXXI, and reproduced, with English translations, in *The Dead Sea Scrolls Reader 3 Parabiblical Texts* (eds. D. W. Parry and E. Tov; Leiden: Brill, 2005).

[38] In the official publication in DJD XXXI:191–99, É. Puech, following J. T. Milik, regards it as a *Testament of Judah*, whereas D. Dimant, "Not the 'Testament of Judah,' but the 'Words of Benjamin': On the Nature of 4Q538," in *Sha'arei Lashon: Studies in Hebrew, Aramaic, and Jewish Languages Presented to Moshe Bar-Asher* (eds. A. Maman et al.; 3 vols.; Jerusalem: Bialik Institute, 2007), 1:10–26, took up Jean Starcky's original identification of the text as being attributed to Benjamin.

[39] The editors, Jonas Greenfield and Michael Stone, split those into six manuscripts, *Aramaic Levi Document^{a-f}* (4Q213, 213a, 213b, 214, 214a, 214b).

[40] E. Tigchelaar, "The Imaginal Context and the Visionary of the Aramaic New Jerusalem," in *Flores Florentino: Dead Sea Scrolls and Other Early Jewish Studies in Honour of Florentino García Martínez* (eds. A. Hilhorst et al.; JSJSup 122; Leiden: Brill, 2007), 257–70.

[41] Cf. for the genre, for example, J. J. Collins, "Testaments," in *Jewish Writings of the Second Temple Period: Apocrypha, Pseudepigrapha, Qumran Sectarian Writings, Philo, Josephus* (ed. M. E. Stone; Assen: Van Gorcum, 1984), 325–55; A. Bingham Kolenkow, "The Literary Genre 'Testament,'" in *Early Judaism and its Modern Interpreters* (eds. R. A. Kraft and G. W. E. Nickelsburg; Philadelphia: Fortress Press, 1986), 259–67.

Above we saw that Dimant distinguished a second group of Aramaic pseudepigraphic texts, which she described as "pseudepigraphic apocalypses and visions attributed to seers in Babylon." Actually, apart from Dan 7, this group would at best comprise the *Prayer of Nabonidus*, and first person Danielic texts like the *Four Kingdom* manuscripts.[42] Whereas it is true that there are many more Aramaic texts that have an Eastern origin or setting, few of those, except Tobit, are formally pseudepigrapha, and even the so-called *Pseudo-Daniel* texts are third person texts, as Dan 1–6. The *Prayer of Nabonidus*, however, is not attributed to a seer, but should be compared to the first person account of Nebuchadnezzar in Dan 4. Rather than labeling those texts as pseudepigraphic, they serve as examples that authors may use fictional first person voices for diverse reasons.

Hebrew examples of new writings ascribed to scriptural figures are mainly writings attributed to Moses,[43] David,[44] and Jeremiah,[45] though rarely the first person voice is attributed to these figures.[46] Here one may question on formal grounds whether these texts should be called pseudepigrapha, and Dimant prefers the label apocrypha.[47] The point is that in the case of both the Aramaic pseudepigrapha, and these Hebrew pseudepigrapha/apocrypha, new texts are attributed to specific figures.

---

[42] Dimant, "Old Testament Pseudepigrapha at Qumran" (see n. 8), 465, refers to *Pseudo-Daniel* and the *Prayer of Nabonidus*, and refers to the Babylonian background of the *Book of Giants* and Iranian elements in *Four Kingdoms*.

[43] These texts are often called Moses pseudepigrapha, even though in those fragmentary texts the name of Moses is not always preserved. Examples are 1Q22 and 4QDM (*Words of Moses*), 4Q376, 4Q408, and 1Q29 (*Apocryphal Moses*), 4Q375 (*Apocryphal Moses*), and 2Q21 (*Apocryphal Moses*). Note that the latter three need not be, in spite of the shared title, the same composition. For a brief overview, cf., for example, E. Tigchelaar, "A Cave 4 Fragment of Divre Mosheh (4QDM) and the Text of 1Q22 1:7–10 and Jubilees 1:9–14," *DSD* 12 (2005): 303–12 (308–9).

[44] See the "non-canonical" psalms in 4Q88 and 11Q5, and perhaps the "apocryphal" psalms of 11Q11.

[45] See the compositions called *Apocryphon of Jeremiah A* (4Q383) and *Apocryphon of Jeremiah C* (4Q385a, 4Q387, 4Q387a, 4Q388, 4Q389, 4Q390), all published by D. Dimant in DJD XXX.

[46] The only clear case is 4Q383 (*apocrJer A*) 1 2 "and I, Jeremiah, wept bitterly." Another example of a Hebrew first person voice pseudepigraphic text is the *Testament of Naphtali* (4Q215), which, in view of all the other Aramaic testaments of the patriarchs, may be a translation from the Aramaic. In none of the Moses texts found at Qumran, is Moses the first person speaker, as he is in the *Testament* or *Assumption of Moses*.

[47] Dimant, "Old Testament Pseudepigrapha at Qumran" (see n. 8), 453, 455.

4. Texts, Pseudepigraphic Figures, and Groups

It is apparent that there are some relationships between the genre or content of texts and the figure to which they are contributed. For example, most of the texts that are connected to Moses deal with law, and it comes as no surprise that heavenly journeys are ascribed to Enoch. However, different kinds of explanations are given as to why authors ascribed their works to particular ancient figures. Collins mentions the older psychological approaches to pseudepigraphy, which presented the theses of "corporate personality" or of identification of the author's visionary alter ego with a famous visionary of the past,[48] which actually are attempts to acquit the pseudepigraphic authors from the charge of deception.

One may also refer to social correspondences between authors and their pseudepigraphic figures. Thus, the authors of the Enochic pseudepigrapha would have been intellectual scribes who had, like Enoch, an encyclopedic interest; the circles behind the Abram-to-Amram works with their priestly and scribal concerns would have been Levitical priests. Yet, Collins counters that "there is no apparent reason why Enoch would have been chosen as the mouthpiece of social criticism," and argues that names such as those of Enoch and Daniel are "use[d] to lend authority to a group or movement in the second century B.C.E.," though he is careful enough not to generalize this for the adoption of pseudepigraphic figures in general.[49] One step further, and probably under the influence of the distinction between Pauline, Petrine, and Johannine communities made in studies of Early Christianity, some scholars entertain the idea of a kind of Enochic community, with the Enochic corpus as its sacred Scripture.[50] Exciting as this suggestion may be, we have no evidence of a community that was primarily based on the Enochic texts, or of a distinctiveness of all Enochic texts. For example, the Enochic *Animal Apocalypse* is closely related in its ideas to the *Damascus Document* and the *Apocryphon of Jeremiah C*.[51]

---

[48] J. J. Collins, *Encounters with Biblical Theology* (Minneapolis: Fortress Press, 2005), 29.

[49] Collins, "Pseudepigraphy and Group Formation" (see n. 13), 47, 48.

[50] Cautiously, G. W. E. Nickelsburg, "The Nature and Function of Revelation in 1 Enoch, Jubilees, and Some Qumran Documents," in *Pseudepigraphic Perspectives* (see n. 9), 91–119 (99). More positively, G. Boccaccini, *Beyond the Essene Hypothesis: The Parting of the Ways Between Qumran and Enochic Judaism* (Grand Rapids, Mich.: Eerdmans, 1998), who refers to the Qumran Community as "the Enochic community of the Dead Sea Scrolls" (165–66), and, without any restriction, D. R. Jackson, *Enochic Judaism: Three Defining Paradigm Exemplars* (LSTS 49; London: T&T Clark, 2004).

[51] Cf., e.g., D. Dimant, "4QApocryphon of Jeremiah: Introduction," in DJD XXX:91–116.

A more recent and different approach was proposed by Najman, who understands works that are connected in some way to an ancient figure (apocryphally, pseudepigraphically, or otherwise), in light of the idea of "discourses that are linked to their founders."[52] In her book Najman focuses almost exclusively on the so-called Mosaic discourse, which includes not only *Jubilees*, and the *Temple Scroll*, but also, in spite of differences, Philo's writings, and reads those texts as participating in a discourse with previous texts attributed to that founding figure. In a note she hints at the possibility of other discourses and mentions the examples of "a Davidic discourse that combines messianism and kingship into texts and subsequent interpretive traditions," "a Solomonic discourse that combines the ever-growing wisdom traditions with a notion of divine revelation and selection," and points at texts associated with Enoch and at Isaiah traditions.[53] It is clear that those other discourses are not in all respects parallel to that of the Mosaic discourse. For example, from a literary and historical perspective, the relation between the "founding figures" and the traditions differs: within the Mosaic discourse, Deuteronomy has a different function than the *Book of Watchers* has in the Enochic collection.

The strength of Najman's model is that it calls attention to the relation of new texts—whether rewritten, apocryphal, pseudepigraphic, or under the author's own name (as with Philo)—to previous texts and traditions, and to the persons to whom those earlier texts are attributed. It also changes the perspective of the classical idea of "pseudepigraphy": authors do not attribute their own work to an ancient figure in order to deceptively authorize it; rather, because they acknowledge the authority of texts and traditions that are connected to those ancient figures (Najman's "founders"), they continue their discourse, and therefore attribute these new works to the founders. More recently, Najman has developed her ideas with respect to pseudonymous attribution, and, with respect to *4 Ezra*, theorizes that "pseudonymous attribution should be seen as a metaphorical device, operating at the level of the text as a whole, whereby the actual author emulates and self-identifies as an exemplar."[54] However, as other explanations, Najman's model of discourses tied to founders does not explain all cases of pseudepigraphy, and in the last part of this paper I wish to add a few additional perspectives, based on the texts found among the Dead Sea Scrolls, to those already discussed above.

---

[52] Najman, *Seconding Sinai* (see n. 28), 12–9 et passim.
[53] Ibid., 17–8 n. 34.
[54] Eadem, "How Should We Contextualize Pseudepigrapha? Imitation and Emulation in *4 Ezra*," in *Flores Florentino* (see n. 40), 529–36 (535).

5. Observations and Conclusions

The large corpus of admittedly largely damaged texts of the Dead Sea Scrolls enables us to regard specific cases of pseudepigraphy in their literary context. The first observation must be that the corpus does not contain a single manuscript or fragment that mentions the name of a contemporary figure, which we would regard as the actual author of a text. In all cases where a text is attributed, implicitly or explicitly, to a specific person, it is to figures from the past, or even to non-human figures, like the first person speech of God in the *Temple Scroll*, or, even more striking, to the archangel Michael himself. Thus, 4Q529 (*Words of Michael*) begins with the title "The words of the book that Michael said to the angels." From our perspective, all those texts are either anonymous, or pseudonymous/pseudepigraphic.[55] This phenomenon is found more broadly in Aramaic and Hebrew literature, and, in contrast to Greek literature, there are only very few cases where the identity of the author is actually included in the text, or otherwise known to us.[56] The example of the exception of Ben Sira underlines the fragmentary nature of our knowledge. Sira's name is only mentioned at the beginning and end of the composition, and we cannot exclude that some other texts had names of authors that have been lost. Still, all the evidence indicates the preponderance of anonymous and pseudonymous texts. If pseudepigraphy would be defined as the phenomenon that an author ascribes his text falsely to another author, *instead of to himself*, in order to enhance its authority and validity, then the term should not be used for Hebrew and Aramaic literature, since authors virtually never ascribed their works to themselves. One may explain this in terms of general cultural attitudes towards individuality and authorship, but perhaps also in terms of cultural literary conventions.

The corpus of Dead Sea Scrolls shows that there is a strong correlation between pseudepigraphic texts with a first-person voice and the Aramaic language. The use of the first-person voice in texts like Tobit and the framework Ahiqar may indicate a typical Aramaic preference for first-person narrative. In that case, the specific voice of a book, which for Bernstein is the criterion for pseudepigraphy, would be in many cases a literary phenomenon related to genre and language. Many questions do remain,

---

[55] One should make a formal distinction between anonymous texts that are later (incorrectly) attributed to a specific author, and texts that are intended by their authors to be connected to an ancient figure.

[56] Perhaps Nehemiah, if we assume he was the author of at least that part of the book of Nehemiah that is called the Nehemiah Memorial; then Ben Sira, and then, centuries later, the *paytan* Yosi ben Yosi. Rabbinic works do refer to the pre-rabbinic works of Ben La'aga and Ben Tagla, but then, their works apparently have not remained.

though, for example why some texts are written in Aramaic and others in Hebrew.[57]

The choice of a first-person voice instead of a third-person also seems to be related to an entirely different aspect, namely the genre and voice of the texts that are already related to the ancient figure. In these cases, the phenomenon of pseudepigraphy is part of a larger phenomenon of parascriptural literature, where new texts contribute to a discourse that has been initiated by already existing texts, and which is related to what Najman calls a founding figure.

On the other hand, most of the Aramaic texts show the phenomenon that texts are attributed to figures that are not connected to writings in the Hebrew Bible. At present, we do not yet have a comprehensive study of all those Aramaic pseudepigrapha, but it would seem that texts are attributed to those figures, for example Levi to Amram, because of their importance as ancestors of Moses and Aaron, and indirectly as perceived founders of the Levitical priesthood. In the case of Kohath and Amram, I would proffer, texts are not attributed to those founding figures in order to authorize the texts, but the other way around. In order to elevate these figures to the position they are entitled to, scriptures are being attributed to them, so that they are fully incorporated in the line from Abraham to Moses and Aaron.

Overall, the different forms of pseudepigraphy we encounter in the scrolls, defy one simple explanation, and should be regarded from different perspectives. I suggest that the first of those is literary and related to genre, determining the choice of voices and expression of fictional authorship. The second perspective regards pseudepigraphic works as a special form of parabiblical or parascriptural texts, where the voice of the earlier scriptures is imitated. The third perspective concerns the different possible kinds of correspondence between factual authors and fictional author, which in previous scholarship have been approached from psychological and sociological points of view. The many kinds of distinctions that previous scholars such as Bernstein and Dimant have made, strongly suggest that we are not dealing with a homogeneous phenomenon at all, but a combination of perspectives, or modes of literature.

---

[57] Dimant, "Old Testament Pseudepigrapha at Qumran" (see n. 8), 464–65, notes that "only at the revelation at Mount Sinai was Hebrew publicly revealed to the people of Israel. So everything related to post-Sinaitic times in the land of Israel had to be formulated in Hebrew, whereas Aramaic was reserved for periods preceding the revelation, or for circumstances of Jews in exile." This is an attractive suggestion, which is, however, not expressed by the references given in 465 n. 92. Some linguistic support for this view may be found in the *Visions of Amram*, where the Hebraisms may suggest an author whose first language was Hebrew, but nevertheless wrote the text because pre-Sinaitic patriarchs were supposed to speak Aramaic.

Appendix: Letters at Qumran

The corpus of Dead Sea Scrolls from Qumran does not contain many letters. Lange lists only three cases, namely *4QLetter? ar* (4Q342), *4QLetter nab* (4Q343), and 4QMMT which he classifies as an "epistolary treatise concerned with religious law."[58] The first two are non-literary, personal letters, and the epistolary character of *MMT*, formerly called *Halakhic Letter*, is disputed.[59]

In addition, the corpus contains fragments of known literary texts such as both Aramaic (4Q204; 4Q212) and Greek (7Q4, 8, 11–14) fragments of the *Epistle of Enoch*, and a few words of verses 43–44 of the *Letter of Jeremiah* (7Q2). Reference to a letter of Jeremiah sent from Egypt to the exile in Babylon is probably included in 4Q389 (*Apocryphon of Jeremiah C*) 1 6, and the remnants of the composition may contain part of the letter.[60] 4Q465, a small papyrus fragment, containing the words "he will send," "the copy of the letter," and "Samson," deserves special attention. The official title of that fragment is *Text Mentioning Samson?*, and the editor mentions Strugnell's view that this is a remnant of a "pseudonymous letter attributed to Samson and perhaps contained riddles or similar wisdom material."[61]

---

[58] Lange, "Annotated List" (see n. 15), 145.

[59] Cf. discussion in H. von Weissenberg, *4QMMT: Reevaluating the Text, the Function, and the Meaning of the Epilogue* (STDJ 82; Leiden: Brill, 2009), 13–4; 144–68 (ch. 4 "The Genre of 4QMMT").

[60] Cf. discussion in Dimant, DJD XXX:222–23, and in L. Doering, "Jeremiah and the 'Diaspora Letters' in Ancient Judaism: Epistolary Communication with the Golah as Medium for Dealing with the Present," in *Reading the Present in the Qumran Library: The Perception of the Contemporary by Means of Scriptural Interpretations* (eds. K. De Troyer and A. Lange; SBLSymS 30; Atlanta: SBL, 2005), 43–72 (65–7).

[61] Erik Larson, in DJD XXXVI:395.

II. Griechisch-römische Kontexte

Göttliche und menschliche Verfasserschaft im Altertum

von

WOLFGANG SPEYER

1. Bewusstseinsgeschichtliche Voraussetzungen

Der Gedanke, der Anfang liege bei der Gottheit und deshalb sei auch jedes menschliche Tun mit der Anrufung der Gottheit zu beginnen, ist der Dichtung der Griechen seit ältesten Zeiten vertraut.[1] Darüber hinaus gehört dieser Gedanke zu den Grundüberzeugungen der religiösen Überlieferung der Völker. In ihm wurzeln geradezu die Ursprünge der Menschheitskulturen. So lautet das übereinstimmende Urteil, der *consensus omnium*: Im Anfang und am Anfang von allem steht der Gott, die Göttin, die Gottheit, das Göttliche.[2] Die Griechen haben zu diesem Thema nicht nur wie die übrigen Völker des Altertums spontane Zeugnisse in bildender Kunst und Literatur hinterlassen, sondern als Erste auch differenzierte Reflexionen entwickelt.[3]

Der geschichtliche Weg, den das menschliche Bewusstsein bis heute durchlaufen hat, führt von einer ursprünglichen *unio magica* und damit einer Fremdbestimmung zu einer Selbstbestimmung des je Einzelnen.[4] Die Fremdbestimmung wurde als Bestimmung durch die geheimnisvollen Mächte des Göttlichen/Dämonischen aufgefasst, die hinter allen und in allen Erscheinungen des Staunen erregenden Universums, des Kosmos oder der Natur oder – jüdisch–christlich–islamisch gesprochen – der Schöpfung, erfahren wurden. Diese Mächte erschienen als die Herrinnen

---

[1] Alcman (um 610 v. Chr.) Frgm. 29 Page / Davies; vgl. J. MARTIN, Arati Phaenomena. Introduction, texte critique, commentaire et traduction, Florenz 1956, 3–11 (v. 1–18).

[2] H. GÖRGEMANNS, Art. Anfang, RAC Suppl. 1 (2001), 401–448; W. SPEYER, Frühes Christentum im antiken Strahlungsfeld, Bd. 2, WUNT 116, Tübingen 1999, Reg.: ‚Anfang'; s. auch u. Anm. 22.

[3] W. JAEGER, Die Theologie der frühen griechischen Denker, Stuttgart 1953 (Nachdruck Darmstadt 1964); H. DÖRRIE, Art. Gottesvorstellung, RAC 12 (1983), 81–154.

[4] C. H. RATSCHOW, Magie und Religion, Gütersloh 1947 (Nachdruck Meisenheim 1955); S. MOWINCKEL, Religion und Kultus, deutsche Übersetzung, Göttingen 1953, 13–27: ‚Das magische Weltbild'.

über Heil und Unheil, Segen und Fluch, Leben und Tod.[5] Das Zeitalter der Fremdbestimmung durch die göttlichen/dämonischen Mächte dauerte hunderttausende Jahre und umfasste das fast gänzlich geschichtslose mythische Zeitalter der Menschheit. Ihm folgten mit der Sesshaftwerdung und dem Ackerbau zu Anfang der Hochkulturen des Vorderen Orients um 10000 v. Chr. das myth-historische und seit dem ersten Jahrtausend v. Chr. in Griechenland das historische Zeitalter, in dem wir heute noch stehen.[6] Dabei ist in dieser dritten Epoche eine Intensivierung des geschichtlichen Erfahrens und Auffassens zu bemerken. Diese ist allerdings nicht geradlinig verlaufen. Ein erster Höhepunkt geschichtlichen Erfahrens und Erfassens ist am Ende des 5. Jh. v. Chr. mit dem Geschichtsschreiber Thukydides erreicht. Der Hellenismus führte diese neu gewonnene Stufe der Historiographie nicht ungebrochen weiter, wie das Aufkommen der tragisch-pathetischen Geschichtsschreibung beweist.[7] Ebenso wenig haben die Römer die von Polybios im Anschluss an Thukydides fortgesetzte kritische Geschichtsschreibung bruchlos übernommen, sondern sie durch ihre moralisierende Geschichtsschreibung überformt, wobei das tragisch-dramatische und zugleich psychagogische Element weiter wirksam blieb.[8]

Eine gewisse Entsprechung findet der Prozess der Emanzipation des Menschen aus einer ursprünglichen Fremdbestimmung durch die übermenschlichen Mächte in jenem bewusstseinsgeschichtlichen Prozess, der von einer fast ausschließlich religiösen Interpretation der Welt zu einer fast ausschließlich profanen Weltdeutung verläuft.[9] Verglichen mit Herodot ist Thukydides bereits der profanere Geschichtsdeuter. Eine ausschließlich profane Weltdeutung hat sich aber im griechisch-römischen Altertum niemals so gebildet wie in der Neuzeit Europas. Gegenüber der religiösen Weltdeutung der Hauptvertreter der vorsokratischen Philosophie, sodann Platons, des Platonismus und der Stoa blieben die Atomisten, die Skeptiker und auch die Epikureer – man denke an den die Religion bekämpfenden römischen Lehrdichter Lukrez – in der Minderzahl. Erst die italienische Renaissance, ferner die philosophisch-wissenschaftliche Aufklärung des 18. Jh. und der Naturalismus sowie Materialismus des 19. und 20. Jh. ha-

---

[5] W. SPEYER, Frühes Christentum im antiken Strahlungsfeld, Bd. 3, WUNT 213, Tübingen 2007, 15–33: ‚Zur Erfahrung der göttlichen Macht in der Religionsgeschichte des Altertums'.

[6] A.a.O. 3 Anm. 6; vgl. Varro bei Censorinus, De die natali 21,1, der bereits von drei Epochen der Menschheit spricht, dem *tempus adelon*, *mythicon* und *historicon*.

[7] E. PLÜMACHER, Lukas als griechischer Historiker, PRE.S 14 (1974), 235–264 (257–260).

[8] A.a.O. 259f.

[9] G. KRÜGER, Religiöse und profane Welterfahrung, WuG, Geisteswiss. Reihe H. 53/54, Frankfurt a.M. 1973.

ben neue Stufen auf dem Weg zu der heute fast ausschließlich herrschenden profanen Welterklärung beschritten.

2. Der ‚göttliche', heilige oder numinose Mensch als der erste mit Eigennamen bekannte Mensch

Eine erkennbare frühe Selbstbestimmung äußerte sich im Hervortreten der damit auch für uns erstmals als myth-historisch fassbaren religiösen Persönlichkeit, also einzelner göttlicher, heiliger oder numinoser Menschen.[10] Diesen dürften bewusstseinsmäßig im späten mythischen und im frühen myth-historischen Zeitalter der mit Namen bekannte einzelne Gott oder die einzelne Göttin sowie der einzelne Heros und die einzelne Heroine vorangegangen sein. In diesem Zusammenhang hat die ‚Ich-bin-Rede' der ägyptischen und der mesopotamischen Götter einen bemerkenswerten Aussagewert; tritt hier doch die einzelne Gottheit einer einzelnen Gottheit oder einem erwählten Menschen gegenüber und offenbart sich.[11] Die ersten sakralen Könige, die Priesterkönige und heiligen Gesetzgeber schwanken noch undeutlich zwischen mythischer und geschichtlicher Wirklichkeit. Sie stehen an den Anfängen der antiken Hochkulturen, während alle übrigen Angehörigen ihres Stammes oder Volkes noch gänzlich im Dunkel der Geschichtslosigkeit und damit der Namenlosigkeit verharren. Der göttliche oder numinose Mensch als König, Herrscher und Gesetzgeber tritt zugleich als der religiöse, sittliche und politisch-militärische Führer der Seinen auf. Dieser numinose Mensch der Frühzeit vereinigte in sich Aufgaben, die in der Folgezeit in verschiedenen Trägern verselbständigt erscheinen. So begegnet bereits sehr früh neben dem Priesterkönig als weiterer Führer der vielen Namenlosen der Dichter-Sänger-Prophet, der oft auch Arzt-Seher war.[12] Wie die Sakralkönige ihren Stammbaum und ihre Weihe auf eine Gottheit, vor allem auf den Himmelsgott, zurückgeführt haben, so auch die heiligen Sänger. In Griechenland liegen derartige Überlieferungen für Orpheus, Musaios, Linos, Bakis, Homer und weitere Dichter-Sänger vor. Apollon, eine Muse oder eine andere Gottheit galten als ihr Vater oder ihre Mutter.[13]

---

[10] W. SCHOTTROFF, Art. Gottmensch I (Alter Orient und Judentum), RAC 12 (1983), 155–234; H. D. BETZ, Art. Gottmensch II (Griechisch-römische Antike und Urchristentum), a.a.O. 234–312.

[11] H. THYEN, Art. Ich-Bin-Worte, RAC 17 (1996), 147–213 (150–158).

[12] P. KETTS, Prosopographie der historischen griechischen Manteis bis auf die Zeit Alexanders des Großen, Diss. Erlangen/Nürnberg 1966.

[13] Hes.theog. 94–96; SPEYER, Frühes Christentum, Bd. 3 (s. Anm. 5), 89–101 (92f.): ‚Gottheit und Mensch, die Eltern des Kunstwerks'.

Gerade in Griechenland können wir die Entwicklung verfolgen, wie aus dem myth-historischen Zeitalter das geschichtliche Zeitalter entstanden ist. Dieser Übergang vollzog sich vom noch gänzlich mythischen Orpheus zu Homer, der selbst ähnlich wie der von ihm beschriebene Trojanische Krieg zwischen Mythos und Geschichte schwankt, und weiter zu Hesiod aus Askra am Helikon, der bereits als Sänger einer geschichtlichen Welt erkennbar ist. Der gleiche Weg führt dann weiter zu den namentlich und geographisch bekannten griechischen Lyrikern, zu den ältesten Philosophen und Geschichtsschreibern. Dieser Übergang von dem einen zum anderen geistigen Zeitalter umfasst die Zeitspanne vom 8. bis ins 5. Jh. v. Chr. Den Schlusspunkt bezeichnen die Atomisten, die Sophisten, Euripides und Thukydides. Ihr Weltbild ähnelt bereits dem der philosophisch-wissenschaftlich aufgeklärten Neuzeit. Es zeichnet sich durch Emanzipation von heiliger Überlieferung in Mythos und Kultus und von Religion aus.[14]

Orpheus und Musaios wirken noch weit mythischer als der bereits das geschichtliche Zeitalter heraufführende Homer bzw. einzelne homerische Sänger, wie der blinde Sänger des homerischen Apollonhymnos aus Chios.[15] Den Griechen galten die Ilias und der Epische Kyklos als Zeugnisse eines geschichtlichen Zusammenhangs, eben des Trojanischen Krieges. Die Zerstörung Trojas datierte Herodot 800 Jahre vor seiner Zeit, also um 1250 v. Chr., und Eratosthenes aus Kyrene (284–202 v. Chr.) in das Jahr 1184/83 v. Chr.[16] Die homerischen Sagen stehen zugleich auch auf der Schwelle der bis dahin allein geltenden Mündlichkeit des Singens und Sagens zu einer beginnenden Schriftlichkeit. Mit der Schrift aber treten die antiken Völker mehr und mehr in das geschichtliche Zeitalter ein.

Für die älteste Stufe geistigen Schaffens ergibt sich eindeutig, dass die Gottheit als die Quelle des Sprechens und Schreibens galt. Wie der erste Vers der Ilias bezeugt, soll die Göttin, also die Muse, den Zorn des Achill, also den Inhalt des Epos, besingen.[17] Der Sänger des Schiffskataloges im zweiten Buch der Ilias vermag dies nur zu tun, wenn ihn darüber die Musen, die als die Töchter der Göttin Erinnerung, Mnemosyne, galten, dazu

---

[14] W. NESTLE, Vom Mythos zum Logos. Die Selbstentfaltung des griechischen Denkens von Homer bis auf die Sophistik und Sokrates, Stuttgart 1940; M. WINIARCZYK, Wer galt im Altertum als Atheist?, Ph. 128 (1984), 157–183; 136 (1992), 306–310; ders., Bibliographie zum antiken Atheismus. 17. Jahrhundert–1990, Bonn 1994.

[15] Hom.Hym. ad Apollinem 166–178.

[16] Hdt. 2,145,4; Eratosthenes. Fragmente der griechischen Historiker 241 (Frgm. 1 Jacoby); vgl. J. STENGER, Art. Troia III, DNP 12/1 (2002), 862–865 (864).

[17] Hom.Il. 1,1; vgl. Hom.Od. 1,1–10; vgl. W. SCHMID, Geschichte der griechischen Literatur Bd. 1,1, HKAW 7,1,1, München 1929 (Nachdruck 1959), 58.60; R. MORTHLEY, Art. Gnosis I (Erkenntnislehre), RAC 11 (1981), 446–537 (450–452); K. THRAEDE, Art. Inspiration, RAC 18 (1998), 329–365 (332–334).

befähigen; denn die Göttinnen sind die Wissenden, die Menschen hingegen die Nichtwissenden.[18]

Der homerische Sänger empfängt von den Musen bereits ein Wissen über bestimmte Vorgänge der Vergangenheit, also ein geschichtliches Wissen, zu dem er selbst unmittelbar keinen Zugang zu besitzen glaubt. Während an dieser Stelle wie in der Ilias als den Gesängen über den Trojanischen Krieg bereits die geschichtliche Dimension erkennbar wird, verbleibt die geistige Welt der Ilias doch noch weitgehend im Rahmen des mythischen Erfahrens. Die das Ganze der Handlung neben der Moira bestimmenden Götter bedeuten in der Ilias und auch noch in der Odyssee viel mehr als in der von Homer abhängigen späteren Epik der Griechen und Römer. Der Weg von einem ursprünglichen mythischen Erleben zu reiner literarischer Fiktion ist in dieser Entwicklung zu erkennen.

Das Sprechen der Gottheit kommt in Griechenland vor allem an den Orakelstätten bis weit in die geschichtliche Zeit vor, an erster Stelle beim Orakel von Delphi, das als der Nabel der Welt angesehen wurde.[19] Hier steht das Sprechen Apollons durch seine Priesterin in der Mitte dieses für das geistige und sittliche Leben Griechenlands so bedeutenden Orakels.[20]

3. Die mythische oder göttliche Verfasserschaft als die älteste Form der Verfasserschaft

Aus dem bisher Mitgeteilten ergibt sich für die älteste Stufe der literarischen Verfasserschaft: Der Dichter-Sänger-Prophet hält sich nicht für den Schöpfer seines Gesanges oder seines literarischen Werkes, sondern er glaubt, Sprachrohr einer Gottheit zu sein. Ob die Muse, ob Apollon, Hermes oder auch Dionysos: Am Anfang dieser geistigen Tätigkeit steht die Gottheit.[21] Diese Überzeugung entspricht auch ganz der von den Griechen reich ausgestalteten Vorstellung von der Gottheit oder vom Heros als dem

---

[18] Hom.Il. 2,484–493; Hes.theog. 52–62; W. HÜBNER, Hermes als musischer Gott. Das Problem der dichterischen Wahrheit in seinem homerischen Hymnus, Ph. 130 (1986), 153–174; M. PUELMA, Der Dichter und die Wahrheit in der griechischen Poetik von Homer bis Aristoteles, Museum Helveticum 46 (1989), 65–100 (66–73).

[19] C. AUFFAHRTH, Art. Omphalos, DNP 8 (2000), 1201f.

[20] J. FONTENROSE, The Delphic Oracle, Berkeley/Los Angeles 1978; ders., Didyma. Apollo's Oracle, Cult and Companions, Berkeley/Los Angeles 1988; V. ROSENBERGER, Art. Orakel III, DNP 9 (2000), 3–7.

[21] Zu Hermes als Erfinder der Rede und als Träger des Logos bzw. als Logos vgl. K. RUPPRECHT, Gott auf Erden. Ein Beitrag zur Horaz-Erklärung und zur Geschichte des Messianismus im Westen, Würzburger Jahrbücher für die Altertumswissenschaft 1 (1946), 67–78 (71f.); J. PÉPIN / K. HOHEISEL, Art. Hermeneutik, RAC 14 (1988), 722–771 (736–738).

ersten Erfinder der einzelnen Künste und Techniken, auf denen die Kultur beruht.[22] Ein entsprechendes Bild zeigen der Alte Orient und Ägypten: Der babylonische Schreibergott Nebo und die Schrifterfinder und Schrifterfinderinnen Thot, Seschat und Isis gehen den menschlichen Schreibern sachlich und zeitlich voraus.[23] Nach diesem allgemein geteilten Glauben des Altertums muss die Gottheit am Anfang aller Kulturerrungenschaften des Menschen stehen.

Dieses Bild bestätigen auch die Überlieferungen über die ältesten religiösen Gesetzgeber. So empfängt König Hammurapi das Gesetz vom Sonnengott Schamasch.[24] Noch die vergleichbare, weit jüngere römische Überlieferung über König Numa und die Quellnymphe Egeria von Aricia zeigt die gleiche gedankliche Struktur.[25] Zu dieser Anschauung passt, was die Bücher Exodus und Deuteronomium über Mose und die vom Finger Gottes geschriebenen Gesetzestafeln mitzuteilen wissen[26]: Mose empfängt von der Gottheit wie König Hammurapi oder ähnlich wie der Pharao Menes, wie König Minos von Kreta, der Spartaner Lykurgos, der Gete Zalmoxis, der Perser Zarathustra und der römische König Numa das Gesetz, auf dem die religiöse, politische und gesellschaftliche Lebensordnung seines Volkes beruht.[27] Für die Tradition des Alten Testamentes war Mose der Verfasser der ersten fünf Bücher dieser Sammlung. Als der religiöse Gesetzgeber, der seine Gesetze nicht selbst erdacht, sondern von der Gottheit erhalten zu haben glaubt, steht er in einer Linie mit den religiösen Gesetzgebern des Alten Orients und der Völker des antiken Mittelmeerraumes. Als Verfasser von Schriften, als deren wahrer Verfasser die Gottheit galt, ist Mose, der nach altisraelitischer Tradition am Beginn der schriftlichen Überlieferung im alten Israel steht, durchaus mit dem viel späteren Homer vergleichbar. Beide Gestalten gehören noch dem myth-historischen Zeitalter an, wie

---

[22] K. THRAEDE, Art. Erfinder II (geistesgeschichtlich), RAC 5 (1962), 1191–1278 (1192–1199).

[23] W. SPEYER, Frühes Christentum im antiken Strahlungsfeld, Bd. 1, WUNT 50, Tübingen 1989, 21–58.495 (34–38): ‚Religiöse Pseudepigraphie und literarische Fälschung im Altertum'.

[24] Ders., Religionsgeschichtliche Studien, Collectanea 15, Hildesheim 1995, Reg.: ‚Hammurapi'.

[25] Quintus Ennius, Annales 2 Frgm. 1,113 (79 Skutsch); Liv. 1,21,3; Plutarch, Vita Numae 4,2,62a; Lact.inst. 1,22,2 (CSEL 19,1,88); SPEYER, Religionsgeschichtliche Studien (s. Anm. 24), 79–86.

[26] Ders., Frühes Christentum, Bd. 1 (s. Anm. 23), 39f.

[27] K. REINHARDT, Poseidonios, PRE 22/1 (1953), 558–826 (638–641); SPEYER, Frühes Christentum, Bd. 1 (s. Anm. 23), 35–37.39–42; ders., Religionsgeschichtliche Studien (s. Anm. 24), 99, und Reg.: ‚Mose'. – Die Vorstellung vom geschriebenen Gotteswort findet sich auch bei Ez 2,9f. innerhalb einer Vision; vgl. Sach 5,1–4; 2Sam 21,12–15.

auch der Inhalt ihrer Schriften beweist. So verkehren einzelne Menschen bei Homer wie bei Mose mit der Gottheit. Man denke an die Paradiesgeschichte über Adam und Eva und die Erzählungen über Noe und Abraham!

Die geschichtlichen Verfasser der Homerischen Lieder sind uns ebenso verborgen wie die der fünf Bücher Mose. So gilt für diese ältesten literarischen Überlieferungen am Anfang der Geschichte der Literatur Griechenlands und Israels bei der Verfasserangabe das In- und Miteinander von Anonymität des oder der uns unbekannt bleibenden geschichtlichen Autoren und der mythischen Verfasserangabe, die sich beispielsweise auf die ‚Muse' oder auf ‚Jahwe' beziehen kann. Auch die Hinweise auf Homer und Mose als Vermittler weisen ins myth-historische Zeitalter, das zwischen Sakralität und beginnender Profanität eigentümlich schillert. In diesem In- und Miteinander von Anonymität, myth-historischer Herkunftsangabe und religiöser ‚Pseudepigraphie', das wohl ein erstes Erwachen des geschichtlichen Sinnes am Anfang der antiken Schriftkulturen kennzeichnet, lag zugleich auch eine traditionsstiftende Kraft, die in der geschichtlichen Literaturepoche noch lange nachzuweisen ist.

Nach dem Selbstverständnis der Epoche, aus der die ältesten Nachrichten über Verfasserschaft zu uns gelangt sind, müssen wir demnach von einer mythischen oder göttlichen Verfasserschaft sprechen. Sie ist gleichbedeutend mit dem Begriff der Offenbarung. Die Griechen, aber auch das alte Israel und das Frühjudentum haben die Übermittlung von Offenbarung an die von der Gottheit erwählten Menschen in zahlreichen Bildern näher entfaltet. Sie reichen von der Übergabe einer himmlischen Schrift, vom Essen einer himmlischen Buchrolle, von der Versetzung eines heiligen Menschen in die himmlische Sphäre und dem Hören der Offenbarung, vom Finden eines heiligen Buches an heiligem Orte, wie in einem Grab oder Tempel, bis hin zu den Formen der Inspiration, des Einwehens des göttlichen Geistes und der Ekstase.[28] Die mythische oder göttliche Verfasserschaft steht somit sachlich und zeitlich am Beginn aller erhaltenen oder erschließbaren Schriften der antiken Hochkulturen mit Einschluss Israels.

---

[28] THRAEDE, Art. Inspiration (s. Anm. 17); W. SPEYER, Bücherfunde in der Glaubenswerbung der Antike, Hyp. 24, Göttingen 1974; ders., Die literarische Fälschung im heidnischen und christlichen Altertum. Ein Versuch ihrer Deutung, HAW I/2, München 1971, 67–70; ders., Frühes Christentum, Bd. 3 (s. Anm. 5), 76–88.

4. Die mythische oder göttliche Verfasserschaft im geschichtlichen Zeitalter

Der geistige Weg führte den Menschen aus der Erfahrung des Mythisch-Religiösen, des Heiligen in seiner furchterregenden Ambivalenz von Segen und Fluch, von Gottheit und Dämon und damit einer Fremdbestimmung durch die göttlich-dämonischen Mächte in eine wachsend profane Geschichtlichkeit seiner selbstverantworteten Kultur und damit zu einer zunächst noch relativ eng begrenzten Autonomie. Ausdruck dieses mehr und mehr geschichtlich geprägten Bewusstseins waren nicht zuletzt die nunmehr im geschichtlichen Zeitalter erkennbaren neuen Möglichkeiten der Verfasserschaft. Neben der bewusst gewählten anonymen Veröffentlichung entsteht nunmehr die individuell erfahrene und verantwortete Eigenleistung des jeweils sich als geschichtlich und damit auch als selbständig und frei fühlenden, sich mit seinem Namen nennenden, bekennenden und signierenden Verfassers, die Orthonymität. Aber auch bei ihr zeigt sich, dass vor allem einzelne Dichter, die sich als Nachfolger der älteren Dichter-Sänger-Propheten fühlten, sogar noch in philosophisch-wissenschaftlich aufgeklärten Epochen an der Vorstellung der Inspiration bald mehr, bald weniger bis in das 20. Jh. festgehalten haben.[29] Als Schatten der Orthonymität begegnet die vorgetäuschte Verwendung eines fremden, meist angesehenen Verfassernamens für das eigene Werk. Neben der selten bezeugten Mystifikation und der Wahl eines falschen Namens als eines reinen Decknamens, um unerkannt zu bleiben, also eines Pseudonyms, kommen die literarische Fälschung und die nicht als Fälschung intendierte pseudepigraphische freie literarische Erfindung vor.[30] Daneben ist aber auch mit der Möglichkeit zu rechnen, dass Schüler und Enkelschüler ihre eigenen Schriften unter dem Namen des Schulgründers oder Schulhauptes verbreitet haben oder dass anonyme Schriften aufgrund ihres Inhaltes dem jeweiligen Schulgründer oder Schulhaupt zugewiesen wurden. Dies gilt es bei der Beurteilung vor allem fachwissenschaftlicher Schriften zu beachten, aber auch bei der Beurteilung religiöser Schriften mit prophetischem oder apokalyptischem, selbst pastoralem Inhalt.

Da wir nur selten etwas Konkretes über die antiken Verfasser von Schriften mit erfundener Herkunftsangabe wissen, können wir meist nur aufgrund von Rückschlüssen und allgemeineren Überlegungen etwas über die Absichten und Ziele pseudepigraphischer Schriften aussagen.

---

[29] Ders., Frühes Christentum, Bd. 1 (s. Anm. 23), 100–139.495 (117–126): ‚Fälschung, pseudepigraphische Erfindung und echte religiöse Pseudepigraphie'.

[30] Ders., Fälschung (s. Anm. 28), 21–31.

Im geschichtlichen Zeitalter der Griechen erschien aus dem zeitlich bewusst erlebten und auch reflektierten Abstand zum myth-historischen Zeitalter jene frühe Zeit eines Offenbarungsempfanges oder der mythischen Verfasserschaft zugleich als die Epoche, die die Grundlage der späteren geschichtlichen Kultur und damit der jeweils eigenen Gegenwart gelegt hat. Die antiken Kulturen, die im Gegensatz zu uns noch eine lebendigere Erinnerung an das myth-historische Zeitalter besaßen, zeichnet deshalb grundsätzlich eine Hochschätzung des Alten und der Alten als des mit der Gottheit verbundenen Ursprünglichen aus. Die Menschen des frühen geschichtlichen Zeitalters waren überzeugt, dass sie die seelisch und geistig tragenden Überlieferungen einem dem Göttlichen noch recht nahen Zeitalter zu verdanken hatten.[31] Damit galten die alten mythischen Schriften als überaus werthaltig und kulturbestimmend. So wie man im 19. Jh. aus einer Sehnsucht für die verlorene religiöse Welt des Mittelalters Bilder und Skulpturen dieser Epoche nachgeahmt und auch gefälscht hat, ähnlich haben meist unbekannte antike Autoren seit dem 4. Jh. v. Chr. bis weit in die römische Kaiserzeit religiöse Schriften mit göttlicher Verfasserschaft in Anlehnung an die alten echten neu geschaffen. In diesen Zusammenhang gehören beispielsweise orphische und pythagoreische Pseudepigrapha. Diese dürften aus neupythagoreischen und neuplatonischen Kreisen stammen, in denen die religiöse Weisheit der Frühzeit geschätzt wurde und in denen auch die religiös-mystische Erfahrung weiter lebendig geblieben war. Mit der Möglichkeit einer subjektiv erlebten göttlichen Verfasserschaft ist hier fallweise durchaus noch zu rechnen.

Auf einem gesonderten Blatt stehen die frühjüdischen Schriften, die für sich göttliche oder prophetische Verfasserschaft beanspruchen. Drängen sich in ihnen auffallend apologetische Absichten vor, so werden wir hier von Fälschungen sprechen müssen; anders dürften wieder die pseudepigraphischen Apokalypsen zu bewerten sein. Bei ihnen dürfte die Möglichkeit echter religiöser Pseudepigraphie neben der literarischen Fiktion zu beachten sein.[32]

---

[31] Plato, Philebos 16c: „die Alten mächtiger als wir und näher bei den Göttern wohnend"; Cicero, De legibus 2,11,27: quoniam antiquitas proxume accedit ad deos; zu Poseidonios: Sen.ep. 90,5: illo ergo saeculo, quod aureum perhibent, penes sapientes fuisse regnum Posidonius iudicat ...; G. PFLIGERSDORFFER, Studien zu Poseidonios, DÖAW Sitzungsbericht 232,5 (1959), 85–99: ‚Entwicklung und Schicksal der Kultur'; Cicero, Tusculanae disputationes 1,26: et primum quidem omni antiquitate [sc. uti possumus], quae quo propius aberat ab ortu et divina progenie, hoc melius ea fortasse quae erant vera cernebat; SPEYER, Frühes Christentum, Bd. 2 (s. Anm. 2), 79f., und Reg.: ‚Hochschätzung der/des Alten'.

[32] Ders., Fälschung (s. Anm. 28), 150–168; M. HENGEL, Anonymität, Pseudepigraphie und „Literarische Fälschung" in der jüdisch-hellenistischen Literatur, in: K. von Fritz (Hg.), Pseudepigrapha I. Pseudopythagorica – Lettres de Platon – Littérature pseudépi-

Betrachten wir die gesamte literarische Hinterlassenschaft der Griechen und Römer nach ihrem Anteil an göttlicher und an menschlicher Urheberschaft, so überwiegt bei weitem der profane Anteil. Dieses Ergebnis wird im Folgenden noch wichtig werden.

5. Die heiligen Offenbarungsträger und die ihnen zugewiesenen Schriften

Der Glanz der sich offenbarenden Gottheit fiel vor allem auf die menschlichen Empfänger der Offenbarung. Der Umgebung erschienen diese als die von der Gottheit Erwählten, als Gottesfreunde und als göttliche oder heilige Menschen, die selbst mit Göttlichkeit, Heiligkeit, Weihe, mit geheimnisvoller Macht und Autorität bekleidet waren.

Ein Großteil der religiösen Literatur der Griechen ist unter dem Namen des Orpheus und ihm verwandter Gestalten, wie Musaios oder Linos, überliefert. Sie alle gehören noch tiefer als Homer oder die homerischen Sänger der Welt des Mythischen an.[33] Die Namen der Offenbarungsempfänger standen für den unbedingten und nicht mehr hinterfragbaren Wert der Offenbarung und damit für Wahrheit. Dies trifft neben Orpheus auch für Homer zu.[34] Viele Griechen fanden in Homer wie in einem alle spätere Differenzierung enthaltenden Anfang ihre gesamte spätere Literatur vereinigt: Homer war für sie ein von den Göttern Erwählter, er galt als der Theologe schlechthin, als der Geschichtsschreiber und Geograph, der Lyriker, Tragiker, Redner und manches andere mehr. Vergleichbares gilt für die ältesten Offenbarungsempfänger im gesamten antiken Mittelmeerraum. Diese Hochschätzung der Weisheit der ältesten religiösen Quellen und ihrer heiligen menschlichen Vermittler erklärt, dass man in geschichtlicher Zeit an diese anzuknüpfen versucht hat, sie weitergedacht und weitergeschrieben und ihnen Antworten auf die Fragen der eigenen Gegenwart in den Mund gelegt hat. Der Abstand zwischen freier literarischer Erfindung und Fälschung erscheint bei dieser Vorgehensweise überaus schmal.

---

graphique juive, EnAC 18, Vandœuvres/Genève 1972, 231–329; E. SCHÜRER, The History of the Jewish People in the Age of Jesus Christ (175 B.C. – A.D. 135), hg. v. G. Vermes u.a., Bd. 3,1, Edinburgh 1986, 240–341.552–558.617–700; Bd. 3,2, Edinburgh 1987, 746–808.

[33] A. BERNABÉ, Poetae epici Graeci 2, 1.2 Orphicorum et Orphicis similium testimonia et fragmenta, München/Leipzig 2004/2005; R. BÖHME, Der Lykomide. Tradition und Wandel zwischen Orpheus und Homer, Bern/Stuttgart 1991, 127f.

[34] Porph.antr. bezieht sich auf Hom.Od. 13,102–112 als auf einen Offenbarungstext; dazu SPEYER, Frühes Christentum, Bd. 3 (s. Anm. 5), 227–230.

Da die Griechen mehr als andere Völker die Literatur in zahlreiche literarische Formen und Gattungen aufgegliedert haben, konnte so der herausragende Repräsentant einer literarischen Gattung oder auch eines wissenschaftlichen Faches zur Autorität werden, dem man nicht nur geistig und formal verwandtes anonymes Gut zuwies, sondern den man auch dazu benutzte, um mit seinem Namen verwandte eigene Erfahrungen und Erkenntnisse zu versehen. Die Schwelle zur vollen literarischen Fälschung lag niedrig. So deckte in geschichtlicher Zeit der Name Orpheus kosmogonische Dichtungen ab, der Name Homer Götterhymnen und heroische Epen, Hesiod genealogische und didaktische Dichtungen, Äsop Fabeln, Hippokrates medizinische Abhandlungen und der nach und nach zum Zauberer gewordene Demokrit magische und alchemistische Schriften.[35] Ferner haben in den Philosophen- und Ärzteschulen Schüler eigene Arbeiten unter dem Namen ihres Lehrers verbreitet. Dies konnte mitunter auch aus Verehrung geschehen.[36] Vielleicht dürfen wir in diesen Zusammenhang einzelne pseudopaulinische Briefe stellen. Motive zur Wahl des Mittels der Pseudepigraphie können sich auch bündeln.

Vergleichbares galt bereits für das Alte Testament. Der Name Mose versammelte unter sich herrenloses, also anonymes Gut von religiösen Rechtssatzungen, zum anderen aber auch ihm untergeschobenes Gut. Ähnliches gilt für das Werk alttestamentlicher Propheten. Prophetenschüler konnten eigene Arbeiten unter den Namen ihres prophetischen Lehrers gestellt haben, wie dies auch in den Malerwerkstätten der Antike und der Neuzeit vorgekommen sein wird.

6. Zur Problematik der Pseudepigraphie im Frühjudentum und im Urchristentum auf dem Hintergrund der Antike und der alttestamentlichen Überlieferungen

Um die in der Forschung kontrovers beurteilte Erscheinung der Pseudepigraphie im Frühjudentum und im Urchristentum annähernd richtig zu verstehen und zu beurteilen, sind einige grundsätzliche Überlegungen anzustellen. Zum einen ist der profane antike Hintergrund zu beachten, zum anderen der religiös geprägte alttestamentliche.

---

[35] Ders., Fälschung (s. Anm. 28), 40.
[36] A.a.O. 34f., mit Hinweis auf Tert.Marc. 4,5,3f. (CChr.SL I,551): eadem auctoritas ecclesiarum apostolicarum ceteris quoque patrocinabitur evangeliis, quae proinde per illas et secundum illas habemus, Iohannis dico atque Matthei, licet et Marcus quod edidit Petri adfirmetur, cuius interpres Marcus. nam et Lucae digestum Paulo adscribere solent. capit autem magistrorum videri quae discipuli promulgarint.

6.1 Der profane antike Hintergrund

Als das schöpferische Zeitalter der Griechen während des 4. Jh. v. Chr. mehr und mehr an sein Ende gekommen war, trat der griechische Geist in eine Periode der Wissenschaftlichkeit, der Gelehrsamkeit, des Sammelns und Sichtens ein. Die Reflexion übernahm gegenüber der spontanen und intuitiven Schöpferkraft die Führung. So kam es im Zeitalter der Makedonen und der hellenistischen Königreiche zu einer Sammlung und Klassifizierung der für vorbildlich gehaltenen Dichter und Redner, aber auch der Geschichtsschreiber und Philosophen der archaischen und klassischen Epoche. In ihnen suchte man die Leitbilder für das eigene nunmehr gelehrte und damit reflektierte und nachahmende Schaffen.[37]

Mit dem Entstehen großer öffentlich zugänglicher Büchersammlungen, der Bibliotheken vor allem in Pella, Antiochien, Pergamon und Alexandrien und deren Ordnung am Anfang des 3. Jh. v. Chr. entstand eine rege philologisch-historische Tätigkeit, die sich in literaturgeschichtlichen und biographischen Studien, in Textausgaben, Kommentaren, Werkverzeichnissen und Katalogen sowie Lexika niederschlug.[38] Die antiken Gelehrten mussten dabei besonders auf die Kritik der Verfasserschaft achten.[39] An der Frage nach der Echtheit oder Unechtheit einer Schrift nahmen auch einzelne Geschichtsschreiber Anteil. Die Anfänge von Kritik und kritischem Sinn lassen sich seit Homer beobachten. Epicharmos aus Megara auf Sizilien (um 550–460 v. Chr.) stellte bereits die Maxime auf: „Sei nüchtern und lerne zu misstrauen; das sind die Gelenke des Geistes."[40] Die antiken Philologen, Literaturwissenschaftler und Gelehrten haben sich deshalb auch als ‚Kritiker', als Richter, als κριτικοί, bezeichnet.[41]

Herodot (um 484–425 v. Chr.) ist für uns der erste und älteste Echtheitskritiker.[42] Seit dieser Zeit begegnen in allen Jahrhunderten des griechischen und römischen Altertums echtheitskritische Äußerungen. Für das Altertum gibt es nur noch Fragmente und Reste dieser gelehrten philologisch-historischen Tätigkeit, die bis in die Spätantike bezeugt ist.

Blicken wir auf die Verfasser der neutestamentlichen Schriften, so sind Paulus und Lukas, deren literarisches Werk umfangmäßig den Hauptbe-

---

[37] R. PFEIFFER, Geschichte der klassischen Philologie. Von den Anfängen bis zum Ende des Hellenismus, Reinbek bei Hamburg 1970, 251–255.

[38] E. A. PARSONS, The Alexandrian Library, London 1952; C. WENDEL, Art. Bibliothek, RAC 2 (1954), 231–274 (239f.); P. M. FRASER, Ptolemaic Alexandria, Bd. 1/3, Oxford 1972. – Zu den Bibliotheken der Hochschulen, Gymnasien und von Privatpersonen vgl. WENDEL, a.a.O. 241–243.

[39] SPEYER, Fälschung (s. Anm. 28), 111–128.

[40] Vorsokratiker 23 B 13 (Diels / Kranz 1[6], 201).

[41] PFEIFFER, Geschichte (s. Anm. 37), Reg. 370: κριτικός.

[42] SPEYER, Fälschung (s. Anm. 28), 114.

stand des Neuen Testaments bildet, Angehörige der hellenistischen Bildungskultur ihrer Zeit. Paulinische Briefe zitieren heidnische Autoren, Paulus ist wie Lukas rhetorisch geschult, wobei Lukas deutlich an die hellenistische tragisch-pathetische Geschichtsschreibung anknüpft.[43] Von dem neuen Ausgangspunkt, dem Glauben an Jesus Christus, setzen Paulus und Lukas die für die Tora und das Judentum werbende Schriftstellerei der hellenistisch gebildeten jüdischen Schriftsteller des 2. und 1. Jh. v. Chr. fort. Sie denken und schreiben für eine griechisch, genauer hellenistisch gebildete Öffentlichkeit. Diese besteht aus Juden der Diaspora, aus ‚Gottesfürchtigen' und an der alttestamentlichen Gottesvorstellung interessierten Heiden.[44] Deshalb dürften Männer wie Paulus und seine Schüler mit Sicherheit auch über die verschiedenen Arten der Pseudepigraphie in ihrem heidnischen und hellenistisch-jüdischen Umfeld Bescheid gewusst haben. Aus der hellenistischen Rhetorenschule waren ihnen die Möglichkeiten bekannt, den Stil jedweden Autors nachzuahmen und so literarische Fiktionen und gegebenenfalls sogar Fälschungen in dessen Art nachzuschaffen.[45] Ferner ist die Nähe Alexandriens, das mit seinen Bibliotheken und Philologen das herausragende griechische Bildungszentrum war, zu Palästina wohl zu beachten. In dieser Stadt wirkte als Zeitgenosse vieler neutestamentlicher Schriftsteller der griechisch gebildete jüdische Theologe Philon.[46] Die frühjüdische Erfindung über das Zustandekommen der Übersetzung der Tora ins Griechische als eines angeblichen Auftragswerkes von Ptolemaios II. Philadelphos, wie sie die gefälschte jüdische apologetische Schrift des ‚Aristeasbriefes' (2. Jh. v. Chr.) kurz beschreibt,[47] war wohl Paulus ebenso wie seinen Schülern bekannt, ohne dass sie diese als Erfindung durchschaut hätten. Paulus zitiert jedenfalls Stellen aus dem Alten Testament nach der Septuaginta-Übersetzung und auffallenderweise nicht aus dem Urtext.

Die meisten Autoren des griechisch geschriebenen Neuen Testamentes gehören mehr der hellenistisch-jüdischen als der aramäisch-jüdischen Kultur an. Viele von ihnen schreiben nach dem Jahr 70 n. Chr., als die Römer das palästinische Judentum weitgehend vernichtet hatten. Auch stammen nicht wenige, wie Paulus und seine Schüler, zu denen Lukas gehört, aus Ländern der hellenistischen Kultur, wobei bereits in der 1. Hälfte des

---

[43] PLÜMACHER, Lukas (s. Anm. 7), 255–261.

[44] SCHÜRER, History, Bd. 3,1 (s. Anm. 32), 150–176; B. WANDER, Gottesfürchtige und Sympathisanten, WUNT 104, Tübingen 1998.

[45] SPEYER, Fälschung (s. Anm. 28), 21f.; zu den fiktiven Reden der Apostelgeschichte des Lukas PLÜMACHER, Lukas (s. Anm. 7), 244–249.

[46] J. MORRIS, The Jewish Philosopher Philo, in: SCHÜRER, History, Bd. 3,2 (s. Anm. 32), 809–889.

[47] O. MURRAY, Art. Aristeasbrief, RAC Suppl. 1 (2001), 573–587.

1. Jh. Rom als Missionsgebiet gewählt wurde, wo der hellenistische Geist gleichfalls seit mehreren Jahrhunderten bestimmend war. So gab es in Rom auch seit 39 und 28 v. Chr. große öffentliche Bibliotheken, die nach dem Vorbild Alexandriens und anderer Bibliotheken des Ostens organisiert waren.[48] Die ersten christlichen Schriftsteller, seien sie Redaktoren und Bearbeiter von älteren mündlichen und schriftlichen Zeugnissen über Jesus wie die Synoptiker, seien sie Verfasser selbständiger Schriften, waren mit den Möglichkeiten der verschiedenen Formen der Verfasserschaft vertraut, wie sie in ihrer Umwelt vorkamen.

Dieses Bild gewinnt noch an Farbe, wenn wir berücksichtigen, dass das Frühjudentum der Diaspora, aus dem Paulus und sein Kreis kommen, seit dem 3. Jh. v. Chr., wenn nicht bereits früher, zahlreiche Einflüsse aus der griechischen Geisteswelt aufgenommen hatte. Die alttestamentlichen Weisheitsbücher, die Septuaginta-Übersetzung, der ‚Aristeasbrief‘, Philon und andere sind dafür ebenso ein Beweis wie die vielfältige frühjüdische pseudepigraphische Literatur.[49]

Wählte ein urchristlicher Schriftsteller statt Anonymität oder Orthonymität eine literarische Maske, so tat er dies nicht naiv, weil es angeblich in seiner Umwelt so Brauch war, sondern mit vollem Bewusstsein der von ihm gewählten Art der Pseudepigraphie, also unter Umständen auch der Fälschung. Dass sein missionarisches oder apologetisches Vorgehen dabei gerechtfertigt scheinen konnte, wird ihm die bei genauer Prüfung sittlich anstößige Maxime nahegelegt haben: ‚Der Zweck heiligt die Mittel‘.

Haben jene frühjüdischen Autoren, die sich der Pseudepigraphie bedient haben, anerkannte Offenbarungsempfänger des Alten Testamentes als Urheber ihrer neuen Schriften ausgegeben, so entsprechend die christlichen Verfasser die Namen Jesu, der Apostel und deren Schüler. In beiden Fällen ging es dabei einmal um den Nachweis einer echten ursprünglichen Überlieferung und damit verbunden um die Werbung für den Glauben an die alttestamentliche bzw. die neue christliche Offenbarung. Da man diese Ziele oftmals nicht allein mit den echten Zeugnissen zu erreichen vermeinte, da auch infolge des Zeitabstandes neue Fragen, neue Schwierigkeiten in Lehre, Kult und Disziplin zu lösen waren, erfanden einzelne Christen angebliche Zeugnisse und gaben ihnen durch die verschiedenen Mittel der Echtheitsbeglaubigung den Anschein geschichtlicher Wahrheit.[50] So sollte eine zurechtgerückte und ergänzte Vergangenheit der Gegenwart mit ihren neuen Fragen und Problemen aufhelfen.

---

[48] WENDEL, Art. Bibliothek (s. Anm. 38), 243–246.

[49] SCHÜRER, History, Bd. 3,1 (s. Anm. 32), 470–700: ‚Jewish literature composed in Greece‘.

[50] SPEYER, Fälschung (s. Anm. 28), 225–231.285–292.

Im Rückbezug auf die Vergangenheit und auf die eigenen zurückliegenden Anfänge als die Lebensquellen der jeweiligen Gegenwart waren sich die Religionen des Altertums einig. Die Hochschätzung des Alten und der Alten war ein bestimmendes einheitsstiftendes Element dieser Kulturen.[51] In dieser Weise argumentierten die Christen eben auch nicht nur mit Worten Jesu und der Schüler Jesu, sondern mit den älteren Worten der alttestamentlichen Propheten und der Tora. Dabei spielten für das christliche Glaubensverständnis die alttestamentlichen Voraussagen eines Messias, den die Christen in Jesus von Nazareth gekommen sahen, also der Weissagungsbeweis, eine zentrale Rolle.[52] Dies erweisen die betreffenden alttestamentlichen Zitate im Neuen Testament. Diese Zitate gehen meist nicht auf den hebräischen Urtext zurück und sind bisweilen auch tendenziös bearbeitet. Hier liegt die Erscheinung der Verfälschung vor.[53]

Überblicken wir die Hinterlassenschaft der urchristlichen Literatur, dann dürfen wir vermuten, wenn nicht sogar sicher behaupten, dass in ihr alle zuvor genannten Möglichkeiten des Zusammenhanges zwischen Verfasser und Werk beggnen werden, wie sie die heidnische hellenistisch-römische und die frühjüdische Literatur entfaltet haben. Dabei werden wir aufgrund der inhaltlichen Nähe des Frühchristentums zum Alten Testament die nächsten Entsprechungen zur christlichen Pseudepigraphie und Fälschung in der Literatur des hellenistischen Frühjudentums finden.

6.2 Der alttestamentliche Hintergrund

Für die Beurteilung der urchristlichen Pseudepigraphie ist neben der antiken religiösen Pseudepigraphie und der antiken historischen und philologischen Kritik auch der alttestamentliche Hintergrund zu berücksichtigen. Das älteste Christentum ist auf dem frühjüdischen Wurzelboden entstanden, der keine in sich geschlossene Größe war, sondern althebräisch und hellenistisch durchformt. Die Vorstellung einer geschichtlichen Offenbarung an Adam bis zu den Propheten, bis zu Johannes dem Täufer und Jesus bestimmte den jüdischen und sodann den christlichen Glauben. Mit dieser Offenbarung, die nach christlicher Auffassung am Ende der Zeit in Jesus Christus gipfelt, ist die Herkunft und damit die Urheberschaft von einem personalen Gott mitgegeben. Da die Offenbarung in den heiligen Schriften, nämlich dem ‚Gesetz', den Propheten, den Geschichtsbüchern Israels und entsprechend in den Evangelien und den übrigen Schriften des Neuen Testamentes, niedergelegt ist, betrifft die Urheberschaft Gottes diese von

---

[51] S.o. Anm. 31.
[52] SPEYER, Fälschung (s. Anm. 28), 234; SCHÜRER, History, Bd. 3,2 (s. Anm. 32), 488–554: ‚Messianism'.
[53] SPEYER, a.a.O. 234–236, und Reg.: ‚Verfälschung'.

Menschen aufgezeichneten Schriften. Die Heiligkeit der Bücher des Alten und des Neuen Testamentes folgt aus dem Begriff der Offenbarung und damit der Urheberschaft Gottes.[54] Ausdruck dieser Auffassung einer göttlichen Verfasserschaft ist die kirchliche Lehre von der Inspiration der von der Kirche anerkannten Offenbarungsschriften.[55] Das *fundamentum in re* für diese dem Selbstverständnis des Christentums und der Kirchen in all ihren verschiedenen geschichtlichen Formen eigentümlichen Auffassung ist zunächst das erfahrene Sprechen Gottes vor allem in den fünf Büchern Mose und den Propheten, also in jenen Teilen des Alten Testamentes, die für den altisraelitischen und jüdischen Glauben sowie auch für den Glauben der Christen bestimmend sind. In den in diesen Büchern antreffbaren Ich-Reden Gottes, vor allem in den Ich-Bin-Worten Jahwes,[56] gründet der jüdische und christliche Glaube an den personalen Gott, der sich zunächst mythischen und myth-historischen, sodann geschichtlichen Personen, angefangen vom Urelternpaar über Noah, Abraham, die Stammväter Israels und Mose bis zu den heiligen Richtern und Königen, den Propheten und schließlich in einzigartiger Weise in Jesus aus Nazareth, geoffenbart hat. Gott redet zu seinen Erwählten, den ‚Gerechten', und dies nicht nur in den Visionen und Auditionen einer Berufung jener Personen. Die Menschen, denen Gottes Wort zuteil wurde, empfanden sich dabei weitgehend als Werkzeug oder als Sprachrohr, wie Mose und die Propheten dies nach ihrem Selbstverständnis waren. Wir finden Ich-Reden Gottes vor allem in der Tora inmitten erzählender Texte, die als geschichtlich/heilsgeschichtlich gelten wollten, und bei den Propheten. Neben den Ich-Reden Gottes begegnet nicht selten als abgeschwächte Form die Er-Rede Gottes. Die religionsgeschichtlich auch außerhalb Israels zu belegende göttliche Stimme vom Himmel gehört gleichfalls in diesen Zusammenhang der Ich-Reden Gottes.[57]

Bei dieser mythischen oder göttlichen Verfasserschaft im Alten und entsprechend auch im Neuen Testament ist davon auszugehen, dass göttliches Reden von einzelnen Menschen immer wieder erfahren werden konnte. Zu einem Vergleich bieten sich die bis zu einem gewissen Grade noch nachprüfbaren neuzeitlichen Visionen, beispielsweise bestimmte Marienerscheinungen des 19. und 20. Jh., an.[58] Viele Menschen haben die ekstati-

---

[54] C. COLPE, Art. Heilige Schriften, RAC 14 (1988), 184–223 (201–210).

[55] C. PESCH, De inspiratione Sacrae Scripturae, Freiburg i. Brsg. ²1925, 38–128; THRAEDE, Art. Inspiration (s. Anm. 17), 343–362.

[56] J. LINDBLOM, Die Vorstellung vom Sprechen Jahwes zu den Menschen im Alten Testament, ZAW 75 (1963), 263–288 (263f.); THYEN, Art. Ich-Bin-Worte (s. Anm. 11), 158–168.

[57] W. SPEYER, Art. Himmelsstimme, RAC 15 (1991), 286–303.

[58] E. BENZ, Die Vision. Erfahrungsformen und Bilderwelt, Stuttgart 1969, 413–417:

schen Zustände, verbunden mit Visionen und Auditionen der Seherin Bernadette Soubirous, 1854 in Lourdes miterlebt.[59] Vergleichbar sind auch die Selbstzeugnisse der Seherkinder von Fatima.[60]

Im Alten Testament wird man bei allen berichteten Gottesworten in der Ich- und Er-Rede, der oft zu belegenden Wendung ‚Spruch des Herrn', zwischen tatsächlich erlebten, „in der Stunde der eigentlichen Gottesbegegnung im Munde Jahwes, und in der von dieser Erstoffenbarung her bestimmten, von ihr aber verschiedenen Stunde, in welcher der Gesandte seinen Auftrag dem Volke weitergibt" zu unterscheiden haben.[61] Eine weitere Unterscheidung betrifft die authentischen Offenbarungsworte und jene, die als Offenbarungsworte weiterverkündet und weitergeschrieben wurden, ohne dass sie im Wortlaut so der Offenbarer gesprochen hat. In diesem Fall kann es verschiedene Möglichkeiten geben, die von einer Paraphrase und Erklärung des Wortes Gottes bis zur Erfindung einer vollständig neuen Gottesrede reichen können, also bis zur freien Erfindung, Fiktion, und gegebenenfalls auch zur Fälschung. Hier wäre nach Kriterien zu suchen, die es erlauben, zwischen erfahrenem und erfundenem Gotteswort zu unterscheiden, falls sich solche überhaupt finden lassen.

Entsprechendes wie für die Gottesrede im Alten Testament gilt für die Worte, die Jesus von den ältesten Zeugen, die wir besitzen, das sind vor allem die vier neutestamentlichen Evangelisten, in den Mund gelegt werden. Hier ist mit der Möglichkeit zu rechnen, dass Worte von Gläubigen über Jesus, also Er-Aussagen, vor allem aus bestimmten Gründen des Glaubens und der Sitten, der Disziplin und des Kultes, Jesus als Ich-Aussagen zugewiesen wurden. So gewann man autoritative Sätze, die auf konkrete Anfragen der damaligen Stunde, wie besonders der Frage nach der Parusieverzögerung, antworten konnten. Vor allem die Ich-Reden und die Ich-Bin-Worte Jesu im vierten Evangelium verlangen nach einer Klärung hinsichtlich ihrer Geschichtlichkeit, oder, wenn diese verneint wird, ihrer vertieften Aussagewahrheit oder ihres Aussagewertes. Die fiktive Wahrheit kann bisweilen einen höheren Wahrheitsgehalt besitzen als die oft vordergründige geschichtliche Wahrheit. Man denke an die dichterische oder die psychologische Wahrheit. Der Evangelist Johannes und sein Kreis dürften theologische und christologische Bekenntnisse und Deutungen im Kleid geschichtlicher Szenen und geschichtlicher Jesusreden gestaltet ha-

---

‚Das visionäre Wort'; 418–440: ‚Die himmlische Musik'. P. DINZELBACHER, Vision und Visionsliteratur im Mittelalter, MGMA 23, Stuttgart 1981.

[59] M. DE ROTON, Art. Lourdes, LThK³ 6 (1997), 1068.

[60] W. BRÜCKNER, Art. Fatima, LThK³ 3 (1995), 1196.

[61] W. ZIMMERLI, Ich bin Jahwe, in: ders., Gottes Offenbarung, TB 19, München 1963, 11–40 (23); THYEN, Art. Ich-Bin-Worte (s. Anm. 11), 161f.

ben. Den Beweis für eine derartige Deutung bietet der Evangelist selbst; denn er spricht im selben Stil und in derselben Ausdrucksweise wie die bei ihm auftretenden Personen, an erster Stelle Jesus und Johannes der Täufer.

Vordergründig und nur geschichtlich betrachtet ist der johanneische Jesus nicht der durch Galiläa ziehende Jesus der Synoptiker. Gehen wir aber von der Erfahrung der ersten Jünger und Jüngerinnen Jesu aus, dass der geschichtliche Jesus infolge seiner von ihnen erfahrenen Auferstehung mehr ist als ein heiliger Mensch, dann verstehen wir die Erfindungen des Johannes wohl richtiger und passender als Erfindungen mit einem tieferen Wahrheitsgehalt. Der vierte Evangelist will durch seine zunächst ungeschichtlich scheinende Darstellung etwas Übergeschichtliches herausarbeiten und zwar Jesu Geheimnis im Lichte der erfahrenen Auferstehung deuten. Dabei geht er in seiner Darstellungsweise weit über die Synoptiker hinaus, indem er sich literarisch und geschichtlich weit größere Freiheiten erlaubt. Johannes sieht Jesu Geheimnis darin, dass Jesus der Gesandte Gottes schlechthin ist, ja dass er das auf diese Erde gekommene Spiegelbild des Schöpfergottes ist. Die zahlreichen Ich-Bin-Worte Jesu in diesem Evangelium verweisen auf die von Johannes angestrebte weitgehende Gleichsetzung vom menschgewordenen Logos mit dem Schöpfergott.[62] Mit dieser seiner Darstellung der Reden Jesu sprengt Johannes die antiken und die neuzeitlichen Vorstellungen über Geschichtlichkeit, genauer über eine nur geschichtliche Echtheit von Worten und Reden Jesu. In der zuvor erwähnten kirchlichen Lehre von der Inspiration der gesamten Heiligen Schrift, vor allem der im Kanon des Neuen Testamentes enthaltenen, für heilig gehaltenen und für heilig erklärten Schriften, ist auf diese mythische oder göttliche Verfasserschaft und damit auf die religiöse und nicht profane Dimension dieser Texte hingewiesen. Diese Heiligkeit folgt letztlich aus dem Inhalt der Offenbarung, vor allem aus der Deutung der geheimnisvollen Person Jesu Christi. Die im Glauben angenommenen Offenbarungsschriften des Alten und des Neuen Testamentes erscheinen dann letztlich wie ihr Inhalt als Schriften einer göttlichen und zugleich einer menschlichen Verfasserschaft. Sie besitzen eine gottmenschliche Herkunft wie Jesus Christus, der *Logos ensarkos* selbst. Rational können aber der *Logos ensarkos* und der *Logos enbiblos* nach den Anteilen des Göttlichen und des Menschlichen nicht voneinander geschieden werden. Eine ausschließlich profane geschichtliche und literaturgeschichtliche Betrachtung nach den Kategorien, wie sie erstmals die Gelehrten der Antike, sodann die italienischen Humanisten und die ihnen folgenden Philologen des 19. und 20. Jh. entwickelt haben, können dem Inhalt und der Gestaltung der Gottesoffenbarung im Alten und Neuen Testament nicht gerecht werden. Hier

---

[62] THYEN, a.a.O. 173–183.

zeigt sich das alles bestimmende Problem von Glaube und Unglaube bzw. von religiöser und profaner Wirklichkeitsdeutung.

Diese Überlegungen beziehen sich auf die Frage der Echtheit oder Unechtheit der Gottesreden im Alten Testament und der Jesusreden vor allem beim vierten Evangelisten. Außerhalb der kanonischen kirchlichen Texte liegen wieder andere Bedingungen vor, wie die Jesusreden in den apokryphen, vor allem in den gnostischen Schriften, nahelegen. Auch wird man zwischen der subjektiven Überzeugung der diese Rede Schreibenden und objektiver Wahrheit im Sinne einer Glaubenswahrheit zu unterscheiden haben. Das Urteil wird je nachdem ausfallen, ob der Urteilende als Gläubiger oder als Ungläubiger spricht, und ob er innerhalb oder außerhalb der Kirche steht.

Auf einer eher sekundären Stufe stehen jene Reden, die Lukas einem der Apostel oder Apostelschüler in den Mund legt. Hier ist vor allem an die Missionsreden zu denken, zu denen die Rede des Paulus auf dem Areopag in herausragender Weise gehört. Bei diesen Reden sind wir vom Zentrum, der Gestalt Jesu, bereits weiter entfernt. Lukas folgt hier der Gepflogenheit der griechischen Geschichtsschreiber, die die Reden der auftretenden geschichtlichen Persönlichkeiten dem Wortlaut nach erfunden haben, dem Sinne nach aber den gegebenen geschichtlichen Bedingungen und Umständen angepasst haben.[63] Bei der literarischen Erfindung von Reden ist also genauer zwischen situationsgebundener und gänzlich freier Erfindung zu unterscheiden. Letztere, gleichsam die Erfindung der Phantasie, dient vor allem zur Unterhaltung oder unter Umständen den Zwecken der Fälschung. Die Erfindung zur reinen Unterhaltung wird in den ersten drei für die Christen so ernsten und schweren Jahrhunderten, in denen es allein um das Überleben ihres Glaubens ging, nicht vorgekommen sein. Erst seit dem 4. Jh. war hierfür die Möglichkeit von den äußeren Bedingungen her gegeben. Erst von dieser Zeit an gab es dafür ein Lesepublikum. Hingegen war die literarische Fälschung seit frühester Zeit ein Kampfmittel im Streit um den wahren Glauben. Fälschung und Gegenfälschung begegnen in allen christlichen Lagern.[64] Hier besteht ein enger Zusammenhang zwischen Mission, also Glaubenswerbung, und literarischer Fälschung.

Zurückblickend ist zu betonen, dass sich bei der Frage nach der Beurteilung der Pseudepigraphie im Altertum zwei gegensätzliche Positionen gezeigt haben, die in der verschiedenen Erfahrung und Deutung der Wirklichkeit wurzeln: eine ältere und ursprünglichere mythische und eine jüngere profane Auffassung. Die Neuzeit lässt seit dem philosophisch-wissen-

---

[63] S.o. Anm. 45.
[64] SPEYER, Fälschung (s. Anm. 28), 238–240.278–285.

schaftlichen Aufklärung des 18. Jh. weithin nur noch die profane Deutung gelten. Deshalb wurde dann vielfach das Religiöse schnell zum Trug von Priestern, machthungrigen Priestern, oder zum Selbstbetrug erklärt. An dieser geistigen Entwicklung ist die sich seit dem späten 18. Jh. vermindernde Erfahrung des Heiligen schuld sowie die damit verbundene grundsätzliche Skepsis gegenüber jeder Art religiöser Erfahrung anderer Zeiten und Menschen. Die profane Deutung sollte nicht in dieser Weise gegen die religiöse ausgespielt werden, sondern beide sind nach dem bekannten Wort Jesu zu den Pharisäern zu berücksichtigen: „Gebt dem Cäsar, was des Cäsars ist, und Gott, was Gottes ist."[65]

---

[65] Mt 22,15–22 (21) par.

Antike (Selbst-)Aussagen über Beweggründe zur Pseudepigraphie

von

MARTINA JANSSEN

Eine Facette im Diskurs über frühchristliche Pseudepigraphie ist die Frage nach der Absicht der Autoren: Warum schreibt beispielsweise der Verfasser der Pastoralbriefe unter dem Namen des Paulus und nicht unter seinem eigenen Namen wie zeitgenössische Autoren (z.B. Ignatius oder Polykarp)?[1] Da die frühchristlichen Verfasser pseudepigraphischer Schriften in der Regel weder in den betreffenden Schriften selbst noch an einem anderen Ort über ihre Entscheidung für ein Autorenpseudonym Auskunft geben,[2] sind die im Laufe der Forschungsgeschichte angestellten Vermutungen über ihre Beweggründe zahlreich und zum Teil gegenläufig. Die Frage nach der autorseitigen Motivation zur Pseudepigraphie ist dabei oft verbunden mit Erwägungen über eine möglicherweise intendierte Durchschaubarkeit der Verfasserfiktion („offene Pseudepigraphie"), die nicht selten eine moralische Bewertung im Blick haben und auf eine kanontheologische Entlastung zielen. Dies schlägt sich nicht zuletzt in dem Bemühen um terminologische Alternativen[3] zu den Begriffen „pseudepigraph" bzw.

---

[1] Die Pseudonymität der Pastoralbriefe galt lange als Forschungskonsens, wird nun aber ebenso wie die Corpus-Hypothese zunehmend zumindest für einzelne Briefe in Frage gestellt; vgl. zur aktuellen Diskussion J. HERZER, Abschied vom Konsens? Die Pseudepigraphie der Pastoralbriefe als Herausforderung an die neutestamentliche Wissenschaft, ThLZ 129 (2004), 1267–1282, und das Themenheft „Die Pastoralbriefe", ThQ 187 (2007). Siehe auch die Beiträge von Timo Glaser und Jens Herzer in diesem Band.

[2] Vgl. G. BARDY, Betrug und Fälschungen in der Literatur der christlichen Antike, in: N. Brox (Hg.), Pseudepigraphie in der heidnischen und jüdisch-christlichen Antike, WdF 484, Darmstadt 1977, 163–184 (168). Eine Ausnahme für die spätere Zeit bietet Salvian von Marseille, der ausführlich über seine Gründe, unter einem Pseudonym zu schreiben, Auskunft gibt; s.u. Anm. 9 u.ö. Sieht man von den zahlreichen häresiologisch motivierten Fälschungsvorwürfen ab (vgl. z.B. Eus.h.e. 7,25,2f.), sind auch rezipientenseitige antikchristliche Erklärungen für Pseudepigraphie bis auf vereinzelte Zeugnisse eher selten (z.B. Tert.bapt. 17,4f.; Canon Muratori, Z. 69f.).

[3] Vgl. z.B. I. H. MARSHALL, A Critical and Exegetical Commentary on the Pastoral Epistles, ICC, Edinburgh 1999, 84: „Since the nuance of deceit seems to be inseparable from the use of the terms ,pseudonymity' and ,pseudepigraphy' and gives them a pejorative sense, we need another term that will refer more positively to the activity of writing

„pseudonym" nieder, denen nach weitläufiger Ansicht eine moralisch negative Konnotation im Sinne von „Lüge, Fälschung" (ψεῦδος) inhärent zu sein scheint.[4] Insgesamt ist die Forschungslage komplex und weit von einem Konsens entfernt; naturgemäß differieren auch die methodischen Zugänge erheblich.[5]

„Was jemand, der damals sich literarisch unter Rückgriff auf apostolische Autorität äußern wollte, schreiben ‚konnte', ‚mußte' und ‚durfte', um auf Anerkennung für sein Werk rechnen zu können, ist keinesfalls mehr nachträglich festzulegen und sicher nicht mit modernen Kriterien zu bestimmen."[6] Dieser von Norbert Brox formulierte methodische Vorbehalt hat auch heute nichts an Relevanz verloren. Um einen hermeneutischen Zirkelschluss zu vermeiden, ist m.E. ein Blick auf die mentalitätsgeschichtlichen Rahmenbedingungen antiker Literaturproduktion angebracht.[7] Deswegen möchte ich im Folgenden *antike* (Selbst-)Aussagen über

---

in another person's name without intent to deceive: perhaps ‚allonymity' and ‚allepigraphy' may be suggested as suitable alternatives." Vgl. zum Problem auch insgesamt M. JANSSEN, Unter falschem Namen. Eine kritische Forschungsbilanz frühchristlicher Pseudepigraphie, ARGU 14, Frankfurt a.M. u.a. 2003, 257–260. Das Bemühen um eine differenzierte Terminologie ist nicht auf die Bibelwissenschaften beschränkt; vgl. z.B. A. GRAFTON, Forgers and Critics. Creativity and Duplicity in Western Scholarship, Princeton 1990, 6.

[4] Eine solches Bemühen um terminologische Alternativen erscheint mir unnötig, da das griechische Wort ψεῦδος als erkenntnistheoretischer Terminus zunächst die Abweichung von der Wirklichkeit/Faktizität in rein ontologischem Sinn bezeichnet und keine Implikationen hinsichtlich der Intentionalität und Moral einschließt. Vgl. dazu z.B. E. FUCHS, Pseudologia. Formen und Funktionen fiktionaler Trugrede in der griechischen Literatur der Antike, BKAW II/91, Heidelberg 1993, 2.10f.191.250.252 u.ö.; W. LUTHER, Weltansicht und Geistesleben, Göttingen 1954, 85ff.; H. PETER, Wahrheit und Kunst. Geschichtsschreibung und Plagiat im klassischen Altertum, Leipzig 1911, 5ff.; L. SCHMIDT, Die Ethik der alten Griechen II, Berlin 1882, 411; W. SPEYER, Die literarische Fälschung im heidnischen und christlichen Altertum. Ein Versuch ihrer Deutung, HAW I/2, München 1971, 21; M. HOSE, Fiktionalität und Lüge. Über einen Unterschied zwischen römischer und griechischer Terminologie, Poetica 28 (1996), 257–274.

[5] Neben mentalitätsgeschichtlichen, literaturwissenschaftlichen und kirchenhistorischen Zugängen sind nicht selten auch kanontheologische Herangehensweisen anzutreffen. Das forschungsgeschichtliche Deutungsspektrum für frühchristliche Pseudepigraphie ist dementsprechend weit. Als mögliche Beweggründe wurden beispielsweise genannt: böswillige Fälschungsabsicht, Inspirationsbewusstsein, Aktualisierung im Sinne fiktiver Selbstauslegung, Polemik, theologische Korrektur, Durchsetzung kirchen- und theologiepolitischer Machtinteressen, literarisches Spiel oder auch fehlerhafte Zuschreibungsprozesse; vgl. dazu insgesamt JANSSEN, Namen (s. Anm. 3).

[6] N. BROX, Die Pastoralbriefe, RNT, Regensburg [5]1989, 59.

[7] Die meisten modernen Klassifizierungsversuche von Pseudepigraphieformen stoßen dabei an Grenzen: Die kategoriale Trennung zwischen imitativer Pseudepigraphie und Fälschung beispielsweise bei R. ZIMMERMANN, Unecht – und doch wahr? Pseudepigraphie im Neuen Testament als theologisches Problem, ZNT 12 (2003), 27–38 (30), ist z.B.

Pseudonymität anführen. Solche autor- oder rezipientenseitigen Erwägungen finden sich ab dem 5. Jh. v. Chr. und häufen sich vom 1. Jh. v. Chr. bis zum 2. Jh. n. Chr. Ab dem 4. Jh. n. Chr. treten dann neben und an die Stelle von eher zufälligen Notizen umfangreiche Abhandlungen wie die der neuplatonischen Aristoteleskommentatoren, die erstmals versuchen, „eine Fälschung als Fälschung ernst zu nehmen und in ihren Intentionen zu verstehen."[8] Auch der neunte Brief des Salvian von Marseille, in dem dieser eine nachträgliche Apologie für die pseudonyme Abfassung seiner unter dem Namen Timotheus veröffentlichten Schrift Ad ecclesiam vorlegt, ist hier zu nennen.[9]

Freilich gilt auch für antike Aussagen, dass sie mitunter nicht deckungsgleich mit den tatsächlichen Motiven sind, sondern den Charakter von Selbststilisierungen oder Hypothesen haben. Ungeachtet dieses Vorbehalts geben die antiken Zeugnisse aber doch Aufschluss darüber, welche Beweggründe für die Entscheidung für ein Autorenpseudonym in der Antike *denkbar* waren und somit auch für einige Bereiche frühchristlicher Pseudepigraphie unter bestimmten Umständen plausible Erklärungsmuster bieten könnten.

1. Falsche Verfasserangaben aus Irrtum

Mitunter ist Pseudepigraphie nicht autorseitig beabsichtigt, sondern resultiert aus den spezifischen buchtechnischen[10] und mentalitätsgeschichtli-

---

schwierig, da imitative Pseudepigraphen auch eine Fälschungsabsicht verfolgen können, bei der die Imitation dann Mittel zum Zweck ist.

[8] C. W. MÜLLER, Die neuplatonischen Aristoteleskommentatoren über die Ursachen der Pseudepigraphie, in: Brox, Pseudepigraphie (s. Anm. 2), 264–271 (268).

[9] Salvian von Marseille verfasste vier kirchenkritische Bücher „an die Kirche" (*Timothei ad Ecclesiam libri quattuor*) unter dem Namen des Paulusschülers Timotheus. Wegen seines Rückgriffs auf dieses apostolische Autorpseudonym vom Bischof Salonius zur Rede gestellt, legt Salvian daraufhin in einem Antwortbrief äußerst vielschichtig und dicht argumentierend seine Motivation offen, die ihn zu einem Pseudonym greifen ließ. Vgl. dazu z.B. N. BROX, Quis ille auctor? Pseudonymität und Anonymität bei Salvian, VigChr 40 (1986), 55–65; A. E. HAEFNER, Eine einzigartige Quelle für die Erforschung der antiken Pseudonymität, in: Brox, Pseudepigraphie (s. Anm. 2), 154–162; N. BROX, Erläuterungen zum Autor und zum Text, in: Salvian von Marseille, Des Timotheus vier Bücher an die Kirche. Der Brief an den Bischof Salonius. Dt. Übersetzung von A. Mayer. Bearbeitet von N. Brox, SKV 3, München 1983, 142–147; JANSSEN, Namen (s. Anm. 3), 147–149.

[10] Vgl. insgesamt SPEYER, Fälschung (s. Anm. 4), 37–44; N. BROX, Falsche Verfasserangaben. Zur Erklärung der frühchristlichen Pseudepigraphie, SBS 79, Stuttgart 1975, 49f. Speziell zum Problem der Mischrollen, in denen Werke mehrerer Verfasser gesammelt waren, was zu Verwechslungen führen konnte, vgl. R. BLUM, Kallimachos und die

chen bzw. rechtlichen[11] Rahmenbedingungen antiker Literaturproduktion, unter denen es leicht zu rezipientenseitigen Fehlzuschreibungen anonymer, orthonymer oder pseudonymer Schriften kommen konnte.[12] Unabsichtliche Falschzuschreibung ereignet sich z.B. aufgrund von Anonymität, durch Verwechslungen[13] oder aus mangelnder Genauigkeit etwa bei Entlehnungen ohne ausreichende Autoren- oder/und Quellenangaben. Etliche antike Autoren sehen dementsprechend eine falsche Verfasserangabe durch verschiedene Irrtümer und Fehlerquellen hervorgerufen. Als häufigster Grund für falsche Zuschreibungen gilt in der Antike die Homonymität[14] von Au-

---

Literaturverzeichnung bei den Griechen. Untersuchungen zur Geschichte der Biobibliographie, AGB 18 (1977), 1–360 (159); zu Fehlzuschreibungen aufgrund abgerissener Titelblätter vgl. T. BIRT, Kritik und Hermeneutik nebst Abriss des antiken Buchwesens, HAW I/3, München ³1913, 224. Oft war zudem im Rollensystem der Titulus/Sibyllos außen an der Rolle angebracht (vgl. T. BIRT, Das Kulturleben der Griechen und Römer in ihrer Entwicklung, Leipzig 1928, 214), was ebenfalls eine mögliche Fehlerquelle darstellen konnte.

[11] Obwohl der Begriff des geistigen Eigentums durchaus bekannt war, unterscheidet sich das antike „Urheberrecht" doch erheblich von dem modernen. Weder eine pauschale Leugnung des Bewusstseins geistigen Eigentums noch das Postulat eines Urheberrechts, das dem modernen gleicht, stellen eine angemessene Interpretation der antiken Rahmenbedingungen dar. Vgl. zu den mentalitätsgeschichtlichen und rechtshistorischen Aspekten, die in der römischen Literatur weitaus besser zu fassen sind als in der griechischen, z.B. W. BAPPERT, Wege zum Urheberrecht, Frankfurt a.M. 1962, 11–50; H. WIDMANN, Herstellung und Vertrieb des Buches in der griechisch-römischen Welt, in: Archiv für Geschichte des Buchwesens LV, in: Börsenblatt des deutschen Buchhandels Nr. 2, 6. Januar 1967, 545–640 (629–632); K. SCHICKERT, Der Schutz literarischer Urheberschaft im Rom der klassischen Antike, Tübingen 2005.

[12] Vgl. dazu exemplarisch A. GUDEMAN, Literarische Fälschungen bei den Griechen, in: Brox, Pseudepigraphie (s. Anm. 2), 43–73; BIRT, Kritik (s. Anm. 10), 240f. Nicht immer ist klar zu unterscheiden zwischen zufälliger Pseudepigraphie im Rahmen fehlerhafter Rezeptionsprozesse und absichtlicher Pseudepigraphie; vgl. exemplarisch zu diesem Problem z.B. BARDY, Fälschungen (s. Anm. 2), 183; A. DIHLE, Die griechische und lateinische Literatur der Kaiserzeit. Von Augustus bis Justinian, München 1989, 101.

[13] Diese sind ganz unterschiedlicher Natur. Auch beim Einstudieren von Komödien durch den διδάσκαλος konnte es vorkommen, dass dieser für den Verfasser gehalten wurde; vgl. SPEYER, Fälschung (s. Anm. 4), 42f. Mitunter kam es im Laufe der Rezeption zu Verwechslungen von Verfasser und Adressat; vgl. zu Beispielen a.a.O. 43.

[14] Zur Homonymität vgl. A. LESKY, Geschichte der griechischen Literatur, Bern ²1963, 388.892 u.ö.; H. HAGEN, Über Litterarische Fälschungen, Hamburg 1889, 68; GUDEMAN, Fälschungen (s. Anm. 12), 69f.; BLUM, Kallimachos (s. Anm. 10), 26–28.283f.291–293 u.ö. Verwechslungsprobleme sind auch im Hinblick auf ähnlich klingende Namen bezeugt. Beispielsweise liefen Werke über Taktik und schwere Waffen unter dem Namen Demokrit, gehen aber wahrscheinlich auf Damokritos zurück; vgl. BLUM, a.a.O. 215. Selbst im Rahmen von Dedikationen konnte Homonymität zum Problem werden; vgl. dazu DIHLE, Literatur (s. Anm. 12), 97, über die „Schrift vom Kosmos". „Sie wurde einem Alexander gewidmet, bei dem es sich vielleicht um Tiberius Iulius Alexander handelt, der aus einer angesehenen jüdischen Familie Alexandriens

toren und Titeln sowie die Gleichnamigkeit der Kommentare. Das Problem der Homonymität ist von zahlreichen antiken Bibliothekaren und Grammatikern explizit thematisiert und von den neuplatonischen Aristoteleskommentatoren als eine der drei Hauptursachen für antike Pseudepigraphie („τρεῖς ἀφορμαὶ τοῦ νοθεύεσθαι") benannt worden.[15] Der Gefahr von Verwechslungen durch Homonymität versuchte man dementsprechend in der Antike vor allem durch Homonymenlexika und Biobibliographien entgegenzuwirken (z.B. Demetrius aus Magnesia),[16] aber auch Erweiterungen in der Proömien- und Sphragistechnik kamen diesbezüglich zum Einsatz.[17]

Diese im Hinblick auf die antike Pseudepigraphie ohne Zweifel wichtige Ursache für falsche Verfasserangaben trägt indes für die Erklärung frühchristlicher Pseudepigraphie nicht viel aus. Fehlerhafte Rezeptionsprozesse spielen im Bereich der Produktion neutestamentlicher Schriften keine exponierte Rolle.[18] Allenfalls wird der Sachverhalt der Homonymität bei der Rezeption einiger frühchristlicher Schriften relevant, wie beispielsweise die altkirchliche Diskussion über den Verfasser der Johannesapokalypse zeigt (Eus.h.e. 7,25,1–27 [14]).[19] Vereinzelt erscheint der Ge-

---

stammte und unter Nero bis zum Präfekten von Ägypten aufstieg. Man glaubte, die Widmung gelte Alexander dem Großen und schrieb das Werk deshalb dessen Lehrer Aristoteles zu."

[15] Vgl. MÜLLER, Aristoteleskommentatoren (s. Anm. 8), 66.

[16] Auch Diogenes Laërtios präsentiert im Anschluss an viele seiner Philosophenviten Homonymenlisten (vgl. z.B. D.L. 5,93f.). Auch ansonsten wird das Problem der Homonymität in der Viten- und Biographieliteratur thematisiert; vgl. Anm. 137.

[17] Nicht wenige Landsleute mit gleichem Namen waren zudem in der gleichen „Branche" tätig (vgl. z.B. drei attische Tragiker mit dem Namen Euripides). Deshalb sicherte man zusätzlich den Verfassernamen durch nähere Bestimmungen wie z.B. den Mutternamen ab. Traditioneller Ort hierfür ist die Sphragis, die in all ihren verschiedenen Formen und Elementen dazu dient, durch Auskunft über Herkunft, Namen und Beschäftigung literarisches Eigentum unverwechselbar identifizierbar zu machen und nicht zuletzt den Autor von anderen Dichtern zu unterscheiden. Dies zeigt deutlich die (sekundäre) Sphragis zu den Bucolica Theokrits, in der Theokrit von einem anderen Dichter abgegrenzt wird: „Ἄλλος ὁ Χῖος, ἐγὼ δὲ Θεόκριτος ὃς τάδ' ἔγραψα εἷς ἀπὸ τῶν πολλῶν εἰμὶ Συρακοσίων, υἱὸς Πραξαγόραο περικλειτᾶς τε Φιλίννας· μοῦσαν δ' ὀθνείαν οὔτιν' ἐφελκυσάμαν." Text: Bucolici Graeci, hg. v. A. S. F. Gow, Oxford 1952, 2.

[18] Vgl. zu einer diesbezüglichen Sonderposition z.B. H.-M. SCHENKE / K. M. FISCHER, Einleitung in die Schriften des Neuen Testament I. Die Briefe des Paulus und Schriften des Paulinismus, Gütersloh 1978, 199–203: Der Erste Petrusbrief, der ursprünglich ein paulinisches Schreiben gewesen sein soll, wurde aufgrund eines „äußeren Mißgeschicks" (203) versehentlich zu einem Petrusbrief.

[19] Homonymität führte nicht selten dazu, dass biblische Personen mit gleichem Namen verwechselt wurden oder miteinander verschmolzen. Dies gilt beispielsweise für Jakobus: Der Herrenbruder verschmilzt mit dem Apostel aus dem Zwölferkreis (vgl. z.B. Augustin, Expositio ad Gal. 12f. [ML 35,2113]); siehe dazu z.B. J. HARTENSTEIN, Die zweite Lehre. Erscheinungen des Auferstandenen als Rahmenerzählungen frühchristli-

danke an Homonymität auch in der modernen Exegese im Hinblick auf die Identifizierung eines (vorgeblichen) Verfassers einer frühchristlichen Schrift. Ein Beispiel stellt der Judasbrief dar, wie die zahlreichen Thesen über die vermutete Identität des Judas zeigen (vgl. schon z.B. Tertullian, De cultu feminarum 1,3 mit Hier.vir.ill 4).[20]

---

cher Dialoge, TU 146, Berlin 2000, 217; F. HAASE, Apostel und Evangelisten in den orientalischen Überlieferungen, NTA 9, Münster 1922, 253; M. HORNSCHUH, Das Apostelbild in der altchristlichen Überlieferung. 2. Die Apostel als Träger der Überlieferung, in: E. Hennecke / W. Schneemelcher (Hg.), Neutestamentliche Apokryphen II. Apostolisches, Apokalypsen und Verwandtes, Tübingen [3]1964, 41–52 (49); B. REPSCHINSKI, Art. Jakobus/Jakkobos (Bruder des Herrn), in: J. Hainz / M. Schmidt / J. Sunckel (Hg.), Personenlexikon des Neuen Testaments, Düsseldorf 2004, 114–117 (114). Auch der Patriarch Jakob wurde mit dem Apostel identifiziert; vgl. dazu z.B. H. LIETZMANN, Petrus und Paulus in Rom. Literarische und archäologische Studien, Berlin u.a. [2]1927, 129. Zu erwähnen ist in diesem Zusammenhang auch die These von A. MEYER, Das Rätsel des Jakobusbriefes, BZNW 10, Gießen 1930, 305. Vgl. zur Synthese aus dem Evangelisten und Apostel Philippus z.B. HARTENSTEIN, a.a.O. 164; W. BAUER, Das Apostelbild in der altchristlichen Überlieferung. 1. Nachrichten, in: Hennecke / Schneemelcher, a.a.O. 11–41 (29); B. KOWALSKI, Art. Philippus/Philippos (Apg), in: Personenlexikon des Neuen Testaments (a.a.O.) 245–247 (246). Zum Zusammenschmelzen der unterschiedlichen „Marias" aus dem Neuen Testament siehe M. JANSSEN, „Deine Lichtkraft hat durch David prophezeit" – Zum Psalmgebet in der Pistis Sophia, in: A. Gerhards / A. Doeker / P. Ebenbauer (Hg.), Identität durch Gebet. Zur gemeinschaftsbildenden Funktion institutionalisierten Betens in Judentum und Christentum, Studien zu Judentum und Christentum 1, Paderborn u.a. 2003, 261–293 (286f.).

[20] Neben der üblichen Gleichsetzung mit dem Apostel und Herrenbruder sind im Gespräch: der gnostische Apostel Judas Thomas (vgl. z.B. H. KÖSTER, Einführung in das Neue Testament im Rahmen der Religionsgeschichte und Kulturgeschichte der hellenistischen und römischen Zeit, Berlin u.a. 1980, 682f.), Judas Barsabas (vgl. z.B. E. E. ELLIS, Prophecy and Hermeneutic in Jude, in: ders., Prophecy and Hermeneutic in Early Christianity, WUNT 18, Tübingen 1978, 221–236 [226f.]), Judas, der erste judenchristliche Bischof von Jerusalem (vgl. z.B. G. KLEIN, Die zwölf Apostel. Ursprung und Gestalt einer Idee, FRLANT 77, Göttingen 1961, 100), der Bischof Justus (J. J. GUNTHER, The Alexandrian Epistle of Jude, NTS 30 [1984], 549–562 [549f.]), ein unbekannter Mann namens Judas (vgl. z.B. J. MOFFATT, The General Epistles. James, Peter and Judas, London [7]1953, 225f.). Letztgenannte Position fügt sich in eine apologetisch motivierte Tendenz der älteren Exegese ein, die in den Autoren der katholischen Briefe nicht eine Referenz auf die Apostel selbst sieht, sondern davon ausgeht, die Briefe seien von unbekannten Menschen geschrieben, die zufällig dieselben Namen wie die Apostel trugen. Damit wären die entsprechenden Schriften als authentische Schriften von dem Beigeschmack einer falschen Verfasserangabe befreit. Vgl. für den Ersten Petrusbrief z.B. R. PERDELWITZ, Die Mysterienreligionen und das Problem des 1. Petrusbriefes. Ein literarischer und religionsgeschichtlicher Vergleich, RVV 11/3, Gießen 1911, 105. Angesichts dieser Position fühlt sich N. BROX, Zur pseudepigraphischen Rahmung des ersten Petrusbriefes, BZ 19 (1975), 78–96 (80), mit Recht an den Philologenwitz erinnert, „welcher wissen will, daß die Odyssee nicht von Homer verfaßt wurde, sondern von einem unbekannten Mann gleichen Namens."

2. Rhetorische und ästhetisch-fiktionale Pseudepigraphie

Nicht immer ist autorseitige Pseudepigraphie mit einer Täuschungsabsicht verbunden. Das Spektrum für „offene Pseudepigraphie" reicht dabei von rhetorischen Schulübungen bis zu ästhetisch-fiktionaler Pseudepigraphie im Bereich der Hochliteratur. Im Fall der berühmten Heroidenbriefe Ovids verweist der Autor selbst in weiteren Werken auf seine Verfasserschaft (Ovid, Ars amatoria 3,339ff.; Ov.am. 2,18,19–26), sodass der fiktionale Charakter dieser literarisch motivierten Pseudgymnie deutlich durchschaubar ist. Eine solche Offenlegung der Verfasserfiktion kann auch nachträglich erfolgen. Zu einem solchen Verfahren greift beispielsweise Salvian von Marseille, der in seinem neunten Brief die Verfasserangabe seiner unter dem Namen „Timotheus" herausgegebenen Schrift Ad ecclesiam nachträglich als fiktiv markiert und gleichzeitig diesen literarischen Kunstgriff rechtfertigt (s.o.). Darüber hinaus finden sich in der antiken Literatur auch implizite Markierungen der Fiktionalität. So läuft Jamblichs Schrift De mysteriis nicht unter dessen realen Namen, sondern ist als Brief des Abammon stilisiert und stellt eine Antwort auf das Schreiben des Porphyrius an den fiktiven Adressaten Anebo dar. Dass es sich um eine Fiktion und gewissermaßen um eine Aufnahme des von Porphyrius mit seinem symbolisch-fiktiven Adressaten begonnenen literarischen Spiels handelt, ist durch ein metafiktionales Signal am Anfang der Schrift klar erkenntlich: Dem Leser wird vorgeschlagen, sich jeden, den er wolle, als Verfasser vorzustellen (Iamb.myst. 1).[21]

Obwohl im Gegensatz zu diesen eindeutigen Beispielen die meisten antiken Schriften nicht autorseitig als fiktiv markiert sind, kommt der nicht auf Täuschung hin angelegten fiktional-ästhetischen Pseudepigraphie in der Antike auch außerhalb der Hochliteratur vermutlich eine hohe Bedeutung zu.[22] Viele Pseudepigraphen sind im Kontext der Prosopopoiie bzw. Ethopoiie[23] entstanden, die im antiken Bildungssystem ihren festen Ort

---

[21] Vgl. auch F. W. CREMER, Die chaldäischen Orakel und Jamblich ‚de mysteriis', Meisenheim a. Glan 1969, 1 Anm. 4. Vgl. zur Identifikation des Verfassers mit Jamblich M. STICHERL, Die Handschriften, Ausgaben und Übersetzungen von Iamblichos de mysteriis. Eine historisch-kritische Studie, TU 62, Berlin 1957, 1–21 u.ö.

[22] Die Entscheidung darüber, ob eine Durchschaubarkeit intendiert ist oder nicht, fällt nicht immer leicht; vgl. dazu z.B. SPEYER, Fälschung (s. Anm. 4), 23.

[23] Oft wurden die Begriffe synonym gebraucht, mitunter wird aber in den antiken Definitionen differenziert; bisweilen kommen zudem flankierende Termini wie Ethologie oder Eidolopoiie zum Einsatz. Vgl. dazu allgemein z.B. R. VOLKMANN, Die Rhetorik der Griechen und Römer in systematischer Übersicht, Leipzig ²1885 (Nachdruck Hildesheim 1963), 280f.498; M. HEINEMANN, Epistulae amatoriae quomodo cohaereant cum elegiis Alexandrinis, Straßburg 1909, 18 Anm. 1; H.-M. HAGEN, Ethopoiia. Zur Geschichte eines rhetorischen Begriffs, Erlangen/Nürnberg 1966, 55ff.; A. N. CIZEK, Imitatio et trac-

hatte und die Theon Aelius von Alexandria wie folgt beschreibt: „προσωποποιία ἐστὶ προσώπου παρεισαγωγὴ διατιθεμένου λόγους οἰκείους ἑαυτῷ τε καὶ τοῖς ὑποκειμένοις πράγμασιν ἀναμφισβητήτως" (Progymnasmata 8 [115.11]).[24] Die Spielarten sind hier vielfältig und reichen von Prosopopoiien sozialer Charaktertypen über individuell-konkrete Personen bis hin zu Verstorbenen, Phantasiefiguren und leblosen, abstrakten Dingen. Etho- bzw. Prosopopoiie ist nicht nur für die Fingierung historischer Reden im Rahmen der Historiographie (z.B. Lukian, De historia conscribenda 58) oder in der (Gerichts-)Rhetorik zur Erzeugung von Ethos und Pathos (z.B. Quintilian, Institutio oratoria 6,1,25) wichtig, sondern spielt auch im Rahmen der Epistolographie eine große Rolle (z.B. Theon, Progymnasmata 115,22).[25] Im Fall fingierter Briefe schlüpft der Autor wie

---

tatio. Die literarisch-rhetorischen Grundlagen der Nachahmung in Antike und Mittelalter, Rhetorik-Forschungen 7, Tübingen 1994, 276–285; T. VEGGE, Paulus und das antike Schulwesen. Schule und Bildung des Paulus, BZNW 134, Berlin u.a. 2006, 155–159; H.-J. KLAUCK, Dion von Prusa. Olympische Rede oder über die erste Erkenntnis Gottes, SAPERE II, Darmstadt 2000, 170f.; H. LAUSBERG, Handbuch der literarischen Rhetorik. Eine Grundlegung der Literaturwissenschaft, München 1960, 407–413 (§§ 820–829).

[24] „Die Prosopopoiie ist die Einführung einer Person, die Worte ausspricht, die zu ihr und zu den vorliegenden Sachverhalten passen ..." Text: M. Patillon / G. Bolognesi, Aelius Theon. Progymnasmata, CUFr. Séries grecque 364, Paris 1997, 70. Vgl. einführend dazu a.a.O. XXXIVff. Übersetzung nach KLAUCK, a.a.O. 172. Dabei geht es nicht allein darum, *was* jemand angesichts einer bestimmten Situation sagen könnte, sondern auch *wie* er es sagen würde; vgl. zu diesem Aspekt der Stilimitation z.B. Pseudo-Longinus, De sublimitate 6.

[25] Vgl. dazu z.B. J. A. SINT, Pseudonymität im Altertum. Ihre Formen und ihre Gründe, Commentationes Aenipontanae 15, Innsbruck 1960, 90ff.113ff.; M. HOSE, Kleine griechische Literaturgeschichte. Von Homer bis zum Ende der Antike, München 1999, 162–167.191–196; VEGGE, Schulwesen (s. Anm. 23), 157f.; K. M. SCHMIDT, Mahnung und Erinnerung im Maskenspiel. Epistolographie, Rhetorik und Narrativik der pseudepigraphen Petrusbriefe, HBS 38, Freiburg i. Brsg. 2003, 99–101; A. J. MALHERBE, Ancient Epistolary Theorists 7, SBL SBibSt 19, Atlanta 1988; S. K. STOWERS, Letter Writing in Greco-Roman Antiquity, LEC 5, Philadelphia 1986, 33; M. L. STIREWALT, Studies in Ancient Greek Epistolography, SBL SBibSt 27, Atlanta 1993, 39–42; H.-J. KLAUCK, Die antike Briefliteratur und das Neue Testament. Ein Lehr- und Arbeitsbuch, UTB 2022, Paderborn u.a. 1998, 144; J. SYKUTRIS, Art. Epistolographie, PRE.S 5 (1931), 185–220 (214); P. A. ROSENMEYER, Ancient Epistolary Fictions. The Letter in Greek Literature, Cambridge 2001, bes. 255–338; H. GÖRGEMANNS, Art. Epistel, DNP 3 (1997), 1162f. (1163); J. SCHNEIDER, Art. Brief, RAC 2 (1954), 564–585 (570); H. U. GÖSSWEIN, Die Briefe des Euripides, BKP 55, Meisenheim a. Glan 1975, 22; J. J. BUNGARTEN, Menanders und Glykeras Brief bei Alkiphron, Bonn 1967, 186f., und den Beitrag von Karl Matthias Schmidt in diesem Band. Auch die Gattung der antiken Briefromane (vgl. auch die Beiträge von Katharina Luchner und Timo Glaser in diesem Band) wurde oft in diesem Kontext verortet; vgl. z.B. SPEYER, Fälschung (s. Anm. 4), 22; R. MERKELBACH, Die Quellen des griechischen Alexanderromans, Zetema 9, München ²1977, 48; HOSE, a.a.O. 192; C. ARNDT, Antiker und neuzeitlicher Briefroman. Ein gattungstypologischer Ver-

ein „Schauspieler" (Philostr.vit.soph. 2,24,1: ὑποκριτής) in die Rolle des fiktiven Autors.[26] Dazu ahmt er dessen Ethos nach, was dem epistulartheoretischen Topos vom Brief als „Spiegel der Seele" entspricht (z.B. Pseudo-Demetrius, De elocutione 227).[27] Das Schema antiker Prosopopoiien „Was hätte x.y. wohl gesagt angesichts ..." ist dabei leicht auf die neutestamentlichen Schriften zu übertragen. „Was hätte Paulus wohl gesagt angesichts der kirchlichen Lage um 100 n. Chr.?"

In der Erforschung der frühchristlichen Literatur wird zu Recht die Relevanz antiker Prosopopoiie betont.[28] Prinzipiell lassen sich auf diesem Hintergrund zunächst Aufschlüsse über die rhetorischen Kenntnisse und das Vorgehen jener Autoren gewinnen, die unter falschem Namen schreiben. Mit diesem Einblick in die technisch-imitative Seite von Pseudepigraphie ist indes noch kein Licht in die Intention und Kommunikationsabsicht der entsprechenden Autoren gebracht. Auch wenn sich vor allem in der Pastoralbriefexegese zur Zeit ein neuer Interpretationsansatz abzeichnet, das *Corpus Pastorale* als „Briefroman" und damit als fiktional-ästhetische Pseudepigraphie zu deuten,[29] werden die neutestamentlichen Pseudepigraphen in der Regel nicht als rhetorische Übungsstücke oder literari-

---

gleich, in: N. Holzberg (Hg.), Der griechische Briefroman. Gattungstypologie und Textanalyse, Classica Monacensia 8, Tübingen 1994, 53–83 (61) u.ö.

[26] Vgl. dazu SYKUTRIS, a.a.O. 194.

[27] Vgl. dazu W. G. MÜLLER, Der Brief als Spiegel der Seele. Zur Geschichte eines Topos der Epistolartheorie von der Antike bis zu Samuel Richardson, AuA 26 (1980), 138–157.

[28] Vgl. z.B. A. STANDHARTINGER, Studien zur Entstehungsgeschichte und Intention des Kolosserbriefes, NT.S 94, Leiden 1999, 37 Anm. 46.

[29] Vgl. dazu R. I. PERVO, Romancing an Oft-Neglected Stone. The Pastoral Epistles and the Epistolary Novel, The Journal of Higher Criticism 1 (1994), 25–47. Diese These wurde positiv aufgenommen (vgl. z.B. KLAUCK, Briefliteratur [s. Anm 25], 244; M. FRENSCHKOWSKI, Pseudepigraphie und Paulusschule. Gedanken zur Verfasserschaft der Deuteropaulinen, besonders der Pastoralbriefe, in: F. W. Horn [Hg.], Das Ende des Paulus. Historische, theologische und literaturgeschichtliche Aspekte, BZNW 106, Berlin/New York 2001, 239–272 [262]; G. HÄFNER, Das Corpus Pastorale als literarisches Konstrukt, ThQ 187 [2007], 258–273 [273]) und von Timo Glaser weiterentwickelt (siehe dazu seinen Beitrag in diesem Band). Auch für den Bereich der apokryphen Literatur wird mit ästhetisch-fiktionalen Funktionen von Pseudepigraphie gerechnet. So gilt beispielsweise der Briefwechsel zwischen Paulus und Seneca mitunter als Übung aus dem Umfeld einer Rhetorenschule; vgl. z.B. C. W. BARLOW, Epistolae Senecae ad Paulum et Pauli ad Senecam <quae vocantur>, PMAAR 10, Rom 1938, 91f.; G. RÖWEKAMP, Art. Paulus-Literatur, in: S. Döpp / W. Geerlings (Hg.), Lexikon der antiken christlichen Literatur, Freiburg i. Brsg. u.a. ³2002, 553–556 (554). Vgl. zu alternativen Intentionen des Briefwechsels: Der apokryphe Briefwechsel zwischen Seneca und Paulus. Zusammen mit dem Brief des Mordechai an Alexander und dem Brief des Annaeus Seneca über Hochmut und Götterbilder. Eingel., übers. u. m. interpret. Essays vers. v. A. FÜRST u.a., SAPERE XI, Tübingen 2006, und den Beitrag von Stefan Krauter in diesem Band.

sche Erfindungen betrachtet. Dennoch scheint sich zunehmend für etliche neutestamentliche Pseudepigraphen eine Deutung als „offene" Pseudepigraphie zu etablieren,[30] mitunter in der Variante, dass die Pseudepigraphie nur für einen Teil der Rezipienten offen war und auch nur für diesen offen sein sollte.[31] Obwohl dieser These im Hinblick auf einige Schriften eine gewisse Plausibilität nicht abzusprechen ist,[32] steht der Vermutung einer „offenen Pseudepigraphie" in den meisten Fällen der kanonhistorische Befund entgegen, da die altkirchlichen Zeugnisse eben jene vermeintlich „offenen" Pseudepigraphen als echte apostolische Schriften auszuweisen scheinen. Zur Lösung dieser Spannung könnte ein Blick auf die fehlerhafte Rezeption antiker Prosopopoiie aufschlussreich sein. Was als rhetorische Übung oder literarische Erfindung gedacht war, konnte nämlich in der Antike unter bestimmten Umständen fälschlicherweise als echt rezipiert werden (vgl. z.B. D.L. 5,92f.).[33] In diesen Fällen liegt eine sekundäre Fehl-

---

[30] Vgl. z.B. KLAUCK, Briefliteratur (s. Anm. 25), 304; T. SCHMELLER, Schulen im Neuen Testament? Zur Stellung des Urchristentums in der Bildungswelt seiner Zeit, HBS 30, Freiburg i. Brsg. 2001, 211.221; G. THEISSEN, Das Neue Testament, München 2002, 85; E. REINMUTH, Hermeneutik des Neuen Testaments, Göttingen 2002, 104–107. Dies betrifft vor allem den Zweiten Petrusbrief; vgl. z.B. A. VÖGTLE, Der Judasbrief. Der 2. Petrusbrief, EKK XXII, Solothurn u.a. 1994, 125–139; R. J. BAUCKHAM, Jude. 2 Peter, WBC 50, Waco 1983, 134 u.ö.; T. L. WILDER, Pseudonymity in the New Testament and Deception. An Inquiry into Intention and Reception, Lanham 2004, 10. Mit der Möglichkeit einer „offenen" Pseudepigraphie der neutestamentlichen Petrusbriefe rechnet auch SCHMIDT, Mahnung (s. Anm. 25), 2f.429–433; siehe auch seinen Beitrag in diesem Band. Auch die Pastoralbriefe werden zunehmend als „offene" Pseudepigraphen verstanden; vgl. z.B. B. S. EASTON, The Pastoral Epistles, New York 1947, 19; MARSHALL, Epistles (s. Anm. 3), 83f.92; H. HEGERMANN, Der geschichtliche Ort der Pastoralbriefe, ThV II (1970), 47–64; H. J. HOLTZMANN, Lehrbuch der neutestamentlichen Theologie I.II., Tübingen 1911, 222f.; KLAUCK, a.a.O. 304; SCHMIDT, a.a.O. 63f. Anm. 179; SCHMELLER, a.a.O. 211.221.
[31] Vgl. für die Pastoralbriefe z.B. SCHMELLER, a.a.O. 229.247; KLAUCK, a.a.O. 304f.; D. G. MEADE, Pseudonymity and Canon. An Investigation into the Relationship of Authorship and Authority in Jewish and Earliest Christian Tradition, WUNT 39, Tübingen 1986, 198.
[32] Die Deutung einer Schrift als „offene" Pseudepigraphie erfolgt oft rein assoziativ oder auf der Ebene von Vermutungen. Hier muss indes ein methodisches Instrumentarium mit sicheren Kriterien entwickelt werden; vgl. dazu die Ansätze bei SCHMIDT, Mahnung (s. Anm. 25), 62ff. Insgesamt sind hier in stärkerem Maße als bisher linguistische und kommunikationstheoretische Methoden zu berücksichtigen und auf die antiken und frühchristlichen Texte anzuwenden; vgl. dazu exemplarisch C. G. LEIDL, Historie und Fiktion. Zum Hannibalbrief (P.Hamb. 129), in: C. Schubert / K. Brodersen (Hg.), Rom und der griechische Osten (FS Schmidt), Stuttgart 1995, 151–169, und den Beitrag von Karl Matthias Schmidt in diesem Band.
[33] Vgl. zu dieser Episode auch SPEYER, Fälschung (s. Anm. 4), 25f.; GUDEMAN, Fälschungen (s. Anm. 12), 53. Eine fehlerhafte Rezeption fiktionaler Briefe in der Antike wurde in der Forschung oft erwogen; vgl. H. GÖRGEMANNS, Art. Epistolographie, DNP 3

inszenierung des fiktionalen Diskurses vor, da der fiktive Autor für den realen Autor gehalten und damit der fiktive Text als faktualer rezipiert wird. Dieser Aspekt könnte auch für einige neutestamentliche Pseudepigraphen von Bedeutung sein, zumal diese aufgrund ihrer Dignität und Normativität ihren primären Rezipientenkreis früh verlassen haben, was zu einer Veränderung der literatursoziologischen Rahmenbedingungen führt und damit Fehlrezeptionen begünstigt. Allerdings ersetzt die Hypothese einer möglicherweise fehlerhaften Rezeption frühchristlicher Pseudepigraphen nicht die Auseinandersetzung mit dem kanonhistorischen Befund und die damit zusammenhängende präzise Erfassung der Kanonkriterien.[34] Die Diskussion über das Verständnis der Autorenzuweisungen im Rahmen des Kanonisierungsprozesses ist nach wie vor kontrovers: Implizieren die Verfasserangaben literarische Authentizität oder sachliche Kontinuität?

3. Pseudepigraphie im Rahmen von Editions- und Fortschreibungsprozessen

Pseudepigraphie ist nicht auf einzelne selbständige Schriften beschränkt, sondern erscheint auch im Rahmen von größeren Textcorpora unterschiedlicher Gattungen wie Biographien (vgl. z.B. Historia Augusta) oder Traktat- und Dialogliteratur (vgl. z.B. Corpus Hermeticum). Vor allem hinsichtlich (pseudepigraphischer) Briefsammlungen oder -romane muss allgemein mit einer pseudepigraphischen Eigendynamik gerechnet werden. Sind solche Erwägungen über sukzessives Wachstum antiker Briefcorpora oft literarkritische Hypothesen neuzeitlicher Forschung, so liegt im Fall des Wachstums der Heroiden des Ovid ein antikes Selbstzeugnis vor: Ovid weist in einer anderen Schrift auf die sekundären Briefkompositionen des Sabinus hin, der Antwortbriefe auf seine Heroidenbriefe verfasst hat: „Quam cito de toto rediit meus orbe Sabinus scriptaque diversis rettulit ille locis! candida Penelope signum cognovit Ulixis; legit ab Hippolyto scripta

---

(1997), 1166–1170 (1168); WILDER, Pseudonymity (s. Anm. 30), 6ff.; SPEYER, Fälschung (s. Anm. 4), 23.178; SINT, Pseudonymität (s. Anm. 25), 95.

[34] Auf der einen Seite steht die in der neutestamentlichen Exegese oft rezipierte (vgl. z.B. BROX, Verfasserangaben [s. Anm. 10], 120ff.) Sicht von Karl Heinz Ohlig: „Das altkirchliche Kriterium der Apostolizität darf nicht vorschnell identifiziert werden mit der Forderung nach apostolischer Herkunft oder Authentizität" (Die theologische Begründung des neutestamentlichen Kanons, Düsseldorf 1972, 8 u.ö.). Auf der anderen Seite steht der Ansatz von Armin Daniel Baum, der literarische Authentizität als exklusives Kanonkriterium versteht; vgl. A. D. BAUM, Literarische Echtheit als Kanonkriterium in der alten Kirche, ZNW 88 (1997), 97–110; ders., Pseudepigraphie und literarische Fälschung im frühen Christentum. Mit ausgewählten Quellentexten samt deutscher Übersetzung, WUNT II/138, Tübingen 2001.

noverca suo. iam pius Aeneas miserae rescripsit Elissae, quodque legat Phyllis, si modo vivit, adest. tristis ad Hypsipylen ab Iasone littera venit; det votam Phoebo Lesbis amata lyram" (Ov.am. 2,18,27–34; vgl. auch Ovid, Epistulae ex Ponto 4,16,13–17).[35]

Abgesehen von der pseudepigraphischen Eigendynamik im Hinblick auf literarische Corpora kann es auch zu Pseudepigraphie im Rahmen von Editionsprozessen kommen. Herausgeber und Verleger greifen dabei auf verschiedene Weise in Editions- und Überlieferungsprozesse ein. Neben Umstellungen, Emendationen, Interpolationen und weiteren Bearbeitungsformen[36] ist auch mit einer redaktionell motivierten Pseudepigraphie zu rechnen. Ein in dieser Hinsicht interessantes Zeugnis liegt mit den griechischen Brutusbriefen vor, die vor allem in der Herausgabe durch Mithridates überliefert sind.[37] Der Herausgeber, „König Mithridates", widmet die Briefsammlung seinem Neffen und komponiert auf der Basis von Geschichtswerken fiktive Antwortbriefe an Brutus hinzu, was er selbst in seinem „cover letter" offen legt und dabei zugleich Einblick in Methode und Schwierigkeiten eines solchen Unternehmens gibt.[38]

Dass Pseudepigraphie im Rahmen von Editions-, Fortschreibungs- und Kanonisierungsprozessen eine Rolle spielt, ist zweifelsohne eine berechtigte Annahme, die auch Licht auf mögliche Motive neutestamentlicher Pseudepigraphie werfen kann. Diesbezügliche Erwägungen mit unterschiedlichem Plausibilitätsgrad finden sich vor allem[39] im Hinblick auf die

---

[35] „Wie schnell kam mein Sabinus zurück aus allen den Ländern. Und hat wiedergebracht Schreiben von hier und von dort. Penelopeia erkannte Odysseus' Siegel mit Freuden, die Stiefmutter durchlas ihres Hippolytos Brief. Seiner Dido hat Aeneas wiedergeschrieben: Auch an Phyllis ist da – lebte sie nur noch! – ein Blatt. Zu Hypsipyle kam ein trauernder Brief von Jason. Sappho, geliebt, kann jetzt, Phöbus, die Leier dir weihn." Text: Ovid, Heroides and Amores. Hg. u. i. Engl. übers. v. G. Showerman, LCL 41, Cambridge/London 1971; Übersetzung: Ovid I. Liebesgedichte. Amores. Lateinisch-deutsch. Eingel., übertr. u. erl. v. H. Naumann, München 1966. Siehe dazu z.B. W. S. TEUFFEL, Geschichte der römischen Literatur II. Neu bearb. v. W. Kroll / F. Skutsch, Leipzig/Berlin ⁶1910, 98–100; P. KROH, Lexikon der antiken Autoren, Stuttgart 1972, 540; F. VOLLMER, Art. Sabinus, PRE 25 (1920), 1598f.

[36] So kam es etwa im Bereich der Fachliteratur auch zu Eingriffen im Hinblick auf die Anordnung der Quellenverzeichnisse; vgl. exemplarisch zur Arbeit des Plinius bei der Herausgabe der Werke seines Onkels z.B. TEUFFEL, a.a.O. 290.

[37] KLAUCK, Briefliteratur (s. Anm. 25), 99. Ob die Briefe des Mithridates authentische Dokumente oder ihrerseits selbst Fälschungen sind, ist für unsere Fragestellung unerheblich; zum Problem siehe z.B. F. RÜHL, Die griechischen Briefe des Brutus, RhM 70 (1915), 315–325 (317–319).

[38] Siehe dazu grundlegend den Beitrag von Robert Matthew Calhoun in diesem Band.

[39] Auch den katholischen Briefen wurde eine hermeneutische Funktion im Rahmen des Kanons zugesprochen: Die ursprünglich anonymen Einzelschriften seien erst während des Kanonisierungsprozesses zu einem Corpus zusammengeordnet und den jeweili-

deuteropaulinischen Schriften: So wurde einerseits im Epheserbrief mitunter eine Einleitung zu einer Paulusbriefsammlung[40] gesehen, andererseits werden die Pastoralbriefe oft als „Schlusspunkt oder ‚Ausrufezeichen' am Ende eines in einer langen Entwicklung stehenden und durch sie abzuschließenden Corpus paulinum"[41] interpretiert. Diese möglichen Begründungen für neutestamentliche Pseudepigraphie gewinnen zudem durch die Tatsache an Relevanz, dass die Vervollständigung von Traditionen und Überlieferungen allgemein ein wichtiger Beweggrund für antike Pseudepigraphie gewesen ist (s.u.).

4. Pseudepigraphie als Spielart literarischer Anonymität

Eine weitere in der Antike bezeugte Funktion von Pseudepigraphie ist die bewusste Verhüllung eines Autors und die dadurch erreichte Anonymisierung einer Schrift. Dies geschah in der Regel weniger im Rückgriff auf verkörpernd-historische Namen als durch den Gebrauch von Kryptonymen, Technonymen, klangsymbolischen oder fiktionalen, d.h. erfundenen Namen.

---

gen fiktiven Autoren zugeschrieben worden; vgl. z.B. A. VON HARNACK, Die Lehre der zwölf Apostel nebst Untersuchungen zur ältesten Geschichte der Kirchenverfassung und des Kirchenrechts, TU 2/1, Leipzig 1886, 106–109 Anm. 2, der von einer „systematischen Correctur durch die Tradition" spricht (109). Bereits nach Augustin, De fide et operibus 14,21 (CSEL 41,62), zielt das *corpus catholicum* auf eine Korrektur eines falsch verstandenen Paulinismus; vgl. auch D. R. NIENHUIS, Not by Paul Alone. The Formation of the Catholic Epistle Collection and the Christian Canon, Waco 2007.

[40] In Aufnahme älterer Ideen hat E. J. Goodspeed vermutet, der Verfasser des Epheserbriefes sei mit dem ersten Redaktor der Paulusbriefsammlung identisch und wolle eine Art Einleitung zum Corpus schaffen; vgl. dazu H. MERKEL, Der Epheserbrief in der neueren Diskussion, ANRW II 25.2 (1987), 3156–3246 (3213); G. LÜDEMANN, Ketzer. Die andere Seite des frühen Christentums, Stuttgart 1995, 278 Anm. 426.

[41] Vgl. P. TRUMMER, Die Pastoralbriefe als Paulustradition, BET 8, Frankfurt a.M. 1978; ders., Corpus Paulinum – Corpus Pastorale. Zur Ortung der Paulustradition in den Pastoralbriefen, in: K. Kertelge u.a. (Hg.), Paulus in den neutestamentlichen Spätschriften. Zur Paulusrezeption im Neuen Testament, QD 89, Freiburg i. Brsg. 1981, 122–145. Nach Peter Trummer schafft der Verfasser der Pastoralbriefe bewusst ein Corpus, weil er sich bereits auf ein Paulusbriefcorpus bezieht und dieses abschließend edieren und interpretieren will; vgl. z.B. TRUMMER, Corpus a.a.O. 123.133 u.ö. Diese Sicht ist oft rezipiert worden; vgl. z.B. J. ROLOFF, Der erste Brief an Timotheus, EKK XV, Zürich 1988, 44; G. THEISSEN, Die Entstehung des Neuen Testaments als literaturgeschichtliches Problem, Heidelberg 2007, 164.166.170; KLAUCK, Briefliteratur (s. Anm. 25), 249. Zum Kanonbewusstsein der Pastoralbriefe und deren hermeneutischer Funktion vgl. weiter MEADE, Pseudonymity (s. Anm. 31), 133f.; F. VOUGA, Der Brief als Form apostolischer Autorität, in: K. Berger (Hg.), Studien und Texte zur Formgeschichte, TANZ 7, Tübingen/Basel 1992, 7–58 (53f.).

Pseudepigraphie als Methode der Anonymisierung diente oft dem Schutz von Autor und Adressat, wenn es um brisante Inhalte und Informationen ging. Dies betrifft zunächst Schriftstücke mit politischem Inhalt,[42] wie z.B. Sueton in seiner Augustusvita bezeugt: Ein Plebejer wurde verbannt, weil er unter dem Namen des jungen Agrippa einen beleidigenden Brief über Augustus geschrieben hatte (Suet.Aug. 51).[43] Naturgemäß veröffentlichte man Schmähschriften gegen Kaiser anonym oder pseudonym, um sich vor den möglichen Konsequenzen zu schützen, sodass im Gegenzug anonyme und pseudonyme Schreiben verboten wurden: „Etiam sparsos de se in curia famosos libellos nec expavit et magna cura redarguit ac ne requisitis quidem auctoribus id modo censuit, cognoscendum posthac de iis, qui libellos aut carmina ad infamiam cuiuspiam sub alieno nomine edant" (Suet.Aug. 55).[44] Die anonymisierende Schutzfunktion von Pseudepigraphie geht indes über die konkrete Herrscherkritik hinaus und betrifft alle Bereiche des politischen Lebens. Davon zeugen exemplarisch die Briefe Ciceros an Atticus (Cicero, Epistulae ad Atticum). In einem Klima, in dem Briefe abgefangen wurden und so manche Information ungewollt durchsickerte (1,13,2),[45] die Vertrauenswürdigkeit eines Briefüberbringers

---

[42] Zu politisch motivierten und polemischen Fälschungen siehe auch SPEYER, Fälschung (s. Anm. 4), 142–146; GUDEMAN, Fälschungen (s. Anm. 12), 63–66; STIREWALT, Studies (s. Anm. 25), 32f.

[43] „Clementiae civilitatisque eius multa et magna documenta sunt. ... Iunium Novatum et Cassium Patavinum e plebe homines alterum pecunia, alterum levi exilio punire satis habuit, cum ille Agrippae iuvenis nomine asperrimam de se epistulam in vulgus edidisset ..." – „Für seine Milde und Leutseligkeit gibt es zahlreiche überzeugende Belege. ... Er hat es zum Beispiel für hinreichend gehalten, Iunius Novatus und Cassius Patavinus, zwei Männer aus dem einfachen Volk, den einen mit Geld, den anderen mit einer leichten Verbannung zu bestrafen; und das, obwohl der erstere im Namen des jungen Agrippa einen äußerst unverschämten Brief über ihn unter die Leute gebracht hat ..." Text und Übersetzung hier und im Folgenden: C. Suetonius Tranquillus, Die Kaiserviten. De Vita Caesarum. Lateinisch-deutsch. Hg. u. übers. v. H. Martinet, Düsseldorf ³2006; vgl. zum Thema auch W. SPEYER, Büchervernichtung und Zensur des Geistes bei Heiden, Juden und Christen, BBW 7, Stuttgart 1981, 57; allgemein zur Zensur siehe auch WIDMANN, Herstellung (s. Anm. 11), 633–636.

[44] „Auch als man über ihn anrüchige Pamphlete in der Kurie verstreut hatte, schreckten ihn diese nicht auf; er verwandte große Sorgfalt darauf, sie zu widerlegen, und ordnete, da nicht einmal die Verfasser ausfindig gemacht werden konnten, lediglich an, daß in Zukunft Untersuchungen über diejenigen durchgeführt würden, die Pamphlete oder Gedichte unter fremden Namen herausgäben, um jemanden in den Schmutz zu ziehen."

[45] „Sunt autem post discessum a me tuum res dignae litteris nostris, sed non committendae eius modi periculo, ut aut interire aut aperiri aut intercipi possint." – „Seit Deiner Trennung von mir sind allerdings Sachen passiert, die einer brieflichen Mitteilung schon wert wären; aber der Brief könnte verlorengehen, geöffnet oder abgefangen werden, und einer solchen Gefahr darf ich ihn nicht aussetzen." Vgl. auch 3,12,2; 10,9[8],1. Text und Übersetzung hier und im Folgenden: M. Tullius Cicero, Atticus-Briefe. Latei-

mitunter ein Problem darstellte und zudem gefälschte Briefe im Umlauf waren (11,17[16],1; vgl. auch Cicero, Epistulae ad familiares 3,11,5), führte die politische Brisanz zu pseudonymer und kodierter Abfassung der entsprechenden Schreiben. „De re p. breviter ad te scribam; iam enim charta ipsa ne nos prodat pertimesco. itaque posthac, si erunt mihi plura ad te scribenda, ἀλληγορίαις obscurabo" (2,20,3).[46] Die Decknamen, die Cicero gezielt für seine anonymisierte Korrespondenz wählt, sind indes keine erfundenen Namen ohne semantische Referenz, sondern rekurrieren auf bekannte Größen aus dem Scipionenkreis; besonders Laelius kommt als dem Freund schlechthin eine verkörpernde Bedeutung zu (s.u.): „Sed haec scripsi properans et me hercule timide. posthac ad te aut, si perfidelem habebo, cui dem, scribam plane omnia, aut, si obscure scribam, tu tamen intelleges. in iis epistulis me Laelium, te Furium faciam; cetera erunt ἐν αἰνιγμοῖς" (2,19,5).[47] Neben politischen Schreiben wurden auch solche Briefe durch Verschlüsselung anonymisiert, die Aufschluss über finan-

---

nisch-Deutsch. Hg. u. übers. v. H. Kasten, München 1959. Das Problem des Briefabfangens erscheint auch sonst häufig; vgl. für den Bereich der christlich-apokryphen Literatur z.B. Epistolae Senecae ad Paulum et Pauli ad Senecam 2, 6. Vgl. zum Problem der Briefüberbringer Cicero, Epistulae ad Atticum 1,13,1; 1,18,2; 1,19,11; 2,19,5, 4,1,1; 4,18(15),3; 10,12(11),1; 15,6(5),4: „Hanc epistulam si illius tabellario dedissem, veritus sum, ne solveret. itaque misi dedita." – „Wenn ich diesen Brief Furius' Kurier mitgebe, wird er ihn wahrscheinlich aufmachen. Somit weiß ich, was ich riskiere." Zu weiterem Material hinsichtlich der Gefahren schriftlicher Korrespondenz siehe W. RIEPL, Das Nachrichtenwesen des Altertums mit besonderer Rücksicht auf die Römer, Leipzig/Berlin 1913, 456–464.

[46] „Über Politik will ich Dir nur einiges wenige schreiben. Ich befürchte nämlich, selbst das Papier könnte uns verraten. Deshalb werde ich in Zukunft, wenn ich Dir ausführlicher schreiben will, meine Ausführungen unter Decknamen tarnen." Korrespondenz über brisante Inhalte wurde nicht nur durch den Gebrauch von Decknamen geschützt. Weitere Sicherungsmaßnahmen waren die nachträgliche Vernichtung kompromittierender Schreiben (10,13[12],3), der Gebrauch von kryptonymen Schriftzeichen (6,6[7],1: graece !) und die Bitte um diskreten Umgang mit vertraulichen Dokumenten; vgl. 1,5: „... nolebam illum nostrum familiarem sermonem in alienas manus devenire ..." – „... und möchte nicht, daß unser vertrautes Zwiegespräch in fremde Hände gerät."

[47] „Soviel für heute in aller Eile und weiß Gott mit aller gebotenen Zurückhaltung. Finde ich einen unbedingt zuverlässigen Überbringer, so schreibe ich Dir demnächst alles mit klaren Worten; wenn nicht, so wirst Du es trotzdem verstehen, auch wenn ich mich dunkel ausdrücke. Alsdann nenne ich mich Laelius, Dich Furius; alles andere wird getarnt." Vgl. auch 2,20,5: „Quod scripseram me Furio scripturum, nihil necesse est tuum nomen mutare; me faciam Laelium et te Atticum neque utar meo chirographo neque signo, si modo erunt eius modi litterae, quas in alienum incidere nolim." – „Wenn ich Dir geschrieben habe, ich wolle Dich in meinen Briefen Furius nennen, so ist bei Dir eine Tarnung doch wohl nicht nötig; mich werde ich Laelius nennen und Dich Atticus, und nicht eigenhändig schreiben, nicht mit meinem Petschaft siegeln, falls es sich um Briefe handelt, die nicht in fremde Hände fallen dürften."

zielle oder private Verhältnisse geben konnten. „Bis ad te antea scripsi de re mea familiari, si modo tibi redditae litterae sunt, Graece ἐν αἰνιγμοῖς" (6,6[7],1).[48]

Einen weiteren Bereich der anonymisierenden Pseudepigraphie stellen amouröse literarische Kontexte dar; auch im Rahmen der apokryph-fiktionalen Literatur des Christentums griff man bei Liebesdingen zu verschlüsselter bzw. anonymer Korrespondenz (PsClem H 5,9f.). Besonders aber in der römischen Dichtung ist die pseudepigraphische Verschlüsselung von Adressaten und literarischen Figuren bezeugt.[49] Als beispielsweise Apuleius vorgeworfen wird, in seinen Schriften einige Knaben mit Pseudonymen benannt zu haben, weist er auf eine entsprechende Praxis in der erotischen Dichtung hin. Im Gegensatz zu dem von ihm negativ als Indiskretion bewerteten Verfahren des Lucilius, die in seinem Werk erscheinenden Knaben mit ihren realen Namen anzuführen (... *pueros directis nominibus carmine suo prostituerit* ...), lobt Apuleius die *modestia* des Vergil, der stattdessen zu Pseudonymen greift.[50] Neben dem Persönlichkeitsschutz und

---

[48] „Zweimal habe ich unlängst über meine Vermögensangelegenheiten an Dich geschrieben – hoffentlich hast Du die betreffenden Briefe erhalten –, und zwar auf Griechisch, unter Decknamen."

[49] So verbirgt sich hinter Catulls Lesbia, der Adressatin seiner Carmina, die Schwester des Publius Clodius Pulcher, Clodia. Dieser Sachverhalt war bereits in der Antike bekannt (Apul.apol. 10; auch Ovid, Tristia 2,427, geht von einem Pseudonym aus) und gilt heute als gesichert; vgl. dazu M. FUHRMANN, Geschichte der römischen Literatur, Stuttgart 1999, 126f.; W. EISENHUT, Catull, München/Zürich ⁹1986, 224; kritisch dagegen N. HOLZBERG, Catull. Der Dichter und sein erotisches Werk, München 2002, 16f. Catull ist kein Einzelfall. Auch Ovid greift im Fall der Perilla auf ein Pseudonym zurück (Ovid, Tristia 3,7); vgl. dazu von M. VON ALBRECHT, Römische Poesie. Texte und Interpretationen, Tübingen/Basel ²1995, 221f. Ähnliches gilt nach Apul.apol.10 für den Neoteriker Ticidas; siehe dazu J. HAMMERSTAEDT, Apuleius. De magia, SAPERE V, Darmstadt 2002, 240. Ein vergleichbarer Gebrauch von Decknamen ist für Horaz bezeugt; vgl. z.B. Terentia als Licymnia (carm. 2,12); siehe dazu z.B. VON ALBRECHT, a.a.O. 338. Zu Stella, der seine Geliebte Violentilla mit dem Namen Asteris bezeichnet und die Martial Ianthis nennt, siehe TEUFFEL, Literatur (s. Anm. 35), 321. Die pseudonyme Verschlüsselung von Liebespartnern ist auch für den homoerotischen Bereich bezeugt; so nennt Vergil seinen Lustknaben Alexander in den Bucolica Alexis (2. Ekloge); siehe auch Apul.apol. 10; Vita Donatiana 9: „... Alexandrum, quem secunda bucolicorum ecloga Alexin appellat ..." (Text: Aeneis und die Vergil-Viten. Lateinisch-deutsch. Hg. u. übers. v. J. Götte, München 1958, 562).

[50] Vgl. Apul.apol. 10: „Eadem igitur opera accusent C. Catullum, quod Lesbiam pro Clodia nominarit, et Ticidam similiter, quod quae Metella erat Perillam scripserit, et Propertium, qui Cunthiam dicat, Hostiam dissimulet, et Tibullum, quod ei sit Plania in animo, Delia in uorsu. et quidem C. Lucilium, quanquam sit iambicus, tamen improbarim, quod Gentium et Macedonem pueros directis nominibus carmine suo prostituerit. quanto modestius tandem Mantuanus poeta, qui itidem ut ego puerum amici sui Pollionis bucolico ludicro laudans et abstinens nominum sese quidem Corydonem, puerum uero

dem Vermeiden von möglichen Kompromittierungen war im poetischen Kontext die Verschlüsselung auch Bestandteil des literarischen Spiels, zumal wenn es sich um Decknamen mit symbolischer Bedeutung handelt.[51]

Ein weiterer Grund für anonymisierende Pseudepigraphie liegt in den Gepflogenheiten des antiken Literaturbetriebs. Dass ein Autor seinen Namen verschwieg, war zwar selten, da in der Antike der Wunsch nach Unsterblichkeit (vgl. z.B. Hor.carm. 3,30,1–6) gerade zum Schutz der Urheberschaft und zur Freude über die weite Verbreitung eigener Schriften führte (vgl. z.B. Martial, Epigrammata 11,3,5; Ovid, Tristia 4,10,128; Plinius ep. 2,10,2; 9,11,2 u.ö.).[52] Aber dennoch gab es Gründe, zu anonymisierenden Pseudonymen zu greifen. Abgesehen von dem Problembereich der inhaltlichen Zensur, die mitunter zu pseudonymer oder anonymer Literaturproduktion zwang,[53] steht hier die Sorge um den literarischen Ruhm an erster Stelle, da schlechte Qualität den Ruf eines Autors nachhaltig gefährden konnte. Dem entspricht die Angst vor schriftstellerischer Unvollkommenheit, die wiederum zu sorgfältiger Herausgabe der eigenen Werke motivierte und bisweilen auch zu regelrechten Publikationshemmungen führte.[54] Diese Haltung wird auch für die Pseudepigraphiefrage

---

Alexin uocat." Text: Apulei Apologia sive pro se magia liber. Hg., eingel. u. komm. v. H. E. Butler / A. S. Owen, Hildesheim 1967.

[51] Der Name der Adressatin der Catull-Briefe, Lesbia, hat eine symbolische Bedeutung als „sexuell aktive und somit höchst schamlose Frau"; dazu siehe HOLZBERG, Catull (s. Anm. 49), 36.

[52] Siehe z.B. GUDEMAN, Fälschungen (s. Anm. 12), 70; WIDMANN, Herstellung (s. Anm. 11), 625–628; SCHICKERT, Schutz (s. Anm. 11), 128–130.

[53] Auch dies kann zum Sujet einer rein literarisch motivierten „offenen" Anonymität werden. Der in Verbannung lebende Ovid hat sich durch seine Ars amatoria Schwierigkeiten eingehandelt. Deshalb empfiehlt er seinen Tristien „heimlich" nach Rom zu gehen („clam tamen intrato!"; vgl. Ovid, Tristia 1,1,63), damit ihre Aufnahme nicht der Zensur zum Opfer falle. Freilich kann jeder erkennen, wessen Werk er vor sich hat („te liquet esse meum!"; vgl. Ovid, Tristia 1,1,62). Text: Ovid, Tristia. Ex Ponto. Hg. u. i. Engl. übers. v. G. P. Goold / A. L. Wheeler, LCL 151, Cambridge/London ²1988. Vgl. weiter zu den „versteckten" Tituli (Tristia 1,1,1–14) in diesem Zusammenhang auch W. SCHUBART, Das Buch bei den Griechen und Römern, Berlin 1907, 91.

[54] Man achtete auf eine sorgfältige Herausgabe seiner Werke und gab sie vor der Veröffentlichung zunächst seinen Freunden zum Lesen; vgl. z.B. Plinius ep. 8,19,2; Vita Focae 29–33; Quintilian, Vorwort zur Institutio oratoria. Auch Atticus liest die Bücher Ciceros anderen (und sich selbst) in einer Generalprobe zur Urteilsbildung vor (Cicero, Epistulae ad Atticum 16,11,1). Mitunter wollte man seine eigenen Werke zurückhalten, weil man sie für unvollkommen hielt. Klassisches Beispiel ist hier Vergils Aeneis, deren vom Autor nicht bzw. nur eingeschränkt gebilligte (posthume) Herausgabe die antike Welt beschäftigte (vgl. z.B. Plinius, Naturalis historia 7,30) und zum beliebten Topos in den Vergilviten und zahlreichen Epigrammen wurde. Generell war man bestürzt, wenn Werke ohne die eigene Einwilligung herausgegeben wurden. Die Klagen über diesen Sachverhalt sind zahlreich und betreffen alle Bereiche antiker Literaturproduktion; vgl.

wichtig.[55] Beispielsweise ließ Aristophanes seine ersten Dramen unter fremden Namen einstudieren,[56] unter denen sie dann vermutlich auch aufgeführt wurden.[57] Darüber hinaus scheint Aristophanes auch für andere Dichter Stücke geschrieben bzw. ihnen Motive geliefert zu haben.[58] An einer Stelle gibt Aristophanes selbst explizit über seine Praxis Auskunft und stellt seine frühere verborgene (οὐ φανερῶς) seiner nun offenen (φανερῶς) Autorschaft gegenüber: „τὰ μὲν οὐ φανερῶς ἀλλ᾽ ἐπικουρῶν κρύβδην ἑτέροισι ποιηταῖς, μιμησάμενος τὴν Εὐρυκλέους μαντείαν καὶ διάνοιαν, εἰς ἀλλοτρίας γαστέρας ἐνδὺς κωμῳδικὰ πολλὰ χέασθαι· μετὰ τοῦτο δὲ καὶ φανερῶς ἤδη κινδυνεύων καθ᾽ ἑαυτόν, οὐκ ἀλλοτρίων ἀλλ᾽ οἰκείων Μουσῶν στόμαθ᾽ ἡνιοχήσας" (Aristophanes, Vespae 1018–1022).[59] Aristophanes greift mit dieser Aussage das Sujet der Inspiration auf, das in der antiken Dichtungstheorie verschiedene

---

z.B. Cicero, Epistulae ad Atticum 13,30(21),4–7; eindrucksvoll sind hier auch Galens Darlegungen „über die eigenen Bücher" und „über die Anordnung der eigenen Bücher." Siehe insgesamt SCHICKERT, Schutz (s. Anm. 11), 54–65.

[55] Mitunter konnten Pseudepigraphie, Plagiat und Fälschung auch zu Schutzbehauptungen werden. Man erklärte misslungene oder verfängliche Schriftstücke schlicht im Nachhinein für gefälscht (vgl. evtl. Cicero, Epistulae ad Atticum 3,12,2). So könnten auch die zahlreichen Klagen Martials, ihm seien unter seinem Namen umherlaufende Epigramme fälschlicherweise untergeschoben, der Versuch einer nachträglichen Zurücknahme von misslungenen, anstößigen oder allzu „martialischen" Inhalten sein; vgl. z.B. Martial, Epigrammata 10,3.

[56] Vgl. generell zu Aristophanes' Praxis, unter einem Pseudonym zu schreiben bzw. seine Werke von anderen einstudieren zu lassen, GUDEMAN, Fälschungen (s. Anm. 12), 70f.; W. SCHMIDT, Geschichte der griechischen Literatur I/4, München 1959, 154f.185; SPEYER, Fälschung (s. Anm. 4), 30; G. KAIBEL, Art. Aristophanes, PRE 2 (1896), 971–994 (973f.); D. MACDOWELL, Aristophanes. Waps, Oxford 1971, 263–265. Ähnlich verfuhr auch Eupolis; vgl. SCHMIDT, a.a.O. 185. Normalerweise übernahmen die Dichter selbst das Einstudieren, aber es sind zahlreiche Ausnahmen bekannt; vgl. auch A. PICKARD-CAMBRIDGE, The Dramatic Festivals of Athens, Oxford ²1968, 84f.

[57] Skeptisch hinsichtlich der These, dass die entsprechenden Stücke auch wirklich unter dem Namen von Kallistratos o.a. liefen, ist KAIBEL, a.a.O. 973f.; vgl. allgemein zum Problem auch BLUM, Kallimachos (s. Anm. 10), 72–86.

[58] Dies geht über das reine Einstudieren durch andere hinaus; vgl. SCHMIDT, Geschichte (s. Anm. 56), 179; KAIBEL, a.a.O. 973. Die Schlüsselstelle Vespae 1018–1022 ist in der Deutung umstritten; vgl. insgesamt auch MACDOWELL, Aristophanes (s. Anm. 56), 263–265; SCHMIDT, a.a.O. 179.185 Anm. 7; KAIBEL, a.a.O. 973.

[59] „... Nicht offen im Anfang, nein, insgeheim als anderer Dichter Gehilfe, da des Eurykles Kunst, weissagenden Geist und Erfindungen wählend zum Vorbild, er heimlich in anderer Bauch sich verbarg und des Komischen viel ihm entströmte. Doch trat er hernach auch offen hervor und wagte sich selbst in die Rennbahn und lenkte der eigenen Musen Gespann, zog er nicht am Gespann der Fremden". Text: Aristophanis Comodiae. Tom. 1, hg. v. F. W. Hall / W. M. Geldart, Oxford 1949; Übersetzung: Die Komödien des Aristophanes, Bd. 2, übers. v. J. J. C. Donne, Naunhof/Leipzig 1938.

Ausprägungen erfährt. Neben der materiellen Inspiration[60] und der Metempsychosis, die vor allem als Illustration des *poeta-redivivus*-Topos erscheint,[61] kommen auch eggastrimythische Vorstellungen zum Einsatz: Ein göttlicher Dämon, ein Python, schlüpft in den Bauch bestimmter Menschen, die dann zu prophezeien beginnen und das von ihnen Verkündete auf den in ihnen und durch sie offenbarenden Dämon zurückführen. Unter den Bauchrednergeistern tat sich besonders Eurykles hervor, der schon bei Platon als Metapher für die „innere Stimme" fungiert und nach dem sich eine ganze Bauchrednerschule benannte (εὐρυκλεῖδαι) (Plato soph. 252c). Wie im Fall des berühmten Bauchredners Eurykles schlüpft nun Aristophanes als offenbarendes *alter ego* in die Person eines anderen, der dann die Werke des Aristophanes als die seinen vorträgt. Aristophanes' pseudonymes Vorgehen entspringt indes keinem irrationalen Inspirationsglauben. Die materielle Inspiration dient dem Dichter vielmehr als Bild, um eine pseudepigraphische Strategie zu veranschaulichen. Die tatsächlichen Gründe für die von ihm gewählte Pseudonymität benennt Aristophanes an anderer Stelle: Selbstzweifel angesichts seiner Jugend (Aristophanes, Nubes

---

[60] Die Vorstellung der materiellen Inspiration schlägt sich nicht zuletzt in dem Topos nieder, dass große Dichter in ihrer Kindheit von Bienen genährt werden, die wegen ihrer hohen geistigen Eigenschaften und wegen der Süßigkeit des von ihnen produzierten Honigs in Beziehung zu den Musen gebracht wurden; vgl. z.B. Plato Ion 534ab; für Vergil z.B. Vita Focae 28–34. Der Inspirationsgedanke kann sich auch auf konkrete literarische Vorbilder beziehen. Dass man sich Inhalte und Autoren im wörtlichen Sinne „einverleibt", ist z.B. bei Artemidor, Onirocriticon 2,45, mit der Metapher des Bücheressens bezeugt; weiter spricht Lukian davon, dass eine Rede wie Ambrosia eingeflößt wird (Nigrinus 11); vgl. zu weiteren Spielarten der materiellen Inspiration im Rahmen antiker Mimesistheorien z.B. (Pseudo-)Longinus, De sublimitate 13,2; Aelian, Varia historia 13,22, oder das Bekenntnis des Aischylos, seine Werke seien Brocken vom Mahl Homers (Athenäus, Deipnosophistes 8,347E). Die Vorstellung der materiellen Inspiration ist dabei geschlossen. So greift Martianus Capella (2,134–146) das Sujet der Einverleibung von Wissen auf, indem er die Kehrseite darstellt: Vor ihrer Hochzeit mit Merkur entleert sich die Philologie all ihres Wissens, indem sie ganze Bücher erbricht.

[61] Die Metempsychosis, die Einkörperung der Seele in den Körper eines anderen, diente oft als Bild der literarischen Positionierung im Kontext antiker Imitationstheorien. Das in den Dichter inkorporierte *alter ego* fungiert als Schlüssel zu Werk und Selbstverständnis des imitierenden Dichters. Bereits das Grabepigramm des Antipatros von Sidon auf Stesichoros bedient sich dieses Sujets (Anthologia Palatina 7,75). Berühmt wird diese Vorstellung jedoch im Bereich der römischen Literatur durch die Metempsychosis, die Ennius für sich in Anspruch nimmt: Ennius schreibt im Stil des Homer, weil dessen Seele in ihm wohnt (Scholia ad. Persius, Prol. 2f.); vgl. A. KAMBYLIS, Die Dichterweihe und ihre Symbolik. Untersuchungen zu Hesiodos, Kallimachos, Properz und Ennius, Heidelberg 1965, 191–204; W. SUERBAUM, Untersuchungen zur Selbstdarstellung älterer römischer Dichter. Livius Andronicus. Naevius. Ennius, Spudasmata 19, Hildesheim 1968, 43–113. Vgl. zu weiteren Beispielen W. STETTNER, Die Seelenwanderung bei Griechen und Römern, Tübingen 1934, 42–44; SUERBAUM, a.a.O. 83–94.

530f.) und Angst vor einem unzufriedenen, unberechenbaren Publikum (Aristophanes, Equites 502f.541) lassen ihn zu dieser literarischen Strategie greifen.[62]

Eine weitere Spielart anonymer Pseudonymität in Verbindung mit der Sorge um die literarische und historische Wirkung bezeugt Xenophon, der seine Anabasis unter dem Pseudonym Themistogenes von Syrakus geschrieben hat und selbst darauf in Hellenika 3,1,2 verweist: Die Darstellung der Ereignisse um Kyros „findet man bei Themistogenes von Syrakus" (Θεμιστογένει τῷ Συρακοσίῳ γέγραπται).[63] Obwohl viele antike Autoren die Anabasis als Werk des Themistogenes ansehen, ist die tatsächliche Verfasserschaft seit der Antike bekannt (vgl. D.L. 2,6,57).[64] Interessant ist die Deutung dieses Sachverhalts durch Plutarch (mor. 345E [Bellone an pace clariores fuerint Athenienses]), wobei offen bleiben muss, ob Plutarch die tatsächliche Intention des Xenophon hinreichend erfasst.[65] Plutarch vermutet, dass Xenophon zu dieser Strategie greift, um größere Glaubwürdigkeit für seine Erzählung zu gewinnen, indem er sich auf sich selbst wie in der dritten Person bezieht und jemand anderes von seinen Taten erzählen lässt. Eine Variante dieser Vorstellung liegt im Fall des Kaisers Hadrian vor, der seine Autobiographie[66] nicht unter eigenem Namen an die Öffentlichkeit gebracht, sondern sie durch gebildete Freige-

---

[62] Im Fall der Überlassung seiner Stücke an seinen Sohn Araros mag auch eine Rolle gespielt haben, diesem einen guten Karrierestart zu ermöglichen; vgl. GUDEMAN, Fälschungen (s. Anm. 12), 70. Dagegen vermutet BLUM, Kallimachos (s. Anm. 10), 85 Anm. 166, Araros habe die Stücke erst nach dem Tod seines Vaters als die eigenen ausgegeben und dann zu seinem Schutz behauptet, sie seien ihm von seinem Vater überlassen worden.

[63] Text und Übersetzung: Xenophon, Hellenika. Griechisch-deutsch. Hg. u. übers. v. G. Strasburger, München 1970. Vgl. zur Stelle HOSE, Literaturgeschichte (s. Anm. 25), 134; GUDEMAN, a.a.O. 70; SPEYER, Fälschung (s. Anm. 4), 30.

[64] Zur Beleglage siehe M. MACLAREN, Xenophon and Themistocles, TAPhA 65 (1934), 240–247 (241). Siehe zur erkannten Pseudepigraphie auch Anm. 68.

[65] „Ξενοφῶν μὲν γὰρ αὐτὸς ἑαυτοῦ γέγονεν ἱστορία, γράψας ἃ ἐστρατήγησε καὶ κατώρθωσε καὶ Θεμιστογένη περὶ τούτων συντετάχθαι τὸν Συρακόσιον, ἵνα πιστότερος ᾖ διηγούμενος ἑαυτὸν ὡς ἄλλον, ἑτέρῳ τὴν τῶν λόγων δόξαν χαριζόμενος." Text: Plutarch's Moralia in Sixteen Volumes. Vol. 4. 263B–351B. Hg. u. i. Engl. übers. v. F. C. Babbitt, LCL 305, Cambridge/London 1962. Vgl. zu den möglichen Motiven auch H. R. BREITENBACH, Art. Xenophon von Athen, PRE 9/A2 (1967), 1644f.; F. DÜRRBACH, L'Apologie de Xenophon dans l'Anabase, REG 23 (1893), 343ff.; C. HÖEG, Xenophontos Kurou Anabasis. Œuvre anonyme ou pseudonyme ou orthonyme?, C&M 11 (1949), 151–179; MACLAREN, a.a.O. 240–247; T. SINKO, Ad fastos Xenophonteos symbolae, Eos 34 (1932/33), 167–183.

[66] Die Autobiographie des Hadrian ist nicht erhalten. Sie wird jedoch in der Historia Augusta, Hadrian 1,1; 3,3.5; 7,2; Septimus Severus 1,6 und bei Cassius Dio 69,11,2 als Quelle genannt und als Hadrians Werk zitiert.

lassene unter deren Namen herausgegeben hat:[67] „Famae celebris Hadrianus tam cupidus fuit, ut libros vitae suae scriptos a se libertis suis litteratis dederit, iubens ut eos suis nominibus publicarent; nam et Phlegontis libri Hadriani esse dicuntur" (Historia Augusta, Hadrian 16,1).[68] Aus dem Mund anderer hat das Lob mehr Gewicht. Eigenlob galt zudem insgesamt als unangebracht; Plutarch widmet sogar eine Schrift dem Thema „wie man, ohne anzustoßen, sich selbst loben kann" (De se ipsum citra invidiam laudando [mor 539A–547Ende]).

Auf einen weiteren Beweggrund für verhüllende Literaturproduktion stößt man möglicherweise in einem Brief von Plinius, in dem dieser die Tugenden des Pompeius Saturninus preist: „Legit mihi nuper epistulas; uxoris esse dicebat: Plautum vel Terentium metro solutum legi credidi. quae sive uxoris sunt, ut adfirmat, sive ipsius, ut negat, pari gloria dignus ..." (Plinius ep. 1,16,6).[69] Plinius erwägt, dass Pompeius seine eigenen Briefe als die seiner Frau ausgibt. Diese Vermutung führt in den Bereich der pseudgymnymen Literaturproduktion, welche in der Antike nicht ungewöhnlich war und sich aus unterschiedlichen Gründen ereignete.[70] Im Fall

---

[67] SPEYER, Fälschung (s. Anm. 4), 31, sieht Analogien zur literarischen Praxis im Frankreich des 18. Jh.

[68] „Auf Verbreitung seines Ruhmes war Hadrian so eifrig bedacht, daß er die Bücher seiner selbstverfaßten Biographie seinen literarisch gebildeten Freigelassenen überantwortete mit dem Auftrag, sie unter ihren Namen zu veröffentlichen; so sollen auch Phlegons Schriften aus Hadrians Feder stammen." Übersetzung hier und im Folgenden: Historia Augusta. Römische Herrschergestalten, Bd. I. Von Hadrianus bis Alexander. Übers. v. J. Straub, Zürich u.a. 1976; Bd. II. Von Maximinus Thrax bis Carinus. Übers. v. J. Straub, Zürich u.a. 1985. Text hier und im Folgenden: The Scriptores Historiae Augustae in Three Volumes. Hg. u. übers. v. D. Magie, LCL 139.149.263, Cambridge/London 1960–1961. Der Plan ging freilich nicht auf; vgl. Anm. 66.

[69] „... Kürzlich hat er mir Briefe vorgelesen, angeblich von seiner Frau. Ich glaubte, Plautus oder Terenz in Prosa zu hören. Mögen sie nun wirklich von seiner Frau sein, wie er behauptet, oder von ihm selbst, was er bestreitet, auf jeden Fall verdient er Anerkennung ..." Text und Übersetzung: C. Plini Caecilii Secundi Epistularum Libri decem. Hg. u. übers. v. H. Kasten, München 1968.

[70] Neben erotischen Briefen wie Ovids Heroiden oder Alkiphrons Hetärenbriefen, in denen die Pseudgymnie ästhetisch-literarisch motiviert ist, dient der fiktive Frauenname als didaktisches Mittel, um weibliche Adressaten zu erreichen, wie vor allem die pseudpythagoreischen Frauenbriefe zeigen; vgl. dazu z.B. A. STÄDELE, Die Briefe des Pythagoras und der Pythagoreer, BKP 115, Meisenheim a. Glan 1980. Dass gerade Frauen über Frauenthemen schreiben, erhöht den Reiz der Fiktion; vgl. W. WILHELM, Die Oeconomica der Neupythagoreer Bryson, Kallikratides, Periktione, Phintys, RhM 70 (1915), 161–223 (186f.). Ein weiteres Beispiel könnte mit der plutarch'schen Schrift περὶ φιλοκοσμίαν vorliegen. Diese einer jungen Frau gewidmete Schrift hat die weibliche Eitelkeit zum Thema. Die Schrift erscheint im Lampriaskatalog als Plutarchschrift. In seinen Conjugalia praecepta 138a–146a führt Plutrach diese Schrift jedoch auf die Urheberschaft seiner Frau Timoxena zurück, was in der Tat passen würde: Plutarch stilisiert

des Pompeius soll der Rückgriff auf ein Pseudgymnym wohl dessen charakterliche Tugenden, allen voran seine Bescheidenheit, illustrieren. Vor allem in der literarischen Anonymität gilt das Zurücktreten des Verfassernamens als literarische Demutsgeste und als Zeichen des guten Tons (Dion Chrysostomus, Oratio 53,10).[71] Auch in der pseudonymen Literaturproduktion ist ein solcher Gedanke bezeugt, wie beispielsweise der neunte Brief des Salvian von Marseille belegt: „Qui sicut *humilitati* praestitit ut alienum, sic timori atque cautellae ut Timothei nomen scriberet" (Salvian ep. 9,17).[72]

Timoxena in seiner Trostschrift anlässlich des Todes ihres gemeinsamen Kindes als eine Frau, die frei von weiblicher Eitelkeit ist (Consolatio ad uxorem 609ab). Wie die Verfasser der pseudpythagoreischen Frauenbriefe wollte Plutarch mit der Zuschreibung an Timoxena eine Frau zu einer Frau über „Frauendinge" sprechen lassen; vgl. bereits dazu U. VON WILAMOWITZ-MOELLENDORFF, Commentariolum grammaticum 3, Göttingen 1889, 27f.: Plutarch greife zu dieser Verfasserfiktion, „ut femina ad feminam scribere videretur."

[71] Dion Chrysostomus, Oratio 53,10: „ὁ δὲ οὕτως ἄρα ἐλευθέριος ἦν καὶ μεγαλόφρων ὥστε οὐδαμοῦ φανήσεται τῆς ποιήσεως αὐτοῦ μεμνημένος, ἀλλὰ τῷ ὄντι ὥσπερ οἱ προφῆται τῶν θεῶν ἐξ ἀφανοῦς καὶ ἀδύτου ποθὲν φθεγγόμενος." – „Homer dagegen war so frei und großmütig, daß er an keiner Stelle seiner Dichtung persönlich in Erscheinung tritt, sondern in der Tat wie die göttlichen Propheten von irgendwoher aus dem Unsichtbaren und Verborgenen spricht." Text: Dio Chrysostom in Five Volumes, Vol. 4. Hg. u. m. engl. Übers. vers. v. H. L. Crosby, LCL 376, Cambridge/London 1962. Übersetzung: Dion Chrysostomos, Sämtliche Reden. Eingel., übers. u. erl. v. W. Elliger, Zürich u.a. 1967. Dion grenzt Homer positiv von jenen Dichtern ab, die ihre Namen auf ihre Abhandlungen setzen; vgl. dazu auch W. SPEYER, Religiöse Pseudepigraphie und literarische Fälschung im Altertum, in: Brox, Pseudepigraphie (s. Anm. 2), 195–263 (199 Anm. 11); D. FRICKENSCHMIDT, Evangelium als Biographie. Die vier Evangelien im Rahmen antiker Erzählkunst, TANZ 22, Tübingen u.a. 1997, 107. Dieser Gedanke findet sich bereits bei Aristoteles, der darauf hinweist, dass die Dichter möglichst wenig in eigener Person reden sollten (Arist.po. 1460a 7–8).

[72] „Wie er in seiner Demut einen fremden Namen schrieb, so aus Furcht und Vorsicht den des Timotheus." Text hier und im Folgenden: Salvien de Marseille, Œuvres. Tome 1. Les Lettres. Les livres de Timothée a l'Église. Eingel., hg. u. m. frz. Übers. vers. v. G. Lagarrigue, SC 176, Paris 1971. Übersetzung hier und im Folgenden: MAYER, Timotheus (s. Anm. 9). Weiter lassen sich etliche Beispiele aus der monastischen Tradition beibringen; vgl. dazu BROX, Auctor (s. Anm. 9), 61–65. Auch Sulpicius Severus zieht es vor, seine Vita Martini ohne Nennung seines Namens zu verbreiten (ML 20,159f.: „Sed tamen, ne nos maneat tam molesta defensio, suppresso, si tibi videtur, nomine libellus edatur. quod ut fieri valeat, titulum fronti erade, ut muta sit pagina; aut, quod sufficit, loquatur materiam, non loquatur auctorem."). Ähnliches ist in der geistlichen und weltlichen Dichtung des Mittelalters zu beobachten, wo die Verhüllung des Autorennamens wegen des Vorbilds der christlichen *humilitas* üblich ist und sich zudem in die Praxis höfischer Servilität einfügt; vgl. dazu insgesamt J. SCHWIETERING, Die Demutsformel mittelhochdeutscher Dichter, Berlin 1921, 27ff.

Im Gegensatz zu den altkirchlichen und apokryphen Befunden[73] tragen die eben angeführten Motive für die neutestamentliche Pseudepigraphie nur mittelbar etwas aus. Schutz, Verhüllung, Bescheidenheit und Strategie werden im Bereich der frühchristlichen Literatur eher bei der Frage der Anonymität relevant. So könnten die Evangelien, abgesehen von theologischen und gattungskritischen Gründen, auch deswegen anonym sein, weil man keine herrscherkritische Biographie schreiben durfte.[74] Hinsichtlich der Anonymität des Hebräerbriefes sind die Erwägungen von Clemens von Alexandrien bezeichnend (Eus.h.e. 6,14,2–4). Er erklärt die Anonymität des in seinen Augen paulinischen Schreibens neben dem Hinweis auf die Bescheidenheit (μετριότης) des Autors damit, dass Paulus um der Wirkung willen seinen eigenen Namen verschwieg, weil er bei den Judenchristen nicht angesehen war. Es handelt sich also um eine Art diplomatischer Anonymität: Der Name soll kein negatives Vorzeichen für die Rezeption sein.[75]

5. Pseudepigraphie als Auftragsarbeit

Mitunter steht hinter einem pseudepigraphischen Dokument eine Auftragsarbeit. Der reale Autor schreibt nicht aus eigenem Antrieb unter einem Pseudonym, sondern tut dies auf Weisung des angeblichen, fiktiven Autors. Es handelt sich dabei gewissermaßen um eine antike Variante des Ghostwritings, die wiederum unterschiedlich motiviert sein kann.

Auftragspseudepigraphie war zunächst ein Geschäftszweig im literarischen Rom der Antike. Bedürftige Dichter schrieben Werke für andere, die diese dann als ihre eigenen herausgaben (Martial, Epigrammata 2,20;

---

[73] Im Bereich der theologischen Lehrstreitigkeiten in der Alten Kirche kam es zu anonymisierender Literaturproduktion. Aus Furcht vor Verfolgungen und Bücherverbrennungen (vgl. zu Beispielen SPEYER, Büchervernichtung [s. Anm. 43], 91f.130) schrieben vor allem heterodoxe Christen unter falschen Namen; vgl. SPEYER, a.a.O. 143f. Nach der Angabe des syrischen Übersetzers hat z.B. Nestorius sein *Liber Heracleides* unter dem Namen Herakleides von Damaskus geschrieben, da er seinen wirklichen Namen verschweigen musste; vgl. F. NAU, Nestorius. Le livre d'Héraclide de Damas, Paris 1910, XVIIf.3.

[74] Vgl. FRICKENSCHMIDT, Evangelium (s. Anm. 71), 507: „Die in der Kaiserzeit spätestens seit Nero lebensbedrohliche Brisanz einer auch nur ansatzweise antityrannisch zu wertenden Biographie ist als möglicher weiterer Grund für die anonyme Abfassung der Evangelien anzusehen."

[75] Vgl. dazu z.B. T. ZAHN, Geschichte des neutestamentlichen Kanons I. Das Neue Testament vor Origenes, Leipzig/Erlangen 1889, 283ff.; E. RIGGENBACH, Der Brief an die Hebräer, KNT 13, Leipzig u.a. 1913, VIIIff. Zum Pseudepigraphiekonzept des Hebräerbriefes siehe auch den Beitrag von Clare Rothschild in diesem Band.

12,[47]46 u.ö.),[76] wofür im Gegenzug die realen Autoren materiell entlohnt wurden. Es handelt sich also gewissermaßen um ein Plagiat im gegenseitigen Einvernehmen, da sich die Ghostwriter ihre geistigen Erzeugnisse gegen Bezahlung „rauben" lassen. Gleiches ist für den Komödienbetrieb bezeugt: So verkaufte der Komiker Platon seine Stücke aus Geldnot.[77] Darüber äußert er sich in seiner nur in Fragmenten erhaltenen Komödie Peisandros (Frgm. 99) und vergleicht sich mit den Arkadern, die als Söldner Siege immer nur für andere und nicht für sich selbst erstritten, wie es laut Suidas heißt: „Ἀρκάδας μιμούμενοι· παροιμία ἐπὶ τῶν ἑτέροις πονούντων ... ταύτῃ τῇ παροιμίᾳ κέχρηται Πλάτων ἐν Πεισάνδρῳ. διὰ γὰρ τὸ τὰς κωμῳδίας αὐτὸς ποιῶν ἄλλοις παρέχειν διὰ πενίαν Ἀρκάδας μιμεῖσθαι ἔφη."[78]

Eine weitere Spielart der Auftragspseudepigraphie führt in den Bereich des Sekretärswesens. Dass antike Herrscher, Philosophen und andere Persönlichkeiten ihre Korrespondenz von Sekretären und Briefschreibern (Epistolographen) zum Teil in professionellen Korrespondenzbüros erledigen ließen, ist reich bezeugt.[79] Die Aufgaben eines antiken Sekretärs waren dabei vielseitig und führten zu unterschiedlichen Beteiligungsformen. Neben dem Niederschreiben eines Diktats, der Fassung von Reden etc. zu Briefen und der Mitautorenschaft kam es mitunter vor, dass Sekretäre völlig eigenständig Schreiben im Namen ihrer Auftraggeber abfassten.[80] So heißt es über den Sophisten Antipater: „Er beschrieb auch die Thaten des Kaisers Severus, von dem er zu seinem Geheimschreiber gemacht wurde und in dessen Namen er Briefe ausfertigte (ὑφ' οὗ μάλιστα ταῖς βασιλείοις ἐπιστολαῖς ἐπιταχθεὶς λαμπρόν τι ἐν αὐταῖς ἤχησεν), die in einem hohen Ton geschrieben waren. Ich urteile so von ihm, dass zwar in seinen Deklamationen und andern Schreibarten viele ihn übertroffen

---

[76] Vgl. dazu SCHICKERT, Schutz (s. Anm. 11), 71f.

[77] Vgl. A. KÖRTE, Art. Platon (Komiker), PRE 20 (1950), 2537–2541 (2540); PICKARD-CAMBRIDGE, Dramatic Festivals (s. Anm. 56), 85; BLUM, Kallimachos (s. Anm. 10), 86f. Dass Dichter und Komödienschreiber mitunter an den Werken anderer mitbeteiligt waren, war auch unabhängig von der finanziellen Frage üblich. Mitunter führte dies nachträglich zu Plagiatsvorwürfen (vgl. den Angriff des Aristophanes, Nubes 533ff. und die Replik des Eupolis, Baptai 415) oder zum Vorwurf der literarischen Unselbständigkeit (Terenz, prol. Adelphoe; Heautontimorumenos).

[78] Text: Comicorum Atticorum Fragmenta, Bd. I, hg. v. T. Kock, Leipzig 1880, 628.

[79] Vgl. z.B. SPEYER, Fälschung (s. Anm. 4), 33f.; SCHNEIDER, Brief (s. Anm. 25), 569; K. DZIATZKO, Art. Brief, PRE 3 (1899), 836–843 (839f.); E. R. RICHARDS, The Secretary in the Letters of Paul, WUNT II/42, Tübingen 1991; STANDHARTINGER, Studien (s. Anm. 28), 92; R. HIRZEL, Der Dialog. Ein literarhistorischer Versuch I, Leipzig 1895, 304 Anm. 2.

[80] Vgl. zu den unterschiedlichen Aufgaben z.B. RICHARDS, a.a.O. 106–111.200 u.ö.; siehe zum Problem auch SCHMIDT, Mahnung (s. Anm. 25), 51–56.

haben, aber in seinen Briefen keiner. Denn so wie ein guter tragischer Schauspieler seine Würde nicht vergisst, so ließ er den Kaiser seiner Hoheit gemäß sich ausdrücken (ἀλλ' ὥσπερ τραγῳδίας λαμπρὸν ὑποκριτὴν τοῦ δραμάτος εὖ ξυνιέντα ἐπάξια τοῦ βασιλείου προσώπου φθέγξασθαι)" (Philostr.vit.soph. 2,24,1).[81] Eine solche Praxis bestätigen sowohl die Kaiserviten des Sueton (vgl. Suet.Dom. 20: „epistulas orationesque et edicta alieno formabat ingenio") als auch die fiktive Biographiensammlung Historia Augusta an etlichen Stellen. So heißt es beispielsweise über den Kaiser Verus, der immer eine Schar gebildeter Männer um sich versammelte: „Nec desunt qui dicant eum adiutum ingenio amicorum, atque ab aliis ei illa ipsa, qualiacumque sunt, scripta." (Historia Augusta, Verus 2,8).[82]

Auch in der alltäglichen Korrespondenz ist Auftragspseudepigraphie bezeugt. Für diesen Sachverhalt sind wiederum die Briefe Ciceros an Atticus aufschlussreich. Cicero gibt Atticus, der auch sonst die Schriften Ciceros auf vielerlei Weise bearbeitet,[83] nicht nur explizit freie Hand, in seinem Namen Briefe zu verfassen, sondern lässt ihn zudem selbst entscheiden, wer einen Brief erhalten soll:[84] „Si qui erunt, quibus putes opus esse meo nomine litteras dari, velim conscribas curesque dandas" (3,15,8).[85] Dieser Beleg ist kein Ausnahmefall; er illustriert vielmehr eine gängige Praxis: „Tu, ut antea fecisti, velim, si qui erunt, ad quos aliquid scribendum a me existimes, ipse conficias" (11,3,3).[86] Sogar Vorkehrungen werden getrof-

---

[81] Übersetzung: Die Werke der Philostrate aus dem Griechischen übersetzt von D. C. Seybold, 2/1, Lemgo 1777, 146. Text: Philostratorum et Callistrati opera, hg. v. F. Dübner, Paris 1849, 255.

[82] „Auch fehlt es nicht an Stimmen, die behaupten, er habe sich von begabten Freunden helfen lassen und von anderen seien für ihn eben jene Erzeugnisse, welcher Art sie auch sein mögen, geschrieben." Über Antonius Pius wird Vergleichbares gesagt; vgl. Historia Augusta, Antionus Pius 11,3: „Orationes plerique alienas esse dixerunt, quae sub eius nomine feruntur; Marius Maximus eas proprias fuisse dicit." – „Die unter seinem Namen gehenden Reden, die nach verbreiteter Behauptung nicht von ihm selbst verfasst wären, erklärt Marius Maximus für des Kaisers geistiges Eigentum."

[83] Atticus korrigiert die Schriften Ciceros (15,26[14],4); er ist Cicero ein Ratgeber in konzeptionellen Fragen (13,26[14,2+15],1f.; 13,27[16],1f.; 13,28[17+18],2; 13,29[19],3f.); er verbessert nachträglich auf Wunsch Ciceros (13,43,3). Insgesamt regelt Atticus die Angelegenheiten von Cicero; vgl. z.B. 5,8,3.

[84] Auch Cicero selbst scheint für andere Reden verfasst zu haben; vgl. Epistulae ad Atticum 15,5(3),2.

[85] „Wenn Du meinst, jemandem in meinem Namen schreiben zu müssen, so tu es bitte und lass die Briefe besorgen!"

[86] „Wenn Du meinst, einigen Leuten müsse ich noch schreiben, so erledige Du das bitte wie bisher." Vgl. auch 11,9(8),2: „Ad quos videbitur, velim cures litteras meo nomine." – „Laß bitte in meinem Namen an geeignete Persönlichkeiten schreiben." Siehe auch 5,8,3; 11,13(12),4; 11,14(13),5.

fen, um die vorgebliche Verfasserschaft glaubwürdig zu machen: „Quibus tibi videbitur, velim des litteras meo nomine; nosti meos familiares. signum requirent aut manum, dices iis me propter custodias ea vitasse" (11,2,4).[87] Mitunter gibt Cicero Gründe für das Delegieren von solchen Schreibarbeiten an, wie z.B. gesundheitliche Einschränkungen: „Ego propter incredibilem et animi et corporis molestiam conficere plures litteras non potui. ... tu velim et Basilo et quibus praeterea videbitur, etiam Servilio conscribas, ut tibi videbitur, meo nomine" (11,6[5],3).[88] Auch andere Gründe sind bekannt. So schreibt Caecilius Rufus offen an Cicero (Epistulae ad familiares 8,1,1 [ep. 74]), dass er aufgrund seiner Zeitknappheit andere dazu abgestellt habe („... quod hunc laborem alteri delegavi ..."), Cicero an seiner statt über alle möglichen Dinge zu berichten und Informationen zusammenzustellen.[89]

Die Befunde hinsichtlich des antiken Sekretärswesens, denen ohne Mühe weitere hinzuzufügen wären, können durchaus etwas zum möglichen Verständnis der *authentischen* paulinischen Briefe austragen.[90] Vorsicht ist dagegen angebracht, mit solchen Stellen neutestamentliche Pseudepigraphie begründen zu wollen, wie es vor allem für die pseudo-paulinische Literatur,[91] aber auch mitunter für den Ersten Petrusbrief erwogen wird (Silvanus-Hypothese [1Petr 5,12]).[92] Zunächst sind chronologische Vorbehalte geltend zu machen: Paulus kann z.B. die Pastoralbriefe – geht man von der konventionellen Datierung gegen Ende des ersten Jahrhunderts aus – nicht selbst in Auftrag gegeben und dazu womöglich noch Stichworte

---

[87] „Schreib bitte im meinem Namen an Dir geeignet erscheinende Persönlichkeiten: Du kennst ja meinen Freundeskreis. Vermissen sie mein Siegel oder meine eigene Hand, so sag' ihnen, ich hätte deren Gebrauch wegen der Kontrolle vermieden." Zur Deutung dieser Stelle RICHARDS, Secretary (s. Anm. 79), 50.108 Anm. 161.

[88] „Wegen meiner kaum glaublichen seelischen und körperlichen Beschwerden habe ich nicht mehr Briefe fertig bekommen. ... Schreib Du bitte in meinem Namen an Basilius und an andere, wo es Dir angebracht erscheint, auch an Servilius, je nachdem, wie Du es für richtig hältst."

[89] Vgl. RICHARDS, Secretary (s. Anm. 79), 51f. Text und Übersetzung hier und im Folgenden: M. Tulli Ciceronis Epistularum ad familiares libri XVI. Lateinisch-deutsch. Hg. u. übers. v. H. Kasten, München 1964.

[90] Solcherlei Überlegungen werden im Fall der paulinischen Literatur durch die 1.-Ps.-pl.-Formulierungen und die Angabe der Mitabsender in den orthonymen Paulusbriefen gestützt (2Kor 1,1; Phil 1,1; Phlm 1; 1Thess 1,1; 1Kor 1,1; Gal 1,2). Zudem erwähnt Paulus selbst eine Mitarbeit von Schreibern und Sekretären (Röm 16,22; vgl. implizit auch 1Kor 16,21; Gal 6,11; Phlm 11).

[91] Vgl. dazu ZIMMERMANN, Pseudepigraphie (s. Anm. 7), 32f.

[92] Als Verfasser gilt dann Silvanus, der mit dem Paulusbegleiter Silas (Apg 15,22–32) identifiziert wird. Vgl. z.B. K. H. SCHELKLE, Die Petrusbriefe. Der Judasbrief, HThK 13, Freiburg i. Brsg. ²1963, 14f.134. Zur berechtigten Kritik an dieser Sichtweise siehe z.B. U. SCHNELLE, Einleitung in das Neue Testament, Göttingen ⁴2002, 447.

und konzeptionelle Überlegungen beigefügt haben. Zur Auftrags- bzw. Sekretärspseudepigraphie gehört aber ein direkter Auftrag, da der Begriff „Sekretärsarbeit" ansonsten zum *umbrella term* für pseudepigraphische Literaturproduktion schlechthin wird. Im Hinblick auf die Auftragspseudepigraphie im Rahmen antiker Sekretärstätigkeit ist weiter relativierend anzumerken, dass diese letztlich selten war. Abgesehen von offiziellen Schreibbüros sind die Hauptbelege bei Cicero zu finden. Dass Atticus mehr war als nur ein Sekretär, sondern ein Vertrauter und Freund, verstärkt zudem den Ausnahmecharakter dieser Belege. Darüber hinaus muss auf die Inhalte und Motive antiker Auftragspseudepigraphie geachtet werden: Atticus hat keine Reden oder literarisch-philosophische Werke unter Ciceros Namen abgefasst, sondern Cicero bei der Korrespondenz entlastet. Die Kaiser und Poeten haben ihre Namen über fremde Werke gesetzt, um literarischen Ruhm zu erlangen, indem sie begabte Männer für sich haben schreiben lassen und diese sich im Gegenzug teilweise dadurch finanzierten. Solche Motive treffen für die neutestamentliche Pseudepigraphie kaum zu. Schließlich fügt sich das Pseudepigraphiekonzept der entsprechenden neutestamentlichen Schreiben nur schwer in eine „Sekretärshypothese" ein. Selbst wenn man in der Mitabsenderangabe in Kol 1,1 und 2Thess 1,1 einen indirekten Hinweis auf den Sekretär und damit den realen Verfasser entdeckt, muss man erklären, warum gerade in diesen Schreiben der eigenständige Gruß des Paulus deutlich hervorgehoben wird (Kol 4,18; 2Thess 3,17).[93]

6. Pseudepigraphie im Spannungsfeld von finanziellen Interessen und Bibliophilie

Die Bibliotheken von Alexandria und Pergamon „gewinnen mit der Zeit ein doppeltes Gesicht. Sie sind ein Paradies für die Fälscher (insbesondere, wenn diese im Stande sind, die Rivalität zwischen den Bibliotheken, das heißt, die zwischen den Herrschenden, die ihre Eigentümer sind, als Hebel benutzen zu können); und sie sind auch der einzige Ort, an dem es möglich ist, Fälscher zu desmaskieren."[94] Die Bibliotheken stellten durch ihre

---

[93] Vgl. dazu ZIMMERMANN, Pseudepigraphie (s. Anm. 7), 33.

[94] So formuliert pointiert L. CANFORA in seinem Kulturkrimi „Die verschwundene Bibliothek. Das Wissen der Welt und der Brand der Bibliothek von Alexandria", Hamburg 1998, 181. Deutlich wird diese Ambivalenz bei Vitruv, De architectura 7 praefatio 3–11: Um seine eigene Quellentransparenz zu verdeutlichen, präsentiert er gewissermaßen eine Negativfolie und berichtet von einem Dichterwettstreit, der nur auf dem Hintergrund des Konkurrenzverhältnisses zwischen den Bibliotheken verständlich ist. Im Verlauf dieses Wettstreits kommt es einerseits zu Plagiaten und Fälschungen, andererseits

archivarische und philologische Arbeit einerseits einen Meilenstein in der Herausbildung der Echtheitskritik dar: Hier kam es zu der systematischen Trennung von echten und unechten Schriften (Echtheitskritik), der Herstellung des unverfälschten Textes (Textkritik) und der Bindung von Autor und Werk (Biobibliographien). Andererseits entstanden gerade im Umfeld von Bibliotheken zahlreiche Fälschungen, über die bereits in der Antike reflektiert wurde.[95] So leistet z.B. Galen eine Aufteilung der Zeit in eine Epoche der Fälschungen und eine Epoche, „als mit Buchaufschriften noch kein Frevel getrieben wurde, sondern jedes Buch die Aufschrift seines tatsächlichen Autors zeigte."[96] Entscheidend für die Zäsur ist das Konkurrenzverhältnis zwischen den Bibliotheken von Alexandria und Pergamon. Nach Galen führten der Konkurrenzkampf der Bibliotheken und die Gewinnsucht der Fälscher gewissermaßen zu einer Interessenkonvergenz. Angebot und Nachfrage regelten sich gegenseitig:[97] Die kulturpolitische Profilierung der Herrschenden (z.B. Ptolemäus) stellte geradezu ein finanzielles Anreizsystem für kriminelle Literaten, Bibliothekare und dergleichen dar, die für Bücher mit gefälschten Verfassernamen (ψευδῶς σύγγραμμα) Bezahlung (μισθός) empfingen (Galen, In Hippocratis de natura hominis commentarium 2 pr.). Dass sich indes in diesem Zusammenhang ganze Fälscherwerkstätten als neuer Industriezweig etablieren konnten, ist zu Recht bestritten worden.[98] Die Anschauung Galens und an-

---

wird deren Aufdeckung erst durch die bibliothekarische Kompetenz der Richter möglich. Vgl. zu Alexandria umfassend P. M. FRASER, Ptolemaic Alexandria I. Text, Oxford 1972, 305–335 (bes. 320–335); siehe auch WIDMANN, Herstellung (s. Anm. 11), 610–619; BLUM, Kallimachos (s. Anm. 10).

[95] Ein ähnliches Phänomen ist im Humanismus anzutreffen; auch hier setzte parallel zu der Echtheitskritik eine große Flut pseudoantiker Schriften ein, die aus Liebe zur Antike resultierte; vgl. W. SPEYER, Italienische Humanisten als Kritiker der Echtheit antiker und christlicher Literatur, Stuttgart 1993. Zu diesem Phänomen in Humanismus und Renaissance vgl. auch HAGEN, Fälschungen (s. Anm. 14), 32.52–59.69–72 u.ö; R. SYME, Fälschung und Betrug, in: Brox, Pseudepigraphie (s. Anm. 2). 295–310 (309).

[96] „... μηδέπω πεπανουργευμένων τῶν ἐπιγραφῶν, ἀλλ' ἑκάστου βιβλίου τὸν ἴδιον γραφέα διὰ τοῦ προγράμματος δηλοῦντος"; vgl. Galen, In Hippocratis de natura hominis commentarium 1,44; u.ö. Vgl. zu den Quellen auch BAUM, Pseudepigraphie (s. Anm. 34), 224–227. Siehe dazu grundlegend MÜLLER, Aristoteleskommentatoren (s. Anm. 8), 264ff. (dort auch Nachweise).

[97] Dies ist nicht auf die Bibliotheken von Alexandria und Pergamon beschränkt, sondern auch für andere Kontexte denkbar. Beispielsweise hat der Brand in Rom unter Nero viele Schriften zerstört; man ist bemüht, den alten Bestand wieder zu bekommen. Vespasian versucht zu diesem Zweck Exemplare aufzustöbern (Sueton, Vespasian 8,5); Domitian stellt zudem fähige Menschen zum Kopieren an (Suet.Dom. 20). In diesen Zusammenhängen könnte es auch zu Fälschungen aus finanziellen Gründen gekommen sein.

[98] Siehe z.B. STANDHARTINGER, Studien (s. Anm. 28), 44; C. W. MÜLLER, Die Kurzdialoge der Appendix Platonica. Philologische Beiträge zur nachplatonischen Sokratik, STA 17, München 1975, 12ff.

derer[99] hat in weiten Zügen den Charakter einer nachträglichen Konstruktion, mittels derer man die Ergebnisse philologischer Echtheitskritik zu erklären versucht. Die „innere Wahrscheinlichkeit" dieser moralisch konnotierten retrospektiven „Hypothese antiker Echtheitskritik" ist dabei „nicht eben groß".[100] Hinzu kommt, dass hohe Preisangaben oft eine literarische Funktion haben und nur selten reale ökonomische Gegebenheiten widerspiegeln.[101]

Gewinnsucht war aber wohl trotz dieser Vorbehalte ein verbreiteter Antrieb zur Fälschung.[102] Auch im Buchhandel fälschte man aus kommerziellen Gründen.[103] Die allgemein antike Ansicht, dass im Alten das Wahre liegt, fand ihren Niederschlag im Leseverhalten und Bildungskanon. Klassiker und alte Bücher standen hoch im Kurs (vgl. z.B. Hor.ep. 2,1,20–27; Plinius, Naturalis historia 13,12; Plinius ep. 1,16,8f.; Gellius, Noctes Atticae 2,3).[104] Auf diese Lust nach Klassikern stellten sich die professionellen Buchhändler ein: Was nicht alt war, wurde häufig künstlich alt gemacht,

---

[99] Die Deutung Galens teilen die neuplatonischen Aristoteleskommentatoren. Insgesamt ist hier die Sicht differenziert: Zum Teil wird die Bücherliebe der Könige betont, zum Teil die Gewinnsucht der Fälscher. Vgl. dazu insgesamt GUDEMAN, Fälschungen (s. Anm. 12), 56f.; siehe auch Anm. 8.

[100] MÜLLER, Kurzdialoge (s. Anm. 98), 13; siehe auch ders., Aristoteleskommentatoren (s. Anm. 8), 265. Es waren z.B. im Fall der Pseudo-Platonica weniger kommerzielle als ideelle Beweggründe, die zur Pseudepigraphie führten. Pseudepigraphische Literaturproduktion resultierte nicht selten aus dem *horror vacui*, zumal wenn es Anspielungen auf Schriften gibt, die nicht erhalten sind; vgl. dazu auch SPEYER, Fälschung (s. Anm. 4), 136–139. Aristoteles soll beispielsweise eine Sammlung von Problemata hinterlassen haben, die nicht erhalten ist. Spätere Aristoteliker füllten diese Lücke mit 70 pseudoaristotelischen Problemata; vgl. auch SINT, Pseudonymität (s. Anm. 25), 105 Anm. 36. Weiter wird Sokrates in Platons Phaidon 60d als Dichter stilisiert, der einen Apollohymnus und äsopische Fabeln verfasst haben soll. In späteren Zeiten entstanden dann solche Sokrates zugeschriebenen literarischen Erzeugnisse (D.L. 1,72; 2,42).

[101] MÜLLER, a.a.O. 16 Anm. 1. Insgesamt waren hohe Preise für Bücher die Ausnahme (15 Anm. 4). Die mitunter in der antiken Literatur anzutreffenden hohen Preise sind größtenteils literarisch-fiktiv, um Wertschätzung o.ä. auszudrücken. Vgl. exemplarisch zum Problem der realen Buchpreise H. WIDMANN, Geschichte des Buchhandels vom Altertum bis zur Gegenwart, Wiesbaden 1952, 14f.; ders., Herstellung (s. Anm. 11), 627f.

[102] HAGEN, Fälschungen (s. Anm. 14), 71f.; GUDEMAN, Fälschungen (s. Anm. 12), 56; SPEYER, Fälschung (s. Anm. 4), 133f.

[103] Vgl. SINT, Pseudonymität (s. Anm. 25), 116f.; MÜLLER, Kurzdialoge (s. Anm. 98), 15 Anm. 4. Reden wurden gefälscht und dazu erfunden, um umfangreichere Ausgaben zu erstellen, mit denen man mehr Geld verdienen konnte; vgl. GUDEMAN, a.a.O. 72f.

[104] Vgl. SCHUBART, Buch (s. Anm. 53), 165ff.; FRENSCHKOWSKI, Pseudepigraphie (s. Anm. 29), 251; BROX, Verfasserangaben (s. Anm. 10), 52f. Insgesamt galt in der Antike: Was alt war, wurde hochgeschätzt; vgl. z.B. SPEYER, Fälschung (s. Anm. 4), 132f.136.263.

wobei sehr unterschiedliche Mittel und Strategien zum Einsatz kamen. Das Spektrum reicht von dem Ältermachen der Handschriften (Dion Chrysostomos, Oratio 21,12 u.ö.), der Abfassung in alten Sprachen und Dialekten[105] bis zur situativen oder personellen Verortung einer Schrift in der Vergangenheit, wobei neben dem Rückgriff auf einen alten Verfassernamen auch spezifische Plausibilisierungsstrategien zum Einsatz kamen.[106] Diese Praktiken waren allerdings so weit verbreitet, dass Schriften wegen ihres alten Charakters geradezu in Verdacht gerieten, gefälscht zu sein. Die vermeintlichen Alters- und Echtheitsbeweise werden so geradezu zu Unechtheitsindikatoren: „Nec mirum debet uideri, quod suspecta habentur, quae sub tantae antiquitatis nomine proferuntur" (Aug.civ.18,38).[107] Lukian spottet dementsprechend über eine solche antiquarische Haltung zu Beginn seiner Schrift „gegen den ungebildeten Büchernarren", welcher den Bücherwurm zum Berater macht, und berichtet in einer anderen Schrift (Lukian, Pseudologistes 30) voller Spott von der Abfassung eines Werkes, das wegen der falschen Autorenangabe einem unkritischen Abnehmer teuer verkauft werden konnte, weil er es für eine alte Schrift hielt: Er zahlte für eine Fälschung der Redekunst des Tisias dreißig Goldstücke.

Trafen auch in der frühchristlichen Kirche das Interesse an Büchern und die Gewinnsucht der Fälscher aufeinander? Regelte die religiös oder lokalpatriotisch motivierte Nachfrage nach apostolischer Literatur ein künstlich produziertes Angebot an gefälschten apostolischen Schriften? Den Marktwert z.B. paulinischer oder petrinischer Schriften in ökonomischer Hinsicht bestimmen zu wollen, bleibt letztlich spekulativ. Aber die von Galen und anderen erwähnte Bücherliebe der Könige und Bibliotheken mag auch für die frühchristliche Literatur relevant sein. Das Bedürfnis nach apostolischen Schriften im frühen Christentum könnte mit dem Interesse der Bibliotheken, Bestände aufzustocken und zu vervollständigen, vergleichbar

---

[105] Vgl. zum Vortäuschen von Übersetzungen aus alten Sprachen und zum Rückgriff auf alte Dialekte oder Schriftzeichen z.B. DIHLE, Literatur (s. Anm. 12), 254; HAGEN, Fälschungen (s. Anm. 14), 34; BIRT, Kulturleben (s. Anm. 10), 194; E. STEMPLINGER, Antiker Volksglaube, Stuttgart 1948, 166; W. SPEYER, Angebliche Übersetzungen des heidnischen und christlichen Altertums, JAC 11/12 (1968/69), 26–41.

[106] Vgl. z.B. das Sujet vom Bücherfund; siehe W. SPEYER, Bücherfunde in der Glaubenswerbung der Antike. Mit einem Ausblick auf Mittelalter und Neuzeit, Hyp. 24, Göttingen 1970.

[107] So Augustin bezüglich der Diskussion über die Echtheit alttestamentlicher Apokryphen, die unter den Namen von biblischen Größen der Vergangenheit im Umlauf waren. Text: Sancti Aurelii Augustini Episcopi de civitate dei, Bd. 2, hg. v. B. Dombart / A. Kalb, Leipzig 1928/29 (Nachdruck Darmstadt 1981). Auch Schriften, die den Anschein besonderer Genauigkeit auf der Ebene der Daten und Fakten erwecken, begegnet man mit einer vergleichbaren Hermeneutik des Verdachts; vgl. SPEYER, Fälschung (s. Anm. 4), 82; G. JACHMANN, Gefälschte Daten, Klio 35 (1942), 60–88 (86).

sein.[108] Die Gemeinden hatten prinzipiell ein Interesse daran, an sie adressierte Paulusbriefe zu besitzen, zu vermehren oder zu aktualisieren, um die jeweilige apostolische Lehre veränderten Umständen und Herausforderungen anzupassen. Man bemühte sich z.b. darum, Briefsammlungen zusammenzustellen (z.b. Corpus Paulinum, Corpus Ignatianum), wobei es möglicherweise auch zu „künstlichen" Vervollständigungen und Aktualisierungen im Zuge einer pseudepigraphischen Eigendynamik kam. Weiter war die Tatsache, dass im Neuen Testament gewisse Schreiben oder Offenbarungen erwähnt, aber nicht überliefert sind, wohl nur schwer hinzunehmen. Dieser *horror vacui* führte wie in der antiken Literatur dazu, Überlieferungslücken durch die Produktion entsprechender Schriften zu schließen, was vor allem an der Auffüllung von 2Kor 12,2–4 und Kol 4,16 deutlich wird.[109] Dies betrifft nicht nur die nachträgliche Abfassung genannter, aber nicht erhaltener Schriften, sondern geht in der apokryphen Literatur weit darüber hinaus. „Leerstellen" im Leben Jesu wie z.b. seine Kindheit oder die Zeit zwischen Auferstehung und Himmelfahrt (Apg 1,3) werden durch textexterne Fortschreibungsverfahren nachträglich „gefüllt", wobei narrative und pseudepigraphische Techniken gleichermaßen zum Einsatz kommen.

---

[108] GUDEMAN, Fälschungen (s. Anm. 12), 50f., sieht in dieser antiquarischen Haltung der Bibliotheken eine Entsprechung zur Entstehung apokrypher Literatur; vgl. auch BARDY, Fälschungen (s. Anm. 2), 169.

[109] Vgl. zu den an 2Kor 12,2–4 anknüpfenden Paulusapokalypsen z.B. G. Lüdemann / M. Janßen, Die Apokalypse des Paulus (NHC V,2). Eingel., komm. u. übers., in: B. Köhler (Hg.), Religion und Wahrheit. Religionsgeschichtliche Studien (FS Wießner), Wiesbaden 1998, 359–368 (360). Der Laodicenerbrief wird schon seit der Antike als Versuch gedeutet, die durch Kol 4,16 entstehende Lücke in der paulinischen Korrespondenz zu schließen. Dies vermuten schon altkirchliche Zeugen wie Theodor von Mopsuestia oder Priszillian; vgl. zu Details RÖWEKAMP, Paulus-Literatur (s. Anm. 29), 553; W. SCHNEEMELCHER, Laodicenerbrief, in: Hennecke / Schneemelcher, Neutestamentliche Apokryphen (s. Anm. 19), 80–84 (81f.); K. PINK, Die pseudo-paulinischen Briefe II, Bib 6 (1925), 179–200 (179–192). *Horror vacui* als Grund für die Entstehung des Laodicenerbriefes legt in der Tat der Schluss des Dokuments nahe, wo explizit auf das Verlesen in Kolossae und damit auf Kol 4,16 Bezug genommen wird. Vgl. zur antik-paganen Literatur Anm. 100.

7. Strategisch-polemische Beweggründe für falsche Verfasserangaben

Pseudepigraphie war als Mittel polemisch-strategischer Auseinandersetzung weit verbreitet, wobei vor allem Namen von zeitgenössischen Personen zum Einsatz kamen, um eben diese zu schädigen. Pausanias berichtet beispielsweise in seinem Reisehandbuch (2,18,5) folgende „absolut nicht unkundige, aber äußerst gehässige (οὐκ ἀμαθέστατα ἀλλὰ καὶ ἐπιφθονώτατα)" Begebenheit:[110] Anaximenes vom Lampsakos schreibt eine Schmähschrift gegen die Athener, Lakedämonier und Thebaner und beschuldigt darin die Städte Athen, Sparta und Theben am politischen Niedergang Griechenlands Schuld zu sein. Diese heute fast vollständig verlorene Schrift trägt den Titel „Trikaranos".[111] Dieser Terminus, der sich nun auf die Athener, Lakedämonier und Thebaner bezieht, wurde bereits von Hesiod zur Charakterisierung eines Ungeheuers verwendet. Anaximenes veröffentlicht seine Schmähschrift nicht unter eigenem Namen, sondern unter dem Namen seines Rivalen Theopomp von Chios, wobei er auf äußerst professionelle Weise dessen Stil nachahmt. Die Aktion glückt. Obwohl Anaximenes die Schrift verfasst hat, wird Theopomp für den Verfasser gehalten. Er ist diskreditiert und der Hass auf ihn wuchs in ganz Griechenland.[112] Ähnliche Strategien wählten scheinbar auch die antiken Philosophen, wie Diogenes Laërtios berichtet: Der Stoiker Diotimos schadete dem ihm verhassten Epikur dadurch, dass er unter dessen Namen 50 schlüpfrige Briefe veröffentlichte. Dieses Vorgehen war zudem kein Einzelfall[113] und fügt sich allgemein in antike Diffamierungsstrategien wie z.B. den Vorwurf des unmoralischen Lebenswandels ein.

Weiter griff man im Rahmen von Anschuldigungen, Prozessen und vergleichbaren Gelegenheiten zu Fälschungen (vgl. auch Iamb.vit.Pyth. 258–

---

[110] Text: Pausanias. Description of Greece, Bd. III. Hg. u. m. engl. Übers. vers. v. W. H. S. Jones, LCL 272, Cambridge/London 1988.

[111] Vgl. E. MEYER, Beschreibung Griechenlands. Pausanias, Zürich 1954, 630. Die Fragmente finden sich in: FGrH 72 (F. JACOBY, Die Fragmente der griechischen Historiker, II. Teil. Zeitgeschichte. A. Universalgeschichte und Hellenika, Berlin 1926, 123f.).

[112] Vgl. dazu GUDEMAN, Fälschungen (s. Anm. 12), 63ff.; HAGEN, Fälschungen (s. Anm. 14), 72.

[113] Vgl. D.L. 10,3: „Διότιμος δ' ὁ Στωικὸς δυσμενῶς ἔχων πρὸς αὐτὸν πικρότατα αὐτὸν διαβέβληκεν, ἐπιστολὰς φέρων πεντήκοντα ἀσελγεῖς ὡς Ἐπικούρου. καὶ ὁ τὰ εἰς Χρύσιππον ἀναφερόμενα ἐπιστόλια ὡς Ἐπικούρου συντάξας." Text: Diogenes Laertius. Lives of the Eminent Philosophers, Bd. II. Hg. u. m. engl. Übers. vers. v. R. D. Hicks, LCL 185, Cambridge/London 2000 ([1]1925); siehe auch SPEYER, Fälschung (s. Anm. 4), 139–142. Auch Pythagoras scheint eine Rede untergeschoben worden zu sein mit dem Ziel, ihn zu diskreditieren (ἐπὶ διαβολῇ Πυθαγόρου: D.L. 8,7). Vgl. ferner Iamb.vit.Pyth. 258–260.

260). Beispielsweise berichtet Philostrat in seiner Vita Apollonia von solchen Vorkommnissen. „Καί τινα ἐπιστολὴν ἀνέπλασαν ... ἐν ᾗ βούλονται τὸν Ἀπολλώνιον ἱκέτην τοῦ Δομετιανοῦ γίγνεσθαι παραιτούμενον ἑαυτὸν τῶν δεσμῶν" (Philostr.vit.ap. 7,35).[114] Während des Prozesses um Apollonius taucht ein Brief auf, den angeblich Apollonius verfasst hat und der wie eine Art Gnadengesuch anmutet. Nach Philostrat stellt dieser gefälschte Brief einen Versuch dar, Apollonius zu diskreditieren, indem man ihn als jemanden stilisiert, der sich unterwirft. Ein solches Apolloniusbild entspricht nicht der Intention der Apolloniusvita des Philostrat: Hier hat Apollonius mit seiner Philosophie Erfolg und entschwindet aus dem Gefängnis, unterwirft sich also gerade nicht. Philostrat erklärt den Brief für unecht und begründet sein Urteil mit stilistischen Argumenten (l. c.). Welches der beiden Apolloniusbilder der Realität entspricht, lässt sich schwer sagen. In jedem Fall belegt die Stelle die Konvention, Briefe zum Nachteil anderer zu fälschen. Einen weiteren Beleg für eine solche Praxis aus der Perspektive des Betroffenen selbst bietet Apuleius, der sich im Kontext seines Prozesses ebenfalls mit einem auf seinen Namen gefälschten Brief auseinandersetzen muss, den sein Ankläger anführt. „Fuit et illa commenticia epistula neque mea manu scripta neque uerisimiliter conficta, qua uideri uolebant blanditiis a me mulierem sollicitatam" (Apul.apol. 87,2–5 [2]).[115] Apuleius versucht die Unechtheit dieses Schreibens mit logischen Einwänden und sprachlichen Argumenten zu erweisen (l. c.).

Die antiken Beispiele bezüglich kompromittierender und schädlicher Briefe unter falschem Namen ließen sich ohne Mühe vermehren,[116] wobei die Pseudepigraphie über die reine Rufschädigung hinausgehen kann.[117]

---

[114] „Auch einen Brief haben sie aufgebracht ... In diesem, so behaupten sie, habe Apollonius den Kaiser um Gnade und Erlösung gebeten." Text und Übersetzung: Philostratos, Das Leben des Apollonios von Tyana. Griechisch-deutsch. Hg., übers. u. erl. v. V. Mumprecht, München/Zürich 1983.

[115] „Und da gab es noch jenen erlogenen Brief, der weder von meiner Hand geschrieben noch glaubwürdig erdacht war, mit welchem sie den Anschein erwecken wollten, dass die Frau von mir durch Schmeicheleien verführt wurde." Text und Übersetzung: Apuleius. De magia. Engel., übers. u. m. interpret. Essays vers. v. J. Hammerstaedt u.a., SAPERE V, Darmstadt 2002.

[116] Siehe auch Anm. 42. Ein weiteres Beispiel sind die vermutlich fingierten Briefe des Menekrates, die in Fragmenten erhalten sind; siehe O. WEINREICH, Menekrates Zeus und Salmoneus. Religionsgeschichtliche Studien zur Psychopathologie des Gottmenschentums in Antike und Neuzeit, TBAW 18, Stuttgart 1933, 95f. Diese Briefe führen ironisch-polemisch die Persönlichkeit des syrakusianischen Arztes vor, der sich wie Zeus aufführte und dessen Jünger ebenfalls Götter imitierten.

[117] Über eine todbringende Brieffälschung berichtet zum Beispiel die Historia Augusta; siehe Historia Augusta, Gordian 10,6ff.; Maximinus 14,4; Herodian 7,6,4–9.

Auch einzelnen neutestamentlichen Pseudepigraphen hat man mitunter polemische Motive unterstellt. Nach Helmut Köster wird im Judasbrief der gnostische Apostel Judas Thomas seiner Würde als Zwilling Jesu entkleidet und als Bruder des Jakobus (Jud 1) zum Autor eines antignostischen Briefes.[118] Auch der Ansicht, der pseudepigraphische Zweite Thessalonicherbrief wolle den authentischen Ersten Thessalonicherbrief verdrängen und dabei gleichzeitig als Fälschung diffamieren (2Thess 2,2), ist zweifelsohne eine polemische Dimension inhärent.[119] Eine direkte Vergleichbarkeit mit den angeführten antiken Belegen liegt indes nicht vor. Zudem richtet sich im Fall der neutestamentlichen Beispiele die Polemik nicht gegen eine Person im Sinne von (posthumem!) Rufmord oder persönlicher Schädigung. Vielmehr zielt die Polemik gegen die fälschlicherweise mit der jeweiligen Person verbundene theologische Lehre: Man will nicht die Apostel als Person in Misskredit bringen, sondern eine theologische Lehrmeinung korrigieren, um so gerade der Person gerecht zu werden.[120]

Im Bereich der altkirchlichen Literatur indes lassen sich dann zahlreiche Briefe mit einer polemischen Intention nachweisen, wie z.B. die auf den Namen des Hieronymus gefälschten Briefe über die Übersetzung des Alten Testaments (Hieronymus, Contra Rufinum 2,24)[121] oder der Briefwechsel zwischen Apollonaris und Basilius, um Letzteren durch seinen angeblichen Umgang mit Apollinaris zu diskreditieren.[122]

---

[118] KÖSTER, Einführung (s. Anm. 20), 682f.

[119] Vgl. zu dieser Position die Angaben bei LÜDEMANN, Ketzer (s. Anm. 40), 274 Anm. 373. Siehe auch die Beiträge von Edgar Krentz und Trevor Thompson in diesem Band.

[120] In der apokryphen Literatur kann dann eine theologische Position durch eine historische Figur symbolisiert werden, die wiederum auf diese Weise zum paradigmatischen Repräsentanten einer Idee wird. Ein Beispiel ist die Petrusapokalypse aus Nag Hammadi, wo im Zuge der Polemik dem Paradeapostel der Orthodoxie kirchenkritisches und gnostisches Denken in den Mund gelegt wird; vgl. ApkPetr 73,18ff.; PistSoph 36 u.ö.; EvMar 17ff.

[121] Hieronymus beklagt sich, dass man Briefe beigebracht habe, die angeblich von ihm stammen würden („quasi meo scriptam nomine") und deren Sinn es sei, seine Übertragung der biblischen Schriften aus dem Hebräischen in Misskredit zu bringen. Hieronymus weist dies zurück und erklärt den Brief für unecht und schlecht gefälscht. „Stilum meum, qualiscumque est, et formam eloquii uir disertissimus exprimere non potuit." Text: Saint Jérôme, Apologie contre Rufin. Hg. u. übers. v. P. Lardet, SC 303, Paris 1983. Vgl. dazu auch M. WOLTER, Art. Pseudonymität II. Kirchengeschichtlich, TRE 27 (1997), 662–670 (666).

[122] BARDY, Betrug (s. Anm. 2), 174.

8. Pseudepigraphie im Kontext antiker Schulen

Der antike Schulbetrieb weist allgemein ein beträchtliches Gefälle zu Pseudepigraphie, Prosopopoiie und Entlehnung auf und gilt in der Pseudepigraphieforschung deswegen weitläufig als „historischer Sonderkontext" für Urheber- und Verfasserfragen.[123] Das prominenteste Beispiel ist die Pseudepigraphie im pythagoreischen Schulbetrieb,[124] wie er vor allem in der Rezeption durch den Neuplatoniker Jamblich dargestellt wird. Jamblich bezeugt in seiner Schrift De vita Pythagorica wiederholt die Praxis einer Schulpseudepigraphie und liefert zudem eine Erklärung für diese spezielle Art von Literaturproduktion. Ein Teil der pythagoreischen Schriften ist aufgrund des mündlichen Vortrags aufgezeichnet, was nicht ohne Konsequenzen für die Verfasserangabe bleibt: „καὶ διὰ τοῦτο οὐδὲ ἑαυτῶν ἐπεφήμιζον αὐτά, ἀλλὰ εἰς Πυθαγόραν ἀνέφερον αὐτὰ ὡς ἐκείνου ὄντα" (Iamb.vit.Pyth. 158).[125] Der Vorlesungsinhalt ist geistiges

---

[123] So z.B. BAUM, Pseudepigraphie (s. Anm. 34), 51–59. Insgesamt trägt die Schulsituation dem kollektiven Urheberrechtsbewusstsein Rechnung. Man stellt disparate Meinungen zusammen, ohne sie auszugleichen, oder nimmt Mängel in der kompositorischen Disposition in Kauf. Auch die Kehrseite der Pseudepigraphie, das Plagiat bzw. die ungenannte Entlehnung und Zitation, findet in gewisser Weise eine „moralische Entlastung" durch das kollektive Urheberrechtsbewusstsein der Schulgemeinschaft. Vgl. exemplarisch für den alexandrinischen Schulbetrieb W. BOUSSET, Jüdisch-hellenistischer Schulbetrieb in Alexandria und Rom. Literarische Untersuchungen zu Philo und Clemens, Justin und Irenäus, FRLANT 23, Göttingen 1915, 5f.: „Es handelt sich bei alledem ja nicht um die weitgehende Aneignung literarischen individuellen Eigentums, um die Ausplünderung von der Literatur angehörigen Büchern, es handelt sich um die Weitergabe von Schulüberlieferung, die nicht so sehr dem einzelnen gehörte, sondern welche die Schule als ihr Eigentum (vgl. das φαμέν der Aristotelesschüler) ansah." Vgl. auch SINT, Pseudonymität (s. Anm. 25), 95–104, in Bezug auf die aristotelische Schule. „Es hing mit der Sonderheit dieses Schulbetriebs zusammen, daß man nicht so sehr nach dem geistigen Eigentum der Einzelpersönlichkeit fragte und wenig darum bemüht war, dieses klar und abgegrenzt zu erhalten" (104). Siehe auch zum Ganzen SPEYER, Fälschung (s. Anm. 4), 34f.
[124] Vgl. GUDEMAN, Fälschungen (s. Anm. 12), 56.58f.; W. BURKERT, Hellenistische Pseudo-Pythagorica, Ph. 105 (1961), 16–43.226–246 (16: „Der Pythagoreismus hat sich anscheinend zumindest zeitweise fast ausschließlich in untergeschobenen Schriften ausgedrückt, so daß man das Apokryphon als seine notwendige innere Form bezeichnen könnte."). Es geht dabei auch um die Legitimation einer Schulrichtung durch pseudepigraphische Schriften (vgl. HOSE, Literaturgeschichte [s. Anm. 25], 197), zumal im Hinblick auf die pythagoreische Schule die antike Ansicht besteht, Pythagoras hätte selbst nichts Schriftliches hinterlassen; vgl. dazu GUDEMAN, a.a.O. 58; MÜLLER, Aristoteleskommentatoren (s. Anm. 8), 268.
[125] „Darum haben die Pythagoreer diese Schriften auch nicht für ihr Eigentum ausgegeben, sondern sie dem Pythagoras als sein Werk zugeschrieben." Text und Übersetzung hier und im Folgenden: Jamblich, Pythagoras. Legende – Lehre – Lebensgestal-

Eigentum des Lehrers. Darum schreibt man den Namen des Lehrers über die Schrift. Eine andere Form von schriftstellerischer Produktion erscheint sogar illegitim und gilt als Plagiat, da es sich um einen geistigen Diebstahl von Vorlesungsinhalten handelt. Wer in der Schule Gehörtes unter eigenem Namen herausgab wie etwa Empedokles, beging das Unrecht des Diebstahls von Vorlesungsmitschriften (λογοκλοπία) und musste mit Konsequenzen rechnen (D.L. 8,54).[126] Doch die Loyalität gegenüber dem Lehrer geht noch weiter. Sogar die eigene geistige Leistung, die eigenen Ideen und die eigenen Schriften werden mitunter dem Lehrer zugeschrieben, da man diesem alles verdankt.[127] Jamblichs Urteil über dieses schulinterne Ethos in der pythagoreischen Gemeinschaft ist positiv: „καλὸν δὲ καὶ τὸ πάντα Πυθαγόρᾳ ἀνατιθέναι τε καὶ ἀπονέμειν καὶ μηδεμίαν περιποιεῖσθαι δόξαν ἰδίαν ἀπὸ τῶν εὑρισκομένων, εἰ μή πού τι σπάνιον· πάνυ γὰρ δή τινές εἰσιν ὀλίγοι, ὧν ἴδια γνωρίζεται ὑπομνήματα" (Iamb.vit.Pyth. 198).[128]

Diese Befunde sind nicht auf den pythagoreischen Schulbetrieb beschränkt, sondern für die antike Schulliteratur typisch.[129] Auch für die

---

tung. Eingel., übers. u. m. interpret. Essays vers. v. M. von Albrecht u.a., SAPERE IV, Darmstadt 2002.

[126] Klagen über Diebstahl und unerlaubte Herausgabe von Vorlesungsmitschriften sind auch außerhalb der pythagoreischen Schule belegt; vgl. z.B. Plato epist. 7,341ab; Plato Parm. 128d; zu Galen siehe auch Anm. 54. Insgesamt vgl. auch STANDHARTINGER, Studien (s. Anm. 28), 41f. Hinzu kommt, dass zwischen internen esoterischen und öffentlichen exoterischen Vorlesungsinhalten unterschieden wurde (Iamb.vit.Pyth. 104). Von der Bedeutsamkeit dieser Thematik zeugt auch ein pseudepigraphischer Brief des Alexander an Aristoteles, in dem er diesem vorwirft, seine Vorlesungen veröffentlicht zu haben: „Οὐκ ὀρθῶς ἐποίησας ἐκδοὺς τοὺς ἀκροαματικοὺς τῶν λόγων." Text: Epistolographi Graeci, hg. v. R. Hercher, Paris 1873, 98; siehe dazu auch SINT, Pseudonymität (s. Anm. 25), 111.

[127] Man kann nach B. L. VAN DER WAERDEN, Pythagoreer. Religiöse Bruderschaft und Schule der Wissenschaft, Zürich u.a. 1979, 71–73, schließen, dass „in gewissen Kreisen von Pythagoreern zur Zeit des Oinopides ... die Neigung bestand, spezifische mathematische und astronomische Entdeckungen dem Pythagoras zuzuschreiben und andere Mathematiker des Plagiats zu bezichtigen" (73). Dies gilt auch für die sokratische Schultradition, wie die bei D.L. 2,60 berichtete Episode vermuten lässt: Weil die Dialoge des Aischines sehr sokratisch anmuten, werden sie wohl ein Plagiat sein, wobei Xantippe zur Helfershelferin des angeblichen Plagiators Aischines wird; vgl. auch SINT, Pseudonymität (s. Anm. 25), 102.

[128] „Edel ist auch, daß sie dem Pythagoras alles zuschrieben und nur ganz selten für ihre Entdeckungen persönlichen Ruhm beanspruchten. Sind es doch verschwindend wenige, von denen man eigene Schriften kennt." Weitere Stellen bei BOUSSET, Schulbetrieb (s. Anm. 123), 9ff. Vgl. dazu VAN DER WAERDEN, Bruderschaft (s. Anm. 127), 71ff.; SPEYER, Fälschung (s. Anm. 4). 34f.

[129] Dies betrifft nicht nur Pseudepigraphie im engeren Sinne, sondern auch die Wahl von literarischen Figuren in dramatischen Textsorten. Mitunter führten Schüler ihre Leh-

epikureische Gemeinschaft ist die Zurückführung alles Wissens auf Epikur eine Selbstverständlichkeit, worauf Seneca hinweist: „Apud istos quidquid Hermarchus dixit, quidquid Metrodorus, ad unum refertur; omnia quae quisdam in illo contubernio locutus est unius ductu et auspiciis dicta sunt" (Sen.ep. 33,4).[130] Dass es aus diesem Gedanken heraus auch zu pseudepigraphischer Literaturproduktion kommen kann, bezeugt dann z.B. Sueton, De grammaticis 7.[131] Dementsprechend können auch die Schriften von Schülern als geistiges Eigentum der Lehrer aufgefasst werden (vgl. auch Tert.Marc. 4,5,3f.).

Abgesehen von dem speziellen „Urheberrecht", das dem literatursoziologischen Ort der antiken Schule inhärent ist, bringen die neuplatonischen Aristoteleskommentatoren einen weiteren Aspekt zur Schulpseudepigraphie ein. Dass die pythagoreischen Schriften alle dem Pythagoras zugeschrieben werden, obwohl dieser nicht eine von ihnen verfasst hat, liegt an der Zuneigung, dem Dank und dem Wohlwollen der Schüler (εὐγνωμοσύνη bzw. εὔνοια).[132] Eine solche Verehrung eines Lehrers und damit eines Vorbilds ist indes nicht an Philosophenschulen gebunden, sondern spielt allgemein in der Antike eine große Rolle.[133] Das Motiv der Liebe,

---

rer auch als Personen in Dialogen ein und machten sie auf diese Weise zu Sprechern ihrer eigenen Gedanken; vgl. dazu HIRZEL, Dialog I (s. Anm. 79), 309 Anm. 3.

[130] Text: L. Annaei Senecae ad Lucilium epistulae morales, hg. v. L. D. Reynolds, Oxford 1965.

[131] Er berichtet über den Grammatiker Marcus Antonio Gnipho Folgendes: „Etsi Ateius Philologus duo tantum volumina ‚De Latino Sermone' reliquisse eum tradit; nam cetera scripta discipulorum eius esse, non ipsius ..." Text: Suetonius in Two Volumes. Hg. u. m. engl. Übers. vers. v. J. C. Rolfe, LCL 38, Cambridge/London 1914 (Nachdruck 1979). Ein weiteres mögliches Beispiel sei genannt: Arrian stilisiert sich im Brief an Gellius als Überlieferer und Herausgeber der Predigten des Epiktet, was sich auch in der Betitelung des Werkes als *Epicteti dissertationes ab Arriano digestae* niederschlägt. Inwieweit Arrian aber lediglich um die Wiedergabe der Reden Epiktets bemüht war bzw. wie sehr er diese selbst gestaltet hat, ist umstritten; vgl. z.B. HOSE, Literaturgeschichte (s. Anm. 25), 207. Aktuell macht J. SELLE, Dichtung oder Wahrheit – Der Autor der Epiktetischen Predigten, Phil 145 (2001), 269–290, anhand mehrerer Beobachtungen plausibel, dass Arrian nicht etwa ein Diktat des Epiktet niedergeschrieben hat, sondern dass er selbst Urheber der epiktetischen Predigen ist: „Es wäre also nicht nur wissenschaftlich korrekt, sondern auch gerecht, statt ‚Epiktet, Diatriben' künftig aufs Titelblatt zu setzen: ‚Arrian, Diatriben Epiktets'" (287f.).

[132] Vgl. MÜLLER, Aristoteleskommentatoren (s. Anm. 8), 268–271.

[133] Dies gilt auch für die Imitation, die die Verehrung eines Vorbilds im Blick haben kann; vgl. dazu A. REIFF, Interpretatio, Imitatio, Aemulatio. Begriff und Vorstellung literarischer Abhängigkeit bei den Römern, Köln 1959, 9f., mit Bezug auf Lukrez 3 proöm. 5f.: „Non ita certandi cupidus quam propter amorem quod te imitari aveo." Mitunter sind die Grenzen zwischen Imitation und Pseudepigraphie auch fließend. Im Bereich der Rhetorik und Literatur legte man sich die Namen seiner Vorbilder in Form eines Attributs zu; vgl. Ausonios, profess. 1,2 („alter rhetoricae Quintiliane togae"); zitiert

Verehrung und Zuneigung als Beweggrund zur pseudonymen Abfassung erscheint auch in den wenigen christlichen Dokumenten, die sich explizit über die Ursachen von Pseudepigraphie oder verwandter Phänomene äußern. So berichtet Tertullian über einen Presbyter, der aufgrund der Abfassung von heterodoxen Paulusakten suspendiert wurde. Nach der Darstellung Tertullians gesteht der Presbyter, die Paulusakten aus Liebe zu Paulus (*amore Pauli*) verfasst zu haben. „Quodsi quae ‚Acta Pauli‘, quae perperam scripta sunt, exemplum Theclae ad licentiam mulierum docendi tinguendique defendunt, sciant in Asia presbyterum, qui eam scripturam construxit quasi titulo Pauli de suo cumulans, convictum atque confessum id se amore Pauli fecisse loco decessisse" (Tert.bapt. 17,5).[134] Ähnlich äußert sich auch der Canon Muratori, Z. 69f. hinsichtlich der Verfasserfrage der Sapientia Salomonis: Die Weisheitsschrift stamme nicht von Salomo, sondern wurde „von Freunden des Salomo zu dessen Ehre (*in honore ipsius*) geschrieben."

Die Verehrung eines Lehrers bzw. einer Gründerfigur im Zusammenhang einer Schulgemeinschaft wurde oft als Erklärung auch der neutestamentlichen, besonders der pseudopaulinischen Pseudepigraphie herangezogen.[135] Dieses Erklärungsmuster birgt indes einige Schwierigkeiten in sich, die zu berücksichtigten sind. Zunächst ist das oben dargestellte Bild für den antiken Schulbetrieb trotz der vereinzelten Belege nicht repräsentativ;[136] selbst in der (neu-)pythagoreischen Schule wurde auf den realen Autor geachtet (Iamb.vit.Pyth. 25). Eine Verwechslung der Autoren etwa im Falle von Homonymität wird im Gegensatz zur Schulpseudepigraphie als schlecht empfunden (οὐ καλῶς, vgl. dagegen Iamb.vit.Pyth. 198:

---

nach REIFF, a.a.O. 20 Anm. 32. Vor allem gab es im Rom der Kaiserzeit zahlreiche weitgehend unbekannte Dichter, die auf epigonale Weise ihren Vorbildern Ovid und Vergil nacheiferten und sich als *poetae ovidianae* und *vergilianae* in ihren Grabinschriften verewigten; vgl. BIRT, Kritik (s. Anm. 10), 239f.

[134] „Wenn irgendwelche ‚Taten des Paulus‘, die einen falschen Titel tragen, das Beispiel der Thecla im Hinblick auf die Vollmacht der Frauen zu lehren und zu taufen als gut und richtig hinstellen, so sollen sie wissen: In Kleinasien wurde ein Priester, der diese Schrift fabrizierte und sie sozusagen durch die Nennung des ehrenvollen Namens des Paulus im Titel eigenmächtig aufwertete, der Fälschung überführt, und er trat, nachdem er erklärt hatte, dies aus Liebe zu Paulus getan zu haben, von seinem Amt zurück." Text und Übersetzung: Tertullian, De baptismo. De Oratione. Übers. u. eingel. v. D. Schleyer, FC 76, Turnhout 2006.

[135] Vgl. z.B. G. STRECKER, Literaturgeschichte des Neuen Testaments, Göttingen 1992, 58; THEISSEN, Testament (s. Anm. 30), 83. Mitunter wurde dies auch mit dem Motiv der Bescheidenheit kombiniert; vgl. z.B. EASTON, Epistles (s. Anm. 30), 19, im Hinblick auf die Pastoralbriefe: „The pseudonymity, in fact, may well have lain only modesty: ‚Whatever I have I owe to Paul; let the credit be given not to me but to him.'"

[136] Vgl. auch FRENSCHKOWSKI, Pseudepigraphie (s. Anm. 29), 248f.

καλὸν δέ).[137] Bei den Belegen hinsichtlich der Schulpseudepigraphie handelt es sich zudem oft um einen nachträglichen Erklärungsversuch für das Vorhandensein zahlreicher pseudpythagoreischer Schriften.[138] Weiter ist zu fragen, wie tragfähig Analogien aus dem pagan-antiken Schulbetrieb für die Erklärung *neutestamentlicher* Pseudepigraphie sind. Zumindest müssen beim Bezug auf solche Belegstellen literatursoziologische Überlegungen zu den Trägergruppen der neutestamentlichen Schriften angestellt werden. Dies gilt umso mehr als die Organisationsstruktur der paulinischen Gemeinden („Paulusschule"?) in der gegenwärtigen Forschung neu zur Diskussion steht, wie beispielsweise die Arbeiten von Thomas Schmeller[139] und Tor Vegge[140] zeigen. Armin Daniel Baum[141] hat zudem einen formalen Gesichtspunkt vorgebracht: (Pseudepigraphische) Paulusbriefe sind als Briefe nicht direkt mit Lehrschriften oder Traktaten zu vergleichen, die einen Großteil des antiken Referenzmaterials aus dem „institutionellen Sonderkontext" Schule ausmachen.

9. Wirkungswille als Motivation zur Pseudepigraphie

Der Autor der Paulusakten hat diese nach eigener Aussage *amore Pauli* verfasst. Tertullian nennt indes noch ein weiteres Motiv: Der Fälscher wollte die Schrift durch den Namen des Paulus vervollkommnen (*quasi titulo Pauli de suo cumulans*), um so größere Wirkung zu erzielen (Tert.bapt. 17,5). Dies ist ein wichtiger Aspekt, der sowohl in Selbstaussagen antiker Autoren als auch in antiken rezipientenseitigen Erklärungen für Pseudepigraphie (vgl. z.B. Gellius, Noctes Atticae 10,12,8) erscheint.[142]

---

[137] So Jamblich über einen Pythagoreer, der zufällig den Namen Pythagoras trug: „ὁμώνυμος μὲν ὢν αὐτῷ, Ἐρατοκλέους δὲ υἱός. τούτου δὴ καὶ τὰ ἀλειπτικὰ συγγράμματα φέρεται καὶ ἡ ἀντὶ ἰσχάδων τοῖς τότε ἀθληταῖς κρεώδους τροφῆς διάταξις. οὐ καλῶς εἰς Πυθαγόραν τὸν Μνημάρχου τούτων ἀναφερομένων." – „Er trug denselben Namen wie der Meister, war aber ein Sohn des Eratokles. Von ihm kennt man Schriften über Leibeserziehung, ebenso auch die Vorschrift, Athleten sollten sich nicht von Feigen, sondern von Fleisch ernähren; denn zu Unrecht schreibt man dies Pythagoras, dem Sohne des Mnemarchos, zu."

[138] Vgl. auch M. FORDERER, Rez. Sint, Gn. 33 (1961), 440–445 (442): „Doch dürften die Schriften, die Iamblich im Auge hatte, in Wirklichkeit neupythagoreisch sein; Pythagoreer wie Philolaos und Archytas schrieben offenbar nicht pseudonym, ebenso wenig wie die bekannten Akademiker, Peripatetiker, Stoiker ..."

[139] S. Anm. 30.

[140] S. Anm. 23.

[141] BAUM, Pseudepigraphie (s. Anm. 34), 60–63.

[142] Vgl. auch die Stellungnahmen der neuplatonischen Aristoteleskommentatoren wie David, In Prophyrii isagogen commentarium 1; siehe MÜLLER, Aristoteleskommentatoren (s. Anm. 8), 268–271.

Der Wirkungswille führte in der Antike häufig zu nicht-orthonymer Literaturproduktion, wobei der Rückgriff auf verkörpernde Pseudonyme und historisch bedeutsame Namen am weitesten verbreitet ist. Durch die *Verbindung* der persönlichen Meinung mit der Autorität eines bekannten Namens *(cum illius auctoritate coniunxit)*[143] wächst das Gewicht einer Schrift.

Signifikante Aussagen finden sich bei Cicero in seiner Schrift Laelius de amicitia und dem dazugehörigen Parallelwerk Cato maior de senectute.[144] Cicero schreibt zwar nicht unter einem Pseudonym oder versucht gar, seine Urheberschaft zu verhüllen, sondern komponiert einen Maskendialog mit berühmten Rednern. Aber auch beim Rückgriff auf eine literarische Figur im Rahmen dramatischer Textsorten spricht der reale Autor durch eine Maske: „Iam enim ipsius Catonis sermo explicabit nostram omnem de senectute sententiam" (Cicero, Cato maior de senectute 1,3).[145] Dies gelingt mitunter so überzeugend, dass Cicero selbst von seiner Fiktion gefangen genommen wird: „Itaque ipse mea legens sic adficior interdum, ut Catonem, non me loqui existimen" (Cicero, Laelius de amicitia 1,4).[146] Eine solche Wirkung wünscht sich Cicero dann auch für die Leser

---

[143] Vgl. Quintilian, Institutio oratoria 10,3,1 über die Methode Ciceros: „Nec inmerito M. Tullius hunc, ‚optimum effectorem ac magistrum dicendi' vocat, cui sententiae personam L. Crassi in disputationibus quae sunt de oratore adsignando iudicium suum cum illius auctoritate coniunxit." – „Nicht zu Unrecht nennt M. Tullius diesen ‚den besten Erzeuger und Lehrer der Rede', ein Gedanke, bei dem Cicero dadurch, daß er ihn in den ‚Gesprächen über den Redner' dem L. Crassus in den Mund legt, sein eigenes Urteil mit der Autorität jenes Mannes verbunden hat." Text und Übersetzung: Marcus Fabius Quintilianus. Ausbildung des Redners. 12 Bücher. Bd. 2. Lateinisch-deutsch. Hg. u. übers. v. H. Rahn, Darmstadt 1975.

[144] Vgl. zur Gemeinsamkeit zwischen den im gleichen Jahr verfassten Schriften K. A. NEUHAUSEN, M. Tullius Cicero, Laelius. Lieferung 2, Heidelberg 1985, 35ff.; HIRZEL, Dialog I (s. Anm. 79), 545f.

[145] Text hier und im Folgenden: Cicero. De Senectute, de amicitia, de divinatione. Hg. u. m. engl. Übers. vers. v. W. A. Falconer, LCL 154, Cambridge/London 1964. Vgl. dazu auch Cicero, Epistulae ad familiares 7,32,2: „… quae sunt a me in secundo libro ‚de oratore' per Antoni personam disputata de ridiculis …" – „… was ich im zweiten Buche ‚De oratore' Antonius über den Witz sagen lasse." Vgl. ähnlich auch die Vita Vossiana Leidensis über Vergil, der u.a. durch die Maske seiner Hirtenfiguren hindurch spricht: „Quod in Virgilio deprehenditur omne; aut enim ex persona sua loquitur aut ex persona alterius, quod dramaticon dicitur, aut ille ipse loquitur et aliae secum personae introductae." – „Alles das trifft man bei Vergil an; denn entweder spricht er in eigener Person oder in der Person eines anderen, <und> das heißt dramatisch, oder er selbst spricht und andere mit ihm eingeführte Personen" (Götte, Vergil-Viten [s. Anm. 49], 628–631).

[146] „… So werde ich auch selbst beim Lesen meiner Schrift manchmal derart gefesselt, daß ich meine, Cato rede da, nicht ich." Text und Übersetzung: M. Tullius Ciceronis Laelius de amicitia. Lateinisch-deutsch. Hg. u. übers. v. M. Faltner, München ³1980.

seiner Schriften: „Tu velim a me animum parumper avertas, Laelium loqui ipsum putes" (Cicero, Laelius de amicitia 1,5).[147] Ciceros Aussagen liefern wichtige Hinweise zum Verständnis einiger Aspekte pseudepigraphischer Literaturproduktion. Hier ist zunächst auf die Wahl der *Kategorie* der Pseudonyme/literarischen Namen hinzuweisen. Wählt man Personen, die der Vergangenheit angehören, oder greift man auf zeitgenössische Charaktere zurück?[148] Prinzipiell ist es nach Cicero für die Überzeugungskraft vorteilhaft, wenn die Dialoganten der Vergangenheit angehören. Anlässlich seines Verfahrens, ausnahmsweise den zeitgenössischen Varro als Sprecher in einem seiner Dialoge einzuführen, äußert sich Cicero wie folgt gegenüber Atticus: „Sic enim constitueram, neminem includere in dialogos eorum, qui viverent ... hoc in antiquis personis suaviter fit, ut et Heraclides in multis et nos VI de re publica libris fecimus. sunt etiam de oratore nostri tres mihi vementer probati" (Epistulae ad Atticum 13,29[19]3f.).[149] Der Gedanke, dass die Wahl von Personen aus der Vergangenheit vorteilhaft ist, erscheint auch im Prolog zu Laelius de amicitia.[150] „Genus autem hoc sermonum positum in hominum veterum auctoritate et eorum inlustrium plus nescio quo pacto videtur habere gravitatis" (Cicero, Laelius de amicitia 1,4).[151] Durch diese Art der Gespräche wird die Autorität der Schrift gesteigert; sie wächst an *gravitas*.[152]

---

[147] „Du aber sollst deine Gedanken ein wenig von mir abwenden und dir vorstellen, Laelius spreche persönlich."

[148] Für die sogenannten Vergangenheitsdialoge ist Heraklides Pontikus ein wichtiger Repräsentant; er verfasste Dialoge, in denen er nicht selbst auftrat, sondern Männer der Vergangenheit anführte. Anders verfuhr Aristoteles; er griff auf zeitgenössische Personen zurück und wählte auch sich selbst als Gesprächspartner. Bei Cicero sind indes beide Dialogtypen bezeugt. Zur prinzipiellen Unterscheidung von Vergangenheits- und Gegenwartsdialogen bei Cicero siehe NEUHAUSEN, Laelius (s. Anm. 144), 123–137.

[149] „Eigentlich hatte ich es mir ja zum Grundsatz gemacht, keinen der Lebenden in meinen Dialogen als Sprecher einzuführen ... Das macht sich sehr gut, wenn die Personen der Vergangenheit angehören; Heraklides hat es z.B. in mehreren seiner Schriften so gemacht, und ich in meinen sechs Büchern vom Staat; ebenso auch in den drei Büchern vom Redner, die ich für besonders gelungen halte."

[150] Vgl. zur Typologie des Proömiums auch NEUHAUSEN, Laelius (s. Anm. 144), 116–122. Der Prolog ist direkt mit der Schrift verbunden, auf sie abgestimmt und inhaltlich mit ihr verknüpft. Hierin unterscheidet er sich von den Prologen, die nur allgemein das Thema der ihnen folgenden Schrift streifen und prinzipiell austauschbar sind (vgl. nur das *volumen prohoemiorum* in Cicero, Epistulae ad Atticum 16,6,4!).

[151] „Die Form der Gespräche aber, aufgebaut auf die Gestalten angesehener und berühmter Männer der Vergangenheit, scheint mir irgendwie ganz besonderen Nachdruck zu besitzen."

[152] Freilich sind Vergangenheitsdialoge auch in diplomatischer Hinsicht vorteilhaft, zumal wenn es um zeitgeschichtlich brisante Inhalte geht; vgl. Cicero, Ad Quintum fratrem 3,5,2. Bei lebenden Dialoganten achtet Cicero dementsprechend darauf, dass die

Aber auch innerhalb der Vergangenheitsdialoge sind prinzipiell Unterschiede möglich. Greift man auf eine historische Person oder eine mythische Größe zurück? Dazu äußert sich Cicero in Cato maior de senectute. Man hätte eine Rede über das Alter nämlich auch einer mythischen Person in den Mund legen können, wie es beispielsweise Ariston von Keos getan hat.[153] Den Rückgriff auf solcherlei mythische Charaktere lehnt Cicero ab, da einer mythischen Person nicht genug Autorität zukommt.[154] „Omnen autem sermonem tribuimus non Tithono, ut Aristo Cius, parum enim esset auctoritatis in fabula, sed M. Catoni seni, quo maiorem auctoritatem haberet oratio" (Cicero, Cato maior de senectute 1,3).[155] Warum nun liegt im Rückgriff auf historische Größen mehr *auctoritas* als in der Verwendung mythischer Charaktere? Im Gegensatz zu Aristons mythischem Maskendialog hätte sich der Vergangenheitsdialog mit historischen Dialoganten in Cato maior de senectute so zutragen können; genau in dieser historischen Möglichkeit liegt die Überzeugungskraft. Eine fiktive Darstellung (*argumentum*) wird von Cicero dementsprechend als „ficta res, quae tamen fieri potuit" definiert (vgl. z.B. Cicero, De inventione 1,27).[156] Mit diesen Aussagen bewegt sich Cicero ganz im Rahmen der rhetorischen Theorie über fiktionale Texte, wie sie schon Aristoteles bezeugt: „Φανερὸν δὲ ἐκ τῶν

---

von den Dialogfiguren vertretenen Meinungen auch zu den jeweiligen Personen passen; vgl. Cicero, Epistulae ad familiares 9,8,1.

[153] Der Peripatetiker Ariston von Keos hat eine Schrift über das Alter geschrieben, die in Fragmenten bei Plutarch überliefert ist. Ariston wählte die mythische Figur Tithonos als Maske für einen Monolog über das Alter. Die Wahl solcher Figuren entsprach dabei seiner literarischen Praxis; vgl. HIRZEL, Dialog I (s. Anm. 79), 332f.

[154] NEUHAUSEN, Laelius (s. Anm. 144), 127f.; HIRZEL, a.a.O. 545f.; vgl. auch Cicero, De finibus 5,13.

[155] „Dabei habe ich aber nicht, wie Ariston aus Keos, das ganze Gespräch dem Tithonos in den Mund gelegt (eine Sage hätte doch zu wenig Nachdruck!), sondern dem greisen Marcus Cato, um den Worten mehr Gewicht zu verleihen." Übersetzung: Cato maior de senectute. Lateinisch-deutsch. Hg. u. übers. v. M. Faltner, München 1963.

[156] Weitere Belege z.B. bei U. LUZ, Fiktivität und Traditionstreue im Matthäusevangelium im Lichte griechischer Literatur, ZNW 94 (1993), 153–177 (167f. Anm. 50); N. HOLZBERG, Historie und Fiktion – Fiktion als Historie, in: Schubert / Brodersen, Rom (s. Anm. 32), 93–101 (93f.); C. W. MÜLLER, Chariton von Aphrodisias und die Theorie des Romans in der Antike, AuA 22 (1976), 111–136 (115 Anm. 3), wiederabgedruckt in: ders., Legende – Novelle – Roman. Dreizehn Kapitel zur erzählenden Prosaliteratur der Antike, Göttingen 2006, 445–475; A. CIZEK, Die „tria genera narrationum" und die Alexanderstoffe. Ein Beitrag zur Poetik des antik-mittelalterlichen Alexanderromans, in: M. Picone / B. Zimmermann (Hg.), Der antike Roman und seine mittelalterliche Rezeption, Basel u.a. 1997, 273–306 (275–288); FUCHS, Pseudologia (s. Anm. 4), 217f.; K. BACKHAUS, Spielräume der Wahrheit. Zur Konstruktivität in der hellenistisch-reichsrömischen Geschichtsschreibung, in: K. Backhaus / G. Häfner (Hg.), Historiographie und fiktionales Erzählen. Zur Konstruktivität in Geschichtstheorie und Exegese, BThSt 86, Neukirchen-Vluyn 2007, 1–29 (5–7).

εἰρημένων καὶ ὅτι οὐ τὸ τὰ γενόμενα λέγειν, τοῦτο ποιητοῦ ἔργον ἐστίν, ἀλλ' οἷα ἂν γένοιτο, καὶ τὰ δυνατὰ κατὰ τὸ εἰκὸς ἢ τὸ ἀναγκαῖον" (Arist.po. 9).[157] Die Dimension der Wahrscheinlichkeit unterscheidet eine Fiktion von einer mythischen Erzählung (*fabula*), „in qua nec verae nec veri similes res continentur" (vgl. z.B. Cicero, De inventione 1,27). Eine Fiktion erreicht also nur dann ihr Ziel, wenn sie glaubwürdig ist,[158] was wiederum nur dann gelingt, wenn sie wahrscheinlich, plausibel und lebensnah ist[159] und das zur Sprache bringt, was zu geschehen pflegt: „Et licebit etiam falso adfingere quidquid fieri solet" (Quintilian, Institutio oratoria 8,3,70).

Die in der antiken Fiktionalitätstheorie breit belegte Forderung nach Wahrscheinlichkeit schließt auch die Ethopoiie/Sermocinatio mit ein.[160] Hinsichtlich der Wahl der Dialogfiguren und literarischen Figuren bedeutet dies, dass jeweils eine zu dem Inhalt passende Person ausgewählt werden soll[161] und dass im Gegenzug eine unpassende Auswahl oder unwahr-

---

[157] „Aus dem Gesagten ergibt sich auch, daß es nicht Aufgabe des Dichters ist mitzuteilen, was wirklich geschehen ist, sondern vielmehr, was geschehen könnte, d.h. das nach den Regeln der Wahrscheinlichkeit oder Notwendigkeit Mögliche." Text und Übersetzung: Aristoteles, Poetik. Griechisch-deutsch. Hg. u. übers. v. M. Fuhrmann, Stuttgart ²1994.

[158] Vgl. dazu grundlegend J. R. MORGAN, Make-Believe and Make believe. The Fictionality of the Greek Novels, in: C. Gill / T. P. Wiseman (Hg.), Lies and Fiction in the Ancient World, Exeter 1993, 175–229; D. C. FEENEY, Epilogue. Towards an Account of the Ancient World's Concept of Fictive Belief, in: Gill / Wiseman, a.a.O. 230–244.

[159] Diese Forderung nach Lebenswirklichkeit schlägt sich auch terminologisch darin nieder, dass πλασματικόν („fingo") und βιωτικαὶ διηγήσεις synonym gebraucht werden; vgl. MÜLLER, Chariton (s. Anm. 156), 116 Anm. 1. Siehe zu der Terminologie bezüglich fiktionaler Literatur auch CIZEK, Alexanderstoffe (s. Anm. 156), 283. Wenn dies beachtet wird, hat eine Fiktion mehr *auctoritas* als ein historischer Text; vgl. dazu z.B. M. STEMBERGER, Auctoritas exempli. Zur Wechselwirkung von kanonisierten Vergangenheitsbildern und gesellschaftlicher Gegenwart in der spätrepublikanischen Rhetorik, in: B. Linke (Hg.), Mos maiorum. Untersuchungen zu den Formen der Identitätsstiftung und Stabilisierung in der römischen Republik, Historia 141, Stuttgart 2000, 141–205 (178f.).

[160] Vgl. z.B. Quintilian, Institutio oratoria 9,2,29f.; siehe auch LAUSBERG, Rhetorik (s. Anm 23), 408 (§ 821): „Inhaltlich braucht die *sermocinatio* nicht historisch wahr zu sein, sie muss nur ‚wahrscheinlich' sein, d.h. insbesondere dem Charakter der entsprechenden Person entsprechen." Siehe auch MÜLLER, Kurzdialoge (s. Anm. 98), 17 Anm. 2: Es gibt ein „eigentümliches Verhältnis, das die antike Literatur zu Brief und Rede als Äußerungen einer historischen Person hat. Maßstab der ‚Wahrheit' ist dabei nicht die dokumentarische Historizität des Wortes, sondern Mentalität und Charakter des Redenden sowie die äußere und innere Situation, aus der heraus gesprochen wird."

[161] A. D. LEEMAN / H. PINKSTER, M. Tullius Cicero, De Oratore libri III. Kommentar. 1. Band, Buch 1,1–165, Heidelberg 1981, 91; NEUHAUSEN, Laelius (s. Anm. 144), 123ff.; R. D. MEYER, Literarische Fiktion und historischer Gehalt in Ciceros de Oratore, Freiburg i. Brsg. 1970, 7ff.

scheinliche Stilisierung als *neque verisimilier confictum* (Apul.apol 87,2) bzw. *imperite absurdeque fictum* (Cic.rep. 2,28) abzulehnen ist.[162] Um beispielsweise die Wahl des Laelius als Sprecher seines Gesprächs über die Freundschaft in Laelius de amicitia zu erläutern, greift Cicero auf das Parallelwerk Cato maior de senectute zurück, in dem das Alter thematisiert wird. Cato scheint deswegen der geeignete Repräsentant für das Thema „Alter" zu sein, weil er aufgrund seines eigenen Alters etwas über dieses Gebiet zu sagen weiß: „Sed ut in Catone Maiore, qui est scriptus ad te de senectute, Catonem induxi senem disputantem, quia nulla videbatur aptior persona, quae de illa aetate loqueretur, quam eius, qui et diutissime senex fuisset et in ipsa senectute praeter ceteros floruisset" (Cicero, Laelius de amicitia 1,4).[163] Gleichermaßen ist Laelius der geeignete „Fachmann" für eine Rede über die Freundschaft, da er im Bewusstsein der Nachwelt durch nichts so lebendig ist wie durch seine Lebensfreundschaft mit Scipio: „Cum accepissemus a patribus maxime memorabilem C. Laeli et P. Scipionis familiaritatem fuisse, idonea mihi Laeli persona visa est, quae de amicitia ea ipsa dissereret, quae disputata ab eo meminisset Scaevola" (Cicero, Laelius de amicitia 1,4).[164] Die Gemeinsamkeit der beiden Schriften be-

---

[162] „Falsum est enim Manili – inquit – id totum, neque solum fictum sed etiam imperite absurdeque fictum; ea sunt enim demum non ferenda mendacia, quae non solum ficta esse sed ne fieri quidem potuisse cernimus." – „Falsch ist nämlich, Manilius, das Ganze und nicht nur erdichtet, sondern dazu töricht und unsinnig erdichtet. Denn die Art Lügen vornehmlich ist unerträglich, von denen wir sehen, nicht nur, daß sie erdichtet sind, sondern daß sie nicht einmal hätten geschehen können" (Cic.rep. 2,28). Text und Übersetzung: Marcus Tullius Cicero, De re publica. Lateinisch-deutsch. Übers. u. hg. v. K. Büchner, Stuttgart 1979. Cicero kritisiert in De re republica 2,28 die anachronistische Behauptung, Numa sei Schüler des Pythagoras gewesen. Weiter bemängelt er in Brutus 218, dass ein fingierter Dialog auf Ereignisse Bezug nimmt, die erst nach dem Dialogzeitpunkt stattfanden; vgl. dazu NEUHAUSEN, Laelius (s. Anm. 144), 126f. Die Forderung nach Angemessenheit führte nicht zuletzt dazu, dass Cicero mitunter die Diaologanten in seinen Dialogen austauschte, wenn ihm die ursprüngliche Wahl παρὰ τὸ πρέπον (Cicero, Epistulae ad Atticum 13,[17]16,1) erschien; siehe auch Cicero, Epistulae ad Atticum 13,(29)19,3f.; 13,17(16),1; 13,39(44),3. Vgl. dazu MEYER, a.a.O. 7–9; NEUHAUSEN, a.a.O. 124–127. Insgesamt erwägt Cicero die Wahl seiner literarischen Figuren äußerst sorgfältig; vgl. z.B. Epistulae ad Atticum 13,24 (12),3f.; 13,26(14,2+15)1f.; 13,29(19),3–6; 13,39(44),3. Dies gilt auch und gerade im Hinblick auf zeitgenössische Personen, die als Sprecher in seinen Dialogen erscheinen; vgl. z.B. Epistulae ad familiares 9,8,1.

[163] „Beim ‚Cato maior', einer Schrift, die ich über das Greisenalter schrieb und dir widmete, machte ich es so, daß ich den greisen Cato als Sprecher auftreten ließ, weil wohl kein anderer geeigneter war, über jene Altersstufe zu reden, als der Mann, der sehr lange in hohem Alter gelebt hat und gerade in seinem hohen Alter so jugendfrisch war wie kaum ein zweiter."

[164] „Da wir nun von unseren Vätern her wissen, daß die Freundschaft zwischen Gaius Laelius und Publius Scipio außerordentlich denkwürdig war, schien mir die Person des Laelius geeignet, zum Thema ‚Freundschaft' eben die Gedanken vorzutragen, die er, wie

steht darin, dass Personen als Sprecher und titelgebende Hauptfiguren ausgesucht werden, die zum Thema passen und es als personale Chiffren gewissermaßen symbolisieren. „Sed ut tum ad senem senex de senectute, sic hoc libro ad amicum amicissimus scripsi de amicitia. tum est Cato locutus, quo erat nemo fere senior temporibus illis, nemo prudentior; nunc Laelius et sapiens – sic enim est habitus –, et amicitiae gloria excellens de amicitia loquetur" (Cicero, Laelius de amicitia 1,5).[165]

In einen weiteren Grenzbereich der Pseudepigraphie führt die spezifische Verfasstheit der lateinischen Literatur, die von der griechischen abhängig ist. Die durchgehende Orientierung an den griechischen Vorbildern führte zur Bezeichnung Roms als *graeca urbs* (Juvenal, Satiren 41) im Sinne eines *victor victus*, wie es Hor.ep. 2,1,156f. in seinem berühmten Diktum formuliert: „Graecia capta ferum victorem cepit et artes intulit agresti Latio."[166] In diesem Zusammenhang nimmt fast jeder lateinische Dichter für sich ein griechisches *alter ego* als Referenzgröße in Anspruch, als dessen Nachfolger und Umformer er sich versteht (vgl. auch Hier.ep. 58,5).[167] Der römische Fabeldichter Phädrus macht z.B. die Fabeln des

---

sich Scaevola erinnerte, auch tatsächlich dargelegt hat." Diese Freundschaft zwischen Scipio und Laelius hat Cicero in Laelius de amicitia und auch in seiner Schrift De re publica idealisiert. In einem Brief an Pompeius Magnus fungiert Laelius zudem als Exemplum für die Freundschaft; vgl. Cicero, Epistulae ad familiares 5,7,3: „... me non multo minorem quam Laelium facile et in re p. et in amicitia adiunctum esse patiare" – „... in mir einen politischen Gesinnungsgenossen und Freund findest, der es mit einem Laelius beinahe aufnehmen kann." In seinen Briefen an Atticus erwägt Cicero sogar, sich den Namen des Laelius als Decknamen zuzulegen, wenn er an seinen Freund über prekäre Sachverhalte schreibt. Atticus erhält dabei im Gegenzug den Decknamen Furius (Philus). Auch dieser war Mitglied des Scipionenkreises und ist einer der Diaolganten in De publica; vgl. auch Anm. 47.

[165] „Wie ich aber damals als Greis an einen Greis über das Greisenalter schrieb, so habe ich die vorliegende Schrift als bester Freund für meinen Freund über die Freundschaft verfaßt. Damals war Cato der Sprecher, nahezu der älteste Mann jener Zeit und auch der weiseste; jetzt soll Laelius über die Freundschaft sprechen – der Weise, wie man ihn nannte, der als Freund berühmt geworden ist."

[166] Zum Panhellenismus vgl. auch S. DÖPP, Aemulatio. Literarischer Wettstreit mit den Griechen in Zeugnissen des ersten bis fünften Jahrhunderts, Göttinger Forum für Altertumswissenschaften 7, Göttingen 2001, 11. Vgl. zum Ganzen auch G. VOGT-SPIRA, Die Kulturbegegnung Roms mit den Griechen, in: M. Schuster (Hg.), Die Begegnung mit dem Fremden. Wertungen und Wirkungen in Hochkulturen vom Altertum bis zur Gegenwart, Colloquium Raurica 4, Stuttgart/Leipzig 1996, 11–33; FUHRMANN, Geschichte (s. Anm. 49), 37–45.

[167] So bezeichnet sich Properz als *Callimachus romanus* (Properz, Elegie 4,1,64); Ennius gilt als *alter Homerus* (Hor.ep. 2,1,50 u.ö.; vgl. auch Cicero, De finibus 1,3,7), Terenz ist der zweite bzw. halbierte Menander (Donat, Commentum Terenti, Vita Terenti 7: „*dimidiatus Menander*"). Die Beispiele ließen sich fast beliebig vermehren und sind auch in die andere Richtung offen (vgl. zu Josephus als *graecus Livius* Hier.ep. 22,35,8). Frei-

Äsop als „Dolmetsch des Äsop"[168] für ein römisches Publikum zugänglich. Dementsprechend nennt er seine Fabeln „*Fabulae Aesopiae*". Die einzelnen Fabelbücher des Phädrus sind durch Pro- und Epiloge gerahmt, die unter anderem Einblick in das Verhältnis zwischen Autor und literarischem Vorbild im Rahmen der identifizierenden Komparation geben. Zunächst versteht sich Phädrus als Überlieferer der Fabeln Äsops: „Aesopus auctor quam materiam repperit, hanc ego polivi versibus senariis" (1 prol 1f.).[169] Die Bearbeitung der äsop'schen Fabeln durch Phädrus in den ersten vier Büchern besteht jedoch nicht allein in deren Aufarbeitung für ein lateinisches Publikum; Phädrus setzt auch inhaltlich eigene Akzente, wie er wiederholt zum Ausdruck bringt.[170] Deutlich übertrifft Phädrus – ganz im Sinne der agonalen Variation eines literarischen Vorbilds (*aemulatio*)[171] – sein Vorbild Äsop: „Quare, Particulo, quoniam caperis fabulis (quas Aesopias, non Aesopi, nomino, quia paucas ille ostendit, ego plures fero, usus vetusto genere, sed rebus novis), quartum libellum, cum vacarit, perleges" (4 prol 10–14).[172] In 4 prol und 4,7/4,22 emanzipiert sich Phädrus explizit von seinem Vorbild, wie es bereits im 3 prol 38f. angedeutet ist.[173] Äsop

---

lich kann ein Dichter auch mehrere Vorbilder haben; vgl. für Vergil z.B. Philagyrius, Vita 1,1.

[168] REIFF, Imitatio (s. Anm. 133), 75.

[169] „Der Stoff, den einst Äsop als Dichter fand, kommt in gefeilten Jamben neu von mir." Text und Übersetzung hier und im Folgenden: Phaedrus, Der Wolf und das Lamm. Fabeln. Lateinisch-deutsch. Hg. u. übers. v. V. Riedel, Leipzig 1989.

[170] Vgl. z.B. 2 prol 8–12: „Equidem omni cura morem servabo senis. sed si libuerit aliquid interponere, dictorum sensus ut delectet varietas, bonas in partes, lector, accipias velim, ita, si rependet illi brevitas gratiam." – „Ich will durchaus des Alten Art bewahren. Doch schlüpft mir einmal Eignes in den Text, um durch den Reiz der Fülle zu erfreuen, so nimm es, lieber Leser, freundlich auf, wofern nur Kürze meine Gabe würzt." Zum Selbstverständnis des Phädrus und seinem Ehrgeiz siehe E. OBERG, Phaedrus-Kommentar, Stuttgart 2000, 15f.

[171] Terminologisch wird zwischen den unterschiedlichen Qualitäten der Transponierung griechischer Autoren in das lateinisch-römische Referenzsystem differenziert; vgl. dazu grundlegend REIFF, Imitatio (s. Anm. 133). Ungeachtet der Frage, ob bereits in den antiken Zeugnissen ein klar unterschiedener Sprachgebrauch dieser Begriffe im Sinne einer systematischen Abstufung von „übersetzen" (*interpretari*), „nachahmen" (*imitari*) und „wetteifern" (*aemulari*) festgestellt werden kann, wohnt vor allem dem Begriff *aemulatio* eine hohe ästhetische Wertung im Sinne einer Selbstbehauptung gegenüber dem literarischen Vorbild inne; siehe z.B. DÖPP, Aemulatio (s. Anm. 166); REIFF, Imitatio (s. Anm. 133), 73–82. Die Unterscheidung zwischen Nachahmung (μίμησις) und Wettkampf (ζῆλος) ist auch ein Kennzeichen des innergriechischen Klassizismus.

[172] „Da nun, Particulo, dich Fabeln freuen – die ich äsop'sche nenne, nicht Äsopens, weil mehr, als jener mich gelehrt, ich bringe, im alten Stil zwar, doch mit neuem Inhalt –, so lies, hast Muße Du, mein viertes Büchlein."

[173] Phädrus weist hier auf den eigenständigen Anteil seiner Arbeit hin: „Ego porro illius semita feci viam, et cogitavi plura, quam reliquerat." – „Ich schreite weiter auf der

fungiert im Folgenden lediglich als Gattungsname (*Aesopas*; vgl. auch 3 prol 29: *Aesopi stilo*), in dessen vorgegebenen Rahmen neue Inhalte gefüllt werden (vgl. auch 4,22). Phädrus entfaltet im Verlauf seiner Fabelbücher immer mehr *cogitatio colorque proprius* (4 prol 7f.) und geht über sein Vorbild hinaus: „Sive hoc ineptum sive laudandum est opus, invenit ille, nostra perfecit manus. Sed *ex*sequamur coeptum propositum ordinem" (4,22,7–9).[174] Im fünften Buch ändert sich dann die gesamte Perspektive. Hat Phädrus zuvor seine eigenen Gedanken Äsop untergeschoben (2 prol 9 „... sed si libuerit aliquid *interponere* ..."), so schiebt er nun Äsop als Dichter unter (5 prol 1: „Aesopi nomen sicubi *interposuero*.").[175] Obwohl das fünfte Buch nur Phädrus-Fabeln enthält, bezeichnet Phädrus auch seine eigenen Produkte als Fabeln des Äsop (*Fabulae Aesopiae*), was in den Bereich der Pseudepigraphie führt. Eine Begründung für dieses Vorgehen findet sich im Prolog zum fünften Buch. Obwohl Phädrus seine Schuld an Äsop beglichen hat, flieht er zum Schein des Alters, um sich nicht dem Neid der Zeitgenossen auszusetzen und um gleichzeitig für sein Werk zu werben. Zur Verdeutlichung seines Vorgehens führt er Entsprechungen aus dem Bereich der bildenden Kunst an: „Aesopi nomen sicubi interposuero, cui reddidi iam pridem quicquid debui, auctoritatis[176] esse scito gratia: Ut quidam artifices nostro faciunt saeculo, qui pretium operibus maius inveniunt, novo si marmori ascripserunt Praxitelen suo, trito Myronem argento, tabulae Zeuxidem. adeo fucatae plus vetustati favet invidia mordax quam bonis praesentibus" (5 prol 1–9).[177]

---

alten Spur, und finde mehr als uns der Dichter gönnte." Vgl. in diesem Zusammenhang zur Aemulatio Äsops nur DÖPP, Aemulatio (s. Anm. 166), 16f.; REIFF, Imitatio (s. Anm. 133), 73–76. Der Prolog zum dritten Buch beginnt zudem im Gegensatz zu den vorherigen nicht mit dem Hinweis auf Äsop, sondern Phädrus nennt sich selbst mit eigenem Namen; vgl. L. NIEDERMEIER, Untersuchungen über die antike poetische Autobiographie, München 1919, 28; OBERG, Phaedrus-Kommentar (s. Anm. 170), 115, der zudem auf den hohen Anteil von Ich-Formen in 3 prol hinweist. Dies entspricht der allgemeinen Tendenz, dass sich die Bedeutung des Phädrus wächst und die des Äsop abnimmt; vgl. auch OBERG, a.a.O. 159.207.

[174] „Das Werk, ob schlecht, ob trefflich, ist Äsops in der Erfindung, doch im Ausbau mein. Ich schreite fort auf der betretnen Bahn." Ein Hinweis auf das neue Selbstverständnis ist auch, dass sich im vierten Buch zwei Fabeln mit dem Titel „Phädrus" finden (4,7; 4,22), in denen Phädrus ähnlich wie sonst in den Pro- und Epilogen über seine Arbeit reflektiert.

[175] Siehe auch OBERG, Phaedrus-Kommentar (s. Anm. 170), 207. Zudem heißt es in der Schlusssentenz in 5 prol 10: „Sed iam ad *fabellam* talis exempli feror." Phädrus stilisiert sich als Urheber der Fabelgleichnisse (*fabella*), ein Terminus, der vorher für Äsop reserviert ist; vorherrschender Begriff für Phädrus' eigene Leistung ist vielmehr *studium* (2 epil 12), *libellus, librum* (3 prol 1.29).

[176] Eventuell wird auf 1 prol 1 (auctor) angespielt; vgl. OBERG, a.a.O. 207.

[177] „Wenn ich Äsop als Dichter unterschiebe, an dem ich längst schon meine Schuld

Der Rückgriff auf ein verkörperndes Pseudonym mit dem Ziel, Wirkung für sein Werk zu erreichen, war indes in der Antike auch Gegenstand der Kritik. Aulus Gellius gibt beispielsweise im zehnten Buch seiner Miszellensammlung Noctes Atticae (10,12) Einblick in einige absurde pseudowissenschaftliche Mitteilungen („multaque vana atque intoleranda auribus"; 10,12,1), die Plinius Secundus fälschlicherweise dem Philosophen Demokrit zuschreibt (vgl. auch Plinius, Naturalis historia 24,160; 28,112 u.ö.). Gellius wirft Plinius Secundus dementsprechend die unkritische Rezeption pseudo-demokrit'scher Schriften vor: Plinius sei auf diejenigen hereingefallen, die den Namen Demokrit für die Verbreitung ihrer Hausfrauenmagie („ita est deridiculae vanitatis!"; 10,12,4) benutzen. Gellius gibt einen Grund für das Vorgehen der Fälscher an. Der falsche, mit Ansehen und Autorität behaftete Name wird als Deckmantel für die eigene, in Gellius' Augen minderwertige Literaturproduktion vorgeschoben („nobilitatis auctoritatisque eius perfugio utentibus"; 10,12,8f.). Die Inanspruchnahme des Namens Demokrit geschieht somit zu Unrecht und wird von Gellius als unwürdig empfunden („... non dignum esse cognomen Democriti puto ..."; 10,12,6).[178]

Der Rückgriff auf apostolische Größen aus Gründen der Steigerung von Autorität ist in der Forschung fast durchgängig zur Erklärung der neutestamentlichen Pseudepigraphie[179] angeführt und zum Teil mit kirchenge-

---

beglich, so ist's um seines großen Namens Klang. Denn mancher Künstler unsrer Tage schreibt, um für sein Werk zu werben, auf ein Bild aus Stein Praxiteles, auf eine Prägung aus Silber Myron, auf die Leinwand Zeuxis. So sehr begünstigt Neid und Hass den Schein des Alters vor dem Gut der Gegenwart." Vgl. hier zum Motiv des Wirkungswillens auch SPEYER, Fälschung (s. Anm. 4), 133.

[178] Text: The Attic Nights of Aulus Gellius in Three Volumes, Bd. II. Hg. u. m. engl. Übers. vers. v. J. C. Rolfe, LCL 195, Cambridge/London 1984.

[179] Dies gilt natürlich auch für die altkirchliche Literatur. In der Alten Kirche wurde heterodoxen Christen oft vorgeworfen, sie würden unter dem Deckmantel apostolischer Verfasserschaft ihren eigenen Schriften zu mehr Autorität verhelfen wollen. So wird z.B. Kerinth unterstellt, er habe seine Apokalypse auf den Namen des Johannes abgefasst, um seine theologischen Interessen mittels eines besser klingenden Namens durchzusetzen (Eus.h.e. 7,25,2f.). Weiter weist Augustin, De consensu evangelistarum 1,10,15f., im Hinblick auf einige Apokryphen, die von Christus an Petrus und Paulus gerichtet sind, auf ein ähnliches Motiv hin: („... qui eiusmodi execrabilibus artibus de tam glorioso nomine pondus auctoritatis dare se posse putauerunt ..." [CSEL 43,15,8f.]). Dieser häresiologische Topos wird von Salvian als Begründung dafür angeführt, warum er seine Bücher an die Kirche nicht unter eigenem Namen geschrieben hat (ep. 9,14–17): Die Geringfügigkeit seiner Person (parvitas personae suae) soll die Bedeutung (auctoritas) nicht negativ beeinflussen. „[D]enn alles, was gesagt wird, steht nur so hoch im Werte wie derjenige, der es sagt (omnia enim admodum dicta tanti existimantur, quantus est ipse qui dixit) (9,15)." Deswegen greift Salvian zu einem Pseudonym. „Die Schrift, die so viel des Guten und Heilsamen in sich trägt, sollte in ihrem Wert nicht etwa durch den

schichtlichen Erwägungen kombiniert worden: Das Autoritätsvakuum der zweiten und dritten Generation machte den Gebrauch von „entliehenen Verfasserangaben"[180] nötig. Dass hierin ein wahrer Kern liegt, ist kaum zu bestreiten. Dennoch zeigen die angeführten Quellen auch, dass der Verweis auf den Wirkungswillen allein nicht ausreicht. Der Wunsch nach Autorität ist immer von Sekundärmotivationen begleitet, die aus den spezifischen kulturellen Präsuppositionen resultieren (vgl. z.B. Phädrus als *Aesopus redivivus* im Rahmen der Kulturbegegnung Roms mit der griechischen Literatur). Zudem ist die Wahl einer literarischen Figur bzw. eines fiktiven Autors nicht beliebig, sondern bestimmten Regeln unterworfen. Das rhetorische Prinzip der Angemessenheit[181] gilt auch für die unterschiedlichen Erscheinungsformen von Pseudepigraphie. Im Hinblick auf die neutestamentliche Literatur ist zu fragen, warum bestimmte Schriften bestimmten Aposteln zugeschrieben wurden. Wo sind die jeweiligen Anknüpfungspunkte? Ist die Inanspruchnahme des jeweiligen Pseudonyms im Rahmen der antiken rhetorischen Theorie angemessen? Ein weiterer Aspekt tritt hinzu. Phädrus will durch seine Referenz auf Äsop nicht nur mehr *auctoritas* für sein Werk erzielen, sondern leistet zugleich eine literaturgeschichtliche Positionierung als *alter Aesopus*. Hier bleibt zu fragen: Inwiefern gehören auch im Fall der neutestamentlichen Pseudepigraphie das gewählte Autorpseudonym und der Wille, sich theologisch zu positionieren, zusammen?

10. Ausblick

1) Das Vorhandensein von in der Antike bezeugten Konventionen und Motiven erhöht zweifelsohne die Plausibilität bestimmter Positionen der Pseudepigraphieforschung. Allerdings ist die antike Literatur kein Steinbruch für Belegstellen. Die Übertragbarkeit auf frühchristliche Kontexte bedarf einer reflektierten Methodik. Hierbei ist auf die Sonderkonditionen der jeweiligen literatursoziologischen Orte, die den einzelnen Gattungen

---

Namen des Verfassers herabgemindert werden (... ne scripta, quae in se habent plurimum salubritatis, minora forsitan fierent per nomen auctoris)" (9,16).

[180] SCHNELLE, Einleitung (s. Anm. 92), 329; vgl. ebd.: „Die ntl. Pseudepigraphie muß als der theologisch legitime und ekklesiologisch notwendige Versuch angesehen werden, die apostolische Tradition in einer sich verändernden Situation zu bewahren und zugleich notwendige Antworten auf neue Situationen und Fragen zu geben. Dabei ist die gesamtkirchliche Perspektive für die pseudepigraphischen Schriften charakteristisch, sie entstanden aus ökumenischer Verantwortung."

[181] Das Prinzip der Angemessenheit ist auch im Bereich der Imitatio leitend; vgl. Quintilian, Institutio oratoria 10,2,14 („quos imitemur"); Pseudo-Longinus, De sublimitate 14,2.

inhärenten Faktoren und die mentalitätsgeschichtlichen Rahmenbedingungen zu achten. Aus diesem Grund scheint eine gewisse Skepsis gegenüber einer pauschalen Deutung neutestamentlicher Pseudepigraphie als Erscheinungsform antiker Sekretärs- oder Schulpseudepigraphie angebracht (s.o.). Vergleichbare Vorbehalte sind verstärkt im Hinblick auf inspirationstheologische Begründungen geltend zu machen:[182] Einerseits belegt das Zeugnis des Aristophanes (s.o.) schon früh die Tendenz, dass Inspirationsvorstellungen zum literarischen Sujet werden können;[183] andererseits war in der Antike das Bewusstsein der Inspiration mit der Nennung des eigenen Namens durchaus vereinbar.[184]

2) Das antike Material eröffnet einen Horizont, um angemessene Fragestellungen zu entwickeln, die sich aus der antiken Geisteshaltung selbst ergeben und nicht aus heutiger Perspektive stammen. Ein Beispiel ist die gezielte Wahl eines angemessenen Pseudonyms, eines „*potissimum nomen*" (Salvian ep. 9,5; Augustin, De consensu evangelistarum 1,10,16).[185]

---

[182] Einflussreich wurde hier die These von Kurt Aland über die „Zeit der echten Pseudonymität", in der der Autor ein „Werkzeug" – gleichsam eine „Feder, die vom heiligen Geist bewegt wird" – ist; vgl. K. ALAND, Das Problem der Anonymität und Pseudonymität in der christlichen Literatur der ersten beiden Jahrhunderte, in: ders., Studien zur Überlieferung des Neuen Testaments und seines Textes, ANTT 2, Berlin 1967, 24–34 [29f.]); siehe dazu auch JANSSEN, Namen (s. Anm. 3), 65–75.

[183] Generell ist der Bezug auf die Musen ein Phänomen der archaischen Epoche; siehe zur Entwicklung der Verfasserpersönlichkeit auch den Beitrag von Wolfgang Speyer in diesem Band. In späterer Zeit verliert im gleichen Atemzug mit der Entdeckung des individuellen Verfassers der Musenanruf seine religiöse Unmittelbarkeit und wird zum literarischen Sujet; vgl. zur Profanisierung der Musen auch Martial, Epigrammata 8,73, der über Catulls Lesbialieder sagt: „Lesbia dictavit, docte Catulle, tibi …" Die Musenvorstellung konnte schließlich ihren Ort auch in der Polemik erobern. In der Vergil-Parodie des Lucan fungiert z.B. Nero als Muse; vgl. DIHLE, Literatur (s. Anm. 12), 131. Vgl. zum Ganzen auch SCHICKERT, Schutz (s. Anm. 11), 118–127.

[184] Vgl. z.B. SPEYER, Pseudepigraphie (s. Anm. 71), 201: „Dies vom Mythos geprägte Verständnis des eigenen Schaffens führte in Griechenland aber nicht notwendig zur religiösen Pseudepigraphie." Wie sich Musenreligion und Bewusstsein individueller Urhebertat im antiken Künstler verbinden können, zeigt exemplarisch Horaz, der als *sacerdos musarum* einerseits sein Werk auf die Musen zurückführt (vgl. z.B. Hor.carm. 4,3,34: „Quod spiro et placeo, si placeo, tuum est."), sich andererseits aber als Urheber preist (z.B. Hor.carm. 3,30,1–6). Vgl. zum antiken Material auch O. FALTER, Der Dichter und sein Gott bei den Griechen und Römern, Würzburg 1934.

[185] Salvian ep. 9,5: „Tria sunt quae in libellis istis de quibus loquimur, quaeri possunt: cur is qui scripsit ad ecclesiam scripserit et utrum alieno nomine an suo; si non suo, cur alieno, et si alieno, *cur Timothei potissimum nomen quod scriberetur elegerit.*" – „Drei Fragen sind es, die bei dem zur Rede stehenden Buch auftauchen können: Warum der Verfasser es an die Kirche gerichtet und ob er unter einem fremden oder unter seinem eigenen Namen geschrieben hat; wenn nicht unter seinem eigenen, warum er unter fremden Namen schrieb; wenn unter fremdem, *warum er gerade den Namen Timotheus wählte.*" Augustin, De consensu evangelistarum 1,10,15f. stellt dementsprechende Über-

Abgesehen von dem Prinzip der Angemessenheit (s.o.) konnte festgestellt werden: Die spezifischen Beweggründe für Pseudepigraphie beeinflussen bereits die Wahl der *Kategorie* von Pseudonymen:[186] Einem historisch-verkörpernden Namen wohnt als *nobilitatis auctoritatisque perfugium* (Gellius, Noctes Atticae 10,12,8f.) eine autorisierende Funktion inne; ein symbolischer Name hat eine inhaltlich-programmatische Funktion, da er semantisch gerade nicht isoliert ist, sondern als „sprechender Name" bereits auf den Inhalt der Schrift hinweist (symbolische Pseudepigraphie);[187] die Wahl eines Kryptonyms ohne semantische Referenz verweist dagegen in den Bereich der literarischen Anonymität; pseudepigraphische Schriften wiederum, die sich eines Namens von Zeitgenossen bedienen – ein Verfahren, das sonst in der Regel wegen der damit verbundenen persönlichen oder politischen Brisanz selten ist –, verfolgen oft eine polemische Zielrichtung. Bei der frühchristlichen Pseudepigraphie handelt es sich in der Regel[188] um historisch-verkörpernde Namen, die nicht selten als Identifikationsfiguren fungieren.

---

legungen über die gezielte und strategisch geschickte Wahl von pseudonymen Adressaten/Offenbarungsempfängern an.

[186] Die Kategorien der Pseudonyme können dabei zu den Typen literarischer Namen in Beziehung gesetzt werden. Zur Typologie literarischer Namen vgl. z.B. H. BIRUS, Vorschlag zu einer Typologie der literarischen Namen, LiLi 17 Heft 67: Namen (1987), 38–51. Birus unterscheidet vier Typen: 1) verkörpernde Namen mit einer Referenz auf eine historische Person und deren Eigenschaften, 2) klassifizierende Namen, die z.B. auf soziale, nationale oder geschlechterspezifische Gruppen referieren und dadurch gezielt bestimmte Assoziationen wecken, sowie 3) klangsymbolische und 4) redende Namen, die jeweils durch ihre ikonischen bzw. etymologischen Merkmale bedeutsam sind. Mit diesen unterschiedlichen Typen literarischer Namen lassen sich nun die unterschiedlichen Klassen fiktiver Autoren- und Adressatennamen korrelieren. Neben Pseudonymen, die keinerlei gezielte Semantisierung aufweisen (anonyme Pseudonymität), eignet anderen Pseudonymen durch ihre Bildhaftigkeit eine sachlich-inhaltliche Verweisfunktion an (symbolische Pseudonymität). Der größte Teil der antiken Pseudonyme ist indes jener Kategorie zuzuordnen, denen eine personal-verkörpernde Verweisfunktion inhärent ist (pseudepigraphische Pseudonymität); vgl. zur Differenzierung in anonyme, pseudepigraphische und symbolische Pseudonymität auch WOLTER, Pseudonymität (s. Anm. 121); siehe auch bereits SPEYER, Fälschung (s. Anm. 4), 30f., der zwischen Pseudonymität unter Rückgriff auf einen erfundenen Decknamen und Pseudepigraphie unterscheidet.

[187] Vgl. dazu M. JANSSEN, „Evangelium des Zwillings?" – Das Thomasevangelium als Thomasschrift, in: J. Frey / E. E. Popkes / J. Schröter (Hg.), Das Thomasevangelium. Entstehung – Rezeption – Theologie, BZNW 157, Berlin/New York 2008, 222–248 (244–246).

[188] Im Bereich der gnostischen Literatur ist zudem verstärkt ein Rückgriff auf Symbolonyme und Phrenonyme zu verzeichnen; vgl. JANSSEN, ebd. Eine weitere Ausnahme stellt die Pseudepigraphie auf den Namen Jesu dar. Diese ist unterschiedlich motiviert und erfährt auch literarisch ganz unterschiedliche Ausprägungen. Neben dem Briefwechsel zwischen Jesus und Abgar (Eus.h.e. 1,13,6–22) erscheint Jesus als literari-

3) Der Rückgriff auf Identifikationsfiguren kann unterschiedliche literarische Ausdrucksformen annehmen. Deswegen ist ein Blick auf der Pseudepigraphie verwandte literarische Formen wie Interpolation, gezielte Autorfiktion bei literarischer Anonymität (Hebräerbrief) oder der Einsatz literarischer Figuren in narrativen oder dramatischen Textsorten aufschlussreich (siehe die Erwägungen Ciceros oben). Dies gilt verstärkt, wenn man von einer ästhetisch-fiktionalen Dimension von Pseudepigraphie ausgeht (Pastoralbriefe als Briefroman).[189] Ein weiterer Aspekt ist zu nennen, nämlich die Interpolation:[190] Wenn man in Kanonisierungsprozessen einen Beweggrund für frühchristliche Pseudepigraphie sieht, erscheint Pseudepigraphie als sich verselbständigte textexterne Fortschreibung, die ähnliche Ziele wie textinterne Interpolationsverfahren verfolgt.

4) Aufgrund des antiken Materials ist es möglich, „moralische" Bewertungsmaßstäbe für Pseudepigraphie zu finden. Abgesehen von transparenter Pseudepigraphie, die als fiktionale Literatur nicht unter den Verdacht moralischer Anrüchigkeit fällt, existieren Formen von Pseudepigraphie, die legitim und sogar lobenswert erscheinen.[191] Geradezu als positiv

---

sche Figur in der apokryphen Dialogliteratur (vgl. dazu M. JANSSEN, Mystagogus Gnosticus? Zur Gattung der „gnostischen Gespräche des Auferstandenen", in: G. Lüdemann [Hg.], Studien zur Gnosis, ARGU 9, Frankfurt a.M. u.a. 1999, 21–260 [125–181]; HARTENSTEIN, Lehre [s. Anm. 19]). Darüber hinaus ist auf das jüngere, aber frömmigkeitsgeschichtlich höchst relevante Motiv des Himmelsbriefes hinzuweisen, in dem Christus über die Heiligung des Sonntags schreibt; vgl. G. RÖWEKAMP, Art. Sonntagsbrief, in: Lexikon der antiken christlichen Literatur (s. Anm. 29), 647; R. STÜBE, Der Himmelsbrief. Ein Beitrag zur allgemeinen Religionsgeschichte, Tübingen 1918.

[189] Dies lässt die etwa von R. Zimmermann angemahnte Unterscheidung zwischen „literarischen Fiktionen" im Sinne einer Wiederbelebung historischer Personen im Roman und literarischer Pseudonymität als problematisch erscheinen; vgl. R. ZIMMERMANN, Lügen für die Wahrheit? Das Phänomen urchristlicher Pseudepigrafie am Beispiel des Kolosserbriefs, in: O. Hochadel / U. Kocher (Hg.), Lügen und Betrügen. Das Falsche in der Geschichte von der Antike bis zur Moderne, Köln u.a. 2000, 257–272 (259).

[190] Dies wurde vereinzelt bereits geleistet; vgl. z.B. MEADE, Pseudonymity (s. Anm. 31).

[191] Eine solche differenzierte Bewertung ist nicht auf Pseudepigraphie beschränkt. So sind auch Entlehnungen nicht automatisch Diebstahl, sondern können – vergleichbar dem Komplimentzitat – auch die Ehrung dessen im Blick haben, von dem entlehnt wird; vgl. z.B. SCHICKERT, Schutz (s. Anm. 11), 68f. Eine vergleichbare Ambivalenz in der Bewertung ist im Hinblick auf die Imitation festzustellen, die sowohl als Diebstahl (vgl. z.B. Hor.ep. 1,3,15ff.) als auch als Wettstreit angesehen werden kann. Für die Frage, ob eine Entlehnung bzw. Transponierung ins Lateinische Diebstahl (*furtum*) oder eine literarische Leistung (*aemulatio*) ist, gibt es klare Kriterien. Abgesehen von dem Grundsatz, dass es um *kunstvolle* Nachahmung und literarischen Wettkampf mit der entsprechenden Referenzgröße gehen muss (vgl. z.B. Horaz, Ars poetica 128–135; Hor.ep. 1,19), spielt auch hier die Frage nach der Transparenz eine Rolle. Der *offene* Bezug auf das literarische Vorbild und die damit verbundenen Prätexte wird dabei durch unterschiedliche Al-

(καλόν) wertet Jamblich die Pseudepigraphie in der (neu-)pythagoreischen Schule (Iamb.vit.Pyth. 198). Sein Urteil ist nicht singulär: Die Begriffe, die bei den verschiedenen rezipientenseitigen Erklärungen von Schulpseudepigraphie erscheinen, sind insgesamt semantisch positiv besetzt (εὐγνωμοσύνη, εὔνοια, *amor, honor*). Allerdings existieren auch für diese Spielart von Pseudepigraphie Regeln. So kommt der Angemessenheit des Pseudonyms eine große Bedeutung zu. Deutlich ist, dass Inhalt und Pseudonym aufeinander bezogen sein sollten. Wird ein Name zu Unrecht in Anspruch genommen, erfährt die pseudepigraphische Vorgehensweise eine negative Wertung (s.o.).[192] Nach einer arabischen Überlieferung[193] teilt Porphyrius das Œuvre des Pythagoras in Fälschungen und 280 echte Schriften auf, wovon 80 auf Pythagoras selbst zurückzuführen sind, 200 indes von seinen Schülern stammen. Porphyrius unterscheidet also zwischen „echten" *Pseud*pythagorica und Fälschungen, die aus inhaltlichen Gründen den Namen des Pythagoras zu Unrecht tragen: *pseudo*pythagoreisch ist also nicht gleich *pseudo*pythagoreisch. Das bedeutet übertragen auf die neutestamentliche Pseudepigraphie: *Pseudo*paulinisch ist nicht gleich *pseudo*paulinisch. Es wäre – im Sinne der antiken Bewertungsmaßstäbe – also immer die sachliche Nähe zu Paulus und damit verbunden die Angemessenheit der Inanspruchnahme des Pseudonyms zu prüfen.[194] Hier-

---

lusions- und Referenzverfahren verwirklicht. Zum Einsatz kommen z.B. titulare Intertextualität (vgl. Ciceros Orationes Philippicae!), die Aufnahme von ersten Sätzen (vgl. Vergils Aeneis, die den Anfangsvers von Homers Odyssee aufnimmt) und griechische Titel: So betitelt etwa Terenz seine Kömodie, die sich an ein Stück von Menander anlehnt, mit dem griechischen Titel Adelphoe und nicht etwa in seiner lateinischen Übersetzung („Fratres"), um diese Anlehnung kenntlich zu machen (Donat, Commentum Terenti, Praefatio ad Terenz, Adelphoe); vgl. dazu auch G. VOIGT-SPIRA, Gellius und die Komödie, in: E. Stärk / ders. (Hg.), Dramatische Wäldchen (FS Lefèvre), Spudasmata 80, Hildesheim u.a. 2000, 683–698 (695). Zur Transparenz des Übernahmeprozesses im Hinblick auf Zitationstechniken siehe z.B. D. GALL, Zur Technik von Anspielung und Zitat in der römischen Dichtung. Vergil, Gallus und die „Ciris", Zet. 100, München 1999, 22 u.ö.

[192] Ein ähnliches Bild bietet die altkirchliche Literatur: Auch Tertullian entlarvt die von ihm erwähnten Paulusakten als unecht, indem er sie am Inhalt der echten Pauluszeugnisse misst. Da dieser „Test" bezüglich der Frage, ob Frauen taufen und lehren dürfen, am authentischen Paulus (vgl. z.B. 1Kor 14,34f.) gewissermaßen negativ ausfällt, tragen die Akten den Namen des Paulus zu Unrecht (Tert.bapt. 17,4f.); vgl. auch im Hinblick auf das Petrusevangelium Serapion von Antiochien (Eus.h.e. 6,12,2–6).

[193] Vgl. dazu z.B. BROX, Verfasserangaben (s. Anm. 10), 73; B. L. VAN DER WAERDEN, Art. Pythagoras, PRE.S 10 (1965), 843–864 (862f.); BAUM, Pseudepigraphie (s. Anm. 34), 54–56.

[194] Insofern scheint die Differenzierung zwischen Deutero- und Tritopaulinen weiterführend. Hier ist der Sprachgebrauch indes uneinheitlich: H. HÜBNER, An Philemon. An die Kolosser. An die Epheser, HNT 12, Tübingen 1997, 272ff., gebraucht die Termini, um eine theologische Entwicklung aufzuzeigen („von Paulus über Deuteropaulus zu

bei gilt indes, dass Identifikationsfiguren keinen statischen Charakter haben, sondern stets einem komplexen Prozess der Konstruktion und Konstituierung unterworfen sind,[195] was freilich nicht mit einer beliebigen Inanspruchnahme verwechselt werden darf.[196] Insgesamt müssen zudem neben der Autorintention auch die Rezeptionsbedingungen und -erwartungen berücksichtigt werden. Die moralische Bewertung von Pseudepigraphie resultiert aus einem Zusammenspiel von Autorintention und erkenntnisleitendem Interesse der Rezipienten.[197] Dies zeigt nicht zuletzt die Spannbreite in der Bewertung von Fälschungen, die auch als solche intendiert sind. Neben breit bezeugter Kritik bis hin zur juristischen Verfolgung der Fälscher werden auch Fälschungen mit offensichtlicher Täuschungsabsicht durchaus ambivalent beurteilt, was nicht zuletzt aus dem komplexen Verhältnis von Lüge und Wahrheit in der Antike resultiert.[198]

5) Pseudepigraphie ist stets ein Wechselprozess zwischen Produktion und Rezeption. Das Zusammenspiel von Autor und Rezipient impliziert dabei auch die Möglichkeit von Fehlrezeptionen, die nicht auf die Ver-

---

Tritopaulus"), andere bezeichnen die Pastoralbriefe im Gegensatz zu den übrigen deuteropaulinischen Schriften als Tritopaulinen, um den größeren Abstand zu Paulus zu markieren; vgl. z.B. L. OBERLINNER, Die Pastoralbriefe. Teil 3. Kommentar zum Titusbrief, HThK.NT XI/2, Freiburg i. Brsg. u.a. 1996, 16 Anm. 1. Vgl. zum Begriff „Tritopaulinen" auch W. SCHENK, Die Briefe an Timotheus I und II und an Titus (Pastoralbriefe) in der neueren Forschung (1945–1985), ANRW II 25.2 (1987), 3404–3495 (3405); TRUMMER, Paulustradition (s. Anm. 41), 228 u.ö.

[195] Vgl. B. Aland u.a. (Hg.), Literarische Konstituierung von Identifikationsfiguren in der Antike, Studien und Texte zu Antike und Christentum 16, Tübingen 2003; siehe dazu auch meine Rezension in: BZ 51 (2007), 151–153.

[196] Vgl. hier im Hinblick auf die Pastoralbriefe die Erwägungen von A. MERZ, Die fiktive Selbstauslegung des Paulus. Intertextuelle Studien zu Intention und Rezeption der Pastoralbriefe, NTOA 52, Göttingen/Freiburg (CH) 2004, 382–387.

[197] Insgesamt ist Echtheit keine „absolute Kategorie". Die Bewertung von Pseudepigraphie hängt nicht zuletzt vom philosophischen, politischen und religiösen Standpunkt des Kritikers ab; vgl. z.B. STANDHARTINGER, Studien (s. Anm. 28), 31.43 u.ö. Siehe auch den Beitrag von Marco Frenschkowski in diesem Band.

[198] Sujets wie die „Medizinerlüge" bzw. „Notlüge" (z.B. Plato polit. 382f.: τό ὡς ἀληθῶς ψεῦδος, vgl. auch Cicero, Brutus 11,42; Lukian, Philopseudes 1) zeugen eindrücklich von diesem Sachverhalt; siehe dazu J. S. ZEMBATY, Plato's Republic and the Greek Morality on Lying, JHP 26 (1988), 517–545. Der Rückgriff auf die heilsame Täuschung erlangte auch im altkirchlichen Bereich eine hohe Bedeutung; vgl. z.B. A. FÜRST, Hieronymus über die heilsame Täuschung, ZAC 2 (1998), 97–112; zu weiterer Literatur siehe JANSSEN, Namen (s. Anm. 3), 45 Anm. 128. Auch Odysseus als hermeneutische Metapher für einen listigen Menschen (Hom.Od. 108f.) ist hier zu nennen; siehe dazu auch PETER, Wahrheit (s. Anm. 4), 4f.: Größen der Vergangenheit rühmen sich ihrer List. Vgl. auch Aischylos, Frgm. 294. Zum Problem der Bewertung von Lüge und Wahrheit siehe auch die Beiträge in Gill / Wiseman, Lies and Fiction (s. Anm. 158), und die in Anm. 4 zitierte Literatur.

wechslung des realen mit dem fiktiven Autor zu reduzieren sind (s.o.). Mitunter ist ein Pseudonym zweideutig, sodass es auch zu Fehlrezeptionen im Hinblick auf die Kategorie der Pseudonyme kommen kann. Glaubt man den Darlegungen Salvians in seinem neunten Brief, so lag bei seiner Schrift Ad ecclesiam eine fehlerhafte Rezeption vor, da der von Salvian intendierte symbolische Name Timotheus („Ehre Gottes") für einen historischen Namen und damit für eine Referenz auf den Paulusschüler Timotheus gehalten wurde (vgl. Salvian ep. 9,17–20). Dies bleibt nicht ohne Folgen für die Bewertung. Die Auffassung, mit Timotheus sei der Paulusschüler gemeint, würde als Zuflucht zu einem historisch-verkörpernden Pseudonym im Sinne einer *nominum commutatio* als *mendacium* (9,18) moralisch anrüchig sein; ein symbolisches Verständnis sei indes als „offene" Pseudepigraphie legitim.

Erkannte Pseudepigraphie?

Ein Essay über Fiktionalität, Antike und Christentum

von

MARCO FRENSCHKOWSKI

1. Vorgedanken zur Pseudepigraphieforschung

Im Buch des Propheten Jeremia heißt es: „Wie könnt ihr sagen: ‚Wir sind weise und haben das Gesetz des Herrn bei uns'? Ist's doch lauter Lüge, was die Schreiber daraus machen" (8,8)[1]. Obwohl Judentum und Christentum Buch- und Offenbarungsreligionen sind, hat es bereits in der Antike Ansätze gegeben, das geschriebene Wort nicht unkritisch zu rezipieren. Und der Verfasser des 2. Thessalonicherbriefes – nach der herrschenden Mehrheitsmeinung selbst ein pseudepigrapher Autor – lässt sich gar auf ein riskantes und moralisch auch nach antiken Vorstellungen äußerst fragwürdiges Spiel in Sachen echte und unechte Briefe ein: „Was nun das Kommen unseres Herrn Jesus Christus angeht und unsre Vereinigung mit ihm, so bitten wir euch, liebe Brüder, dass ihr euch in eurem Sinn nicht so schnell wankend machen noch erschrecken lasst – weder durch eine Weissagung noch durch ein Wort oder einen Brief, die von uns sein sollen –, als sei der Tag des Herrn schon da. Lasst euch von niemandem verführen, in keinerlei Weise; denn zuvor muss der Abfall kommen und der Mensch der Bosheit offenbart werden, der Sohn des Verderbens" (2Thess 2,1–3). Die innere Rechtfertigung des Autors lag offenbar – sehr allgemein gesprochen

---

[1] Zur Bandbreite der Deutungen s. etwa G. FISCHER, Jeremia 1–25, HThK.AT 30/I, Freiburg i. Brsg. u.a. 2005, 335, und v.a. W. L. HOLLADAY, Jeremiah 1, Hermeneia, Philadelphia 1986, 281–283. Undeutlich ist, ob „Tora" bereits ein Buch (Josias Deuteronomium?) oder allgemeiner „Gesetzesweisung" meint, doch ist Ersteres wahrscheinlicher. Schwerlich richtet sich der Vers gegen jede Form schriftlicher Torafixierung, wie gelegentlich vertreten. Die antiken Übersetzungen divergieren bereits beträchtlich, und die Graeca verkehrt die kaum erträgliche Aussage in ihr Gegenteil (vgl. a.a.O. 281). Just. dial. 71 behauptet jüdische „Verfälschungen" der Schrift; das Thema spielt auch in der Häretikerpolemik eine Rolle: A. BLUDAU, Die Schriftfälschungen der Häretiker. Ein Beitrag zur Textkritik der Bibel, NTA XI/5, Münster 1925.

– in der Bedeutung der Sache, die er zur Sprache zu bringen hatte.[2] Auch kann er davon überzeugt gewesen sein, dass er die „echte Stimme" des Paulus zum Ausdruck bringt, das, was die apostolische Botschaft in der neuen Gemeindesituation gewesen sein würde. Er rechnet jedenfalls nicht damit, dass seine Pseudepigraphie ohne weiteres als solche durchschaubar ist, zugleich jedoch mit einem selbstverständlichen Wissen seiner Leser darum, dass es so etwas wie „Briefe mit falschen Verfasserangaben" gibt.[3] Tatsächlich ist die Echtheit seiner Schrift in der Alten Kirche offenbar niemals angezweifelt worden, auch z.B. von Markion nicht, der den 2Thess seinem Apostolos zurechnet, obwohl unsere Verse 2,1f. nicht direkt für seine Paulusausgabe bezeugt sind.[4] Das ist bemerkenswert, denn in Hinsicht auf andere paulinische Pseudepigraphen war die Kirche durchaus fä-

---

[2] Das folgende Essay ist eine Fortsetzung meiner Studie „Pseudepigraphie und Paulusschule. Gedanken zur Verfasserschaft der Deuteropaulinen, insbesondere der Pastoralbriefe" (in: F. W. Horn [Hg.], Das Ende des Paulus. Historische, theologische und literaturgeschichtliche Aspekte, BZNW 106, Berlin/New York 2001, 239–272). Das dort Gesagte wird hier vorausgesetzt, doch sind kleinere Überschneidungen nicht zu vermeiden.

[3] Eine besondere Pikanterie besteht in der Möglichkeit, dass der von 2Thess als „gefälscht" angegriffene Brief der echte 1Thess gewesen sein könnte. So z.B. A. LINDEMANN, Der Abfassungszweck des zweiten Thessalonicherbriefes, ZNW 68 (1977), 35–47; W. TRILLING, Der zweite Brief an die Thessalonicher, EKK XIV, Zürich u.a. 1980, 76f. S. SCHREIBER, Der Zweite Thessalonicherbrief, in: M. Ebner / S. Schreiber (Hg.), Einleitung in das Neue Testament, KST 6, Stuttgart 2008, erwägt 446 im (buchstäblich) Kleingedruckten diese Möglichkeit, um dagegen 440–443.446–448 2Thess als frühe „Auslegung des 1 Thess" (440) zu verstehen, als pseudepigraphe „Nachjustierung" (ebd.), die sich gegen gewisse Fehlentwicklungen in den paulinischen Gemeinden wende. Sogar von „ersten Schritten einer schriftlichen Paulus-Hermeneutik" (448) ist die Rede, die sich nicht gegen 1Thess wenden könne, da sie sich sonst ihrer eigenen Autoritätsbasis entziehe (ebd.). Damit widerspricht er aber der Deutung, die er wenige Seiten zuvor für möglich gehalten hat. 2Thess 2,2 wendet sich (faktisch) gegen 1Thess oder nicht: beides gleichzeitig ist nicht möglich. Das gilt auch dann, wenn 2Thess natürlich einen „in bestimmter Weise" verstandenen 1Thess (446) meinte, der etwa sekundär (und fälschlich) zur Legitimierung einer unapokalyptisch-präsentischen Eschatologie oder aber einer übersteigerten Naherwartung verwendet wurde. 2Thess würde sich dann gegen eine umlaufende Interpretation des älteren Briefes richten, wenn auch kaum (wie immer wieder vermutet) in Thessalonich selbst, wo die Unechtheit des 1Thess schwerlich plausibel zu machen war. Mit dieser Unklarheit blendet Schreiber aber wie viele Ausleger im Ergebnis die Massivität des expliziten Fälschungsvorwurfes in 2Thess 2,2 aus. Allerdings ist es nicht sicher, dass sich der Vers auf 1Thess bezieht (obwohl ich keine konkurrenzfähige Alternative sehe). Ähnlich wie Schreiber auch U. SCHNELLE, Einleitung in das Neue Testament, Göttingen [6]2007, 366f. („Ein Vorgehen, das einem ntl. Autor nicht unterstellt werden sollte!" – Warum?).

[4] U. SCHMID, Marcion und sein Apostolos, ANTT 25, Berlin/New York 1995, 336; A. VON HARNACK, Marcion. Das Evangelium vom fremden Gott, Leipzig [2]1924 (zusammen mit: Neue Studien zu Marcion), Darmstadt 1985, 114*.

hig, sie als Fälschungen zu durchschauen (z.B. Epiphanius von Salamis, haer. 38,25 (GCS 31,64,19–65,1 Holl/Drummer) über ein kainitisches ἀναβατικὸν Παύλου, oder allgemein Aug.civ. 15,23); dazu weiter später.

Mit der Etablierung der Einsicht, dass nicht wenige frühchristliche und altkirchliche Schriften unter falschen Verfassernamen auf uns gekommen sind, war zwar ein wichtiger Baustein zu einer Kulturgeschichte des christlichen Altertums gegeben, aber es öffneten sich zahlreiche weitere Fragen.[5]

---

[5] Aus der Literatur: K. ALAND, The Problem of Anonymity and Pseudonymity in Christian Literature of the First Two Centuries, JThS 12 (1961), 39–49 = Das Problem der Anonymität und Pseudonymität in der christlichen Literatur der ersten beiden Jahrhunderte, in: ders., Studien zur Überlieferung des Neuen Testaments und seines Textes, ANTT 2, Berlin 1967, 24–34; ders., Falsche Verfasserangaben? Zur Pseudonymität im frühchristlichen Schrifttum, ThRv 75 (1979), 1–10 (Rez. zu Brox, Verfasserangaben); ders., Noch einmal: Das Problem der Anonymität und Pseudonymität in der christlichen Literatur der ersten beiden Jahrhunderte, in: E. Dassmann / K. S. Frank (Hg.), Pietas (FS Kötting) JAC.E 8, Münster 1980, 121–139; auch in: B. Köster / H. U. Rosenbaum / M. Welte (Hg.), Supplementa zu den neutestamentlichen und kirchengeschichtlichen Entwürfen (FS Aland), Berlin 1990, 158–176; H. R. BALZ, Anonymität und Pseudepigraphie im Urchristentum. Überlegungen zum literarischen und theologischen Problem der urchristlichen und gemeinantiken Pseudepigraphie, ZThK 66 (1969), 403–436; R. J. BAUCKHAM, Pseudo-Apostolic Letters, JBL 107 (1988), 469–494; A. D. BAUM, Literarische Echtheit als Kanonkriterium in der alten Kirche, ZNW 88 (1997), 97–110; ders., Pseudepigraphie und literarische Fälschung im frühen Christentum. Mit ausgewählten Quellentexten samt deutscher Übersetzung, WUNT II/138, Tübingen 2001 (mit nützlicher, aber leider bei weitem nicht vollständiger Quellensammlung antiker Stellungnahmen zum Thema); P. F. BEATRICE, Forgery, Propaganda and Power in Christian Antiquity. Some Methodological Remarks, in: W. Blümer u.a. (Hg.), Alvarium (FS Gnilka), JAC.E 33, Münster 2002, 39–51; N. BROX, Falsche Verfasserangaben. Zur Erklärung der frühchristlichen Pseudepigraphie, SBS 79, Stuttgart 1975; ders. (Hg.), Pseudepigraphie in der heidnischen und jüdisch-christlichen Antike, WdF 484, Darmstadt 1977 (Sammlung älterer Aufsätze zum Thema, z.T. leider nur in Auszügen); D. A. CARSON, Pseudonymity and Pseudepigraphy, in: C. A. Evans / S. E. Porter (Hg.), Dictionary of New Testament Background, Downers Grove 2000, 857–864; J. D. G. DUNN, Pseudepigraphy, in: R. P. Martin / P. H. Davids (Hg.), Dictionary of the Later New Testament and its Developments, Leicester 1997, 977–984; E. E. ELLIS, Pseudonymity and Canonicity of New Testament Documents, in: ders., History and Interpretation in New Testament Perspective, Biblical Interpretation Series 54, Leiden 2001, 17–29; FRENSCHKOWSKI, Pseudepigraphie und Paulusschule (s. Anm. 2); P. GERLITZ, Art. Pseudonymität I. Religionsgeschichtlich, TRE 27 (1997), 659–662; M. HENGEL, Anonymität, Pseudepigraphie und „Literarische Fälschung" in der jüdisch-hellenistischen Literatur, in: K. von Fritz (Hg.), Pseudepigrapha I. Pseudopythagorica – Lettres de Platon – Littérature pseudépigraphique juive, EnAC 18, Vandœuvres/Genève 1972, 231–308 = (erweitert) in: M. HENGEL, Judaica et Hellenistica. Kleine Schriften I. Unter Mitarbeit von R. Deines, J. Frey, C. Markschies, A. M. Schwemer mit einem Anhang von H. Bloedhorn, WUNT 90, Tübingen 1996, 196–251; A. HÖLTER, Art. Fälschung II. A-B, DNP 10 (2001), 1076–1079; C. K. HORN, Pseudonymity in Early Christianity. An Inquiry into the Theory of Innocent Deutero-Pauline Pseudonymity, Diss. Southwestern Baptist Theol. Seminary 1996 (Ann Arbor,

Diese beziehen sich einmal auf die Produktion von Pseudepigraphie, aber auch auf ihre Rezeption. Beide Gesichtspunkte gehören zusammen: Wie ist das kulturelle Milieu zu bestimmen, in dem Pseudepigraphie geschrieben und gelesen wird? Ist sie einfach Ausdruck eines allgemeinantiken Schwankens in Hinsicht auf die Zuschreibung geistiger Produkte, oder hat sie spezifische Gründe, die eventuell in jedem Fall einzeln zu eruieren sind? Gibt es jüdische, christlich-großkirchliche, gnostische Besonderhei-

---

University of Michigan); M. JANSSEN, Unter falschem Namen. Eine kritische Forschungsbilanz frühchristlicher Pseudepigraphie, ARGU 14, Frankfurt a.M. u.a. 2003 (exzellente Forschungsgeschichte); F. LAUB, Falsche Verfasserangaben in neutestamentlichen Schriften, TTZ 89 (1982), 228–242; T. D. LEA, Pseudonymity and the New Testament, in: D. A. Black / D. S. Dockery (Hg.), New Testament Criticism and Interpretation, Grand Rapids 1991, 535–559; D. G. MEADE, Pseudonymity and Canon. An Investigation into the Relationship of Authorship and Authority in Jewish and Earliest Christian Tradition, WUNT 39, Tübingen 1986; B. M. METZGER, Literary Forgeries and Canonical Pseudepigrapha, JBL 91 (1972), 3–24; P. POKORNÝ, Das theologische Problem der neutestamentlichen Pseudepigraphie, EvTh 44 (1984), 486–496; ders., Art. Pseudepigraphie I. Altes und Neues Testament, TRE 27 (1997), 645–655; H. J. RIEDL, Anamnese und Apostolizität. Der Zweite Petrusbrief und das theologische Problem neutestamentlicher Pseudepigraphie, RSTh 64, Frankfurt a.M. u.a. 2005; M. RIST, Pseudepigraphy and the Early Christians, in: D. Aune (Hg.), Studies in New Testament and Early Christian Literature (FS Wikgren), NT.S 33, Leiden 1972, 75–91; G. SCHÖLLGEN, Pseudapostolizität und Schriftgebrauch in den ersten Kirchenordnungen. Anmerkungen zur Begründung des frühen Kirchenrechts, in: ders. (Hg.), Stimuli. Exegese und ihre Hermeneutik in Antike und Christentum (FS Dassmann), JAC.E 23, Münster 1996, 96–121; J. A. SINT, Pseudonymität im Altertum. Ihre Formen und ihre Gründe, Commentationes Aenipontanae 15, Innsbruck 1960; W. SPEYER, Religiöse Pseudepigraphie und literarische Fälschung im Altertum, JAC 8/9 (1965/66), 88–125 (= Brox, a.a.O. 195–263); ders., Die literarische Fälschung im heidnischen und christlichen Altertum. Ein Versuch ihrer Deutung, HAW I/2, München 1971 (grundlegend; vgl. die Rezensionen von H. HUNGER, ByZ 63 [1973], 387–389, und W. G. KÜMMEL, ThR 38 [1974], 64f.); ders., Fälschung, pseudepigraphische freie Erfindung und ‚echte religiöse Pseudepigraphie', in: von Fritz, a.a.O. 331–366 = W. SPEYER, Frühes Christentum im antiken Strahlungsfeld. Ausgewählte Aufsätze, WUNT 50, Tübingen 1989, 100–139; ders. / M. HEIMGARTNER, Art. Pseudepigraphie, DNP 13 (1999), 509–512; G. STEMBERGER, Pseudonymität und Kanon. Zum gleichnamigen Buch von David G. Meade, JBTh 3 (1988), 267–273; ders., Art. Pseudepigraphie II. Judentum, TRE 27 (1997), 656–659; F. TORM, Die Psychologie der Pseudonymität im Hinblick auf die Literatur des Urchristentums, SLA 2, Gütersloh 1932 (eine der wenigen religionspsychologischen Studien zum Thema; sollte nicht übersehen werden. Zur Kritik vgl. JANSSEN, a.a.O. 37–46); M. WOLTER, Die anonymen Schriften des Neuen Testaments. Annäherungsversuch an ein literarisches Phänomen, ZNW 79 (1988), 1–16; T. L. WILDER, Pseudonymity, the New Testament, and Deception. An Inquiry into Intention and Reception, Lanham 2004; M. WOLTER, Art. Pseudonymität II. Kirchengeschichtlich, TRE 27 (1997), 662–670; R. ZIMMERMANN, Unecht – und doch wahr? Pseudepigraphie im Neuen Testament als theologisches Problem, ZNT 12 (2003), 27–38. Daneben enthalten viele Einleitungen Exkurse zum Thema.

ten? War sie in der Antike, zumindest in bestimmten Bildungsschichten bzw. für bestimmte Textgruppen, als solche durchschaubar, also vielleicht gar eine stillschweigende Übereinkunft zwischen Autoren und Publikum? Galt sie – wenn erkannt – durchgehend als Betrug, oder konnte sie als Stilmittel gewertet werden, das dann eventuell bei Bekanntwerden der Pseudepigraphie ein Werk nicht desavouierte? Diese Fragen sind mittlerweile zumindest partiell beantwortet, wobei sich ein überaus differenziertes Bild ergibt, das für keine der genannten Fragen eine allgemeingültige Antwort erlaubt, sondern jeweils sorgfältiger Unterscheidung der Genres und literarischen Milieus bedarf. Es kann daher nicht mehr einfach (wie immer wieder geschehen) aus allgemeinen Beobachtungen oder z.B. solchen zur Pseudepigraphie in den Philosophenschulen auf die neutestamentlichen Autoren zurückgeschlossen werden. Doch ergibt sich aus dem Umfeld des NT ein Raum von Plausibilitäten, die sorgfältig beachtet werden wollen, zumal sie weitab von denen der literarischen Moderne liegen.

In der Diskussion über die neutestamentlichen Pseudepigraphen wurde das wissenschaftliche Binnengespräch über die in Frage stehenden einzelnen Texte immer komplexer (zumal es immer wieder abweichende Hypothesen gab),[6] während gleichzeitig der tatsächliche Vergleich mit dem konkreten pseudepigraphen Schrifttum der Umwelt früher Christen nicht selten stärker in den Hintergrund trat,[7] vor allem wurde das Phäno-

---

[6] In Verfasserschaftsfragen fällt, um Walter Bauer zu zitieren, „die sichere Entscheidung nur dem Ignoranten leicht." Ders., Heinrich Julius Holtzmann, in: ders., Aufsätze und kleine Schriften, hg. v. G. Strecker, Tübingen 1967, 308. Daher kann die Diskussion um die Tatsächlichkeit eines Vorliegens von Pseudepigraphie bei ntl. Schriften nur selten (vielleicht nie) als abgeschlossen betrachtet werden.

[7] Nur eine kurze Zwischenbemerkung können wir der These Udo Schnelles zuwenden, die frühchristliche Pseudepigraphie sei ein zeitlich befristetes Phänomen: „Die ntl. Pseudepigraphie ist zeitlich deutlich eingrenzbar, die meisten pseudepigraphischen Schriften entstanden zwischen 60 und 100 n. Chr., wobei die Protopaulinen und die Ignatius-Briefe die jeweilige Grenze bilden. Der genannte Zeitraum stellt innerhalb der Geschichte des Urchristentums eine Epoche des Umbruchs und der Neuorientierung dar" (Einleitung in das Neue Testament [s. Anm. 3], 323). Diese sachlich offenkundig unzutreffende These (die meisten Deuteropaulinen z.B. sind ja nach diesem Zeitfenster entstanden, vom Alexandriner- und Laodizenerbrief über den 3Kor, den Briefwechsel Paulus-Seneca und die Visio Pauli bis zu den zahlreichen gnostischen Deuteropaulinen) resultiert wohl aus der Konzentration des Blicks nur auf die kanonische Literatur. Dennoch wird sie wiederholt in ders., Theologie des Neuen Testaments, Göttingen 2007, 499. Vgl. zur Kritik FRENSCHKOWSKI, Pseudepigraphie und Paulusschule (s. Anm. 2), 241f. Leider entgeht auch G. THEISSEN, Die Entstehung des Neuen Testaments als literaturgeschichtliches Problem, Heidelberg 2007, 148–154, dieser Gefahr nicht, indem er ebenfalls von einer „pseudepigraphen Phase" des Urchristentums spricht, in der „Nachahmungsliteratur" produziert worden sei. Auch hier ist die Alte Kirche aus dem Blick geraten, in der sich diese „Phase" ungebrochen fortgesetzt hätte, natürlich nur als ein Teil der immer komplexer werdenden christlichen Literaturproduktion. Theißens Unterscheidung zwi-

men Pseudepigraphie selbst als im Grunde nicht weiter erklärungsbedürftiges Stilmittel einer zweiten und dritten Generation hingenommen. Freilich hat es immer wieder Gegenbewegungen gegeben, aber in neutestamentlichen Einleitungen und Kommentaren wird doch nach wie vor sehr viel mehr diskutiert, ob ein Text pseudepigraph ist oder nicht, als z.B. wie genau und in welchem Milieu eine eventuelle Pseudepigraphie zu verstehen sein könnte, und wie sie sich eventuell von der Pseudepigraphie anderer Texte unterscheidet. Es wurde damit sehr viel Energie auf die Fragen verwendet, ob oder ob nicht eine bestimmte Schrift pseudepigraph ist, jedoch deutlich weniger auf das Problem, was diese Pseudepigraphie für das Milieu, die geistige Welt ihrer Autoren und Leser, besagt. Gewisse allgemeine Auskünfte („Schulzusammenhänge", „Neuinterpretation", „Adaption für die Fragen der Gegenwart", „geisterfüllte Aktualisierung") dienten oft eher der nachträglichen theologischen Legitimierung als der tatsächlichen historischen Forschung und argumentieren nicht selten mit sehr allgemeinen Plausibilitäten. Hinzu treten viele unbeantwortete Detailfragen. Wie wurde Pseudepigraphie verbreitet, wie erreichte sie den entstehenden christlichen Büchermarkt, der offensichtlich subkulturellen Charakter hatte, also bis in das 4. Jh. anderen Gesetzen unterlag als der profane antike Büchermarkt (über den wir einiges an Informationen besitzen)? Zu diesen Fragen wird noch viel Forschung erforderlich sein.

Die folgenden Beobachtungen und Gedanken wollen das Gespräch über Pseudepigraphie an einer Reihe von begrenzten Teilthemen stärker an eine Diskussion der antiken Parallelen und der sich aus ihnen ergebenden Fragen anbinden. Ein erheblicher Teil der theologischen Literatur zum Thema ist den Bemühungen gewidmet, den Begriff „Fälschung" für pseudepigraphe Literatur zu umgehen. Dies kann im historisch-kritischen Diskurs nur so geschehen, dass überprüft werden muss, inwiefern Pseudepigraphie in gewissen antiken Kontexten ethisch akzeptabel gewesen sein könnte. Doch soll im Folgenden nicht diese vielfach verhandelte Frage der moralischen Wertung im Mittelpunkt stehen, sondern die weit seltener untersuchte Vorfrage der faktischen Zurkenntnisnahme von Pseudepigraphie in antiken Literaturen, und von hier ein Bogen geschlagen werden zu den divergierenden Fiktionalitätsdiskursen von Christen und Heiden. Wir betrachten jeweils nur einige exemplarische Fälle, um ein Fundament zu legen für die allgemeineren Beobachtungen, in die das vorliegende Essay einmündet und die vielleicht einen kleinen Beitrag zur Wegrichtung künftiger Pseudepigraphieforschung leisten können.

---

schen charismatischer und pseudepigrapher Phase scheint mir zu schematisch, obwohl sie ohne Frage etwas sehr Wichtiges sieht und vielleicht nur der Weiterentwicklung und Präzisierung in Hinsicht auf die nachntl. Zeit bedarf.

2. Haben frühe Christen die Pseudepigraphie weiter Teile ihrer Literatur durchschaut?

Aber haben denn die Christen überhaupt gewusst, dass erhebliche Teile ihres Schrifttums unter fingiertem Verfassernamen umliefen? Wenn wir nach erkannter Pseudepigraphie unter Christen fragen, müssen wir mit der Beobachtung beginnen, dass frühe Christen sehr oft, ja im Allgemeinen, Pseudepigraphie aus ihren eigenen Reihen, vor allem in ihrem Kanon *nicht* als solche erkannt haben. In manchen Fällen ist das ganz erstaunlich. Wir wollen den Blick nicht gleich auf das Neue Testament richten, sondern beginnen mit einen scheinbar harmlosen Beispiel: dem apokryphen Briefwechsel Paulus-Seneca. Die Tatsache, dass sich der berühmteste stoische Philosoph seiner Zeit und der Apostel zur gleichen Zeit in Rom aufgehalten haben, hat offenbar schon früh die Spekulation genährt, ob sich die beiden nicht getroffen haben könnten. „Seneca saepe noster" (Tert.an. 20,1) genoss unter Christen eine beträchtliche Hochachtung, die sich ungebrochen ins Mittelalter fortsetzte.[8] Ein ganz besonders unbegabter, geist- und witzloser Schreiberling hat aus dieser Denkmöglichkeit (Paulus und Seneca könnten sich in Rom kennengelernt haben) Mitte des 4. Jh. oder sogar etwas später einen Briefwechsel zwischen beiden mit insgesamt 14 Briefen gebastelt.[9] Diese Briefe sind vollständig inhaltsleer und bieten insbesondere keine Theologie.[10] Zu anderen Deuteropaulinen stehen sie insofern in einigem Kontrast, auch zu nachneutestamentlichen wie dem Laodizenerbrief. Alfons Fürst hat sie sehr zutreffend als „Freundschaftsbillets" bezeichnet,[11] deren einziger Daseinszweck eben ihre Existenz ist. Sie sollen keine Inhalte transportieren, sondern den Sachverhalt einer Beziehung zwischen Seneca und Paulus als solchen behaupten bzw. inszenieren. Daraus ergibt sich natürlich eine „hidden agenda", die aber nicht unbedingt

---

[8] W. TRILLITZSCH, Seneca im literarischen Urteil der Antike. Darstellung und Sammlung der Zeugnisse, 2 Bd., Amsterdam 1971, hier 1,120–221; 2,362–419. Zum Thema Seneca und das Christentum vgl. auch G. SCARPAT, Il pensiero religioso di Seneca e l'ambiente ebraico e cristiano, Brescia ²1983.

[9] Der apokryphe Briefwechsel zwischen Seneca und Paulus zusammen mit dem Brief des Mordechai an Alexander und dem Brief des Annaeus Seneca über Hochmut und Götterbilder. Eingel., übers. u. m. interpret. Essays vers. v. A. FÜRST u.a., SAPERE XI, Tübingen 2006.

[10] Ich halte es für übertrieben, wenn A. Fürst aus Brief 1 und 14 eine gnostisierende Neigung des Autors extrahieren will (a.a.O. 36 Anm. 1; 62–64 Anm. 204.206.208). Die von ihm angeführten Stellen sind vage Berührungen ohne großes Gewicht, wie er selbst auch sieht (vgl. 10–21 seine Diskussion von Inhalt und Intention).

[11] A.a.O. 16.

theologischer Art ist. Eher geht es um die (durchaus erfolgreiche)[12] Vereinnahmung Senecas für das entstehende christliche Bildungswesen, und umgekehrt um den Versuch, Paulus bildungsbürgerlich (sit venia verbo) aufzuwerten. Dennoch ist das Niveau der Briefe sprachlich und gedanklich gering. Erasmus von Rotterdam – der ihre Pseudepigraphie durchschaut hatte – schreibt dazu: „His epistolis non video quid fingi possit frigidius aut ineptus; et tamen quisque fuit autor, hoc egit ut nobis persuaderet ut Senecam fuisse Christianum" (ep. 2092 von 1515),[13] um dann die gegen eine Echtheit sprechenden Argumente zu benennen. Aber wie wurden sie von ihren ersten christlichen Lesern aufgenommen? Laktanz kannte diesen Briefwechsel noch nicht, obwohl er derjenige lateinische Kirchenschriftsteller ist, der Seneca am häufigsten zitiert und wohl am höchsten einschätzt.[14] (Dies ist ein entscheidendes Argument gegen eine frühere Datierung.) Hieronymus und Augustinus sind die Ersten, die den Briefwechsel erwähnen, und beide können sich nicht zu einer klaren Ablehnung durchringen. Hieronymus nimmt Seneca gar in seine Galerie christlicher Autoren auf – ein Kuriosum, das direkt auf unser doppeltes Pseudepigraphon und die Unwilligkeit des Kirchenvaters zu deutlicher Kritik an diesem zurückgeht: „Lucius Annaeus Seneca Cordubensis, Sotionis Stoici discipulus et patruus Lucani potae, continentissimae vitae fuit. Quem non ponerem in catalogo sanctorum, nisi me illae epistolae provocarent quae leguntur a plurimis, Pauli ad Senecam aut Senecae ad Paulum, in quibus, cum esset Neronis magister et illius temporis potentissimus, optare se dicit eius esse loci apud suos cuius sit Paulus apud Christianos. Hic ante biennium quam Petrus et Paulus martyrio coronarentur a Nerone interfectus est" (vir.ill. 12). „Ille epistolae" könnte darauf hindeuten, dass die Briefe erst kürzlich in den Blick der lesenden Christen geraten sind. Hieronymus lässt eine gewisse Distanz spüren (leguntur a plurimis): Offenbar ist ihm das geringe Niveau der Briefe bewusst, aber die Konsequenz einer wirklichen Infragestellung ihrer Autorschaft zieht er nicht. Ähnliches gilt für Augustinus wenige Jahre später. „Merito ait Seneca, qui temporibus apostolorum fuit, cuius etiam quaedam ad Paulum apostolum leguntur epistolae: Omnes odit, qui malos odit" (ep. 153,14; das Senecazitat ist offenbar spurios und stammt auch nicht aus einem bekannten Pseudepigraphon). Auch Augustin zeigt keine rechte Begeisterung für das Machwerk. Aber weder Hieronymus noch Augustin ziehen Pauli und Senecas Autorschaft konsequent in

---

[12] „Die Fälschung der Briefe hat vielleicht dazu beigetragen, den echten Seneca zu retten", A. MOMIGLIANO, Bemerkungen über die Legende vom Christentum Senecas, in: ders., Ausgewählte Schriften 2, Stuttgart 1999, 69 (zuerst italien. als: Note sulla leggenda del cristianesimo di Seneca, Rivista di Storia Italiana 62 [1950], 325–344).

[13] Text bei FÜRST, Der apokryphe Briefwechsel (s. Anm. 9), 74.

[14] R. M. OGILVIE, The Library of Lactantius, Oxford 1978, 73–77.

Frage; man spürt nur ihr Unbehagen. Andere frühe Zeugnisse scheint es nicht zu geben.[15]

Diese Beobachtung ließe sich leicht verallgemeinern. Kritischer Umgang mit Quellen war kein Kennzeichen der entstehenden christlichen Bildungskultur. Nennen wir noch ein Beispiel aus dem Umfeld Augustins. In seiner Diskussion mit Manichäern in Nordafrika – mit den Lehrern Fortunatus und Faustus – wird einmal auch die Verfasserschaft biblischer Texte zum Problem. Für den gebildeten Lehrer Faustus ist gute Kenntnis beider Testamente selbstverständlich; er zitiert z.B. ausgiebig aus dem Corpus Paulinum, um die Postionen des älteren Manichäers Adimantus (Adda, Manis Hauptmissionar im Westen) zu verteidigen. Dabei rechnet er auch mit der Möglichkeit von Textkorruptionen (Augustinus, contra Faustum Manichaeum 11,1). Faustus wendet gegen die Christen ein, sie würden das Alte Testament willkürlich-selektiv lesen, aber auf der vollständigen Gültigkeit des Neuen Testaments bestehen (contra Faustum Manichaeum 32,1).

Auf diese Gedanken hin fährt Faustus fort (wir zitieren leichterer Lektüre zuliebe die einzige vollständige englische Übersetzung): „If there are parts of the Testament of the Father which we are not bound to observe (for you attribute the Jewish law to the Father, and it is well known that many things in it shock you, and make you ashamed, so that in heart you no longer regard it as free from corruption, though, as you believe, the Father Himself partly wrote it for you with His own finger while part was written by Moses, who was faithful and trustworthy), the Testament of the Son must be equally liable to corruption, and may equally well contain objectionable things; especially as it is allowed not to have been written by the Son Himself, nor by His apostles, but long after, by some unknown men, who, lest they should be suspected of writing of things they knew nothing of, gave to their books the names of the apostles, or of those who were thought to have followed the apostles, declaring the contents to be according to these originals. In this, I think, they do grievous wrong to the disciples of Christ, by quoting their authority for the discordant and contradictory statements in these writings, saying that it was according to them that they wrote the Gospels, which are so full of errors and discrepancies, both in facts and in opinions, that they can be harmonized neither with themselves nor with one another. This is nothing else than to slander good men, and to bring the charge of dissension on the brotherhood of the disciples. In reading the Gospels, the clear intention of our heart perceives the errors, and, to avoid all injustice, we accept whatever is useful, in the

---

[15] Sammlung der Zeugnisse bei FÜRST, Der apokryphe Briefwechsel (s. Anm. 9), 68–71.

way of building up our faith, and promoting the glory of the Lord Christ, and of the Almighty God, His Father, while we reject the rest as unbecoming the majesty of God and Christ, and inconsistent with our belief" (32,2).[16] Augustinus antwortet darauf: „We give to the whole Old Testament Scriptures their due praise as true and divine; you impugn the Scriptures of the New Testament as having been tampered with and corrupted. Those things in the Old Testament which we do not observe we hold to have been suitable appointments for the time and the people of that dispensation, besides being symbolical to us of truths in which they have still a spiritual use, though the outward observance is abolished; and this opinion is proved to be the doctrine of the apostolic writings. You, on the other hand, find fault with everything in the New Testament which you do not receive, and assert that these passages were not spoken or written by Christ or His apostles. In these respects there is a manifest difference between us. When, therefore, you are asked why you do not receive all the contents of the New Testament, but, while you approve of some things, reject a great many in the very same books as false and spurious interpolations, you must not pretend to imitate us in the distinction which we make, reverently and in faith, but must give account of your own presumption" (contra Faustum Manichaeum 32,8). Etwas weiter kommt Augustinus auf das Thema zurück: „Why, then, do you not accept everything in the New Testament? Is it because the books have not the authority of Christ's apostles, or because the apostles taught what was wrong? You reply that the books have not the authority of the apostles. That the apostles were wrong in their teaching is what Pagans say. But what can you say to prove that the publication of these books cannot be traced to the apostles? You reply that in many things they contradict themselves and one another. Nothing could be more untrue; the fact is, you do not understand. In every case where Faustus has brought forward what you think a discrepancy, we have shown that there was none; and we will do the same in every other case. It is intolerable that the reader or learner should dare to lay the blame on Scriptures of such high authority, instead of confessing his own stupidity. ... Your only answer to this would be, that you could not possibly alter documents already in the possession of all Christians; for at the very outset of such an attempt, it would be met by an appeal to older copies. But if this proves that the books could not be corrupted by you, it also proves that they could not be corrupted by any one. The first person who ventured to do such a thing would be convicted by a comparison of older manuscripts;

---

[16] Diese und die folgenden Übersetzungen stammen aus der Fassung der Nicene and Post-Nicene Fathers IV. St. Augustine. The Writings against the Manichaeans and against the Donatists, New York 1887 (c. Faust. übers. v. R. Stothert). Die lateinische Fassung findet sich PL 42 und CSEL 25,1, hg. v. J. Zycha.

especially as the Scripture is to be found not in one language only, but in many. As it is, false readings are sometimes corrected by comparing older copies or the original language. Hence you must either acknowledge these documents as genuine, and then your heresy cannot stand a moment; or if they are spurious, you cannot use their authority in support of your doctrine of the Paraclete, and so you refute yourselves" (32,16).

Man sieht sehr deutlich, wie die beiden Kontrahenten aneinander vorbeireden. Die Autoritätsgläubigkeit Augustins scheint den schlichten Vorwurf der Pseudepigraphie gar nicht ernsthaft aufzugreifen, sondern zieht sich auf das Problem der Textkritik zurück: Die christlichen Texte sind solide überliefert, wie ihre breite Streuung und große Zahl plausibel macht. Freilich – nach einer längeren Ausführung zu anderen Fragen – kommt Augustinus doch noch einmal auf die Verfasserschaftsfrage zurück:

„We can now answer the question, how we know that these books were written by the apostles. In a word, we know this in the same way that you know that the books whose authority you are so deluded as to prefer were written by Manichæus. For, suppose some one should raise a question on this point, and should contend, in arguing with you, that the books which you attribute to Manichæus are not of his authorship; your only reply would be, to ridicule the absurdity of thus gratuitously calling in question a matter confirmed by successive testimonies of such wide extent. As, then, it is certain that these books are the production of Manichæus, and as it is ridiculous in one born so many years after to start objections of his own, and so raise a discussion on the point; with equal certainty may we pronounce it absurd, or rather pitiable, in Manichæus or his followers to bring such objections against writings originally well authenticated, and carefully handed down from the times of the apostles to our own day through a constant succession of custodians.

We have now only to compare the authority of Manichæus with that of the apostles. The genuineness of the writings is equally certain in both cases. But no one will compare Manichæus to the apostles, unless he ceases to be a follower of Christ, who sent the apostles. Who that did not misunderstand Christ's words ever found in them the doctrine of two natures opposed to one another, and having each its own principle? Again, the apostles, as becomes the disciples of truth, declare the birth and passion of Christ to have been real events; while Manichæus, who boasts that he leads into all truth, would lead us to a Christ whose very passion he declares to have been an illusion. The apostles say that Christ was circumcised in the flesh which He took of the seed of Abraham; Manichæus says that God, in his own nature, was cut in pieces by the race of darkness. The apostles say that a sacrifice was offered for Christ as an infant in our nature, according to the institutions of the time; Manichæus, that a member, not of humanity, but of the divine substance itself, must be sacrificed to the whole host of demons by being introduced into the nature of the hostile race. The apostles say that Christ, to set us an example, was baptized in the Jordan; Manichæus, that God immersed himself in the pollution of darkness, and that he will never wholly emerge, but that the part which cannot be purified will be condemned to eternal punishment. The apostles say that Christ, in our nature, was tempted by the chief of the demons; Manichæus, that part of God was taken captive by the race of demons. And in the temptation of Christ He resists the tempter; while in the captivity of God, the part taken captive cannot be restored to its origin even after victory. To conclude, Manichæus, under the guise of an improvement, preaches another gospel, which is the doctrine of devils; and the apostles, after the doctrine of Christ, enjoin that whoever preaches another gospel shall be accursed" (32,21f.). Das folgende Buch 33 beginnt mit einem völlig neuen Thema, kommt aber ebenfalls in Kap. 6 noch einmal auf die Pseudepigraphiefrage zurück. Die lange Zeugenkette verbürge die Echtheit der neutestamentlichen Bücher: Augustin kontrastiert mit den Schriften des Corpus Hippocraticum, von denen manche echt, andere unecht seien, was sich aber schon aus ihrer Bezeugung und dem inhaltlichen Vergleich mit den echten Texten leicht erschließen lasse.[17] Zum Problem wurde das Thema für Augustin nicht wirklich. Wir haben diese Aussagen etwas ausführlicher im Kontext zitiert, weil sie zeigen, wie ein stabiler Kanon- und Orthodoxiediskurs bestimmte Fragen nicht mehr zugelassen hat.

Blicken wir im Kontrast kurz auf den bekanntesten, immer wieder zitierten Fall einer durchschauten Pseudepigraphie, den des Salvian von Marseille (geb. vor 400, gest. um 480).[18] Dieser – Asket, aber kein Kleriker – hatte unter dem Pseudonym „Timotheus" vier Bücher Reichtumskritik an die „Herrin Kirche" geschrieben, also eine Verteidigung des asketischen Lebens gegen die sich etablierende Kirche Galliens. Ein befreundeter Bischof, Salonius, hatte das durchschaut und Salvian auf die Sache angesprochen. Salvian verteidigt sich (ohne die Fälschung förmlich einzugestehen)

---

[17] Leider steht nur dieser Abschnitt aus contra Faustum Manichaeum mit Text und Übersetzung auch in der Textsammlung bei BAUM, Pseudepigraphie und literarische Fälschung (s. Anm. 5), 206–209.
[18] Hauptquelle über sein Leben ist Gennadius, vir.ill. 68. Für das Folgende vgl. v.a. Salvian von Marseille, Des Timotheus vier Bücher an die Kirche. Der Brief an den Bischof Salonius. Dt. Übersetzung von A. Mayer. Bearbeitet von N. Brox, SKV 3, München 1983 (mit einem Anhang zu Leben und Werk des Salvian von N. Brox). Neueste Textausgabe ist G. Lagarrigue, Salvien de Marseille. Œuvres tome I. Les lettres. Les livres de Timothée à l'Église. Introduction, texte critique, traduction et notes, SC 176, Paris 1971.

ausführlich in einem erhaltenen Brief an Salonius (ep. 9).[19] Hauptargument ist, der Wert des Buches solle nicht unter der Unwürdigkeit des wahren Verfassers in Mitleidenschaft geraten. Eifer und Liebe für Gottes Sache hätten ihn zu seinem Schritt bewogen. Andererseits solle das Buch nicht der Eitelkeit des Verfassers dienen, sondern der Ehre Gottes (was mit dem Hauptargument schlecht zusammengeht).[20] Was Salvian nicht sagt, ist, dass er sich selbst auf diese Weise aus der Schusslinie gegen sein kirchenkritisches Buch nimmt.[21] Die Verfasserangabe wäre im Grunde nur eine Art Metapher, keine Fälschung. Sofort ist deutlich, dass Salvian in Erklärungsnotstand gerät. Von einer problemlosen Akzeptanz oder sofortigen, konsensuellen Durchschaubarkeit seines Stilmittels kann keine Rede sein. Er muss sich gegen den Vorwurf der Fälschung wehren und tut dies mit gewundenen, damals wie heute nicht völlig überzeugenden Argumenten.

Weniger Beachtung hat merkwürdigerweise gefunden, dass Salvian andernorts selbst gegen Schriftfälschungen der Häretiker polemisiert. So schreibt er gegen die arianischen Vandalen und Goten: „Es könnte jemand sagen ..., sie, die Häretiker, lesen dasselbe wie wir, haben dieselben Propheten Gottes, dieselben Apostel, dieselben Evangelisten ... Wie soll das dasselbe sein, was ehedem bös gesinnte Verfasser böswillig untergeschoben und böswillig überliefert haben (quae ab auctoribus quondam malis et male sunt interpolata at male tradita)? Schon deshalb ist es nicht dasselbe, weil das nicht vollständig dasselbe sein kann, was in irgendeinem Teile verfälscht ist (vitiata), denn keine Unversehrtheit (incolumitatem) hat, was die Vollkommenheit verloren hat" (De gubernatione Dei 5,2, hg. v. Pauly 102f.).[22] Wir haben also eventuell den gleichen Fall wie (vielleicht) im 2Thess vor uns: einen Fälscher, der gegen Fälschungen polemisiert. Ähnliches gilt ja für den 3. Korintherbrief, der vielleicht vom gleichen kleinasiatischen Verfasser wie die Paulusakten stammt: Auch dieser pseudepigraphe Paulus wehrt sich gegen Veränderung seiner Worte.[23] Ebenso beschwert sich der fiktionale Petrus der pseudo-clementinischen Homilien brieflich (!) über Verfälschungen seiner Worte (PsClem H, ep. Petri 2, 4–7,

---

[19] Übersetzt bei Salvian v. Marseille, a.a.O. 125–133.

[20] Interessant ist, dass Salvian beiläufig die moderne (sachlich unwahrscheinliche) Deutung der Widmung des lukanischen Doppelwerkes als Fiktion vorwegnimmt (ebenfalls ep. 9). Vgl. dazu v.a. C. HEIL / T. KLAMPFL, Theophilus (Lk 1,3; Apg 1,1), in: C. G. Müller (Hg.), „Licht zur Erleuchtung der Heiden und Herrlichkeit für dein Volk Israel". Studien zum lukanischen Doppelwerk (FS Zmijewski), BBB 151, Hamburg 2005, 7–28.

[21] So Brox in seinem Erläuterungsteil zu Salvian v. Marseille, Des Timotheus vier Bücher (s. Anm. 18), 147.

[22] Vgl. BLUDAU, Die Schriftfälschungen der Häretiker (s. Anm. 1), 54, dessen Übersetzung ich auch zitiere. Zu Salvian vgl. noch bes.: N. BROX, Quis ille auctor? Pseudonymität und Anonymität bei Salvian, VigChr 40 (1986), 55–65.

[23] M. Testuz, Papyrus Bodmer X–XII, Cologny/Genève 1959, 7–45.

hg. v. B. Rehm / J. Irmscher / F. Paschke). Für die Psychologie der Verfasser ist das sehr aufschlussreich. Sie wähnen sich mit ihren Sachanliegen so sehr im „Recht", dass ihnen die Absurdität dieses Verhaltens nicht in den Blick kommt. Es berührt uns ja auch ähnlich merkwürdig, wenn sich z.B. gerade Rufinus in seiner Vorrede zu Origenes περὶ ἀρχῶν über Verfälschungen des Origenes durch Häretiker echauffiert, die er mit seinen massiven Texteingriffen wieder zurechtrücke (1 praef. Rufini 4–6, hg. v. H. Görgemanns / H. Karpp). Die gewundene, unkonkrete Ausdrucksweise des Salvian zeigt m.E. auch, dass er gar keine spezifischen Beispiele im Sinn hat, sondern allgemein sagen will: Alles, was die Häretiker benutzen, muss a priori verfälscht sein.[24] Die Zahl der Timotheus-Apokryphen ist auch sonst bis ins Mittelalter sehr hoch; Salvian wählt den Namen mit Bedacht.[25]

Bis in eine sehr späte Zeit der Alten Kirche konnte die Behauptung einer Verfasserschaft in apostolischer Zeit noch rezipiert werden, wenn nur der Inhalt der gerade herrschenden Theologie entsprach. Ein berühmtes Beispiel ist das Corpus Dionysiacum, das wohl Ende des 5., Anfang des 6. Jh. im Namen des Dionysios Areopagita (Apg 17,34) auftrat und zudem noch dem Paulusschüler Timotheus gewidmet war. Obwohl dieses mystische Textcorpus spätneuplatonische Philosophie voraussetzt, wurde seine Autorschaft lange Zeit kaum in Zweifel gezogen. Mit großem Raffinement werden hier an verschiedenen Stellen Bezüge auf Personen der neutestamentlichen Zeit in den Text einbezogen, um die Verfasserfiktion aufrechtzuerhalten. Johannes Philoponus, Johannes von Skythopolis, Gregor der Große, Leontius von Byzanz und der erste Kommentator Maximus Confessor hielten die Texte bereits für echt, z.T. mit wütendem Ungestüm gegen Andersdenkende (Zweifel äußerte immerhin Hypatius von Ephesus).[26]

Es hat freilich auch schon früher – aber eben nur auffallend vereinzelt – Fälle deutlich durchschauter und entlarvter (nicht einfach nur abstrakt wegen Heterodoxie behaupteter) Pseudepigraphie gegeben. Erinnern wir kurz an den bekanntesten Fall. Tertullian[27] berichtet: „Quodsi quae Acta Pauli, quae perperam scripta sunt, exemplum Theclae ad licentiam mulierum do-

---

[24] Zum durchgehenden Vorwurf der Alten Kirche, Häretiker hätten die Schrift verfälscht, vgl. BLUDAU, Die Schriftfälschungen der Häretiker (s. Anm. 1), passim, der zeigt, dass dieser Vorwurf in vielen Fällen freie Erfindung ist bzw. sich auf Textvarianten bezieht, die auch andernorts gut bezeugt sind.

[25] Eine (freilich nicht vollständige) Übersicht gibt H. VON LIPS, Timotheus und Titus. Unterwegs für Paulus, BG 19, Leipzig 2008, 159–189.

[26] Vgl. zusammenfassend B. R. SUCHLA, Art. Dionysius Areopagita, Lexikon der antiken christlichen Literatur ([3]2002), 203–205.

[27] Allgemein zu ihm und zu Datierungsfragen s. meine Übersicht: Art. Tertullian, BBKL 11 (1996), 695–720, um neuere Literatur ergänzt auch: www.bautz.de/bbkl/t/tertullian_q_s_f.shtml.

cendi tinguendique defendunt, sciant in Asia presbyterum, qui eam scripturam construxit quasi titulo Pauli de suo cumulans, convictum adque confessum id se amore Pauli fecisse loco decessisse" (bapt. 17,5).[28] Diese Passage ist nicht zuletzt von Bedeutung, weil sie ein für alle mal die Legende von der problemlosen Akzeptanz von Pseudepigraphie in einem christlichen Umfeld widerlegen sollte: Solche Akzeptanz gab es in begrenztem Umfang in der antiken Philosophie, aber nicht in der Alten Kirche.[29] Der der Fälschung überführte Presbyter brachte zwar eine Verteidigung vor (er habe aus Liebe zu Paulus gehandelt), musste aber doch von seinen kirchlichen Ämtern zurücktreten. Völlig deutlich ist, dass es für Tertullian selbst sicher nicht vorstellbar war, weite Teile seines Neuen Testamentes seien ebenfalls pseudepigraph. Diese Möglichkeit ist ihm offenbar nie in den Sinn gekommen, was heißt, dass sie auch in den nordafrikanischen Gemeinden seines Umfeldes nicht diskutiert wurde: Sonst hätte er schwerlich so schreiben können, wie er es in De baptismo tut. Die beliebte Schutzbehauptung einer moralischen Unbedenklichkeit der Pseudepigraphie für frühchristliche Autoren erledigt sich damit von selbst.[30] Auch Euseb hat gefälschte orthodoxe Schriften nicht für kanonfähig gehalten (häretische selbstverständlich ohnehin nicht).[31] Tertullian war mit dem Problem der gefälschten Texte allerdings noch in einem ganz anderen Kontext konfrontiert. Sein antimarkionitisches Magnum opus war selbst vor einer förmlichen Veröffentlichung in nichtautorisierten Abschriften in Umlauf geraten und textlich verändert worden, und zwar durch einen ehemaligen „Bruder" (Christen), der dann zum Apostaten geworden sei: „Si quid retro gestum est nobis aduersus Marcionem iam hinc uiderit. Nouam rem adgredimur ex uetere. Primum opusculum quasi properatum pleniore

---

[28] Hier zitiert nach der Fassung von W. P. J. Borleffs, CCL 1, Turnhout 1954, 291f., die auch in der Ausgabe von D. Schleyer, FC 76, Turnhout 2006, 204–206, abgedruckt ist. Über die schwierigen textkritischen Fragen der ganzen Passage s. dessen Exkurs a.a.O. 280–287.

[29] Tatsächlich ist der einzige explizite Beleg für eine moralische Akzeptanz durchschauter Pseudepigraphie bei einem christlichen Autor Canon Muratori (s. im Text). Natürlich könnte man meinen, zumindest die Verfasser der Pseudepigraphen müssten diese für unbedenklich gehalten haben, das ist aber ein angesichts des Fehlens sonstiger Zeugnisse problematischer Schluss. Das „moralische" Problem bedarf sehr eingehender und differenzierter Darstellung schon für den antiken Befund, die hier nicht gegeben werden kann.

[30] Zu dieser hier nicht vertieften Frage vgl. FRENSCHKOWSKI, Pseudepigraphie und Paulusschule (s. Anm. 2), 240–253, und v.a. JANSSEN, Unter falschem Namen (s. Anm. 5), 263–268; auch BAUM, Pseudepigraphie und literarische Fälschung (s. Anm. 5), passim.

[31] Eus.h.e. 3,25,4–7 und dazu A. D. BAUM, Der neutestamentliche Kanon bei Eusebios (hist. eccl. III.25.1-7) im Kontext seiner literaturgeschichtlichen Arbeit, EThL 73 (1997), 307–347 (320–334).

postea compositione rescideram. Hanc quoque nondum exemplariis suffectam fraude tunc fratris, dehinc apostatae, amisi, qui forte descripserat quaedam mendosissime et exhibuit frequentiae. Emendationis necessitas facta est innouationis. Eius occasio aliquid adicere persuasit. Ita stilus iste nunc de secundo tertius et de tertio iam hinc primus hunc opusculi sui exitum necessario praefatur, ne quem uarietas eius in disperso reperta confundat" (Marc. 1,1f.; CChr I,441).[32] Tertullian ist verärgert über die Freiheiten, die sich ein „falscher Bruder" mit seinen Texten genommen hatte. Der Abschnitt erlaubt einen wichtigen Einblick in die Verselbständigung von Texten gegenüber ihrem Autor selbst zu dessen Lebzeiten, ein wichtiger Unterschied antiker und moderner Literaturproduktion. Eine andere gelegentlich zur Sache genannte Stelle gehört jedoch nicht hierher. Marc. 4,5,4 schreibt Tertullian: „capit autem magistrorum videri quae discipuli promulgarint" (CChr I,551) „Es darf als Werk des Lehrers angesehen werden, was seine Schüler publiziert haben." Er denkt dabei freilich an das Markus- und Lukasevangelium, hinter denen er die Autorität des Petrus und Paulus sieht. Es geht also gar nicht um Pseudepigraphie, sondern um die Autorität der Schriften von (angeblichen) Apostelschülern. Daraus lassen sich allenfalls indirekte Schlüsse auf eine Wahrnehmung von Pseudepigraphie ziehen.

Ein ähnlich wie für Adversus Marcionem gelagerter Fall liegt indes vielleicht bei Bischof Dionysios von Korinth vor, dessen umfangreichen Briefwechsel wir leider nur aus dem hier allerdings ausführlichen Referat des Eusebius kennen. In diesem Rahmen begegnet ein bemerkenswertes Zitat, das Eusebius sicher auch deshalb bringt, weil es ein Problem größerer Bedeutung reflektiert: „Bezüglich der Fälschung seiner Briefe bemerkte Dionysios: Auf die Bitte von Brüdern hin, zu schreiben, habe ich Briefe verfaßt. Die Apostel des Teufels haben dieselben mit Unkraut angefüllt, indem sie einiges strichen, anderes hinzufügten. Ihnen gilt das Wehe. Man kann sich daher nicht darüber wundern, dass einige sich erkühnt haben, selbst die Schriften des Herrn zu fälschen, da sie es sogar bei nicht so wertvollen Schriften versuchten" (Eus.h.e. 4,23,12, übers. v. Ph. Haeuser / H. A. Gärtner). Leider erfahren wir keine Details darüber, welche Eingriffe in seine Texte den Bischof erzürnten. Tertullian und Dionysios sind also darin Leidensgenossen, dass sich bereits Zeitgenossen an ihren Schriften zu schaffen machten, wie es ähnlich auch Galen erging (s.u.). Das dürfte auch für die neutestamentlichen Pseudepigraphen interessant sein: Sie könnten also problemlos bereits zu Lebzeiten des Apostels entstanden sein

---

[32] Vgl. M. FRENSCHKOWSKI, Der Text der Apostelgeschichte und die Realien antiker Buchproduktion, in: T. Nicklas / M. Tilly (Hg.), The Book of Acts as Church History. Apostelgeschichte als Kirchengeschichte, BZNW 120, Berlin/New York 2003, 87–107 (87 Anm. 1).

(natürlich existieren in vielen Fällen Argumente für spätere Datierungen, aber Pseudepigraphen sind nicht grundsätzlich „spät"). Dazu nur ein paganes Beispiel: Der Stoiker Diotimos, ein Gegner Epikurs, versuchte erfolgreich, diesen zu desavouieren, indem er unter dessen Namen 50 obszöne Briefe erscheinen ließ, wogegen dieser sich nur mit Mühe wehren konnte (D.L. 10,3). Bei Christen hören wir noch öfters von Fälschungen zu Lebzeiten der Betroffenen.[33] Cyprian schließt einmal aus der Beschaffenheit des Papyrus wie des Inhalts, ein ihm aus Rom zugekommenes Schreiben könne nicht echt sein (ep. 9,2; CSEL 3,2,489). Mit diesen Beobachtungen ist es möglich, Pseudepigraphie in manchen Fällen sehr dicht an die angeblichen Autoren heranzurücken.

Von der besagten kritischen Tertullianstelle abgesehen, ist Canon Muratori der älteste Text, in dem sich ein altkirchlicher Autor eindeutig und diesmal erstaunlich positiv mit dem Phänomen der Pseudepigraphie auseinandersetzt.[34] Der Text verdient daher unsere gesteigerte Aufmerksamkeit, zumal er immer wieder im Zusammenhang der Pseudepigraphieforschung zum Kronzeugen gemacht wurde. Wir müssen prüfen, ob das legitim ist. Die leider an Anfang und Ende verstümmelte kommentierte Liste[35] unklarer Provenienz empfiehlt für die gottesdienstliche Lesung

---

[33] Die bekannten Fälle sind aufgelistet bei SPEYER, Die literarische Fälschung (s. Anm. 5), 192–195.

[34] Aus der Literatur: A. C. SUNDBERG, Canon Muratori. A Fourth Century List, HTR 66 (1973), 1–41; G. M. HAHNEMAN, The Muratorian Fragment and the Development of the Canon, Oxford 1992 (dort 6f. die neueste Ausgabe des Textes, nach der hier zitiert wird); W. HORBURY, The Wisdom of Solomon in the Muratorian Fragment, JThS 45 (1994), 149–159; H. VON CAMPENHAUSEN, Die Entstehung der christlichen Bibel, Tübingen 1968, 282–303; J. CAMPOS, Epoca del Fragmento Muratoriano, Helmantica 11 (1960), 485–496; N. A. DAHL, Welche Ordnung der Paulusbriefe wird vom muratorischen Fragment vorausgesetzt?, ZNW 52 (1961), 39–53; E. FERGUSON, Canon Muratori. Date and Provenance, StPatr 18 (1982), 677–683; C. E. HILL, The Debate over the Muratorian Fragment and the Development of the Canon, WThJ 57 (1995), 437–452; J.-D. KAESTLI, La place du Fragment de Muratori dans l'histoire du canon. À propos de la thèse de Sundberg et Hahneman, CrSt 15 (1994), 609–634; M. FRENSCHKOWSKI, Art. Muratorisches Fragment, RGG[4] 5 (2002), 1587f.; J. VERHEYDEN, The Canon Muratori. A Matter of Dispute, in: J.-M. Auwers / H. J. De Jonge (Hg.), The Biblical Canons, BEThL 163, Leuven 2003, 487–556; C. MARKSCHIES, Kaiserzeitliche christliche Theologie und ihre Institutionen, Tübingen 2007, 228–236. Der umfassendste Kommentar bleibt T. ZAHN, Geschichte des Neutestamentlichen Kanons, 2 Bd., Leipzig 1888–1892 = Hildesheim 1975, hier Bd. 2, 1–143; auch ders., Art. Kanon Muratori, PRE 9 (1901), 796–806.

[35] Auch der auf Canon Muratori in der Handschrift (Codex Ambrosianus I.101 supp.) folgende Auszug aus Ambrosius, De Abraham (dazu später ein zweiter Auszug aus der gleichen Schrift) ist Fragment ohne Überschrift, Einleitung oder Subscriptio. Es ist also unklar, ob schon die Vorlage verstümmelt war, oder ob der Abschreiber noch einen längeren Text vorliegen hatte. Die Handschrift selbst, die vor allem lateinische Chrysosto-

offenbar vier Evangelien in der Reihenfolge Mt/Mk/Lk/Joh (Mt und Anfang Mk nicht erhalten; ausführliche Entstehungslegende zu Joh, das dem Zebedaiden zugeschrieben wird), Apg, 13 Paulusbriefe, nämlich (wie Apk 2f.) an sieben Gemeinden (1/2Kor, Eph, Phil, Kol, Gal, 1/2Thess, Röm; daneben ist eine chronologische Reihenfolge 1/2Kor, Gal, Röm bezeugt) und vier Briefe an Einzelpersonen (Phlm, Tit, 1/2Tim), weiter Judas und zwei Johannesbriefe (welche?), SapSal (deren Pseudepigraphie bekannt ist, dazu sofort) sowie Apk und ApkPetr; Herm dagegen sei als Werk der jüngeren Vergangenheit (Datierung unter dem Episkopat des Pius von Rom) nicht apostolisch, wohl aber für die private Lektüre geeignet. Hebr, 1/2Petr, Jak und ein Johannesbrief werden nicht erwähnt. Als häretisch verworfen werden markionitische Deuteropaulinen an die Laodizäer und Alexandriner, Schriften des Arsinous, Valentin, Miltiades und Basilides (der fälschlich als Stifter der Kataphryger = Montanisten gilt) sowie Psalmen des Markion. Die erhaltene lateinische Fassung stammt aus dem späten 4. oder frühen 5. Jh.;[36] ein griechisches Original ist möglich (falls sich ein Übersetzungsfehler zur Weisheit Salomos findet, s.u.; daneben jedoch ein nur lateinisch mögliches Wortspiel). Die Angaben zu Herm und v.a. auch das Profil der antihäretischen Front legen eine Abfassung Ende des 2. Jh. nahe. Gegen diese Datierung haben Sundberg und Hahneman eine Spätdatierung (4. Jh.) vorgeschlagen, die sich nicht durchsetzen konnte.[37] Canon Muratori ist ein bemerkenswertes Dokument der Bemühung um

---

mustexte, einige Glaubensbekenntnisse und anderes in etwas wirrer Folge enthielt, war vielleicht als eine „Art monastisches Handbuch zur Bibel" (MARKSCHIES, a.a.O. 230) gedacht. Ein interner Gliederungsversuch im Text (Z. 4 und 9 sind in roter Tinte geschrieben) wurde offenbar nicht weitergeführt. HORBURY, a.a.O., hat wahrscheinlich zu machen versucht, dass Canon Muratori an einem verbreiteten Schema orientiert ist, bei dem alt- und neutestamentliche Apokryphen nach Abschluss der kanonischen Texte gemeinsam besprochen wurden. Dann wäre damit zu rechnen, dass vor dem mit Lukas beginnenden Text nicht nur Matthäus und Markus, sondern auch die atl. Schriften besprochen wurden. Das ist nicht wirklich erweislich, wenn es auch in der Tat erklären könnte, warum die Weisheit Salomos inmitten von ntl. Schriften diskutiert wird.

[36] Zur lateinischen Übersetzung und ihrer Datierung s. CAMPOS, Epoca del Fragmento Muratoriano (s. Anm. 34); HAHNEMAN, The Muratorian Fragment (s. Anm. 34), 10–14.

[37] Die von Sundberg und Hahneman vertretene Spätdatierung (um 400) darf als durch Verheyden widerlegt angesehen werden, obwohl sie in der amerikanischen Forschung noch einige Anhänger hat. So auch z.B. T. J. Kraus / T. Nicklas (Hg.), Das Petrusevangelium und die Petrusapokalypse, GCS NF 11, Berlin/New York 2004, 88; HORBURY, The Wisdom of Solomon (s. Anm. 34), 158 (spätes 2. oder frühes 3. Jh.); FERGUSON, Canon Muratori (s. Anm. 34), 677–683; P. HENNE, La datation du Canon de Muratori, RB 100 (1993), 54–75; MARKSCHIES, Kaiserzeitliche christliche Theologie (s. Anm. 34), 228–236 (sehr vorsichtig: „Die Mehrzahl der Argumente spricht nach wie vor für eine Datierung um 200 n. Chr., obwohl der exakte historische Hintergrund und die präzise literarische Form des Textes unklar bleiben" [234]).

eine verbindliche Sichtung der für die Kirche ausschlaggebenden Bücher. Verschiedene Vorschläge zur Identifizierung des Verfassers (Hippolyt, Victor, Zephyrin, neuerdings Victorin von Pettau[38] u.a.) sind unerweislich. Kein altkirchlicher Autor zitiert Canon Muratori, was freilich für die meisten handschriftlich erhaltenen unabhängigen (also nicht literarisch tradierten) Kanonlisten gilt. Erst nachträglich haben einige von ihnen einen quasi-offiziellen Anstrich erhalten, insbesondere das Decretum Gelasianum und die Auflistung im 39. Osterfestbrief des Athanasius von 367 n. Chr.[39] Der Gebrauch der 1. Ps. pl. (recipimus) im Canon Muratori darf in dieser Hinsicht sicher nicht überbewertet werden.[40] Formal ähnelt Canon Muratori weniger den späteren Kanonlisten, sondern eher der längeren Diskussion kanonischer und apokrypher Texte bei Eusebius. Eine Abfassung direkt in Rom, die Harnack vertreten hatte (der gar an ein amtliches Dokument dachte), ist wegen der distanzierten Art der Erwähnung Roms („In urbe Roma conscripsit", Z. 74f.) nicht wahrscheinlich. Es ist etwas misslich, dass dieser in seiner Herkunft unklare Text zu einem Hauptgewährsmann der frühen Kanongeschichte gemacht wurde, die dadurch einen Fixpunkt erhält, der in Wahrheit keiner ist.

Wir wollen uns nun mit einer Passage zur Pseudepigraphie eingehender beschäftigen. Der besagte Abschnitt lautet (in präziser Transkription, welche das fehlerhafte Küchenlatein schmerzlich deutlich macht): „epistola sane Iude et superscriptio Iohannis duas In catholica habentur Et Sapientia ab amicis salomonis in honorẽ ipsius scripta apacalypse etiam Iohanis et Petri tantum recipimus quam quidam ex nostris legi In eclesia nolunt Pastorem uero nuperrime e temporibus nostris In urbe roma herma consc-

---

[38] J. J. ARMSTRONG, Victorinus of Pettau as the Author of the Canon Muratori, VC 62 (2008), 1–34.

[39] Auch dieser wird (wie Canon Muratori) in seiner Bedeutung für die Alte Kirche gerne überschätzt. Man sollte nicht übersehen, dass der relevante Text griechisch nur zufällig bei dem Kanoniker Theodor Balsamon und an eher entlegener Stelle in syrischer und koptischer Übersetzung erhalten ist. Er wurde von den Zeitgenossen des Athanasius keineswegs als abschließendes oder auch nur entscheidendes Wort zur Sache wahrgenommen, wie sich aus den fehlenden Zitaten ergibt (obwohl uns Zitate der anderen Osterfestbriefe begegnen; vgl. ZAHN, Geschichte des ntl. Kanons 2 [s. Anm. 34], 203–209). Die alexandrinischen Osterfestbriefe dienen primär der Mitteilung des jährlichen Ostertermins gleich nach dem Epiphanienfest, ein Vorrecht, das die Patriarchen der Stadt seit Nicäa besitzen. Als gleichsam „offiziell", gar apostolisch geben sich dagegen die Kanonlisten in den apostolischen Konstitutionen (180–184).

[40] Die traditionelle Bezeichnung Canon Muratori bringt immerhin zum Ausdruck, dass es sich um ein strukturiertes Dokument handelt, das eine Reihe irgendwie doch autoritativer Aussagen zum Thema machen will. Ich ersetze sie daher nicht, wie mehrfach vorgeschlagen, durch ein nichtssagendes „Muratorisches Fragment" oder ähnlich, auch wenn der formale Charakter des Textes unklar bleibt.

ripsit ..."[41] (Z. 68–75). Die Weisheit Salomos werde also in der Kirche gelesen, obwohl sie von Freunden Salomos zu seinen Ehren geschrieben sei. Ob dem Autor dabei das wahre Alter der Schrift im Kontrast zu Salomo bewusst war? Für unsere Fragestellung zentral ist natürlich, dass die Pseudepigraphie hier nicht negativ beurteilt wird, allenfalls einer freundlichen Apologie bedarf. Selbstverständlich darf man nicht mit einem modernen Problembewusstsein rechnen: Die Pastoralbriefe etwa oder die fraglos pseudepigraphe Petrusapokalypse werden nicht hinterfragt. Allerdings ist es umstritten, ob der lateinische Text das griechische Original (wenn es eines gab) korrekt wiedergibt. Schon Samuel Prideaux Tregelles hatte die kluge Idee, es könnte hier ursprünglich gestanden haben ὑπὸ Φίλωνος statt ὑπὸ φίλων (ab amicis).[42] Das hätte ein ungeschickter Übersetzer missverstanden, vor allem, wenn er von der Tradition nichts wusste, welche in Philon den Verfasser der Weisheit Salomos sah. Der jüdische Religionsphilosoph Philon galt in altkirchlicher Zeit tatsächlich öfters als Autor dieser Schrift. Zitiert zuerst im 1. Clemensbrief, dann von Irenäus und vor allem sehr häufig von Clemens Alexandrinus benutzt, gilt die Weisheit als philonisch z.B. für Personen, von denen Hieronymus spricht (Prologus in libros Salomonis, PL 28,1308A bzw. Vulgata II 957, hg. v. R. Weber / R. Gryson; auch in Dan. 9)[43], und auch für Julian von Eclanum, der daneben an Sirach als potentiellen Autor denkt (bei Augustin, opus imperfectum contra Iulianum 4,123; PL 45,1420). Augustin hielt zuerst Jesus Sirach für den Verfasser, meinte aber später, die Frage sei unentscheidbar.[44] Dass die Weisheit nicht von Salomo stammen könne, „war damals allgemeine Überzeugung der Leute von einiger gelehrter Bildung geworden"[45]. Cassiodor (Institutiones divinarum et saecularium litterarum 1,5,5, hg. v. R. A. B. Mynors[46], auch FC 39/1,148) und Isidor von Sevilla (Etymologiarum libri viginti 6,2,30, hg. v. W. M. Lindsay) sind Hieronymus

---

[41] HAHNEMAN, The Muratorian Fragment (s. Anm. 34), 7, ohne Berücksichtigung der durch einen zeitgenössischen Korrektor bereits verbesserten Fehler.

[42] S. P. TREGELLES, Canon Muratorianus. The Earliest Catalogue of the New Testament, Oxford 1867, 53f., der erwähnt, dass unabhängig auch William Fitzgerald diese Idee vertreten hat.

[43] Vielleicht ist an Hegesippus zu denken. Vgl. HORBURY, The Wisdom of Salomon (s. Anm. 34), 157, sowie P. E. BRUNS, Philo Christianus. The Debris of a Legend, HThR 66 (1973), 141–145. Allgemein über Philon bei Hieronymus s. D. T. RUNIA, Philo in Early Christian Literature. A Survey, CRI III/3, Assen 1993, 312–319.

[44] Diskussion der relevanten Passagen bei A.-M. LABONNARDIÈRE, Biblia Augustiniana. A. T. Le livre de la Sagesse, Paris 1970, 46–57.

[45] ZAHN, Geschichte des ntl. Kanons 2 (s. Anm. 34), 1, 101 mit Belegen (vgl. 257f. Anm. 1).

[46] Auch FC 39/1, 148f., leider mit einer verfehlten Fußnote (Nr. 96), in der Philo Alexandrinus mit Philo von Carpasia verwechselt wird.

gefolgt. Doch steht daneben eine Vielzahl von Stimmen, welche die Verfasserschaft Salomos nicht problematisieren.[47] Diese Meinungsverschiedenheit scheint dem Ansehen der Weisheit kaum geschadet zu haben. Im Canon Muratori hat die ganze Konjektur viel für sich; tatsächlich scheint sonst auf den ersten Blick der Plural „amici" im überlieferten Text sinnlos: Warum sollte die Weisheit mehrere Verfasser haben? Dass Wilhelm Schneemelcher in seiner Übersetzung des Canon Muratori diese Verbesserung – die zum Beispiel auch Hans von Campenhausen für genial und ganz fraglos richtig gehalten hat[48] – nicht einmal erwähnt, ist sehr merkwürdig. Doch existieren immerhin auch bedenkenswerte Einwände, die vor allem von William Horbury vorgebracht wurden. Die Rede von den „Freunden Salomos" könnte nämlich an eine im Hellenismus beliebte Wendung von den Königsfreunden anknüpfen, die auch in der LXX in den Text eingetragen wird (Spr 25,1: οἱ φίλοι Ἐζεκίου τοῦ βασιλέως τῆς Ἰουδαίας).[49] Die Vulgata spricht Hhld 5,1 von den amici des Königs (LXX: πλησίοι).[50] Richtig bleibt, dass der Canon Muratori ein als solches durchschautes Pseudepigraphon für eine lesenswerte Schrift hält. Aber dieser Fall ist in der Frühzeit singulär, eher Ausnahme als Regel.[51]

Natürlich nahm die Großkirche grundsätzlich die Existenz von Fälschungen wahr. In ihrer Kritik an gnostischer Literatur etwa setzen Häresiographen regelmäßig die Pseudepigraphie der von ihnen angegriffenen Literatur voraus. So schreibt Epiphanius über die Kainiten: „Wiederum andere erdichten ein anderes Büchlein auf den Namen des Paulus, voll von heimlichen Dingen, das auch die sogenannten Gnostiker gebrauchen, das sie ‚Aufstieg des Paulus' nennen" (Epiph.haer 38,2,5).[52] Das literarische Phänomen als solches war ihnen also vertraut: Sie kamen im Allgemeinen

---

[47] ZAHN, Geschichte des ntl. Kanons 2 (s. Anm. 34), 1, 99f.

[48] VON CAMPENHAUSEN, Die Entstehung der christlichen Bibel (s. Anm. 34), 284f. Anm. 199; 287 mit Anm. 207. Ähnlich E. SCHÜRER, The History of the Jewish People in the Age of Christ (175 B.C. – A.D. 135), hg. v. G. Vermes u.a., Bd. 3,1, Edinburgh 1986, 574; C. LARCHER, Études sur le Livre de la Sagesse, Paris 1969, 40; HAHNEMAN, The Muratorian Fragment (s. Anm. 34), 14.201f.215.

[49] Die weitergehende These von TREGELLES, Canon Muratorianus (s. Anm. 42), dass sich Canon Muratori auf Proverbien und nicht auf die Weisheit Salomos beziehe, hat keine weiteren Freunde gefunden.

[50] Vgl. zu weisen „Freunden Salomos" auch Flav.Jos.Ant. 8,143–149; Apion. 1,109–120; Theophilus, Ad Autolycum 3,22; Euseb, chronicon 1,17,1–13 und Weiteres zur Sache bei HORBURY, The Wisdom of Salomon (s. Anm. 34), bes. 151.

[51] BAUM, Pseudepigraphie und literarische Fälschung (s. Anm. 5), 116–118, lässt die Frage einer Fehlübersetzung in Canon Muratori unentschieden.

[52] Übersetzung W. Förster, in: Carl Andresen (Hg.), Die Gnosis I. Zeugnisse der Kirchenväter, Zürich/Stuttgart 1969, 59. Viele weitere Beispiele bei SPEYER, Die literarische Fälschung (s. Anm. 5), 201–208.260–265 u.ö.

nur nicht auf die Idee, es auf die kanonischen Schriften anzuwenden. Ebenso nahm man natürlich Fälle von Urkundenfälschung und ähnliche Delikte zur Kenntnis. Als ein Knecht Stilichos gefälschte Tribunatsurkunden ausfertigte und die Sache aufflog, verfluchte ihn Ambrosius, so dass ein unreiner Geist ihn hin- und herriss. So erzählt Paulinus von Nola, Vita Ambrosii 43. Für uns ist v.a. bemerkenswert, dass die Episode noch jahrhundertelang Interesse fand (Eugippius, Vita Severini 36,2).[53] Selbstverständlich gab es ein Gespür für Fälschungen, aber in der Rezeption des eigenen religiösen Traditums kam es verhältnismäßig wenig zum Tragen. Alles Orthodoxe gilt als echt, alles Häretische als unecht. Athanasius z.B. kann schreiben: „Die Häretiker teilen ihren Erzeugnissen gerne alte Zeiten zu, damit sie jene als alt ausgeben können und einen Vorwand haben, die Einfältigen zu täuschen" (ep. 39; MPG 26,1440A). Neutestamentliche Pseudepigraphie freilich hat er nicht durchschaut. Die Echtheitskritik ist also vorkritisch: Sie richtet sich nur auf das „Andere".[54] Ähnlich hatte offenbar schon Serapion von Antiochien das Petrusevangelium erst für unecht erklärt, als ihm dessen inhaltliche Heterodoxie ins Bewusstsein trat (Eus.h.e. 6,12,2–6).[55]

Auf die im engeren Sinn neutestamentliche Epoche können wir nur zurückschließen, da (außer 2Thess 2,2) direkte christliche Zeugnisse fehlen, ob und wie Pseudepigraphie wahrgenommen wurde. Mit an Sicherheit grenzender Wahrscheinlichkeit dürfte aber nach allem, was wir sehen können, Gerd Theißen Recht zu geben sein, der schreibt: „Ausschließen können wir, dass es ein stillschweigendes Einverständnis zwischen Autoren und Lesern gab, religiöse Pseudepigraphie sei als *pia fraus* (fromme Täuschung) legitim." Aber inwiefern stimmen auch seine nächsten beiden Sätze: „Fälschungen wurden in der Antike abgelehnt. Man erwartete, dass der Inhalt eines Textes auf den Autor zurückging, dem der Text zuge-

---

[53] Ebenso fand der Fall eines eventuellen Brieffälschers am Hofe Herodes d. Gr. noch lange Interesse (Flav.Jos.Bell. 1,529). Vgl. die Diskussion bei A. SCHALIT, König Herodes. Der Mann und sein Werk. Berlin 1969, 619f.

[54] Ähnlich schon SPEYER, Die literarische Fälschung (s. Anm. 5), 201–210.

[55] Zu den Schwierigkeiten der Interpretation dieser Passage vgl. jedoch BAUM, Pseudepigraphie und literarische Fälschung (s. Anm. 5), 100–103. Ganz singulär ist die Nachricht bei Hieronymus, einige Personen hielten den Philemonbrief für unecht, nicht erbaulich und daher unkanonisch. Hieronymus entgegnet darauf, „numquam in toto orbe a cunctis ecclesiis fuisse receptam, nisi Pauli apostoli crederetur" (in Philemonem prologus; MPL 26,637C).

schrieben wurde. Nur im Wortlaut durfte er abweichen"[56]? Dieser Frage wollen wir uns jetzt etwas ausführlicher zuwenden.[57]

3. In welchem Umfang war Pseudepigraphie in antiker Bildungskultur als solche erkennbar?

Es ist seit je bekannt, dass offenbar spätestens seit frühhellenistischer Zeit in philosophischen Schulzusammenhängen Pseudepigrapha im Namen eines Meisters produziert worden sind. „Der Pythagoreismus hat sich anscheinend zumindest zeitweise fast ausschließlich in untergeschobenen Schriften ausgedrückt, so dass man das Apokryphon als seine notwendige innere Form bezeichnen könnte."[58] Immer wieder zitiert in Pseudepigraphiestudien wurden v.a. die neuplatonischen Aussagen zur Sache, die in der Tat auch deutlich demonstrieren, dass dies *in gewissen Zirkeln* eine grundsätzlich durchschaubare literarische Erscheinung war. An Jamblich, De vita Pythagorica 29,157f. (159–161 von Albrecht). 31,198 (197 von Albrecht); David, In Porphyrii isagoge commentarium 1; Olympiodorus, prolegomena (CAG XII/1,13,4–14,4 A. Busse) und ähnliche Texte wurde in der Literatur daher gerne immer wieder erinnert.[59]

Darf man aber von solchen Konventionen der philosophischen Bildungselite auf die ganz anders geartete soziale und kulturelle Welt der frühen Christen oder auch nur der Alten Kirche zurückschließen? Dagegen sprechen schwerwiegende Argumente, die wir zum Teil schon in Augenschein genommen haben. Anton Vögtle und andere haben freilich gemeint,

---

[56] THEISSEN, Die Entstehung des Neuen Testaments (s. Anm. 7), 153f., der sich in seiner Formulierung eng an BAUM, Pseudepigraphie und literarische Fälschung (s. Anm. 5), 193, anschließt.

[57] Undiskutiert muss hier die von A. D. Baum aufgeworfene These bleiben, erkannte Pseudepigraphie hätte in der Alten Kirche zum Ausschluss aus dem Kanon geführt. Baum bringt plausible Argumente für seine These, unterschätzt aber m.E. die ganz unterschiedliche literarkritische Brille, mit der kanonische und nichtkanonische Literatur wahrgenommen wurde.

[58] W. BURKERT, Hellenistische Pseudopythagorica, in: ders., Kleine Schriften III Mystica, Orphica, Pythagorica, hg. v. F. Graf, Hyp. Suppl. 2/3, Göttingen 2006, 236 (zuerst Ph. 105 [1961], 16–43.226–246). Namen einiger Autoren von Ps.-Pythagorica hat Porphyrios in einem nur arabisch erhaltenen Text überliefert; vgl. SPEYER, Die literarische Fälschung (s. Anm. 5), 130 mit Anm. 11. Fälschungen pythagor. Literatur durch einen gewissen Cleemporus bestreitet Plinius, Naturalis historia 24,159 mit dem Argument, dieser Autor habe bekannte Bücher unter eigenem Namen publiziert.

[59] Alle diese Texte mit Übersetzung auch bei BAUM, Pseudepigraphie und literarische Fälschung (s. Anm. 5). Die Jamblich-Passagen werden z.B. von THEISSEN, Die Entstehung des Neuen Testaments (s. Anm. 7), 162, als Kronzeugen zitiert.

auch im frühen Christentum sei Pseudepigraphie grundsätzlich durchschaut worden.[60] Aber diese These ist als unzulässige Verallgemeinerung schon kritisiert worden. Ihre Unhaltbarkeit erweist sich sehr schlicht schon daran, dass kein frühchristlicher oder altkirchlicher Autor die Pseudepigraphie z.B. der Pastoralbriefe tatsächlich durchschaut hat. Das gilt selbst da, wo die junge Kirche stärker in gebildete Kreise hineinwächst, wo also nach Vögtle eine solche allgemeine Akzeptanz von Pseudepigraphie am ehesten zum Tragen hätte kommen müssen.

Kann auch in anderen als schulphilosophischen Kontexten Pseudepigraphie zumindest in manchen Fällen als stillschweigendes Einverständnis zwischen Schreibenden und Lesenden interpretiert werden? Dieses Einverständnis müsste ja gerade bei religiösen Texten nicht einmal „bewusst" sein. Es könnte sozusagen an der Grenze der bewussten Wahrnehmung existieren, als eine Art Konfabulation, eine gemeinsame „Geschichte", die systemisch erzeugt wird, also im komplexen Verhältnis zwischen Erwartungen und Erfüllungsbedürfnissen, Lesenden, Schreibenden, Umfeld und allgemeinem geistigen Klima. Das erscheint grundsätzlich plausibel, ist aber nur sehr schwer zu verifizieren. Allgemeine Plausibilitäten ersetzen hier leider keine Belege. Immerhin helfen manche Grenzfälle, das Phänomen Pseudepigraphie in seinem Umfeld besser zu verstehen. Wir betrachten dazu in lockerer Folge einige kaiserzeitliche Beispiele „umspielter" Verfasserschaft, die uns zu unserer Hauptthese führen werden.

Lukian betreibt in seiner unterhaltsamen ethnologisch-religionsgeschichtlichen Schrift „De Dea Syria" inhaltlich und vor allem auch sprachlich (Pseudo-Jonismen) Herodot-Imitation.[61] Inwiefern seine Absicht dabei zumindest auch ironischer Natur ist, bleibt umstritten. Interessant seine Berufung auf Autopsie in Kap. 1, die sich auf Lukian selbst bezieht, aber eben doch auch an Herodots bekannte Aussagen erinnert.[62] Als was haben Lukians Leserinnen und Leser dieses Werk rezipiert? Als ein geistreiches Spiel mit ironischen Obertönen? Hier bewegen wir uns auf der höchsten Ebene antiker Bildungskultur, in einem Milieu, in dem ironische Distan-

---

[60] A. VÖGTLE, Der Judasbrief. Der 2. Petrusbrief, EKK XXII, Solothurn u.a. 1994, 122–131; auch ders., Die Schriftwerdung der apostolischen Paradosis nach 2 Petr 1,12–15, in: H. Baltensweiler (Hg.), Neues Testament und Geschichte (FS Cullmann), Zürich 1972, 297–305. Speziell zum 2Petr ging Vögtle voran R. J. BAUCKHAM, Jude, 2 Peter, WBC 50, Waco 1983, 158–162, sowie 134: „an entirely transparent fiction". Vgl. auch ders., Pseudo-Apostolic Letters (s. Anm. 5), 469–494, und zur Diskussion v.a. JANSSEN, Unter falschem Namen (s. Anm. 5), 182–185.
[61] Vgl. jetzt zu allen Fragen J. L. Lightfoot, Lucian On the Syrian Goddess. Edited with Introduction, Translation and Commentary, Oxford 2003.
[62] Vgl. a.a.O. 290.

zierungen und Imitationen nachvollziehbar sind.[63] Der gebildete Leser weiß, dass er nicht Herodot liest – und findet sein ästhetisches Vergnügen doch an der erneuten Begegnung mit der klassischen griechischen Stimme über die kulturelle Welt der „anderen".

Hier spielt der Autor mit dem Wissen der Leser. Andere Fälle zeigen die Probleme, die bei unklaren Verfasserschaftsverhältnissen entstehen können. Die wohl interessanteste Passage über Komplikationen in Hinsicht auf Verfasserschaft antiker Bücher und ihre Rezeption im 1./2. Jh. der Kaiserzeit ist zwar schon öfters herangezogen worden, aber doch nur selten im Zusammenhang ihrer Relevanz für die christliche Literatur. Sie steht bei dem Arzt Galen (2. Jh.). Ich zitiere die Passage aus dem Vorwort seiner Schrift De libris propriis hier in einer neueren Übersetzung: „The validity of your advice regarding the cataloguing of my extant books, Bassus, has been proved by events. I was recently in the Sandalarium, the area of Rome with the largest concentration of booksellers, where I witnessed a dispute as to whether a certain book for sale was by me or someone else. The book bore the title: Galen the doctor. Someone had bought the book under the impression that it was one of mine; someone else – a man of letters – struck by the odd form of the title, desired to know the book's subject. On reading the first two lines he immediately tore up the inscription, saying simply: ‚This is not Galen's language – the title is false'. Now, the man in question had been schooled in the fundamental early education which Greek children always used to be given by teachers of grammar and rhetoric. Many of those who embark on a career in medicine or philosophy these days cannot even read properly, yet they frequent lecture on the greatest and most beautiful field of human endeavour, that is, the knowledge provided by philosophy and medicine. This kind of laziness existed many years ago, but it had not yet reached the extreme state it has now. For this reason – and also because my books have been subject to all kinds of mutilations, whereby peoples in different countries publish different texts under their own names, with all sorts of cuts, additions, and alterations – I decided it would be best, first to explain the cause of these mutilations, and secondly to give an account of the content of each of my genuine works. Well, as for the fact of my books being published by many people under their own names, my dearest Bassus, you know the reason yourself: it is that they were given without inscription to friends or pupils,

---

[63] Vgl. über Lukian als Autor von Pastiches und Parodien allgemein J. BOMPAIRE, Lucien écrivain. Imitation et création, Paris 1958 (Nachdruck 2000), 599–655. Der Satiriker hat sich z.B. auch an einer Heraklit-Imitation versucht. Vgl. dazu G. STROHMAIER, Übersehenes zur Biographie Lukians, Ph. 120 (1976), 117–122. Die Autorschaft Lukians an De Dea Syria ist gelegentlich bestritten worden; dagegen s. Lightfoot, a.a.O. 184–208.

having been written with no thought for publication, but simply at the request of those individuals who had desired a written record of lectures they had attended. When in the course of time some of these individuals died, their successors came into possession of the writings, and began to pass them off as their own ...[64] Taking them from their owners, they returned to their own countries, and after a short space of time began to perform the demonstrations in them, each in some different way. All these were eventually caught, and many of those who then recovered the works affixed my name to them. They then discovered discrepancies between these and copies in the possession of other individuals, and so sent them to me with the request that I correct them."[65]

Im Folgenden erläutert Galen noch den Sachverhalt, dass er viele Bücher ohne Titel umlaufen ließ, die dann im Zuge ihrer Verbreitung mit verschiedenen Titeln versehen wurden, während andere Autoren von vornherein Sorge dafür getragen hätten, dass auch Gelegenheitsschriften nicht ohne Titel kopiert wurden. Der Hauptinhalt der Schrift, die mit diesem Passus beginnt, ist dann ein kurzes Resümee seiner bislang publizierten Schriften, ohne Frage auch im Sinne einer Eigenwerbung. Der auf den ersten Blick erstaunlichste Aspekt dieser Passage ist die Leichtigkeit, mit der offenbar wissenschaftliche (!) Texte lebender Autoren unter falschen Namen umlaufen konnten, ja bewusst unter falschem (eigenem) Namen verbreitet werden konnten. Dazu gehört ohne Frage eine gewisse Schamlosigkeit und Skrupellosigkeit, aber es scheint dabei doch nicht allzuviel „kriminelle Energie" im Spiel gewesen zu sein. Das Ganze war offenbar eher ein Kavaliersdelikt. Die Hemmschwelle zur Aneignung von Texten war offenbar unter den von Galen beschriebenen Rahmenbedingungen gering. Allerdings sind das Genre der Texte (modern gesprochen: Vorlesungsskripte) und das Milieu ihrer Rezeption zu bedenken. Vielleicht lässt sich der Vorgang mit der Leichtigkeit vergleichen, mit der Pfarrerinnen und Pfarrer Bausteine für Predigten, ja ganze Predigten übernehmen.[66] Galen – der hier sehr schön den Schritt zur professionellen Autorschaft erkennen lässt – ringt im Grunde um das, was wir ein Copyright nennen würden. Bekanntlich ist auch heute ein juristischer Streit um die Frage

---

[64] Kleine Textlücke im griechischen Text.

[65] Galen, Selected Works. Translated with an Introduction and Notes by F. N. Singer. Oxford/New York 1997, 3f. Der Text findet sich auch bei BAUM, Pseudepigraphie und literarische Fälschung (s. Anm. 5), 226–231.

[66] Von der Übernahme von Predigten aus dem Internet, ohne die Gemeinde darauf hinzuweisen, dass dies eine „fremde" Predigt ist, habe ich mehrfach von Kollegen im Pfarramt im vertrauten Gespräch gehört. In einem mir bekannten Fall hat es zu einem erheblichen Konflikt geführt, als in einer Gemeinde dem Kirchenvorstand zufällig auffiel, dass gehaltene Predigten 1:1 aus einer Internetressource stammten.

nicht ganz selten, ob ein Werk Teil der Public Domain ist oder nicht.[67] Galen setzt als konsensfähig voraus, dass der Vorgang der Aneignung unrecht ist. Finanzielle Gesichtspunkte scheinen dabei keine Rolle gespielt zu haben: Im Normalfall existiert in der Antike noch kein Autorhonorar, obwohl es deutliche Ansätze zu einem Verlagswesen gegeben hat. Auch der augusteische Architekturhistoriker Vitruv erwähnt De architectura 7 praefatio 3, dass Autoren aus Ruhmsucht fremde Schriften als ihre eigenen ausgeben, also das Gegenteil der üblichen Pseudepigraphie. Galen kennt auch – wenn auch nicht für sein eigenes Schrifttum – Fälle, bei denen ein echtes hippokratisches Buch sekundär mit einem Pseudepigraphon verbunden wurde, dessen Namen er zu vermuten wagt (der Arzt Polybus).[68]

Besonders interessant sind für uns solche Fälle, bei denen wir uns in einem subkulturellen, eventuell sehr spezifischen oder gar in sich geschlossenen Milieu bewegen, welches soziologisch insofern analogiefähig sein könnte für das frühe Christentum.[69] Das gilt für die bisher genannten Fälle nicht. Betrachten wir wieder ein Beispiel. Unter Demokrits Namen liefen eine große Zahl magisch-okkulter, paradoxographer, pseudo-medizinischer und hortologischer Schriften um (wohl das größte magische Corpus der älteren griechischen Literatur).[70] Verfasser war aber nicht Demokrit, sondern der Thaumatograph mit pythoreisierenden Neigungen Bolos von Mendes. Bolos war wohl Ägypter, der in griechischer Sprache schrieb, vermutlich unter Ptolemäus VIII. Euergetes (145–116 v. Chr.).[71] Columella schreibt im 1. Jh. n. Chr.: „Sed Aegyptiae gentis auctor memorabilis Bolus Mendesius cuius commenta quae appellantur Graece Χειρόκμητα, sub nomine Democriti falso produntur ..." (7,5,17). Diese Cheirokmeta enthielten medizinische, pharmakologische und veterinärmedizinische Nach-

---

[67] Das Problem existiert allerdings nur im amerikanischen Recht, da das deutsche Recht keine wirkliche Analogie zum Begriff der frei verfügbaren Public Domain hat. Der rechtefreie Nachdruck bzw. die Gemeinfreiheit sind sachlich etwas anderes. Anders als im deutschen Recht kann z.B. ein Werk im amerikanischen Recht sofort mit Erscheinen Teil der Public Domain werden, wenn Autor und Verlag dies beschließen.

[68] Galen, In Hippocratis de natura hominis commentarium 2 pr. (Corpus Medicorum Graecorum V,9,1,54 hg. v. J. Mewaldt); Text und Übersetzung auch bei BAUM, Pseudepigraphie und literarische Fälschung (s. Anm. 5), 224–227. Der Text ist auch wichtig, weil er zeigt, dass kleinere Rollen zu einer größeren zusammenrediert werden konnten, wie es für 2Kor vermutet wurde.

[69] Es ist eines der wenigen Defizite des grundlegenden Werkes von SPEYER, Die literarische Fälschung (s. Anm. 5), dass er solche Differenzierungen kaum vornimmt.

[70] H. Diels / W. Kranz (Hg.), Die Fragmente der Vorsokratiker 2, [6]1952 (Nachdruck Hildesheim 1985, zuerst Berlin 1903), Nr. 68 Frgm. 298a–C8, p. 207–230.

[71] So nach der Argumentation von P. M. FRASER, Ptolemaic Alexandria I, Oxford 1972 = 2001, 440–444, hier 440 (mit Fußnoten Bd. 2. Oxford 1972 = 2001, 640–646), der auch zeigt, dass es vermutlich Bolos war, dessen Vorbild spätere Autoren dazu brachte, unter dem Namen des Demokrit zu schreiben.

richten. Columella zitiert sie sowohl unter dem Namen des Bolos als auch unter dem des Demokrit (1,7; 11,3,64 etc.). Am bekanntesten war unter den Pseudodemokritea eine Schrift über kosmische Sympathien und Antipathien, deren Spuren wir weit in die Kaiserzeit hinein verfolgen können.[72] Diogenes Laërtios kannte wohl weitere unechte Schriften, obwohl er die Cheirokmeta unter den echten nennt (9,13; textkritisch unsicher). Plinius hielt Letztere für sicher echt: „Democriti certe chirocmeta esse constat" (Naturalis historia 24,160) und zitiert sie mehrfach (21,62; 24,160–166 vgl. 156; 26,18f.; 27,141 u. vielleicht öfter, falls das volumen de effectu herbarum 25,13 identisch ist). In einer umfangreichen Passage kritisiert ein Jahrhundert später Aulus Gellius, Noctes Atticae 10,12,1–8 die Leichtgläubigkeit des älteren Plinius in dieser Frage: natürlich stammten diese Schriften nicht von Demokrit, der ja gerade als kritischer Geist berühmt und allem Aberglauben abgeneigt war. Die Suda zählt dann zahlreiche Schriften unter Bolos auf, trennt aber fälschlich den Demokriteer und den Pythagoreer (B 481 und 482, hg. v. A. Adler 1,489f.). Unabhängig von der kontrovers diskutierten Frage, welche Pseudodemokritea tatsächlich von Bolos stammen, haben wir hier den Fall, dass ein antikes Textcorpus unter dem Namen eines hochangesehenen Autors (Demokrit genoss das gleiche Ansehen wie etwa Aristoteles) pseudepigraph produziert war und der Name des wahren Verfassers als bekannt galt: Und dennoch wurde das Corpus unter dem Namen Demokrits weitertradiert.[73] Die Christen nahmen die Debatte offenbar nicht zur Kenntnis und behandelten das vielgelesene Corpus gefälschter Demokritea weiterhin explizit als demokriteisch (z.B. Tatian, Oratio ad Graecos 17,1; Clemens, Stromateis 1,15,69,4; Lydus, De ostentis, hg. v. C. Wachsmuth 2. ed. p. 157,18 aus dem Calendarium des Clodius Tuscus). Überhaupt bleibt der Name Demokrit in der kaiserzeitlichen Literatur vielfach mit Magie verbunden (vgl. etwa die Paignia-

---

[72] T. WEIDLICH, Die Sympathie in der antiken Literatur, Stuttgart 1894, 13–35 (13f. werden hier leider mehrfach Vitruv und Columella verwechselt).

[73] Vgl. außer T. Weidlich auch M. WELLMANN, Art. Bolos 3), PRE 3/1 (1897), 676f.; ders., Die Physika des Bolos Demokritos und der Magier Anaxilaos aus Larissa, Teil 1, Abh. Berlin phil.-hist. Kl. 1928/7; ders., Die Georgica des Demokritos, APAW PH. 1921/4; I. HAMMER-JENSEN, Art. Pseudo-Demokrit, PRE.S 4 (1924), 219–223; H. STECKEL, Art. Demokritos, PRE.S 12 (1970), 191–223 (193f.199f.); BURKERT, Hellenistische Pseudopythagorica (s. Anm. 58), 265–268.272f. Einschränkend dazu allerdings W. KROLL, Bolos und Demokritos, Hermes 69 (1934), 228–232 (auch der echte Demokrit könnte für die hortologischen Zitate in den Geoponica und andernorts verantwortlich sein; und Bolos konnte schwerlich nachdemokriteische Autoren wie Theophrast zitieren, wenn er als Demokrit auftrat. Aber dagegen stehen das präzise Zeugnis des Columella und der Gesamtbefund); J. H. WASZINK, Art. Bolos, RAC 2 (1954), 502–508. Leider behandelt I. BODNÁR, Art. Demokritos (1) von Abdera, DNP 3 (1997), 455–458, die pseudo-demokriteischen Schriften nicht.

Sammlung PGM VII,167–186). Es scheint in solchen Fällen eine Art Nichtwahrhabenwollen gegeben zu haben, einen okkulten Fundamentalismus, der von den kritischen Einwänden der wissenschaftlichen Literatur keine Kenntnis nehmen wollte.[74] Damit stellt sich die Frage, ob es dieses Phänomen auch in anderen Kontexten gegeben hat, also ein subkulturelles Festhalten an Verfasserschaftsfiktionen, die in einem größeren Rahmen als solche bekannt waren.

Betrachten wir einen weiteren weniger oft diskutierten Fall der unmittelbar neutestamentlichen Zeit, in dem Pseudepigraphie als vermutlich durchschaubares und nachweislich auch tatsächlich durchschautes Stilmittel auftritt. Wir sprechen von Dorotheus von Sidon, der im 1. Jh. n. Chr. das bedeutendste astrologische Lehrgedicht seiner Zeit schrieb. Lange war dieser sogenannte „Pentateuch" (das Werk war explizit als Fünfrollenwerk in Hexametern konzipiert) nur in Fragmenten bekannt,[75] obwohl seine Spuren allenthalben in den späteren Klassikern der antiken Astrologie wahrzunehmen sind. So schon bei dem wenig erforschten Astrologen Manethon[76], der ebenfalls noch ins 1./2. Jh. gehört, bei dem elegischen Dichter Anubio (Verfasser des einzigen griechischen Lehrgedichtes zur Astrologie, das auch in den Pseudoclementinen öfters erwähnt wird[77]) und bei den großen Astrologen Firmicus Maternus und Hephaistion von Theben. In byzantinischer Zeit benutzten ihn etwa noch Rhetorius im 7. Jh. und später ausführlich Konstantin Porphyrogennetos. Seit 1976 ist nun eine vollständige Fassung dieses Werkes bekannt, die David Pingree nach der arabischen Version einer Pahlavi-Übersetzung aus dem 4. Jh. herausgegeben hat.[78] Die

---

[74] In der reichen arabischen Demokritos-Überlieferung ist er ganz mit Bolos verschmolzen; M. ULLMANN, Die Natur- und Geheimwissenschaft im Islam, HdO I Erg. VI/2, Leiden u.a. 1972, 402f.428f.

[75] V. STEGEMANN, Die Fragmente des Dorotheus von Sidon. Quellen und Studien zur Geschichte und Kultur des Altertums und des Mittelalters, Reihe B, Heft 1, 2 Bd., Heidelberg 1939–1943.

[76] A. Koechly, Manethonis Apotelesmaticorum qui feruntur libri VI, Leipzig 1858 (enthält auch die damals bekannten Fragmente des Dorotheus und des Anubio). Manethon der Astrologe ist ein Autor „von einer fast beispiellosen Barbarei" (W. KROLL, Art. Manethon 2), PRE 14/1 [1928], 1102–1106, hier 1102) und natürlich nicht mit dem älteren Verfasser der berühmten Aegyptiaca zu verwechseln.

[77] D. Obbink, Anubio Carmen astrologicum elegiacum, BT, München/Leipzig 2006 (v.a. die Testimonia).

[78] D. Pingree, Dorothei Sidonii Carmen astrologicum. Interpretationem Arabicam in linguam Anglicam versam una cum Dorothei fragmentis et Graecis et Latinis, Leipzig 1976. Es existiert von diesem Buch auch eine um den arabischen Text gekürzte Ausgabe Abingdon 2005, welche die Seitenzahlen der Teubner-Ausgabe mit abdruckt (und Pingrees Vorwort ins Englische übersetzt). Das 3./4. Jh. war eine Zeit eifriger Übersetzungen von Fachbuchtexten aus dem Griechischen ins Pahlavi, die dann später ins Arabische weiterübersetzt und zu einer wichtigen Quelle islamischer Wissenschaft wurden.

Pahlavi-Fassung hat ihre Spuren in einigen Einschüben und iranischen Fremdworten im arabischen Text hinterlassen und ist auch anderweitig bezeugt.[79] Trotz dieser komplexen Überlieferungslage handelt es sich um ein wichtiges „Sachbuch" des 1. Jh. n. Chr. Dank des Fachbuchcharakters des Werkes ist sein Inhalt trotz der Übersetzung gut erkennbar. Dorotheus tritt als weit gereister Ägypter vor seine Leser, der aus ägyptischen und babylonischen Quellen schöpfen will, und an seinem Lebensabend die Summe seines Wissens seinem Sohn Hermes (!) mitteilt (Proömium des 1. Buches). In der Einleitung des 5. Buches[80] behauptet Dorotheus gar, König von Ägypten zu sein, womit er als fiktionale Gestalt der vorrömischen Zeit auftritt, tendenziell sogar der mythischen Geschichte Ägyptens, die der Name Hermes evoziert. Dies ist die Verfasserfiktion. Aber im 1. Buch teilt Dorotheus Horoskope mit (die zu den ältesten erhaltenen in der antiken Literatur überhaupt gehören), welche sich auf acht Daten weitgehend des 1. Jh. n. Chr. beziehen, und zwar zwischen dem 29. März 7 v. Chr. und dem 2. August 43. Dies war für astrologisch gebildete Leser durchschaubar. Tatsächlich wusste man, dass der Autor ein Sidonier war, kein Ägypter. Firmicus Maternus erwähnt dies Mathesis 2,29,2, und später weiß es z.B. Michael Italicus.[81] Es scheint mir eindeutig, dass die wenig entfaltete Verfasserfiktion ein durchschaubares und auf Durchschaubarkeit berechnetes Stilmittel war. Damit ist in solchen Büchern wohl öfters zu rechnen.

Blicken wir noch auf ein etwas späteres Beispiel. Jamblich, De mysteriis gibt sich als Antwortschrift eines ägyptischen Priesters Abammon auf den Fragenkatalog, den Porphyrios an seinen (Abammons) Schüler Anebo geschrieben hatte (Epistula ad Anebo). Es wird also sozusagen von Jamblich (etwa 240–325 n. Chr.) für seine Antwort auf ein Buch aus der Generation seiner Lehrer eine höhere, zudem exotisch-ägyptische Autorität beschworen. Anebo antwortet nicht selbst, sondern sein Lehrer übernimmt diese Aufgabe. Es besteht aber kein Zweifel, dass De mysteriis ein Werk des Jamblich ist, und es wurde auch so verstanden. Die Pseudepigraphie ist hier in der Tat durchschaubares literarisches Spiel, Evokation halbfiktiver Autoritäten.[82]

Vgl. D. PINGREE, Māshā'allāh. Some Sasanian and Syriac Sources, in: G. F. Hourani (Hg.), Essays on Islamic Philosophy and Science, Albany 1975, 5–24.

[79] Zu allen Details s. D. Pingree im Vorwort seiner Ausgabe.

[80] Die Bucheinteilung nach einem Fünferschema ist bewusst geplant, wie der Autor uns mehrfach mitteilt.

[81] Appendix I und Appendix III E 1 in Pingrees Teubner-Ausgabe.

[82] Vgl. ausführlicher zu diesem Werk M. FRENSCHKOWSKI, Offenbarung und Epiphanie 1, WUNT II/79, Tübingen 1995, 311–314.

Parallel erwacht das kritische Denken in Hinsicht auf Verfasserschaftsfragen ebenfalls vor allem im gelehrten Milieu des Neuplatonismus. Der Plotinschüler Amelius schrieb ein umfängliches Werk gegen den gnostischen Zostrianos in 40 Büchern, und Porphyrios entlarvte die auch von Christen gelesenen graecoiranischen Apokalypsen in Gestalt eines Zoroaster-Buches: „[I]ch, Porphyrios, habe zahlreiche Gegengründe gegen das Buch des Zoroaster festgestellt; ich wies nach, daß das Buch gefälscht und jung ist und erst von den Gründern der Sekte fingiert um glauben zu machen ihre Lehren stammten vom alten Zoroaster, die sie doch erst von eigenen Gnaden in Geltung gesetzt hatten" (Porphyrios, Vita Plotini 81, übers. v. R. Harder). Porphyrios bewegt sich darin in den Bahnen der intellektuellen Gnostiker-Kritik seines Lehrers Plotin, den er mit Amelius auch gegen Plagiatsvorwürfe verteidigt (l. c. 82). Porphyrius war es bekanntlich auch, der als Erster die wahren Abfassungsverhältnisse des Danielbuches unter Antiochos IV. Epiphanes durchschaute,[83] worin ihm die Christen sehr zu ihrem Schaden nicht gefolgt sind. Hieronymus referiert Porphyrios zwar ausführlich in seinen Commentarii in Danielem, lässt sich aber von den völlig zutreffenden Argumenten des Philosophen nicht beeindrucken und erklärt diesen vielmehr zum „calumniator ecclesiae" (2,48, hg. v. Glorie CCSL LXXV A p. 796). Immerhin versucht Hieronymus (l. c. 9,21, hg. v. Glorie CCSL LXXV A p. 914 = FrGH 260 Fr. 49a) den präzisen Punkt zu benennen, ab dem sich eine „christliche" Lektüre des Daniel von derjenigen durch den Philosophen unterscheidet, wie er überhaupt ein intensives, wenn auch voreingenommenes (etwas anachronistisch formuliert: fundamentalistisches) Gespräch mit dem Heiden führt. Doch berührt uns dabei unangenehm, dass Hieronymus seinem Gegner immer wieder – modern formuliert – Naivität vorwirft, weil er die Überlegenheit der biblischen Offenbarung nicht erkennen könne: „Hactenus Porphyrius utcumque se tenuit et tam nostrorum imperitis quam suorum male eruditis imposuit" (l. c. 12,1, hg. v. Glorie CCSL LXXV A p. 936 = FrGH 260 Fr. 57).[84] Wir erinnern an diese wohlbekannten Sachverhalte nur en passant, um in den

---

[83] Vgl. SPEYER, Die literarische Fälschung (s. Anm. 5), Index s.v. Porphyrius; P. M. CASEY, Porphyry and the Origin of the Book of Daniel, JThS 27 (1976), 15–33; vgl. ders., Porphyry and Syrian Exegesis of the Book of Daniel, ZNW 81 (1990), 139–142. Das Material zur Danielinterpretation des Porphyrios liegt gesammelt vor bei M. STERN, Greek and Latin Authors on Jews and Judaism 2, Jerusalem 1980, 423–483 (455–476). Allgemein über Porphyrios vgl. meine Übersicht BBKL 7 (1994), 839–848, sowie zu seinem kulturellen Hintergrund seitdem besonders F. MILLAR, Porphyry, Ethnicity and Alien Wisdom, in: ders., Rome, the Greek World, and the East. III. The Greek World, the Jews, and the East, Chapel Hill 2006, 331–335 (zuerst in kürzerer Form 1997). Millar zeigt insbesondere, dass Porphyrios die biblischen Texte wahrscheinlich nur auf Griechisch lesen konnte.

[84] Die zitierten Texte auch bei STERN, a.a.O. Nr. 464f. 464n. 464t.

Blick nehmen zu können, wie auch durchaus niveauvolle, gebildete Denker wie Hieronymus aufgrund des subkulturellen Charakters ihrer ererbten Tradition „blinde Flecke" aufweisen, und dies nun gerade in Pseudepigraphiefragen. Dabei interessiert an dieser Stelle weniger der Scharfblick des gelehrten Neuplatonikers als das Unvermögen des gebildeten Christen, historische Argumente in ihrer Tragweite und Plausibilität zu durchschauen, wenn es um die Pseudepigraphie kanonischer Texte geht. Ganz ähnlich vorkritisch diskutiert Tertullian das apokryphe Henochbuch – um seine Echtheit ausdrücklich zu verteidigen (die ja auch der Judasbrief ohne Frage voraussetzt);[85] Noah hätte es mit sich auf der Arche gehabt (De cultu feminarum 1,3,1–3).[86] Augustin verteidigt seine Echtheit, da es sonst Judas nicht hätte zitieren können, auch wenn es über die langen Zeiträume vielleicht nicht völlig authentisch bewahrt worden sein mochte und daher nicht selbst kanonisch sei (civ. 15,23; 18,38). Und der doch hochgebildete Origenes verteidigt (Epistula ad Africanum) sachlich unzutreffend die Historizität und Echtheit der Susannaepisode gegen Julius Africanus (Epistola ad Originem),[87] usw. Solche Stimmen sind nicht selten. Wir nennen nur Beispiele.

Dennoch nahmen Christen natürlich Anteil an literaturwissenschaftlichen Echtheitsfragen, sobald sie sich auf der dazu erforderlichen Bildungshöhe bewegten. Julius Africanus, der erste christliche Chronograph, ist auch der Erste gewesen, der sich zu homerischen Athetierungen geäußert hat (Kestoi Frgm. 5 Vieillefond = P.Oxy. 412). Aber wie in jeder echten Subkultur stellten sie die Fragen der Mainstreamkultur nur selektiv. Andere Motive sind wirksam. Vor allem ist die Tendenz zu erkennen, alle relevanten Texte der jeweils bedeutendsten Autorität zuzuschreiben (daher halten Tertullian, Cyprian und nach dem Zeugnis des Hilarius von Poitiers und des Augustin auch andere westliche Autoren gar Sirach für ein Werk Salomos[88], etc.).

---

[85] Zur Rezeption des Henochbuches und den widersprüchlichen Aussagen zu seiner Echtheit in der Alten Kirche s. H. J. LAWLOR, Early Citations from the Book of Enoch, JP 25 (1897), 164–225; J. C. VANDERKAM, 1 Enoch, Enochic Motifs, and Enoch in Early Christian Literature, in: ders. / W. Adler (Hg.), The Jewish Apocalyptic Heritage in Early Christianity, CRI III/4, Minneapolis 1996, 33–101.

[86] Text mit Übersetzung auch bei BAUM, Pseudepigraphie und literarische Fälschung (s. Anm. 5), 254f.

[87] Beide Texte mit franz. Übersetzung bei N. de Lange (Hg.), SC 302, Paris 1983, 514–521 (Julius Africanus). 522–573 (Origenes); vgl. die knappe Diskussion bei BAUM, Pseudepigraphie und literarische Fälschung (s. Anm. 5), 105f.

[88] Tertullian, Scorpiace 7,1; Cyprian, Ad Quirinum testimoniorum libri tres 2,1; 3,6.12.35.51.53.95f.109.113; Ad Fortunatum 9; De opere et eleemosynis 5; ep. 3,2; Hilarius von Poitiers, Tractatus super Psalmos 140,5 (CSEL 22,792,11–13 hg. v. A. Zingerle); vgl. Aug.doctr.chr. 2,8,13.

4. Zwei frühchristliche Beispiele: die Pastoralbriefe und der Judas- sowie 2. Petrusbrief

Blicken wir nun wieder zurück auf die neutestamentliche Epoche, und zwar auf zwei frühchristliche Beispiele, um einerseits die Relevanz dieser Fragen für die Erforschung konkreter pseudepigrapher Schriften in den Blick zu nehmen, andererseits weitere Beobachtungen zusammenzustellen, die uns erlauben werden, einige Gedanken hinsichtlich frühchristlicher und antiker Fiktionalitätsdiskurse überhaupt zu formulieren. Speziell zur Pseudepigraphie der Pastoralbriefe habe ich andernorts versucht, die Verfasserschaftsfragen einer Klärung näher zu bringen. Gegen die dabei vorgeschlagene Lösung (Timotheus und Titus gemeinsam oder einer von beiden als Überlebende[r] des „Paulusteams" als Verfasser) ist eingewandt worden, dass 1Tim 6,12f. den Tod des Apostelschülers voraussetzten.[89] Doch könnte man sich diese Sätze auch sehr gut als Worte eines alten Mannes vorstellen, der weiß, dass er bald sterben wird, sein geistliches Erbe zu Papier bringt – in Reverenz seinem alten Meister gegenüber – und sich zugleich selbst auf die Vollendung seines Lebens einstellt. Aber das mag hier auf sich beruhen: Mehr als Wahrscheinlichkeitsurteile werden nicht möglich sein. Für die Pastoralbriefe hängt die Frage nach ihrem prägenden Zweck wesentlich an der Identifikation der Gemeinschaft bzw. Lehre, gegen die sie offenbar polemisieren. Man hat wegen 1Tim 6,20 mehrfach einen Bezug auf Markions Antithesen diskutiert, der aber inhaltlich und wohl auch chronologisch nicht recht passen will – wenn der Autor das Werk auch weder gelesen noch verstanden haben müsste, um darauf polemisch anzuspielen, und die Antithesen schon lange vor Markions römischer Exkommunikation 144 n. Chr. entstanden sein könnten. Auch hierzu ist also vielleicht das letzte Wort noch nicht gesagt. Oft wird nach wie vor sehr allgemein von „gnostischen Irrlehrern (wohl Wanderpredigern)"[90] gesprochen. Bentley Layton hat gemeint, dass sich 2Tim 2,18 schon auf den gnostischen Brief an Rheginus bezieht.[91] Aber natürlich finden sich gnostische Usurpationen der Auferstehungsbegrifflichkeit (bei radikaler inhaltlicher Umdeutung) auch sonst, z.B. EvThom 51. Wir müs-

---

[89] Rezension des Bandes durch A. M. SCHWEMER, ThLZ 127 (2002), 909–912.

[90] So jetzt wieder VON LIPS, Timotheus und Titus. Unterwegs für Paulus (s. Anm. 25), 156; SCHNELLE, Einleitung in das Neue Testament (s. Anm. 3), 381f., denkt an eine Frühform christlicher Gnosis, in die jüdische Elemente eingeflossen seien.

[91] B. LAYTON, The Gnostic Treatise on Resurrection from Nag Hammadi. Edited with Translation and Commentary, HDR 12, Missoula 1979, 1. Als Denkmöglichkeit auch erwogen bei H.-M. SCHENKE, „Der Brief an Rheginus" (NHC I,4), in: ders. / H.-G. Bethge / U. U. Kaiser (Hg.), Nag Hammadi Deutsch, Bd. 1: NHC I,1–V,1, GCS NF 8, Berlin/New York 2001, 49.

sen das hier nicht klären: Unbestreitbar dürfte sein, dass die Pastoralbriefe eine komplexe ekklesiologische Agenda aufweisen, die sich in der Tat als Vergegenwärtigung eines paulinischen Erbes verstehen lässt. Auch die vielschichtigen Personalnotizen der Pastoralbriefe tragen zu einer hohen Literarizität bei, indem sie sie der Welt des antiken Romans annähern.[92] Pseudepigraphie ist dabei nur ein Stilmittel neben anderen, um eine Interpretation und Korrektur des Pauluserbes für die Gegenwart zu inszenieren und zu legitimieren. Weiterführende Fragen zu den Entstehungsverhältnissen der Pastoralbriefe hat in jüngerer Zeit v.a. Jens Herzer gestellt.[93] Dabei ist die Einheitlichkeit und Zusammengehörigkeit der Pastoralbriefe erneut zum Problem geworden, ebenso ihre Reihenfolge (1Tim – 2Tim – Tit? Tit – 1Tim – 2Tim? Oder, so Herzer, Tit – 2Tim und dann mit Abstand 1Tim?[94]). 1Tim zeigt Eigentümlichkeiten stilistischer und theologischer Art, die ihn von 2Tim und Tit abheben. Herzer untersucht dabei u.a. die Affinitäten zur Popularphilosophie, die Eschatologie, die Verwendung von Konzepten wie εὐσέβεια und ἐπιφάνεια, das Verständnis und die Präsenz der einzelnen kirchlichen Ämter (Verhältnis Presbyter-Episkopos) und andere Aspekte, mit der resultierenden Frage, inwiefern jeder der drei Pastoralbriefe ein theologisch unterschiedliches Profil zeigt. Identität der Gegner wäre dann zu beweisen, nicht vorauszusetzen. Aus solchen Beobachtungen (die auch von anderen formuliert wurden) könnten sich Konsequenzen für die Pseudepigraphiefrage ergeben, bis zu einer Lösung mit drei verschiedenen Verfassern.[95] Ein solches Extremmodell dürfte aber wohl die Gemeinsamkeiten unterbewerten. Herzers Beobachtungen scheinen sich zu dieser Frage noch nicht zu einer präzisen Theorie verfestigt zu haben. In jedem Fall zeigen sie, in wie hohem Maße auch hier scheinbar stabile Konsense fragwürdig geworden sind.[96]

---

[92] R. I. PERVO, Romancing an Oft-Neglected Stone. The Pastoral Epistles and the Epistolary Novel, The Journal of Higher Criticism 1 (1994), 25–47.

[93] J. HERZER, Abschied vom Konsens? Die Pseudepigraphie der Pastoralbriefe als Herausforderung an die neutestamentliche Wissenschaft, ThLZ 129 (2004), 1267–1282 (Sammelrezension neuerer Kommentare); ders., „Das Geheimnis der Frömmigkeit" (1 Tim 3,16). Sprache und Stil der Pastoralbriefe im Kontext hellenistisch-römischer Popularphilosophie – eine methodische Problemanzeige, ThQ 187 (2007), 309–329; ders., Rearranging the ‚House of God'. A New Perspective on the Pastoral Epistles, in: A. Houtman / A. de Jong / M. Misset-van de Weg (Hg.), Empsychoi Logoi – Religious Innovations in Antiquity (FS van der Horst), AGAJU 73, Leiden/Boston 2008, 547–566.

[94] HERZER, Rearranging the ‚House of God' (s. Anm. 93), 564.

[95] So W. A. RICHARDS, Difference and Distance in Post-Pauline Christianity. A Epistolary Analysis of the Pastorals, Studies in Biblical Literature 44, New York u.a. 2002.

[96] Ähnliches gilt für die schwierige Frage der Rezeption der Past im 2. Jh. Ein maximalistisches Modell vertritt C. LOOKS, Das Anvertraute bewahren. Die Rezeption

Vergleicht man 2Thess, die Pastoralbriefe und andererseits etwa Eph, wird sehr deutlich, wie unterschiedlich jeder Fall von Pseudepigraphie beurteilt werden muss. Nicht nur divergiert die entfaltete Theologie,[97] sondern der literarische Charakter der Texte und ihre Autorenfiktion sind kaum vergleichbar. Langfristig wird die Forschung eine Typologie von Formen von Pseudepigraphie entwickeln müssen, in der das literarische Raffinement der Pastoralbriefe von der quasi „mythischen" Pseudepigraphie der Henochliteratur und diversen anderen Typen auch begrifflich deutlicher unterschieden werden kann.[98] Theologische und literaturgeschichtliche Unterschiede wären dabei deutlich zu trennen. Ein Kriterium einer solchen Typologie könnte das Maß sein, in dem die Verfasserfiktion im Brief konkretisiert wird – von der nur angedeuteten Umsetzung im Epheserbrief (als dessen Verfasser Tychikus – Eph 6,21 – wohl nicht in Frage kommt, weil der Autor diesen Namen einfach nur aus Kol 4,7 übernommen haben könnte) bis zu der romanhaften Auffüllung mit Details, die wir in den Pastoralbriefen beobachten (zur Typologiefrage vgl. weiter unten).

Wenden wir uns in einem nächsten Schritt zwei anderen Texten zu, die sich in einem komplexen, schwer genau in den Griff zu bekommenden Intertextualitätsverhältnis bewegen, welches irgendwie mit ihrer Pseudepigraphie zusammenhängen muss: Judas und 2Petr.[99] Woher nimmt der Autor des 2Petr das Recht, Judas weithin in sein Schreiben zu integrieren?[100] Diese Freiheit setzt ja mehrerlei voraus: Der Verfasser kannte Judas, und hat zugleich fest damit gerechnet, dass sein Publikum Judas nicht

---

der Pastoralbriefe im 2. Jahrhundert, München 1999, der aber auch die Unsicherheit der Belege sieht (122).

[97] Sehr schön formuliert Gerd Theißen: „Jeder von ihnen öffnet eine kleine theologische Welt für sich" (Die Entstehung des Neuen Testaments [s. Anm. 7], 178 Anm. 31).

[98] Ein anderer Spezialfall wäre der Hebräerbrief, falls sich die ehemals von Adolf von Harnack begründete, in jüngerer Zeit unermüdlich von Ruth Hoppin verteidigte These durchsetzen sollte, dass dieser Brieftraktat ein Werk der Priscilla ist (Priscilla's Letter. Finding the Author of the Letter to the Hebrews, San Francisco 1997). Dafür existieren eine Reihe ernstzunehmender Argumente, die freilich nur im Ensemble ihre Plausibilität entfalten. Ich hoffe, die Frage an anderer Stelle ausführlich diskutieren zu können.

[99] Die im Folgenden ausgeführten Gedanken gelten mutatis mutandis auch für Kolosser- und Epheserbrief, deren Pseudepigraphie ja ebenfalls intertextuell vernetzt ist, obwohl sie mit einiger Sicherheit nicht vom selben Verfasser stammen.

[100] Aus der reichen Literatur wird im Folgenden v.a. verwiesen auf: R. J. BAUCKHAM, Jude and the Relatives of Jesus in the Early Church, Edinburgh 1990; VÖGTLE, Der Judasbrief. Der 2. Petrusbrief (s. Anm. 60); R. HEILIGENTHAL, Zwischen Henoch und Paulus. Studien zum theologiegeschichtlichen Ort des Judasbriefes, TANZ 6, Tübingen 1992; T. J. KRAUS, Sprache, Stil und historischer Ort des zweiten Petrusbriefes, WUNT II/136, Tübingen 2001.

kannte (dieser Punkt wird leicht übersehen). Außerdem galt ihm Judas nicht als heiliger oder sakrosankter Text – durchschaute er also dessen Pseudepigraphie? Oder hat der Autor des 2Petr Judas gerade deshalb integriert, weil ihm dies ein „besonderer" Text war, der mit einer besonderen Autorität versehen war? Aber er verwendet ja keine Zitationsformeln oder sonstige Zitationssignale. Man wird also nicht umhin können, von einem Vorgang der Aneignung unter Verschleierung der wahren Verfasserschaft zu sprechen. Auch hier wird man m.E. eher niederschwellig von einem unausgeprägten Gespür für eine solche Aneignung eines Textes auszugehen haben: Vielleicht haben Formulierungen und Zusammenhänge aus dem Judasbrief dem Verfasser des 2Petr einfach so gut gefallen, dass er sich ohne weitere Hintergedanken berechtigt sah, sie zu übernehmen. Dennoch bleibt der Punkt, dass er offenbar nicht damit gerechnet hat, dass sein Akt der Aneignung als solcher erkannt werden würde. Diese Beobachtungen sind umso bemerkenswerter, als der Verfasser des 2Petr wohl mit einiger Sicherheit bei seinen Lesern Kenntnis des 1Petr voraussetzt und auf diesen verweist (2Petr 3,1). Auch die in ihrer Form singuläre explizite Bezugnahme auf das Corpus Paulinum muss bedacht werden (2Petr 3,15f.). Leider wissen wir weder sicher, welche Paulusbriefe der Autor kennt bzw. voraussetzt, noch ob er den 1Petr für einen echten Petrusbrief gehalten hat. Letzteres dürfte aber doch wahrscheinlich sein; nur dann macht der Bezug wirklich Sinn und kann sein eigenes Schreiben legitimieren. Wir haben also mindestens einen weiteren Fall nicht durchschauter Pseudepigraphie vor uns, eventuell verbunden mit einem anders gelagerten Fall, bei dem diese durchschaut wurde oder zumindest der integrierte Text als „verfügbare Größe" erscheint. Die etwas halbherzige Verteidigung paulinischer Theologie in 2Petr ist umso bemerkenswerter, wenn sich andererseits der Jakobusbrief gegen Paulus selbst oder eine Richtung der Paulusschule wendet, wie sie uns etwa im Kolosserbrief entgegentritt. Der Verweis auf Judas als Bruder des Jakobus in Jud 1 (und vielleicht damit wohl eigentlich auf den Jakobusbrief, mit dem Bekanntschaft aber nicht textlich nachzuweisen ist) könnte den Judasbrief als Pseudepigraphon in pauluskritischen Kreisen verorten.[101] Ein solcher Zusammenhang ist schon vielfach vermutet worden. Dann würde verständlich, warum der insgesamt – mit Einschränkungen – doch paulusfreundliche 2Petr Judas als in „seinen Kreisen"

---

[101] Nach HEILIGENTHAL, a.a.O. 165, vertrat der pseudepigraphe Autor des Judasbriefes „eine frühe, jüdisch gefärbte antiochenische Gemeindetheologie. Seine Trägerkreise sind in dem Milieu christlichen Diasporapharisäertums zu suchen." Abgesehen von der Begrifflichkeit (die Theologie eines Menschen jüdischer Herkunft ist nicht „jüdisch gefärbt", sondern jüdisch), wird hier mit vielen Unbekannten hantiert, nicht zuletzt einem Diasporapharisäertum, dessen Existenz durch nichts erwiesen ist. Er will den Brief als „christliche Henochliteratur" verstehen.

nicht weiter bekannt behandeln kann. Die Pseudepigraphie des Judasbriefes selbst scheint mir aber nicht wirklich sicher zu sein; auch das soll hier nicht weiter diskutiert werden. Wir bewegen uns also in einem komplizierten literarischen Netzwerk an Intertextualitäten, die zugleich mit theologischen Affinitäten, aber auch massiven Distanzierungen verbunden sind. Pseudepigraphie ist ein Mittel der Durchsetzung von theologischen Positionen im Widerstreit mit theologischen Gegnern: In keinem Fall ist sie einfach nur „Stilmittel", sondern konstituiert Legitimitätsstrukturen in Konfliktsituationen.

Wie auch immer, in jedem Fall sah sich der Autor des 2Petr (dessen Pseudepigraphie kaum widerlegbar ist) berechtigt, Judas ohne weiteren Verweis in seine Schrift zu integrieren. Der Text war für ihn als Baustein seiner eigenen Schrift „verfügbar": nicht nur faktisch, sondern auch ideologisch. Beide Autoren (derjenige des Judasbriefes und derjenige des 2Petr) stammen aus ganz unterschiedlichen theologischen Milieus. Dennoch wäre es denkbar, dass der Verfasser des 2Petr damit rechnete, dass Judas auf einer Fiktion beruht. Bekanntlich übernimmt er den Text auch nicht vollständig, sondern streicht die Bezüge auf apokryphe Schriften. Das zeigt eine nicht unkritische Lektüre. Judas ist für ihn „Material", aber keine sakrosankte Autorität, und vermutlich auch kaum „Heilige Schrift", zumal Zitationsformeln fehlen. Was bedeutete dann für 2Petr die Verfasserschaftsangabe des Judas? Inwiefern gab sie den Text für seine eigene Benutzung „frei"? Welche Stellung gegenüber der Familie Jesu kommt in 2Petr zum Tragen?[102] Diese Fragen zu stellen, heißt leider noch nicht, sie beantworten zu können.

Der Judasbrief selbst war – nach allem, was wir sehen können – in seiner Verfasserschaft nicht unumstritten, wobei jedoch offenbar nicht an Pseudepigraphie gedacht wurde. Das Decretum Gelasianum zählt unter den kanonischen Schriften des NT auf „Iudae Zelotis apostoli epistula una", und eine Varia lectio liest dazu sogar noch „sed ista publice in ecclesia non legitur".[103] Eine gewisse Zurückhaltung dem Schreiben gegenüber mag es

---

[102] Diese Frage stellt auch BAUCKHAM, Jude and the Relatives of Jesus in the Early Church (s. Anm. 100), nicht. Übrigens diskutiert selbst Bauckhams exzellente Studie über die leiblichen Verwandten Jesu in der Alten Kirche keineswegs alle einschlägigen Überlieferungen. Nicht behandelt wird z.B. die Tradition über Servatius von Tongern, der nach einer interessanten Notiz ein Abkömmling der Familie Jesu war, und noch die mittelalterliche Legenda aurea 142 bzw. 212 kennt ihn als „in quarto gradu attinens Christo Iesu" (954 hg. v. Graesse). Vgl. M. LEJEUNE, De legendarische Stamboom van Sint Servaas, Publ. de la Societé historique et archéologique de la Limburg 77, Maastricht 1941, 283–332. Eine Sammlung aller auch legendarischer Nachrichten über die Familie Jesu bis ins frühe Mittelalter ist ein dringendes Desiderat.

[103] E. von Dobschütz, Das Decretum Gelasianum de libris recipiendis et non recipiendis, TU 38/4, Leipzig 1912, 28.

also gegeben haben. Judas- und 2. Petrusbrief sind allerdings beide schon im späten 2. Jh. recht gut bezeugt; jedenfalls lässt sich aus ihrer frühen Bezeugung nichts Sicheres für ihre Entstehung entnehmen.[104] An den Apostel Judas als Verfasser denkt schon Tertullian, De cultu feminarum 1,3,3, während Hieronymus den Brief dem Herrenbruder Judas zuschreibt (vir.ill. 4), was der Autor offenbar auch selbst suggerieren will (vgl. zur Person Hegesipp bei Eus.h.e. 3,19,1–20,6). An andere Träger des Namens Judas hat man erst in der Neuzeit gedacht. Fragmente aus den Anmerkungen zu Judas in Clemens' Hypotyposen sind bei Cassiodor erhalten, und Didymus Alexandrinus schrieb einen lateinisch erhaltenen Kommentar, der auch 2Petr und andere katholische Briefe umfasste, etc.[105] Die frühe papyrologische Bezeugung ist allerdings eher kümmerlich, wenn auch von erheblichem Interesse: 2Petr ist, wenn ich recht sehe, im 2. Jh. gar nicht und im 3. Jh. nur in P^{72} (= P. Bodmer VII/VIII) erhalten, wenn dieser wichtige Papyrus nicht gar erst aus dem 4. Jh. stammt, der auch Judas umfasst.[106] Die ntl. Schriften sind dabei aber nur Teile einer großen, ehemals von Martin Bodmer aufgekauften Sammelhandschrift, die ursprünglich vielleicht 190 Seiten von nahezu quadratischem Format aufwies und zu den wunderlichsten frühchristlichen Zeugnissen gehört. Die Sammlung, die schwerlich liturgischen Zwecken diente, sondern eine typische Privatabschrift gewesen sein dürfte, enthielt eine Nativ. Mariae (heute Protevangelium Jacobi genannt, P. Bodmer V), 3Kor sowie eine ebenfalls pseudepi-

---

[104] Biblia Patristica. Index des citations et allusions bibliques dans la littérature patristique 1, Paris 1986, 530f.536f.; T. WASSERMAN, The Epistle of Jude. Its Text and Transmission, Stockholm 2006; Novum Testamentum Graecum Editio Critica Maior IV. Die Katholischen Briefe. Teil 2, 4. Lief., hg. v. B. Aland u.a., Stuttgart 2005, bes. B 134f. (Liste der Kirchenväterzitate).

[105] C. KANNENGIESSER, Handbook of Patristic Exegesis 1, Leiden/Boston 2004, 362. Didymus' Verfasserschaft ist nicht ganz über jeden Zweifel erhaben, wird aber mehrheitlich aufrecht erhalten. Der Text ist ediert in F. Zoepfl (Hg.), Didymi Alexandrini in epistulas canonicas brevis ennarratio, NTA 4/1, Münster 1914. In Übersetzung sind alle Reste altkirchlicher Judaskommentare gesammelt in: P. R. JONES, The Epistle of Jude as Expounded by the Fathers – Clement of Alexandria, Didymus of Alexandria, the Scholia of Cramer's Catena, Pseudo-Oecumenius, and Bede, TSR 89, Lewiston 2001.

[106] 1Petr ist in sahidischer Übersetzung bereits in Codex Crosby-Schøyen 193 wohl noch aus dem 3. Jh. erhalten: J. E. GOEHRING, The Crosby-Schøyen Codex MS 193 in the Schøyen-Collection, Leuven 1990. Überschrift und Subscriptio (ΠЄΠΙ СΤΟΛΗ ΜΠЄΤΡΟС „der Brief des Petrus") beweisen, dass dieser Codex nur einen Petrusbrief als kanonischen Text kennt. Nur Koh, 1Joh und 2Petr dagegen enthält ein jüngst publizierter Codex in fajumischem Koptisch (Dialekt V4) aus der 1. Hälfte des 4. Jh.: H.-M. Schenke in Zusammenarbeit mit R. Kasser, Papyrus Michigan 3520 und 6868(a). Ecclesiastes, Erster Johannesbrief und Zweiter Petrusbrief in fayumischem Dialekt, TU 151, Berlin/New York 2003.

graphe Antwort der Korinther auf 2Kor (P. Bodmer X), die 11. Ode Salomos (P. Bodmer XI), den Judasbrief (P. Bodmer VII), Melitons Passahomilie (P. Bodmer XIII), einen weiteren hymnischen Text, den Othmar Perler auch Meliton zuschreiben wollte (P. Bodmer XII), die Phileasapologie (P. Bodmer XX), Psalm 33 und 34 LXX (P. Bodmer IX) und schließlich 1Petr und 2Petr (P. Bodmer VIII).[107] Dabei waren vier, eventuell sogar sechs Abschreiber beteiligt; die einzelnen Texte wurden Anfang des 4. Jh. sorgfältig zusammengefügt, doch stammen die Abschriften selbst außer Phileas und den beiden Psalmen aus dem 3. Jh. Was besondere Hervorhebung verdient, ist natürlich, dass das ganze „Corpus" 1Petr/2Petr/Jud hier in einem Umfeld von Texten tradiert wird, die zu dieser Zeit längst als apokryph galten, und die jedenfalls keinen kanonischen Charakter hatten. Obwohl wie gesagt auch zwei Psalmen miteingebunden waren, ist der nicht-kanonische Grundcharakter der Handschrift (auf der Ebene der Textzusammenstellung letzter Hand) auffällig. Die immer nur partielle und zerstückelte Publikation des Codex unter verschiedenen Papyrussiglen hat eine Wahrnehmung seiner Bedeutung gerade als Sammlung lange Zeit sehr behindert.[108] In welchem Sinn 1/2Petrus und Judas für den Veranstalter der Sammlung überhaupt Heilige Schriften waren, ist alles andere als deutlich. Judas ist zudem weit weniger sorgfältig abgeschrieben als 1/2Petrus. Aber was bedeutet dieser Befund?[109] Auch sonst ist vieles an der Handschrift merkwürdig, wozu hier nur auf die exzellente Diskussion von Tobias Nicklas und Tommy Wasserman verwiesen werden kann. Diese haben die kuriose Textauswahl der Handschrift mit der Schwierigkeit zu erklären versucht, überhaupt an Büchertexte heranzukommen. Wirkliche inhaltliche Leitlinien der Auswahl lassen sich – obwohl verschiedentlich vorgeschlagen – nicht plausibel machen.[110] James M. Robinson will einen Zusammenhang mit einer Mönchsgemeinschaft des Pachomius herstellen, aus der das Gesamtpaket der Dishna Papyri (gemeinhin auch Bodmer Papyri

---

[107] Edition: M. Testuz, Papyrus Bodmer VII–IX. Cologny/Genève 1959; C. M. Martini, Beati Petri Apostoli Epistulae. Ex Papyro Bodmeriana VIII, Mailand 1968. Vgl. auch zur ersten Orientierung den (nicht unproblematischen) Druck bei P. W. Comfort / D. P. Barrett (Hg.), The Complete Text of the Earliest New Testament Manuscripts, Grand Rapids 1999, 468–490. Allgemein zu den Bodmerpapyri vgl. die Übersicht A. PIETERSMA, Art. Bodmer Papyri, AncBDict 1 (1992), 766f.

[108] So sehr treffend K. HAINES-EITZEN, Guardians of Letters. Literacy, Power, and the Transmission of Early Christian Literature, Oxford 2000, 96.

[109] Vgl. auch T. NICKLAS, Der ‚lebendige Text' des Neuen Testaments. Der Judasbrief in P 72 (P. Bodmer VII), ASE 23 (2005), 69–88; HAINES-EITZEN, a.a.O. 96–104.

[110] Dazu in eingehender Diskussion T. NICKLAS / T. WASSERMAN, Theologische Linien im Codex Bodmer Miscellani?, in: T. J. Kraus / T. Nicklas (Hg.), New Testament Manuscripts. Their Texts and Their World, Leiden 2006, 161–188.

genannt) vermutlich stammt.[111] Doch viele Fragen bleiben. „Das Manuskript bleibt rätselhaft."[112]

Judas 4f.7f. ist außerdem auf dem offenbar als Amulett verwendeten Miniaturcodex P. 78 = P.Oxy. 2684 bezeugt (3. Jh.),[113] der nur 2,9 x 5,3 cm misst. Dieser ganze Befund zum Judas- und 2. Petrusbrief ist doch recht eigentümlich und unterscheidet sich deutlich z.b. von der Überlieferung der Paulusbriefe. Der 2. Petrusbrief wurde vielleicht auch echtheitskritisch diskutiert, wenn wir darüber auch nur wenig wissen: „Simon Petrus ... scripsit duas epistulas, quae catholicae nominantur; quarum secunda a plerisque eis negatur propter stili cum priore dissonantiam" (Hier.vir.ill. 1). Man beachte, wie Hieronymus sich in seinem eigenen Urteil zurückhält. Eus.h.e. 3,3,1 hatte den 1Petr für fraglos kanonisch erklärt, den 2Petr zwar für unkanonisch, aber „gleichzuhalten"; auch hier also deutliche Zurückhaltung.

Ein wesentlicher und erklärungsbedürftiger Unterschied zwischen Judas und 2Petr ist dabei die divergierende Haltung gegenüber den Apokryphen. Dass 2Petr die Apokryphenanspielungen des Judas nicht übernimmt, zeigt, dass er dem Brief nicht völlig unkritisch gegenübersteht. Von Bedeutung ist möglicherweise eine Passage im Berliner Koptischen Buch (P. Berlin 20915), die jüngst in den Mittelpunkt des Interesses gerückt ist. Sie zitiert vielleicht dasselbe Mosesapokryphon wie Judas[114], aber sicher ist die Sache nicht. Tertullian benutzt die Henochanspielungen in Judas als Beleg dafür, dass „Enoch" (gemeint ist die heute äthiopischer Henoch genannte Schrift, die er wohl in griechischer Fassung kannte) tatsächlich von dem Vorweltpatriarchen Henoch stammt (De cultu feminarum 1,3,3). Viele Details beider Briefe bleiben rätselhaft; wir merken jedoch, dass wir uns in einer literarischen Subkultur bewegen, in der Verfasserschaftsangaben

---

[111] Vgl. J. M. ROBINSON, The Pachomian Monastic Library at the Chester Beatty Library and the Bibliothèque Bodmer, Institute for Antiquity and Christianity: Occasional Papers 19, Claremont 1990, 19 Inv. 6. Diese wichtige kleine Schrift Robinsons mit ihrem Textverzeichnis ermöglichte zum ersten Mal einen wirklichen Gesamteindruck der pachomischen Bibliothek. Sie ist neuerdings auch im Internet zugänglich unter: http://tinyurl.com/6kf3vy.

[112] NICKLAS / WASSERMAN, Theologische Linien im Codex Bodmer Miscellani? (s. Anm. 110), 188 (Schlusssatz der Studie).

[113] T. WASSERMAN, P 78 (P.Oxy. XXXIV 2684). The Epistle of Jude an Amulet?, in: Kraus / Nicklas, New Testament Manuscripts (s. Anm. 110), 137–160. Zum Gebrauch biblischer Texte als Amulette in der Alten Kirche vgl. M. FRENSCHKOWSKI, Art. Magie, RAC (im Druck). Vgl. insgesamt auch die tabellarische Übersicht über den Gesamtbefund frühchristlicher Textzeugen bei L. HURTADO, The Earliest Christian Artifacts. Manuscripts and Christian Origins, Grand Rapids/Cambridge 2006, 209–229.

[114] Das Berliner „Koptische Buch" (P 20915). Eine wiederhergestellte frühchristlich-theologische Abhandlung, bearb. v. G. Schenke Robinson (...), CSCO 611, Leuven 2004, 140 vgl. XII.

weithin offen waren für vielschichtige Fiktionalität. Ob die vielfältigen kanongeschichtlichen Besonderheiten der Katholischen Briefe auch damit zusammenhängen, dass man sich zum Teil über ihre fiktive Herkunft im Klaren war? Aber für eine solche Annahme fehlen eindeutige Zeugnisse. David R. Nienhuis hat jüngst den Jakobusbrief als bewusst gestaltete Einführung in ein Corpus der Katholischen Briefe deuten wollen: „It was written to forge together a Jerusalem Pillars letter collection to balance the emphasis of the Pauline collection, defend the authority of the Jewish scriptures, and uphold the continuity of the covenants – in short, to protect against the theological distortions that tended to arise whenever readers championed Paul alone."[115] Anders gesagt: Die Zusammenstellung der Katholischen Briefe richte sich gegen jenes theologische Klima, dessen wichtigster Vertreter Markion war, und der Jakobusbrief sei zur Abrundung dieser Sammlung entstanden. Auch Theißen sieht in den Katholischen Briefen kanongeschichtlich ein „Gegengewicht"[116] gegen das langsam wachsende Corpus Paulinum. Das sind ingeniöse Vermutungen, die aber leider nichts darüber aussagen, ob die Kompilatoren etwas über die Pseudepigraphie der von ihnen zusammengestellten Briefe wussten. Insgesamt scheint das eher unwahrscheinlich; es bleibt bei Einzelstimmen, die sich weniger auf die Echtheit als die Kanonizität richten.

Die zum hier vorausgesetzten Verhältnis Judas-2Petr umgekehrte Annahme, dass nämlich der Judasbrief vom 2. Petrusbrief abhängig sei und sich Formulierungen aus diesem geliehen habe, hat wenig, was sie empfehlen könnte. Obwohl sie einige Anhänger hatte – u.a. Theodor Zahn[117], dessen Urteil ernst zu nehmen ist – wollen wir diese Denkmöglichkeit hier nicht verfolgen und diese Diskussion den Einleitungen überlassen.[118] Ist die Pseudepigraphie dieser Briefe eine „harmlose Raffiniertheit"? Das wird man nicht sagen können. Wir bewegen uns in einem Milieu, in dem theologische Parteinahmen durch Pseudepigraphie untermauert wurden, wohl wissend, dass diese wahrscheinlich nicht durchschaut werden würde. Die frühe christliche Rezeption besagt, dass sich die Echtheitsannahme wenn

---

[115] D. R. NIENHUIS, Not by Paul Alone. The Formation of the Catholic Epistle Collection and the Christian Canon, Waco 2007, 238.

[116] THEISSEN, Die Entstehung des Neuen Testaments (s. Anm. 7), 181.

[117] T. ZAHN, Einleitung in das Neue Testament, 2 Bd., Leipzig ³1906/7 (Nachdruck mit einem Vorwort von R. Riesner, Wuppertal/Zürich 1994), Bd. 2, 43–112.

[118] Dazu m.E. abschließend WASSERMAN, The Epistle of Jude. Its Text and Transmission (s. Anm. 104), 73–98 (auch zu methodischen Problemen solcher Vergleiche); KRAUS, Sprache, Stil und historischer Ort des zweiten Petrusbriefes (s. Anm. 100), 368–376. Wasserman zeigt a.a.O. 99–102 auch, dass sich die Texte von Judas und 2Petrus in der Textgeschichte gegenseitig beeinflusst haben (etwa wie v.a. Matthäus die Überlieferung der anderen Synoptiker stark beeinflusst hat).

auch doch nicht ungebrochen, so doch mehrheitlich durchsetzen konnte. Was besagt dies über den kulturellen Ort von Schreibern und Empfängern?

5. Christentum und Pseudepigraphie, oder: Waren Christen naiver?

Wir stehen also vor der grundlegenden Spannung, dass Pseudepigraphie in gewissem Umfang durchschaubar war und durchschaut wurde, anders gesagt tatsächlich tradierbares literarisches Stilmittel war, andererseits jedoch von den Christen mehrheitlich in Hinsicht auf ihr eigenes literarisches Traditum, v.a. ihre kanonische Literatur nicht als solches wahrgenommen wurde. Gewisse vereinzelte kritische Stimmen waren eher theologisch motiviert als literarisch-stilistisch, und konnten sich auch kein anhaltendes Gehör verschaffen. Selbst völlig unglaubwürdige Pseudepigraphen wie der Briefwechsel Paulus-Seneca fanden bereitwillig Glauben und spielen in der Kanondebatte nur deshalb keine Rolle, weil sie dafür zu spät auf die Bühne traten. Plakativ lässt sich sagen, dass Christen Verfasserschaftsfragen gegenüber nicht weiter argwöhnisch waren, wenn ihnen der Inhalt eines Buches unbedenklich erschien.[119] Waren Christen also – sit venia verbo – naiver als ihre Umwelt? Ganz so einfach ist die Sache sicher nicht. Wir müssen einmal sozial- und bildungsgeschichtlich differenzieren. In der frühen Zeit, sicher im 1. Jh., aber auch noch weit darüber hinaus, bewegt sich das Christentum mehrheitlich noch in großem Abstand zu jener Bildungs- und Literaturwelt, in der Verfasserschaftsfragen zum Problem werden und diskutiert werden konnten.

G. Theißen und in Ansätzen auch H.-J. Klauck haben präziser die Bildungsdistanz zwischen Autoren und Publikum zur Erklärung der genannten Beobachtungen herangezogen. „Die neutestamentlichen Autoren mochten zu literaturfähigen gebildeten Kreisen gehören, die Adressaten der urchristlichen Schriften gehörten sicher in der Mehrzahl zu literaturfernen Schichten. Die Gattungserwartungen, die man in diesen Kreisen voraussetzen konnte, waren minimal. Anerkannt war unter ihnen die personale Autorität Jesu und der Apostel. Was von ihnen stammte, war für die einfachen Glaubenden akzeptabel. Deshalb wurden die Paulusbriefe nach-

---

[119] Diese Beobachtung ist zu trennen von der spezifischen kanongeschichtlichen Theorie Armin Daniel Baums (Pseudepigraphie und literarische Fälschung [s. Anm. 5], passim), erkannte Pseudepigraphie habe in der Alten Kirche als Hinderungsgrund für kanonische Geltung gegolten, auch wenn die betreffende Schrift „orthodox" war. M.E. stellt die gelehrte Arbeit Baums – aus der vieles zu lernen ist – die Sache trotz vieler Einsichten auf den Kopf: Angesichts kanonischer Texte stellte sich der unterentwickelte kritische Sinn gar nicht erst ein, der Pseudepigraphie hätte erkennen können.

geahmt. Daher wurden Evangelien geschrieben. Beides geschah, um literarische Kommunikation in einem an sich unliterarischen Milieu zu ermöglichen."[120] Theißen fährt fort: „In der ersten Phase urchristlicher Literatur konnten wir die Aneignung kommunikativer Oberschichtformen durch literaturferne Kreise beobachten. In der zweiten Phase beobachten wir den umgekehrten Prozeß: das Eindringen der mündlichen Kultur einfacher Menschen in die Literatur, einerseits im Botenbewusstsein der Autoren, andererseits in der begrenzten Gattungskompetenz der Adressaten. Beides erklärt die Pseudepigraphie des guten Gewissens."[121] Dies bedeutet dann in Konsequenz: „War den ersten Christen bewusst, dass viele urchristliche Schriften pseudonym waren? Gab es ein heimliches Einverständnis darüber? ... Im Blick auf die Gemeinden insgesamt wird man diese Frage zwar verneinen müssen, im Blick auf kleine Gruppen gebildeter Christen muss man sie jedoch bejahen."[122] Damit ist sicher etwas Richtiges gesehen, m.E. ist aber doch noch ein weiterer Aspekt zu bedenken. Bildungsabstand ist ein wichtiger Faktor, aber er erklärt nicht den gesamten Befund. Ein Christ wie Tatian, Oratio ad Graecos 17,1 in seiner Kritik am superstitiösen Sympathieglauben weiß nichts von der Pseudepigraphie der ps.-demokritéischen Magica, die er diskutiert, und die doch zu seiner Zeit längst bekannt war (s.o.). Wir begegnen hier dem gleichen Bildungsabstand, der auch heutige fundamentalistische Christen oft schlicht nicht wahrnehmen lässt, dass in der wissenschaftlichen Forschung ein „Pseudepigraphieproblem" existiert. In der heutigen Diskussion wird Unkenntnis nach wie vor öfters mit systemischem Konservativismus verwechselt; das mag es auch in der Antike gegeben haben. Dieser Bildungsabstand hängt aber nicht am Niveau der Bildung, sondern an ihrem subkulturellen Charakter.

Theißens Modell bringt noch nicht hinreichend zur Geltung, warum in bestimmten Kontexten gerade auch gebildete christliche Autoren offenkundige Pseudepigraphie nicht durchschauten. Das frühe Christentum ist ein subkulturelles Phänomen: Nicht alle Konsense der antiken Bildungskultur können auf es übertragen werden. Subkulturen zeichnen sich gegenüber Mainstream-Kulturen dadurch aus, dass sie deren Inhalte nur selektiv rezipieren, aber völlig eigene Leitideen und Sensibilitäten besitzen, welche die Auswahl von kulturellen Inhalten der Mainstream-Kultur faktisch steuern. Ausdrucksformen der Mainstream-Kultur werden vor allem übernommen, wenn sie zur Legitimierung des „Eigenen" nützlich sind. Dabei disambiguieren sie: Was in einer Mainstream-Kultur eine vielschichtige, von Ambivalenzen umspielte Sache ist, wird in einer Subkultur eindeutig bzw.

---

[120] THEISSEN, Die Entstehung des Neuen Testaments (s. Anm. 7), 159.
[121] A.a.O. 159f.
[122] A.a.O. 160. Ähnlich auch H.-J. KLAUCK, Die antike Briefliteratur und das Neue Testament. Ein Lehr- und Arbeitsbuch, UTB 2022, Paderborn 1998, 304.

eindimensional. Menschen können durchaus an einem hohen gesellschaftlichen Status partizipieren, aber dennoch subkulturell agieren. Die Mainstream-Kultur ihrerseits nimmt ihre Devianzformen in Subkulturen oft nur sehr eingeschränkt zur Kenntnis.

Im Umfeld eines Augustinus und Hieronymus gilt eine Distanz zur Bildungswelt natürlich kaum mehr. Hier begegnen sich pagane und die mittlerweile etablierte christliche Bildungskultur auf Augenhöhe.[123] Dennoch bleibt die Fähigkeit zur kritischen Reflexion des eigenen Traditums unterentwickelt: Das subkulturelle Erbe wirkt nach. Wesentliche Gründe hierfür sind nicht schwer zu finden. Die Absicherung des Glaubensinhalts im Kanon hat daran gehindert, seine Schriften als literarische Produkte wahrzunehmen. Generell haben Christen zwar nur wenig zwischen Echtheitsfragen und Legitimität bzw. Autorität einer Schrift unterscheiden können. Man stellte daher an das kanonische Corpus Paulinum nicht die gleichen Fragen, die man z.B. im Kontext paganer Traditionen durchaus zu reflektieren wusste.

Sicher sind auch Unterschiede der Region und des Milieus zu bedenken. Dazu ein Beispiel aus der jüngsten Diskussion. Alfons Fürst hat zu zeigen versucht, dass sich das Christentum in Alexandrien zuerst in einer ausgesprochen intellektuellen Klientel und in Lehrer-Schüler-Verhältnissen etabliert habe und erst allmählich traditionelle Gemeinden entstanden.[124] In einem solchen Umfeld freier Lehrer wäre eine anders geartete Diskussion über autoritative Schriften denkbarer als in entstehenden kirchlichen Hierarchien. Dieser Sicht des alexandrinischen Christentums stehen allerdings einige Bedenken entgegen. Fürst arbeitet in hohem Maße mit dem Argumentum e silentio: Eine gemeindliche Einbindung von Lehrerpersönlichkeiten wie Basilides, Herakleon, Pantainos werde nicht recht sichtbar, während doch schon Clemens – von dem wir schlicht sehr viel mehr Text besitzen – deutlich auch in einer Gemeinde existiert. Vor allem aber unterschätzt er m.E. den subkulturellen Charakter der alexandrinischen christlichen Intellektuellen.[125] Es kommt nicht allein auf „Bildung" an, um an ei-

---

[123] Vgl. jetzt zusammenfassend P. GEMEINHARDT, Das lateinische Christentum und die antike pagane Bildung, Studien und Texte zu Antike und Christentum 41, Tübingen 2007, der die spannungsreiche Koexistenz antiker Bildungskultur und entstehender christlicher Bildung in vielen Details für den Westen des Imperiums nachzeichnet (allerdings auf die hier zur Debatte stehende Frage nicht eingeht).

[124] A. FÜRST, Christentum als Intellektuellen-Religion. Die Anfänge des Christentums in Alexandria, SBS 213, Stuttgart 2007.

[125] Ein weiteres Problem ist, dass Fürst mit einer ausgebildeten kirchlichen Hierarchie rechnet, in die Clemens und Pantainos noch nicht, Heraklas aber schon sehr wohl eingebunden gewesen seien (Origenes wurde ja erst in Palästina zum Priester geweiht). Die bekannte Merkwürdigkeit, dass Clemens zwar allgemein von Hirten, Vorstehern, Bischöfen, Presbytern und Diakonen spricht (Paidagogos 1,37,3; 3,63,1; 97,2; Stromateis

ner entwickelten Kultur zu partizipieren, sondern auch auf die Grundeinstellung dieser Kultur gegenüber. Christen haben sich nie ungebrochen als Träger des antiken Bildungserbes verstehen können. Für unsere Frage ist aber gerade dieser subkulturelle Charakter wichtig, der dazu führt, dass Einsichten, Fragen und Problembewusstsein des intellektuellen Mainstreams von Christen nur selektiv rezipiert werden. Der „freie, intellektuelle christliche Lehrerstand" des 2. Jh. sei im 3. Jh. verschwunden, was mutatis mutandis wieder auf ein Amt vs. Charisma-Szenario hinführt, wie in der ehemaligen Sohm-Harnack-Debatte, wenn auch nun in „intellektueller" Variante. Dazu wäre viel zu sagen. Lehrer-Schüler-Verhältnisse wurden auch nachträglich konstruiert, so zwischen Clemens und Origenes (Eus.h.e. 6,6; Hier.vir.ill. 38,7).[126] Sicher ist Fürst darin Recht zu geben, dass mit regional und sozial ganz unterschiedlichen Intensitäten einer „intellektuellen" christlichen Kultur zu rechnen ist. In einem Milieu, in dem das Christentum als Philosophenschule galt, wäre es jedenfalls auch gut möglich, dass die Konventionen der Philosophen in Sachen Pseudepigraphieakzeptanz übernommen wurden. Für sichere Aussagen fehlen uns aber auch hier die Belege. Und auch Christen, die ihre Religion als eine Philosophie verstanden, haben in anderen sozialen und kulturellen Bezügen gelebt als die traditionellen Philosophenschulen: nämlich solchen subkultureller Art.[127] Das ändert sich erst sehr langsam im 4. Jh.

Was könnten im Kontext dieses Referenzrahmens weitere Besonderheiten frühchristlicher Pseudepigraphie sein, die sie vielleicht etwa auch von jüdischer und hellenistisch-römischer unterscheiden? Wir entwickeln dazu die oben angedeutete Typologie von Pseudepigraphien einen Schritt weiter, indem wir nach ihrem „Gestus" fragen. Pseudepigraphie verweist fiktiv auf eine grundsätzlich als real angesehene Autorität. Der dabei zur Geltung kommende Gestus kann aber ein solcher einer Nahdeixis, einer

---

3,90,1; 4,108,1; 6,106,2; 6,107,2) und anschauliche Gottesdienstschilderungen bietet (Paidagogos 3,79,3–81,3), aber an keiner Stelle einen Bischof von Alexandrien nennt, wird m.E. von Fürst unterbewertet (nur 48 in einem Nebensatz). Die Möglichkeit, dass es ein breites Gemeindeleben gegeben haben könnte, das nicht katholisch-hierarchisch organisiert war, tritt m.E. zu wenig in den Blick. Die Frage, wie sich das Bischofsamt in Alexandrien durchgesetzt hat und welche Anerkennung es genoss, bleibt jedenfalls offen.

[126] Es wäre schlechterdings unverständlich, warum Origenes Clemens nicht ein einziges Mal erwähnt haben sollte, wenn er sein Schüler gewesen wäre. FÜRST, Christentum als Intellektuellen-Religion (s. Anm. 124), 59f., will dennoch eine vage Beziehung gelten lassen, da es eine Reihe möglicher Textbenutzungen des Clemens durch Origenes gibt (wenn auch nie mit Namensnennung). Das Verhältnis beider Autoren bleibt einigermaßen rätselhaft.

[127] Arbeiten über altkirchliche Rezeption philosophischer Traditionen fragen m.E. viel zu wenig, was alles nicht oder nur verkürzt übernommen wird.

Ferndeixis oder einer mittleren Deixis sein. Damit übertragen wir Begriffe aus der Sprachwissenschaft. Eine Nahdeixis verweist auf Naheliegendes (z.B. das dt. Demonstrativpronomen „dieser, dieses"), eine Ferndeixis auf Fernerliegendes („jener, jenes"), eine mittlere Deixis steht zwischen diesen beiden Möglichkeiten (in den indogermanischen Sprachen im Fall der Demonstrativpronomina selten, in anderen Sprachfamilien aber sehr häufig). Man könnte etwas frei von mythischer, legendärer und geschichtlicher Deixis sprechen. Pseudepigraphie im Namen Henochs, Abrahams oder Moses' ist eine quasi-mythische Ferndeixis; im hellenistischen Raum entsprechen ihr im Gestus Schriften unter den Namen des Orpheus, Musaeus, Linus,[128] Hermes Trismegistus oder Bakis. Eine legendäre (natürlich nicht weniger fiktionale) „mittlere Deixis" betrifft Gestalten wie Esra, Baruch oder Jeremia, die nicht in mythische Ferne entrückt sind, aber doch auch nicht der unmittelbaren Vergangenheit angehören, und mit denen die Adressaten oft eine gemeinsame Lebenssituation teilen (Daniel: Diaspora). Das lässt sich im Gestus gut mit den pseudoplatonischen Briefen oder den ebenfalls pseudepigraphen Kynikerbriefen[129] vergleichen, die gleichsam Lebensstile durch Verweis auf eine jüngere Vergangenheit absichern, legitimieren und inszenieren. Ein Gestus der Nahdeixis dagegen weist auf Autoritäten der allerjüngsten Vergangenheit, die eventuell den Adressaten noch als Menschen vertraut waren, oder allenfalls durch zwei oder drei Generationen von diesen getrennt sind. Eine Nahdeixis versucht, einen drohenden Bruch zwischen jüngster Vergangenheit und unmittelbarer Gegenwart zu verhindern; sie verarbeitet öfters auch Generationenkonflikte.

Das früheste Christentum produziert ausschließlich Pseudepigraphen im Gestus der Nahdeixis (Paulus, Jakobus, Petrus ...), das hellenistische Judentum ausschließlich solche der Ferndeixis (Moses, Henoch, Noah, Salomon), das frühkaiserzeitliche Judentum ergänzend auch solche einer mittleren Deixis (Esra, Baruch, Sibyllen, in gewisser Hinsicht auch noch Daniel). Erst in nachkanonischer Zeit beginnen Christen, in ihrer Pseudepigraphenproduktion am Gestus der Ferndeixis zu partizipieren, aber auch hier vor allem in Ergänzung schon vorliegender jüdischer Schriften (Testamente der 12 Patriarchen, christl. Fassung; christl. Sibyllen; 4Esra; AcsJes etc.). Diese Beobachtungen scheinen mir von großer Bedeutung.

---

[128] Der schiere Umfang der v.a. unter diesen drei fiktionalen Namen stehenden Literaturproduktion wird jetzt mit dem Abschluss der monumentalen dreibändigen Ausgabe von Albert Bernabé sichtbar: Orphicorum et Orphicis similium testimonia et fragmenta. Fasciculus 1–3. Poetae Epici Graeci testimonia et fragmenta II, BT, München/Leipzig 2004–2007. Der Index fontium (3,329–373) lässt die vielfache Vernetzung mit christlicher Literatur erkennen.

[129] E. Müseler, Die Kynikerbriefe, Bd. 2. Kritische Ausgabe mit deutscher Übersetzung, SGKA N.F. 1/7, Paderborn u.a. 1994.

Sie sind vor allem deshalb auffällig, weil Christen ansonsten von Anfang an durchaus am Altersbeweis beteiligt waren, mit dem alle Religionen der Antike ihre Ehrwürdigkeit durch eine Behauptung größeren Alters abzusichern versuchen und um Status konkurrieren.[130] Ein Altersbeweis ist immer komparativ (Moses sei älter als Homer, etc.), und für die Apologeten ist er eine Stütze ihrer Beweisführung. Freilich schon Paulus leistet einen Altersbeweis für sein Glaubensverständnis, indem er Abraham zum ersten Christen und damit sein Evangelium für älter als das thoraobservante Judentum erklärt.[131] Es ist in der Theologie nicht üblich, die Inanspruchnahme Abrahams als Altersbeweis wahrzunehmen, aber dieser Zusammenhang scheint mir evident. Gerade im Kontrast dazu ist der durchgehende Gestus der Nahdeixis in der frühchristlichen pseudepigraphen Literatur so aufschlussreich: Die jüngste Vergangenheit ist autoritative Offenbarungszeit, nicht die ferne Vergangenheit.[132] Auch nichtchristliche und christliche Gnosis unterscheiden sich hierin: Während jene wie das hellenistische Judentum die Ferndeixis bevorzugt (Seth, Zostrianos etc.), partizipiert diese an der frühchristlichen Bevorzugung der Nahdeixis (Thomas, Philippus, Johannes, dazu Sukzessionsfiktionen wie jene um Theudas und Glaukias, die angeblichen Schüler des Paulus und Petrus). Wieder können wir die komplexen Zusammenhänge nur skizzieren, um Fragen anzudeuten, die in der künftigen Pseudepigraphieforschung weiterer Diskussion bedürfen.

Für die gnostische Literatur tritt die Besonderheit hinzu, dass diese weithin Züge der Traditions- und nicht nur der Autorenliteratur aufweist. Es ist ja eine grundlegende Einsicht, dass sich Autorenliteratur und Traditionsliteratur (wie die rabbinischen Sammlungen) in der Antike grundsätzlich anders verhalten und im Literaturbetrieb auch anders behandelt werden. Traditionsliteratur ist von spezifischer struktureller Flexibilität, die

---

[130] P. PILHOFER, Presbyteron kreitton. Der Altersbeweis der jüdischen und christlichen Apologeten und seine Vorgeschichte, WUNT II/39, Tübingen 1990.

[131] In diesem Typ von fiktionalem Altersbeweis ist Paulus später der Islam gefolgt, der explizit Abraham nicht als Juden oder Christen, sondern als Muslim (Koran, Sure 3,65–70 vgl. 2,140) bzw. Hanifen für sich in Anspruch nimmt und mit dieser Argumentationsfigur den Islam für älter als Christentum und Judentum erklärt. Vgl. zur Sache auch M. FRENSCHKOWSKI, Das früheste Zeugnis einer abrahamischen Ökumene. Zum antiken interreligiösen Abrahamkult von Mamre, Sacra Scripta 5 (2007), 117–129 (127f.). Von heutigen Mandäern (iraqischen Migranten in Deutschland) habe ich mehrfach gehört, dass für sie ihre Religion selbstverständlich älter als Judentum, Christentum und Islam sei: ein fiktionaler Altersbeweis, der zur bloßen Behauptung geschrumpft ist, aber umso massiver aufrecht erhalten wird.

[132] Im rabbinischen Judentum entwickelt sich sehr allmählich mit der zunehmenden Produktion von fiktiven Überlieferungen angesehener Lehrmeister ein Typ der mittleren Deixis, der die apokryphe Ferndeixis der älteren hellenistischen Zeit weithin verdrängt. Eine wirkliche pseudepigraphe Nahdeixis ist im antiken Judentum sehr selten.

sowohl ihre Bausteine als auch ihren Gesamtaufbau betrifft. Sie funktioniert gewissermaßen nach dem Baukastenprinzip.[133] Was besagt diese Unterscheidung für die Pseudepigraphieforschung? Könnte man sagen, um eine Arbeitsthese zu formulieren, dass sich in der gnostischen Pseudepigraphie Dynamiken und Entwicklungen der Traditionsliteratur in die Autorenliteratur eindrängen? Für die gnostische Literatur trifft dies jedenfalls in höherem Maße zu als für die neutestamentliche Pseudepigraphie, denn die Textvarianten der neutestamentlichen Bücher sind um vieles geringer als z.B. die Abstände zwischen den Fassungen des gnostischen Johannesapokryphons oder anderer gnostischer Texte, die wir in mehreren Versionen besitzen. Dieser Sachverhalt geringer Textstabilität ist für die gnostischen Pseudepigrapha sehr auffällig und bedarf der Erklärung. Auch der neuerschlossene gnostische Codex Tchacos macht das wieder gut erkennbar: Der Brief des Petrus an Philippus (CT 1) divergiert stark von NHC VIII/2, ebenso die erste Jakobusapokalypse (CT 2) von ihrer Parallele NHC V/3. Das Judasevangelium (CT 3) – der Text, durch den Codex Tchacos berühmt wurde – ist nicht identisch mit der Fassung, die bereits früher aus dem Referat des Irenäus (haer. 1,31,1) bekannt war (zu CT 4 ist keine Parallele erhalten).[134] Wie sind diese Variationen zu erklären? Die Texte waren offenbar nicht „sakrosankt". Die Abschreiber bzw. Herausgeber der Codices – die bewusst geplante Zusammenstellungen sind – haben sich offenbar für berechtigt gehalten, an den Texten zu arbeiten. Diese sind esoterisch-gnostische meditative und reflexive Schriften, aber nicht „geistiges Eigentum" oder stabile Heilige Schriften. Es ist mir überhaupt fraglich, inwiefern die gnostischen Lehrer eigene Canones definiert haben (einzige Ausnahme ist der Religionsgründer Mani)[135]. Wie haben also die Abschreiber gnostischer Texte deren Literarizität bestimmt, wenn sie sich

---

[133] Doch kann auch Traditionsliteratur weitgehend textstabil sein, was insbesondere für die Gesetzesliteratur (die juristischen Corpora) gilt, die immerhin dennoch Glossen und Einschübe aufweisen. Vgl. das „Zitiergesetz" Valentinians III. aus dem Jahr 426, das festlegt, dass die Schriften einer Reihe klassischer Juristen (Papinian, Paulus, Scaevola etc.) die Dignität von Gesetzen haben sollten, „vorausgesetzt, daß die Texte ihrer Bücher wegen ihrer altersbedingten Unsicherheit durch Collationierung mehrerer Codices bestätigt sei" (si tamen eorum libri propter antiquitatis incertum codicum collatione firmentur) (Codex Theodosianus 1,4,3).

[134] J. Brankaer / H.-G. Bethge (Hg.), Codex Tchacos. Texte und Analysen, TU 161, Berlin/New York 2007, dazu die etwas ältere Editio princeps R. Kasser / G. Wurst / M. W. Meyer / F. Gaudard (Hg.), The Gospel of Judas together with the Letter of Peter to Philipp, James and A Book of Allogenes from Codex Tchacos. Critical Edition, Washington 2007.

[135] Nur in der manichäisch-gnostischen Tradition existieren eigene Kanonlisten. Zu diesen vgl. etwa die vergleichende Auflistung von Michael H. Browder im Appendix zu: P. Bryder (Hg.), Manichaean Studies. Proceedings of the First International Conference of Manichaeism August 5–9, 1987 (...), LSAAR 1, Lund 1988, 292.

für berechtigt hielten, in hohem Maße in die Textgestalt einzugreifen? Offenbar waren die Texte für sie Exponenten einer okkulten, eben „gnostischen" Wahrheit, nicht in erster Linie Produkte von „Autoren". Das Pseudepigraphieproblem ist hier anders gelagert als für die reine Autorenliteratur. (Natürlich existiert auch ausgesprochene gnostische Autorenliteratur, z.B. im Fall Valentins, aber diese ist im Allgemeinen nicht pseudepigraph.) Für die Großkirche ergibt sich als weitere Fragestellung, wie sich Pseudepigraphie unterscheidet, wenn ihre Produkte relativ textstabil sind (wie alle neutestamentlichen Beispiele), oder wenn sie wie Traditionsliteratur grundsätzlich in divergierenden Fassungen umläuft.

6. Fiktionalitätsdiskurse in Antike und Christentum

Wir haben damit verschiedene Bausteine und Fragen benannt, mit deren Hilfe nun in einem letzten Schritt das vielschichtige Bild frühchristlicher Pseudepigraphie in allgemeine Fiktionalitätsdiskurse einzuzeichnen bleibt. Angesichts der Offenheit vieler Probleme kann dies nur behutsam und tastend geschehen. Pseudepigraphie ist insofern ein Spezialfall von Fiktionalität, als sie sich nicht auf den Text als Ganzen bezieht. Sie erzeugt also einen Text, der fiktionale und nichtfiktionale Eigenschaften vereint. Textpragmatisch erzeugt sie ein Zusammenspiel zwischen Autor und Lesenden im Rahmen herrschender Fiktionalitätsdiskurse.[136] Wie wir jedoch gesehen haben, trifft eine Durchschaubarkeit, an der Autoren und Rezipienten gleichermaßen teilnehmen, auf das frühe Christentum im Allgemeinen nicht zu. Wir können nun an dieser Stelle die sich ergebenden Fragen nicht in eine allgemeine Diskussion mit neueren Fiktionalitätstheorien integrieren, und müssen es bei einer Problemskizze belassen. Unser Problem reicht in jedem Fall tiefer als bisher sichtbar geworden und kann m.E. nur in einer Annäherung an die fundamentalen Fiktionalitätsdiskurse der Antike weitergeführt werden. Dazu definieren wir in einem ersten Schritt allgemein: Wir nennen einen Text *fiktional*, wenn wir ihn als den einzigen Zugang zu seiner Binnenwelt ansehen; wir nennen ihn *nichtfiktional*, wenn wir in ihm

---

[136] Für einen solchen konsequent literaturgeschichtlichen Blick, in dem sich Echtheitsfragen in Fiktionalitätsdiskurse auflösen bzw. entschärfen, s. jetzt auch P. A. ROSENMEYER, Ancient Epistolary Fictions. The Letter in Greek Literature, Cambridge 2001 (eine grundlegende Arbeit, die freilich leider die christliche Briefproduktion nicht diskutiert); auch: R. Morello / A. D. Morrison (Hg.), Ancient Letters. Classical and Late Antique Epistolography, Oxford 2007, eine Sammlung von Studien, die v.a. die divergierenden kommunikativen Situationen ausleuchten, in denen literarische Briefe formuliert werden, dabei auch solche Fälle, die seltener im Blick sind, wie die antike Wissenschaft und Medizin.

nicht den einzigen Zugang zu der „Welt" sehen, die er beschreibt bzw. evoziert.[137]

Um die Sache auf eine sehr plakative These zuzuspitzen, hatten Christen immer Schwierigkeiten, sich vorzustellen, eine Sache sei ausschließlich fiktiv bzw. fiktional (nicht: eine Sache sei erlogen – das war problemlos vorstellbar, weil in einem schlichten binären Wahrheitsdiskurs verortbar). *Christliche Subkultur hat die Fiktionalitätsdiskurse der Antike reduziert.* Die Götter der Heiden sind nicht einfach nichtexistent: sie sind Dämonen. Erklärungsmodelle wie der Euhemerismus oder der stoische Naturalismus wurden von Christen begierig aufgegriffen, weil sie die mythischen Geschichten der alten Überlieferungen nicht einfach zu Fiktionen machten. Daher konnte der „Goldene Esel" des Apuleius erregte Debatten darüber auslösen, ob die in ihm erzählte Verwandlung eines Menschen in einen Esel real oder Illusion sei: Was kaum in den Blick gerät, ist ihr *fiktionaler Charakter* in einem Roman (Aug.civ. 18,18, ein sehr lehrreicher Text für unsere Frage). Christliche Romane wie die Pseudoclementinen, die apokryphen Apostelakten, die Visio Zosimi[138] oder auch die Anfänge der hagiographischen Literatur wurden in einem Maße als Berichte über Tatsächliches gelesen, das so ungeheuerlich ist, dass wir es in unserer Wahrnehmung der Alten Kirche gerne übersehen. Für die Anfänge der Hagiographie, wie sie etwa in den Mönchsviten[139] vorliegen, überrascht immer wieder das völlige Fehlen jeder kritischen Instanz, die andere Kategorien als Wahrheit und Lüge wahrnehmen könnte. Diese Wahrheitsdiskurse weitergehend zu dokumentieren, liegt jenseits der Möglichkeiten dieses Essays. Der für unser Thema diskursgeschichtlich wichtige Aspekt ist da-

---

[137] Vgl. sehr ähnlich L. DANNEBERG, Weder Tränen noch Logik. Über die Zugänglichkeit fiktionaler Welten, in: U. Klein / K. Mellmann / S. Metzger (Hg.), Heuristiken der Literaturwissenschaft. Einladung zu disziplinexternen Perspektiven auf Literatur, Paderborn 2006, 35–83.

[138] Über diesen bemerkenswerten Reisebericht, der phantastisch-utopische Elemente in einem asketischen Milieu realisiert, im Kontext der o. skizzierten diskursgeschichtlichen Fragestellung s. M. FRENSCHKOWSKI, Vision als Imagination. Beobachtungen zum differenzierten Wirklichkeitsanspruch frühchristlicher Visionsliteratur, in: N. Hömke / M. Baumbach (Hg.), Fremde Wirklichkeiten. Literarische Phantastik und antike Literatur, Kalliope 6, Heidelberg 2006, 339–366 (354–361), und insgesamt demnächst J. DOCHHORN, in: JSHRZ, Supplementa. Interessant ist in diesem Kontext auch, dass der romanhafte Charakter altkirchlicher Erzähltexte oft umstritten ist, etwa im Fall der Narratio des Ps.-Nilos. S. M. LINK, Die ‚Erzählung' des Ps.-Neilos. Ein spätantiker Märtyrerroman. Einleitung, Text, Übersetzung, Kommentar, Beiträge zur Altertumskunde 220, München/Leipzig 2005, 8–24.

[139] S. zum Fiktionalitätsproblem in der frühen Hagiographie auch M. FRENSCHKOWSKI, Art. Vita, in: Enzyklopädie des Märchens. Handwörterbuch der historischen und vergleichenden Erzählforschung (im Druck).

bei gar nicht, dass der Supranaturalismus der Alten Kirche Dinge und Geschehnisse für wirklich gehalten hat, bei denen uns das fraglich erscheint – sondern umgekehrt, dass das Spektrum der Fiktionalität zusammenschmolz. Wir fragen also nicht, was alles die Alte Kirche für real gehalten hat, sondern wie weniges sie für irreal hielt, genauer gesagt, *wie ihr die Kategorie der schlichten Fiktion abhanden kam*. Diese Reduktion der Fiktionalität steigert sich bis ins Mittelalter, von dessen Gelehrten C. S. Lewis in einer berühmten Formulierung sagen konnte: „They are bookish. They are indeed very credulous of books. They find it hard to believe that anything an old *auctour* has said is simply untrue."[140] Dass die Ereignisse in Ovids und Vergils Dichtungen historisch sind, ist einem solchen Kontext selbstverständlich, obwohl man ihren religiösen Referenzrahmen nicht teilte.[141] Und Augustin muss wie angesprochen die alten Geschichten über Tierverwandlungen einschließlich der scheinbar autobiographischen Passagen des Apuleius mit einer elaborierten Theorie über Trancevisionen erklären: Was nicht in Frage kommt, ist die Geschichten als Fiktionen zu verstehen, weil ihm diese Kategorie entgleitet (l. c.). Nicht zuletzt seit der berühmten „Literaturtheorie im deutschen Mittelalter" des kürzlich verstorbenen Schweizer Mediävisten Walter Haug (1927–2008)[142] ist das Problem der reduzierten Fiktionalität in der Mediävistik breit diskutiert worden, aber seine Wurzeln in der Alten Kirche sind bisher noch zu wenig bedacht.[143]

In dieser hier nur skizzierten Reduktion der Fiktionalitätsdiskurse sehe ich den letzten Grund für die nur rudimentär ausgeprägte Pseudepigraphiekritik der Alten Kirche. Man lebte mit Wahrheit und Lüge, Orthodoxie und Häresie.[144] Die Zwischentöne der Literatur gingen verloren. Natürlich besitzt auch die Alte Kirche subtile Literatur, aber sie selbst konnte diese nur eingeschränkt als solche wahrnehmen. In welchem Maße z.B. selbst autobiographische Literatur eben *Literatur* ist, wurde ihren Autoren nur wenig

---

[140] C. S. LEWIS, The Discarded Image. An Introduction to Medieval and Renaissance Literature, Cambridge 1964, 11.

[141] S. FREUND, Vergil im frühen Christentum, SGKA N.F. 16, Paderborn u.a. 2000, bietet das Material, diskutiert die hier angesprochenen Fragen aber nicht.

[142] W. HAUG, Literaturtheorie im deutschen Mittelalter. Von den Anfängen bis zum Ende des 13. Jahrhunderts, Darmstadt 1985.²1992 (Neuausgabe mit neuem Vorwort Darmstadt 2009).

[143] Wichtige Beobachtungen zur Sache unter einer angrenzenden Leitfrage (Historisierung von Fiktionen in der Spätantike) bietet G. W. BOWERSOCK, Fiction as History. Nero to Julian, Sather Classical Lectures 58, Berkeley 1994.

[144] So auch SPEYER, Die literarische Fälschung (s. Anm. 5), 201: „Die Kritik der Christen war also dogmatisch bestimmt. Ihre Echtheitskritik arbeitete so fast ausschließlich mit den Begriffen ‚Rechtgläubig' und ‚Häretisch'."

bewusst.[145] Frühchristliche Literatur ist zudem bis weit in die Zeit der Alten Kirche subkulturelle Literatur. Diese Feststellung hat quantitative und qualitative Aspekte und ist keineswegs trivial. Aus ihr folgt von selbst, dass eine Erforschung frühchristlicher Literatur den intensiven Kontakt zur Erforschung anderer literarischer Subkulturen suchen muss und Aussagen aus dem kulturellen Mainstream nur begrenzt übertragbar sind. Diese Feststellung darf nun wiederum keineswegs vermengt werden mit derjenigen nach dem präzisen soziologischen Ort dieser Literatur in der Struktur antiker Gesellschaften; Subkulturen sind in Unterschichten wie Oberschichten gleichermaßen heimisch. Aber damit betreten wir einen Fragehorizont, der endgültig für ein Essay zu weit ist.

---

[145] T. KRÄMER, Augustinus zwischen Wahrheit und Lüge. Literarische Tätigkeit als Selbstfindung und Selbsterfindung, Hyp. 170, Göttingen 2007.

Pseudepigraphie und antike Briefromane

von

KATHARINA LUCHNER

Demosthenes schreibt Bittgesuche an die Athener. Themistokles klagt Freunden und Bekannten die Unbilden seiner Laufbahn. Platon korrespondiert, mal freundlicher, mal weniger freundlich, mit dem Alleinherrscher von Syrakus. Euripides fragt besorgt nach Sophokles' Wohlergehen nach überstandenem Seesturm. Ein Redner, ein Politiker und Feldherr, ein Philosoph und ein Tragödiendichter, allesamt berühmte Namen, schreiben Briefe. Aber sind diese Briefe tatsächlich vom historischen Redner, Politiker und Feldherrn, Philosophen, Tragödiendichter verfasst? Und wenn nein: Wer hat diese Briefe aus welchem Grund für welches Publikum dann geschrieben und hat dies überhaupt eine einzelne Person getan? Und wenn ja: Lässt sich ein Prinzip erkennen, nach dem diese einzelne Person, der Autor, der seinen Namen nicht nennt, diese Briefe zu einer Sammlung zusammengestellt hat? Und wenn wiederum ja: Handelt es sich bei diesem Prinzip um so etwas wie die Errichtung einer narrativen Einheit, etwa in Form einer Erzählung in Etappen? Und kann man diese Erzählung dann also ‚Briefroman' nennen? – Die Reihe der Fragen ließe sich beliebig verfeinern, etwa indem man zusätzlich zur Frage nach dem Autor noch die Frage eines möglichen Redaktors und/oder mehrerer Überarbeitungsstufen ein und derselben Briefsammlung mit einbezöge.[1] Sie ließe sich, zumal an ihrem Ende, beliebig fortsetzen, wenn man die möglichen Spielarten romanhaften Erzählens in der Antike einbeziehen wollte.[2] Und sie führte

---

[1] So ist für etliche und gerade die berühmteren Briefsammlungen nicht nur die Anordnung der Einzeltexte in den Handschriften uneinheitlich, sondern es lässt sich auch zeigen, dass ein ursprünglicher Kern nachträglich erweitert und teilweise modifiziert wurde, so beispielsweise im Fall der Phalaris-Briefe; vgl. hierzu S. MERKLE / A. BESCHORNER, Der Tyrann und der Dichter. Handlungssequenzen in den Phalaris-Briefen, in: N. Holzberg (Hg.), Der griechische Briefroman. Gattungstypologie und Textanalyse, Classica Monacensia 8, Tübingen 1994, 116–168 (165–168), sowie insgesamt zum Nachleben der Briefe V. HINZ, Nunc Phalaris doctum protulit ecce caput. Antike Phalarislegende und Nachleben der Phalarisbriefe, Beiträge zur Altertumskunde 148, München u.a. 2001. Zu deren forschungsgeschichtlicher Bedeutung s.u. Abschnitt 1.

[2] Einen raschen Überblick gewinnt man in G. Schmeling (Hg.), The Novel in the Ancient World, Mnemosyne Suppl. 159, Leiden u.a. 1996, darin für unsere Fragestellung

schließlich in äußerst unwegsames Gelände, wenn man versuchte, die Merkmale der Textsorte ‚Brief' auf einer abstrakteren als der rein formalen Ebene genauer zu bestimmen.[3]

Mitten hinein in das Feld dieser Fragen begibt sich, wer sich dem Problemkomplex ‚Pseudepigraphie und Briefroman' aus klassisch philologischer Perspektive nähert. Eine wesentliche Ursache für die zahlreichen Unwägbarkeiten liegt darin, dass die antike Literaturtheorie den Forschenden hier nahezu sich selbst überlässt: So ist das Wort ‚*pseudepigraphos*' zwar antik,[4] eine Theorie pseudepigraphen Schreibens besäße man aber nur dann, wenn man bereit wäre, alles, was die antike Rhetorik zum literarischen Produktionsfeld ‚Ethopoiie', ‚Prosopopoiese' etc. zu sagen hat, hierfür zu vereinnahmen. Denn das Einüben dieser Techniken bildet sicherlich eine Voraussetzung, bisweilen wohl sogar einen *stimulus* für das, was wir unter pseudepigrapher Literatur, zumal in Briefform, verstehen.[5] Es kann aber kaum mehr als ein erster Ausgangspunkt für die Beurteilung der Texte sein. Ähnliches gilt bekanntlich für ‚Brief' und ‚Roman': Sieht man von den Handreichungen und Typologisierungen der späteren Antike ab,[6] die allesamt die klare Unterscheidbarkeit einer Textsorte ‚Brief' bereits voraussetzen, so kommt man über Augustinus' viel zitiertes „*habet quis ad quem scribat*"[7] kaum hinaus. Vollends verlassen sieht man sich bei dem,

---

besonders wichtig N. HOLZBERG, Novel-like Works of Extended Prose-Fiction II, 619–653.

[3] Immer noch ein guter Ausgangspunkt für die Beschäftigung mit antiker Epistolographie ist J. SYKUTRIS, Art. Epistolographie, PRE.S 5 (1931), 185–220; hilfreich sind auch J.-D. GAUGER, Art. Brief, Lexikon des Hellenismus (2005), 209–212; S. K. STOWERS, Letter-Writing in Graeco-Roman Antiquity, Philadelphia 1986; J. L. WHITE, Light from Ancient Letters, Philadelphia 1981; M. L. STIREWALT, Studies in Ancient Greek Epistolography, SBLRBS 27, Atlanta 1993.

[4] Der Begriff ψευδεπίγραφος ist zuerst inschriftlich im 2. Jh. v. Chr., dann bei Dionysios von Halikarnass, Demosthenes 57 bezeugt; vgl. LSJ s.v. 2020: „with false subscription or title, not genuine". Ich benutze ‚pseudepigraph', mangels einer etablierten, prägnanten Alternative, wertungsfrei im Sinne von ‚nicht mit der realen Verfasserschaft übereinstimmende Zuweisung an einen Autor'.

[5] Vgl. den Überblick bei G. NASCHERT, Art. Ethopoeia, Historisches Wörterbuch der Rhetorik 2 (1994), 1512–1516, sowie R. CRIBIORE, Gymnastics of the Mind. Greek Education in Hellenistic and Roman Egypt, Princeton u.a. 2005, 215–219, zum Verfassen von Briefen im Schulunterricht.

[6] Letztere sind bequem zugänglich in A. J. Malherbe (Hg.), Ancient Epistolary Theorists, SBL SBibSt 19, Atlanta 1988.

[7] Vgl. Augustinus, Retractationes 2,20. Die Unterscheidbarkeit der Textsorte ‚Brief' für den antiken Rezipienten erfolgte wohl schon früh anhand eben solcher pragmatischer Standards: Durchgängig formelhafte Elemente in Briefen sind seit der zweiten Hälfte des 5. Jh. v. Chr. erkennbar; vgl. GAUGER, Art. Brief (s. Anm. 3), 210, der hierzu auf R. BUZÓN, Die Briefe der Ptolemäerzeit. Ihre Struktur und ihre Formeln, Diss. Heidelberg 1984, verweist. – J. L. WHITE, The Greek Documentary Letter Tradition Third

was wir heute ‚Roman' zu nennen gewohnt sind: Hier hat die Antike bekanntlich nicht einmal den Begriff, geschweige denn, dass uns Anweisungen zur Abfassung oder gar theoretische Überlegungen zur Gattung vorlägen. Noch stärker als sonst sieht sich der Interpret hier also auf eigene, d.h. aus späteren Literaturen und Forschungsgeschichten stammende Definitionen und Setzungen verwiesen. Die Abgrenzungen des Genres blieben dem entsprechend trotz der mittlerweile reichen Forschung zu einzelnen Ausprägungen des antiken Romans oftmals eher vage. So lautet etwa eine Definition in einem der neueren Standard-Nachschlagewerke: „In der griech.[ischen] Lit.[eratur] wird mit ‚Roman' eine Reihe fiktiver Prosatexte bezeichnet, welche durch zwei thematische Grundkonstanten (Liebe und Abenteuer) und eine Reihe von Topoi miteinander verbunden sind."[8]

Century BC to Third Century AD, Semeia 22 (1981), 89–106 (91), definiert, ebenfalls ganz für den antiken Horizont (hier: dokumentarischer Briefe), ausgehend von (einer) der epistolographischen Grundsituation(en), Briefe als Kommunikation über räumliche Trennung hinweg; der überzeugendste neuere Definitionsversuch stammt von M. Trapp (Hg.), Greek and Latin Letters. An Anthology with Translation, Cambridge 2003, 1; R. K. GIBSON / A. D. MORRISON, Introduction: What is a letter?, in: R. Morello / A. D. Morrison (Hg.), Ancient Letters. Classical and Late Antique Epistolography, Oxford 2007, 1–16, kommen m.E. nicht wirklich über ihn hinaus. – Nicht eingehen kann ich hier auf die alte Kontroverse ‚(realiter abgeschickter) Brief' vs. ‚(literarische) Epistel', wie sie seit G. A. DEISSMANN, Licht vom Osten. Das Neue Testament und die neuentdeckten Texte der hellenistisch-römischen Welt, Tübingen [4]1923 (zuerst ebd. 1908), immer wieder geführt wurde; für die hier behandelten Texte ist sie ohnehin kaum von Bedeutung, da diese, unabhängig von Verfasserfrage und Sitz im Leben, allesamt den Willen zu literarischer Stilisierung eindeutig aufweisen.

[8] So M. FUSILLO, Art. Roman II Griechisch, DNP 10 (2001), 1108–1114 (1108). Fusillo fährt ebd. fort: „Neben dem Fehlen eines ant. Gattungsbegriffs ‚Roman' erfuhr dieser auch keinerlei theoretische Kodifikation; daher der Charakter einer ‚offenen Form', welche alle lit. Gattungen der Ant. aufnahm und durch Übertragung ins Alltägliche, Private und Sentimentale transformierte." Für die Übertragung dieses allgemeinen Begriffs vom antiken Roman auf ein Genre Briefroman ist diese formale ‚Offenheit' zwar von Vorteil, hierfür misslich aber ist die inhaltliche Festlegung: In der Regel versteht man unter ‚antikem Roman' ausschließlich den idealisierenden und komisch-realistischen Roman; vgl. N. HOLZBERG, Der antike Roman, Darmstadt [3]2006, hier v.a. 38f. Nur konsequent schließt Holzberg deshalb eine „fiktive Selbstbiographie" (36) wie die Pseudoclementinen oder eine Erzählung wie die Historia Apollonii Regis (ebd.) von der Gattung ‚Roman' in antiker Perspektive aus; zu dieser Problematik auch ders., Novel-like Works (s. Anm. 2). – Die Briefsammlungen der ‚berühmten Männer' stehen nun aber, mit Ausnahme der erotischen Briefe, solcher Literatur thematisch fast durchgängig näher als Liebes- oder Abenteuererzählungen, ein komisch-realistisches Moment fehlt ihnen fast ganz. Indem man von ‚Briefromanen' spricht, errichtet man deshalb entweder eine neue Sonderkategorie des antiken Romans oder muss sich fragen, ob man den Romanbegriff nicht insgesamt einer (noch) weiteren und damit (noch) weniger trennscharfen Definition zuführen will. Die Verwendung des Begriffes ist somit *per se* problematisch. Da er aber als etabliert gelten kann, behalte ich ihn im Folgenden bei.

In diesem Sinne wird im Folgenden eine selektive Annäherung an ein komplexes Feld versucht, deren Fokus ich auf den Begriff der Pseudepigraphie einerseits und den der Frage nach der ‚Romanhaftigkeit' der uns vorliegenden Briefsammlungen im Sinne der Gattungsfrage[9] andererseits gelegt habe. Ich beschränke mich, wie schon die Eingangsbeispiele nahelegen, dabei gänzlich auf die in griechischer Sprache überlieferte Literatur,[10] überschreite hierbei nirgends die Grenze der Spätantike und nähere mich dem Gegenstand in drei Schritten: Nach einer kurzen Skizze der Sonderrolle von Briefen für die Forschung zur Pseudepigraphie innerhalb (nicht nur?) der Klassischen Philologie (1.), folgt eine kurze Bestandsaufnahme der vorliegenden Texte zusammen mit Streiflichtern auf neuere Impulse der Pseudepigraphie-Forschung (2.), sowie zuletzt eine konkrete Annäherung an die Gattung ‚Briefroman' am Beispiel der Platon- und Chion-Briefe (3.). Der ‚Ausblick' fasst zusammen und formuliert weiterführende Überlegungen (4.).

1. Pseudepigraphie und Briefe – Wie alles begann und wie dies bis heute nachwirkt

Gleichsam am Anfang der Erforschung pseudepigrapher Literatur nach modernen Maßstäben der Philologie steht eine Untersuchung von Briefsammlungen. Ihr Verfasser hat das Ziel seiner Bemühungen unter anderem folgendermaßen formuliert:

„I am willing ... to examine some ... impostures ... out of the ... school of Sophists. It will be no unpleasant labour to me, nor, I hope, unprofitable to others, to pull off the disguise from those little pedants, that have stalked about so long in the apparel of heroes."

So Richard Bentley in seiner berühmten „Dissertation upon the Epistles of Phalaris, Themistocles, Socrates, Euripides etc."[11] aus dem Jahr 1697 in

---

[9] Hierbei lege ich einen an Jauß orientierten Gattungsbegriff zugrunde, der sich über die grundsätzlich kommunikative Bedeutung auch literarischer Werke und somit vor allem als je spezifischer ‚Erwartungshorizont' des Rezipienten konstituiert; vgl. z.B. H. R. JAUSS, Theorie der Gattungen und Literatur des Mittelalters, in: ders. u.a. (Hg.), Grundriß der romanischen Literaturen des Mittelalters, GRLMA I, Heidelberg 1973, 107–138.

[10] Dies ergibt sich aus der Tatsache, dass uns für die Antike in lateinischer Sprache zwar zahl- und umfangreiche Briefsammlungen vorliegen, jedoch keine Texte, die sich einer Gattung ‚Briefroman' zuordnen ließen.

[11] Der volle Titel lautet: A Dissertation upon the Epistles of Phalaris, Themistocles, Socrates, Euripides, etc. and upon the Fables of Aesop; zu den verschiedenen Versionen des Titels sowie den Unterschieden zwischen erweiterter und revidierter Fassung vgl. das

der Einleitung zu seiner Analyse der Themistokles-Briefe.[12] Bentleys Dissertation hat (zusammen mit den späteren „Remarks upon a Late Discourse of Free-Thinking" von 1713)[13] für die Beschäftigung (nicht nur) der Klassischen Philologie mit (nicht nur) pseudepigrapher Literatur nicht mehr zu hintergehende methodische Maßstäbe gesetzt. Bentleys Interesse war freilich ein ganz und gar zeitgebundenes: Die im Titel genannten Brief*corpora* waren zu einem zentralen Streitobjekt in der Auseinandersetzung zwischen ‚Ancients' und ‚Moderns' im England des ausgehenden 17. Jahrhunderts[14] geworden: Für die ‚Ancients' repräsentierten sie beispielhaft die Überlegenheit der griechisch-römischen Autoren sowie der antiken Kultur überhaupt. Für Bentley war der Erweis ihrer ‚Unechtheit' nicht nur ein Sieg ‚moderner' wissenschaftlicher Methode über bloße Schwärmerei (‚rhetoric'), sondern vor allem ein entscheidender Schlag gegen einen in seinen Augen unqualifizierten und somit lähmenden Umgang mit der Vergangenheit insgesamt.[15]

Bentleys Verdienste können wohl kaum überschätzt werden. Freilich wurde, ebenfalls für Jahrhunderte, sein teilweise polemischer Gestus (vgl. das obige Zitat) mit fortgeschrieben. Die als schulmeisterlich-sophistische ‚Pedanten' inkriminierten Rhetoren, Sophisten oder, in heutiger Diktion, schlicht: Schriftsteller, die unter dem Namen eines Prominenten der großen Vergangenheit Griechenlands Briefe verfassten, hatten in Bentleys Augen vor allem „forgery", „cheat" und „imposture",[16] allesamt wenig ehrenhafte Motive, im Sinn. Der deutsche Begriff ‚Fälschung'[17] ist vergleichbar nega-

---

Vorwort zu Dyces Gesamtausgabe (A. Dyce [Hg.], The Works of Richard Bentley, collected and edited, Bd. I: Dissertation upon the Epistles of Phalaris, Bd. II: Dissertations upon the Epistles of Phalaris, &c., and Epistola ad Millium, Bd. III: Theological Writings, London 1836.1838 [Nachdruck New York 1966], v.ixff.), nach der hier durchgängig zitiert wird.

[12] BENTLEY, Dissertation (s. Anm. 11), Bd. II, 182.

[13] Wieder in zweiter Auflage 1743; vgl. a.a.O. Bd. III.

[14] Zum geistesgeschichtlichen Kontext vgl. für das Beispiel der Phalaris-Briefe HINZ, Phalarislegende (s. Anm. 1), 344–358.371–382 (nur Dissertation), sowie allgemeiner J. M. LEVINE, The Battle of Books. History and Literature in the Augustan Age, Ithaca 1991, 1–84, und A. E. BURLINGAME, The Battle of Books in its Historical Setting, New York 1969.

[15] Vgl. hierzu LEVINE, a.a.O. 267–413 (267): „... it was clear, that the controversy was above all about history, about how to read and understand past authors, and about how to recapture and represent past customs, institutions, and events."

[16] Diese Begriffe verwendet Bentley durchgängig; vgl. z.B. BENTLEY, Dissertation (s. Anm. 11), Bd. I, 82 („forge", ähnlich a.a.O. 289.389.430).156 („cheat", ähnlich a.a.O. 271, Bd. II, 82).165 („Sophist", „guilty of sophistry").255 („imposture", ähnlich Bd. II, 126.157), u.ö.

[17] Ähnliches gilt für den Begriff des ‚Plagiats'. Beide Begriffe finden sich vor allem in älterer Literatur durchgängig. Dies dokumentiert E. STEMPLINGER, Das Plagiat in der

tiv konnotiert. Bentleys im Letzten moralisch gefärbter Blick trifft einen je variierenden Teil der uns erhaltenen Briefcorpora aber bis zum heutigen Tag, und dies unabhängig davon, ob Bentley selbst eine bestimmte Briefsammlung in sein Verdikt mit einbezog oder nicht. So galten Bentley beispielsweise die unter Platons Namen überlieferten Briefe wohl allesamt als ‚echt' (im Sinn der Verfasserschaft durch den historischen Platon)[18] und doch liest man beispielsweise noch im Jahr 2005 mit Bezug auf eben jene Briefe:[19]

„Letters as a genre are particularly open to suspicions about authenticity, since they were relatively easy to *forge in order to sell* to libraries of the Hellenistic period, ... and because the rhetorical schools employed, as an exercise, the composition of letters of famous people."

Und wenig später, noch deutlicher, über den berühmten Siebten Brief aus derselben Sammlung:

„The Seventh Letter is ... so long and complicated that it is hard to imagine either that someone composed it in order *to make a little profit* [sc. indem er sein Werk einer Bibliothek verkauft] or that it can be a school exercise" (Hervorhebung von mir).

Bentleys Verachtung für die ‚kleinen Pedanten', die er als Verfasser der von ihm untersuchten Briefe „entlarven" („to pull off the disguise")[20] wollte, klingt hier nach, vermischt mit der (spätestens) seit der römischen Kaiserzeit (und Bentley)[21] immer wieder angeführten, sicher zu einseiti-

---

Griechischen Literatur, Leipzig/Berlin 1912, sowie F. DORNSEIFF, Echtheitsfragen antikgriechischer Literatur, Berlin 1939.

[18] Sowohl in beiden Fassungen der Dissertation als auch in den Remarks hat Bentley nirgends den geringsten Zweifel an der Verfasserschaft geäußert. Er verteidigt vielmehr neben Plato epist. 2 und 6 (BENTLEY, Dissertation [s. Anm. 11], Bd. II, 83 = 170f., und 97f. = 172), den heute überwiegend für ‚unecht' gehaltenen Plato epist. 13 mit den Worten: „That letter is as genuine as any of the rest [sc. genuine]" (Remarks III [s. Anm. 13], 410).

[19] C. A. HUFFMAN, Archytas of Tarentum. Pythagorean, Philosopher and Mathematician King, Cambridge 2005, 42. Huffmans Monographie ist in jeder anderen Hinsicht ein unentbehrliches Buch; die Briefliteratur *per se* steht nicht im Zentrum seines Interesses.

[20] Vgl. das Zitat oben 236.

[21] Schon BENTLEY, Dissertation (s. Anm. 11), Bd. I, 82 Anm. *h*, zitiert den *locus classicus* dieser Deutung: Galen, In Hippocratis de natura hominis commentarium 15,105.109 Kühn (Corpus Medicorum Graecorum V,9,1,55.57 hg. v. Mewaldt), um daraus zu folgern: „... to forge and counterfeit books ... was then most of all in fashion, when the Kings of Persia and Alexandria, rivalling one another in the magnificence and copiousness of their Libraries, gave great rates for any treatises that carried the names of celebrated authors. ... But what was then done chiefly for lucre, was afterwards done out of glory and affectation, as an exercise of style and an ostentation of wit. In this the tribe of the Sophists are principally concerned" (82f.). Vgl. auch Bentleys weitere Diskussion der Stelle a.a.O. 84–87. – Kritisch hierzu bereits C. W. MÜLLER, Die Kurzdialoge der Appendix Platonica. Philologische Beiträge zur nachplatonischen Sokratik, STA 17,

gen, rein materialistischen antiken Begründung für hellenistische ‚Fälschungen' allgemein.

Derart rein negativ wertende Begründungsmodelle für die Existenz antiker Briefcorpora finden sich in der neueren Forschung meist dort, wo die Briefe selbst gerade nicht im Zentrum des Forschungsinteresses stehen und deshalb die Mühen einer Neubewertung für den Forscher offenbar in keinem Verhältnis zum argumentativen Gewinn für sein eigentliches Anliegen gestanden hätten. Trotzdem sieht man sich nicht selten auf eben solche ‚Nebenerträge' der Forschung verwiesen, wenn man eine der Briefsammlungen unter dem Namen der ‚famous men' zu seinem Forschungsgegenstand macht. Die Briefform an sich hat nämlich in den letzten Jahrzehnten innerhalb der Klassischen Philologie zwar zunehmend an Beliebtheit gewonnen.[22] Doch profitieren von diesem Trend vor allem die umfangreichen Briefcorpora der römischen Republik bzw. der Spätantike beider Reichshälften[23] einerseits sowie andererseits die schon von ihren antiken Verfassern durch die Sprecherwahl eindeutig als fiktiv ausgewiesenen Briefsammlungen.[24] Die ‚Letters of famous men' genießen dem gegenüber eher bescheidenes Interesse: Einzelne, zumal philosophiegeschichtlich relevante Texte, wie beispielsweise der bereits erwähnte Siebte Brief aus dem *Cor-*

München 1975, 13f.: „Nichts berechtigt dazu, gerade die hellenistischen Zentren der philologischen Kritik für besonders anfällige Opfer literarischer Täuschungen zu halten." Vgl. a.a.O. 12–15 mit Anm. die Auflistung der Vertreter dieses Ansatzes in der älteren Forschung.

[22] Einen Überblick über Tendenzen der Forschung von dokumentarischen bis hin zu fiktionalen Briefen geben GIBSON / MORRISON, Introduction (s. Anm. 7).

[23] Für den griechischsprachigen Bereich betrifft dies vor allem folgende Corpora (hier wie im Folgenden gebe ich die Seitenzahlen in R. Hercher [Hg.], Epistolographi Graeci, Paris 1873 [Nachdruck Amsterdam 1965], zur ersten Orientierung für Überblicke über die neuesten Ausgaben s.u. Anm. 33): Julian Apostata, 4. Jh. n. Chr. (ca. 87 Briefe an Bekannte, Freunde, Gruppen, Hercher 337–391, einzelne Briefe verdächtigt), Libanios, 4. Jh. n. Chr. (ca. 1500 Briefe an Administration, Freunde, Bekannte, Schüler etc., fehlt bei Hercher), Synesios von Kyrene 4./5. Jh. n. Chr. (ca. 156 Briefe an Verwandte, Freunde, Administration, Hercher 638–739), Prokop von Gaza, 5./6. Jh. n. Chr. (160 Briefe an Verwandte, Freunde etc., Hercher 533–598), Aineias von Gaza, um 500 n. Chr. (25 Briefe an Schüler und Freunde, Hercher 24–32), Dionysios von Antiocheia, 6. Jh. n. Chr. (85 Briefe, teilw. ohne Adressat, Hercher 260–274).

[24] Die wichtigsten Sammlungen chronologisch nach Verfassern sind: Alkiphron, 2. Jh. n. Chr. (4 Bücher, 118 Briefe: Fischer-, Bauern-, Parasiten-, Hetärenbriefe, Hercher 44–97), Lukian, 2. Jh. n. Chr. (4 Saturnalische Briefe, u.a. an Kronos, Hercher 392–398), Aelian, 2./3. Jh. n. Chr. (20 Bauernbriefe, Hercher 17–23), Philostratos, 2./3. Jh. n. Chr. (73 Briefe, meist erotisch, Hercher 468–489), Aristainetos, 5. Jh. n. Chr. (2 Bücher erotische Briefe, Hercher 133–171), Theophylaktos Simokates, 6./7. Jh. n. Chr. (85 Moral-, Bauern-, Hetärenbriefe, Hercher 763–762).

pus Platonicum[25] oder der im Rahmen der *Pseudopythagorica* gewichtige Lysis-Brief[26], finden zwar immer wieder und bis in einzelne Details hinein Beachtung. Die Sammlungen, innerhalb derer diese Texte überliefert sind, werden aber meist mittels des Verdiktes der ‚Unechtheit' im Sinne der nicht realen Verfasserschaft durch den im Präskript Genannten rasch beiseite geschoben.

Auch dies lässt sich, soweit ich sehe, als oft unbewusste Spätfolge Bentleys begreifen: Wo er kritische Untersuchung anstelle bloßer Schwärmerei gefordert hatte und als Ergebnis seiner Untersuchung für *einzelne, bestimmte Sammlungen* deren späte Entstehung wahrscheinlich machen konnte, wurde in der Folge in verzerrender Übersteigerung das Verdikt der ‚Unechtheit' im Sinne der Nicht-Verfasserschaft durch die im Präskript genannte historische Person nahezu blindlings auf andere Briefsammlungen, ja Briefsammlungen überhaupt, übertragen. In diesem Sinne klagt bereits Blass (1893),[27] dass derartige Urteile

„ohne stattgehabte wirkliche Untersuchung ... einigermassen an die Anklageschrift gegen den hingerichteten Lord Hastings bei Shakespeare erinnern".

Und wie eine späte Antwort darauf liest sich Szlezáks (1985)[28] Mahnung:

„... wie in der Rechtssprechung die Verhaftung eines Mannes in Gesellschaft von Verbrechern ihn noch nicht als Verbrecher erweist, so ist selbstverständlich auch im epistolographischen Corpus der Antike jedes Stück gesondert zu prüfen."[29]

Briefsammlungen unterliegen also in weiten Teilen der Forschung meist unausgesprochen einem Vor-Urteil, das im Gegensatz zu sonst angewendeten methodischen Grundüberzeugungen steht: Wo sonst die allgemeine Übereinkunft besteht, dass im Hinblick auf die Verfasserschaft eines Tex-

---

[25] Bezeichnenderweise behandelt der neueste Kommentar zu den Platon-Briefen ausschließlich den Siebten Brief; vgl. R. KNAB, Platons Siebter Brief. Einleitung, Text, Übersetzung, Kommentar, Spudasmata 110, Zürich 2006. Zur den Plato epist. auch unten 3.1.

[26] Vgl. die Anmerkungen bei A. Städele (Hg.), Die Briefe des Pythagoras und der Pythagoreer, BKP 115, Meisenheim a. Glan 1980.

[27] Vgl. F. BLASS, Die Attische Beredsamkeit, III.1: Demosthenes, Leipzig ²1893, das folgende Zitat a.a.O. 439 im Blick auf die Demosthenes-Briefe.

[28] Vgl. T. A. SZLEZÁK, Platon und die Schriftlichkeit der Philosophie. Interpretationen zu den frühen und mittleren Dialogen, Berlin u.a. 1985, darin: ‚Anhang III: Zum siebten Brief' (389).

[29] Dem ließen sich noch zahlreiche ähnliche Zitate an die Seite stellen. So klagt etwa auch I. Düring (Hg.), Chion of Heraclea. A Novel in Letters. Edited with Introduction and Commentary, AUG 57.5, Göteborg 1951 (Nachdruck New York 1979), 7, im Blick auf die Chion-Briefe: „Ever since Bentley published his famous Dissertations upon the Epistles of Phalaris and other epistolographers, epistolary literature has enjoyed a constantly bad reputation. All these letters were considered spurious and that was the end of it."

tes stets die Beweislast aufseiten dessen liegt, der sich gegen die durch die Überlieferung gegebenen Daten wendet, scheint es im Fall der Briefcorpora der ‚famous men' beinahe umgekehrt zu sein und sich derjenige in eine Rechtfertigungssituation zu begeben, der die Verfasserangaben der Überlieferung übernimmt.

Hinzu kommt ein zweites. Wo die Forschung des 19. Jh. Impulsen wie dem von Blass (s. obiges Zitat) gefolgt ist, hat sie zwar gewissenhaft die Bentleyschen methodischen Vorgaben abgearbeitet, d.h. stilistische Merkmale gesammelt und verglichen, die inhaltliche Konsistenz innerhalb der Sammlung bzw. mit dem Werk des Autors, so es vorliegt, überprüft, sowie den Abgleich mit der biographischen und/oder historischen Parallelüberlieferung vollzogen. Dennoch ließ sich, sieht man einmal von einzelnen Briefen oder Briefgruppen ab, aufgrund des Mangels an gesichert erschlossenem Vergleichsmaterial desselben literarischen Genres kaum einmal wirkliche Sicherheit hinsichtlich der Verfasserschaft erzielen. Und selbst dort, wo man sich im Laufe der Zeit einig war, dass eine Verfasserschaft durch den im Präskript Genannten unwahrscheinlich ist, schwanken die Datierungen oftmals um mehrere Jahrhunderte.[30] Bereits die rein positivistische Grundeinschätzung der Briefsammlungen ist somit in vielen Fällen nach wie vor ungewiss, was dazu führt, dass die ‚Letters of famous men' gerade aufgrund dieser Unsicherheit oftmals von dem neuen Interesse an (vor allem:) fiktiven Briefsammlungen[31] nicht in vollem Umfang profitieren konnten. So spart etwa Rosenmeyer in ihrer Monographie „Ancient Epistolary Fictions" (2001)[32] die unter dem Namen Platons überlieferten Briefe, an sich eine der berühmtesten und wirkmächtigsten Sammlungen dieser Art, komplett aus, da ihr die Verfasserfrage nach wie vor ungeklärt scheint.

---

[30] Vgl. hier den Überblick unten Anm. 34f.

[31] Vgl. v.a. die Sammlung von C. D. N. Costa (Hg.), Greek Fictional Letters. A Selection with Introduction, Translation and Commentary, Oxford 2001, sowie Trapp, Greek and Latin Letters (s. Anm. 7).

[32] P. A. ROSENMEYER, Ancient Epistolary Fictions. The Letter in Greek Literature, Cambridge 2001.

2. Briefsammlungen oder Briefromane – Wie soll man pseudepigraphe Briefsammlungen lesen?

Besser steht es dementsprechend für diejenigen Sammlungen der ‚Letters of famous men', bei denen in der Forschung wenigstens ein gewisser Konsens hinsichtlich ihres pseudepigraphen Charakters besteht oder es wenigstens in Teilen der Forschung als etabliert gilt, dass größere Teile der Sammlung pseudepigraph sind. Nimmt man hier die Edition von Hercher (1873)[33] als Grundlage für einen ersten Überblick, so finden sich dort insgesamt 14 Sammlungen, die heute als höchstwahrscheinlich durchgängig pseudepigraph gelten,[34] bei sieben weiteren rechnet man eher mit einer Mischung von pseudepigraphen und *realiter* vom angegebenen Verfasser geschriebenen Briefen.[35] Fügt man diesen beiden Gruppen einerseits die

---

[33] Hercher, Epistolographi Graeci (s. Anm. 23). – Die Angaben der folgenden Anmerkungen fassen die *communis opinio* der Forschung zu den einzelnen Sammlungen zusammen. Auf ausführliche bibliographische Nachweise musste ich aus Platzgründen verzichten; ersten Zugang gewinnt man aber jeweils leicht, wenn man die Überblicksbibliographie in Holzberg, Briefroman (s. Anm. 1), 169–190, heranzieht und diese ggf. ergänzt durch die Angaben in H.-J. KLAUCK, Die antike Briefliteratur und das Neue Testament, UTB 2022, Paderborn u.a. 1998, 96–106 (zu den Sammlungen).107–109 (zu den unselbständig überlieferten Briefen), und R. NICKEL, Lexikon der antiken Literatur, Zürich 1999, v.a. 330–350 (unter dem lat. Titel *epistulae* geführte Sammlungen).

[34] Nach heutigem Forschungsstand wahrscheinlich pseudepigraph sind die Briefsammlungen unter den Namen folgender Personen (die Aufzählung führt jeweils Namen, historisches Lebensdatum, Zahl, Seiten bei Hercher, Epistolographi Graeci [s. Anm. 23], und in der Regel angesetztes Abfassungsdatum): Anacharsis, 6. Jh. v. Chr. (9 [Sammlung] + 1 [bei D.L. 1,105] Brief, Hercher 102–105, verfasst: 3. Jh. v. Chr.?), Phalaris, 6. Jh. v. Chr. (148 Briefe v.a. popularphilosophischen Inhalts, Hercher 409–469, verfasst: 400 n. Chr.?), Themistokles, 6./5. Jh. v. Chr. (21 Briefe, Hercher 741–762, verfasst: 1./2. Jh. n. Chr.?), Heraklit von Ephesos, um 500 v. Chr. (7 + 2 [Briefe *an* Heraklit] Briefe, Hercher 280–288, verfasst: 1. Jh. n. Chr.?), Hippokrates, 5. Jh. v. Chr. (27 bzw. 24 Briefe an Städte und Bekannte, Hercher 289–318, verfasst: 5. Jh. bis ?), Euripides, 5. Jh. v. Chr. (5 Briefe an Archelaos, Sophokles, Hercher 275–279, verfasst: augusteisch?), Lysias, 5./4. Jh. v. Chr. (7 Briefe, 6 davon erotisch, Status ungeklärt, da nur fragmentarisch, fehlt bei Hercher), Pythagoras und die Pythagoreer, 5./4. Jh. v. Chr. (ca. 11 Briefe, Hercher 601–608, verfasst: 4./5. Jh. n. Chr.?), Sokrates und die Sokratiker, 5./4. Jh. (35 Briefe zur Illustration der Sokratiker untereinander, Hercher 609–635, verfasst 1./2. Jh. n. Chr.?), Aischines, 4. Jh. v. Chr. (12 Briefe an Freunde und Bekannte, verfasst: ?), Chion von Herakleia, 4. Jh. v. Chr. (17 Briefe an Bekannte und Freunde, Hercher 194–206, verfasst: 1. Jh. v. Chr. / 1. Jh. n. Chr.?), Diogenes, der Kyniker, 4. Jh. v. Chr. (51 Briefe an Städte, Freunde, Schüler etc., Hercher 235–258, verfasst: 2. Jh. v. Chr. bis 2. Jh. n. Chr.?), Krates, 4. Jh. v. Chr. (36 Briefe an Städte, Freunde, Schüler etc., Hercher 208–217, verfasst: 1. Jh. v. Chr. bis 2. Jh. n. Chr.?), Brutus, 1. Jh. v. Chr. (70 Briefe an Städte, mit Antworten eines Redaktors, Hercher 177–191, verfasst: ?).

[35] Nach heutigem Forschungsstand vermutlich eine Mischung pseudepigrapher und nicht-pseudepigrapher Stücke liegt vor bei bzw. im Status höchst umstritten sind (zur

nicht selbständig überlieferten Briefe Alexanders des Großen und die der Sieben Weisen hinzu,[36] so ergibt sich eine Zahl von ca. 25 uns kenntlichen Sammlungen von ‚Letters of famous men'.

Vor allem diese Briefsammlungen sind es, anhand derer die Forschung über das Problem pseudepigrapher Epistolographie einerseits bzw. das des Briefromans andererseits nachgedacht hat. Dabei hat man aus der oben skizzierten, hermeneutisch unbefriedigenden, da in gewisser Weise ‚ans Ende' gelangten Ausgangssituation in den letzten Jahrzehnten verschiedene Auswege gesucht, von denen hier nur einige wenige umrisshaft skizziert seien.

Einen der radikalsten Versuche, der speziell für die griechische Epistolographie entwickelt wurde und daher auch nur allzu deutlich entlang der oben skizzierten Fronten der Briefforschung verläuft, bietet Stirewalt (1993). Er wendet sozusagen einen semantischen ‚Trick' an, indem er das Problemfeld ‚Fälschung vs. Fiktion' durch Umdefinition der es bezeichnenden Begriffe gleichsam verschwinden macht:[37] So scheidet er scharf zwischen ethisch zu inkriminierender ‚Fälschung' („forgery") einerseits und Fiktion, Schulübung, bloßen Zufällen der Überlieferung andererseits. Auf dieser Basis kommt er zu dem Ergebnis, dass gefälschte Briefe aus der Antike gar nicht oder nur in äußerst geringem Umfang erhalten seien. Damit bleibt er nicht nur völlig eben dem von ihm zu Recht bemängelten, moralisierenden Problemhorizont verhaftet.[38] Man wird ihm außerdem entgegnen müssen, dass man wohl kaum den bloßen Tatbestand einer ‚Fälschung' (im traditionellen Sinne) für jeden einzelnen Text der gesamten Antike ausschließen kann. Nachweisbar dürfte eine solche ‚Fälschung' aber in der Regel kaum sein: Schwerlich lässt sich eine echte ‚Täuschungsabsicht' unterscheiden von anderen Motivationen, gar vom Spiel mit ver-

---

Reihenfolge vgl. die vorangehende Anm. 34): Platon, 5./4. Jh. v. Chr. (13 Briefe v.a. an Dionysios II, Dion und Dions Freunde, Hercher 492–532, verfasst: Lebenszeit bis spätestens 1. Jh. n. Chr.), Xenophon, 5./4. Jh. v. Chr. (7 Briefe, teilw. in Sokrates-Briefen, teilw. Exzerpte, Hercher 788–791, verfasst: kaiserzeitlich?), Aristoteles, 4. Jh. v. Chr. (6 Briefe an makedonische Herrscher und Theophrast, Hercher 172–174, verfasst: Lebenszeit / ?), Demosthenes, 4. Jh. v. Chr. (6 Briefe an Volk und Rat von Athen, Hercher 219–234, verfasst: Lebenszeit / ?), Isokrates, 5./4. Jh. v. Chr. (9 Briefe an Makedonenherrscher u.a., Hercher 319–336, verfasst: Lebenszeit / ?), Dion Chrysostomos, 1./2. Jh. n. Chr. (5 Briefe an Lehrer, Bekannte, Hercher 259, verfasst: Lebenszeit / ?), Apollonios von Tyana, 1. Jh. n. Chr. (ca. 100 Briefe an Bekannte, Freunde, Städte, verfasst: Lebenszeit / ?).

[36] Sie sind für die Erforschung der Gattung ‚antiker Briefroman' bedeutend, s. KLAUCK, Die antike Briefliteratur (s. Anm. 33), 107–110.

[37] STIREWALT, Studies (s. Anm. 3), 27–42.

[38] So KLAUCK, Die antike Briefliteratur (s. Anm. 33), 96: „Mit diesem moralisierenden Zugriff lassen sich Fragen um Authentizität und Inauthentizität antiker Briefe und Briefsammlungen nicht adäquat bearbeiten."

schiedenen Ebenen des Fiktionalen. Da aber das Kriterium für die Frage ‚Fälschung oder nicht?' letztlich in der uns jenseits des Textes nicht mehr ermittelbaren inneren Haltung des Verfassers liegt, muss ein solcher Fragehorizont hermeneutisch unbefriedigend bleiben.

Nur konsequent ist vor diesem Hintergrund ein anderer Versuch, diesmal der Pseudepigraphie-Forschung allgemein, das skizzierte Problemfeld gleichsam durch Suspension des Autors aufzuheben. Einen Überblick über die verschiedenen Spielarten dieser Richtung vermittelt ein Tagungsband aus dem Jahr 2000.[39] Hier wird zuerst das Phänomen der Autorschaft allgemein für die Antike als kontingente und damit zweitrangige Kategorie postuliert.[40] Diese relative Schwächung der Autorposition ermöglicht es dann in einem zweiten Schritt, die Verfertigung eines *Pseudepigraphons* als nur mehr symbolischen Akt der Zuweisung eines Textes an den Vertreter einer bestimmten Denkrichtung (im weitesten Sinne) zu begreifen.[41] Bei einem *Pseudepigraphon* handle es sich um eine

„attribuzione simbolica all'autore/archegeta, in una cultura di tipo tradizionalistico, oggetivistica e mitizzante".[42]

Dass es hier darum geht, eine Alternative zum moralisierenden und deshalb unüberprüfbaren Kriterien unterworfenen Blick auf pseudepigraphe Literatur zu finden, diesmal indem man den Autor, dem ein Werk zugewiesen wird, gleichsam zu einer Art allgemeiner kultureller Chiffre macht, liegt auf der Hand. Zweifelhaft scheint freilich, ob es für die Annahme einer symbolischen Setzung tatsächlich einer derartigen Schwächung des individuellen Profils eines Autors bedarf. Sie lässt sich ja wohl nur für ganz vereinzelte Stationen des gesamten von der antiken Literaturgeschichte abgedeckten Spektrums an Personen und Zeiträumen plausibel behaupten.[43] Der Versuch, die Zuschreibung an einen anderen als den rea-

---

[39] G. CERRI, La Letteratura Pseudepigrafa nella Cultura Greca e Romana. Atti di un incontro di studi, Napoli 15–17 gennaio 1998, AION 22, 2000, Napoli 2000.

[40] So wörtlich CERRI, a.a.O. 539: Autorschaft als „aspetto contingente e, quindi, secondario".

[41] Eine ähnliche Tendenz lässt sich in der Biographie-Forschung feststellen, um mit der Fülle an legendarischem Material, das sich nicht zuletzt oftmals eben gerade in (nach heutiger Überzeugung) pseudepigraphen Briefen findet, umzugehen; vgl. z.B. T. SCHIRREN, Philosophos Bios. Die antike Philosophenbiographie als symbolische Form. Studien zur Vita Apollonii des Philostrat, Bibliothek der Altertumswissenschaften N.F. 2. Reihe. 115, Heidelberg 2005, der offensichtlich von CERRI, a.a.O., unabhängig ist. Bedauerlicherweise wird der Symbolbegriff bei Cerri anders als bei Schirren nicht weiter definiert, so dass man wohl von einem normalsprachlichen Verständnis auszugehen hat.

[42] CERRI, a.a.O. 539.

[43] Ein denkbares Beispiel für eine solche Zuweisung von Schriften zu einem gleichsam zu einer Art ‚Markenzeichen' gewordenen Autor könnte man etwa im Corpus Hippocraticum sehen, in das ab der Lebenszeit des Namensgebers bis in die nachchristlichen

len Verfasser als symbolische Handlung zu begreifen, hat jedoch den Vorzug, dass sich in diesem Rahmen nahezu das gesamte Spektrum möglicher Motivationen pseudepigrapher Literatur subsumieren lässt. Der Verfasser eines *Pseudepigraphons* verfolgte durch seine Zuweisung dann immerhin eine bestimmte Intention, nach der sich als Teil eines übergeordneten kulturell-intellektuellen Diskurses sinnvoll fragen lässt.

Auf dieser allgemeinsten Ebene lässt sich der letztgenannte Ansatz mit einer weitaus älteren Richtung der Beschäftigung mit (diesmal wieder) pseudepigraphen Briefen in eine Linie setzen. Ein wesentlicher Teil, zumal der deutschsprachigen Forschung zu pseudepigraphen Briefsammlungen, verdankt sich nämlich eben dem Impuls, einer derartigen Sammlung eine einheitliche, von deren Verfasser[44] verfolgte, Intention zuzuweisen. Die Sinnzuweisung an einen einzelnen pseudepigraphen Text wurde hier gleichsam vom einzelnen Mitglied der Sammlung auf diese als Ganzes transferiert.

Dieser Transfer hat, soweit ich sehe, in der Briefforschung des 20. Jh. wiederholt und in systematischer Weise zunächst vor allem für die Platon-Briefe stattgefunden. Hier war Immisch[45] der Erste, der in einer ausführlichen Analyse die Existenz und Anlage der Briefsammlung durch eine inhaltliche Kategorie, hier – wie bei dem Namensgeber Platon naheliegend – durch eine einheitliche philosophische Intention, zu erklären suchte. Diese These konnte sich nun zwar für die Platon-Briefe nicht durchsetzen. Grundgedanke (einheitliche Aussageintention für die gesamte Sammlung) und Grundimpuls (gegen eine rein biographisch-historische Lesart der Briefe als ‚Quelle') der These fanden aber ihre Fortsetzung. So übernahm Dornseiff[46] den antihistorischen Impuls sowie die Suche nach einer die Sammlung einenden Aussage, fügte dem seinerseits eine Abgrenzung von

---

Jahrhunderte hinein in einem Prozess fortschreitender Kanonisierung von Wissen neue Texte einbezogen wurden; vgl. J. JOUANNA, Hippocrates. Trans. M. B. DeBevoise, Baltimore u.a. 1999 (zuerst französisch 1992), 56–71 (‚Writings in Search of an Author'); die Hippokrates-Briefe stellen in dieser Sammlung eher eine Randerscheinung dar; vgl. zu diesen ROSENMEYER, Ancient Epistolary Fictions (s. Anm. 32), 217–224.

[44] Auch hier verzichte ich der Einfachheit halber darauf, zwischen Verfasser bzw. Verfassern und Redaktor/-en zu unterscheiden; das Grundproblem, ob der Sammlung eine einheitliche Intention unterliegt, die vom Rezipienten wahrgenommen werden soll, besteht in beiden Fällen.

[45] Vgl. O. IMMISCH, Der erste platonische Brief, Ph. 72 (1913), 1–41.

[46] Vgl. F. DORNSEIFF, Platons Buch ‚Briefe', Hermes 69 (1934), 223–226, sowie ders., Echtheitsfragen (s. Anm. 17), 31–36 (‚Exkurs über die Platonbriefe'); Dornseiff rezipiert IMMISCH, a.a.O., v.a. vermittelt durch E. HOWALD, Die Briefe Platons, Zürich 1923; vgl. DORNSEIFF, Echtheitsfragen, 31. HOWALD, a.a.O. 14f., geht ohne weitere Erläuterungen für das 4. Jh. von „geschichtliche[n] Briefromanen" aus, deren „älteste überlieferte Probe" die Platon-Briefe seien. Diese Grundannahme entbehrt jeder weiteren Evidenz.

der politisch-philosophischen Lesart hinzu, und kam so zu seiner These von einem ‚Buch Briefe', das aus „eine[r] Brieffolge mit seiner [sc. Platons] eigenen Person als Helden"[47] bestehe. Die Festlegung auf Platon als autobiographisch tätigen Autor hat Dornseiff in der späteren der genannten Arbeiten wieder zurückgenommen.[48] Die Formulierung vom ‚Helden' wie auch Dornseiffs übrige Ausführungen zeigen aber, dass damit die ‚Roman-These' für die Platon-Briefe erstmals ausgesprochen und durchgespielt worden war. Von Dornseiffs ‚Buch Briefe' wiederum führt eine direkte Linie zu Holzbergs[49] Überlegungen zum antiken Briefroman, die bis heute die ausführlichste Darstellung der Genre-Problematik speziell der griechischsprachigen *Brief*romane darstellen, und von dort wiederum zu Rosenmeyers[50] allgemeinerer Untersuchung fiktionaler Briefe der Antike.

Schon die schiere Genese eingehenderer Beschäftigung mit der Gattung ‚antiker Briefroman' macht deutlich, dass sich in der Forschung der Wille zu einer vom antiken Autor angestrebten einheitlichen Intention hinter den Sammlungen lange vor einer systematischen Untersuchung aller uns erhaltenen Texte etabliert hatte. Und so besteht heute zwar weitgehend Übereinstimmung, dass es bereits in der Antike Werke gab, die, bis auf die Wahl des jeweiligen ‚Helden',[51] dem, was man seit etwa der frühen Neuzeit als ‚Briefroman' zu rezipieren gewohnt ist, immerhin in wesentlichen Aspekten entsprechen.[52] Hinsichtlich der Gattungsmerkmale bzw. -grenzen aber herrscht nach wie vor solche Unsicherheit, dass nicht einmal über den mit dem Begriff ‚Briefroman' zu bezeichnenden Kanon an Texten Einigkeit besteht. So geht etwa Holzberg[53] von insgesamt sieben uns noch kenntlichen Briefromanen (die Briefe Platons, des Euripides, des Aischines, des Hippokrates, Chions, des Themistokles, des Sokrates und der Sokratiker)

---

[47] So DORNSEIFF, Platons Buch (s. Anm. 46), 226.

[48] Vgl. ders., Echtheitsfragen (s. Anm. 17), 31: „Daß es [sc. das Briefbuch Plato epist.] von Platon selbst stammt, möchte ich nicht mehr behaupten."

[49] Vgl. Holzberg, Briefroman (s. Anm. 1).

[50] S. Anm. 32.

[51] Bei den ‚Helden' neuzeitlicher Briefromane handelt es sich in aller Regel gerade nicht um historische Persönlichkeiten, sondern um frei erfundene Figuren; vgl. ROSENMEYER, Ancient Epistolary Fictions (s. Anm. 32), 196–201; für einen breiter angelegten Gattungsvergleich s. C. ARNDT, Antiker und neuzeitlicher Briefroman. Ein gattungstypologischer Vergleich, in: Holzberg, Briefroman (s. Anm. 1), 53–83.

[52] Vgl. beispielsweise J. STENGER, Eine Aufforderung zum Tyrannenmord? Die Doppelbödigkeit der Briefe des Chion, Antike und Abendland 51 (2005), 120–136 (120): „Nachdem man lange Zeit der Überzeugung war, daß der Roman in Briefform eine genuine Schöpfung der Neuzeit sei, hat sich inzwischen die Ansicht durchgesetzt, daß es zumindest in der griechischen Antike durchaus vergleichbare Werke gab."

[53] S. N. HOLZBERG, Der griechische Briefroman. Versuch einer Gattungstypologie, in: ders., Briefroman (s. Anm. 1), 1–52 (5), ebenso ARNDT, Antiker und neuzeitlicher Briefroman (s. Anm. 51).

aus und zieht zusätzlich vier weitere Gruppen von Briefen als möglicherweise ‚romanhaft' in Erwägung (die Briefe der Sieben Weisen, Xenophons, Alexanders des Großen sowie Teile der Briefe des Phalaris), während etwa Rosenmeyer (2001) allein die Chion-Briefe als ‚epistolary novel' gelten lassen möchte. Ursache dieses Dissenses ist nicht nur die oben skizzierte Unsicherheit hinsichtlich des fiktionalen Anteils an den genannten Corpora. Gerade auch die jeweils unterschiedliche, stets aus neuzeitlichen Formen abgeleitete Vorstellung von einer antiken Gattung ‚Briefroman' bedingt die verschiedene Einordnung der genannten Texte.

Um in dieser Frage substantielle Fortschritte zu erzielen, bedürfte es einer erneuten Untersuchung *aller* Briefsammlungen,[54] die heute als (relativ) sicher vollständig fiktional gelten. Da dies hier nicht geleistet werden kann, beschreite ich im Folgenden einen anderen Weg, der kaum mehr als eine weitere Schärfung des Problemhorizontes erbringen kann: Da Holzbergs[55] Ausführungen immer noch den ausführlichsten Versuch einer umfassenderen Gattungstypologie darstellen, lege ich sie im Folgenden in leicht modifizierter Form (s.u.) zugrunde und wende sie exemplarisch und gleichsam versuchsweise auf die forschungsgeschichtlich wichtigen Platon-Briefe einerseits sowie die von der Mehrzahl der Forscher übereinstimmend als ‚romanhaft' empfundene Sammlung der Chion-Briefe[56] andererseits an. In der spezifischen Differenz beider Sammlungen lassen sich erste Möglichkeiten einer weiteren Präzisierung der Gattung festmachen.

Zu diesem Zweck seien hier Holzbergs Analysen vorab noch einmal knapp zusammengefasst: Holzberg übernimmt von Dornseiff[57] den antihistorischen Impuls und stellt ebenfalls das ‚Nicht-Historisch-Philosophische' in den Mittelpunkt seiner Deutung.[58] Ohne die Dominanz des politischen Themas in den von ihm untersuchten Briefsammlungen zu leugnen, versteht er die Briefe vor allem als „an ein Unterhaltung und Erbauung suchendes Lesepublikum"[59] gewandt. Hatte schon Dornseiff für sein ‚Buch

---

[54] Eine solche hat auch ROSENMEYER, Ancient Epistolary Fictions (s. Anm. 32), in ihren Ausführungen zum Briefroman (169–252) nicht vorgenommen.

[55] S. Anm. 1.

[56] Auch im Hinblick auf die Chion ep. besteht keine völlige Einigkeit; vgl. die Vorbehalte bei Costa, Greek Fictional Letters (s. Anm. 31), xviiif., und Trapp, Greek and Latin Letters (s. Anm. 7), 30.

[57] DORNSEIFF, Echtheitsfragen (s. Anm. 17), und ders., Platons Buch (s. Anm. 46).

[58] Vgl. v.a. seine Einleitung in Holzberg, Briefroman (s. Anm. 1), XIf.

[59] So ebenfalls in der Einleitung a.a.O. IX. Forschungsgeschichtlich ist Holzbergs Impuls nachvollziehbar, doch darf dies nicht so gemeint sein, dass biographisch-historische bzw. doxographische Informationen gegen eine auf ‚Unterhaltung' zielende Ausrichtung der Sammlungen ausgespielt werden: Gerade ein hellenistisches oder kaiserzeitliches Publikum (und von einem solchen muss man nach heutigem Forschungsstand für die meisten uns erhaltenen Sammlungen ausgehen, vgl. o. Anm. 34f.) fühlte sich wohl just

Briefe' „planmäßig entwickelt[e] ... Motive" sowie auch einen „aufs kunstvollste und bewußteste komponiert[en] ... Gang der Handlung" und eine besondere Ausrichtung auf das *ēthos* (‚Charakter') des Ich-Sagenden postuliert,[60] so übernimmt Holzberg (1994) diese Elemente weitgehend und macht sie zum Baustein eines größer angelegten „Versuch[es] einer Gattungstypologie"[61] des griechischen Briefromans. Er lässt damit die enge Textbasis, die Dornseiff[62] zugrunde gelegt hatte, hinter sich. So gut wie keine Rolle spielt außerdem für Holzberg (1994) die Ausrichtung der Darstellung hin auf das *ēthos* des Helden. In diesem einen Punkt möchte ich, abweichend von Holzberg, Dornseiffs Beobachtung nicht aufgeben, da mir dieses Merkmal in den uns erhaltenen Briefsammlungen ebenfalls durchgängig vorzuliegen scheint (*mein Merkmal 1: ēthos*). Gerechtfertigt scheint mir dies zusätzlich durch zweierlei: Zum einen, wenn man die Rolle bedenkt, die, wie bemerkt, das Verfassen von Briefen für den Schulbetrieb (Einübung in Ethopoiie) hatte,[63] und zum anderen, weil man das Schreiben über den bedeutenden Einzelnen in Briefform auch in Beziehung setzen kann zu Formen biographischen Schreibens im Hellenismus, die ebenfalls eine starke *ēthos*-Zentriertheit aufweisen.[64]

Für den von Holzberg entwickelten Begriff des ‚Briefromanes' sind folgende weiteren Merkmale kennzeichnend, die er nach den Bereichen „Er-

---

dann am besten ‚unterhalten', wenn es auch in seinen Bildungshorizonten angesprochen wurde.

[60] Vgl. den Titel des Aufsatzes von DORNSEIFF, Platons Buch (s. Anm. 46), sowie für die Zitate a.a.O. 223f.

[61] So HOLZBERG, Gattungstypologie (s. Anm. 53), 1.

[62] DORNSEIFF, Platons Buch (s. Anm. 46), bezieht sich ausschließlich auf die Plato epist., s. Anm. 46.

[63] S.o. 234 mit Anm. 5.

[64] Dieser Punkt bedürfte ausführlicherer Darlegung als es hier möglich ist, zumal biographisches Schreiben in Hellenismus (und Klassik) gattungsmäßig ähnlich schwierig zu fassen ist wie die oben verhandelten Genres. Für einen Überblick vgl. jetzt M. Erler / S. Schorn (Hg.), Die Griechische Biographie in Hellenistischer Zeit. Akten des internationalen Kongresses vom 26.–29. Juli 2006 in Würzburg, Beiträge zur Altertumskunde 245, Berlin u.a. 2007. – Untersucht man die uns erhaltenen Fragmente etwa eines Aristoxenos, Antigonos von Karystos, Hermipp von Smyrna und Satyros von Kallatis, so lässt sich in ihrem biographischen Schreiben in je unterschiedlicher Weise eine Ausrichtung hin auf das *ēthos* des Darzustellenden zeigen, deren ursprüngliche Wurzel die Frage nach der rechten Lebensform darstellt. Alle vier behandeln vor allem Philosophen und Schriftsteller, verschränken dabei biographische und doxographische Nachrichten und bringen so Details in ihre Darstellung ein, die in der Gesuchtheit der Information (Fiktion?) teilweise stark an die biographischen Details der fiktionalen Briefsammlungen erinnern. So kennt etwa Hermipp den Namen der Hetäre des Isokrates ebenso wie die Höhe seines Honorars oder diejenigen Gegenstände, die Dionysios I. von dessen Erben erworben hat (Hermipp F 42.43.84 Bollansée). Ich hoffe, diesen Punkt an anderer Stelle genauer darzulegen.

zählstruktur", „Stoffbehandlung" und „Motive" unterscheidet[65]: Konstituierend für einen Briefroman ist nach Holzberg, dass die Sammlung als Ganzes eine narrative Einheit bildet, in der „die einzelnen Briefe in ihrer Abfolge eine Handlung nachzeichnen" (a.a.O. 1). Er geht von „wie eine fortlaufende Erzählung strukturierten Briefbücher[n]" aus.[66] Holzberg rechnet also, resümierend gesagt, mit der Errichtung eines narrativen Kontinuums (*Merkmal 2*).[67] Um unter diesen Begriff auch Sammlungen subsumieren zu können, deren nicht-chronologische Anlage dem Kriterium der ‚Handlung in der Abfolge' (s.o.) nur schwer entspricht, nimmt er zusätzlich eine „Erzählweise der sukzessiven Aufklärung" unter „Verwendung von Techniken einer ausgeklügelten Enthüllungsdramaturgie"[68] an (*Merkmal 3*). Außerdem bestimmt Holzberg „Motive" (a.a.O. 51), die allen von ihm untersuchten Sammlungen zugrunde liegen, wie etwa ‚der Briefschreiber und ein Machthaber', ‚Frage nach der Sinnfälligkeit politischer Betätigung', ‚Wert des Geldes', ‚der Briefschreiber und seine Freunde und Feinde' (*Merkmal 4*). Zusammenfassend formuliert hat man es somit nach Holzberg dann mit einem Briefroman und nicht mit einer nach anderen als romanhaften oder etwa bloß konservatorisch bedingten Kriterien zusammengestellten Briefsammlung zu tun, wenn die Struktur den Charakter einer ‚fortlaufenden Erzählung' aufweist, die durch eine ‚Erzählweise der sukzessiven Aufklärung' erfolgt und zusätzlich durch bestimmte Motive bzw. Motivketten zusammengehalten wird. Der pseudepigraphe Charakter der Sammlungen ist in diesem Ansatz dadurch gleichsam ‚aufgehoben', dass Holzberg das Augenmerk des Lesers vor allem auf den unterhaltenden Charakter der Texte und damit deren fiktionales Potential lenkt.[69]

---

[65] Vgl. zum Folgenden v.a. das Resümee in HOLZBERG, Gattungstypologie (s. Anm. 53), 49–52.

[66] So HOLZBERG, a.a.O. 2, ebenso ders., Briefroman (s. Anm. 1), X („bilden die ... Episteln in ihrer Abfolge den Verlauf einer Handlung ab"), und wieder im Resümee: „In allen sieben Briefromanen *folgen die Briefe in der Weise aufeinander*, daß sie die von dem Briefschreiber reflektierten Ereignisse, die während der Zeit der Abfassung der Briefe geschehen, *chronologisch nachzeichnen*" (ders., Gattungstypologie [s. Anm. 53], 50, Hervorhebung von mir).

[67] Holzberg, das sei betont, spricht in abschwächender (?) Weise von ‚Widerspiegelung bzw. Nachzeichnung eines *Handlungs*kontinuums', so a.a.O. 4: „ein Handlungskontinuum nachzeichnende[n] griechische[n] Briefbücher", ebenso 52 Anm. 156, s.a. a.a.O. 13: „Briefsequenzen ..., die ein Handlungskontinuum widerspiegeln". Ebenso wieder ders., Der antike Roman (s. Anm. 8), 32, als Merkmal der Phalaris ep.: Diese Sammlung „unterscheidet sich ... von den bisher genannten Briefbüchern [sc. die auch 1994 untersuchten sieben Sammlungen], daß sie kein *Handlungskontinuum*, sondern nur Gruppen thematisch zusammengehöriger Briefe aufzuweisen hat" (Hervorhebung von mir).

[68] Beide Zitate ders., Gattungstypologie (s. Anm. 53), 9.

[69] Nicht näher eingehen kann ich auf Holzbergs daraus resultierende Behandlung der in einer ganzen Reihe von Briefen unserer Sammlungen vorkommenden Anachronismen;

3. Briefsammlungen oder Briefromane? – Am Beispiel der Platon- und der Chion-Briefe

3.1 Die Platon-Briefe

Unter Platons Namen ist uns innerhalb der Tetralogienordnung seiner Werke eine Sammlung von dreizehn Briefen erhalten.[70] Die Verfasserfrage ist bis heute höchst umstritten.[71] Dementsprechend besteht keine Einigkeit über die Datierung, wenn auch Teile der Sammlung heute meist als ‚alt' (im Sinne einer relativen Nähe zur Lebenszeit Platons gelten).[72] Die

---

vgl. z.B. a.a.O. 44 Anm. 135 (zu den Socrates ep.): „Aber danach [sc. ob der Verfasser bewusst oder aus Unkenntnis gegen die übliche Chronologie verstieß] zu fragen, ist ohnehin müßig, da es sich ... bei diesem Text ebenso wie bei den anderen Briefromanen um fiktionale Literatur handelt." Es bedürfte m.E. einer genaueren Untersuchung, ob die in den Briefsammlungen begegnenden Abweichungen von der Chronologie auf ähnliche Lizenzen hindeuten wie sie der griechische Roman (in Nicht-Brief-Form) kennt.

[70] Ich lege die Ausgabe von Moore-Blunt (Platonis Epistulae recogn. J. Moore-Blunt, Leipzig 1985) zugrunde. Die Sekundärliteratur, zumal zu einzelnen Briefen, ist Legion. Eine neuere Monographie oder ein neuerer Kommentar zur gesamten Sammlung jedoch fehlen; KNAB, Platons Siebter Brief (s. Anm. 25), behandelt ausschließlich den Siebten Brief. – Stellvertretend sei deshalb verwiesen auf L. Brisson (Hg.), Platon. Lettres. Traduction, introduction, notices, notes, Paris ⁴2004 (zuerst ebd. 1987), und M. Isnardi Parente (Hg.), Platone. Lettere. Trad. di M.G. Ciani, o.O. 2002, die auch weiterführende Literatur angeben. Die m.E. immer noch beste Gesamtdarstellung der Sammlung bietet G. P. PASQUALI, Le lettere di Platone, Florenz ²1961; hilfreich sind zur Sprache v.a. F. NOVOTNÝ, Platonis Epistulae commentariis illustratae, Brno 1930, zu philosophischen Fragen sowie zum historischen Hintergrund G. R. MORROW, Plato's Epistles. A Translation with Critical Essays and Notes, Indianapolis u.a. ²1962; L. EDELSTEIN, Plato's Seventh Letter, PhAnt 14, Leiden 1966; K. VON FRITZ, Platon in Sizilien und das Problem der Philosophenherrschaft, Berlin 1968; SZLEZÁK, Platon und die Schriftlichkeit (s. Anm. 28); J. TRAMPEDACH, Platon, die Akademie und die zeitgenössische Politik, Hermes.E 66, Stuttgart 1994. H. LÄNGIN, Erzählkunst und Philosophie in den Platon-Briefen, GrB 22 (1998), 101–115, schreibt Holzbergs These (a.a.O.) von den Plato epist. als Briefroman aus.

[71] Vgl. die Überblickstabelle in Brisson, a.a.O. 70: Weitgehende Einigkeit besteht heute dahingehend, dass sich um einen frühen und möglicherweise vom historischen Platon verfassten Kern der Sammlung (Plato epist. 7 + Plato epist. n) eine ansonsten pseudepigraphe Sammlung konstituiert hat. Allenfalls Briefgruppen innerhalb der Sammlung, keinesfalls aber die Sammlung insgesamt, stammen dann von einem einzigen Autor. Die Frage nach einer einheitlichen Intention, die die Anlage der Sammlung bedinge, verlagert sich vor diesem Hintergrund auf die Ebene eines planvoll sammelnden Redaktors.

[72] HOLZBERG, Gattungstypologie (s. Anm. 53), 47f., selbst erwägt, dass es sich um das älteste der von ihm untersuchten Briefcorpora handeln könne, was mir plausibel scheint; die zeitlich untere Grenze ergibt sich durch die Aufnahme in die Tetralogienordnung, d.h. spätestens im 1. Jh. n. Chr.

Sammlung ist monologisch angelegt, Platon durchgängig als Absender der Briefe vorausgesetzt. Die Briefe richten sich an den sizilischen Alleinherrscher Dionysios II (Plato epist. 1, 2, 3, 13), an Dion (Plato epist. 4), Dionysios' zeitweiligen Schwager und Schüler Platons, an dessen politische Weggefährten und Verwandte (Plato epist. 7, 8), einen sonst unbekannten Aristodoros, wohl einen Freund Dions (Plato epist. 10), den unteritalischen Pythagoreer Archytas (Plato epist. 9, 12), an Leodamas, wohl den Aristotelesschüler und Mathematiker (Plato epist. 11), sowie an Perdikkas III, den älteren Bruder Philipps II (Plato epist. 5) und eine aus den Platonschülern Erastos und Koriskos sowie dem Kleinfürsten Hermeias bestehende Gruppe (Plato epist. 6).[73] Den Hintergrund der meisten Briefe (Plato epist. 1–4, 7–10, 12, 13) bilden die Ereignisse um Platons Aufenthalte in Syrakus 366 und 361/0 v. Chr.: Der Platon der Briefe hatte vergeblich versucht, Dionysios II, den bei seinem ersten Aufenthalt am Hof noch jungen Alleinherrscher von Sizilien, zu einer Reform seiner Herrschaft zu bewegen und wird schließlich zum hilflosen Zeugen eines tief greifenden Zerwürfnisses zwischen Dionysios und Dion. Dieses führt zu Dions Verbannung, seinem späteren Marsch auf Syrakus und, in letzter Konsequenz, zu seiner Ermordung im Jahre 354, nach der seine Parteigänger und Freunde in bürgerkriegsähnlichen Wirren zurückbleiben.[74]

Hauptmerkmal der Sammlung ist – auf den ersten Blick – die Diversität der in ihr enthaltenen Texte. Dies gilt bereits für den Umfang: Der Siebte Brief sprengt jedes quantitative Maß und erreicht mit seinen 809 Zeilen[75] etwa die Länge eines der kleineren Dialoge (des Autors) Platon. Der Umfang der restlichen Briefe bewegt sich zwischen wenigen Zeilen (Plato epist. 10, 12) über etwa 20 bis 30 Zeilen (Plato epist. 1, 4, 5, 6, 9, 11) bis hin zu mehrere Seiten umfassenden Schreiben (ca. 120–160 Zeilen, Plato epist. 2, 3, 8, 13). Sieht man einmal von der Mittelstellung des Siebten Briefes ab, bildet somit die schiere Textlänge kein Kriterium für die Stellung eines Textes in der Sammlung. Auch andere denkbare Anordnungsprinzipien versagen.[76] Offenbar liegt weder eine alphabetische Ordnung

---

[73] Zur Prosopographie vgl. D. NAILS, The People of Plato. A Prosopography of Plato and other Socratics, Indianapolis u.a. 2002, jeweils *sub voce*.

[74] Vgl. hierzu TRAMPEDACH, Platon (s. Anm. 70), 111–122.

[75] Hier wie im Folgenden gezählt nach der Ausgabe von Moore-Blunt, Platonis Epistulae (s. Anm. 70).

[76] Die Reihenfolge der handschriftlichen Überlieferung, d.h. die unserer Ausgaben, weicht von derjenigen ab, die Diogenes Laërtios für die Briefsammlung innerhalb der Tetralogienordnung gibt. Vgl. D.L. 3,61: „Ein Brief an Aristodoros, zwei an Archytas, vier an Dionysios, einer an Hermeias, Erastos, Korsikos, einer an Leodamas, einer an Dion, einer an Perdikkas, zwei an die Vertrauten Dions". Doch ist mir auch für diese alternative Reihung kein durchgängiger Ordnungswille erkennbar: Nach den ersten fünf Nennungen erwartet man eine alphabetische Anordnung, die dann offensichtlich von den

nach Adressatennamen noch eine Ordnung nach geographischer Herkunft oder ‚Profession' des Adressaten vor: Zwar lässt sich am Beginn der Sammlung mit den drei Briefen an Dionysios II und dem Brief an Dion (Plato epist. 1–4) eine Art ‚Sizilien'-Gruppe ausmachen,[77] doch folgen auf diese die ‚unsizilischen' Briefe 5 und 6, dann die beiden wiederum ‚sizilischen' Briefe an die ‚Freunde und Verwandten Dions' (Plato epist. 7, 8), die ebenfalls sizilisch grundierten Briefe an Archytas und Aristodoros (Plato epist. 9, 10), bevor, wiederum gleichsam unterbrochen durch den Brief an Leodamas (Plato epist. 11), ein zweiter Brief an Archytas (Plato epist. 12) und schließlich ein weiterer an Dionysios II (Plato epist. 13) die Sammlung beschließen. Ebenso wenig findet das je von den Einzelbriefen vorausgesetzte Datum in der Anordnung der Briefe seinen Niederschlag. Die Reihenfolge der Briefe nach diesem Datum wäre nämlich etwa Plato epist. 9 und 12 (nach 387), 13 (365?), 5 (zwischen 365 und 359), 6 (gegen 360), 1 (noch 360), 2 und 3 (nach 360), 4 (357/6), 10 (vor 354), 7 (354/3), 8 (353/2) und zuletzt 6 (351/0).[78]

Blickt man angesichts dieses für eine einheitliche Intention eines Redaktors wenig ermutigenden Befundes Orientierung suchend an Anfang und Ende der Sammlung, so begegnet man dort einerseits (in Plato epist. 1: An Dionysios II) einem tödlich gekränkten Platon, der Dionysios nach seiner Heimkehr vom letzten Besuch in Syrakus wutentbrannt ein seiner Ansicht nach viel zu geringes Reisegeld vor die Füße wirft (Plato epist. 1: 309c1–d2) und dies zum Anlass nimmt, seinen Adressaten in gnomenhaft ausgewählten Dichterzitaten vor der Einsamkeit des Tyrannen zu warnen (ab 309d2 bis Ende). Der letzte Brief der Sammlung (Plato epist. 13), ebenfalls an Dionysios adressiert, hingegen zeigt einen ‚Platon der kleinen Dinge', der als treuer Sachwalter der finanziellen Angelegenheiten des Dionysios auf dem Festland agiert (Plato epist. 13: ab 361b4), nicht nur zu diesem selbst, sondern auch zu dessen Familie freundschaftliche Beziehungen unterhält (361a1–6) und außerdem nicht geringen Stolz über seine Rolle als Empfehlungsbriefe schreibender Vermittler zum Hofe zu verspü-

---

letzten drei Einträgen nicht eingehalten wird; unter diesen drei Einträgen findet sich an letzter Stelle auch der von uns als ältester Kern vorausgesetzte Plato epist. 7, so dass die Ordnung offensichtlich auch nicht der Entstehung der Sammlung geschuldet ist. Der bloße Befund einer zweifachen Überlieferung der Anordnung wirft aber m.E. *per se* ein bedenkliches Licht auf alle Versuche, für eine Interpretation zu starkes Gewicht auf die bloße Reihenfolge der Briefe zu legen.

[77] HOLZBERG, Gattungstypologie (s. Anm. 53), 13, spricht von „Sizilien-Roman"; ebd. auch zu seinem Verständnis der Anordnung der übrigen Briefe, s.a. unten 254.

[78] Aus manchen Briefen lassen sich kaum sichere Daten ihrer vorausgesetzten Abfassung gewinnen; vgl. hierzu sowie zu den im Haupttext genannten Daten die jeweiligen Einträge bei Brisson, Platon, und Isnardi Parente, Platone (beide s. Anm. 70).

ren scheint (363b1–5).[79] Dazwischen begegnet man Platon unter anderem als geheimnisvoll raunendem Welterklärer (neo?-)pythagoreischer Ausrichtung (Plato epist. 2: An Dionysios II),[80] ganz auf die konkreten Verhältnisse in Syrakus bezogenem Realpolitiker (Plato epist. 3: An Dionysios)[81] sowie als tief enttäuschtem philosophischen Lehrer (Plato epist. 7: An Dions politische Weggefährten und Verwandte).[82]

Das *ēthos* der (!) Platons dieser Briefe ist, zumal wenn man das intellektuelle Profil der je entworfenen Persönlichkeit mit einbezieht, m.E. kaum miteinander vereinbar (*Merkmal 1*). Seine Diversität kann allenfalls für den Platon der Plato epist. 1 und 13 durch das als wesentlich früher vorausgesetzte Datum des 13. Briefes vor dem finalen Zerwürfnis, dem Plato epist. 1 erst folgen soll, erklärt werden. Akzeptiert man diese Erklärung und lässt sich auf dieser Grundlage (etwa: ‚erster und letzter Brief des Corpus ‚passen' zusammen') auf eine fortlaufende Lektüre der Sammlung ein, bleibt m.E. dennoch schwierig, was man aus einem solchen Anfang und Ende zu machen hat: Hebt der ‚Roman' gleichsam mit einem Paukenschlag der Entrüstung an, trägt dann die eigentlichen, tieferen Gründe dieser Entrüstung vor allem in den Schilderungen von Plato epist. 7 und 8 nach,[83] um dann am Ende mit einem Blick auf Platons Verdienste um Dionysios zu schließen? Sollte dieses Ende dann zeigen, wie guten Willens Platon war? Und dies ein wehmütig tragisches Licht auf alles zuvor Geschehene werfen? Hätte ein derartiges Ende nicht irgendeiner motivischen Vorbereitung bedurft, um den von vorne nach hinten lesenden Rezipienten nicht völlig zu überfordern, zumal der nirgends direkt annoncierte zeitliche Sprung zum unmittelbar vorhergehenden Brief (Plato epist. 12: An Archytas) gut zwanzig Jahre beträgt?[84] – Eine gleichsam konsequent linear verfahrende Lesart (*Merkmal 2*), das zeigen schon diese wenigen Andeu-

---

[79] Anders, nämlich als Reflex platonfeindlicher Tradition (‚Platon als Parasit'), versteht diesen Brief K. GAISER, Platone come kolax in una lettera apocrifa (13a epist.), Sandalion 4 (1981), 71–94.

[80] Vgl. v.a die dort entwickelte Lehre von den ‚Drei Königen' (Plato epist. 2: ab 312d7) mit den Warnungen vor schädlicher Vulgarisierung des Mitgeteilten ab 314a1, dem rätselhaften Sprechen vom ‚jungen, schönen Sokrates' (314c2) sowie v.a. der in der gesamten antiken Briefliteratur nahezu singulären Aufforderung, den Brief nach der Lektüre zu verbrennen (314c3–5). Hierzu J. M. RIST, Neophythagoreism and Plato's Second Letter, Phronesis 10 (1965), 78–81.

[81] Hier verfasst Platon sogar ‚Proömien' zu einem Gesetzgebungswerk für Syrakus (Plato epist. 3: 316a2).

[82] V.a. im Umfeld des sog. ‚Philosophischen Exkurses' (Plato epist. 7: 342a6–344d2); hierzu SZLEZÁK, Platon und die Schriftlichkeit (s. Anm. 28).

[83] Dabei bleibt das explizit rein pekuniäre Motiv des Ersten Briefes singulär und wäre dann gleichsam nur noch als ‚Tropfen, der das Fass zum Überlaufen brachte' zu verstehen.

[84] S. zur Datierung der Briefe oben 252.

tungen, kann m.E. keine hinreichend große Anzahl von Merkmalen des Textes integrieren, um als Interpretationsansatz befriedigend zu sein.

Eine solche streng lineare Lesart nimmt Holzberg aber für die Plato epist. auch nicht vor.[85] Er geht vielmehr vom längsten Brief der Sammlung, dem Siebten Brief, aus und begreift ihn als strukturelles (als Symmetrieachse) und inhaltliches Zentrum der Sammlung.[86] Dieser Siebte Brief werde durch die Anfangsgruppe der Plato epist. 1 bis 4 gleichsam vorbereitet; die sozusagen ‚ortsfremden', nicht-sizilischen Plato epist. 5 und 6 dienten der Überbrückung „hinterszenischen Geschehens", Plato epist. 8 stelle eine Art „Epilog" zu Plato epist. 7 dar.[87] Auf diese Weise bildeten Plato epist. 1–8 einen „Sizilien-Roman", der Rest der Sammlung (Plato epist. 9–13) ist „nur thematisch miteinander verknüpft".[88]

Dass der Siebte Brief eine zentrale Stellung einnimmt, ist unbestreitbar. Ebenso wird man für den impliziten Hinweis dankbar sein, dass ein möglicher Redaktor der Sammlung durchaus auch an einen ‚second reader' mit zusätzlicher Deutungskompetenz gedacht haben mag. Alles weitere aber erscheint mir zweifelhaft: Es ist m.E. unbefriedigend, die zweifach um Plato epist. 7 angeordnete Gruppierung der Briefe (jeweils sechs Briefe davor und danach), einerseits als bewusst eingesetztes Instrument der Rezipientenlenkung hin auf das Ziel der ‚Erzählung' zu deuten,[89] dann aber die in dieser Ordnung angelegte Symmetrie preisgeben zu müssen, da Plato epist. 9–13 gerade *nicht* in das postulierte, narrative Kontinuum integriert werden können.[90] Gerät die für die Sammlung als Ganzes angesetzte

---

[85] So auch noch einmal explizit im Resümée seiner Deutung HOLZBERG, Gattungstypologie (s. Anm. 53), 13: „Obwohl alle in der zweiten Hälfte des Buches [sc. der Plato epist.] enthaltenen Briefe außer Nr. 8 die mit Nr. 1 beginnende chronologische Reihe nicht mehr fortsetzen, sollte man keine Bedenken tragen, das Buch als Ganzes zur Gruppe der griechischen Briefromane zu zählen." Vgl. ebd.: „mit dieser symmetrischen Strukturierung [sc. dürfte der Autor bzw. Redaktor] eine bestimmte Intention verbunden haben."

[86] So HOLZBERG, a.a.O. 12: „Hier laufen alle Handlungsfäden zusammen", a.a.O. 51: der „erklärende Brief".

[87] So HOLZBERG, a.a.O. 50 bzw. 51, ähnlich a.a.O. 16, wo epist. 5 und 6 die Funktion der ‚Überbrückung eines Zeitsprunges' zugewiesen wird.

[88] So a.a.O. 13 und 51 (erstes Zitat) bzw. 50 (zweites Zitat).

[89] Dies übernimmt HOLZBERG (a.a.O. 13: „daß dem langen 7. Brief je sechs erheblich kürzere Briefe vorausgehen und folgen") von DORNSEIFF, Platons Buch (s. Anm. 46), 224: „Hier haben wir 12 Briefe, die den großen siebenten umrahmen, mit zwei gleichen Hälften."

[90] Vgl. HOLZBERG, a.a.O. 13: „Zwar ist ab Brief 9 *kein fortlaufendes Geschehen* erkennbar, im Gegenteil: Brief 10 setzt offenbar voraus, daß Dion noch lebt, und Brief 13 ist an den noch in Syrakus herrschenden Tyrannen Dionysios gerichtet. Aber es existiert *eine Fülle von motivischen Bezügen* zwischen dem ‚Sizilien-Roman' und dem übrigen Briefbuch" (Hervorhebung von mir). Einen solchen motivischen Bezug stellt für

Architektur als einheitsstiftendes Moment ins Wanken, bleiben noch die Motivketten (*Merkmal 4*) innerhalb der Sammlung. Die inhaltlichen Gemeinsamkeiten zwischen den Briefen reichen nun tatsächlich bis in einzelne Wendungen.[91] Selbst wenn man einmal davon absieht, dass es sich hierbei schlicht um Spuren der Entstehung eines Briefes der Sammlung aus einem anderen (im Sinne von: ‚Brief y wurde aus einem einzelnen Motiv von Brief x herausgesponnen') handeln könnte,[92] scheint mir auch dies kein ausreichendes Kriterium dafür, dass wir die Plato epist. als narratives Kontinuum oder auch nur bewusst komponierte narrative Einheit lesen sollen. Zu Recht nennt Holzberg diese ‚Gemeinsamkeiten' nämlich „Motive" oder „Themen".[93] Er impliziert damit selbst, dass es sich hierbei eben nicht um durch die Abfolge von Plato epist. 1 bis 13 fortlaufend erzählte oder sukzessiv ergänzte Handlungsstränge handelt, sondern um inhaltliche Überschneidungen zwischen einzelnen Briefen. Ob diese aber für einen Autor, der sich im Themenfeld ‚Platon in Sizilien' bewegt, überhaupt zu vermeiden waren, scheint mir – zumal vor dem Hintergrund antiplatonischer Polemik[94] – fraglich. Die mit dem Problem der gemeinsamen ‚Motive' verknüpfte These, dass diese durch bewusste Selektion eines zwischen den Briefen angelegten Informationsflusses nur „schrittweise immer deutlicher heraus[ge]arbeitet"[95] würden, vernachlässigt zudem die (von Holzberg selbst herausgestellte) Tatsache, dass den Platon-Briefen histori-

---

Holzberg etwa dar, dass in Plato epist. 5/6 die Motive ‚Verhältnis Philosoph/Herrscher' und ‚Freunde wichtiger als Geld und Macht' vorherrschen, was seiner Meinung nach „eng verwandt" sei mit Plato epist. 9 („daß der Dienst am Vaterland für jeden Pflicht ist") und Plato epist. 11 („Platon gibt seinem an einer Koloniegründung beteiligten Schüler Laodamas politische Ratschläge"). Durch die Verquickung der Kriterien ‚fortlaufendes Geschehen' und ‚gemeinsames Motiv' verliert Holzbergs Instrumentarium m.E. die hermeneutische Schärfe. Ähnliches gilt für das im Anschluss zusätzlich eingeführte Kriterium eines alle Briefe verbindenden „Romanhelden" in Auseinandersetzung „mit einem Problem, das ihn geistig und seelisch *in allen Briefen* beschäftigt" (alle Zitate ebd., Hervorhebung von mir).

[91] In diesem Sinne leitet HOLZBERG, a.a.O. 9, eine Stelle aus Plato epist. 1 aus Plato epist. 7 ab, s. aber Anm. 92.

[92] Dies lässt sich für Plato epist. 1 mit Bezug auf Plato epist. 7 insgesamt plausibel vermuten; vgl. Brisson, Platon (s. Anm. 70), 76f. mit Anm. 79.

[93] So HOLZBERG, Gattungstypologie (s. Anm. 53), 10, wo als ‚wichtigste Themen' benannt werden: „der Verlauf seiner [sc. Platons] einstigen Bemühungen um eine philosophische und politische Unterweisung des Dionysios, die mit Dions Rachekampagne verbundene Entwicklung und Platons geistiger Anteil an der Aktion, schließlich die Überlegungen des Philosophen zur Erkenntnistheorie".

[94] Für die zahlreichen antiplatonischen Anekdoten vgl. A. SWIFT RIGINOS, The Anecdotes Concerning the Life and Writing of Plato, Leiden 1976.

[95] So HOLZBERG, Gattungstypologie (s. Anm. 53), 10.

sche Abläufe zugrunde liegen.[96] Gerade was die Sizilien-Reisen betrifft, ist nun aber die Überlieferung durch die Jahrhunderte besonders reich.[97] Für die Hauptlinien des Geschehens[98] kann somit anders als bei fiktionalen Texten ohne historischen Ausgangspunkt kaum ein völlig ahnungsloser ‚first reader' vorausgesetzt werden.[99]

Die Interpretation der Sammlung als narratives Kontinuum scheint mir somit auch unter den im beschriebenen Sinne gelockerten Kriterien für Kontinuität für die Platon-Briefe unhaltbar, ebenso eine methodisch eindeutig nachweisbare Verzahnung der einzelnen Texte durch gemeinsame Motive, so man beides bereits für einen antiken „Autor bzw. Redaktor"[100] zugrunde legt.[101] (Ein interessantes Leseexperiment für den modernen Rezipienten bleibt sie freilich allemal.)

---

[96] Vgl. a.a.O. 1ff. Dort könnte man noch schärfer zwischen ‚historischem Roman in Briefform' und ‚romanhafter Biographie in Briefform' scheiden. Wie Holzberg zu Recht betont, spielt in den Briefen oftmals das, was er „Innenleben der in den Briefen ‚ich' Sagenden" (2) nennt, eine große Rolle; dies hatte schon DORNSEIFF, Platons Buch (s. Anm. 46), 236, bemerkt. Übersetzt man diesen Aspekt in das, was wir ēthos-Bezogenheit genannt haben, rückt dies die Briefe – unabhängig von ihrer möglichen Herkunft aus einem Geschichtswerk – eindeutig in größere Nähe zur Biographie.

[97] Vgl. SWIFT RIGINOS, The Anecdotes (s. Anm. 94), 70–92.

[98] Manche der historischen Grundlinien des Geschehens fallen mit dem zusammen, was HOLZBERG, Gattungstypologie (s. Anm. 53), als „Themen" bezeichnet, s.o. Anm. 93.

[99] Dies scheint HOLZBERG, a.a.O. 8, anzunehmen. Anders HUFFMAN, Archytas of Tarentum (s. Anm. 19), 39, mit Bezug auf die Hauptlinien des Geschehens in Plato epist. 7: „even if the letter is primarily a literary rather than a historical document, its originality is in its interpretation of the events rather than in the invention of them."

[100] So HOLZBERG, a.a.O. 13 und wieder 47.

[101] Zwar geht auch HOLZBERG (a.a.O. 47f.) von einem bereits vor, d.h. unabhängig von jeder ‚fortlaufenden Erzählung' existierenden Kern der Sammlung aus, um den herum dann sekundär der ‚Briefroman' errichtet worden sei. Für das Entstehen der Sammlung selbst zieht er keine andere Intention in Betracht, erwägt aber umgekehrt, dass bei diesem Redaktionsakt Briefe eigens verfasst wurden, um eben das Ganze eines ‚Romans in Briefen' zu erzeugen.

3.2 Die Chion-Briefe[102]

Auch die Sammlung der Chion-Briefe trägt in ihrem Titel den Namen einer historischen Person, wiederum den eines Philosophen: Chion aus Herakleia am Pontos, ein Platonschüler, war 353/2 v. Chr. an der Ermordung des Klearchos, des Tyrannen seiner Heimatstadt, beteiligt, überlebte jedoch selbst den Anschlag nicht.[103] Die 17 Briefe der Sammlung richten sich vor allem an seinen Vater Matris (Chion ep. 1–8, 10–15). Hinzu kommen einzelne Briefe an seinen Freund Bion (Chion ep. 9), den später von ihm ermordeten Klearchos (Chion ep. 16) und seinen Lehrer Platon (Chion ep. 17). Die Sammlung gilt heute allgemein als Schöpfung eines einzigen, anonymen Autors, der gemäß sprachlicher und inhaltlicher Kriterien in der Regel in das 1. Jh. n. Chr. eingeordnet wird.[104] Wie die Plato epist. enthält auch diese Sammlung ausschließlich Briefe, die der namensgebende Absender verfasst haben soll. Der fiktive Abfassungszeitraum der Briefe deckt in etwa die letzten fünf Jahre vor Chions Tod im Jahre 352 v. Chr.

---

[102] Die Zitation der Briefe folgt durchgängig der Ausgabe von Düring, Chion of Heraclea (s. Anm. 29), nach Briefnummer, Seiten- und Zeilenzahl; er wird nicht ersetzt, ist jetzt aber zu ergänzen durch P.-L. Malosse (Hg.), Lettres de Chion d'Héraclée. Texte rév., trad. et comm., Cardo 1, Salerno 2004. Ein neuerer Kommentar der Chion ep. 3, 13, 14 und 16 findet sich auch bei Costa, Greek Fictional Letters (s. Anm. 31), 179–186, von Chion ep. 17 bei Trapp, Greek and Latin Letters (s. Anm. 7), 217–219. – Die wichtigsten neueren Beiträge zu den Chion ep. neben HOLZBERG, a.a.O. 28–32, sind A. BILLAULT, Les lettres de Chion d'Héraclée, REG 90 (1977), 29–37; B. ZUCCHELLI, A proposito dell'epistolario di Chione di Eraclea, Paideia 41 (1986), 13–24; D. KONSTAN / P. MITSIS, Chion of Heraclea. A Philosophical Novel in Letters, in: M. C. Nussbaum (Hg.), The Poetics of Therapy, Hellenistic Ethics in its Rhetorical and Literary Context, Apeiron 23.4, Edmonton u.a. 1990, 257–279; ROSENMEYER, Ancient Epistolary Fictions (s. Anm. 32), 237–252; STENGER, Tyrannenmord (s. Anm. 52). – Die Arbeiten von H. M. HOWE, The Authenticity of the Letters of Chio of Heraclea (Resümée in:), TAPhA 73 (1942), xxixf., und Q. CATAUDELLA, Sull'autenticità delle lettere di Chione di Eraclea, Memorie della Classe di Scienze morali e storiche della Accademia nazionale die Lincei 24 (1980), 649–751, sowie ders., Revisioni e riscoperte. Chione di Eraclea, Cultura e Scuola XX 79 (1981), 79–84, zielen darauf ab, die Authentizität der Chion ep. (im Sinne der Verfasserschaft durch den historischen Chion) zu erweisen und konnten sich in der Forschung nicht durchsetzen, da sprachliche Kriterien gegen eine so frühe Abfassungszeit der Texte sprechen, so bereits K. BURK, De Chionis epistulis, Diss. Gießen/Darmstadt 1912, und wieder Düring, a.a.O. 14–16.108–116; BILLAULT, a.a.O. 30–32, ebenso ZUCCHELLI, a.a.O.

[103] Zur Prosopographie sowie den historischen Vorgängen vgl. TRAMPEDACH, Platon (s. Anm. 70), 88–90, sowie die Einleitung in Malosse, a.a.O. Einen Kommentar zu den biographischen Testimonien bietet Düring, a.a.O. 9–13.

[104] So bereits BURK, De Chionis epistulis (s. Anm. 102), aufgrund sprachlicher Beobachtungen und wieder Düring, a.a.O. 14–16.108–116; BILLAULT, Les lettres (s. Anm. 102), 30–32; STENGER, Tyrannenmord (s. Anm. 52), 121.

ab:[105] Dabei entfallen auf den fünfjährigen Aufenthalt in Athen acht Briefe (Chion ep. 5–12), während die letzten fünf Briefe (Chion ep. 13–17) in den letzten Monaten vor Chions Tod geschrieben sein sollen.[106]

Auch die Briefe dieser Sammlung divergieren hinsichtlich ihres Umfanges beträchtlich: So umfasst der längste Brief 87 (Chion ep. 16), der kürzeste nur 7 Zeilen (Chion ep. 8).[107] Insgesamt aber sind die Schwankungen im Umfang weit geringer als bei den Platon-Briefen.[108] Ein quantitierendes Anordnungskriterium liegt auch in dieser Sammlung nicht vor; die geringe Anzahl von Adressaten, unter denen Matris stark überrepräsentiert ist (s.o.), machen außerdem die Frage nach einer Anordnung nach Maßgabe der Adressaten (alphabetisch nach Namen, nach geographischer Herkunft etc.) von vornherein hinfällig.

Dem die Sammlung schlicht von vorne nach hinten durchlesenden (Erst-)Rezipienten wird jedoch schnell klar, dass er damit wohl eben das tut, was der Verfasser nicht nur stillschweigend intendiert hat, sondern seinem Leser durch deutlich wahrnehmbare Rezeptionssignale anempfiehlt. So signalisiert der Beginn des Ersten Briefes (wie auch Chion ep. 2–4: An Matris) zwar lediglich, dass der Leser hier in einen bereits bestehenden Briefwechsel eines Ichs auf Reisen mit hineingenommen wird (Chion ep. 1: 44,2–4), und der Zweite Brief setzt durch seine Form als Empfehlungsschreiben gleichsam nochmals neu ein. Dann aber beginnt eine enge inhaltliche Verklammerung, indem die äußeren Umstände, unter denen Chion seine Briefe verfasst bzw. versendet, durchgängig in die Briefe eingeschrieben werden:[109] So erfährt der Leser gegen Ende von Chion ep. 2, dass Chion

„nun sehr gerne absegeln würde, aber immer noch auf einen günstigen Wind wartet (ἀνέμου δ' οὐκ ἐπιτυγχάνω)" (Chion ep. 2: 46,6f. = Briefende).

Gleich zu Beginn des Dritten Briefes liest man (Chion ep. 3: 46,9f.):

„Sehr dankbar bin ich den Winden (τοῖς ἐπισχοῦσιν ἡμᾶς ἀνέμοις), die uns aufgehalten haben, und einen weiteren Aufenthalt in Byzanz erzwungen ..."

---

[105] Vgl. STENGER, a.a.O. 121.130.

[106] Vgl. für die Analyse der zeitlichen Struktur STENGER, a.a.O. 124f.126.

[107] Hier wie im Folgenden beziehe ich mich auf die Ausgabe von Düring, Chion of Heraclea (s. Anm. 29).

[108] Nach Chion ep. 16 ist derjenige Brief der längste, der Chions Vorhaben, Philosophie zu studieren, darlegt (Chion ep. 3: 72 Z.), gefolgt von demjenigen, der den ‚Schlussblock' (Ereignisse außerhalb Athens) einleitet (Chion ep. 14: 52 Z.), und demjenigen, der die Anfangsgruppe (auf der Reise) abschließt (Chion ep. 4: 42 Z.). Ein paar der übrigen Briefe sind ungefähr 25 Zeilen lang (Chion ep. 7, 13, 15, 17), der überwiegende Teil der Briefe ist aber kürzer und zählt 10/5 Zeilen (Chion ep. 1, 2, 5, 6, 9, 10, 11, 12).

[109] Für eine Interpretation der Anfangsbriefe mit leicht anderer Akzentsetzung vgl. ROSENMEYER, Ancient Epistolary Fictions (s. Anm. 32), 237–239.

Ähnlich kündigt der Sprecher am Ende dieses längeren Briefs an (Chion ep. 3: 50,20f.):

„Wisse, dass ich jetzt bald absegeln kann (ἤδη πρὸς τῷ πλεῖν ὄντα); denn im Hinblick auf die Winde steht es jetzt weit besser (τὰ τῶν ἀνέμων αἰσιώτερα)."

Am Beginn des nächsten Briefes wird das Motiv ‚Ausfahrt des Schiffes' zunächst nur indirekt weitergeführt; an dessen Ende liest man dann aber wieder explizit (Chion ep. 4: 54,2f.):

„Zur Zeit sind wir in Chios und hatten die ganze Fahrt überaus günstige Winde (πάνυ ἐπιεικῶς τῶν ἀνέμων ἡμῖν ... χρησαμένων)",

um dann als erste Worte von Chion ep. 5 zu erfahren (Chion ep. 5: 54,8f.):

„Wir sind in Athen angekommen (Ἀφίγμεθα ἐς Ἀθήνας)."

M.E. eindeutig wird hier der Rezipient von Anfang an in eine Reisesituation mit hineingenommen, entlang deren Stationen die Briefe abgesandt werden, d.h. die Reihenfolge der Briefe wird eigens als gemäß der Chronologie der (fiktiven) Abfassungszeitpunkte ausgewiesen. Der Verfasser der Briefe hat damit in den ersten fünf Briefen einen linearen Rezeptionsmodus entlang eines narrativen Kontinuums etabliert und dieser Rezeptionsmodus bleibt für die gesamte Sammlung bis hin zum letzten Brief gültig.

Die Verklammerung innerhalb der restlichen Sammlung ist zwar nirgends mehr so deutlich und lückenlos wie zu deren Beginn.[110] Auch muss der Leser teilweise erhebliche chronologische Sprünge zwischen den einzelnen Briefen zur Kenntnis nehmen. Doch werden diese meist noch einmal eigens in den Briefen annonciert oder indirekt thematisiert.[111] Mit zunehmender Lektüre gewinnt zudem die Gesamtanlage an Kontur und verleiht so der Sammlung formale Kohärenz. Hier hat Holzberg[112] m.E. überzeugend dafür argumentiert, dass sich durch den in den Briefen je vorausgesetzten Ortswechsel eine dreiteilige, wohl symmetrische Struktur ergibt: So schildern die Chion ep. 1–4 Chions Reise nach Athen, die folgenden neun Briefe (Chion ep. 5–13) zeichnen, deutlich markiert durch den Adressatenwechsel in Chion ep. 5 (An Platon), seinen Athener Aufent-

---

[110] Vgl. aber beispielsweise den Übergang von Chion ep. 7 zu 8 (58,12f.), den Einleitungssatz von Chion ep. 12: 62,1, ebenso den von Chion ep. 14: 64,28f. etc.

[111] Hierzu STENGER, Tyrannenmord (s. Anm. 52), 130: „[Es] deuten Anspielungen darauf hin, daß die vorliegenden siebzehn Briefe keineswegs die gesamte Korrespondenz ausmachen, die Chion in gut fünf Jahren geführt hat. Zwar könnte man zu dieser Erkenntnis auch auf Grund der Relation von Anzahl und Dauer gelangen, doch macht der Text des öfteren selbst darauf aufmerksam" (mit Belegen ebd.).

[112] Vgl. HOLZBERG, Gattungstypologie (s. Anm. 53), 30; ihm folgt zuletzt STENGER, a.a.O. 125f. ROSENMEYER, Ancient Epistolary Fictions (s. Anm. 32), 245, interpretiert den Aufbau der Sammlung anders.

halt nach, während die letzten vier (Chion ep. 14–17) auf Ereignisse außerhalb von Athen Bezug nehmen. Zusätzlich sind teilweise innerhalb der Sammlung weit auseinander stehende Einzelbriefe motivisch verzahnt. So hat Holzberg[113] beispielsweise sicherlich richtig gesehen, dass die (im nicht-terminologischen Sinne:) ‚Kampf-Szenen' des Vierten (Chion steht in Perinthos gegen die Thraker) und 13. Briefes (Chion wehrt ein Attentat des Leibwächters des Klearchos ab) nicht nur bewusst je ans Ende eines der Haupthandlungsblöcke gesetzt sind, sondern dass sie auch eine sich stetig steigernde Linie anlegen, die schließlich in der Ankündigung des Attentats und des daraus resultierenden eigenen Sterbens in dem den letzten Hauptblock (und damit die gesamte Sammlung) beschließenden Brief seinen Höhepunkt findet. Umgekehrt verweist der Traum des 17. Briefes (Chion ep. 17: 78,11f.: eine hoch gewachsene wunderschöne Frau bekränzt Chion mit Siegerbinden und Ölzweigen), den Chion im Kontext seines Vorhabens, den Tyrannen zu morden, erzählt, als gleichsam ‚glückliches Ende', noch einmal zurück ganz an den Anfang der Sammlung, geht doch auf diese Weise der dort geäußerte Lebenswunsch Chions in Erfüllung.[114]

Und schließlich hat der Verfasser immer wieder Informationsknotenpunkte angelegt, an die er im weiteren Verlauf seiner Erzählung, d.h. in den Folgebriefen, zusätzliche Präzisierungen in oftmals ergänzender und fortführender, bisweilen auch vertiefender Funktion anknüpfen lassen kann (Holzbergs ‚Erzählstrategie des sukzessiven Enthüllens'[115]): So erfährt der Leser in Chion ep. 1, dass Chion sich auf Reisen in der Nähe von Byzanz befindet.[116] Ziel der Reise ist Athen, wo Chion, wie Chion ep. 3 deutlich macht, Philosophie studieren will.[117] Durch die Begegnung mit Xenophon, ebenfalls in Chion ep. 3, wird dieser Wunsch auch gleich personell konkretisiert (der Sokrates-Schüler)[118] und gleichzeitig das die gesamte restliche Sammlung durchziehende Grundthema ‚der tapfere Philosoph' angelegt.[119] Es wird, ab der Peripetie (Chion erfährt von Klearchos' Macht-

---

[113] Wiederum HOLZBERG, a.a.O. 30; mit leicht anderem Akzent STENGER, a.a.O. 125.

[114] Vgl. HOLZBERG, ebd.

[115] Vgl. a.a.O. 29f. STENGER, Tyrannenmord (s. Anm. 52), 127, stellt die in den Chion ep. angewandte „Antizipationstechnik" heraus.

[116] Vgl. Chion ep. 1: 45,2f.

[117] Vgl. v.a. Chion ep. 3,5: 48,25f.: „Wisse, dass ich jetzt unbedingt nach Athen fahren will, um dort Philosophie zu studieren (με νῦν προθυμότερον εἰς Ἀθήνας πλευσεῖσθαι φιλοσοφήσαντα)."

[118] Vgl. Chion ep. 3,3: 48,2–24: Chion ist gleichsam ganz bezaubert von Xenophons Erscheinung, die bis in physische Details hinein geschildert wird.

[119] Zutreffend weist STENGER, Tyrannenmord (s. Anm. 52), 128, darauf hin, dass die alte Frage der Wahl zwischen *vita contemplativa* und *activa* in den Chion ep. einer eher harmonisierenden Lösung zugeführt werden soll. Dass diese Lösung dann durch die nar-

ergreifung)[120] in immer schnellerem Tempo, Chion schließlich zum Tyrannenmörder machen. Dass Chion bei Platon Philosophie studieren wird, erfährt der Leser in Chion ep. 5. Vergleichbares lässt sich für Chions Charakter, sein *ēthos*, an dessen Vervollkommnung ihm nach eigener Auskunft so viel liegt, zeigen: Schon der Chion der ersten Briefe zeigt von seiner charakterlichen Anlage her die Grundkonstante, die schließlich über die Stationen Xenophon-Erlebnis, Philosophiestudium, Entschluss, der Heimat zu helfen, persönliche Bedrohung durch den Tyrannen zum willigen Aufsichnehmen des eigenen Todes am Ende der Sammlung führt. In einzelnen Punkten wohnt dem Chion der früheren Briefe gegenüber dem der letzten zwar bisweilen ein gewisses ‚Noch nicht' inne. Insgesamt aber erfährt sein *ēthos* eher eine Schärfung und Konturierung hin auf ein konkretes Ziel, als dass sich der Leser an irgendeiner Stelle der Brieffolge plötzlich mit einem ihm bislang völlig unbekannten, nirgendwo zuvor wenigstens potentiell angelegten Charakterzug konfrontiert sähe.[121]

Die Chion-Briefe bilden somit ein von der ersten Zeile an klar als solches ausgewiesenes narratives Kontinuum. Die klare Gesamtanlage der Sammlung, motivische Verknüpfungen und die Anlage von Informationsketten, deren Konkretheit mit Fortschreiten der Handlung zunimmt, verleihen der Sammlung zusätzlich Kohärenz.

---

rativen Strategien gleichsam konterkariert werde (vgl. a.a.O. 134f.: „Die Verbindung von *vita contemplativa* und *vita activa*, die im Briefroman als Ideal beschworen wird, gestaltet sich in der Praxis nicht so problemlos, wie Chion meint"), so dass auch eine „distanziert-reflektierende" Lesart der Sammlung möglich sei, ist mir hingegen nicht völlig überzeugend. Gerade wenn man mit KONSTAN / MITSIS, Chion of Heraclea (s. Anm. 102), den philosophischen Hintergrund der Briefe und zumal die wohl eindeutig Platon- bzw. Sokrates- und Sokratikerfreundliche Haltung des Verfassers mit einbezieht, scheint mir dies eher für eine (den modernen Interpreten vielleicht als ‚platt' befremdende) rein positiv-identifikatorische Rezeption zu sprechen. Die Gesamtdeutung der Chion ep. ist umstritten; für eine politische Deutung im Sinne einer Art ‚Pamphlets' gegen Domitian (der dann mit dem zu ermordenden Tyrannen zu identifizieren wäre) vgl. BILLAULT, Les lettres (s. Anm. 102).

[120] Den Begriff verwendet STENGER, a.a.O. 125, für den Umschwung der Handlung zwischen den Chion ep. 11 und 12 und macht dies vor allem daran fest, dass ab diesem Zeitpunkt Chions Gedanken vor allem auf Zukünftiges gerichtet seien, während er sich zuvor vor allem erinnere; zudem verlagere sich das in den Briefen Dargestellte zunehmend von äußeren Geschehnissen hin zum inneren Erleben des Sprechers (126).

[121] Ich halte es deshalb nicht für zutreffend, wenn STENGER, a.a.O. 128, den von ihm zu Recht unterstrichenen Aspekt des „Heranreifens" Chions dann als ‚Entwicklung' fasst; vgl. ebd. Anm. 47: „Man könnte im weiteren Sinne von einem Entwicklungsroman in Briefform sprechen." Das hierfür nötige neuzeitliche Menschenbild scheint mir zu weit (auch noch) von dem kaiserzeitlichen Kontext der Chion ep. entfernt.

Schon die hier nur skizzenhaft nachgezeichneten Charakteristika der Platon- und der Chion-Briefe haben wohl anschaulich gemacht, mit wie in jeder Hinsicht unterschiedlichen Briefsammlungen wir es hier zu tun haben. Diese Verschiedenartigkeit *per se* müsste noch kein Indiz dafür sein, dass sich die beiden Sammlungen nicht derselben literarischen Gattung ‚Briefroman' zuordnen lassen, zumal aller Wahrscheinlichkeit nach mehrere Jahrhunderte zwischen ihrer jeweiligen Entstehungszeit liegen. Unbestreitbar ist aber m.E., dass die Chion-Briefe den von Holzberg entworfenen (und von uns hier in leichter Modifikation übernommenen) Merkmalen einer Gattung ‚Briefroman' weit zwangloser entsprechen als dies bei den Platon-Briefen der Fall ist.

Will man hinsichtlich der Gattungsfrage eine Entscheidung treffen, dann muss man also spätestens an diesem Punkt entscheiden, wie klar man die Linien dessen, was man als Erwartungshorizont des Rezipienten eines antiken Briefromans voraussetzen kann, definieren möchte. In diesem Sinne versteht sich die abschließende Zusammenfassung.

4. Zusammenfassung und Ausblick: Vorläufige Annäherung an eine schwierige Gattung

Diejenigen Briefsammlungen der griechischsprachigen Literatur, an denen sich die Frage nach einer antiken Gattung ‚Briefroman' entzündet hat, tragen in der Regel den Namen eines meist prominenten Intellektuellen oder Politikers der klassischen bzw. nachklassisch-hellenistischen Zeit.[122] Das Hauptinteresse der Texte liegt auf dem Erleben dieser prominenten Person, sie ist der Absender und damit durchgängig der Sprecher oder Erzähler in den Texten. ‚Held' und Sprecher der Darstellung fallen somit in der Regel in eins. Nur im Ausnahmefall, wie etwa bei den Chion-Briefen (s.o. 3.2), handelt es sich um eine weniger bekannte Person, deren Erlebnisse dann aber meist stark auf die prominenten Zeitgenossen hin perspektiviert werden, beispielsweise durch Treffen mit diesen, maßgeblicher Prägung des Protagonisten durch diese etc.[123] Bei dieser Sprecherkonstellation hat nicht nur die Persönlichkeitszeichnung größere Spielräume. Der unbekanntere ‚Held' erlaubt zusätzlich den Blick des Zeitgenossen auf die in den anderen Briefen zu Sprechern gemachten Persönlichkeiten, so dass sich für den Rezipienten das identifikatorische Potential im Sinne einer stellvertretenden Autopsie des Helden ergibt.

---

[122] Vgl. oben die Einleitung sowie v.a. Anm. 34.
[123] So beispielsweise in den Chion-Briefen; vgl. oben Anm. 118.

Blicken wir von dieser Grundkonstellation noch einmal zurück an den Beginn unserer Überlegungen und Bentleys Verärgerung über die mangelnde Authentizität der Briefsammlungen im Sinne einer Übereinstimmung von überliefertem Absendernamen und Verfasserschaft durch die historische Person (s.o. 236f.). Angesichts der Tatsache, dass in den uns erhaltenen Sammlungen anders als bei den antiken ‚Romanen' durchweg historische Persönlichkeiten in den Fokus des Interesses rücken, lag forschungsgeschichtlich zunächst ein vor allem biographisch-historischer Blick auf die Briefe und damit die Diskussion um ihre ‚Echtheit', wiederum im Sinne der Verfasserfrage, nahe. Oder anders ausgedrückt: Der Blick der Forschung verengte sich fast ausschließlich auf die Frage ‚Pseudepigraphon oder nicht' (s.o. 240ff.). Die wenig differenzierte Rezeption Bentleys führte hier oftmals zu unzulässiger Verallgemeinerung einerseits (‚*alle* Briefsammlungen sind unecht') bzw. zu einer methodisch nicht fruchtbar zu machenden moralischen Inkriminierung der als Pseudepigrapha klassifizierten Sammlungen (‚der Fälscher hat *schnöde Absichten*') andererseits.

Der Ansatz, die Briefsammlungen als ‚Brief*romane*' zu lesen, lässt sich vor diesem Hintergrund vor allem auch als Versuch verstehen, die Interpretation der Briefsammlungen aus einer zweifachen Enge zu befreien: Zum einen evoziert der Begriff des ‚Romans', wie unklar seine Abgrenzung im Einzelnen in diachroner Sicht auch immer sein mag, den Gebrauch fiktiver Elemente bis hin zu völliger Fiktionalität und nimmt damit der Forderung nach historischer Genauig- und Korrektheit die Schärfe. An ihre Stelle tritt die Frage nach literarästhetischen Gestaltungsprinzipien. Zum anderen verbindet sich mit der Zuweisung ‚Roman' die Vorstellung einer größeren Erzähleinheit in Prosa. Die These einer gemäß nachvollziehbaren, vor allem auch ästhetischen Kriterien organisierten literarischen Einheit wird so vom Einzelbrief auf den gesamten Sammlungszusammenhang ausgeweitet. Bei diesem letzten Schritt ist es nun die entscheidende Frage, ein wie hohes Maß an schon im Text bzw. in der Anordnung der Einzeltexte angelegten narrativen Zusammenhanges, zumal narrativer Kontinuität, man erwartet oder umgekehrt: ein wie hohes Maß an erst im Kopf des Lesers zu erzeugender Kontinuität man toleriert, um die Zuweisung ‚Roman' an unsere Sammlungen noch als sinnvoll im Sinne hermeneutischer Trennschärfe des Gattungsbegriffes zu akzeptieren.

Mir scheint es angezeigt, in diesem Punkt die Grenzen des *antiken* Romans, nicht die seiner modernen oder postmodernen Nachfolger mit ihrer oft bis zu prismenhaft zersplitterten Montagen reichenden Erzähltechnik zugrunde zu legen.[124] Derartig radikale Zertrümmerungen und Neuarrangements des zu Erzählenden finden sich, soweit ich sehe, in der gesamten griechischen Literatur der Antike nur äußerst selten.[125] Die narrativen Mittel des antiken ‚Romans' bleiben dem gegenüber völlig im Rahmen dessen, was man in anachronistisch-moderner Sicht als ‚konventionell' bezeichnen würde: So kennt der antike ‚Roman' Vor- und Rückverweise, auch die Strategie enthüllender Erzählweise, in der Einzelinformationen nachgetragen, Irrtümer aufgelöst, überraschende Wendungen erzielt werden können etc. Das volle Spektrum narrativer Strategien bildet sich, soweit wir sehen, ohnehin erst im Laufe der Gattungsgeschichte aus[126] und erreicht somit seinen Höhepunkt nicht vor der Literatur der hohen Kaiserzeit. Überträgt man diesen Befund auf eine antike Gattung ‚Briefroman', so ergeben sich schon aus dieser literarhistorischen Perspektive gewisse Beschränkungen für diejenigen unserer Briefsammlungen, deren übrige Charakteristika sie (mindestens in Teilen) in eine wesentlich frühere Zeit verweisen (z.B. die Platon-Briefe): Wenn man diese Sammlungen nur unter das Genre ‚Briefroman' subsumieren kann, indem man narrative Strategien ansetzt, die in ihrer Komplexität und unannoncierten Forderung an die Rekonstruktionsleistung des Lesers diejenigen der spätesten Vertreter der Gattung ‚Roman' noch übertreffen würden, scheint dies zweifelhaft. In aller Regel gibt es nämlich etwa auch bei den raffiniert erzählten griechischen Romanen im Gefolge der sogenannten ‚Zweiten Sophistik', beispielsweise Achilleus Tatios' Leukippe und Kleitophon oder Longos' Daphnis und Chloe,[127] eine

---

[124] Ebenso verfährt Holzberg für eine Gattungsdefinition des antiken Romans an sich; vgl. HOLZBERG, Der antike Roman (s. Anm. 8), 38 (als Resümée einer Zusammenschau verschiedener romanhafter Prosaformen): „Würde man nun von dem neuzeitlichen Gattungsbegriff ‚Roman' ausgehen …, hätte man wohl keine Schwierigkeiten, alle diese Texte als Romane zu definieren. In der Antike dagegen dürfte es weder Leser noch Literaturtheoretiker gegeben haben, die auch nur auf den Gedanken gekommen wären, die [sc. zuvor verhandelten Formen] … als Spielart ein und desselben literarischen Genos zu betrachten. Man sollte daher, wenn man vom ‚antiken Roman' spricht, darunter nur die idealisierenden und die komisch-realistischen Romane verstehen."

[125] Denken ließe sich hier etwa an einen Text wie die *Hieroi logoi* des Aelius Aristides, in denen in ‚Traumbuchhaften' Sequenzen Stücke autobiographischen Erinnerns aneinander montiert werden; vgl. hierzu M. KORENJAK, ‚Unbelievable Confusion'. Weshalb sind die ‚Hieroi Logoi' des Aelius Aristides so wirr?, Hermes 133.2 (2005), 215–234.

[126] Vgl. HOLZBERG, Der antike Roman (s. Anm. 8), 21: „Kompliziertere narrative Techniken wie Ich-Erzählung, Retrospektive oder Verschachtelung, ja Verrätselung der Handlung, die sich von der Darstellungsweise der Historiographie entfernen, … werden vom antiken Roman erst im Laufe der Gattungsgeschichte entwickelt."

[127] Achilleus Tatios' Roman ist die einzige Ich-Erzählung unter den vollständig erhaltenen idealisierenden Romanen, sein zeitliches Verhältnis zu Longos' Daphnis und Chloe ist umstritten. Die Forschungsliteratur zu beiden Romanen ist Legion; für eine

deutlich vernehmbare Erzählerstimme, die den Leser durch die Narration geleitet. Lösen sich mehrere Erzählerstimmen für verschiedene Ebenen des Geschehens ab, wie dies etwa bei Heliodors Aithiopika der Fall ist, bleiben solche Sprecherwechsel stets nachvollziehbar und treffen den Rezipienten nicht unangekündigt.[128] Und selbst dort, wo, wie im Falle eines sich vom Menschen zum Tier und wieder zurück verwandelnden Ich-Erzählers, so im sog. Eselsroman, auf den ersten Blick kaum eine Kontinuität der Erzählerstimme gegeben scheint, bleibt diese dem Rezipienten trotzdem klar unterscheidbar als leitende Instanz und so in ihrer Sicht auf die Welt als einheitliche Entität wahrnehmbar.[129]

Überträgt man die damit umrissene narrative Konstellation sowie das Sprecherprofil auf den Briefroman, so bestätigt dies die oben von uns angewendeten ‚Merkmale 2' und ‚1': Formale Grundbedingung für das Vorliegen eines antiken Briefromans ist dann, dass sich ein narratives Kontinuum nicht nur im Kopf des nachrechnenden Lesers ergibt, sondern die Briefe der Sammlung derart angeordnet und begrifflich und/oder motivisch miteinander verzahnt sind, dass eine lineare Lektüre bereits vom antiken Verfasser[130] durch Rezeptionssignale als intendierter Lesemodus annon-

---

erste Einführung sowie weiterführende Literatur vgl. wiederum HOLZBERG, a.a.O. 116–123.123–130. Für einen Überblick über Tendenzen der Narratologieforschung zum antiken Roman vgl. J. MORGAN, ‚Part Nine. The Novel', in: I. J. F. de Jong / R. Nünlist / A. Bowie (Hg.), Narrators, Narratees, and Narratives in Ancient Greek Literature, Studies in Ancient Greek Literature, Bd. 1, Mnemosyne Suppl. 257, Leiden 2004, 479–543 (493–506 zu Achilleus Tatios.507–522 Longos).

[128] Bei den Aithiopika handelt es sich um den am komplexesten erzählten idealisierenden griechischen Roman: Zwei verschiedene Erzähler erzählen unterschiedliche Handlungsstränge, in die ihrerseits wiederum Berichte anderer eingelegt sind; vgl. hierzu MORGAN, a.a.O. 523–543. Vor allem der „hochentwickelten Erzählkunst" (HOLZBERG, Der antike Roman [s. Anm. 8], 130) des Heliodor dankt ders., Gattungstypologie (s. Anm. 53), einen großen Teil der von ihm auch für seinen Begriff des Briefromans zugrunde gelegten narrativen Strategien.

[129] Die wohl recht umfangreiche Urfassung des griechischen Eselsromans ist uns nur noch indirekt durch den Vergleich einer im Werk des Lukian erhaltenen Kurzform mit Apuleius' Metamorphosen fassbar; es scheint aber so gut wie sicher, dass die Lukios-Handlung (d.h. die eigentliche Eselsgeschichte) bis unmittelbar vor der Rückverwandlung in einen Menschen denjenigen unserer Fassungen entsprach. Eine forschungsgeschichtlich besonders wirksame narratologische Untersuchung stellt J. J. WINKLER, Auctor and Actor. A Narratological Reading of Apuleius' ‚The Golden Ass', Berkeley 1985, dar.

[130] Akzeptiert man dieses zugegebenermaßen verhältnismäßig eng gefasste Kriterium, ist in letzter Konsequenz ein Briefroman ohne eine einheitsstiftende *Verfasser*instanz nicht denkbar: Zwar ist es weiterhin vorstellbar, dass ein späterer *Redaktor* eine ihm vorliegende Sammlung von Briefen nach dem Vorbild von ihm bereits bekannten Briefromanen umgestaltet, d.h. die Reihenfolge der nicht von ihm verfassten Briefe ändert. Geht dieser Redaktor aber nicht so weit, entweder selbst Briefe hinzuzudichten, wie dies

ciert wird. Hinzu tritt eine erste inhaltliche Erwartung, nämlich die eines zwar gegebenenfalls gewissen Schwankungen unterworfenen, insgesamt aber konsistent angelegten *ēthos* des Sprechers und Helden,[131] der, im Unterschied zu den nicht in Briefform abgefassten Romanen, stets ausgehend von einer historischen Persönlichkeit gestaltet wird. Hieran anschließen lässt sich eine zweite inhaltliche Erwartung, die teilweise mit unserem obigen ‚Merkmal 4' (Vorkommen bestimmter Motive) konvergiert bzw. dies leicht modifiziert: In den uns vorliegenden Briefsammlungen handelt es bei dieser historischen Persönlichkeit meist um Intellektuelle. Oftmals sieht man sie im Konflikt mit ihrem Umfeld oder den Mächtigen ihrer Zeit und somit in sozialem, meist politischem Kontext im weitesten Sinn. Das Vorherrschen bestimmter Motive ergibt sich m.E. aus dieser inhaltlichen Grundanlage. Was narrative Techniken angeht, hat Holzberg mit dem, was er „Erzählweise der sukzessiven Aufklärung" nennt (*Merkmal 3*),[132] sicherlich Wichtiges gesehen. Eine genauere Bestimmung weiterer narrativer Strategien, die gerade für den Briefroman der Antike typisch sind, bedürfte einer umfassenderen Untersuchung als sie hier geleistet werden konnte.

Nicht viele der oben (Anm. 34) angeführten, heute meist als ganz oder überwiegend pseudepigraph akzeptierten Briefsammlungen werden, das sei hier zuletzt im Sinne eines Ausblicks für künftige Untersuchungen bemerkt, sich in einen derart abgesteckten Gattungsrahmen einpassen lassen.[133] Manche von ihnen ‚werden' somit – forschungsgeschichtlich betrachtet – von Briefromanen wieder zu schlichten Briefsammlungen. Bedauerlich ist dies nicht, lassen sich doch diese Sammlungen, gerade auch dort, wo sie, wie etwa die Sokratiker-Briefe, multiperspektivisch angelegt sind, dann ihrerseits aus ihrer Nähe zu anderen Genres verstehen, wie etwa – im Blick auf ihre Form – zu Briefsteller-Büchern oder – im Blick auf ihren Inhalt – zu Anekdotensammlungen oder Teilen der Hypomnemata-Literatur als Sonderformen biographisch-doxographischen Schreibens. Doch dies bleibt weiterer Forschung vorbehalten.

---

vermutlich bei den Brutus-Briefen der Fall ist, oder in den Text der vorliegenden Briefe einzugreifen, ergibt sich daraus nach den von uns festgelegten Merkmalen kein Briefroman, da die eine lineare Lektüre festlegenden Rezeptionssignale fehlen (müssen).

[131] ROSENMEYER, Ancient Epistolary Fictions (s. Anm. 32), 233, bezeichnet die Kriterien „consistency in characterization" und „logical chronology" (ebd.) als „Richardsonian". Mit Blick auf den (nicht in Briefform abgefassten) antiken Roman scheint es mir nicht zutreffend, just diese beiden Merkmale auf einen neuzeitlichen Vertreter des Genres zu beziehen, auch wenn es bemerkenswert bleibt, dass offenbar antike und neuzeitliche Texte, die sich dem Genre zuordnen lassen, in diesen Punkten übereinstimmen.

[132] HOLZBERG, Gattungstypologie (s. Anm. 53), s. auch o. 249.

[133] Ob ROSENMEYER, Ancient Epistolary Fictions (s. Anm. 32), 233, Recht hat, deshalb ausschließlich die Chion ep. als „epistolary novel" zu akzeptieren, bleibt ebenfalls weiterer Untersuchung vorbehalten.

Erzählung im Fragment

Ein narratologischer Ansatz zur Auslegung pseudepigrapher Briefbücher

von

TIMO GLASER

Die berühmte Definition des Briefes als „die eine Hälfte eines Dialogs"[1] sowie seine inhaltliche Qualifizierung als „Spiegel der Seele"[2] verführen immer wieder dazu, Briefe für eine historo- bzw. biographische Rekonstruktion der genannten Personen bzw. der erwähnten historischen Begebenheiten auszuwerten.[3] Entsprechend ist in der Forschung die vornehmliche Fragestellung die nach der Echtheit des betreffenden Briefes und seine

---

[1] εἶναι γὰρ τὴν ἐπιστολὴν οἷον τὸ ἕτερον μέρος τοῦ διαλόγου, so Demetrius, De elocutione 223, der hier die Meinung des Herausgebers der Aristoteles-Briefe, Artemon, wiedergibt.

[2] *Locus classicus* Demetrius, De elocutione 227: „The letter should be strong on characterization, like the dialogue; everyone in writing a letter more or less composes an image of his own soul. One can indeed see the writer's character in any other kind of writing, too, but in none so clearly as in the letter" (Übers. M. TRAPP, Greek and Latin Letters. An Anthology with Translation, Cambridge Greek and Latin Classics, Cambridge u.a. 2003, 181). Zum Topos vgl. W. G. MÜLLER, Der Brief als Spiegel der Seele. Zur Geschichte eines Topos der Epistolartheorie von der Antike bis zu Samuel Richardson, AuA 26 (1980), 138–157.

[3] Wie problematisch es sein kann, wenn die Briefe die einzige Quelle zum Leben des Verfassers sind, zeigt z.B. M. HOSE, Synesios und seine Briefe. Versuch der Analyse eines literarischen Entwurfs, Würzburger Jahrbücher für die Altertumswissenschaft N.F. 27 (2003), 125–141 (128); auch die Ignatius-Briefe stellen mehr Fragen, als dass sie Antworten auf die Biographie des vermeintlichen Bischofs von Antiochien geben könnten; vgl. R. HÜBNER, Thesen zur Echtheit und Datierung der sieben Briefe des Ignatius von Antiochien, ZAC 1 (1997), 44–72; ebenfalls sperrig für eine historo- resp. biographische Auswertung seines Exils erweisen sich die Briefe des Johannes Chrysostomos, die zwar stets zur Rekonstruktion herangezogen werden, bisher allerdings keine eingehende Untersuchung erfahren haben; vgl. W. MAYER, John Chrysostom. Deconstructing the Construction of an Exile, in: T. K. Kuhn / E. W. Stegemann (Hg.), „Was von Anfang an war". Neutestamentliche und kirchengeschichtliche Aufsätze (FS Brändle), Basel 2006 (= ThZ 62.2 [2006]), 248–258 (249f.).

rhetorische Analyse gewesen, die Rückschluss auf den Gebrauchswert des Briefes innerhalb seines Kommunikationsgeschehens zulasse.[4] Im Rahmen solch rhetorischer Analysen ist auch die literarische Qualität der Briefe sowie der in ihnen durchgeführten *narratio*[5] Gegenstand der Untersuchung gewesen.

1. Pseudepigraphe Briefsammlungen und der antike Briefroman

Zu wenig Berücksichtigung findet dabei jedoch die Bedeutung der Überlieferung des Einzelbriefes in Sammlungen, obgleich der Korpuscharakter Auswirkungen auf die Interpretation des Briefes zeitigt. Durch die Einbettung eines Briefes in eine Sammlung von Briefen verschiebt sich das Aussagepotential des Briefes, was nicht zuletzt daher rührt, dass die zusammengestellten Briefe sich gegenseitig ergänzen und kommentieren sowie das Briefbuch eine vom expliziten Autor nicht-intendierte neue, größere Leserschaft gewinnt.[6]

---

[4] Hier steht die epistolographische Forschung unter dem bleibenden Einfluss Richard Bentleys (A Dissertation upon the Epistles of Phalaris, Themistocles, Socrates, Euripides, and Others. And the Fables of Aesop, London 1697), dessen erklärtes Ziel es war: „It will be no unpleasant labour to me, nor, I hope, unprofitable to others, to pull off the disguise from those little Pedants, that have stalked about so long in the apparel of Hero's" (79).

[5] Die Nähe der *narratio* zur fiktionalen Erzählung hebt auch schon Quintilian, Institutio oratoria 4,2,31 hervor: „*narratio est rei factae aut ut factae utilis ad persuadendum expositio* / Die Erzählung ist ja eine zum Überreden nützliche Darlegung eines tatsächlichen oder scheinbar tatsächlichen Vorgangs" (Marcus Fabius Quintilianus. Ausbildung des Redners, 2 Bde., übers. v. H. Rahn, TzF 2/3, Darmstadt ²1988).

[6] Das gilt selbst dann, wenn die Briefe von ihrem Autor gesammelt und publiziert werden, ist doch dann für die Interpretation der Herausgeber vom Verfasser des Briefes zu unterscheiden. Für pseudepigraphe Briefe als Teil von Sammlungen echter Briefe hat Annette Merz eine solche (rezeptionsästhetische) Fragestellung in die Pseudepigraphieforschung eingebracht; vgl. A. MERZ, Die fiktive Selbstauslegung des Paulus. Intertextuelle Studien zur Intention und Rezeption der Pastoralbriefe, NTOA 52, Göttingen/Freiburg (CH) 2004; dies., Amore Pauli. Das Corpus Pastorale und das Ringen um die Interpretationshoheit bezüglich des paulinischen Erbes, ThQ 187 (2007), 274–294. Eine weitere Form von Briefsammlung ist die Zusammenfügung von Einzelbrief(fragment)en zu einem neuen, scheinbar integren Brief. Wie die so konstruierte Briefsammlung den Leseakt beeinflusst, ist anhand der Philipper- und Korintherkorrespondenz durch Günther Bornkamm herausgearbeitet worden; vgl. G. BORNKAMM, Die Vorgeschichte des sogenannten zweiten Korintherbriefes, in: ders., Geschichte und Glauben 2, Gesammelte Aufsätze 4, BEvTh 53, München 1971, 162–194; ders., Der Philipperbrief als paulinische Briefsammlung, in: ders., a.a.O. 195–205.

Dieser Aspekt ist zunächst von gleicher Bedeutung für orthonyme wie pseudonyme Briefe. Hinsichtlich Letzterer bleibt an einer primär unter rhetorischem Vorzeichen stehenden Untersuchung problematisch, dass zumeist vorausgesetzt wird, dass die Briefe ihre Autorität durch die gelungene Täuschung gewinnen, dass kaum gefragt wird, wie die Briefe *unabhängig* von der Frage ihrer Authentizität wirken, und dass schließlich trotz des pseudonymen Charakters für die Briefe ein direkter Kommunikationsakt postuliert wird.[7]

Eine narratologische Lektüre epistolographischer Texte – sowohl von Einzelbriefen als auch von Briefsammlungen – stellt die Frage nach dem Kommunikationsakt vorerst zurück (ebenso wie die Frage nach der Authentizität von in einem Brief/in einer Briefsammlung möglicherweise enthaltenen authentischen Textteilen) und geht den Implikationen dessen nach, dass Briefe zunächst autodiegetische Erzählungen sind – bzw. im Fall von Pseudepigraphen: vorgetäuschte Autodiegesen.[8] Damit wird Briefliteratur in die Nähe romanhafter Literatur gebracht und zuweilen sogar als ‚Briefroman' bezeichnet.[9] Erst mit der gattungskritischen Untersuchung von Niklas Holzberg erfuhr der Briefroman jedoch den Status einer eigenständigen, abgrenzbaren Gattung, nachdem zuvor nur angele-

---

[7] Vgl. auch A. STANDHARTINGER, Studien zur Entstehungsgeschichte und Intention des Kolosserbriefs, NT.S 44, Leiden u.a. 1999, v.a. 57: „Wichtig ist jedoch die Feststellung, daß die Abfassung eines pseudepigraphen Schreibens für eine konkret existierende Gemeinde im Rahmen antiker Pseudepigraphie sehr ungewöhnlich wäre."

[8] In diese Richtung weist schon der Ansatz von N. R. PETERSEN, Rediscovering Paul. Philemon and the Sociology of Paul's Narrative World, Philadelphia 1985, und dann v.a. der von W. G. DOTY, Imaginings at the End of an Era. Letters as Fictions, Semeia 69/70 (1995), 83–110, der die Paulusbriefe von modernen Briefromanen her liest: „Revising some goals of the critical imagination, primitive Christian letters are explored as constructs, ‚fictions,' ... Insights from literary criticism of the epistolary novel tradition raise questions about the literary dynamics of early-Christian letters as well as about biblical criticism" (83).

[9] Diese Benennung erfahren dabei nicht nur Briefsammlungen, sondern auch Einzelbriefe: So bezeichnete M. HENGEL, Anonymität, Pseudepigraphie und „Literarische Fälschung" in der jüdisch-hellenistischen Literatur, in: ders., Judaica et Hellenistica. Kleine Schriften I. Unter Mitarbeit von R. Deines, J. Frey, C. Markschies, A. M. Schwemer mit einem Anhang von H. Bloedhorn, WUNT 90, Tübingen 1996, 196–251 (245), den Aristeasbrief einmal als einen Briefroman wegen der in ihm mitgeteilten romanhaften Erzählung über die Entstehung der Septuaginta. Zu einem kurzen Überblick über die Forschungsgeschichte zum antiken Briefroman vgl. N. HOLZBERG, Vorwort, in: ders. (Hg.), Der griechische Briefroman. Gattungstypologie und Textanalyse, Classica Monacensia 8, Tübingen 1994, IX–XV (IX–XIII); T. GLASER, Paulus als Briefroman erzählt. Studien zum antiken Briefroman und seiner christlichen Rezeption in den Pastoralbriefen, NTOA 76, Göttingen u.a. 2009.

gentlich der Edition[10] von einzelnen pseudepigraphen Briefsammlungen oder in Aufsätzen zu solchen die Gattungsfrage gestreift worden war.[11]

Wenn nun die Gattung des Briefromans für die Erforschung antiker Briefliteratur fruchtbar gemacht werden soll, stellt sich die Frage, inwiefern sich eine Sammlung von (pseudepigraphen) Briefen von einem Briefroman unterscheidet, was das spezifisch ‚romanhafte' Element in solch einer Sammlung von Briefen sein muss.

Verdienstvoll hat sich Niklas Holzberg um eine Herausarbeitung von Gattungskriterien des antiken griechischen Briefromans bemüht, die hilfreich sind, Besonderheiten von Briefsammlungen und von der Art, wie sie ihre Erzählung aufbauen, zu erkennen; sein dahinter stehendes Gattungskonzept jedoch – eine Differenzierbarkeit von ‚novels proper' und ‚fringe novels' – ist meines Erachtens problematisch,[12] zumal er die Gattungskriterien aus zuvor aufgrund bestimmter Gemeinsamkeiten ausgewählten Briefbüchern[13] deduziert hat, so dass der Verdacht naheliegt, dass das ausgewählte Material – die idealen „historischen Romane in Briefform"[14] – zu begrenzt ist, um umfassend die Poetik des Briefromans zu erfassen, der sich auch in der Neuzeit als ein „proteusartiges Genus"[15] zeigt, das nur schwer zu greifen ist – u.a. aufgrund der Kombination zweier in sich nur schwer zu fassender Gattungen: des Briefes[16] und des Ro-

---

[10] Hier sind bes. I. Düring (Hg.), Chion of Heraclea. A Novel in Letters. Edited with Introduction and Commentary, AUG 57.5, Göteborg 1951, und N. A. DOENGES, The Letters of Themistokles, Monographs in Classical Studies, New York 1981, zu nennen. Zu weiterer Literatur vgl. A. BESCHORNER, Griechische Briefbücher berühmter Männer. Eine Bibliographie, in: Holzberg, a.a.O. 169–190.

[11] H. KUCH, Rez. Holzberg, AAW 49 (1996), 77–81 (78): „Daß die Briefromane aus neuerer Zeit antike Vorläufer haben, ist zwar keine ganz neue, aber doch eine wichtige Erkenntnis." Skeptisch bleibt hier O. HODKINSON, Rez. Malosse, Lettres de Chion d'Héraclée, Bryn Mawr Classical Review 2005.02.42 (http://ccat.sas.upenn.edu/bmcr/2005/2005-02-42.html): „Of course it would be anachronistic to say that the author set out to write an epistolary novel, since he did not have a fully formed genre in which to write (although there were what may be termed early, less developed examples of the genre)".

[12] Vgl. N. HOLZBERG, The Genre. Novels Proper and the Fringe, in: G. Schmeling (Hg.), The Novel in the Ancient World, Mn.S 159, Leiden u.a. 1996, 11–28. Zu meinem dagegen entwickelten Gattungskonzept, das sich an Wittgensteins Sprachtheorie der Familienähnlichkeiten anschließt vgl. GLASER, Paulus (s. Anm. 9).

[13] Die Briefe Platons, des Euripides, des Aischines, des Hippokrates, Chions, des Themistokles, des Sokrates und der Sokratiker.

[14] N. HOLZBERG, Der griechische Briefroman. Versuch einer Gattungstypologie, in: ders., Briefroman (s. Anm. 9), 1–52 (2–4).

[15] So K. KLOOCKE, Formtraditionen – Roman und Geschichte. Dargestellt am Beispiel des Briefromans, in: H.-W. Ludwig (Hg.), Arbeitsbuch Romananalyse, Literaturwissenschaft im Grundstudium 12, Tübingen ⁶1998, 189–207 (205).

[16] Zur Offenheit des Briefes als Gattung vgl. TRAPP, Letters (s. Anm. 2), v.a. 1–5.

mans[17] – und sich sowohl in seiner Form als auch in seinem Inhalt und seinen Aussageabsichten entsprechend den kulturellen, gesellschaftlichen, ästhetischen und individuellen Umständen und Erfordernissen modifizieren lässt.[18]

Aufgrund dessen lässt sich bezüglich des (antiken) Briefromans nur eine sehr basale Definition der Gattung vornehmen: Ein Briefroman ist ein Text, in dem die Geschichte primär[19] durch Briefe aufgebaut wird.

2. Handlungsaufbau in Brieferzählungen

Zunächst ist Briefliteratur ein Stück Autodiegese, eine Art von Ich-Erzählung. Und entgegen dem Vorurteil, dass der Brief „Spiegel der Seele" sei, hat die Forschung mittlerweile immer stärker erkannt, dass auch in einem echten Brief der Briefschreiber ein Bild seiner selbst konstruiert und damit eher eine Art von Maske zeichnet, als dass er seinem Adressaten ein Spiegelbild präsentiert.[20]

---

[17] Zum antiken Roman vgl. H. KUCH, Die Herausbildung des antiken Romans als Literaturgattung. Theoretische Positionen, historische Voraussetzungen und literarische Prozesse, in: ders. u.a. (Hg.), Der antike Roman. Untersuchungen zur literarischen Kommunikation und Gattungsgeschichte, Veröffentlichungen des Zentralinstituts für Alte Geschichte und Archäologie der Akademie der Wissenschaften der DDR 19, Berlin 1989, 11–51 (18–28).

[18] Ebenso problematisch ist es, Gattungskriterien neuzeitlicher Briefromane auf antike Briefbücher zu applizieren, da auch deren Poetik von einem relativ begrenzten Korpus idealisierter Liebesbriefromane ausgeht; vgl. C. ARNDT, Antiker und neuzeitlicher Briefroman. Ein gattungstypologischer Vergleich, in: Holzberg, Briefroman (s. Anm. 9), 53–83 (56 Anm. 11).

[19] Mit ‚primär' ist die Frage angesprochen, inwiefern Briefe durch (Rahmen)erzählungen ergänzt werden können. J. SYKUTRIS, Art. Epistolographie, PRE.S 5 (1931), 185–220 (213f.), meinte hier ein Differenzmerkmal zwischen antiken und modernen Briefromanen ausmachen zu können. Aufgrund der Überlieferungslage lässt sich hier kaum eine eindeutige Antwort ausmachen, die fließenden Übergänge zwischen nichtbrieflichem Roman und Briefroman, wie sie etwa durch Sophie von LaRoches Fräulein von Sternheim vorgeführt werden, lassen an einer solch grundlegenden Aussage m.E. jedoch Zweifel aufkommen. Von der Handlungsstruktur unterscheidet sich etwa Goethes Werther nicht von der Abgarerzählung: Nach dem Aufbau einer Erzählung durch Briefe wird nach dem Tod des Protagonisten die Erzählung nichtbrieflich weitergeführt und zum Ende gebracht.

[20] Vgl. z.B. P. A. ROSENMEYER, Ancient Epistolary Fictions. The Letter in Greek Literature, Cambridge 2001, 5: „Whenever one writes a letter, one automatically constructs a self, an occasion, a version of the truth. Based on a process of selection and selfcensorship, the letter is a construction, not a reflection, of reality"; vgl. a.a.O. 10f.; TRAPP, Letters (s. Anm. 2), 3f. Dass die Grenzen zwischen echtem Brief und fiktionalem Brief mitunter kaum mehr auszumachen sind, darauf hat G. MANN, Der Brief in der Weltliteratur, Neue Rundschau 86 (1975), 631–649 (648), hingewiesen: „Briefe des 19. Jahrhunderts,

In dieser Hinsicht unterscheidet sich ein pseudonymer Brief nicht von einem authentischen, wohl aber in seinem Wirklichkeitsbezug. Während der echte Brief direkt auf die Kommunikationssituation zwischen Sender und Empfänger einwirken will, vermag der fingierte Brief dies nicht. Der Verfasser mag sich zwar durch die Wahl eines Pseudonyms dessen Autorität aneignen und auf den Empfänger einwirken, er vermag jedoch nicht, die reziproke Beziehung zwischen dem genannten Verfasser und dem Empfänger zu beeinflussen. Insofern spiegelt der Brief mit fingierter Verfasserangabe ein Kommunikationsgeschehen vor, das er nicht konstruieren kann. Ähnlich verhält es sich mit solch fingierten Briefen, die als ‚doppeltpseudonym' bezeichnet werden,[21] wenn sowohl der genannte Verfasser wie der genannte Empfänger nicht mit den realen identisch sind.[22]

Mit diesen beiden Aspekten zeigt sich der grundlegende fiktionale Charakter von Briefliteratur, sowohl der orthonymen[23] als vor allem aber auch der pseudonymen; entsprechend hat Patricia Rosenmeyer darauf hingewiesen, dass „epistolary technique always problematizes the boundary between reality and fiction".[24] Wie Käte Hamburger herausgearbeitet hat, ist es jedoch ein wesentliches Kennzeichen jeder Form von Ich-Erzählung, „daß sie sich selbst als Nicht-Fiktion, nämlich als historisches Dokument setzt. Dies tut sie aber auf Grund ihrer Eigenschaft als Ich-Erzählung."[25]

Für fiktionale Briefliteratur heißt dies zunächst, dass sie als Ich-Erzählung den Anschein von echter Brieflichkeit zu erwecken sucht, u.a. durch den gesamten in der Erforschung der Pseudepigraphie herausgearbeiteten ‚Beglaubigungsapparat', wie etwa Unterschriftenimitation, Nachahmung

---

die aus einem Roman eben dieser Zeit sein könnten, reale Briefwechsel, die einen eigentlichen Briefroman bilden."

[21] Vgl. W. STENGER, Timotheus und Titus als literarische Gestalten. Beobachtungen zur Form und Funktion der Pastoralbriefe, Kairos 16 (1974), 252–267 (253).

[22] Ebenso DOTY, Imaginings (s. Anm. 8), 92.104–106.

[23] Dieser Charakter verstärkt sich noch einmal, wenn ursprünglich echte Briefe gesammelt und ediert werden; vgl. etwa MANN, Brief (s. Anm. 20), 633, über die Briefe Carl Jakob Burckhardts („man merkt die Absicht und wird verstimmt"). Für die Antike lässt sich etwa durch eine Auswertung der Diskrepanzen zwischen den ersten neun Briefbüchern des Plinius, die er selbst herausgegeben hat, und dem zehnten Buch seiner Briefe, das erst postum herausgegeben wurde, der Wille zur Selbstdarstellung durch vermeintlich ‚echte' Briefe herausarbeiten; vgl. etwa M. LUDOLPH, Epistolographie und Selbstdarstellung. Untersuchungen zu den ‚Paradebriefen' Plinius des Jüngeren, Classica Monacensia 17, Tübingen 1997. Einen Überblick über antike edierte Briefkorpora bietet TRAPP, Letters (s. Anm. 2), 12–33.

[24] P. A. ROSENMEYER, The Epistolary Novel, in: J. R. Morgan / R. Stoneman (Hg.), Greek Fiction. The Greek Novel in Context, London u.a. 1994, 146–165 (147); vgl. auch DOTY, Imaginings (s. Anm. 8), 85 Anm. 3.

[25] K. HAMBURGER, Die Logik der Dichtung, München ³1987, 273; vgl. überhaupt 272–297.

von Sprache und Stil, Einfließenlassen von Personalia oder – sofern Herausgeberkommentare vorhanden sind – der Beteuerung, dass das vorliegende Werk aus aufgefundenen, echten Briefen bestehe.[26]

Eine damit gegebene Notwendigkeit ist die Differenzierung zwischen externem und internem Leser mit einem jeweils unterschiedlichen Vorwissen, die der Autor vornehmen muss. Da der Brief normalerweise die Fortführung eines bestehenden „Gespräches", also Ausschnitt aus einem Kommunikationsakt miteinander Bekannter ist,[27] verfügen beide Kommunikationspartner über ein gemeinsames Wissen, auf das in der Briefkommunikation zurückgegriffen werden kann, das jedoch nicht explizit vergegenwärtigt werden muss. Der externe, reale Leser dagegen verfügt nicht über dieses Wissen, so dass die Herausforderung für den Verfasser eines fiktionalen Briefverkehrs darin besteht, dieses Wissen zu vermitteln, ohne dass die Fiktion eines realen Briefverkehrs gesprengt würde.

Der Autor hat hierbei die Möglichkeiten, zwischen Überdetermination und Unterdetermination von Textaussagen jeweils im Hinblick auf den externen oder den internen Leser abzuwägen, so dass sich folgende vier Optionen ergeben:

---

[26] Solche modernen Herausgeberkommentare etwa in Goethes Werther: „Was ich von der Geschichte des armen Werthers nur habe auffinden können, habe ich mit Fleiß gesammelt." In Choderlos des Laclos' Liaisons dangereuses dienen die Vorworte der Stiftung von Verwirrung über den Echtheitsgrad: Während der ‚Sammler der Briefe' beteuert (*Préface du rédacteur*), dass er hier echte Briefe versammelt habe, merkt der Herausgeber an (*Avertissement de l'éditeur*), dass es sich dennoch wohl eher um einen Briefroman handeln dürfte (*nota bene*: Beide einleitenden Texte sind von Choderlos de Laclos geschrieben, d.h. sowohl *rédacteur* als auch *éditeur* sind fiktionale Figuren des Romans, die vor Romanbeginn auftreten). Aber auch in der Antike lassen sich solche ‚Herausgeberkommentare' finden, z.B. in dem Exilbriefbuch Ovids, wenn er schreibt: „Nicht, daß entstünde ein Buch, nein, daß sein Brief einem jeden zukommt, das war mein Zweck, darum bemühte ich mich. Dann hab' ich ordnungslos die gesammelten irgend verbunden: nicht von mir sind des Werks Dichtungen etwa gewählt" Ov.ep. 3,9,51 (Publius Ovidius Naso. Briefe aus der Verbannung. Tristia – Epistulae ex Ponto, lateinisch-deutsch. Übers. v. W. Willige, München u.a. 1990); so auch Plinius ep. 1,1. Ähnlich ist m.E. auch die Anmerkung Eusebs zu bewerten, der behauptet, den Jesus-Abgar-Briefwechsel im edessischen Archiv gefunden zu haben (h.e. 1,13,5). Gegen eigene Forschungsarbeiten Eusebs in Edessa spricht, dass in seiner sonstigen Kirchengeschichte keine weiteren Notizen über die edessische Kirche zu finden sind. Damit ist noch nicht gesagt, dass dieser ‚Briefroman' auch von Euseb selbst verfasst ist, bleibt aber möglich (evtl. unter Rückgriff auf Quellen; vgl. Die Abgarlegende/Das Christusbild von Edessa, griechisch/lateinisch-deutsch, übers. u. eingel. v. M. Illert, FC 45, Turnhout 2007, 18–20.30–33).

[27] Der Brief wird bestimmt als Gespräch zwischen Freunden, z.B. Pseudo-Libanius, De forma epistulari 2: „A letter, then, is a kind of written conversation that takes place between two parties who are in different places, and fulfils some practically useful purpose; one will say in it just what one would say if face to face with the addressee" (Übers. TRAPP, Letters [s. Anm. 2], 189).

1. absolut notwendiges Wissen, über das der interne Leser bereits verfügt, das der externe Leser vermittelt bekommen muss, weil sonst der Briefverkehr oder Teilaussagen unverständlich bleiben[28] (Textaussagen sind – aus Sicht des internen Lesers – überdeterminiert);
2. (scheinbar) notwendiges Wissen, über das der interne Leser bereits verfügt, das dem externen Leser aber unbekannt bleibt: Dadurch verstärkt sich der Eindruck, Einblick in real geführte Briefkorrespondenz zu bekommen (Textaussagen sind – aus Sicht des externen Lesers – unterdeterminiert);
3. notwendiges Wissen, das der interne Leser nicht in den an ihn adressierten Briefen mitgeteilt bekommt, wohl aber der externe (durch Briefe an andere Personen; Textaussagen sind – aus Sicht des internen Lesers – unterdeterminiert);
4. und schließlich kann diese Differenzierung dazu führen, dass der Briefschreiber dem internen Leser neue Informationen übermittelt, über die der externe Leser bereits verfügt (Textaussagen sind – aus Sicht des externen Lesers – überdeterminiert).[29]

Zugleich ergibt sich aus dem Abwägen von Über- und Unterdetermination eine Möglichkeit, die Fiktion aufzudecken, indem danach gesucht wird, wo sich für den internen Leser überflüssige Informationen finden, die jedoch für den externen Leser notwendig sind (Option 1). Solche überdeterminierten Aussagen werden dabei oft zusätzlich vom Verfasser ‚gerechtfertigt', um die Fiktion eines echten Briefwechsels trotz des Verstoßes gegen die Plausibilität aufrechtzuerhalten.

So schreibt Chion z.B. an seinen Vater in Heraklea über den Charakter des Tyrannen Klearch, dass er ὠμός/grausam und μισούμενος/verhasst sei, besinnt sich dann jedoch und merkt an: „Aber dies ist dir natürlich bekannt."[30] Ein weiteres Beispiel dieser Art,

---

[28] Dies betrifft auch Aussagen, durch die dem impliziten Leser weitere Informationen geboten werden, die er nicht unbedingt bräuchte, die aber dem Briefverkehr und den an ihm beteiligten Personen ‚Leben einhauchen' (wie durch die Näherbestimmung bekannter Personen, s.u.).

[29] Diese Erzähltechnik kann etwa dazu eingesetzt werden, um die Geschichte bis zu diesem Punkt für den externen Leser zusammenzufassen – gerade hinsichtlich der fragmentierten Erzählweise von Briefromanen kann dies für den externen Leser hilfreich sein, die Gesamtgeschichte nicht aus dem Blick zu verlieren. Wenn die mitgeteilten Informationen andererseits in einzelnen Punkten von dem (möglichen) Vorwissen des externen Lesers abweichen, kann dies etwa dazu eingesetzt werden, um den Leser mit einer neuen Perspektive auf bereits Bekanntes zu konfrontieren, wie es etwa Lukian in seinen Wahren Geschichten (2,35) mit dem von Odysseus an Circe geschriebenen Brief tut (vgl. ROSENMEYER, Fictions [s. Anm. 20], 133f.), oder um über die Verlässlichkeit des Briefschreibers als Ich-Erzähler zu informieren und damit seinen Charakter zu erhellen (s.u. zu Chion ep. 3 und 16).

[30] Ep. 15,3: ἀλλὰ ταῦτα μὲν καὶ σοὶ δηλαδὴ φανερά.

Erzählung im Fragment 275

wie ein Autor für den internen Leser überflüssige Informationen an die externen Leser weitergibt, findet sich im vierten Aischinesbrief, den der verbannte Redner an einen Freund schreibt. Nachdem er Pindar erwähnt hat, fährt er fort: „Aber errege ja nicht Lachen durch die Frage, Wer denn Pindar sey? Denn ich denke, du hast mit mir bei dem Lehrer Mantias einst dieses Gedicht kennen gelernt; und wenn du dich an Nichts mehr von Mantias her erinnerst, so hörst du wenigstens immer" den Namen Pindar in den Volksversammlungen fallen und eine Bildsäule in Athen erinnere an den großen Dichter aus Theben, der die Athener besungen hat.[31] Und weiter führt er als Begründung für die ausführliche Erzählung an: „Und wenn ich nicht allzugut wüßte, daß du ein Verächter der Dichter bist …, so hätte ich es für hinreichend gehalten, dich daran zu erinnern, und bloß die Worte des Pindar über die Diagoreer anzuführen; nun aber weiß ich, daß ich umsonst mit dir von dieser Leier sprechen würde. Es scheint mir demnach nothwendig, dir die Sache ausführlich zu erzählen" (ep. 4,4f.). – Hier schiebt der Verfasser die Bildungsvergessenheit seines Adressaten als Vorwand vor, um ausführlich von Pindar, seinem Lob der Athener und der Schulzeit bei Mantias zu berichten.[32]

Ein anderes Beispiel aus dem gleichen Briefroman ist der zweite Brief, den der gerade erst aus Athen Verbannte an Ktesiphon schreibt. Der verlorene ‚Kranzprozess' gegen eben diesen Ktesiphon war Grund für das Exil des Aischines, darauf spielt der Redner an, wenn er schreibt: „der Unfall, den ich durch dich erlitten" (ep. 2,1) – erst weiter unten im Brief wird dieser ‚Unfall'/συμφορά näher erläutert: ich, „der aus dem Vaterlande verbannt, seiner bürgerlichen Ehre, seiner Rechte im Staate, seiner Mitbürger und Freunde beraubt ist" (ep. 2,2). Das alles musste Ktesiphon natürlich wissen, der externe Leser dagegen konnte dies noch nicht wissen und ihm war – nachdem er im ersten Brief von der Abreise des Aischines von Athen nach Rhodos gelesen hatte – auch noch nicht klar, dass es sich hierbei um das Exil des Redners handelte: Der Empfänger des ersten Briefes (Philokrates) wusste dies natürlich, ebenso wie Ktesiphon um die Bedeutung des Exils für einen Exilanten wusste. Aber diese Informationen sind unbedingt notwendig für die externen Leser, damit sie wissen, dass es sich hier um einen Exilbriefroman handelt und nicht um die Erzählung einer Bildungsreise (wie sie in dem Roman in ep. 10 erzählt wird[33]). Die Erwähnung des durch Ktesiphon verursachten Unglücks setzt freilich Leser voraus, die den Namen Ktesiphon und die Verbannung des Aischines in dessen Biographie richtig einordnen können, für die die bloße Anspielung ausreichend ist. Für die anderen jedoch findet sich in ep. 7,2 eine weitere Aufklärung, wenn er erklärt, „daß mir Dieses widerfahren ist, weil ich die Gesetze vertheidigen wollte, und dafür kämpfte, daß Niemand gegen dieselben bekränzt würde."

---

[31] Ep. 4,2f. Übersetzung hier und im Folgenden: Aeschines Rhetor/Aeschines der Redner, übers. v. J. H. Bremi, Griechische Prosaiker in neuen Übersetzungen 53, Stuttgart 1828/29.

[32] Mit diesem dürfte wohl der athenische Rhetor und Politiker gemeint sein; vgl. zu diesem Demosthenes, Reden 39 und 40. Zur Zuschreibung eines Lehrers des Aischines in der biographischen Tradition (v.a. Sokrates, Plato und Isokrates bzw. Leodamas werden hier angeführt) vgl. J. F. KINDSTRAND, The Stylistic Evaluation of Aeschines in Antiquity, AUU. SGU 18, Uppsala 1982, 68–75.

[33] Zu dieser Bildungsreise nach Troja vgl. T. GLASER, Vom Nutzen und Schaden klassischer Bildung (im Exil). Homerimitation in den Exilbriefromanen des *Aeschines orator* und *Werthers*, in: A. Standhartinger / H. Schwebel / F. Oertelt (Hg.), Kunst der Deutung – Deutung der Kunst. Beiträge zu Bibel, Antike und Gegenwartsliteratur (FS von Blumenthal), Ästhetik – Theologie – Liturgik 45, Münster u.a. 2007, 39–49.

Auch ist der zweite Brief weiter sehr ausführlich in der Schilderung der Abschiedsszene – Ktesiphon war dabei und bedarf dieser ausführlichen Beschreibung seiner „düsteren Miene, die so aussah, als hättest du Thränen vergossen" (ep. 2,1), seiner Art, mit Aischines zu reden, „daß ich überzeugt war, Alles, was du sagest, sey ungeheuchelte Wahrheit" (ep. 2,1), nicht. Für den realen Leser dagegen sind solche Beschreibungen notwendig, um die zugrunde liegende Situation zu verstehen: dass Ktesiphon vorgetäuscht habe, er würde das Schicksal seines politischen Gegners ernsthaft betrauern und sich dessen Familie während des Exils annehmen.

Ein weiteres Beispiel für Option 1 ist die Näherbestimmung bekannter Personen:

So wie Aischines seinen Leser nicht darüber im Unklaren lässt, wie der Name des gemeinsamen Lehrers gewesen ist, wer sich also hinter Mantias verbirgt, so verdanken wir auch dem Paulus des 2Tim die Namen von Großmutter und Mutter des Timotheus: Lois und Eunike (1,5). Vergleichbar ist hier auch die Näherqualifizierung des Onesiphorus in 2Tim 1,16–18, von dem Paulus sagt, dass er ihn oft in Rom im Gefängnis besucht habe. Paulus erinnert dort Timotheus auch daran, dass er selbst am besten wisse, was Onesiphorus in Ephesus alles geleistet habe, und trägt ihm am Ende des Briefes auf, „das Haus des Onesiphorus" zu grüßen (4,19). Ob in der Formulierung impliziert ist, dass dieser nicht mehr lebt oder noch nicht wieder in Ephesus zurück ist, wurde zwar erwogen, ist aber unwahrscheinlich.[34] Es muss also als vorausgesetzte Geschichte zwischen diesen Notizen gedacht werden, dass Onesiphorus nach Rom gekommen ist, sich dort um den gefangenen Paulus gekümmert hat, und dann wieder nach Ephesus zurückgekehrt ist, bevor Paulus 2Tim geschrieben hat. Timotheus muss daher vermittels Onesiphorus bestens über Paulus, seine Lage und damit auch die Fürsorge des Onesiphorus um Paulus gewusst haben. Sie in 2Tim 1,16f. zu nennen, wäre überflüssig für Timotheus, für den Leser der Briefe jedoch nicht. Gleiches gilt für die Näherbestimmung der Häresie in 2Tim 2,16–18: Paulus warnt Timotheus vor der Irrlehre von Hymenaios und Philetus, „die von der Wahrheit abgeirrt sind und sagen, die Auferstehung sei schon geschehen, und bringen einige vom Glauben ab." All dies muss der in Ephesus weilende Timotheus natürlich gewusst haben. Zwar zitiert auch Paulus in den echten Briefen Positionen seiner Gegner in den Gemeinden, wiederholt also das den Adressaten längst Bekannte; der Unterschied besteht allerdings darin, dass dort Paulus theologisch gegen die jeweiligen Positionen argumentiert, in 2Tim dagegen unterbleibt eine solche Argumentation. Hier bleibt es bei dem ‚Zitat' und die theologische Relevanz erwächst nicht aus der Situation in Ephesus, sondern aus der Situation des gefangenen Paulus, insofern der 2Tim allenthalben das Thema Tod und Verfolgung aufgreift.

Dies ist natürlich kein eindeutiges Kennzeichen für den fiktionalen Charakter der Briefe, es fällt aber auf, dass in den überlieferten Papyrusbriefen die dem Absender und dem Adressaten bekannten Personen i.d.R. nicht näher charakterisiert werden.

So wird z.B. in P.Oxy. 744, ein Brief vom 17. Juni 1 v. Chr., den ein Ehemann an seine Frau schreibt, nicht deutlich, wer Berus „meine Herrin", wer Apollonarin und wer

---

[34] Vgl. A. WEISER, Der zweite Brief an Timotheus, EKK XVI/1, Düsseldorf u.a. 2003, 140.

Aphrodisias ist.[35] Ähnlich der Trostbrief der Eirene (P.Oxy. 115, 2. Jh. n. Chr.), in dem der Name des Betrauerten, seine Beziehung zu den Trauernden Taonnophris und Philon sowie die Beziehung zwischen Eirene und Didymas unerklärt bleiben: „Ebenso bin ich in Trauer (und) weine über den Seligen, wie ich über Didymas geweint habe."[36] Ein weiterer Familienbrief ist der Brief des Apion (der den Soldatennamen Maximus angenommen hat) an seinen Vater (BGU 423, 2. Jh. n. Chr.), in dem er ihn bittet, seine Schwester, seine Nichte und seinen Bruder zu grüßen, die namenlos bleiben. Erst durch einen zweiten Brief desselben Soldaten erfahren wir den Namen seiner Schwester, an die er einige Zeit später schreibt (BGU 632). In diesem Brief finden sich zwar auch folgende Zeilen: „Es] grüßt Dich [meine] Lebensgefährtin [A]uphidia und [M]aximos [m]ein [Sohn], [dessen] Gebur[tstag] der dreißigste [E]peip ist nach Hel[lenischem Kalende]r, und Elpis und Fortu[nata]."[37] Die Näherbestimmung der Auphidia und des Maximos fallen hier auf, möglicherweise erklärt sich die des letzteren mit Angabe des Geburtsdatums aus der erst kürzlich erfolgten Geburt (im Gegensatz dazu scheinen Elpis und Fortunata zwei schon ältere und damit der Schwester bekannte Töchter zu sein). Ob nun Auphidia der Schwester deswegen auch noch nicht bekannt ist und vorgestellt werden muss, bleibt offen. Jedenfalls ist diese Näherbestimmung eine Ausnahme in dem Brief, direkt vor dem zitierten Satz heißt es: „Grüße den Maximos vielmals und Kopres meinen Herr[n]." Hier wieder lässt sich nur vermuten, wer damit gemeint sein soll.[38]

Wenn solche echten Briefe durch Zufall in die Hände anderer als der expliziten Leser gelangen, bleiben die Angaben unterdeterminiert und laden zur Spekulation ein – was nichts anderes ist als das Konstruieren einer Geschichte aus den dürftigen Angaben eines Briefes, um die Geschichte, aus der der Brief erwachsen ist, zu verstehen. So kommentiert Deißmann sein Vorgehen bei der Interpretation der Papyrusbriefe: „Habe ich zuviel zwischen den Zeilen dieses Briefes gelesen? Ich glaube nicht. Bei Briefen will das zwischen den Zeilen Stehende mitbegriffen sein."[39] Solche Unbestimmtheit in Privatbriefen Genannter kann sich natürlich auch in fingierten Briefen finden, um dadurch den Anschein der Echtheit zu forcieren (Option 2).

So lässt Euripides über den aus Seenot geretteten Sophokles die mit ihm geretteten Chionides und Laprepes grüßen sowie die Söhne des Kratinos (ep. 2,2). Wer sich hinter die-

---

[35] G. A. DEISSMANN, Licht vom Osten. Das Neue Testament und die neuentdeckten Texte der hellenistisch-römischen Welt, Tübingen [4]1923, 136, vermutet hinter Berus die Schwiegermutter, hinter Apollonarin das (einzige?) Kind der beiden und hinter Aphrodisias eine Freundin der Familie.
[36] Übersetzung nach DEISSMANN, a.a.O. 143.
[37] Nach der Rekonstruktion und Übersetzung von DEISSMANN, a.a.O. 150.
[38] DEISSMANN, a.a.O. 152 Anm. 8 u. 9, vermutet, dass Maximos der Neffe des Briefschreibers, der nach ihm so benannt wurde, und dass Kopres sein Schwager sei.
[39] A.a.O. 149f., ähnlich auch F. PREISIGKE, Familienbriefe aus alter Zeit, PrJ 108 (1902), 88–111 (108): „Es ist der Phantasie weitester Spielraum gelassen, um aus diesen wenigen Zeilen sich den weiteren Zusammenhang zurechtzulegen." Vgl. TRAPP, Letters (s. Anm. 2), 194f.

sen Namen ‚versteckt', bleibt unklar und reizt zu historischem Puzzlespiel.[40] Hier findet sich allerdings auch das Gegenteil, dass für den genannten Empfänger notwendige Informationen ausbleiben, weil sie für den realen Leser ohnehin unwichtig wären: Zu Anfang des Briefromans schreibt Euripides an den Makedonenkönig Archelaos u.a. bezüglich zweier in Pella gefangen gehaltener junger Männer, Söhne eines angesehenen alten Mannes aus Pella: „Was aber die jungen Leute aus Pella betrifft, so habe ich früher schon brieflich Fürbitte bei Dir eingelegt" (ep. 1,2). U.a. an dieser Stelle nimmt Bentley Anstoß und sieht einen Beleg für den unechten Charakter der Briefe: „'tis a plain violation of good Sense, to petition for a Man without telling his Name: as if Pella the royal City had no Old Man in it but one."[41] So argumentiert er für die Unwahrscheinlichkeit der Fiktion, dass diesem Brief ein – wie es an der Stelle heißt – Brief vorausgegangen sein könnte, in dem die fehlenden Informationen dem Archelaos mitgeteilt worden seien.[42] Für die Leser des Briefromans freilich erweckt die Notiz diesen Eindruck einer vorausgegangenen Näherbestimmung.

In den Pastoralbriefen wiederum werden zahlreiche Personennamen genannt, die für den realen Leser unbekannt bleiben; einige der Personen kann er durch anderweitiges (intertextuelles) Wissen identifizieren (z.B. Priska und Aquila oder Erastos und Trophimus aus 2Tim 4,19f.), andere bleiben völlig unbekannt (z.B. Eubulos, Pudens, Linus und Claudia aus 2Tim 4,21; Artemas oder Zenas aus Tit 3,12f.); wieder andere werden durch das Briefbuch selbst weiter in ihrem Charakter ausgemalt (wie Hymenaios und Alexander in 1Tim 1,20; 2Tim 2,17f.; 4,14f.; oder Tychikus in Tit 3,12 und 2Tim 4,12).

Ein weiteres literarisches Stilmittel in Brieffiktion, um Option 2 anzuwenden, ist der Verweis auf außerhalb des Briefbuches geführte Kommunikation, die das gemeinsame Wissen, das dem expliziten Leser nicht mitgeteilt wird, begründet.

So findet sich z.B. der Verweis auf Briefe, die nicht in die Sammlung aufgenommen sind: In einem Brief an seinen Vater schreibt Chion: „It happened that he made an attempt on me shortly after I had sent you the letter informing you of my illness."[43] Hier wird eine genaue Zeitangabe für ein von dem Tyrannen Klearchos beauftragtes Attentat auf Chion verbunden mit dem subtilen Hinweis, dass der externe Leser zwar Einblick in eine (vermeintlich) reale Briefkorrespondenz zwischen Chion und seinem Vater erhält, aber dennoch zwischen beiden mehr Informationen ausgetauscht wurden, als der Leser

---

[40] Vgl. die Bestimmungsversuche bei H.-U. GÖSSWEIN, Die Briefe des Euripides, BKP 55, Meisenheim a. Glan 1975, jeweils im Kommentar zu den Stellen. Die folgenden Zitate aus den Briefen nach der Übersetzung Gößweins.

[41] BENTLEY, Dissertation (s. Anm. 4), 125.

[42] Im ersten Brief lehnt Euripides ein (seiner Meinung nach viel zu großes) Geldgeschenk des Makedonenkönigs ab, das ihm ein Bote überbracht hatte. Bentley argumentiert nun, dass Archelaos, wenn er sich so großzügig gezeigt habe, sicherlich die beiden Jünglinge, da sie (wie Euripides im Brief auch schreibt) kein nennenswertes Verbrechen begangen hätten und es zukünftig auch nicht tun würden, freigelassen hätte, wovon der Bote dem Euripides hätte berichten können. Dass Euripides ein zweites Mal bitten müsse (und Archelaos gewährt ihm diese Bitte; vgl. ep. 3), erscheine damit ganz unglaubhaft.

[43] Ep. 13,1: καὶ μικρὸν ὕστερον ἢ γραφῆναί σοι τὴν περὶ τῆς νόσου παρ' ἡμῶν ἐπιστολὴν ἐπεχείρησεν ... Die Übersetzung der Zitate aus dem Chionbriefroman stammt von Düring, Chion (s. Anm. 10).

weiß.[44] Neben solch einem Verweis auf andere Briefe gelten natürlich auch die Rückverweise auf die gemeinsame Zeit als Erklärung, wie in den Pastoralbriefen Paulus den Titus erinnert: „Deswegen ließ ich dich in Kreta, dass du vollends ausrichten solltest, was noch fehlt, und überall in den Städten Älteste einsetzen, wie ich dir befohlen habe" (Tit 1,5), oder an Timotheus adressiert: „Du weißt, wie ich dich ermahnt habe, in Ephesus zu bleiben, als ich nach Mazedonien zog" (1Tim 1,3).

Diese Beispiele aus antiken Briefromanen zur Über- und Unterdetermination von Informationen und zur Diskrepanz zwischen dem Wissen des externen und internen Lesers beleuchten die grundlegende narrative Technik von Briefromanen: In ihnen bieten die Briefe Schlaglichter auf eine Geschichte, die beiden Briefpartnern bekannt ist und deshalb nur angedeutet werden muss, wohingegen der reale Leser diese Geschichte durch die Andeutungen der Briefe rekonstruieren bzw. auf sein Hintergrundwissen zurückgreifen muss, um die Notizen der Briefe zu sinnvollen Aussagen zu ergänzen. Von der Produktivität solcher Erzähltechnik zeugen die Kommentare, in denen versucht wird, die Genannten zu identifizieren und die dahinter stehenden Geschichten zu rekonstruieren.

Neben dieser gemeinsamen Geschichte, auf die beide Briefpartner zurückblicken können, gibt es jedoch auch noch die Geschichten, in die nur einer der Briefpartner verwickelt ist, und die er demgemäß dem anderen Briefpartner mitteilt – in der Typologie des Briefromans sind solche Episoden als statische Elemente des Briefromans bezeichnet worden,[45] weil hier innerhalb eines Briefes eine Erzählung geboten wird. Das Gegenstück dazu sind die dynamischen Momente eines Briefromans, in denen durch den Briefverkehr eine Handlung initiiert bzw. vorangetrieben wird:[46] Diese wird dann in der Regel nicht in den Briefen selbst erzählt, sondern kommentiert und alludiert. Hier findet die Geschichte zwischen den Briefen statt, die Ereignisse sind den Handelnden und Briefschreibenden bekannt, können aber nur aus ihren Anspielungen in den Briefen von den Lesenden rekonstruiert werden. Dabei ist der Ich-Erzähler keineswegs immer eine verlässliche Erzählfigur, kann er die Darstellung in den Briefen doch auch nutzen, um seine Briefpartner zu täuschen und die Handlung dadurch entsprechend zu beeinflussen bzw. zu ermöglichen. Den externen Lesern ist dabei nicht immer bewusst, dass es sich bei dem aktuellen Brief um einen

---

[44] Zudem – so ROSENMEYER, Novel (s. Anm. 24), 155 – soll dadurch plausibel gemacht werden, weshalb in der Sammlung nur so wenig Briefe enthalten sind, obwohl sie eine Zeitspanne von etwas über fünf Jahren abdecken.

[45] Zum ‚statischen' und ‚dynamischen' Briefroman vgl. F. JOST, The Epistolary Novel. An Unacted Drama, in: J. P. Strelka (Hg.), Literary Theory and Criticism, 1: Theory (FS Wellek), Bern u.a. 1984, 335–350 (344–348). Er fasst damit den Briefroman als Ganzen, diese Aspekte lassen sich jedoch auch auf einzelne Handlungssequenzen innerhalb eines Briefromans übertragen. Vgl. dazu auch ARNDT, Briefroman (s. Anm. 18), 68–71.

[46] Vgl. ROSENMEYER, Novel (s. Anm. 24), 146.

Täuschungsbrief handelt, kann doch z.B. erst durch einen späteren Brief diese Täuschung aufgedeckt werden.[47] Solche Art von Täuschungs- und Offenbarungsbriefen sind in den *Liaisons dangereuses* das dominierende Element, finden jedoch auch bereits in der Antike Anwendung; in den Chionbriefen etwa wird dieser Erzählmodus gleich zweimal eingesetzt.

Einmal schreibt der junge Philosoph einen falschen Empfehlungsbrief an seinen Vater (ep. 8), einmal einen Täuschungsbrief an den Tyrannen seiner Heimatstadt (ep. 16). In beiden Fällen geht dem Täuschungsbrief ein Aufklärungsbrief voraus (adressiert an seinen Vater, ep. 7 und 15), der für den realen Leser den Sinn hat, den nachfolgenden Brief verstehen und damit den Charakter Chions richtig schätzen zu können.[48] So schreibt Chion einen Empfehlungsbrief an seinen Vater: „The man who delivers this letter is Archepolis of Lemnus, going to Pontus as a merchant. He asked me to introduce him to you and I acceded with pleasure to his request. ... I believe that he is also a honest merchant, for he devoted himself to the study of philosophy before he took to commerce."[49] Was es mit diesem μέτριον ἔμπορον auf sich hat, erfährt sein Vater – und der implizite Leser – bereits mit dem vorausgehenden Brief, in dem beide über den Charakter des Empfohlenen aufgeklärt werden und die Dechiffrierung des ‚Empfehlungsbriefes' ermöglicht wird: „Archepolis who professes to be of Lemnian origin, is an untrustworthy and obscure fellow ... Unworthy as he is, I did not want to treat him as Bellerophon was treated,[50] and so I gave him another letter, not containing any lies of that kind, whereas I entrust this letter to Lysis who will bring it to you. ... I have told you this about him frankly and undisguisedly, but to other persons I do not want to say anything evil about him. I think it just to state my mind to you frankly and unambiguously, undisguised by words."[51]

Ein zweitesmal bieten die Chionbriefe solche Abfolge von Aufklärungs- und Täuschungsbrief, wenn der junge Held seinem Vater schreibt, dass er dem Tyrannen seiner Heimatstadt, Klearchus, einen Täuschungsbrief geschrieben habe: „I congratulate my city that the tyrant allows himself to be lulled by what you said to him about me. I shall follow your advice and write myself too, leading him as far astray from the truth as possi-

---

[47] Dies entspricht Option 3 aus der obigen Typologie: Die Angaben sind für den expliziten Leser unterdeterminiert, der implizite Leser erhält (durch einen späteren oder früheren Aufklärungsbrief) die fehlenden Informationen.

[48] Vgl. K. LATTE, Rez. Düring, Gn. 25 (1953), 45–47 (47).

[49] Ep. 8: Ὁ ἀποδιδούς σοι τὸ γράμμα Ἀρχέπολις ὁ Λήμνιος ἐμπορευόμενος εἰς τὸν Πόντον ἐδεήθη μου ὅπως αὐτὸν συστήσαιμί σοι, ἐγὼ δὲ ἄσμενος ἐδεξάμην· ... πείθομαι δὲ καὶ μέτριον αὐτὸν ἔμπορον εἶναι· καὶ γὰρ φιλοσοφήσας πρότερον εἶτα ἐμπορεύεται.

[50] Zum Bellerophon-Brief (Il. 6,167–170) und seiner Bedeutung für die antike Briefliteratur vgl. ROSENMEYER, Fictions (s. Anm. 20), 39–44.

[51] Ep. 7: Ἀρχέπολις Λήμνιος μέν ἐστιν, ὡς λέγει, τὸ γένος, φαῦλος δὲ καὶ ἀτέκμαρτος ἄνθρωπος ... οὗτος ἐπιλαθόμενος τῶν βλασφημιῶν προσῆλθέ μοι καὶ ἐδεήθη σοι γράψαι περὶ αὐτοῦ, ἐγὼ δὲ ἐκείνῳ μέν, ἵνα μὴ ἀναξίῳ ὄντι Βελλεροφόντου σχῆμα περιθῶ, ἑτέραν ἐπιστολὴν ἔδωκα, οὐδὲ ἐκεῖ τι ὁμοίως ψευσάμενος, ταύτην δὲ προαναγομένῳ Λύσιδι ἐνεχείρισα. ... τάδε περὶ αὐτοῦ λελυμένως καὶ ἀπροκαλύπτως ἐδήλωσα, πρὸς ἄλλον μὲν οὐδέν ποτε βλασφημήσας τῶν ὄντων οὐδένα, πρὸς σὲ δὲ τὸν ἐμὸν νοῦν ὑπὸ μηδενὸς παραμπεχόμενον λόγον ἁπλοῦν καὶ σαφῆ δικαιῶν εἶναι.

ble."[52] Er schließt den Brief: „I send you here a copy of my letter to Clearchus which, on purpose, I have written in an exalted tone in order to make him despise me as a pure windbag."[53] Mit diesem Schlusssatz geht der reale Leser dann dazu über, den folgenden Brief an Klearch zu lesen, in dem der junge Philosoph den Tyrannen davon zu überzeugen versucht, dass er keine Gefahr für Klearch darstelle, da er als Schüler Platons keine politischen Ambitionen habe, sondern einzig in der *theoria*, die die Ruhe voraussetze, seine Bestimmung sehe: „While I was studying philosophy in Athens, my father and some of our common friends wrote to me that I was suspected by you and asked me to refute these calumnies. ... I had intercourse with a man who is a lover of a quiet life and I was instructed in a most godlike doctrine. The very first precept of his was: seek stillness. For that is the light of philosophy, whereas politics and meddlesomeness wrap it in gloom and make the way to philosophy hard to find for those who search."[54] In beiden Beispielen ist der Grund angegeben, wie die Täuschungsbriefe ihren Weg in die Briefsammlung des Vaters gefunden haben, einmal ein an ihn direkt adressierter Brief (ep. 8), einmal eine Kopie des echten Briefes an Klearch (ep. 16). Darüber hinaus ist der Brief an Klearch (v.a. ep. 16,4–7) auch ein Beispiel für Option 4, insofern der Tyrann hier über das aufgeklärt wird, was der externe Leser in den vorausgehenden 15 Briefen miterleben konnte. Ein weiteres Beispiel ist ep. 3, in dem Chion seinem Vater von seiner ‚Konversion' zur Philosophie erzählt, die veranlasst ist durch die Begegnung mit Xenophon, der in Byzanz seine Soldaten davon abgehalten hatte, die Stadt zu plündern. Hier erlebte Chion, wie die Philosophie zu einem nützlichen Staatsmann erziehen kann – und der externe Leser erfährt die negative Sicht, die Sicht der Byzantier auf die Folgen des freudigen θάλαττα, θάλαττα der Truppen Xenophons (Anabasis 4,7,24), die dieser Anabasis 7,1 mitteilt.[55]

Um den Aufbau einer Geschichte in Briefromanen zusammenzufassen: Es ist für Briefromane typisch, dass es keinen stringenten *plot* gibt, dass die Erzählung nicht durch ein Handlungskontinuum aufgebaut wird, sondern dass allein Schlaglichter auf eine Geschichte geboten werden. So hat Christiane Arndt den Gedanken des Handlungskontinuums aufgrund der Beobachtung von mitunter langen Intervallen zwischen den einzelnen Brie-

---

[52] Ep. 15,1: Ἐπὶ μὲν τῷ συμπείθεσθαι τὸν τύραννον οἷς περὶ ἐμοῦ πρὸς αὐτὸν ἔλεγες, συγχαίρω τῇ πατρίδι, γράψω δὲ καὶ αὐτός, ὡς συνεβούλευσας, ἀπάγων αὐτὸν ἀπὸ τἀληθοῦς ὡς μάλιστα ἔνεστι.
[53] Ep. 15,3: ἔπεμψα δέ σοι καὶ τὸ ἀντίγραφον τῆς πρὸς τὸν Κλέαρχον ἐπιστολῆς, διθυραμβικωτέραν ποιήσας ἐπίτηδες αὐτήν, ἵν' ἡμῶν καταφρονῇ ὡς λογομανούντων τελέως.
[54] Ep. 16,1.5: Ἐν Ἀθήναις μοι φιλοσοφίας χάριν διατρίβοντι τῶν τε κοινῶν τινες φίλων καὶ ὁ πατὴρ ἔγραψαν ὡς δι' ὑποψίας εἴην πρός σε, καὶ τὰς αἰτίας ἐκέλευον ἀπολύσασθαι ... ἀλλ' ἀνδρὶ ἡσυχίας ἐραστῇ διελεγόμην, τὸν ἔγγιστα θεῷ λόγον παιδευόμενος. καί μοι πρῶτον ὑπ' αὐτοῦ παρηγγέλθη ἡσυχίαν ποθεῖν· ταύτην γὰρ τοῦ κατὰ φιλοσοφίαν λόγου φῶς εἶναι, τὴν δὲ πολιτείαν καὶ πολυπραγμοσύνην ὥσπερ ζόφον τινὰ ἐπικαλύπτειν καὶ ἀνεύρετον ποιεῖν τοῖς ἐρευνῶσιν.
[55] Dass Chion seinem Vater in diesem Brief zudem erklärt, wer Xenophon sei und dass er von einem Feldzug des Kyros zurückgekommen sei, ist natürlich im Hinblick auf den externen Leser geschrieben (somit ein weiteres Beispiel für Option 1), Matris wird dieses Wissen aufgrund der Bedrohung von Heraklea durch das griechische Söldnerheer gehabt haben (vgl. Anabasis 6,2).

fen und der Fragmentarizität relativiert und sieht den „Geschehenszusammenhang eher durch Stationen punktuell"[56] hergestellt.

Briefromane sind fragmentierte Erzählungen und gleichen damit einem Detektivroman:[57] Der Verfasser bietet den Lesern Indizien eines Falles an, die Lösung desselben müssen sie selbst vornehmen, d.h. die Geschichte, die hinter den Briefen steht, rekonstruieren. Stärker als andere Prosagattungen involvieren Briefromane damit die Leser, wie überhaupt auch der Brief stärker die Leser einbindet, weil er den Akt des Schreibens und Lesens durchgängig gegenwärtig hält und damit den Leser an seine Rolle als Leser erinnert.[58] Dieser wird parallel zum Lesen auf Spurensuche geschickt – sowohl innerhalb des Textes: damit wird er aufgefordert, Querbeziehungen zwischen den einzelnen Briefen, zwischen den an verschiedenen Orten genannten Personen herzustellen sowie die durch die zeitliche Erstreckung der Korrespondenz geöffnete Zeitspanne mit Handlungen, mit Hintergrundgeschehen[59] auszufüllen. Daneben wird der Leser aber auch angeregt, außerhalb des Textes Spuren zu sammeln, indem er etwa internymischen Referenzen nachgeht oder diese erinnert.[60]

3. Verarbeitung von Traditionen in Briefromanen

Die Ausnutzung der Dichotomie von externem und internem Leser zum Aufbau der Erzählung ist die grundlegende narrative Strategie in Briefromanen. Eine daraus erwachsene zweite zentrale narrative Strategie, v.a. für historisch orientierte Briefromane, ist die Verarbeitung von (Personal-) Traditionen im Briefbuch. Da zum einen dem externen Leser nicht alles erzählt werden kann, muss er auf solch externes Wissen zurückgreifen und kann dies mit der Darstellung des Briefbuches in Beziehung setzen. Zum

---

[56] KUCH, Rez. Holzberg (s. Anm. 11), 80, bezogen auf ARNDT, Briefroman (s. Anm. 18), 74f.

[57] Vgl. J. DERRIDA, Die Postkarte von Sokrates bis an Freud und jenseits (übers. v. H.-J. Metzger), 2 Bde., Berlin 1982/87, Bd. 1, 234; DOTY, Imaginings (s. Anm. 8), 86; ARNDT, Briefroman (s. Anm. 18), 76 (und Anm. 76). Vgl. auch M. TRAPP, Biography in Letters. Biography and Letters, in: B. McGing / J. Mossman (Hg.), The Limits of Ancient Biography, Swansea 2006, 335–350 (342).

[58] Vgl. auch O. HODKINSON, ‚Novels in the Greek Letter'. Inversions of the Written-Oral Hierarchy in the *Briefroman* ‚Themistokles', in: V. Rimell (Hg.), Seeing Tongues, Hearing Scripts. Orality and Representation in the Ancient Novel, Ancient Narrative. Supplementum 7, Groningen u.a. 2007, 257–278 (260–266).

[59] Vgl. HOLZBERG, Versuch einer Gattungstypologie (s. Anm. 14), 50f.

[60] Zur Internymität von Literatur vgl. W. G. MÜLLER, Namen als intertextuelle Elemente, Poetica 23 (1991), 139–165.

anderen ermöglicht die Konzeption als Ich-Erzählung jedoch auch, umläufige Traditionen (durch den Brief als vermeintlich authentischere Quelle) zu korrigieren bzw. zu ergänzen.

3.1 Der Briefroman des Aischines

Der Briefroman des Aischines beginnt mit der Erwähnung seiner Abreise: „Wir lichteten abends in Munichia bei starkem Nordwestwind die Anker und gelangten gegen Mittag nach Koressos auf Keos" (ep. 1,1). Im Verlauf der anschließenden Briefe erfahren die Leser den Anlass der Schifffahrt: die Verbannung des Aischines aus Athen. Was es mit der Verbannung auf sich hat, wird nach und nach in den einzelnen Briefen offen gelegt: Man liest von Gegnern in Athen und erfährt von der Reaktion der Öffentlichkeit auf seine Parteinahme für Philipp und Alexander von Makedonien. Während Aischines anfangs noch voller Hoffnung war, später nach Athen zurückkehren zu können, so muss er am Ende erkennen, dass er sich die ganze Zeit über getäuscht hatte.[61] In seinem Abschiedsbrief an die Athener bittet er sie schließlich nur noch ausschließlich für seine Kinder, dass ihnen erlaubt sei, nach seinem bevorstehenden Tod in die Heimat zurückzukehren (ep. 12,14–16). Dieser letzte Brief ist zugleich eine Apologie seiner politischen Betätigung und beginnt entsprechend programmatisch mit einer Selbstvorstellung: „Ich begann politisch aktiv zu werden mit 33 Jahren"[62]: Hier verteidigt sich der Redner ein letztes Mal gegen den Vorwurf, er habe als Gesandter Athens in Makedonien aus Eigennutz wider die Interessen seiner Polis gehandelt.

In den antiken Biographien wird erzählt, dass der verbannte Redner nach Rhodos gefahren sei, nachdem er Athen verlassen musste. Es lassen sich hier jedoch zwei unterschiedliche Stränge der biographischen Tradition unterscheiden: Der älteste Strang (der zuerst durch Cicero bezeugt ist) ist bestimmt vom Interesse an der Rhetorik. Hier heißt es, dass der Redner ohne Umweg nach Rhodos gekommen sei, wo er den dritten Stil der Rhetorik, die Mischung von attischem und asianischem Stil, eingeführt habe, der die rhodische Redekunst prägt.[63]

---

[61] Zum Aischinesbriefroman als einem Entwicklungsroman vgl. GLASER, Nutzen (s. Anm. 33).

[62] Ep. 12,1: Ἐγὼ προσῆλθον τῷ πολιτεύεσθαι γεγονὼς ἔτη τρία καὶ τριάκοντα ...

[63] Diese Differenzierung der Stile scheint Cicero eingeführt zu haben (vgl. Brutus 13,51; Orator 8,25), wenngleich erst Quintilian (Institutio oratoria 12,10,18f.) Aischines als Urheber des rhodischen Stils benennt; vgl. KINDSTRAND, Evaluation (s. Anm. 32), 80–83.

Der zweite biographische Strang, der wie der Briefroman selbst ins 2. Jh. n. Chr. zu datieren ist,[64] rekurriert auf Demosthenes,[65] den Gegenspieler des Aischines, und bringt den Verbannten in die Nähe zu Alexander: Aischines sei, so heißt es, von Athen zunächst nach Ephesus zu Alexander geflohen; erst nach dessen Tod habe er sich dann auf Rhodos niedergelassen.[66]

Der Verfasser des Aischinesbriefromans hat beide Stränge aufgenommen und miteinander verflochten aus einem ‚apologetischen' Interesse heraus:[67] Aischines ist ohne Umweg nach Rhodos gegangen und kämpft gegen die Vorwürfe an, nicht loyal zu Athen gestanden zu haben und nur auf eigenen Vorteil bedacht gewesen zu sein: „Und wie sie [sc. die Verbannten] die Widerfahrnisse ertragen und wie sie gegen ihr eigenes Vaterland gesonnen sind, das wird hinreichend deutlich. Bin ich nun, der ich mein eigenes Vaterland Philipp übergeben ... und immer die Makedonen hoffiert haben soll, als ich als Verbannter schnellstmöglich von euch fortgesegelt bin, zu Alexander hin ...?"[68]

Aus diesem Grund zeichnet der Autor Aischines, wie er nach Rhodos kam, wie ihm die Rhodier ein kleines Grundstück zuteilten und wie er dort unter bescheidenen Umständen lebte. So imaginiert er den berühmten Redner, wie dieser sich gegen die Angriffe verteidigte und die Schande des Exils würdevoll und loyal zu Athen bis an sein Lebensende ertrug. Dazu

---

[64] Apollonios, Vita Aeschinis; Philostr.vit.soph. 1,18 (509); Ps.-Plutarch, Vitae decem oratorum.

[65] Zur Infragestellung der Loyalität des Aischines durch Demosthenes vgl. z.B. Aischines, Reden 3,66.215 und Demosthenes, Reden 18,51f.

[66] So in der Überlieferung bei Ps.-Plutarch und Phot.bibl. 61,20a,22–26,264. Philostrat andererseits erzählt, dass Aischines zu Alexander wollte, von dem er wusste, dass er in Susa war. Als er jedoch in Ephesus vom Tod des Königs erfahren hatte, sei er nach Rhodos geflohen, um nicht in die Thronkämpfe verstrickt zu werden.

[67] Dass allerdings Aischines mehr als 400 Jahre nach seinem Tod keine aktuelle Apologie für seine vermeintliche Makedonenfreundschaft bedurfte, wird in der Forschung nicht immer hinreichend deutlich; vgl. z.B. E. MIGNOGNA, Cimone e Calliroe. Un „romanzo" nel romanzo. Intertestualità e valenza strutturale di Ps.-Eschine *epist.* 10, Maia 48 (1996), 315–326 (315 Anm. 1): „Il corpus di 12 lettere ... costituiscono un autoritratto fittizio, nel quale l'io narratore, oltre a tracciare un quadro della sua vita di esule, tende a offrire un bilancio giustificatorio della propria attività politica"; J. A. GOLDSTEIN, The Letters of Demosthenes, New York u.a. 1968, 78: „writer of literary or propagandistic fiction".

[68] Ep. 12,6f.: καὶ γὰρ καὶ ὅπως φέρουσι τὰς συμφοράς, καὶ ὡς διάκεινται πρὸς τὰς ἑαυτῶν πατρίδας, ἐξετάζονται σαφῶς. Ἆρ' οὖν καὶ Φιλίππῳ προδοὺς τὴν ἐμαυτοῦ πατρίδα, καὶ παραπρεσβεύσας τοιαῦτα κατὰ τῆς πόλεως, καὶ ἀεὶ θεραπεύσας Μακεδόνας, ἐπειδὴ τάχιστα φεύγων παρ' ὑμῶν ᾠχόμην, πρὸς Ἀλέξανδρον ἀπηλλάγην, χάριν τε ὧν παρεσχόμην αὐτῷ κομιούμενος καὶ προμηθείας δηλονότι τευξόμενος παρ' αὐτοῦ;

greift der Autor verschiedene, widersprüchliche Personaltraditionen auf, die er zur Inszenierung seiner Geschichte frei kombiniert und mit seiner fingierten Ich-Erzählung kritisch kommentiert bzw. berichtigt.

Der folgende Briefroman zeigt eine andere Art, wie eine Gegengeschichte zugleich mit ihrer Geschichte aufgebaut werden kann.

3.2 Der Briefroman des Euripides

Antike wie moderne Biographien und historische Abrisse behaupten, dass der Dichter Euripides etwa 407 v. Chr. nach Pella, an den Hof des makedonischen Königs Archelaos gegangen und dort etwa eineinhalb Jahre später gestorben sei. Der kurze, fünf Briefe umfassende Roman aus dem 2. Jh. n. Chr. greift diese Situation auf und versucht zu erklären, wieso der Dichter in die Fremde gezogen ist.[69]

Der Roman beginnt mit der brieflichen Ablehnung der Einladung des Archelaos an den noch in Athen weilenden Dichter. Im Laufe der Briefkorrespondenz (ep. 3–5) kann der Leser verfolgen, wie Euripides seinen bleibenden Einfluss auf den Herrscher nutzt, um ihn sowie seine Herrschaft zu bessern. Den letzten Brief schließlich schreibt der Dichter aus Pella an einen Freund nach Athen, der ihn über kursierende Gerüchte informiert, nach denen Euripides aus Macht- und Geldsucht an den Königshof gegangen sein soll. Jedoch liegt, wie gelegentlich angenommen wird, in dieser Apologie ebenso wenig wie im Fall des Aischines das Zentralmotiv des Briefromans,[70] vielmehr scheint es dem Autor um ein Spiel mit Personaltraditionen zu gehen, durch das die Erzählung um Euripides aufgebaut wird. So kann erst, wenn diese narrative Technik erkannt ist, die Aussage, die hinter dem Roman steht, angemessen erfasst werden.

Dieses Spiel findet im Briefroman mehrfach Anwendung und wird besonders in drei Aspekten augenfällig: hinsichtlich des Euripidesbildes, hinsichtlich seiner Beziehung zu Sophokles und hinsichtlich des vermeintli-

---

[69] Dass Euripides tatsächlich in Pella gewesen ist, wird allgemein als historisch zuverlässig bezeugt angesehen; vgl. z.B. E. N. BORZA, In the Shadow of Olympus. The Emergence of Macedon, Princeton 1990, 172–177; A. GAVRILOV, Euripides in Makedonien, Hyperboreus 2,2 (1996), 38–53; D. KOVACS, Euripides. Cyclops, Alcestis, Medea, LCL 12, Cambridge 1994, 20f. Allerdings ist die einzige halbwegs vertrauenswürdige Quelle dafür Arist.pol. 1311b 30–34. Dass aber die ganze Szenerie auch schon bei Aristoteles und in der Gnomen-Tradition frei erfunden ist, zeigt überzeugend S. SCULLION, Euripides and Macedon, or: The Silence of the Frogs, CQ 53 (2003), 389–400, durch eine Analyse der Frösche des Aristophanes.

[70] So aber z.B. GÖSSWEIN, Euripides (s. Anm. 40), 23.30; B. KNOX, Rez. Gößwein, The Classical Journal 73 (1977), 179; F. JOUAN / D. AUGER, Sur le corpus des ‚Lettres d'Euripide‘, Mélanges Edouard Delebecque, Aix-en-Provence 1983, 183–198 (190).

chen Zentralmotivs, der Apologie des Dichters gegen den Vorwurf der Tyrannenfreundschaft.

Ein Vergleich des Euripidesbildes des Romans mit dem der biographischen Tradition zeigt auf, wie die Briefe das weit verbreitete Bild des Dichters durch eine Ich-Erzählung kommentieren, ohne explizit darauf einzugehen. Die biographische Tradition über den Dichter bezieht sich primär auf seine Stücke sowie auf die des Aristophanes. Auf diese Weise schafft sie ein mysteriös-romantisches Bild eines Einsiedlers, der in einer Höhle am Meer wohnt, Menschen meidet, Frauen hasst und von ihnen gehasst wird: Dieser exzentrische Charakterkopf stecke hinter den genialen Bühnenstücken, die ihn zum beliebtesten Dichter der Nachwelt werden ließen.[71]

Der Briefroman entwirft ein dem entgegenstehendes Bild des Tragikers: Er zeichnet ihn nicht als Misanthropen, sondern als einen vorbildlichen Bürger, der unter Menschen lebt, ein Bewusstsein für seine gesellschaftliche Verantwortung zeigt und kaum als Bühnendichter sichtbar wird.[72]

Ausdrücklich gemacht wird dagegen die Verschiebung des traditionellen Euripidesbildes hinsichtlich der Beziehung des Euripides zu Sophokles, seinem Dichterkollegen und Rivalen. Im letzten Brief schreibt er diesbezüglich: [D]enn gegen diesen allein war ich, wie man vielleicht weiß, nicht immer gleichmäßig eingestellt. Ihn habe ich zwar nie gehaßt, sondern immer bewundert, aber nicht immer in gleicher Weise geliebt, sondern in dem zeitweiligen Glauben, er sei ein Mensch von übertriebenem Ehrgeiz (φιλοτιμότερον), sah ich ihn scheel an; als aber er den Zwist aus der Welt schaffen wollte, habe ich ihn mit offenen Armen aufgenommen."[73] Ähnlich, allerdings mit anderem Fokus, heißt es im Genos, wenn der antitypische Charakter beider Dichter herausgestellt wird: „It was for this reason that he was rather proud (φιλοτιμίαν) and pardonably stood aloof from the majority, showing no ambition as regards his audience. Accordingly this fact hurt him as much as it helped Sophocles."[74]

---

[71] Vgl. JOUAN / AUGER, a.a.O.

[72] Am deutlichsten in ep. 5,1: „... indem sie mich bei jeder Gelegenheit nötigen, stets in meiner gewohnten Sphäre zu entwerfen (φροντίζειν) und zu dichten (ποιεῖν), so daß, wie mir scheint, Archelaos ein gern, aber nicht ohne Mühe gewährtes Entgelt sich bezahlen läßt für die Geschenke, die er mir gleich bei der Ankunft machte ... "

[73] Ep. 5,5f.: ὃν ἐγὼ ἐμίσησα μὲν οὐδέποτε, ἐθαύμασα δὲ ἀεί, ἔστερξα δὲ οὐχ ὁμοίως ἀεί, ἀλλὰ φιλοτιμότερον μέν τινα εἶναί ποτε δόξας ὑπεῖδον, βουληθέντα δὲ ἐκλύσασθαι τὰ νείκη προθυμότατα ὑπεδεξάμην.

[74] § 34. Euripidea. Übers. v. D. Kovacs, Mn.S 132, Leiden u.a. 1994, 8f.: ὅθεν καὶ πλέον τι φρονήσας εἰκότως περιίστατο τῶν πολλῶν, οὐδεμίαν φιλοτιμίαν περὶ τὰ θέατρα ποιούμενος. διὸ τοσοῦτον αὐτὸν ἔβλαπτε τοῦτο ὅσον ὠφέλει τὸν Σοφοκλέα.

Der Vorwurf der *philotimia* bzw. der Widerstand, danach zu streben, ist aus zwei unterschiedlichen Perspektiven formuliert. Auf diesem Hintergrund wird der zweite Brief verständlich, der ansonsten unverbunden zur Archelaos-Geschichte des Briefromans steht: Euripides wird als enger Freund des Sophokles porträtiert, der sich um ihn kümmert und dessen Interessen vertritt, solange Sophokles außerhalb Athens ist.[75] Der Briefroman zeigt beide Dichter in vorbildlicher Harmonie, während die biographische Tradition sie als Antitypen stilisiert hat.[76] So heißt es über Sophokles in dessen Vita: „Und, um es kurz zu sagen, die Anmut seines Wesens war so groß, daß er überall und von allen geliebt wurde." Und wenige Paragraphen später: „Mit so großer Liebe aber hing er an Athen, daß er seine Vaterstadt nicht verlassen mochte, wiewohl viele Könige ihn zu sich beriefen."[77]

Dieser Gegentypus wird besonders durch die Darstellung in der als Dialog geschriebenen Euripidesbiographie des Satyrus (3. Jh. v. Chr.) deutlich, die nur in Fragmenten erhalten ist (P.Oxy. 9,1176): „Everyone became his enemy, the men because he was so unpleasant to talk to, the women because of his abuse of them in his poetry. He ran into great danger from both sexes."[78] Später heißt es (Frgm. 39,15): „He, partly in annoyance at the ill-will of his fellow-citizens ...", bevor sein Verlassen Athens und die Reise nach Makedonien erzählt werden (Frgm. 39,17–19).

Bisher arbeitet der Briefroman zum Aufbau des Euripidesbildes mit der Technik, wie sie auch im vorausgehenden Aischinesbriefroman angewandt wurde: mit dem Aufbau eines Gegenbildes gegen eine bekannte, umläufige Vorstellung.[79] Eine Besonderheit des Euripidesbriefromans ist jedoch, dass

---

[75] Vgl. Xenophon, Memorabilia 2,3,12. Diese Bedeutung der kleinen Szene verkennt BENTLEY, Dissertation (s. Anm. 4), 127, vollständig, wenn er schreibt: „Must Euripides, his Rival, his Antagonist, tell him, That his Orders about family affairs were executed: as if He had been employ'd by him, as Steward of his Houshold?"

[76] Dieser antitypische Charakter beider ist bereits in den Fröschen des Aristophanes angelegt (V. 76–82.787–793).

[77] § 7. Sophokles, Dramen. griechisch-deutsch. Übers. v. W. Willige, München/Zürich ²1985: Καὶ ἁπλῶς εἰπεῖν τοσαύτη τοῦ ἤθους αὐτῷ γέγονε χάρις ὥστε πάντῃ καὶ πρὸς ἁπάντων αὐτὸν στέργεσθαι. § 10: Οὕτω δὲ φιλαθηναιότατος ἦν ὥστε πολλῶν βασιλέων μεταπεμπομένων αὐτὸν οὐκ ἠθέλησε τὴν πατρίδα καταλιπεῖν.

[78] Frgm. 39,10 Übers. Kovacs, Euripidea (s. Anm. 74), 21: ἀπήχθοντ' αὐτῶι πάντες οἱ μὲν ἄνδρε[ς] διὰ τὴν δυ[σ]ομιλίαν, α[ἱ δὲ] γυναῖκε[ς δ]ιὰ τοὺς ψ[ό]γους τοὺς ἐν τοῖς ποιήμασιν· ἦλθεν δ' εἰς κίνδυνον ἀφ' ἑκατέρου τῶν γενῶν μέγαν.

[79] Bezüglich der Beziehung zu Sophokles wird die Veränderung gegenüber der Tradition im Briefroman explizit gemacht, unkommentiert bleibt dagegen die Neuschreibung der Beziehung des Euripides zu Kephisophon, der als Adressat des letzten Briefes als enger Freund des Euripides auf die Bühne tritt und nicht als dessen Nebenbuhler um seine Frau; vgl. D. KOVACS, De Cephisophonte Verna, Ut Perhibent, Euripidis, ZPE 84 (1990), 15–18.

er eine Gegengeschichte aufbaut, zu der es bislang noch keine Geschichte gegeben hat, dass diese überhaupt erst durch die Erzählung ihrer Gegengeschichte entsteht.

Ein zentrales Motiv des Romans ist die Apologie des Dichters gegen die gegen ihn erhobenen Vorwürfe anlässlich seiner Entscheidung, an den Hof des makedonischen Königs zu ziehen. Die fünf Briefe geben in unterschiedlichen Graden Zeugnis für den Vorteil, den ein Herrscher aus dem Verkehr mit Intellektuellen ziehen kann. Allerdings ist solch ein Vorwurf in der gesamten biographischen Tradition zu Euripides nicht erhalten.[80]

Möglicherweise deutet Satyrus, Frgm. 39,17 auf solch einen Vorwurf gegen Euripides. Dort berichtet ein Gesprächsteilnehmer (A) vom Protest, den Euripides gegen Athen in Form eines Chorstücks vorgebracht habe: „There are golden wings about my back and the winged sandals of the Sirens are fitted on my feet, and I shall go aloft far into the heavens, there with Zeus ..." An diesem Punkt bricht das Fragment ab, aber der Text des nächsten Fragments (39,18) liest: „... began the songs. Or do you not know that it is this that he says? (Diodora:) What do you mean? (A:) In saying ‚mingle my flight with Zeus' he hints metaphorically at the monarch and at the same time increases the man's preeminence. (Di.:) It seems to me that you speak with more subtlety than truth. (A:) You may understand it as you like. At any rate, he went over and spent his old age in Macedonia, enjoying very high honor with the king; ..."[81] Die „goldenen Flügel" (χρύσεαι πτέρυγες) mögen auf den Vorwurf der Geldsucht hinweisen. Jedoch wäre dies der einzige Zeuge aus der gesamten Tradition und bleibt aufgrund des fragmentarischen Charakters stark hypothetisch. Zudem zweifelt die Gesprächsteilnehmerin Diodora die Glaubwürdigkeit dieser Interpretation an, was ein Indiz dafür sein könnte, dass der Verfasser selbst nicht an die Richtigkeit dieser Aussage glauben konnte. Zumindest wird deutlich, dass Kritik am Aufenthalt des Euripides in Pella und der Vorwurf der Macht- und Geldgier nicht weit verbreitet waren und höchstens den gebildeteren Lesern des Romans hätten bekannt sein können.

So wird im Briefroman nun allein durch die Apologie (v.a. in ep. 5) dieser Vorwurf literarisch gestaltet, d.h. durch den Aufbau der Gegengeschichte wird gleichzeitig ihre Geschichte konstruiert. Sobald dieses ‚Spiel mit Geschichten' als das zentrale Motiv des Werkes erkannt wird, wird einsichtig, weshalb der Autor des Romans darauf verzichten kann, einen

---

[80] Aristophanes, Frösche 83–85 kann als vergleichbarer Vorwurf gegen Agathon gelesen werden, der „zum Festmahl der Seeligen" gegangen ist (Ἐς μακάρων εὐωχίαν V.85), was in einigen Scholien interpretiert wird als die goldenen Tafeln des Archelaos (vgl. Scholia in Aristophanem. Pars III. Ib Scholias recentiora in Aristophanis Ranas edidit M. CHANTRY, Groningen 2001, zur Stelle).

[81] Übers. Kovacs, Euripidea (s. Anm. 74), 25.

positiven Grund dafür anzuführen, weshalb Euripides zum König gegangen ist.[82]

3.3 Die Pastoralbriefe als Paulusbriefroman

Die Affinität der Pastoralbriefe[83] zu erzählender Literatur ist schon häufig beobachtet worden: Jerome D. Quinn etwa hat sie als den Abschluss des lukanischen Doppelwerkes angesehen,[84] Dennis R. MacDonald mit den Paulus- und Theklaakten in Zusammenhang gebracht[85] und Richard I. Pervo sie schließlich als eine Art von Briefroman gelesen, vergleichbar den Chion- und Sokratikerbriefen.[86] V.a. die Fokussierung auf die Person des Paulus sticht in ihnen hervor,[87] so dass sie auch als „Paulushagiographie" bezeichnet worden sind,[88] und ihre vermeintlich unerfindlichen Personalnotizen wecken immer wieder das Interesse der Forschung,[89] die

---

[82] In ep. 5 argumentiert Euripides allein gegen die vorgebrachten Vorwürfe, obwohl er dem Leser zugleich eine positive Begründung in Aussicht stellt: „Wenn aber einer von denen, die würdig sind, über Euripides etwas zu sagen oder zu hören, mich wegen der Reise zu Archelaos beschuldigen, weil er zwar weiß, was ich früher hinsichtlich meiner Ablehnung einer Emigration nach Makedonien sagte, aber nicht weiß, was mich danach nötigte zu gehen, so halte diesen für wert ihm mitzuteilen, was du weißt, mein Kephisophon; und auf diese Weise wird er über die Motive nicht mehr im unklaren sein" (ep. 5,2).

[83] Zur neueren Kritik an dem Korpuscharakter der Pastoralbriefe und der Verteidigung dessen vgl. G. HÄFNER, Das Corpus Pastorale als literarisches Konstrukt, ThQ 187 (2007), 258–273.

[84] Vgl. J. D. QUINN, The Last Volume of Luke. The Relation of Luke-Acts to the Pastoral Epistles, in: C. H. Talbert (Hg.), Perspectives on Luke-Acts, Perspectives in Religious Studies, Special Studies Series 5, Danville u.a. 1978, 62–75 (68–70); zur geläufigen Praxis, ein literarisches Œuvre mit einem Briefbuch zu beenden; vgl. jetzt auch M. KORENJAK, Abschiedsbriefe. Horaz' und Ovids epistolographisches Spätwerk, Mn. 58 (2005), 46–61.218–234.

[85] Vgl. D. R. MACDONALD, The Legend and the Apostle. The Battle for Paul in Story and Canon, Philadelphia 1983.

[86] Vgl. R. I. PERVO, Romancing an Oft-Neglected Stone. The Pastoral Epistles and the Epistolary Novel, The Journal of Higher Criticism 1 (1994), 25–47 [URL: http://www.depts.drew.edu/jhc/pervope.html], dessen These positive Aufnahme gefunden hat, z.B. H.-J. KLAUCK, Die antike Briefliteratur und das Neue Testament. Ein Lehr- und Arbeitsbuch, Paderborn u.a. 1998, 243–246; vgl. ausführlich GLASER, Paulus (s. Anm. 9).

[87] „In den Pastoralbriefen wird die Person des Paulus dem Leser bewußt nahe gebracht und lieb gemacht", U. LUZ, Erwägungen zur Entstehung des „Frühkatholizismus", ZNW 65 (1974), 88–111 (100).

[88] So R. COLLINS, The Image of Paul in the Pastorals, LTP 31 (1975), 147–173 (147.168.173); E. DASSMANN, Der Stachel im Fleisch. Paulus in der frühchristlichen Literatur bis Irenäus, Münster 1979, 165–168.

[89] Vgl. dazu N. BROX, Zu den persönlichen Notizen der Pastoralbriefe, BZ.NF 13

gerade in diesen Reste authentischer Pauluskorrespondenz zu finden hofft, bzw. den Zweiten Timotheusbrief, der das lebhafteste Paulusbild zeichnet, als authentischen Paulusbrief ansieht.[90]

Wie eingangs argumentiert, ist die Vorspiegelung von Authentizität Kennzeichen jeder Form von Autodiegese und entsprechend lässt sich in den Pastoralbriefen die Diastase von externem und internem Leser narratologisch zum Aufbau der Erzählung nutzen, welche auch deutlich auf die Implikation solch einer Diastase eingehen: Der Verweis auf eine dem Brief vorausgehende Kommunikation zwischen Apostel und Delegaten (Tit 1,5; 1Tim 1,3)[91] expliziert, dass die externen Leser, anders als die internen Leser Timotheus und Titus, nur einen Bruchteil dessen erfahren, was nötig wäre, um die den Briefkommunikationsakt umgebende Situation angemessen zu erfassen.

Ähnlich wie in den Briefromanen um Aischines und Euripides wird auch in den Pastoralbriefen die Spätzeit des ‚Helden' erzählt, die bis an seinen bevorstehenden Tod heranführt. Und ebenso wie dort wird auch hier das wesentliche Kennzeichen des Briefschreibers ausgeblendet: Aischines tritt nicht als Redner auf, Euripides nur in einer Randbemerkung als Dichter, und dass Paulus Briefe an Gemeinden geschrieben hat (wie aus den anderen Paulusbriefen bekannt), entfällt ebenso wie seine Missionstätigkeit im engeren Sinn (welche in Apg im Mittelpunkt der Paulusdarstellung steht, da in ihr auf den gegenwärtigen Paulus fokussiert wird, weshalb sie auch seine Briefschreiberei außer Acht lassen kann).

In dem Buch der Pastoralbriefe kann der Leser die Entwicklung einer Geschichte verfolgen: die Geschichte von Paulus, dem Ich-Erzähler, an drei Punkten seines Lebensweges (Tit–1Tim–2Tim); er erzählt von Timotheus in zwei verschiedenen Situationen seiner Biographie (1Tim–2Tim) und ebenso von Titus (Tit–2Tim 4,10). Die Momentaufnahmen, die der Ich-Erzähler zur Zeit des Briefschreibens vermittelt, sind in allen drei Fällen nicht identisch: Auch wenn Tit und 1Tim ähnlich sind, so bieten beide doch Einblicke in zwei gegensätzliche geographische Räume mit je spezifischen Gemeindestrukturen und Konflikten[92] und unterscheiden sich grundlegend von den in 2Tim erzählten Widerfahrnissen des Paulus. Diese

---

(1969), 76–94 (76): „In jedem Plädoyer für die Echtheit wird auf den unbedingten Eindruck einer echten Ursprünglichkeit, großer Unmittelbarkeit, persönlicher Herzlichkeit und absoluter Unerfindlichkeit verwiesen, den die betreffenden Passagen bei jedem unbefangenen Leser erwecken."

[90] J. MURPHY-O'CONNOR, Paul. A Critical Life, Oxford 1996; J. HERZER, Abschied vom Konsens? Die Pseudepigraphie der Pastoralbriefe als Herausforderung an die neutestamentliche Wissenschaft, ThLZ 129 (2004), 1267–1282, sowie sein Aufsatz im vorliegenden Sammelband.

[91] 2Tim 1,4 könnte eine vergleichbare Funktion einnehmen; vgl. weiter V.6.13.15.18.

[92] Vgl. dazu PERVO, Stone (s. Anm. 86), 38–45.

Grundgeschichte wird primär in der jeweiligen Briefrahmung aufgebaut, wo der Briefschreiber Auskunft über seine gegenwärtige Situation gibt. Aber auch in den Hauptteilen der Briefe sind ‚Erzählsplitter' auszumachen, die den Lesern den Eindruck einer konsistenten Handlung suggerieren und ihn dazu veranlassen, aus dem *plot* der Briefe eine *story* zu rekonstruieren.

Der erste Schritt dahin besteht darin, die Abfolge der Briefe zu klären. Anders als andere Formen von Prosaliteratur geben Briefbücher keine feste Lesereihenfolge vor, sondern ähnlich Gedichtbüchern ermöglichen sie den Lesern durch ihre szenische Kompositionstechnik, bei einem beliebigen Brief anzufangen, und sie können in der Handschriftenüberlieferung ohne weiteres ihre Positionen wechseln. So sind denn auch nicht inhaltliche Aspekte wie geographische Angaben oder die Beobachtung thematischer Entfaltungen zur Begründung einer vom Autor intendierten Lesereihenfolge hinreichend, sondern die kompositorischen Hinweise sind eher formaler Art.[93] So zeichnen sich Briefromane häufig dadurch aus, dass im Eröffnungssatz die Hauptthemen des Romans *in nuce* enthalten sind. Das ungewöhnlich lange Tit-Präskript enthält nun bereits die zentralen Schlagwörter der Pastoralbriefe (wie πίστις, εὐσέβεια, σωτήρ), die Vorstellung von Paulus als *Knecht Gottes* und *Apostel* sowie das bedeutsame Thema der *Erkenntnis der Wahrheit*. Dass 1Tim auch nicht Tit vorausgehen kann, wird m.E. zudem durch das Ende von 1Tim deutlich markiert, das ein Scharnier zwischen 1Tim und 2Tim darstellt. Hier ist nicht nur der fehlende Briefschluss von Belang,[94] sondern über Stichworte wird 1Tim 6,20f. mit 2Tim 1 verknüpft, neben der namentlichen Anrede noch besonders durch die Mahnung, die παραθήκη zu bewahren (φυλάσσειν 2Tim 1,12.14). Die Schlussstellung von 2Tim ist kaum fraglich, wenn die drei Briefe als Einheit gelesen werden; wie der Vergleich mit antiken Briefromanen zeigt, ist 2Tim deutlich als Abschiedsbrief des Paulus vor seiner erwarteten Hinrichtung geschrieben (4,6–8.16–18), und auch wenn in Briefromanen die historische Abfolge zugunsten der dramatischen Gestaltung nicht immer eingehalten werden muss, so ist es doch üblich, dass ein solcher Brief das Ende der Sammlung markiert und dass nach einem Abschiedsbrief keine weiteren Briefe des internen Verfassers folgen.

---

[93] So argumentiert HÄFNER, Corpus (s. Anm. 83), 270.272, für die Abfolge 1Tim–Tit–2Tim mit der räumlichen Bewegung des Paulus von Ephesus über Makedonien (1Tim), über Nikopolis (Tit) nach Rom (2Tim), und mit der erläuternden Funktion, die 1Tim für Tit habe. Für ihn heißt es allerdings, wenn Tit erst nach der Lektüre des 1Tim verstehbar ist, dass dann dieser jenem vorausgehen müsse, was freilich kein valides Argument für Briefromane ist, die sich häufig durch eine Enthüllungsdramatik auszeichnen; vgl. ROSENMEYER, Novel (s. Anm. 24), 161: „For an epistolary novelist, the initial withholding of information from the external reader is a generic necessity"; vgl. auch HOLZBERG, Versuch einer Gattungstypologie (s. Anm. 14), 9.50f.

[94] Darauf verweist HÄFNER, Corpus (s. Anm. 83), 270.

Um seine Paulusgeschichte zu erzählen, greift der Verfasser der drei Briefe ähnlich wie die Verfasser der Aischines- und Euripidesbriefromane auf andere Erzählungen zurück, ohne sich durch sie gebunden zu fühlen. Die Freiheit, mit der Traditionen verarbeitet werden, hat in der Forschung zu zahlreichen Versuchen geführt, die Notizen der Pastoralbriefe mit dem aus den anderen Paulusbriefen oder der Apostelgeschichte Bekannten zu harmonisieren, um zumindest einen hypothetischen Ort in der Paulusbiographie für diese drei Briefe zu finden.

In 1Tim ist es die bewusste Zusammenstellung der Personen- und Ortsnamen Paulus, Timotheus, Makedonien und Ephesus (1Tim 1,1–3; vgl. auch 3,14f.; 4,13), die denjenigen Lesern, denen das Leben des Paulus wie aus Apg oder anderen Briefen bekannt ist, den Brief an Timotheus in eine scheinbar vertraute Geschichte hineingeschrieben erscheinen lässt. Der Vergleich mit diesen Parallelgeschichten zeigt jedoch, dass die zugrunde liegende Situation weder eindeutig erhebbar[95] noch mit denen aus Apg 19f. und 1Kor 16 harmonisierbar ist. Da die Briefe den Anschein vermitteln, autodiegetische Erzählungen und damit grundsätzlich vertrauenswürdig zu sein, werden die Leser auf die Spur gesetzt, ihr vorgängiges Wissen mit den neuen Informationen aus (vermeintlich) erster Hand zu vereinbaren, z.B. indem die anderen Erzählungen als nur ungenau oder falsch qualifiziert werden[96] oder indem unbesetzte Flecken in der Biographie gesucht werden, so dass die Briefe als Zeugnisse dieser ansonsten unbekannten Zeit angesehen werden können.

Anders geht der Autor bei der Gestaltung der Erzählung von Tit vor: Hier greift er nicht frei auf eine bekannte Episode aus der Paulusbiographie zurück, sondern besetzt bisher freie geographische Räume mit Pauluserzählungen, wenn er den Apostel mit Kreta und Nikopolis (womit sicherlich das Actium gegenüberliegende gemeint ist) zusammenbringt.[97] Mit beiden Erzählungen informiert der Autor den Leser, dass sein Wissen über Paulusbiographie unvollständig und/oder fehlerhaft gewesen ist.

Mithilfe dieser fiktiven Szenarien wird Paulus als stetig reisender Missionar in Szene gesetzt, der, nachdem er seine Gemeinden verlassen hat,

---

[95] Z.B. ist aus dem Text nicht herauslesbar, ob Paulus selbst in Ephesus gewesen ist oder Timotheus von einem ungenannten Ort in die Metropole Kleinasiens geschickt hat; vgl. J. D. QUINN / W. C. WACKER, The First and Second Letters to Timothy, Eerdmanns Critical Commentary, Michigan u.a. 2000, 69–72.

[96] Allerdings sind Briefe in der Antike durchaus nicht als autodiegetische Erzählungen mit einem höheren Wahrheitsgehalt angesehen worden, weshalb sie nur gelegentlich von Historio- resp. Biographen herangezogen worden sind; vgl. TRAPP, Biography (s. Anm. 57), 336–339.

[97] Dass die Szenerie des Tit auf dem Hintergrund der Kretaepisode von Apg 27 gestaltet ist, scheint unwahrscheinlich zu sein, da es in Tit keinen Hinweis darauf gibt, dass Paulus in Gefangenschaft ist.

weiterhin um sie Sorge trägt und mit ihnen Kontakt hält. Dass Paulus sich um Gemeindeaufbau und Gemeindestrukturen Gedanken gemacht und gegen Gegner gekämpft hat, war bekannt. Dass er dies mithilfe von Abgeordneten getan hat, die er in den Gemeinden (zumindest zeitweise) installiert hat, ist etwas Neues, die besondere Vision des Verfassers dieses Paulusbriefromans.

Der Briefroman erzählt die Geschichte von der missionarischen, eher: gemeindeorganisatorischen Aktivität des Paulus bis zum Vorabend seines Todes. Wie in einem monologischen Briefroman nicht anders zu erwarten, kann der Tod selbst nicht erzählt, sondern nur in der Erwartung des Briefschreibers antizipiert werden. Da es in der frühchristlichen Paulustradition kaum eine Erzählung über den Tod des Apostels gibt, füllt der Brief damit eine weitere Leerstelle der Paulusbiographie.

In Fortführung der aus den Paulusbriefen bekannten theologischen Kontroversen zeichnet der Autor des Briefromans Paulus stark als den von vielen Seiten Bedrängten, der sich sowohl inner- wie außergemeindlicher Gegner erwehren muss, am Ende seines Lebens von allen verlassen worden ist (vgl. 2Tim 4,9–20) und dessen Lebensprojekt (aus Tit und 1Tim), die gelingende Inkulturation christlicher Existenz in die Gesellschaft, sich als gescheitert erweist (vgl. Tit 3,1f.; 1Tim 2,1f. mit 2Tim 3,11f.). Solch ein Fokus auf das Scheitern mitsamt der Hervorhebung von Verlassenheit und Anfeindung (bei gleichzeitigem Verweis auf das umgebende soziale Netz) ist ein gängiger Topos gerade von Exil- und Gefangenenliteratur (so beklagt etwa auch Aischines allenthalben seine Verlassenheit und fordert zum Besuch auf, vgl. z.B. ep. 6 und 8; ebenso Ovid in seinen beiden Exildichtungen Tristia und Epistulae ex Ponto oder Johannes Chrysostomos in seinen Exilbriefen) und kann nicht ohne weiteres als historische Reminiszenz ausgewertet werden.[98]

Mit diesem Ende entlässt der Autor die Leser in die nachpaulinische Zeit: Er gestaltet mit seinem Briefroman durchgängig den abwesenden Paulus. Dafür eignet sich die Gattung des Briefes besonders gut, thematisiert der Brief doch die Dialektik von An- und Abwesenheit.[99] So wie die Gemeinden zuvor ohne Paulus leben mussten, wie es der Autor erzählt, so müssen sie es nun weiterhin. Aus diesem Grund endet der Briefroman, wie so viele andere Briefromane, mit einem Abschiedsbrief vom Vorabend des Todes des Ich-Erzählers.

---

[98] So aber z.B. M. GÜNTHER, Die Frühgeschichte des Christentums in Ephesus, ARGU 1, Frankfurt a.M. u.a. ²1998, v.a. 80–85.206.

[99] Vgl. MANN, Brief (s. Anm. 20), 639f.

***

Liest man die Pastoralbriefe auf dem generischen Hintergrund des Briefromans, kann man erkennen, wie der Autor durch den gewählten fragmentarischen Erzählmodus den Leser in die Konstruktion eines eigenen Paulusbildes hinein nimmt, unabhängig davon, über wie viel Hintergrundwissen zu Paulus er bereits verfügt. Das Vexierspiel mit internem und externem Leser spiegelt dem realen Leser dabei stets vor, Einblick in reale Kommunikation zu erhalten – selbst wenn er weiß, dass er einen fiktionalen Briefverkehr liest, wie anhand der zeitgenössischen Rezeption des modernen Briefromans zu beobachten ist. Um das (so) vorhandene Hintergrundwissen der Leser zu aktivieren, stehen dem Autor diverse Möglichkeiten zur Verfügung, vorgängige Traditionen aufzugreifen, zu bearbeiten, zu kommentieren oder sogar erst zu erschaffen. Inwiefern der Autor damit in real geführte Diskussionen um die Hauptperson eintritt und wie er auf seine Leserschaft einwirken will, kann nicht durch eine rhetorische Analyse der Briefe allein herausgearbeitet werden, da dadurch reale und fiktionale Kommunikationsebene vertauscht werden.

The *Letter* of Mithridates

A Neglected Item of Ancient Epistolary Theory

by

ROBERT MATTHEW CALHOUN

Among the several kinds of literary forgeries in antiquity, arising from diverse motives, that of producing spurious epistles seems to have been most assiduously practiced. There is scarcely an illustrious personality in Greek literature or history from Themistocles down to Alexander, who was not credited with a more or less extensive correspondence. Probably the most famous are the 148 Greek epistles supposedly written by Phalaris, tyrant of Acragas (Agrigentum) in the sixth century B.C. ... As is well-known, these were brilliantly and vigorously exposed in 1697–99 by Bentley *as a worthless forgery*, composed probably by a sophist of the second century A.D.[1]

I generally follow the citation conventions of *The SBL Handbook of Style* (eds. P. H. Alexander et al.; Peabody, Mass.: Hendrickson, 1999). Additional abbreviations include: *AET* = A. J. Malherbe, ed. & trans., *Ancient Epistolary Theorists* (SBLSBS 19; Atlanta: Scholars Press, 1988); *BNP* = H. Cancik and H. Schneider, eds., *Brill's New Pauly: Encyclopaedia of the Ancient World: Antiquity* (11+ vols.; Leiden: Brill, 2002–); *EG* = R. Hercher, ed. & trans., *Epistolographi Graeci* (Paris: A. Firmin Didot, 1874); *LAL* = J. L. White, *Light from Ancient Letters* (FF; Philadelphia: Fortress Press, 1986), cited by § for texts; *RG* = L. Spengel and C. Hammer, eds., *Rhetores Graeci vol. I* (Leipzig: Teubner, 1894), L. Spengel, ed., *Rhetores Graeci vol. II* (Leipzig: Teubner, 1853), and idem, ed., *Rhetores Graeci vol. III* (Leipzig: Teubner, 1853), cited by volume and page; Torraca = L. Torraca, ed. & trans., *Marco Giunio Bruto: Epistole Greche* (Collana di Studi Greci 31; Naples: Liberia Scientifica Editrice, 1959) (cf. the edition and Latin translation at *EG* 177–78). I thank Elizabeth Asmis, Hans-Josef Klauck, Margaret M. Mitchell, David Martinez, Clare K. Rothschild, Janet Spittler and Trevor Thompson for their comments and criticisms on portions of this project, and for encouragement that promoted its completion. David Monaco gave special assistance with Torraca's Italian; all translations of Italian herein are his. I also thank those present at the Early Christian Studies Workshop (University of Chicago) on October 20, 2008, and at the SBL Corpus Hellenisticum Novi Testamenti Section on November 24, 2008, for lively discussion.

[1] B. M. Metzger, "Literary Forgeries and Canonical Pseudepigrapha," *JBL* 91 (1972): 1–24 (9–10, emphasis added). Cf. A. Gudeman, "Literary Frauds among the Greeks," in *Classical Studies in Honour of Henry Drisler* (New York: MacMillan & Co., 1894), 52–74 (64–5). For further discussion of epistolary forgery, see M. Luther Stirewalt, *Studies in Ancient Greek Epistolography* (SBLRBS 27; Atlanta: Scholars Press, 1993), §2, "Forgery and Greek Epistolography."

So wrote Bruce Metzger in his SBL presidential address of 1971, a seminal overview of literary forgeries, apocrypha and pseudepigrapha. However, his description of the correspondence of Phalaris as "worthless" needs qualification. If he means "not useful as historical sources for the life and reign of Phalaris," he is of course correct. But the letters are an extremely valuable resource for investigations of the literature of the Second Sophistic, since they are widely admired instances of epistolary craftsmanship that eventually became regarded as authentic. The exposure of their false attribution in no way renders them "worthless," only pseudepigraphic, and thus illuminating for questions beyond the periods and individuals that are their putative topics—not unlike the deutero-Pauline and Pastoral letters of the New Testament.

The corpus of Greek letters attributed to Marcus Junius Brutus has experienced a fate similar to that of Phalaris.[2] The few scholars who have written about the letters have generally focused upon their authenticity and utility as historical sources.[3] The case against their authenticity gains

---

[2] In fact, several of the authors cited in the next note begin their essays the same way that I begin mine here—by referring to Bentley and his analysis of the correspondence of Phalaris. Cf. the remarks of Bentley on the Brutan corpus (quoted by Torraca at vi–vii): "Some of the greek Sophists had the Success and Satisfaction to see their Essays in that Kind pass with some Readers for the genuine works of those they endeavor'd to express. This, no doubt, was great content and joy to them; being as full as testimony of their Skill in Imitation, as the birds gave to the Painter when they peck'd at his grapes. One of them, indeed, has dealt ingeneously, and confess'd that he feign'd the answers to Brutus, only as a trial of Skill: but most of them took the other way, and concealing their own names, putt off their copies for originals ..."

[3] In addition to Torraca's edition, Italian translation and commentary, the bibliography of twentieth century studies dedicated to the corpus, or addressing it with more than a few sentences, includes the following items: F. Rühl, "Die griechischen Briefe des Brutus," *RhM* 70 (1915): 315–25; T. O. Achelis, "Erasmus über die griechischen Briefe des Brutus," *RhM* 72 (1917–18): 633–38; C. Cichorius, "Die griechischen Brutusbriefe und ihre Verfasser," in *Römische Studien* (ed. idem; Leipzig, Berlin: Teubner, 1922), 434–38; R. E. Smith, "The Greek Letters of Brutus," *CQ* 30 (1936): 194–203; J. Deininger, "Brutus und die Bithynier: Bemerkungen zu den sog. griechischen Briefen des Brutus," *RhM* 109 (1966): 356–72; E. Rawson, "Cassius and Brutus: The Memory of the Liberators," in *Past Perspectives* (eds. I. S. Moxon, J. D. Smart and A. J. Woodman; Cambridge: Cambridge University Press, 1986), 101–19 (107–8); J. Moles, "Plutarch, Brutus and Brutus' Greek and Latin Letters," in *Plutarch and His Intellectual World* (ed. J. Mossman; London: Duckworth, 1997), 141–68 (143–48). H.-J. Klauck (*Ancient Letters and the New Testament* [Waco, Tex.: Baylor University Press: 2006], 113) gives a brief description of the corpus and calls the letters "spurious." As far as I know, no German, French or English translation of the corpus and its cover letter has appeared. (Incidentally, some of those who commented on earlier drafts of my essay found the adjective "Brutan" distracting, but, if previous scholarship on the corpus provides the best guide, it is correct; see, e.g., Moles, ibid., 143–44.)

strength in part from the cover letter by a Mithridates, the second editor of the corpus: he claims to have composed historically plausible responses on behalf of the cities with whom the "real" Brutus corresponded. If Mithridates forges responses, why not the "original" letters as well?[4] Would not the whole conceit of wanting to "improve" the corpus serve to enhance the "authenticity" of the "original" compositions of Brutus? Such questions need not occupy us here, since the utility of the corpus does not solely derive from its potential value for reconstructing Brutus' activities as a general in Asia Minor. Instead it lies in two areas: (1) the discussion of the aims and methods of the pseudepigrapher/editor in his cover letter; and (2) the high estimation of the letters very soon after their initial publication as epistolary stylistic models. In both areas the corpus and its cover letter contribute helpfully to our understanding of ancient epistolary theory, especially as it pertains to the pseudepigraphy of letters. My goals in this short study are to offer an annotated English translation of the *Letter* of Mithridates,[5] along with translations of four testimonia (from Plutarch, Philostratus, Photius and the *Suda*) regarding the corpus, to wrestle briefly with a few matters pertaining to dating and authorship, and to point to some ways that it and the Brutan corpus add to our knowledge of epistolary theory and pseudepigraphy.

---

[4] See, e.g., W. Speyer, *Die literarische Fälschung im heidnischen und christlichen Altertum* (Handbuch der Altertumswissenschaft I/2; München: Beck, 1971), 138: "Neuerdings glaubt man, daß bereits Plutarch [who cites the letters as authentic] einem literarischen Trug zum Opfer gefallen sei." Cf. Torraca xxx.

[5] In my translation of the *Letter*, I strive to render the Greek literally in order to make my interpretive decisions clear. Admittedly, this decision does not make for smooth English at several points, because Mithridates' Greek text is often muddled and difficult to construe. I explain my decisions further in the annotations.

1. Texts and Translations

The *Letter* of Mithridates[6]

Μιθριδάτης βασιλεῖ[7] Μιθριδάτῃ τῷ ἀνεψιῷ χαίρειν.

[1] τὰς Βρούτου ἐθαύμασα πολλάκις ἐπιστολάς, οὐ μόνον δεινότητος καὶ συντομίας χάριν, ἀλλὰ καὶ ὡς ἡγεμονικοῦ φρονήματος ἐχούσας χαρακτῆρα· [2] ἐοίκασι γὰρ οὐδὲν νομίζειν καλόν, εἰ μὴ καὶ μεγαλοψυχίας ἔχοιτο. [3] ἐγὼ δ᾽ ἃ μὲν περὶ τῶν τοιούτων φρονῶ λόγων οὐδ᾽ ἐν τῷ δὲ ἀξιῶ διαμφισβητεῖν· [4] ἀποφαίνοντος δὲ σοῦ δυσαποκρίτως αὐτὰς ἔχειν, ᾠήθην δεῖν πεῖραν ποιήσασθαι τῆς ἀντιγραφῆς καὶ πορίσασθαι λόγους, οἵους εἰκὸς ἦν ἕκαστον ἀποκρίνασθαι τῶν ἐπεσταλκότων. [5] ἦν δὲ δυσεύρετος ἡ ἐπιβολὴ κατ᾽ ἄγνοιαν τῆς τότε περὶ τὰς πόλεις τύχης τε καὶ γνώμης· [6] οὐ μὴν ταύτῃ γε ἀνῆκα τὴν ὁρμήν, ἀλλὰ τὰ μὲν ἐξ ἱστοριῶν ἐπιλεξάμενος, τὰ δὲ ταῖς δευτέραις καὶ τρίταις ἐπιστολαῖς ὑποσημαίνεσθαι περὶ τῶν προτέρων συνεὶς οὐχ ἥκιστα παρέζευξα καὶ τὸν ἐξ ἐπινοίας κατάλογον. [7] φύσει δέ πως δυσχερὲς ἀποβαίνει τὸ εἰς ἀλλοτρίαν συνδραμεῖν εὐστοχίαν, ὁπότε καὶ ἰδίαν χαλεπὸν ἀναλογῆσαι. [8] ὁ γοῦν Βροῦτος μυρίας ὡς εἰκὸς ἄνδρα πολλοῖς ἔθνεσι πολεμοῦντα διαπρεσβευσάμενος ἐπιστολάς, εἴτε ἰδίας εἴτε τινὸς τῶν εἰς ταῦτα μισθοῦ δοκίμων, μόνας ἐξέδωκε τὰς εὐφόρως γραφείσας διὰ τὸ ἀρκέσαι ταῖς ὀλίγαις μόλις τὴν διόρθωσιν. [9] ὁπότε οὖν ἐκεῖνος ἠσθένησεν ἑαυτὸν ἐν πᾶσι μιμήσασθαι, πῶς οἷόν τε ἡμᾶς ἑτέρῳ ἐξομοιωθῆναι καὶ τῇ κατὰ σφᾶς ὁμοτονῆσαι προθέσει; [10] ἀλλά πως γλυκὺ πάθος ἐλπίς, οὐ τῇ ἐπιτυχίᾳ δελεάζουσα μόνον, κολακεύουσα δὲ καὶ τὸ ἀπότευγμα, δι᾽ ἣν οὐδενὸς ἄλλου λείπεσθαι δικαιῶ μάλιστά σοι χαριεῖσθαι. [11] ἐπεὶ κἀκεῖνό με οὐ λέληθεν, ὅτι ὁ μὲν πολλοῖς ἀνδράσι καὶ δήμοις γράφων εἰκότως ἑνὸς ἐξείχετο χαρακτῆρος, ὁ δὲ[8] ὑπὲρ πολλῶν διαλεγόμενος, ἐὰν μὲν ἀλλάσσῃ τὸν τύπον, ἀποπεπλανῆσθαι δόξει τοῦ σκοποῦ, τῇ δὲ αὐτῇ προσέχων ἰδέᾳ καὶ ἀπίθανος φανήσεται καὶ ἕωλος. [12] ἔτι πρὸς τούτοις ἐνθυμητέον, ὡς ἡγεμόνος μὲν ἴδιον οἴονταί τινες τὰ γέμοντα ὑπεροψίας ἐπιστέλλειν τοῖς ὑπηκόοις, ἡμῖν δ᾽ ἡ αὐθάδης ἀντιγραφὴ κατάγνωσιν ὡς ἠλιθίοις φέρει, τὸ δὲ ταπεινὸν οὐκέτ᾽ ἀναλογεῖ πρὸς τὴν ὁμοίαν ἀπόκρισιν. [13] ὅμως δ᾽ οὖν τὰ δυσχερῆ καίπερ τοσαῦτα ὄντα προεκλογισάμενος οὐδὲν ἧττον ὑπέστην τὸ ἔργον, βραχὺ μὲν ἐμαυτῷ γύμνασμα συντάξας, σοὶ δὲ οὐ μέγα κτῆμα, ἀλλὰ τοῖς πολλοῖς τάχα καὶ εὐκαταφρόνητον· [14] φιλεῖ γὰρ τὰ πρὸ τῆς πείρας θαυμαστὰ μετὰ τὴν ἐκ τοῦ συντελέσματος γνῶσιν ῥᾴδια εἶναι παραθεωρεῖσθαι.

---

[6] Text per Torraca 5–6. I have numbered each of the sentences for ease of reference. I intend my annotations to supplement those of Torraca (73–9), whose commentary includes rich citation of ancient rhetorical theory. One should note that a block of 13 MSS (out of 33) of the Brutan corpus omits the *Letter* altogether, including one of the two earliest, Ambrosianus 81 (x CE; the other that has it is Heidelbergensis Palatinus gr. 398, x CE), although all include Mithridates' responses on behalf of the cities. The MSS also display considerable instability in the sequence of letters; see the data at Torraca xlvii–xlviii.

[7] *EG:* βασιλεύς, following four xiv–xv century MSS (Torraca 5); evidently the other extant copies of the *Letter* read βασιλεῖ, including one xvi century MS that moves it after Μιθριδάτῃ.

[8] Instead of ὅτι ὁ μὲν ... ὁ δὲ ... *EG* has ὅτι ὃ μὲν ... ὃ δὲ ... See n. 41 below.

Mithridates[9] to [my] cousin[10] the king Mithridates, greetings.[11]

---

[9] Μιθριδάτης. "The personal name Μιθραδάτης is Persian—coins ... attest to the original spelling. Inscriptions ... sporadically give Μιθριδάτης, even contemporary ones ..., which is the form found in most later documents ... and manuscripts" (*BNP* 9:77–8, s.v. "Mithridates"). Throughout this study I refer to the author as "Mithridates" with no commitment to the factuality of the name; see the discussion of authorship below.

[10] ἀνεψιῷ. LSJ renders ἀνεψιός as "first cousin" (137, s.v.; also BDAG 78, s.v.; *EG, consobrinus*; É. des Places, review of Torraca, *L'Antiquité classique* 30 [1961]: 225–26), although most scholars take it here to mean "nephew" (Smith, "Greek Letters" [see n. 3], 194; Cichorius, "Die griechischen Brutusbriefe" [see n. 3], 434; Speyer, *Die literarische Fälschung* [see n. 4], 138; Torraca 53; cf. Rühl, "Die griechischen Briefe" [see n. 3], 317: "Vetter oder Neffen"; see n. 68 below). The text later portrays the addressee as younger, in need of instruction, and the object of the author's paternalistic indulgence. The didactic nature of the *Letter* (and of the collection as well) thereby comes into focus, paralleling instructional literature of various kinds from the ancient Near East and the Greco-Roman world. Such literature often presupposes a father-son relationship. Cf., e.g., M. Lichtheim, *Ancient Egyptian Literature* (3 vols.; Berkeley, Calif.: University of California Press, 1973–80), 1:58, 136; Prov 2:1 (בני, υἱέ), Sirach prol. 5 (ὁ πάππος μου Ἰησοῦς); 1 Tim 1:2 (Τιμοθέῳ γνησίῳ τέκνῳ ἐν πίστει); 2 Tim 1:2 (Τιμοθέῳ ἀγαπητῷ τέκνῳ); Titus 1:4 (Τίτῳ γνησίῳ τέκνῳ κατὰ κοινὴν πίστιν); *C.H.* IV (Hermes to Tat, n.b. 3, ὦ πάτερ ... ὦ τέκνον) and V (Hermes to Tat his son); PGM IV.478/9 (χρὴ οὖν σε, ὦ θύγατερ, λαμβάνειν etc., and see the comments by H. D. Betz, *The "Mithras Liturgy"* [STAC 18; Tübingen: Mohr Siebeck, 2003], 96–7). Note especially Cicero's *De partitione oratoria*, a dialogue between the author and his son on rhetorical matters, and cf. the cover letters of didactic texts like *Rhetorica ad Alexandrum* (1420a–21b, a forgery), Quintilian's *Institutio Oratoria* (a letter *Tryphoni suo*, his publisher) and Epictetus' *Dissertationes* (Ἀρριανὸς Λουκίῳ Γελλίῳ).

[11] Μιθριδάτης ... χαίρειν. Unlike many of the literary letters that frequently have only the recipient's name in the dative, the text has the full formula that one commonly finds in the documentary papyri. Epistolary prescripts in these letters tend toward simplicity, e.g., *LAL* §3 (iii BCE, Καλλικλῆς Ἁρμούθηι χαίρειν), §23 (iii BCE, Ζήνων Κρότωι χαίρειν), cf. [Libanius], *Epistulares characteres* 51, *AET* 44, ὁ δεῖνα τῷ δεῖνι χαίρειν), but they sometimes also include details about the relationship between the author and the recipient, e.g., §35 (ii BCE, Διονύσιος Ἡφαιστίωνι τῶι ἀδελφῶι χαίρειν), §40 (ii BCE, Σαραπίων Πτολεμαίωι καὶ Ἀπολλωνίῳ τοῖς ἀδελφοῖς χαίρειν), §§41–42 (ii BCE, Ἀπολλώνιος Πτολεμαίωι τῷ πατρὶ χαίρειν), §67 (i BCE, Διογέν[η]ς Διονυσίωι τῶι ἀδελφῶι πλεῖστα χα(ίρειν) καὶ ὑγιαίνειν, and note the other familial terms in this letter). In more official contexts the use of titles and other appellatives naturally increases, as in §88 (i CE, Τιβέριος Κλαύδιος Καῖσαρ Σεβαστὸς Γερμανικὸς Αὐτοκράτωρ ἀρχ<ι>ιερεὺς μέγιστος δημαρχικῆς ἐξουσίας ὕπατος ἀποδεδιγμένος Ἀλεξανδρέων τῇ πόλει χαίρειν); cf. the prescripts of Paul's authentic letters. Similar situations occasionally pertain in the case of prescripts of the literary letters, when they have them, e.g., Hippocrates, *ep.* 1 (βασιλεὺς βασιλέων μέγας Ἀρταξέρξης Παίτῳ χαίρειν, *EG* 289), and 13 (Ἱπποκράτης Διονυσίῳ χαίρειν, *EG* 294). In the Brutan collection, each letter specifies the author and addressee, but omits χαίρειν. If these letters are authentic, the headings are surely not the original prescripts, but are instead aids for the reader to keep track of which letter is whose. Such appears to be the conventional method in collections which have multiple (putative) authors, as in the imaginative letters

[1] I have often admired[12] the letters of Brutus, not only on account of [their] forcefulness and conciseness,[13]

---

of Aelian and Alciphron, samples of which C. D. N. Costa helpfully collects, translates and comments upon in his *Greek Fictional Letters* (Oxford: Oxford University Press, 2001).

[12] ἐθαύμασα πολλάκις. This phrase or something like it occurs at a couple of points in the introductory formulas of passages by authors that were later singled out as stylistically exemplary, e.g., Xenophon, *Mem.* 1.1.1, πολλάκις ἐθαύμασα, τίσι ποτὲ λόγοις Ἀθηναίους ἔπεισαν οἱ γραψάμενοι Σωκράτη ὡς ἄξιος εἴη θανάτου τῇ πόλει; Isocrates, *Paneg.* 1, πολλάκις ἐθαύμασα τῶν τὰς πανηγύρεις συναγαγόντων καὶ τοὺς γυμνικοὺς ἀγῶνας καταστησάντων, ὅτι etc. See also [Aelius Aristides], *Ars rhetorica* 2.21 (per Patillon's edition; per Spengel/Hammer, 2.2.11, *RG* 2.519) and 2.36 (2.3.5, *RG* 2.525) on Xenophon; Aristotle, *Rhet.* 3.9.7, 1409b on Isocrates (illustrating περιόδος); Alexander Rhetor, *De figuris* 2.1 (*RG* 3.28, illustrating περιόδος), ibid. 2.17 (*RG* 3.35, illustrating ζεῦγμα) both on Isocrates, and cf. Epictetus, *Diatr.* 3.23.30 and Gal 1:6.

[13] δεινότητος καὶ συντομίας χάριν. Epistolary theorists often identify brevity, at the levels of both content and style, as a necessity, e.g., Demetrius, *Eloc.* 228 (τὸ δὲ μέγεθος συνεστάλθω τῆς ἐπιστολῆς, ὥσπερ καὶ ἡ λέξις); Philostratus, *De epistulis* lines 14–19 (*AET* 42–43); Julius Victor (iv CE), *Ars rhetorica* 27 (*AET* 62–63). Rhetorical theorists perceive it as a primary "virtue" or "excellence" (ἀρετή) for style in general—so the Stoics (Diogenes Laertius 7.59), Philodemus (see R. N. Gaines, "Qualities of Rhetorical Expression in Philodemus," *TAPA* 112 [1982]: 71–81), and Dionysius of Halicarnassus (*Thuc.* 22–23, *Pomp.* 3, *Lys.* 4, *Is.* 3, and cf. *Dem.* 58). Brevity also befits the style of the διήγησις (narrative) ([Aristotle], *Rhet. Alex.* 1438a; Cicero, *Part. or.* 31–32; [Cicero], *Rhet. Her.* 1.8.14; Quintilian, *Inst.* 4.2.31–33; Theon of Alexandria, *Progymnasmata* 4, *RG* 2.79; Aphthonius, *Progymnasmata* 2, *RG* 2.22; and many others). On brevity as a proper feature of epistolary style, Artemon, the editor of Aristotle's correspondence, observes that ἐν δὲ ταῖς ἐπιστολαῖς φαίνεται κατωρθωκὼς τὸν ἐπιστολιμαῖον χαρακτῆρα, ὃν καὶ σύντομον εἶναι δεῖ καὶ σαφῆ καὶ ἀπηλλαγμένον πάσης περισκελοῦς συνδέσεώς τε καὶ φράσεως (V. Rose, ed., *Aristotelis qui ferebantur librorum fragmenta* [Leipzig: Teubner, 1886], 411). Demetrius closely associates brevity and forcefulness at *Eloc.* 7: the former enables the latter because of a formal similarity to the abrupt manner that one uses to address a slave (τῶν δὲ μικρῶν κώλων κἂν δεινότητι χρῆσίς ἐστι· δεινότερον γὰρ τὸ ἐν ὀλίγῳ πολὺ ἐμφαινόμενον καὶ σφοδρότερον, διὸ καὶ οἱ Λάκωνες βραχυλόγοι ὑπὸ δεινότητος· καὶ τὸ μὲν ἐπιτάσσειν σύντομον καὶ βραχύ, καὶ πᾶς δεσπότης δούλῳ μονοσύλλαβος, τὸ δὲ ἱκετεύειν μακρὸν καὶ τὸ ὀδύρεσθαι). (See also *Eloc.* 8–9, 137, 241–243 on συντομία, βραχύτης, βραχυλογία; cf. Plutarch, *Phoc.* 5.2–3 and the literature cited by Torraca at 74.) Demetrius' observation explains the rest of Mithridates' expression of admiration: Brutus' style powerfully conveys his ἦθος as an authoritative figure. The imprint of one's letters with one's own character comes up occasionally in discussions about epistolary style as well, e.g., Philostratus on Marcus Aurelius (τὸ ἑδραῖον τοῦ ἤθους ἐντετύπωτο τοῖς γράμμασι), but also much earlier: Seneca, *Ep.* 40.1 (*AET* 28, *nam quo uno modo potes, te mihi ostendis*), and Demetrius, *Eloc.* 227 (σχεδὸν γὰρ εἰκόνα τῆς ἑαυτοῦ ψυχῆς γράφει τὴν ἐπιστολήν). I discuss rhetorical and epistolary theory on brevity in much greater detail in my dissertation, "Paul's Definitions of the Gospel in Romans 1," ch. 3, "The Ancient Rhetorical Theorists on Brevity" (University of Chicago, in progress).

but also for possessing the style[14] of a leader's mind.[15] [2] For they seem to make use of nothing elegant[16] unless it might adhere[17] to greatness of soul.[18] [3] Now what I think about such texts[19] I do not deem worth disputing in this context.[20] [4] But since you de-

---

[14] χαρακτῆρα. This term eventually comes to mean "style," probably in extension of its meanings "imprint" or "stamp" (LSJ 1977, s.v.). Earlier authors, for example Aristotle in his *Rhetorica* and the author of the *Rhetorica ad Alexandrum*, prefer λέξις; χαρακτήρ may not have yet acquired this meaning when these treatises appeared, although Diogenes Laertius (6.15) indicates that Antisthenes (v–iv BCE) wrote a study called περὶ λέξεως ἢ περὶ χαρακτήρων. Dionysius often qualifies χαρακτήρ with a genitive, λέξεως (e.g., *Lys.* 11, *Isocr.* 20) or λόγων (e.g., *Lys.* 1), meaning something like "type" (cf. n. 42 re ἰδέα). In later theoretical literature, χαρακτήρ as "stylistic type" slides into virtual equivalence with other terms referring to style or diction, λέξις, ἑρμηνεία, and φράσις. The present sentence could certainly tolerate the rendering "... as having the *impression* of a leader's mind." While the context makes it sufficiently clear that Brutus' style is what Mithridates has in mind, he probably selects χαρακτήρ for its potential to mean both. Cf. 11 below, where χαρακτήρ reappears.

[15] ἡγεμονικοῦ φρονήματος. ἡγεμών can refer simply to a leader or military commander, but Greek authors also use the word to translate *princeps*, i.e., the Emperor, or as a label for Roman regional governors (LSJ 763, s.v. ἡγεμών and ἡγεμονικός; BDAG 433, s.v. ἡγεμών 2 for further literature). Cf. 12, ἡγεμόνος ἴδιον τὰ γέμοντα ὑπεροψίας ἐπιστέλλειν. The way the sentence runs, the author appears first to identify the basis upon which people generally admire Brutus' letters ("not only" συντομία καὶ δεινότης), but he wishes to add another to their list of virtues ("but also" ὁ ἡγεμονικοῦ φρονήματος χαρακτήρ), supported by the following sentence (γάρ).

[16] ἐοίκασι ... καλόν. Or, "they seem to regard nothing as elegant"; cf. *EG: nihil enim honestum putare videntur*.

[17] ἔχοιτο. The change of subjects of the main verbs between the first and second clauses evidently prompted some scribes to correct ἔχοιτο to the plural ἔχοιντο (Torraca 5). ἔχοιτο can be middle or passive; I opt for the former, with αὐτό as understood from οὐδέν in the previous clause. For ἔχεσθαι τινός meaning "to cling to," see LSJ, s.v., C.2, and cf. the usage of ἐξέχεσθαι in 11.

[18] μεγαλοψυχίας, "greatness of soul," may convey a positive quality ("magnanimity") or a negative one ("arrogance"). Aristotle defines it thus (*Rhet.* 1.9.11, 1366b): μεγαλοψυχία δὲ μεγάλων ποιητικὴ εὐεργημάτων; and the Stoics, according to Diogenes Laertius (7.93, placing it as a secondary virtue) thus: τὴν δὲ μεγαλοψυχίαν ἐπιστήμην ἢ ἕξιν ὑπεράνω ποιοῦσαν τῶν συμβαινόντων κοινῇ φαύλων τε καὶ σπουδαίων. The context of 3 lends the word significant ambiguity. On the one hand, Mithridates is praising Brutus δεινότητος καὶ συντομίας χάριν; on the other hand, a ἡγεμονικὸν φρόνημα might come across as high-handed and harsh, as the author admits in 12. As with χαρακτήρ, the author again deliberately selects a word that yields plural senses in its context.

[19] λόγοι. I interpret λόγοι as referring to the individual letters (note αὐτάς in 4), hence "texts" (LSJ 1059, s.v. VI.3.e). λόγοι could also mean Mithridates' laudatory remarks in 2.

[20] ἐγὼ ... διαμφισβητεῖν. The author temporarily sets aside his assessment of Brutus' style (μέν) in order to introduce his rationale for expanding the corpus with his own compositions (δέ, 4). Depending on how strongly one takes διαμφισβητεῖν, some debate may have existed about the stylistic merits of Brutus' letters, or even that the author and

clare them to be hard to answer,[21] I supposed that I must make an attempt at response,[22] and furnish texts of a sort as was probable for each of those who had written letters [back to Brutus] to have said in reply. [5] But the [proper] approach was difficult to find because of [my] ignorance of both the fortune and opinion around the cities at that time.[23] [6] At this point[24] I surely did not neglect the impulse, but by reading over materials from the histories,[25]

---

his addressee previously disagreed about this (see 4). The testimonia speak of Brutus' Greek letters as praiseworthy with no intimation that such assessments present any controversy.

[21] ἀποφαίνοντος ... ἔχειν. Mithridates confirms that both he and his addressee possess copies of an older version of the corpus. One may only guess at the reason why the addressee would have complained of their answerability. Perhaps he is saying that he finds their style objectionable, or that they are so severe, even devastating, that he cannot imagine how the cities managed to find the words for their replies. Or maybe someone, possibly the author as his instructor, set him the task of crafting responses as an exercise in προσωποποιία. If this were the case, however, Mithridates would in effect be conceding that he assigned a project so far beyond his student's capabilities that he had considerable trouble achieving it himself. One may thus reasonably surmise that criticism of Brutus from the younger Mithridates prompts the elder to take on a self-imposed challenge to his own abilities in research and rhetoric.

[22] On ἀντιγραφή as an epistolary reply, see LSJ 154 s.v., also *Let. Aris.* 51 (καὶ τὰ μὲν πρὸς τὴν τοῦ βασιλέως ἐπιστολὴν τοιαύτης ἐντύγχανεν ἀντιγραφῆς ὑπὸ τῶν περὶ τὸν Ἐλεάζαρον); Athenaeus, *Deipn.* 14.40 (Kraibel) (Ἀπολλόδωρος δ' ἐν τῇ πρὸς τὴν Ἀριστοκλέους Ἐπιστολὴν Ἀντιγραφῇ «ὃ νῦν», φησίν, «ἡμεῖς λέγομεν ψαλτήριον, τοῦτ' εἶναι μάγαδιν»). Cf. Arrian, *Anab.* 2.14.4 (πρὸς ταῦτα ἀντιγράφει Ἀλέξανδρος ... παραγγείλας τὴν ἐπιστολὴν δοῦναι Δαρείῳ); Origen, *frg. 1 Cor.* 33 (line 14) (ἔγραψαν οὖν περὶ τούτου ἐπιστολὴν οἱ ἐν Κορίνθῳ τῷ ἀποστόλῳ, καὶ πρὸς τὴν ἐπιστολὴν ταύτην ἀντιγράφει ὁ ἀπόστολος τὰ προγεγραμμένα, text per C. Jenkins, "Origen on 1 Corinthians III," *JTS* 9 [1908]: 500–14 [500]).

[23] ἦν ... γνώμης. Mithridates' remarks imply that the letters' historical value may not have been the primary stimulus for their preservation, and he may further imply that they do not supply sufficient historical detail even for their interpretation. The ignorance that he confesses confirms some remoteness in time from the events in question (τότε), enough at least for the histories referred to in 6 to have appeared. If he were living in Asia Minor within a few decades of Brutus' activities there (in other words, if he were a relative or near descendant of Mithradates VI of Pontus), one may suppose that memories of Brutus' actions and public opinion about them would have been fresh enough to deserve mention in his list of sources (cf. the αὐτόπται at Luke 1:2).

[24] On the usage of ταύτῃ in this manner, see LSJ 1276, s.v. οὗτος, C.III.4.a–b; ταύτῃ could also refer back to ἄγνοιαν in the previous sentence.

[25] ἐξ ἱστοριῶν. Mithridates does not specify which histories he uses (on ἐπιλέγεσθαι meaning "to read," see LSJ 643, s.v., III.2); those who doubt the authenticity of Brutus' letters on account of disagreements between them and the extant histories (e.g., Smith, "Greek Letters" [see n. 3], 198–201) need to reckon with the likelihood that Mithridates has some which are no longer available, and that he may have edited the letters' headings to conform with his findings. We simply cannot determine the extent of his editorial work without having access to a previous recension or whatever histories consulted by him that are no longer extant. Cf. the remarks of K. Meister (*BNP* 6:419, s.v. "Histo-

and above all by bringing together[26] things in the second and third letters in order to make observations about the earlier ones, I too welded together an account from [my] ingenuity.[27] [7] But, naturally, how difficult it turns out [to be] to contend with another person's skill when it is hard even to keep up one's own![28] [8] Now Brutus, although he dispatched[29] countless letters (as is reasonable for a man who wages war against many

---

riography" II.C): "While the progress of historiography in the classical period is easily comprehensible and limited to a few authors, its development in the Hellenistic period is complicated and confusing. According to Dionysius of Halicarnassus (Comp. 4.30), an entire day would not suffice to list all of the authors. In fact, the spectrum of historiography is characterized by an enormous wealth of production, variety of topics, and breadth of presentation." See also A. Dihle, *A History of Greek Literature from Homer to the Hellenistic Period* (trans. C. Krojzl; London/New York: Routledge, 1994), 289–303; W. R. Connor, "Historical Writing in the Fourth Century B.C. and in the Hellenistic Period," in *The Cambridge History of Greek Literature, I. Greek Literature* (eds. P. E. Easterling and B. M. W. Knox; Cambridge: Cambridge University Press, 1985), 458–71.

[26] συνείς. The verb συνιέναι in this context offers several possible renderings (see LSJ 1718, s.v.). "To bring together" captures the idea of collecting items of information from the available sources for the purpose of making observations (ὑποσημαίνεσθαι). It can also mean "to take notice of" and "to understand," here with the sense of "to infer."

[27] οὐ μὴν ... κατάλογον. After declaring that he would not be deterred from his task, Mithridates describes his process of historical induction, i.e., the correlation of information gleaned from the histories with that given by the letters themselves in order to fill lacunae in the overall narrative, and from his surmises to take up the *personae* of the cities' letter-writers. References to similar historiographic methods for the composition of speeches appear at a couple of points in the ancient sources, particularly the famous passage of Thucydides (1.21.1–4), often cited in connection with the speeches in Acts. Note also Lucian, *Historia conscribenda* 58: ἢν δέ ποτε καὶ λόγους ἐροῦντά τινα δεήσῃ εἰσάγειν, μάλιστα μὲν ἐοικότα τῷ προσώπῳ καὶ τῷ πράγματι οἰκεῖα λεγέσθω, ἔπειτα ὡς σαφέστατα καὶ ταῦτα. πλὴν ἐφεῖταί σοι τότε καὶ ῥητορεῦσαι καὶ ἐπιδεῖξαι τὴν τῶν λόγων δεινότητα. See further H. J. Cadbury, *The Making of Luke-Acts* (New York: Macmillan, 1927), 184–93; M. Dibelius, "The Speeches in Acts and Ancient Historiography," in idem, *Studies in the Acts of the Apostles* (ed. H. Greeven; trans. M. Ling; London: SCM, 1956), 138–85; S. E. Porter, "Thucydides 1.22.1 and Speeches in Acts: Is There a Thucydidean View?" *NovT* 32 (1990): 121–42 with more bibliography.

[28] φύσει ... ἀναλογῆσαι. τὸ συνδραμεῖν, functioning here as the subject of the main verb ἀποβαίνει, can mean "to run together" (i.e., to commingle), "to encounter" in both hostile and friendly senses, "to agree" or "to concur," and "to race" (LSJ 1728, s.v. συντρέχειν). Mithridates seems to be making a transition from difficulties presented by insufficient data to problems inherent in matching the stylistically superior talents (εὐστοχία) of a literary master. He wants his contributions to the corpus to attain the same level, but he candidly admits that he most likely failed (ὁπότε καὶ ἰδίαν ἀναλογῆσαι, for ἀναλογεῖν meaning "to keep up" see LSJ 111, s.v.; note also 10, ἐλπὶς κολακεύουσα τὸ ἀπότευγμα). Therefore the rendering "to contend with" (cf. Torraca 53, "gareggiare") seems most appropriate for τὸ συνδραμεῖν in this context.

[29] διαπρεσβευσάμενος, "to send emissaries." In effect Mithridates is classifying Brutus' correspondence as diplomatic letters, carried by envoys who read and interpreted them for their addressees. Regarding ancient diplomatic correspondence, see C. B. Wel-

nations)—whether by his own hand or by one of those approved for hire for these matters[30]—published[31] only those which were written easily,[32] because [his] correction[33] was scarcely adequate for [just those] few.[34] [9] Therefore when that man was unable to imi-

---

les, *Royal Correspondence in the Hellenistic Period: A Study in Greek Epigraphy* (New Haven, Conn.: Yale University Press, 1934); Stirewalt, *Studies* (see n. 1), 6–10; M. M. Mitchell, "New Testament Envoys in the Context of Greco-Roman Diplomatic and Epistolary Conventions: The Example of Timothy and Titus," *JBL* 111 (1992): 641–62; Klauck, *Ancient Letters* (see n. 3), 77–82.

[30] εἴτε ... δοκίμων. Mithridates concedes that a Roman military governor at a time of war may not have had the time or inclination to compose his own letters. Brutus could in fact be accruing the credit for the extraordinary work of his secretary. This remark coordinates with Philostratus' similar statement, στρατηγῶν δὲ Βροῦτος ἢ ὅτῳ βροῦτος ἐς τὸ ἐπιστέλλειν ἐχρῆτο (see below), in a manner which helps to determine the date of the *Letter*. Although the diction between these two passages diverge, the idea is close enough to suppose that Philostratus has read the collection in its present form *with its cover letter*, setting a possible *terminus ante quem* of the third century CE for Mithridates' republication of the corpus.

[31] ἐξέδωκε. For other instances of ἐκδιδόναι meaning "to publish," see Aristotle, *Poet.* 15, 1454b (εἴρηται δὲ περὶ αὐτῶν ἐν τοῖς ἐκδεδομένοις λόγοις ἱκανῶς); Diogenes Laertius 2.11 (πρῶτος δὲ Ἀναξαγόρας καὶ βιβλίον ἐξέδωκε συγγραφῆς); Irenaeus, *Haer.* 3.1.1 (ἔπειτα Ἰωάννης, ὁ μαθητὴς τοῦ Κυρίου, ὁ καὶ ἐπὶ τὸ στῆθος αὐτοῦ ἀναπεσών, καὶ αὐτὸς ἐξέδωκεν τὸ εὐαγγέλιον, ἐν Ἐφέσῳ τῆς Ἀσίας διατρίβων); cf. Acts 15:30 (οἱ μὲν οὖν ἀπολυθέντες κατῆλθον εἰς Ἀντιόχειαν, καὶ συναγαγόντες τὸ πλῆθος ἐπέδωκαν τὴν ἐπιστολήν). Mithridates assumes, or has information, that Brutus released his own letters. Given that he was having a busy couple of years between 44 and his death in 42, it may seem incredible that he would take the time to edit and release even a few of his letters (see, e.g., Smith, "Greek Letters" [see n. 3], 195). One must not, however, discount the determination of a person with literary pretensions. His contemporary Cicero prepared many works for publication while maintaining a full calendar of litigation and politics. Brutus' knowledge of the risks to his own life involved with his final campaigns may have moved literary ambitions up his list of priorities.

[32] εὐφόρως means "easily" (LSJ 737, s.v. εὔφορος 5); Mithridates seems to be talking about letters that require little editorial attention. Torraca (53) translates "scritte con spontanea immediatezza" ("written with spontaneous immediacy").

[33] διόρθωσιν. Torraca (76) points out that this is a technical term of Alexandrian philology.

[34] ὁ γοῦν Βροῦτος ... διόρθωσιν. The basic idea is ὁ γοῦν Βροῦτος ἐξέδωκεν μόνας τὰς εὐφόρως γραφείσας, "Now Brutus published only those [letters] which were written easily." A concessive participial phrase, μυρίας διαπρεσβευσάμενος ἐπιστολάς, "although he dispatched countless letters," agrees with ὁ βροῦτος. Buried within this phrase is ὡς εἰκὸς ἄνδρα πολλοῖς ἔθνεσι πολεμοῦντα. Finally we have διὰ τὸ ἀρκέσαι ταῖς ὀλίγαις μόλις τὴν διόρθωσιν. The subject of the infinitive could be τὴν διόρθωσιν, "because the correction was scarcely enough for a few"; or it could be Βροῦτος, yielding "he barely achieved correction for a few." The net result of either option for the overall meaning of the sentence is essentially the same: Brutus only managed to prepare a few letters for publication.

tate himself in every detail [as he edited his archive],[35] how is it possible for us both to take on the likeness of another[36] and to sing in harmony[37] with our own[38] intention? [10] But how sweet an emotion is hope that not only entices success but soothes failure;[39] because of it I claim my right to fall short of nobody else in order to indulge you most.[40]

---

[35] ὁπότε ... μιμήσασθαι. Mithridates seems to describe Brutus' editorial process as one of ἑαυτὸν μιμήσασθαι, a peculiar notion to say the least. I suppose him to mean that Brutus, in his "corrections," would need to put himself back into the moments that prompted each item and adjust the style and content for a wider readership while consistently maintaining his own authorial voice. The amount of work involved with such a project supposedly prevented him from issuing a more comprehensive collection. Cf. Torraca 53, "se già quegli non riusci ad essere sempre uguale a se stesso" ("if already he did not succeed at always being equal to himself").

[36] ἑτέρῳ (coordinating with ἐκεῖνος in the previous clause) most likely refers to someone other than Brutus, indicating a return to the subject of the difficulty of composing responses.

[37] ὁμοτονῆσαι. According to LSJ (1228, s.v.), this word means "to have the same pitch" or "accent with" (τινί). It and the related adjective ὁμότονος appear often in ancient grammatical texts that discuss accents, e.g., Athenaeus, Deipn. 9.62 (Kraibel): δεῖ δὲ ὀξυτονεῖν τὴν λέξιν, ἐπειδὴ τὰ εἰς ΟΣ λήγοντα τῶν ὀνομάτων ὁμότονα ἐστι, κἂν μεταλημφθῇ εἰς τὸ Ω παρ' Ἀττικοῖς· ναὸς νεώς, κάλος κάλως. Obviously Mithridates is using ὁμοτονεῖν metaphorically. Whereas Brutus has only his own style to contend with in editing his letters, Mithridates must both (τε) conform to someone else's style and (καί) to his own πρόθεσις: it is like trying to sing two songs at the same time. Origen deploys the term in a musical metaphor to explain one of the kinds of εἰρηνοποιός who receive a blessing in Matt 5:9 (Comm. Matt. frg. 3): the one παριστὰς τὴν συμφωνίαν καὶ τὴν εἰρήνην τούτων, i.e., of apparent discrepancies in the scriptures. Such a person ἀποτελέσει φθόγγον μουσικῆς θεοῦ, ἀπὸ ταύτης μαθὼν ἐν καιρῷ κρούειν χορδὰς νῦν μὲν νομικάς, νῦν δὲ συμφώνως αὐταῖς εὐαγγελικάς, καὶ νυνὶ μὲν προφητικάς, ὅτε δὲ τὸ εὔλογον ἀπαιτεῖ, τὰς ὁμοτονούσας ἀποστολικὰς αὐταῖς, οὕτω δὲ καὶ ἀποστολικὰς εὐαγγελικαῖς.

[38] σφᾶς. σφεῖς is normally third person plural, but it can also be first person plural (LSJ 1739–40, s.v. B.IV) as seems to be the case here; so also EG: propositum nostrum prorsus assequamur. It could also refer back to ἑτέρῳ, with the implication that the second clause restates the first: "to take on the likeness of another, and to sing in tune with their own intention." The apparent change in number from singular (ἑτέρῳ) to plural (κατὰ σφᾶς; cf. ἡμᾶς earlier in the sentence, and ἡμῖν in 12) leads me to think that a change in person occurs as well, although LSJ (s.v. B.II) mentions that the dative and accusative forms σφι(ν) and σφε can mean "him" or "her."

[39] ἀλλὰ πως γλυκὺ ... ἀπότευγμα. Mithridates reiterates what he says above in 6, οὐ μὴν ταύτῃ γε ἀνῆκα τὴν ὁρμήν, with a concisely expressed sentiment in a form not unlike a maxim of his own composition (note the author's characteristic πως). Cf. on 14 below.

[40] δι' ἣν ... χαριεῖσθαι. Affection for his addressee plays no small role in motivating Mithridates toward the completion of his task. χαριεῖσθαι, a future infinitive of purpose, generally supports the premise that his addressee is younger and the object of his paternalistic indulgence, while δικαιῶ indicates that such indulgence is his privilege to claim.

[11] And yet it has not escaped my attention that the one[41] who was writing to many men and districts suitably adhered to one style, but someone else arguing on behalf of others, if he varies the type [of style], will seem to have strayed from his aim; but by cleaving to the same form [of style] he will appear both unpersuasive and stale.[42] [12] One must still consider in addition to these points that some suppose the distinguishing mark of a leader to be to send letters full of contempt to [his] subordinates;[43] but in our view the rash response [to such missives] brings [with it] the contempt due to fools, but humility is no longer proportionate[44]

---

[41] ὁ μὲν ... ὁ δὲ ... Torraca is probably correct in his accenting of the omicrons, taking them as definite articles with the participles γράφων and διαλεγόμενος instead of relative pronouns, ὃ μὲν ... ὃ δὲ ..., as *EG* has them.

[42] ἐπεὶ κἀκεῖνο ... ἕωλος. Mithridates now returns to the topic of style with which the *Letter* began. He addresses Brutus' authorial voice (ὁ μέν) as opposed to any one of those persons (ὁ δέ) who take on the responsibility of responding to the missives on behalf of his city, and whom Mithridates sets out to imitate in his reconstructions. ἰδέα eventually comes to mean "stylistic type," most famously in Hermogenes' περὶ ἰδεῶν λόγου (see the introduction of C. W. Wooten, trans., *Hermogenes' On Types of Style* [Chapel Hill, N.C.: University of North Carolina Press, 1987]; D. A. Russell, *Criticism in Antiquity* [2d ed.; London: Bristol Classical Press, 1995], 139–43; G. A. Kennedy, *A New History of Classical Rhetoric* [Princeton, N.J.: Princeton University Press, 1994], 208–17 [215–17]), and such seems to be its valence here. That τόπος and ἰδέα have more or less equivalent meanings in this context is indicated by αὐτῇ, "the *same* form [of style]." Ultimately Mithridates is speaking to the problems that confront *him* as he adopts the χαρακτήρ of Brutus' respondents: if on the one hand he mixes it up to reflect the diversity of individual *personae* writing for the cities, he sacrifices a level of consistency in these various responses that matches Brutus' consistent *persona* and thereby "wanders off" from his aim (ἀποπεπλανῆσθαι δόξει τοῦ σκοποῦ) of creating letters that have parity of skill with Brutus' (7). If on the other hand he adheres too closely to the same type of style (τῇ αὐτῇ προσέχων ἰδέᾳ) throughout, he risks flattening everyone into the same mold, hence appearing "unpersuasive and stale" (ἀπίθανος καὶ ἕωλος). A similar problem no doubt confronted ancient historians in the composition of their characters' speeches.

[43] τὰ γέμοντα ... ὑπηκόοις. The brevity and severity of Brutus' letters may seem unlikely as characteristics of real communications between him and the cities. Rawson ("Cassius and Brutus" [see n. 3], 107), e.g., writes: "One needs only to look at the various epistles that survive on stone from Roman generals to Greek cities ... to see how implausible the exaggeratedly brief, unremittingly gnomic and antithetic notes attributed to Brutus are ..." The curt tone and compressed content may not, however, be too unusual in the letters sent from superiors to their inferiors giving orders or demanding explanations of failures, e.g., the ὑπόμνημα preserved in a letter from Panakestor to Zenon (iii BCE, *LAL* §18): Ἀπολλώνιος. κατεπλησσόμην τὴν ὀλιγωρίαν σου ἐπὶ τῶι μηθὲν γεγραφέναι μήτε περὶ τῆς συντιμήσεως μήτε περὶ τῆς συναγωγῆς τοῦ σίτου. ἔτι οὖν καὶ νῦν γράψον ἡμῖν ἐν οἷς ἕκαστά ἐστιν. N.b. the long reply from Apollonius which follows. Also, why should Greek cities want to make monuments out of threatening communiqués from Roman officials?

[44] ἀναλογεῖ. This verb makes its second appearance in this text, and while its meaning seems clear enough in 7, it is more obscure here. The idea apparently pertains to *proportion*: when one receives an official letter that conveys the intention to humiliate

for a response in kind.⁴⁵ [13] In spite of all this, then, after I tallied up the difficulties at the outset (although they are so many), I nevertheless set upon the task, composing [what is] for myself a brief exercise, and for you no great acquisition—but for many perhaps it is even easily despised.⁴⁶ [14] For things that are admirable prior to [their] attempt are typically easy to be overlooked⁴⁷ [when viewed] alongside the knowledge [acquired] from [their] completion.⁴⁸

---

through contempt, automatic concession and the sacrifice of all dignity and autonomy fail to maintain any historical probability. It simply strikes the author as implausible that any Greek city would tolerate such scorn with docility. Cf. the apt rendering of *EG: nec tamen humilitas ad similia responsa quadrat.*

⁴⁵ ἔτι ... ἀπόκρισιν. The author again states two extremes that he must avoid in his compositions, on one side rashness (ἡ αὐθάδης ἀντιγραφή) and on the other humility (τὸ ταπεινόν).

⁴⁶ ὅμως ... εὐκαταφρόνητον. Mithridates has outlined all of τὰ δυσχερῆ, and he now begins to draw his letter to a close with some self-deprecation. He interestingly refers to οἱ πολλοί who will read his compositions. The *Letter* thus partly functions as a dedication for a published collection, in a manner similar to Luke 1:1–4 and other such literary dedications. γύμνασμα, an educational technical term, contributes to his apology for its deficiencies: he belittles his work as a "brief exercise," of marginal worth to his addressee beyond any enjoyment it may impart (cf. 10), and "negligible" or even "contemptible" (εὐκαταφρόνητον) for anyone else that might read it. On literary dedications, especially in the form of letters, see L. C. A. Alexander, *The Preface of Luke's Gospel: Literary Convention and Social Context in Luke 1.1–4 and Acts 1.1* (SNTSMS 78; Cambridge: Cambridge University Press, 1993), chs. 4 and 5 on "scientific prefaces," esp. 50–6. Her survey and analysis of the ancient literature in these chapters, and in ch. 3 on "historical prefaces" as well, will retain lasting value even if one disagrees with her conclusions on how to classify Luke 1:1–4 (e.g., D. E. Aune, "Luke 1.1-4: Historical or Scientific *Prooimion*?" in *Paul, Luke and the Graeco-Roman World: Essays in Honour of A. J. M. Wedderburn* [eds. A. Christopherson et al.; JSNTSup 217; Sheffield: Sheffield Academic Press, 2002], 138–48). See also L. C. A. Alexander, "The Preface to Acts and the Historians," in *Acts in its Ancient Literary Context* (ed. eadem; Library of New Testament Studies 298; London/New York: T&T Clark, 2005), 21–42. On εὐκαταφρόνητος, see LSJ 717, s.v., and add to the literature cited there this passage from Dionysius, *Lys.* 12, in which he determines that the speeches of Lysias supposedly written for Iphicrates are spurious and in fact written by the latter: καὶ γὰρ πολέμια δεινὸς ὁ ἀνὴρ καὶ ἐν λόγοις οὐκ εὐκαταφρόνητος, ἥ τε λέξις ἐν ἀμφοῖν πολὺ τὸ φορτικὸν καὶ στρατιωτικὸν ἔχει καὶ οὐχ οὕτως ἐμφαίνει ῥητορικὴν ἀγχίνοιαν ὡς στρατιωτικὴν αὐθάδειαν καὶ ἀλαζονείαν. Note that the brash (cf. ἡ αὐθάδης ἀντιγραφή!) and boastful ἦθος of this speaker in no way renders him εὐκαταφρόνητος.

⁴⁷ παραθεωρεῖσθαι. On this word meaning "to overlook," see Dionysius, *Is.* 18, regarding the differences in style (χαρακτήρ) between Isaeus and Lysias: εἰ δέ τις παραθεωροίη ταῦτα ὡς μικρὰ καὶ φαῦλα, οὐκ ἂν ἔτι γένοιτο ἱκανὸς αὐτῶν κριτής. It could also mean here "to be compared," on which see the next note.

⁴⁸ φιλεῖ ... παραθεωρεῖσθαι. A couple of epistolary theorists mention the suitability of citing proverbs or creating maxims from scratch in one's letters (see n. 82 below). Mithridates has taken such advice to heart, since this sentence is the second such maxim of his own composition. He picks up a couple of words from earlier in the letter (cf. ἐθαύμασα, 1; πεῖραν, 4), and we find here his first reference to anything about the pro-

Plutarch (i-ii CE), *Brutus* 2.5-8.[49]

Ῥωμαϊστὶ μὲν οὖν ἤσκητο πρὸς τὰς <δι>εξόδους καὶ τοὺς ἀγῶνας ἱκανῶς ὁ βροῦτος, Ἑλληνιστὶ δὲ τὴν ἀποφθεγματικὴν καὶ Λακωνικὴν ἐπιτηδεύων βραχολογίαν ἐν ταῖς ἐπιστολαῖς ἐνιαχοῦ παράσημός ἐστιν. οἷον ἤδη καθεστηκὼς εἰς τὸν πόλεμον γράφει Περγαμηνοῖς· «ἀκούω ὑμᾶς Δολοβέλλᾳ δεδωκέναι χρήματα· ἃ εἰ μὲν ἑκόντες ἔδοτε, ὁμολογεῖτε ἀδικεῖν· εἰ δ' ἄκοντες, ἀποδείξατε τῷ ἐμοὶ ἑκόντες δοῦναι.» πάλιν Σαμίοις· «αἱ βουλαὶ ὑμῶν ὀλίγωροι, αἱ ὑπουργίαι βραδεῖαι. τί τούτων τέλος ἐννοεῖσθε;» καὶ [περὶ Παταρέων] ἑτέραν· «Ξάνθιοι τὴν ἐμὴν εὐεργεσίαν ὑπεριδόντες τάφον ἀπονοίας ἐσχήκασι τὴν πατρίδα, Παταρεῖς δὲ πιστεύσαντες ἑαυτοὺς ἐμοὶ οὐδὲν ἐλλείπουσι διοικοῦντες τὰ καθ' ἕκαστα τῆς ἐλευθερίας. ἐξὸν οὖν καὶ ὑμῖν ἢ τὴν Παταρέων κρίσιν ἢ τὴν Ξανθίων τύχην ἑλέσθαι.» τὸ μὲν οὖν τῶν παρασήμων γένος ἐπιστολίων τοιοῦτόν ἐστιν.

In Latin Brutus was indeed competently trained for expositions and trials, but in Greek he is sometimes distinguished[50] when he pursues apophthegmatic and Spartan brevity in his letters. For example, when he had already set out for battle, he writes to the Pergamenes: "I hear that you have given supplies to Dolobella. If you gave them voluntarily, confess to acting unjustly; but if involuntarily, prove it by giving them voluntarily to me" [*ep.* 1]. Again, to the Samians: "Your counsels are contemptuous, your compliances are late. What do you intend as a result of these?" [*ep.* 69]. And another:[51] "The Xanthians,

---

ject being "easy" (cf. δυσεύρετος, 5; δυσχερές, χαλεπόν, 7; δυσχερῆ, 13). One may understand the gist of this maxim a couple of different ways. He may be saying either that he has extracted what insight he could from the exercise and cares not at all about anyone's assessment of the final product; or, that what initially seemed θαυμαστόν has produced γνῶσις which he shares with his addressee and any other reader who happens to pick up his volume, and he urges them to view the product in this light. Such is evidently how Torraca (54) understands the sentence: "Infatti, le cose degne di ammirazione prima che uno tenti di realizzarle quando sono riguardata dopo l'esecuzione, sogliono essere disprezzate come facili" ("In fact the things worthy of admiration before one attempts to realize them, when they are regarded after their execution, would ordinarily be despised as easy"). M. M. Mitchell (in her comments on an earlier draft of this essay) tentatively proposed: "For things that are admired before they are tried are wont to be judged lightly when compared with the knowledge that comes from finishing them." There is a third option, which would make this sentence less of a maxim. The question is: who is doing the "overlooking"—or "comparing" (another possible meaning for παραθεωρεῖν, LSJ 1310, s.v.)? The two options above would associate Mithridates himself with the infinitive ("easy to be overlooked *by me*"). But he may mean οἱ πολλοί, translating loosely: "For the things which οἱ πολλοί admire about the letters prior to my attempt at adding responses are easy to compare unfavorably with whatever insight that they may acquire from reading the finished product, with the result that my work is easily despised."

[49] Text per K. Ziegler, ed., *Plutarchi Vitae Parallelae* (vol. 2.1; Leipzig: Teubner, 1964), 137.

[50] παράσημος here means "distinguished," not "counterfeit" as Moles ("Plutarch" [see n. 3], 145) unconvincingly argues in order to support his claim that Plutarch adopts some measure of skepticism toward the authenticity of the corpus.

[51] I omit from the translation [περὶ Παταρέων] as unsupported in Ziegler's apparatus and obvious from the context. Regarding ἑτέραν, Smith ("Greek Letters" [see n. 3], 194)

by ignoring my philanthropy, have had their homeland as a tomb for their folly, but the Patareans, by entrusting themselves to me, lose nothing of their freedom as they manage each their own affairs. Hence it is possible for you too to choose either the decision of the Patareans or the fate of the Xanthians" [*ep.* 25]. Such indeed is the type of his distinguished little letters.

Philostratus (iii CE), *De epistulis, AET* 42.1–9.[52]

τὸν ἐπιστολικὸν χαρακτῆρα τοῦ λόγου μετὰ τοὺς παλαιοὺς ἄριστά μοι δοκοῦσι διεσκέφθαι φιλοσόφων μὲν ὁ Τυαννεὺς καὶ Δίων, στρατηγῶν δὲ Βροῦτος ἢ ὅτῳ Βροῦτος ἐς τὸ ἐπιστέλλειν ἐχρῆτο, βασιλέων δὲ ὁ θεσπέσιος Μάρκος ἐν οἷς ἐπέστελλεν αὐτός, πρὸς γὰρ τῷ κεκριμένῳ τοῦ λόγου καὶ τὸ ἑδραῖον τοῦ ἤθους ἐντετύπωτο τοῖς γράμμασι, ῥητόρων δὲ ἄριστα μὲν Ἡρώδης ὁ Ἀθηναῖος ἐπέστελλεν, ὑπεραττικίζων δὲ καὶ ὑπερλαλῶν ἐκπίπτει πολλαχοῦ τοῦ πρέποντος ἐπιστολῇ χαρακτῆρος.

After the ancients, [the following persons] seem to me to observe best the epistolary style of discourse: of philosophers, the Tyanan [Apollonius] and Dio; of generals, Brutus or whomever Brutus used for the purpose of writing letters; of kings, divine Marcus in the things he himself wrote in letters, for in addition to him being distinguished in speech the steadfastness of his character has also been stamped on his letters; of rhetors, Herodes the Athenian wrote letters best, but by over-Atticizing and over-speaking he often falls from the style which is suitable for letters.

Photius (ix CE), *Epistula* 207.10–16, Ἀμφιλοχίῳ μητροπολίτῃ Κυζίκου.[53]

τίσιν οὖν ἐπιστολαῖς ὁμιλητέον, καὶ τίσι τὸν ἐπιγνωσθέντα ἡμῖν διὰ τῆς τέχνης χαρακτῆρα ἐφαρμόζοντες τὴν γυμνασίαν συλλεξόμεθα; ἔστιν μὲν καὶ ἄλλο πλῆθος ἄπειρον· ἔχεις δ', ἵνα μηδὲ μακρὸν ᾖ σοι τὸ τῆς γυμνασίας στάδιον, τὰς εἰς Φάλαριν ἐκεῖνον οἶμαι τὸν Ἀκραγαντῖνον τύραννον ἀναφερομένας ἐπιστολὰς καὶ αἷς Βροῦτος ὁ Ῥωμαίων στρατηγὸς ἐπιγράφεται καὶ τὸν ἐν βασιλεῦσι φιλόσοφον καὶ τὸν σοφιστὴν ἐν ταῖς πλείσταις Λιβάνιον.

So with what letters should one be familiar, and with what [letters] shall we assemble the exercise by fitting [it] to the style that became known to us through [their] art? There is

---

avers: "The verb in the first two cases has no direct object; we are told to whom Brutus writes, and the letter is then quoted in full; in the third case not only are we not told to whom the letter is written, we find γράφει governing ἑτέραν; the reason for this is that the recipients are the same as in the foregoing example, namely the Samians, and ἑτέραν has its proper force of 'a second letter,' instead of 'another,' i.e., ἄλλην. Yet in our collection this letter is addressed to the Lycians." Essentially Smith argues that because the third letter has unidentified recipients, ἑτέραν *must* mean that Plutarch's source has it addressed to the Samians (with the result that the credibility of Mithridates' collection suffers). It is indeed possible, perhaps even likely, that Mithridates changed some of the headings in his re-publication of Brutus' letters, but the omission of the recipient city in this sentence neither proves nor even supports that proposition.

[52] Malherbe takes the text from C. L. Kayser, ed., *Flavii Philostrati Opera* (vol. 2; Leipzig: Teubner, 1871, repr. 1964), 257–58.

[53] Text per B. Laourdas and L. G. Westerink, eds., *Photii Patriarchae Constantinopolitani Epistulae et Amphilochia* (vol. 2; Leipzig: Teubner, 1984), 106–7.

indeed another boundless multitude, but in order that the course of exercise may not be long for you, you have, I suppose, the letters attributed to Phalaris, the Acragantan tyrant;[54] and those which Brutus, the general of the Romans, inscribes; and Libanius, the sage among kings and the sophist in most [of his letters].

Suda (x CE), s.v. B §561.[55]

Βροῦτος, στρατηγὸς Ῥωμαίων, ἔγραψεν Ἐπιστολὰς καὶ τῶν Πολυβίου τοῦ ἱστορικοῦ Βίβλων ἐπιτομήν. θαυμάζεται δὲ εἰς τὴν τῶν ἐπιστολῶν ἰδέαν, ἤγουν χαρακτῆρα.

Brutus, a general of the Romans, wrote *Letters* and an epitome of the books of Polybius the historian. He is admired for the quality, this is to say the style, of his letters.

2. Authorship and Date

The most basic question about the *Letter* of Mithridates pertains to whether it is itself a pseudepigraphon.[56] There are several possible answers: (1) the author hides his own identity, and intends to deceive his readers; (2) he hides his identity, but in a transparent fashion in order to make it clear that he writes pseudonymously; (3) the letter is an authentic communication between two royal persons named Mithridates; (4) the letter is an authentic communication either between two ordinary persons of that name, or between others whose names are lost.

In weighing the first two answers, we need to reckon with the question of why the author would construct a Mithridates and put this fictitious person between himself and his readers. If the author wants to deceive his readers (option 1), he most likely would do this to conceal the fact that he composes not only the replies of the cities but the letters of Brutus as well. Bentley speculates that the authors of such forgeries derive pleasure from successful deception, "being as full as testimony of their Skill in imitation, as the birds gave to the painter when they peck'd at his grapes."[57] It is likely, however, that an edition of Brutus' letters existed prior to Mithridates' labors. Plutarch quotes three of the letters verbatim, and implies that he selects a few from many (τὸ μὲν οὖν τῶν παρασήμων γένος

---

[54] Cf. the entry for Phalaris at *Suda* s.v., Φ 43, 4.694: Φάλαρις, Ἀκραγαντῖνος, τυραννήσας δὲ Σικελίας ὅλης κατὰ τὴν νβ´ ὀλυμπιάδα. ἔγραψεν ἐπιστολὰς πάνυ θαυμασίας, ed. Adler (see the next note).

[55] Text per A. Adler, ed., *Suidae Lexicon* (5 vols.; Teubner, 1928–30; repr. 1971), 1:498.

[56] For other discussions of authorship, see Rühl, "Die griechischen Briefe" (see n. 3), 317–18; Smith, "Greek Letters" (see n. 3), 202–3; Cichorius, "Die griechischen Brutusbriefe" (see n. 3), 434–38; Torraca xxviii–xxxi.

[57] See n. 2 above.

ἐπιστολίων τοιοῦτόν ἐστιν). He thus has a corpus of some kind. But he seems unaware of the cover letter and responses. Both he and Mithridates praise the letters for their brevity, but with different technical terminology (βραχυλογία and συντομία). Plutarch also focuses exclusively on Brutus' "Spartan brevity" while Mithridates mentions it in passing as one of two stylistic reasons that his letters enjoy such high esteem. Both authors offer independent confirmation of a general admiration of the corpus, and thus attest to its prior existence. It therefore seems improbable that we have a situation of pure pseudepigraphic deception, since it is difficult to ascertain why the author would do this apart from a desire to mask his pseudepigraphy not only of the responses of the cities, but of the letters of Brutus themselves.[58]

So if the pseudepigrapher has an edition of Brutus' letters, he may have a different reason for concealing his identity, and may be using a different strategy, that of recognized pseudonymity in lieu of anonymity. This fictional scenario enables "Mithridates" to excuse the author's temerity in supplementing a collection that was generally regarded as excellent just the way it was, while giving him a platform to outline his real objectives, methods and hardships in completing the project. His intimations of doubt about the quality of his compositions may not be feigned, so "Mithridates" deflects any disgrace for failure. For this strategy of pseudonymity to work, he must give *unambiguous* clues to his readers so that they may see through the fiction—clues which the *Letter* does not seem to provide. The text lacks ostentatious personal details,[59] elaborations of the relationship between author and addressee,[60] or other features that would signal προσωποποιία. The only substantive indication of pseudonymity occurs in the greeting, which labels the addressee (or the author in some manu-

---

[58] In connection with the first option, another possible—but, to my mind, very unlikely—scenario arises, involving a three-stage evolution of the corpus: (1) the composition (real or feigned) of the letters of Brutus; (2) the subsequent pseudepigraphic composition of the responses; and (3) the composition of the *Letter* of Mithridates and its placement at the head of the corpus. The only reason I can come up with for someone to write such a cover letter would be that its real author inferred that the responses are not authentic, probably because he believed them to be of inferior quality to letters of Brutus. He thus imagines a scenario for their production, encodes this scenario in his pseudepigraphon, explains why the responses should be preserved, and apologizes for their stylistic deficiencies. After considering this possibility, I rejected it; the *Letter* furnishes a sufficiently plausible scenario both for its own composition and for that of the responses, so the third stage seems unnecessary in order to explain the corpus as we have it.

[59] Cf. 1 Tim 1:12–17, 2:7, 3:14–15, 2 Tim 3:10–11, 4:6–18. See further L. R. Donelson, *Pseudepigraphy and Ethical Argument in the Pastoral Epistles* (HUT 22; Tübingen: Mohr Siebeck, 1986), 23–42.

[60] Cf. 2 Tim 1:3–7.

scripts) a king. Yet nothing about the body of the *Letter* projects the royal ἦθος of the author or addressee that the greeting leads one to expect. Mithridates presents himself foremost as a scholar or educator who engages in a rhetorical exercise that he offers as a gift to his addressee. In this respect the *Letter* contrasts markedly with the obviously pseudepigraphic missive purporting to be from Aristotle to Alexander the Great at the beginning of the *Rhetorica ad Alexandrum*. In the first paragraph, for example, "Aristotle" justifies his desire to create the best rhetorical handbook possible thus:

ὥσπερ γὰρ ἐσθῆτα σπουδάζεις τὴν εὐπρεπεστάτην τῶν λοιπῶν ἀνθρώπων ἔχειν, οὕτω δύναμιν λόγων λαβεῖν ἐστί σοι πειρατέον τὴν εὐδοξοτάτην· πολὺ γὰρ κάλλιόν ἐστι καὶ βασιλικώτερον τὴν ψυχὴν ἔχειν εὐγνωμονοῦσαν ἢ τὴν ἕξιν τοῦ σώματος ὁρᾶν εὐειματοῦσαν. καὶ γὰρ ἄτοπόν ἐστι τὸν τοῖς ἔργοις πρωτεύοντα φαίνεσθαι τῶν τυχόντων τοῖς λόγοις ὑστερίζοντα.

For just as you are zealous to have attire more beautiful than the rest of humanity, so also you must strive to acquire the most distinguished power of words. For it is much more noble and royal to have a sensible soul than to see a well-dressed outward appearance of the body. For it is also absurd that the one who holds first place in actions should appear to fall behind those who have proven successful in words. (*Rhet. Alex.* 2–3, 1420a)

Mithridates in contrast appeals to his affection for his addressee as a primary motive for his labors, as well as to the lure of a challenge to his own abilities in rhetoric and research that arises from his cousin's remark, that the letters are "hard to answer" (δυσαποκρίτως ἔχειν, 4). The contrast between the superior appearance and abilities of Alexander on the one hand, and those of ordinary people on the other, is also something the *Letter* conspicuously lacks: in other words, Mithridates, unlike "Aristotle," makes no explicit connection between the status or responsibilities of the addressee and the relevance of the texts discussed in the cover letter.[61] "Aristotle" furthermore exaggerates his own philosophical ἦθος later in his letter, advising "Alexander" regarding politics, and discussing λόγος as the great dignity of humanity above the animals and as the source of good living and governance. The only ἦθος that Mithridates seems concerned to

---

[61] This statement prompted some controversy on one occasion when I presented the paper orally. The point at issue is whether Mithridates directs the question of how he should respond to Brutus' scornful letters (navigating a course between rashness and humility) toward his cousin as a client king, because the latter must himself write letters to Roman officials. If such is the case, the first and second options acquire an increased persuasiveness. On the other hand, Mithridates does not explicitly underscore the relevance of the question for his cousin. He instead treats it as a problem inherent within the γύμνασμα. Also, he neither describes his responses as compositional models of the kinds of letter that his cousin will have occasion to write, nor does he put Brutus forward as a model of how his cousin should address his own subordinates.

imprint upon the text is that of an affectionate teacher. These observations cast suspicion neither on the authenticity of the *Letter* as a whole nor the scenario that it projects,[62] rather upon the authenticity of the prescript. It thus seems safe to conclude, both from the text's failure to develop the royal ἦθος of the author or addressee and from the absence of other features that would make pseudonymity transparent, that the text is not pseudonymous.

In order to assess the remaining two possibilities, we must consider the greeting further. It could be original in its entirety, and factual in its ascription of royalty to the author and/or addressee, regardless of the lack of mention of this topic within the body of the letter. The fact that all manuscripts read βασιλεῖ or βασιλεύς could be taken as confirming this.[63] Or a scribe may have added βασιλεῖ (or βασιλεύς) as a "clarification," giving a substantial promotion to an ordinary person named Mithridates. Or possibly no part of the prescript is authentic; it replaces one now lost or imaginatively fills a lacuna. Many kings in Hellenistic and Roman times bore the name of Mithridates,[64] but it also shows up in Athens and Thrace in inscriptions,[65] and in Egypt in papyri,[66] so it was a personal name for ordinary people as well. The problem with "King" Mithridates in the prescript emerges from the fact that none of the known kings of this name springs

---

[62] Cf. Smith, "Greek Letters" (see n. 3), 203: "Mithridates may be in fact an Eastern dynast; he may equally well be a sophist using a pen name. There seems to be no ground for denying his existence or for doubting the words of his introduction."

[63] See n. 7 above.

[64] For an overview, see the numerous entries in *BNP* 9:77–85, s.v. Mithridates.

[65] Athens, dating a catalogue of ephebes: ἐπὶ Μιθριδάτου ἄρχοντος καὶ ἱερέως Δρού[σου] ὑπάτου ... (*IG* II² 1968, ca. 41–54 CE). Thrace, in an inscribed epigram from Philippopolis: ἐμοὶ γενέτης Μιθριδάτης καὶ μήτηρ Χρήστη (G. Mihailov, ed., *Inscriptiones Graecae in Bulgaria Repertae*, vol. 3, *Inscriptiones inter Haemum et Rhodopem Repertae* [Serdicae: Bulgarian Academy of Letters, 1961], 86, §1022, ca. ii–iii CE per P. M. Fraser and E. Matthews, eds., *A Lexicon of Greek Personal Names* [4 vols.; Oxford: Clarendon Press, 1987–2005], 4:236).

[66] P.Prince. 2, col. V (a tax register, 25 CE), Μιθραδάτη(ς); and 13, col. XII (an account register, ca. 35 CE), Μιθραδ(άτης) (A. C. Johnson and H. B. von Hoesen, eds., *Papyri in the Princeton University Collection* [Johns Hopkins University Studies in Archaeology 10; Baltimore: Johns Hopkins Press, 1931], 10, 89). P.Petr. III.58.e, col. I (a list of payments made by sureties), Μιθραδάτου (J. P. Mahaffy and J. G. Smyly, eds., *The Flinders Petrie Papyri* [Dublin: Academy House, 1905], 3:170). See further F. Preisigke, *Namenbuch: Enthaltend alle griechischen, lateinischen, ägyptischen, hebräischen, arabischen und sonstigen semitischen und nichtsemitischen Menschennamen, soweit sie in griechischen Urkunden (Papyri, Ostraka, Inschriften, Mumienschildren u.s.w.) Ägyptens sich vorfinden* (repr.; Amsterdam: Hakkert, 1967), 217, s.v., and D. Foraboschi, *Onomasticon Alterum Papyrologicum* (Mailand: Instituto Editorale Cisalpino, 1967), 197, s.v.

forward as a plausible candidate.[67] The one element that can help to link author or addressee with a historical figure, ἀνεψιός, is erroneously assumed by scholars to mean "nephew" instead of "first cousin."[68] Conrad Cichorius, for example, initially rules out Mithridates VIII of the Bosporus (d. 68 CE),[69] and settles on a Mithridates of Armenia who ascended the throne in 35 CE, suffered imprisonment in Rome in 38, then regained his rule in 51. Combining the evidence from an inscription (dated to 75) with a notice from Tacitus, he argues that Mithridates II of Iberia (active in the

---

[67] In addition to the candidates discussed below, Speyer (*Die literarische Fälschung* [see n. 4], 138) cautiously refers to the addressee as "König Mithridates (von Parthien?)"; a Mithridates indeed founded the Parthian empire in the 2d century BCE, whose nephew of the same name succeeded him in 123/4 (*BNP* 9:83–4). The dates make these two unlikely. Torraca (xxxi) tentatively suggests the Parthian Mithridates IV (reigned 130–47 CE) as addressee, proposing that the author fictitiously passes himself off as his uncle.

[68] "Nephew" is ἀδελφιδέος (LSJ 20, s.v.) or ἐξάδελφος (LSJ 581, s.v. II). ἀνεψιός as "cousin" goes back to Homer, e.g., *Il.* 9.464, 15.422, 554 (R. J. Cunliff, *A Lexicon of the Homeric Dialect* [Norman/London: University of Oklahoma Press, 1963], 37, s.v.; B. Snell, *Lexikon des frühgriechischen Epos* [3+ vols.; Göttingen: Vandenhoeck & Ruprecht, 1955], 1:821, s.v., also quoting a scholion of Didymus: ἀδελφῶν υἱοί. ὡς Ἀχιλλεὺς καὶ Αἴας). W. Pape (*Griechisch-Deutsches Handwörterbuch* [3d ed.; ed. M. Sengebusch; 2 vols.; Graz: Akademische Druck- u. Verlagsanstalt, 1954], 1:228, s.v.) gives the translation "Geschwistersohn" ("nephew"), citing Andocides, *De mysteriis* 47, a list of the speaker's relatives whom Diocletes "denounced," beginning with Charmides son of Aristoteles: οὗτος ἀνεψιὸς ἐμός· ἡ μήτηρ <ἡ> ἐκείνου καὶ ὁ πατὴρ ὁ ἐμὸς ἀδελφοί. Andocides also refers to Critias as ἀνεψιὸς καὶ οὗτος τοῦ πατρός· αἱ μητέρες ἀδελφαί. Obviously these persons are cousins. See also Pollux, *Onom.* 3.28: πάλιν τοίνυν ἀδελφῶν παῖδες ἀνεψιοί, εἴτ' ἐκ πατραδέλφων εἶεν εἴτ' ἐκ μητραδέλφων, καὶ εἴτ' ἐξ ἀδελφοῦ ἢ ἀδελφῆς, εἴτ' ἐκ δυοῖν ἀρρένων ἀδελφῶν, εἴτ' ἐκ δυοῖν θηλειῶν ἀδελφῶν· κατὰ ταῦτα δὲ καὶ αἱ θήλειαι ἀνεψιαί. (For further literature, see BDAG 78, s.v., with refs. to papyri and inscriptions.) The word ἀνεψιός has an etymological relation to Latin *nepos*, German Neffe, and English nephew (see the data at Snell, ibid., 1:821, and H. Frisk, *Griechisches Etymologisches Wörterbuch* [3 vols.; Heidelberg: Carl Winter Universitätsverlag, 1960], 1:106, s.v.). Clear attestations of ἀνεψιός as "nephew" do not appear until late antiquity (E. A. Sophocles, *Greek Lexicon of the Roman and Byzantine Periods* [repr. Hildesheim/New York: Georg Olms, 1975], 166, s.v.; E. Trapp et al., eds., *Lexikon zur byzantinischen Gräzität* [Wien; Österreichische Akademie der Wissenschaften, 2001–], 1:106, s.v.).

[69] This date is per I. von Bredow, *BNP* 9:82–3, s.v. Mithridates §8; Cichorius ("Die griechischen Brutusbriefe" [see n. 3], 435) gives 69. This Mithridates attracts Cichorius' attention because he wrote ethnographic and geographic accounts to which Pliny refers, and thus seems to have the literary credentials to edit the Brutan corpus. However: "Gleichwohl kann Mithridates von Bosporus als Verfasser der Briefe meiner Ansicht nach nicht in Betracht kommen. Wir kennen von ihm keinen Neffen namens Mithridates, aber selbst wenn er einem solchen gehabt haben sollte, so wäre dieser doch als Adressat ausgeschlossen" (ibid.).

late first century) is his nephew.[70] Cichorius surmises that the uncle's sojourn in Rome promoted his interest in Roman culture and history,[71] hence his desire to pass an enhanced collection of Brutus' letters to his namesake. Another possibility is Mithridates II of Commagene (reigned 36–20 BCE) who had a nephew of the same name. Augustus elevated the younger to the throne in 20 as a παιδίσκος, after the elder had his brother, the father of the younger, assassinated.[72] Both of these proposals would be possible, except that they rely upon a lexically questionable interpretation of ἀνεψιός to form a bridge between the prescript with the very thin historical record.[73] The confusion about the precise King Mithridates whom the prescript envisions, coupled with the fact that the text does not carry this ἦθος forward, leads one to the conclusion that βασιλεῖ/-εύς is an early scribal intrusion into the original prescript,[74] Μιθριδάτης Μιθριδάτῃ τῷ

---

[70] Cichorius, "Die griechischen Brutusbriefe" (see n. 3), 436: "Aus dem Kaukasus, aus der Gegend von Tiflis, haben wir eine interessante Inschrift vom Jahre 75 n. Chr. (C.I.L. III 6052, Ath. Mitt. XXI 472, Dittenberger Or. Gr. inscr. sel. 379), die äußerste, die wir aus dem Nordosten besitzen. Sie betrifft den Bau von Festungen durch römische Soldaten im Auftrag Vespasians und seiner Söhne, offenbar in Zusammenhang mit dem damaligen Alanenkriege und zwar βασιλεῖ Ἰβήρων Μιθριδάτῃ βασιλέως Φαρασμάνου καὶ Ἰαμάσδει τῷ υἱῷ. Der hier genannte König ist ein Sohn des Königs Pharasmanes, der mindestens seit 35 und mindestens bis 60 n. Chr. (Tacitus, Ann. 14,26) regiert hatte, d.h. des Bruders jenes armenischen Königs Mithridates." The inscription is reprinted at SEG 20 (1964): 35, §112. The entries on Mithridates by M. Schottky at BNP 9:84–5, s.v. Mithridates §§20, 22, agree with Cichorius that the Iberian Mithridates is the nephew of the Armenian.

[71] Ibid.: "Sodann würde der lange Aufenthalt in Rom auch bei ihm ein Interesse für rein römische Dinge erklärlich erscheinen lassen. Literarische Tätigkeit eines armenischen Königs könnte nichts Befremdliches haben, war doch schon im ersten vorchristlichen Jahrhundert König Artavasdes als Schriftsteller in griechischer Sprache hervorgetreten; vgl. Plut. Crass. 33, wonach er καὶ τραγωδίας ἐποίει καὶ λόγους ἔγραψε καὶ ἱστορίας, ὧν ἔνιαι διασώζονται."

[72] On these kings, see R. D. Sullivan, "The Dynasty of Commagene," ANRW II 8: 775–83; n.b. the genealogy laid out at 743. Sullivan draws the conclusion that III is the nephew of II from a remark by Cassius Dio (54.9.3): τῷ τε Ἡρώδῃ Ζηνοδώρου τινὸς τετραρχίαν, καὶ Μιθριδάτῃ τινὶ τὴν Κομμαγηνήν, ἐπειδὴ τὸν πατέρα αὐτοῦ ὁ βασιλεὺς αὐτῆς ἀπεκτόνει, καίτοι παιδίσκῳ ἔτ᾽ ὄντι ἐπέτρεψε (quoted from ibid., 780, nn. 199, 202). "His father was probably not the well-known Mithridates II," Sullivan reasons, "since Dio leaves him nameless and describes the child with 'tis.'" Therefore: "The king responsible would be Mithridates II, still ruling after the removal of his brother nine years before. On chronological grounds, the dead father should be yet another son of Antiochus I" [i.e., the father of Mithridates II].

[73] Cf. Deininger, "Brutus und die Bithynier" (see n. 3), 370–71.

[74] The initial intrusion may have occurred because an early scribe mistook the author for the famous Mithridates VI of Pontus (d. 63 BCE), whom E. Olshausen (BNP 9:81, s.v. Mithridates §6) describes thus: "[Mithridates'] outward appearance, his physical and mental abilities, and his character are regularly portrayed to us by the literary sources in a

ἀνεψιῷ χαίρειν. An equally strong possibility is that the whole prescript is not part of the original composition.

We may therefore eliminate the third option, that the addressee or author is a "King" Mithridates. The fourth has as the strongest point in its favor the plausibility of the scenario as the author presents it: he issues a "second edition" of Brutus' letters with his own replies in order to please his addressee. The stimulus was a remark from the latter about the letters: ἀποφαίνοντος δὲ σοῦ δυσαποκρίτως αὐτὰς ἔχειν (4). Mithridates frankly confesses his own difficulties in executing his goal, and seems uncertain of the results. Insofar as the *Letter* functions as a literary dedication, he seeks to explain to his addressee—and to anyone else who picks up the volume—what he is doing and why. He offers his explanations in simple terms that in no way exaggerate his own or his addressee's importance.

Regarding the dates of the original Brutan corpus and Mithridates' second edition and *Letter*, the testimonia provide some hints but no conclusive results. The *terminus post quem* for the original corpus is easily fixable to the late 40s BCE. Philostratus supplies a tentative *terminus ante quem* of the third century CE for the revised corpus, since he echoes Mithridates' surmise that Brutus delegated his correspondence in a way that suggests (but does not definitively confirm) that he has read the *Letter*.[75] As noted above, Plutarch seems to know the Brutan letters from the original corpus, not Mithridates' edition. If the latter comes to replace the initial version, as the testimony of Philostratus and the manuscripts imply, it must therefore have appeared sometime between Plutarch and Philostratus, during the second century CE. If Brutus indeed authored the letters attributed to him, he may have published them himself (as Mithridates assumes) or a friend may have selected and published them posthumously, producing a date

---

somewhat hymnical way. ... [T]all and powerful in stature, a passionate huntsman, an energetic and persevering horseman, charioteer and soldier, often wounded, seldom sick, he was intelligent and clever, a gifted speaker, an excellent orator, educated in the Greek manner, a bibliophile, scholarly, particularly interested in toxicology, knowledgeable about art and lover of music."

[75] Philostratus, listing exemplary letter writers: στρατηγῶν δὲ Βροῦτος ἢ ὅτῳ Βροῦτος ἐς τὸ ἐπιστέλλειν ἐχρῆτο; and Mithridates 8: εἴτε ἰδίας εἴτε τινὸς τῶν εἰς ταῦτα μισθοῦ δοκίμων. Philostratus' remark stands out because another person on his list would be a likely candidate as someone to have delegated his correspondence, namely the Emperor Marcus Aurelius, whom he praises thus: πρὸς γὰρ τῷ κεκριμένῳ τοῦ λόγου καὶ τὸ ἑδραῖον τοῦ ἤθους ἐντετύπωτο τοῖς γράμμασι, i.e., for one of the reasons that Mithridates also lauds Brutus' letters, ὡς ἡγεμονικοῦ φρονήματος ἐχούσας χαρακτῆρα. It thus seems probable that it would occur to Philostratus to mention a secretary for Brutus, but not for Marcus, because his edition of the former notes this possibility as well.

somewhere in the late first century BCE. But they may indeed be pseudepigrapha, in which case a lapse of time becomes necessary for successful deception in order to prevent disauthentication by those who knew firsthand that Brutus did not write them (first century CE).

3. The Style of the *Letter*

The *Letter* supplies a few indications that its author may have written it as a rhetorical-epistolary exercise. Mithridates not only remarks upon stylistic theory as it pertains to Brutus' letters and uses rhetorical and epistolary technical terms throughout,[76] he also studiously adheres to the standard doctrines that one finds elsewhere. Taking into account that he elevates his style (perhaps more than his rhetorical skill can support) in order to conform to the conventions of literary prefaces, he keeps his letter short and to the point, and he writes with a tone that is neither too formal nor too familiar,[77] and without conspicuous Atticism.[78] With a couple of exceptions (11–12) the sentences are generally not heavy with excessive cola; nor do final cola give the impression of periodic rounding,[79] although Mithridates does show a fondness for antitheses.[80] He expresses affectionate sentiments (11, 13), keeping the letter easily within the confines of "friendly"

---

[76] E.g., δεινότης and συντομία in 1; χαρακτήρ in 1 and 11; διαπρεσβεύεσθαι, ἐκδιδόναι and διόρθωσις in 8; ὁμοτονεῖν in 9; ἰδέα in 11; and γύμνασμα in 13.

[77] Demetrius, *Eloc*. 224: δεῖ γὰρ ὑποκατεσκευάσθαι πως μᾶλλον τοῦ διαλόγου τὴν ἐπιστολήν. Gregory of Nazianzus, *Ep*. 51 (*AET* 58): χρὴ φεύγοντα τὸ λογοειδές, ὅσον ἐνδέχεται, μᾶλλον εἰς τὸ λαλικὸν ἀποκλίνειν. Julius Victor, *Rhet*. 27 (*AET* 62), *orationem proprius sermo explicet*.

[78] Philostratus, *Ep*. lines 9–11 (*AET* 42): δεῖ γὰρ φαίνεσθαι τῶν ἐπιστολῶν τὴν ἰδέαν ἀττικωτέραν μὲν συνηθείας, συνηθεστέραν δὲ ἀττικίσεως καὶ συγκεῖσθαι μὲν πολιτικῶς, τοῦ ἁβροῦ μὴ ἀπάδειν. [Libanius], *Ep. char*. 47: ἡ γὰρ ὑπὲρ τὸ δέον ὑψηγορία καὶ τὸ ταύτης καὶ τὸ ὑπεραττικίζειν ἀλλότριον τοῦ τῶν ἐπιστολῶν καθέστηκα χαρακτῆρος, ὡς πάντες οἱ παλαιοὶ μαρτυροῦσι.

[79] Overall Mithridates' style is hypotactic. He likes to place his main clauses near the beginning of his multi-clause sentences (1, 2, 7, 10, 11), but he delays the main clause to the end in one instance (8). Within clauses, the finite verb often stands near the beginning (ἐθαύμασα in 1; ἐοίκασι in 2; ᾠήθην and ἦν in 4; ἦν in 5; ἐξέδωκε in 8; φιλεῖ in 14), and infinitives near the end (ἔχειν in 4; συνδραμεῖν and ἀναλογῆσαι in 7; μιμήσασθαι and ὁμοτονῆσαι in 9; χαριεῖσθαι in 10; ἐπιστέλλειν in 12; παραθεωρεῖσθαι in 14). He furthermore at a few points balances his clauses with the figure of ἰσόκωλον (the first two clauses of 1: 14 syllables each; the last two clauses of 12: 21 and 20 syllables respectively; the last three clauses of 13: 12, 7, and 14 respectively).

[80] Philostratus, *Ep*. lines 15–16 (*AET* 42): τῶν δὲ ἐς μῆκος προηγμένων ἐπιστολῶν ἐξαιρεῖν χρὴ κύκλους.

correspondence.[81] He offers a couple of maxims of his own composition.[82] He also clearly understands what he writes both in the *Letter* and in his additions to the corpus to be a gift to his addressee.[83] He so thoroughly conforms to the canons of epistolary style that one must conclude that he intends to do so. But why would he write his cover letter as a "textbook" example of epistolary style? The testimonia provide some assistance toward an answer. All four in chorus underscore how highly the ancients regarded Brutus' letters: Plutarch calls them "distinguished" (παράσημα ἐπιστόλια), they make Philostratus' and Photius' short lists of stylistic exemplars, and the *Suda* echoes Mithridates' expressions of "admiration" (θαυμάζειν) of his ἰδέα and χαρακτήρ. If these four communicate a consensus opinion that spans from the initial publication of the corpus through the tenth century, it surely received study from aspiring *litterati*—not only for its exhibition of excellent epistolary style but also for its "apophthegmatic and Spartan brevity" (as Plutarch phrases it). While the ancients may have read the Greek letters of Brutus for their historical value as well as for the great importance of their author, they appear to have preserved them mainly for their literary worth. The concessions of Mithridates and Philostratus that Brutus might have appointed someone in his retinue to compose his official correspondence reflects an ancient custom practiced by other important persons.[84] But it also signals a notable measure of indifference toward the identity of the author as such.[85] Philostratus and Photius

---

[81] [Demetrius], *Typoi epistolikoi* 1 (*AET* 32), s.v. φιλικὸς χαρακτήρ; [Libanius], *Ep. char.* 11, 58 (*AET* 68, 74), s.v. φιλικὴ ἐπιστολή. Most early theory presupposes that correspondence occurs between friends, but it eventually expands to accommodate the genre's manifold uses.

[82] Demetrius (*Eloc.* 232) warns against this, although he approves of proverbs: αἵ τε φιλικαὶ φιλοφρονήσεις καὶ πυκναὶ παροιμίαι. Gregory (*Ep.* 51.5, *AET* 60) recommends γνῶμαι, παροιμίαι and ἀποφθέγματα if not overused; Ps.-Libanius agrees (παροιμίαι, *Ep. char.* 50, *AET* 72).

[83] Demetrius, *Eloc.* 224: ἡ δὲ (ἐπιστολὴ) γράφεται καὶ δῶρον πέμπεται τρόπον τινά.

[84] For a discussion of the roles of secretaries in ancient correspondence, see E. R. Richards, *The Secretary in the Letters of Paul* (WUNT II/42; Tübingen: Mohr Siebeck, 1991), ch. 1, "The Secretary in Greco-Roman Antiquity"; cf., however, the withering review by H. D. Betz, *JTS* 43 (1992): 618–20.

[85] Smith ("Greek Letters" [see n. 3], 195) seemingly misses this point when he writes: "If Brutus employed secretaries for the purpose of writing to the allies and subjects, then it is clearly useless for us to attempt to discern any outstanding similarity of style between the various letters ... Yet these letters were clearly deemed to bear the stamp of Brutus' individuality on them. ... It is certainly not improbable that Brutus employed secretaries; yet, if he did, and that is what Mithridates and Philostratus thought, then we cannot expect any particularly individual characteristics of Brutus to be discernable." Smith says all this to underscore that ancient authors recognize that the letters may not be

furthermore speak of Brutus the same way Dionysius of Halicarnassus speaks of Lysias or Demosthenes in his *Critical Essays*: as a master of his chosen literary form who deserves close scrutiny with the objective of careful imitation. Mithridates may therefore seek to enhance further the utility of the corpus as an educational text. Striving to model the other principles of epistolary composition in his cover letter—especially those which are absent in Brutus' own letters by virtue of their extreme brevity—makes sense from this point of view. He writes a "textbook" letter because he writes the introduction to a kind of textbook: between the cover letter and the letters themselves, the corpus includes both discussion of the principles of epistolary style and models of their execution.[86] The fact that the *Letter* partakes of several epistolary categories—"friendly" letter, di-

---

authentically Brutan (ibid., 196). In response, I would first call attention to Smith's reference to plural *secretaries*; Mithridates and Philostratus refer only to one (τινός, ὅτῳ respectively), probably reflecting their perception of the corpus' unity of style and authorial voice throughout. Second, if a secretary did write the letters, the impressiveness of his stylistic achievement significantly increases from an ancient perspective, since in addition to their remarkable brevity, they powerfully capture the ἦθος not of the person who wrote them but the one on whose behalf they are written. Third, Brutus would certainly have given his secretary explicit instructions regarding content and tone, and would have reviewed them before dispatch. I agree with Smith that the external evidence does not confirm the authenticity of the corpus, but it does not disconfirm it either, since the sources have no interest in the question whatsoever.

[86] To clarify what I mean by "a kind of textbook," I am suggesting neither that the corpus serves a function parallel to rhetorical τεχναί or the epistolary handbooks, nor that teachers assigned it as a manual for elementary students. Instead, like the Demosthenean and Lysian corpora for speeches, the Brutan corpus with its supplements provide a convenient volume for study by those who strive for mastery of brevity in epistolary contexts. Artemon, the editor of Aristotle's correspondence and probably the very first to address epistolary style at a theoretical level, may exert considerable influence over Mithridates. We know only a little about what he says (presumably in his own introductory cover letter to the Aristotelian epistolary corpus) but Demetrius reveals that he dealt with proper epistolary style: Ἀρτέμων μὲν οὖν ὁ τὰς Ἀριστοτέλους ἀναγράψας ἐπιστολάς φησιν, ὅτι δεῖ ἐν τῷ αὐτῷ τρόπῳ διάλογόν τε γράφειν καὶ ἐπιστολάς· εἶναι γὰρ τὴν ἐπιστολὴν οἷον τὸ ἕτερον μέρος τοῦ διαλόγου (*Eloc.* 223). Demetrius for his part implies that he is not convinced of Aristotle's comprehensive merit as a stylistic exemplar, at some points praising him (*Eloc.* 230, 233) and at others blaming him (225, 234). But he confirms the admiration of Aristotle's letters in general opinion (230, Ἀριστοτέλης γοῦν ὃς μάλιστα ἐπιτετευχέναι δοκεῖ τοῦ [αὐτοῦ] ἐπιστολικοῦ). It is probably pointless to speculate about what else Artemon's cover letter might have included, although it bears noting that Demetrius certainly is arguing with *someone* (maybe several someones) here and there in his discussion, and Artemon as the only one named seems like the most likely candidate. Mithridates does something more than just collect or re-publish Brutus' letters, however; he contributes new compositions of his own and therefore takes up most of his letter explaining them. But by beginning the *Letter* with the topic of Brutus' admirable style he may follow Artemon's example.

dactic letter, literary dedication and preface, and perhaps royal/diplomatic letter—contributes to its many obscurities, because Mithridates is trying to do too many things at once, frustrating his overall pedagogical objective. Several scribes evidently decide that the *Letter* adds nothing to the corpus, so they omit it from their copies.[87]

4. Implications

Regarding the relevance of Mithridates' labors for contemporary research, one should first take note of the consistent interest in style exhibited both by him and by the testimonia. The *Letter* confirms several observations found elsewhere in rhetorical and epistolary theory: that letters should exhibit brevity in style and content;[88] that brevity and forcefulness (συντομία and δεινότης) are closely associated stylistic features;[89] and that epistolary pseudepigrapha were regarded as "exercises" (γυμνάσματα) and challenges to one's rhetorical skill.[90] The letters of Brutus thus would have wielded considerable influence over other ancient letter-writers, especially those who sought a comparable quasi-gnomic brevity and authoritarian tone. If someone hoping to obtain a sophisticated and sensitive understanding of rhetorical theory must follow the ancient custom of studying exemplary speeches, the same premise applies to the related discipline of epistolary theory. The sources identify Brutus as one such outstanding letter-writer, so the epistles attributed to him deserve close scrutiny alongside those of other named stylistic exemplars. Mithridates and Plutarch furthermore identify the main reason why Brutus is exemplary: brevity. In his capacity as a general, the need to communicate efficiently calls forth his extraordinary skill. The letters indeed powerfully convey a picture of the man in action. The reader imagines him reflecting for a moment, then dictating to his secretary a few carefully selected lines that evocatively capture the substance of a threat or demand. Then, as Brutus turns his mind to other pressing matters of the campaign, the secretary seals the missive and hands it off to a messenger, who thunders away on horseback to deliver it. Such is why Philostratus names Brutus as the para-

---

[87] See n. 6 above.
[88] See n. 13.
[89] Within n. 13, see my brief discussion of Demetrius, *Eloc.* 7.
[90] Cf. Theon, *Progymnasmata* 8 (per Patillon; *RG* 2.115), who views exercises in letter-writing as part of προσωποποιία: ὑπὸ δὲ τοῦτο τὸ γένος τῆς γυμνασίας πίπτει καὶ τὸ τῶν παρηγορικῶν λόγων εἶδος, καὶ τὸ τῶν προτρεπτικῶν, καὶ τὸ τῶν ἐπιστολικῶν.

digm of letters στρατηγῶν. His unusual abilities in brevity make him a worthwhile study for anyone who desires the same skill.

Mithridates' discussion of his methods of creating pseudepigraphic letters additionally throws some useful light on other such texts. His *Letter* is in fact the only extant text from antiquity wherein an author overtly acknowledges his authorship of pseudepigrapha (apart from someone defending himself after his forgery was detected),[91] and sets forth his methods of doing so.[92] Mithridates confirms his approach as an intensified form of ἠθοποιΐα or προσωποποιΐα, towards approximations of what Brutus' correspondents would really have written back, based on substantial historical spade-work and presented in a style that seeks to match the excellence of Brutus' achievement. He strives to create compositions that accurately capture both *what* their putative authors would say and *how* they would say it. In this connection Mithridates also tackles the problem of propriety (11–12). He acknowledges the common opinion that a Roman general has the right τὰ γέμοντα ὑπεροψίας ἐπιστέλλειν τοῖς ὑπηκόοις. As the samples quoted by Plutarch amply demonstrate, the letters are indeed harsh and threatening. Their style and content force their addressees into a subservient posture. The persons that Mithridates sets out to imitate must plot a course between rashness and humility in order both to acknowledge the superiority of Brutus and to maintain their dignity as sovereign states. The difficulty increases from Mithridates' point of view because of the plurality of the respondents in contrast to Brutus' single authorial voice. His γύμνασμα unites challenges to style and to content in a context of addressing a superior in a delicate situation.

For scholars of the New Testament and early Christian literature, the remarks of Mithridates on the production of pseudepigraphic letters should

---

[91] I am referring to Salvian of Marseille, *ep.* 9 (G. Lagarrigue, ed. & trans., *Salvien de Marseille: Œvres* [2 vols.; SC 176; Paris: Les Éditions du Cerf, 1971], 1:120–33); he apparently forged a tract under Timothy's name. When his bishop surmises that he is the real author, he writes a letter in response justifying the forgery. See further A. E. Haefner, "A Unique Source for the Study of Ancient Pseudonymity," *AThR* 16 (1934): 8–15 (with a partial English translation); M. Kiley, *Colossians as Pseudepigraphy* (Biblical Seminar; Sheffield: JSOT, 1986), 21–2; Donelson, *Pseudepigraphy* (see n. 59), 21–2.

[92] Mithridates' replies fall into the broad category of what Costa calls "fictional letters," which divide into three classes: (1) "letters which form part of fictional or historical narratives" (i.e., Acts 23:26–30); (2) "comic" or "imaginary" letters, which "aim to portray character and various levels of society, or to evoke a past age" (i.e., the fictional letters of Aelian, Alciphron and Philostratus); and (3) letters "attributed to famous philosophers and other historical characters," which often have a didactic aim (Costa, *Greek Fictional Letters* [see n. 11], xiv–xv). Mithridates' project partakes of both the first and third categories, insofar as he uses the histories to construct a narrative of his own, but he chooses to allow his responses to stand alongside Brutus' original compositions with no exposition of the background.

hold a comparable importance to what Thucydides has to say about the composition of speeches in historical narrative,[93] since both directly address at a theoretical level phenomena that actually occur in Christian texts. The main area of the *Letter*'s relevance pertains to the relationship it highlights between author, source materials, and pseudepigraphic end-product. The history of scholarship of the New Testament might lead us to think of "sources" primarily as texts which an author directly appropriates into his own, quoting or adapting them without attribution. But we might better think of sources as *resources*. Mithridates has the original compositions of Brutus which he takes as stylistic models and as points of departure for his replies.[94] He also conducts research on the cities on whose behalf he composes responses in order to flesh out the ἦθος of each and to determine the overall historical narrative. He thus deploys his sources toward plausibility in content and excellence in style. Insofar as the epistolary pseudepigrapha of the New Testament had analogous aims and confronted challenges like those outlined by Mithridates, what kinds of sources were available to their authors and how do they use them?

The epistle of James furnishes an instructive test case. Some scholars have speculated that its body was not originally attributed to James at all.[95] Much of the material therein has the ring of traditional exhortation; in other words, one or more sources may have been woven into the text. The attribution of the document to James in the epistolary prescript depends on a generally known ἦθος. Both the author and the target audience need to recognize him as the sort of person who delivered such teachings as we find in the letter, and who would furthermore say things like δεῖξόν μοι τὴν πίστιν σου χωρὶς τῶν ἔργων, κἀγώ σοι δείξω ἐκ τῶν ἔργων μου τὴν πίστιν (2:18), an apparent rejoinder to the teachings of Paul.[96] This

---

[93] See n. 25 above.

[94] To underscore a point I made in the introduction, whether or not the "original" letters of Brutus are authentic does not matter to the present point: Mithridates treats them as authentic, and the testimonia admire their style and set them forth as authentic.

[95] E.g., Johannes Weiß writes: "The first preliminary consideration for understanding this highly significant piece of writing appears to me to be that one shall perceive clearly that the epistolary address ... is an ornamentation imposed by a collector who wishes thereby to assign it a place in a collection of primitive apostolic writings" (*Earliest Christianity: A History of the Period A.D. 30–150* [ed. & trans. F. C. Grant; 2 vols.; New York: Harper & Row, 1959], 2:743).

[96] L. T. Johnson (*The Letter of James* [AB 37A; New York: Doubleday, 1995], 118–21; see also R. J. Bauckham, *James: Wisdom of James, Disciple of Jesus the Sage* [New Testament Readings; London: Routledge, 1999], 11–28) argues for the authenticity of James, based upon the following observations: (1) "James lacks any of the classic signs of late, pseudonymous authorship" (i.e., obvious προσωποποιία or evidence of later theological disputes); (2) "James reflects the social realities and outlooks appropriate to a sect in the early stages of its life"; (3) the letter has similarities with Q and (4) similar-

general knowledge implies sources other than those within the text itself: orally transmitted recollections of James' character and teachings, historical/legendary accounts like Acts, and the letters of Paul to which the text responds on its alleged author's behalf.[97] The author almost certainly lacks any actual writings of James which he can utilize as stylistic guides,[98] however, so he must imagine what James' distinctive authorial voice would sound like both to himself and his readers: with the brevity of a sage, he imparts items of instruction organized by catchword association,

---

ities with Paul; (5) "the Letter of James contains a number of incidental details that could be taken as evidence for a Palestinian provenance"; and (6) Johnson argues that *1 Clement* depends upon James, which suggests an earlier dating than scholars normally assign. Setting aside item 6, items 2 through 5 could very well indicate pseudepigraphic strategy—precisely the sort of προσωποποιία that Johnson denies in item 1. For example, the main affinities between Q and James are in format (the way that they lay out their instructions), and in the agrarian imagery that projects a scenario wherein a teacher sits outdoors and points to the surrounding natural phenomena (which are by no means unique to Palestine) (for further investigation, see P. J. Hartin, *James and the Q Sayings of Jesus* [JSNTSup 47; Sheffield: Sheffield Academic Press, 1991]). The noted affinities with Paul are primarily topical and stylistic. It thus seems possible that the author has both some version of Q and the corpus Paulinum as resources for the synthesis of an ἦθος for James, the brother of Jesus and the peer apostle of Paul. On this point, see M. M. Mitchell, "The Letter of James as a Document of Paulinism?" in *Reading James with New Eyes: Methodological Reassessments of the Letter of James* (eds. R. L. Webb and J. S. Kloppenborg; Library of New Testament Studies 342; London: T&T Clark, 2007), 75–98. The discussion of πίστις in ch. 2 also contributes significantly to James' ἦθος: readers of the corpus Paulinum know from Gal 1–2 that πίστις was a source of contention between the apostolic leadership. A letter of "James" would reasonably weigh in on the topic in a way that does not *refute* Paul's position but adds nuance to James' own. His interest in "the poor" (2:1–7) could also factor into characterization, since Paul's delivery of a collection εἰς τοὺς πτωχοὺς τῶν ἁγίων τῶν ἐν Ἰερουσαλήμ (Rom 15:26) would presumably be given to James as that church's leader for dispersal (cf. Gal 2:10).

[97] Note also the prescript: Ἰάκωβος θεοῦ καὶ κυρίου Ἰησοῦ Χριστοῦ δοῦλος; cf. Rom 1:1, Phil 1:1, where Paul describes himself as a "slave of Jesus Christ."

[98] Patrick J. Hartin has argued that James, while not the literal author of the letter, remains responsible for its content: a disciple publishes it "with the intention of handing on the traditions and teaching of James to communities outside Palestine who were united with the community of Jerusalem in their bonds with the house of Israel" ("The Religious Context of the Letter of James," in *Jewish Christianity Reconsidered: Rethinking Ancient Groups and Texts* [ed. M. Jackson-McCabe; Minneapolis: Fortress Press, 2007], 203–31 [206]; also idem, *James* [SP 14; Collegeville, Minn.: Liturgical Press, 2003], 21–5). Hartin's theory is, of course, possible. But if it captures what actually occurred, pseudepigraphic methods such as those I discuss nevertheless come into play. The disciple must render James' ἦθος with a high degree of accuracy, since some readers of the letter would have personally known James and could (dis)authenticate it.

using simple yet elegant Greek style.[99] This interaction between the author/editor and his sources constitutes an integral feature of the text's persuasive strategy, that the teachings in the epistle command obedience not only because of their intrinsic merit but also because of the authority of the person who utters them.[100]

Comparisons of the deutero-Pauline letters and the Pastorals also helpfully display differing interplays of authors, sources and pseudepigraphic end-products. The authors of Ephesians, Colossians and 2 Thessalonians clearly possess authentic letters of Paul. They apply themselves to the imitation of his style as they rework some of his favorite themes.[101] The

---

[99] The author often leads his clauses with verbs, a nod to the style of the LXX (e.g., in ch. 1, αἰτείτω in vv. 5–6; μὴ γὰρ οἰέσθω in v. 7; καυχάσθω in v. 9; ἀνέτειλεν in v. 11; μὴ πλανᾶσθε in v. 16; etc.), but he organizes his clauses variously and makes rich use of participles, infinitives and subordinate clauses. He furthermore does not get carried away with the semitizing flavor of the style; he uses many other conjunctions than καί and δέ (cf. Mark, Revelation). Rhetorical figures also adorn his composition. A brief stylistic analysis of a portion of his remarks on πίστις will illustrate some of these points. The author asks in 2:14, τί τὸ ὄφελος, ἀδελφοί μου, ἐὰν πίστιν λέγῃ τις ἔχειν ἔργα δὲ μὴ ἔχῃ; μὴ δύναται ἡ πίστις σῶσαι αὐτόν; He artfully pulls πίστιν away from the infinitive for which it acts as subject (ὑπέρβατον), and ἔργα similarly comes first in its clause. The first and last clauses also have five and six syllables each (ἰσόκωλον). The second question contrastingly has ἡ πίστις nestled between the main verb and its complementary infinitive. Vv. 15–17 present a complex conditional construction with a three-part protasis, and an apodosis of three words that circles back to the point where he starts, τί τὸ ὄφελος; The lopsided nature of this sentence gives a sarcastic bite to its end. The author next draws elements of the vocabulary and syntax together in a succinct statement (v. 17): οὕτως καὶ ἡ πίστις, ἐὰν μὴ ἔχῃ ἔργα, νεκρά ἐστιν καθ' ἑαυτήν. As he turns to the tactics of diatribe in vv. 18–19, the diction remains clipped in order to convey scorn, again using ἰσοκώλον: σὺ πίστιν ἔχεις (5 syllables), κἀγὼ ἔργα ἔχω (6), δεῖξόν μοι τὴν πίστιν σου χωρὶς τῶν ἔργων (12), κἀγώ σοι δείξω ἐκ τῶν ἔργων μου τὴν πίστιν (13). The author creates an antithetical σύγκρισις between "you" and "me," but the final σύγκρισις in v. 19 veers toward *ad hominem* attack, likening "your" faith to that of τὰ δαιμόνια, who at least have the wit to "tremble." The good quality of the author's Greek contributes to scholars' suspicion of the text's authenticity; M. Dibelius (*James* [rev. H. Greeven; ed. H. Koester; trans. M. A. Williams; Hermeneia; Philadelphia: Fortress Press, 1975], 17), e.g., simply cannot believe that a native speaker of Aramaic could have composed the text. For further discussion of the style of James, see J. H. Ropes, *A Critical and Exegetical Commentary on the Epistle of St. James* (ICC; New York: Charles Scribner's Sons, 1916), 24–7; P. H. Davids, "The Epistle of James in Modern Discussion," *ANRW* II 25.5:2621–45, 3639–40; Johnson, *Letter of James* (see n. 96), 7–11.

[100] Cf. Dibelius (*James* [see n. 99], 11), who points out that "the admonitions in the letter give the impression of authority, and yet the author's right to speak in this way is never explicitly justified."

[101] This is especially evident in the introductory sections of the letters, which echo Paul's style and vocabulary in his title (ἀπόστολος Χριστοῦ Ἰησοῦ διὰ θελήματος

canons and categories of the ancient rhetorical theorists (which were in part designed to facilitate imitation of the literary masters) have an important application in the analysis of these pseudepigrapha.[102] But whereas Mithridates directs his skills in imitation toward a rhetorical exercise that will earn him admiration, the authors of the deutero-Paulines use their skills to deceive:[103] they want their compositions to be read as if they were Paul's, so they adopt his authentic compositions as guides both of style and content. The Pastorals in contrast seem much less concerned with reproducing Paul's style,[104] and instead invest greater energy on elaborating his ἦθος in relation to his "addressees" Timothy and Titus.[105] The author(s) could intend the readers to notice the distinctive style, and to deduce their character as pseudonymous,[106] although it is difficult to discern why this

---

θεοῦ, Eph 1:1, Col 1:1, cf. 1 Cor 1:1, 2 Cor 1:1); adscriptions (τοῖς ἁγίοις τοῖς οὖσιν [ἐν Ἐφέσῳ] καὶ πιστοῖς ἐν Χριστῷ Ἰησοῦ, Eph 1:1; τοῖς ἐν Κολοσσαῖς ἁγίοις καὶ πιστοῖς ἀδελφοῖς ἐν Χριστῷ, Col 1:1, cf. Rom 1:7, Phil 1:1; also τῇ ἐκκλησίᾳ Θεσσαλονικέων ἐν θεῷ πατρὶ ἡμῶν καὶ κυρίῳ Ἰησοῦ Χριστῷ, 2 Thess 1:1, cf. 1 Thess 1:1); his greeting χάρις καὶ εἰρήνη (passim); forms of εὐχαριστεῖν at the headings of the thanksgiving sections, which are themselves a characteristic feature of the Pauline epistle (Col 1:3, 2 Thess 1:3, Eph 1:16, cf. Rom 1:8, 1 Cor 1:4, Phil 1:3, 1 Thess 1:2); benedictions (Eph 1:3, cf. 2 Cor 1:3); and the topoi of ὑπὲρ ἡμῶν προσεύχεσθαι (Col 1:9, 2 Thess 1:11, cf. Phil 1:4) or μνείαν ποιοῦσθαι ἐπὶ τῶν προσευχῶν (Eph 1:16, cf. Rom 1:9, Phil 1:3–4, 1 Thess 1:2, Phlm 4). Studious imitation of Paul's style and vocabulary in the opening sections would be crucial for convincing readers of the letters' authenticity.

[102] Trevor Thompson is investigating this matter in his dissertation (University of Chicago, in progress).

[103] My description of the authors' objective as "to deceive" reflects a *historical assessment*, not an *ethical* one. The authors who adopt Paul's ἦθος seem to have believed themselves justified in doing so, and presumably would not have regarded their deception as ethically incorrect.

[104] Again, the introductory sections render this point evident, in Paul's title (ἀπόστολος Χριστοῦ Ἰησοῦ κατ' ἐπιταγὴν θεοῦ σωτῆρος ἡμῶν καὶ Χριστοῦ Ἰησοῦ τῆς ἐλπίδος ἡμῶν, 1 Tim 1:1; ἀπόστολος δὲ Ἰησοῦ Χριστοῦ κατὰ πίστιν ἐκλεκτῶν θεοῦ καὶ ἐπίγνωσιν ἀληθείας τῆς κατ' εὐσέβειαν, Titus 1:1, and continuing on for two more verses; 2 Tim 1:1 comes much closer, with the addition of διὰ θελήματος θεοῦ, although he adds more prepositional phrases that recall the other two Pastoral prescripts, κατ' ἐπαγγελίαν ζωῆς τῆς ἐν Χριστῷ Ἰησοῦ); greeting (χάρις ἔλεος εἰρήνη, 1 Tim 1:2, 2 Tim 1:2, cf. Titus 1:4, χάρις καὶ εἰρήνη; all three have ἀπὸ θεοῦ πατρός); and thanksgiving (χάριν ἔχω, 1 Tim 1:12, 2 Tim 1:3). The noticeable relaxation of imitation as compared with the deutero-Paulines clearly signals less concern with capturing Paul's style as a pseudepigraphic tactic.

[105] Scholars generally agree that the Pastorals have one author (or multiple authors working together). See, e.g., I. H. Marshall, *A Critical and Exegetical Commentary on the Pastoral Epistles* (ICC; Edinburgh: T&T Clark, 1999), 1–2.

[106] I. Howard Marshall has proposed something similar. He argues that 2 Timothy has an authentic Pauline fragment as its basis, and that a group that includes Timothy and

situation should be this case. Or perhaps the *need* to imitate Paul so assiduously as a pseudepigraphic strategy may have diminished.[107] Mithridates' *Letter* has a contribution to make here as well, in his supposition that Brutus may have employed a secretary to compose his correspondence. We know that Tertius "wrote" Romans (16:22, ἀσπάζομαι ὑμᾶς ἐγὼ Τέρτιος ὁ γράψας τὴν ἐπιστολὴν ἐν κυρίῳ),[108] but we do not know whether he merely fair-copied a draft, or took oral dictation, or even adopted Paul's ἦθος as he composed the letter under his supervision. Similarly, an unresolved (indeed, unresolvable) question is how great a role Paul's co-senders played in the composition of his letters. But the appearances of such persons in the prescripts and postscripts prompt suppositions like that of Mithridates, although with a different emphasis. Mithridates perceives a unity in style and authorial voice in the Brutan corpus, whether Brutus is the real author or not. The contributions of secretaries and co-senders to Paul's letters might in contrast promote the expectation of a *lack* of stylistic unity, and a *plurality* of authorial voices, creating a plausible opening for pseudepigraphic expansion of his corpus and allowing some flexibility should the pseudepigraphers' efforts at imitation not prove as persuasive as they hoped.[109] This situation might even render the need for rigorous stylistic imitation moot by the time the Pastorals come along.

We can at this point discern another implication of Mithridates' *Letter*: the development of the corpus Paulinum seems to have a parallel in the Brutan corpus, since in both cases pseudepigraphic compositions were

---

Titus amplifies this original piece: "The letters were intended to give Pauline backing to Timothy and Titus ... in their work of calling the congregations back from false teaching and practice. They are examples not of pseudonymity but of allonymity. Their composition was accordingly in no sense deceptive, in that it was known that these were fresh formulations of Pauline teaching to take account of the changing situation" (*Critical and Exegetical Commentary* [see n. 105], 92). In response, I ask why Timothy and Titus would require *transparently "allonymous"* texts in order to accomplish the correction that Marshall envisions, given that Paul mentions them repeatedly as his most trusted associates. Why should the readers of the Pastorals afford any more authority to Timothy and Titus speaking as "Paul" than they would to them speaking in their own voices?

[107] The author may slyly allude to some of his sources—or pretend to possess sources that he does not in fact have—when he urges Timothy to bring his "notebooks," τὰ βίβλια μάλιστα τὰς μεμβράνας (2 Tim 4:13).

[108] For further discussion of Tertius, see Richards, *Secretary* (see n. 84), 170–72.

[109] Richards and I draw opposite conclusions regarding the implications of Paul using secretaries. Whereas I argue that pseudepigraphers notice and exploit this fact to expand the corpus, Richards sees an explanation for how all thirteen letters could be "written" by Paul (ibid., ch. 3, "The Role of the Secretary in the Letters of Paul").

added to existing collections. Several copies of the latter circulated without its cover letter,[110] and someone encountering it without Mithridates' explanation of his project would likely have perceived his additions as the real replies of the cities.[111] New editions of Paul's correspondence would similarly provide the ideal concealment for the various pseudo-Pauls to revive Paul's voice without arousing suspicion of their activities of forgery.[112] Their pseudepigrapha indeed may have ensured that his authentic letters did not fall into obscurity, insofar as they establish the continuing relevance of his letters by producing fresh syntheses of his teachings and by directing attention to the ways they speak to contemporary problems and controversies. Mithridates' sources furthermore imply more items of correspondence than the Brutan corpus supplies; as he says in 4, ἀποφαίνοντος δὲ σοῦ δυσαποκρίτως αὐτὰς ἔχειν, ᾠήθην δεῖν πεῖραν ποιήσασθαι τῆς ἀντιγραφῆς καὶ πορίσασθαι λόγους, οἵους εἰκὸς ἦν ἕκαστον ἀποκρίνασθαι τῶν ἐπεσταλκότων. Neither he nor his addressee doubt that the cities wrote back to Brutus. The question, indeed the challenge, derives from what they would have written given the letters which they received. Mithridates thus has the corpus, and he has the names of Brutus' correspondents; what he lacks is a clear sense of the identities of the latter and the events in play, so he turns to the histories. One can detect similar processes in the cases of Pauline pseudepigrapha, both within and beyond the canon. In Philippians Paul writes from prison, perhaps in Rome. He has with him both friends (Timothy and Epaphroditus, 2:19–30; also unnamed ἀδελφοί, 4:21) and enemies (1:12–18). He intimates that the end of his life approaches (1:21–26). In Philemon, Paul calls himself in the prescript a δέσμιος Χριστοῦ Ἰησοῦ (1), and later a πρεσβύτης νυνὶ δὲ καὶ δέσμιος Χριστοῦ Ἰησοῦ (9). Such remarks invite speculation: what other letters might he have sent from prison, and what would he as an "old man" look-

---

[110] See n. 6 above. As far as I know, we have no instances of other authors from antiquity quoting Mithridates' replies as if they were the actual replies of the cities.

[111] We have here an illustration of how copyists can frustrate the goal of an author to have his compositions recognized as pseudepigrapha. It would be as if the fictional letters of Alciphron became detached from his name and mistaken for the letters of ordinary fourth-century Athenians.

[112] Indeed, it is difficult to explain how Hebrews came to be regarded as a letter of Paul so early in its transmission history if its author did not intend this to be the case. Inclusion of the letter in a new edition of the corpus Paulinum would be his way of ensuring the impression of Pauline authorship. Note particularly 13:23, γινώσκετε τὸν ἀδελφὸν ἡμῶν Τιμόθεον ἀπολελυμένον μεθ' οὗ ἐὰν τάχιον ἔρχηται ὄψομαι ὑμᾶς. Clare K. Rothschild investigates Hebrews as a pseudepigraphon in her new study, *Hebrews as Pseudepigraphon. The History and Significance of the Pauline Attribution of Hebrews* (WUNT 235; Tübingen: Mohr Siebeck, 2009).

ing back on his life's work have said?[113] The author of Colossians steps into this gap,[114] with a quasi-testamentary letter that gives general exhortations (including a "household table")[115] and epitomes of Paul's doctrinal instruction elsewhere,[116] and he makes sure that the readers locate the letter along a known biographical timeline. The author also draws upon a familiar cast of characters: "Paul" sends Onesimus with Tychicus to the Colossians (4:7–9), and his συναιχμάλωτος Aristarchus greets them (4:10).[117] He furthermore mentions some of the same people that appear in the postscript of the letter to Philemon,[118] but with some interesting elaborations. Mark becomes ὁ ἀνεψιὸς Βαρναβᾶ;[119] Epaphras ὁ ἐξ ὑμῶν, δοῦλος Χριστοῦ [Ἰησοῦ], πάντοτε ἀγωνιζόμενος ὑπὲρ ὑμῶν ἐν ταῖς προσ-

---

[113] Cf. the essay by L. G. Perdue, "The Death of the Sage and Moral Exhortation from Ancient Near Eastern Instructions to Graeco-Roman Paraenesis," in *Paraenesis: Act and Form* (eds. idem and J. G. Gammie; Semeia 50; Atlanta: Scholars Press, 1990), 81–109.

[114] Note 1:24–25, νῦν χαίρω ἐν τοῖς παθήμασιν ὑπὲρ ὑμῶν καὶ ἀνταναπληρῶ τὰ ὑστερήματα τῶν θλίψεων τοῦ Χριστοῦ ἐν τῇ σαρκί μου ὑπὲρ τοῦ σώματος αὐτοῦ, ὅ ἐστιν ἡ ἐκκλησία, ἧς ἐγενόμην ἐγὼ διάκονος κατὰ τὴν οἰκονομίαν τοῦ θεοῦ τὴν δοθεῖσάν μοι εἰς ὑμᾶς πληρῶσαι τὸν λόγον τοῦ θεοῦ. Cf. Eph 3:1, τούτου χάριν ἐγὼ Παῦλος ὁ δέσμιος τοῦ Χριστοῦ [Ἰησοῦ] ὑπὲρ ὑμῶν τῶν ἐθνῶν.

[115] Cf. Eph 5:21–6:9. See J. T. Fitzgerald, "Haustafel," *RGG*[4] 3:1485–86; J. E. Crouch, *The Origin and Intention of the Colossian Haustafel* (FRLANT 109; Göttingen: Vandenhoeck & Ruprecht, 1972).

[116] One can see the author synthesizing themes and language from several of Paul's letters in 2:6–13. In v. 6 he uses the metaphor of "walking" (ὡς οὖν παρελάβετε τὸν Χριστὸν Ἰησοῦν τὸν κύριον, ἐν αὐτῷ περιπατεῖτε), cf. Rom 6:4 (ἡμεῖς ἐν καινότητι ζωῆς περιπατήσωμεν), 8:4 (ἐν ἡμῖν τοῖς μὴ κατὰ σάρκα περιπατοῦσιν ἀλλὰ κατὰ πνεῦμα), Gal 5:16 (πνεύματι περιπατεῖτε), also 1 Cor 3:3, 7:17. V. 7 features the metaphor of "building upon" (ἐποικοδομούμενοι ἐν αὐτῷ), cf. 1 Cor 3:9–15, as well as "abounding" (περισσεύοντες ἐν εὐχαριστίᾳ), cf. Rom 5:15 (ἡ χάρις τοῦ θεοῦ καὶ ἡ δωρεὰ ἐν χάριτι τῇ τοῦ ἑνὸς ἀνθρώπου Ἰησοῦ Χριστοῦ εἰς τοὺς πολλοὺς ἐπερίσσευσεν), 15:13 (εἰς τὸ περισσεύειν ὑμᾶς ἐν τῇ ἐλπίδι ἐν δυνάμει πνεύματος ἁγίου), 1 Cor 15:58 (περισσεύοντες ἐν τῷ ἔργῳ τοῦ κυρίου πάντοτε). V. 8 raises the issue of φιλοσοφία (cf. 1 Cor 1–2) and τὰ στοιχεῖα τοῦ κόσμου (Gal 4:3, 9). The term πλήρωμα in v. 9 appears in several other passages, but with a different sense than here (Rom 11:12, 25; 13:10, and note εὐσχημόνως περιπατεῖν, 13; 15:29; Gal 4:4). The metaphor of κεφαλή (v. 10) is central to Paul's argument in 1 Cor 11:2–16. Vv. 11–13 concentrate several metaphors from Romans, including a non-literal περιτομή (Rom 2:25–29), being "buried" and "raised with Christ" in baptism (Rom 6) and being "co-enlivened" (cf. 6:8, συζήσομεν αὐτῷ). For more analysis, see E. P. Sanders, "Literary Dependence in Colossians," *JBL* 85 (1966): 28–45.

[117] Cf. Acts 27:2.

[118] Phlm 23–24: ἀσπάζεταί σε Ἐπαφρᾶς ὁ συναιχμάλωτός μου ἐν Χριστῷ Ἰησοῦ, Μᾶρκος, Ἀρίσταρχος, Δημᾶς, Λουκᾶς, οἱ συνεργοί μου. Cf. E. Lohse, *Colossians and Philemon* (ed. H. Koester; trans. W. R. Poehlmann and R. J. Karris; Hermeneia; Philadelphia: Fortress Press, 1971), 170–77, esp. the table at 175–76.

[119] Acts 12:12, 25; 15:37–39.

ευχαῖς;[120] and Luke ὁ ἰατρὸς ὁ ἀγαπητός.[121] Does the author fabricate these details or take them from other sources available to him (and his readers)? Either way, he positions the letter relative to other known events (Paul's imprisonment and eventual execution) and persons as part of his pseudepigraphic strategy. The Pastorals intensify the testamentary character of Colossians further, with "Paul" the old man addressing his protégés Timothy and Titus, again as a "prisoner" (2 Tim 1:8). One may also mention pseudepigraphic epistles outside of the New Testament which take references to "lost" epistles of the corpus Paulinum as a point of departure, particularly *3 Corinthians* (1 Cor 5:9, 7:1) and the *Epistle to the Laodiceans* (Col 4:16).[122]

---

[120] Cf. 1:7–8, καθὼς ἐμάθετε ἀπὸ Ἐπαφρᾶ τοῦ ἀγαπητοῦ συνδούλου ἡμῶν, ὅς ἐστιν πιστὸς ὑπὲρ ὑμῶν διάκονος τοῦ Χριστοῦ, ὁ καὶ δηλώσας ἡμῖν τὴν ὑμῶν ἀγάπην ἐν πνεύματι.

[121] Cf. the closing greetings of 1 Peter, which refer to Silvanus (a co-sender of First Thessalonians) and "Mark my son." Cf. also 2 Tim 4:19–21 (Prisca and Aquila, Onesiphorus, Erastus, Trophimus, Eubulus, Pudens, Linus, Claudia), Titus 3:12–14 (Artemas, Tychicus, Zenas, Apollos).

[122] The latter is a transparently clumsy pastiche, but the former—which dates to the second century, per J. K. Elliott (*The Apocryphal New Testament: A Collection of Apocryphal Christian Literature in an English Translation* [Oxford: Clarendon Press, 1993], 353–54)—is less so, at least from an ancient point of view. Stephan (1 Cor 1:16) and the πρεσβύτεροι Daphnus, Eubolus (2 Tim 4:21?), Theophilus (Luke 1:3?) and Zenon address Paul regarding the arrival of two heretical teachers at Corinth, a Simon (Magus, Acts 8?) and a Cleobius (?). These individuals seem to teach a composite of heresies (text below per M. Testuz, ed., *Papyrus Bodmer X–XII* [Cologny-Genève: Bibliotheca Bodmeriana, 1959], 30–45, with the editor's recommended corrections in square brackets and my own addition of accents): Marcionism (οὐ δεῖν, φησίν, προφήτ[αι]ς χρῆσθαι, 1:10; οὐδ' εἶναι θεὸν παντοκράτορα, 11; οὐδ' εἶναι τὴν πλάσιν τὴν τῶν ἀνθρώπων τοῦ θεοῦ, 13; οὐδ' εἶναι τὸν κόσμον θεοῦ ἀλλὰ ἀγγέλων, 15), the problem that Paul deals with in 1 Cor 15 (οὐδὲ ἀνάστασιν εἶναι σαρκός, 12), and Docetism (οὐδ' ὅτι εἰς σάρκα ἦλθεν ὁ κύριος οὐδ' ὅτι ἐκ Μαρίας ἐγεννήθη, 14). On the other hand, these assertions could cover a broad range of heretical movements, past, present and future. The response of "Paul" blends diction and ideas from the corpus Paulinum with those found in other NT texts in order to produce a workable doctrinal synthesis. But the efforts toward προσωποποιία (incomplete as they are) remain consistent throughout. For example, the prescript reads Παῦλος ὁ δεσμ[ί]ος Χριστοῦ Ἰησοῦ τοῖς ἐν Κορίνθῳ ἀδελφοῖς ἐν πόλλοις ὢν ἀστοχήμασι (!) χαίρειν (!!). "Paul" therefore locates himself as a prisoner with a familiar phrase, but strangely does not give his typical greeting. Another interesting passage pertains to the question of Christ's birth, which expands Rom 1:3–4: ὁ κύριος ἡμῶν Χριστὸς Ἰησοῦς ἐκ Μαρ[ί]ας ἐγεννήθη ἐκ σπέρματος Δαυὶδ πνεύματος ἁγίου ἀπὸ οὐράνου παρὰ τοῦ πατρὸς ἀποσταλέντος εἰς αὐτήν, 2:5. The real Paul never mentions Mary by name nor directly betrays any knowledge of the Virgin Birth, but early Christians would presuppose that he both knew about and taught such things, something that the author of *3 Corinthians* helpfully renders explicit.

I have thus in the present essay offered an annotated English translation of the *Letter* of Mithridates. I have also established that the author is probably not a king or addressing a king, that he is the same person who expanded the Brutan corpus, and that he did so sometime during the second century CE. I examined the testimonia, showing how they exhibit a consistent interest in Brutus' style, and that his letters were influential as models of epistolary composition. Mithridates indeed writes both his *Letter* and his pseudepigraphic additions to the corpus in order to enhance its pedagogical utility. And finally I pointed out some ways that Mithridates illuminates the epistolary pseudepigrapha of the New Testament, especially the relationship of sources, authors and end-products. He supplies a much-needed window into the processes behind the composition of these texts and their inclusion in the canon.

III. Frühchristliche Kontexte

Pseudonymity and the New Testament Canon

by

HARRY Y. GAMBLE

A broad consensus of modern critical scholarship holds that, of the twenty-seven items of early Christian literature that ultimately came to constitute the canon of the New Testament, only eight appear under the names of their actual authors, namely, the seven authentic letters of the apostle Paul and the Apocalypse of John of Patmos. Thus in respect of authorship the contents of the New Testament are by heavy preponderance either pseudonymous or anonymous. Among the Pauline epistles, Ephesians and the Pastoral letters (1–2 Timothy and Titus) are certainly pseudonymous, and most also consider 2 Thessalonians and Colossians to be pseudonymous. Among the catholic epistles, those commonly taken to be pseudonymous are James, 1–2 Peter and Jude.

Beyond these ten pseudonymous items, the New Testament also contains no fewer than nine anonymous documents: the four Gospels, the Acts of the Apostles, 1–2–3 John, and Hebrews. These writings, though naming no author, began at an early time to be associated by tradition with specific authors—the four Gospels with Matthew, Mark, Luke and John respectively, Acts with Luke, the Johannine epistles with the same John as the Gospel, and Hebrews with Paul. In this way anonymous writings acquired pseudonymous attributions, a phenomenon sometimes called "secondary" or "extrinsic" pseudonymity.

This essay considers the significance of the presence of pseudonymous writings within the New Testament canon. It will not be much concerned with the many issues that surround the production of pseudonymous writings, but will concentrate instead upon the history of their reception in the early church and their eventual inclusion in the canon. The recognition that the New Testament contains pseudonymous documents both raises historical questions about the formation of the New Testament canon and poses theological questions about the nature of the canon and its authority. But it is essential to distinguish these two sets of questions and to answer them separately, for otherwise the issues become hopelessly confused. Hence in the following we will first consider the historical problems, and then give some brief attention to the more theological concerns.

1. Pseudonymity and the History of the Canon

The New Testament canon is the outcome of a lengthy process extending from the second through the fifth centuries. Because this process is only partially documented in ancient sources, all reconstructions must be in some measure hypothetical and tentative. The main outlines of the history of the canon are nevertheless relatively clear. The following sketch is not intended to be comprehensive, but aims rather to highlight the role of authorship, including pseudonymous authorship, in the development of the canon.

The New Testament canon that finally emerged in the late fourth and early fifth centuries consists in the main of three smaller collections, each of which had its own earlier and independent history, namely, the Pauline corpus, the fourfold Gospel, and the catholic epistles. Only two writings of the New Testament do not belong to one of these smaller and earlier collections, namely the Acts of the Apostles and the Apocalypse of John. For the question of the role of pseudonymity in the history of the canon it is helpful to discuss these smaller collections individually.

1.1 The Pauline Corpus

The letters of Paul are not only the earliest extant Christian writings, but were also the earliest to be collected. Already near the beginning of the second century collections of Paul's letters were available over a broad area. Clement of Rome, Ignatius of Antioch, Polycarp of Smyrna and the author of 2 Peter were each acquainted with aggregates of Paul's letters, though it is not possible to determine precisely which or how many such letters each knew. Small and partial collections of Paul's letters may have arisen still earlier as individual letters of the apostle were exchanged among his communities (cf. Col 4:16), but of these we have no clear evidence.

We have definite knowledge, however, that at least two large-scale editions of the collected letters of Paul were current by the middle of the second century.[1] One is the edition evidenced by Marcion (ca. 140), which comprised ten letters in the order Galatians, 1–2 Corinthians, Romans, 1–2 Thessalonians, Laodiceans (= Ephesians), Colossians, Philippians and Philemon. The other edition lies behind most early Greek manuscripts, including the earliest extant manuscript of the *Corpus Paulinum*, P[46] (ca. 200). This edition offered the letters in a different order: Romans, (Hebrews), 1–2 Corinthians, Ephesians, Galatians, Philippians, Colossians, 1–

---

[1] An "edition" (ἔκδοσις) is to be distinguished from a mere "collection" by reason of deliberate, unifying formal features that represent its contents as a coherent whole.

2 Thessalonians. Manuscripts with this latter arrangement normally also include, after these letters to churches, the "personal letters," in the order 1–2 Timothy, Titus and Philemon. In this edition the Pauline letters are arranged by decreasing length, Romans being the longest and standing at the head, 1 Corinthians being the next longest and standing second, etc.

There is also good evidence, though less direct, of yet a third early edition of the letters of Paul. A number of ancient Christian sources express the idea that Paul had written to seven churches and, because the number seven symbolized totality or universality, that Paul therefore addressed the church at large.[2] This conception almost certainly reflects an actual early edition of the Pauline letters that presented them as "letters to seven churches." Although no seven-churches edition has survived as such, its traces can be seen whenever the letters are enumerated according to deceasing length *and* letters to the same community are taken together as a length-unit: Corinthians (1–2), Romans, Ephesians, Thessalonians (1–2), Galatians, Philippians and Colossians (+ Philemon). Construing Paul's letters in this way places the emphasis not upon the number of letters Paul wrote but upon the number of *churches* to which he wrote. This offers a strong indication that there was once a "seven churches" edition of Paul's letters that presented ten letters, but as addressed to exactly seven churches, and thus to Christendom as a whole.

There are reasons to think that this seven-churches edition was the earliest edition of the collected letters of Paul. First, it offers a solution to a problem that was early felt with regard to Paul's letters, namely their particularity: because Paul had written to individual communities about matters of local and immediate concern, it was uncertain what relevance, value and authority those letters might have for other communities.[3] A seven-churches edition of Paul's letters connoting their ecumenical relevance seems to have been designed to meet this problem. Second, there are strong reasons to suppose that the edition used by Marcion was derived from such a seven-churches edition.[4] In Marcion's edition the letters are

---

[2] T. Zahn, *Geschichte des neutestamentlichen Kanons* (Erlangen: Deichert, 1892), 2:73–5, K. Stendahl, "The Apocalypse of John and the Epistles of Paul in the Muratorian Canon," in *Current Issues in New Testament Interpretation* (eds. W. Klassen and G. F. Snyder; New York: Harper & Row, 1962), 239–45, and N. A. Dahl, "The Particularity of the Pauline Epistles as a Problem in the Ancient Church," in *Neotestamentica et Patristica: Freundesgabe O. Cullmann* (NovTSup 6; Leiden: Brill, 1962), 261–71.

[3] N. A. Dahl, ibid. This difficulty must already have been felt in the first century, for old textual variants, which probably predate any collections, show that the specific addresses of some of Paul's letters (e.g., 1 Cor 1:2; Rom 1:7, 15; cf. Eph 1:1) were sometimes omitted in favor of more generalized designations of intended readers.

[4] See particularly H.-J. Frede, *Altlateinische Paulus-Handschriften* (VL 24/2; Freiburg i. Brsg.: Herder, 1969), 290–303 ("Die Ordnung des Paulusbriefe und der Platz des

not arranged by decreasing length, for Galatians stands at the beginning and Laodiceans (= Ephesians) follows the Thessalonian letters. But leaving aside those exceptions, the rest of the letters *are* ordered by decreasing length, with the two Corinthian letters, the two Thessalonian letters, and Colossians-Philemon being taken together as length-units. Since the principle of diminishing length is not consistently followed and has no constitutive importance for Marcion's edition, the presence of its clear vestiges shows the indebtedness of Marcion's edition to an earlier edition that did adhere to this principle. And, since letters to the same community are counted together, that earlier edition must have given particular emphasis to the number of communities addressed by Paul, and is likely therefore to have been precisely the seven-churches edition. Like the seven-churches edition, Marcion's edition contained only community letters, with Philemon construed among them as a companion letter to Colossians, both understood to be addressed to the same community. If Marcion's edition is indebted to it, then a seven-churches edition of Paul's letters must go back at least to the very early second century, and perhaps reaches back into the first.

For present purposes, these early editions of the Pauline corpus yield some useful insights. Of chief importance is the fact that all of the earliest recoverable editions of the collected letters of Paul already contained some documents now considered pseudonymous: Ephesians, Colossians and 2 Thessalonians. At least one of these—Ephesians (though not 2 Thessalonians)—was indispensable to the idea that Paul wrote to precisely seven churches: without it, Paul wrote to only six churches. But Colossians had its own importance in this collection, since the very brief letter to Philemon does not specifically mention Colossae and could not be taken as addressed to that church unless it was accompanied by Colossians.[5] Thus the inclusion of Ephesians and Colossians along with the authentic letters was essential to the conception and construction of a seven-churches edition. Finally, because Ephesians, Colossians and 2 Thessalonians belonged to all three early forms of the Pauline corpus and were in no way differentiated from other letters, all of these letters must have entered into the

---

Kolosserbriefs im Corpus Paulinum," esp. 295–97); N. A. Dahl, "The Origin of the Earliest Prologues to the Pauline Letters," *Semeia* 12 (1978): 233–77; J. J. Clabeaux, *A Lost Edition of the Letters of Paul: A Reassessment of the Text of the Pauline Corpus Attested by Marcion* (CBQMS 21; Washington: Catholic Biblical Association, 1989), and U. Schmid, *Marcion und sein Apostolos: Rekonstruktion und historische Einordnung der Paulusbriefausgabe* (ANTF 25; Berlin: de Gruyter, 1995). For a summary, see H. Gamble, *Books and Readers in the Early Church* (New Haven, Conn.: Yale University Press, 1995), 59–62.

[5] The personalia in Colossians (4:9, 12, 14–15; cf. Phlm 2, 23) provide the necessary basis for the Colossian address of Philemon.

stream of textual transmission and dissemination along with the authentic letters. Thus all ten of these letters were from the outset universally received and recognized as authentically Pauline. There is no evidence that anyone in the ancient church called into question the authorship of any of the Pauline community letters.

The pseudonymous letters that belonged to the *Corpus Paulinum* in its earliest editions are also those that stand in the closest relationships, whether of form, style or content, to the authentic letters: Colossians, Ephesians and 2 Thessalonians. Neither claim can be made, however, for the remaining Pauline pseudepigrapha, 1–2 Timothy and Titus. Since these are personal letters addressed to individuals, naturally they would have found no place in the old seven-churches edition, nor did they belong to Marcion's edition.[6] In all likelihood they were also absent from our earliest extensive manuscript of Paul's letters, P^{46}.[7] To all appearances, these three letters were at some point, probably around the middle of the second century, added to the pre-existing collection of Paul's community letters, perhaps in connection with a new, revised and expanded edition of the *Corpus Paulinum*.[8] The first explicit witnesses to their presence are Athenagoras, Irenaeus and Tertullian toward the end of the second century.[9] Reservations were indeed expressed in the ancient church about the authority of the Pastoral epistles, but this had nothing to do with doubts about authorship. Rather, for some the fact that these letters were addressed to individuals seemed to preclude their catholic relevance and authority far more even than the particularity of the community letters.[10] Yet it may have

---

[6] Even if the Pastorals were composed before the middle of the second century (as most suppose), there is no good evidence for the view that Marcion knew but rejected them, as Tertullian claims (*Marc.* 5.21).

[7] The manuscript lacks its final leaves, but in the opinion of the original editor, they were insufficient to have accommodated the Pastorals. See F. G. Kenyon, *The Chester Beatty Biblical Papyri*, Fasc. 3, Supplement (London: Emery Walker, 1936), x–xi. For a recent discussion of the question, also concluding to the original absence of the Pastorals, see E. J. Epp, "Issues in the Interrelation of New Testament Textual Criticism and Canon," in *The Canon Debate* (eds. L. M. McDonald and J. A. Sanders; Peabody, Mass.: Hendrickson, 2002), 485–515 (495–500).

[8] P. Trummer, "Corpus Paulinum – Corpus Pastorale: Zur Ortung der Paulustradition in den Pastoralbriefen," in *Paulus in den neutestamentlichen Spätschriften: Zur Paulusrezeption im Neuen Testament* (ed. K. Kertelge; Freiburg i. Brsg.: Herder, 1981), 122–45; M. Wolter, *Die Pastoralbriefe als Paulustradition* (FRLANT 146; Göttingen: Vandenhoeck & Ruprecht, 1981).

[9] Athenagoras, *Supplicatio* 37.1; Irenaeus, *Haer.* 1 (preface); 2.14.7; 3.3.4; 3.14.1; Tertullian, *Idol.* 11; *Apol.* 31; *Cor.* 8, 10, 15; *An.* 2, 16.

[10] Dahl, "The Particularity of the Pauline Epistles" (see n. 2), 263–66. The author of the Muratorian Canon (lines 61–63) finds it necessary to give a separate justification for the Pastoral epistles, viz. that they are acknowledged by the catholic church "for the or-

been precisely their private and personal character that enabled these pseudonymous letters to be added, without suspicion of authorship, to the earlier editions, for it could offer some explanation of their delayed appearance as part of the Pauline corpus.

The only other document to bid strongly for inclusion among the letters of Paul was Hebrews which, though actually anonymous, might seem implicitly a Pauline letter by reason of its letter-like conclusion (13:22–25). And indeed Hebrews, in spite of its anonymity, was from an early time taken to be a Pauline letter in some areas, most notably in Egypt: in P^{46} Hebrews stands among the community letters of Paul, and by virtue of its length, holds the second place after Romans. This is intelligible in an Egyptian manuscript belonging to the end of the second century, for Clement of Alexandria (following Pantaenus [Eusebius, *Hist. eccl.* 6.14.2–4]) considered it to have been composed by Paul in Hebrew and translated into Greek by Luke, and Origen, though he doubted the Pauline authorship of Hebrews on grounds of style, and conjectured either Clement of Rome or Luke as its author, nevertheless deferred to eastern tradition that held it to be Pauline (Eusebius, *Hist. eccl.* 6.25).[11] Apart from the early acquaintance with Hebrews that seems to be shown for Rome by *1 Clement*, there was in the West no early or general recognition of Hebrews as a Pauline letter or as any part of the Pauline corpus. After Clement, Tertullian, who attributes the authorship of Hebrews to Barnabas (*Pud.* 20), is its sole Western witness prior to the fourth century when the West finally acquiesced in its canonical standing, yet without embracing it as fully Pauline: in Western manuscripts Hebrews commonly stands at the end of the Pauline corpus, after both the community letters and the personal letters, a token of long-standing Western doubts about its authorship. While the case of Hebrews is interesting in itself, its fate serves to show, by contrast, how fully and consistently the letters of Paul, including pseudonymous ones, were from the beginning recognized and received as genuinely Pauline. So far as we know, no question was ever raised about the authenticity of any of them.[12]

---

dering of ecclesiastical discipline." It perhaps deserves mention that Tatian accepted only the letter to Titus (Jerome, *Comm. Tit. Praefatio*), not 1–2 Timothy, probably for encratite reasons (R. M. Grant, "Tatian and the Bible," *StPat* 1 [1957]: 297–306).

[11] This judgment persisted in the East: in later Egyptian MSS. Hebrews is typically positioned within the Pauline letters after the letters to the churches but before the personal letters—a uniquely Alexandrian position. See W. H. P. Hatch, "The Position of Hebrews in the Canon of the New Testament," *HTR* 29 (1936): 133–51.

[12] The eventual inclusion of both the Pastoral Epistles and Hebrews in the Pauline corpus resulted in a total of fourteen letters of the apostle, so that even though the original idea that Paul had written to seven churches was superseded, the larger collection nevertheless retained the symbolic significance of the number seven ($2 \times 7 = 14$).

Given the early and broad dissemination of Paul's collected letters and the high esteem for Paul as *the* apostle in the second century, it is not surprising that many subsequent pseudonymous writings were produced in his name. These included one or two letters to the Laodiceans,[13] a letter to the Alexandrians (otherwise unknown), a letter known as 3 Corinthians (which came to be incorporated into the Acts of Paul and Thecla),[14] an Apocalypse of Paul, and a body of correspondence between Paul and his contemporary, the Roman philosopher Seneca. Although all of these Pauline pseudepigrapha had some circulation and use in the early church, only 3 Corinthians was ever to gain any canonical recognition, and that was limited to the Syrian and Armenian churches. The pseudonymous character of all these seems to have been recognized by most in the ancient church, sometimes promptly, and their value discounted, but it cannot be said that they were discounted exclusively or primarily for that reason, for by the time of their appearance the scope of the Pauline corpus had become firmly enough established to preclude additions.

In sum, the history of the Pauline corpus reveals a very mixed pattern of reception toward Pauline pseudepigrapha: some pseudonymous writings (Ephesians, Colossians, 2 Thessalonians) belonged to the collection of community letters in their earliest editions, some pseudonymous writings (1–2 Timothy, Titus) were subsequently added to the community letters without known objection on grounds of authorship, one anonymous document (Hebrews) was associated with the community letters of Paul (early and more closely in Egypt, much later and less closely in the West) despite long-standing doubts about its Pauline authorship, and a number of later Pauline pseudepigrapha never acquired general recognition as genuinely Pauline.

---

[13] There is one preserved Pauline pseudepigraphon "To the Laodiceans" (in Latin) which is a brief and clumsy pastiche of excerpts from other letters, apparently intended to supply an otherwise unknown Pauline letter mentioned in Col 4:16. The Muratorian Canon (lines 63–64) mentions a letter to the Laodiceans "forged in Paul's name for the heresy of Marcion," but this is unlikely to be the Laodicean letter that we possess. Further, Marcion knew our Ephesians as a letter to the Laodiceans (*Marc.* 5.11, 17), although Epiphanius (*Pan.* 42.9.4; 42.12.3) mentions among the letters used by Marcion both Ephesians and Laodiceans. On the whole question see G. Hahneman, *The Muratorian Fragment and the Development of the Canon* (Oxford: Clarendon Press, 1992), 196–200.

[14] 3 Corinthians, like Laodiceans, may possibly have been fabricated to supply another presumably lost letter of Paul to the Corinthians (cf. e.g., 1 Cor 5:9).

1.2 The Fourfold Gospel

For present purposes much briefer attention can be given to the emergence of another component collection of the New Testament canon, the four Gospels. Here primary pseudonymity is not at issue since all four are anonymous documents. Nevertheless, during the course of the second century a secondary pseudonymity was attached to these narratives by means of traditions attributing their authorship to specific individuals, "Matthew" and "John" to disciples/apostles of Jesus, "Mark" and "Luke" to disciples of Peter and Paul respectively. These attributions came to be incorporated, not into the texts of the Gospels, but into their superscriptions, which were taken to designate their actual authors. Precisely when this occurred and why has been and remains a matter of debate.[15] These traditions of attributed authorship do not seem to have arisen all at once or all together, but gradually and independently in relation to different Gospels.

Irenaeus, writing about 180, provides our earliest evidence for a collection of these four Gospels, and is the first to argue for its exclusive authority (*Haer.* 3.11.8). How much earlier this collection may have been made is arguable. The reception of these Gospels prior to Irenaeus' time is not well-documented. According to Eusebius (*Hist. eccl.* 3.39.15–16), Papias, about a half century before Irenaeus (ca. 130), was acquainted with the Gospel of Mark, considered its author to be an associate of Peter, defended it against criticisms arising probably from unfavorable comparison with one or more other Gospels, and seems also to have known a Gospel (presumably our Matthew) associated with the name of Matthew. It is not clear what other Gospels, if any, he may have known. Marcion (ca. 140) had an exclusive preference for a Gospel that bore enough resemblance to Luke for his later opponents to identify it as Luke, although Marcion himself seems not to have known this Gospel by any title or author. Justin (ca. 150), who habitually refers to Gospel documents as "memoirs (ἀπομνημονεύματα) of the apostles and those who followed them," yet without ever naming them, seems to have relied mainly upon a Gospel harmony of some sort that drew especially on Matthew and Luke, and he may have

---

[15] The early appearance of the superscriptions, already in the late first or early second century (and possibly originally with the publication of Mark), and thus independently of any collection of Gospels, has been urged by M. Hengel, "The Titles of the Gospels and the Gospel of Mark," in *Studies in the Gospel of Mark* (ed. idem, London: SCM, 1985), 64–84; cf. idem, *The Four Gospels and the One Gospel of Jesus Christ* (Harrisburg: Trinity Press International, 2000), 48–115. But all of Hengel's evidence comes from the late second century. For criticism, see F. Bovon, "The Synoptic Gospels and the Canonical Acts of the Apostles," *HTR* 81 (1988): 19–36. The evidence is not sufficient to support such early dating of the superscriptions, and it remains likely that their peculiar form originated with the creation of a collection of Gospels, on which see below.

been unacquainted with John.[16] Justin's student Tatian (ca. 170) was certainly acquainted with all four of these Gospels, but conflated their texts into a single narrative and made additions from other sources, and thus did not think of these four in the same way as Irenaeus. Moreover, as Irenaeus acknowledges (*Haer.* 3.1.7), various Christian groups had been accustomed to use only single Gospels. Thus it appears that a collection of four Gospels attributed to Matthew, Mark, Luke and John did not come into being before about the middle of the second century.[17] Despite the strong advocacy of Irenaeus, the four-fold Gospel did not immediately secure universal acceptance and use. Tatian's *Diatessaron* enjoyed broad and long use, especially in the Syrian church, and other Gospels were variously in use in particular communities.

Beyond offering the earliest evidence for the collection of four Gospels and the first argument for its exclusive authority, it is important, though less often noticed, that Irenaeus is also the first Christian writer actually to name all four of these Gospels, which he does in accordance with their superscriptions, and also the first to state for each the tradition of authorship that had developed by his time (*Haer.* 3.1.1). Although the traditions of authorship for Mark and Matthew seem to go back ultimately to Papias, those for Luke and John appear to have arisen rather later and to have been less well-established. Irenaeus is the first to speak of Luke as a companion of Paul (*Haer.* 3.1.1; cf. 3.14.1), and this is in all likelihood his own inference from his reading of the Pauline letters and of Acts.[18] Soon after Irenaeus, Clement of Alexandria also shows acquaintance with these four

---

[16] Justin, if he quotes the Gospel of John at all, does so only once (*Apol.* 1.61.4), and it remains doubtful to most that Justin knew, or at any rate valued, this Gospel. M. R. Hillmer, "The Gospel of John in the Second Century" (PhD diss., Harvard University, 1966), 51–73, and H. Koester, *Ancient Christian Gospels* (Philadelphia: Trinity Press, 1990), 246, 360, deny Justin's knowledge of the Fourth Gospel, while J. Prior, "Justin Martyr and the Fourth Gospel," *SecCent* 9 (1992): 153–69, thinks Justin knew it but did not regard it as apostolic or authoritative. More recently C. E. Hill, *The Johannine Corpus in the Early Church* (Oxford: Oxford University Press, 2004), 312–42, has argued for Justin's knowledge, use and high valuation of John as an apostolic Gospel. In that case, however, Justin's silence about this Gospel becomes wholly inexplicable.

[17] For a date around the middle of the first century see T. C. Skeat, "Irenaeus and the Four-Gospel Canon," *NovT* 34 (1992): 194–99, and idem, "The Oldest Manuscript of the Four Gospels," *NTS* 43 (1997): 1–34, followed by G. N. Stanton, "The Fourfold Gospel," *NTS* 43 (1997): 317–46. A still earlier date is proposed, although on different grounds, by T. Heckel, *Vom Evangelium des Markus zum viergestaltigen Evangelium* (WUNT 120; Tübingen: Mohr Siebeck, 1999). Hengel, despite claiming that the traditional superscriptions are very early, thinks the collection of four Gospels emerged only late in the second century and as a product of the Roman church (*The Four Gospels* [see n. 15], 136–40).

[18] A. Gregory, *The Reception of Luke and Acts in the Period Before Irenaeus* (WUNT II/169; Tübingen: Mohr Siebeck, 2003).

Gospels by name and as a collection. The authorship of the Gospel of John, however, was still liable to question in Rome in the early third century by opponents of Montanism.[19]

How far did their authorial attributions contribute to the development of the collection of these four Gospels and its inclusion in the New Testament canon? It is noteworthy that Gospels are not, as a rule, cited by name during the first half of the second century. Indeed, apart from the testimony of Papias preserved by Eusebius, no Gospel is mentioned by the name of its ostensible author before Theophilus of Antioch (ca. 170), who refers to the Gospel of John (*Autol.* 2.22). This alone suggests that authorial attributions had little significance for most of the second century. Yet sources belonging to the late second and early third century consistently acknowledge these four by name and support this acknowledgment by appeal to the traditions linking them with their presumed authors, hence as "handed down to us by the apostles." These traditions all manifest legendary, polemical or apologetical features, and aim at legitimizing the authority and use of the Gospel in question by asserting its apostolic origin, whether direct or indirect. Such traditions probably arose during the earlier period when different Gospels were individually in use among various Christian communities and competed with each other for recognition. Indeed, the impulse to promote the authority of a particular Gospel can sometimes be seen in the texts of the Gospels themselves. The secondary epilogue of the Gospel of John (ch. 21) stands in sponsorship of the Gospel by asserting that the "disciple whom Jesus loved" is the one who "has written these things" (21:20, 24), and the author of the Gospel of Luke suggests in his prologue (1:1–4) that his narrative, though admittedly one among many, is orderly, well-informed, and conveys truth to the reader. Direct claims to authority are made under apostolic pseudonyms in the Gospel of Peter and the Gospel of Thomas, and the traditions of the authorship of Matthew, Mark, Luke and John must originally have served no other purpose. Especially noteworthy is the tradition, found in one form in Clement of Alexandria (Eusebius, *Hist. eccl.* 6.14.7) and a more elaborate form in the Muratorian Canon, that John, urged by his fellow-disciples, wrote a "spiritual Gospel," a legend that is clearly meant to urge the authority of the Gospel of John despite its large and troublesome disparities with other Gospels.[20]

---

[19] For the dispute about the Fourth Gospel (and the Apocalypse) in Rome led by Gaius and the "alogoi," (Irenaeus, *Haer.* 3.11.9, Epiphanius, *Pan.* 51.4.5–12.6, Dionysius Bar Salibi, *In Apocalypsin* 1), see R. E. Heine, "The Role of the Gospel of John in the Montanist Controversy," *SecCent* 6 (1987): 1–19.

[20] Eusebius (*Hist. eccl.* 3.24.7–13) offers another tradition but for the same purpose, maintaining, that the Gospel of John recounts events before John the Baptist was imprisoned, while the other Gospels speak of events after John's imprisonment.

While modern scholarship considers the traditional authorial ascriptions of the Gospels historically unsupportable, they had gained strong credit in the early church by the end of the second century and thereafter encountered little dispute. Although it cannot be determined how far these traditions of authorship were influential in promoting the use of the Gospels of Matthew, Mark, Luke and John, they clearly played a significant role in the authorization of the collection of these four and in its achievement of canonical standing. Nevertheless, it cannot be claimed that these ascriptions of authorship were the decisive factor, for these Gospels were also the ones that seem to have enjoyed the longest and most widespread use in the second century (even though the Gospel of John seems to have had its earliest popularity in Gnostic circles). Moreover, the fact that other Gospels explicitly claiming apostolic authorship, such as the Gospel of Thomas and the Gospel of Peter, had early currency but failed to gained canonical recognition also indicates that putative authorship was not in itself a conclusive consideration.

1.3 The Corpus of Catholic Epistles

By contrast with the Pauline letters and the Gospels, both of which were shaped into fixed collections in the course of the second century, the corpus of seven letters comprising the so-called catholic epistles (James, 1–2 Peter, Jude, 1–2–3 John) did not come into being before the late third or early fourth century. It is first attested in the early fourth century by Eusebius, who speaks of "the seven letters called catholic" (*Hist. eccl.* 2.23.25). It was in connection with the contents of this collection that the issue of authenticity most exercised the early church. Although 1 John is anonymous, and 2 and 3 John are effectively anonymous, written by someone who calls himself "the elder," the remaining four items of this collection explicitly claim apostolic authorship by James, Peter and Jude.

Of these seven letters, only 1 Peter and 1 John appear to have been much known and used in the second and third centuries, being taken as products of their supposed apostolic authors and frequently cited, though not always by name. But the rest had a very limited and uneven history of reception. Of 2 Peter nothing at all is heard before Origen, who notes its disputed status (Eusebius, *Hist. eccl.* 6.25.8), and Origen is also the first to mention "the epistle of James that is in circulation," seeming to imply doubt about it (*Comm. Joh.* 19.23.152 and 20.10.66). The two smaller Johannine letters (2–3 John) likewise had a sparse and erratic history of reception. Clement of Alexandria refers to 1 John as "[John's] larger epistle," implying a knowledge at least of 2 John (*Strom.* 2.15.66), and Irenaeus quotes both 1 and 2 John, yet oddly as if from a single letter (*Haer.* 3.16.5–8). Origen was aware of all three Johannine letters, mentioning "an epistle of very few lines [= 1 John] and, it may be, also a second and a third, for not everyone says these are genuine" (Eusebius, *Hist. eccl.* 6.25.10). Origen apparently shared such doubts since he never quotes 2 or 3 John. His student Dionysius distinguished the author of 2–3 John from the author of the Gospel and 1 John (Eusebius, *Hist. eccl.* 7.25.11). As to Jude, its earliest witness in the West is Tertullian, who firmly attributed it to the "apostle Jude" (*Cult. fem.* 1.3.1–3), and it is listed in the Muratorian Canon, but it was apparently unknown to Irenaeus. In the East it was known but little used by Clement of Alexandria (*Strom.* 2.11, *Paed.* 3.8.44ff.), but known and often cited by Origen, who only once expressed some doubt about it ("if anyone were to accept the epistle of Jude": *Comm. Matt.* 17.30.9–10). It is especially noteworthy that early in the fourth century Eusebius unequivocally designated James, Jude, 2 Peter and 2–3 John as ἀντιλεγόμενα ("disputed") (*Hist. eccl.* 3.25.3). Thus with the exceptions of 1 Peter and 1 John, the authenticity of all the catholic epistles was broadly in doubt well into the fourth century.[21]

It is remarkable that despite early hesitancy about their authority, despite their limited and sporadic use, and despite Eusebius' statement that five of the catholic epistles were disputed, the collection of all seven nevertheless found a place in canon lists that begin to appear soon after the middle of the fourth century—in Egypt with Athanasius' Easter Letter of 367, in Asia Minor with the Council of Laodicea of 363, and in Africa with the Synod of Carthage in 397, for example. This can hardly be taken to mean that all doubts about the authenticity of the catholic epistles had suddenly been overcome.[22] To the contrary, it can only be assumed that those long-standing reservations were not overcome but were only set aside, and the apostolic authorship of all the catholic epistles, whether pseudony-

---

[21] It is to be noted also that the catholic epistles were consistently absent in all the earliest Syrian witnesses, and that only with the fifth century and the Peshitta do we find three of the catholic epistles included: James, 1 Peter and 1 John.

[22] The variable status of the catholic epistles even in the late fourth century can be seen in the remark of Amphilochius of Iconium (Iambi ad Selucum), "Of the catholic epistles some say we should accept seven, but others say only three should be accepted - one of James, one of Peter and of those of John one. But some accept three (of John) and besides these two of Peter, and that of Jude, a seventh." Amphilochius himself seems not to have acknowledged 2 Peter, 2–3 John and Jude. It is sometimes said that another late 4th century writer, Didymus the Blind, did not accept all the catholic epistles, and considered 2 Peter as a forgery (falsata), a judgment based on a Latin commentary commonly attributed to Didymus (In epistolam S. Petri Secundam Enn., PG 39 1774A). But it is clear from the Toura commentaries that Didymus did accept 2 Peter as genuine: see B. Ehrman, "The New Testament Canon of Didymus the Blind," *VC* 37 (1983): 1–21. Ehrman also shows, however, that Didymus included in his canon of authoritative scripture the Epistle of Barnabas, the Shepherd of Hermas, the Didache and probably 1 Clement.

mously claimed or merely attributed, was simply presumed. Questions about authorship were now judged less important than the value of a collection of seven catholic epistles that could be assigned to apostolic figures, for such a collection could furnish the church with texts representing apostles both other than Paul and earlier than Paul—especially the "pillar apostles" Peter, James and John (cf. Gal 2:9)—and could serve to supplement and counterbalance the long-standing and imposing corpus of the Pauline letters.[23] Hence in the case of the catholic epistles it is especially clear that in the later stages of the formation of the canon issues of authenticity were superseded by the theological usefulness of a more comprehensive apostolic witness than was afforded by Paul's letters alone or the Gospels.

1.4 Acts and the Apocalypse

Finally, with respect to the two canonical documents that belonged to none of the three collections discussed so far, namely Acts and the Apocalypse, brief remarks will suffice. Although we hear nothing of Acts before Irenaeus (*Haer.* 3.12.1–15), the obvious relationship between Acts and the Gospel attributed to Luke, a relationship emphasized by Irenaeus, served to identify also the author of Acts, and there was no more dispute about the authorship of Acts than of the Gospel. The situation with the Apocalypse was more complicated. Despite the early identification of the author of the Apocalypse with John the apostle, a sophisticated argument against that identification was made by Dionysius of Alexandria (ca. 250) in opposition to Egyptian chiliasts. Excerpts of his argument preserved by Eusebius (*Hist. eccl.* 7.24–25) mention an earlier rejection of the Apocalypse by some who thought it was written not by the apostle but by Cerinthus. Dionysius demurred from that conclusion, but he made detailed comparisons between the Apocalypse and the Fourth Gospel and 1 John in order to show that the Apocalypse was not written by John the apostle. His aim was not to expose the Apocalypse as pseudonymous, but only to show that it was misattributed. His denial of its apostolic authorship did not cause him to repudiate the Apocalypse; for him, its authority and usefulness did not depend finally on its authorship. Yet Dionysius' argument effectively undermined the standing of the Apocalypse among later Eastern Christians, and its authority remained doubtful in the East well into the fourth century.

---

[23] This has now been argued thoroughly and effectively by D. R. Nienhuis, *Not by Paul Alone: The Formation of the Catholic Epistle Collection and the Christian Canon* (Waco, Tex.: Baylor University Press, 2007). See previously D. Lührmann, "Gal. 2:9 und die katholischen Briefe," *ZNW* 72 (1981): 65–87.

2. The Significance of Pseudonymity in the History of the Canon

This relatively brief and selective overview of the history of the canon has aimed to show that, although the early church both desired and generally assumed the apostolic origins of its authoritative literature, the significance of authorship was highly variable both over time and with regard to different writings. Confidence in apostolic authorship was most consistent in connection with the letters of Paul, slower to develop and somewhat more tenuous with regard to the Gospels, and for a long time was at best weak for the majority of the catholic epistles. Moreover, doubts about the authorship of Hebrews and of the Apocalypse were never fully resolved, and yet did not finally serve to exclude either from canonical standing. Hence it cannot be said that the issue of authenticity always played the same role or that full confidence in apostolic authorship was the *sine qua non* for an authoritative writing.

If, beyond the documents that ultimately found their way into the canon, we consider the larger range of early Christian literature, the role of authorship appears to have been similarly variable. A number of writings explicitly claiming apostolic authorship failed to gain canonical standing (for example, the *Didache*, the *Gospel of Peter*, the *Gospel of Thomas*, the *Apocalypse of Peter*); a few anonymous writings which were sometimes (mis-)attributed to an apostolic author were ultimately discounted (for example, the *Epistle of Barnabas, 1 Clement*); and still other writings which did not claim apostolic authorship nevertheless enjoyed significant early use and authority alongside authentically or pseudonymously apostolic ones (for example, the *Shepherd of Hermas*).[24] Such instances indicate that authorship *per se* was by no means the only issue that conditioned the early church's regard for its literature.[25]

---

[24] The *Shepherd of Hermas* was regarded authoritative scripture by Irenaeus (*Haer.* 4.20.2), Clement of Alexandria (*Strom.* 1.1.1; 1.85.4; 1.181.1; 2.3.5; etc.), and by Tertullian in his pre-Montanist period (*Or.* 16; cf. *Pud.* 10), without any presumption of apostolic authorship, and was highly regarded also by most Christian writers up to the fourth century. Origen (*Comm. Rom.* 10.31) was the first to conjecture its apostolic authorship, attributing it to the Hermas mentioned in Rom 16:14, an idea echoed by Eusebius (*Hist. eccl.* 3.3.6) and Jerome (*Vir. ill.* 10).

[25] It is worth noting that in some major early biblical codices such documents yet found a place: Codex Sinaiticus (4th century) includes both *Barnabas* and the *Shepherd of Hermas* (and possibly held still other documents, since the last leaves of the codex are lost), and Codex Alexandrinus (5th century) has *1–2 Clement*. Codex Vaticanus (5th century) has lost its leaves after Heb 11:4, and it cannot be known what more it might have contained. Moreover, the catalogue of biblical books (4th century) associated with the Codex Claromontanus lists the *Shepherd of Hermas*, the *Acts of Paul* and the *Apoca-*

The variable relationship between authorship and authority in the history of the canon raises two questions: first, whether and how far early Christian communities were invested in issues of authorship, and second, whether and how far they were capable of adjudicating such issues and undertook to do so.

That in the early church apostolic authorship was a powerful *desideratum* for writings taken to be authoritative is clearly shown by the esteem accorded to writings that were believed to be of apostolic origin, by the tendency to associate anonymous writings with apostolic figures, and by the rich production of apostolic pseudepigrapha, especially in the second century. These developments were consequences of the early Christian regard for the "apostolic age" as the normative period of revelation and authoritative teaching. The demise of the apostolic generation required the early church to find means of appropriating and perpetuating the authority of the apostles and the teaching associated with them.[26] It did so by developing and relying upon three closely correlative conceptions: apostolic tradition (teaching), apostolic succession (office) and apostolic writings (authoritative scriptures), all of which became effectively operative, even if not fully formalized and consolidated, during the second century. Because all three of these *loci* of authority were conceived as deriving from "the apostles" they were understood to be not merely compatible but fundamentally unitary, each in accord with the others and thus mutually re-enforcing. Hence writings of apostles were expected to be in conformity with traditions of teaching that, even if unwritten, were likewise taken to derive from the apostles, and to be in use in churches that stood prominently in succession to the apostles. It is not surprising therefore to see in the history of the canon a lively interplay of authorship, content and use. This interplay is nicely illustrated in relation to the issue of pseudonymity.

Although it is sometimes asserted that in the early church writings believed to be pseudonymous were dismissed out of hand on the basis of authorship alone, the evidence commonly adduced fails to support this claim. Often mentioned in this connection is the case of the Gospel of Peter. According to Eusebius (*Hist. eccl.* 6.12.2–6), in the late second century the

---

lypse of Peter. None of these is included in Codex Claromontanus itself, but they must have belonged to a manuscript known to the writer of the catalogue.

[26] On the normative nature of the apostolic period see the comments of N. Brox, "Zum Problemstand in der Erforschung der altchristlichen Pseudepigraphie," in *Pseudepigraphie in der heidnischen und jüdisch-christlichen Antike* (ed. idem; Wege der Forschung 484; Darmstadt: Wissenschaftliche Buchgesellschaft, 1977), 311–34, and the extended discussion by Wolter, *Die Pastoralbriefe als Paulustradition* (see n. 8), 95–130. Whether or not one chooses to speak of a "vacuum of authority" or a "crisis of continuity" with the demise of the apostolic period, the desire to maintain a material connection with the apostolic generation is everywhere evident.

Gospel of Peter was being read in the community of Rhossus, a practice to which Serapion, the bishop of Antioch, initially had no objection. When it was subsequently brought to his attention that the Gospel of Peter contained objectionable elements, Serapion examined it and disallowed its use, asserting that "we receive both Peter and the other apostles as Christ, but writings which falsely bear their names (τὰ δὲ ὀνόματι αὐτῶν ψευδεπίγραφα) we reject, as men of experience, knowing that such were not handed down to us." Here it appears that the effective reason for Serapion's repudiation of the Gospel of Peter was not in the first place recognition of its pseudonymous character, but rather what he perceived as its heterodox content. A negative judgment about content, coupled with an appeal to traditional usage, overrode a prior presumption of apostolic authorship. We may imagine that the same considerations would have been in effect for the evaluation of other Gospels: no matter what the assumptions about authorship, defective content and/or an absence of broad use counted heavily against authoritative status. Frequent reference is also made to Tertullian's account (*Bapt.* 17) of an Asian presbyter who wrote the Acts of Paul "thinking to add to Paul's reputation" but was found out and, though protesting that he had done it "for the love of Paul," was deposed from his office. The episode is often taken to show that pseudonymous authorship was condemned as such, but the context makes it clear that, even if he disapproved of pseudonymous composition, Tertullian rejected the Acts of Paul because it taught that a woman might teach and baptize.[27] Another but much later example involving pseudonymous authorship is provided by Salvian of Marseilles (400–480), who defended an encyclical letter entitled "From Timothy to the Whole Church."[28] Salvian's bishop, Salonius, discovered that the document had been pseudonymously composed by Salvian himself, and let it be known that such forgeries were unacceptable. While the bishop apparently opposed to pseudonymous authorship in principle, Salvian's response emphasized the importance of giving greater weight to the substance of what is written than to the one who wrote it. None of these examples, then, demonstrates that pseudonymous authorship was judged inherently objectionable by the early church, but they do show that in disputes over the authority of particular documents there was always an eye to content.

Of course, in the larger history of the canon many documents were judged to be spurious and were rejected. In most cases we do not know the

---

[27] It would not appear that Tertullian was objecting to pseudonymity in this case, since the *Acts of Paul* itself was not pseudonymous but anonymous, though 3 Corinthians is pseudonymous.

[28] For the text, see J. O'Sullivan, *The Writings of Salvian the Presbyter* (New York: Cima Press, 1947), 260–61.

circumstances or grounds for their rejection, but the question of literary authenticity was often involved. The Muratorian Canon, for example, states that "a letter to the Laodiceans and another to the Alexandrians, forged in the name of Paul for the heresy of Marcion, and several others, cannot be accepted in the catholic church, for gall cannot be mixed with honey" (lines 64–67). Although these writings are labeled as pseudonymous (*Pauli nomine ficte*), they are also alleged to be heterodox, and they may have been ruled out for either reason, or for both reasons. The Muratorian Canon also rejects the *Shepherd of Hermas*, maintaining that it is not to be read "either among the prophets, whose number is complete, nor among the apostles, for it is after their time" (lines 73–80). Here the issue is not strictly authorship, but the fact that the *Shepherd* post-dates the apostolic period, which perhaps implies that it cannot be taken to convey apostolic teaching. On the other hand, the Muratorian Canon (lines 69–72) approves the use of other writings that are certainly pseudonymous, namely the *Apocalypse of Peter*, concerning which it is conceded that "some do not want it to be read [publicly] in the church," and the Wisdom of Solomon, said to be "written by friends of Solomon in his honor,"[29] which presumably means pseudonymously. The considerations at work in the Muratorian Canon include authorship, but content and tradition are also taken fully into account.

An extremely important piece of evidence for the history of the canon generally and for the significance of pseudonymity within it is Eusebius's famous catalogue of "writings of the new covenant" (*Hist. eccl.* 3.25). In it Eusebius sorts early Christian literature into three categories: (1) books that are "acknowledged" (ὁμολογούμενα), (2) books that are "disputed" (ἀντιλεγόμενα) and "not genuine" (νόθα), and finally, (3) books "that are promoted by the heretics under the name of the apostles."[30] With this

---

[29] Or, according to a popular conjecture, "the Wisdom of Solomon, written by Philo in his honor," but in that case it would still be a matter of pseudonymity.

[30] The precise nature of Eusebius' classification has long been debated, above all whether Eusebius provides four categories (acknowledged, disputed, spurious, and heretical) or only three (acknowledged, disputed, heretical). Recent opinion has strongly inclined toward seeing here only three categories (considering ἀντιλεγόμενα and νόθα as synonymous terms). For this judgment, see G. A. Robbins, "Eusebius' Lexicon of Canonicity," *StPat* 25 (1993): 134–41; idem, "*Peri ton endiathekon graphon:* Eusebius and the Formation of the Christian Bible" (PhD diss., Duke University, 1986); A. D. Baum, "Der neutestamentliche Kanon bei Eusebius (*Historia ecclesiastica* 3.25.1–7) im Kontext seiner literaturgeschichtlichen Arbeit," *ETL* 73 (1997): 307–48; idem, "Literarische Echtheit als Kanonkriterium in der alten Kirche," *ZNW* 88 (1997): 97–110, and E. Kalin, "The New Testament Canon of Eusebius," in *The Canon Debate* (see n. 7), 386–404. Robbins thinks that Eusebius regarded all the writings classified as ἀντιλεγόμενα as spurious, but that he nevertheless distinguishes between those that some

classification Eusebius mainly has in view the question of literary authenticity, and the terms he employs throughout are among those commonly used in ancient discussions of literary authenticity.[31] To the first category of "acknowledged" writings Eusebius (*Hist. eccl.* 3.25.1–2) assigns the four Gospels, Acts, the letters of Paul (among which Eusebius reckons Hebrews; cf. 3.3.5), 1 John, 1 Peter and, "if it seems desirable," the Apocalypse. All these he calls not only "acknowledged" (ὁμολογούμενα) but also "true and genuine" (ἀπλάστους καὶ ἀληθεῖς, *Hist. eccl.* 3.25.6), and thus shows that it is a matter of literary authenticity. Among the books that are "disputed" (ἀντιλεγόμενα) and "not genuine" (νόθα) Eusebius (*Hist. eccl.* 3.25.3–5) lists James, Jude, 2 Peter and 2–3 John, the *Acts of Paul*, the *Shepherd of Hermas*, the *Apocalypse of Peter*, the *Epistle of Barnabas*, the *Didache*, once again the Apocalypse of John ("if this view prevail"), and finally the *Gospel of the Hebrews*. "All these," he says, "belong to the disputed books" (ἀντιλεγόμενα). Lastly, among heretical writings Eusebius (*Hist. eccl.* 3.25.6) names "Gospels such as those of Peter and Thomas and Matthias, and some others besides, or Acts such as those of Andrew and John and the other apostles." Of these last he goes on to say (*Hist. eccl.* 3.25.7) that their "type of phraseology differs from the apostolic style, and the opinion and tendency of their contents is widely divergent from true orthodoxy and clearly shows that they are forgeries (ἀναπλάσματα) of heretics." As such, they should not even be considered among the spurious writings (ἐν νόθοις).

In this famous passage the question of authorship has large prominence. The "acknowledged" writings are those regarded as genuine, that is, actually written by those who claim to be their authors or to whom they have been attributed. The "disputed" writings are those whose literary authenticity is doubted, that is, whose putative authorship is suspect. Of the heretical writings, their authorship is not only suspect but undoubtedly false. Eusebius' catalogue therefore offers gradations of literary authenticity: undoubted, doubtful and false. Those that stand in doubt Eusebius excludes from the "acknowledged" writings, which he also calls "encovenanted"

---

thought to be genuine and those that none considered genuine. Baum also thinks that Eusebius makes a distinction within the ἀντιλεγόμενα category, by which he expresses his own opinion that some are genuine. Kalin (ibid., 394–97) argues persuasively that Eusebius neither intends nor makes any significant differentiation within the category of ἀντιλεγόμενα and that in Eusebius' usage ἀντιλεγόμενα and νόθα "are essentially two different terms for the same category." Cf. Nienhuis (*Not by Paul Alone* [see n. 23], 63–8), who thinks that Eusebius "believed the ἀντιλεγόμενα and the νόθα to be of the same larger group" but that the two are differentiated by the fact that James, 2 Peter, 2–3 John and Jude are "known by most."

[31] For the terminology, see esp. Baum, ibid., 309–10.

(ἐνδιαθήκους), even though they may have been widely known. As a result, his catalogue of fully authoritative literature contains only twenty-two items. But even though Eusebius' terminology has to do mainly with literary authenticity, the issue of authorship is for him inseparable from the question of content and traditional recognition within the church. The importance of content is clear from the comment in 3.25.7 about heretical books: it is their content that shows they are forgeries. The importance of traditional use is evident from his comment in 3.25.6, to the effect that with the division between the "acknowledged books" and the "disputed books" he has sought to distinguish between those "which, *according to the tradition of the church* (κατὰ τὴν ἐκκλησιαστικὴν παράδοσιν) are true, genuine and accepted, and those which, by contrast to these, are not encovenanted but are disputed." Thus it appears that the principal bases for Eusebius' judgments about literary authenticity was content, that is, agreement with what he understood as apostolic and orthodox teaching, and tradition, that is, what writings had been in broad and common Christian use from early times. For Eusebius, authorship, content and usage were co-inherent factors in determining the scope of authoritative scripture.

Another text that merits mention in this connection is the *Apostolic Constitutions*, composed in the fourth century. Although itself a pseudonymous composition, the *Apostolic Constitutions* (6.3.16) nevertheless inveighs against pseudonymous compositions, admonishing its readers

that you not accept those books that carry our name but are written by the ungodly. For you are not to attend to the names of the apostles, but to the nature of things and to their settled opinions. For we know that Simon and Cleobius and their followers have written poisonous books under the name of Christ and his disciples and carry them about in order to deceive you ... And among the ancients also some have written apocryphal books of Moses and Enoch and Adam and Isaiah and David and Elijah and of the three patriarchs, pernicious and repugnant to the truth. The same things even now have the wicked heretics done.

We see here an acute sensitivity to the currency of pseudonymously apostolic writings and a strong opposition to them. But this is accompanied by the insistence that what matters is not whether a document carries an apostolic name, but whether it is orthodox and thus comports with what was understood to be apostolic teaching. Here the criterion for judging authorship is content, not vice versa. And similarly, in the fourth century Cyril of Jerusalem takes content as a sound indication of authorship when he lists the canonical books (*Catechetica* 4.36) and stipulates "the four Gospels alone, for the rest are falsely inscribed and harmful (ψευδεπίγραφα καὶ βλαβερά)," adding that "the Manichees also wrote a Gospel according to Thomas which, tinged with the fragrance of an evangelical title, corrupts the souls of the more simple-minded."

If we now consider together these rather disparate bits and pieces of evidence, several conclusions can be drawn about the significance of pseudonymity within the history of the canon. First, for most of the second century Christian communities were disinclined to question the authorship of writings that had come into general circulation and customary use. Explicit claims of authorship were commonly taken at face value and, where explicit claims were lacking, traditions ascribing authorship were generally accepted. Little or no suspicion of pseudonymity seems to have found expression. Second, as Christian literature proliferated, much of it pseudonymous, and as that literature reflected an ever broader diversity of ideas and practices, questions inevitably arose about which documents should be valued as authoritative by Christian communities. Such disputes are first evident in the late second century and persisted through the third and in the fourth century. Third, in all discussions about the authorship and authority of particular texts, the question of authorship never stood alone. It was regularly accompanied by a concern about content, and not merely whether the content of a document was useful or edifying, but above all whether it was orthodox, that is, in conformity with the faith and practice of the church, which was itself understood to be "apostolic." Thus it can be seen that from the late second century onward pseudonymity came to be closely associated with heterodox content, so that a negative judgment about content sufficed to demonstrate pseudonymous authorship: what was not orthodox could not be apostolic. Fourth, yet a further factor in judging the authorship and authority of any given text was the history of its actual use so far as that was known. Naturally this consideration came into play only gradually as common usages developed, and so it belongs mainly to the third and fourth centuries. Because authorship alone appears not to have been the decisive issue in the determination of the canonical status of any writing, the significance of pseudonymity for the history of the New Testament canon should not be overestimated.

That some pseudonymous writings succeeded in gaining broad acceptance and were ultimately incorporated into the New Testament canon need not be taken to mean that the church willingly or knowingly embraced pseudonymous literature. It may very well be true that in antiquity generally and in the early church "no one ever seems to have accepted a document as religiously and philosophically prescriptive which was known to be forged."[32] Nor is it necessary to assume that Christians of the early centuries were simply naïve and easily fooled into thinking that pseudonymous writings were genuine. It needs to be recognized that in the an-

---

[32] L. R. Donelson, *Pseudepigraphy and Ethical Argument in the Pastoral Epistles* (HUT 22; Tübingen: Mohr Siebeck, 1986), 11.

cient world it was not an easy matter to tell the difference between authentic and spurious works. By the middle of the second century the actual origins of most documents in Christian use had probably been lost to view and lay beyond any direct knowledge or determination. In this connection, far more attention needs to be given to the fact that the very methods by which ancient literature was published and entered into the process of reproduction and circulation served to quickly distance texts from their authors and to obscure the circumstances of their origins.[33] Under such conditions it was natural and necessary for Christian communities to rest their judgments on content, accustomed usages and received tradition.

Of course, well-educated Christian thinkers who were acquainted with the literary-critical methods developed and employed in ancient scholarship had some advantage in evaluating issues of authorship and authenticity.[34] Clement and Origen (Eusebius, *Hist. eccl.* 6.14.2–3; 6.25.11–14) put just such methods to use in discussing the authorship of Hebrews, carefully comparing its vocabulary, style and thought with the letters of Paul, and concluding that Hebrews could not have been written directly by Paul. Origen elsewhere (*Princ.* praef. 8) remarked about *The Teaching of Peter* that it "is not included among the books of the church, and I can show that it is not a writing of Peter nor of anyone else who was inspired by the spirit of God," and although he does not say how he would show this, we may suppose he would have employed the same sorts of observations that he applied to Hebrews. Dionysius of Alexandria's demonstration (Eusebius, *Hist. eccl.* 7.25) that the author of the Apocalypse was not the author of the Gospel and 1 John provides another example of the careful application of the methods of ancient literary criticism. The rejection of the Apocalypse and of Hebrews by the learned Roman churchman Gaius (Eusebius, *Hist. eccl.* 3.28.1–2; 6.20.3) probably depended at least in part on similar arguments.

Still, a knowledge and use of critical methods by some Christian thinkers to judge authorship did not consistently lead them to defensible conclusions. Clement of Alexandria took the *Apocalypse of Peter*, among other anonymous or pseudonymous writings,[35] to be genuine (Eusebius, *Hist.*

---

[33] Gamble, *Books and Readers in the Early Church* (see n. 4), 82–143.

[34] On the use of critical methods in antiquity and early Christianity, see W. Speyer, *Die literarische Fälschung im heidnischen und christlichen Altertum: Ein Versuch ihrer Deutung* (Handbuch der Altertumswissenschaft I/2; München: Beck, 1971), 181–86, and R. M. Grant, *Heresy and Criticism: The Search for Authenticity in Early Christian Literature* (Louisville, Ky.: Westminster John Knox, 1993).

[35] On the generous breadth of Clement's conception of authoritative writings, see J. Ruwet, "Clement d'Alexandrie: Canon des écritures et apocryphes," *Bib* 29 (1948): 77–99, 240–68, 391–408, and J. A. Brooks, "Clement of Alexandria as a Witness to the Development of the New Testament Canon," *SecCent* 9 (1992): 41–55.

eccl. 6.14.1), as did Hippolytus and the author of the Muratorian Canon. Origen accepted as genuine the *Acts of Paul* and the *Didache*, not to mention Susanna, despite the critical arguments made against it by Julius Africanus. In fact, many of the most highly literate Christian writers accepted as genuine various patently pseudonymous works. To mention only the most telling instances, a report ostensibly written by Pontius Pilate to the Emperor Tiberius and attesting to the miracles and resurrection of Jesus was regarded as genuine by Justin (*Apol.* 1.35, 48), Tertullian (*Apol.* 5) and Eusebius (*Hist. eccl.* 2.2.1–6), and the pseudepigraphical correspondence between Paul and Seneca was considered authentic by both Jerome (*Vir. ill.* 12) and Augustine (*Epistulae* 153). Such instances show that, despite the availability of classical methods of criticism, they were neither consistently used nor rigorously applied, and so did not reliably lead to accurate differentiations between genuine and spurious writings. In this light it is no wonder that some pseudonymous writings escaped suspicion, came to be highly valued and widely used, and eventually found inclusion in the canon of Christian scriptures.

If it is reasonably clear that the early church had genuine misgivings about pseudonymous writings and rejected those it knew or strongly suspected to be pseudonymous, it nevertheless needs to be emphasized that the issue of literary authenticity seems to have held less interest for the early church than is commonly supposed. It is a mistake to imagine that every document in Christian use was subjected to careful critical scrutiny aimed at certifying its literary authenticity. This was not done, and could not be done. Rather, writings that had early come into customary and widespread use, whether on the presumption of their authenticity or for other reasons, were largely immune to second-guessing about their authorship: established usage among Christian communities was itself sufficiently probative. Questions of literary authenticity normally arose only in particular circumstances, mainly when it was necessary to defend the authority of a writing already widely held to be authoritative, to challenge the authority of a document suspected of heterodox content or liable to heterodox interpretation, or to investigate the pedigree of a writing that was newly-known or not well-known. Yet even when authorship was in question, that issue never stood alone, in isolation from other considerations. Instead, what we see in the early church is a progressive confluence and conflation of ideas about authorship, content, antiquity and use: each was understood to presume and imply the others. Certainly the concept of "apostolicity" was not predicated exclusively on direct authorship by an apostle. Without excluding that possibility, the conception of what was apostolic could be and was also construed more broadly: it could signify authorship by followers or successors of the apostles, or derivation from the period of the apostles, or merely essential agreement with what the church regarded as apostolic teaching. In the history of the canon each of these construals seems to have been operative at various times and in connection with different documents.[36]

Thus, while it is to be granted that apostolicity was an important consideration in the early church's valuation of its literary heritage, it must also be said that no document attained authority or secured canonical standing merely on the basis of presumed literary authorship by an apostle. Content played an equally important role, most especially whether a given writing concurred with the tradition of the church's faith and practice (that is, was orthodox) and was broadly relevant and useful (that is, "catholic"). Ultimately, however, and amid the interplay of all such considerations, the most powerfully effective factor in bringing early Christian literature to canonical status was traditional usage. Here we are dealing not with abstract principles or criteria, but with actual practice. In the nature of the case, traditional use could only arise over time, and effective appeal could be made to it only as the church gained retrospect on its past. But it is already a prominent consideration for Irenaeus in the second century and Origen in the third century, and it is decisive for Eusebius in the early fourth. Whether a document had been in broad, consistent and public use in most Christian communities, above all in liturgical reading, and had been recognized and cited as authoritative by earlier Christian writers, was a matter of large import. The force of traditional use is readily seen in the fact that the four Gospels, the letters of Paul, 1 Peter and 1 John, all of which were widely and continuously employed as Christian scripture at least from the middle of the second century, never suffered any challenges to their authenticity or authority, whereas the additional documents that were finally to gain canonical standing had significantly less long and broad histories of use, and correspondingly their authenticity and/or authority was more open to question.

In light of the many factors that were at work in the history of the canon and the actual course of the development of the canon so far as it can be reconstructed, it is not remarkable but rather to be expected that numerous pseudonymous writings and misattributed anonymous writings should have found their way into the corpus of Christian scripture.

---

[36] K.-H. Ohlig, *Die theologische Begründung des neutestamentlichen Kanons in der alten Kirche* (Düsseldorf: Patmos-Verlag, 1972), 57–156. According to Ohlig, the fundamental sense of "apostolicity" is "Urkirchlichkeit"—what is characteristic of the early church. See also the comments of D. Farkasfalvy, "The Ecclesial Setting of Pseudepigraphy in Second Peter and its Role in the Formation of the Canon," *SecCent* 5 (1985): 3–29, who rightly notes that the concept of what was apostolic was as much theological as literary or historical.

3. Canonical Pseudepigrapha as a Theological Problem

Modern discussions of the relation of pseudonymity and canon have been characterized not only by historical but also by theological concerns, and some brief attention may be given to these.[37] At the root of the theological issues is the nature of pseudonymity itself. The principal question is whether and to what extent the practice of pseudonymous authorship was deceptive: was pseudonymity regarded in antiquity as an essentially harmless literary convention that, at least from certain motives or in some circumstances, might be legitimately exercised, or was it understood as a thoroughly deceitful and hence morally reprehensible undertaking that was in all instances unacceptable. How this question is answered has made a large difference for the way in which the relation of pseudonymity and canon has been evaluated.

It is recognized on all sides that pseudonymous authorship was widely practiced in the ancient world—in Judaism, in early Christianity and in their larger Greco-Roman environment—but there is little consensus about how this practice was understood. Writing under the name of another occurred in many different contexts, in relation to multiple genres of literature, and for a variety of motives, and there is no single conception of the pseudepigraphical enterprise that can cover all cases.[38] It is undeniable, however, that irrespective of context, genre or motive, pseudonymous writings are in their very nature deceptive, misleading the reader about the identity of the author, a point that has been re-emphasized in some recent studies.[39] This issue, more than any other, has rendered the idea of canonical pseudepigrapha problematical, but how the problem is conceived and discussed depends heavily on confessional differences.

---

[37] For general discussions of pseudonymity as a theological issue see, in addition to the studies cited in the following notes, M. Janßen, *Unter falschem Namen. Eine kritische Forschungsbilanz frühchristlicher Pseudepigraphie* (ARGU 14; Frankfurt a.M.: Peter Lang, 2003), 263–68, and K. Clarke, "The Problem of Pseudonymity in Biblical Literature and its Implications for Canon Formation," in *The Canon Debate* (see n. 7), 440–68 (457–68).

[38] For the variety of settings, genres and motives see the concise discussion by B. M. Metzger, "Literary Forgeries and Canonical Pseudepigrapha," *JBL* 91 (1972): 3–24, and, in greater detail, Speyer, *Die literarische Fälschung* (see n. 34), and Brox, *Pseudepigraphie* (see n. 26).

[39] J. Duff, *A Reconsideration of Pseudepigraphy in Early Christianity* (PhD thesis, Oxford, 1998), T. L. Wilder, *New Testament Pseudonymity and Deception: An Inquiry into Intention and Reception* (Lanham, Md.: University Press of America, 2004), and idem, "Pseudonymity and the New Testament," in *Interpreting the New Testament: Essays on Method and Issues* (eds. D. A. Black and D. S. Dockery; Nashville: Broadman & Holman, 2001), 296–335.

Those of a conservative Protestant persuasion have been particularly reluctant to admit that any of the canonical documents may be pseudonymous. Characterizing pseudepigraphic writings as "forgeries," "frauds" or "fictions," they often insist that explicit claims of authorship by an apostolic figure be taken as factually accurate. This position is motivated by two considerations. First, because it is a deceptive device pseudonymity is thought to be at odds with the moral values of early Christianity, which included a commitment to truthfulness. Second, and yet more important, because scripture is regarded as the inspired, truthful and irrefragable medium of divine revelation, rooted in the direct witness of the apostles, it cannot be in any respect misleading. To acknowledge that any scriptural document makes a false claim of authorship would both disqualify it from providing apostolic witness and put it at odds with the truthfulness of scripture, and thus deprive it of authority. On these premises scriptural authority and pseudonymous authorship are seen as mutually exclusive.[40] Beyond disputing the idea of canonical pseudepigrapha, some conservative scholars have gone so far as to propose that if any canonical document could be shown to be pseudonymous it should be excluded from the canon.[41] This approach to the problem is obviously determined by dogmatic theological presuppositions about the nature of the scriptural canon rather than by any careful historical assessments of the evidence either for

---

[40] The idea is categorically expressed by J. Packer, *Fundamentalism and the Word of God* (Grand Rapids, Mich.: Eerdmans, 1958), 184: "We may lay it down as a general principle that when biblical books specify their own authorship, the affirmation of their canonicity involves a denial of their pseudonymity." Among those maintaining a similar view are J. S. Candlish, "On the Moral Character of Pseudonymous Books," *Expositor* 4 (1891): 91–107, 262–79; D. Guthrie, "The Development of the Idea of Canonical Pseudepigrapha in New Testament Criticism," in *The Authorship and Integrity of the New Testament* (eds. K. Aland et al.; TC 4; London: SPCK, 1965), 14–39; E. E. Ellis, "Pseudonymity and Canonicity of New Testament Documents," in *Worship, Theology and Ministry in the Early Church* (eds. M. J. Wilkins and T. Paige; JSNTSup 87; Sheffield: JSOT Press, 1992), 212–24; E. J. Schnabel, "Der biblische Kanon und das Phänomen der Pseudonymität," *JEvTh* 3 (1989): 59–96; idem, "History, Theology and the Biblical Canon: An Introduction to Basic Issues," *Them* 20 (1995): 16–24; T. D. Lea, "Pseudonymity and the New Testament," in *New Testament Criticism and Interpretation* (eds. D. A. Black and D. S. Dockery; Grand Rapids, Mich.: Zondervan, 1991), 535–59; S. Porter, "Pauline Authorship and the Pastoral Epistles: A Response to R. W. Wall's Response," *BBR* 6 (1996): 133–38; A. D. Baum, *Pseudepigraphie und literarische Fälschung im frühen Christentum: Mit ausgewählten Quellentexten samt deutscher Übersetzung* (WUNT II/138; Tübingen: Mohr Siebeck, 2001), esp. 179–91.

[41] Candlish, ibid., 95–7; Schnabel, ibid., 87–91, 96; Ellis, ibid., 224; Baum, ibid., 171–85, 191; Porter, ibid., 133–38. P. Pokorný, "Das theologische Problem der neutestamentlichen Pseudepigraphie," *EvTh* 44 (1984): 486–96 (496), would force the issue.

pseudonymity or for the history of the canon.[42] On such presuppositions "canonical pseudepigrapha" is an oxymoron, and such a category cannot exist.

Other scholars, including some of relatively conservative perspective, both Protestant and Catholic, find it hard to deny the evidence that at least some canonical documents are pseudonymous, and have sought to understand pseudonymity in terms that are less theologically problematic. Primarily, this means conceiving of pseudonymous authorship in a fashion that mitigates or minimizes the element of deception. This may be done in various ways, depending on what cultural, literary, historical or theological influences are thought to have been at work. Some, noting the frequency of pseudonymous attribution in the prophetic, apocalyptic and wisdom literature of Judaism, have suggested that in Judaism pseudonymity was a conventional literary device by means of which traditions were articulated, interpreted or developed in the name of an ancient figure of authority with whom such traditions were typically associated, and that early Christian pseudonymity was merely a carry-over from its Jewish cultural environment.[43] On such a basis it can be claimed that there is a "biblical mode" of pseudonymity in which literary attribution is "an assertion of authoritative tradition, not literary origins."[44] By placing the emphasis not on authorship *per se* but upon the authority, value and vitality of the tradition that is pseudonymously sponsored, the issue of literary attribution is relativized. It may be thought that pseudonymity was a familiar and transparent fiction, readily recognized and accepted as such, and/or that the pseudonymous author did not intend merely to appropriate falsely the identity of another but genuinely to speak on behalf of an authoritative figure and as an advocate of a tradition or traditions associated with that figure. Thus the element of deceit is mitigated, either by convention or intention or both, and

---

[42] In regard to the history of the canon, conservative Protestants refuse to regard the canon as a creation of the church or as a function of developing ecclesiastical tradition, and represent it rather as the church's recognition of and acquiescence in the self-authenticating authority of those documents that embody the apostolic witness. Only so do they believe that scripture can retain its independence of and priority over tradition, and therefore its exclusively normative role (*sola scriptura*).

[43] This position is developed by D. G. Meade, *Pseudonymity and Canon: An Investigation into the Relationship of Authorship and Authority in Jewish and Earliest Christian Tradition* (WUNT 39; Tübingen: Mohr Siebeck, 1986).

[44] Meade, ibid., 105, 186, 193, etc. Meade's argument is characterized by a steady apologetic toward a conservative view of scripture. He is concerned to differentiate between deception at the level of literary attribution and deception at the level of "(doctrinal) truth," viewing the former as conventional but the latter as unacceptable (197).

the phenomenon of pseudonymous authorship, legitimized by reference to biblical literature itself, is naturalized within the canon.[45]

Others, however, find nothing distinctive in Jewish pseudepigraphy, and regard both Jewish and early Christian pseudonymity merely as particular manifestations of a wider ancient practice of which Greco-Roman literature offers many examples. In some Greco-Roman contexts pseudonymous authorship appears to have been conventional and innocuous: students in rhetorical schools practiced pseudonymous writing by composing "speeches in character" of famous orators (προσωποποιία), followers of Pythagoras composed philosophic and scientific works under his name, ascribing to him all that they knew, and medical treatises were routinely attributed pseudonymously to Hippocrates. Many regard early Christian pseudepigraphy as closely parallel to such practices: traditions of Christian teaching were similarly elaborated, interpreted and deployed under the name of an authoritative figure. To the extent that this was culturally conventional, genuinely deceptive motives are minimized. Yet it is ordinarily conceded that already by the early Hellenistic period there was a clear and widespread sense of "intellectual property" (*geistiges Eigentum*) and a corresponding disapproval of pseudonymous authorship.[46] Thus most scholars acknowledge that an element of deception remains intrinsic to pseudonymity, even if it is a matter of "the noble lie" (*pia fraus*).[47] In that case, it can be imagined that the possibility of a pseudonymous work finding acceptance depended, at least in part, on the author's ability to induce credence and prevent the detection of the authorial fiction.[48] While it is true that some pseudonymous writings (e.g., Colossians, Ephesians, the Pastorals, 2 Peter) plead for credence by the introduction of personal remarks, others (e.g., James, Jude) make no effort to evince authenticity beyond the mere assertion of the pseudonym in the address. Thus it appears that elaborate techniques of pseudonymity were not necessarily required.

Whether Jewish or Greco-Roman practice is considered the primary influence, and whether or not deceptive intent is minimized or emphasized, pseudonymous composition in early Christianity has its fundamental motive in the desire both to furnish and to warrant teaching that was taken to

---

[45] Ibid., 198–99. This approach has proven attractive to some conservative commentators who acknowledge the existence of canonical pseudepigrapha.

[46] Speyer, *Die literarische Fälschung* (see n. 34), 175–76, Brox, *Falsche Verfasserangaben: Zur Erklärung der frühchristlichen Pseudepigraphie* (SBS 79; Stuttgart: KBW Verlag, 1975), 68–70.

[47] On deception for a good purpose, an idea that goes back to Plato (*Resp.* 2.376E–3.392C, and 3.414C–E, 5.459D) and was known among Christian Platonists (Clement of Alexandria, *Strom.* 7.9; Origen, *Cels.* 4.18–19), see Brox, ibid., 83–4.

[48] Donelson, *Pseudepigraphy and Ethical Argument* (see n. 32), 23–66. Donelson emphasizes the deliberate and artful detail of pseudonymous deception in the Pastorals.

be authoritative by the writer and intended to be authoritative for the reader. Because the early church regarded the apostolic past as both the source and the norm of authoritative teaching, pseudonymously apostolic authorship was a ready means for the extension of apostolic authority into the post-apostolic period, and for the interpretive contemporization and application (*Vergegenwärtigung*) of teachings that had, or were believed to have, apostolic sanction. In current scholarship this is the most widely-held conception of the role of pseudonymity in the early church, especially in relation to the canonical pseudepigrapha.[49] On these terms, special recourse is sometimes made on behalf of the canonical pseudepigrapha to a "school-hypothesis": it is supposed that such compositions arose among nearer or more distant devotees of a body of teaching associated with an apostolic or otherwise authoritative figure, and aimed to perpetuate, promote and activate that teaching in fresh circumstances.

The plausibility and usefulness of understanding early Christian pseudepigraphy in this way depends upon whether it can be shown that pseudonymous writings do in fact presuppose and develop traditions that are indebted to their fictive authors. For example, Colossians, Ephesians and 2 Thessalonians manifest a clear dependence, both literary and theological, upon Pauline teaching as we find it in the authentic letters of the apostle. Their pseudonymous authors stand self-consciously in continuity with an identifiably Pauline tradition, whereas far less continuity is to be seen in the Pastoral epistles.[50] The school-hypothesis has more plausibility for the deutero-Pauline letters than for other canonical pseudepigrapha, both because we have Paul's authentic letters as a reference point and because of the historical circumstances of the Pauline mission, which involved a con-

---

[49] Among many, see H. Balz, "Anonymität und Pseudepigraphie im Urchristentum: Überlegungen zum literarischen und theologischen Problem der urchristlichen und gemeinantiken Pseudepigraphie," *ZThK* 66 (1969): 403–36; P. Pokorný, "Das Theologische Problem" (see n. 41); E. Reinmuth, "Zur neutestamentlichen Paulus-Pseudepigraphie," in N. Walter, idem and P. Lampe, *Die Briefe an die Philipper, Thessalonicher und an Philemon* (NTD 8/2; Göttingen: Vandenhoeck & Ruprecht, 1998), 190–200; Wolter, *Die Pastoralbriefe als Paulustradition* (see n. 8), and idem, "Pseudonymität II," *TRE* 27:662–70; J. Zmijewski, "Apostolische Paradosis und Pseudepigraphie im Neuen Testament," *BZ* 23 (1979): 161–71; M. Kiley, *Colossians as Pseudepigraphy* (Sheffield: JSOT Press, 1986). H. J. Riedl, *Anamnese und Apostolizität: Der zweite Petrusbrief und das theologische Problem neutestamentlicher Pseudepigraphie* (RST 64; Frankfurt a.M.: P. Lang, 2005), offers a variation on this theme by emphasizing the notion of "remembrance" as the interpretive key for early Christian pseudepigraphy: it aims not so much to interpret the tradition in a new situation as to transport the reader into a participation in (past) revelatory events.

[50] Donelson, *Pseudepigraphy and Ethical Argument* (see n. 32), suggests that the author of the Pastorals "appears to be a Paulinist not in theology but in name only; he is defending a man he knows mostly by reputation and legend" (60).

siderable number of associates and assistants of Paul who are likely to have continued to promote his teaching and authority after the apostle's death.[51] Such an explanation is more difficult to sustain for other pseudonymous letters. It is highly questionable, for example, whether the author of 2 Peter can be said to appropriate or re-present any tradition distinctively associated with Peter himself (notwithstanding his acquaintance with 1 Peter, which is itself certainly pseudonymous), or whether anything in James has ultimate roots in actual teachings of James as distinct from common Jewish-Christian paraenesis.[52] In these and other instances we have neither sources that can provide a touchstone for the teaching of the fictive authors nor indications of *Sitze im Leben* for the transmission and development of traditions associated with them.

Hence in most, perhaps all, cases outside the Pauline corpus, pseudonymous authorship is nothing else than it appears to be, namely the use of a revered apostolic name in order to assert the authority of teaching that was believed to be of value by its author, irrespective of its actual origins. Although the element of deception cannot be expunged from it, the production of pseudonymous literature in the early church needs to be seen in the larger context of the struggle to define the substance and norms of Christian teaching, a struggle that belonged mainly, though not exclusively, to the second century. All forms of early Christianity—heterodox and proto-orthodox alike—regarded the apostolic past as the source and norm of authoritative teaching and sought to root their teachings in it, laying claim to apostolic warrant, and so pseudonymous compositions were produced on all sides. It ought to be considered, therefore, whether pseudonymously apostolic writings may not have been an instrument of necessity in the hands of the proto-orthodox, and one without which they would have been at a decided disadvantage in defining what constituted Christian faith and practice.

Although the phenomenon of early Christian pseudonymity, and more specifically of canonical pseudepigrapha, may be rationalized in various ways, some of which are theologically more problematic than others, the

---

[51] On Pauline pseudepigrapha and the idea of a Paul-school, see M. Frenschkowski, "Pseudepigraphie und Paulusschule: Gedanken zur Verfasserschaft der Deuteropaulinen, insbesondere der Pastoralbriefe," in *Das Ende des Paulus: Historische, theologische und literaturgeschichtliche Aspekte* (ed. F. W. Horn; BZNW 106; Berlin: de Gruyter, 2001), 239–72, with reference to earlier literature.

[52] For an effort to identify a Petrine tradition, see Meade, *Pseudonymity* (see n. 43), 161–90, and for a survey of efforts to describe a James-tradition, see Nienhuis, *Not By Paul Alone* (see n. 23), 99–161, and for Petrine and Johannine traditions, see Wolter, *Die Pastoralbriefe als Paulustradition* (see n. 8), 104–12. Attempts to delineate such traditions come to thin results, which consist only of a few themes, not substantive traditions of teaching.

history of the New Testament canon cannot be reduced to or explained as a process of literary authentication.[53] For the same reason, literary authenticity cannot be made the measure of canonicity. It was undoubtedly the desire and the intention of the ancient church to honor and defer to literature that was apostolic. It did so not by rigorous and careful scrutiny of authorial claims and attributions, but by finally stipulating those writings that, in consequence of their long and wide use within Christian communities, had decisively shaped and informed its faith and guided its practice, and among those writings there were some that passed under a false claim of authorship.

In sum, traditions and presumptions about authorship had their role to play in the canonization of the New Testament, but it was a role correlative with, and ultimately subordinate to, the usages of Christian literature that had become common, traditional and habitual in Christian communities. It was because of such use that this literature had become integral and indispensable to the self-understanding of the church. Canonization served both to make that use *de jure* and to secure that self-understanding. To make authorship the exclusive or even the principal criterion of canonical status is to give literary authenticity, and thus also pseudonymity, a significance it did not have and could not have had in the early church.

---

[53] This is the whole effect of the study of Baum, *Pseudepigraphie* (see n. 40), which is based on a conservative Protestant conception of the canon of scripture that precludes a fully critical evaluation of the evidence. Such an approach will be persuasive only to those who share his theological presuppositions.

Von Paulus zu „Paulus"

Paulinische Pseudepigraphie-Forschung als literaturgeschichtliche Aufgabe

von

EVE-MARIE BECKER

1. Die literaturgeschichtlichen Aspekte der Pseudepigraphie-Forschung

Neutestamentliche Schriften, so auch die paulinischen Briefe, sind als Teil der antiken Literaturgeschichte zu betrachten. Der Weg zu einer literaturgeschichtlichen Betrachtung der pseudepigraphen neutestamentlichen Texte wurde in erheblichem Maße durch Literar- und Echtheitskritik gebahnt.

Zugleich markiert die sog. Pseudepigraphie-Forschung in historischer Hinsicht nicht nur die Anfänge der modernen neutestamentlichen Exegese, sondern ist seit diesen Anfängen, die auf die paulinischen Briefe konzentriert waren, auch literaturgeschichtlich geprägt, wie die folgende forschungsgeschichtliche Übersicht verdeutlichen wird. In literaturgeschichtlicher Hinsicht zielt die Pseudepigraphie-Forschung im Bereich der Paulus-Exegese nämlich besonders darauf, die literarische Echtheit von Paulusbriefen zu prüfen (s. 1.1), die Phänomene literarischer Orthonymität und Pseudepigraphie bei den Paulusbriefen vor dem Hintergrund der hellenistischen Literatur insgesamt zu untersuchen (s. 1.2) sowie die Schreib- und Sammlungsbedingungen mutmaßlicher pseudepigrapher Paulusbriefe zu rekonstruieren (s. 1.3). Allerdings wird die literaturgeschichtliche Prägung der Pseudepigraphie-Forschung vielfach durch theologisch-hermeneutische Diskurse verdeckt. Der folgende Beitrag möchte demgegenüber die Bedeutung der literaturgeschichtlichen Aspekte für die paulinische Pseudepigraphie-Forschung im Kontext antiker Literatur (s. 2.) letztlich auch in theologiegeschichtlicher Hinsicht aufzeigen (s. 3.).

1.1 Kanon- und Echtheitskritik

Die paulinische Pseudepigraphie-Forschung geht im 18. Jh. zunächst maßgeblich aus der bibelhermeneutisch motivierten Kritik am Kanonprinzip hervor.[1] Die Kanonkritik verfolgte dogmatische Interessen, indem sie zur kritischen Auseinandersetzung mit der sog. Inspirationslehre führte. Sie war literarkritisch orientiert und insofern auch literaturgeschichtlich relevant, als sie sich in der Folge auf Autoren-, und d.h. Echtheitskritik konzentrierte: So wurde mit der Kanon-Kritik Johann Salomo Semlers (1771–1775)[2] zunächst die Authentizität von Verfassern und Verfasserangaben hinterfragt.[3] Ferdinand Christian Baur entwickelte gerade dadurch die historisch-kritische Methode weiter,[4] dass er in seinen Studien zu den Pastoralbriefen (1835)[5] deren paulinische Verfasserschaft[6] bleibend infrage stellte. Ähnliche Überlegungen hatten bereits Friedrich D. E. Schleiermacher (1807) im Blick auf den 1. Timotheusbrief[7] und J. E. Christian Schmidt (1798/1801) in Bezug auf den 2. Thessalonicherbrief formuliert.[8]

---

[1] Vgl. O. MERK, Anfänge neutestamentlicher Wissenschaft im 18. Jahrhundert, in: ders., Wissenschaftsgeschichte und Exegese. Gesammelte Aufsätze zum 65. Geburtstag, hg. v. R. Gebauer u.a., BZNW 95, Berlin/New York 1998, 1–23 (12ff.). – Vgl. hierzu auch den Artikel Kanon, Lexikon der Bibelhermeneutik (im Druck).

[2] Vgl. J. S. SEMLER, Abhandlung von freier Untersuchung des Canon; nebst Antwort auf die tübingische Vertheidigung der Apocalypsis, Halle 1771. – Vgl. zu Semler auch: W. RAUPP, Art. Semler, Johann Salomo, BBKL 14 (1998), 1444–1473.

[3] Vgl. MERK, Anfänge (s. Anm. 1), 17ff. – Nach Merk liegen dieser Untersuchung zwei hermeneutische Grundthesen zugrunde: erstens die Annahme, dass das Wort Gottes und die Heilige Schrift nicht identisch seien. „Daraus ergibt sich als Konsequenz: Nicht alle Teile des Kanons können inspiriert sein ... In den Schriften des Kanons begegnet uns Gottes Wort im Menschenwort" (13f.). Zweitens: „Die Zugehörigkeit einer Schrift zum Kanon ist ... eine rein historische Frage ... Jeder einzelne Christ kann die historischen Umstände überprüfen ..." (14f.).

[4] Vgl. zur Übersicht: U. KÖPF, Art. Baur, Ferdinand Christian, RGG[4] 1 (1998), 1183–1185. Vgl. auch: K. SCHOLDER, Art. Baur, Ferdinand Christian (1792–1860), TRE 5 (1980), 352–359; F. W. BAUTZ, Art. Baur, Ferdinand Christian, BBKL 1 (1990), 427f.

[5] Vgl. F. C. BAUR, Die sogenannten Pastoralbriefe des Apostels Paulus aufs neue kritisch untersucht, Stuttgart/Tübingen 1835.

[6] Vgl. zur Forschungsgeschichte auch: W. G. KÜMMEL, Einleitung in das Neue Testament, Heidelberg [21]1983, 326ff.

[7] Vgl. F. D. E. SCHLEIERMACHER, Ueber den sogenannten ersten Brief des Paulos an den Timotheos. Ein kritisches Sendschreiben an J. C. Gass, Berlin 1807. – BAUR, Pastoralbriefe (s. Anm. 5), 1ff. verweist kritisch auf Schleiermacher, indem er betont, auch die geschichtlichen Entstehungsbedingungen der Briefe müssten berücksichtigt werden. Baur geht es also darum, zu einem „geschichtlich begründeten Resultat zu kommen" (7).

[8] Vgl. dazu J. E. C. SCHMIDT, Vermutungen über die beiden Briefe an die Thessalonicher, Bibliothek für Kritik und Exegese des NT. Tom. 2 Fasc. 3, Hadamar 1801, 380–386. – Hinweise dazu auch bei KÜMMEL, Einleitung (s. Anm. 6), 228. Vgl. auch B. RI-

Jedoch wird erstmals bei Baur den Merkmalen von apostolischer Authentizität deutlich das *Phänomen der Pseudepigraphie* im Blick auf alle drei Pastoralbriefe[9] gegenübergestellt.[10] Im Bereich der Bibelexegese sind also Kanonkritik und Echtheitskritik untrennbar miteinander verbunden. Auch in den klassischen Altertumswissenschaften spielt die Echtheitskritik im Laufe des 19. Jh. eine zunehmend wichtigere Rolle: Der Altphilologe Friedrich Blass gibt im ersten Band des „Handbuchs der klassischen Altertumswissenschaft" (1892) den Stand der philologischen Forschung am Ende des 19. Jh. wieder. Blass nennt hier die Anlässe des kritischen Zweifels im Umgang mit pseudepigrapher griechischer und römischer Literatur und die Kriterien der sog. ‚Echtheitskritik'.[11] In den Zusammenhang literarhistorischer Arbeiten zur paulinischen Pseudepigraphie-Forschung gehört in gewissem Sinne auch William Wredes Monographie zur ‚Echtheit des 2. Thessalonicherbriefs' (1903).[12] Denn Wrede richtet hier das Augenmerk auf das literarische Verhältnis des 1. Thessalonicherbriefs zum 2. Thessalonicherbrief als Schlüsselfrage der ‚Echtheitskritik'.[13]

Trotzdem etablierte sich die Pseudepigraphie-Forschung in der Paulus-Exegese nur sehr schwer als eine dezidert literaturgeschichtliche Fragestellung. Denn es ist die oben genannte ursprünglich kanon-, d.h. bibelkritische Fundierung der Pseudepigraphie-Forschung, die dazu führt, dass in der Exegese des 19. und 20. Jh. bis in die Gegenwart hinein die Diskus-

---

GAUX, Saint Paul. Les Épîtres aux Thessaloniciens, Paris/Gembloux 1956, 124f. (124 Anm. 2).

[9] Nach BAUR, Pastoralbriefe (s. Anm. 5), 5 Anm. *, wurde die Echtheit aller drei Pastoralbriefe erstmals von Johann Gottfried Eichhorn (Einleitung in das Neue Testament, Bd. III/1, Leipzig 1812, bes. 317–328), infrage gestellt.

[10] Baur selbst geht a.a.O. wie folgt vor: Als Argumente für die nicht-apostolische Verfasserschaft der drei Pastoralbriefe nennt er die Auseinandersetzung mit Häretikern (8ff.), Einzelmotive, die auf eine späte Abfassungszeit hinweisen wie 1Tim 2,11 (40ff.). Baur bedenkt sodann die Entstehungsverhältnisse der Briefe (54ff.), nimmt weitere nachapostolische Elemente in den Blick (97ff.) und wertet äußere Zeugnisse aus (136ff.). Ausmaß und Schärfe von Baurs Kritik an der Authentizität der Paulusbriefe sind allerdings forschungsgeschichtlich überholt; vgl. auch KÖPF, Art. Baur (s. Anm. 4), 1185.

[11] Vgl. F. BLASS, Art. Hermeneutik und Kritik, HKAW 1, München 1892, 149–295 (269ff.289ff.). Als Anlässe des ‚kritischen Zweifels' nennt Blass: „Sprachliche Anstösse ..., Anstösse des Gedankens und der verletzten Individualität ..., Historische und technische Anstösse ..." (274ff.). – Vgl. auch: A. D. BAUM, Pseudepigraphie und literarische Fälschung im frühen Christentum. Mit ausgewählten Quellentexten samt deutscher Übersetzung, WUNT II/138, Tübingen 2001, 21ff.

[12] Vgl. W. WREDE, Die Echtheit des Zweiten Thessalonicherbriefs, TU 9/2, Leipzig 1903.

[13] Dabei kommt Wrede zum Urteil: „Das literarische Verhältnis des Briefes zum ersten Thessalonicherbrief bleibt ohne die Annahme der Fälschung völlig unverständlich" (a.a.O. 114).

sionen über die literarische Authentizität der Paulusbriefe theologisch-dogmatisch kontrovers geführt wurden und werden.[14] So ist die Pseudepigraphie-Forschung auch ein Thema der neutestamentlichen Hermeneutik[15] und sogar der dogmatischen Schriftlehre.[16] Hier kommt ein weiterer theologisch-hermeneutischer Aspekt hinzu, der eine literaturgeschichtliche Würdigung des Phänomens der Pseudepigraphie schwierig macht: Seit dem 19. Jh. wird in der Philologie, besonders aber in der Theologie, die Frage nach der Vereinbarkeit von ‚literarischer Fälschung' mit dem ‚Wahrheitsgehalt' der (neutestamentlichen) Texte (*pia fraus*) als eine ‚ethisch-moralische' Fragestellung[17] debattiert. Selbst Gelehrte wie Adolf Deißmann haben immer wieder gezeigt, dass die Feststellung von Pseudepigraphie in der Paulus-Exegese nachhaltig zu z.T. äußerst polemischen und emotionalen Diskussionen führen kann. Deißmanns Beschreibung der Situation der Paulus-Forschung (1911)[18] ähnelt dabei den Überlegungen, die

---

[14] Vgl. etwa: D. L. STAMPS, Art. Pauline Letters, Dictionary of Biblical Criticism and Interpretation (2007), 265–270 (265f.) – Vgl. auch z.B. P. H. TOWNER, The Letters to Timothy and Titus, NICNT, Grand Rapids/Cambridge 2006, der zuletzt an der Authentizität der Pastoralbriefe festhält.

[15] Obwohl Kanonkritik und Echtheitskritik von ihren Ursprüngen her, besonders aber bei Semler, bibelhermeneutische Fragen sind (s.o., vgl. MERK, Anfänge [s. Anm. 1], z.B. 16: „Die Hermeneutik ist die Mutter der neutestamentlichen Wissenschaft im 18. Jahrhundert"), sind die jüngeren Entwürfe zu einer neutestamentlichen Hermeneutik – wie P. STUHLMACHER, Vom Verstehen des Neuen Testaments. Eine Hermeneutik, NTD Erg. 6, Göttingen ²1986, 128ff. (Abschnitt zu Semler); H. WEDER, Neutestamentliche Hermeneutik, Zürich ²1989; K. BERGER, Hermeneutik des Neuen Testaments, UTB 2035, Tübingen/Basel 1999 – kaum mit dem Phänomen der Pseudepigraphie befasst. Vgl. aber O. WISCHMEYER, Hermeneutik des Neuen Testaments. Ein Lehrbuch, NET 8, Tübingen/Basel 2004, 34f.37f. Vgl. auch F. TORM, Nytestamentlig Hermeneutik, Kopenhagen ²1938, 174ff.

[16] Ansätze zu systematisch-theologischen Überlegungen finden sich auch bei P. POKORNÝ, Art. Pseudepigraphie I. Altes und Neues Testament, TRE 27 (1997), 645–655 (654).

[17] So z.B. J. S. CANDLISH, Über den moralischen Charakter pseudonymer Bücher (1891), wiederabgedruckt in: N. Brox (Hg.), Pseudepigraphie in der heidnischen und jüdisch-christlichen Antike, WdF 484, Darmstadt 1977, 7–42; G. BARDY, Betrug und Fälschungen in der Literatur der christlichen Antike (1936), wiederabgedruckt in: Brox, a.a.O. 163–184. – Vgl. dazu auch W. SPEYER, Die literarische Fälschung im heidnischen und christlichen Altertum. Ein Versuch ihrer Deutung, HAW I/2, München 1971, 94ff., der aus altertumswissenschaftlicher Sicht den Sachverhalt wie folgt beschreibt: „Die literarische Fälschung ist ... ein Sonderfall der Lüge, näherhin des Betruges" (94). – In der jüngsten exegetischen Diskussion vgl. R. ZIMMERMANN, Unecht – und doch wahr? Pseudepigraphie im Neuen Testament als theologisches Problem, ZNT 12 (2003), 27–38.

[18] „Noch immer geht in gewissen Kreisen der Wahn um, die Wissenschaftlichkeit eines Bibelforschers sei prozentual nach dem Verhältnis seiner Unechtheitsverdikte auszurechnen ..., und ein gutes Teil der Martyrien des historischen Paulus haben die überlieferten Paulusbriefe im neunzehnten Jahrhundert unschuldig nacherleben müssen ...",

wenig später der bekannte Altphilologe Franz Dornseiff (1939) im Blick auf pagane Texte und Textcorpora vorträgt.[19] Auch diese Diskussionen dauern an,[20] obwohl Wissenschaftler wie Günter Stemberger zu Recht in Hinsicht auf das Phänomen der Pseudepigraphie zu Bedenken gaben: „Pauschalurteile wie *pia fraus* oder fehlender Begriff geistigen Eigentums tragen wenig zur Erklärung des Phänomens und seiner Vielfalt sowie der Wahl der jeweiligen Verfassernamen bei ..."[21]

1.2 Religionswissenschaftliche und philologische Zugänge im 20. Jh.

Im 20. Jh. war die Pseudepigraphie-Forschung trotz der genannten Diskurse innerhalb und außerhalb der neutestamentlichen Wissenschaft besonders durch philologische und religionswissenschaftliche Untersuchungen

---

A. DEISSMANN, Paulus. Eine kultur- und religionsgeschichtliche Skizze, Tübingen 1911, 10. Wichtig ist hier aber, dass Deißmann seine Zweifel an der Feststellung von ‚pseudopaulinischen' Briefen mit deren unliterarischem Charakter begründet: „Bei literarischen Episteln vielleicht anwendbar, sind die vulgären Fragezeichen der Studierstube bei unliterarischen Briefen nicht einleuchtend ..." (ebd).

[19] „Ein wohlmeinender Fachgenosse hat mir geraten, ich täte am besten, wenn ich jetzt endlich auch mal eine Schrift für unecht erklärte, sonst heißt es: Ach, für den D. ist ja alles immer echt! Diesen Rat kann ich leider diesmal nicht befolgen und z.Z. die Zahl der antiken Pseudepigrapha nicht vermehren, ich habe in dieser Richtung nichts vorrätig. Aber ich versichere, daß ich das dichterisch großartige syrische Testament Adams nicht für authentisch halte und das Buch Henoch nicht für ein Werk seines Enkels, des Sohnes Kains ...", F. DORNSEIFF, Echtheitsfragen antik-griechischer Literatur. Rettungen des Theognis, Phokylides, Hekataios, Choirilos, Berlin 1939, 1. Im Folgenden zählt Dornseiff eine Reihe alttestamentlicher, frühjüdischer, pagan-antiker und frühchristlicher Texte auf, die er für pseudonym oder anonym, d.h. für *nicht* literarisch authentisch hält (1). Dornseiff kommt zu dem Schluss: „... Ich bin also kein Panauthentiker, kein blinder Überlieferungsanbeter. Auch kein Panunitarier ... Man kann ... nicht verlangen, daß die Echtheit nachgewiesen wird. Aber wenn die Einwände gegen die Echtheit als haltlos erwiesen sind, muß eine Schrift für echt angesehen werden ... Aus dieser kurzen Übersicht [über die Forschungs- und Geistesgeschichte] geht hervor, daß die Empfänglichkeit oder Immunität gegenüber Argumenten weitgehend von den geistigen Strömungen abhängig war und demnach wohl auch ist. Es mag Leute geben, die daraus den Schluß ziehen, man solle also das Ganze an den Nagel hängen, da die Vergangenheit unerkennbar bleibe. Ich möchte daraus nur folgern, daß die auf die genannten geistigen Moden zurückgehenden Vorurteile abzulegen sind. Unsere eigenen Scheuklappen mag die Folgezeit belächeln" (1–4).

[20] Vgl. dazu die Hinweise bei R. ZIMMERMANN, Art. Pseudepigraphie/Pseudonymität, RGG[4] 6 (2003), 1786–1788 (1788), oder auch M. FRENSCHKOWSKI, Pseudepigraphie und Paulusschule. Gedanken zur Verfasserschaft der Deuteropaulinen, insbesondere der Pastoralbriefe, in: F. W. Horn (Hg.), Das Ende des Paulus. Historische, theologische und literaturgeschichtliche Aspekte, BZNW 106, Berlin/New York 2001, 239–272 (250ff.).

[21] G. STEMBERGER, Art. Pseudepigraphie II. Judentum, TRE 27 (1997), 656–659 (656).

bestimmt.[22] Walter Bauers Beitrag zu „Rechtgläubigkeit und Ketzerei im ältesten Christentum" (1934) hat in diesem Zusammenhang die Aufmerksamkeit auf die diffizile Unterscheidung von ‚Kirchenlehre' und ‚Häresie' schon im frühen Christentum gerichtet. Demnach kann ‚Häresie' nicht einfach als Abwandlung des ‚Echten' verstanden werden.[23] Diese Bewertung wirkt sich auch auf die Verhältnisbestimmung von orthonymer und pseudepigrapher Schriftstellerei im Bereich der Paulus-Exegese aus.[24]

Doch stellt sich die Pseudepigraphie-Forschung im 20. Jh. nicht allein als text- oder textcorporabezogene Echtheitskritik dar, sondern sie widmet sich dem Phänomen der Pseudepigraphie umfassend. Frederik Torm hat – zeitgleich zu Arnold Meyers Beitrag „Religiöse Pseudepigraphie als ethisch-psychologisches Problem" im „Archiv für die gesamte Psychologie" (1932)[25] – in seiner Untersuchung „Die Psychologie der Pseudonymität im Hinblick auf die Literatur des Urchristentums" (1932) die psychologischen Voraussetzungen und Umstände pseudonymen Schreibens in den Blick genommen.[26] Dabei kommt Torm zu einer differenzierten Bewertung des Phänomens der Pseudepigraphie, die sich an den verschiedenen Genera der Literatur orientiert.[27] Im Bereich der klassischen Altertumswissenschaften ist auf die oben schon erwähnte Studie Franz Dornseiffs (1939)

---

[22] Vgl. hier auch die Darstellung bei L. R. DONELSON, Pseudepigraphy and Ethical Argument in the Pastoral Epistles, HUTh 22, Tübingen 1986, 9–23.

[23] Vgl. W. BAUER, Rechtgläubigkeit und Ketzerei im ältesten Christentum, BHTh 10, Tübingen 1934, bes. 1–5.

[24] S. dazu unten.

[25] Vgl. A. MEYER, Religiöse Pseudepigraphie als ethisch-psychologisches Problem, AGPs 86 (1932), 171–190; später: ZNW 35 (1936), 262–279; wiederabgedruckt in: Brox, Pseudepigraphie (s. Anm. 17), 90–110.

[26] Vgl. F. TORM, Die Psychologie der Pseudonymität im Hinblick auf die Literatur des Urchristentums, SLA 2, Gütersloh 1932. – Das Erlanger Exemplar unter der Signatur S 10,599 ist ein Geschenk des Verfassers an Prof. D. Althaus. – Die Bedeutung der frühchristlichen Pseudepigraphie für die Psychologie des frühen Christentums findet zuletzt bei G. THEISSEN, Erleben und Verhalten der ersten Christen. Eine Psychologie des Urchristentums, Gütersloh 2007, keine Erwähnung. – Vgl. auch die Rezension von A. MEYER (1933): Besprechung von: Frederik Torm, Die Psychologie der Pseudonymität im Hinblick auf die Literatur des Urchristentums, wiederabgedruckt in: Brox, Pseudepigraphie (s. Anm. 17), 149–153.

[27] TORM, a.a.O. 53ff. Bei den jüdischen apokalyptischen Schriftstellern z.B. kommt Torm zu folgender Einschätzung: „Es bleibt also dabei, daß wir, wenn uns die Psychologie der Pseudonymität bei den jüdischen apokalyptischen Schriftstellern einigermaßen verständlich werden soll, hauptsächlich uns vor Augen halten müssen, daß ekstatische Neigungen das Vermögen zum Unterscheiden zwischen eigenen und angeeigneten Gedanken in der Regel abschwächen und daher nach und nach ein mystisches Einheitsgefühl hervorrufen zwischen der eigenen und einer anderen Persönlichkeit, von welcher das eigene Seelenleben beeinflußt, ja überwältigt wird" (23f.).

hinzuweisen.[28] In den 60er und 70er Jahren sind eine Vielzahl von Untersuchungen zur antiken und frühchristlichen Pseudepigraphie hinzugekommen. Hier sind besonders die Monographien von Josef A. Sint (1960),[29] Wolfgang Speyer (1971)[30] und Norbert Brox (1975)[31] zu nennen. Neben der von Norbert Brox in „Wege der Forschung" (1977) herausgegebenen Sammlung von Beiträgen zur antiken und frühchristlichen Pseudepigraphie aus den Jahren 1891–1973[32] sind eine Reihe weiterer Aufsätze zum Thema entstanden, so etwa von Kurt Aland (1961/1967)[33] und Horst R. Balz (1969).[34] Weitere wichtige Beiträge stammen von Martin Hengel und Wolfgang Speyer und sind 1972 unter dem Titel „Pseudepigrapha I" im Rahmen der Fondation Hardt erschienen.[35] Bis zum Ende des 20. Jh. sind darüber hinaus Beiträge zu Einzelfragen antiker und frühchristlicher Pseudepigraphie entstanden, so etwa zum Paulus-Seneca-Briefwechsel von Alfons Fürst (1998).[36]

---

[28] Vgl. DORNSEIFF, Echtheitsfragen (s. Anm. 19).

[29] Vgl. J. A. SINT, Pseudonymität im Altertum. Ihre Formen und ihre Gründe, Commentationes Aenipontanae 15, Innsbruck 1960.

[30] Vgl. SPEYER, Die literarische Fälschung (s. Anm. 17).

[31] Vgl. N. BROX, Falsche Verfasserangaben. Zur Erklärung der frühchristlichen Pseudepigraphie, SBS 79, Stuttgart 1975.

[32] Ders., Pseudepigraphie (s. Anm. 17).

[33] Vgl. K. ALAND, The Problem of Anonymity and Pseudonymity in Christian Literature of the First Two Centuries, JThS 12 (1961), 39–49; deutsche Übersetzung: Das Problem der Anonymität und Pseudonymität in der christlichen Literatur der ersten beiden Jahrhunderte, in: ders., Studien zur Überlieferung des Neuen Testaments und seines Textes, ANTT 2, Berlin 1967, 24–34.

[34] Vgl. H. R. BALZ, Anonymität und Pseudepigraphie im Urchristentum. Überlegungen zum literarischen und theologischen Problem der urchristlichen und gemeinantiken Pseudepigraphie, ZThK 66 (1969), 403–436.

[35] Vgl. M. HENGEL, Anonymität, Pseudepigraphie und „Literarische Fälschung" in der jüdisch-hellenistischen Literatur, in: K. von Fritz (Hg.), Pseudepigrapha I. Pseudopythagorica – Lettres de Platon. Littérature pseudépigraphique juive, Vandœuvres/Genève 1972, 231–308; W. SPEYER, Fälschung, pseudepigraphische freie Erfindung und „echte religiöse Pseudepigraphie", in: von Fritz, a.a.O. 333–366.

[36] A. FÜRST, Pseudepigraphie und Apostolizität im apokryphen Briefwechsel zwischen Seneca und Paulus, JAC 41 (1998), 77–117. – E. NORDEN (Die Römische Literatur. Anhang: die Lateinische Literatur im Übergang vom Altertum zum Mittelalter, hg. v. B. Kytzler, Stuttgart/Leipzig [7]1998 [erg. Nachdruck der 3. Aufl. 1927], 75) bewertete diesen Briefwechsel wie folgt: „... der uns erhaltene Briefwechsel des Philosophen mit dem Apostel Paulus hat, so kindlich die Fälschung auch ist ..., doch etwas Rührendes und ist, etwa wie die christliche Paraphrase der vierten vergilischen Ekloge ..., ein religionsgeschichtlich nicht ganz bedeutungsloses Dokument". – Vgl. jetzt auch: Der apokryphe Briefwechsel zwischen Paulus und Seneca. Zusammen mit dem Brief des Mordechai an Alexander und dem Brief des Annaeus Seneca über Hochmut und Götterbilder. Eingel., übers. u. m. interpret. Essays vers. v. A. FÜRST u.a., SAPERE XI, Tübingen 2006.

Wenigstens die soeben genannten monographischen Arbeiten sollen kurz skizziert werden: Josef A. Sint untersucht pseudonymes Schrifttum in der Antike und unterscheidet dabei vor allem zwischen „Schrifttum aus mythischen und religiösen Triebkräften" einerseits und „Schriften aus literarischen Gestaltungskräften" andererseits.[37] Bei seiner Darstellung der Briefliteratur bemüht sich Sint um eine literaturgeschichtliche Differenzierung, indem er zwischen ‚Privatbriefen', ‚biographisch-politischen Briefen' und ‚Lehrbriefen' unterscheidet, ohne hierbei allerdings explizit die neutestamentliche oder gar die paulinische Briefliteratur in den Blick zu nehmen.[38] Wolfgang Speyer widmet sich in seiner Arbeit vor allem der Unterscheidung von ‚Pseudepigraphie' und ‚literarischer Fälschung'.[39] Er kommt dabei zu der einschlägig gewordenen Definition, die zu einer wichtigen terminologischen und sachlichen Differenzierung des Phänomens der Pseudepigraphie beigetragen hat: „Die Fälschung kann als eine besondere Erscheinungsform der Pseudepigraphie bestimmt werden."[40] Diese Definition ermöglicht es, das Phänomen paulinischer Pseudepigraphie nicht primär aus ethisch-moralischer Sicht zu bewerten. Speyer indes geht es in dieser Untersuchung im Wesentlichen darum, die Gründe, Ziele und Techniken literarischer Fälschung im paganen Altertum, dem frühen Judentum und dem frühen Christentum kriteriologisch zusammenzustellen. Sein Interesse gilt dabei *nicht* der Feststellung inner-neutestamentlicher oder speziell paulinischer Pseudepigraphie,[41] auch wenn er sie andernorts als Möglichkeit nicht ausschließt.[42] Norbert Brox hingegen nimmt in seiner Monographie in besonderer Weise die frühchristliche Pseudepigraphie in den Blick. Dabei äußert er sich auch zu pseudepigrapher Literatur innerhalb des Neuen Testaments.[43] Zu den ‚Fälschungen' im Bereich der paulinischen Briefliteratur rechnet Brox vor allem die Pastoralbriefe und den

---

[37] SINT, Pseudonymität (s. Anm. 29), 17ff.90ff.

[38] A.a.O. 108ff.

[39] Vgl. auch W. SPEYER, Religiöse Pseudepigraphie und literarische Fälschung im Altertum, wiederabgedruckt in: Brox, Pseudepigraphie (s. Anm. 17), 195–263.

[40] SPEYER, Die literarische Fälschung (s. Anm. 17), 13. Die Definition lautet weiter: „Die Begriffe literarische Fälschung und Pseudepigraphie verhalten sich dann wie Species und Genus zueinander. Ein Pseudepigraphon ist ein literarisches Werk, das nicht von dem Verfasser stammt, dem es der Titel (die Subscriptio), der Inhalt oder die Überlieferung zuweisen ... Eine Fälschung liegt dann vor, wenn der wirkliche Verfasser mit dem angegebenen nicht übereinstimmt und die Maske als Mittel gewählt wurde, um Absichten durchzusetzen, die außerhalb der Literatur, das heißt der Kunst, lagen. Nur wo Täuschungsabsicht, also dolus malus vorliegt, wird der Tatbestand der Fälschung erfüllt. Insofern gehört die Fälschung zur Lüge, und zwar zur vorsätzlichen Lüge ..."

[41] SPEYER, a.a.O. 171f., verweist lediglich auf den 2Petr.

[42] Vgl. ders., Religiöse Pseudepigraphie (s. Anm. 39), 249f.

[43] Vgl. BROX, Falsche Verfasserangaben (s. Anm. 31), 18ff.

2Thess. Brox unterscheidet hier durchaus wertend zwischen zwei Typen von Paulusbrief-Fiktion: nämlich ‚harmlosen Elementen der Paulusbrief-Fiktion', wie der „Nachahmung des paulinischen Stils", einerseits – es handelt sich hier um „unbedingt historisch und unmittelbar echt anmutende Angaben" – und inhaltlichen Aussagen, die sich der literarischen Autorität des Paulus bedienen, andererseits – es handelt sich hier um Angaben, die „ganz bewußt und künstlich so gestaltet [sind], dass sie die geeigneten Vehikel oder die Provokationen für bestimmte, von vornherein intendierte Aussagen darstellen".[44] Diese Unterscheidung ist aus literaturgeschichtlicher Sicht nicht einleuchtend.

1.3 Jüngste literaturgeschichtliche Fragen

Marco Frenschkowski hat in einem Beitrag zu „Pseudepigraphie und Paulusschule" von 2001 zu einer neuen Diskussion über das gegenwärtig unter den Exegeten scheinbar bestehende Einvernehmen über das ‚Dass' paulinischer Pseudepigraphie angeregt und dabei eine explizit literaturgeschichtliche Perspektive gewählt, auf die auch Gerd Theißen zuletzt hingewiesen hat.[45] Frenschkowski allerdings fragt speziell unter dem Stichwort der ‚Paulus-Schule' nach den institutionellen Rahmenbedingungen, die die fingierte Abfassung von Paulusbriefen erfordert haben können.[46] Er weist damit auf einen wichtigen, sonst gern übersehenen literaturgeschichtlichen Aspekt paulinischer Pseudepigraphie hin.[47] Dabei wird der Faktor der ‚Schultradition' in den Altertumswissenschaften inzwischen als *ein* möglicher literarischer Umstand für das Phänomen antiker Pseudepigraphie gewertet. H. J. Rose und P. J. Parsons nennen in Anlehnung an Josef A.

---

[44] A.a.O. 20.
[45] Vgl. FRENSCHKOWSKI, Pseudepigraphie (s. Anm. 20); G. THEISSEN, Die Entstehung des Neuen Testaments als literaturgeschichtliches Problem. Vorgetragen am 27.11.2004, Schriften der Philosophisch-historischen Klasse der Heidelberger Akademie der Wissenschaften Bd. 40 (2007), Heidelberg 2007, bes. 148ff. – Zu jüngsten Untersuchungen zur Pseudepigraphie vgl. BAUM, Pseudepigraphie (s. Anm. 11); A. MERZ, Die fiktive Selbstauslegung des Paulus. Intertextuelle Studien zur Intention und Rezeption der Pastoralbriefe, NTOA 52, Göttingen/Freiburg (CH) 2004; J. HERZER, Abschied vom Konsens? Die Pseudepigraphie der Pastoralbriefe als Herausforderung an die neutestamentliche Wissenschaft, ThLZ 129 (2004), 1267–1282.
[46] FRENSCHKOWSKI, Pseudepigraphie (s. Anm. 20), bes. 254ff. – Zur Bedeutung der Paulus-Schule im Blick auf die Annahme der Pseudepigraphie vgl. auch G. THEISSEN, Das Neue Testament, München 2002, 85; ders., The New Testament. History, Literature, Religion, London/New York 2003, 130f.
[47] Zu den literaturgeschichtlichen Implikationen der Pseudepigraphie-Forschung vgl. auch C. MORESCHINI / E. NORELLI, Early Christian Greek and Latin Literature. A Literary History, vol. 1: From Paul to the Age of Constantine, Peabody 2005, 20ff.

Sint[48] insgesamt sechs Faktoren, die mit der Entstehung von pseudepigrapher Literatur in der Antike in Zusammenhang stehen können:

(a) „A tendency to ascribe anonymous pieces to a well-known author of the genre."
(b) „Works by the followers of a philosopher tended to be credited to their master" – hier begegnet der schon genannte Faktor der Schultradition.
(c) „Rhetorical exercises in the form of speeches, letters, etc., supposed to be by well-known persons, now and then were taken for their real works."
(d) „The existence of deliberate forgeries, made to sell."
(e) „Various mechanical accidents of copying ..."
(f) „But the most frequent cases are of rather late date and connected with the craze for producing evidence of the doctrine one favoured being of great age."[49]

Bei diesen genannten Faktoren lässt sich faktisch nur (b), „Works by the followers of a philosopher tended to be credited to their master",[50] auf die Deutero- und Tritopaulinen anwenden: Es liegen keine Indizien dafür vor, die pseudepigraphen Paulusbriefe seien zunächst anonym geschrieben worden [(a)],[51] sie seien als rhetorische Übungen verfasst und später (nur zufällig) in einen pseudepigraphen Status geraten [(c)],[52] oder sie seien aus kommerziellen Gründen gefälscht worden [(d)]. Auch gibt es keine Anhaltspunkte dafür, die Deutero- und Tritopaulinen seien zufällig im Ab-

---

[48] S.o. – SINT, Pseudonymität (s. Anm. 29), nennt einige dieser Aspekte bes. a.a.O. 115ff. im Rahmen seiner Darstellung der pseudonymen Briefliteratur.
[49] H. J. ROSE / P. J. PARSONS, Art. Pseudepigraphic Literature, OCD³ revised (2003), 1270.
[50] S.o.
[51] Dagegen spricht, dass die Briefform von Anfang an die Nennung von Absender und Adressat voraussetzt: Die Nennung des Absenders (*superscriptio*) ist hierbei als zentrales Element des Präskripts bzw. des Briefanfangs zu werten.
[52] S. die vorhergehende Anm. – Das Interesse an rhetorischen Übungen könnte aber z.B. im Hintergrund der pseudepigraphen Abfassung der unechten Platon-Briefe stehen; vgl. dazu z.B. E. HOWALD, Nachwort, in: ders. (Hg.), Platon. Der siebente Brief, RUB 8892, Stuttgart 1964, 57–72 (57). Zu diskutieren ist in diesem Zusammenhang auch, inwiefern das Phänomen der Sammlung der pseudepigraphen Platon-Briefe diese gattungstypologisch in die Nähe des ‚Briefromans' stellt; vgl. z.B. N. HOLZBERG, Der griechische Briefroman. Versuch einer Gattungstypologie, in: ders. (Hg.), Der griechische Briefroman. Gattungstypologie und Textanalyse, Classica Monacensia 8, Tübingen 1994, 1–52. – Unter (c), unter (b) oder unter (f) könnte auch die Abfassung ps.-aristotelischer, in Briefform gekleideter Abhandlungen wie De mundo gehören, worauf Ps.-Demetrius, De elocutione 4,234 Hinweis gibt. Vgl. dazu D. J. FURLEY, On the Cosmos, in: E. S. Forster / D. J. Furley (Hg.), Aristotle. On Sophistical Refutations, On Coming-To-Be and Passing-Away, On the Cosmos, LCL, London/Cambridge 1965, 331–409 (338f.).

schreibeprozess mit der paulinischen Verfasserschaft versehen [(e)][53] oder aber erst in großem zeitlichen Abstand zu Paulus verfasst worden [(f)].[54] So scheinen Frenschkowskis Überlegungen zum Zusammenhang von paulinischer Pseudepigraphie und Paulus-Schule auch in Hinsicht darauf, wie er das in der Forschung höchst umstrittene Phänomen der ‚Paulus-Schule'[55] beschreibt, in sich zunächst einleuchtend: „Das, was man gerne vage die Schule des Paulus nennt, ist nichts anderes als das ehemalige Missionsteam des Apostels."[56] Eine spezifische Nähe zu dem äußerst vielfältigen Phänomen von Philosophenschulen wird hier in Frage gestellt. Ob, wie Frenschkowski meint, die Pastoralbriefe dann direkt auf Paulusmitarbeiter wie Timotheus zurückgeführt werden können,[57] ist Teil einer komplexen Debatte,[58] die hier nicht weiter vertieft werden kann.

Aus meiner Sicht ist diese Überlegung aus technischen und organisatorischen Gründen mit Skepsis zu betrachten: Im Blick auf die verschiedenen Aspekte, die mit der gemeindlichen Tradierung und ‚Bearbeitung' der ‚authentischen' Paulusbriefe bis ca. zum Ende des 1. Jh. verbunden sind, scheint es mir sinnvoller, bereits im Blick auf die authentischen Paulusbriefe die einzelnen Bearbeitungs*vorgänge* wie etwa Abschrift, Kompila-

---

[53] Eine ähnliche Überlegung zum Phänomen antiker Pseudepigraphie stellt SPEYER, Die literarische Fälschung (s. Anm. 17), 41, in abschreibetechnischer Hinsicht an. Aber auch hier gelten die vorhergehenden Überlegungen.

[54] Dies z.B. gilt aber für den pseudepigraphen Briefwechsel zwischen Paulus und Seneca. Vgl. dazu: FÜRST, Pseudepigraphie (s. Anm. 36).

[55] Der Begriff ‚Paulus-Schule' (1880) begegnet erstmals bei H. J. HOLTZMANN (Die Pastoralbriefe. Kritisch und exegetisch behandelt, Leipzig 1880, 110.117). Vgl. auch H. CONZELMANN, Die Schule des Paulus, in: G. Bornkamm / G. Klein (Hg.), Theologia crucis – signum crucis (FS Dinkler), Tübingen 1979, 85–96. – Vgl. zur neueren Diskussion auch T. SCHMELLER, Schulen im Neuen Testament? Zur Stellung des Urchristentums in der Bildungswelt seiner Zeit, HBS 30, Freiburg i. Brsg. u.a. 2001; T. VEGGE, Paulus und das antike Schulwesen. Schule und Bildung des Paulus, BZNW 134, Berlin/New York 2006, bes. 501ff.

[56] FRENSCHKOWSKI, Pseudepigraphie (s. Anm. 20), 259. – Vgl. ähnlich auch die Überlegungen bei B. HEININGER, Die Rezeption des Paulus im 1. Jahrhundert. Deutero- und Tritopaulinen sowie das Paulusbild der Apostelgeschichte, in: O. Wischmeyer (Hg.), Paulus. Leben – Umwelt – Werk – Briefe, UTB 2767, Tübingen/Basel 2006, 309–340 (309f.).

[57] Vgl. FRENSCHKOWSKI, Pseudepigraphie (s. Anm. 20), 263ff.

[58] Vgl. dazu zuletzt z.B. die Beiträge von J. SCHRÖTER, Kirche im Anschluss an Paulus. Aspekte der Paulusrezeption in der Apostelgeschichte und in den Pastoralbriefen, ZNW 98 (2007), 77–104; J. HERZER, ‚Das Geheimnis der Frömmigkeit' (1Tim 3,16). Sprache und Stil der Pastoralbriefe im Kontext hellenistisch-römischer Popularphilosophie – eine methodische Problemanzeige, ThQ 187 (2007), 309–327, sowie die weiteren Beiträge in ThQ 187 (2007): Themenheft zu den Pastoralbriefen. – Diese Frage hängt eng mit der Datierung der Pastoralbriefe zusammen; vgl. dazu auch die entsprechenden Beiträge in diesem Band.

tion und redaktionelle Bearbeitung der Briefe terminologisch und sachlich zu differenzieren.[59] Eine solche Unterscheidung basiert vor allem auf der differenzierten Wahrnehmung des ‚Kopisten' als eines eigenständigen Funktionsträgers im Prozess der Tradierung antiker und so auch frühchristlicher Literatur,[60] die für die Epistolographie-Forschung inzwischen grundlegend geworden ist.[61] Daher sollte meines Erachtens sachlich (a) zwischen einem Tradentenkreis der Paulusbriefe und (b) einer Gruppe theologisch motivierter pseudepigrapher Briefeschreiber unterschieden werden.[62] Vor diesem Hintergrund stellen die Mitarbeiter des Paulus (z.B. Timotheus und Titus), die in den authentischen Paulusbriefen z.T. auch als ‚co-sender' fungieren (z.B. 2Kor 1,1),[63] dann eine weitere, durchaus eigenständige Gruppe (c) innerhalb einer solchen vermuteten ‚Paulus-Schule' dar.

Worin aber könnte das Schreibinteresse derjenigen liegen, die sich als eine solche Gruppe theologisch motivierter pseudepigrapher paulinischer Briefeschreiber (a) charakterisieren lassen? Für Alfons Fürst besteht die Intention der Pseudepigraphie, wie sie im apokryphen Briefwechsel zwischen Paulus und Seneca begegnet, zunächst darin, „bestimmte Absichten oder Lehren unter dem Deckmantel einer anerkannten Autorität zu propagieren".[64] Ruben Zimmermann schlägt entsprechend vor, im Blick auf die neutestamentlichen Schriften, so auch die Paulusbriefe, von einer ‚imitativen Pseudepigraphie' zu sprechen, „bei der Schriften inhaltlich und stilistisch *normativen* Werken anerkannter *Autoritäten* nachempfunden wur-

---

[59] Vgl. E.-M. BECKER, Schreiben und Verstehen. Paulinische Briefhermeneutik im Zweiten Korintherbrief, NET 4, Tübingen/Basel 2002, 56ff.

[60] Vgl. dies., Letter Hermeneutics in 2 Corinthians. Studies in Literarkritik and Communication Theory, JSNT.S 279, London/New York 2004, 53ff.; H. Y. GAMBLE, Books and Readers in the Early Church. A History of Early Christian Texts, New Haven/London 1995, bes. 98ff. – Vgl. für den Bereich der neutestamentlichen Textgeschichte: B. ALAND, Neutestamentliche Handschriften als Interpreten des Textes? P[75] und seine Vorlagen in Joh 10, in: D.-A. Koch u.a. (Hg.), Jesu Rede von Gott und ihre Nachgeschichte im frühen Christentum (FS Marxsen), Gütersloh 1989, 379–397; K. ALAND, Repertorium der Griechischen Christlichen Papyri II. Teil 1, PTS 42, Berlin/New York 1995, z.B. 95. – Vgl. für den Bereich der Altertumswissenschaften etwa: L. CASSON, Libraries in the Ancient World, New Haven/London 2001, z.B. 103f.; H. BLANCK, Das Buch in der Antike, München 1992, z.B. 124f.

[61] Vgl. etwa J. M. LIEU, Art. Letters, The Oxford Handbook of Biblical Studies (2006), 445–456 (452f.).

[62] Vgl. BECKER, Schreiben (s. Anm. 59), bes. 59f.

[63] Vgl. a.a.O. 147ff.

[64] FÜRST, Pseudepigraphie (s. Anm. 36), 80. Fürst betont in diesem Zusammenhang allerdings, dass der Rückgriff auf die Apostolizität weniger über deren ursprüngliche Bedeutung aussagt, als vielmehr Einblick in die „kirchliche Gegenwart des 4. Jahrhunderts" gibt (116).

den".[65] Allerdings ist bei dieser Charakterisierung paulinischer Pseudepigraphie zu fragen, *ob* und von *wem* zum Zeitpunkt der Abfassung der sog. Deutero- und Tritopaulinen Paulus als eine solche allgemein ‚anerkannte Autorität' verstanden und seine Briefe als ‚normative Werke' gelesen wurden: Wenn sich die pseudepigraphen Briefeschreiber literarisch-formal auf die Autorität des Paulus stützen, scheint das Phänomen der Pseudepigraphie in theologiegeschichtlicher Hinsicht doch eher anzuzeigen, dass es am Ende des 1. Jh. n. Chr. im Zuge konkurrierender Autoritätsansprüche[66] überhaupt erst um die Fortschreibung und Durchsetzung paulinischer Autorität ging. Dementsprechend stellen Normativität und Autorität weniger die Voraussetzung als das Ziel paulinischer Pseudepigraphie dar, was – wenn wir Andreas Lindemann folgen – spätestens dann erreicht ist, wenn sich christliche Autoren wie der Verfasser des 1. Clemensbriefes „auf Paulus berufen und seine Briefe für ihre Argumentation in Anspruch nehmen".[67]

Zudem ist auch in literarischer und thematischer Hinsicht zwischen den verschiedenen Briefen der sog. Deutero- und Tritopaulinen zu differenzieren: Während der Zweck mindestens der Pastoralbriefe in der konkreten Gemeindegestaltung und -leitung liegt, sind der Epheser- und Kolosserbrief eher ‚theologisch' motiviert – der 2. Thessalonicherbrief ist im Blick auf sein Verhältnis zum 1. Thessalonicherbrief hier sogar als Sonderfall zu betrachten (s.u.). So erschließt sich das Phänomen paulinischer Pseudepigraphie nicht nur von der literarischen Nachahmung mit dem Ziel der Durchsetzung paulinischer Autorität her, sondern konstituiert sich auf der Basis literarischer Einzelformen und theologischer, ekklesiologischer oder ethischer Einzelthemen, wie sie in den Deutero- und Tritopaulinen anzu-

---

[65] ZIMMERMANN, Art. Pseudepigraphie (s. Anm. 20), 1787 (Hervorhebung durch Verf.in).

[66] Einige Beispiele: Vgl. 2Thess im Konflikt mit (der Auslegung des) 1Thess, s. dazu unten; vgl. 2Petr 3,15f. in Konflikt mit den Paulusbriefen; vgl. die Thematik der ‚Werk-Gerechtigkeit' in Jak 2,14ff. und Röm 4,13ff. bzw. Gal 3,6ff.; vgl. die literarischen und theologischen Unterschiede bei der Abfassung der Evangelien zeitgleich zur Abfassung der Deutero- und Tritopaulinen; vgl. die sieben Sendschreiben in Apk 2f. als möglichen Konkurrenzfaktor zu den Paulusbriefen. – Zu diesen Überlegungen auch: E.-M. BECKER, Amt und Autorität im frühesten Christentum – aus evangelischer Sicht, in: V. A. Lehnert / U. Rüsen-Weinhold (Hg.), Logos – Logik – Lyrik. Engagierte exegetische Studien zum biblischen Reden Gottes (FS Haacker), ABG 27, Leipzig 2007, 71–86 (84–86).

[67] A. LINDEMANN, Die Rezeption des Paulus im 2. Jahrhundert, in: Wischmeyer, Paulus (s. Anm. 56), 341–357 (342). „Während die Autoren der pseudopaulinischen Briefe in die Maske des Apostels schlüpfen …, beziehen sich die … späteren Autoren ausdrücklich zurück auf Paulus als Autorität, wobei sie offensichtlich voraussetzen können, dass auch die Adressaten ihrer Schriften diese Autorität anerkennen" (342).

treffen sind, d.h. die Schreibintentionen sind für jedes einzelne Stück ganz individuell.

An dieser Stelle ließe sich nun weiter fragen, *wie* der Vorgang der Inkorporation fingierter Paulusbriefe in die protokanonischen Paulusbrief-Sammlungen technisch vorzustellen ist.[68] Hier wären Fragen z.B. nach antikem ‚Urheberrecht'[69], nach der frühchristlichen Kanonisierungsgeschichte insgesamt[70] oder auch schreib- und kopiertechnische Fragen bei der Erstellung der frühesten Briefcorpora[71] von Bedeutung, und zwar wiederum für jeden Text individuell. Die folgenden Ausführungen setzen demgegenüber einen anderen Schwerpunkt: Es geht darum, das Phänomen der Orthonymität der authentischen Paulusbriefe einerseits und der Pseudepigraphie der sog. pseudepigraphen Paulusbriefe andererseits, das besonders in religionsgeschichtlicher Hinsicht diskutiert worden ist (s.o. 1.2), nun in seiner dezidiert literaturgeschichtlichen Bedeutung zu würdigen.

2. Die Paulusbriefe im Spannungsfeld von anonymer, pseudepigrapher und orthonymer antiker Literatur

Die in der Pseudepigraphie-Forschung vorgetragenen Überlegungen zum religionsgeschichtlichen Hintergrund, den philologischen Bedingungen und der literaturgeschichtlichen Funktion antiker Pseudepigraphie tragen zur Klärung des Verhältnisses von Anonymität, Pseudepigraphie[72] und Or-

---

[68] So auch die Forderung bei FRENSCHKOWSKI, Pseudepigraphie (s. Anm. 20). – Vgl. dazu auch den Ansatz bei D. TROBISCH, Die Paulusbriefe und die Anfänge der christlichen Publizistik, München 1994, bes. 88ff., der bereits mit einer Autorenrezension der Paulusbriefe, d.h. einer Bearbeitung durch Paulus selbst („Paulus als Redakteur") rechnet.

[69] Vgl. dazu z.B. BROX, Verfasserangaben (s. Anm. 31), 68ff.; SPEYER, Die literarische Fälschung (s. Anm. 17), 93.175f.

[70] Vgl. dazu etwa die Überlegungen bei H. LIETZMANN, Geschichte der Alten Kirche. Mit einem Vorwort von C. Markschies, 2 Bd., Berlin/New York 1999, II, 88f., oder GAMBLE, Books (s. Anm. 60), 100ff. – Vgl. auch einzelne Beiträge in: L. M. McDonald / J. A. Sanders (Hg.), The Canon Debate, Peabody ²2004. – Speziell das Verhältnis von neutestamentlicher Pseudonymität und Kanongeschichte versucht D. G. MEADE, Pseudonymity and Canon. An Investigation into the Relationship of Authorship and Authority in Jewish and Earliest Christian Tradition, WUNT 39, Tübingen 1986, bes. 194ff., wie folgt zu beschreiben: „Attribution, in the context of canon, must be primarily regarded as a statement (or assertion) of authoritative tradition" (216 [im Original kursiv]).

[71] Vgl. dazu noch einmal BECKER, Schreiben (s. Anm. 59), 56ff.

[72] Die Begriffe Pseudepigraphie und Pseudonymität sind nicht einfach synonym zu gebrauchen. Bei der Pseudonymität wird ein fiktiver Autor gewählt, bei der Pseudepigraphie wird das Werk einem realen Autor zugeschrieben.

thonymität antiker Literatur bei.[73] Ich werde diese Ergebnisse kurz resümieren (2.1) und dann auf den Briefeschreiber Paulus beziehen (2.2).

2.1 Anonymität, Pseudonymität, Pseudepigraphie und Orthonymität in der antiken Literatur

In seinem Artikel „Pseudepigraphie" stellt Wolfgang Speyer zur grundlegenden Erklärung des Phänomens der antiken *Pseudepigraphie* fest: „In vielen frühen Kulturen wird ein Vorrang der göttlichen vor der menschlichen Urheberschaft ... angenommen. Das begründet P[seudepigraphie] als älteste Form der Schriftstellerei: Ein Gott oder ein göttlicher Mensch der mythischen Urzeit gilt als Verf[asser]."[74] Man könnte hier – ebenso mit Speyer – vom Phänomen ‚religiöser Pseudepigraphie' sprechen.[75] Mit dem Aufkommen der *Orthonymität* seit der Autorenpersönlichkeit Hesiod (vgl. theog. 22f.) tritt die nunmehr noch oder wieder anzutreffende Pseudepigraphie (z.B. pseudo-platonische Schriften) in verschiedenen Formen und mit unterschiedlichen Funktionen auf, die Speyer im Folgenden benennt[76] und auf die ich oben schon hingewiesen habe.[77] So ließe sich also für den Bereich paganer Literatur verallgemeinernd sagen: Seit der Ablösung religiöser Pseudepigraphie durch die schriftstellerische Orthonymität (Hesiod), die von nun an dominant wird, fungiert die dann auftretende Pseudepigraphie in der griechischen Literatur gleichsam als eine spezifische literarische Form der *mimesis* bereits bestehender literarischer Formen und Gattungen.[78] Das Phänomen der Pseudepigraphie ist in dieser Phase der Literaturgeschichte nicht allein religiös, sondern vor allem literarisch-mimetisch motiviert.

---

[73] Zur möglichen Differenzierung der Begrifflichkeiten vgl. jedoch M. KILEY, Colossians as Pseudepigraphy, Sheffield 1986, 15–17. Zur Begriffsbestimmung vgl. insgesamt auch H.-J. KLAUCK, Die antike Briefliteratur und das Neue Testament. Ein Lehr- und Arbeitsbuch, UTB 2022, Paderborn u.a. 1998, 301–303.

[74] W. SPEYER, Art. Pseudepigraphie I. Allgemein, DNP 10 (2001), 509f. (509) – mit Verweis auf K. THRAEDE, Art. Erfinder II (geistesgeschichtlich), RAC 5 (1962), 1191–1278.

[75] Vgl. SPEYER, Religiöse Pseudepigraphie (s. Anm. 39), 197f.

[76] Vgl. ders., Art. Pseudepigraphie (s. Anm. 74), 510.

[77] S. oben Anm. 49 den OCD-Artikel.

[78] Zum Phänomen der *mimesis* vgl. die Überlegungen bei M. FUHRMANN, Die Dichtungstheorie der Antike. Aristoteles – Horaz – ‚Longin'. Eine Einführung, Darmstadt ²1992, 85ff. – Die Lexeme μιμητής (1Thess 1,6; 2,14) und μιμεῖσθαι (2Thess 3,7.9) begegnen auch in den Thessalonicher-Briefen. Dieses Element lässt sich ggf. auch über eine ethische Deutung hinaus (vgl. O. MERK, Nachahmung Christi. Zu ethischen Perspektiven in der paulinischen Theologie, in: ders., Wissenschaftsgeschichte [s. Anm. 1], 302–336) in literaturgeschichtlicher Hinsicht begreifen.

Martin Hengel hat für den Bereich der frühjüdischen Literatur das Vorherrschen von *anonymer* und *pseudonymer* Literatur wie folgt zu erklären versucht: „Die Unterordnung unter die transsubjektive Tradition blieb stärker als der Drang, die Person des Schriftstellers zur Geltung zu bringen. In der eigentlichen Offenbarungsliteratur bei Apokalypsen und Testamenten war die Autorität einer religiösen Schrift außerdem von der Bindung an eine Autorität der Vergangenheit abhängig."[79] Daraus folgt: Im Bereich frühjüdisch-hellenistischer Literatur[80] muss eher das orthonyme Schreiben[81] Philos oder des Josephus oder zuerst Ben Siras erklärt werden als die allgemein übliche Abfassung anonymer oder pseudonymer Schriften, wie wir sie in überwiegendem Maße in der sog. deuterokanonischen bzw. parabiblischen Literatur finden.[82] So lässt sich zusammenfassend sagen:

– *Anonym* verfasste Literatur versteht sich in der Unterordnung unter eine transsubjektive religiöse oder literarische Tradition.
– *Pseudonym* verfasste Literatur steht in der Tradition religiöser Offenbarungsliteratur, die sich eines mythischen oder prähistorischen Autorennamens bedient. *Pseudepigraph* verfasste Literatur dient der literarisch-mimetischen Nachahmung einer bestehenden Autoren- oder Literaturtradition mit u.U. verfälschender Absicht (*dolus malus*).
– *Orthonym* verfasste Literatur dient der Entdeckung und Artikulation der individuellen Autoren-Persönlichkeit und ihrer eigenen Autoritätsfunktion.

2.2 Orthonymität und Pseudonymität/Pseudepigraphie bei Paulus

Vor dem Hintergrund der pagan-antiken *und* der frühjüdischen Geschichte des Umgangs mit Autorennamen ist also im Falle des Briefeschreibers Paulus der Umstand am interessantesten, *dass* sich Paulus mit Namen nennt – und *nicht, dass* es im frühesten Christentum zur Abfassung an-

---

[79] HENGEL, Literatur (s. Anm. 35), 305. – Vgl. auch die Beobachtungen von MEADE, Pseudonymity and Canon (s. Anm. 70), zum Phänomen der Pseudonymität in prophetischer (17ff.), weisheitlicher (44ff.) und apokalyptischer (73ff.) Literatur, die er als „claim" oder „assertion" to/of „authoritative tradition" versteht (43.72.102).

[80] Vgl. dazu schon E. SCHÜRER, The History of the Jewish People in the Age of Jesus Christ (175 B.C. – A.D. 135), hg. v. G. Vermes u.a., Bd. 3,1, Edinburgh 1986, 470ff.; SPEYER, Religiöse Pseudepigraphie (s. Anm. 39), 209f. – Vgl. zur frühhellenistischen Entwicklung frühjüdischer Literatur M. HENGEL, Judentum und Hellenismus. Studien zu ihrer Begegnung unter besonderer Berücksichtigung Palästinas bis zur Mitte des 2. Jhs. v. Chr., WUNT 10, Tübingen ³1988, 202ff.

[81] Vgl. dazu auch O. WISCHMEYER, Die Kultur des Buches Jesus Sirach, BZNW 77, Berlin/New York 1995, 136ff.

[82] Vgl. dazu J. MAIER, Zwischen den Testamenten. Geschichte und Religion in der Zeit des zweiten Tempels, NEB Erg. 3, Würzburg 1990, 65ff.

onymer oder pseudepigrapher Literatur gekommen ist. Oder anders gesagt: *Paulus* ist die Ausnahme – nicht die anonyme oder pseudepigraphe frühchristliche Literatur. Durch sein orthonymes Schreiben markiert Paulus eine literaturgeschichtliche Zäsur im Übergang von der frühjüdischen zur frühchristlichen Literatur, an die spätere Autoren (z.B. Ignatius) anknüpfen können. Daher gilt für das weitere Vorgehen auch: Die literarische und theologische Bedeutung von Pseudepigraphie im Bereich paulinischer Briefe lässt sich nur vor dem Hintergrund paulinischen orthonymen Schreibens einordnen und verstehen.

2.2.1 Orthonymität bei Paulus

Mit der Nennung seines Namens gibt sich Paulus als eine historische Person *und* als literarischer Autor,[83] also gleichsam als ‚Autorenpersönlichkeit'[84], zu erkennen und agiert nicht als anonym bleibender Vermittler religiöser Traditionen. Die orthonyme Autorschaft hebt Paulus aus dem Umfeld der frühchristlichen, überwiegend nicht orthonym schreibenden Schriftsteller markant heraus,[85] deutet auf sein Selbstverständnis als historische und literarische Person und stellt ihn in die Nähe der jüdischhellenistischen Autoren Philo und Josephus. Warum und in welcher Form

---

[83] Vgl. dazu O. WISCHMEYER, Paulus als Autor, in: dies., Von Ben Sira zu Paulus. Gesammelte Aufsätze zu Texten, Theologie und Hermeneutik des Frühjudentums und des Neuen Testaments, hg. v. E.-M. Becker, WUNT 173, Tübingen 2004, 289–307; dies., Paulus als Ich-Erzähler. Ein Beitrag zu seiner Person, seiner Biographie und seiner Theologie, in: E.-M. Becker / P. Pilhofer (Hg.), Biographie und Persönlichkeit des Paulus, WUNT 187, Tübingen 2005/2009, 88–105; E.-M. BECKER, Autobiographisches bei Paulus. Aspekte und Aufgaben, in: dies. / Pilhofer, a.a.O. 67–87.

[84] Vgl. dazu insgesamt die Beiträge in: dies. / Pilhofer, a.a.O.

[85] Im Falle des Apokalyptikers Johannes, der unter Umständen (M. HENGEL, Die johanneische Frage. Ein Lösungsversuch, mit einem Beitrag zur Apokalypse von J. Frey, WUNT 67, Tübingen 1993, 311ff., geht davon aus, dass die Johannes-Apokalypse im Kern auf den Presbyter zurückgehe, insgesamt aber in einem längeren editorischen Prozess entstanden sei. J. Freys Überlegungen hingegen zielen darauf, die Schrift als Pseudepigraphon zu verstehen, das nur in der redaktionellen Rahmung auf ‚Johannes' zurückzuführen sei [425]. Vgl. zur kritischen Darstellung dieser Überlegungen auch F. W. HORN, Johannes auf Patmos, in: ders. / M. Wolter [Hg.], Studien zur Johannesoffenbarung und ihrer Auslegung [FS Böcher], Neukirchen-Vluyn 2005.2009, 139–159 [144f.]) als einziger weiterer neutestamentlicher orthonymer Autor verstanden werden kann, ist die Charakteristik der Orthonymität diffiziler. Hier sind besonders Gattungsfragen (Apokalyptik und Prophetie) zu diskutieren, aber auch die Bedeutung der in Apk 1,9 genannten Topographie; vgl. dazu E.-M. BECKER, Patmos – ein *utopischer* Ort? Apk 1,9–11 in auslegungs- und kulturgeschichtlicher Hinsicht, Saec. 59 (2008), 81–106; dies., „Patmos". En nøgle til fortolkningen af Johannes' Åbenbaring, Dansk Teologisk Tidsskrift 70 (2007), 260–275 (267f.).

benennt und betont Paulus seine schriftstellerische Orthonymität? Ich nenne einige Beispiele:

- *Autograph:* In 1Kor 16,21; Gal 6,11 betont Paulus sein autographisches Verhältnis zum geschriebenen Brief (Rezeption dieses Motivs auch in 2Thess 3,17, s.u.).
- *Briefrezeption:* In 1Thess 5,27 formuliert Paulus sein Interesse an einer breiten gemeindlichen Rezeption seines Briefes.
- *Autobiographie:* In zahlreichen autobiographischen Passagen nutzt Paulus die Briefform *erstens* dazu, seine Person und seinen apostolischen Dienst sowie die Geschichte seines Wirkens schriftlich zu dokumentieren (z.B. Gal 1f.). *Zweitens* möchte Paulus Einfluss auf seinen Status und seine Rolle in den Gemeinden nehmen (z.B. 2Kor 12). *Drittens* dienen autobiographische Elemente der Planung und Vorbereitung von künftigen Besuchen, Reisen und gemeindlichem Wirken (z.B. Phlm 21f.).
- So sind die paulinischen Briefe eine wichtige historische Quelle für die Rekonstruktion der Biographie des Paulus.[86] Allerdings gilt dies mit Einschränkung auch für die Deutero- und Tritopaulinen. Das methodologische Verhältnis von historischer Biographie-Forschung und literarischer Echtheitskritik ist also komplex: Die (auto-)biographischen und chronologischen Angaben in den echten Paulusbriefen *einerseits* und in den unechten Briefen *andererseits* lassen sich zwar unterscheiden und dienen z.B. im Falle von Widersprüchen als mögliches Kriterium der literarischen Echtheitskritik. Zugleich aber können biographische Angaben in den pseudepigraphen Paulusbriefen (z.B. als Reminiszenzen) auch einen historischen Quellenwert haben.[87] Die historische Biographie-Forschung wird die Frage nach der literarischen Authentizität von Briefen also nur dann ausführlich problematisieren, wenn diese Briefe als historische Quellen fraglich sind.
- *Apostolische Parusie:* Die Epistolographie-Forschung hat gezeigt, dass und wie antike Briefe – so auch die Paulusbriefe – als Mittel einer auch brieftheoretisch begründeten personalen Präsenz im Falle persönlicher Abwesenheit fungieren.[88] Bei den Paulusbriefen wird hier von ‚apostoli-

---

[86] Vgl. ausführlich BECKER, Autobiographisches (s. Anm. 83).

[87] Vgl. dazu die Überlegungen zu den platonischen Briefen bei M. D. DETTENHOFER, Briefe und Biographien, in: M. Maurer (Hg.), Aufriß der Historischen Wissenschaften, Bd. 4: Quellen, RUB 17030, Stuttgart 2002, 82–101 (84).

[88] Vgl. dazu K. THRAEDE, Einheit, Gegenwart, Gespräch. Zur Christianisierung antiker Brieftopoi, Diss. Bonn 1967, 40ff.; ders., Grundzüge griechisch-römischer Brieftopik, Zet. 48, München 1970, 39ff. u.ö.; H. KOSKENNIEMI, Studien zur Idee und Phraseologie des griechischen Briefes bis 400 n. Chr., Helsinki 1956, 38ff. Zur Darstellung des Phänomens auch BECKER, Schreiben (s. Anm. 59), 32f.

scher Parusie' gesprochen.[89] Paulus ist also auf das orthonyme Briefeschreiben als *eines* Mediums authentischer personaler Präsenz förmlich angewiesen.

– *Namensnennung:* Paulus leitet sämtliche Briefe mit der Nennung seines Namens Παῦλος ein. Dieser Name wird in jedem Brief in spezifischer Form syntagmatisch erweitert, was ggf. Einblicke in die jeweilige Schreibsituation erlaubt (z.B. co-sender [z.B. 1Thess], Gefangenschaft [z.B. Phlm]):

– Παῦλος καὶ Σιλουανὸς καὶ Τιμόθεος (1Thess 1,1)
– Παῦλος κλητὸς ἀπόστολος Χριστοῦ Ἰησοῦ (1Kor 1,1)
– Παῦλος ἀπόστολος Χριστοῦ Ἰησοῦ (2Kor 1,1)
– Παῦλος δοῦλος Χριστοῦ Ἰησοῦ (Röm 1,1)
– Παῦλος ἀπόστολος (Gal 1,1)
– Παῦλος καὶ Τιμόθεος δοῦλοι Χριστοῦ Ἰησοῦ (Phil 1,1)
– Παῦλος δέσμιος Χριστοῦ Ἰησοῦ καὶ Τιμόθεος ὁ ἀδελφός (Phlm 1).

Nun ist die Namensnennung allein zwar kein exklusives Kriterium für die Feststellung von literarischer Authentizität, denn diese Form der *superscriptiones* wird in den pseudepigraphen Paulusbriefen imitiert (s.u.). Wichtig aber ist, dass Paulus mit seiner orthonymen Namensnennung in Briefen die Tradition anonym oder pseudepigraph verfasster, religiöser Offenbarungsliteratur verlässt und eine eigene, autorenbezogene literarische Brieftradition begründet, die später dann pseudepigraph fortgeführt wird.

Dass Paulus die Orthonymität wählt, steht offenbar mit seiner kulturellen und sprachlichen Prägung durch die hellenistische literarische Kultur in Zusammenhang, hat aber auch theologische Gründe, die Speyer in seinem Beitrag zur ‚religiösen Pseudepigraphie' pointiert formuliert hat: „Paulus besaß genug Ansehen, da er sich von Christus berufen wußte. Er hatte es nicht nötig, seine Schriften etwa als von Jesus stammend auszugeben."[90] Paulus setzt also an die Stelle religiöser Pseudepigraphie oder schriftstellerischer Anonymität das Kennzeichen der literarischen Orthonymität und der eigenen persönlichen Autorität, die er von Christus ableitet (1Kor 9,1; 15,8; Gal 1,16).

2.2.2 *Apostolizität, Pseud-Apostolizität und Pseudepigraphie*

Schon innerhalb der authentischen Paulusbriefe wird deutlich, dass sich der Missionar, Gemeindeleiter, Theologe und Briefeschreiber Paulus in

---

[89] Vgl. etwa BROX, Falsche Verfasserangaben (s. Anm. 31), 112.
[90] SPEYER, Religiöse Pseudepigraphie (s. Anm. 39), 253f.

Auseinandersetzung mit Gegnern, d.h. vor allem gegnerischen Missionaren befindet (z.B. 2Kor 10–13). In 2Kor 11,13 bringt Paulus den Konflikt mit den korinthischen Gegnern sogar auf den Begriff der ψευδοαπόστολοι, die als ἐργάται δόλιοι, μετασχηματιζόμενοι εἰς ἀποστόλους Χριστοῦ charakterisiert werden.[91] In den späteren pseudopaulinischen Briefen kommt es zu einer Auseinandersetzung mit ,Irrlehrern' und ,Irrlehre' (bes. Kol 2,8ff., 2Thess 2; 1Tim 1,3ff.; 6,3ff.: ἑτεροδιδασκαλεῖν; 2Tim 2,14ff.; Tit 1,10ff.: φρεναπάται). Diese Auseinandersetzung begegnet auch außerhalb des *Corpus Paulinum* in den sog. katholischen Briefen (vgl. Jud 3ff.; 2Petr 2; 1Joh 4; 2Joh 7ff.).[92] Am Ende des 1Tim werden die Konflikte mit Gegnern und gegnerischen Lehren auf den Begriff ψευδώνυμος gebracht (1Tim 6,20: ... καὶ ἀντιθέσεις τῆς ψευδωνύμου γνώσεως).[93] Vor diesem Hintergrund ist bemerkenswert, dass die Deutero- und Tritopaulinen – mit Ausnahme des 2Thess und des Tit 1,1 (δοῦλος) – in der *superscriptio* die ἀπόστολος-Bezeichnung, wie sie in 1Kor und 2Kor sowie im Gal anzutreffen ist (s.o.), aufgreifen. Diese Beobachtung zeigt, dass besonders der ἀπόστολος-Titel[94] zumindest in Teilen der deutero- und tritopaulinischen Briefe literarisch *und* theologisch als Garant für die Sicherung und Fortsetzung des paulinischen Erbes dient. Hier ließe sich angesichts zunehmender Lehr- und Autoritätskonflikte von einer adaptierenden Fortführung eines bereits etablierten apostolischen Briefformulars sprechen.

Doch hat dieser Vorgang insofern auch paradox wirkende Züge, als hier die ,pseud'-epigraphe Fortschreibung paulinischen Briefeschreibens offenbar u.a. gegen ,pseud'-apostolische Gestalten und Irrlehrer gewendet wird. Diese ,Paradoxie' ist aus unserer modernen Sicht kaum aufzulösen. Sie weist vielmehr darauf hin, dass sich die paulinische Pseudepigraphie kaum durch Kategorien wie sachlich-theologische Richtigkeit oder ethisch-moralische Integrität bewerten lässt, sondern so wie schon die paulinische Gegnerpolemik wesentlich als eine literarische Strategie zu verstehen ist. Aus der Sicht der frühchristlichen Verfasser freilich stellt Pseudepigraphie in literarischer Hinsicht kein Problem dar: Denn nur solche Paulusbriefe

---

[91] Vgl. zu den Gegnern des Paulus auch den Exkurs bei M. E. THRALL, A Critical and Exegetical Commentary on the Second Epistle to the Corinthians, 2 Bd., ICC, Edinburgh 1994/2000, 671ff.

[92] Vgl. zum 2Petr zuletzt auch H. J. RIEDL, Anamnese und Apostolizität. Der zweite Petrusbrief und das theologische Problem neutestamentlicher Pseudepigraphie, Frankfurt a.M. u.a. 2005.

[93] Zur Semantik vgl. H. BALZ, Art. ψευδόχριστος κτλ., EWNT 3 (²1992), 1193–1195; H. BIETENHARD, Art. ὄνομα κτλ., ThWNT V (1954), 242–283 (282f.).

[94] Vgl. dazu auch J. FREY, Paulus und die Apostel. Zur Entwicklung des paulinischen Apostelbegriffs und zum Verhältnis des Heidenapostels zu seinen ,Kollegen', in: Becker / Pilhofer, Biographie (s. Anm. 83), 192–227 (194ff.).

sind als ‚Fälschung' zu enttarnen, die mit ‚häretischen Lehren' in Zusammenhang gebracht werden (vgl. z.B. Canon Muratori, Z. 63–65: ... *Pauli nomine fincte ad heresem marcionis* ...).

2.2.3 Ein pseudepigrapher Sonderfall: 2Thess

In diesem Zusammenhang möchte ich abschließend einen Blick auf den 2Thess werfen, der im Rahmen der paulinischen Pseudepigraphie einen Sonderfall darstellt. Der 2Thess ist nicht nur deswegen ein pseudepigrapher Sonderfall, weil seine literarische Authentizität bis in die gegenwärtige Forschung hinein umstritten ist.[95] Dementsprechend variieren auch die Datierungsvorschläge (zwischen ca. 50–90 n. Chr.) erheblich.[96] Doch auch der Umstand, dass wir es im Falle von 1Thess und 2Thess – ähnlich wie bei 1Kor und 2Kor – mit einer Gemeindekorrespondenz zu tun haben, wirft die schon bei Wrede (s.o.) diskutierte Frage nach dem literarischen und literaturgeschichtlichen Verhältnis beider Briefe zueinander auf. Sollte der 2Thess im Unterschied zum 1Thess pseudepigraph verfasst worden sein, würden beide Briefe das in der kanonischen Paulusbrief-Sammlung einmalige[97] Phänomen einer pseudepigraphen Fortschreibung paulinischer Gemeindekommunikation darstellen.

In diesem Zusammenhang sind zwei Beobachtungen zur literarischen Konzeption von 2Thess bedeutsam.[98] *Erstens:* Bei den epistolographischen Formalia wie der *superscriptio* (2Thess 1,1) bemüht sich der Verfasser nicht nur um eine identische Wiedergabe von 1Thess (vgl. 1Thess 1,1). Vielmehr wird darin, dass der Autor auf dem apostolischen Autograph

---

[95] Zur Geschichte der älteren Forschung vgl. etwa H. J. HOLTZMANN, Lehrbuch der historisch-kritischen Einleitung in das Neue Testament, Freiburg i. Brsg. 1885, 229ff. – Zur Forschungsgeschichte bis zu Beginn des 20. Jh. vgl. die umfassende Darstellung bei E. VON DOBSCHÜTZ, Die Thessalonicher-Briefe, KEK 10, Göttingen 1909, 31ff. – Zur jüngeren und jüngsten Forschung vgl. J. A. D. WEIMA / S. E. PORTER, An Annotated Bibliography of 1 and 2 Thessalonians, NTTS 26, Leiden u.a. 1998, 51–64.

[96] Hier existieren drei Positionen: (1) Die Befürworter der Authentizität des 2Thess rechnen mit einer Abfassung in zeitlicher Nähe zum 1Thess. (2) Die Befürworter der pseudepigraphen Abfassung von 2Thess datieren den Brief vielfach auf das Ende des 1. Jh. (3) P. Vielhauer und O. Merk vertreten die Meinung, beim 2Thess handele es sich um den ältesten, vielleicht noch zu Lebzeiten des Paulus geschriebenen deuteropaulinischen Brief. Vgl. zur Darstellung der Forschungspositionen auch E.-M. BECKER, Ὡς δι' ἡμῶν in 2 Thess 2,2 als Hinweis auf einen verlorenen Brief, NTS 55 (2009), 55–72.

[97] Ein weiteres Beispiel außerhalb der neutestamentlichen Paulusbrief-Sammlung wäre vor allem der sog. 3Kor; vgl. dazu W. SCHNEEMELCHER, Paulusakten, in: ders. (Hg.), Neutestamentliche Apokryphen. II Apostolisches, Apokalypsen und Verwandtes, Tübingen [6]1997, 193–241 (231–234). – Vgl. dazu auch A. F. J. KLIJN, The Apocryphal Correspondence Between Paul and the Corinthians, VigChr 17 (1963), 2–23.

[98] Vgl. dazu ausführlich BECKER, Ὡς δι' ἡμῶν in 2 Thess 2,2 (s. Anm. 96).

(2Thess 3,17), der nicht in 1Thess zu finden ist und vergleichsweise emphatisch über die autographischen Hinweise in 1Kor 16,21 oder Gal 6,11 hinausgeht, insistiert, gerade der literarische Versuch des mutmaßlich pseudepigraphen Verfassers des 2Thess erkennbar, seiner literarischen Fiktion zu Authentizität zu verhelfen. *Zweitens*: Die Schlüsselstellen für die Beurteilung des literarischen und sachlich-theologischen Verhältnisses von 2Thess zu 1Thess sind 2Thess 2,2 und 2,15.[99] Im Unterschied zu einem Großteil der Exegeten, die in beiden Sätzen einen direkten Bezug auf 1Thess erkennen und den 2Thess daher als einen Beitrag zur Korrektur oder Aktualisierung der Naherwartung in 1Thess 4f. verstehen wollen,[100] scheinen mir beide Verse auf unterschiedliche Prätexte zu verweisen: Während sich 2Thess 2,2 auf eine fälschlich in Umlauf geratene, nicht mehr erhaltene briefliche Fehlinterpretation von 1Thess bezieht, zielt 2Thess 2,15 in explizitem Rückbezug auf den 1Thess auf eine sachgerechte *relecture* von 1Thess. Dementsprechend gibt es für den Verfasser des 2Thess offenbar drei Typen von Pauluslehre und Paulusbriefen, nämlich: (1) ‚richtige' Pauluslehre (wie den 1Thess), die in literarisch authentischer, d.h. orthonymer Form vorliegen kann (vgl. den Hinweis in 2Thess 2,15); (2) sachlich ‚richtige' Pauluslehre (wie den 2Thess), die in literarisch nicht-authentischer, d.h. pseudepigrapher Form vorliegen kann (vgl. als Indiz 2Thess 3,17); (3) ‚falsche' Pauluslehre (u.U. in Form eines verlorenen Briefs, worauf 2Thess 2,2 hinweist).[101] Wenn hier also die These formuliert ist, der 2Thess sei als eine sachlich-authentische Fortführung des 1Thess zu verstehen, ist damit die literarische Authentizität von 2Thess logisch zwar nicht auszuschließen. Sie wird damit aber auch nicht wahrscheinlicher, da *sachlich-theologische Authentizität* und *literarische Authentizität* nicht zusammenfallen müssen.

Diese Beobachtungen machen insgesamt den frühchristlichen Prozess pseudepigraphen Briefeschreibens literaturgeschichtlich durchsichtig. Denn sie zeigen, dass die Beurteilung von ‚richtiger' oder ‚verfälschender' paulinischer Lehre nicht mit der Beurteilung von literarischer Authentizität oder Pseudepigraphie gleichzusetzen ist. Zugleich wird bereits innerhalb der neutestamentlichen Briefliteratur erkennbar, dass und wie sich der

---

[99] 2Thess 2,1f.: ¹ Wir bitten euch aber, Brüder, was die Parusie unseres Herrn Jesus Christus und unsere Zusammenführung mit ihm betrifft, ² dass ihr euch nicht schnell in (eurem) Sinn ins Wanken bringen noch erschrecken lasst – weder durch Geist, noch durch Wort, noch durch einen Brief, scheinbar (ὡς δι' ἡμῶν) durch uns (gewirkt) –, wie (ὡς) (ὅτι): ‚Der Tag des Herrn ist schon gegenwärtig.' 2Thess 2,15: Also nun, Brüder, steht fest und haltet die Überlieferungen fest, in denen ihr unterwiesen wurdet – sei es durch ein Wort oder durch einen Brief von uns.

[100] Ähnlich kritisch zuletzt auch T. ROH, Der zweite Thessalonicherbrief als Erneuerung apokalyptischer Zeitdeutung, NTOA 62, Göttingen/Freiburg (CH) 2007, bes. 9ff.

[101] Vgl. noch einmal ausführlich BECKER, Ὡς δι' ἡμῶν in 2 Thess 2,2 (s. Anm. 96).

Kampf um die Durchsetzung der ‚richtigen' paulinischen Lehre als eine literarische Aufgabe darstellt.

3. Die literatur- und theologiegeschichtliche Funktion ‚paulinischer' Pseudepigraphie

So lassen sich der paulinischen Pseudepigraphie verschiedene literarische Funktionen zuschreiben, die ich abschließend besonders im Hinblick auf ihre theologiegeschichtlichen Implikationen für eine neutestamentliche Literaturgeschichte resümieren werde. Dabei wird deutlich, dass und wie sich die theologiegeschichtliche Bedeutung paulinischer Pseudepigraphie von ihrer literaturgeschichtlichen Funktion erschließen lässt.

(a) Die Sicherung literarischer und apostolischer Kontinuität: Nach dem Tod des Paulus wird die Sicherung paulinischer Lehr- und Weisungsautorität unter dem Namen des ‚Paulus' bedeutsam. Dabei kann auch eine personale und literarische Kompensation des Todes Pauli wichtig geworden sein. Denn die paulinische Pseudepigraphie führt gewissermaßen das paulinische παρών-ἀπών-Motiv epistolographisch weiter und verhilft daher dem Apostel Paulus auch nach seinem Tod zu personaler Präsenz in den Gemeinden. Die räumliche Distanz zwischen dem abwesenden und dem anwesenden Apostel, die bereits ein wichtiges Thema des 2Kor ist, wird durch das pseudepigraphe Briefeschreiben nun sogar über den Tod des Paulus hinaus zu kompensieren gesucht.[102]

(b) Die Aktualisierung und Deutung paulinischer Lehre: Die paulinische Pseudepigraphie dient – wie etwa Samuel Vollenweider herausstellt – der Aktualisierung paulinischer Lehre[103]: „Gegenüber dem oft aufgebotenen Degenerationsproblem empfiehlt sich der Ansatz, die Paulusrezeption der nachapostolischen Zeit mit den Stichworten Fortschreiben, Relektüre und Kontextualität zu umschreiben: Das Potential des pln. Erbes wird in jeweils neuen gesch[ichtlichen] Situationen aktualisiert."[104] Dabei kann es auch – wie 2Petr 3,15 indiziert – um die Notwendigkeit zur Interpretation und Deutung, ggf. auch *retractatio*, paulinischer Lehre gehen. Der 2Thess hingegen könnte ein Beispiel für einen komplexen, pseudepigraph verfassten Diskursbeitrag über die ‚richtige' (wie der 2Thess) oder ‚verfälschende' (s. der Hinweis in 2Thess 2,2) Fortführung paulinischer Lehre sein.

---

[102] Vgl. ähnlich S. VOLLENWEIDER, Art. Paulus, RGG⁴ 6 (2003), 1035–1065 (1054).
[103] Vgl. ebd.
[104] Ebd.

(c) Die Sicherung und Entwicklung des Paulusbildes als ‚Identifikationsmodell': „Die Gruppe der sechs pseudonymen Paulusbriefe ... leihen [sic] sich die literarische und gemeindeleitende Autorität des Paulus, um die Gemeinden nach seinem Tode leiten und weiterentwickeln zu können. Zugleich entwickeln sie parallel zum Paulusbild der Apostelgeschichte ihrerseits das Paulusbild weiter ..."[105] Im Bereich der paulinischen Pseudepigraphie kann daher von einer literarischen Fingierung des Paulus als Theologen und Briefeschreiber gesprochen werden.[106] Zugleich wird der Apostelbrief selbst literarisch fingiert: Das literarische Instrument des Apostelbriefs wird offenbar als so gewichtig (vgl. schon 2Kor 10) und erfolgreich empfunden, dass die Paulusschüler dies Instrument nicht nur verwenden, indem sie die Paulusbriefe kopieren und sammeln, sondern auch pseudepigraph weiterentwickeln und dabei erfolgreich sind (s. die Kanonisierung der Deutero- und Tritopaulinen).

(d) Die theologisch-hermeneutische Leistung: Aus kirchengeschichtlicher Sicht ist mit dem Phänomen paulinischer Pseudepigraphie eine weit reichende theologiegeschichtliche Weiche gestellt: „Die Paulushermeneutik der Deutero- und Tritopaulinen setzt den christlichen Kontinuitätsstrom der christlichen theologischen Hermeneutik aus sich heraus."[107] So gesehen, beginnt die Hermeneutik paulinischer Briefe textintern in den Paulusbriefen selbst[108] und setzt sich textextern in den Deutero- und Tritopaulinen und/oder anderen frühchristlichen Schriften (z.B. 2Petr) fort. Dieser textexterne hermeneutische Deutungsprozess dauert bis in die Gegenwart an und ist bleibend unabgeschlossen.

---

[105] HEININGER, Rezeption (s. Anm. 56), 310. – VOLLENWEIDER, ebd., spricht hier von der Herstellung eines ‚Identifikationsmodells'. – THEISSEN, Entstehung (s. Anm. 45), 148, hingegen reduziert die Pseudepigraphie auf den Aspekt der ‚Nachahmung' und meint: „Die pseudepigraphe Literatur war weder schöpferisch noch standen Autor und Leserschaft in Interaktion".

[106] Zum Motiv der Schaffung von Identifikationsfiguren in der Antike vgl. auch C. RONNING, Soziale Identität – Identifikation – Identifikationsfigur. Versuch einer Synthese, in: B. Aland u.a. (Hg.), Literarische Konstituierung von Identifikationsfiguren in der Antike, Studien und Texte zu Antike und Christentum 16, Tübingen 2003, 233–251.

[107] W. WISCHMEYER, Die Rezeption des Paulus in der Geschichte der Kirche, in: O. Wischmeyer, Paulus (s. Anm. 56), 358–368 (358).

[108] Vgl. dazu zuletzt E.-M. BECKER, Text und Hermeneutik am Beispiel einer textinternen Hermeneutik, in: O. Wischmeyer / S. Scholz (Hg.), Die Bibel als Text. Beiträge zu einer textbezogenen Bibelhermeneutik, NET 14, Tübingen/Basel 2008, 193–215.

Paulus versus Paulus

Der Epheserbrief als Korrektur des Kolosserbriefes

von

MARTIN HÜNEBURG

Meinem Vater, Gotthelf Hüneburg, zum fünfzigjährigen Ordinationsjubiläum

Die Diskussion zur Pseudepigraphie im NT wird gegenwärtig immer noch wesentlich bestimmt durch den Aspekt ihrer ethischen und (kanon-)theologischen Bewertung.[1] In Folge dieser – häufig noch auf die Alternative legitimes Mittel oder bewusste Täuschung – eingeschränkten Fragestellung tritt die immer wieder geforderte differenzierte Betrachtung[2] des Phänomens selbst in den Hintergrund.[3] Dabei zeigt bereits ein Blick auf den engeren Bereich der mit dem Namen des Paulus verbundenen Pseudepigraphie[4] die Unausweichlichkeit solcher differenzierten Herangehensweise, weisen diese Briefe doch nicht nur inhaltlich-theologisch ein breites Spektrum auf, sondern unterscheiden sich v.a. auch erheblich in der Art, in der ihre Verfasser als „Paulus" ihren Adressaten gegenübertreten. Dies betrifft sowohl die Art der Plausibilisierungsstrategien wie die Verwendung autographer Subskriptionen oder die Art und den Umfang von persönli-

---

[1] Charakteristisch dafür ist etwa die Arbeit von A. D. BAUM, Pseudepigraphie und literarische Fälschung im frühen Christentum. Mit ausgewählten Quellentexten samt deutscher Übersetzung, WUNT II/138, Tübingen 2001.

[2] N. BROX, Falsche Verfasserangaben. Zur Erklärung der frühchristlichen Pseudepigraphie, SBS 79, Stuttgart 1975; M. JANSSEN, Unter falschem Namen. Eine kritische Forschungsbilanz frühchristlicher Pseudepigraphie, ARGU 14, Frankfurt a.M. u.a. 2003.

[3] Vgl. dazu die Behandlung des Pseudepigraphieproblems in vielen Einleitungsbüchern oder Exkursen in den Kommentaren mit ihren generalisierenden Erklärungsmodellen. Auch M. FRENSCHKOWSKI, Pseudepigraphie und Paulusschule. Gedanken zur Verfasserschaft der Deuteropaulinen, insbesondere der Pastoralbriefe, in: F. W. Horn (Hg.), Das Ende des Paulus. Historische, theologische und literaturwissenschaftliche Aspekte, BZNW 106, Berlin/New York 2001, 239–272, stellt zwar zunächst fest (251): „Die Ursachen der Pseudepigraphie sind vielfältig", erklärt dann aber – sicher im Blick auf die ntl. Pseudepigraphie – die Ursache als „epigonales Bewußtsein" und als Autorisierungsproblem. „Die Normen liegen immer in der Vergangenheit."

[4] 2Thess, Kol, Eph und Past.

chen Angaben, als auch den Sprachgebrauch und die Weise des Rückgriffs auf die paulinische Theologie.

Der Epheserbrief[5] erscheint innerhalb der paulinischen Pseudepigraphie als besonders geeignet, Licht auf den Facettenreichtum des Phänomens zu werfen. Was ihn von den anderen Deuteropaulinen unterscheidet, ist sein weitgehender Verzicht auf den Ausbau der Verfasserfiktion und das Fehlen eines erkennbaren Abfassungszweckes. Diese Besonderheit verlangt um so mehr nach einer Erklärung, wenn in Betracht gezogen wird, dass AuctEph, wie heute kaum noch bestritten, den ebenfalls pseudepigraphen Kolosserbrief[6] als Vorlage verwendet hat[7] und die Kenntnis dieses Briefes wahrscheinlich sogar voraussetzt.[8] Angesichts dieser engen Beziehung der beiden Briefe zueinander stellt sich die Frage, wie die völlig unterschiedliche Art ihrer pseudepigraphischen Gestaltung zu erklären ist.

Während Kol um die Darstellung einer im paulinischen Leben situierten Kommunikationssituation bemüht ist und durch die zahlreichen, dem Phlm entnommenen Namen bei der Gestaltung seiner bemerkenswert umfangreichen Grußliste die paulinische Verfas-

---

[5] Eph wird hier als Pseudepigraphon vorausgesetzt. Zwar mehren sich wieder die Stimmen, die für die Authentizität der Verfasserangabe plädieren, ohne jedoch neue Argumente einführen zu können. Gerade der Kommentar von H. HOEHNER, Ephesians. An Exegetical Commentary, Michigan 2006, 2–61, zeigt in seiner umfassenden Diskussion der Verfasserfrage das Problem der Auseinandersetzung deutlich. Hoehner kann zwar darauf verweisen, dass nahezu jede Beobachtung, die zur Begründung nichtpaulinischer Verfasserschaft angeführt wird, auch in den Homologumena nachweisbar ist, ignoriert dabei jedoch völlig, dass sich aus diesen Einzelbeobachtungen ein Gesamtbild ergibt, das letztlich gegen Paulus als Verfasser spricht.

[6] Die pseudepigraphische Verfasserschaft des Kol ist zwar stärker umstritten als die des Eph, kann aber m.E. durch die Untersuchung von W. BUJARD, Stilanalytische Untersuchungen zum Kolosserbrief als Beitrag zur Methode von Sprachvergleichen, StUNT 11, Göttingen 1973, trotz mancher berechtigter Kritik daran, als gesichert gelten.

[7] F. C. SYNGE, Philippians and Colossians. Introduction and Commentary, TBC, London 1951, und J. COUTTS, The Relationship of Ephesians and Colossians, NTS 4 (1958), 201–207, vertreten ein umgekehrtes Abhängigkeitsverhältnis. Beide können aber die von C. MITTON, The Epistle of the Ephesians and its Authorship, Origin and Purpose, Oxford 1951, 68–74, genannten Gründe nicht widerlegen. Nach E. BEST, Who Used Whom? The Relationship of Ephesians and Colossians, NTS 43 (1997), 72–96, erklärt sich die Nähe beider Briefe „most easily on the assumption of distinct authors who were members of the same Pauline school and had discussed together the Pauline theology they had inherited." HOEHNER, Eph (s. Anm. 5), 31 Anm. 5, hält die von Mitton genannten literarischen Beziehungen für „not as formidable as it might first appear". Allerdings geht es ihm darum, dieses Argument zu schwächen, um die Authentizität des Eph behaupten zu können. Diskutiert wird jedoch die Frage, ob AuctEph Kol vorliegen hatte oder ihn aus einer allgemeinen Kenntnis heraus verwendete (vgl. dazu Anm. 19).

[8] Dafür spricht etwa die Selbstverständlichkeit, mit der die von AuctCol durch seine Interpretation des Hymnus 1,15–20 geschaffene σῶμα-κεφαλή-Ekklesiologie in 1,20–23 eingeführt wird.

serschaft seinen Lesern glaubhaft zu machen versucht, sind im Eph die persönlichen Angaben stark zurückgedrängt. Hingewiesen wird lediglich auf die Gefangenschaft des Paulus (3,1; 4,1). Die Selbstbezeichnung als ἐλαχιστότερος πάντων in 3,8 ist formelhaft. Bis auf die Nennung des Tychikus durch die nahezu wörtliche Übernahme von Kol 4,7f. werden auch keine anderen Namen mehr genannt. Dass AuctEph die den Anlass des Kol bildende Auseinandersetzung mit der kolossischen Philosophie auslässt, ist an sich nicht auffällig, sondern wäre als Folge veränderter Umstände zu verstehen. Jedoch nennt er gerade keinen anderen Anlass, der ihn zur Abfassung seines Briefes bewog. Er vermeidet nicht nur persönliche Angaben, sondern verzichtet auch auf die Nennung von Gegnern oder die Darstellung von Kontroversen; er scheint vielmehr überhaupt keine Auseinandersetzung irgendwelcher Art zu führen. Das ganze Schreiben wirkt so seltsam situationslos. Im Brief werden zwar verschiedene, v.a. ekklesiologische Themen angesprochen, die gegenüber Kol neu sind oder über ihn hinausgehen, dies geschieht jedoch in einer Weise, die gerade nicht auf akute Problemlagen rückschließen lässt.[9]

Die Versuche, nachdem das religionsgeschichtliche Bemühen um eine Rekonstruktion von Gegnerpositionen[10] als gescheitert betrachtet werden muss, aus diesen Themen den theologiegeschichtlichen Ort des Eph zu erheben[11] und von daher die Frage nach dem Abfassungsgrund zu beantworten, stoßen deshalb auf zwei Probleme. Sie müssen sowohl die unpolemische Gestalt des Briefes selbst erklären[12] als auch die intensive Nutzung

---

[9] Dass, wie häufig behauptet, eine Spannung zwischen Juden- und Heidenchristen den Anlass für die Abfassung von Eph gegeben haben soll, ist ganz unwahrscheinlich. Weder wird ein Streitpunkt genannt, noch spielen mögliche Streitthemen eine Rolle. AuctEph zeigt auch kein Interesse an dem gegenwärtigen Judentum.

[10] Auch wenn es gelänge, einen religionsgeschichtlichen Hintergrund zu beschreiben, der es erlaubte, Eph als Reaktion auf eine bestimmte Herausforderung zu verstehen, bliebe die Frage, warum AuctEph an keiner Stelle Ross und Reiter wenigstens andeutungsweise nennt.

[11] Eine zusätzliche Erschwernis kommt dadurch hinzu, dass keine Klarheit über die Adressaten besteht. Die Unsicherheit bei der vieldiskutierten Frage, ob ἐν Ἐφέσῳ in Eph 1,1 sekundär ergänzt oder ursprünglich vorhanden, dann getilgt und später wieder eingefügt wurde, lässt es in Anbetracht der Einsicht in die äußerst differenzierte religionsgeschichtliche Situation Kleinasiens kaum geraten erscheinen, den Brief auf dem Hintergrund einer rekonstruierten ephesinischen Situation zu interpretieren, wie dies z.B. R. SCHWINDT, Das Weltbild des Epheserbriefes, WUNT 148, Tübingen 2002, versucht.

[12] Dies wird deutlich bei den Versuchen von K. M. FISCHER, Tendenz und Absicht des Epheserbriefes, Berlin 1973, Eph als Auseinandersetzung mit dem sich in Kleinasien durchsetzenden monarchischen Episkopat und heidenchristlichen Vorbehalten gegenüber Judenchristen zu verstehen, wie auch der These von E. FAUST, Pax Christi – Pax Caesaris, NTOA 24, Göttingen/Freiburg (CH) 1993, Eph gestalte die universale Ekklesia als Gegenentwurf zu den imperialen Ansprüchen Roms. Beide gewinnen ihre Textbasis im Wesentlichen aus Eph 2,11–22. A. LINDEMANN, Bemerkungen zu den Adressaten und zum Anlaß des Epheserbriefes, ZNW 67 (1976), 235–251, sieht in 6,10–17 einen Reflex auf eine Verfolgungssituation und versteht Eph deshalb als Trostbrief. Nach G. VAN KOOTEN, Cosmic Christology in Paul and the Pauline School. Colossians and Ephesians in the Context of Graeco-Roman Cosmology, with a New Synopsis of the Greek Texts,

des Kol[13] bei gleichzeitiger Berücksichtigung der besonderen Ausprägung seines pseudepigraphischen Stiles.

Die offensichtliche Nähe der beiden pseudopaulinischen Schreiben zueinander hat dazu geführt, in ihnen einen gemeinsamen Strang der Paulusrezeption zu sehen.[14] Dabei ist die Beziehung von Eph zu Kol keineswegs unproblematisch.[15] Die Frage, der im Folgenden nachgegangen werden soll, heißt also: Besteht ein Zusammenhang zwischen der Rezeption des Kol durch AuctEph und seiner speziellen Form der Pseudepigraphie und lässt sich daraus ein Hinweis auf seinen Abfassungszweck gewinnen?

1. Zur pseudepigraphischen Technik

Eph nimmt einen erheblichen Anteil an Kolosserstoff auf.[16] Nach der Berechnung von Mitton handelt es sich um 34% des Kol, nach Pokorný[17] sogar um fast die Hälfte, die wörtlich, und zwei Drittel, die inhaltlich aufgenommen werden. Demnach stammen zwischen 26,5% und 50% des Wortbestandes von Eph aus dem Kol.[18] Die Differenz resultiert aus der unterschiedlichen Bewertung von Parallelen. Dennoch kann das Zahlenverhältnis der Berührungen im Wortlaut allein noch nicht viel besagen. Interessant ist hier vielmehr, wie diese Übernahmen erfolgen. Zumeist sind es

---

WUNT II/171, Tübingen 2003, geht es dem Verfasser um eine Weiterführung der Christologie des Kol. Nicht deutlich wird bei diesen Ansätzen, wie etwa der umfangreiche paränetische Teil des Briefes zu erklären ist.

[13] H. GESE, Das Vermächtnis des Apostels, WUNT II/92, Tübingen 1997, 266: „... eine schlüssige Erklärung für diese enge Anlehnung konnte bis heute nicht gefunden werden." S. RANTZOW, Christus Victor Temporis. Zeitkonzeptionen im Epheserbrief, WMANT 123, Neukirchen 2008, 270: „Warum er [sc. AuctEph] diesen Brief so stark rezipiert hat, ist bis heute unklar."

[14] In diesem Zusammenhang wird die Theorie einer Paulusschule modifiziert durch die Annahme verschiedener Flügel einer Schule bzw. verschiedener Schulen, die durch Eph/Kol einerseits und Past andererseits repräsentiert werden. Unsicher ist dabei die Stellung des 2Thess.

[15] Vgl. aber schon W. OCHEL, Die Annahme der Bearbeitung des Kolosser-Briefes im Epheser-Brief in einer Analyse des Epheser-Briefes untersucht, Marburg 1934, 72f., der bereits aus der Ähnlichkeit beider Briefe darauf schließt, Eph wolle Kol verdrängen.

[16] Nach A. KENNY, A Stylometric Study of the New Testament, Oxford 1986, 99, sind Kol und Eph die beiden Briefe des NT mit dem höchsten Verwandtschaftsgrad.

[17] P. POKORNÝ, Der Brief des Paulus an die Epheser, THKNT 10/2, Berlin 1992, 3.

[18] MITTON, Epistle (s. Anm. 7), 57 und die Synopse 316–321; R. REUTER, Synopse zu den Briefen des Neuen Testaments. Teil I: Kolosser-, Epheser-, II. Thessalonicherbrief, ARGU 5, Frankfurt a.M. u.a. 1997, 540–619; VAN KOOTEN, Cosmic Christology (s. Anm. 12), 239–289.

nämlich nur kleinere Wortgruppen von selten mehr als vier bis fünf Wörtern, die sich in direkter Folge in Eph wiederfinden. Deutliche Ausnahmen bilden mit dem Präskript und der sog. Tychikusnotiz (Eph 6,21f./Kol 4,7f.) nur zwei eher formale Elemente. Alle anderen Übernahmen weisen dagegen z.T. erhebliche Eingriffe auf. AuctEph stellt gelegentlich Verse um, wandelt Zitate ab, erweitert oder strafft seine Vorlage. Zumeist aber schafft er neue Kontextualisierungen, indem er Wendungen von verschiedenen Stellen des Kol miteinander verbindet. Bei diesem, von Mitton als Conflation bezeichneten, Vorgehen handelt es sich demnach um die für AuctEph charakteristische Arbeitsweise.[19] Sie zeigt, dass er seinen Prätext nicht mechanisch verwendet oder einfach ausschreibt, sondern theologisch transformiert. Nach der weithin akzeptierten These von H. Merklein fungiert die Verschiebung der Antithetik von unten/irdisch versus oben/himmlisch (Kol) zu heidnisch versus christlich (Eph) dabei als Transformationsregel.[20]

Angesichts dieser klaren Tendenz des Verfassers, seinen Prätext zu transformieren und so neue Aussagen zu gewinnen, überrascht es aber zu sehen, wie sehr Eph und Kol in ihrem Aufbau übereinstimmen. Van Kooten hat für den Kol unter epistolographischen und inhaltlichen Gesichtspunkten eine neunteilige Struktur ausgemacht. Diese Disposition findet sich in gleicher Abfolge fast vollständig in Eph wieder.[21] Ausgelassen wird lediglich der Komplex der Auseinandersetzung mit der kolossischen Philosophie Kol 2,8–3,4. Zugleich werden mit 2,11–22; 4,1–16 und 6,10–17 drei neue Teile in den von Kol vorgegebenen Rahmen eingefügt. Aber auch wenn Kol 2,8–3,4 nicht als thematische Einheit rezipiert wird, werden wesentliche Gedanken daraus in andere Zusammenhänge aufgenommen.

Insgesamt zeigt sich, dass AuctEph den die Kapitel 1–3 umfassenden theologisch-lehrhaften Teil wesentlich stärker bearbeitet und neu gestaltet, während er die Paränese zwar erweitert, letztlich aber erheblich konservativer mit ihr verfährt.

Über diese Kolosserrezeption hinaus nimmt AuctEph weitere Traditionen auf. Bemerkenswert ist dabei, dass er auch ausdrücklich auf das Alte

---

[19] MITTON, Epistle (s. Anm. 12), 63, schließt daraus, dass AuctEph den Kol nicht als literarische Vorlage verwendete, sondern aus seiner Kenntnis des Briefes heraus arbeitete. Ähnlich auch H. MERKEL, Der Epheserbrief in der neueren exegetischen Diskussion, ANRW II 25.4 (1987), 3156–3246 (3213f.), und H. MERKLEIN, Eph 4,1–5,20 als Rezeption von Kol 3,1–17 (zugleich in Beitrag zur Pragmatik des Epheserbriefes), in: P.-G. Müller / W. Stenger (Hg.), Kontinuität und Einheit (FS Mußner), Freiburg i. Brsg. 1986, 194–210 (195). Dafür spricht ein solcher Umgang aber gerade nicht.
[20] MERKLEIN, a.a.O.
[21] VAN KOOTEN, Cosmic Christology (s. Anm. 12), 223f.

Testament zurückgreift.[22] In diesem Punkt ist die Abweichung von seiner Vorlage besonders deutlich. Denn es gehört zu den Auffälligkeiten des Kol, dass er trotz seiner Paulusimitation keinerlei erkennbare Bezüge auf das AT herstellt.[23] In Eph wird zwar lediglich Ps 68,19 in Eph 4,8 mit einer Zitationsformel eingeführt, aber weitere Zitate finden sich in 1,22 (Ps 8,7), 4,25f. (Sach 8,16 und Ps 4,4), 5,31 (Gen 2,24) und 6,2f. (Ex 20,12 bzw. Dtn 5,16). Sonst begegnen verschiedene Anspielungen.[24] Von Paulus klar unterschieden ist allerdings der Einsatz des AT. AuctEph verwendet es nicht argumentativ-begründend, sondern illustrativ. Dies kann jedoch kaum als programmatischer Unterschied gedeutet werden, sondern eher als stilistische Eigenart, die sich auch im Umgang mit anderen Vorlagen findet.

Neben der Aufnahme alttestamentlicher Traditionen und verschiedener frühchristlicher Formeln und Wendungen greift AuctEph schließlich auch auf andere Paulusbriefe zurück. Anklänge finden sich an alle Homologumena.[25] Ob es sich dabei jedoch um Kenntnis und literarische Nutzung einzelner Briefe oder den Soziolekt einer Schultradition handelt, ist allerdings umstritten.[26] Die Schwierigkeit hier zu entscheiden besteht darin, dass nur an wenigen Stellen direkt zitiert wird. Trotzdem erscheint die Nähe zu verschiedenen Paulusbriefen,[27] gerade auch dann, wenn es sich nicht um geprägte Wendungen handelt, eng genug, um ein literarisches Abhängigkeits-

---

[22] Vgl. M. BARTH, Traditions in Ephesians, NTS 30 (1984), 3–25 (3f.); A. T. LINCOLN, The Use of the OT in Ephesians, JSNT 14 (1982), 16–57; T. MORITZ, A Profound Mystery. The Use of the Old Testament in Ephesians, NT.S 85, Leiden 1996.

[23] Neuerdings meint zwar C. A. BEETHAM, Echoes of Scripture in the Letter of Paul to the Colossians, Biblical Interpretation Series 96, Leiden/Boston 2008, insgesamt neun „Echoes" und zwei „Allusions" erkennen zu können. Aber unabhängig davon, ob es sich in jedem Fall tatsächlich um einen Schriftbezug handelt, bleibt die Frage, ob darin ein bewusster Rückgriff auf die Schrift als Autorität gesehen werden kann und ob er als solcher wahrgenommen werden konnte.

[24] Z.B. Jes 57,19 in Eph 2,17 und Jes 59,17 und dessen Verarbeitung in SapSal 5,17–23 als Hintergrund von Eph 6,10–20.

[25] Vgl. die Synopsen bei MITTON, Ephesians (s. Anm. 7), 98–158; GESE, Vermächtnis (s. Anm. 13), 76–78; REUTER, Synopse (s. Anm. 18), 247–531; VAN KOOTEN, Cosmic Christology (s. Anm. 12), 239–289.

[26] A. LINDEMANN, Paulus im ältesten Christentum. Das Bild des Apostels und die Rezeption der paulinischen Theologie in der frühchristlichen Literatur bis Marcion, BHTh 58, Tübingen 1979, 122–130, hält die Indizien für eine literarische Abhängigkeit lediglich im Fall von 1Kor für stark genug. J. GNILKA, Der Epheserbrief, HThK.NT X/2, Freiburg i. Brsg. 1971, 22, rechnet mit einer Kenntnis aller Paulusbriefe mit Ausnahme des 2Thess.

[27] Dies gilt mit hoher Wahrscheinlichkeit für 1Kor, 2Kor, 1Thess und Röm. Vgl. dazu außer den genannten Synopsen auch die Nachweise bei GESE, Vermächtnis (s. Anm. 13), 54–85, der die gleiche Wahrscheinlichkeit auch für Phlm annimmt.

verhältnis anzunehmen. Vorzugsweise begegnen solche Anspielungen in Verbindung mit Kolosserstellen. Die Rezeption erfolgt damit in ähnlicher Weise in Form von Conflations, wie dies auch bei den Einzeltexten des Kol der Fall war. Diese Übereinstimmung in der Art des Umgangs spricht dafür, dass AuctEph auch Kol für einen authentischen Paulusbrief gehalten hat. Tatsächlich aber erreicht er durch diese Verbindung eine wechselseitige Interpretation, indem er nichtpaulinische Traditionen „paulinisiert"[28] und sachlich zugleich über Paulus hinausführt.[29]

Dieses schon früh – freilich unter dem Gesichtspunkt der Verfasserfrage[30] – als problematisch empfundene In- und Nebeneinander von Übernahme und eigenständiger Gestaltung lässt fragen, warum AuctEph nicht einen eigenen neuen Text schafft. Die hier erwogenen Möglichkeiten differieren erheblich. Verwendet AuctEph den Kol nur als Vorlage, um seine eigene Theologie zu autorisieren?[31] Ist er ein eigenständiger Theologe, der sich durch die Absenderangabe und Übernahme des pln Briefformulares bewusst in paulinische Tradition stellt? Beabsichtigt er eine Paulinisierung unpaulinischer Elemente?[32] Geht es ihm um eine abschließende, objektivierende Neuformulierung paulinischer Theologie?[33] Oder zielt er im Gegenteil auf eine Fortsetzung der „Dynamik der paulinischen Theoriebildung"[34], die durchaus auch die Form einer kritischen Auseinandersetzung annehmen kann.[35]

---

[28] Dieser von H. MERKLEIN, Paulinische Theologie in der Rezeption des Kolosser-und Epheserbriefes, in: K. Kertelge (Hg.), Paulus in den neutestamentlichen Spätschriften. Zur Paulusrezeption im Neuen Testament, QD 89, Freiburg i. Brsg. u.a. 1981, 25–69 (63), eingeführte Begriff bezeichnet den Umdeutungsprozess vorwiegend hellenistisch-judenchristlicher Traditionen mit Hilfe paulinischer Gedanken.

[29] Vgl. dazu beispielsweise H. ROOSE, Die Hierarchisierung der Leib-Metapher im Kolosser- und Epheserbrief als „Paulinisierung". Ein Beitrag zur Rezeption paulinischer Tradition in pseudo-paulinischen Briefen, NT 47 (2005), 117–141.

[30] So hat man daraus Argumente sowohl für als auch gegen die paulinische Verfasserschaft des Eph gewonnen. Zur Diskussion des Verhältnisses von Rezeptionsverhalten und Verfasserfrage vgl. J. SCHMID, Der Epheserbrief des Apostels Paulus. Seine Adresse, Sprache und literarischen Beziehungen untersucht, BSt(F) 22,3–4, Freiburg i. Brsg. 1928.

[31] LINDEMANN, Paulus (s. Anm. 26), 129f.; SCHWINDT, Weltbild (s. Anm. 11), 54: AuctEph lehnt sich an Kol an, da dieser in seinem Umfeld Autorität besitzt. Nach A. T. LINCOLN, Ephesians, WBC 42, Dallas 1990, LXVIII, nimmt AuctEph den Kol zum Vorbild, weil er darin das Werk eines Paulusschülers sieht.

[32] Vgl. oben Anm. 28.

[33] GESE, Vermächtnis (s. Anm. 13), 250–276: „theologischer Abschluß der paulinischen Tradition" und „theologisches Vermächtnis der Paulusschule".

[34] RANTZOW, Christus Victor Temporis (s. Anm. 13), 271.

[35] J. BERENSON MCLEAN, Ephesians and the Problem of Colossians. Interpretation of Texts and Traditions in Eph 1:1–2:10, Ann Arbor 1996. VAN KOOTEN, Cosmic Christology (s. Anm. 12), 202, betrachtet Eph „as a full-scale critical commentary on Col, in particular on its cosmology and cosmic Christology".

Der eben dargestellte Befund lässt vermuten, dass es ihm wohl kaum nur darum geht, eine Vorlage für seine Verfasserfiktion zu nutzen. Sein ganzes Rezeptionsverhalten, die nahezu vollständige Übernahme des Kol in Verbindung mit der Conflation von Einzeltexten, scheint vielmehr auf eine Überarbeitung des Kol durch Einbeziehung anderer Paulusbriefe und des AT zu zielen. Dann aber kann vermutet werden, dass es letztlich der Kol selbst ist, dem sein Interesse gilt, weil er es für notwendig hält, ihn neu zu interpretieren.[36] Um die Frage zu beantworten, was ihn dazu bewogen haben könnte, muss zunächst geklärt werden, mit welchen Positionen des Kol er sich auseinandersetzt.[37]

2. Die Bearbeitung des Kolosserbriefs

2.1 Die Neugestaltung des Briefeinganges

AuctEph stellt der zur paulinischen Brieftopik gehörenden und an Kol orientierten Eucharistie und Fürbitte in 1,15–23 eine Eulogie voran. Diese Änderung gegenüber seiner Vorlage ist deswegen so bemerkenswert, weil es für eine solche Briefeingangseulogie[38] außer in 2Kor 1,3–10 keine Vorbilder gibt[39] und er die Eucharistie des Kol nicht ersetzt, sondern beide aufeinander folgen lässt. Eine solche unmittelbare Verbindung ist völlig singulär.[40] Da mittlerweile ein weitgehender Konsens darüber besteht, dass es sich bei Eph 1,3–14 um ein vom Autor selbst formuliertes Stück handelt[41] und er dabei wahrscheinlich auf 2Kor 1,3ff. zurückgreift,[42] stellt sich

---

[36] Etwas zurückhaltender H. HÜBNER, An Philemon. An die Kolosser. An die Epheser, KEK 8, Göttingen 1997, 11: „Man kann fast von einer theologischen Überarbeitung des Kol durch den Schreiber des Eph sprechen. In gewisser Hinsicht ist der Eph so etwas wie eine editio secunda des Kol."

[37] Damit soll nicht bestritten werden, dass AuctEph außer diesen Auseinandersetzungen auch Theologumena des Kol weiterführt.

[38] Begriff von N. A. DAHL, Adresse und Proömium des Epheserbriefes, ThZ 7 (1951), 241–264 (250–264).

[39] Vgl. noch 1Petr 1,3. Zwar wird der Brief Hierams an Salomo in 2Chr 2,11f. ebenfalls mit einer Eulogie eingeleitet, jedoch zeigt die Parallele in 1Kön 5,21, dass es sich um eine sekundäre Verbindung handelt. Vgl. auch die Zitation von 2Chr in Flav.Jos.Ant. 8,53 und bei Eupolemos (Eus.praep. 9,34). Die Briefeingangseulogie gehört nicht zur Brieftopik. Anders allerdings DAHL, a.a.O. 250f.

[40] LINCOLN, Eph (s. Anm. 31), 52: „This is a feature which makes Ephesians unique in the Pauline Corpus."

[41] A.a.O. 14: „an ad hoc composition on the part of the author in elevated liturgical language".

[42] Dafür spricht trotz der inhaltlichen Unterschiede nicht so sehr die gattungstypische Einleitung εὐλογητὸς ὁ θεὸς καὶ πατὴρ τοῦ κυρίου ἡμῶν Ἰησοῦ Χριστοῦ als vielmehr

die Frage nach dem Grund für diese ungewöhnliche Konstruktion. Das Bemühen um Vollständigkeit bei der Rezeption möglicher Briefeingänge[43] dürfte jedoch kaum das Richtige treffen. Weiterführend ist vielmehr der Blick auf die Verbindung von Eulogie und Briefkorpus. Das häufig zitierte aber einseitig allein an philologischen Kriterien orientierte dictum Nordens, Eph 1,3–14 sei „das monströseste Satzkonglomerat"[44], ist längst einer positiveren Einschätzung gewichen. Die zahlreichen Beziehungen lassen erkennen, dass wesentliche Themen hier bereits angesprochen sind, die im Briefkorpus dann entfaltet werden. Die Eulogie erweist sich so als sorgfältig komponiertes Stück mit der Funktion einer Briefeinleitung.[45] Die folgende Eucharistie behält aber ihrerseits ebenfalls den Charakter einer Eröffnung, indem hier erstmals Auferstehung, Erhöhung und Kirche genannt werden. Lincoln schließt daraus zu Recht: „In this way the thanksgiving has a complementary introductory role to the berakah, giving sharper focus to the themes already introduced or only implicit."[46] Sind aber Eulogie und Eucharistie in dieser Weise komplementär zu sehen, so bilden sie zusammen das Vorzeichen, von dem her der gesamte Brief gelesen werden muss. Das verschärft noch einmal die Frage, warum AuctEph diese Briefeinleitung in Eulogie und Eucharistie aufteilt.

Durch das einleitende εὐλογητὸς ὁ θεός wird das Gewicht, das bei der Eucharistie auf dem Glauben der Gemeinde liegt, auf das Handeln Gottes verschoben. Erst mit dem καὶ ὑμεῖς in 1,13 werden die Adressaten direkt angeredet. Insofern erhalten die Aussagen einen allgemeinen und objektiven Charakter. Zugleich aber wird auch durch die Wahl der Gattung, der bekanntlich die jüdische Berakah zugrunde liegt, auf die Verankerung im Judentum hingewiesen.[47]

Auch wenn AuctEph sich damit bereits im Briefeingang deutlich von Kol abhebt, greift er zu dessen Gestaltung auf Formulierungen aus diesem

---

mehr die Verbindung mit dem auf die Eingangseulogie folgenden Motiv der Versiegelung und Geistgabe als ἀρραβών in Eph 1,13f. und 2Kor 1,22.

[43] So aber P. SCHUBERT, Form and Function of the Pauline Thanksgivings, Berlin 1939, 44. Ähnlich auch LINDEMANN, Paulus (s. Anm. 26), 122, der vermutet, der „Verfasser wolle es besonders ‚richtig' machen".

[44] A. NORDEN, Agnostos Theos. Untersuchungen zur Formgeschichte religiöser Rede, Leipzig 1913, 253.

[45] R. HOPPE, Erinnerung an Paulus. Überlegungen zur Eulogie des Epheserbriefes (Eph 1,3–14), in: M. Theobald / R. Hoppe (Hg.), „Für alle Zeiten zur Erinnerung" (Jos 4,7). Beiträge zu einer biblischen Gedächtniskultur, SBS 209, Stuttgart 2006, 281–299 (282f.), vergleicht die Eulogie im Anschluss an M. Theobald mit Beethovens zweiter Leonoren-Ouvertüre, „die die wesentlichen Motive der Fidelio-Oper beinhaltet und so auf die gesamte Handlung vor allem in ihrem vorwärtsdrängenden Duktus vorausweist".

[46] LINCOLN, Eph (s. Anm. 31), 53.

[47] So auch HOPPE, Erinnerung (s. Anm. 45), 283.

Brief zurück. So nimmt er die für Kol zentrale Aussage von der Versöhnung durch Christus Kol 1,14.20.22 bereits in 1,4–7 auf.

Eph 1,4.7	Kol 1,22.14.20
ἐξελέξατο ἡμᾶς ἐν αὐτῷ πρὸ καταβολῆς κόσμου	παραστῆσαι ὑμᾶς
εἶναι ἡμᾶς ἁγίους καὶ ἀμώμους κατενώπιον αὐτοῦ ἐν ἀγάπῃ	ἁγίους καὶ ἀμώμους καὶ ἀνεγκλήτους κατενώπιον αὐτοῦ,
ἐν ᾧ ἔχομεν τὴν ἀπολύτρωσιν διὰ τοῦ αἵματος αὐτοῦ, τὴν ἄφεσιν τῶν παραπτωμάτων ...	ἐν ᾧ ἔχομεν τὴν ἀπολύτρωσιν, τὴν ἄφεσιν τῶν ἁμαρτιῶν
	καὶ δι' αὐτοῦ ἀποκαταλλάξαι ... εἰρηνοποιήσας διὰ τοῦ αἵματος τοῦ σταυροῦ αὐτοῦ ...

Mit dieser Neukontextualisierung verändert er die Aussage von Kol jedoch grundlegend. Die in Kol 1,14.20 allein auf das Kreuz bezogene Versöhnung wird jetzt in den Zusammenhang der Schöpfung gerückt. Die Versöhnungsaussage des Kol wird unter Rückgriff auf Röm 8,29 von der Erwählung her interpretiert. Der Segen zeigt sich in der ἐν αὐτῷ = im präexistenten Christus erfolgten Erwählung πρὸ καταβολῆς κόσμου. Der Status der Glaubenden als ἁγίους καὶ ἀμώμους ergibt sich jetzt als Konsequenz aus der Erwählung, Vorherbestimmung, Versöhnung und Einsetzung zu Erben. Auch das Christusgeschehen wird so zurückgebunden an die Vorzeitlichkeit göttlichen Handelns. Von der Notwendigkeit einer Bewährung des Heilsstandes der Gemeinde ist an dieser Stelle keine Rede mehr. Dieser erscheint gegenüber Kol deswegen auch nicht als gefährdet, da er in der vorzeitlichen Erwählung (1,4.11) gegründet ist. Durch die Streichung von παραστῆσαι und ἀνεγκλήτους wird außerdem der forensische Charakter aufgehoben.[48] AuctEph rezipiert hier also v.a. die Rahmenteile des Kolosserhymnus, durch die AuctCol seine christologische Grundlegung interpretiert und auf seine Adressaten bezieht. Durch diese Transformation stellt er das die Gemeinde begründende Christusgeschehen in einen heilsgeschichtlichen Zusammenhang, der so zum Verstehenshorizont des Briefes insgesamt wird.

Hier klingt auch bereits die in 2,11ff. entfaltete Israelthematik an, denn mit der Erwählungsaussage wird eine Vorstellung auf die Adressaten des Schreibens (ἐξελέξατο ἡμᾶς) übertragen, die fest mit Israel verbunden ist.[49] Die im AT als geschichtliches Handeln Gottes verstandene Erwäh-

---

[48] BERENSON MCLEAN, Ephesians (s. Anm. 35), 23–32.
[49] Dtn 7,6; 14,2 u.ö. Vgl. auch 1Kor 1,27 im Blick auf die Kirche.

lung wird hier als präexistentes Geschehen beschrieben.[50] Ihre geschichtliche Umsetzung erfolgt im Christusgeschehen (V.7: διὰ τοῦ αἵματος αὐτοῦ), von dem her die Zeit nun interpretiert wird als Verheißung einerseits und Durchdringung der Welt bis zur Zusammenfassung aller Dinge (V.10) andererseits.

2.2 Die Gemeinde und ihr Heil

Die soteriologischen Aussagen werden von AuctCol im Anschluss an das Christus-Enkomion Kol 1,15–20 entfaltet und strukturiert durch das Einst-Jetzt-Schema auf die Gemeinde appliziert. Ihr Zielpunkt ist mit V.23 die Mahnung zum Bleiben im Glauben. Sie bereitet, wie die variierende Aufnahme des Verses in 2,7 zeigt,[51] die Auseinandersetzung von 2,6–23 vor, die – unabhängig davon, was unter dieser φιλοσοφία zu verstehen ist[52] – den Anlass für die Abfassung des Kol liefert. Die Auseinandersetzung selbst wird vom AuctEph zwar nicht übernommen, die in diesem Zusammenhang stehenden Aussagen werden jedoch deswegen nicht insgesamt einfach gestrichen. Die Aussagen über den Heilsstand der Christen werden vielmehr bearbeitet und in andere Zusammenhänge eingebaut.

Eph 2,1.5f.

καὶ ὑμᾶς ὄντας νεκροὺς τοῖς
παραπτώμασιν καὶ ταῖς ἁμαρτίαις
ὑμῶν, ...

καὶ ὄντας ἡμᾶς νεκροὺς τοῖς
παραπτώμασιν συνεζωοποίησεν τῷ
Χριστῷ, χάριτί ἐστε σεσῳσμένοι

καὶ συνήγειρεν καὶ συνεκάθισεν ἐν τοῖς
ἐπουρανίοις ἐν Χριστῷ Ἰησοῦ,

Kol 2,13.12

καὶ ὑμᾶς νεκροὺς ὄντας [ἐν] τοῖς
παραπτώμασιν καὶ τῇ ἀκροβυστίᾳ τῆς
σαρκὸς ὑμῶν, συνεζωοποίησεν ὑμᾶς σὺν
αὐτῷ, χαρισάμενος ἡμῖν πάντα τὰ
παραπτώματα.

συνταφέντες αὐτῷ ἐν τῷ βαπτισμῷ, ἐν ᾧ
καὶ συνηγέρθητε διὰ τῆς πίστεως ...

---

[50] Vgl. aber Jub 2,19f. Dort wird die Erwählung des Samens Jakobs vorzeitlich den Engeln mitgeteilt. Bei JosAs 8,9 handelt es sich möglicherweise um eine christliche Interpolation.

[51] 1,23: ... τῇ πίστει τεθεμελιωμένοι καὶ ἑδραῖοι, 2,7: ἐρριζωμένοι καὶ ἐποικοδομούμενοι ἐν αὐτῷ καὶ βεβαιούμενοι τῇ πίστει ...

[52] Die in völlig unterschiedliche Richtungen weisenden Vorschläge zeigen die Schwierigkeit, hier zu einer näheren Bestimmung zu kommen, nur zu deutlich. Jeder Rekonstruktionsversuch stößt auf erhebliche Schwierigkeiten methodischer und materialer Art. Weder ist die Abgrenzung der mit dieser Philosophie zu verbindenden Aussagen deutlich, noch ist klar, in welchem Maße AuctCol ihr Selbstverständnis getroffen hat oder überhaupt treffen wollte. Vgl. dazu die Kritik der neueren Vorschläge bei H. HÜBNER, Die Diskussion um die deuteropaulinischen Briefe seit 1970. I: Der Kolosserbrief II, ThR 68 (2003), 395–440 (395–411), und den Beitrag von Nicole Frank in diesem Band.

Die enge Beziehung zwischen den beiden Texten ist von Best[53] u.a. durch einen unabhängig voneinander vollzogenen Rückgriff auf ein Traditionsstück erklärt worden. Dies erscheint aber schon wegen des Gesamtbefundes der Abhängigkeit des Eph von Kol zweifelhaft. Vollends unwahrscheinlich wird die Annahme durch das Fehlen jedes hymnischen Stiles und die Verzahnung mit den anderen Briefteilen.

AuctEph formuliert vielmehr in 2,1ff. wiederum unter Rückgriff auf Kol seine soteriologische These, ohne diese jedoch in den Horizont einer Kontroverse zu stellen. Die durch περιπαθήσατε (2,2)/περιπαθήσωμεν (2,10) gebildete inclusio verweist vielmehr auf eine paränetische Zielrichtung. Umso bemerkenswerter ist es, dass er bei der Darstellung des Heilsstandes in 2,6f. durch die Einfügung einer dritten συν-Aussage noch über Kol hinausgeht. Christen sind durch die Taufe[54] nicht nur mit Christus lebendig gemacht und auferweckt, sondern bereits auch mit in den Himmel versetzt. Mit dieser Änderung gegenüber Kol verstärkt er den Gedanken der Suffizienz des von Gott vorzeitlich geplanten Werkes Christi. Die Gläubigen sind damit prinzipiell nicht mehr durch die Mächte und Gewalten dieses Aions angreifbar.[55] Durch die Aufnahme einer schlagwortartigen Zusammenfassung paulinischer Theologie in 2,8.10 weist er seine Position als übereinstimmend mit den sonst von Paulus her bekannten Positionen aus.[56] Zugleich lenkt er so den Blick voraus auf sein sich daraus ergebendes, gegenüber Kol neues Verständnis der Paränese.

---

[53] E. BEST, A Critical and Exegetical Commentary on Ephesians, ICC 1998, Edinburgh 1998, 199f. Vgl. auch FISCHER, Tendenz (s. Anm. 12), 121–131. Hier bestehen jedoch große Differenzen hinsichtlich einer Abgrenzung und Einordnung des angenommenen Traditionsstückes.

[54] Dass 2,1–10 auf die Taufe referiert, wird besonders in 2,5 deutlich. Der Rückgriff auf Röm 6 spiegelt sich möglicherweise auch in der Einfügung von ἁμαρτίαι in 2,1; vgl. Röm 6,11 und beachte den einfachen Dativ.

[55] Vgl. POKORNÝ, Eph (s. Anm. 17), 103.

[56] H. HÜBNER, Glossen in Eph 2, in: H. Frankemölle / K. Kertelge (Hg.), Vom Urchristentum zu Jesus (FS Gnilka), Freiburg i. Brsg. 1989, 392–406 (402ff.), hat aus dem von Paulus erheblich abweichenden Verständnis der guten Werke und der sich damit ergebenden Spannung zur Rettung aus Gnade geschlossen, dass es sich bei 2,8–10 um eine sekundäre Glosse im Eph handele. Die Aussage fügt sich dafür jedoch zu gut in den Argumentationszusammenhang ein.

Eph 4,21f.; 3,17; 5,6; 3,19

... καὶ ἐν αὐτῷ ἐδιδάχθητε, καθώς ἐστιν ἀλήθεια ἐν τῷ Ἰησοῦ, ἀποθέσθαι ὑμᾶς κατὰ τὴν προτέραν ἀναστροφήν ...

κατοικῆσαι τὸν Χριστὸν διὰ τῆς πίστεως ἐν ταῖς καρδίαις ὑμῶν, ἐν ἀγάπῃ ἐρριζωμένοι καὶ τεθεμελιωμένοι,

Μηδεὶς ὑμᾶς ἀπατάτω κενοῖς λόγοις

γνῶναί τε τὴν ὑπερβάλλουσαν τῆς γνώσεως ἀγάπην τοῦ Χριστοῦ, ἵνα πληρωθῆτε εἰς πᾶν τὸ πλήρωμα τοῦ θεοῦ.

Kol 2,6f.8.9f.

ὡς οὖν παρελάβετε τὸν Χριστὸν Ἰησοῦν τὸν κύριον, ἐν αὐτῷ περιπατεῖτε,

ἐρριζωμένοι καὶ ἐποικοδομούμενοι ἐν αὐτῷ καὶ βεβαιούμενοι τῇ πίστει καθὼς ἐδιδάχθητε ...

Βλέπετε μή τις ὑμᾶς ἔσται ὁ συλαγωγῶν διὰ τῆς φιλοσοφίας καὶ κενῆς ἀπάτης ...

ὅτι ἐν αὐτῷ κατοικεῖ πᾶν τὸ πλήρωμα τῆς θεότητος σωματικῶς, καὶ ἐστὲ ἐν αὐτῷ πεπληρωμένοι, ὅς ἐστιν ἡ κεφαλὴ πάσης ἀρχῆς καὶ ἐξουσίας.

Die christologisch begründete Aufforderung zur Gestaltung des Lebenswandels wird aus dem Zusammenhang der Bewahrung des Heilsstandes in die Paränese versetzt. Die Gefahr der Täuschung durch leeren Betrug besteht nicht mehr im Blick auf die Soteriologie, sondern das Ethos. Schon diese Neufassung lässt deutlich werden, dass der umfangreiche paränetische Teil des Briefes nicht einfach als traditionell abgetan werden kann, sondern als wesentliches Anliegen des Verfassers betrachtet werden muss.

2.3 Kirche und Israel

Die in 2,1–10 formulierte soteriologische These des Eph wird im Folgenden noch einmal ekklesiologisch entfaltet.[57] Dabei ist es auffällig, dass die in den Kolosserrahmen eingebauten ekklesiologischen Aussagen von AuctEph mit der Israelthematik verbunden werden. Ausgangspunkt der Überlegung ist die ἐν τῷ αἵματι τοῦ Χριστοῦ erreichte Versöhnung mit Gott, die aus den (gott-)fernen Heiden (τὰ ἔθνη ἐν σαρκί, οἱ λεγόμενοι ἀκροβυστία) Nahe werden lässt.[58] Diese vertikale Ausrichtung der Versöhnung wird jetzt aber außerdem noch horizontal als Aufhebung des Gegensatzes von Juden und Heiden (τὰ ἀμφότερα 2,14) interpretiert. 2,11f. nimmt das bisher vom Gegensatz einst/tot/Welt versus jetzt/lebendig/Himmel bestimmte soteriologische Kontrastschema auf und fasst es neu: ποτὲ ... καιρῷ ἐκείνῳ χωρὶς Χριστοῦ – νυνὶ δὲ ἐν Χριστῷ. Die Vergangenheit der Adressaten wird hier als Zeit ohne Christus zur Existenz Israels ins Verhältnis gesetzt und durch eine Reihe von vier Appositionen, von

---

[57] Diese ekklesiologische Neuformulierung umfasst nicht nur 2,11–22, sondern schließt auch noch die Aussagen über die Rolle des Paulus ein.
[58] Vgl. Jes 57,19 und 52,7.

denen je zwei durch καί verbunden sind, näher bestimmt:[59] χωρὶς Χριστοῦ = ἀπηλλοτριωμένοι τῆς πολιτείας τοῦ Ἰσραὴλ καὶ ξένοι τῶν διαθηκῶν τῆς ἐπαγγελίας - ἐλπίδα μὴ ἔχοντες καὶ ἄθεοι ἐν τῷ κόσμῳ. Die Defizite der Existenz χωρὶς Χριστοῦ werden jedoch nicht aufgehoben durch die Inkorporation der Heiden in Israel,[60] denn die Versöhnungsaussage in V.16 und der nur durch Christus vermittelte Zugang zu Gott (V.18) gelten trotz der Charakterisierung als Nahe in V.17 auch im Blick auf Israel, sondern durch die Verbindung beider zu einer neuen Schöpfung (ἵνα τοὺς δύο κτίσῃ ἐν αὐτῷ εἰς ἕνα καινὸν ἄνθρωπον), zum Leib Christi. Die Aussagen zum Status ἐν Χριστῷ greifen auf die Defizitaussagen zurück,[61] zeigen aber zugleich, dass es nicht bloß um eine Angleichung geht, sondern eine deutliche Überbietung vorliegt:

ἀπηλλοτριωμένοι τῆς πολιτείας τοῦ Ἰσραήλ	συμπολῖται τῶν ἁγίων[62]
ἄθεοι ἐν τῷ κόσμῳ	οἰκεῖοι τοῦ θεοῦ

Angesichts dieses Befundes erscheint die Einführung des Themas Israel in doppelter Hinsicht bemerkenswert. Zum einen richtet sich das Interesse von AuctEph ausschließlich auf das – letztlich ebenso versöhnungsbedürftige – Israel vor Christus,[63] ohne die für Paulus so entscheidende Frage nach der Zukunft Israels auch nur anklingen zu lassen. Zum anderen sind keine Anzeichen für einen zwischen Juden und Christen oder Juden- und Heidenchristen bestehenden Konflikt erkennbar, die diesen Gedankengang herausfordern würden.[64] Kritik am gegenwärtigen Israel findet sich nicht.

---

[59] Der Kontrast zu ἐν Χριστῷ spricht dafür, χωρὶς Χριστοῦ als umfassendes Prädikat zu verstehen.

[60] So etwa dezidiert M. BARTH, Ephesians 1–3, AncB 34, Garden City 1974, zur Stelle.

[61] Vgl. auch die Wiederaufnahme von ξένοι in V.19.

[62] Wie die ἅγιοι zu identifizieren sind, ist umstritten. Genannt werden: der himmlische Hofstaat, Juden, Judenchristen, Christen allgemein. M.E. zwingt der Sprachgebrauch von 1,1 und 1,4 dazu, auch hier an Christen allgemein zu denken. Das Argument SELLINS, Der Brief an die Epheser, KEK 8, Göttingen 2007, 232f., συμπολῖται setze als Relationsbegriff Bürger und neu Hinzugekommene voraus, ist nicht zwingend.

[63] Nach HÜBNER, Eph (s. Anm. 36), 182, erweckt die Formulierung ὁ ποιήσας τὰ ἀμφότερα ἕν in 2,14 den Eindruck, ganz Israel gehöre zur Einheit der Kirche.

[64] Anders z.B. FISCHER, Tendenz (s. Anm. 12), der mit wachsenden Vorbehalten gegenüber Judenchristen rechnet, und C. ROETZEL, Jewish Christian – Gentile Christian Relations. A Discussion of Ephesians 2,15a, ZNW 74 (1983), 81–89. Jedoch erscheint die häufig als Erklärung angeführte Behauptung, derartige Konflikte spielten zur Zeit der Abfassung von Eph bereits keine Rolle mehr, angesichts der vorhandenen Quellen als kaum überzeugend. M. Y. MACDONALD, The Politics of Identity in Ephesians, JSNT 26 (2004), 419–444, rechnet mit einem Interesse des Epheserautors am wechselnden Geschick Israels zur Zeit Domitians angesichts eigener Identitätsprobleme.

Themen, die in der Auseinandersetzung zwischen Juden- und Heidenchristen eine Rolle spielen, werden nicht benannt, die von Kol her gegebenen Ansatzpunkte sämtlich ausgelassen. Auch die Erklärung, AuctEph ginge es lediglich darum, Heidenchristen die Bedeutung ihres Statuswechsels deutlich zu machen, kann kaum überzeugen. Warum entfaltet AuctEph also die Ekklesiologie als Überwindung der Trennung von Juden und Heiden und welche Bedeutung hat das Israel vor Christus für ihn?

Die Aussagen von V.12 lassen einen Umkehrschluss zu bzw. fordern diesen geradezu heraus.[65] Danach erscheint Israel, trotz der für alle geltenden Aussage der Zornverfallenheit in 2,1–3 καὶ ἤμεθα τέκνα φύσει ὀργῆς ὡς καὶ οἱ λοιποί im Unterschied zu den ἔθνη als Bündnispartner Gottes und – gut paulinisch – Träger der Verheißung. Dass darauf tatsächlich der Schwerpunkt liegt, zeigt das Verhältnis zu Röm 9,4f., woran AuctEph möglicherweise anknüpft.[66] Von den dort von Paulus parallel genannten Privilegien Israels begegnen in Eph lediglich αἱ διαθῆκαι und αἱ ἐπαγγελίαι wieder, jedoch verbunden zu αἱ παραθῆκαι τῆς ἐπαγγελίας. Inhalt der (verschiedenen) Bundessetzungen ist die eine Verheißung, die in Christus erfüllt ist. Nicht nur das Fehlen der νομοθεσία in der Reihe der Vorzüge spricht dafür, dass es hier um eine Neudefinition Israels ohne Rekurs auf das Gesetz geht. Der ἐν Χριστῷ gegebene neue Status wird erreicht durch die Vernichtung (καταργήσας) des Gesetzes,[67] das mit der Näherbestimmung τὸ μεσότοιχον τοῦ φραγμοῦ[68] anders als bei Paulus ausschließlich von seiner Funktion als Identitätssicherung durch Abgrenzung gegenüber den Heiden her erfasst ist. Bereits die einführende Umschreibung Israels als περιτομὴ ἐν σαρκὶ χειροποίητος zielte mit ihrer negativen Konnotation[69] nicht auf eine Vorabrelativierung der nachfolgend

---

[65] Die Möglichkeit eines solchen Umkehrschlusses wird von LINDEMANN, Bemerkungen (s. Anm. 12), 249, vehement bestritten. Seiner Meinung nach „geht es dem Vf. des Eph ausschließlich darum, die Vergangenheit der angeredeten (Heiden-)Christen unter Aufbietung aller Argumente als ‚heillos' zu kennzeichnen." Aber selbst wenn im Blick auf Israel keine positiven Aussagen gemacht werden, lässt sich die Beschreibung des Seins χωρὶς Χριστοῦ durch die folgende Apposition ἀπηλλοτριωμένοι τῆς πολιτείας τοῦ Ἰσραήλ kaum anders als ein gegenüber Israel defizienter Status verstehen. Die Aussagen von V.12 gelten gerade nicht, wie Lindemann meint, „pauschal für alle Christen", da ausdrücklich Heidenchristen angeredet werden.

[66] Dafür spricht v.a. das ungewöhnliche Vorkommen von διαθήκη im Plural (V.12).

[67] Von einer Vernichtung des Gesetzes redet Paulus gerade nicht. Vgl. Röm 3,31 und 7,2.6.

[68] Vgl. Aristeas 139.142. Rabbinische Belege bei Bill I 867 und III 587f.

[69] χειροποίητος begegnet im AT als Kennzeichnung von Götterbildern. Die Bezeichnung der Beschneidung als χειροποίητος und ἐν σαρκί setzt die Vorstellung einer geistlichen Beschneidung als der eigentlichen voraus, die ἀχειροποίητος erfolgt. Vgl. Röm 2,28f., Phil 3,3 und Kol 2,11.

genannten Vorzüge,[70] sondern wie auch die Bezeichnung der Heiden als τὰ ἔθνη ἐν σαρκί οἱ λεγόμενοι ἀκροβυστία darauf, die mit dem Gesetz verbundenen Unterscheidungen als irrelevant zu erweisen. Dass schließlich in 3,6 die Heiden ἐν Χριστῷ als συγκληρονόμα καὶ σύσσωμα καὶ συμμέτοχα τῆς ἐπαγγελίας bezeichnet werden, scheint zwar auf den ersten Blick hinter 2,5f. und 2,19 zurückzufallen, betont aber noch einmal das Anliegen, die Bedeutung Israels als Träger der Verheißung gerade auch im Blick auf die Ekklesia herauszustellen. Sie ist hier von der Ekklesia als dem καινὸς ἄνθρωπος her gedacht, die damit als Zielpunkt einer im vorzeitlichen Ratschluss Gottes begründeten Verheißungsgeschichte erscheint.[71] Für die Leser des Eph ergibt sich daraus die Einsicht, dass die Ekklesia trotz ihrer Qualität als neue Schöpfung Gottes in Christus Teil einer Geschichte ist, in der sich der vorzeitliche Erwählungswillen Gottes durchsetzt, der letztlich auf die kosmisch-universale Einheit zielt, für die die Kirche paradigmatisch steht.[72] Die für AuctEph bleibende Bedeutung Israels, als Träger der Verheißung Repräsentant der Heilsgeschichte zu sein, spiegelt sich darin, dass das Alte Testament im Unterschied zu Kol wieder als Referenz- und Beleginstanz verwendet wird.

Dass der in den Zusammenhang von Kol eingebaute ekklesiologische Abschnitt mit seiner Herausstellung der Einheit der Ekklesia und der Bedeutung Israels für die Kirche in Reaktion auf die Vorgaben des Kol erfolgt, zeigt sich in der Neufassung wesentlicher Begriffe des Kol. Die wegen ihres letzten Gliedes singuläre Verbindung τὸν νόμον τῶν ἐντολῶν ἐν δόγμασιν in Eph 2,15 spielt an auf Kol 2,14.[73] Dort ist der Dativ δόγμασιν zwar innerhalb des Syntagmas τὸ καθ' ἡμῶν χειρόγραφον τοῖς δόγμασιν sowohl syntaktisch als auch semantisch[74] schwer zu deuten, sicher ist jedenfalls, dass es um die Trennung zwischen Gott und Menschen geht, die durch das Kreuz überwunden wird. Im Eph sind die δόγματα eindeutig Explikation des Gesetzes, das Juden und Heiden trennt. Noch deutlicher wird dies im Blick auf den für Kol und Eph in gleicher Weise zentralen Mysteriumsbegriff. In beiden Briefen ist damit der zentrale Inhalt der paulinischen Verkündigung an die Heiden bezeichnet, dessen Bekanntmachung bereits Teil der neuen Christuswirklichkeit ist. Während aber Kol

---

[70] SELLIN, Eph (s. Anm. 62), 194.

[71] Für Paulus zielt die Verheißung auf die Offenbarung der Gerechtigkeit Gottes in Christus (Röm 3,21). Deshalb ist er gezwungen den Israel-Begriff zu problematisieren (Gal 3; Röm 9). Vgl. dazu H. MERKLEIN, Christus und die Kirche. Die theologische Grundstruktur des Epheserbriefes nach Eph 2,11–18, SBS 66, Stuttgart 1973, 72–76.

[72] A. T. LINCOLN, The Church and Israel in Ephesians 2, CBQ 49 (1987), 605–624 (618).

[73] SELLIN, Eph (s. Anm. 62), 216.

[74] Sellin sieht ebd. darin einen Terminus der kolossischen Philosophie für die Speisevorschriften. Zahlreiche Exegeten beziehen den Ausdruck aber auf das atl. Gesetz.

1,26f. Χριστὸς ἐν ὑμῖν, ἡ ἐλπὶς τῆς δόξης, durch seinen Kontext ganz auf den Aspekt der durch Christus gewirkten Versöhnung mit Gott ausgerichtet ist, geht es in Eph 3,6 ausdrücklich um die Einbeziehung der Heiden in die Verheißung Israels. AuctEph nimmt also nicht nur Begriffe aus Kol auf und interpretiert sie durch Kontextualisierung, sondern füllt sie auch inhaltlich ausdrücklich neu.

2.4 Die Rezeption der Paränese

Das Anliegen des Eph ist lange Zeit von dem ekklesiologisch ausgerichteten ersten Teil her bestimmt worden, wobei die paränetischen Passagen vernachlässigt wurden bzw. im Schatten des ekklesiologischen Themas als mitgeschleppte Tradition galten. Dagegen haben sie neuerdings zu Recht wieder stärkere Beachtung und Gewichtung erfahren.[75] Musste es doch auffallen, dass AuctEph nicht nur die Paränese des Kol nahezu vollständig übernimmt, sondern diese auch z.T. erheblich erweitert.[76] Trotzdem ist es nicht so sehr der beträchtliche Umfang, welcher der Paränese ihr Gewicht verleiht,[77] sondern die auch gegenüber Kol deutlich stärkere Verzahnung beider Briefteile. AuctEph bindet sie in 4,1 nicht nur mit der an Röm 12,1 erinnernden Formulierung παρακαλῶ οὖν ἐγὼ ὑμᾶς + Inf. zurück an den ersten Teil des Briefes und macht sie durch die Wiederaufnahme der Bezeichnung ὁ δέσμιος aus 3,1 als Teil der paulinischen οἰκονομία kenntlich, er schafft auch zahlreiche innertextuelle Verflechtungen,[78] die auf einen engen Zusammenhang von Ekklesiologie und Paränese im Verständnis des Autors hinweisen.[79] Daraus ergibt sich wiederum gegenüber Kol eine Neubestimmung der Funktion der Paränese.

---

[75] H. MERKLEIN, Eph 4,1–5,20 (s. Anm. 19). U. LUZ, Überlegungen zum Epheserbrief und seiner Paränese, in: H. Merklein (Hg.), Neues Testament und Ethik (FS Schnackenburg), Freiburg i. Brsg. u.a. 1989, 376–396; G. SELLIN, Die Paränese des Epheserbriefes, in: ders., Studien zu Paulus und zum Epheserbrief, Göttingen 2009, 180–198; R. HOPPE, Ekklesiologie und Paränese in Eph 4,17–5,20, in: M. Wolter (Hg.), Ethik als angewandte Ekklesiologie. Der Brief an die Epheser, Rom 2005, 139–162.

[76] Nach LUZ, a.a.O. 377, liegt das Interesse von AuctEph auf der Paränese des Kol.

[77] SELLIN, Paränese (s. Anm. 75), 180f., verweist auf die quantitative Verschiebung gegenüber Röm, Gal und 1Thess, die ein ähnliches Nacheinander von Indikativ und Imperativ aufweisen wie Eph.

[78] Entfremdung von Gott: 4,18 vgl. 2,12; Wandel im alten Leben: 4,22 vgl. 2,3; 1,13; Anziehen des neuen Menschen: 4,24 vgl. 2,10.15 und die Beschreibung des neuen Menschen als gerecht und heilig/heilig und untadelig in 1,4; Apolytrosis/Versiegelung: 4,30 vgl. 1,7.13f.; Tod-Leben = Wandel in Sünden 2,1 vs. Wandel in guten Werken 2,10 vgl. Wandel nach Maßstäben der Heiden 4,17 vs. Leben als Kinder des Lichtes 5,8. Vgl. dazu auch HOPPE, Ekklesiologie (s. Anm. 75), 145–147.

[79] Nach HÜBNER, Eph (s. Anm. 36), 198, ist „AuctEph gar nicht in der Lage, Paränese untheologisch und unchristologisch zu denken".

Über die Abgrenzung der Paränese in Kol besteht keine Übereinstimmung.[80] M.E. muss Kol 3,1-4 zum vorangegangenen lehrhaften Teil gerechnet werden. Die Parallelität von 2,20 und 3,1 εἰ ἀπεθάνετε σὺν Χριστῷ und εἰ οὖν συνηγέρθητε τῷ Χριστῷ fassen in antithetischer Weise noch einmal die Position des Verfassers gegen die Philosophie zusammen und bilden so seine Antwort auf die Forderung μὴ οὖν τις ὑμᾶς κρινέτω ἐν ... (2,16). Erst mit dem Imperativ νεκρώσατε οὖν τὰ μέλη τὰ ἐπὶ τῆς γῆς (3,5) setzen dann die einzelnen Mahnungen ein. Das Ethos des Kol ist demnach bestimmt von der alleinigen Ausrichtung nach oben. Diese wird kontrastiert mit der Forderung sich von allem Irdischen zu lösen. Die Paränese gewinnt so den Charakter eines Gegenentwurfes zu jedem welthaften Verhalten.

Eph gestaltet seine Paränese dagegen ausdrücklich als Kontrast zur heidnischen Lebensweise.[81] Wie Gerhard Sellin gezeigt hat, ist die Paränese von 4,1-6,9 zyklisch aufgebaut und hat ihre Achse in 5,1f.[82] Es verdient weiterhin Beachtung, dass der Forderung in 4,17 nach einem Lebenswandel μηκέτι ... καθὼς καὶ τὰ ἔθνη in 4,1-6 und 4,7-16 eine Grundlegung voransteht,[83] die AuctEph unter Einbeziehung von Kol 3,12-15 weitgehend frei[84] geschaffen hat. Daraus ergibt sich ein hermeneutischer Schlüssel für das Verständnis der Paränese insgesamt. Das geforderte Verhalten zielt auf die Wahrung der Einheit (ἑνότης 4,3.13) der Ekklesia,[85] die begründet ist in der Einheit Gottes. Insofern ist solcher Wandel imitatio nach dem Vorbild Christi (5,1f.). Durch die Wiederaufnahme des Gedankens der Berufung in 4,1.4 wird der Bezug zur Eingangseulogie 1,11 hergestellt. Zugleich wird so auch der Gedanke von 2,10 wieder aufgenommen, dass der Wandel in guten Werken die Konsequenz des vorgängigen Handelns Gottes ist. Die Paränese erscheint so letztlich als Umsetzung der vorzeitlichen Erwählung. Umgekehrt formuliert: Die Erwählung findet ihre Gestalt im Ethos. Rudolf Hoppe kommt deshalb zu

---

[80] Die meisten Kommentare lassen die Paränese mit 3,1 einsetzen.

[81] 4,17: τοῦτο οὖν λέγω καὶ μαρτύρομαι ἐν κυρίῳ, μηκέτι ὑμᾶς περιπατεῖν, καθὼς καὶ τὰ ἔθνη περιπατεῖ ἐν ματαιότητι τοῦ νοὸς αὐτῶν.

[82] SELLIN, Paränese (s. Anm. 75), 192-195 (195); vgl. auch ders., Eph (s. Anm. 62), 304f.: A: 4,1-16 (Einheit in der Vielfalt), B: 4,17-24 (Der alte und der neue Mensch), C: 4,25-32 (Dualistisch-katalogische Mahnungen), D: 5,1f. (Prinzip: Nachahmung Gottes am Modell Christi), C': 5,3-14 (Dualistisch-katalogische Mahnungen), B': 5,15-20 (Das törichte [des alten] und das geisterfüllte Leben [des neuen Menschen]), A': 5,21-6,9 (Die Familie als Zelle und Bild der Einheit).

[83] περιπατεῖν in 4,1 und 4,17.

[84] Eph 4,7-16 weist keine Beziehungen zu Kol auf.

[85] 4,7-16 führt den Gedanken der Einheit weiter, insofern die Vielfalt des Leibes auf das Maß der Gabe Christi zurückgeführt wird, die letztlich auf die Einheit des Glaubens und der Erkenntnis (4,13) und sein Wachsen (4,16) zum ἀνὴρ τέλειος (4,13) zielt.

dem Schluss, die „Frage nach der Gestaltungskraft zu einer dem erkannten Gotteswillen entsprechenden Lebensführung [ist] ein notwendiger Bestandteil der Ekklesiologie selbst. ... Die Paränese ist ... als eine Darstellung der Ekklesiologie im eigentlichen Sinne zu verstehen."[86]
Dass dabei AuctEph anders als AuctCol die alttestamentlich-jüdische Tradition nicht unter die Torheit des alten Lebens verrechnet, zeigt sich an der positiven Verwendung atl. Vorstellungen und direkter Zitate. So wird etwa die Aufforderung an die Kinder, sich ihren Eltern unterzuordnen in 6,2 nicht nur durch die Zitation von Ex 20,12/Dtn 5,15 erweitert, es wird vielmehr ausdrücklich darauf hingewiesen, dass mit diesem Gebot eine Verheißung verbunden ist. Auch die abschließenden Mahnungen 6,10–20 transportieren noch einmal – vermittelt durch das atl. Bild von der Waffenrüstung Gottes – Grundsätzliches über die Situation der Gemeinde. Aufgenommen wird dabei die Vorstellung einer Herrschaft der ἀρχαὶ καὶ ἐξουσίαι (καὶ δυνάμεις) über die Welt, wie sie bereits in 1,21; 2,2 und 3,10 begegnete. Aber anders als bei den beiden Prätexten Jes 59,16f. und SapSal 5,17–23 ist es hier nicht Gott selbst, der die Rüstung anlegt, um Widersacher zu bekämpfen, sondern die Gemeinde, die so in diesen Kampf einbezogen ist.[87] Diese Kennzeichnung der Wirklichkeit der Gemeinde verstärkt nicht nur den appellativen Charakter, sondern verweist zugleich noch einmal abschließend auf die ekklesiologische Vorstellung von der Durchsetzung des Herrschaftsanspruches Gottes durch das Wachsen des Leibes Christi.
AuctEph bezieht sich also auch im paränetischen Teil seines Briefes positiv auf Israel als Teil der Identität der Kirche. Insofern ist der Einwand Hoppes gegen Merklein, die Absicht einer Erinnerung an die Israelidentität sei überzogen, da die Thematik nach 4,17 nicht mehr erkennbar wäre, nicht haltbar.[88]

---

[86] HOPPE, Ekklesiologie (s. Anm. 75), 147.
[87] Vgl. dazu E. HAAG, Die Waffenrüstung Gottes nach Jesaja 59. Zur Vorgeschichte einer neutstamentlichen Paränese, TThZ 115 (2006), 26–49.
[88] HOPPE, Ekklesiologie (s. Anm. 75), 143.

3. Versuch einer Ortsbestimmung des Eph

3.1 Die rhetorische Situation

Eph zeigt zwar keine Anzeichen einer Auseinandersetzung mit Gegnern, dennoch ist deutlich geworden, dass er in einen Diskurs eingebunden ist, dessen Konturen durch seine Beziehungen zu Kol einigermaßen erkennbar werden. Ob AuctEph sich dabei zu diesem Diskurs durch seine Lektüre des Kol selbst oder durch theologische Positionen, die sich auf Kol stützen, herausgefordert sieht, lässt sich nicht entscheiden. Aber die Art, wie er den Kol rezipiert, zeigt, dass er seinen Prätext weder als bloßes Muster für die Abfassung eines „paulinischen" Briefes verwendet hat, noch als Vorlage verstanden haben kann, auf deren Basis weiterdenkend er dann eigene Akzente setzt. Er will also nicht paulinische Theologie unter veränderten Umständen weiterschreiben oder zum Abschluss bringen. Vielmehr geht er in einer Weise mit dem Kol um, die das Bestreben deutlich werden lässt, trotz einer unbestreitbaren Nähe und Übereinstimmung in verschiedenen Vorstellungen deutliche Korrekturen vorzunehmen. Solche Korrekturen betreffen nicht etwa nur Einzelaussagen, sondern berühren das in der Theologie des Kol begründete Grundanliegen.

Kernpunkt für AuctEph ist seine Vorstellung von der einen Kirche, die sich sowohl räumlich in kosmisch-universaler Weite als auch zeitlich in heilsgeschichtlicher Dimension erstreckt. Während er erstere Vorstellung mit Kol teilt, sieht er den letzteren Gedanken von dort her gefährdet. Anliegen des Kol ist es, die durch die Versöhnungstat Christi am Kreuz bewirkte Identität der Ekklesia als eschatologische Heilsgemeinschaft zu schützen, die er durch die „Philosophie" infrage gestellt sieht, da diese darüber hinaus weitere Bedingungen einfordert. Ihr setzt er die soteriologische Suffizienz des Christusgeschehens entgegen. Die Aufforderung zum Bleiben im Glauben (1,23) zielt deshalb auf das Bewahren des in der Taufe geschehenen radikalen Existenzwechsels mit der Konsequenz der Loslösung von allen Bindungen an das bisherige Leben (3,2.5). Von diesem Ansatz her kommt er zu einer Perhorreszierung der vorchristlichen Vergangenheit insgesamt. AuctCol konzentriert dabei den geschichtlichen Aspekt des Heilshandeln Gottes auf das Eintreten des Gekreuzigten in die Geschichte. Die Frage nach dessen Vorgeschichte bleibt offen. Offen bleibt damit aber auch die Frage nach dem Gott Israels. Problematisch wird dies, zumindest in den Augen von AuctEph, durch die in der Auseinandersetzung mit der „Philosophie" ausdrücklich abgelehnten Verhaltensweisen. Denn die lassen sich – freilich in malam partem – als jüdische identity marker lesen.

Die in Kol 2,8.20 wahrscheinlich aus Gal 4,3.9 übernommene Wendung[89] τὰ στοιχεῖα τοῦ κόσμου hat bei Paulus ihren Ort in der Auseinandersetzung mit judaisierenden Tendenzen und fungiert als zusammenfassender Ausdruck für den Rückfall unter das Gesetz, den er, wie dann auch in Eph, mit der Beachtung bestimmter Zeiten verbindet und so in die Nähe heidnischer Kulte rückt. Die Anspielungen auf Speisevorschriften und als Reinheitsgebote verstehbare Berührungstabus lassen sich ebenso wie der Vorwurf der Engelverehrung[90] auf jüdische Gebräuche beziehen.

Damit aber verfällt im Kontext von Kol auch die Israeltradition insgesamt dem Verdikt einer Gefährdung des Heilsstandes der Gemeinde.[91] Genau an diesem Punkt greift AuctEph korrigierend ein, indem er das Christusgeschehen und die daraus folgende Existenz der Kirche protologisch im Heilsratschluss Gottes verankert und die paulinische Sicht auf Israel als Träger der Verheißung in seiner eigenen Interpretation geltend macht.

3.2 Die pseudepigraphische Gestaltung

Welche Konsequenzen ergeben sich nun aus den bisherigen Ausführungen für das Verständnis der Pseudepigraphie des Eph? AuctEph steht trotz seiner Nähe zu Kol zentralen Punkten dieses Schreibens so kritisch gegenüber, dass er sich veranlasst sieht, einer ihm gefährlich erscheinenden Tendenz entgegenzusteuern. Trotzdem polemisiert er an keiner Stelle gegen ihn. Auch Formulierungen, die 2Thess 2,2 vergleichbar wären, finden sich bei ihm nicht. All dies spricht dafür, dass er in Kol einen echten Paulusbrief sieht. Damit befindet er sich aber in der prekären Lage, sich mit ebenfalls von Paulus stammenden oder sich auf Paulus berufenden Positionen auseinandersetzen und diese kritisieren zu müssen. Dieser Herausforderung begegnet er durch eine tief greifende Bearbeitung von Kol. Dazu übernimmt er jedoch nicht nur einen erheblichen Teil des Wortbestandes von Kol, sondern bindet sich außerdem noch eng an dessen Aufbau. Im Schlussteil seines Briefes übernimmt er schließlich die für ihn eigentlich belanglose Tychikusnotiz nahezu wörtlich aus Kol 4,7f. So schafft er eine für seine Rezipienten erkennbare Nähe zu Kol. Zugleich lässt er aber alle weiteren persönlichen Notizen und situativen Angaben aus.[92] Diese Verän-

---

[89] Dafür spricht etwa auch die Verbindung mit τὸ πλήρωμα τοῦ χρόνου/τὸ πλήρωμα τῆς θεότητος im Blick auf die Sendung Christi.
[90] C. E. ARNOLD, The Colossian Syncretism. The Interface Between Christianity and Folk Belief at Colossae, WUNT II/77, Tübingen 1995, 32–60, mit Verweis auf Or.Cels. 1,27; 5,6; 6,30; Kerygma Petri zitiert nach Or.comm. in Joh. 13,17 und Clemens, Stromateis 6,5,41.
[91] Dass die Lösung von den jüdischen Wurzeln zum Problem wird, zeigt in der Mitte des 2. Jh. nicht zuletzt der aus Kleinasien stammende Markion.
[92] Dies könnte möglicherweise auch das Fehlen einer konkreten Adressatenangabe erklären, die trotz der daraus folgenden grammatisch schwierigen Form der Adscriptio textkritisch zu bevorzugen ist.

derung gegenüber seiner Vorlage spricht für das Bemühen, das Anliegen möglichst allgemein zu formulieren. Auch diese Besonderheit der Pseudepigraphie des Eph kann wiederum durch dessen Verhältnis zu Kol verständlich gemacht werden.

Da Kol bereits eine Generalisierung seiner Theologie als wahres paulinisches Erbe[93] vornimmt und AuctEph ihn als Brief des Paulus nicht verdrängen kann,[94] versucht er, ihn durch eine enge Anlehnung bei allgemeinerer Formulierung als einen in einer konkreten Situation begründeten Spezialfall erscheinen zu lassen, um ihn so zu neutralisieren.

Das Selbstverständnis des AuctEph scheint in der Formulierung 3,3f. durchzuklingen. Er versteht sich als Exeget des Paulus aufgrund seiner Einsicht in das Mysterium. So kann er die Rolle des Apostels verstärken,[95] indem er die Bedeutung seiner οἰκονομία für die Heiden als Teil der Heilsgeschichte herausstellt und ihn als alleinigen Absender erscheinen lässt, ohne deswegen selbst als „Paulus" weiter in Erscheinung zu treten. Die Autorität des Paulus besteht in der Ausfüllung dieser οἰκονομία, nicht im Wortlaut seiner Briefe. So ist für ihn ein solcher kritischer Umgang mit einem Brief des Apostels möglich.[96]

4. Ergebnis

Die Pseudepigraphie des Eph mit ihrer besonderen Gestalt erklärt sich nicht allgemein als Weiterführung des paulinischen Erbes angesichts von Herausforderungen durch veränderte Zeiten, sondern genauer als die Positionierung innerhalb eines in der Rezeptionsgeschichte der paulinischen Theologie selbst verlaufenden Diskurses, in dem sich AuctEph bemüht, einer von Paulus ausgehenden Gefahr durch seine Paulusexegese zu begegnen. Deshalb unterscheidet sie sich auch wesentlich von der pseudepigraphischen Gestaltung des Kol. Damit bestätigt diese Untersuchung, dass das Aufkommen pseudepigraphischer Schriften im frühen Christentum hinsichtlich ihrer Ursachen und Ziele nicht als ein einheitliches Phänomen zu erfassen ist. Die unterschiedliche Durchführung der pseudepigraphischen Fiktion verdankt sich am wenigsten auctorialer Individualität, sondern ist

---

[93] Vgl. die Aufforderung zum Austausch von Briefen (4,16) und die Hervorhebung der Bedeutung des Apostels und seines Schülers für Laodikeia (4,13) und für alle, die ihn nicht selbst gesehen haben (2,1).

[94] Vgl. dazu die Aussagen zu Paulus in 3,1–10.

[95] Vgl. aber 2,20: Apostel und Propheten im Plural.

[96] Zum Exegeseverständnis von AuctEph vgl. BERENSON MCLEAN, Ephesians (s. Anm. 35), 214f.

vielmehr eine Folge der Gründe und der Funktion dieser Art der Textproduktion, auf die hin jede Schrift für sich befragt werden muss. Auch die Frage einer Paulusschule ist angesichts dieser Ortsbestimmung des Eph neu zu überdenken.

Der Kolosserbrief und die „Philosophia"

Pseudepigraphie als Spiegel frühchristlicher Auseinandersetzungen um die Auslegung des paulinischen Erbes

von

NICOLE FRANK

Betrachtet man die exegetische Forschungsgeschichte zur Frage neutestamentlicher Pseudepigrapha, so nimmt der Brief an die Kolosser in mehrfacher Hinsicht eine gewisse prototypische Stellung ein. Zum einen gilt der Kolosserbrief nach heutigem Stand der Forschung als ältestes uns überliefertes paulinisches Pseudepigraphon;[1] zum anderen scheint er durch die ausgiebige inhaltliche Auseinandersetzung mit einer gegnerischen *Philosophia* (Kol 2,8.16–23) auch gleichsam eine paradigmatische Rekonstruktion der Genese frühchristlicher pseudepigrapher Schriften zu erlauben: Die Verfasserfiktion erhält ihre Legitimation durch die akute Notwendigkeit, einer kursierenden Irrlehre mit dem Anspruch apostolischer Autorität entgegentreten zu können. Der klassische Disput über Legitimität resp. Illegitimität pseudepigrapher Verfasserschaftszuschreibung[2] kann somit gewissermaßen auf die Ebene einer unmittelbaren Bedrohungssituation heruntergebrochen werden, innerhalb derer, zugespitzt formuliert, die Lageeinschätzung „Gefahr im Verzug" besondere Maßnahmen rechtfertigt.

---

[1] Auf eine eingehende Rekapitulation der Forschungsdiskussion zu Verfasserschaft und Datierung des Kol soll an dieser Stelle verzichtet werden; die entsprechenden Abwägungen sind in den vergangenen Jahrzehnten ausgiebig erörtert worden. Zur Frage der deuteropaulinischen Autorschaft sei hier in erster Linie auf die sprachanalytische Studie von Walter Bujard verwiesen, die bis heute als grundlegend für die Forschung zum Kolosserbrief gelten kann (siehe W. BUJARD, Stilanalytische Untersuchungen zum Kolosserbrief als Beitrag zur Methodik von Sprachvergleichen, StUNT 11, Göttingen 1973); eine ausführliche forschungsgeschichtliche Übersicht bieten u.a. Wolter (M. WOLTER, Der Brief an die Kolosser. Der Brief an Philemon, ÖTBK 12, Gütersloh/Würzburg 1993, 27–43) und Pokorný (P. POKORNÝ, Der Brief des Paulus an die Kolosser, ThHK 10/1, Berlin 1987, 1–18).

[2] Zur Geschichte dieser theologischen Auseinandersetzung siehe insbesondere den umfassenden forschungsgeschichtlichen Überblick bei M. JANSSEN, Unter falschem Namen. Eine kritische Forschungsbilanz frühchristlicher Pseudepigraphie, ARGU 14, Frankfurt a.M. 2003.

So einleuchtend es prima facie erscheinen mag, Intention und Abfassungshintergründe des ältesten paulinischen Pseudepigraphons auf einen so schlüssigen Nenner zu bringen, so greift diese Annahme doch, wie im vorliegenden Beitrag zu zeigen sein soll, textanalytisch zu kurz und vermag dem grundsätzlichen theologischen Anspruch von Kol 2 nicht gerecht zu werden. Im Folgenden soll daher in drei Schritten entfaltet werden, dass Kol 2,16–23 nicht eine spezifische Irrlehre im Umfeld von Kolossä im Blick hat, sondern gerade vor dem Hintergrund der pseudepigraphen Abfassungssituation als umfassende Handreichung für den christlichen Umgang mit abweichenden Lehrmeinungen zu verstehen ist (1), und sich darin gegenüber den Protopaulinen durch eine deutlich restriktivere Position auszeichnet (2). Diese wird ihrerseits untermauert durch eine entsprechend zugespitzte Lesart paulinischer Theologie im Hinblick auf die Frage christlicher Glaubensgemeinschaft und Heilsgewissheit (3).

Im Zentrum steht somit nicht die exegetisch mitunter ebenso überstrapazierte wie eindimensionale Diskussion um Echtheit/Unechtheit bzw. Legitimität/Illegitimität von Pseudepigraphie, sondern vielmehr die Rekonstruktion der hierbei wirksamen literarischen Mechanismen und Strategien: Welches (fiktionale) Bild zeichnet der Kolosserbrief im Blick auf seine Selbstverortung innerhalb eines bestimmten situativen Kontextes, der auf textueller Ebene durch die Koordinaten Autor – Adressaten – Gegner vorstrukturiert und definiert wird?

1. Zur (fiktiven) Situierung des Kolosserbriefes

Basierend auf der Annahme des pseudepigraphen Charakters sprechen viele textimmanente wie textexterne Faktoren klar dagegen, Adressaten wie implizite Gegner des Kolosserbriefes tatsächlich im Sinne konkreter Gruppierungen im Umfeld von Kolossä zu lokalisieren. Bereits die briefliche Selbstverortung des Kol weist eine auffällige „epistolographische Diskontinuität"[3] auf, indem neben Kolossä (Kol 1,2: τοῖς ἐν Κολοσσαῖς ἁγίοις καὶ πιστοῖς ἀδελφοῖς ἐν Χριστῷ) mit den mehrfachen Verweisen auf die Gemeinde von Laodizea (Kol 2,1; 4,13.16) ein weiterer Adressatenkreis des Schreibens genannt wird; vgl. Kol 4,16: καὶ ὅταν ἀναγνωσθῇ παρ' ὑμῖν ἡ ἐπιστολή, ποιήσατε ἵνα καὶ ἐν τῇ Λαοδικέων ἐκκλησίᾳ ἀναγνωσθῇ.[4] Zugleich zeichnet sich der Kolosserbrief grund-

---

[3] F. VOUGA, Der Brief als Form der apostolischen Autorität, in: K. Berger (Hg.), Studien und Texte zur Formgeschichte, TANZ 7, Tübingen/Basel 1992, 7–58 (49).

[4] Auf Grundlage dessen vermutet Lindemann, dass Laodizea die eigentliche Adressatengemeinde des Kolosserbriefes bildet, während die fiktive Adressierung an Kolossä der Authentizitätsfiktion des Schreibens geschuldet ist: „Der Autor wollte seinen Lesern

sätzlich durch eine universell-umfassende Perspektivierung aus; vgl. Kol 1,6: ἐν παντὶ τῷ κόσμῳ. Dabei wird die kosmologische Reichweite von Schöpfungs- und Erlösungsgeschehen im Blick auf τὰ πάντα ἐν τοῖς οὐρανοῖς καὶ ἐπὶ τῆς γῆς (1,16) bzw. εἴτε τὰ ἐπὶ τῆς γῆς εἴτε τὰ ἐν τοῖς οὐρανοῖς (1,20) ebenso universell ausgedeutet wie der Verkündigungsanspruch ἐν πάσῃ κτίσει τῇ ὑπὸ τὸν οὐρανόν (1,23) und die apostolische Tätigkeitscharakterisierung καταγγέλλομεν νουθετοῦντες πάντα ἄνθρωπον καὶ διδάσκοντες πάντα ἄνθρωπον ἐν πάσῃ σοφίᾳ, ἵνα παραστήσωμεν πάντα ἄνθρωπον τέλειον ἐν Χριστῷ (1,28). Gleichzeitig erfährt der postulierte Skopus des apostolischen Wirkens eine schrittweise Ausweitung von der konkreten Gemeinde in Kolossä über die Nachbargemeinde von Laodizea bis hin zur universellen Gesamtheit derer, mit denen den Apostel keine persönliche Bekanntschaft verbindet; vgl. Kol 2,1: Θέλω γὰρ ὑμᾶς εἰδέναι ἡλίκον ἀγῶνα ἔχω ὑπὲρ ὑμῶν καὶ τῶν ἐν Λαοδικείᾳ καὶ ὅσοι οὐχ ἑόρακαν τὸ πρόσωπόν μου ἐν σαρκί.

Während somit bereits der so formulierte Selbstanspruch des Kolosserbriefes deutlich über Kolossä hinaus verweist, spricht insbesondere auch die pseudepigraphe Abfassungssituation gegen eine geographische Verortung der intendierten Adressatenschaft innerhalb des Lykostals. Nach verschiedenen historiographischen Zeugnissen, u.a. bei Tacitus (Annales 14,27,1), Orosius (Historiae adversum Paganos 7,7,11) und in der Eusebschen Chronik des Hieronymus, wurden Kolossä, Laodizea und Hierapolis durch ein oder mehrere starke Erdbeben um 60–62 n. Chr. gänzlich zerstört;[5] zusätzliche Untermauerung erhalten diese Berichte durch die Tatsa-

---

den Eindruck vermitteln, Paulus habe mit Blick auf Kolossä einst (also um das Jahr 60) Stellung genommen zu einer Entwicklung, wie sie sich jetzt in ganz ähnlicher Weise in ihrer eigenen Gemeinde zeigt" (A. LINDEMANN, Die Gemeinde von „Kolossä". Erwägungen zum „Sitz im Leben" eines pseudopaulinischen Briefes, in: ders., Paulus, Apostel und Lehrer der Kirche. Studien zu Paulus und zum frühen Paulusverständnis, Tübingen 1999, 187–210 [193]. Siehe zu dieser Position ferner auch R. WILSON, A Critical and Exegetical Commentary on Colossians and Philemon, ICC, London/New York 2005, 183). Problematisch erscheint diese Annahme jedoch angesichts der mutmaßlichen Zerstörung der gesamten Region um 60 n. Chr. durch ein Erdbeben (s.o.), das nach den Textzeugnissen bei Eusebius, Tacitus und Orosius neben Kolossä auch Laodizea in Mitleidenschaft gezogen hatte.

[5] Nach anderen Quellen wird die Zerstörung der Region auf das Jahr 64 datiert und damit mutmaßlich in unmittelbarer zeitlicher Nähe zum Tod Pauli, der – bei aller auch in diesem Punkt verbleibenden Unsicherheit der Chronologie – während der Christenverfolgung unter Nero ebenfalls um 64 n. Chr. vermutet wird. Zur Quellenlage der Erdbeben-Berichte und deren kritischer Bewertung vgl. auch U. LUZ / J. BECKER, Die Briefe an die Galater, Epheser und Kolosser, NTD 8/1, Göttingen 1998, 184, und E. LOHSE, Die Briefe an die Kolosser und an Philemon, KEK 9/2, Göttingen 1968, 37f., sowie WOLTER, Kolosser (s. Anm. 1), 34, und O. LEPPÄ, The Making of Colossians. A Study on the Formation and Purpose of a Deutero-Pauline Letter, Vantaa 2000, 18.

che, dass Kolossä im Zeitraum danach keinerlei literarische Bezeugung mehr findet. Die Existenz einer christlichen Gemeinde in Kolossä ist daher zum Zeitpunkt der Abfassung des Kolosserbriefes, der als frühestes paulinisches Pseudepigraphon zeitlich gemeinhin relativ früh nach dem Tod des Apostels angesetzt wird,[6] eher unwahrscheinlich, was für die Annahme spricht, dass die fiktive Adressierung eines Schreibens an die Gemeinde von Kolossä vielmehr der Authentizitätsfiktion des Briefes dient, indem er gleichsam vor die Zerstörung und damit in die Lebenszeit Pauli hinein rückdatiert wird: „Ein toter Paulus und ein zerstörter Ort waren offenbar die gegebenen Voraussetzungen für diese älteste Pseudepigraphie."[7] Und selbst bei begründeter Skepsis gegenüber der Zerstörungsthese spricht die pseudepigraphe Abfassungssituation per se gegen eine Verortung der intendierten Adressaten in diesem Umfeld, da die Autorenfiktion ihrerseits die Adressatenfiktion voraussetzt: „Denn sollte der Brief wirklich für die Gemeinde in Kolossae bestimmt gewesen sein, wird die Autorfiktion problematisch: Wie sollte in diesem Fall das unvermittelte Auftauchen eines der Gemeinde bisher unbekannten Paulusbriefes an sie erklärt werden? Denn es ist doch wohl damit zu rechnen, daß man in Kolossae auch in den 70er Jahren noch gewusst hat, ob es einen Paulusbrief an die dortige Gemeinde gegeben hat oder nicht. Trotz der bleibenden Unsicherheit ist darum anzunehmen, daß außer der Autorenangabe auch die Adresse des Kol fiktiv ist."[8]

Dieselbe sachlogische Rekonstruktion gilt entsprechend auch für die Lokalisierung der ‚Gegner' im Kolosserbrief. Kol 2,8.16–23 als Referenz auf eine spezifische Gruppierung im Umfeld der intendierten Adressaten zu werten, würde voraussetzen, dass der pseudepigraphe Autor des Schreibens sich brieflich mit einer häretischen Strömung auseinandersetzt, die zu Lebzeiten Pauli in der Umgebung von Kolossä zu verorten gewesen sein müsste, wenn die Authentizitätsfiktion des Schreibens nicht gebrochen werden sollte, und dabei zugleich eine aktuelle Bedrohungslage abbildet,

---

[6] Die meisten Datierungen gehen von einer Abfassung um ca. 70 n. Chr. aus; siehe dazu z.B. WOLTER, a.a.O. 35f., und LEPPÄ, a.a.O. 368, sowie ferner U. SCHNELLE, Einleitung in das Neue Testament, UTB.W 1830, Göttingen [4]2002, 337, und H.-J. KLAUCK, Die antike Briefliteratur und das Neue Testament. Ein Lehr- und Arbeitsbuch, UTB 2022, Paderborn u.a. 1998, 242. Den zweiten chronologischen Eckpunkt neben dem Tod des Apostels bildet dabei die Abfassung des Epheserbriefes, der Kol als literarische Vorlage voraussetzt.

[7] W. SCHENK, Der Kolosserbrief in der neueren Forschung (1945–1985), ANRW II 25.4 (1987), 3327–3364 (3335). Vgl. ferner auch I. MAISCH, Der Brief an die Gemeinde von Kolossä, Theologischer Kommentar zum Neuen Testament 12, Stuttgart 2003, 21f., und POKORNÝ, Kolosser (s. Anm. 1), 17, sowie WOLTER, a.a.O. 35f., und LEPPÄ, a.a.O. 20.

[8] WOLTER, ebd.

die zum Zeitpunkt der Briefabfassung eine solche autoritative Stellungnahme erforderlich machte.

Gerade angesichts des ebenso disparaten wie stichwortartigen Charakters der in Kol 2,16–23 genannten Elemente der *Philosophia* erscheint es m.E. deutlich naheliegender, dass auch die Gegnerpolemik demselben universellen Anspruch folgt, wie er oben bereits für die grundsätzliche Ausrichtung des Kol ἐν παντὶ τῷ κόσμῳ skizziert wurde: Kol 2,16–23 will als allgemeine Handreichung für den Umgang mit abweichenden Lehren und Praktiken rezipiert werden und weist daher bewusst kein spezifisches Referenzprofil im Hinblick auf eine konkrete Gruppierung auf. In diese Annahme fügt sich auch der forschungsgeschichtliche Befund der mannigfaltigen Identifizierungsversuche der kolossischen Philosophia schlüssig ein,[9] denn alle Rekonstruktionsversuche einer konkreten Gruppierung, wahlweise im Umfeld antiker philosophischer Schulen,[10] mysterienreligiöser

---

[9] Ähnlich auch A. STANDHARTINGER, Studien zur Entstehungsgeschichte und Intention des Kolosserbriefs, NT.S 94, Leiden 1999, 284: „Die vielen religionsgeschichtlichen Identifizierungen ... machen m.E. deutlich, daß sich die Andeutungen des Kol nicht zu einem kohärenten Bild einer bestimmten theologischen oder philosophischen Richtung integrieren lassen."

[10] Basierend auf der in Kol 2,8 gewählten Bezeichnung als φιλοσοφία wurde verschiedentlich versucht, die Gegnergruppierung(en) des Kol innerhalb zeitgenössischer Philosophenschulen zu verorten und Kol 2,16–23 wahlweise als Referenz auf mittelplatonisches, stoisches oder kynisches Gedankengut zu deuten; vgl. u.a. G. H. VAN KOOTEN, Cosmic Christology in Paul and the Pauline School. Colossians and Ephesians in the Context of Graeco-Roman Cosmology, with a New Synopsis of the Greek Texts, WUNT II/171, Tübingen 2003, 17.21, R. E. DEMARIS, The Colossian Controversy. Wisdom in Dispute at Colossae, JSNT.S 96, Sheffield 1994, 100–103, und T. W. MARTIN, By Philosophy and Empty Deceit. Colossians as Response to a Cynic Critique, JSNT.S 118, Sheffield 1996, 45f.120f. Siehe ferner auch E. SCHWEIZER, Altes und Neues zu den „Elementen der Welt" in Kol 2,20; Gal 4,3.9, in: K. Aland / S. Meurer (Hg.), Wissenschaft und Kirche (FS Lohse), TAzB 4, Bielefeld 1989, 111–118 (111f.). Problematisch ist dabei zum einen die Einschätzung, dass die Bezeichnung als φιλοσοφία „ohne Zweifel eine Selbstbezeichnung der gegnerischen Lehre" bildet (so G. BORNKAMM, Die Häresie des Kolosserbriefes, in: ders., Das Ende des Gesetzes. Paulusstudien. Gesammelte Aufsätze Bd. 1, BEvTh 16, München ²1966, 139–156 [143]), denn der Kontext von Kol 2,8 lässt deutlich erkennen, dass die Wortwahl hier abwertend-polemisch fungiert und somit vielmehr den Standpunkt des Autors spiegelt als das Selbstverständnis einer bestimmten Gruppierung: Βλέπετε μή τις ὑμᾶς ἔσται ὁ συλαγωγῶν διὰ τῆς φιλοσοφίας καὶ κενῆς ἀπάτης. Zum anderen ist auch eine vorschnelle Gleichsetzung mit dem heutigen Verständnis von Philosophie insofern inadäquat, als der zeitgenössische Begriffsgebrauch ein erheblich breiteres Bedeutungsspektrum aufweist, das u.a. auch Referenzen auf das Judentum einschließt (vgl. Aristeas 256; 4Makk 5,22–24; Philo mut. 223; cont. 26; Flav.Jos.Ant 18,11.23). Siehe dazu v.a. J. D. G. DUNN, The Colossian Philosophy. A Confident Jewish Apologia, Bib 76 (1995), 153–181 (157); zur Bedeutungsoffenheit des Begriffsgebrauchs von φιλοσοφία vgl. auch WOLTER, Kolosser (s. Anm. 1), 120f.,

Kultgemeinschaften,[11] mystisch-asketischer[12] oder gnostischer Strömungen angesiedelt,[13] verblieben in der Forschungsgeschichte zum Kolosserbrief bis dato ohne greifbares Ergebnis, geschweige denn eine kohärente religionsgeschichtliche Verortung, die alle entsprechenden inhaltlichen Referenzen von Kol 2,16–23 überzeugend abzudecken vermag, so dass im Zuge der exegetischen Auseinandersetzung mit dem Gegnerprofil des Kolosser-

---

sowie A. LINDEMANN, Der Kolosserbrief, ZBK.NT 10, Zürich 1983, 39, und M. Y. MACDONALD, Colossians and Ephesians, Sacra Pagina Series 17, Collegeville 2000, 97.

[11] Der mysterienkultische Ansatz geht wesentlich auf die Arbeit von Dibelius zurück, der das neutestamentliche Hapaxlegomenon ἐμβατεύειν (Kol 2,18) auf Grundlage der Metamorphosen des Apuleius von Madaura (Metamorphoses 11,23) als terminus technicus mysterienreligiöser Initiationsriten deutete: „Man wird also wohl auch hier in ἐμβατεύειν einen kultischen Terminus der Mysteriensprache zu erkennen haben und wird dann schließen dürfen, daß die ‚Philosophen' von Kolossae selbst davon Gebrauch gemacht haben, d.h. daß der von ihnen propagierte Kult κατὰ τὰ στοιχεῖα τοῦ κόσμου Mysterienform hatte" (M. DIBELIUS, An die Kolosser, Epheser, an Philemon, HNT 12, Tübingen ³1953, 35f.). Da dieser Ansatz, der in der Folge auch von Lohse, Bornkamm und Lindemann aufgegriffen und weiterentfaltet wurde (vgl. LOHSE, Kolosser [s. Anm. 5], 189, und BORNKAMM, a.a.O. 141–148, sowie LINDEMANN, a.a.O. 48f.), jedoch weitgehend auf der Annahme einer exklusiv mysterienkultischen Verwendung von ἐμβατεύειν basiert, kann der primäre Ausgangspunkt dieser Deutung durch die Studie von Francis, der ἐμβατεύειν anhand einer Auswertung antiker Rechtspapyri als gängigen juristischen Terminus des Besitzstandes ausweisen konnte, als widerlegt betrachtet werden; vgl. F. O. FRANCIS, The Background of EMBATEUEIN (Col 2:18) in Legal Papyri and Oracle Inscriptions, in: ders. / W. A. Meeks (Hg.), Conflict at Colossae. A Problem in the Interpretation of Early Christianity Illustrated by Selected Modern Studies, SBibSt 4, Missoula 1975, 197–207 (198).

[12] Seit der Arbeit von Francis, der die vormals auf eine mysterienkultische Lesart verengte Diskussion um Kol 2,18 in einen weiteren Sinne visionärer Erfahrungen öffnete (s. Anm. 11), wird der Ansatz, die kolossische Philosophia als mystisch-judaistische Bewegung mit asketischen und visionären Zügen zu klassifizieren, von einer Vielzahl neutestamentlicher Exegeten geteilt (Dunn, Yates, Sappington, Rowland, Bandstra, Sumney, Evans, Royality). Zentral ist dabei neben einer entsprechenden visionären Lesart des ἃ ἑόρακεν ἐμβατεύων (Kol 2,18) insbesondere die Wertung der asketischen Anklänge in Kol 2,16–23 im Sinne asketischer Vorübungen der visionären Erfahrungssuche, die ihr Ziel in einem Einblick in die Verehrungstätigkeit von Engelwesen findet (θρησκεία τῶν ἀγγέλων [Kol 2,18] in einem Verständnis als Genitivus subjectivus; siehe dazu auch Anm. 19).

[13] Der gnostische Ansatz der Gegnerklassifizierung in Kol (Bornkamm, Pokorný u.a.) wertet in erster Linie die terminologischen Referenzen auf φιλοσοφία (2,8) und σοφία (2,23) als Indikatoren gnostischer Vorstellungswelt und deutet auf Grundlage dessen auch weitere genannte Elemente wie die Redeweise von Weltelementen (2,8: στοιχεῖα τοῦ κόσμου) und Engeln (2,18: θρησκεία τῶν ἀγγέλων) im Sinne gnostischer Archonten aus. In Verbindung mit anderen, stärker judaistisch konnotierten Motiven v.a. von Kol 2,16 (μὴ οὖν τις ὑμᾶς κρινέτω ἐν βρώσει καὶ ἐν πόσει ἢ ἐν μέρει ἑορτῆς ἢ νεομηνίας ἢ σαββάτων) wird jene gnostische Prägung der *Philosophia* traditionell synkretistisch im Sinne jüdischer Gnosis resp. gnostischem Judaismus gedeutet.

briefes eine bemerkenswerte selbstkritische Ernüchterung eingetreten ist – „Perhaps we should simply admit – although New Testament scholars seem reluctant ever to do so – that this puzzle is insoluble."[14]

2. „Lasst euch von niemandem verurteilen" – Argumentationsmuster der kolossischen Gegnerpolemik

Mit der Ermahnung, *sich von niemandem verurteilen zu lassen* (μὴ οὖν τις ὑμᾶς κρινέτω), beginnt in Kol 2,16 der Kernbereich der kolossischen Gegnerpolemik, die zuvor bereits in Kol 2,8 antizipiert wurde: *Gebt acht, dass niemand euch ein Verführer werde* (βλέπετε μή τις ὑμᾶς ἔσται ὁ συλαγωγῶν) *durch Philosophie und leeren Trug* (διὰ τῆς φιλοσοφίας καὶ κενῆς ἀπάτης), *gemäß der Lehren der Menschen und der Elemente der Welt* (κατὰ τὴν παράδοσιν τῶν ἀνθρώπων, κατὰ τὰ στοιχεῖα τοῦ κόσμου), *und nicht gemäß Christus* (καὶ οὐ κατὰ Χριστόν). Dieses Schema negierter Imperative im Blick auf einen indefiniten Gegner[15] erfolgt noch ein weiteres Mal in Kol 2,18 – mit der Ermahnung, sich von niemandem *den Siegpreis nehmen zu lassen* (μηδεὶς ὑμᾶς καταβραβευέτω).[16]

Mit diesem Dreiklang bestärkender Ermahnungen – *lasst euch nicht verführen, lasst euch nicht verurteilen, lasst euch nicht den Siegpreis nehmen* – ist die argumentative Ausrichtung der Gegnerpolemik bereits deut-

---

[14] J. M. G. BARCLAY, Colossians and Philemon, Sheffield 2001, 53.

[15] In diesem Formschema negierter Imperative macht Wolter eine strukturelle Parallelität zu den Protopaulinen aus (vgl. Röm 14,3; 1Kor 3,18.21; 10,24; Gal 6,17), sieht jedoch insofern eine Abweichung von der paulinischen Verwendung vorliegen, als in Kol die Vertreter der gegnerischen Position außerhalb der Gemeinde lokalisiert würden (vgl. WOLTER, Kolosser [s. Anm. 1], 140; siehe auch a.a.O. 163); eine Folgerung, die sich aus dem Textbefund m.E. zumindest nicht zwangsläufig nahelegt. So könnte etwa die Kritik in Kol 2,19, die Gegner hielten sich nicht an das Haupt (οὐ κρατῶν τὴν κεφαλήν), in der Logik der Haupt-Leib-Bildlichkeit von Kol 1,18 (αὐτός ἐστιν ἡ κεφαλὴ τοῦ σώματος τῆς ἐκκλησίας) durchaus als Indiz dafür betrachtet werden, dass jene Teil des σῶμα Χριστοῦ und damit der christlichen Gemeinschaft sind. Vgl. zur Frage der innerresp. außergemeindlichen Lokalisierung der Gegner ferner auch E. PERCY, Die Probleme der Kolosser- und Epheserbriefe, SHVL 39, Lund 1946, 142, sowie LUZ, Kolosser (s. Anm. 5), 218, und R. M. ROYALTY, Dwelling on Visions. On the Nature of the so-called „Colossians Heresy", Bib 83 (2002), 329–357 (352).

[16] Während die Nominalform βραβεῖον in 1Kor 9,24 und Phil 3,14 jeweils in der Kombination λαμβάνει bzw. διώκω εἰς τὸ βραβεῖον belegt ist, bildet καταβραβεύειν ein Hapaxlegomenon, das auch in der außerbiblischen Literatur nur wenige Belege findet; siehe zur Quellenlage u.a. F. O. FRANCIS, Humility and Angelic Worship in Col 2:18, in: ders., Colossae (s. Anm. 11), 163–195 (163), und PERCY, Kolosser (s. Anm. 15), 143f.

lich vorstrukturiert.[17] Im Zentrum steht die Bestärkung und Versicherung christlicher Glaubensüberzeugung und Heilsgewissheit gegenüber drohender Verunsicherung durch abweichende Lehren und Praktiken. Den Kern der inhaltlichen Kritik jener Lehren nimmt Kol 2,8 vorweg (*gemäß der Lehren der Menschen und der Elemente der Welt, und nicht gemäß Christus*), wobei jene Kritik – m.E. bewusst – in einer so grundsätzlichen Weise formuliert ist, dass sie auf ein weites Spektrum möglicher Konflikt- und Bedrohungskonstellationen hin übertragbar ist. In Kol 2,16–23 wird jener „leere Trug" vermeintlicher Heilslehren im Folgenden facettenreich verbildlicht. Als potentielle Konflikt- bzw. Kritikpunkte nennt der Kolosserbrief Fragen des Essens und Trinkens und der Einhaltung von Festtagen (2,16),[18] sowie darüber hinaus falsche Demut, Engelsverehrung,[19] visionäre

---

[17] Eine interessante intertextuelle Parallele in der neueren deutschen Literatur stellt die Adaption dieses Dreiklangs in Bertolt Brechts Hauspostille von 1926/27 dar, deren Schlusskapitel das Gedicht „Gegen Verführung" bildet. Den Auftakt der Einzelstrophen formen hier jeweils die Ermahnungen „Laßt euch nicht verführen!" (Z. 1), „Laßt euch nicht betrügen!" (Z. 6) und „Laßt euch nicht vertrösten!" (Z. 11), bevor in der abschließenden vierten Strophe erneut das Leitmotiv der ersten („Laßt euch nicht verführen"; Z. 16) wieder aufgegriffen wird. Zugleich wird der religiöse Prätext der Heilszusage jeweils konsequent ironisch gebrochen – „Es gibt keine Wiederkehr" (Z. 2), „Laßt Moder den Erlösten" (Z. 13), „Ihr sterbt mit allen Tieren / Und es kommt nichts nachher" (Z. 19f.); entsprechend firmiert der Text in einigen Manuskripten auch unter dem Titel „Luzifers Abendlied" (obige Zitation folgt der Suhrkamp-Gesamtausgabe: Die Gedichte von Bertolt Brecht in einem Band, Frankfurt a.M. [8]1995, 260).

[18] Entgegen der vorherrschenden Auslegung von Kol 2,16, die hier eine kritische Referenz auf die Praktiken der *Philosophia* ausmacht, hat Troy Martin überzeugend veranschaulicht, dass der Bezugspunkt jener Speise- und Festtagsvorschriften keineswegs eindeutig ist und Kol 2,16 durchaus auch als Verteidigung der innergemeindlichen Praxis gegen Kritik von außen gelesen werden kann (vgl. MARTIN, Philosophy [s. Anm. 10], 127, sowie ders., But Let Everyone Discern the Body of Christ [Colossians 2:17], JBL 114 [1995], 249–255 [255], und ders., Pagan and Judeo-Christian Time-Keeping Schemes in Gal 4.10 and Col 2.16, NTS 42 [1996], 105–119 [107]) – eine Lesart, die in jüngster Zeit auch bei Wolter in Erwägung gezogen wird (vgl. M. WOLTER, Kolosser 1,24–2,23 [3,4], in: B. Standaert [Hg.], „Le Christ tout et en tous" [Col 3,11]. L'épître aux Colossiens, SMBen.BE 16, Rom 2003, 29–68 [52]).

[19] Der Verweis auf die θρησκεία τῶν ἀγγέλων (Kol 2,18) bildet einen der umstrittensten Punkte der Exegese von Kol 2,16–23. Sowohl ein Verständnis als Genitivus subjectivus (durch Engelwesen praktizierte Gottesverehrung) als auch die Deutung als Genitivus objectivus (durch Menschen praktizierte Engelsverehrung) wird in der exegetischen Forschung bis heute vertreten und bestimmt insofern maßgeblich die Rekonstruktionsversuche der gegnerischen Lehre, wobei sich die Lesart der Gottesverehrung durch Engel insbesondere in das Konzept mystischer Visionserfahrungen schlüssig einfügt (s. Anm. 12). Gegen ein solches Verständnis der θρησκεία τῶν ἀγγέλων als Genitivus subjectivus spricht textimmanent jedoch die Begriffsverwendung in Kol 2,22f., wo θρησκεία eindeutig auf menschliche Verehrungspraxis referiert (κατὰ ... διδασκαλίας τῶν ἀνθρώπων, ἅτινά ἐστιν λόγον μὲν ἔχοντα σοφίας ἐν ἐθελοθρησκίᾳ καὶ ταπεινο-

Erfahrungen,[20] Aufgeblasenheit und Selbstgefälligkeit (2,18), das Auferlegen menschlicher Satzungen, Lehren und Gebote (2,20–22), vermeintliche Weisheit, selbstgemachte Religiosität und körperliche Kasteiung (2,23). Wenngleich das solchermaßen skizzierte Szenario deutlich plastischer wird als die abstrakte Mahnung von Kol 2,8 (s.o.), so unterbleibt doch jede klare Identifizierbarkeit einer konkreten Zielgruppe der Polemik. Judaistisch konnotierte Stichworte wie σαββάτων[21] finden sich unverbunden neben mystisch-visionären Anklängen (θρησκεία τῶν ἀγγέλων, ἃ ἑόρακεν ἐμβατεύων), asketischen Elementen (ἀφειδία σώματος) und Motiven tendenziell gnostischer resp. philosophischer Prägung (φιλοσοφία, ἅτινά ἐστιν λόγον μὲν ἔχοντα σοφίας). Wie unter 1. bereits ausgeführt, lässt sich diese Diversität und Deutungsoffenheit schlüssig als Konsequenz der pseudepigraphen Abfassungssituation erklären. Wenn wir davon ausgehen, dass der Kolosserbrief qua pseudepigrapher Fiktion nicht nur in eine fiktive, in die Lebenszeit Pauli rückdatierte Situation hineinspricht, sondern im Rahmen dieser fiktionalen Selbstverortung gleichzeitig den Anspruch erhebt, innerhalb eines zeitgenössischen Rezeptionskontextes eine Handreichung für tatsächliche Konflikt- und Bedrohungskonstellationen zu bieten, so bildet gerade eine möglichst umfassende Bandbreite unterschiedlichster Anklänge die beste Gewähr dafür, auf ein breites Spektrum verschiedener Rezeptionskontexte hin Anwendung bzw. Übertragung finden zu können. In diesem Sinne konstatiert auch Standhartinger treffend: „Aufgrund des fiktiven Charakters pseudepigrapher Briefe ist daher auch nicht anzunehmen, daß im Kol eine bestimmte reale Oppositionsgruppe beschrieben wird. Sollte überhaupt eine Oppositionsgruppe thematisiert

---

φροσύνη [καὶ] ἀφειδίᾳ σώματος, οὐκ ἐν τιμῇ τινι πρὸς πλησμονὴν τῆς σαρκός). Eine Analogie des Begriffsgebrauchs von Kol 2,18 und 2,23 wird zudem dadurch unterstrichen, dass in beiden Fällen die Verknüpfung von θέλων und θρησκεία vorliegt.

[20] Zum Verständnis von ἃ ἑόρακεν ἐμβατεύων siehe auch Anm. 11. Unabhängig vom postulierten Vorstellungshintergrund der so umschriebenen religiösen Erfahrung ist auch die syntaktische Konstruktion grammatisch uneindeutig – ἃ kann sich sowohl als Relativergänzung auf ταπεινοφροσύνῃ καὶ θρησκείᾳ τῶν ἀγγέλων beziehen als auch als Objekt zu ἐμβατεύων oder φυσιούμενος gelesen werden. Zu verschiedenen syntaktischen Auflösungsversuchen von Kol 2,18 vgl. u.a. FRANCIS, Embateuein (s. Anm. 11), 198, und WOLTER, Kolosser (s. Anm. 1), 147f., sowie PERCY, Kolosser (s. Anm. 15), 171f., und C. ROWLAND, Apokalyptic Visions and the Exaltation of Christ in the Letter to the Colossians, JSNT 19 (1983), 73–83 (75f.).

[21] Diese judaistische Konnotation im Sinne eines paganen Hintergrundes umzudeuten, indem σάββατον als Referenz auf den Sabazios-Kult gewertet wird (so etwa bei MAISCH, Kolossä [s. Anm. 7], 186), ist angesichts der Tatsache, dass die hier vorliegende Trias von Festtagen, Neumond und Sabbat (ἐν μέρει ἑορτῆς ἢ νεομηνίας ἢ σαββάτων) als alttestamentlicher Topos vielfach belegt ist (vgl. Ez 45,17; Jes 1,13; 1Chr 23,31; 2Chr 8,13; Jdt 8,6), m.E. wenig überzeugend.

sein, dann in einer der Pseudepigraphie entsprechenden offenen und mehrfach deutbaren Weise."[22]

Setzt man eine solche bewusste Mehrdeutigkeit voraus, so stellt sich unter dem Gesichtspunkt der grundsätzlichen Frage nach Intentionalität und literarischer Strategie pseudepigrapher Schriften zwangsläufig die Frage nach dem semantischen Mehrwert, den dieses früheste paulinische Pseudepigraphon beansprucht. Vereinfacht gesprochen: Welchen „Gebrauchswert" bietet Kol 2,16–23 im Hinblick auf den christlichen Umgang mit konkurrierenden Heilslehren, der nicht bereits durch die diesbezüglichen theologischen Handreichungen der authentischen Paulinen abgedeckt wäre? Meines Erachtens kann ein solches Novum, das über den Befund der antihäretischen Mahnungen in den Protopaulinen hinausgeht, tatsächlich in Kol 2,16–23 ausgemacht werden, und es zielt weniger auf den – faktisch diffusen – Gegenstand der Ausführungen im Sinne eines neuen Bedrohungs- bzw. Konfliktprofils, sondern vielmehr auf die Art des Umgangs mit entsprechenden Szenarien. Diese Neuakzentuierung zeigt sich deutlich im direkten Vergleich mit den paulinischen Ausführungen in Römer- und Erstem Korintherbrief, die sich in sachlicher Analogie zu Kol 2 der Frage der Speisegebote und der asketischen Lebensführung widmen, wie im Folgenden anhand des intertextuellen Vergleichs der jeweiligen Argumentationsstrategien veranschaulicht werden soll.

2.1 Die Frage der Speisegebote und ihre Behandlung in Kol, Röm und 1Kor

Den Auftakt der kolossischen Gegnerpolemik bildet mit Kol 2,16 die kategorische Zurückweisung von Kritik (μὴ οὖν τις ὑμᾶς κρινέτω) in Fragen von Speis und Trank, Festtagen, Neumonden und Sabbat (ἐν βρώσει καὶ ἐν πόσει ἢ ἐν μέρει ἑορτῆς ἢ νεομηνίας ἢ σαββάτων). Die engste inhaltliche Parallele innerhalb der Protopaulinen stellen die Ausführungen in Röm 14 dar,[23] auch dort eingeleitet mit der Mahnung μὴ κρινέτω (Röm 14,3; ähnlich auch 14,4.5.13.20), dem zentralen Begriffspaar βρῶσις καὶ πόσις (14,17) mit zahlreichen weiteren lexikalischen Variationen des Wortfeldes von Speis und Trank – βρῶμα (14,15.20), ἐσθίειν (14,3.6.21), πίνειν (14,21) –, und analog zu Kol 2,16 kommt auch hier als zweiter Themenbereich die Frage der Festtage zur Sprache (14,5f.). Intertextuell signifikant ist dabei, dass hier zwar einerseits dieselbe Parallelität von Speisegeboten und Festtagen zum Ausdruck kommt wie in Kol 2,16 (vgl.

---

[22] STANDHARTINGER, Kolosserbrief (s. Anm. 9), 181; ähnlich auch MACDONALD, Colossians (s. Anm. 10), 119f.

[23] Siehe dazu auch H. HÜBNER, An Philemon, an die Kolosser, an die Epheser, HNT 12, Tübingen 1997, 86.

Röm 14,6: ὁ φρονῶν τὴν ἡμέραν κυρίῳ φρονεῖ καὶ ὁ ἐσθίων κυρίῳ ἐσθίει), andererseits jedoch gerade das wesentliche Charakteristikum der Mahnungen in Röm 14, d.h. die reziproke Perspektive der Argumentation, im Kolosserbrief keinen Niederschlag findet. So hebt Röm 14,3 nachdrücklich die wechselseitige Akzeptanz unterschiedlicher Speisepraktiken hervor (ὁ ἐσθίων τὸν μὴ ἐσθίοντα μὴ ἐξουθενείτω, ὁ δὲ μὴ ἐσθίων τὸν ἐσθίοντα μὴ κρινέτω, ὁ θεὸς γὰρ αὐτὸν προσελάβετο) und Röm 14,13 fordert explizit Rücksichtnahme gegenüber abweichenden Überzeugungen und Praktiken ein (μηκέτι οὖν ἀλλήλους κρίνωμεν· ἀλλὰ τοῦτο κρίνατε μᾶλλον, τὸ μὴ τιθέναι πρόσκομμα τῷ ἀδελφῷ ἢ σκάνδαλον).

Diese Perspektive der wechselseitigen Rücksichtnahme ist der kolossischen Gegnerpolemik grundsätzlich fremd. Hier steht perspektivisch nicht die *Vermittlung* unterschiedlicher Positionen im Blickpunkt, sondern vielmehr die *Abgrenzung*, wie bildhaft auch anhand der anatomischen Metaphorik von Kol 2,19 greifbar wird (οὐ κρατῶν τὴν κεφαλήν, ἐξ οὗ πᾶν τὸ σῶμα διὰ τῶν ἁφῶν καὶ συνδέσμων ἐπιχορηγούμενον καὶ συμβιβαζόμενον αὔξει τὴν αὔξησιν τοῦ θεοῦ). Auch ein weiteres Bildmotiv im Kontext der Gegnerpolemik zeigt deutlich die Unterschiede in der Argumentationsstruktur der Mahnungen von Röm 14 und Kol 2 auf – das Motiv der Oikodome,[24] das als Metapher der Einheit und Gemeinschaft in Röm 14f. die Grundlage der Forderung nach gegenseitiger Rücksichtnahme bildet: ἕκαστος ἡμῶν τῷ πλησίον ἀρεσκέτω εἰς τὸ ἀγαθὸν πρὸς οἰκοδομήν (Röm 15,2; vgl. auch Röm 14,19: Ἄρα οὖν τὰ τῆς εἰρήνης διώκωμεν καὶ τὰ τῆς οἰκοδομῆς τῆς εἰς ἀλλήλους). Der hier erkennbare argumentative Aufbau, im Kontext der Diskussion um unterschiedliche Speisepraktiken unter Berufung auf das Motiv der Oikodome gegenseitige Rücksichtnahme einzufordern, findet sich neben Röm 14f. in vergleichbarer Form auch in 1Kor 8,1–13 und 1Kor 10,23–11,1, und stellt somit ein wiederkehrendes Schema der Auseinandersetzung mit der Frage unterschiedlicher religiöser Praktiken dar, wobei jeweils die gegenseitige Toleranz und Rücksichtnahme im Zentrum der Argumentation steht. Eben dieser Fokus fehlt in der kolossischen Gegnerpolemik nicht nur gänzlich, sondern wird zugleich auch aus dem Bild der Oikodome eliminiert. Dies wird wiederum deutlich, wenn man den direkten Vergleich mit den authentischen Paulinen hinzuzieht. Neben den oben angeführten Belegen in Röm 14,19 und 15,2, bei denen die Bezugsgröße der Oikodome jeweils die Ausrichtung auf den Nächsten (πλησίον – Röm 15,2) resp. die Gegenseitigkeit (ἀλλήλους – Röm 14,19) bildet, kommt dieser Aspekt der Rezipro-

---

[24] Zum paulinischen Motiv der Oikodome als ekklesiologischer Metapher siehe v.a. P. VIELHAUER, Oikodome. Das Bild vom Bau in der christlichen Literatur vom Neuen Testament bis Clemens Alexandrinus, in: ders., Aufsätze zum Neuen Testament, Bd. 2: Oikodome, TB, Neues Testament 65, München 1979, 1–168 (85–100).

zität als dominierendes Merkmal der Oikodome analog auch in 1Thess 5,11 und 1Kor 10,23f. zum Tragen (διὸ παρακαλεῖτε ἀλλήλους καὶ οἰκοδομεῖτε εἰς τὸν ἕνα, καθὼς καὶ ποιεῖτε bzw. πάντα ἔξεστιν ἀλλ᾽ οὐ πάντα οἰκοδομεῖ. μηδεὶς τὸ ἑαυτοῦ ζητείτω ἀλλὰ τὸ τοῦ ἑτέρου). Als ekklesiologische Metapher[25] schließt die Oikodome in der paulinischen Verwendung also jene Orientierung am Nächsten (πλησίον), am Anderen (ἕτερος), am Miteinander (ἀλλήλους) ganz wesenhaft ein. Dieser Aspekt entfällt im Kolosserbrief gänzlich – das Verhältnis der Gemeindemitglieder untereinander weicht hier einer ausschließlichen Konzentration auf das Verhältnis des Einzelnen zu Christus; eine „Individualisierung" des Oikodome-Motives,[26] bei der die christozentrische Ausrichtung an die Stelle der Ausrichtung auf das zwischenmenschliche Miteinander tritt: ὡς οὖν παρελάβετε τὸν Χριστὸν Ἰησοῦν τὸν κύριον, ἐν αὐτῷ περιπατεῖτε, ἐρριζωμένοι καὶ ἐποικοδομούμενοι ἐν αὐτῷ καὶ βεβαιούμενοι τῇ πίστει (Kol 2,6f.). Diese christozentrische Ausdeutung der Oikodome wird auch durch die entsprechende Neuakzentuierung der Annahmeformel unterstrichen, denn die solchermaßen personalisierte Verwendungsweise von παραλαμβάνειν (παρελάβετε τὸν Χριστὸν Ἰησοῦν) weicht auffallend von der paulinischen Begriffsverwendung ab, die ausschließlich abstrakte Objekte wie die Annahme des Evangeliums und christlicher Unterweisungen kennt (vgl. 1Kor 15,1; Gal 1,9; 1Thess 2,13; Phil 4,9; 1Thess 4,1).

Was bedeuten diese intertextuellen Beobachtungen im Hinblick auf die (Selbst-)Verortung der kolossischen Gegnerpolemik innerhalb der paulinischen Tradition, in die sich der Kolosserbrief qua Autorenfiktion dezidiert einreiht – und somit als genuiner Bestandteil des paulinischen Schrifttums rezipiert werden möchte? Mit der Frage von Speise- und Festtagspraktiken greift der Autor des Kol eine Diskussion auf, die offenkundig bereits zu Lebzeiten Pauli virulent war und ihren Niederschlag in den paulinischen Korrespondenzen gefunden hatte. Während bei Paulus dabei jedoch eine vermittelnde Position erkennbar ist, deren argumentatives Gewicht auf der gegenseitigen Rücksichtnahme und Akzeptanz liegt, zeichnet sich im Kolosserbrief eine Veränderung des Umgangs mit vergleichbaren Konfliktsituationen ab. Das integrative Moment, das in den Protopaulinen seine Grundlegung in der Oikodome findet, weicht im Kolosserbrief einem konfrontativen Umgang.

---

[25] Neben jenem Gebrauch als ekklesiologische Metapher fungiert das Oikodome-Motiv bei Paulus an anderer Stelle auch als Verbildlichung missionarischer Tätigkeit (vgl. 1Kor 3,6–11; 2Kor 10,8; 13,10; 12,19); siehe zur Unterscheidung dieser Verwendungsformen auch a.a.O. 72.85.

[26] A.a.O. 99.

2.2 Asketische Lebensführung in den Proto- und Deuteropaulinen

Der Bereich der Körperlichkeit wird in Kol 2,16–23 mithilfe verschiedener Motive versprachlicht. Entgegen der christologisch-ekklesiologischen Verwendung des σῶμα-Motives in 2,17 (τὸ δὲ σῶμα τοῦ Χριστοῦ) und 2,19 (τὸ σῶμα ... αὔξει τὴν αὔξησιν τοῦ θεοῦ) wird σῶμα in 2,23 in abwertender Weise als Umschreibung körperlicher Kasteiung gebraucht (ἀφειδίᾳ σώματος).[27] Konträr dazu fungiert σάρξ jeweils als ironisch-abwertende Kennzeichnung leiblicher Gesinnung (vgl. 2,18.23: νοῦς τῆς σαρκός, πλησμονὴ τῆς σαρκός) – d.h. gerade das gegnerische Insistieren auf körperliche Askese wird hier als fleischliche Gesinnung und leibliche Befriedigung gebrandmarkt. In der Form eines Gegnerzitats werden in Kol 2,21ff. diesbezügliche Forderungen aufgegriffen (μὴ ἅψῃ μηδὲ γεύσῃ μηδὲ θίγῃς) und inhaltlich zurückgewiesen. Mit μηδὲ γεύσῃ klingt dabei erneut der Bereich der Speiserestriktionen an, während μὴ ἅψῃ und μηδὲ θίγῃς eine stärker sexuelle Konnotation erkennen lassen, wie der Vergleich mit 1Kor 7,1 zeigt (καλὸν ἀνθρώπῳ γυναικὸς μὴ ἅπτεσθαι). Analog zu Kol 2,21 liegt dabei auch in 1Kor 7,1 eine Zitation vor, d.h. ein Verweis auf eine von anderer Seite erhobene Forderung, doch der argumentative Kontext ist ein gänzlich anderer: Im Gegensatz zur strikten Zurückweisung asketischer Forderungen in Kol 2,20–23 qualifiziert Paulus in 1Kor 7,1 das Ideal sexueller Enthaltsamkeit als grundsätzlich positiv (καλόν) und trägt erst im Folgevers eine alternative Option nach – das monogame Eheleben (διὰ δὲ τὰς πορνείας ἕκαστος τὴν ἑαυτοῦ γυναῖκα ἐχέτω καὶ ἑκάστη τὸν ἴδιον ἄνδρα ἐχέτω). Dieser Gegenentwurf zur asketischen Lebensweise wird bei Paulus jedoch ausdrücklich als „Erlaubnis, nicht Gebot" ausgewiesen (7,6: τοῦτο δὲ λέγω κατὰ συγγνώμην οὐ κατ᾽ ἐπιταγήν), und der unmittelbar folgende Vers verdeutlicht, dass damit keine Abwertung eines asketischen Lebensentwurfes intendiert ist, sondern dessen

---

[27] Die abwertende Referenz auf asketische Praktiken als ἀφειδίᾳ σώματος bildet dabei ein Hapaxlegomenon des Kolosserbriefes und auch die dementsprechend negativ konnotierte Verwendung von ταπεινοφροσύνη (Kol 2,23) ist im Kontext des Corpus Paulinum singulär. So begegnet ταπεινοφροσύνη bzw. ταπεινός in den Protopaulinen ausschließlich in positiv besetzter Bedeutung – sowohl als Selbstcharakterisierung Pauli (vgl. Phil 4,12; 2Kor 7,6; 10,1) als auch in der Form der direkten Aufforderung zu einer demütigen Lebensweise (vgl. Phil 2,3; Röm 12,16), wie sie sich ähnlich auch in Kol 3,12 findet: ἐνδύσασθε οὖν, ὡς ἐκλεκτοὶ τοῦ θεοῦ ἅγιοι καὶ ἠγαπημένοι, σπλάγχνα οἰκτιρμοῦ χρηστότητα ταπεινοφροσύνην πραΰτητα μακροθυμίαν. Innerhalb der Gegnerpolemik hingegen wird ταπεινοφροσύνη in abwertender Weise im Kontext der Leibesfeindlichkeit gebraucht (ταπεινοφροσύνῃ καὶ ἀφειδίᾳ σώματος); eine Begriffsverwendung, die ihre Parallele in der alttestamentlichen Sprachtradition findet (vgl. Jes 58,3.5; Esr 8,21; Ps 35,13; Lev 16,29.31) und im vorliegenden Kontext als Referenz auf Askese resp. Fastenpraxis zu deuten ist. Vgl. dazu u.a. auch LUZ, Kolosser (s. Anm. 5), 216f.

grundsätzliche Richtigkeit vielmehr unter Verweis auf das Beispiel des Apostels bestätigt wird (7,7: θέλω δὲ πάντας ἀνθρώπους εἶναι ὡς καὶ ἐμαυτόν· ἀλλὰ ἕκαστος ἴδιον ἔχει χάρισμα ἐκ θεοῦ, ὁ μὲν οὕτως, ὁ δὲ οὕτως).

Was bedeutet dies im Blick auf die anti-asketische Polemik des Kolosserbriefes? Gegenüber der diplomatischen und vermittelnden Haltung Pauli im Umgang mit verschiedenen menschlichen Lebensentwürfen weist der Kolosserbrief asketische Forderungen kategorisch und kompromisslos zurück – dies alles sind menschliche Lehren und Gebote (κατὰ τὰ ἐντάλματα καὶ διδασκαλίας τῶν ἀνθρώπων), die nichts wert sind (οὐκ ἐν τιμῇ τινι). Somit zeigt sich auch in der Frage asketischer Praktiken derselbe argumentative Paradigmenwechsel, wie er bereits anhand der Speisegebote aufgewiesen werden konnte: An die Stelle des paulinischen Primats gegenseitiger Rücksichtnahme und Toleranz tritt eine strikte Zurückweisung entsprechender Forderungen und Praktiken.

Vor den Hintergrund der pseudepigraphen Abfassung des Kolosserbriefes sind dabei zwei Aspekte bemerkenswert, die Licht auf die Abfassungssituation und -intention des ersten pseudopaulinischen Schreibens werfen: Der intertextuelle Befund macht einerseits deutlich, dass mit den genannten Themen- bzw. Problemfeldern Fragestellungen aufgegriffen und fortgeführt werden, die bereits zu Lebzeiten Pauli offenkundig lebhafte Diskussionen in den christlichen Gemeinden hervorgerufen hatten, wie die einleitende Anmerkung von 1Kor 7,1 erkennen lässt (περὶ δὲ ὧν ἐγράψατε). Gleichzeitig zeigt Kol 2,16–23 andererseits eine signifikante Veränderung in der Art des Umgangs mit entsprechenden Konfliktpotentialen, eine klare Verschärfung der Tonlage, die greifbar macht, dass jene Fragestellungen in nachpaulinischer Zeit neue Antworten erforderlich machten und die ausgleichende und vermittelnde Position des Apostels nicht mehr als angemessene Reaktion auf eine sich verändernde Situation betrachtet wurde. Angesichts dieser Herausforderung ermöglicht das Mittel der pseudepigraphen Verfasserschaftsfiktion, jene Veränderungen und neuen Erfordernisse in die paulinische Tradition einzutragen und damit „den Abwesenden je neu in die Gegenwart sprechen" zu lassen.[28]

Dass in der Frage asketischer Praktiken tatsächlich ein solcher grundsätzlicher Konfliktherd vorlag, der in nachpaulinischer Zeit in einer neuen Weise akut wurde und nun restriktivere Antworten nötig machte, zeigt die Tatsache, dass die diesbezügliche Verschärfung der Diskussion ein Merkmal ist, das gerade die Deutero- und Tritopaulinen auszeichnet. So findet die ἀφειδία σώματος von Kol 2,23 ihr inhaltliches Pendant in 1Tim 4,8

---

[28] S. VOLLENWEIDER, Paulus zwischen Exegese und Wirkungsgeschichte, in: M. Mayordomo (Hg.), Die prägende Kraft der Texte. Hermeneutik und Wirkungsgeschichte des Neuen Testaments (FS Luz), SBS 199, Stuttgart 2005, 142–159 (156f.).

(σωματικὴ γυμνασία), wobei die damit bezeichnete körperliche Kasteiung jeweils in analoger Weise als wertlos resp. nutzlos qualifiziert wird: οὐκ ἐν τιμῇ τινι (Kol 2,23); πρὸς ὀλίγον ἐστὶν ὠφέλιμος (1Tim 4,8). Eine ähnlich abwertende Konnotation der Unterwerfung unter Fragen der Körperlichkeit könnte zudem auch dem sekundär zugefügten „Ketzerschluss" des Römerbriefes zugrunde liegen (Röm 16,18: δουλεύουσιν ... τῇ ἑαυτῶν κοιλίᾳ).[29] Die dabei jeweils auffallende verbale Schärfe, mit der die angesprochenen Praktiken verurteilt werden, lässt erkennen, von welcher Härte die Auseinandersetzung um Fragen körperlicher Askese geprägt war. Weitgehend spekulativ verbleibt hingegen die Frage, was letztlich jene Verschärfung der Auseinandersetzung bedingt haben könnte. Denkbar ist sowohl eine Zuspitzung von Konflikten, die bereits zu Lebzeiten Pauli virulent waren als auch eine gänzlich neue anti-asketische Konfliktkonstellation. Und im Kontext des Kolosserbriefes verdient auch die Überlegung Aufmerksamkeit, ob die Diskussion um körperlichen Rigorismus nicht vielmehr den oberflächlich erfassbaren Ausdruck tiefer liegender Konfliktpotentiale repräsentiert.

Betrachtet man die Form der Mahnungen von Kol 2,16–23, so wird deutlich, dass qua Formulierung nicht die gegnerischen Praktiken im Zentrum der Kritik stehen, sondern deren argumentative Funktionalisierung – als Anlass der Kritik an der abweichenden Lebensweise der Christen (2,16), als Mittel der Verunsicherung christlicher Heilsgewissheit (2,18), als Grund einer prahlerisch-überheblichen Selbstgefälligkeit (2,18).[30] Genau dieser Haltung tritt der Autor des Kolosserbriefes entgegen, indem er sie als Schein-Weisheit und selbstbezogene Frömmigkeit entlarvt (2,23: ἅτινά ἐστιν λόγον μὲν ἔχοντα σοφίας ἐν ἐθελοθρησκίᾳ).

Das positive Gegenbild, das der Kolosserbrief diesem Streben nach körperlicher Schonungslosigkeit und Selbstkasteiung entgegensetzt, ist, wie im Folgenden zu zeigen sein wird, das Bild der christlichen Heilsgemeinschaft des σῶμα Χριστοῦ, in dem die Gläubigen durch die Teilhabe an Christi Tod und Auferstehung dem Machtbereich jedweder menschlicher Satzungen, Gebote und vermeintlich heilsrelevanter religiöser Übungen entstorben sind: εἰ ἀπεθάνετε σὺν Χριστῷ ἀπὸ τῶν στοιχείων τοῦ κόσμου, τί ὡς ζῶντες ἐν κόσμῳ δογματίζεσθε; (Kol 2,20).

---

[29] Zur literarkritischen Diskussion um Röm 16,17–20.25–27 vgl. z.B. M. THEOBALD, Der Römerbrief, EdF 294, Darmstadt 2000, 18f., und H. BALZ, Art. Römerbrief, TRE 29 (1998), 291–311 (292f.).

[30] Ähnlich auch J. L. SUMNEY, Those Who „Pass Judgement". The Identity of the Opponents in Colossians, Bib 74 (1993), 366–388 (386f.); vgl. ferner E. SCHWEIZER, Askese nach Kol 1,24 oder 2,20f?, in: H. Merklein (Hg.), Neues Testament und Ethik (FS Schnackenburg), Freiburg i. Brsg. 1989, 340–348 (346f.).

2.3 Das positive Gegenbild: die Heilsgemeinschaft des σῶμα Χριστοῦ (Kol 2,19f.)

Umrahmt von den antihäretischen Mahnungen bildet das Motiv des σῶμα Χριστοῦ in 2,19f. den positiven Gegenpol und zugleich die christologische Grundlage der Ausführungen von Kol 2,16–23. Hier wird das Bild einer christlichen Gemeinschaft als Leib Christi gezeichnet, die sich nicht an menschlichen Satzungen und religiösen Pflichtübungen orientiert, sondern ausschließlich an dem Haupt jenes Leibes, das diesen stützt und zusammenhält: ἡ κεφαλή, ἐξ οὗ πᾶν τὸ σῶμα διὰ τῶν ἁφῶν καὶ συνδέσμων ἐπιχορηγούμενον καὶ συμβιβαζόμενον αὔξει τὴν αὔξησιν τοῦ θεοῦ (Kol 2,19). Diese Teilhabe am σῶμα Χριστοῦ schließt die Partizipation an Tod und Auferweckung Christi ein, und damit die letztgültige Freiheit von jeglichen weltlichen Satzungen: εἰ ἀπεθάνετε σὺν Χριστῷ ἀπὸ τῶν στοιχείων τοῦ κόσμου, τί ὡς ζῶντες ἐν κόσμῳ δογματίζεσθε; (Kol 2,20) In der Bildlichkeit dieser beiden Verse kommen zwei wesentliche theologische Charakteristika des Kolosserbriefes zum Tragen, die zuvor bereits in Kol 1,15–20 und 2,12–14 entfaltet wurden – die ekklesiologische Haupt-Leib-Metaphorik einerseits und die Betonung der gegenwärtigen Heilswirklichkeit der Christen andererseits. Dabei lässt der Kolosserbrief in beiden Punkten erneut signifikante Neuakzentuierungen gegenüber dem Befund der Protopaulinen erkennen:

1. Gegenüber dem paulinischen Motiv des σῶμα Χριστοῦ (vgl. insbesondere 1Kor 12,12–27) trägt der Kolosserbrief durch die Verknüpfung von κεφαλή und σῶμα eine hierarchisierende Komponente in die ekklesiologische Leib-Christi-Metaphorik ein:[31] καὶ αὐτός ἐστιν ἡ κεφαλὴ τοῦ σώματος τῆς ἐκκλησίας (Kol 1,18). Diese bildhafte christozentrische Zuspitzung wird nun in Kol 2,19 inhaltlich weiter ausgeführt – Christus ist das Haupt, das dem Leib Bestand, Zusammenhalt und Wachstum sichert (ἐξ οὗ πᾶν τὸ σῶμα διὰ τῶν ἁφῶν καὶ συνδέσμων ἐπιχορηγούμενον καὶ συμβιβαζόμενον αὔξει τὴν αὔξησιν τοῦ θεοῦ).

Mit dem Bild der den Leib zusammenhaltenden Bänder (διὰ τῶν ἁφῶν καὶ συνδέσμων) knüpft Kol 2,19 dabei, wie in der motivgeschichtlichen Untersuchung van Kootens anschaulich aufgezeigt werden konnte, an zeitgenössische Vorstellungen vom Zusammenhalt des Weltleibes in der Tradition mittelplatonischer und stoischer Kosmologie an (vgl.

---

[31] Zum Begriff der „Hierarchisierung" im Kontext der Haupt-Leib-Metaphorik von Kol 1,18 siehe H. ROOSE, Die Hierarchisierung der Leib-Metapher im Kolosser- und Epheserbrief als „Paulinisierung". Ein Beitrag zur Rezeption paulinischer Tradition in den pseudo-paulinischen Briefen, NT 47 (2005), 117–141 (132): „Während Paulus die Leib-Metapher ‚demokratisch' verwendet und mit ihr die Binnenstruktur der Gemeinde beschreibt, hierarchisiert der Verfasser des Kolosserbriefes die Metapher. Ihm geht es um die Ausrichtung der Gemeinde als Leib auf ihr Haupt (Christus)."

Plato Tim. 31b–32b; Plutarch, De animae procreatione 1016f–1017a; Marc Aurel, Meditationes 6,38; 7,9).[32] Dies entspricht der bereits im Kontext der Haupt-Leib-Metaphorik von 1,18 dominierenden kosmologischen Bildlichkeit des ‚Christushymnus' in Kol 1,15–20 (siehe dazu auch die Ausführungen unter 1.). Dass mit dem Motiv des vom Haupt ausgehenden körperlichen Wachsens (ἐξ οὗ πᾶν τὸ σῶμα ... αὔξει) zudem antike Vorstellungen embryonalen Wachstums aufgenommen werden, die ihrerseits ihren Anknüpfungspunkt in der platonischen Kosmologie finden (vgl. Plato Tim. 44d; 69c), wurde in jüngster Zeit bei Tieleman herausgearbeitet.[33]

Der Leib Christi wird hier somit als hierarchisches Konzept entworfen, das von oben, von seinem Haupt her, zusammengehalten wird. Dies steht in klarem Gegensatz zum ‚demokratischen' Gefüge des σῶμα Χριστοῦ bei Paulus, wo der Zusammenhalt des Leibes von seinen Gliedern her gedacht wird und auch das Haupt keine exponierte Stellung einnimmt, sondern vielmehr durch den Zusammenhalt der anderen Glieder gestützt wird: νῦν δὲ πολλὰ μὲν μέλη, ἓν δὲ σῶμα. οὐ δύναται δὲ ὁ ὀφθαλμὸς εἰπεῖν τῇ χειρί· χρείαν σου οὐκ ἔχω, ἢ πάλιν ἡ κεφαλὴ τοῖς ποσίν χρείαν ὑμῶν οὐκ ἔχω (1Kor 12,20f.).[34] Dieses Gefüge, das gerade durch die Gleichwertigkeit seiner Glieder bestimmt ist, weicht in Kol 2,19 einer christozentrischen Ausrichtung auf das Haupt, wodurch das demokratische Konstrukt des σῶμα Χριστοῦ, wie es in 1Kor 12 den Zusammenhalt des Leibes garantiert, in ein hierarchisches transformiert wird.

Analog entfällt, wie unter 2.1 bereits deutlich wurde, auch im Hinblick auf das Motiv der οἰκοδομή jenes Moment der Gegenseitigkeit der Glieder zugunsten einer christozentrischen Blickrichtung (vgl. Kol 2,6f.: ὡς οὖν παρελάβετε τὸν Χριστὸν Ἰησοῦν τὸν κύριον, ἐν αὐτῷ περιπατεῖτε, ἐρριζωμένοι καὶ ἐποικοδομούμενοι ἐν αὐτῷ). Insofern kann hier eine deuteropaulinische Neuakzentuierung konstatiert werden, die über die Verwendung einzelner Motive hinausgeht und folglich als konzeptionell betrachtet werden muss: Beide innerhalb der kolossischen Gegnerpolemik adaptierten ekklesiologischen Konzepte paulinischer Prägung, οἰκοδομή *und* σῶμα Χριστοῦ, erfahren gegenüber ihrem ursprünglichen Gebrauch eine christozentrische Zuspitzung; der Kirchenbegriff des Kol ist nicht nur

---

[32] Vgl. VAN KOOTEN, Christology (s. Anm. 10), 30–53. Zur Adaption des Bändermotives in der frühchristlichen Literatur siehe ferner auch M. LAPIDGE, A Stoic Metaphor of Late Latin Poetry. The Binding of the Cosmos, Latomus 39 (1980), 817–837 (821–824).

[33] Vgl. T. TIELEMAN, Head and Heart. The Pauline Corpus Considered against the Backdrop of Graeco-Roman Medicine and Philosophy [bislang unveröffentlichter Vortrag, gehalten auf der Jahrestagung der SBL in San Diego am 18.11.2007]. Zur motivgeschichtlichen Verankerung von Kol 2,19 in der Bildwelt antiker anatomischer Vorstellungen siehe u.a. auch H. BLANKE, Eine Auslegung von Kolosser 1 und 2, Aurich 1987, 216, und J. B. LIGHTFOOT, Saint Paul's Epistles to the Colossians and to Philemon, The Epistles of Saint Paul 3, London 1904, 196–199.

[34] Vgl. dazu neben ROOSE (s. Anm. 31) auch LINDEMANN, Kolosserbrief (s. Anm. 10), 49.

ein universeller (siehe die Ausführungen unter 1.),[35] sondern auch ein hierarchischer, der nicht das wechselseitige Miteinander der Glieder, sondern die Ausrichtung auf das Haupt hin zur Grundlage christlichen Zusammenlebens macht.

2. Im unmittelbaren Anschluss an die Haupt-Leib-Motivik von 2,19 formuliert Kol 2,20 die lebenspraktische Konsequenz für die in der Heilsgemeinschaft des σῶμα Χριστοῦ eingeschlossenen Gläubigen: Durch die Teilhabe an Christi Tod sind die Christen den weltlichen Gesetzmäßigkeiten gestorben (εἰ ἀπεθάνετε σὺν Χριστῷ ἀπὸ τῶν στοιχείων τοῦ κόσμου)[36] und damit befreit von allen Geboten, die im weltlichen Dasein Gültigkeit beanspruchen (τί ὡς ζῶντες ἐν κόσμῳ δογματίζεσθε;). Wie radikal der Kolosserbrief den Gedanken der Partizipation am Schicksal Christi ausbuchstabiert, zeigt hier in erster Linie die Aussage von Kol 2,12, die im vorliegenden Kontext durch die Formel des Mitsterbens anaphorisch wieder aufgegriffen wird: συνταφέντες αὐτῷ ἐν τῷ βαπτισμῷ, ἐν ᾧ καὶ συνηγέρθητε διὰ τῆς πίστεως τῆς ἐνεργείας τοῦ θεοῦ τοῦ ἐγείραντος αὐτὸν ἐκ νεκρῶν.

Die hier gebrauchte Bildlichkeit des Mitsterbens und Mitauferstehens findet zahlreiche Parallelen in den Protopaulinen (vgl. 1Thess 4,14–17; 1Kor 15,12–22; 6,14; Röm 4,24f.; 6,2–8; 8,9–11; 2Kor 4,14), auffällig sind jedoch vor allem die deutlichen Berührungspunkte mit Röm 6. Insbesondere im Blick auf Röm 6,4 sind die lexikalischen wie inhaltlichen Überschneidungen mit Kol 2,12 so signifikant, dass in diesem Punkt ein breiter exegetischer Konsens über das Vorliegen eines literarischen Abhängigkeitsverhältnisses besteht[37]:

---

[35] Zum universellen Kirchenverständnis des Kol siehe z.B. WOLTER, Kolosser (s. Anm. 1), 82, J. GNILKA, Der Kolosserbrief, HThK.NT X/1, Freiburg i. Brsg. 1980, 106, und R. HOPPE, Paulus in nachpaulinischen Schriften, in: A. Bilgri / B. Kirchgessner (Hg.), Liturgia semper reformanda (FS Schlemmer), Freiburg i. Brsg. 1997, 36–47 (42f.), sowie A. DE OLIVEIRA, Christozentrik im Kolosserbrief, in: K. Scholtissek (Hg.), Christologie in der Paulus-Schule. Zur Rezeptionsgeschichte des paulinischen Evangeliums, SBS 181, Stuttgart 1999, 72–103 (103), LINDEMANN, Kolosserbrief (s. Anm. 10), 30, und MAISCH, Kolossä (s. Anm. 7), 51.

[36] Über das Verständnis der στοιχεῖα τοῦ κόσμου in Kol 2,8.20 besteht in der Exegese der kolossischen Gegnerpolemik bis heute kein mehrheitsfähiger Konsens; das Spektrum der zeitgenössischen Begriffsverwendung schließt die Referenz auf die physikalischen Grundelemente ebenso ein wie den allgemeineren Bezug auf Grundlagen, Grundstoffe und Grundprinzipien unterschiedlichster Art. Vgl. zur Quellenlage u.a. SCHWEIZER, Elemente (s. Anm. 10), und D. RUSAM, Neue Belege zu den στοιχεῖα τοῦ κόσμου (Gal 4,3.9; Kol 2,8.20), ZNW 83 (1992), 119–125 (122f.).

[37] Umstritten verbleibt hingegen, inwieweit diese literarische Abhängigkeit als direkte Text-Text-Beziehung zu verstehen ist, oder aber als indirekte, über eine gemeinsame Vorlage vermittelte Intertext-Relation (zu den unterschiedlichen Rekonstruktionen der

Röm 6,4.8: συνετάφημεν οὖν αὐτῷ διὰ τοῦ βαπτίσματος εἰς τὸν θάνατον, ἵνα ὥσπερ ἠγέρθη Χριστὸς ἐκ νεκρῶν διὰ τῆς δόξης τοῦ πατρός, οὕτως καὶ ἡμεῖς ἐν καινότητι ζωῆς περιπατήσωμεν. ... εἰ δὲ ἀπεθάνομεν σὺν Χριστῷ, πιστεύομεν ὅτι καὶ συζήσομεν αὐτῷ.

Kol 2,12: *συνταφέντες αὐτῷ ἐν τῷ βαπτισμῷ, ἐν ᾧ καὶ συνηγέρθητε διὰ τῆς πίστεως τῆς ἐνεργείας τοῦ θεοῦ τοῦ ἐγείραντος αὐτὸν ἐκ νεκρῶν·*

Die Parallelität beider Tauformeln ist offenkundig; umso augenscheinlicher ist in Anbetracht der großen Übereinstimmung die auffallende Abweichung, die Kol 2,12 auszeichnet: Wo Röm 6,4.8 temporal klar zwischen dem in der Vergangenheit verorteten Mitgestorben- resp. Mitbegraben-Sein (ἀπεθάνομεν σὺν Χριστῷ / συνετάφημεν οὖν αὐτῷ) und der in der Zukunft zu erwartenden Auferstehung der Gläubigen unterscheidet (πιστεύομεν ὅτι καὶ συζήσομεν αὐτῷ / ἵνα ὥσπερ ἠγέρθη Χριστός ... οὕτως καὶ ἡμεῖς ἐν καινότητι ζωῆς περιπατήσωμεν), entfällt im Kolosserbrief diese temporale Abstufung[38]: Sowohl die Auferstehung Christi als

---

Textgenese siehe z.B. U. SCHNELLE, Gerechtigkeit und Christusgegenwart. Vorpaulinische und paulinische Tauftheologie, GTA 24, Göttingen 1983, 89, und A. J. M. WEDDERBURN, Baptism and Resurrection. Studies in Pauline Theology against its Graeco-Roman Background, WUNT 44, Tübingen 1987, 70–84). Dabei bilden in erster Linie die prägnanten Berührungspunkte zwischen frühchristlicher Tauftheologie und -praxis einerseits und den Initiationsriten antiker Mysterienkulte andererseits die Grundlage für eine lange exegetische Tradition, die Motivik des Mitsterbens und -auferstehens als christianisierte Adaption einer ursprünglich mysterienkultischen Formel zu deuten. Eine entsprechende rituell nachempfundene Teilhabe an Tod und Auferstehung einer Gottheit findet sich etwa in Osiris-, Isis-, Adonis-, Attis-, und Mithraskult; darüber hinaus weisen insbesondere die Mysterien um Isis und Osiris zahlreiche weitere Analogien zur christlichen Taufe auf. Vgl. u.a. D. ZELLER, Die Mysterienkulte und die paulinische Soteriologie (Röm 6,1–11). Eine Fallstudie zum Synkretismus im Neuen Testament, in: H. P. Siller (Hg.), Suchbewegungen. Synkretismus – kulturelle Identität und kirchliches Bekenntnis, Darmstadt 1991, 42–61, und G. WAGNER, Das religionsgeschichtliche Problem von Römer 6,1–11, AThANT 39, Zürich 1962, 11–49; zur Grundlegung dieses Ansatzes siehe v.a. R. REITZENSTEIN, Die hellenistischen Mysterienreligionen nach ihren Grundgedanken und Wirkungen (Fotomechanischer Nachdruck der dritten Auflage von 1927), Darmstadt 1956. Unabhängig von der Frage der religionsgeschichtlichen Ableitung aus einer vorpaulinischen mysterienkultischen Sprachtradition ist m.E. jedoch die intertextuelle Beziehung zwischen Kol 2,12 und Röm 6,4 als direkte literarische Abhängigkeit zu werten; gerade angesichts der signifikanten Neuakzentuierung der Auferstehungsaussage in Kol 2,12 (siehe obige Ausführungen), die als präsentische Umwidmung eschatologischer Aussagen Pauli ein wiederkehrendes Charakteristikum des Kolosserbriefes repräsentiert (vgl. auch 1Kor 15,24 gegenüber Kol 2,10.15).

[38] Die verschiedentlich unternommenen exegetischen Versuche, jene Unterschiedlichkeit der temporalen Ausgestaltung durch eine gegenwartsbezogene Lesart der Auferstehungsaussagen von Röm 6 aufzulösen – so z.B. Eckstein und Agersnap (vgl. S. AGERSNAP, Baptism and the New Life. A Study of Romans 6.1–14, Aarhus 1999, 290–293, und H.-J. ECKSTEIN, Auferstehung und gegenwärtiges Leben nach Röm 6,1–11. Präsentische Eschatologie bei Paulus?, ThBeitr 28 [1997], 8–23 [21.20.23]; ähnlich auch

auch die der auf ihn Getauften ist bereits gegenwärtige Heilsrealität (συνηγέρθητε); der eschatologische Vorbehalt rückt zugunsten der Bekräftigung des gegenwärtigen Heilszustandes in den Hintergrund.[39]

Dass die Formel des Mitgestorben-Seins später innerhalb der kolossischen Gegnerpolemik wiederaufgegriffen wird (Kol 2,20: εἰ ἀπεθάνετε σὺν Χριστῷ), bildet dabei ein deutliches Indiz, dass diese präsentische Neuakzentuierung vor dem textpragmatischen Hintergrund jener Auseinandersetzung mit konkurrierenden Heilslehren zu verstehen ist. Denn gerade angesichts der Versicherung, dass die Auferstehung in Christus bereits gegenwärtige Heilsrealität der Gläubigen ist, erweisen sich jegliche religiösen Forderungen, die von anderen Gruppierungen als heilsrelevant propagiert werden könnten, als gegenstandslos.[40] Aus der Perspektive einer solchen Beruhigung und Bestärkung der Adressaten vor dem Hintergrund potentieller oder realer Verunsicherung durch religiöse Forderungen konkurrierender Heilslehren stellt die Betonung der Heilsgegenwart einen textimmanent schlüssigen Paradigmenwechsel „ins enthusiastische Präsens" dar.[41] Denn im Gegensatz zur paulinischen Argumentationsstruktur in Röm 6 (ähnlich auch 1Kor 15) steht hier eben nicht die Betonung des eschatologischen Vorbehalts im Vordergrund, die einem heilsenthusiastischen Taufverständnis entgegengestellt wird, sondern vielmehr die Betonung des gegenwärtigen Heilszustandes, die der strikten Zurückweisung gegnerischer Forderungen geschuldet ist: Aufgrund des Heilsgeschehens in der Taufe, durch das den Christen die Auferstehungswirklichkeit bereits im Hier und Jetzt zugesprochen ist (συνηγέρθητε), kann entsprechenden Satzungen und Geboten (vgl. Kol 2,14.20) keinerlei soteriologische Qualität

---

PERCY, Kolosser [s. Anm. 15], 110) –, verbleiben m.E. wenig überzeugend. So signalisiert bereits das einleitende πιστεύομεν ὅτι in Röm 6,8 deutlich den futurisch-eschatologischen Charakter des συζήσομεν als Hoffnung auf eine noch ausstehende Auferstehung der Gläubigen (siehe dazu u.a. auch P. STUHLMACHER, Der Brief an die Römer, NTD 6, Göttingen/Zürich 1998, 84, und J. D. G. DUNN, Romans 1–8, WBC 38a, Dallas 1988, 318.322.332), und Wilckens hebt in seinem Römerkommentar zu Recht hervor, dass Röm 6,4.8 grundsätzlich durch eine kontrastierende Struktur bestimmt ist, innerhalb derer den präsentischen Versbestandteilen jeweils futurisch-eschatologische Aussagen gegenübergestellt werden (vgl. U. WILCKENS, Der Brief an die Römer, Teilbd. 2: Röm 6–11, EKK VI/2, Zürich 1980, 15f.).

[39] Ähnlich auch R. HOPPE, Epheserbrief. Kolosserbrief, SKK.NT 10, Stuttgart 1987, 100.131, POKORNÝ, Kolosser (s. Anm. 1), 108, und H. LUDWIG, Der Verfasser des Kolosserbriefs – Ein Schüler des Paulus, Göttingen 1974, 170.177f., sowie G. SELLIN, „Die Auferstehung ist schon geschehen". Zur Spiritualisierung apokalyptischer Terminologie im Neuen Testament, NT 25 (1983), 220–237 (232–237), und LINDEMANN, Kolosserbrief (s. Anm. 10), 53.

[40] Vgl. WOLTER, Kolosser (s. Anm. 1), 38, sowie LINDEMANN, Kolosserbrief (s. Anm. 10), 53, und LUDWIG, Kolosserbrief (s. Anm. 39), 170.

[41] HOPPE, Paulus (s. Anm. 35), 41.

mehr zukommen; die entsprechende Aktualisierung des Taufverständnisses in Kol 2,12 ist daher die stimmige Konsequenz aus dem solchermaßen veränderten situativen Rahmen, innerhalb dessen jene Verkündigung des neuen Lebens in und durch die Taufe erfolgt und der eine Neuakzentuierung gegenüber der protopaulinischen Tauftheologie erforderlich machte.

Was bedeutet dieser intertextuelle Befund für die Frage der pseudepigraphen Selbstverortung des Kolosserbriefes im Kontext des paulinischen Erbes bzw. innerhalb der pseudopaulinischen Briefkonstitutions-Koordinaten Autor – Adressaten – Gegner? Betrachten wir die vorhergehenden Ausführungen, so lassen sich auf Basis dieses epistolographischen Koordinatensystems drei wesentliche Charakteristika des Kol festhalten: Der Kolosserbrief beansprucht durch seine (pseudonyme) apostolische Autorität eine Richtlinienfunktion in Fragen christlicher Gemeindepraxis. Durch den globalen Adressierungsanspruch (εἰς ὑμᾶς, καθὼς καὶ ἐν παντὶ τῷ κόσμῳ) wird diese als überindividuell gültige Leitlinie ausgewiesen – und mit demselben generellen Anspruch werden jedwede religiösen Forderungen, die seitens konkurrierender Heilslehren an die Christen herangetragen werden könnten, als gegenstandslos zurückgewiesen. Die argumentative Grundlage bildet dabei die exklusive Bezogenheit der Gläubigen auf Christus als Haupt des σῶμα Χριστοῦ, innerhalb dessen die Glieder dieses Leibes durch ihre Teilhabe an der Auferstehungswirklichkeit Christi in die gegenwärtige Heilsrealität in Christus mit hineingenommen und somit dem Zwang aller menschlichen Satzungen und Gebote entzogen sind.

Und an genau diesem Punkt wird die pseudepigraphe Briefkonstitution zum bedeutungstragenden Moment der Argumentation: Mit dem ekklesiologischen Leib-Christi-Motiv wie auch der Formel des Mitsterbens und Mitauferstehens werden prominente paulinische Topoi aufgegriffen und in ganz spezifischer Weise vor einem neuen situativen Hintergrund ausgedeutet. Der Vielfalt der in Kol 2,16–23 genannten religiösen Praktiken und Forderungen wird eine exklusive Bezogenheit des σῶμα Χριστοῦ auf Christus als Haupt entgegengesetzt, die in dieser Form keine motivische Parallele in den Protopaulinen kennt. In selber Weise wird jeder vermeintlichen Heilsrelevanz derartiger Forderungen das „umfassende Heilsperfektum"[42] der in Christus bereits im Hier und Jetzt Auferweckten entgegengestellt – eine deutliche präsentische Neuakzentuierung der entsprechenden Formeln bei Paulus. Und doch trägt der Kolosserbrief gerade durch die enge Anlehnung an paulinische Sprachlichkeit und Motivik die jeweilige semantische Ausgestaltung dieser Motive qua Verfasserfiktion in

---

[42] SCHNELLE, Tauftheologie (s. Anm. 37), 80.

das zugrunde liegende orthonyme Schriftgut ein und präsentiert damit die argumentativen Grundpfeiler der kolossischen Gegnerpolemik als genuine Selbstauslegung Pauli. Für Vertreter einer paulinischen Diplomatie in Fragen unterschiedlicher religiöser Praktiken in Anlehnung an Röm 14; 1Kor 7.8.10 bleibt in dieser Auslegung des paulinischen Erbes, die beansprucht, Selbst-Auslegung Pauli zu sein, kein Platz.

A Stone that *Still* Won't Fit

An Introductory and Editorial Note for Edgar Krentz's "A Stone that Will Not Fit"

by

TREVOR THOMPSON

In December of 1983, the Thessalonians Seminar of the Society of Biblical Literature devoted its fifth and final year to the study of Second Thessalonians after four years of focus on First Thessalonians. At that time, the two landmark works of Wolfgang Trilling were only beginning to exert an influence outside of Germany.[1] The published work of English-speaking scholars on Second Thessalonians overwhelmingly supported the authenticity of the text. Among commentaries, Gerhard Krodel's remarks in the *Proclamation Commentary* series stood alone in opposing Paul's authorship.[2] The Thessalonians Seminar asked Edgar Krentz ("A Stone that Will Not Fit: The Non-Pauline Authorship of Second Thessalonians") and John Hurd ("Concerning the Authenticity of Second Thessalonians") to offer competing papers on the question of authenticity. Neither the paper by Krentz nor the paper by Hurd was immediately published.[3] Yet, both papers—as evidenced by repeated citation (see below)—exerted an important influence upon the other members of the Seminar and those who subsequently received copies of the respective papers.

The editorial decision to publish the full version of Krentz's paper in this volume follows the publication of Hurd's paper in 1998 and thus allows later readers to hear both sides of the conversation.[4] Inclusion here

---

[1] W. Trilling, *Untersuchungen zum zweiten Thessalonicherbrief* (ETS 27; Leipzig: St. Benno, 1972), and idem., *Der zweite Brief an die Thessalonicher* (EKKNT 14; Zürich: Benziger Verlag, 1980).

[2] G. Krodel, "2 Thessalonians," in *Ephesians, Colossians, 2 Thessalonians, the Pastoral Epistles* (ed. idem; Proclamation Commentaries; Philadelphia: Fortress Press, 1978), 73–96. In 1992, M. D. Goulder noted, "Until 1980 almost all commentators held to Pauline authenticity: including E. von Dobschütz, M. Dibelius, Rigaux and Best" ("Silas in Thessalonica," *JSNT* 48 [1992]: 87–106 [96 n. 2]).

[3] Summarized and abbreviated portions of Krentz's paper appeared nine years later in E. Krentz, "Thessalonians, First and Second Epistles to the," *ABD* 6:515–23.

[4] J. C. Hurd, "Concerning the Authenticity of 2 Thessalonians," in *The Earlier Letters*

also recognizes the paper's historic influence and fills a recognized lacuna in the history of North American Second Thessalonians research. Beyond citation in Krentz's own work,[5] his paper has been referenced in important secondary literature on the Thessalonian letters.[6] Moreover, the significance of the paper is not limited to the past. It remains the most comprehensive and detailed argument against the authenticity of Second Thessalonians in English. Krentz's succinct and effective summaries of the arguments and conclusions of Wilhelm Bornemann,[7] William Wrede,[8] Heinrich J. Holtzmann,[9] and Trilling have continuing relevance amidst current debates concerning authenticity. While most German scholars are now in agreement that Second Thessalonians is not a genuine text,[10] scholars in North America remain divided on the issue. Since 1983, numerous English commentaries have appeared. Some treat Second Thessalonians as a pseudepigraphic text[11] while others continue to read the document as an

---

of Paul – and Other Studies (Arbeiten zur Religion und Geschichte des Urchristentums 8; Frankfurt a.M.: Peter Lang, 1998), 135–61.

[5] E. Krentz, "Traditions Held Fast: Theology and Fidelity in 2 Thessalonians," in *The Thessalonian Correspondence* (ed. R. F. Collins; BETL 87; Leuven: Leuven University Press, 1990), 505–15 (505 n. 2).

[6] Essay: H. Koester, "From Paul's Eschatology to the Apocalyptic Schemata of 2 Thessalonians," in *The Thessalonian Correspondence* (see n. 5), 441–58 (455 n. 67). Monographs: R. F. Collins, *Letters That Paul Did not Write: The Epistle to the Hebrews and the Pauline Pseudepigrapha* (GNS 28; Wilmington, Del.: Michael Glazier, 1988), 218; G. S. Holland, *The Tradition that You Received from Us: 2 Thessalonians in the Pauline Tradition* (HUT 24; Tübingen: Mohr Siebeck, 1988), 160. Commentary: R. K. Jewett, *The Thessalonian Correspondence: Pauline Rhetoric and Millenarian Piety* (Foundations & Facets: New Testament; Philadelphia: Fortress Press, 1986), 15–6.

[7] W. Bornemann, *Die Thessalonicher-Briefe* (5th & 6th ed.; KEK 10; Göttingen: Vandenhoeck & Ruprecht, 1894).

[8] W. Wrede, *Die Echtheit des zweiten Thessalonicherbriefs* (TUGAL 24; Leipzig: J. C. Hinrichs, 1903).

[9] H. J. Holtzmann, "Zum zweiten Thessalonicherbrief," *ZNW* 2 (1901): 97–108.

[10] U. Schnelle, *Einleitung in das Neue Testament* (5th ed.; Göttingen: Vandenhoeck & Ruprecht, 2005), 372, "Über den pseudepigraphischen Charakter des 2 Thess herrscht in der neueren Exegese ein weitgehender Konsens." Cf. P.-G. Müller, *Der Erste und Zweite Brief an die Thessalonicher* (RNT; Regensburg: Friedrich Pustet, 2001), 227–45. Among French scholars in the mid-twentieth century, B. Rigaux affirmed the letter's authenticity (*Les Épîtres aux Thessaloniciens* [EBib; Paris: J. Gabalda, 1956]). C. Masson famously denied authenticity but then treated the text in his comments as a genuine missive from Paul (*Les Deux Épîtres de Saint Paul Aux Thessaloniciens* [CNT 11a; Paris: Delachaux & Niestlé, 1957]). More recent French scholarship seems to be moving toward reading the text as a pseudepigraphon. E.g., S. Légasse, *Les Épîtres de Paul Aux Thessaloniciens* (LD Commentaires 7; Paris: Cerf, 1999) and R. Burnet, *Épîtres et Lettres, Ier-IIe Siècle: De Paul de Tarse À Polycarpe de Smyrne* (LD; Paris: Cerf, 2003), 245–56.

[11] Krodel, "2 Thessalonians" (see n. 2); M. J. J. Menken, *2 Thessalonians* (New Testament Readings; London and New York: Routledge, 1994); B. Thurston, *Reading Colos-*

authentic letter by Paul.[12] The recent commentary by Abraham Malherbe in support of authenticity within *The Anchor Bible* series confirms the ongoing vitality of the debate.[13]

In the years since Krentz's presentation, the basic contours of the discussion about authenticity have remained essentially unchanged. In general, scholars who support Paul's authorship question the value and validity of the operative criteria used in discussions of authenticity[14] and attempt to construct an historical situation which can account for the remarkable similarities and notable differences between the two letters. Among the proposed historical situations, the following are worthy of note. Charles A. Wanamaker revives the thesis that Second Thessalonians was written be-

---

sians, *Ephesians & 2 Thessalonians: A Literary and Theological Commentary* (New York: Crossroad, 1995); E. J. Richard, *First and Second Thessalonians* (SP; Collegeville, Minn.: The Liturgical Press, 1995); B. R. Gaventa, *First and Second Thessalonians* (IBC; Louisville, Ky.: Westminster John Knox, 1998); V. P. Furnish, *1 Thessalonians & 2 Thessalonians* (ANTC; Nashville: Abingdon Press, 2007); L. McKinnish Bridges, *1 & 2 Thessalonians* (Smyth and Helwys Bible Commentary 17; Macon, Ga.: Smyth & Helwys, 2008). A few commentaries are currently being written which interpret Second Thessalonians as a pseudonymous document: H. Koester, *1 & 2 Thessalonians* (Hermeneia; Minneapolis: Fortress Press, forthcoming); E. E. Johnson, *1 and 2 Thessalonians* (NTL; Louisville, Ky.: Westminster John Knox, forthcoming).

[12] C. A. Wanamaker, *The Epistles to the Thessalonians: A Commentary on the Greek Text* (NIGTC; Grand Rapids, Mich.: Eerdmans, 1990); L. Morris, *The First and Second Epistles to the Thessalonians* (NICNT; Grand Rapids, Mich.: Eerdmans, 1991); D. J. Williams, *1 and 2 Thessalonians* (NIBCNT; Peabody, Mass.: Hendrickson, 1992); J. A. Weatherly, *1 & 2 Thessalonians* (College Press NIV Commentary; Joplin, Mo.: College Press, 1996); M. W. Holmes, *1 & 2 Thessalonians* (NIV Application Commentary; Grand Rapids, Mich.: Zondervan, 1998); G. L. Green, *The Letters to the Thessalonians* (Pillar New Testament Commentary; Grand Rapids, Mich.: Eerdmans, 2002); G. K. Beale, *1–2 Thessalonians* (IVP New Testament Commentary Series; Downers Grove, Ill.: InterVarsity Press, 2003); B. Witherington III, *1 and 2 Thessalonians: A Socio-Rhetorical Commentary* (Grand Rapids, Mich.: Eerdmans, 2006); G. D. Fee, *The First and Second Letters to the Thessalonians* (NICNT, Grand Rapids, Mich.: Eerdmans, 2009). S. Kim is in the process of completely revising F. F. Bruce's commentary on the Thessalonian letters within the *Word Biblical Commentary* series.

[13] A. J. Malherbe, *The Letters to the Thessalonians: A New Translation with Introduction and Commentary* (AB 32B; New York: Doubleday, 2000).

[14] For example, concerning the noted official tone of Second Thessalonians, Jewett, *The Thessalonian Correspondence* (see n. 6), 11–2, writes, "The difficulty is in drawing appropriate conclusions from such data; since Trilling rejects any situation explanations, the elements of differentiation drive him to the conclusion of inauthenticity. But can one apply such a method elsewhere in the Pauline corpus?" Similarly, in regard to arguments of vocabulary and style, Green, *The Letters to the Thessalonians* (see n. 12), 60–1, asserts, "Moreover, they [Trilling, etc.] put forward no objective criteria regarding what types of stylistic variations would indicate that the two writings did not come from the same hand."

fore First Thessalonians.[15] Michael Goulder asserts, relying in part upon the veracity of the Acts account, that Silvanus/Silas remained in Thessalonica after Paul's departure and offered a different message which, among other items, stressed the immortality of the believer and the call to cease work.[16] Silvanus later joined Paul in Corinth where Paul "browbeat him into joining in the two Thessalonian letters."[17] Malherbe argues that Second Thessalonians, written soon after First Thessalonians, was targeted to a group that had only read a copy of Paul's earlier letter (First Thessalonians) accompanied by amplification, glossing, commentary, and/or oral explanation.[18] Colin Nicholl maintains the probable authenticity of Second Thessalonians by synthesizing the epistolary situations of the two letters as "two stages of a single rapidly developing eschatological crisis ultimately rooted in an unfortunate interpretation of the unexpected deaths."[19] George H. van Kooten dates the composition of Second Thessalonians to the first year of Nero's disappearance, between June 68 and July 69, and proposes a solution to the discussion of authenticity by connecting the "I" of 2 Thess 2:5 with Silvanus or Timothy. Thus, with Paul in Nero's custody and after one of his co-workers had visited the Thessalonians, the three took up the pen and wrote to the Thessalonians.[20]

---

[15] E.g., Wanamaker, *The Epistles to the Thessalonians* (see n. 12), 37–45. Cf. T. W. Manson, "St. Paul in Greece: The Letters to the Thessalonians," *BJRL* 35/2 (1953): 428–47, and R. W. Thurston, "The Relationship Between the Thessalonian Epistles," *ExpTim* 85 (1973): 52–6.

[16] Goulder, "Silas in Thessalonica" (see n. 2), 105, connects the message of Silvanus with the message of the Jerusalem church as expressed in the Gospel of Matthew. "Now it is Matthew who shows the outworking of this doctrine of the present kingdom in just the practical ways which we have seen to be issue in the Thessalonian letters ... We are meeting the Jerusalem theology—the kingdom which has arrived, the call to cease work, the demand for a higher sexual righteousness, the immortality of the believer, the full requirement of the Law—in the preaching of Silas. It is this which evokes the various crises which result in the two Thessalonian letters."

[17] Ibid., 104.

[18] Among those convinced by Malherbe's arguments on authenticity see J. R. C. Cousland, "The Letters to the Thessalonians, by Abraham J. Malherbe," *JBL* 121/2 (2002): 380–83. Among those not convinced by Malherbe see H.-D. Betz, "The Letters to the Thessalonians: A New Translation with Introduction and Commentary," *JR* 84/2 (2004): 272–74.

[19] C. R. Nicholl, *From Hope to Despair in Thessalonica: Situating 1 and 2 Thessalonians* (SNTSMS 126; Cambridge: Cambridge University Press, 2004), 197.

[20] G. H. van Kooten, "'Wrath Will Drip in the Plains of Macedonia': Expectations of Nero's Return in the Egyptian *Sibylline Oracles* (Book 5), 2 Thessalonians, and Ancient Historical Writings," in *The Wisdom of Egypt: Jewish, Early Christian, and Gnostic Essays in Honour of Gerard P. Luttikhuizen* (eds. A. Hilhorst and G. H. van Kooten; Leiden/Boston: Brill, 2005), 177–213 (211–13). As a middle ground between the dueling alternatives, K. Donfried proposes Timothy as the probable author of Second Thessalo-

Those who deny Paul's authorship of Second Thessalonians rely upon the same basic arguments provided in Krentz's paper. However, over the last twenty-five years, some portions of the inauthenticity argument have been extended or clarified. Daryl Schmidt calls new attention to the syntactical complexity of the opening thanksgiving in 2 Thess 1:3–12. Drawing upon Noam Chomsky's theory of generative linguistics,[21] he identifies twenty-two dependent/embedded clauses in the opening thanksgiving. The final embedded sentence is fifteen syntactical levels removed from the main/matrix sentence. Schmidt notes that this level of syntactical complexity "is unmatched in the Pauline corpus and has its closest parallel in Eph, and secondly in Col, two members of the Pauline corpus often considered 'pseudepigraphic.'"[22] He further compares the frequency of coordinating conjunctions other than copulative καί (e.g., ἀλλά, δέ, διό, γάρ, ἤ, οὖν) and subordinating conjunctions (e.g., ἐάν, εἰ, ἵνα, καθώς, ὅπως, ὅτε, ὅτι, ὡς). With the aid of GramCord software, Schmidt's comparison confirms the stylistic proximity of Second Thessalonians to Ephesians and Colossians.[23] The publication of Michael Ernst's exhaustive stylistic analysis of Second Thessalonians according to the canons of ancient rhetoric further strengthens the argument from literary style against the letter's authenticity.[24]

---

nians which was sent to "a specific situation in Thessalonica." K. P. Donfried, *Paul, Thessalonica, and Early Christianity* (Grand Rapids, Mich.: Eerdmans, 2002), 49–67 (53–6). Reprint of K. P. Donfried, "2 Thessalonians and the Church of Thessalonica," in *Origins and Method: Towards a New Understanding of Judaism and Christianity* (ed. B. H. McLean; Sheffield: Sheffield Academic Press, 1993), 128–44.

[21] D. Schmidt, *Hellenistic Greek Grammar and Noam Chomsky: Nominalizing Transformations* (SBLDS 62; Chico, Calif.: Scholars Press, 1981).

[22] Idem, "The Syntactical Style of 2 Thessalonians: How Pauline Is It?" in *The Thessalonians Correspondence* (see n. 5), 383–93 (385). Cf. idem, "The Authenticity of 2 Thessalonians: Linguistic Arguments," in *SBLSP 1983* (ed. K. H. Richards; Chico, Calif.: Scholars Press, 1983), 289–96.

[23] Schmidt, "The Syntactical Style of 2 Thessalonians: How Pauline Is It?" (see n. 22), 387, "In 2 Thess the use of subordinating conjunctions (37.7 per 1000 words) is almost as great (within 9%) as the use of non-copulative coordinating conjunctions (41.3). The only Pauline letters with higher rates are Eph, where they are almost equal (within 4.5%), and Col, where subordinators actually are greater in number."

[24] M. Ernst, *Distanzierte Unpersönlichkeit: Analyse von Sprache und Stil des Zweiten Thessalonicherbriefes im Vergleich mit paulinischen Texten* (Salzburg: Institut für Neutestamentliche Bibelwissenschaft, 1998), 144, "Die Untersuchung konnte deutlich machen, daß nicht Paulus der Verfasser des 2 Thess ist. Nicht aufgrund inhaltlicher Aussagen oder wegen der literarischen Nähe zu 1 Thess kann diese Aussage getroffen werden, sondern vor allem aufgrund des Stilvergleichs." Although published in 1998, this volume is an essentially unchanged edition of the author's Habilitationsschrift accepted by the Katholisch-Theologische Fakultät der Universität Salzburg in 1986.

Glenn Holland focuses on the apocalyptic material in Second Thessalonians and calls attention to the "device of attributing the apocalyptic revelation to a revered figure of the past" within early Christian literature and its implications for the authenticity of Second Thessalonians. In Revelation and in the so-called Synoptic Apocalypse (i.e., Mark 13, Matt 24, and Luke 21), Jesus is the source of the apocalyptic material. The same pattern is evident in 1 Thess 4:13–18 by the attribution to a "word of the Lord" (1 Thess 4:15). 2 Thess 1:7–10 and 2:3–12, in contrast, lack specific appeal to a figure of the past. Rather, Paul is the source of the apocalyptic material (2:5). According to Holland, Paul in Second Thessalonians is the revered figure of the past supplying apocalyptic revelation and therefore not the actual author of the text.[25]

In regard to the Christology of Second Thessalonians, Maarten J. J. Menken argues for an evident transformation from Paul's Christology. He specifically notes the "idiosyncratic and one-sided appropriation" of Paul's Christological titles in the author's preference for the exalted κύριος, the use of Jesus as the first or only subject in supplications and statements of confidence, and the application of Septuagint κύριος texts to Jesus primarily—though not exclusively—within eschatological contexts.[26]

As a testimony to the paper's enduring relevance and its historic significance, E. Krentz's "A Stone that Will Not Fit" is presented here—apart from a few minor alterations—in the form provided to the members of the Thessalonians Seminar in 1983.

---

[25] G. S. Holland, "'A Letter Supposedly from Us': A Contribution to the Discussion About the Authorship of 2 Thessalonians," in *The Thessalonian Correspondence* (see n. 5), 394–402 (401), "If one assumes that Paul is himself the author of 2 Thessalonians, it is very difficult to account for the lack of an appropriate reference to a religious figure from the past as the authority for the apocalyptic information he conveys."

[26] M. J. J. Menken, "Christology in 2 Thessalonians: A Transformation of Pauline Tradition," *EstBib* 54 (1996): 501–22. Cf. R. F. Collins, "'The Gospel of Our Lord Jesus' (2 Thess 1,8): A Symbolic Shift of Paradigm," in *The Thessalonian Correspondence* (see n. 5), and G. Hotze, "Die Christologie des 2. Thessalonicherbriefes," in *Christologie in der Paulus-Schule: Zur Rezeptionsgeschichte des paulinischen Evangeliums* (ed. K. Scholtissek; Stuttgart: Verlag Katholisches Bibelwerk, 2000), 124–48.

A Stone that Will Not Fit

The Non-Pauline Authorship of Second Thessalonians

by

EDGAR KRENTZ

The authorship of Paul (with Silvanus and Timothy) is clearly claimed by 2 Thess 1:1. The letter goes out of its way to assure the reader that Paul is the primary author by mentioning his personally written signature as a sign of authenticity (3:17), and at least once presents him as speaking in the first person (2:5). It is possibly cited (or at least loosely referred to) already in Pol. *Phil* 11.3 (cf. 2 Thess 1:4) and 11.4 (cf. 2 Thess 3:15).[1] After that it is listed in the Canon Muratori, was apparently included in Marcion's canon, and was cited by Justin Martyr (*Dial.* 110), the Epistle of Vienne and Lyons (Eusebius, *Hist. eccl.* 5.1), Irenaeus, *Haer.* 3.7.2, Clement of Alexandria, *Strom.* 5, p. 554 Sylburg, and by Tertullian, *Res.* 24. Its authenticity was not questioned until modern times.

The story of that challenge to Pauline authorship is told well in a number of publications. The history falls into three major periods. The first was initiated by Johann E. C. Schmidt,[2] who challenged the authenticity of 2 Thess 2:1–12 on the basis of its eschatology. Heinrich J. Holtzmann[3] summarized and evaluated the debate in 1892: no anti-Jewish polemic as in the authentic Pauline letters; reflections of First Corinthians and Revelation; non-Pauline form of the language; the letter is basically an "erweiternde, z. Th. steigernde Wiederholung" of parallels from the first let-

---

[1] G. Milligan, *St Paul's Epistles to the Thessalonians: The Greek Text with Introduction and Notes* (London: Macmillan & Co., 1908), lxxvi–lxxvii.

[2] The history is surveyed in detail down to 1894 by W. Bornemann, *Die Thessalonicher-Briefe* (5 & 6 ed.; KEK 10; Göttingen: Vandenhoeck & Ruprecht, 1894), 492–537 on authenticity, 538–708 on the history of interpretation; through 1955 by B. Rigaux, *Les Épîtres aux Thessaloniciens* (EBib; Paris: J. Gabalda, 1956), 308–40; through 1972 by W. Trilling, *Untersuchungen zum zweiten Thessalonicherbrief* (ETS 27; Leipzig: St. Benno, 1972), 11–45. Trilling reprints Schmidt's basic position as an appendix to his work ibid., 159–61.

[3] H. J. Holtzmann, *Lehrbuch der historisch-kritischen Einleitung in das Neue Testament* (3d ed.; Freiburg i. Brsg.: Mohr Siebeck, 1892), 213–17.

ter; the lack of Old Testament citations. He devoted most space to the divergent eschatology as the major argument.

The second stage of the argument was introduced by Holtzmann[4] in 1902 and William Wrede[5] one year later. The earlier eschatological argument had made much use of the Nero redivivus myth as the basis of 2 Thess 2:1–12,[6] a view discredited by the work of Wilhelm Bousset[7] on Jewish Apocalyptic. Holtzmann and Wrede laid stress on the literary relationship of Second Thessalonians to First Thessalonians, stressing the similarity in structure, the repetition of First Thessalonians in Second Thessalonians, and the indications that Second Thessalonians must be literarily the later. These two formulated the questions that dominated the discussion in the commentaries of George Milligan, Ernst von Dobschütz,[8] James Frame,[9] Martin Dibelius,[10] William Neil,[11] Denys Whiteley,[12] and Ernest Best.[13] The same can be said of the New Testament Introductions of James Moffatt,[14] Paul Feine / Johannes Behm,[15] Alan Hugh McNeile /

---

[4] Idem, "Zum zweiten Thessalonicherbrief," *ZNW* 2 (1901): 97–108.

[5] W. Wrede, *Die Echtheit des zweiten Thessalonicherbriefs* (TUGAL 24; Leipzig: J. C. Hinrichs, 1903).

[6] This view was given brief new life by G. Hollmann, "Die Unechtheit des zweiten Thessalonicherbriefes," *ZNW* 5 (1904): 28–38.

[7] W. Bousset, *The Antichrist Legend: A Chapter in Christian and Jewish Folklore* (trans. A. H. Keane; American Academy of Religion Texts and Translations Series 24; London: Hutchinson, 1896), 128.

[8] E. von Dobschütz, *Die Thessalonicher-Briefe* (KEK 10; Göttingen: Vandenhoeck & Ruprecht, 1909), 32–49.

[9] J. E. Frame, *A Critical and Exegetical Commentary on the Epistles of St. Paul to the Thessalonians* (ICC; New York: C. Scribner's Sons, 1912), 28–39 on language, 39–54 on authenticity.

[10] M. Dibelius, *An die Thessalonicher I, II, An die Philipper* (3d ed.; HNT 11; Tübingen: Mohr Siebeck, 1937), 57–8.

[11] W. Neil, *The Epistle of Paul to the Thessalonians* (MNTC; London: Hodder & Stoughton, 1950).

[12] D. E. H. Whiteley, *Thessalonians in the Revised Standard Version* (New Clarendon Bible; London: Oxford University Press, 1969), 11–8.

[13] E. Best, *The First and Second Epistles to the Thessalonians* (BNTC; New York: Harper & Row, 1972), 37–59. The commentaries of G. Wohlenberg, *Der erste und zweite Thessalonicherbrief* (2d ed.; Kommentar zum Neuen Testament 12; Leipzig: A. Deichert, 1909); A. Oepke, "Die Briefe an die Thessalonicher," in *Die kleineren Briefe des Apostels Paulus* (9th ed.; ed. idem; NTD 8; Göttingen: Vandenhoeck & Ruprecht, 1962); L. Morris, *The First and Second Epistles to the Thessalonians* (NICNT; Grand Rapids, Mich.: Eerdmans, 1959); A. L. Moore, *1 and 2 Thessalonians* (NCB; London: Nelson, 1969), contributed little or nothing original to the discussion of authenticity.

[14] J. Moffatt, *An Introduction to the Literature of the New Testament* (3d ed.; Edinburgh: Clark, 1918), 76–82.

[15] P. Feine, *Einleitung in das Neue Testament* (11th ed.; ed. J. Behm; Heidelberg: Quelle & Meyer, 1956), 134–39.

Charles Williams,[16] Alfred Wikenhauser,[17] Wilhelm Michaelis,[18] Willi Marxsen,[19] and Werner Kümmel.[20] All of the above, but for Marxsen, decide for the authenticity of Second Thessalonians, usually with some hesitation.

The third stage in the study of the authorship of Second Thessalonians was introduced by the work of Wolfgang Trilling in 1972. His *Untersuchungen zum zweiten Thessalonicherbrief* reviewed the entire history of research since Schmidt.[21] He then examined the style of the letter, did a form-critical analysis, and considered the theological character of the letter to conclude that the vocabulary is in general Pauline, but the style and rhetoric of the letter, and all other factors point to non-Pauline authorship. He has since become the first to write a major commentary on the letter based on the theory of non-Pauline origins[22] and has summed up both works in a recent article drawing conclusions for early church history.[23] His work has had significant influence. Gerhard Krodel[24] fundamentally accepts and expands his conclusions in his recent *Proclamation Commentary*, while Helmut Koester finds his early convictions about the date and

---

[16] A. H. McNeile, *An Introduction to the Study of the New Testament* (2d ed.; rev. C. S. C. Williams; Oxford: Clarendon Press, 1953), 131–32.

[17] A. Wikenhauser, *New Testament Introduction* (trans. Joseph Cunningham; New York: Herder & Herder, 1958), 368–72.

[18] W. Michaelis, *Einleitung in das Neue Testament: Die Entstehung, Sammlung und Überlieferung der Schriften des Neuen Testaments* (3d ed.; Bern: Berchtold Haller, 1961), 230–31.

[19] W. Marxsen, *Introduction to the New Testament: An Approach to its Problems* (trans. G. Buswell; Philadelphia: Fortress Press, 1968), 37–44.

[20] W. G. Kümmel, *Introduction to the New Testament* (rev. ed.; trans. H. Clark Kee; Nashville: Abingdon Press, 1975), 265–69. The mention of New Testament Introductions could be endless, if one sought to be absolutely complete. D. Guthrie, *New Testament Introduction: The Pauline Epistles* (Chicago: InterVarsity Press, 1961), 184–94, also argues for authenticity, as does R. H. Fuller, *A Critical Introduction to the New Testament* (Studies in Theology 55; London: G. Duckworth, 1966), 57–9. E. Lohse, *The Formation of the New Testament* (ed. M. E. Boring; Nashville: Abingdon, 1981), 85–7, is one of the few who argues against authenticity. There were scattered smaller journal articles in this period.

[21] Trilling, *Untersuchungen zum zweiten Thessalonicherbrief* (see n. 2).

[22] Idem, *Der zweite Brief an die Thessalonicher* (EKKNT 14; Zürich: Benziger Verlag, 1980).

[23] Idem, "Literarische Paulusimitation im 2. Thessalonicherbrief," in *Paulus in den neutestamentlichen Spätschriften: Zur Paulusrezeption im Neuen Testament* (ed. K. Kertelge; Freiburg i. Brsg.: Herder, 1981), 146–56 (146–51).

[24] G. Krodel, "2 Thessalonians," in *Ephesians, Colossians, 2 Thessalonians, the Pastoral Epistles* (ed. idem; Proclamation Commentaries; Philadelphia: Fortress Press, 1978), 73–96.

provenance of Second Thessalonians[25] supported, as his recent New Testament Introduction suggests.[26] Andreas Lindemann[27] and John Bailey[28] both argue in similar fashions (though Bailey makes no reference to Trilling's work), while the most recent English commentaries of Frederick Fyvie Bruce[29] and I. Howard Marshall[30] show that any defense of authenticity must now take Trilling into account. In short, the question of the authorship of the letter is once again opened.

The Thessalonians Seminar of SBL has posed the question of the authorship of Second Thessalonians in a unique fashion. After studying First Thessalonians for five years, the members decided to ask the question: What effect does our discussion of the first letter have on our understanding of the second? Has it highlighted the difference between the two even more? Or is our analysis of the relation between the two tilted more in favor of the authenticity of the second through our examination of the first?

This paper defends the thesis that our study makes the maintenance of the authenticity more difficult. The argument will survey the results of the last two centuries of work on the question and then seek to correlate that with the results of our seminar. There will probably be little that is new in the survey. But that is to be expected in a matter which has had two scholars of the competency of Wrede and Trilling treat the matter in depth.

1. The Problem Raised: Linguistic Data

1.1 Vocabulary Data

1. No certain conclusions can be gained on the basis of *hapax legomena*. There are only ten of them in Second Thessalonians: ἀτακτεῖν (3:7), ἀτάκτως (3:6, 11), ἐγκαυχᾶσθαι (1:4), ἔνδειγμα (1:5), ἐνδοξάζεσθαι

---

[25] H. Koester, "ΓΝΩΜΑΙ ΔΙΑΦΟΡΟΙ: The Origin and Nature of Diversification in the History of Early Christianity," *HTR* 58/3 (1965): 279–318; repr.: *Trajectories Through Early Christianity* (eds. J. M. Robinson and idem; Philadelphia: Fortress Press, 1971), 114–57. The specific reference is to pages 153–54 in the latter publication.

[26] Idem, *History and Literature of Early Christianity* (Introduction to the New Testament 2; Philadelphia: Fortress Press, 1982), 241–46.

[27] A. Lindemann, "Zum Abfassungszweck des Zweiten Thessalonicherbriefes," *ZNW* 68 (1977): 35–47 (35 n. 4, et passim).

[28] J. A. Bailey, "Who Wrote II Thessalonians?" *NTS* 25 (1978–79): 131–45.

[29] F. F. Bruce, *1 & 2 Thessalonians* (WBC 45; Waco, Tex.: Word Books, 1982), xxxii–xliii. Bruce curiously lists Trilling's works in his bibliography, but does not mention them in his discussion of the authenticity of 2 Thess.

[30] I. H. Marshall, *1 and 2 Thessalonians* (NCB; Grand Rapids, Mich.: Eerdmans, 1983), 23–45. Marshall devotes pages 29–40 to an examination of Trilling's work, an indication of its importance.

(1:10), καλοποιεῖν (3:13), περιεργάζεσθαι (3:11), σημειοῦσθαι (3:14), τίνειν (1:9), and ὑπεραυξάνειν (1:3).[31] Not much can be made of this. As Milligan points out, five of the terms occur in the Septuagint; none of the others is that unusual.

2. The list of terms that are in Second Thessalonians and are Pauline *hapax legomena*, i.e., elsewhere in the New Testament, but not in Paul, is perhaps more significant. The terms, together with the books of the New Testament in which they are found, follows: ἀναιρεῖν (Matt – 1x, Luke – 2x, Acts – 19x, Heb – 1x), ἀποστασία (Acts – 1x), ἄτοπος (Luke – 1x, Acts – 2x), δίκη (Acts – 1x, Jude – 1x), ἐπισυναγωγή (Heb – 1x), θροεῖσθαι (Matt – 1x, Mark – 1x), καταξιοῦσθαι (Luke – 1x, Acts – 1x), μιμεῖσθαι (Heb – 1x, 3 John – 1x), σαλεύειν (Matt – 2x, Mark – 1x, Luke – 4x, Acts – 4x, Heb – 3x), σέβασμα (Acts – 1x), φλόξ (Luke – 1x, Acts – 1x, Heb – 1x, Rev – 3x). To these should be added the words that occur in Ephesians and the Pastorals (deutero-Pauline): ἀξιοῦν (1 Tim – 1x, Heb – 2x), ἐπιφανεία (Pastorals – 5x), ἡσυχία (Acts – 1x, 1 Tim – 2x), κρίσις (Matt – 12x, Luke – 4x, John – 11x, Acts – 1x, 1 Tim – 1x, Heb – 2x, Jas – 3x, 2 Pet – 4x, 1 John – 1x, Jude – 3x, Rev – 4x), μήτε (1 Tim – 2x). Bornemann's[32] suggestion that the language of Second Thessalonians has close affinity to that of Luke-Acts (especially, says Bornemann, to Acts 20:17–35) seems to have some validity.

3. There is finally a list of terms which do not appear in Second Thessalonians, but appear in all, or almost all, other Pauline letters (excluding the Pastorals).[33] The terms are not of equal significance. Particularly striking are prepositions and particles, whose occurrence would not be affected by subject matter: ἀγαπητός (not in Gal), αἰών (not in 1 Thess), ἁμαρτία (not in Phil), ἄν (not in Eph, Col, 1 Thess), ἀνήρ (not in Phil, 1 Thess), ἀποθνῄσκειν (not in Eph), ἀπόστολος, γινώσκειν, γνωρίζειν (not in 1 Thess), ἐγείρειν, ἐγώ, ἔθνος (not in Phil), ζητεῖν (not in Eph), καλός, κηρύσσειν (not in Eph), λαλεῖν (not in Gal), μᾶλλον (not in Col), μέν, νεκρός, πολύς, σύν, σῶμα, τέκνον, τίς (interrogative). Especially significant terms are underscored. (This listing should, of course, be balanced by a list of terms used with absolutely expected consistency, etc., δέ, διά, καρδία, κατά, κύριος, etc.) It is striking that ἄν does not occur even

---

[31] K. Aland et al., *Spezialübersichten* (vol. II of *Vollständige Konkordanz zum griechischen Neuen Testament*; Berlin/New York: De Gruyter, 1978), 456. Cf. also Milligan, *St Paul's Epistles to the Thessalonians* (see n. 1), liii, and Frame, *A Critical and Exegetical Commentary on the Epistles of St. Paul to the Thessalonians* (see n. 9), 30.

[32] Bornemann, *Die Thessalonicher-Briefe* (see n. 2), 471; cf. Milligan, ibid., liii–liv.

[33] I drew up the list here and in I.A.2 on the basis of a rapid reading of the frequency lists in Aland et al., *Spezialübersichten* (see n. 31), 2–305. A significant item or two may have been overlooked.

where one expects it, after ἕως in 2 Thess 2:7 (it does appear in 1 Cor 4:5, but is similarly absent in 1 Tim 4:13).

4. There are only two words that Second Thessalonians shares with First Thessalonians that are unique in the Pauline corpus: Θεσσαλονικεύς (1 Thess 1:1, 2 Thess 1:1, the only times Paul uses the term for an inhabitant of a city rather than the city name itself) and κατευθύνειν (1 Thess 3:11, 2 Thess 3:5). The similarity in the use of the proper noun is more striking than the other usage.

5. Can any conclusions be drawn from all this? Nothing definite! Ernst von Dobschütz comments that the list of *hapax legomena* is a good proof of the "Wert der Hapaxerei,"[34] citing Eduard Reuss's pun on the *Hexerei*. The list of unique terms in Paul suggests that one should check out an affinity with possibly later New Testament works (Luke-Acts, Heb, Eph). The non-occurrence of a few key terms at least raises the question of variation from Pauline usage. More than that cannot be said. (Grayston and Herdan,[35] who use statistical linguistics, suggest that the vocabulary of both First and Second Thessalonians is Pauline, with fewer *hapax legomena* than one would expect [expect ninety and find only fifty eight]. They also suggest that their study implies that too many words and phrases in the two letters are the same to preclude some kind of relationship; one letter must be based on the other. Their study does not suggest which is prior).

1.2 Pauline Terms in a Non-Pauline Sense

A number of terms frequent in Paul seem to be used in Second Thessalonians in an unusual, though not necessarily impossible, sense for Paul. We list a sample of them. At times they are also of theological significance. θλῖψις in 2 Thess 1:4–6 is viewed as the basis for retribution of the persecutors; in 2 Thess 1:6–10 it is used to confirm the election of the Thessalonians.[36] In 2 Thess 1:5 the βασιλεία τοῦ θεοῦ is viewed as something future; in Rom 14:17, 1 Cor 4:20, 1 Thess 2:12 it is something present (though in the phrase "inherit the kingdom," one can make a case for a future ideas; cf. 1 Cor 6:9, 10; 15:50 [15:24 is obscure]; Gal 5:21).[37] ἀποκάλυψις in 2 Thess 1:7 is used of the parousia of Jesus; only 1 Cor 1:7 is close to this. Elsewhere the term is used of the revelation of the wrath of

---

[34] Von Dobschütz, *Die Thessalonicher-Briefe* (see n. 8), 39.

[35] K. Grayston and G. Herdan, "The Authorship of the Pastorals in the Light of Statistical Linguistics," *NTS* 6 (1959–60): 1–15.

[36] Koester, *History and Literature of Early Christianity* (see n. 26), 244.

[37] H. Braun, "Zur nachpaulinischen Herkunft des zweiten Thessalonicherbriefes," *ZNW* 44 (1952/53): 152–56 (152–53).

God (Rom 2:5) or of the revelation of some specific item (1 Cor 14:6, 20; Gal 1:12; 2:2) or of some form of mystical experience (2 Cor 12:1, 7). In 2 Thess 1:11 κλῆσις apparently has a future orientation (in the light of the preceding verses), while "call" in 1 Thess 4:7 refers to the life which the Christian lives in the world.[38] The ties to baptism and the proclamation of the Gospel present in Gal 1:6, 15; 5:13; 1 Cor 1:26; 7:20 are absent in Second Thessalonians. Nor is it tied to the use of charismata in the present life, as in Rom 11:29. In 2 Thess 2:14 the writer speaks of the δόξα of our Lord Jesus Christ (cf. also 1:10, 12). Elsewhere it is God who has δόξα (Rom 1:23; 3:7, 23; 4:20; 5:2; 6:4; 1 Cor 10:31, etc.). The closest Paul comes to speaking of Christ's or Jesus' glory is when he speaks of Jesus reflecting the glory of God (2 Cor 3:18, 4:4 interpreted in 4:6). First Thessalonians is in the Pauline tradition when it speaks of "his kingdom and glory" (2:12). At this point Second Thessalonians diverges from the major Pauline emphasis.[39] In 2 Thess 2:17 and 3:3 στηρίζω is used of being set in every good work and word, while 1 Thess 3:2 and 13 uses it of establishment concerning the faith and in sanctification before God at the parousia. Second Thessalonians sounds more prosaically ethical. That impression is confirmed by the contrast in the use of στήκω: in 1 Thess 3:8 the Thessalonians are described as standing ἐν κυρίῳ, while in 2 Thess 2:15 the term is set parallel to "holding on to the traditions." These terms are of varying theological significance; they suggest a somewhat different orientation regarding eschatology and Christology than one finds in the major Pauline letters. Of course, here too the old saw applies: μία χέλιδων ἔαρ οὐ ποιεῖ. How many swallows does it take?[40]

1.3 Peculiar Phraseology

Frame presents an extensive list (though not exhaustive) of phrases and turns of thought. He regards them as "more significant" than the examination of isolated words.[41] Trilling reproduces these lists in a more convenient format.[42] They are given below:

---

[38] Wrede, *Die Echtheit des zweiten Thessalonicherbriefs* (see n. 5), 75.

[39] Holtzmann, "Zum zweiten Thessalonicherbrief" (see n. 4), 102.

[40] Cf. John C. Hurd's proposal about quantifying scholarship's arguments in his paper to the Seminar in 1979, "Certain Uncertain Certainties in New Testament Studies," 4–6. I look forward to learning more about this from his paper for this session.

[41] Frame, *A Critical and Exegetical Commentary on the Epistles of St. Paul to the Thessalonians* (see n. 9), 32–4; Rigaux, *Les Épîtres aux Thessaloniciens* (see n. 2), 85–7, largely reproduces Frame's lists.

[42] Trilling, *Untersuchungen zum zweiten Thessalonicherbrief* (see n. 2), 49–50.

(a) Phrases in Second Thessalonians, but not elsewhere in NT

διδόναι ἐκδίκησις τινι 1:8
ἐκ μέσου γίνεσθαι 2:7
ἐν παντὶ τρόπῳ 3:16 (cf. Phil 1:18)
εὐδοκεῖν τινι 2:12 (LXX)
εὐχαριστεῖν ὀφείλομεν 1:3; 2:13
ἡγεῖσθαι ὡς 3:15 (LXX)
στηρίζειν καὶ φυλάσσειν 3:3
τίνειν δίκην 1:9 (classics)
ἀπάτη ἀδικίας 2:10
ἄτοπος καὶ πονηρός 3:2
ἐνέργεια πλάνης 2:11
κατευθύνειν τὰς καρδίας 3:5 (LXX)
περιπατεῖν ἀτάκτως 3:6, 11
πιστεύειν τῇ ἀληθείᾳ 2:12
πιστεύειν τῷ ψεύδει 2:11
πίστις ἀληθείας 2:13 (cf. Phil 1:27)
σαλευθῆναι ἀπὸ τοῦ νοός 2:2

(b) The influence of apocalyptic may be felt in

ἀγγέλων δυνάμεως 1:7
ἀνελεῖ τῷ πνεύματι τοῦ στόματος 2:8 (LXX)
ὁ ἄνθρωπος τῆς ἀνομίας 2:3
ὁ ἀντικείμενος κτλ 2:4 (LXX)
ἀπὸ τῆς δόξης τῆς ἰσχύος 1:9 (LXX)
ἡ ἐπιφάνεια τῆς παρουσίας 2:8
ὁ κατέχων ἄρτι 2:7
τὸ κατέχον 2:6
τὸ μυστήριον τῆς ἀνομίας 2:7
ὄλεθρος αἰώνιος 1:9
ὅταν ἔλθῃ 1:10 (LXX)

(c) The following may have been coined by Paul

ἡ ἀγάπη τῆς ἀληθείας 2:10
ἐλπίς ἀγαθή 2:16
εὐδοκία ἀγαθωσύνης 1:11
τὸ μαρτύριον ἡμῶν 1:10 (cf. 2:14)
παράκλησις αἰωνία 2:16
τρέχειν καὶ δοξάζεσθαι 3:1
ἡ ὑπομονὴ τοῦ Χριστοῦ 3:5

(d) The following have a distinctively Pauline flavor

ἐν θεῷ πατρὶ ἡμῶν 1:1
τὸ εὐαγγέλιον τοῦ κυρίου ἡμῶν Ἰησοῦ 1:8
ὁ θεὸς ὁ πατὴρ ἡμῶν 2:16
ὁ κύριος τῆς εἰρήνης 3:16 (cf. I.5:23)
πιστὸς δέ ἐστιν ὁ κύριος 3:2

A number of comments can be made. It is surprising that more of these phrases are not to be found in the Septuagint. The writer is capable of using familiar words in unfamiliar ways. Frame is probably correct in his suggestion that the terms in list (d) have a Pauline ring, though we shall see later that some of them are nevertheless unlikely for Paul. The list in (a) has few linguistic impossibilities for Paul; εὐχαριστεῖν ὀφείλομεν (2 Thess 1:3, 2:13) is one that will get our attention. Trilling[43] points out that the heading given to list (b) suggests that the subject matter (apoca-

---

[43] Ibid., 50.

lyptic) accounts for the language by itself; he suggests that other factors (figures of speech, σχήματα λέξεως, especially the recurrent parallelism, and the frequent plerophoria)[44] also play a role and may therefore give a broader base for understanding the linguistic peculiarities in these expressions. The hesitancy in the title to list (c) suggests that these expressions are truly singular in the Pauline corpus and deserve close attention. But, as in the case of the vocabulary stock, a consideration of idiomatic expressions, singular phraseology, and turns of thought by itself cannot decide questions of authorship.

1.4 The Style and Rhetoric of Second Thessalonians

Johannes Weiß[45] years ago called for the use of rhetorical analysis as a tool in deciding questions of authorship:

The question of authenticity is all too often decided on the basis of biblical-theological and linguistic, that is word-statistical data and one has not asked often enough about the undoubtedly critical passages whether Paul, whose emphases and rhythm we ought to know quite precisely, is speaking.[46]

Weiß made a major contribution with his study of Paul's rhetoric, concentrating on the use of parallelism (especially antithetic parallelism in Hebraistic mode and aspects of the artistic Greek rhetorical parallelism), and applying his findings to the interpretation of Romans. He makes little use of First and Second Thessalonians. He sums up Paul's style as follows:[47]

---

[44] See below.

[45] J. Weiß, "Beiträge zur Paulinischen Rhetorik," in *Theologische Studien: Herrn wirkl. Oberkonsistorialrath Professor D. Bernhard Weiss zu seinem 70. Geburtstage dargebracht* (eds. C. R. Gregory et al.: Göttingen: Vandenhoeck & Ruprecht, 1897), 165–247.

[46] Ibid., 166, "Die Echtheitsfragen sind oft allzusehr nur nach biblischtheologischen und sprachlichen d.h. wörterstatistischen Gesichtspunkten entschieden worden und nicht genug hat man gefragt, ob in den kritisch zweifelhaften Stücken Paulus redet, dessen Diktion, dessen Tonfall und Rhythmus wir doch eigentlich ganz genau kennen sollten."

[47] Ibid., 167, "Es ist anerkannt, dass Paulus nicht periodisch schreibt. Man braucht nur den Hebräerbrief zu vergleichen, den auch Blass zur eigentlichen Kunstprosa rechnet, und man wird den Unterschied merken. Das Grundelement der Rede des Apostels ist der einzelne kurze Satz, der nur selten mit anderen zu einer größeren, wirklichen Periode verbunden wird. Die Regel ist entweder das asyndetische Nebeneinander, das namentlich in der lebhaften Rede sehr häufig ist oder die lockere Anreihung durch Copula, antithetische oder vergleichende Partikeln. Appositionen, oft mit Participiis conjunctis, sehr selten mit absoluten Genitiven. Zur anreihenden, nicht periodisierten Rede gehören auch die Sätze mit ὅτι, ἵνα, ὅπως, ὥστε, etc., wenn, was fast immer der Fall ist, der Hauptsatz sie nicht periodisierend umklammert und so zu einem runden Schluss führt ... Aber was dem Paulus so an Kunstprosa fehlt, ersetzt er, wenigstens in den sorgfältiger geschriebenen

It is generally recognized that Paul does not write in periodic style. One only has to compare the Letter to the Hebrews, which Blass also counts as using truly artistic prose, and one will note the difference. The basic element of the apostle's speech is the individual, short sentence, which only rarely is united with another into a larger, authentic period. The normal rule is either placing sentences next to each asyndetically, which happens very often in lively speech or the simple ordering via the copula, antithetical or comparative particles. Appositions, often with conjunctive particles, rarely with genitive absolutes. The sentences with ὅτι, ἵνα, ὅπως, ὥστε, etc. also belong to to parallel, not periodic speech, since (what is almost always the case) the major clause does not surround it in periodic style and thus lead to a rounding off conclusion. ... Still, what Paul lacks in artistic prose, he replaces, at least in the carefully written letters, with a certain rhetorical movement, which works decidedly impressive and often through symmetry, rhythm, emotion and oral effect in a not inartistic manner. It is the oral type of the Cynic-Stoic diatribe.

Weiß was followed by Paul Wendland,[48] Rudolf Bultmann,[49] and Eduard Norden,[50] who examined Paul's rhetoric in the light of the diatribe style (Wendland and Bultmann) and the conventions of ancient rhetoric (Norden). Their work remains largely definitive yet today, since few have mastered ancient rhetoric and applied it to the study of the New Testament.

1. First Thessalonians is well described by Weiß in the extract above; but Second Thessalonians breaks the description at several points. First Thessalonians has many short sentences. Longer sentences (e.g., 1 Thess 1:6, 7) often make use of ὥστε (1 Thess 1:7, 8; 4:18). Adverbial participles are frequent, e.g., 1 Thess 1:2–4. Comparisons are drawn or prior knowledge appealed to by the term καθώς (13 times). Picture language is used

---

Briefen, durch eine gewisse rhetorische Bewegung, die entschieden packend und häufig durch Symmetrie, Rhythmus, Schwung und Vollklang nicht unkünstlerisch wirkt. Es ist die rednerische Art der kynisch-stoischen Diatribe." Not every long sentence in Greek is a period. For the understanding of the Greek period cf. Aristotle, *Rhet.* 3.9, Demetrius, *Eloc.* 10–18; for the different kinds of periods, l. c. 19–21. The classic summary of ancient rhetoric for this period is R. Volkmann, *Rhetorik der Griechen und Römer in Systematischer Übersicht* (2d ed.; Leipzig: B. G. Teubner, 1885). Paul's style according to Dionysius' canons would fall between λέξις διαλελυμένη and the περίοδος διαλογική; cf. Demetrius, *Eloc.* 21. Cf. also E. Norden, *Die antike Kunstprosa vom VI. Jahrhundert v. Chr. bis in die Zeit der Renaissance* (2 vols.; Leipzig/Berlin: B. G. Teubner, 1915–18), 1:42 n. 2 et passim.

[48] P. Wendland, *Die hellenistisch-römische Kultur in ihren Beziehungen zu Judentum und Christentum: Die urchristlichen Literaturformen* (2d & 3d ed.; HNT 2; Tübingen: Mohr Siebeck, 1912), 75–81, 342–58.

[49] R. Bultmann, *Der Stil der paulinischen Predigt und die kynisch-stoische Diatribe* (FRLANT 13; Göttingen: Vandenhoeck & Ruprecht, 1910). Note also the generative study of P. Wendland, "Philo und die kynisch-stoische Diatribe," in *Beiträge zur Geschichte der griechischen Philosophie und Religion* (eds. idem and O. Kern; Berlin: Reimer, 1895), 2–75.

[50] Norden, *Die antike Kunstprosa* (see n. 47), 2:498–510.

from everyday life, the contest (ἀγών, 2:2), the wet nurse at home (2:7), the father with his children (2:11, 12), the wriggling of a dog (σαίνεσθαι, 3:2). There is frequent reference to the readers, addressed directly. There is relatively little use of the Old Testament. The style is colloquial, familiar, and similar to that of other Pauline letters. (It does not make extensive use of the rhetorical question; 2:19 is the only example.)

Second Thessalonians contrasts strongly; there is almost nothing of the diatribe about it. It makes sparing use of picture language. Rigaux[51] lists a long series for First Thessalonians, but finds only two pictures in the second letter: ἄνεσις (rest) in 2 Thess 1:6 and the verb τρέχειν of the word of the Lord in 3:2. Trilling[52] comments that this fact is "ohne Zweifel ein Indiz für die Unechtheit."

Second Thessalonians has longer sentences. Von Dobschütz[53] describes the manner of composition of the long sentences as "kettenartige Verknüpfung," referring to the way in which the long sentence in 2 Thess 1:3–12 is put together. (Holtzmann[54] calls this sentence "ein Ungetüm von Satzbildung" and points out that the style is close to that of Second Peter.) In contrast to First Thessalonians, the second letter makes little use of comparisons (καθώς only twice, 1:3, 3:1), of γάρ (23 times in 1 Thess, only five in 2 Thess), of ὥστε (1:4, 2:4). Where First Thessalonians frequently uses participial constructions, Second Thessalonians uses more frequent relative clauses. Where First Thessalonians uses περί (8x), Second Thessalonians prefers ὑπέρ (1:4, 6; 2:1).

The difference in the length of sentences is nowhere more strikingly clear than in a comparison of the parenetic sections in the two letters. 1 Thess 4:7–10 is really a series of short sentences joined by conjunctions. The same is true of 1 Thess 5:1–11. The short sentences in 1 Thess 5:16–22 are each indented as a separate paragraph in Aland's 26th edition. Second Thessalonians appears different; there are only two short sentences in the parenetic section (2 Thess 3:2b, 17)[55]—and only two short parenetic imperatives (2:15, 3:14) to balance the series in 1 Thess 5:16–22.

2. The sentences are also different in structure. 1 Thess is largely run-on sentences. It correlates well with Weiß's description of diatribe style. What von Dobschütz called the "kettenartige Verknüpfung" is caused by what

---

[51] Rigaux, *Les Épîtres aux Thessaloniciens* (see n. 2), 90.

[52] Trilling, *Untersuchungen zum zweiten Thessalonicherbrief* (see n. 2), 56.

[53] Von Dobschütz, *Die Thessalonicher-Briefe* (see n. 8), 42, following Bornemann, *Die Thessalonicher-Briefe* (see n. 2), 328. Moffatt, *An Introduction to the Literature of the New Testament* (see n. 14), 79, and Rigaux, ibid., 93, say similar things.

[54] Holtzmann, "Zum zweiten Thessalonicherbrief" (see n. 4), 98.

[55] Trilling, *Untersuchungen zum zweiten Thessalonicherbrief* (see n. 2), 64.

Trilling calls a "poverty of expression."[56] Terms are repeated soon after their introduction, or related stems occur soon. Trilling's list is extensive and can simply be reproduced here (from pages 62, 63):

θεὸς πατὴρ ἡμῶν καὶ κύριος Ἰ. Χρ. 1,2–2 (cfr. θεὸς ἡμῶν καὶ κύριος Ἰ. Χρ. 1,12 und ὁ κύριος ἡμῶν Ἰ. Χρ. καὶ θεὸς ὁ πατὴρ ἡμῶν 2,16); εὐχαριστεῖν ὀφείλομεν τῷ θεῷ πάντοτε περὶ ὑμῶν 1,3; 2,13; θλίψις, θλίβοντες, θλιβόμενοι 1,4.6.6.6; ἀποκάλυψις 1,7; 2,3.6.8; ὑπακούω 1,8; 3,14; ἐνδοξάζω 1,10.12; δοξάζειν 3,1; δόξα 1,9; 2,14; πιστεύω, πίστις, πιστός 1,4.10.10.11; 2,11.12.13; 3,2.3; ἡμέρα 1,10; 2,2; προσεύχεσθαι 1,11; 3,1; ἀξιόω, καταξιόω 1,5.11; κλῆσις, καλεῖν 1,11; 2,14; εὐδοκία, εὐδοκεῖν 1,11; 2,12; ἔργον, ἐργάζεσθαι, περιεργάζεσθαι 1,11; 2,17; 3,8.10.11.12; δύναμις 1,7.11; 2,9; ὄνομα 1,12; 3,6; χάρις 1,2.12; 2,16; 3,18; παρουσία 2,1.8.9; πνεῦμα 2,2.8.13; λόγος 2,2.15.17; 3,1.14; ἐπιστολή 2,2.15; 3,14.17; ἐξαπατᾶν, ἀπάτη 2,1.10; ἀνομία, ἄνομος 2,3.7.8; κατέχω 2,6.7; ἐνέργεια 2,7.11; ψεῦδος 2,9.11; ἀδικία 2,10.12; ἀγάπη 1,3; 2,10.13.16; ἀλήθεια 2,10.12.13; κρίσις 1,5; 2,12; εὐαγγέλιον 1,8; 2,14; παραδόσις 2,15; 3,6; παράκλησις, παρακαλεῖν 2,16.17; 3,12; καρδία 2,17; 3,5; στηρίζω 2,17; 3,3; πᾶς, πάντες, πάντοτε, διὰ παντός 1,3.4.10; 2,9.17; 3,2.6.16.16. 16.17.18; 1,3.11; 2,13; παραγγέλλω 3,4.6.10.12; ποιεῖν 3,4.4; οἶδα 2,6; 3,7; ἀτάκτως, ἀτακτεῖν 3.6.7.11; περιπατεῖν 3,6.11; μιμεῖσθαι 3,7.9; εἰρήνη 1,3; 3,16.16; ἄρτον φαγεῖν, ἐσθίειν 3,8.12. cfr. 10.

The repetition runs throughout the letter. It is clearly a stylistic peculiarity of the author. Paul can, of course, also use such a device. 1 Cor 13:4 uses ἡ ἀγάπη frequently, while 1 Cor 13:7 does the same with πάντα. But these are examples of anaphora. It is quite different in tone and effect.

3. Weiß called attention to the significance of parallelism in the study of Paul's style.[57] He distinguished three forms of "hebraizing" parallelism: synonymous, synthetic, and antithetic. The last, he says, is "unendlich viel häufiger ... bei Paulus."[58] Trilling's list of antithetical statements in Second Thessalonians follows:[59]

ὑπεραυξάνει ἡ πίστις ὑμῶν καὶ πλεονάζει ἡ ἀγάπη ἑνὸς κτλ	(1:3)
ἀνταποδοῦναι τοῖς θλίβουσιν ὑμᾶς θλῖψιν καὶ ὑμῖν τοῖς θλιβομένοις ἄνεσιν μεθ' ἡμῶν	(1:6–7)
τοῖς μὴ εἰδόσιν θεὸν καὶ τοῖς μὴ ὑπακούουσιν τῷ εὐαγγελίῳ κτλ	(1:8)
ἀπὸ προσώπου τοῦ κυρίου καὶ ἀπὸ τῆς δόξης τῆς ἰσχύος αὐτοῦ	(1:9)

---

[56] Ibid., 62. Wendland, *Die urchristlichen Literaturformen* (see n. 48), 359, observed earlier: "Dieses Gedankenarmut zeugende Verfahren kann ich Paulus nicht zutrauen."

[57] Weiß, "Beiträge zur Paulinischen Rhetorik" (see n. 45), 168–84.

[58] Ibid., 174. Cf. Bultmann, *Der Stil der paulinischen Predigt und die kynisch-stoische Diatribe* (see n. 49), 76–81 (79).

[59] Trilling, *Untersuchungen zum zweiten Thessalonicherbrief* (see n. 2), 52–3; Krodel, "2 Thessalonians" (see n. 24), 82–3.

(ὅταν ἔλθῃ) ἐνδοξασθῆναι ἐν τοῖς ἁγίοις αὐτοῦ καὶ θαυμασθῆναι ἐν πᾶσιν τοῖς πιστεύσασιν	(1:10)
ἵνα ὑμᾶς ἀξιώσῃ τῆς κλήσεως ὁ θεὸς ἡμῶν καὶ πληρώσῃ πᾶσαν εὐδοκίαν ἀγαθωσύνης κτλ	(1:11)
Ἰησοῦ ἐν ὑμῖν, καὶ ὑμεῖς ἐν αὐτῷ	(1:12)
ὑπὲρ τῆς παρουσίας ... Ἰησοῦ Χριστοῦ καὶ ἡμῶν ἐπισυναγωγῆς ἐπ' αὐτόν	(2:1)
ὅτι ἐὰν μὴ ἔλθῃ ἡ ἀποστασία πρῶτον καὶ ἀποκαλυφθῇ ὁ ἄνθρωπος τῆς ἀνομίας	(2:3)
ὃν ὁ κύριος ... ἀνελεῖ τῷ πνεύματι τοῦ στόματος αὐτοῦ καὶ καταργήσει τῇ ἐπιφανείᾳ τῆς παρουσίας αὐτοῦ	(2:8)
ἐν πάσῃ δυνάμει καὶ σημείοις καὶ τέρασιν ψεύδους καὶ ἐν πάσῃ ἀπάτῃ ἀδικίας	(2:9–10a)
οἱ μὴ πιστεύσαντες τῇ ἀληθείᾳ ἀλλὰ εὐδοκήσαντες τῇ ἀδικίᾳ	(2:12)
ὁ ἀγαπήσας ἡμᾶς καὶ δοὺς παράκλησιν αἰωνίαν	(2:16)
παρακαλέσαι ὑμῶν τὰς καρδίας καὶ στηρίξαι ἐν παντὶ ἔργῳ κτλ	(2:17)
ἵνα ὁ λόγος τοῦ κυρίου τρέχῃ κτλ καὶ ἵνα ῥυσθῶμεν ἀπὸ τῶν ἀτόπων κτλ	(3:1–2)
ὃς στηρίξει ὑμᾶς καὶ φυλάξει ἀπὸ τοῦ πονηροῦ	(3:3)
ὅτι οὐκ ἠτακτήσαμεν ἐν ὑμῖν κτλ ἀλλ' ἐν κόπῳ καὶ μόχθῳ ἐργαζόμενοι κτλ	(3:7–8)
οὐχ ὅτι οὐκ ἔχομεν ἐξουσίαν ἀλλ ἵνα ἑαυτοὺς τύπον δῶμεν ὑμῖν	(3:9)

Weiß makes almost no use of the Thessalonian letters in his article. The only reference he makes to Second Thessalonians points to 3:1–2 as an example of synonymous parallelism via a doubled ἵνα.[60] (He regards this as typically Pauline, referring to Rom 7:13; Gal 3:14; 2 Cor 11:12; Phil 1:9f.; 1 Cor 9:13; and Rom 15:2, 31 as other examples.) Rigaux[61] treats parallelism very summarily, suggesting that the two letters are similar in their usage. He suggests that 1 Thess 5:15, 19–20, and 2 Thess 1:8, 10, 11; 3:1 are the best short examples.

---

[60] Weiß, "Beiträge zur Paulinischen Rhetorik" (see n. 45), 171.
[61] Rigaux, *Les Épîtres aux Thessaloniciens* (see n. 2), 88. The two examples from First Thessalonians occur as part of a parenetic chain and so are probably not germane.

Trilling's list is thus a great advance over all earlier investigations, as Krodel recognizes. It makes clear, as Trilling says, that parallelism is one of the key stylistic features of the letter. It is primarily synonymous parallelism, more rarely synthetic, almost never antithetic. It thus runs contrary to the conclusion of Weiß about Pauline style.[62] Trilling calls attention also to the conclusion of Weiß that Paul often makes use of some Greek rhetorical devices, e.g., anaphora, parison, etc.,[63] something that Second Thessalonians does not do.

> Parallelism is also a recognized formal characteristic in Greek rhetoric and in many cases we certainly will need to think more directly on these analogies than on the biblical custom.[64]

Second Thessalonians thus uses parallelism as a mode of securing a "certain breadth and gravity of expression."[65] That character is reinforced by another characteristic of the second letter.

4. Rigaux[66] calls attention to the development of thought (by threes or twos). First Thessalonians, according to him, has sixteen such triadic groupings: 1:2–4, 3, 5; 2:5, 9, 10, 12, 14; 3:13, 16; 4:4–6, 11, 16; 5:12–13, 16–17, 23. In contrast Second Thessalonians has only four 2:2, 3–4, 9, 16. And not all of these are persuasive. 2 Thess 2:9 is certain. But 2:3, 4 is made up of two dyads, while in 2:16 ἐν χάριτι is in different grammatical relationship to the verb from παράκλησιν αἰωνίαν and ἐλπίδα ἀγαθήν.[67] In short, the triadic arrangement is almost entirely absent from Second Thessalonians. Rigaux also lists the dyads. There are seventeen in his list for First Thessalonians: 1:1; 2:2, 9 (3:10 parr.), 12; 3:2 (two dyads), 7, 12; 4:1 (two dyads), 4, 6 (two), 15, 17; 5:1, 3, 6+10, 11. In Second Thessalonians he lists 1:1, 3, 4, 8, 9, 10, 11; 2:1, 2, 4, 14, 17; 3:8, 12.[68] The difference here is less striking than in the case of the triads. Trilling[69] nevertheless argues that in the second letter "tragen jedoch gerade diese Wortgruppen zu dem feierlich-distanzierten Gepräge bei und sind im Zusammenhang mit dem für II [Thess] typischen hebraisierenden Parallelismenstil zu be-

---

[62] Trilling, *Untersuchungen zum zweiten Thessalonicherbrief* (see n. 2), 52.
[63] Ibid., 53.
[64] Weiß, "Beiträge zur Paulinischen Rhetorik" (see n. 45), 184: "Auch in der griechischen Rhetorik ist der Parallelismus eine bekannte Form und in sehr vielen Fällen werden wir sicherlich eher an diese Analogien zu denken haben, als an die biblische Gewöhnung."
[65] The expression belongs to Bornemann, *Die Thessalonicher-Briefe* (see n. 2), 463: "eine gewisse Breite und Schwerfälligkeit der Ausdrucksweise."
[66] Rigaux, *Les Épîtres aux Thessaloniciens* (see n. 2), 89.
[67] Trilling, *Untersuchungen zum zweiten Thessalonicherbrief* (see n. 2), 55.
[68] Rigaux, *Les Épîtres aux Thessaloniciens* (see n. 2), 89–90.
[69] Trilling, *Untersuchungen zum zweiten Thessalonicherbrief* (see n. 2), 55.

urteilen." Its significance can only be measured by contrasting the prevalence of dyads with the absence of triads, and by recognizing that the dyads are of a piece with the parallelism, a form of formal expression.

5. There are other marks of the style of Second Thessalonians that Trilling has isolated. Both parallelism and dyads are related to the tendency toward fullness of expression (plerophoria) that expresses itself in other ways. These include the following:

The use of compounds when a simple word would do:
ὑπεραυξάνει	(1:3)
ἐν ὑμῖν ἐγκαυχᾶσθαι	(1:4)
εἰς τὸ καταξιωθῆναι	(1:5)
ἐνδοξασθῆναι	(1:10; cf. 1:12)

These terms are all hapax legomena.[70]

The frequent use of πᾶς, πάντες, πάντοτε, ἐν παντὶ τρόπῳ:
ἑνὸς ἑκάστου πάντων ὑμῶν εἰς ἀλλήλους	(1:3)
ἐν πᾶσιν τοῖς διωγμοῖς ὑμῶν	(1:4)
ἐν πᾶσιν τοῖς πιστεύσασιν	(1:10)
κατὰ μηδένα τρόπον	(2:3)
ἐν πάσῃ δυνάμει	(2:9)
ἐν πάσῃ ἀπάτῃ	(2:10)
πάντες οἱ μὴ πιστεύσαντες	(2:12)
ἀπὸ παντὸς ἀδελφοῦ	(3:6)
διὰ παντὸς ἐν παντὶ τρόπῳ	(3:16)
ἐν πάσῃ ἐπιστολῇ	(3:17)
μετὰ πάντων ὑμῶν	(3:18; cf. 1:11; 2:4, 13, 17; 3:2)[71]

Trilling comments that the occurrences are more general and widely distributed than in Paul. Aland's statistics suggest that he is pressing the evidence a bit.[72] πᾶς occurs in Rom 71x, in 1 Cor 112x, in 2 Cor 52x, in Gal 15x, in Eph 52x, in Col 39x, in Phil 33x, in 1 Thess 18x, in 2 Thess 16x. Only over against First Thessalonians does the number appear high.

Substantive chains are also frequent:
ἀγγέλων δυνάμεως αὐτοῦ	(1:7)
ἀπὸ τῆς δόξης τῆς ἰσχύος αὐτοῦ	(1:9, LXX Citation)
εὐδοκίαν ἀγαθωσύνης	(1:11)
ἔργον πίστεως ἐν δυνάμει	(1:11)
τῷ πνεύματι τοῦ στόματος αὐτοῦ	(2:8, LXX Citation)
ἐν πάσῃ ἀπάτῃ ἀδικίας	(2:10)
ἐνέργειαν πλάνης	(2:11)

---

[70] Ibid., 58.
[71] Ibid., 58–9.
[72] Aland et al., *Spezialübersichten* (see n. 31), 214.

ἐν ἁγιασμῷ πνεύματος καὶ πίστει ἀληθείας	(2:13)
εἰς περιποίησιν δόξης	(2:14)

as are also adjectival expressions:[73]

τῆς δικαίας κρίσεως	(1:5)
ὄλεθρον αἰώνιον	(1:9)
παράκλησιν αἰωνίαν καὶ ἐλπίδα ἀγαθήν	(2:16)
ἐν λόγῳ ἀγαθῷ	(2:17)
ἀπὸ τῶν ἀτόπων καὶ πονηρῶν ἀνθρώπων	(3:2)
(cf. ἐγκακήσητε – καλοποιοῦντες)	(3:13)

Both contribute to the feeling of full, extended language, with a certain formal, official air.

There is also some hendiadys, both of verbs and nouns, the result of parallelism or the use of dyads:[74]

ὁ ἀντικείμενος καὶ ὑπεραιρόμενος	(2:4)
παραγγέλλομεν καὶ παρακαλοῦμεν	(3:12)
θεὸν ἢ σέβασμα	(2:4)
ἐν παντὶ ἔργῳ καὶ λόγῳ ἀγαθῷ	(2:17)
ἐν κόπῳ καὶ μόχθῳ νυκτὸς καὶ ἡμέρας	(3:8; cf. 1 Thess 2:9)

6. Trilling[75] also points to a series of striking phrases that may not be unique in style, but nevertheless are unusual:

εὐχαριστεῖν ὀφείλομεν	(1:2; 2:13)
τὴν ἀγάπην τῆς ἀληθείας	(2:10; cf. 2:12)
τὸ μυστήριον τῆς ἀνομίας	(2:7)
cf. ὁ ἄνθρωπος τῆς ἀνομίας	(2:3)
ὁ υἱὸς τῆς ἀπωλείας	(2:3)
ὁ κύριος τῆς εἰρήνης	(3:16)
ὑπακούει τῷ λόγῳ ἡμῶν	(3:14)
τὰς παραδόσεις ἃς ἐδιδάχθητε	(2:15)
cf. παρελάβοσαν	(3:6)

He also points out that Second Thessalonians likes words from particular stems: δόξα and δοξάζειν (1:9, 10; cf. 1:12; 2:14; 3:1), ἄξιος and ἀξιοῦν (1:3, 5, 11), the δικ* (1:5, 6, 8, 9; 2:10, 12), and the stem τασσ* (3:6, 6, 11).

7. Certain things characteristic of Paul's style are not found. Most of them are characteristic of the diatribe style. There are no parentheses. What parenesis there is deals with only one topic. There is no playing on prepositions, as there is in Gal 1:11, 12 or Rom 11:36. There are no indi-

---

[73] Trilling, *Untersuchungen zum zweiten Thessalonicherbrief* (see n. 2), 59.
[74] Ibid., 60.
[75] Wrede, *Die Echtheit des zweiten Thessalonicherbriefs* (see n. 5), 60–1.

cations of Greek initial or end rhyme, unless ἐν παντὶ ἔργῳ καὶ λόγῳ ἀγαθῷ is regarded as such (2 Thess 2:17).

1.5 Conclusions

James Moffatt[76] said that, "In parts the style resembles nothing to be met elsewhere in the letters of Paul." The letter has a certain "formality of official tinge," a "curious poverty of expression, and even a lack of point." Moffatt only echoes what almost every commentator says. There is "unleugbar eine kleine Differenz" of this letter from other Pauline letters.[77] In many respects the letter is higher and more elevated in tone, almost hymnic, and closer to Ephesians than to the other letters of Paul (von Dobschütz). Bornemann[78] sums up well:

So the letter has from beginning to end an impersonal, thematic character. It is no less a letter in the normal sense. It is an official, formal, ethical-religious communication of the apostle to his congregation, a writing that has more similarity to a prophetic speech or to a sermon than to a private letter, in spite of its letter form.

The style of the letter is of one piece, independent of Paul's normal mode of writing. It runs through the entire letter. And the linguistic, stylistic peculiarities are precisely what raise the problem of authenticity. Two solutions are possible. One must either account for Paul's variant style from the situation he faced or from the amanuensis he used,[79] or one must accept the conclusion that another mind produced the letter, *tertium non datur*. It must as firmly be stated that the linguistic data *per se* compel neither solution. They raise the question, but do not answer it.[80]

---

[76] Moffatt, *An Introduction to the Literature of the New Testament* (see n. 14), 80.

[77] Von Dobschütz, *Die Thessalonicher-Briefe* (see n. 8), 41.

[78] Trilling, *Untersuchungen zum zweiten Thessalonicherbrief* (see n. 2), 63, citing Bornemann, *Die Thessalonicher-Briefe* (see n. 2), 468: "So trägt der Brief einen durch und durch unpersönlichen, sachlichen Charakter. Er ist nichts weniger als ein Brief im gewöhnlichen Sinne. Er ist ein offizielles, feierliches, sittlich-religiöses Sendschreiben des Apostels an seine Gemeinde, ein Schreiben, das mit einer prophetischen Rede oder mit einer Predigt trotz seiner Briefform mehr Ähnlichkeit hat als mit einem Privatbrief."

[79] Moffatt, *An Introduction to the Literature of the New Testament* (see n. 14), 80, suggests that the contribution of Silvanus, a prophet, might account for the tone. He does not suggest why Silvanus' contribution should not have affected First Thessalonians in the same manner, i.e., does not account for the difference between First Thessalonians and Second Thessalonians.

[80] Trilling, *Untersuchungen zum zweiten Thessalonicherbrief* (see n. 2), 65, draws too rapid a conclusion in the summation, "II [Thess] ist ein gemessenes Lehrschreiben, thematisch eng begrenzt, in der Gedankenführung der einzelnen Teile zielstrebig fortschreitend, im Aufbau des Ganzen aber wenig geschickt, im Ausdruck manchmal umständlich gedrechselt, in Perioden (besonders 1,3–12!) und Sätzen oft mühsam geschraubt, überladen und schwerfällig—wenn auch der Stil im ganzen nicht banal oder primitiv wirkt,

2. Toward a Solution

2.1 The Argument from Structure

2.1.1 Similarity of Outline

When the two Thessalonian letters are compared, striking similarities and divergences present themselves. The first similarity is the structural similarity. Bailey[81] shows the similarity in a brief table.

	II Thess	I Thess
A. Letter Opening	1.1–12	1.1–10
1. Prescript	1.1f.	1.1
2. Thanksgiving	1.3ff.	1.2–10
B. Letter Body	2.1–16	2.1–3.13
1. Thanksgiving in the middle	2.13	2.13
2. Benediction at the end	2.16	3.11–13
C. Letter close	3.1–18	4.1–5.28
1. Paraenesis	3.1ff.	4.1–5.22
2. Peace wish	3.16	5.23f.
3. Greetings	3.17	5.26
4. Benediction	3.18	5.28

A number of items deserve comment. The two letters have strikingly common features in their structure. Both have a long thanksgiving after the prescript. In each case the prescript introduces the material that will be discussed, under a different aspect in each case, to be sure, in the letter body. The letter body is in each case interrupted by a thanksgiving and concludes with a volitive optative that expresses the request that God and the Lord Jesus do something. In each letter a parenetic section follows, followed by a prayer wish that the God (Lord) of peace would do something. Greetings and a blessing conclude each letter.

The similarities go beyond the structure. Here only the structural ones will be highlighted. The prescripts are almost verbally identical; they are the only two in the Pauline corpus in which Paul is not named as apostle. They are the only two in which the people are addressed as "inhabitants of" the city (Θεσσαλονικεῖς), and not as the church in a place or those called saints, or some such expression. No other letters have such prayers of thanks in the body of the letter. The benedictions at the end of the body

---

sondern eher gewählt, manchmal kunstvoll bis künstlich. Originaler Stil des Paulus ist das allerdings nicht. Doch möchte man eher an eine von der Sache und von dem Zweck des Schreibens bestimmte, von I [Thess] inspirierte und I [Thess] teilweise bewusst steigern wollende selbstständige literarische Leistung als an sklavische Imitation von I [Thess] denken."

[81] Bailey, "Who Wrote II Thessalonians?" (see n. 28), 133.

both have the verb στηρίζειν and ὑμῶν τὰς καρδίας as direct object—a combination nowhere else in Paul. The benedictions at the end are virtually identical.[82]

There are differences. Second Thessalonians is much shorter than First Thessalonians. The body of the letter is much smaller, though the letter opening is of a size. The eschatological material in First Thessalonians is in the parenetic section; in Second Thessalonians it is in the body of the letter. Best[83] uses this to argue that the two outlines are dissimilar, because in Second Thessalonians the main theological argument falls before the second thanksgiving, and not after it as in 1 Thess 4:13–5:11. He also objects that there are three occurrences εὐχαριστεῖν in First Thessalonians (1:3, 2:13, 3:9), but only two in Second Thessalonians (1:3, 2:13). But there are not three thanksgiving prayers. The similarity of structure remains. Best also assumes (incorrectly) that doctrine is the main concern in both letters.

2.1.2 Congruence of Language and Order (Wrede)

Bornemann[84] had already pointed out that the similarity of the two letters went beyond their structure in general. It extended, he said, "auch auf bestimmte Gedankenreihen, Satzglieder, Wendungen und Ausdrücke." He pointed to 2 Thess 1:1–2; 2:13–17, and 3:1, 3–12 to argue that the writer of the second letter knew the first letter and was dependent on it in some manner. Holtzmann[85] argued that the literary relationship of the two was the key to the solution of their interrelationship. After pointing out that 1 Thess 1:1 and 2 Thess 1:1–2 were identical (except that Second Thessalonians showed a tendency to lengthen), Holtzmann found in 2 Thess 1:3–12 a key to understanding. The prayer of thanksgiving, he argued really ended at 2 Thess 1:4. The true theme of the letter is to be found in 2 Thess 1:6–10, a passage close to Second Peter in rhetoric and thought. He concludes that basically only 2 Thess 2:2–9, 11, 12 is new in the letter (in contrast to First Thessalonians), with anticipatory material in 1:5, 6, 9, 12, and a few verses that make up the epistolary framework (2:15; 3:2, 13, 14, 17). The rest of the letter is excerpt, paraphrase, and rewriting of First Thessalonians. Holtzmann pointed in the right direction, but his article was too short to be persuasive.

Wrede provided the massive demonstration required in the long first chapter of his monograph: "Literarisches Verhältnis des 2. zum 1. Thess.-

---

[82] Ibid., 133.
[83] Best, *The First and Second Epistles to the Thessalonians* (see n. 13), 53.
[84] Bornemann, *Die Thessalonicher-Briefe* (see n. 2), 473.
[85] Holtzmann, "Zum zweiten Thessalonicherbrief" (see n. 4), 98–104.

brief."[86] His argument, though one may quibble at this or that detail, remains massively persuasive in this chapter. He first gives a rapid overview of the parallels in tabular form.[87] He concludes that the material in this table is of very different quality. Indeed, the relationship of the two letters is different from that of Jude and Second Peter or Polycarp to First Peter. Parallels comes from all over the first letter. On first glance the interrelationship appears so complex that it is opaque. At the same time, no two other Pauline letters have such massive interrelationships. In some way they must be mastered as a totality.

It is in considering the structure that Wrede finds light. Two major passages in First Thessalonians do not appear to correspond to any passage in Second Thessalonians: 1 Thess 2:1–6 and 2:7–3:10. But every paragraph of the second letter has a conceptually related section in the first. Individual points of contact in one paragraph are found in a corresponding paragraph in the other letter. He lays this out in a table:[88]

2 Thess 1:3–12	in der einen Stelle
Εὐχαριστεῖν — τῷ θεῷ πάντοτε περὶ ὑμῶν — ἡ πίστις — ἡ ἀγάπη — der Gedanke vom Rühmen v. 4 — τῆς ὑπομονῆς — πίστεως — θλίψεσιν — πᾶσιν τοῖς πιστεύσασιν (?) — προσευχόμεθα πάντοτε περὶ ὑμῶν — ἔργον πίστεως	1 Thess 1:2–8
2:15–3:5	1 Thess 3:11 (8) – 4:2
στήκετε (1 Thess 3:8) — τὰς παραδόσεις ἃς ἐδιδάχθητε (1 Thess 4:1) — αὐτὸς δὲ ὁ κύριος ἡμῶν Ἰησοῦς Χριστὸς καὶ ὁ θεὸς ὁ πατὴρ ἡμῶν — ὑμῶν τὰς καρδίας — στηρίξαι — Τὸ λοιπόν — ἃ παραγγέλλομεν — κατευθύναι — ὑμῶν τὰς καρδίας.	
3:6–12	1 Thess 4:1–12
Παραγγέλλομεν ὑμῖν, ἀδελφοί, ἐν (ὀνόματι τοῦ) κυρίου Ἰησοῦ — περιπατοῦντος — κατὰ τὴν παράδοσιν ἣν παρελάβοσαν παρ' ἡμῶν — γὰρ οἴδατε — πῶς δεῖ — παρηγγέλλομεν (praeter.) ὑμῖν — ἐργάζεσθαι — παραγγέλλομεν καὶ παρακαλοῦμεν ἐν κυρίῳ Ἰησοῦ Χριστῷ — μετὰ ἡσυχίας ἐργαζόμενοι — [τὸν] ἑαυτῶν [ἄρτον] (?)	4:3–9 kommen aber dabei nicht in Frage, also in Wahrheit: 4:1, 2, 10–12. Im Wesentlichen korrespondieren dabei 1 Thess 4:1,2 & 2 Thess 3:6–7 1 Thess 4:10–12 & 2 Thess 3:10–12
3:1–3	1 Thess 5:24–25
προσεύχεσθε, ἀδελφοί, περὶ ἡμῶν — πιστὸς δέ ἐστιν ὁ κύριος, ὅς ...	

---

[86] Wrede, *Die Echtheit des zweiten Thessalonicherbriefs* (see n. 5), 3–36.
[87] Ibid., 4–12.
[88] Ibid., 19.

Wrede points out that very precise parallels occur between the two letters. (a) The thanksgiving of the opening is picked up in each in a similar manner: καὶ ἡμεῖς in 1 Thess 2:13, ἡμεῖς δέ in 2 Thess 2:13. But in the context in Second Thessalonians the emphatic "we" draws a contrast to the preceding. It is not necessary for the verb in v. 13. The "we" should refer to those who are not going to be judged for their unbelief, but elected to salvation. The "we" that refers to Paul, Silas, and Timothy should not be so emphatically stated. It must come from 1 Thess 2:13, where it makes excellent sense.[89] The phrase αὐτὸς ὁ θεός (2 Thess, κύριος) with optative occurs in each letter twice in corresponding locations (2 Thess 2:16 = 1 Thess 3:11; 2 Thess 3:16 = 1 Thess 5:23). The phrase occurs nowhere else in Paul; the volitive optative is rare. In the first passage in each letter there is a double subject (with differing order), in the second a single subject. (c) In both letters a form of λοιπόν follows (1 Thess 4:1, 2 Thess 3:1), in precisely the same location.

Wrede next argues that a significant number of the parallels appear in the same order. He shows this with a table on pp. 24–27, reproduced below. In the tables italics indicate parallels in order.

2 Thess	1 Thess
1:1–2 Παῦλος κτλ τῇ ἐκκλησίᾳ Θεσσαλονικέων ἐν θεῷ πατρί	*1:1 Παῦλος κτλ τῇ ἐκκλησίᾳ Θεσσαλονικέων ἐν θεῷ πατρὶ*
- καὶ κυρίῳ Ἰησοῦ Χριστῷ· χάρις κτλ.	*καὶ κυρίῳ Ἰησοῦ Χριστῷ· χάρις κτλ.*
1:3 Εὐχαριστεῖν - τῷ θεῷ πάντοτε περὶ ὑμῶν - ἡ πίστις πλεονάζει ἡ ἀγάπη εἰς ἀλλήλους,	*1:2–3 Εὐχαριστοῦμεν τῷ θεῷ πάντοτε περὶ ὑμῶν - τῆς πίστεως τῆς ἀγάπης*
	3:12 πλεονάσαι τῇ ἀγάπῃ εἰς ἀλλήλους
1:4 Rühmen der Thessalonicher unter den Gemeinden.	*1:7f. Der Glaube der Thessalonicher berühmt in aller Welt.*
	2:19 στέφανος καυχήσεως ἢ οὐχὶ καὶ ὑμεῖς
ἐν ταῖς ἐκκλησίαις τοῦ θεοῦ (?)	2:14 τῶν ἐκκλησιῶν τοῦ θεοῦ (?)
τῆς ὑπομονῆς - πίστεως - διωγμοῖς - θλίψεσιν	*1:3 τῆς ὑπομονῆς*
	1:6 ἐν θλίψει
	2:14f. Verfolgungen.
1:5 εἰς τὸ καταξιωθῆναι - *τῆς βασιλείας τοῦ θεοῦ* (vgl. 1:11 ἀξιώσῃ τῆς κλήσεως)	2:12 περιπατεῖν ἀξίως τοῦ θεοῦ τοῦ καλοῦντος - *βασιλείαν*
1:7 ἐν τῇ ἀποκαλύψει τοῦ κυρίου Ἰησοῦ ἀπ' οὐρανοῦ μετ' ἀγγέλων αὐτοῦ	*3:13 ἐν τῇ παρουσίᾳ τοῦ κυρίου - Ἰησοῦ μετά - τῶν ἁγίων αὐτοῦ*
	4:16 ἀπ' οὐρανοῦ
1:8 ἐκδίκησιν - τοῖς μὴ εἰδόσιν θεόν	4:5–6 τὰ μὴ εἰδότα τὸν θεόν - ἔκδικος
1:10 ἐν τοῖς ἁγίοις αὐτοῦ	3:13 τῶν ἁγίων αὐτοῦ
1:10 ἐν πᾶσιν τοῖς πιστεύσασιν (?)	*1:17 πᾶσιν τοῖς πιστεύουσιν (?)*

---

[89] Ibid., 20–1.

(2 Thess)
1:11 προσευχόμεθα πάντοτε
περὶ ὑμῶν
ἔργον πίστεως
2:1 Ἐρωτῶμεν δὲ ὑμᾶς, ἀδελφοί
τῆς παρουσίας τοῦ κυρίου - ἡμῶν
ἐπισυναγωγῆς ἐπ' αὐτόν
2:5 Οὐ μνημονεύετε - ἔτι ὢν πρὸς ὑμᾶς -
ἔλεγον ὑμῖν

2:13–14 Ἡμεῖς - εὐχαριστεῖν τῷ θεῷ
πάντοτε
περὶ ὑμῶν, ἀδελφοὶ ἠγαπημένοι ὑπὸ
κυρίου - εἵλατο ὑμᾶς ὁ θεός - εἰς
σωτηρίαν ἐν ἁγιασμῷ -
ἐκάλεσεν εἰς περιποίησιν δόξης τοῦ
κυρίου ἡμῶν Ἰησοῦ Χριστοῦ

2:15 στήκετε
τὰς παραδόσεις ἃς ἐδιδάχθητε - ἡμῶν
2:16 Αὐτὸς δὲ ὁ κύριος ἡμῶν
Ἰησοῦς Χριστὸς καὶ ὁ θεὸς ὁ πατὴρ
ἡμῶν -
2:17 παρακαλέσαι ὑμῶν τὰς καρδίας -
στηρίξαι (opt.)

3:1 Τὸ λοιπόν
προσεύχεσθε, ἀδελφοί, περὶ ἡμῶν

3:3 πιστὸς ὁ κύριος, ὅς
3:4 ἃ παραγγέλλομεν
3:5 (ὁ κύριος) κατευθύναι
τὰς καρδίας
3:6–7 Παραγγέλλομεν ὑμῖν - ἐν
(ὀνόματι) τοῦ κυρίου Ἰησοῦ Χριστοῦ -
ἀτάκτως περιπατοῦντος - κατὰ τὴν
παράδοσιν ἣν παρελάβοσαν παρ' ἡμῶν
- αὐτοὶ γὰρ οἴδατε - πῶς δεῖ -
ἠτακτήσαμεν

3:8 ἐν κόπῳ καὶ μόχθῳ νυκτὸς καὶ
ἡμέρας ἐργαζόμενοι πρὸς τὸ μὴ
ἐπιβαρῆσαί τινα ὑμῶν
3:9 τύπον - τὸ μιμεῖσθαι ἡμᾶς
3:10 καὶ γὰρ ὅτε ἦμεν πρὸς ὑμᾶς

(1 Thess)
1:2 πάντοτε περὶ ὑμῶν τῶν προσευχῶν
ἡμῶν
1:3 ἔργου τῆς πίστεως
5:12 Ἐρωτῶμεν δὲ ὑμᾶς, ἀδελφοί
4:14–15, 17 ἄξει σὺν αὐτῷ - τὴν
παρουσίαν τοῦ κυρίου - εἰς ἀπάντησιν
3:4 ὅτε πρὸς ὑμᾶς ἦμεν, προελέγομεν
ὑμῖν
(cf. 2:9 μνημονεύετε)
2:12–13 καλοῦντος - εἰς δόξαν - ἡμεῖς
εὐχαριστοῦμεν τῷ θεῷ
ἀδιαλείπτως
1:2 Εὐχαριστοῦμεν τῷ θεῷ πάντοτε περὶ
πάντων ὑμῶν
1:4 ἀδελφοὶ ἠγαπημένοι ὑπὸ θεοῦ - τὴν
ἐκλογήν
4:7 ἐκάλεσεν ὁ θεός - ἐν ἁγιασμῷ
5:9 ἔθετο ὁ θεός - εἰς περιποίησιν
σωτηρίας τοῦ κυρίου ἡμῶν Ἰησοῦ
Χριστοῦ

3:8 στήκετε
4:1 καθὼς παρελάβετε παρ' ἡμῶν
3:11 Αὐτὸς δὲ ὁ θεὸς καὶ πατὴρ ἡμῶν
καὶ ὁ κύριος ἡμῶν Ἰησοῦς -

3:13 εἰς τὸ στηρίξαι ὑμῶν τὰς καρδίας
3:2 εἰς τὸ στηρίξαι ὑμᾶς καὶ
παρακαλέσαι
4:1 Λοιπόν
5:25 Ἀδελφοί, προσεύχεσθε καὶ περὶ
ἡμῶν
5:24 πιστὸς ὁ καλῶν ὑμᾶς, ὅς
4:2 παραγγελίας ἐδώκαμεν
3:11 κατευθύναι
3:13 τὰς καρδίας
4:1–2 ἐρωτῶμεν ὑμᾶς καὶ
παρακαλοῦμεν ἐν κυρίῳ Ἰησοῦ (entspricht jedoch 3:12 noch genauer als 3:6) -
καθὼς παρελάβετε παρ'
ἡμῶν - πῶς δεῖ περιπατεῖν - οἴδατε γὰρ
5:14 τοὺς ἀτάκτους
2:1 Αὐτοὶ γὰρ οἴδατε (?)
2:9 κόπον - καὶ τὸν μόχθον· νυκτὸς καὶ
ἡμέρας ἐργαζόμενοι πρὸς τὸ μὴ
ἐπιβαρῆσαί τινα ὑμῶν
1:6–7 μιμηταὶ ἡμῶν - τύπον
3:4 καὶ γὰρ ὅτε πρὸς ὑμᾶς ἦμεν

(2 Thess)	(1 Thess)
3:10–12 παρηγγέλλομεν ὑμῖν –	*4:10–12 παρακαλοῦμεν – ἡσυχάζειν – τὰ*
ἐργάζεσθαι – περιπατοῦντας ἀτάκτως –	*ἴδια (?) – ἐργάζεσθαι – ὑμῖν*
ἐργαζομένους	*παρηγγείλαμεν – περιπατῆτε.*
– παραγγέλλομεν καὶ παρακαλοῦμεν ἐν	
κυρίῳ Ἰησοῦ Χριστῷ	*5:14 τοὺς ἀτάκτους*
– μετὰ ἡσυχίας ἐργαζόμενοι	*4:1 ἐρωτῶμεν ὑμᾶς καὶ παρακαλοῦμεν*
– ἑαυτῶν (?) [ἄρτον]	*ἐν κυρίῳ Ἰησοῦ*
3:15 (μὴ ὡς ἐχθρὸν) ἡγεῖσθε –	*5:13–14 ἡγεῖσθαι (ἐν ἀγάπῃ) –*
νουθετεῖτε (sc. die *ἄτακτοι*)	*νουθετεῖτε τοὺς ἀτάκτους*
3:16 Αὐτὸς δὲ ὁ κύριος τῆς εἰρήνης	*5:23 Αὐτὸς δὲ ὁ θεὸς τῆς εἰρήνης*
3:18 ἡ χάρις κτλ.	*5:28 ἡ χάρις κτλ.*

Nine points of contact between the letters appear in the same order.

Wrede makes a number of additional comments. The two addresses are striking because both have no addition to the name Paul, both use the *nomen gentilicum* instead of the place name, both use ἐν θεῷ πατρί, a phrase not attested elsewhere in Paul. A second parallel, out of order because the section in First Thessalonians is not used in Second Thessalonians, is even more striking: the reproduction of 1 Thess 2:9 in 2 Thess 3:8.

These parallels and those in the table are to a large degree not dependent on a specific historical situation. They are not determined by the situation in the congregation addressed. That led Wrede to parody those explanations that use either historical situation or coincidental memory to account for the parallels. His words are worth citing *in extenso*.

A coincidence it must be, that expression and linguistic material agree too strongly, where no explanation for it lies in the nature of the questions taken up; a coincidence, that the address of the first letter not only is especially close to that of the second, but returns word for word, and that Paul in 3:8 uses a dozen words almost painfully precise in the same form and sequence as in I [Thess] 2:9; a coincidence, that he never describes new pages in the life of the congregation, and that he has scarcely one new thought to offer outside of 2:1–12. A coincidence it must be, that he involuntarily once again falls into a similar arrangement of his thoughts as he had months before; a coincidence that the reminiscences heap up in discrete specific sections, that correlate with the earlier document; a coincidence that one must accept this in all the parts of the letter. A coincidence it must be, that the appearance arises as a result, that the composer follows with the exception of some units, the sequence of the first letter. A coincidence that striking similarities in remarkably analogous places arise, and that precisely here—and elsewhere—flourishes, arrangements, sentence forms meet [the reader] that otherwise would be scarcely conceivable in the letters of the apostle, and actually cannot be found in them. A coincidence finally and the true coincidence, that all these coincidences come together.

There is no such coincidence. Therefore the supposition must be false that presumes it exists. This is the decisive fact, that to be sure indirectly, but as it seems to me, is extremely strong, indeed compelling proof.[90]

The cogency of Wrede's parallels is almost universally accepted, his historical conclusions are not. Thus Best[91] recognizes the similarity of vocabulary and structure and the difference in tone and summarizes Wrede's findings briefly, but well. But he argues that the similarity of structure, not as perfect as Wrede holds, does not implicate non-Pauline authorship. The smaller points of similarity, Best holds, even argue for the same author. Marshall[92] argues against Wrede on the grounds that we do not know how Paul's mind worked, when two letters to the same church needed to be written in a short space of time. And he finds Zahn's suggestion that Paul may have worked from a retained draft copy of First Thessalonians a less hypothetical reconstruction than pseudepigraphy. When *obscura* and *obscuriora* are used as categories it is difficult to find agreement. I find such reasoning not too helpful.

Others seek to disallow the position by a kind of statistical argument. Milligan,[93] for example, suggests that the parallels at most make up only one third of Second Thessalonians. If you deduct the salutation, transitional phrases, and the close, what is left that is parallel is not often in the same section. It is more likely to hold that the same author has freely han-

---

[90] Ibid., 29–30: "Zufall muss es sein, dass Wendungen und Wortmaterial auch dort so stark übereinstimmen, wo in der Natur der behandelten Fragen keinerlei Erklärung dafür liegt; Zufall, dass die Adresse des ersten Briefes der des zweiten nicht nur besonders ähnelt, sondern in ihr bis aufs Wort wiederkehrt, und dass Paulus 3,8 ein Dutzend Wörter fast peinlich genau in der gleichen Form und Folge bringt wie I.2,9; Zufall, dass er neue Seiten des Gemeindelebens nicht einmal streift, und dass er seiner Gemeinde außer 2,1–12 kaum einen neuen Gedanken zu bieten hat. Zufall muss es sein, dass er unwillkürlich wieder in eine ganz ähnliche Gruppierung der Gedanken verfällt wie Monate zuvor; Zufall, dass die Reminiscenzen sich in bestimmten Einzelabschnitten häufen, die denen des früheren Schreibens entsprechen; Zufall, dass man das fast in allen Teilen des Briefes wahrnehmen muss. Zufall muss es sein, dass der Schein entsteht, als folge der Verfasser mit Ausschluss gewisser Abschnitte, dem Gange des ersten Briefes; Zufall, dass an sich schon bemerkenswerte Ähnlichkeiten an merkwürdig analogem Orte auftreten, und dass gerade hier—und anderswo—Floskeln, Fügungen, Satzformen begegnen die sonst in den Briefen des Apostels zwar leicht denkbar wären, aber sich tatsächlich nicht in ihnen finden; Zufall endlich und der eigentliche Zufall, dass alle diese Zufälle zusammentreffen. Einen solchen Zufall gibt es nicht. Deshalb muss die Annahme falsch sein, die ihn voraussetzt. Dies ist das ausschlaggebende Faktum, der zwar indirekte, aber wie mir scheint, äußerst starke, ja zwingende Beweis."
[91] Best, *The First and Second Epistles to the Thessalonians* (see n. 13), 37, 50–4.
[92] Marshall, *1 and 2 Thessalonians* (see n. 30), 31.
[93] Milligan, *St Paul's Epistles to the Thessalonians* (see n. 1), lxxxiii.

dled the same material. Finally, he concedes, it is an interesting, but insoluble problem.

There are other arguments that have been added to Wrede's that suggest the author was not Paul. Bailey has called attention to two passages.[94] 2 Thess 1:1–2 uses the phrase "God our Father and the Lord Jesus Christ" twice. Nowhere else does such a doubling occur. It suggests a copier working in an un-Pauline manner. Trilling adds that this correlates with the writer's fondness for parallelism.[95] Delling[96] shows that all the parallels in the Pauline corpus come from the wish for grace. Only in the Thessalonian letters in the language "our God" found frequently. Delling's insight supports Bailey's view.

Bailey refers to a second passage that shows later (and non-Pauline) use. The phrase ἔργον πίστεως occurs in Paul only in 1 Thess 1:3 and 2 Thess 1:11. In the first letter it refers to faith as God's work; in the second, parallel to εὐδοκία ἀγαθωσύνης, it describes a way of life. The phrase is used in a non-Pauline sense.

Bailey finally refers to two changes that suggest the language of a later period.[97] In 2 Thess 1:3 and 2:13 the εὐχαριστοῦμεν of First Thessalonians is changed to εὐχαριστεῖν ὀφείλομεν. The phrase is unknown elsewhere in the New Testament, but is found in *1 Clem.* 38.4 and *Barn.* 5.3. The verb καταξιόομαι in 2 Thess 1:5 is used with the kingdom. Elsewhere Paul uses the verb κληρονομεῖν (1 Cor 6:9f., 15:50, Gal 5:21). καταξιόομαι, says Bailey, is frequent in the Apostolic Fathers (e.g., *1 Clem.* 41.4, 50.2, Ignatius, *Eph.* 20.1, *Mag.* 1.2, etc.). Once again Paul's language is replaced with later terminology.

2.1.3 Conclusion

Wrede's argument still stands. It has been reinforced by subsequent detailed investigation, not overturned. It is a powerful argument for the non-Pauline origin of Second Thessalonians.

---

[94] Bailey, "Who Wrote II Thessalonians?" (see n. 28), 135.

[95] Trilling, *Untersuchungen zum zweiten Thessalonicherbrief* (see n. 2), 68–9.

[96] G. Delling, "Zusammengesetzte Gottes- und Christusbezeichnungen in den Paulusbriefen," in *Studien zum Neuen Testament und zum hellenistischen Judentum: Gesammelte Aufsätze 1950–1968* (eds. T. Holtz, F. Hahn and N. Walter; Göttingen: Vandenhoeck & Ruprecht, 1970), 417–24 (417–19).

[97] Bailey, "Who Wrote II Thessalonians?" (see n. 28), 134.

2.2 The Argument from Theological Content

Second Thessalonians introduces no new themes into the correspondence with Thessalonica. That is in itself remarkable. But there are many places where there are differences in emphasis or nuance that suggest that the second letter's author either comes from a later age or did not, at least, completely agree with Paul.

2.2.1 The Variation in Eschatology

The topic has been so frequently discussed that only a brief mention is necessary here. Second Thessalonians is the only letter in which eschatology is the major topic of the letter. That in itself is not enough to suggest non-Pauline origins. But aspects of the eschatology suggest a strong difference from other Pauline letters. The eschatological passages elsewhere make some use of apocalyptic motifs, e.g., the present age and the coming age (Gal 1:4), or of the periodization of events in history (1 Cor 15:21–28). But fundamentally Paul's eschatology uses apocalyptic motifs without being thoroughly apocalyptic. The same is true of First Thessalonians. The passage about the dead in Christ is formed from motifs without being thoroughly apocalyptic. The passage about the dead in Christ is formed from motifs out of the ruler cult (παρουσία, ἀπάντησις, etc.). The section on times and seasons (1 Thess 5:1–11) combines the prophetic 'Day of the Lord' motif with antithetical light-dark language.

Second Thessalonians is unusual in being close to the Apocalypse in its language. Holtzmann[98] calls attention to the idea of rewards and punishments coming from God (1:5, 6; cf. Rev 6:10f.; 7:14; 11:18; 13:6), the phrases ἄγγελοι δυνάμεως (1:7, cf. Rev 19:14), πῦρ φλογός (1:8, cf. Rev 19:12), and ὄλεθρος αἰώνιος (1:9, cf. Rev 20:10), all in the first chapter (1:5–11). In 2 Thess 2:1–12 he calls attention to ὁ υἱὸς τῆς ἀπωλείας and ἡ ἀποστασία in 2:2–3; cf. Rev 13:4, 8, 12, 14, 15, and 17:18 εἰς ἀπώλειαν ὑπάγει). 2 Thess 2:4 is paralleled by Rev 13:6, 12, 14, 15 and 19:20. The σημεῖα of 2:9 are similar to those in Rev 13:2, 12, 14; 16:13; 19:20. In short, Second Thessalonians is apocalyptic in language and conception.

The differences go beyond language. Paul never makes use of time calculation devices from apocalyptic, except in 2 Thess 2:1–12. They are not found in 1 Cor 15:20–28. 1 Thess 5:1–2 expressly refutes time speculation, and bases the refusal on prior oral teaching. 2 Thess 2:1–12 expressly

---

[98] Holtzmann, "Zum zweiten Thessalonicherbrief" (see n. 4), 103; cf. Moffatt, *An Introduction to the Literature of the New Testament* (see n. 14), 76–82.

teaches it, and appeals to prior oral teaching.[99] They thus appeal to contradictory earlier teaching. Whiteley[100] calls this a "flat contradiction." The "sudden destruction" of 1 Thess 5:3 does not leave time for the preliminary signs. One might say the two things to different audiences, at different times, and under changing conditions; but hardly to the same church at the same time. I omit the question of whether an essentially Gentile church (as is presupposed in 1 Thess 1:9–10) could have such detailed knowledge of Jewish apocalyptic. (There is no doubt that apocalyptic thinking was possible this early in Paul's ministry. It is the historical situation that makes it unlikely.)

The direction of the argument in Second Thessalonians is contradictory to that in First Thessalonians. The parousia in First Thessalonians is anticipated very soon (cf. 1 Thess 4:15); in Second Thessalonians the parousia is being pushed off into the (distant?) future. First Thessalonians offers prayers for survival in the parousia (5:23), since the parousia is a basis for comfort (4:18, 5:11). In Second Thessalonians the prayers are directed to an on-going life (ὑπομονή, 3:5) lived in peace (3:16) and right action (2:16, 17). The anticipated parousia of the Lord Jesus is one of power exercised in judgment and destruction (2 Thess 2:8). God will reward the faithful with rest along with the apostle.[101] The parousia may be a source of help, but not of comfort.

Attention was called above to the use of ἀποκάλυψις in 1:7 in a sense not normal in Paul (see. p. 445).

Braun[102] stresses that the judgment (δικαία κρίσις) in 1:5 is punishment of the persecutors for their persecution, reward of the persecuted for this persecution. Thus the familiar judgment scene before the βῆμα (Rom 14:10–12, 2 Cor 5:10, etc.) is not present. People here are not rewarded for their good or evil deeds, but only for their role in Christian persecution, a sort of *quid pro quo* arrangement. Braun has probably overdrawn his case here, though Second Thessalonians does seem open to a moralistic tendency (cf. 2:17).

---

[99] Hollmann, "Die Unechtheit des zweiten Thessalonicherbriefes" (see n. 6), 33; Bailey, "Who Wrote II Thessalonians?" (see n. 28), 135–37.

[100] Whiteley, *Thessalonians in the Revised Standard Version* (see n. 12), 14.

[101] Braun, "Zur nachpaulinischen Herkunft des zweiten Thessalonicherbriefes" (see n. 37), 155. The near parousia is also found in Phil 4:5; 1 Cor 7:29, 31, and Rom 13:11–12. Cf. Krodel, "2 Thessalonians" (see n. 24), 75; Best, *The First and Second Epistles to the Thessalonians* (see n. 13), 54, seeks to build a bridge between the eschatology of the two letters by pointing out that the Lord is invoked in prayer, pointing to 1 Cor 16:22 as evidence. But it is an acclamation there, not a prayer.

[102] Braun, ibid., 152.

2.2.2 The Expanded Role of the Kyrios

Many scholars have pointed to the difference in the role of the κύριος in Second Thessalonians over against First Thessalonians. What First Thessalonians ascribes to God or predicates of God, Second Thessalonians credits to Christ.[103]

Where 1 Thess 1:4 describes the Thessalonians as ἠγαπημένοι ὑπὸ θεοῦ, 2 Thess 2:13 calls them ἠγαπημένοι ὑπὸ κυρίου. When 1 Thess 5:24 grounds a prayer wish (5:23) it does so in the fidelity of the one who calls (πιστὸς ὁ καλῶν ὑμᾶς); it follows standard Pauline usage: 1 Cor 1:9, 10:13b, 2 Cor 1:18. 2 Thess 3:3 grounds its prayer wish in the fidelity of the Lord (πιστὸς δέ ἐστιν ὁ κύριος). Von der Osten-Sacken in a form critical study of these πιστός sayings in Paul decided that they have a standard form: πιστός plus καὶ θεός, followed by a ὅτι clause that gives the eschatological basis for the conviction of fidelity.[104] Second Thessalonians does not have the καί, the ὅτι, or the eschatological orientation. Its form is thus unique in the Pauline corpus.

Where 1 Thess 5:23 invokes the "God of peace," 2 Thess 3:16 calls on the ὁ κύριος τῆς εἰρήνης. The former is the standard Pauline phrase (Rom 15:33, 16:20, 1 Cor 14:33, 2 Cor 13:11, Phil 4:9). Where First Thessalonians speaks of God and the Lord Jesus Christ (3:11f.), Second Thessalonians reverses the order and puts the Lord first (2:16, 3:5).

We called attention to the use of δόξα terminology for the Lord above (p. 445).[105] It should not surprise one therefore that 2 Thess 1:12 calls Jesus "our God and Lord." The anarthrous κυρίου suggest that θεοῦ and κυρίου are a hendiadys governed by the single article before θεοῦ. Second Thessalonians is written under the influence of a developing honorific Christology that elevates Jesus above his Pauline status.

---

[103] Holtzmann, "Zum zweiten Thessalonicherbrief" (see n. 4), 102; Wrede, *Die Echtheit des zweiten Thessalonicherbriefs* (see n. 5), 74; Braun, ibid., 157; Trilling, *Untersuchungen zum zweiten Thessalonicherbrief* (see n. 2), 128–29; idem, "Literarische Paulusimitation im 2. Thessalonicherbrief" (see n. 23), 151–52; Krodel, "2 Thessalonians" (see n. 24), 83; Bailey, "Who Wrote II Thessalonians?" (see n. 28), 139. Note the frequency of reference to κύριος in the letter: "Our Lord Jesus Christ": 2:1, 14, 16; 3:8 (cf. 1 Thess 2:2, 12; 3:6, 12). "Our Lord Jesus": 1:8, 12. "The Lord": 1:9; 2:2, 13; 3:1, 3, 4, 5, 16.

[104] P. von der Osten-Sacken, "Gottes Treue bis zur Parusie: Formgeschichtliche Beobachtungen zu 1 Kor 1:7b–9," *ZNW* 68 (1977): 176–99 (181–82).

[105] See also Holtzmann, "Zum zweiten Thessalonicherbrief" (see n. 4), 102.

2.2.3 Absent Motifs

Some Pauline themes are naturally expected in a Pauline letter, but are absent here. Krodel[106] points out that the motif of "joy" is absent. There is no mention of the kerygma of the cross and resurrection. Jesus' resurrection is not the beginning of the eschatological end drama as in 1 Cor 15:20–28. The Spirit plays almost no role in the letter (contrary to 1 Thess 1:15, 4:8, 5:19–20). In 2:2 the term is used to note direct revelation: in 2:8 it is the destructive power of the Lord exercised on the man of lawlessness. 2:13 is the clearest reflection of the Pauline insight about the Spirit, but it is less specific about the Spirit as eschatological power than is Paul. It is not surprising that almost all baptismal imagery is absent from the letter.

3. Characteristics that Support a Later Date

The eschatology and the christology suggest a later date. Other elements do the same. As Vawter has pointed out, there are no glaring anachronisms that betray the author's hand and make Pauline authorship impossible.[107] But there are indications of a changed situation, even if not anachronistic.

3.1 The Impersonal, Formal Tone

Moffatt[108] is typical: the letter has a "certain formality or official tinge." It contrasts strongly with the first letter in this respect. There Paul talks of their initial reception of the word, of his personal experiences in Thessalonica, of his grief at not being able to return, of his joy over their fidelity. Here all is different. The personal notes are minimal: mention of the names in 1:1; a reference to a letter ὡς δι' ἡμῶν in 2:2; a reference to Paul's being with them in the past (2:5), reference to the παραδόσεις which he taught them, whether by word or by epistle; his working night and day (3:7–10). There is no expression of sorrow over their separation, no mention of plans for the future. There are no new personal data. The names are shared with First Thessalonians, as is the reference to work. The seven uses of the term ἀδελφοί are almost the only recognition of personal relationship.

There is even more. Paul twice speaks of "the obligation to give thanks" (1:3, 2:13), as though it is necessary or at least "proper" (καθὼς ἄξιόν

---

[106] Krodel, "2 Thessalonians" (see n. 24), 83.

[107] B. Vawter, *Introduction to the Pauline Letters: First and Second Thessalonians* (2d ed.; New Testament Reading Guide 6; Collegeville, Minn.: Liturgical Press, 1960), 36.

[108] Moffatt, *An Introduction to the Literature of the New Testament* (see n. 14), 79.

ἐστιν, 1:3). The word command (παραγγέλλειν) appears four times (3:3, 6, 10, 12); elsewhere in Paul it occurs only twice in First Corinthians and once in First Thessalonians.[109]

Years ago Theodor Zahn[110] noted that there "is no expression of anger at this insolent deceit" (referring to the spurious letter of 2:2). Zahn makes nothing of his comment. Yet this absence of emotion is striking. The Paul of Galatians, of 2 Cor 11, of Phil 3, even of First Corinthians can scarcely be recognized in this bloodless author who shows neither anger at the deceit nor joy over the fidelity of the persecuted. Instead he presents an apocalyptic *quid pro quo* comfort. The only explanation is that he has no personal, direct contact with the presumed addressees, i.e., is removed from them in time and/or space. The Thessalonians are "lay figures," much like Prometheus on the rock in Aeschylus' play, necessary for the scenery, but not required to move, feel, or think. It is not surprising that the prayers in the letter are general, formal, and impersonal, applicable to any Christian at any time and place.[111]

3.2 The Stress on Authority: A Later Age

Twice the letter refers to the παράδοσις. In 2:15 standing firm is equated to holding the traditions taught by Paul through word or letter. In 3:6 the readers are commanded to stay away from Christians who do not "walk according to the tradition which they received from us." The contrast to earlier Paul could not be more striking. Paul spoke of κατὰ πνεῦμα (Rom 8:4, cf. Gal 5:25) or "walking straight πρὸς τὴν ἀλήθειαν τοῦ εὐαγγελίου (Gal 2:14). A dynamic criterion is replaced in Second Thessalonians by the received tradition. The analogy to the faithful words of Pastoral Epistles is clear. Paul's authority is now transmitted by traditions, whether oral or written. (See the two references to λόγος and ἐπιστολή, 2:2, 15.) The lesser role of the πνεῦμα in the letter correlates with this. One no longer "puts all things to the test and holds fast to the good" (1 Thess 5:21, in the context of πνεῦμα and προφητεία, vv. 19, 20), one consults the tradition.

Paul "commands" in this letter, not exhorts. His parenesis is παραγγελία, not παράκλησις. His person becomes a norm also. In 1 Thess 2:9 his work was designed to remove a burden from them. In 2 Thess 3:7 the Thessalonians are told that he gave them a model that must (δεῖ) be imitated. This was not an abdication of authority (Paul has ἐξουσία,

---

[109] Bailey, "Who Wrote II Thessalonians?" (see n. 28), 137.

[110] T. Zahn, *Introduction to the New Testament* (trans. J. Moore Trout et al.; 3 vols.; New York: C. Scribner's, 1909), 1:235.

[111] Trilling, *Untersuchungen zum zweiten Thessalonicherbrief* (see n. 2), 94–5.

2 Thess 3:9), but a deliberate choice to give them a model.[112] Second Thessalonians claims that Paul ate no one else's bread (3:8), a claim that directly contradicts Phil 4:15f., in a manner that First Thessalonians does not.[113]

The elevation of Paul's tradition and authority argue for the composition of the letter at a time when the church was stabilizing its existence by received norms.

3.3 The Sign in His Own Hand

Three times in the Pauline corpus there is reference to Paul's signature in his own hand. In 1 Cor 16:21 it comes in a series of greetings, without any specific stress. Gal 6:11 mentions Paul's large script, but not as a mark of authenticity. In both cases the signatures are marks of Paul's personal feelings for his addressees. 2 Thess 3:17 is different. Only here does Paul use his signature as a mark of authentication. (All of the other six occurrences of σημεῖον refer either to miraculous happenings or to evidence of the Spirit's activity.) Paul refers to it as an habitual trait, in every letter. Yet only Second Thessalonians (and no other letter) has it. The conclusion seems clear. As Bailey states,[114] "iii.17 makes more sense as the product of the pseudonymous author who wished by it to allay any suspicions of inauthenticity which his letter might arouse." The author of Second Thessalonians doth protest too much, methinks.

The reference does illuminate the mention of word and epistle in 2:15. It suggests that 2:2 either refers to an otherwise unknown spurious letter of Paul, or to an interpretation of First Thessalonians that the writer regards as false.

4. The Purpose and Situation

The letter is pseudonymous and later than Paul's own lifetime. It is much more semitic in thought than is First Thessalonians. The work of the seminar has reinforced the hellenistic character of the first letter. That *obiter dictum* reflects both the papers of Malherbe and me on the letter. It agrees with John Townsend that Second Thessalonians reflects Jewish apocalyp-

---

[112] Idem, "Literarische Paulusimitation im 2. Thessalonicherbrief" (see n. 23), 155; Moffatt, *An Introduction to the Literature of the New Testament* (see n. 14), 80; Krodel, "2 Thessalonians" (see n. 24), 84.

[113] Bailey, "Who Wrote II Thessalonians?" (see n. 28), 139.

[114] Trilling, *Untersuchungen zum zweiten Thessalonicherbrief* (see n. 2), 102–8; Bailey, ibid., 138.

tic. It accepts Peter Berkovitz's examination of events lying behind First Thessalonians and agrees that there is no room historically for what must have happened for Second Thessalonians to be authentic.

It is not necessary for me to pass all the theories of origins for the letter in review. I agree fundamentally with Wendland's view[115] that the letter originated at a time when enthusiasm that misinterpreted Paul was disturbing the church. I do not find it necessary, with Lindemann, to feel that it is designed to replace First Thessalonians, nor do I see in the letter the anti-gnostic cast that Koester[116] suggests. But I find Koester's suggestion of a renaissance of apocalyptic persuasive and helpful. The Apocalypse also finds enthusiasm a threat (cf. Rev 2:20). Second Thessalonians shows us a late "Paulinist" rethinking Paul in terms of apocalyptic and the growing body of orthodox tradition and apostolic authority.

---

[115] Wendland, *Die urchristlichen Literaturformen* (see n. 56), 360–61; Wrede, *Die Echtheit des zweiten Thessalonicherbriefs* (see n. 5), 78.

[116] Lindemann, "Zum Abfassungszweck des Zweiten Thessalonicherbriefes" (see n. 27), 35–47; Koester, *History and Literature of Early Christianity* (see n. 26), 244.

As If Genuine

Interpreting the Pseudepigraphic Second Thessalonians

by

TREVOR THOMPSON

Scholars who interpret Second Thessalonians as an early Christian pseudepigraphon consider at least some element in the text to be false.[1] As a document that is neither from the ascribed authors (i.e., Paul, Silvanus, and Timothy) nor to the attributed addressees (i.e., the Thessalonians),[2] any attempt to reconstruct the actual *Sitz im Leben*[3] for the text faces the inter-

---

[1] The compelling arguments against the authenticity of Second Thessalonians will not be rehearsed here. See the essay of Edgar Krentz in this volume.

[2] For Second Thessalonians as a "double pseudepigraphon" (i.e., neither from Paul, Silvanus, and Timothy nor to the Thessalonians) see M. M. Mitchell, "Thessalonicherbriefe," *RGG*[4] 8:360–61. Some interpret the letter as being addressed to a real congregation or community other than the Thessalonians: I. Havener, "2 Thessalonians," in *The Collegeville Bible Commentary: Based on the New American Bible with Revised New Testament* (eds. D. Bergant and R. J. Karris; Collegeville, Minn.: Liturgical Press, 1989), 1172; E. J. Richard, *First and Second Thessalonians* (SP; Collegeville, Minn.: The Liturgical Press, 1995), 28; P. F. Esler, "2 Thessalonians," in *The Oxford Bible Commentary* (eds. J. Barton and J. Muddiman; Oxford: Oxford University Press, 2001), 1218. Others maintain that the letter was actually for the Thessalonians: L. McKinnish Bridges (*1 & 2 Thessalonians* [Smyth and Helwys Bible Commentary 17; Macon, Ga.: Smyth & Helwys, 2008], 194–213) asserts—with appeal to the reconstructions of the community behind the Gospel of John offered by R. E. Brown and J. L. Martyn—that Second Thessalonians was written to "the same intimate group of artisan believers" as First Thessalonians (193–94) and "was written by a disciple of Paul who continues to minister in the Thessalonian community after Paul's ministry had ended" (201). It is unclear how to connect a document written by someone in Thessalonica to the Thessalonians with her additional comment, "To place the name of the missionary leader Paul on the letter assured the letter's delivery and acceptance by the anxious congregation" (199). Cf. B. Thurston, *Reading Colossians, Ephesians & 2 Thessalonians: A Literary and Theological Commentary* (New York: Crossroad, 1995), 162; E. E. Johnson, "2 Thessalonians," in *Women's Bible Commentary: Expanded Edition with Apocrypha* (eds. C. A. Newsom and S. H. Ringe; Louisville, Ky.: Westminster John Knox, 1998), 442; B. Roberts Gaventa, "Thessalonians, Second Letter to the," in *Eerdmans Dictionary of the Bible* (ed. D. N. Freedman; Grand Rapids, Mich.: Eerdmans, 2000), 1299–1300.

[3] *Sitz im Leben* is used here in its less technical sense as a synonym for "historical set-

pretive challenge of working with a literary fable. In the more than two hundred years since Johann E. C. Schmidt first raised questions about the identity of the author,[4] there has been little reflection upon the complex issues involved in employing the pseudepigraphic Second Thessalonians to restore the circumstances and events surrounding the letter's composition. Rather, the history of research has been dominated by the question of authenticity.[5] As a result of the sustained focus on the genuineness of the text, a modified hermeneutical lens for reading Second Thessalonians as a pseudepigraphon has not been developed.

This essay will seek to demonstrate that, in the absence of a nuanced hermeneutic, many interpreters who regard Second Thessalonians as a pseudepigraphon commonly read parts of the text as if it were a genuine document.[6] Although not acknowledged as such, commentators seem to borrow the basic reading assumptions (e.g., a real letter sent from an author to an intended audience) and interpretative approaches (e.g., use of the

---

ting." An argument for a more restricted use of *Sitz im Leben* is available in S. Byrskog, "A Century with the *Sitz im Leben*: From Form-Critical Setting to Gospel Community and Beyond," *ZNW* 98 (2007): 1–27. He strictly defines *Sitz im Leben* as, "that recurrent type of mnemonic occasion within the life of early Christian communities when certain people cared about the Jesus tradition in a special way and performed and narrated it orally and in writing" (20).

[4] J. E. C. Schmidt, "Vermuthungen über die beyden Briefe an die Thessalonicher," in *Kritische Geschichte der neutestamentlichen Schriften* (ed. idem; Hadamer: Neue Gelehrtenbuchhandlung, 1801), 380–86.

[5] Notable studies in the history of the debate include: F. H. Kern, "Über 2 Thess. 2,1–12. Nebst Andeutungen über den Ursprung des zweiten Briefes an die Thessalonicher," *Tübinger Zeitschrift für Theologie* 2 (1839): 145–214; H. J. Holtzmann, "Zum zweiten Thessalonicherbrief," *ZNW* 2 (1901): 97–108; W. Wrede, *Die Echtheit des zweiten Thessalonicherbriefs* (TU 24; Leipzig: J. C. Hinrichs, 1903); G. Hollmann, "Die Unechtheit des zweiten Thessalonicherbriefes," *ZNW* 5 (1904): 28–38; G. Milligan, *St Paul's Epistles to the Thessalonians: The Greek Text with Introduction and Notes* (London: Macmillan & Co., 1908); J. E. Frame, *A Critical and Exegetical Commentary on the Epistles of St. Paul to the Thessalonians* (ICC; New York: C. Scribner's Sons, 1912); H. Braun, "Zur nachpaulinischen Herkunft des zweiten Thessalonicherbriefes," *ZNW* 44 (1952/53): 152–56; C. Masson, *Les Deux Épîtres de Saint Paul aux Thessaloniciens* (CNT; Paris: Delachaux & Niestlé, 1957); E. Best, *The First and Second Epistles to the Thessalonians* (BNTC; New York: Harper & Row, 1972); W. Trilling, *Untersuchungen zum zweiten Thessalonicherbrief* (ETS 27; Leipzig: St. Benno, 1972); idem, *Der zweite Brief an die Thessalonicher* (EKKNT 14; Zürich: Benziger Verlag, 1980); A. Lindemann, "Zum Abfassungszweck des Zweiten Thessalonicherbriefes," *ZNW* 68 (1977): 35–47; R. K. Jewett, *The Thessalonian Correspondence: Pauline Rhetoric and Millenarian Piety* (Philadelphia: Fortress Press, 1986); A. J. Malherbe, *The Letters to the Thessalonians: A New Translation with Introduction and Commentary* (AB 32B; New York: Doubleday, 2000).

[6] This essay is part of a larger project on early Christian pseudepigraphy, "The Search for an Author and Addressee: Ancient Authenticity Criticism and the Interpretation of 2 Thessalonians" (provisional title for in-progress University of Chicago dissertation).

text as a clear window into the life and experiences of the author and addressees) from the analysis of authentic Pauline texts to reconstruct the *Sitz im Leben* for the pseudepigraphic Second Thessalonians. The result of this approach is a long-standing interpretive tension. As exemplified below, in the mid-nineteenth century work of Ferdinand C. Baur, a methodological disconnect exists between, on the one hand, the identification of Second Thessalonians as a pseudepigraphon and, on the other, the use of certain key passages (e.g., 2 Thess 1:4, 2:2, 3:6–12) as a relatively transparent window into the real world of the actual author and first readers.[7] This tension becomes more evident in the move made by some scholars to treat those passages in Second Thessalonians about the ascribed authors (i.e., Paul, Silvanus, and Timothy) as autobiographical remarks from the actual author. Primarily although not exclusively evident in the recent exegetical comments of North American scholars, these interpreters read the narrated experiences of Paul, Silvanus, and Timothy in Second Thessalonians (e.g., 2 Thess 2:5, "Do you not remember that while I was still with you I was telling you these things?"[8]) as real events experienced by the actual author.

1. F. C. Baur and Second Thessalonians: The Search for the *Sitz im Leben*

In his landmark two-volume work on Paul published in 1845,[9] Baur famously denied the authenticity of every letter attributed to Paul in the New Testament with the exception of Galatians, First Corinthians, Second Co-

---

[7] The number of actual authors remains an unanswerable question. Throughout the remainder of the paper, the singular "author" will be used for purposes of expediency.

[8] 2 Thess 2:5, οὐ μνημονεύετε ὅτι ἔτι ὢν πρὸς ὑμᾶς ταῦτα ἔλεγον ὑμῖν;

[9] F. C. Baur, *Paulus, der Apostel Jesu Christi: Sein Leben und Wirken, seine Briefe und seine Lehre. Ein Beitrag zu einer kritischen Geschichte des Urchristentums* (Stuttgart: Becher & Müller, 1845). The second edition was published posthumously by his son-in-law, Edward G. Zeller, in two volumes: F. C. Baur, *Paulus, der Apostel Jesu Christi. Sein Leben und Wirken, seine Briefe und seine Lehre. Ein Beitrag zu einer kritischen Geschichte des Urchristenthums* (2d ed.; ed. E. G. Zeller; Leipzig: Fues's Verlag [R. Reisland], 1866–67). In addition to the two short works published as appendixes to the first edition, Zeller included a third item, an article written by Baur on the Thessalonian correspondence which originally appeared in *Theologische Jahrbücher*: F. C. Baur, "Die beiden Briefe an die Thessalonicher, Ihre Aechtheit und Bedeutung für die Lehre von der Parusie Christi," *Theologische Jahrbücher* 14 (1855): 141–68. Two-volume English Translation of the second German edition: F. C. Baur, *Paul, The Apostle of Jesus Christ: His Life and Works, His Epistles and His Doctrine* (2d ed.; trans. A. Menzies; London: Williams & Norgate, 1873–75). The quotation of Baur's text is, unless otherwise noted, from the second edition. The English translations of Baur's work rely upon the translation of Menzies unless otherwise noted.

rinthians, and Romans. Concerning the Thessalonian correspondence, Baur challenges Paul's authorship of First Thessalonians based upon the lack of a specific epistolary occasion, the apparent dependence upon First Corinthians, Second Corinthians, and Romans,[10] the post-70 CE perspective of 1 Thess 2:14–16, and the non-Pauline details about the resurrection of the dead and the second coming of Christ in 1 Thess 4:14–18.[11] In regard to Second Thessalonians, he challenged its authenticity based upon the use of Jewish sources—especially Daniel—in 2 Thess 2:3–12,[12] notable differences between 1 Cor 15:23–52 and 2 Thess 2:3–12, the absence of original material, dependence upon First Thessalonians,[13] exaggerated, strange and far-fetched expressions,[14] and the elevated importance of writing and epistolary communication (e.g., 2 Thess 2:2, 15; 3:17).[15]

Ten years later in 1855, Baur returned to the Thessalonian correspondence in response to the criticism of Richard A. Lipsius who argued against Baur in favor of the genuineness of First Thessalonians.[16] His renewed analysis of the two letters emphasizes the importance of situating First and Second Thessalonians within a particular historical context in order to establish their chronology and to resolve questions about their authenticity.[17] For Baur, the documents themselves serve as the primary witnesses to the *Sitz im Leben* in which they were crafted. He finds the

---

[10] E.g., 1 Thess 1:5 and 1 Cor 2:4; 1 Thess 1:6 and 1 Cor 11:1; 1 Thess 1:8 and Rom 1:8; 1 Thess 2:5 and 2 Cor 7:2.

[11] Baur, *Paulus* (see n. 9), 2:94–9. English Translation (ET): Baur, *Paul* (see n. 9), 2:85–90.

[12] Baur, *Paulus* (see n. 9), 2:100. Consistent with Baur's understanding of Christian origins according to Hegelian dialectic, he writes, "On the other hand, however, we must remember that here is a man who resolutely broke through the limits of the national consciousness, and rose to a point of view essentially different from the Jewish to whom, therefore, we must beware of ascribing more sympathy with Jewish ways of thinking than there is good evidence for. We must not overlook the fact that in this matter of the second coming of Christ, as much as in anything else, the strongest repulsion (abstoßenden Gegensatz) must have been discovered between the Pauline view of Christianity and the Judaeo-Christian view." ET: 2:90.

[13] 2 Thess 3:1–2 and 1 Thess 5:25; 2 Thess 3:5 and 1 Thess 3:11–13, 5:24; 2 Thess 3:6–12 and 1 Thess 2:6–12, 4:11; 2 Thess 3:16 and 1 Thess 5:23.

[14] E.g., 2 Thess 1:3, ὅτι ὑπεραυξάνει ἡ πίστις ὑμῶν καὶ πλεονάζει ἡ ἀγάπη ἑνὸς ἑκάστου πάντων ὑμῶν εἰς ἀλλήλους. 2 Thess 1:10, ὅτι ἐπιστεύθη τὸ μαρτύριον ἡμῶν ἐφ' ὑμᾶς. 2 Thess 2:10, τὴν ἀγάπην τῆς ἀληθείας οὐκ ἐδέξαντο.

[15] Baur, *Paulus* (see n. 9), 2:99–107. ET: 2:90–7.

[16] The critique: R. A. Lipsius, "Über Zweck und Veranlassung des ersten Thessalonicherbriefs," *TSK* 27 (1854): 905–34. The response: F. C. Baur, "Die beiden Briefe an die Thessalonicher" (see n. 9).

[17] Baur, *Paulus* (see n. 9), 2:350. "What has to be done first of all, however, is to find a point from which to determine the historical situation (die Zeitverhältnisse) to which the Epistles belong." ET: 2:323.

strongest clues to the historical occasion within 2 Thess 2. In contrast to his earlier position which emphasized elements of Jewish thought in the apocalyptic material, Baur here highlights important sustained parallels between 2 Thess 2 and Revelation, and proposes using the latter as an explanatory guide for the former.[18] By using Revelation as a lens through which to interpret the apocalypse of 2 Thess 2, Baur identifies the enigmatic ὁ ἄνθρωπος τῆς ἀνομίας[19] with the Antichrist figure in Revelation whom he regards as the Emperor Nero.[20] Baur then reads the remainder of 2 Thess 2:3–12 as a description of Nero's character and actions. More specifically, Baur takes the phrase εἰς τὸ μὴ ταχέως σαλευθῆναι in 2 Thess 2:2 as evidence that, at the time when Second Thessalonians was composed, an event had already occurred which resulted in the readiness of some "to be excited and led away." He connects this occurrence with the reported tumult in Greece and Asia Minor caused by the appearance of a false-Nero shortly after the death of Galba.[21] Baur regards Vespasian as the ὁ κατέχων of 2 Thess 2:7 and thus situates the composition of Second Thessalonians in the early years of his reign.[22] As a result, he argues

---

[18] Baur's lexical connections: (1) 2 Thess 1:7, ἀγγέλων δυνάμεως αὐτοῦ and Rev 19:18, τὰ στρατεύματα ἐν τῷ οὐρανῷ; (2) 2 Thess 1:8, ἐν πυρὶ φλογός and Rev 19:12, φλὸξ πυρός; (3) τὸ γὰρ μυστήριον ἤδη ἐνεργεῖται τῆς ἀνομίας and Rev 17:5, καὶ ἐπὶ τὸ μέτωπον αὐτῆς ὄνομα γεγραμμένον, μυστήριον, Βαβυλὼν ἡ μεγάλη, Rev 17:7, ἐγὼ ἐρῶ σοι τὸ μυστήριον τῆς γυναικὸς καὶ τοῦ θηρίου τοῦ βαστάζοντος αὐτήν; (4) 2 Thess 2:8, τῷ πνεύματι τοῦ στόματος αὐτοῦ and Rev 19:15, καὶ ἐκ τοῦ στόματος αὐτοῦ ἐκπορεύεται ῥομφαία ὀξεῖα (cf. 19,20); (5) 2 Thess 2:9, ἡ παρουσία κατ᾽ ἐνέργειαν τοῦ σατανᾶ ἐν πάσῃ δυνάμει and Rev 13:2, καὶ ἔδωκεν αὐτῷ ὁ δράκων τὴν δύναμιν αὐτοῦ καὶ τὸν θρόνον αὐτοῦ καὶ ἐξουσίαν μεγάλην; (6) 2 Thess 2:9, σημείοις καὶ τέρασιν ψεύδους and Rev 13:13, ποιεῖ σημεῖα μεγάλα, Rev 19:20, ὁ ποιήσας τὰ σημεῖα ἐνώπιον αὐτοῦ; (7) 2 Thess 2:11, ἐνέργειαν πλάνης and Rev 13:14, καὶ πλανᾷ τοὺς κατοικοῦντας ἐπὶ τῆς γῆς (cf. Rev 19:20), ἐν οἷς ἐπλάνησεν τοὺς λαβόντας τὸ χάραγμα τοῦ θηρίου). Baur, *Paul* (see n. 9), 2:325, "In all these particulars the Epistle to the Thessalonians and the Apocalypse are substantially agreed; and there are some other points in the Epistle which appear inexplicable until the Apocalypse explains them" (Baur, *Paulus* [see n. 9], 2:353).

[19] ὁ ἄνθρωπος τῆς ἁμαρτίας in Baur following some early MSS (e.g., A D F G).

[20] Baur asserts connections between particular historical persons and figures in the text following the conclusions of Kern, "Ueber 2 Thess. 2,1–12" (see n. 5), esp. 193–214.

[21] Tacitus *Hist.* 2.8.

[22] Baur, *Paulus* (see n. 9), 2:356–59. ET: 2:328–31. More recently, G. H. van Kooten, "'Wrath Will Drip in the Plains of Macedonia': Expectations of Nero's Return in The Egyptian *Sibylline Oracles* (Book 5), 2 Thessalonians, and Ancient Historical Writings," in *The Wisdom of Egypt: Jewish, Early Christian, and Gnostic Essays in Honour of Gerard P. Luttikhuizen* (eds. A. Hilhorst and idem; Leiden/Boston: Brill, 2005), 177–213, argues for a similar historical reconstruction. However, for van Kooten, τὸ κατέχον (2:6)/ὁ κατέχων (2:7) refer to the "abstract force of Vindex and Galba as well as the individual figure of Galba" (ibid., 204). He dates Second Thessalonians between June 68

strongly against Paul's authorship of Second Thessalonians and maintains—a reversal of his earlier position—Second Thessalonians was written before First Thessalonians.

Near the end of the analysis, Baur recognizes a potential objection to his historical reconstruction:

> But, it may be objected, how could another writer make the apostle say these things if he could not possibly have said them himself? How could a later writer make him speak of Nero as Antichrist, when this theory could have had no evidence nor reason at the time when the Epistle was represented as having been written?[23]

In effect, has not the author of Second Thessalonians committed the error of anachronism by having the ascribed authors (i.e., Paul, Silvanus, and Timothy) offer an apocalyptic narrative dependent upon post-Pauline speculation concerning Nero's possible postmortem return? Meeting this objection, Baur points to the skill of the author in composing a letter in the personality of another:[24]

> The answer to this question is found in the precautions taken by the writer himself to meet it, if it should arise. This precisely is the very special character of such a letter, determined mainly by the double personality of the author. The writer is the apostle and yet at the same time another person. The form of the Epistle is from the pretended. The content is from the real author. These two have to be made to harmonize in some way.[25]

According to Baur, the author does not forget "the part he was playing."[26] Rather, the writer of Second Thessalonians maintains a healthy distance

---

and July 69 and reads the "I" of 2 Thess 2:5 as either Silvanus and Timothy "because Paul would have been in Nero's custody in Rome for many years at this stage" (212).

[23] Baur, *Paul* (see n. 9), 2:334. "Allein, wird man freilich auch hier einwenden, wie kann ein Anderer den Apostel sagen lassen, was der Apostel selbst nicht sagen konnte, wie kann ein Späterer ihn von Nero als dem Antichrist reden lassen, wenn doch zu der Zeit, in welcher der Apostel dem Brief geschrieben haben soll, alle Voraussetzungen dieser Vorstellung noch gar nicht vorhanden waren?" (Baur, *Paulus* [see n. 9], 2:363).

[24] Baur's recognition and description of a pseudepigrapher's skill is uncommon in the history of New Testament research on pseudepigraphy.

[25] Baur, *Paul* (see n. 9), 2:334–35. "Zur Beantwortung dieser Frage darf man nur darauf achten, wie der Verfasser des Briefs selbst diese Frage nicht unberücksichtigt gelassen hat. Dies eben ist der eigene durch die Doppelpersönlichkeit des Verfassers bedingte Charakter eines solchen Briefs. Der Schreibende ist der Apostel und doch zugleich ein Anderer, seine Form hat der Brief von dem angeblichen, seinem Inhalt von dem wahren Verfasser, beides muss daher erst in Einklang gebracht werden" (Baur, *Paulus* [see n. 9], 2:363). Following the advice of Klauck, the second sentence from Menzies' translation has been altered above. Menzies translates, "in such a point we see very distinctly how the character of such an Epistle is insensibly determined by the double personality of the writer." The punctuation and sentence division also differs from Menzies' translation.

[26] Baur, *Paulus* (see n. 9), 2:363, "Der Verfasser des Briefs sei aus seiner angenommenen Rolle gefallen." ET: 2:335.

from the historical Paul by depicting the character and actions of Nero in such a general way that the description would not unambiguously evoke the figure of Nero.[27] As such, the actual author avoids *explicit* reference to events or figures after the death of Paul so as to avoid over-stepping the line of Paul's probable authorship.[28]

Consistent with his interpretive dictum, Baur's exegetical analysis of Second Thessalonians carefully separates the identities of the actual author from those of the ascribed authors and avoids collapsing them into one indistinguishable persona. According to Baur, the actual author repeatedly maintains that the content of Second Thessalonians corresponds to the message "which the apostle had told his readers by word of mouth, when he was present with them" (2 Thess 2:5, 3:10).[29] Although not fully explained by Baur, his reading of 2:5 and 3:10 exhibits sensitivity to the subtle ways in which pseudepigraphic texts interact with readers on multiple levels. The actual readers were to believe that obscure material in Second Thessalonians had been more fully explicated in the referenced oral teaching of Paul (2:5) and that these texts were readily understood by the original readers ("die ursprünglichen Leser").[30] Similarly, he reads 2 Thess 3:7 as an appeal for imitation of Paul's example and enactment of "the principles enunciated by him in his own Epistles."[31]

---

[27] Although rightly offered by Baur as proof of the author's pseudepigraphic skill, the generalized portrait of the figure described in 2 Thess 2:3–12 problematizes definitive identification with any specific historical figure(s).

[28] Baur, *Paulus* (see n. 9), 2:363, "Man sieht in dem Brief nicht undeutlich, nach mehr oder minder kennbaren Merkmalen, die Verhältnisse einer über den Apostel hinausgehenden Zeit, und doch ist auch wieder alles so gehalten, dass die Grenzlinie der Möglichkeit oder Wahrscheinlichkeit der apostolischen Abfassung nicht zu auffallend überschritten ist, das Specielle, Concrete, geschichtlich Individuelle ist so viel möglich wieder verallgemeinert, wie hier an der Vorstellung des Antichrists zu sehen ist." ET: 2:335.

[29] Cf. Baur, *Paulus* (see n. 9), 2:364, "Dasselbe Bestreben, das Nichtapostolische an die Persönlichkeit des angeblichen apostolischen Verfassers anzuknüpfen, so viel möglich in der Sphäre derselben zu bleiben, zeigt sich in der wiederholten Bemerkung, der Apostel habe das, was er in dem Briefe schreibt, auch schon mündlich bei seiner Anwesenheit den Lesern gesagt. Vgl. 2,5. 3,10." ET: 2:335.

[30] Baur, *Paulus* (see n. 9), 2:364, "Wenn also auch das Eine oder Andere in dem Briefe dunkel bleibt, so muss man sich eben das mündlich Gesagte als den Commentar dazu denken, und sich mit der Voraussetzung beruhigen, die ursprünglichen Leser haben schon gewusst, was der Apostel meinte." ET: 2:335.

[31] Baur, *Paulus* (see n. 9), 2:360, "In einem solchen Zusammenhang, in welchem vom Arbeiten zur Selbsterhaltung, und von dem Bestreben, Andern auf keine Weise zur Last zu fallen, die Rede ist, ist nichts motivirter, als die Hinweisung auf des Apostels eigenes Beispiel, und die von ihm selbst in seinen Briefen ausgesprochenen Grundsätze." ET: 2:332. In regard to Paul's epistolary principles, Baur observes echoes of 1 Cor 9:3–12 in 2 Thess 3:7–9, 1 Cor 5:9–11 in 2 Thess 3:14, and 2 Cor 13:11 in 2 Thess 3:16.

Yet, despite his insistence on recognizing the dual personality of the writer and the nuanced reading of texts concerning the ascribed authors, Baur's approach to other texts in Second Thessalonians does not exhibit the same hermeneutical sensitivity. As a result, he employs parts of the text as a transparent window to situate the document in a specific historical setting and reconstruct the situation surrounding its composition. By reading select portions of Second Thessalonians as if the document were genuine, Baur asserts, apparently on the basis of ch. 1, that the readers were suffering.[32] Also, as noted above, he concludes with reference to εἰς τὸ μὴ ταχέως σαλευθῆναι in 2 Thess 2:2 that the text was composed shortly after the tumult caused by the appearance of the first false-Nero during the early years of Vespasian's reign. He further posits, on the basis of 2 Thess 2:2, the existence of "some movement that had arisen among the Christians" which promoted the view that "the Parousia is coming now."[33] In arguing against the authenticity of Second Thessalonians, Baur regards the mention of "attributed Pauline letters (untergeschobene paulinische Briefe)"[34] as evidence that, at the time when Second Thessalonians was written, pseudo-Pauline letters circulated and it was therefore necessary to distinguish genuine texts from those documents forged in Paul's name.[35] For Baur, the existence of these pseudo-Pauline letters serves as a decisive proof against the Pauline origin of Second Thessalonians.[36] Finally, he reads the exhortations in 2 Thess 3 as a direct response to those who acted on the belief "that all things were on the verge of dissolution"[37] by abandoning their own labor and becoming a financial burden to others.

---

[32] Baur, *Paulus* (see n. 9), 2:356, "Der Verfasser ist von vorn herein mit Gedanken an die Parusie Christi, an das bei derselben über die ungläubige Welt erfolgende Strafgericht und an die Herrlichkeit erfüllt, welche die Gläubigen zum Lohn für ihre Drangsale zu erwarten haben." ET: 2:328.

[33] Baur, *Paulus* (see n. 9), 2:356. ET: 2:328.

[34] Baur, *Paulus* (see n. 9), 2:106. Cf. Menzies' "pretended Pauline ones." ET: 2:95.

[35] Cf. Baur's remarks on 2 Thess 3:17b, "Not only is this quite un-Pauline in comparison with 1 Cor.; it is an unmistakable proof (unzweideutiges Kriterium) that our Epistle was written at a time when spurious apostolic writings (unächte apostolische Briefe) were known to be in circulation, and there was cause for inquiry into the genuineness of each production" (Baur, *Paulus* [see n. 9], 2:105–6. ET: 2:95).

[36] Baur's logic seems to proceed as follows: (1) An ἐπιστολή is mentioned in 2 Thess 2:2; (2) Baur assumes, without argument, that the ἐπιστολή in 2 Thess 2:2 refers to real pseudonymous letters; (3) He asserts as a claimed historical fact that pseudonymous letters did not circulate during Paul's lifetime; (4) Therefore, he concludes that the mention of pseudo-Pauline letters by the author of Second Thessalonians is anachronistic and that the letter comes from a time after Paul.

[37] Baur, *Paulus* (see n. 9), 2:360, "Das Letztere war das Hauptübel, das aus der Meinung entstand, es löse sich jetzt alles auf." ET: 2:331–32.

Baur does not stand alone in his use of these texts to reconstruct the document's *Sitz im Leben*. Scholars repeatedly turn to 2 Thess 1:4, 2:2, and 3:6–12 in their respective attempts to situate the text within a particular historical context.[38] Among recent interpreters see Maarten Menken,[39] Earl Richard,[40] Pheme Perkins,[41] Philip Esler,[42] and Victor Furnish.[43]

---

[38] The repeated efforts to locate the author and intended addressees of this document with some precision is perhaps a testimony to the influence of interpreters who read Second Thessalonians as an authentic Pauline letter. In that, they frequently demand a plausible alternative life-setting from interpreters who read the letter as a pseudepigraphon. For example, E. J. Goodspeed (*An Introduction to the New Testament* [Chicago: University of Chicago Press, 1937], 19–20) writes, "We must not be content to set aside an ancient writing as not authentic; some better place in the history of early Christian literature must then be found for it, for we are seeking to interpret these documents, and to do that we must discover their place in history—the date and circumstances of their composition. No one has found a better place or date for II Thessalonians than Corinth about A.D. 50."

[39] M. J. J. Menken, *2 Thessalonians* (New Testament Readings; London/New York: Routledge, 1994), 15, "It is not a general tract, but a writing in which two specific problems are tackled. The first is the commotion caused by the message that 'the day of the Lord has come' (2.2), a message which the author of the letter condemns as false (2.1–12). The second is the disorderly conduct of a group of Christians, which amounts to a refusal to work for a living (3.6–12)."

[40] Richard, *First and Second Thessalonians* (see n. 2), 28, "From the outset one learns that the community is undergoing hard times at the hands of people who will undergo divine punishment (1:4–10) ... In fact, the author speaks of doomsday preachers who are active within the community via ecstatic pronouncements, extended preaching, and use of a letter allegedly by Paul. These have brought about a radical change in members' perspectives, from a firm adherence to the community's venerable traditions (2:15) to a full-blown apocalypticism (2:2). They are spending their time and energy discussing these issues, trying to influence their neighbors, and are neglecting their personal, community, and spiritual duties (3:6–12)."

[41] P. Perkins, "1 and 2 Thessalonians," in *Harper Collins Bible Commentary* (rev. ed.; ed. J. L. Mays; San Francisco: HarperSanFrancisco, 2000), 1131, "2 Thessalonians is written to deal with two problems that have arisen in the church: first, misinterpretations of teachings that claim to be Pauline and yet insist that 'the day of the Lord is already here' (2:2), and, second, the conduct of persons who reject Paul's teaching about working and living quietly (3:6–12). Both of these themes were addressed in the parenesis (exhortation) of 1 Thessalonians (on the 'day of the Lord,' 4:13–5:11); on working and not living 'idly,' 4:11; 5:14). In addition, the church continues to suffer tribulations (1:5–10; cf. 1 Thess. 1:6; 2:14–16), which may contribute to the confusion about Paul's teaching."

[42] Esler, "2 Thessalonians" (see n. 2), 1214, "The three substantive issues of local context recognized in the letter are the existence of some form of oppression being suffered by the addressees (1:4–6), the disturbance caused by the message that 'the day of the Lord has come' (2:1–12), and the disorderly conduct of certain Christ-followers who are refusing to work for a living."

[43] V. P. Furnish, *1 Thessalonians & 2 Thessalonians* (ANTC; Nashville: Abingdon Press, 2007), 138, "The author is concerned primarily to refute those who claim that the

Despite his recognition of the interpretative challenges generated by a pseudepigraphic text and the double personality of its author ("Doppelpersönlichkeit des Verfassers"), the result of Baur's two different reading approaches creates an obvious tension. On the one hand, he treats those passages which discuss the ascribed authors' tenure and teaching among the attributed addressees as opaque windows offering no information about the life and experiences of the actual author. On the other hand, he regards those passages which mention persecution, opposed teaching, or proper behavior as transparent windows providing valuable information concerning the actual *Sitz im Leben* of Second Thessalonians. The former reading approach seems to accord well with the identification of Second Thessalonians as a pseudepigraphon while the latter exhibits some of the same interpretative assumptions and reading strategies evident in his treatment of genuine Pauline texts.

As an example of the latter, Baur unhesitatingly reads μήτε δι' ἐπιστολῆς ὡς δι' ἡμῶν (2 Thess 2:2) as evidence for the existence of pseudonymous Pauline letters circulating at the time Second Thessalonians was written.[44] Similarly, he interprets Paul's reference to an ἐπιστολή in 1 Cor 5:9 as an indication of a real letter sent to the Corinthians from Paul prior to our First Corinthians.[45] Notably, in both of these instances, Baur uses the text as a clear window through which he is able to project the actual existence of a real document based solely upon its mention in another written text. The world of the written texts thus moves from page to reality. In the case of 1 Cor 5:9, interpreters rightly and consistently posit the existence of an earlier Corinthian letter based upon the apparent logical inference that no valid historical or rhetorical reason exists for Paul to refer to an earlier imaginary letter within a later missive to the same group of

---

end-time events are already taking place (2:1–12), and, secondarily, to encourage responsible conduct within the believing community (3:6–12). He also wants to console the addressees as they continue to undergo persecution, but his consolation take the form of instruction (1:5–10)."

[44] Cf. E.-M. Becker, "Ὡς δι' ἡμῶν in 2 Thess 2.2 als Hinweis auf einen verlorenen Brief," *NTS* 55 (2009): 55–72.

[45] Ἔγραψα ὑμῖν ἐν τῇ ἐπιστολῇ μὴ συναναμίγνυσθαι πόρνοις. Baur, *Paulus* (see n. 9), 1:341, "Das Missverständniss, das er 5,9f. zu berichtigen hatte in Betreff des μὴ συναναμίγνυσθαι πόρνοις, wozu er die Korinther in einem frühern Briefe vor unserem ersten ermahnt hatte, hätte kaum entstehen können, wenn über diese Sache zuvor schon mündlich verhandelt worden wäre." ET: 1:318. The content of that letter was apparently misunderstood and Paul was thus required to exegete his own preceding missive. Cf. M. M. Mitchell, "The Corinthian Correspondence and the Birth of Pauline Hermeneutics," in *Paul and the Corinthians: Studies on a Community in Conflict. Essays in Honour of Margaret Thrall* (eds. T. J. Burke and J. K. Elliott; Leiden/Boston: Brill, 2003), 17–53.

Christ-believers. In the case of 2 Thess 2:2, the methodological basis for positing the existence of a text based solely upon its mention in a pseudepigraphon remains unclear.

2. Beyond Baur: Situating the Author

The methodological inconsistency demonstrated above in Baur's reading of Second Thessalonians has, in the last twenty-five years, become more apparent in the work of some scholars who extend the reading strategy to additional portions of Second Thessalonians. Drawing upon the interpretive assumptions and strategies used in genuine Pauline documents, they treat passages about the ascribed authors (i.e., Paul, Silvanus, and Timothy) as autobiographical remarks from the actual author. These interpreters, despite identifying Second Thessalonians as a pseudepigraphon, regard the narrated circumstances of Paul, Silvanus, and Timothy in Second Thessalonians as portraying the real world of the actual author. Thus, the epistolary document written in the name of Paul, Silvanus, and Timothy to the Thessalonians neither provides information about the historical Paul and his colleagues nor serves as a fictitious literary stage for Paul's epistolary activity. Baur's double personality of the author ("Doppelpersönlichkeit des Verfassers") collapses into a single persona ("Einzelpersönlichkeit").

Within the world created in Second Thessalonians, the texts used to situate the actual author refer to the epistolary past (2 Thess 1:10; 2:5, 14, 15; 3:6, 7–10) and the epistolary present (1:4; 3:1–2, 11). More specifically, the former texts include references to the initial reception of the attributed writers' εὐαγγέλιον/μαρτύριον (1:10, 2:14), apocalyptic teaching delivered to the ascribed addressees (2:5), traditions (παραδόσεις) passed on by word or letter (2:15, 3:6), and the behavior of the attributed authors while among the ascribed addressees (3:7–10). The latter includes the boast of the attributed authors (1:4), a request for prayer (3:1–2), and mention of reported behavior among the ascribed addressees (3:11).

Although a relatively recent development, the extension of an old—albeit methodologically suspect—reading strategy to additional passages in Second Thessalonians is not limited to one or two interpreters. Rather, it is found in the work of a number of different scholars. In the pages that follow, this essay will demonstrate the broad currency of this reading by ample citation in the text and notes.

3. The Epistolary Past

3.1 2 Thess 1:10

The typical Pauline thanksgiving is replaced in 2 Thess 1:3 by an obligatory thanksgiving (εὐχαριστεῖν ὀφείλομεν τῷ θεῷ πάντοτε περὶ ὑμῶν)[46] which develops into a long and meandering sentence.[47] Near the end of the thanksgiving, the author asserts in a parenthesis "our testimony to you was believed" (ὅτι ἐπιστεύθη τὸ μαρτύριον ἡμῶν ἐφ' ὑμᾶς – 2 Thess 1:10).[48] For Menken ἡμῶν does not refer to the ascribed authors (i.e., Paul, Silvanus, and Timothy), but to the actual author and his testimony to the church. Menken writes, "The clause shows that the addressed community is supposed to belong to 'all who have believed.' The community has believed the testimony of the sender of the letter, a testimony which is identical to 'the gospel of our Lord Jesus Christ' (1.8)."[49] This reading of 2 Thess 1:10 merges the epistolary identities of the ascribed authors and the actual author.

3.2 2 Thess 2:5

Following a brief injunction to avoid possible deception (2 Thess 2:3a),[50] the author of Second Thessalonians continues with the beginning of a conditional sentence. The protasis,[51] which introduces ὁ ἄνθρωπος τῆς ἀνομίας, lacks the anticipated apodosis.[52] Rather, the writer further de-

---

[46] Cf. 2 Thess 2:13, ἡμεῖς δὲ ὀφείλομεν εὐχαριστεῖν τῷ θεῷ πάντοτε περὶ ὑμῶν.

[47] For a syntactical analysis of this sentence see D. Schmidt, "The Syntactical Style of 2 Thessalonians: How Pauline Is It?" in *The Thessalonian Correspondence* (ed. R. F. Collins; BETL 87; Leuven: Leuven University Press, 1990), 383–93.

[48] The precise syntax of the ὅτι clause is not clear. At issue is whether ἐφ' ὑμᾶς goes with ἐπιστεύθη or τὸ μαρτύριον ἡμῶν. The latter option is preferred by most interpreters. See the helpful discussion in J. E. Frame, *Epistles of St. Paul to the Thessalonians* (see n. 5), 221, 236–38.

[49] Menken, *2 Thessalonians* (see n. 39), 92. See also A. Smith, *The Second Letter to the Thessalonians* (NIB 11; Nashville: Abingdon Press, 2000), 747, "Because the church believed his testimony and on that basis acquired a fate distinct from the unbelievers (1:10), he can consider presumably dissident thought (2:3–12) and behavior (3:6–15)—whether within or outside the church—as falsehood that should not be believed or supported." Similarly, he notes, "the church 'believed' the writer's testimony (v. 10)," (746) and later, "The peroration's use of 1 Thessalonians reinforces both the theme about belief in the writer's gospel or testimony and the theme of standing firm" (770).

[50] μή τις ὑμᾶς ἐξαπατήσῃ κατὰ μηδένα τρόπον. The subjunctive of prohibition in the third person is rare in the NT.

[51] 2 Thess 2:3b, ὅτι ἐὰν μὴ ἔλθῃ ἡ ἀποστασία πρῶτον καὶ ἀποκαλυφθῇ ὁ ἄνθρωπος τῆς ἀνομίας.

[52] Frame, *Epistles of St. Paul to the Thessalonians* (see n. 5), 250, plausibly argues

scribes the figure just introduced and the projected result of his action (2:3c–4). The description then breaks off with the question (2 Thess 2:5): "Do you not remember that while I was still with you I was telling you these things?"[53] In her recent commentary, Linda McKinnish Bridges maintains that this question does not evoke Paul's actual oral instruction while among the Thessalonians or even instruction fictitiously attributed to Paul. Rather, it calls to mind the actual words of the author while among the readers. She writes, "The author uses his personal relationship with the members of the congregation to reinforce this teaching. The use of the imperfect tense implies that the teachings happened more than once."[54] When read in this way, the actual author of Second Thessalonians refers to time spent among the audience.

3.3 2 Thess 2:14–15

The author of Second Thessalonians, following the model of First Thessalonians, introduces a second thanksgiving at 2:13–14.[55] Within the thanksgiving, it is affirmed that, "[God] called you through our gospel" (εὐαγγελίου ἡμῶν – 2 Thess 2:14). Consistent with the reading of 2 Thess

---

that the apodosis would have read ἡ ἡμέρα τοῦ κυρίου οὐκ ἐνστήσεται. Cf. Best, *The First and Second Epistles to the Thessalonians* (see n. 5), 280–81; Richard, *First and Second Thessalonians* (see n. 2), 325–26; Malherbe, *The Letters to the Thessalonians* (see n. 5), 418.

[53] 2 Thess 2:5, οὐ μνημονεύετε ὅτι ἔτι ὢν πρὸς ὑμᾶς ταῦτα ἔλεγον ὑμῖν; Cf. 2 Thess 3:10, καὶ γὰρ ὅτε ἦμεν πρὸς ὑμᾶς and 1 Thess 3:4, καὶ γὰρ ὅτε πρὸς ὑμᾶς ἦμεν, προελέγομεν ὑμῖν ὅτι μέλλομεν θλίβεσθαι, καθὼς καὶ ἐγένετο καὶ οἴδατε.

[54] Cf. McKinnish Bridges, *1 & 2 Thessalonians* (see n. 2), 238. Cf. Smith, *The Second Letter to the Thessalonians* (see n. 49), 757–58, "Then the sentence is interrupted by a parenthetical clause about the writer's earlier words while he was with the church." Also, Havener, "2 Thessalonians" (see n. 2), 1174–75, "The author reminds them that they were told (oral tradition) about these things when the author was still with them." Note also the tension in Menken's comments. Menken, *2 Thessalonians* (see n. 39), 107, writes, "A statement such as this also belongs, of course, to the pseudonymous fiction, and it seems to have been derived from 1 Thessalonians 3.4." Inexplicably, on the very next page of his commentary (108), Menken opts for a very different reading which accords with that of McKinnish Bridges. Menken asserts, "In a passage that concerns the timing of the events of the end, the adverb 'now' at the beginning of 2.6 can be supposed to have its normal temporal sense. It qualifies 'you know'; the present knowledge of the addressees is primarily contrasted with the author's teaching when he was still with the congregation (2.5)."

[55] 2 Thess 2:13–14, ἡμεῖς δὲ ὀφείλομεν εὐχαριστεῖν τῷ θεῷ πάντοτε περὶ ὑμῶν, ἀδελφοὶ ἠγαπημένοι ὑπὸ κυρίου, ὅτι εἵλατο ὑμᾶς ὁ θεὸς ἀπαρχὴν εἰς σωτηρίαν ἐν ἁγιασμῷ πνεύματος καὶ πίστει ἀληθείας, εἰς ὃ [καὶ] ἐκάλεσεν ὑμᾶς διὰ τοῦ εὐαγγελίου ἡμῶν, εἰς περιποίησιν δόξης τοῦ κυρίου ἡμῶν Ἰησοῦ Χριστοῦ. Cf. 1 Thess 2:13.

1:10 and 2:5 above, Menken treats the good news as the message of the actual writer, "It [God's calling] is the realization in history of God's decree of election 'from the beginning,' through the preaching, by 'Paul' and his companions, of the good news about Christ (cf. Rom. 8:30)."[56] Similarly, the command to hold onto the traditions (παραδόσεις) taught through "our word or letter" (εἴτε διὰ λόγου εἴτε δι' ἐπιστολῆς ἡμῶν – 2 Thess 2:15),[57] is read by Bonnie Thurston as an appeal to the traditions passed on by the actual author:

In their dangers and persecutions, the Thessalonian Christians must stand fast (*stekête*), that is, be stalwart and resolute in trials, and must hold fast (*krateite*) to that which is passed on ... the teaching of the writer and his colleagues.[58]

3.4 2 Thess 3:6–10

With reference to the tradition mentioned in 2 Thess 3:6 (παραγγέλλομεν ... στέλλεσθαι ὑμᾶς ἀπὸ παντὸς ἀδελφοῦ ἀτάκτως περιπατοῦντος καὶ μὴ κατὰ τὴν παράδοσιν ἣν παρελάβοσαν παρ' ἡμῶν), the example set

---

[56] Cf. Menken, *2 Thessalonians* (see n. 39), 121. Near the beginning of this commentary, Menken writes, "In 2 Thess 2.2, the author of the letter, who presents himself as Paul (I shall refer to him as 'Paul'), tells his addressees not to panic" (33). Among the other descriptive titles used for the figure behind Second Thessalonians (e.g., an anonymous Christian, someone, sender, the writer of our letter, author, our author, a post-Pauline author, an author in the Pauline tradition, the author of the letter, the author of Second Thessalonians, the author of the second letter, etc.), Menken's 'Paul' is one of the most used designations in his commentary (33, 35, 63, 70, 71, 72, 73, 74, 75, 76, 77, 92, 93, 94, 96, 104, 109, 110, 113, 125, 128, 129, 130, 131, 132, 136, 137, 140, 141, 143). For Menken, 'Paul' is not the historical Paul but is the actual author whose real behavior and thought are attributed to the historical Paul in Second Thessalonians. Cf. Smith, *The Second Letter to the Thessalonians* (see n. 49), 761, "The thanksgiving here also links God's call of the church to the writer's proclamation (v.14)." See E. Krentz, "Through a Lens: Theology and Fidelity in 2 Thessalonians," in *Pauline Theology. Vol. 1: Thessalonians, Philippians, Galatians, Philemon* (ed. J. M. Bassler; Minneapolis: Fortress Press, 1991), 58, "God has called them by the writer's gospel 'so that you may obtain the glory of our Lord Jesus Christ.'" Also, Thurston, *Reading Colossians, Ephesians & 2 Thessalonians* (see n. 2), 183–84.

[57] Reading the personal pronoun, ἡμῶν, with both substantives. See Frame, *Epistles of St. Paul to the Thessalonians* (see n. 5), 283–84.

[58] Thurston, *Reading Colossians, Ephesians & 2 Thessalonians* (see n. 2), 183–84. Cf. Smith, *The Second Letter to the Thessalonians* (see n. 49), 761–62, "This is a critical link because the writer will later ask the church to stand firm and hold fast to traditions that he taught them (v.15). It is also critical because a part of the audience's problem is its potential dissuasion from the writer's truth, even though the church came to belief through the writer." Also, Menken, *2 Thessalonians* (see n. 39), 71, "'Paul' concludes in 2.15 that the congregation has to stand firm and to hold fast to the traditions they have been taught by his word or letter."

forth in 3:7–9,[59] and the citation of a community rule in 3:10, Abraham Smith writes:

> This initial set of verses gives a specific command (v. 6) and a specific example drawn from the writer's previous visit and ongoing life while he was with the church (3:7–10). On the one hand, the writer does not wish the church to be influenced by the conduct of those who depart from the writer's tradition (v. 6) ... On the other hand, the writer lifts up his own visit as a model for the church (vv. 7–10).[60]

Once again, rather than a reference to time spent by the historical Paul among the Thessalonians or even a literary creation of a fictive tenure by Paul among the Thessalonians, Smith and others read it as an account of the actual author's tenure and teaching with the church.

4. The Epistolary Present

4.1 2 Thess 1:4

The protracted initial thanksgiving of Second Thessalonians contains a result clause in 1:4 which reports boasting among the assemblies of God (ὥστε αὐτοὺς ἡμᾶς ἐν ὑμῖν ἐγκαυχᾶσθαι ἐν ταῖς ἐκκλησίαις τοῦ θεοῦ ὑπὲρ τῆς ὑπομονῆς ὑμῶν καὶ πίστεως ἐν πᾶσιν τοῖς διωγμοῖς ὑμῶν καὶ ταῖς θλίψεσιν αἷς ἀνέχεσθε). Consistent with the reading of those texts which describe the ascribed authors' tenure among the attributed addressees, Charles H. Giblin comments, "The reason is twofold: the increase of their faith and love (v 3cd) and the writer's grounds for taking credit

---

[59] Cf. 2 Thess 3:8, οὐδὲ δωρεὰν ἄρτον ἐφάγομεν παρά τινος, ἀλλ' ἐν κόπῳ καὶ μόχθῳ νυκτὸς καὶ ἡμέρας ἐργαζόμενοι πρὸς τὸ μὴ ἐπιβαρῆσαί τινα ὑμῶν with 1 Thess 2:9, μνημονεύετε γάρ, ἀδελφοί, τὸν κόπον ἡμῶν καὶ τὸν μόχθον· νυκτὸς καὶ ἡμέρας ἐργαζόμενοι πρὸς τὸ μὴ ἐπιβαρῆσαί τινα ὑμῶν ἐκηρύξαμεν εἰς ὑμᾶς τὸ εὐαγγέλιον τοῦ θεοῦ.

[60] Smith, *The Second Letter to the Thessalonians* (see n. 49), 767–68. See also his comments on 3:11–12, "With the play on words, in the exhortation directed to the erring ones, the writer clarifies the contrast between 'the disorderly ones' (*ataktoi*) and his own 'model' behavior ... What they do, in contrast to the model of the writer, does not aid the larger church, and thus they must be admonished 'in the Lord Jesus Christ' (v. 12)" (768). Note Menken, *2 Thessalonians* (see n. 39), 133, "The conjunction 'for' at the beginning of 3.7 shows that 'Paul' now advances his arguments to buttress the command of 3.6. The arguments concern his stay, in the past, with the community: then, as they know, he demonstrated both by his own behavior (3.7–9) and by his words (3.10) that one has to work for a living." However, in the paragraph which proceeds the sentences just quoted, Menken seems to offer a very different reading of 3:6–12, "It is striking that in his argument in 3.6–12, he does not revert to the first letter, but—fictitiously, of course—to Paul's founding visit to the community." Cf. Thurston, *Reading Colossians, Ephesians & 2 Thessalonians* (see n. 2), 189, 191–93.

among the churches of God for their patient endurance and fidelity in the persecutions and tribulations, which they are undergoing."[61] When read in this way, the boast in 2 Thess 1:4 is thus neither an assertion about the historical Paul nor a component of the epistolary fiction. It is rather an autobiographical comment from the actual author.[62]

4.2 2 Thess 3:1–2

2 Thess 3:1–2 contains a two-fold prayer request on behalf of the ascribed authors for the advancement of the word of the Lord (3:1, ἵνα ὁ λόγος τοῦ κυρίου τρέχῃ καὶ δοξάζηται καθὼς καὶ πρὸς ὑμᾶς) and rescue "from improper and evil human beings" (3:2, ἵνα ῥυσθῶμεν ἀπὸ τῶν ἀτόπων καὶ πονηρῶν ἀνθρώπων). Gerhard Krodel writes, "Having prayed for the Thessalonians (2:16–17), the author now asks them to pray for him (3:1). Reciprocal prayers express the church's unity between the missionary-preacher and his people."[63] Thus, by using the prayer request as a transpar-

---

[61] C. H. Giblin, *The Second Letter to the Thessalonians* (*NJBC*; Englewood Cliffs, N.J.: Prentice Hall, 1990), 873. Smith, ibid., 745–46, "The recognition of the believer's endurance and faith is enhanced by the writer's insistence that he boasts about them to the churches of God." Also note, E. Krentz, "Traditions Held Fast: Theology and Fidelity in 2 Thessalonians," in *The Thessalonian Correspondence* (see n. 47), 505–15 (512), "The writer speaks of boasting 'on behalf of your endurance and faith (ὑπὲρ τῆς ὑπομονῆς ὑμῶν καὶ πίστεως) in all your persecutions and afflictions' (2 Thess 1,4)." Cf. Menken, *2 Thessalonians* (see n. 39), 83; Thurston, *Reading Colossians, Ephesians & 2 Thessalonians* (see n. 2), 168; Simon Légasse, *Les Épîtres de Paul Aux Thessaloniciens* (LD Commentaires 7; Paris: Cerf, 1999), 362–63; McKinnish Bridges, *1 & 2 Thessalonians* (see n. 2), 217.

[62] A similar interpretative strategy seems to inform Smith's reading of the reported prayer in 1:11–12 (εἰς ὃ καὶ προσευχόμεθα πάντοτε περὶ ὑμῶν, ἵνα ὑμᾶς ἀξιώσῃ τῆς κλήσεως ὁ θεὸς ἡμῶν καὶ πληρώσῃ πᾶσαν εὐδοκίαν ἀγαθωσύνης καὶ ἔργον πίστεως ἐν δυνάμει, ὅπως ἐνδοξασθῇ τὸ ὄνομα τοῦ κυρίου ἡμῶν Ἰησοῦ ἐν ὑμῖν, καὶ ὑμεῖς ἐν αὐτῷ, κατὰ τὴν χάριν τοῦ θεοῦ ἡμῶν καὶ κυρίου Ἰησοῦ Χριστοῦ). Smith, ibid, 746, notes, "And the writer prays that God will complete in the church 'every ... work of faith' (v.11)." There is, however, a tension in Smith's commentary on this point. Two pages prior, he writes, "The other sentence is short (vv. 11–12), reporting the content (v. 11) and purpose (v. 12) of Paul's intercessory prayer report" (744). The subject of the prayer is, on the one hand, the writer, but, on the other hand, Paul.

[63] G. Krodel, "2 Thessalonians," in *The Deutero-Pauline Letters: Ephesians, Colossians, 2 Thessalonians, 1–2 Timothy, Titus* (ed. idem; Proclamation Commentaries; Minneapolis: Fortress Press, 1993), 51. Cf. Smith, ibid., 765, "The second concern of the prayer request is more directly related to the writer. He may be a towering figure in the eyes of the church, but continuing use of the first-person plural pronouns ('we' and 'us') and the prayer request for deliverance from opposition suggest that he is not a lone hero. Furthermore, he *and* his church stand in opposition to others ('for not all have faith,' v. 2), a somber, but realistic, recognition of the old age's presence and of the division of sides squared off against each other in the writer's apocalyptic perspective." Similarly,

ent window, the prayer request from and for the Paul, Silvanus, and Timothy of the text in the midst of opposition is in fact a prayer request from and for the actual author who is facing opposition.

4.3 2 Thess 3:11

In 2 Thess 3:11 (ἀκούομεν γὰρ τινας περιπατοῦντας ἐν ὑμῖν ἀτάκτως, μηδὲν ἐργαζομένους ἀλλὰ περιεργαζομένους) the ascribed authors attribute the source of information about the behavior addressed in 3:6–12 to an oral report. Richard asserts, "By means of an authoritative 'we have heard' (see 1 Cor 11:18 where the closest parallel is 'I hear'), the author claims personal knowledge of the community's situation."[64] The "we hear" in 2 Thess 3:11 is read as the actual author's auditory activity.

Menken, *2 Thessalonians* (see n. 39), 63, "It is further clear from 2 Thessalonians itself that both the author and the addressees of the letter are suffering persecution (1.4; 3.2)." On page 74, Menken writes, "The author asks the congregation to pray for him that his preaching may be successful and that he may be saved 'from wicked and evil people; for faith is not everyone's business' (3.1–2)." Thurston, *Reading Colossians, Ephesians & 2 Thessalonians* (see n. 2), 185, "Here the writer requests petitions for the success of his apostolic work in the midst of serious opposition and for personal deliverance from those who oppose the gospel. The request for prayer for himself shifts at v. 4 to a form of entreaty to the letter's recipients." Cf. Giblin, *The Second Letter to the Thessalonians* (see n. 61), 875. More cautious, E. Krentz, "Thessalonians, First and Second Epistles to the," *ABD* 6:515–23, "Improper and evil people' are impeding Paul's (their?) missionary work (2 Thess 3:1–2)" (518). However, his comments from an earlier article are more in line with those of Smith. Krentz, "Traditions Held Fast" (see n. 61), 504–5, "The writer is himself experiencing such opposition; he asks for prayers that he might be delivered from 'evil and pernicious people' (τῶν ἀτόπων καὶ πονηρῶν ἀνθρώπων, 2 Thes 3,2), clearly opponents of 'the word of the Lord' (2 Thes 3,1) and without faith, as are the persecutors who are not obedient to the gospel."

[64] Richard, *First and Second Thessalonians* (see n. 2), 382. Also, Menken, *2 Thessalonians* (see n. 39), 136, "After the digression on his exemplary conduct and word, 'Paul' returns to the topic broached in 3:6: the behaviour of the disorderly ones. He first refers to news that has reached him: 'For we hear that some are living among you in a disorderly way, not doing any work but being busybodies' (3.11). The fact that news reached 'Paul' (in what form, is not clear), explains why he made the preceding digression; therefore, he starts with 'for.'" Cf. Furnish, *1 Thessalonians & 2 Thessalonians* (see n. 43), 178, and P.-G. Müller, *Der Erste und Zweite Brief an die Thessalonicher* (RNT; Regensburg: Friedrich Pustet, 2001), 302.

5. Concluding Observations

The use of passages in the pseudepigraphic Second Thessalonians in order to reconstruct the document's *Sitz im Leben* is without a clearly defined method and results in interpretive inconsistencies. The identification of Second Thessalonians as a pseudepigraphon turns our confident affirmations—based in a reading of the text—about the background of the document into complex and involved questions: Where if anywhere in the text does the identity of the actual author emerge from behind the mask of the ascribed authors and their narrated context? Do the historical reminiscences and past experiences of the ascribed authors resonate with the real experiences of the actual author? If so, to what extent and how would we know? Was there an actual persecution against Christians raging among perceived readers (1:4–10)? Was a real letter being circulated in the name of Paul, Silvanus, and Timothy (2:2)? Did some source truly claim that the Day of the Lord had come (2:2)? Was the actual author being maltreated (2 Thess 3:2)? Were idle individuals causing trouble by their refusal to work (2 Thess 3:7–13)? In terms of reconstructing a *Sitz im Leben* through the window of Second Thessalonians, does deception ever end and truth begin?

In order to move forward, Second Thessalonians research needs to develop a rigorous hermeneutical model which adequately takes into consideration the interpretive complexities of working with a pseudepigraphon. Baur's concept of the author's double personality, when consistently applied, provides a promising new beginning. In addition, a focus on the process of producing a pseudepigraphon in antiquity can offer new ways for thinking about how Second Thessalonians was composed to meet the goals of its actual author.

Fiktion oder Täuschung?

Zur Diskussion über die Pseudepigraphie der Pastoralbriefe

von

JENS HERZER

Seit Friedrich Daniel Ernst Schleiermacher 1807[1] die Echtheit des Ersten Timotheusbriefes in Zweifel gezogen und Ferdinand Christian Baur fast 30 Jahre später[2] diesen Zweifel zur grundlegenden Voraussetzung für die Interpretation aller drei Pastoralbriefe erklärt hatte, ist es zu keiner einhelligen Auffassung über diese Briefe mehr gekommen – es sei denn, man beschränkt das, was man in der Forschung Konsens nennt, auf diejenigen Gelehrten, die der Grundannahme Baurs bis heute folgen.[3] Schon für Adolf von Harnack stand allerdings fest: „Das Rätsel, das über diesen Briefen schwebt, hat noch niemand wirklich gelöst und ist auch mit unseren geschichtlichen Hilfsmitteln unlösbar."[4] Angesichts der disparaten Forschungslage ist der Schluss unausweichlich, dass sich daran trotz aller Bemühungen bis heute nichts geändert hat. Dieser Einsicht gilt es beim Entwickeln von Erklärungsmodellen für die Pastoralbriefe mit methodischer Vorsicht Rechnung zu tragen. Der Titel des vorliegenden Versuches, die Pseudepigraphie der Pastoralbriefe vor dem Hintergrund der Geschichte dieses interpretatorischen Paradigmas zu beschreiben, zeigt das Spannungsfeld an, in dem sich ein solches Unterfangen bewegt. Erklärungsversuche unter der Voraussetzung der Pseudepigraphie der drei Briefe haben es mit dem Problem zu tun, sich zwischen theologisch legitimer, literarischer Fiktion einerseits[5] und zweifelhafter, mit Täuschungsabsicht

---

[1] F. D. E. SCHLEIERMACHER, Ueber den sogenannten ersten Brief des Paulos an den Timotheos. Ein kritisches Sendschreiben an J. C. Gass, Berlin 1807.

[2] F. C. BAUR, Die sogenannten Pastoralbriefe des Apostels Paulus aufs neue kritisch untersucht, Stuttgart/Tübingen 1835.

[3] Vgl. J. HERZER, Abschied vom Konsens? Die Pseudepigraphie der Pastoralbriefe als Herausforderung an die neutestamentliche Wissenschaft, ThLZ 129 (2004), 1267–1282.

[4] A. VON HARNACK, Die Briefsammlung des Apostels Paulus und die anderen vorkonstantinischen christlichen Briefsammlungen. Sechs Vorlesungen aus der altkirchlichen Literaturgeschichte, Leipzig 1926, 14.

[5] Vgl. dazu bes. die unter den gegebenen Voraussetzungen konsequente und umfassende Interpretation von A. MERZ, Die fiktive Selbstauslegung des Paulus. Intertextuelle

verbundener Fälschung andererseits[6] entscheiden zu müssen. Der kanonische Rang der Pastoralbriefe scheint dabei nahezulegen, das erstere Modell zu bevorzugen – ungeachtet der konkreten literarischen Merkmale der Briefe, die bereits auf einen ersten oberflächlichen Blick zutage treten und darauf hindeuten, dass es sich dabei um unterschiedliche und im Einzelfall keinesfalls unproblematische Weisen im Umgang mit pseudepigraphischen Stilmitteln handelt.[7]

Da die Pastoralbriefe auf ihre Weise am Phänomen der Pseudepigraphie in der Antike partizipieren, soll es im Folgenden wesentlich um methodische Klärungen bzw. Bestandsaufnahmen der Diskussion zum Thema der Pseudepigraphie sowie um daraus folgende Problemanzeigen und Perspektiven im Blick auf die Pastoralbriefe gehen. Mehr ist angesichts der Komplexität der aktuellen Diskussionslage kaum zu leisten, aber wenn dies erreicht werden kann, dann ist schon viel gewonnen. Der vorliegende Band macht immerhin deutlich, dass Pseudepigraphie nicht pauschal abgehandelt werden kann, sondern ein so komplexes Phänomen darstellt, dass vor dem Hintergrund dieser Komplexität jede Schrift – und wegen des unbestreitbar autoritativen Anspruches besonders jede neutestamentliche Schrift – für sich betrachtet und beurteilt werden muss.

1. Forschungsgeschichtliche Bemerkungen zur Diskussion um die neutestamentliche Pseudepigraphie

Gleichsam als Bestandsaufnahme der Situation vor rund 100 Jahren sei den folgenden Ausführungen erneut ein Zitat von Adolf von Harnack vorangestellt:

„Als ich vor 57 Jahren das theologische Studium begann, galt nur der Theologe als ein kritischer Kopf, der nicht mehr als vier Paulusbriefe als echt bestehen ließ. Seitdem ist es anders geworden. Neben I. und II. Kor., Galat., Röm. ist jetzt auch die Echtheit von I. Thess., Koloss., Philipp., Philem. so gut wie allgemein anerkannt. Kontrovers sind noch von den Gemeindebriefen – von den Pastoralbriefen wird später kurz zu reden sein – II. Thess. und Ephes. Ich verkenne nicht, daß hier Schwierigkeiten bestehen, be-

---

Studien zur Intention und Rezeption der Pastoralbriefe, NTOA 52, Göttingen/Freiburg (CH) 2004.

[6] Vgl. die Problemanzeige bei M. FRENSCHKOWSKI, Pseudepigraphie und Paulusschule. Gedanken zur Verfasserschaft der Deuteropaulinen, insbesondere der Pastoralbriefe, in: F. W. Horn (Hg.), Das Ende des Paulus. Historische, theologische und literaturgeschichtliche Aspekte, BZNW 106, Berlin/New York 2001, 239–272.

[7] Vgl. dazu vor allem N. BROX, Zu den persönlichen Notizen der Pastoralbriefe, in: ders. (Hg.), Pseudepigraphie in der heidnischen und jüdisch-christlichen Antike, WdF 484, Darmstadt 1977, 272–294. Vgl. ders., Falsche Verfasserangaben. Zur Erklärung der frühchristlichen Pseudepigraphie, SBS 79, Stuttgart 1975.

sonders in Hinsicht auf Ephes.; allein sie sind m.E. nicht unüberwindlich, und die inneren Momente, die für die Echtheit sprechen, geben den Ausschlag. Dazu kommt, daß die Sammlung so alt ist, daß die Annahme, einer der Briefe sei eine Fälschung, große Bedenken erregen muß. Nicht, als ob nicht bereits falsche Briefe im Umlauf gewesen sein können …, aber daß falsche Briefe von *Gemeinden* in ältester Zeit widerspruchslos hingenommen worden sind, darin liegt die Schwierigkeit."[8]

Diese Äußerung weist nicht zuletzt darauf hin, wie schwierig es im Einzelfall ist, die pseudepigraphische Abfassung einer neutestamentlichen Schrift zu erweisen bzw. – etwas vorsichtiger formuliert – plausibel zu machen. Stellt man dem aktuellere Äußerungen zum Thema gegenüber, so scheint es, dass die vorsichtige Annäherung, wie sie noch für von Harnack erforderlich schien, längst nicht mehr selbstverständlich zum wissenschaftlichen Diskurs über Pseudepigraphie gehört.

1.1 Der Ausgangspunkt für eine kritische Neuorientierung

Als geradezu klassisch für eine nach wie vor weit verbreitete Auffassung im Blick auf das so genannte „Zeitalter der Pseudepigraphie" (wie Karl-Martin Fischer die Zeit zwischen 60 und 100 n. Chr. bezeichnet hatte[9]) kann wohl gelten, was Udo Schnelle in der „Einleitung in das Neue Testament" schreibt – und ein Einleitungswerk, zumal ein solches, das inzwischen als „Standardwerk" bezeichnet werden kann, präsentiert in erster Linie den breiteren, d.h. weithin akzeptierten Konsens der Forschung:

„Die literarische Form der Pseudepigraphie war im letzten Drittel des ersten christlichen Jahrhunderts das wirksamste Mittel, um die neu aufgebrochenen Probleme aus der Sicht der Verfasser der Pseudepigraphen im Sinn der von ihnen jeweils in Anspruch genommenen Autoritäten zu lösen. Die moralische Kategorie der Fälschung ist deshalb ungeeignet, die Zielsetzungen der Pseudepigraphie zu erfassen."[10]

Die Absicht der Fiktion – auch dies als weitgehender Konsens der Forschung – besteht danach in der Sicherung und Bewahrung der apostolischen Tradition in einer sich verändernden Situation, aus „ökumenischer Verantwortung" heraus und damit in „gesamtkirchliche[r] Perspektive".[11]

---

[8] VON HARNACK, Briefsammlung (s. Anm. 4), 11.
[9] K. M. FISCHER, Anmerkungen zur Pseudepigraphie im Neuen Testament, NTS 23 (1977), 76–81.
[10] U. SCHNELLE, Einleitung in das Neue Testament, Göttingen [6]2007, 325.
[11] Ebd., ausdrücklich gegen M. FRENSCHKOWSKI (s. Anm. 6). Schnelle hält es daher für sachgemäßer, statt von falschen „von ‚entliehenen Verfasserangaben' zu sprechen, bei denen die apostolische Autorität als Bürge für die Gültigkeit des Gesagten auftritt" (ebd. in Anlehnung an und Modifikation von BROX, Verfasserangaben [s. Anm. 7], 105). Vgl. ferner M. WOLTER, Die anonymen Schriften des Neuen Testaments. Annäherungsversuch an ein literarisches Phänomen, ZNW 79 (1988), 1–16, der den Stand der Forschung folgendermaßen zusammenfasst: „Die neutestamentliche Forschung hat sich in den letzten Jahren vor allem mit den pseudonymen Schriften befaßt und versucht, eine

Bereits in der Einleitung von Adolf Jülicher in der Bearbeitung von Erich Fascher lässt sich als Ergebnis der Debatte des 19. Jh. Ähnliches lesen[12] und man könnte viele andere Beispiele ergänzend hinzufügen.[13] Petr Pokorný etwa begründet die positive Intention falscher Verfasserangaben mit der theologischen Aussage, Gott habe „sich auch zu den fiktiven Pseudepigraphen bekannt, ähnlich wie er sich zu Jakob in Bethel bekannte".[14] Ruben Zimmermann bietet trotz seiner berechtigten Kritik an Pokornýs Erklärung eine sehr ähnliche und pauschale Lösung: „Auch wenn den eigentlichen Autoren pseudepigrapher Schriften im NT die ‚falsche Verfasserangabe' bewusst war, handelten sie nicht mit Täuschungsabsicht im Sinne einer bewussten Irreführung der Adressaten. Im Gegenteil. Die Verfasserangabe sollte nicht hinters Licht führen, sondern zum Licht hin."[15] Solche Formulierungen – Marco Frenschkowski hat sie als „binnentheologische Schönfärberei"[16] bezeichnet – machen immerhin deutlich, dass es in der

---

historische und theologische Erklärung zu finden. Am weitesten gekommen ist in dieser Hinsicht Norbert Brox, der davon ausgeht, daß es mit Ausnahme des Judasbriefes durchweg die Apostel sind, die als Verfasser der neutestamentlichen Pseudepigraphen fingiert werden. Dementsprechend sieht er – und dem stimme ich zu – die falschen Verfasserangaben dem Zweck dienen, die Kontinuität der apostolischen Tradition in der Zeit nach dem Tod der Apostel sicherzustellen. Es geht in den pseudonymen Schriften insofern darum, die Autorität der Apostel in ihrer jeweiligen Gegenwart verbindlich zu Gehör zu bringen."

[12] Die neutestamentlichen Autoren hätten „in bester Absicht und mit reinem Gewissen einem Apostel Worte in den Mund gelegt, die sie gerne mit apostolischer Autorität ihren Zeitgenossen zugerufen wissen wollten, und sich nicht im Geringsten als Lügner und Betrüger gefühlt" (A. JÜLICHER / E. FASCHER, Einleitung in das Neue Testament, Tübingen [7]1931, 54).

[13] Vgl. P. J. ACHTEMEIER / J. B. GREEN / M. M. THOMPSON, Introducing the New Testament, its Literature and Theology, Grand Rapids/Cambridge 2001, 560: „Pseudonymity appears to have been primarily a literary technique, and not one meant to deliberately deceive its readers." Vgl. in diesem Sinne auch B. M. METZGER, Literary Forgeries and Canonical Pseudepigrapha, JBL 91 (1972), 3–24 (21f.); D. A. DESILVA, An Introduction to the New Testament. Contexts, Methods and Ministry Formation, Downers Grove 2004, 685; P. POKORNÝ / U. HECKEL, Einleitung in das Neue Testament. Seine Literatur und Theologie im Überblick, UTB 2798, Tübingen 2007, 619–623; u.a.

[14] Sc. zu Jakob, der sich sein Erstgeburtsrecht durch die Täuschung seines Vaters erschlich, P. POKORNÝ, Art. Pseudepigraphie I. Altes und Neues Testament, TRE 27 (1997), 645–655 (654); vgl. dazu M. JANSSEN, Unter falschem Namen. Eine kritische Forschungsbilanz frühchristlicher Pseudepigraphie, ARGU 14, Frankfurt a.M. 2003, 240f.

[15] R. ZIMMERMANN, Unecht – und doch wahr? Pseudepigraphie im Neuen Testament als theologisches Problem, ZNT 12 (2003), 27–38 (35); s. dazu auch unten Anm. 25 sowie S. 501.

[16] FRENSCHKOWSKI, Pseudepigraphie (s. Anm. 6), 242. Vgl. dazu den vehementen Einspruch bei SCHNELLE, Einleitung (s. Anm. 10), 325 Anm. 12.

Frage nach der Einschätzung und Beurteilung von Pseudepigraphie nicht mehr darum gehen kann, sich auf einen kritischen Konsens zu verlassen. Aus der Annahme der Pseudepigraphie bestimmter Schriften folgt stets die Notwendigkeit, von dieser Voraussetzung her nicht nur eine schlüssige Interpretation der entsprechenden Schriften vorzunehmen, sondern im Zuge dieser Interpretation immer auch die *Legitimität* und *Plausibilität* der Fiktion bzw. der Fälschung zu erweisen. Angesichts dieser Problematik wird deutlich, wie sehr Walter Bauer mit seiner zugegebenermaßen polemisch zugespitzten Äußerung Recht hatte, dass in Verfasserschaftsfragen „die *sichere* Entscheidung nur dem Ignoranten leicht" falle.[17] Vor dem Hintergrund dessen, was auf dem Gebiet der altertumswissenschaftlichen Pseudepigraphieforschung bisher geleistet wurde, erweist sich die oben zitierte Auffassung zur Legitimität von Pseudepigraphie *in dieser Form* als unzutreffend;[18] ganz abgesehen von der Tatsache, dass bisher keineswegs plausibel gemacht werden konnte, warum und inwiefern Pseudepigraphie „im letzten Drittel des ersten christlichen Jahrhunderts das wirksamste Mittel"[19] zur Lösung der anstehenden Probleme gewesen sei. Ist speziell die neutestamentliche Pseudepigraphie tatsächlich ein so einheitlich zu beurteilendes Phänomen, wie zumeist behauptet bzw. vorausgesetzt wird? Wie „wirksam" im Sinne der ihnen unterstellten Absichten waren die als pseudepigraphisch eingestuften Schriften? In welchem Verhältnis steht ihre Wirksamkeit zu (zeitgenössischen!) Schriften jener lokal und überregional wirkenden Autoritäten, die unter ihrem eigenen Namen Probleme lösten? Und nicht zuletzt: In welchem Verhältnis steht die Wirksamkeit der als pseudepigraphisch eingestuften Schriften zur unumstrittenen und fortdauernden Wirksamkeit der authentischen Schriften des reklamierten Autors, von denen sie sich offenbar so grundlegend unterscheiden, dass man sie ihm absprechen muss? Die Fragen ließen sich vermehren. Die darauf zum Teil gegebenen Antworten setzen durchweg die Richtigkeit der be-

---

[17] W. BAUER, Heinrich Julius Holtzmann, in: ders., Aufsätze und kleine Schriften, hg. v. G. Strecker, Tübingen 1967, 308 (Hervorhebung J.H.).

[18] Vgl. auch H.-J. KLAUCK, Die antike Briefliteratur und das Neue Testament. Ein Lehr- und Arbeitsbuch, UTB 2022, Paderborn u.a. 1998, 303, der zu Recht einwendet: „Man darf nicht so weit gehen und behaupten, daß Pseudepigraphie in der Antike ein allgemein verbreiteter und anerkannter Vorgang gewesen sei, an dem niemand Anstoß nahm. Es gab im Gegenteil sehr wohl ein Gefühl für geistige Urheberschaft und für bewußte Fälschung."

[19] SCHNELLE, Einleitung (s. Anm. 10), 329; vgl. auch P. F. BEATRICE, Forgery, Propaganda, and Power in Christian Antiquity. Some Methodological Remarks, in: W. Blümer u.a. (Hg.), Alvarium (FS Gnilka), JAC.E 33, Münster 2002, 39–51; vgl. dazu JANSSEN, Unter falschem Namen (s. Anm. 14), 209–212; zur Kritik vgl. auch ZIMMERMANN, Unecht – und doch wahr? (s. Anm. 15), 28.33.

haupteten Auffassung von Pseudepigraphie voraus und schon damit ist ihre Überzeugungskraft infrage gestellt.[20]

1.2 Problematische Alternativen

Freilich darf eine Kritik an der Annahme neutestamentlicher Pseudepigraphie nicht ihrerseits zu Ignoranz der offenkundigen Probleme führen, um Pseudepigraphie im Neuen Testament grundsätzlich abzulehnen. Die Kontroverse um die Berechtigung der Annahme, dass es auch im Neuen Testament Pseudepigraphie gibt, hat die Diskussion seit Anfang des 19. Jh. erschwert und eine phänomenologisch differenzierende Wahrnehmung der Problematik behindert. Die Bestreitung von Pseudepigraphie im Neuen Testament wurde nicht zuletzt dadurch belastet, dass man die Kategorie der Moral ins Spiel brachte, die etwa so zusammengefasst werden kann: Vom ethischen Anspruch neutestamentlicher Autoren her sei es ausgeschlossen, dass diese auf das Mittel der Fälschung, d.h. auf bewusste Täuschung zur Durchsetzung ihrer Ziele zurückgegriffen hätten.[21] Angesichts dessen, was in christlicher Tradition mit hohem moralischem Anspruch tatsächlich an Pseudepigraphie vorliegt (z.B. Epheserbrief, katholische Briefe), ist dieses Argument nicht nur naiv, sondern muss auch konkrete Tatbestände nivellieren bzw. ignorieren, um den aufgestellten Prämissen gerecht zu werden. Dies kann somit kein ernsthafter Beitrag zu einer konstruktiven Diskussion sein. Im Gegenzug dazu hilft es aber auch nicht, wenn man – um dem moralischen Einwand zu entgehen – *bestreitet*, dass Pseudepigraphie im Neuen Testament *auch* Fälschung sein kann und aus diesem Grund nur pauschal behauptet, sie sei ein legitimes und allseits akzeptiertes Mittel antiker Schriftstellerei gewesen. Es überzeugt in diesem Zusammenhang auch nicht, die platonische Idee der „guten Lüge" bzw. die Vorstellung von der *pia fraus* oder des *dolus bonus* zu bemühen, wonach das Schreiben unter falschem Namen durch die gute Absicht gerechtfertigt wäre,[22] oder eben – wie etwa in dem bereits zitierten TRE-Artikel von Petr

---

[20] Martina Janßen hat vieles davon als eine „kritische Forschungsbilanz" anschaulich dargestellt und die Schwächen vieler Erklärungsversuche aufgezeigt (Unter falschem Namen [s. Anm. 14]). Zugleich wird daran sehr gut deutlich, wie viel oft an kreativer Phantasie nötig ist, um den Sinn und die Geltung des jeweils vorausgesetzten Paradigmas zu erweisen und die Texte entsprechend zu interpretieren (das gilt selbstverständlich keineswegs pauschal für alle dort referierten Arbeiten!).

[21] Vgl. in diesem Sinne z.B. F. TORM, Die Psychologie der Pseudonymität im Hinblick auf die Literatur des Urchristentums, SLA 2, Gütersloh 1932; G. HOLTZ, Die Pastoralbriefe, ThHK 13, Berlin 1980, 12f.

[22] Verwiesen wird hierbei in der Regel auf die Ausführungen zur erlaubten Lüge bei Xenophon, Memorabilia 4,2,14–18; Plato rep. 382C.389B.459C oder auch Cicero, Brutus 11,42; vgl. dazu W. SPEYER, Die literarische Fälschung im heidnischen und christlichen

Pokorný – Pseudepigraphie im Neuen Testament theologisch zu legitimieren.[23]

In diese geistlich-theologische Kategorie von Legitimierungsversuchen gehört auch die Erklärung, die Angabe eines anderen Verfassers beruhe auf einem Inspirationsbewusstsein, durch welches im Zusammenhang der Traditionssicherung und Traditionsweitergabe die Fiktion gerechtfertigt und geradezu notwendig sei.[24] Auch dieses Argument hat eine lange Tradition[25] und entspricht etwa dem, was Wolfgang Speyer als „echte religiöse Pseudepigraphie" beschrieben hat (freilich in Bezug auf ganz andere Schriften und gerade nicht auf die neutestamentlichen Brieffälschungen!).[26] Es bleibt aber gerade für die besonders strittigen Fälle wie den 2Thess oder die Pastoralbriefe ein reines Postulat, das in den konkreten Texten nur schwer zu verifizieren ist.[27] Nicht überzeugend ist ferner die konsequente Ableitung

---

Altertum. Ein Versuch ihrer Deutung, HAW I/2, München 1971, 94–97, der die Legitimität dieser „Lösung" im Kontext der antiken christlichen Schriftstellerei zu Recht bezweifelt; ferner BROX, Verfasserangaben (s. Anm. 7), 71.83f.

[23] S.o. Anm. 14.

[24] Vgl. z.B. P. GERLITZ, Art. Pseudonymität I. Religionsgeschichtlich, TRE 27 (1997), 659–662. Zur Funktion der Traditionssicherung s.o. Anm. 11.

[25] Vgl. etwa A. MEYER, Religiöse Pseudepigraphie als ethisch-psychologisches Problem (1932), in: Brox, Pseudepigraphie (s. Anm. 7), 90–110, der vom pseudonymen Autor annimmt: „... er kennt und spürt noch eine Macht, die mehr ist und mehr gibt als bloß fortgepflanzte Tradition, mehr auch als poetische Inspiration dem Dramatiker eingibt, den Geist Gottes und Christi" (108). Weiterhin etwa auch R. F. MERKEL, Kirchen- und religionsgeschichtliche Fälschungen, Süddeutsche Monatshefte 33 (1935–1936), 693–699 (vgl. dazu JANSSEN, Unter falschem Namen [s. Anm. 14], 50–53). Pointiert formuliert, die Dinge jedoch völlig auf den Kopf stellend und dadurch regelrecht *ad absurdum* geführt wird dieser geistliche Begründungszusammenhang vor allem bei K. ALAND, Das Problem der Anonymität und Pseudonymität in der christlichen Literatur der ersten beiden Jahrhunderte, in: ders., Studien zur Überlieferung des Neuen Testaments und seines Textes, ANTT 2, Berlin 1967, 24–34: „Wer der Christenheit jener Zeit allgemeingültige Weisungen gibt, tut das aus dem Heiligen Geist, er ist nur die Feder, die vom Geist bewegt wird. Derartige Schriften, sobald sie über den Charakter eines Briefes im engsten Sinne hinausgehen, können den eigentlichen Verfasser gar nicht nennen. Anonymität bzw. Pseudonymität sind m.E. keine Erscheinungen der frühchristlichen Literatur, die wir erklären oder gar rechtfertigen müßten, gerade umgekehrt ist es: Wir brauchen eine Erklärung, wenn der wirkliche Verfasser sich mit Namen nennt" (30). Zur berechtigten Kritik daran vgl. bereits H. R. BALZ, Anonymität und Pseudepigraphie im Urchristentum. Überlegungen zum literarischen und theologischen Problem der urchristlichen und gemeinantiken Pseudepigraphie, ZThK 66 (1969), 304–436 (419f.). Zustimmend zu Aland neuerdings z.B. A. STANDHARTINGER, Studien zur Entstehungsgeschichte und Intention des Kolosserbriefs, NT.S 94, Leiden u.a. 1999, 47.

[26] SPEYER, Fälschung (s. Anm. 22), 36f. (zur Definition von „echter religiöser Pseudepigraphie"); vgl. auch dessen Beitrag in diesem Band.

[27] Zum 2Thess vgl. A. J. MALHERBE, The Letters to the Thessalonians. A New Translation with Introduction and Commentary, AncB 32B, New York u.a. 2000, 349–375, der

neutestamentlicher Pseudepigraphie aus dem Phänomen der Fortschreibung und textergänzenden und textproduzierenden Interpretation in der alttestamentlichen und frühjüdischen Überlieferung, wie sie Eckard Reinmuth vorgeschlagen hat.[28] Trotz der berechtigten Forderung, dass jede der frühchristlichen Schriften „in ihrer speziellen Ausprägung gesondert betrachtet werden muß", ließen sich nach Reinmuth vor dem Hintergrund der biblischen Überlieferung „allgemeine literaturtheoretische und -historische Aussagen zum Phänomen der neutestamentlichen Pseudepigraphie treffen und auf die pseudo-paulinischen Texte anwenden".[29] Dass die dabei vorausgesetzte Kontinuität pseudepigraphischer bzw. pseudonymer Textproduktion vom Alten zum Neuen Testament gerade *aufgrund* der je konkret zu betrachtenden literaturtheoretischen Umstände so nicht aufrecht zu erhalten ist, wurde bereits durch Speyers Klassifikation nachgewiesen.[30] Die Fiktion eines 4. Esrabuches oder der syrischen Baruchapokalypse mit derjenigen pseudepigraphischer Paulusbriefe zu vergleichen, ist schon deshalb nicht überzeugend, weil sie literarische Formen miteinander vermischt, die auf ganz unterschiedlichen Ebenen zu beurteilen sind.[31] Die auf diesen „gewachsenen literarischen Konventionen" beruhende Legitimität *jeder* pseudepigraphischen Fiktion im Neuen Testament nennt Reinmuth einen „selbstverständlich gültigen hermeneutischen Kontrakt[.] zwischen Auto-

---

insgesamt kumulative Beweisführungen – wie sie auch für die Arbeit an den Pastoralbriefen charakteristisch sind – für methodisch unzureichend hält. Zur neueren Diskussion um den 2Thess vgl. auch den Beitrag von Trevor Thompson in diesem Band.

[28] E. REINMUTH, Der zweite Brief an die Thessalonicher, NTD 8/2, Göttingen 1998, 190–202 (Exkurs: Zur neutestamentlichen Paulus-Pseudepigraphie), bes. 196.

[29] A.a.O. 191.

[30] Vgl. SPEYER, Fälschung (s. Anm. 22); aber auch M. HENGEL, Anonymität, Pseudepigraphie und „Literarische Fälschung" in der jüdisch-hellenistischen Literatur, in: ders., Judaica et Hellenistica. Kleine Schriften I. Unter Mitarbeit von R. Deines, J. Frey, C. Markschies, A. M. Schwemer mit einem Anhang von H. Bloedhorn, WUNT 90, Tübingen 1996, 196–251 (= K. von Fritz [Hg.], Pseudepigrapha I. Pseudopythagorica – Lettres de Platon – Littérature pseudépigraphique juive, EnAC 18, Vandœuvres/Genève 1972, 231–308).

[31] Vgl. REINMUTH, Thessalonicher (s. Anm. 28), 194: „Dabei sind freilich auch Unterschiede nicht übersehbar. So beziehen sich die im NT gewählten Pseudonyme regelmäßig auf Personen der jüngsten Vergangenheit, im frühjüdischen Bereich indessen auf solche der ferneren Geschichte." Dennoch setzt er fort: „Das kann als Hinweis auf das frühchristliche Selbstverständnis interpretiert werden, Gegenwart und Zukunft in der Vollmacht des eschatologisch wirkenden Geistes zu erfassen" (ebd.). Die Intention der Pseudonymität frühjüdisch-apokalyptischer Schriften wird dabei zum Verstehenshintergrund neutestamentlicher Pseudepigraphie *erklärt*, auch wenn dieser Grundsatz dann im Einzelnen zu differenzieren ist. Vgl. auch Malherbes Urteil im Blick auf 2Thess: „2 Thessalonians is not an apocalypse but a letter that has concrete circumstances in view ..." (Thessalonians [s. Anm. 27], 373). Das gilt natürlich auch für den Vergleich der Pastoralbriefe mit derartiger Literatur.

ren und Adressaten".[32] Den Begriff der Fälschung vermeidet er daher konsequent.

1.3 Konsequenzen und mögliche Neuansätze

Diese knappen Bemerkungen können keinesfalls das gesamte Spektrum der Positionen zur neutestamentlichen Pseudepigraphie erfassen. Die Übergänge sind oft fließend und schwer darstellbar. Als ein erstes Fazit ergibt sich dennoch Folgendes: Keine der benannten (und sich zum Teil ausschließenden) Perspektiven ist geeignet, das Problem und das Phänomen der neutestamentlichen Pseudepigraphie zu beschreiben und zu erklären. Sie kann weder als selbstverständlich legitim verstanden bzw. zum geistlich legitimierten Sonderfall erklärt werden (so z.B. Schnelle, Pokorný), noch kann sie *pauschal* – wie bei Marco Frenschkowski[33] – als Fälschung bezeichnet werden, noch ist es gerechtfertigt, die Berechtigung der Kategorie „Fälschung"[34] abzulehnen oder gar innerneutestamentliche Pseudepigraphie aus „moralischen" Gründen generell zu bestreiten. Die entscheidende Frage ist vor allem diejenige nach *verlässlichen Kriterien, deren Relevanz und Geltung intersubjektiv im fachwissenschaftlichen Diskurs plausibel gemacht werden können*. Eine wesentliche Voraussetzung für die Kriterienfrage ist die differenzierte Wahrnehmung der *Durchführung* der pseudepigraphischen Fiktion in den konkreten Texten und daraus folgend die Unterscheidung verschiedener Arten von Pseudepigraphie (und nicht

---

[32] REINMUTH, Thessalonicher (s. Anm. 28), 196; vgl. auch die berechtigten kritischen Bemerkungen bei JANSSEN, Unter falschem Namen (s. Anm. 14), 192f.: Gerade im Fall des 2Thess werde „Traditions- oder Schulbewusstsein … zur inhaltlichen *Konfrontation*" (193, Hervorhebung J.H.). Vgl. auch deren Beitrag in diesem Band.

[33] Vgl. FRENSCHKOWSKI, Pseudepigraphie (s. Anm. 6), 251: „Es bleibt dabei, daß Pseudepigraphie eine bewußte und planmäßig durchgeführte Täuschung ist, welche – wenn sie erkannt worden wäre – damalige Leser im allgemeinen ebenso vor den Kopf gestoßen hätte wie heutige"; vgl. a.a.O. 262 zu den Pastoralbriefen: „geplante und raffinierte Fälschungen".

[34] Vgl. dezidiert SCHNELLE, Einleitung (s. Anm. 10), 325. In Duktus und Konkretion vergleichbar bei REINMUTH, Thessalonicher (s. Anm. 28), passim; vgl. auch bes. STANDHARTINGER, Kolosserbrief (s. Anm. 25), 31, wobei die Behauptung, Speyer begründe den Gebrauch des Begriffes Fälschung (sc. ausschließlich) mit dem Hinweis auf die Echtheitskritik des Altertums, so nicht stimmt. Seine Darstellung der Echtheitskritik und ihrer Methoden ist darüber hinaus sehr viel differenzierter, als Standhartinger dies referiert und kann daher auch nicht einfach in wenigen Zeilen erledigt werden – zumal sie selbst dann auf die Bedeutung von Echtheitskritik hinweist (40). Kaum weiterführend sind in diesem Kontext – vor allem hinsichtlich der Intention der pseudonymen Autoren – die ansonsten instruktiven Ausführungen Standhartingers (31–40) zu literarischen Schulübungen im antiken Bildungssystem als „Voraussetzungen für die Entstehung pseudepigrapher Werke" (40), da nicht deutlich wird, wie von daher Intention und gewählte Mittel der pseudonymen Autoren plausibel werden sollen.

nur zwischen Anonymität und Pseudonymität!) *auch im Neuen Testament*.[35] Die Bedeutung einer solchen Unterscheidung ist insbesondere durch die Arbeiten von Josef A. Sint (1960)[36] und vor allem Wolfgang Speyer (1971)[37] als *conditio sine qua non* für die Erörterung der Problematik aufgewiesen worden, hat aber bisher kaum zu einer differenzierten Anwendung auf innerneutestamentliche[38] Pseudepigraphen geführt.[39] Speyer hatte seine umfassende monographische Darstellung der profanen und christlichen Pseudepigraphie der Antike einen „Versuch der Deutung" genannt. Dieser Versuch besteht im Wesentlichen darin, den zunächst wertfreien Begriff „Pseudepigraphie" so zu differenzieren, dass man dem Phänomen und seinen unterschiedlichen literarischen Formen gerecht werden kann.[40] Erst auf dieser Grundlage ist es möglich, ein Urteil darüber zu

---

[35] Auch die – unter kirchengeschichtlicher Perspektive – vorgenommene Unterscheidung von M. WOLTER, Art. Pseudonymität II. Kirchengeschichtlich, TRE 27 (1997), 662–670, in „pseudepigraphische Pseudonymität", „anonyme Pseudonymität" und „symbolische Pseudonymität" hilft im Blick auf das Neue Testament nicht weiter, da die neutestamentlichen (mit den altkirchlichen) Pseudepigraphen generell unter der Rubrik „pseudepigraphische Pseudonymität" subsummiert werden, wobei es im Kontext innerkirchlicher Auseinandersetzungen darum ging, „die Ursprungsnorm ihrer jeweiligen Gegenwart mit dem Anspruch auf Verbindlichkeit zur Sprache zu bringen" und somit um die „authentische Bewahrung der identitätsstiftenden Tradition" (664f.).

[36] J. A. SINT, Pseudonymität im Altertum. Ihre Formen und ihre Gründe, Commentationes Aenipontanae 15, Innsbruck 1960. Ein Problem bei Sint ist jedoch, dass er unter der Feststellung, religiöse Pseudepigraphie stelle ein besonders großes Problem hinsichtlich ihrer Legitimität dar (159), zu deren Begründung ebenfalls eine nur hypothetisch zu behauptende geistliche Haltung „echter religiöser Ergriffenheit" unterstellen muss, so „daß von bewußter Täuschung keine Rede sein kann, ja daß ihm [sc. dem pseudonymen Autor] die moralische Wahrheitsfrage gar nicht erst zum Problem wird und er darum seine Entlarvung nicht befürchten konnte" (163).

[37] SPEYER, Fälschung (s. Anm. 22), passim; vgl. ders., Art. Fälschung, literarische, RAC 7 (1969), 236–277; ders., Religiöse Pseudepigraphie und literarische Fälschung im Altertum (1967), in: Brox, Pseudepigraphie (s. Anm. 7), 195–263.

[38] Der Begriff „*inner*neutestamentliche Pseudepigraphen" legt sich in diesem Zusammenhang aus literaturgeschichtlichen Gründen nahe, insofern auch *außer*neutestamentliche Schriften auf Grund ihrer literarischen Ursprungsrelation als „neutestamentliche" Apokryphen und Pseudepigraphen bezeichnet werden.

[39] Eine Ausnahme ist bis zu einem gewissen Grad die Monographie von A. D. BAUM, Pseudepigraphie und literarische Fälschung im frühen Christentum. Mit ausgewählten Quellentexten samt deutscher Übersetzung, WUNT II/138, Tübingen 2001, obwohl er dazu tendiert, Pseudepigraphie im Neuen Testament eher negativ zu beurteilen und daher versucht, die Echtheit der neutestamentlichen Pseudepigraphen zu plausibilisieren. Leider ist er in dieser Hinsicht an vielen Stellen nicht eindeutig genug und bemüht stattdessen gern die Kirchenväter (vgl. 148).

[40] Vgl. SPEYER, Fälschung (s. Anm. 22), 311: „Wichtig ist, daß klare Begriffe angewendet werden. Schon die antiken Echtheitskritiker haben nicht deutlich genug zwischen Irrtum, Fälschung und literarisch gemeinter Erfindung unterschieden."

fällen, unter welchen Kriterien und aufgrund welcher Merkmale eine Schrift etwa in den Bereich einer anerkannten „Schulpseudepigraphie" einzuordnen ist,[41] die keine Täuschungsabsicht verfolgt und bei der die Verwendung des Pseudonyms innerhalb eines soziologisch abgrenzbaren Kontextes auf einen offenen Konsens zurückgeführt werden kann, oder ob es sich um eine literarische (z.b. romanhaft fiktive) Schrift[42] oder um eine Fälschung handelt, die notwendig auf die Täuschung der Adressaten etwa durch Echtheitsbeglaubigungen (z.B. Unterschriftsfälschung), persönliche Angaben und dergleichen[43] angewiesen ist, weil sie sonst nicht akzeptiert werden würde. Dabei ist zu berücksichtigen, dass bei Schriften, die in einem offenen Konsens pseudepigraphisch entstanden sind, im Verlauf der Überlieferung und der Verselbständigung der offene Konsens keine Rolle mehr spielt und ursprünglich daran nicht beteiligte Kreise das Pseudonym nicht mehr als solches wahrnehmen und insofern gewissermaßen erst indirekt bzw. irrtümlich[44] „getäuscht" werden. Das Vorhandensein einer *ursprünglichen* Täuschungsabsicht bzw. die Funktion der Täuschung machen also den Unterschied in der positiven oder negativen Beurteilung der jeweiligen Schrift aus.[45] Darin aber liegt historisch das eigentliche Problem, da diese Absicht in der Regel nur schwer verifizierbar ist und hier schnell mit Unterstellungen (positiver wie negativer Art) gearbeitet wird, die ihrerseits wiederum von bestimmten interpretatorischen Voraussetzungen beeinflusst sind.

Norbert Brox kommt das Verdienst zu, unter anderem Speyers Ergebnisse für die Beurteilung der neutestamentlichen Pseudepigraphie fruchtbar gemacht und damit wichtige Impulse für die weitere und differenzierte Beschäftigung mit diesem Phänomen im Bereich der neutestamentlichen Forschung gegeben zu haben.[46] Vor allem auf die Notwendigkeit, die Frage nach dem geistigen Eigentum oder auch dem Begriff der Fälschung ernst zu nehmen, hat auch Brox deutlich hingewiesen. Allerdings hat sich im Ergebnis seiner Arbeiten eine Tendenz entwickelt, die zu den oben beschriebenen und angesichts der Forschungen in den 1970er Jahren erstaun-

---

[41] Nach SPEYER, a.a.O. 32–35, gehört dies zur „Pseudepigraphie außerhalb der Fälschung", wobei die sog. „[m]ythische oder ‚echte religiöse Pseudepigraphie'" (35) als eigene Kategorie innerhalb dieser Rubrik behandelt wird. Dieser Abschnitt fällt bei Speyer relativ kurz aus, da diese Art der Pseudepigraphie kein eigentliches Problem darstellt.
[42] Vgl. a.a.O. 21–25.
[43] Vgl. a.a.O. 44–84.
[44] Vgl. a.a.O. 24.33.
[45] A.a.O. 94: „... die Täuschungsabsicht, die jenseits eines literarischen Zweckes liegt, (macht) ein Pseudepigraphon zur Fälschung."
[46] Vgl. bes. BROX, Verfasserangaben (s. Anm. 7), passim.

lich wenig differenzierten Auffassungen von neutestamentlicher Pseudepigraphie geführt hat.

Das mag auch daran liegen, dass Brox speziell im Blick auf die Pastoralbriefe zwar gesehen hat, dass die literarische Gestaltung durch übermäßige persönliche Notizen ein Problem darstellt, dies aber dadurch abmildert, dass er – entgegen der Klassifikation von Speyer – die fiktiven Angaben zu einem „Kabinettstück" einer noch legitimen Pseudepigraphie erklärt: „Traditionen, Namen, Erinnerungen aus der Umgebung des Paulus und sicher auch ausgesprochene Erfindungen werden im pseudepigraphischen Paulusbrief zu sehr variablen Mitteln, das fiktive Dokument literarisch und sachlich so auszustatten, daß es erfolgreich wird. Die Pastoralbriefe stellen nach Programm und Vielseitigkeit der Ausführung innerhalb des Neuen Testaments diesbezüglich wohl das Kabinettstück dar."[47] Peter Trummer hat dies noch verschärft, um letztlich ebenfalls die Art der Pseudepigraphie der Pastoralbriefe als „noch" legitim erscheinen zu lassen. Insbesondere der 2. Timotheusbrief zeige, dass und inwiefern „eine sich als legitim verstehende[.] ‚kirchliche[.]' Pseudepigraphie" an ihre „Grenzen und (ihr) Ende" gekommen sei. „Dies gilt sowohl hinsichtlich der zeitlichen wie sachlichen Entwicklung, aber auch der literarischen Durchführung: Sie [sc. die Pastoralbriefe] treiben die Fiktion und literarische Form bis ins äußerste, sie betreiben ‚totale Pseudepigraphie' und sind wohl überhaupt das ‚Kabinettstück' einer ntl Pseudepigraphie."[48] Solche Auffassungen sind zu vereinfachend, als dass sie dem damit beschriebenen Phänomen gerecht würden, denn die Merkmale, die Brox aufzählt, gehören alle in den Bereich der Fälschung, wenn sie denn tatsächlich unter den Vorzeichen der Pseudepigraphie verstanden werden sollten. Brox selbst hat dies immerhin deutlich gesehen: „Der Autor [sc. der Pastoralbriefe] führt seine Fiktion sehr überlegt und einfallsreich durch, das heißt, ihm liegt deutlich am Gelingen der Täuschung, um seinen Briefen ihre Wirkung zu sichern."[49] „Man kann nicht mit theologischen Motivationen darüber hinwegeilen, daß die sog. Past des Neuen Testaments ... vom literarischen Unternehmen her eine methodisch angelegte Täuschung, eine bewußte und künstlerisch raffiniert durchgeführte Autoritätsanmaßung darstellen."[50]

---

[47] A.a.O. 24.

[48] P. TRUMMER, Corpus Paulinum – Corpus Pastorale. Zur Ortung der Paulustradition in den Pastoralbriefen, in: K. Kertelge (Hg.), Paulus in den neutestamentlichen Spätschriften. Zur Paulusrezeption im Neuen Testament, QD 89, Freiburg i. Brsg. u.a. 1981, 122–145 (129: alle Zitate); ähnlich L. R. DONELSON, Pseudepigraphy and Ethical Argument in the Pastoral Epistles, HUT 22, Tübingen 1986, 55. Was hier noch als äußerste Möglichkeit akzeptabler Pseudepigraphie bezeichnet wird, avanciert etwa bei STANDHARTINGER, Kolosserbrief (s. Anm. 25), 54, zur am „kunstvollsten" durchgeführten „Imagination des fiktiven Absenders".

[49] BROX, Verfasserangaben (s. Anm. 7), 178; anders wiederum STANDHARTINGER, Kolosserbrief (s. Anm. 25), 55: „Dabei dienen die persönlichen Notizen nicht nur zur Beglaubigung der pseudepigraphen Briefe, sondern zur exemplarischen Demonstration der philosophischen bzw. theologischen Lehre (vgl. I Tim 1,16; II Tim 1,13, vgl. auch I Tim 4,12; Tit 2,7)." Die *petitio principii* ist nicht zu übersehen; die genannten Belege lassen gerade keinen Zusammenhang mit den (fiktiven) persönlichen Notizen erkennen.

[50] N. BROX, Zum Problemstand in der Erforschung der altchristlichen Pseudepigraphie (1973), in: ders., Pseudepigraphie (s. Anm. 7), 310–334 (324); vgl. dazu E. E. ELLIS, The Making of the New Testament Documents, Biblical Interpretation Series 39, Leiden u.a. 1999, 324.

Angesichts dieser Einsicht bleibt unklar, warum Brox an einem positiven Verständnis dieser Art von Pseudepigraphie festhalten konnte; wirkungsgeschichtlich war dies allerdings äußerst bedeutsam. Das Problem jedoch wird nicht einfach dadurch erledigt, dass man den Begriff der Fälschung vermeidet.

Ruben Zimmermann hat demgegenüber im Blick auf die Frage der neutestamentlichen Pseudepigraphie bereits wichtige Fragen gestellt und sehr zu Recht vereinfachende Lösungen als unzureichend bezeichnet.[51] Allerdings wird auch in seiner knappen Darstellung deutlich, wie unzureichend vor allem die bereits erkannten Differenzierungen auf die Betrachtung der Pastoralbriefe angewendet wurden. Zimmermann konzediert selbst, dass etwa die für bestimmte neutestamentliche Pseudepigraphen (er nennt 2Thess, Kol und Eph) sinnvolle Kategorie der „imitativen Pseudepigraphie" im Schulkontext der Paulusschule[52] gerade für die Pastoralbriefe *nicht* ausreicht.[53] Sein Lösungsversuch der Beschreibung des „spannungsvolle[n] Zusammenhang[es] zwischen fiktiver und realer Briefkommunikation bei den Pastoralbriefen" entspricht der These Frenschkowskis, die Adressaten seien in Wirklichkeit als die Verfasser anzusehen. „Die auffällige Autorisierung des Adressaten (2Tim 3,10f.; 4,1–8), die jenseits der in den Briefen genannten Ämter liegt, könnte so letztlich der Selbstlegitimation des eigentlichen Verfassers dienen, der als Stellvertreter des Paulus beauftragt wurde und sich als solcher verstand. Die Pseudepigraphie könnte somit gerade als eine literarische Erfüllung dieses Stellvertretungsauftrags erklärt werden."[54] Auch hier gelten die Pastoralbriefe als eine kompositorische Einheit, und die Frage nach legitimer literarischer Fiktion und illegitimer Fälschung wird nicht mehr gestellt bzw. für die Pastoralbriefe einseitig und ohne Wahrnehmung der literarischen Eigenheiten zugunsten der legitimen Fiktion entschieden. In Verkennung der literarischen Gegebenheiten kann daher nun in deutlichem Gegensatz zum Urteil von Brox resümiert werden: „Die fiktive Verfasserangabe erfolgte nicht mit Täuschungsabsicht, vielmehr stand eine theologische Intention, eine bestimmte Rezeptionsabsicht im Vordergrund, bei der die gegenwärtige Gültigkeit der Botschaft zum Ausdruck gebracht werden sollte ... In welchem Maße die Adressaten diese fingierte Kommunikation durchschauten, wird unerheblich, sofern sie die Relevanz eines traditionellen Textes für ihre gegenwärtige Situation anerkannten."[55] Das geht nicht nur nicht über bisherige Erklärungsversuche hinaus, sondern mutet den impliziten Adressaten der Pastoralbriefe etwas zu, was sie den Texten selbst beim besten Willen nicht entnehmen konnten, wenn sie die Fiktion nicht durchschauten.

Auch wenn bei Speyers Ansatz vielleicht manche Begriffe – insbesondere derjenige der sog. „Schulpseudepigraphie" – weiter zu präzisieren wären, ist eine *grundsätzliche* Kritik an dessen Differenzierungen, wie sie etwa Angela Standhartinger vorgenommen hat,[56] kaum angemessen. Speyers Nachweis der Vielfältigkeit des Phänomens sowie der Schwierigkeit einer Begründung im konkreten Fall darf keinesfalls zu der Schlussfolgerung

---

[51] ZIMMERMANN, Unecht – und doch wahr? (s. Anm. 15), 27f.
[52] In Anlehnung an FRENSCHKOWSKI, Pseudepigraphie (s. Anm. 6), sowie G. THEISSEN, Die Entstehung der urchristlichen Pseudepigraphie, in: ders., Das Neue Testament, München 2002, 82–85.
[53] ZIMMERMANN, Unecht – und doch wahr? (s. Anm. 15), 33.
[54] A.a.O. 34.
[55] A.a.O. 35.
[56] STANDHARTINGER, Kolosserbrief (s. Anm. 25), 30f.

führen, die leider oft daraus gezogen wurde, dass nämlich die bloße *Verbreitung des Phänomens* der Pseudepigraphie ihre *selbstverständliche Legitimität und Akzeptanz* einschließe.[57] Man ist fast geneigt zu sagen, das Gegenteil sei der Fall: Die Akzeptanz und Legitimität pseudepigraphischer Schriften ist in bestimmten literarischen Genres unter literaturhistorischen Aspekten eher als eine Ausnahme anzusehen und erfordert ganz bestimmte Voraussetzungen.

2. Die Pseudepigraphie der Pastoralbriefe – Die Entwicklung eines Paradigmas

Nach der Erörterung grundlegender Aspekte im Blick auf die Beurteilung von Pseudepigraphie im Neuen Testament sei diesem Abschnitt folgende These vorangestellt: Die für den aktuellen Konsens[58] charakteristische Beurteilung der Pastoralbriefe als eines pseudepigraphisch verfassten Korpus dreier zusammengehöriger Schriften eines einzelnen Verfassers zum Zweck der Traditionssicherung und -weitergabe in (spät)nachapostolischer Zeit beruht auf einem idealistischen Paradigma des 19. Jh., welches – angestoßen von Friedrich D. E. Schleiermachers Arbeit zum Ersten Timotheusbrief[59] – zunächst von Ferdinand C. Baur[60] entwickelt und schließlich von Heinrich J. Holtzmann[61] in der kritischen Forschung etabliert wurde.

2.1 Die Anfänge der pseudepigraphischen Beurteilung der Pastoralbriefe: F. D. E. Schleiermacher und F. C. Baur

Im Detail kann an dieser Stelle die komplexe Entwicklung dieses Paradigmas[62] der neuzeitlichen Pastoralbriefinterpretation nicht vorgeführt wer-

---

[57] So zu Recht FRENSCHKOWSKI, Pseudepigraphie (s. Anm. 6), 249.

[58] Über die Problematik, im Blick auf die Beurteilung der Pastoralbriefe von einem Konsens zu sprechen, vgl. HERZER, Abschied (s. Anm. 3).

[59] SCHLEIERMACHER, Brief des Paulos an den Timotheos (s. Anm. 1).

[60] BAUR, Pastoralbriefe (s. Anm. 2).

[61] H. J. HOLTZMANN, Die Pastoralbriefe kritisch und exegetisch behandelt, Leipzig 1880, 7 und passim.

[62] Mit der Einführung des Begriffes „Paradigma" in diesem Zusammenhang soll zugleich auf die Notwendigkeit seiner Konkretion hingewiesen werden, die ihn zur *Beschreibung eines Phänomens hinsichtlich seiner ideengeschichtlichen Verankerung* geeignet macht; vgl. zum Problemfeld W. Kinzig / V. Leppin / G. Wartenberg (Hg.), Historiographie und Theologie. Kirchen- und Theologiegeschichte im Spannungsfeld von geschichtswissenschaftlicher Methode und theologischem Anspruch, AKThG 15, Leipzig 2004, darin insbesondere U. MUHLACK, Theorie der Geschichte. Schwerpunkte in der gegenwärtigen Diskussion der Geschichtswissenschaften, 19–37, der darauf hinweist, dass jeder konkreten Geschichtsschreibung eine methodentheoretische Reflexion inhärent ist

den, so dass einige Schlaglichter genügen müssen. Nachdem Johann Ernst Christian Schmidt (1772–1831) in seiner „Historisch-kritischen Einleitung in das Neue Testament" von 1804[63] m.W. zum ersten Mal[64] Bedenken gegenüber der Echtheit des Ersten Timotheusbriefes geäußert hatte (die ihm allerdings nicht stark genug waren, entsprechende Konsequenzen zu ziehen), liefert Friedrich Schleiermacher wenige Jahre später eine ausführliche Begründung dafür, indem er im Wesentlichen inhaltlich-stilistische

---

und dass umgekehrt jede Theoriebildung nicht losgelöst von konkreter historischer Arbeit geschehen darf. Der Begriff des Paradigmas, wie er von Thomas S. Kuhn Mitte der 60er Jahre des 20. Jh. geprägt wurde, spielt dabei eine nicht unerhebliche Rolle (25f.). Mit Recht beklagt Muhlack, „dass sozusagen jeder thematische oder methodische Einfall als Paradigmawechsel daherkommt" (26). Seine These in Bezug auf die Inflation von Paradigmenwechseln geht von Kuhns Klassifikation aus, dass jedes Paradigma eine Grundausrichtung der Forschung bedeutet, die konkrete Forschungsprozesse aus sich heraus setzt, „bis sie durch eine andere traditionsstiftende Leistung abgelöst wird" (25; vgl. dazu T. S. KUHN, Die Struktur wissenschaftlicher Revolutionen, Frankfurt a.M. 1967, 28–43). Muhlacks These lautet daher: „Das für die gegenwärtige Geschichtswissenschaft maßgebliche Paradigma ist durch die Grundlegung der modernen Geschichtswissenschaft seit der Wende vom 18. zum 19. Jahrhundert gegeben; sie hat einen Problemhorizont eröffnet, dem auch wir noch angehören." Dies wird man nicht grundsätzlich bestreiten können; die Frage ist aber, was sich daraus für konkrete – und fortschreitende – Forschungsprozesse ergibt.

[63] J. E. C. SCHMIDT, Historisch-kritische Einleitung in das Neue Testament, Gießen 1804/5.

[64] Abgesehen von Auseinandersetzungen zwischen unterschiedlichen Gruppen in der Alten Kirche; auch dort waren die Pastoralbriefe gelegentlich Gegenstand der Kritik. Zu nennen wäre hier die Nichtannahme der Pastoralbriefe durch Marcion, wobei der Negativbefund oft mit Unkenntnis erklärt wird; vgl. etwa die Äußerung Tertullians (Marc. 5,21); dazu C. LOOKS, Das Anvertraute bewahren. Die Rezeption der Pastoralbriefe im 2. Jahrhundert, Münchener Theologische Beiträge, München 1999, 221–228. A. VON HARNACK, Marcion – Das Evangelium vom fremden Gott. Eine Monographie zur Geschichte der Grundlegung der katholischen Kirche, Berlin 1960 (= TU 45, Leipzig ²1924), 170*–172*, bezweifelt den Wert der Aussage Tertullians zu Marcion gänzlich; vgl. auch U. SCHMID, Marcion und sein Apostolos. Rekonstruktion und historische Einordnung der marcionitischen Paulusbriefausgabe, ANTT 25, Berlin/New York 1995, bes. 284–298. Nach dem Zeugnis des Hieronymus hat Tatian (ca. 120–173) einige Paulusbriefe verworfen und nur den Titusbrief anerkannt, vermutlich weil Tatian als Anhänger der Enkratiten asketisch lebte und die Ehe ablehnte (vgl. dagegen 1Tim 4,1–5; 5,3–16). Nur vermuten kann man daher, dass sich unter den abgelehnten Schriften auch der Erste und Zweite Timotheusbrief befanden, da Hieronymus nicht überliefert, *welche* Paulusbriefe Tatian ablehnte; vgl. dazu schon BAUR, Pastoralbriefe (s. Anm. 2), 137. In der Vorrede zu Hieronymus' Kommentar über den Titusbrief heißt es: „Aber Tatian, der Vater der Enkratiten, der auch selbst einige Briefe des Paulus verworfen hat, glaubte, daß dieser am allermeisten, das heißt, der des Apostels an Titus, verkündet, öffentlich gemacht werden muß; die Erklärung des Marcion und anderer, die mit ihm in dieser Frage übereinstimmen, achtete er gering" (PL 26,555, Übers. zit. n. LOOKS, a.a.O. 262).

Gründe geltend macht.[65] Johann Gottfried Eichhorn (1752–1827) bezieht in seiner Einleitung von 1812[66] diese Sicht unter nunmehr *historischen* – nicht stilistischen – Gesichtspunkten auf alle drei Pastoralbriefe.[67] Der ‚schwäbische Mustertheologe'[68] Ferdinand Christian Baur ist es dann, der in Abgrenzung von konservativ kirchlichen Gegentendenzen[69] die sich in der kritischen Forschung durchsetzende und mehrheitlich nicht mehr hinterfragte Sicht der drei Briefe als pseudepigraphische Schreiben begründet, die zudem als ein zusammengehörendes Ganzes zu behandeln seien. Den – wie er es nennt – „objektiven" Grund für die Unechtheit aller drei Briefe sah Baur in der Charakterisierung der Gegner als Gnostiker des 2. Jh. und verband dieses konkret mit der markionitischen Gnosis.[70] Darauf weist für

---

[65] Vgl. A. SCHWEITZER, Geschichte der Paulinischen Forschung von der Reformation bis auf die Gegenwart, Tübingen 1911, 6: „Eigentlich ist nicht der Kritiker, sondern der Aesthetiker Schleiermacher am I Tim. irre geworden."

[66] J. G. EICHHORN, Einleitung in das Neue Testament III/1, Leipzig 1812.

[67] Vgl. BAUR, Pastoralbriefe (s. Anm. 2), 5 Anm. *, sowie die ausführliche Darstellung bei L. T. JOHNSON, The First and Second Letters to Timothy. A New Translation with Introduction and Commentary, AncB 35A, New York u.a. 2001, 42–54.

[68] Vgl. H. GRAF REVENTLOW, Epochen der Bibelauslegung, Bd. IV: Von der Aufklärung bis zum 20. Jahrhundert, München 2001, 269.

[69] Vgl. dazu U. KÖPF, Ferdinand Christian Baur als Begründer einer konsequent historischen Theologie, ZThK 89 (1992), 440–461 (447–450); sowie z.B. F. C. BAUR, Abgenöthigte Erklärung gegen einen Artikel der evangelischen Kirchenzeitung, herausgegeben von D. E. W. Hengstenberg, Prof. der Theol. an der Universität zu Berlin. Mai 1836, in: ders., Historisch-kritische Untersuchungen zum Neuen Testament. Mit einer Einführung von Ernst Käsemann, Ferdinand Christian Baur – Ausgewählte Werke in Einzelausgaben, Bd. 1, hg. v. K. Scholder, Stuttgart/Bad Cannstatt 1963, 267–320 (= TZTh 1836, 179–232). Zu Ernst Wilhelm Hengstenberg als „einflussreichste[m] Vertreter der Neuorthodoxie in Deutschland" vgl. REVENTLOW, Epochen (s. Anm. 68), 278–290 (281). Die im Titel der Schrift von Baur erwähnte Evangelische Kirchenzeitung war ein Organ der Erweckungsbewegung, das Hengstenberg, der u.a. auch scharfsinnig „[d]ie Authentie des Pentateuch" (so den Titel eines zweibändigen Werkes von 1836–1839) unter der Verfasserschaft des Mose erweisen wollte, im Kampf gegen den aufklärerischen Rationalismus instrumentalisierte; vgl. REVENTLOW, a.a.O. 281.

[70] Vgl. dazu bes. F. C. BAUR, Die christliche Gnosis oder die christliche Religions-Philosophie in ihrer geschichtlichen Entwicklung, Tübingen 1835 (Nachdruck 1967). Diese Arbeit und ihre These, die Pastoralbriefe von dem Phänomen der Gnosis her zu erklären, beruht auf Baurs im Anschluss an die Hegelsche Philosophie der Geschichte gewonnene Grundüberzeugung vom Urchristentum als einer sich in zwei Gegensätzen entwickelnden Bewegung, wie er sie in seiner programmatischen Schrift „Die Christuspartei in der korinthischen Gemeinde, der Gegensatz des petrinischen und paulinischen Christentums in der ältesten Kirche, der Apostel Petrus in Rom" (TZTh 1831, 61–206 [Ausgewählte Werke I, 1963, 1–146]), entwickelt hat. „Auf Grund der inzwischen gewonnenen Kriterien bestritt Baur für die Pastoralbriefe die Verfasserschaft des Paulus: Die antignostische Tendenz der Briefe verweise sie eindeutig in eine spätere Zeit. Die kleine Schrift [sc. über die Pastoralbriefe] ist ein Musterbeispiel der sogenannten Ten-

Baur nicht nur die Erwähnung der „fälschlich so genannten Gnosis" in 1Tim 6,20 hin, sondern die durchgängige Beschreibung der Gegner als gnostische Häretiker.[71] Wenn die Gnosis ein Phänomen des 2. Jh. ist (darin hatte Baur gegen andere Auffassungen immerhin Recht!) und alle drei Briefe als Einheit verstanden werden müssen, dann müssen sie unter der gegebenen Voraussetzung aus dem 2. Jh. stammen.[72] Trotz der frühen Einwände von Richard Rothe (1799–1867), der die Gnosis bereits Mitte des 1. Jh. ansetzen und so die Echtheit der Pastoralbriefe verteidigen wollte,[73] ist bis auf die Verortung der Gnosis im 2. Jh. keine der Voraussetzungen Baurs überzeugend. Das betrifft vor allem die bis heute weithin anerkannte Hypothese, alle drei Briefe müssten als kompositorische Einheit verstanden und demzufolge auch als solche interpretiert werden. In dieser Hinsicht war für Baur die ausschließlich auf den Ersten Timotheusbrief bezogene Argumentation Schleiermachers ohne „Haltpunkt"[74], denn „wir bleiben mit dem Briefe, wie er ist, doch immer mehr oder minder in der Nähe des Apostels, und die Unmöglichkeit, daß er der Verfasser des Briefes sey, ist nicht so groß, daß die Voraussezung des Gegentheils ihr nicht auch wieder wenigstens Gleichgewicht halten könnte."[75] Baur räumt immerhin ein, bei aller Verwandtschaft der Pastoralbriefe könne „doch nicht geläugnet werden, daß es sich mit dem ersten dieser Briefe in kritischer Hinsicht im Ganzen auch wieder anders verhält, als mit den beiden andern, und der von Schleiermacher in Beziehung auf jenen geführte negative Beweis kann in Beziehung auf diese wenigstens nicht auf dieselbe Weise

---

denzkritik und ihrer historischen Absicht" (K. SCHOLDER, Art. Baur, Ferdinand Christian [1792–1860], TRE 5 [1980], 352–359 [355]).

[71] Zur Interpretation der Pastoralbriefe vor dem Hintergrund der Gnosis vgl. J. HERZER, Juden – Christen – Gnostiker. Zur Gegnerproblematik der Pastoralbriefe, BThZ 25 (2008), 143–168.

[72] BAUR, Pastoralbriefe (s. Anm. 2), passim; ders., Ueber den Ursprung des Episcopats in der christlichen Kirche. Prüfung der neuestens von Hrn. D. Rothe hierüber aufgestellten Ansicht (1838), in: ders., Historisch-kritische Untersuchungen (s. Anm. 69), 321–505 (= TZTh 1838, 1–185), 335f.

[73] R. ROTHE, Die Anfänge der christlichen Kirche und ihrer Verfassung (1837). Vgl. dazu die monographische Replik von BAUR, Ueber den Ursprung des Episcopats (s. Anm. 72). Zu Rothe vgl. H. KRÖTKE, Selbstbewußtsein und Spekulation. Eine Untersuchung der spekulativen Theologie Richard Rothes unter besonderer Berücksichtigung des Verhältnisses von Anthropologie und Theologie, hg. v. H.-W. Schütte, TBT 103, Berlin/New York 1999. – M. BAUMGARTEN, Die Aechtheit der Pastoralbriefe, mit besonderer Rücksicht auf den neuesten Angriff von Herrn Dr. Baur, Berlin 1837, hatte ebenfalls gegen Baur für die Echtheit der Pastoralbriefe argumentiert, allerdings wollte er gegen die Gnosistheorie in den Häretikern eine kabbalistische Art des Judentums sehen; vgl. dazu BAUR, a.a.O. 337f.

[74] Ders., Pastoralbriefe (s. Anm. 2), 3.

[75] A.a.O. 4.

geführt werden"[76]. Erst unter der Voraussetzung, dass alle drei Briefe zusammengehören, kann Baur auch den Zweiten Timotheusbrief und den Titusbrief für unecht *erklären*.[77] Dennoch gilt: „Den sichersten Standpunkt für diese Untersuchung muß der erste Brief geben."[78]

2.2 Die Voraussetzungen der Theorie Ferdinand Christian Baurs

Baur ist der Erste, der aus *inhaltlichen und literarischen* Gesichtspunkten die Pastoralbriefe als Einheit verstehen will und dabei im Blick auf die Unechtheit aller drei Briefe von der erwiesenen Unechtheit des Ersten Timotheusbriefes ausgehen *muss*, *obwohl* er die Unterschiede zwischen dem Ersten Timotheusbrief auf der einen und dem Zweiten Timotheusbrief und dem Titusbrief auf der anderen Seite festhält. Eine wirklich überzeugende Voraussetzung oder gar Begründung für die Behauptung der Einheitlichkeit ergibt sich daraus allerdings nicht. Baur liefert eine solche Begründung auch nicht, sondern setzt sie als gegeben voraus, und dies ist dann auch in der Baur folgenden Forschung nicht infrage gestellt worden.[79] Der Versuch, gegen diese kritischen Ansätze an der Echtheit der Pastoralbriefe festzuhalten oder diese gar zu *erweisen*, hat sich daher in der Regel auch auf alle drei Briefe bezogen, was freilich ebenso auf die fragwürdige Voraussetzung der Einheitlichkeit hinsichtlich der Verfasserschaft gründet.[80]

Ein Problem der Entstehung von Baurs Theorie und ihrer späteren Rezeption ist, dass die Ergebnisse seiner historisch-kritischen Arbeit sehr deutlich unter dem Einfluss des Idealismus stehen, der – verbunden mit den Namen Schelling und Hegel – im 19. Jh. die Entwicklung eines bestimmten Geschichtsbildes prägte, das unter dem Stichwort des sogenannten „Historismus" nicht nur eine sich stetig entfaltende Idee von Geschichte zugrunde legte,[81] sondern auch von dem „Ideal vermeintlicher

---

[76] Ebd.

[77] Ebd.

[78] A.a.O. 5; vgl. auch a.a.O. 54.

[79] Vgl. etwa L. OBERLINNER, Die Pastoralbriefe. Kommentar zum Ersten Timotheusbrief, HThK.NT XI/2.1, Freiburg i. Brsg. u.a. 1994, XLII: „Da die Abfassung als zusammengehöriges Briefkorpus anzunehmen ist, ist die Frage nach der Reihenfolge der Entstehung der einzelnen Briefe kaum mehr zu klären und letztlich für die Interpretation belanglos."

[80] Dabei spielen dann zumeist historische Argumente eine entscheidende Rolle. Selbst Baur hielt Eichhorns *historische* Argumente gegen die Echtheit *aller drei* Briefe nicht für überzeugend; vgl. BAUR, Pastoralbriefe (s. Anm. 2), 5–7 Anm. *: „Ist alles dieß etwas anderes, als dieselbe Hypothesensucht, die Eichhorn an den Vertheidigern der Aechtheit dieser Briefe rügt …?"

[81] Zu Begriff, Grundlagen und Kritik des Historismus vgl. z.B. M. MURRMANN-KAHL, Die entzauberte Heilsgeschichte. Der Historismus erobert die Theologie 1880–1920, Gütersloh 1992, bes. 75–204, der den grundlegenden Anstoß Friedrich Nietzsches für die

Objektivität"[82] ausging. Auch für Baur war diese Vorgabe maßgeblich, und das unter diesen Voraussetzungen gewonnene geschichtliche Bild der Gnosis war für ihn entscheidend für die Beurteilung der Pastoralbriefe.[83]

Es war kein Geringerer als der Harnack-Schüler Ernst Troeltsch, der Baurs Beeinflussung durch die Philosophie Hegels würdigte, indem er ihn mit von Harnack in eine gemeinsame Tradition der „großen idealistisch-historischen Denkweise der deutschen Philosophie und Historie vom Anfang des letzten Jahrhunderts"[84] verortet und im Blick auf Baur festhält: „Baurs Werk ist gegründet auf die besondere Fassung des Entwicklungsgedankens in der Hegelschen Dialektik. Er stellt die Geschichte des Christentums als die Selbstentfaltung und Selbstbewegung der christlichen Idee und die christliche Idee selbst als den Höhepunkt der in der Universal- und Religionsgeschichte sich entfaltenden reli-

---

Kritik des Historismus herausstellt (168ff.; vgl. F. NIETZSCHE, Unzeitgemäße Betrachtungen – Zweites Stück: Vom Nutzen und Nachteil der Historie für das Leben [1874], in: ders., Werke in drei Bänden, Bd. 1: Menschliches – Allzumenschliches und andere Schriften, hg. v. R. Toman, Köln 1994, 153–242). Auch wenn der Traktat Nietzsches eher Ausdruck eines Lebensgefühls denn konkrete wissenschaftliche Kritik ist und es ihm vor allem um die Bedeutung des historischen Fragens für das gegenwärtige Leben geht und diese letztlich in Frage stellt, da bloßes historisches Wissen das Leben zerstöre und töte (vgl. 187), so bringt doch der scharfe – und sarkastische – Blick des Philosophen das Grundproblem auf den Punkt, was angesichts des Erscheinungsdatums 1874 durchaus erstaunlich ist: „Jene naiven Historiker nennen ‚Objektivität' das Messen vergangener Meinungen und Taten an den Allerwelts-Meinungen des Augenblicks: hier finden sie den Kanon aller Wahrheiten; ihre Arbeit ist, die Vergangenheit der zeitgemäßen Trivialität anzupassen. Dagegen nennen sie jede Geschichtsschreibung ‚subjektiv', die jene Popularmeinungen nicht als kanonisch nimmt. Und sollte nicht selbst bei der höchsten Ausdeutung des Wortes Objektivität eine Illusion mit unterlaufen? Man versteht dann mit diesem Worte *einen Zustand im Historiker*, in dem er ein Ereignis in allen seinen Motiven und Folgen so rein anschaut, daß es auf sein Subjekt gar keine Wirkung tut: man meint jenes ästhetische Phänomen, jenes Losgebundensein vom persönlichen Interesse, mit dem der Maler in einer stürmischen Landschaft, unter Blitz und Donner, oder auf bewegter See sein inneres Bild schaut und dabei seine Person vergißt. Man verlangt also auch vom Historiker die künstliche Beschaulichkeit und das völlige Versunkensein in die Dinge: *ein Aberglaube jedoch ist es, daß das Bild, welches die Dinge in einem solchermaßen gestimmten Menschen zeigen, das empirische Wesen der Dinge wiedergebe.* ... Dies wäre eine Mythologie, und eine schlechte obendrein ..." (197f., Hervorhebung J.H.).

[82] REVENTLOW, Epochen (s. Anm. 68), 270.

[83] Vgl. a.a.O. 270f.

[84] E. TROELTSCH, Adolf von Harnack und Ferdinand Christian Baur, in: Festgabe von Fachgenossen und Freunden A. von Harnack zum siebzigsten Geburtstag dargebracht, Tübingen 1921, 282–291 (283). Vgl. auch das euphorische Votum von E. TROELTSCH, Der Historismus und seine Probleme, Gesammelte Schriften 3, Aalen 1977 (= Tübingen 1922), 271, u.a. in Bezug auf die Namen Baur, Strauß, aber auch Ranke: „Daß die deutsche Historie die Welt das historische Denken gelehrt, dankt sie, wenn nicht Hegel selbst, so doch seiner Epoche, deren Quintessenz er ja nur zu systematisieren und zu rationalisieren versuchte."

giös-metaphysischen Idee überhaupt dar."[85] Karl Bauer urteilt, Baurs Arbeiten zu den Paulusbriefen seien „gleichsam die Ausführung der in der ‚Christuspartei' gegebenen Skizze. Der Semlersche Gegensatz zwischen Judaismus und Paulinismus war hier durch die Hegelschen Kategorien in Bewegung gesetzt zu einem dialektischen Prozeß, dessen einzelne Stadien durch die Schriften des Kanons bezeichnet waren."[86]

Das Bemerkenswerte der Objektivitätsvorstellung Baurs ist *einerseits*, dass er sie anhand überaus wichtiger Überlegungen zum Verhältnis von Geschichte und Geschichtsschreibung gewinnt, wie sie für den nachaufklärerischen sog. Historismus maßgeblich und für den Erkenntnisfortschritt der historischen Wissenschaften entscheidend waren und bis heute von ihrer grundlegenden Relevanz nichts verloren haben.

„Seitdem es auch eine Kritik des Erkennens ... gibt ..., muss auch Jeder, der nicht ohne alle philosophische Bildung zur Geschichte herankommt, wissen, dass man zwischen den Dingen, wie sie an sich sind, und wie sie uns erscheinen, zu unterscheiden hat, und dass sie zu Erscheinungen für uns eben dadurch werden, dass wir nur durch das Medium unseres Bewusstseins zu ihnen gelangen können. Hierin liegt der grosse Unterschied zwischen der rein empirischen und der kritischen Betrachtungsweise, und die letztere, welche eben darum die kritische heisst, weil es ihre Aufgabe ist, was an den Gegenständen des geschichtlichen Erkennens entweder objektiv oder subjektiv ist, streng zu scheiden und auseinanderzuhalten, will so wenig an die Stelle des Objektiven etwas bloss Subjektives setzen, dass ihr vielmehr alles daran gelegen ist, nichts, was nur subjektiver Natur ist, für die reine Objektivität der Sache zu halten; sie will nur mit geschärfterem Auge der Sache auf den Grund ihres Wesens gehen."[87]

---

[85] TROELTSCH, a.a.O. 284. Vgl. weiterhin z.B. R. BULTMANN, Theologie des Neuen Testaments, Berlin ³1959, 591ff.; E. E. ELLIS, Ferdinand Christian Baur and His School, in: ders., Making (s. Anm. 50), 435–445 (441f.); ähnlich REVENTLOW, Epochen (s. Anm. 68), 269–278, der den Einfluss der idealistischen Philosophie Schellings auf Baur besonders hervorhebt.

[86] K. BAUER, Art. Baur 2. Ferdinand Christian und die Tübinger Schule, RGG² 1 (1927), 818. Vgl. weiterhin auch K. SCHOLDER, Ferdinand Christian Baur als Historiker, EvTh 21 (1961), 435–458; ders., Art. Baur (s. Anm. 70); ders., Ursprünge und Probleme der Bibelkritik im 17. Jahrhundert. Ein Beitrag zur Entstehung der historisch-kritischen Theologie, FGLP X/33, München 1966; U. Köpf (Hg.), Historisch-kritische Geschichtsbetrachtung. F. C. Baur und seine Schüler, 8. Blaubeurer Symposion, Contubernium. Tübinger Beiträge zur Universitäts- und Wissenschaftsgeschichte 40, Ostfildern 1994; ders., Art. Baur, Ferdinand Christian, RGG⁴ 1 (1998), 1183–1185; K. NOWAK, Vernünftiges Christentum. Über die Erforschung der Aufklärung in der evangelischen Theologie Deutschlands seit 1945, ThLZ.F 2, Leipzig 1999, 26–36. – Unter der Überschrift „Die Kirchengeschichte als Verwirklichung der ‚Idee' der Kirche" behandelt P. MEINHOLD, Geschichte der kirchlichen Historiographie, Orbis Academicus III/5, München 1967, 170–195, die Voraussetzungen und Bedingungen des historischen Urteils Baurs.

[87] F. C. BAUR, Lehrbuch der christlichen Dogmengeschichte, Tübingen 1858, VIIf.; vgl. auch ders., Die Epochen der kirchlichen Geschichtsschreibung, Tübingen 1852, 3: „Die geschichtliche Darstellung scheint daher hier nur die einfache Aufgabe zu haben, dem objektiv gegebenen Gange zu folgen, um alles so aufzufassen und zusammenzustellen, wie es der Objektivität der Sache selbst entspricht."

Andererseits aber ist diese Verhältnisbestimmung zwischen objektiver Geschichte und subjektiver Geschichtsschreibung verbunden mit jenem idealistischen, geschichtsphilosophisch geprägten Bild einer sich entwickelnden Geschichte, die für Baur einen „Standpunkt der Objectivität"[88] bot und in deren Konsequenz Baurs sog. „Tendenzkritik" steht, die seine Beurteilung der biblischen Schriften – und eben insbesondere der paulinischen Briefe – prägt. Durch die Verbindung mit der Gnosis können speziell die Pastoralbriefe dem authentischen Paulus bereits von ihrer *inhärenten Tendenz* nicht zugeschrieben werden. Baur hielt bekanntermaßen ohnehin nur vier Paulusbriefe für echt (Röm, 1Kor, 2Kor, Gal) und gab damit u.a. den Anlass für Bruno Bauers Echtheitskritik, der schließlich *alle* Paulusbriefe zu Fälschungen einer späteren Zeit erklärte.[89]

Der „positive" Konstruktivismus, auf den Baurs Vorstellung von objektiver Geschichtsdarstellung zurückgeht, gründet – das hat Klaus Scholder gezeigt – in Barthold Georg Niebuhrs Überlegungen zum Verhältnis von („negativer") Quellenkritik und („positiver") Konstruktion: „... die Trennung der Fabel, die Zerstörung des Betrugs, mag dem Kritiker genügen ... Der Historiker aber bedarf Positives: er muß wenigstens mit Wahrscheinlichkeit Zusammenhang und eine glaublichere Erzählung an der Stelle derjenigen entdecken, welche er seiner Überzeugung opfert."[90] Als Ziel dieses Konstruktivismus bestimmt Scholder „das reine und wahre Bild der Geschichte"[91], das den sog. Historismus und eben insbesondere auch Baur bestimmt, wofür Scholder die aus seiner Sicht negative Bestimmung als „Positivismus" für ungeeignet hält, dem historischen Bemühen um die Darstellung geschichtlicher Gesamtzusammenhänge gerecht zu werden, allerdings nicht ohne selbst einem gewissen Idealismus das Wort zu reden.[92] Natürlich ist auch die Behandlung der Pastoralbriefe bei Baur diesem Paradigma verpflichtet.[93]

---

[88] Ders., Die christliche Gnosis (s. Anm. 70), 668f.
[89] Vgl. B. BAUER, Kritik der paulinischen Briefe (1850–1852), Nachdruck Aalen 1972.
[90] B. G. NIEBUHR, Römische Geschichte I, o.O. 1811, IXf., zit. n. SCHOLDER, Baur als Historiker (s. Anm. 86), 438.
[91] SCHOLDER, ebd.
[92] A.a.O. 439–442; im Anschluss an Wilhelm von Humboldt und Leopold Ranke hält Scholder an der Bedeutung der Vorstellung von der „‚Idee' hinter allem Geschehen" fest.
[93] Vgl. BAUR, Pastoralbriefe (s. Anm. 2), IV; sowie zu Recht SCHOLDER, a.a.O. 446, immerhin nicht ohne darauf hinzuweisen, dass zumindest andere Eingriffe in die Überlieferung „zum Teil zweifellos über das Ziel hinausschießen" (447). Die damit verbundene Aufgabe der Vorstellung von einer Heilsgeschichte, die Scholder als wesentliches Problem ansieht, spielt für unseren Zusammenhang im Blick auf die Pastoralbriefe keine Rolle; vgl. dazu auch E. REINMUTH, Neutestamentliche Historik. Probleme und Perspek-

In vielen Bereichen der neutestamentlichen Forschung ist die Problematik dieser Anfänge der historisch-kritischen Wissenschaft erkannt und folgerichtig modifiziert und revidiert worden – ohne dass damit die grundlegenden Verdienste dieses kritischen Aufbruches zu leugnen wären.[94] Hinsichtlich der Frage nach der neutestamentlichen Pseudepigraphie im Allgemeinen und den Pastoralbriefen im Besonderen steht dieser – wenn man so will „postmoderne" – Paradigmenwechsel noch aus.

2.3 Heinrich Julius Holtzmanns Verständnis der Pastoralbriefe

Baurs grundlegende Sichtweise der Pastoralbriefe ist durch den in liberaler Tradition stehenden Exegeten Heinrich Julius Holtzmann (1832–1910; sein wohl bekanntester Schüler war Albert Schweitzer[95]) endgültig in der Forschung etabliert worden.[96] In seinem zu einem Standardwerk gewordenen Kommentar über die Pastoralbriefe von 1880 hat Holtzmann erneut sprachlich-stilistische Untersuchungen als Hauptgrund ausgewiesen und der historischen Problematik nur eine zweitrangige Rolle zuerkannt.[97] Holtzmann

---

tiven, ThLZ.F 8, Leipzig 2003, 11–16, unter der Überschrift: „Das Scheitern der Heilsgeschichte".

[94] Vgl. J. SCHRÖTER, Von der Historizität der Evangelien. Ein Beitrag zur gegenwärtigen Diskussion um den historischen Jesus, in: ders. / R. Brucker (Hg.), Der historische Jesus. Tendenzen und Perspektiven der gegenwärtigen Forschung, BZNW 114, Berlin/New York 2002, 163–212; ders., Neutestamentliche Wissenschaft jenseits des Historismus. Neuere Entwicklungen in der Geschichtstheorie und ihre Bedeutung für die Exegese urchristlicher Schriften, ThLZ 128 (2003), 855–866. Vgl. auch ders., Konstruktion von Geschichte und die Anfänge des Christentums. Reflexionen zur christlichen Geschichtsdeutung aus neutestamentlicher Perspektive, in: ders. / A. Eddelbüttel (Hg.), Konstruktion von Wirklichkeit. Beiträge aus geschichtstheoretischer, philosophischer und theologischer Perspektive, TBT 127, Berlin/New York 2004, 202–219 (217–219), im Blick auf den konstruktivistischen Charakter von Geschichte: „Jede historische Konstruktion ist vielmehr [sc. gegen Droysen] ein hypothetischer, falsifizierbarer Entwurf, Wirklichkeit zu verstehen, historische Wahrheit deshalb eine regulative Idee, der sich diese Entwürfe anzunähern suchen" (219). Vgl. auch insbesondere REINMUTH, a.a.O. bes. 35–47.

[95] Vgl. REVENTLOW, Epochen (s. Anm. 68), 297.

[96] Vgl. K. BAUER, Art. Baur (s. Anm. 86), 819: Gegenüber Baur wies „Karl Hase (,Die Tübinger Schule. Sendschreiben an Herrn Dr. von Baur', 1855) mit Recht auf die von B. verkannte Spannung zwischen Idee und historischer Wirklichkeit hin. Doch haben Männer wie Hausrath, H. J. Holtzmann, Keim, O. Pfleiderer, Weizsäcker u.a. in veränderter Form die Tübinger Position verteidigt."

[97] HOLTZMANN, Pastoralbriefe (s. Anm. 61), 84–118. Die Hochschätzung Baurs bei Holtzmann – trotz kritischer Bemerkungen im Detail – lässt sich klar zeigen; vgl. z.B. a.a.O. 9f., wo zugleich eine illustre Schar von Kollegen genannt wird, in deren Reihe sich Holtzmann offenbar sieht: „Der eigentliche Begründer des kritischen Urteils ist aber Baur in einem glänzend geschriebenen Werke, das zugleich für den damaligen Uebergangsstand seiner theologischen Ueberzeugungen ausserordentlich bezeichnend ist und von

hat damit zwar einerseits das idealistische Geschichtsparadigma Baurs in gewisser Weise relativiert.[98] Andererseits aber wird aus dem Kommentar – trotz seines exegetischen Feingespürs im Detail – der eigentliche Grund für die Berechtigung der pseudepigraphischen Beurteilung der Pastoralbriefe unmissverständlich deutlich, der nicht minder Zeichen eines ungebrochenen idealistischen Geschichtsbewusstseins ist, das demjenigen Baurs nicht nachsteht:

„Man trete an unsere Briefe heran, unmittelbar nach einer gründlichen Lectüre der Römer-, Galater- oder Korintherbriefe [nota bene: Das ist der ‚paulinische Kanon' Baurs! J.H.], und das plötzlich veränderte, bedeutend niederer gestellte Niveau der ganzen Denkart wird sich unabweisbar geltend machen. Zwar kennt man das Horazische Quandoque bonus dormitat Homerus, man weiss auch, dass Göthe neben Faust zuweilen ‚Quark' producirt hat. Aber bei einem so stark ausgeprägten originalen Geiste wie Paulus erwartet man mit Recht in allen grösseren Auslassungen, die er schriftlich fixirte, ‚seines Geistes einen Hauch zu verspüren'. Ein Mann, welcher von der Ursprünglichkeit seines inneren Gehaltes selbst ein so bestimmtes Bewusstsein verräth (Gal. 1,11f. 2,2f. 2Kor. 4,2. 11,4), wird Allem, was er in irgend einer Weise amtlich oder beruflich schreibt, auch den unverkennbaren Stempel seines Geistes aufdrücken. Nun braucht man aber noch keineswegs der Ansicht Schwab's zu sein, dass nur leeres Stroh in den Pastoralbriefen stecke, um die auch von ihm concedirten ‚Glanzstellen' doch als secundären Charakters, als Nachwirkungen paulinischer Lectüre zu recognosciren und zu finden, dass in Bezug auf Gewicht des Gehaltes, Grossartigkeit und Geschlossenheit des Gedankenganges selbst die zweifelhaften Paulinen hoch über jenen stehen."[99]

Hengstenberg sogleich als Prolog zur Verleugnung aller Paulusbriefe charakterisiert wurde ... Seither ist die Unechtheit der Pastoralbriefe nicht blos in der älteren und eigentlichen Tübinger Schule eine ausgemachte Sache gewesen ... sondern auch Bruno Bauer, Hilgenfeld, Ewald, Mangold, Meyer ... Schenkel, Hausrath, Pfleiderer, Pierson, Renan, Immer, Beyschlag, Bahnsen sind demselben Urtheil beigetreten." Baur ist übrigens auch der erste Autor, der im Kommentar Holtzmanns zitiert wird (2). Die von Holtzmann präsentierte Forschungsgeschichte zeigt, dass keine der bis heute vertretenen Positionen wirklich neu ist, sondern die gedanklichen Konstruktionen bereits im 19. Jh. alle Möglichkeiten von Kritik und Gegenkritik und ihren jeweiligen Begründungszusammenhängen abgeschritten haben.

[98] Vgl. REVENTLOW, Epochen (s. Anm. 68), 297f., der jedoch ausdrücklich den maßgeblich von Leopold von Ranke vertretenen „Historismus" als zeitgenössische Vorgabe festhält, dessen Grundprinzip die Frage nach der größtmöglichen Objektivität gewesen sei (zu „zeigen, wie es eigentlich gewesen", L. VON RANKE, Werke Bd. 33/34, Leipzig ²1874, VII). Dazu REVENTLOW, ebd.: „Der Glaube an eine in der Geschichtswissenschaft erreichbare Objektivität – heute wissen wir, daß sie eine Illusion war – beherrschte von da an das gesamte 19. Jahrhundert."

[99] HOLTZMANN, Pastoralbriefe (s. Anm. 61), 60f. Holtzmann notiert es zwar nicht ausdrücklich, aber die als Zitat markierte Bemerkung, alle größeren Auslassungen des Paulus müssten „seines Geistes einen Hauch verspüren" lassen, ist wahrscheinlich dem Gedicht „Bertran de Born" des schwäbischen Romantikers Johann Ludwig Uhland entlehnt, dessen letzte Zeile lautet: „Weg die Fesseln! Deines Geistes hab' ich einen Hauch ver-

Die Pastoralbriefe reichen nach Holtzmann an die hohe Theologie eines Paulus nicht heran, sie ermangeln des „Stempels seines Geistes" und würden die geschichtliche Größe des Apostels relativieren, ja regelrecht zunichte machen, würde man sie ihm zuschreiben wollen. Über die Frage der Legitimität der Fiktion reflektiert Holtzmann nicht mehr. Auf die relative Berechtigung seiner Einschätzung wird am Schluss zurückzukommen sein.

2.4 Zwischenbilanz

Die Wirkung Holtzmanns auf die nachfolgende Forschung über die Pastoralbriefe ist evident und braucht nicht nachgewiesen werden.[100] Dem im 19. Jh. entwickelten Paradigma der Interpretation der Pastoralbriefe, dessen Entstehung forschungsgeschichtlich aufgezeigt werden kann, liegt nicht nur ein bestimmtes Verständnis von Geschichte im Allgemeinen zugrunde, sondern auch ein Verständnis von der Geschichte des frühen Christentums und der Entstehung seiner Literatur im Besonderen – vom Einfluss binnenkirchlicher und konfessioneller Auseinandersetzungen auf die wissenschaftliche Diskussion[101] und schließlich auch der Dimension der Wissenssoziologie[102], wie sie bereits in dem Eingangszitat bei von Harnack unmissverständlich zum Ausdruck kommt, ganz zu schweigen.

Die Folgezeit ist bis in die Gegenwart geprägt von dem Versuch, dieses idealistische Paradigma der Beurteilung der Pastoralbriefe – seine nicht mehr zu hinterfragende Gültigkeit und Berechtigung voraussetzend – auf unterschiedlichste Weise unter Rückgriff auf ebenso idealtypische Anschauungen von Pseudepigraphie zu begründen. Erst in den 60er und 70er Jahren des letzten Jahrhunderts gab es – wie oben gezeigt – neue Impulse in der Pseudepigraphieforschung, die jedoch nicht oder nicht konsequent dazu geführt haben, die Voraussetzungen jenes Paradigmas der Pastoralbriefinterpretation auf ihre Berechtigung und ihren Sinngehalt erneut zu prüfen.

---

spürt" (L. UHLAND, Bertran de Born, in: ders., Gedichte, Stuttgart/Tübingen ⁹1835 [1815], 345).

[100] Vgl. O. MERK, Art. Holtzmann, Heinrich Julius (1832–1910), TRE 15 (1986), 519–522 (521).

[101] Das beginnt bereits mit den Reaktionen auf Schleiermachers Arbeit zum 1Tim; die harsche Kritik, die Baur seitens konservativer kirchlicher Kräfte entgegenschlug, hat u.a. seine Berufung nach Halle verhindert; vgl. SCHOLDER, Art. Baur (s. Anm. 70), 356.

[102] Zu Begriff und Methode der Wissenssoziologie, die sich mit den sozialen Voraussetzungen und Prozessen des Wissens bzw. der Konstruktion von Wirklichkeit befasst; vgl. P. LAMPE, Die Wirklichkeit als Bild. Das Neue Testament als ein Grunddokument abendländischer Kultur im Lichte konstruktivistischer Epistemologie und Wissenssoziologie, Neukirchen-Vluyn 2006, bes. 63–65; ders., Wissenssoziologische Annäherung an das Neue Testament, NTS 43 (1997), 347–366; J. KREINRATH, Art. Wissenssoziologie, RGG⁴ 8 (2005), 1663f.

Die grundlegende Kritik an den Voraussetzungen eines forschungsgeschichtlichen Paradigmas muss sich in der konkreten Auseinandersetzung mit den infrage stehenden Texten erweisen. Es muss einsichtig gemacht werden, in welche Aporien die auf dem Paradigma beruhenden Erklärungsversuche führen und welche positiven Möglichkeiten sich unter anderen Voraussetzungen ergeben können. Das ist in einem solchen Rahmen natürlich nur begrenzt möglich, so dass materialiter im Folgenden exemplarische Hinweise genügen müssen. Speziell im Blick auf die Pseudepigraphie der Pastoralbriefe hat sich bereits abgezeichnet, dass die zur Diskussion stehenden grundlegenden Alternativen nicht tragfähig sind, weder die Behauptung einer unproblematischen und legitimen pseudepigraphischen Abfassung der drei Briefe, noch die pauschale Annahme der bewussten und damit konsequenterweise illegitimen Fälschung, noch die diesen beiden entgegengesetzte Behauptung der authentischen paulinischen Verfasserschaft.

Die Unterschiedlichkeit und Widersprüchlichkeit der Begründungsversuche in die eine wie die andere Richtung sind daher zunächst einmal Indikator des offensichtlichen Problems, den Charakter der Pastoralbriefe nicht nur zu beschreiben, sondern auch zu begründen. Dieses Problem ist der Grund dafür, dass es bisher zu keinem inhaltlichen Konsens in der Beurteilung der Pastoralbriefe kommen konnte, insbesondere hinsichtlich der Intention und Absicht der pseudepigraphischen Schreiben, der Begründung der Wahl der literarischen Gestaltungsmittel sowie nicht zuletzt der Profilierung der Adressaten und deren Situation. Es nützt daher auch wenig, die Plausibilität des jeweils entworfenen Gesamtbildes zu optimieren. Wenn das Vorzeichen stimmt, ist alles plausibel zu machen – vorausgesetzt, man stimmt dem gesetzten Vorzeichen zu. Entscheidend für die Plausibilität historischer und literarhistorischer Rekonstruktionen ist also stets die intersubjektive Verständigung (um nicht zu sagen: Einigung) über die zugrunde liegenden und als gültig anerkannten Voraussetzungen sowie über die Frage, welche Schlussfolgerungen daraus legitimerweise gezogen werden können.

3. Konkretisierung der Kritik

Eine umfassende Bearbeitung der relevanten Aspekte, die für eine differenzierte Beurteilung der Pastoralbriefe notwendig wären, ist an dieser Stelle nicht zu leisten.[103] Es wurde bereits mehrfach darauf hingewiesen,

---

[103] Dabei muss im Vordergrund stehen, das je eigene Profil der drei Briefe so präzise wie möglich herauszuarbeiten, um sowohl die Gemeinsamkeiten als auch die Unter-

dass eines der größten Probleme für die gegenwärtige Interpretation der Pastoralbriefe die Hypothese eines dreifachen Briefkorpus ist, wie es seit Holtzmann die Forschung beherrschte[104] und in neuerer Zeit wirkungsvoll von Peter Trummer etabliert wurde.[105] Mit dieser Korpus-Hypothese ist nicht nur das nur spekulativ zu beantwortende Problem der Dreizahl der Briefe verbunden. Unter der Voraussetzung einer bewussten Komposition eines *Corpus pastorale*[106] durch einen einzelnen Autor ist darüber hinaus notwendig anzunehmen, dass er mit dieser Komposition eine bestimmte Abfolge der Schriften und somit einen bestimmten Rezeptionsvorgang im Blick hatte. Es muss daher nicht nur plausibel gemacht werden, warum es drei Schriften an zwei Adressaten sind, sondern auch, warum es drei so unterschiedliche Schriften sind, wobei zwei – 1Tim und Tit – dann auch wieder vom zumeist vorausgesetzten Anliegen her, nämlich der Etablierung von Gemeindestrukturen, unter der Korpus-These sehr nahe beieinander liegen, jedoch ihrerseits in der Grundidee nicht kohärent sind. Weiterhin bleibt strittig, in welcher Weise diese drei Schriften gelesen werden sollen, damit die dem Autor zu unterstellenden Absichten nicht nur deutlich werden, sondern auch ihre Wirkung entfalten; ganz abgesehen von der Frage, wie unter diesen Voraussetzungen für die (im Blick auf die Verfasserschaft getäuschten!) Rezipienten deutlich werden soll, worauf der Verfasser hinaus will.

Im Folgenden sollen zwei Aspekte herausgegriffen werden, die über die Interpretation einzelner Topoi hinausgehend für die pseudepigraphische Beurteilung der Pastoralbriefe stets eine wichtige Rolle gespielt haben und

---

schiede angemessen interpretieren zu können und sie nicht zugunsten einer bestimmten Theorie entweder zu nivellieren oder übermäßig zu betonen. Verwiesen sei daher auf folgende Versuche, dies an zentralen Punkten durchzuführen: J. HERZER, „Das Geheimnis der Frömmigkeit" (1Tim 3,16). Sprache und Stil der Pastoralbriefe im Kontext hellenistisch-römischer Popularphilosophie – eine methodische Problemanzeige, ThQ 187 (2007), 309–329; ders., Rearranging the ‚House of God'. A New Perspective on the Pastoral Epistles, in: A. Houtman / A. de Jong / M. Misset-van de Weg (Hg.), Empsychoi Logoi – Religious Innovations in Antiquity (FS van der Horst), Ancient Judaism and Early Christianity 73, Leiden 2008, 547–566; ders., Juden – Christen – Gnostiker (s. Anm. 71), passim.

[104] Vgl. HOLTZMANN, Pastoralbriefe (s. Anm. 61), 53: Die Pastoralbriefe seien „unzertrennlichere Drillinge, als Epheser- und Kolosserbrief Zwillinge sind".

[105] P. TRUMMER, Die Paulustradition der Pastoralbriefe, BET 8, Frankfurt a.M./Bern 1978, 73f.; ders., Corpus Paulinum (s. Anm. 48), passim; vgl. aber bereits A. E. BARNETT, Paul Becomes a Literary Influence, Chicago 1941, 222.251; J. L. HOULDON, The Pastoral Epistles, London 1989 (= 1976), 18f.

[106] Vgl. dazu H. VON LIPS, Von den „Pastoralbriefen" zum „Corpus Pastorale". Eine Hallische Sprachschöpfung und ihr modernes Pendant als Funktionsbestimmung dreier neutestamentlicher Briefe, in: U. Schnelle (Hg.), Reformation und Neuzeit. 300 Jahre Theologie in Halle, Berlin/New York 1994, 49–71.

nach wie vor spielen. Im Ergebnis – soviel sei hier bereits gesagt – werden diese Überlegungen die anderweitig bereits mehrfach begründete These unterstützen, dass die Pastoralbriefe nicht sinnvoll als einheitliches Briefkorpus interpretiert werden können und dieses Interpretationsparadigma aufgegeben werden muss. Die differenzierte Wahrnehmung der formalen literarischen, der sprachlichen und der inhaltlichen Unterschiede legen vielmehr nahe, jeden Brief individuell zu betrachten, um auf dieser Grundlage eine neue Verhältnisbestimmung vorzunehmen und die Frage nach Pseudepigraphie und Authentizität neu zu stellen.

3.1 Der Ertrag gattungskritischer Beobachtungen zur Plausibilisierung der Pseudepigraphie der Pastoralbriefe

Als bedeutendes Problem für die Interpretation der Pastoralbriefe stellt sich die Frage nach der Gattungsbestimmung und ihres Einflusses auf die Gesamtbeurteilung der Briefe. Sieht man in den Pastoralbriefen ein pseudepigraphisch abgefasstes Korpus, dann bekommt die Bestimmung der zu dieser literarischen Komposition gewählten Gattung bzw. die Kombination verschiedener Gattungen ein umso größeres Gewicht, da damit zugleich gemäß der von Speyer erarbeiteten Kriterien (s.o.) die konkrete literarische Gestaltung und somit die Art der pseudepigraphischen Fiktion plausibel gemacht werden muss.

Die Frage nach der Briefgattung und nach der konkreten Gestaltung der formalen Gattungsmerkmale gehört zu den kompliziertesten Problemen nicht nur der Pastoralbriefe, sondern antiker Briefe überhaupt. In der Forschung besteht Einigkeit darüber, dass auch in antiken Briefen Echtheit oder Unechtheit anhand der Gattungsbestimmung oft schwer oder gar nicht zu entscheiden sind.[107] Schon die Zuordnung einzelner Briefe zu Einzelgattungen oder Gattungen von Sammlungen ist mitunter problematisch. David Trobisch etwa unterscheidet – etwas vereinfachend[108] – zwischen Einzelbrief und redaktionellen Briefsammlungen, wobei er für Letztere den Vergleich mit *literarischen* Briefsammlungen für entscheidend hält.[109] Erst die Brief*sammlung* erlange literarischen Charakter, weil sie ursprüngliche Privatbriefe (mit Überarbeitungen) einem größeren Publikum zugänglich mache und so die Briefe ihren privaten Charakter verlieren.[110] Die Frage wäre, was daraus für die Beurteilung des einzelnen Briefes im Blick auf seine Echtheit – und damit eben auch im Blick auf seine Interpretation – folgt. Werden Briefe gesammelt und ediert, kommen kleinere Ergänzungen zum gesammelten Bestand, aber auch neue und damit pseudepigraphisch verfasste Briefe hinzu.

---

[107] Zum Ganzen vgl. z.B. K. BERGER, Hellenistische Gattungen im Neuen Testament, ANRW II 25.2 (1984), 1031–1432; KLAUCK, Briefliteratur (s. Anm. 18), passim; ELLIS, Making (s. Anm. 50), 50f.

[108] Vgl. ELLIS, a.a.O. 50.

[109] D. TROBISCH, Die Entstehung der Paulusbriefsammlung. Studien zu den Anfängen christlicher Publizistik, NTOA 10, Göttingen/Freiburg (CH) 1989, 85–88.

[110] A.a.O. 88.

Doch nach welchen Kriterien kann im Blick auf eine derartige Zusammenstellung von Einzelbriefen eine Unterscheidung zwischen echt und unecht vorgenommen werden? Welche Funktion kommt dabei der Bestimmung von Gattungen zu? Gibt es vielleicht sogar Aspekte, die im Rahmen einer solchen Sammlung in Abhängigkeit vom Kontext und der Intention der Sammlung die Notwendigkeit einer Unterscheidung in echt und unecht obsolet werden lassen bzw. zumindest relativieren, z.B. bei der Sammlung in einem relativ geschlossenen Schulkontext? Gerade dies wäre für die Pastoralbriefe eine interessante Frage, wobei freilich präzise nach *der Art* der Durchführung, also formkritischen Kriterien, gefragt werden muss. Darüber hinaus ergibt sich mit der Voraussetzung eines Wachstums von Briefsammlungen bereits die Möglichkeit, innerhalb einer solchen Sammlung zwischen echten und unechten Briefen zu unterscheiden, was auch für die (Unter-)Gruppe der Pastoralbriefe nicht von vornherein ausgeschlossen werden kann.

3.2 Die Pastoralbriefe und die antike Brieftheorie

Bei der Beurteilung solcher formaler Aspekte kann man sich zunächst nach den Kriterien antiker Brieftheoretiker richten, die für bestimmte Briefgattungen konkrete Merkmale formulieren. Wie solche Kriterien im Einzelnen – z.B. die Verwendung formaler Stereotypen und Floskeln – aussehen, hat Abraham Malherbe in einer kleinen Studie anschaulich gemacht.[111] Man *kann* damit rechnen, dass ein pseudepigraphisch schreibender Verfasser sich nach solchen Kriterien richtet und daran erkennbar ist. Das wird bei den Pastoralbriefen etwa im Blick auf die Verwendung persönlicher Notizen vorausgesetzt. Doch ist diese Voraussetzung, dass sich ein pseudepigraphischer Autor nach gewissen Regeln verhält, tatsächlich selbstverständlich? Ein solches Kriterium ist bei Weitem nicht differenziert *genug*, weil es nicht berücksichtigt, dass brieftheoretische Kriterien natürlich auch für „echte" Briefe gelten, d.h. auch authentisch abgefasste Briefe Stereotypen, Floskeln und nicht zuletzt – je nach Brieftyp – natürlich auch persönliche Elemente enthalten.[112] Es ist daher fraglich, ob aus der – noch dazu stets unsicheren – Gattungsbestimmung überhaupt Anhaltspunkte für die Begründung pseudepigraphischer Fiktion gewonnen werden können. Malherbe hat darüber hinaus auf die notwendige Unterscheidung zwischen *aktueller Praxis* des Briefeschreibens und antiker Brief*theorie* aufmerksam gemacht. Man müsse sorgfältig unterscheiden zwischen „echten" Briefen, die ohne fiktiven Hintergrund aus aktuellem Anlass geschrieben werden

---

[111] A. J. MALHERBE, Ancient Epistolary Theorists, SBL SBibSt 19, Atlanta 1988.

[112] Vgl. dazu vor allem BERGER, Gattungen (s. Anm. 107), 1132–1138. Berger weist besonders auf das Vorbildmotiv als Kennzeichen echter Briefe hin (1134f.).

und sich meist unbewusst und selbstverständlich brieflicher Stilelemente bedienen, woraus sich dann auch *Mischformen* verschiedener Gattungsmerkmale erklären, und *literarisch konzipierten* Briefen, für die nicht nur fiktive Elemente konstitutiv sind, sondern die in viel höherem Maße brieftheoretische Kriterien reflektieren und vor allem auch stilistisch variieren.[113] Im Blick auf die Frage nach Pseudonymität oder Authentizität ist daraus jedoch noch nichts abzuleiten und erst recht nicht zu begründen. Dabei beeinflusst der rhetorische bzw. im weiteren Sinne kulturelle Bildungsstand des Verfassers den Grad der brieftheoretischen Reflexion. Auch konkrete inhaltliche Anliegen können zu stilistischen Brüchen führen, so dass oft kaum eindeutig zu entscheiden ist, ob ein literarischer bzw. literarisch fingierter, ein gefälschter oder ein aktueller authentischer Brief vorliegt. Hinzu kommt weiterhin – wie bereits angedeutet – die notwendige Unterscheidung zwischen *literarischen* Einzelbriefen und *literarischen* Briefsammlungen, die wiederum eigenen Kriterien unterliegen, an denen auch die Pastoralbriefe als pseudepigraphisch konzipierte Briefsammlung von drei Briefen gemessen werden müssten – wenn man sie denn unter diesem Vorzeichen betrachten will.

Diese Überlegungen deuten an, wie komplex die Beurteilung der Pastoralbriefe im Rahmen antiker Brieftheorie und -praxis tatsächlich ist und dienen daher zunächst nur zur Präzisierung der Problembeschreibung. Die Komplexität des Problems führt oft zu einseitigen und dadurch wenig brauchbaren Bestimmungen sowohl des einzelnen Briefes wie des dreifachen Korpus, wie etwa der Versuch Alfons Weisers zur Gattungsbestimmung des 2Tim zeigt: „So führt die Untersuchung der Form- und Gattungsmerkmale zu dem Ergebnis, dass 2Tim ein *testamentarisches Mahnschreiben* in Form eines *Freundschaftsbriefes* ist, dessen hauptsächlich *symbuleutischen* Ausdrucksformen auch *epideiktische* zugeordnet sind."[114] Demgegenüber werden die Gattungen des 1Tim und Tit zumeist mit den sogenannten *mandata principis* verglichen, d.h. autoritativen Mandatsbriefen aus dem Kontext politisch-ideologischer Machtausübung,[115]

---

[113] MALHERBE, Theorists (s. Anm. 111), 4, im Blick auf das „Handbuch" Τύποι Ἐπιστολικοί des Ps.-Demetrios von Phaleron (zwischen 200 v. Chr. und 300 n. Chr.): „The exact relationship of this manual to the actual practice of letter writing is difficult to determine."

[114] Vgl. A. WEISER, Der zweite Brief an Timotheus, EKK XVI/1, Neukirchen-Vluyn 2003, 44 (Hervorhebungen J.H.).

[115] Vgl. M. WOLTER, Die Pastoralbriefe als Paulustradition, FRLANT 146, Göttingen 1988, 164f.; JOHNSON, Letters to Timothy (s. Anm. 67), 139f. Die Inanspruchnahme des Tebtunis Papyrus Nr. 703, der Anweisungen eines ägyptischen Beamten an einen Untergebenen enthält, für die Identifizierung des Genres von 1Tim durch Johnson ist von M. M. MITCHELL, PTEBT 703 and the Genre of 1 Timothy. The Curious Career of a Ptolemaic Papyrus in Pauline Scholarship, NT 44 (2002), 344–370, einer grundlegenden

wobei auch dies in seiner Bedeutung für die Frage nach der Pseudepigraphie umstritten bleibt. Was soll damit gesagt bzw. begründet sein? Welche Bedeutung hat diese unterschiedliche Bestimmung für die Beurteilung eines mutmaßlichen *Corpus pastorale* (Trummer)?[116] Nach den Maßstäben antiker Brieftheorie könnte man auch sagen: Es handelt sich bei den Pastoralbriefen (sowohl bei den je einzelnen wie auch im Korpus insgesamt) um einen schlechten Stilmix, wie dies etwa Margaret Mitchell formuliert hat: „... the Pastorals are an odd mix of the personal and the public, of church order and personal exhortation, of instruction and command, of the particular and the general."[117] Der pseudepigraphische Charakter der Pastoralbriefe lässt sich daher anhand von Gattungsmerkmalen ohne weiteres weder entscheiden noch begründen, zumal dabei auch die dreifache Verhältnisbestimmung zwischen Gattung des einzelnen Briefes, dem dreiteiligen Korpus sowie dessen Verortung im Kontext der Paulusbriefsammlung zu klären wäre.

Wenn man darüber hinaus der These von Peter Trummer folgen will, wonach die Pastoralbriefe als Abschluss einer Neuedition des *Corpus Paulinum* verfasst wurden,[118] wird die Notwendigkeit einer solchen Differenzierung noch deutlicher. Entsprechend Trummers These könnten sie nämlich – und das ist vielfach getan worden – zunächst unabhängig von der Form des einzelnen Briefes als dreiteiliges Korpus formal der Gattung der antiken Briefsammlungen zugeordnet werden, von denen einige auch mit pseudepigraphischem Material erhalten sind, so z.B. die Sokrates- und Sokratikerbriefe, die Platonbriefe, die Briefe des Cicero, bzw. auch der Gattung des Briefromans, zu der etwa die Briefe Alexanders des Großen oder die Chionbriefe gerechnet werden. Innerhalb der christlichen Tradition wäre hier etwa der Briefwechsel zwischen Paulus und Seneca (ca. 4. Jh.)[119] zu nennen.

Kritik unterzogen worden. Mitchell hebt zu Recht hervor, dass PTEBT 703 *kein* Brief ist, und daher die Bestimmung als „mandata principis letter" durch Johnson falsch und für den Vergleich mit den Pastoralbriefen ungeeignet ist. Mit Wolter verweist Mitchell lediglich auf die „vergleichbare Kommunikationsstruktur" beider Texte (362.368; vgl. WOLTER, a.a.O. 163.169f.).

[116] S.u.
[117] MITCHELL, Genre (s. Anm. 115), 344.
[118] S.o. 514.
[119] Vgl. hierzu: Der apokryphe Briefwechsel zwischen Seneca und Paulus zusammen mit dem Brief des Mordechai an Alexander und dem Brief des Annaeus Seneca über Hochmut und Götterbilder, eingel., übers. u. m. interpret. Essays vers. v. A. FÜRST u.a., SAPERE XI, Tübingen 2006; ders., Pseudepigraphie und Apostolizität im apokryphen Briefwechsel zwischen Seneca und Paulus, JAC 41 (1998), 77–117; C. RÖMER, Der Briefwechsel zwischen Seneca und Paulus, in: W. Schneemelcher (Hg.), Neutestamentli-

3.3 Die Pastoralbriefe und der antike Briefroman

Insbesondere Richard I. Pervo hat versucht, die Pastoralbriefe auf dem Hintergrund der Gattung des antiken Brief*romans* zu verstehen und damit deren legitimen pseudepigraphischen Charakter zu begründen.[120] Auch wenn man prinzipiell bezweifeln kann, ob die Pastoralbriefe – wie dabei *notwendig* vorausgesetzt werden muss! – tatsächlich als Briefkorpus verfasst wurden (s.u.) und ob es in der Antike eine Gattung „Briefroman" überhaupt gab,[121] nennt Pervo als deren spezifischen Merkmale: Pseudonymität, historische Verankerung, Ausrichtung auf bestimmte Charakterzüge, philosophische bzw. moralische Absicht, Integrität und Kohärenz der Sammlung sowie, als entscheidendes Kriterium, die *Präsentation einer Erzählung*.[122] Als Beispiele zieht Pervo die Briefe des Chion und die Sokratikerbriefe heran. Abgesehen davon, dass selbst diese Beispiele die *idealtypisch konstruierten* Gattungsmerkmale nicht hinreichend repräsentieren, ist auch der darauf beruhende Vergleich mit den Pastoralbriefen letztlich nicht überzeugend. Dabei spielt nicht zuletzt die relativ geringe Zahl der drei Pastoralbriefe gegenüber der deutlich höheren in den herangezogenen Briefsammlungen eine Rolle.[123] Insbesondere jedoch das ent-

---

che Apokryphen in deutscher Übersetzung, Bd. II: Apostolisches, Apokalypsen und Verwandtes, Tübingen ⁶1997, 44–50; sowie den Beitrag von Stefan Krauter in diesem Band.

[120] Vgl. dazu R. I. PERVO, Romancing an Oft-Neglected Stone. The Pastoral Epistles and the Epistolary Novell, The Journal of the Higher Criticism 1 (1994), 25–47, der die Parallelen zwischen den Pastoralbriefen und antiken Briefromanen herausstellt; sowie die Dissertation von T. GLASER, Paulus als Briefroman erzählt. Studien zum antiken Briefroman und seiner christlichen Rezeption in den Pastoralbriefen, NTOA 76, Göttingen u.a. 2009 (vgl. dessen Beitrag in diesem Band). Vgl. auch SPEYER, Fälschung (s. Anm. 22), 22; FRENSCHKOWSKI, Pseudepigraphie (s. Anm. 6), 262.

[121] PERVO, Romancing (s. Anm. 120), 27, nennt als – wohl kaum ernst gemeintes – Argument: „Epistolary novels obviously existed, for they are discussed in Pauly-Wissowa." Zum Problem der Gattung Briefroman vgl. N. Holzberg (Hg.), Der griechische Briefroman. Gattungstypologie und Textanalyse, Classica Monacensia 8, Tübingen 1994; sowie den Aufsatz von Katharina Luchner im vorliegenden Band.

[122] PERVO, a.a.O. 29f. Vgl. dazu die Kriterien bei N. HOLZBERG, Der griechische Briefroman. Versuch einer Gattungstypologie, in: ders., a.a.O. 1–52 (49–52).

[123] Die Sokratikerbriefe umfassen immerhin 35 Einzelschreiben, die Chionbriefe 17 (die Datierungen schwanken jeweils zwischen dem 1. und 3. Jh.). Beide Sammlungen sind einer Persönlichkeit zugeordnet, die zum Zeitpunkt der Abfassung bereits in gleichsam mythischer Vergangenheit liegt: Bei Sokrates (469–399 v. Chr.) handelt es sich um 400–600 Jahre, beim Platonschüler Chion (Mitte 4. Jh. v. Chr.) immerhin um 300–500 Jahre. – Hierbei würde sich auch die Frage stellen, inwiefern die Pastoralbriefe als Briefroman in die Paulusbriefsammlung zu integrieren sind und ob die „Romanhandlung" durch diese intertextuelle Verortung nicht auch verändert würde oder überhaupt erst dadurch zustande käme. Aber dies bleibt genauso hypothetisch wie die Theorie, durch die solche Fragen erst aufkommen.

scheidende Element der *fortlaufenden Erzählung* kann für die Pastoralbriefe nicht plausibel herausgearbeitet werden. Was Pervo am Schluss als Intention der Pastoralbriefe beschreibt, ist so hypothetisch und inkohärent, dass es letztlich sogar den von ihm selbst gesetzten Voraussetzungen nicht gerecht wird.[124]

Während man jedoch im Blick auf die genannten paganen Beispiele nicht im eigentlichen Sinn von pseudepigraphischen *Kompositionen* sprechen kann, sondern von Sammlungen ausgehen muss, die durch pseudepigraphisches Material ergänzt wurden, handelt es sich beim Briefwechsel zwischen Paulus und Seneca wahrscheinlich um eine bewusste pseudepigraphische Komposition, deren Intention zwar nicht eindeutig bestimmt werden kann, die aber immer wieder als christliches Beispiel für ein literarisch fiktives Briefkorpus angeführt wird. Doch damit ist die Vergleichsmöglichkeit zu den Pastoralbriefen schon erschöpft, denn auch im Briefwechsel zwischen Paulus und Seneca liegt – wie bei den meisten pseudepigraphischen Briefen innerhalb anderer Sammlungen – nun tatsächlich ein rein *literarisches* Produkt vor, also im guten Sinne eine literarische „Erfindung"[125], die keine erkennbaren *gewichtigen, d.h. in ideologischer Weise durchzusetzenden* Absichten verfolgt und zu diesem Zwecke täuschen müsste.[126] Der entscheidende Unterschied zu den Pastoralbriefen ist nicht nur, dass es sich um einen regelrechten Brief*wechsel* handelt, sondern auch, dass z.B. persönliche Notizen und Anspielungen außer allgemeinen stilistischen Floskeln gerade *nicht* in der Weise wie etwa in 2Tim und Tit vorkommen.[127]

---

[124] PERVO, Romancing (s. Anm. 120), 43–45. Obwohl zuvor festgestellt wurde, dass die Pastoralbriefe am besten mit den Chionbriefen zu vergleichen sind (36), schreibt Pervo: „The PE are rather more successfully read as a work like the Socratic Epistles, granting that the latter are, *so to speak, letters written by Timotheus and Titus rather than to them*", da die Sokratikerbriefe von den Schülern, nicht von der Schulautorität stammen (45).

[125] Diesen Begriff benutzt SPEYER, Fälschung (s. Anm. 22), 21f. u.ö.

[126] Vgl. SPEYER, a.a.O. 178.258, der hier leider nicht ganz entschieden ist; vgl. auch RÖMER, Briefwechsel (s. Anm. 119), 45. A. FÜRST, Einführung, in: ders., Der apokryphe Briefwechsel (s. Anm. 119), 3–22, stellt fest: „Ohne die Existenz der genannten Einzelthemen in Abrede stellen zu wollen, gilt es die Einsicht ernstzunehmen, dass dieser Briefwechsel als ganzer eigentümlich inhaltslos ist. Auch aus der Philosophie Senecas und der Theologie des Paulus finden sich nur dürftige Spuren, die durchweg bis zur Banalität verformt sind und nichts weiter demonstrieren als den Dilettantismus des Verfassers. Eine verbreitete Intention antiker Pseudepigraphie, nämlich bestimmte Ansichten oder Lehren unter dem Deckmantel einer anerkannten Autorität zu propagieren, lässt sich am Text dieser Briefe nicht verifizieren. Die auffällige Eigenheit des Briefwechsels zwischen Seneca und Paulus ist die, dass es in ihm offenbar gar nicht um Inhalte geht, sondern um die Namen der Korrespondenten und nur um diese" (11).

[127] Bemerkenswert ist allenfalls die Mahnung des Seneca in Brief XIII, Paulus solle

3.4 Die Pastoralbriefe und philosophische Schulpseudepigraphie

Unter dem Aspekt der Verwendung pseudepigraphischer Stilmittel ist weiterhin ein Vergleich der Pastoralbriefe insbesondere mit den Sokratikerbriefen oder auch den pseudopythagoreischen Briefen[128] aufschlussreich, deren pseudepigraphische Absicht es ist, ein philosophisches Leben nach dem Beispiel des Sokrates oder Pythagoras zu propagieren.[129] Charakteristisch für solche Briefe aus dem philosophisch-literarischen Schulbetrieb ist nun tatsächlich *nicht* die Täuschungsabsicht, sondern die *Anknüpfung an vorhandene Schreiben gleicher Art*, der *sparsame Rückgriff auf bekannte Aspekte aus dem Leben des Lehrers* und zugleich eine *Verallgemeinerung persönlicher Züge*, um *Charakteristisches* herauszuheben. Die Tendenz zur Verallgemeinerung dient dabei vor allem der Verschärfung bzw. Zuspitzung von Grundpositionen, die auch zur Klärung bzw. Interpretation strittiger und in der bisherigen Überlieferung nicht eindeutig formulierter Themen beitragen sollen. Zu berücksichtigen wäre darüber hinaus auch, dass in Schultraditionen fingierte Briefe zu Übungszwecken verfasst werden, einerseits um verschiedene Briefstile einzuüben, andererseits um dabei die Lehren des Schuloberhauptes wiederzugeben bzw. weiterzuentwickeln.[130] Die Absicht, den *Eindruck* der Echtheit zu vermitteln und damit zu täuschen, die bei den Pastoralbriefen in der Regel als Merk-

---

doch mehr „auf den reinen lateinischen Stil" achten. Gerade an einer solchen Notiz wird deutlich, wie Schulpseudepigraphie „funktioniert". Die eigentliche Absicht, die Tertullian bekanntlich hinter diesem Briefwechsel erkennt, ist kaum von ideologisch-autoritärem Charakter, wohl aber durchaus positiv: „Seneca saepe noster" (Tert.an. 20,1); vgl. dazu A. FÜRST, Seneca – ein Monotheist? Ein neuer Blick auf eine alte Debatte, in: ders., Der apokryphe Briefwechsel (s. Anm. 119), 85–107 (85–88). – Unter diesem Gesichtspunkt, d.h. der literarischen Charakteristik der Pastoralbriefe, die sie durch die ungewöhnlich hohe Zahl an persönlichen Notizen erhalten, versteht Speyer sie demgegenüber als „Gegenfälschungen", weil sie mit dem Mittel der Täuschung im Kontext der Ketzerbekämpfung ideologische Interessen durchsetzen wollen; vgl. SPEYER, Fälschung (s. Anm. 22), 279. Leider ist dies zu wenig differenziert, vor allem im Blick auf die Einschätzung der Gegnerpolemiken in Tit und 1Tim, die nicht – wie Speyer dies offenbar voraussetzt – auf einen Nenner zu bringen sind; unter den gegebenen Voraussetzungen aber ist Speyer hier konsequent und nimmt Frenschkowskis Einschätzung vorweg (s.o. Anm. 33).

[128] Vgl. BROX, Verfasserangaben (s. Anm. 7), 72f.; KLAUCK, Briefliteratur (s. Anm. 18), 303; STANDHARTINGER, Kolosserbrief (s. Anm. 25), 55; ZIMMERMANN, Unecht – und doch wahr? (s. Anm. 15), 30.

[129] Vgl. DONELSON, Pseudepigraphy (s. Anm. 48), 41; SPEYER, Fälschung (s. Anm. 22), 136f.; zum Ganzen B. FIORE, The Function of Personal Example in the Socratic and Pastoral Epistles, AnBib 105, Rom 1986, bes. 101–164.

[130] Vgl. dazu SPEYER, a.a.O. 34f. Der Abschnitt zur pseudepigraphischen Produktion innerhalb von Schulkontexten fällt bei Speyer leider sehr kurz aus, vermutlich deshalb, weil hierbei kein eigentliches Problem vorliegt.

mal der pseudepigraphischen Fiktion angesehen wird, steht bei der Schulpseudepigraphie nicht im Vordergrund und ist im Schulkontext auch nicht plausibel.[131] Das bedeutet aber konkret, dass *innerhalb eines Schulkontextes* die Verfasserfiktion gerade nicht unentdeckt bleiben muss, um das Schreiben akzeptabel zu machen, d.h. dass die Fiktion tatsächlich legitim und unproblematisch ist, weil sie auf einem offenen Konsens beruhen konnte. Darauf hatte erstaunlicherweise bereits Schleiermacher aufmerksam gemacht.[132] Gerade dies wird oft auch für die Pastoralbriefe insgesamt reklamiert, wobei aber die Frage bestehen bleibt, ob bzw. inwiefern die drei Schreiben aufgrund ihrer unterschiedlichen stilistischen Merkmale tatsächlich gleichermaßen vor diesem Hintergrund verstanden werden können. An dieser Stelle ist man leider über die Behauptung, dass dies so sei, nicht hinausgekommen. Die Pastoralbriefe sind jedoch gerade im Blick auf Briefgestaltung so unterschiedlich, dass man hier auch nicht viel weiterkommen wird, wenn man diese Unterschiede nicht stärker in die Diskussion einbezieht. Dies betrifft sowohl inhaltliche als auch formale Aspekte hinsichtlich der Gestaltung des Briefformulars und der Verwendung von persönlichen Notizen, die etwa im 1Tim im Unterschied zum (unter pseudepigraphischer Perspektive immer problematischen, da auf Fälschung hindeutenden!) Überfluss solcher Notizen der beiden anderen Briefe (fast) vollständig fehlen – bis dahin, dass noch nicht einmal die bei Paulus auch sonst üblichen Schlussgrüße aufgeführt werden. Darin steht der 1Tim in der literarischen Anlage (nicht im Inhalt!) dem Epheserbrief nahe, der nicht zuletzt aus diesem Grund plausibel als Schulpseudepigraphon im oben beschriebenen Sinn angesehen werden kann.[133] Allerdings wäre dabei auch zu klären, ob und inwiefern man überhaupt von einer „Paulusschule"

---

[131] Mit Hinweis auf die pseudopythagoreischen Schriften oder rhetorische Schulübungen urteilt ähnlich KLAUCK, Briefliteratur (s. Anm. 18), 303: „Am ehesten war man noch geneigt, im Kontext von festen Schultraditionen (Philosophenschulen, Ärzteschulen) hinzunehmen, wenn Literatur späterer Schulmitglieder unter dem Namen des Schulhauptes erschien." Ähnlich FIORE, Example (s. Anm. 129), 163. Vgl. dazu auch den Aufsatz von Marco Frenschkowski in diesem Band.

[132] F. D. E. SCHLEIERMACHER, Der christliche Glaube nach den Grundsätzen der evangelischen Kirche im Zusammenhange dargestellt, Bd. 2, hg. v. R. Schäfer, Berlin 2003 (= 1830/31), 332f.: „Ja auch gleich bei ihrer Erscheinung könnte eine Schrift den Namen eines Andern als ihres eigentlichen Verfassers an der Spitze getragen haben; wenn dabei nur eine von dem sittlichen Gefühl des Verfassers übereinstimmend mit dem sittlichen Gemeingefühl seiner Zeitgenossen für unschuldig geachtete Fiktion zum Grunde gelegen, könnte auch ein so beschaffenes Buch immer authentisch sein als Theil der Bibel. Nur wenn eine solche Bezeichnung ein absichtliches Irreleiten gewesen wäre, würde diese Schrift nicht berufen sein können, die normale Darstellung des Christenthums zu ergänzen."

[133] S. dazu unten die Thesen 6 und 7 in der Zusammenfassung.

sprechen kann, in der man die Produktion pseudonymer „Schulschriften" verortet.[134]

3.5 Sprache und Stil als Indikatoren pseudepigrapischer Verfasserschaft

Ein wichtiger Ausgangspunkt der neuzeitlichen Kritik an der Echtheit der Pastoralbriefe waren zunächst wortstatistische und stilistische sowie später stylometrische Erhebungen, die vor allem seit den 60er Jahren des 20. Jh. durch zum Teil computeranalytische Methoden verfeinert wurden.[135] Statistische Erhebungen, insbesondere die von Kenneth Grayston und Gustav Herdan[136], sind bis in neueste Untersuchungen hinein immer wieder Ausgangspunkt für die Begründung pseudopaulinischer Verfasserschaft gewesen und müssen daher hinsichtlich ihres grundsätzlichen Wertes erörtert werden.[137]

---

[134] Vgl. hierzu neuerdings wieder T. VEGGE, Paulus und das antike Schulwesen. Schule und Bildung des Paulus, BZNW 134, Berlin u.a. 2006, bes. 498f., der in Aufnahme und Fortführung einer älteren These von H. CONZELMANN, Die Schule des Paulus, in: C. Andresen / G. Klein (Hg.), Theologia crucis – signum crucis (FS Dinkler), Tübingen 1979, 85–96, versucht zu begründen, dass Paulus selbst aufgrund seiner Vertrautheit mit und seiner Prägung durch hellenistisch-philosophische Schulbildung die Entstehung einer eigenen „Schule" betrieben bzw. eine solche „gegründet" habe.

[135] Vgl. neben den Autoren des 19. Jh. bes. K. GRAYSTON / G. HERDAN, The Pastorals in the Light of Statistical Linguistics, NTS 6 (1959–1960), 1–15; K. BEYER, Semitische Syntax im Neuen Testament, StUNT 1, Göttingen 1962, 232.295.298; P. F. JOHNSON, The Use of Statistics in the Analysis of the Characteristics of Pauline Writings, NTS 20 (1974), 92–100; A. KENNY, A Stylometric Study of the New Testament, Oxford 1986; D. L. MEALAND, Positional Stylometry Reassessed. Testing a Seven Epistle Theory of Pauline Authorship, NTS 35 (1989), 266–286; ders., The Extent of the Pauline Corpus. A Multivariate Approach, JSNT 59 (1995), 61–92; K. J. NEUMANN, The Authenticity of Pauline Epistles in the Light of Stylostatistical Analysis, SBLDS 120, Atlanta 1990; G. K. BARR, A Computer Model for the Pauline Epistles, Literary and Linguistic Computing 16 (2001), 233–250. Kritisch gegenüber solchen Analysen bereits B. M. METZGER, A Reconsideration of Certain Arguments against the Pauline Authorship of the Pastoral Epistles, ET 70 (1958–1959), 91–94; W. MICHAELIS, Die Pastoralbriefe und Wortstatistik, ZNW 28 (1929), 69–76; T. A. ROBINSON, Grayston and Herdan's ‚C' Quantity Formula and the Authorship of the Pastoral Epistles, NTS 30 (1984), 282–288; G. LEDGER, An Exploration of Differences in the Pauline Epistles Using Multivariate Statistical Analysis, Literary and Linguistic Computing 10 (1995), 85–97, sowie (ohne konkreten Bezug zu biblischen Texten) M. L. HILTON / D. I. HOLMES, An Assessment of Cumulative Sum Charts for Authorship Attribution, Literary and Linguistic Computing 8 (1993), 73–80, als Kritik an A. Q. MORTON / S. MICHAELSON, The QSUM Plot Internal Report CSR-3-90, Edinburgh 1990; vgl. dies., Last Words. A Test of Authorship for Greek Writers, NTS 18 (1972), 192–208.

[136] GRAYSTON / HERDAN, Linguistics (s. Anm. 135).

[137] Vgl. z.B. W. G. KÜMMEL, Einleitung in das Neue Testament, Heidelberg [21]1983, 328f.; I. BROER, Einleitung in das Neue Testament, Bd. 2, Würzburg 2001, 534f.;

Gemäß der oft herangezogenen und in ihrer Methodik kaum infrage gestellten Statistik von Richard Morgenthaler enthalten die Pastoralbriefe mit 335 Hapaxlegomena mehr als der doppelt so lange Römerbrief.[138] Das Vorkommen von Gräzismen in den Pastoralbriefen wird von Klaus Beyer ungleich höher veranschlagt als in anderen Paulusbriefen.[139] Dabei ist jedoch zu bedenken, dass die Verwendung von Hapaxlegomena und Sondergutvokabeln stets auch thematisch durch Aufnahme traditionell geprägter Wendungen[140] oder durch Begriffe und Vorstellungen[141] bedingt ist, die durch gegnerische Positionen vorgegeben sind – ein häufig erwähnter inhaltlicher Vorbehalt, der in der Statistik nicht oder nicht hinreichend abgebildet und im Übrigen oft ignoriert wird.[142] Bereits in der einflussreichen

---

SCHNELLE, Einleitung (s. Anm. 10), 371; sowie N. BROX, Die Pastoralbriefe, RNT, Regensburg ⁴1969, 46–49; J. ROLOFF, Der erste Timotheusbrief, EKK XV, Neukirchen-Vluyn 1988, 28–31, der die vor allem gegen P. N. HARRISON, Paulines and Pastorals, London 1964, vorgebrachten Einwände durch die Analyse von Grayston / Herdan widerlegt sieht; OBERLINNER, 1Timotheus (s. Anm. 79), XXXVII u.a.; sowie neuerdings A. D. BAUM, Semantic Variation within the Corpus Paulinum. Linguistic Considerations Concerning the Richer Vocabulary of the Pastoral Epistles, TynBul 59 (2008), 271–292.

[138] Vgl. R. MORGENTHALER, Statistik des neutestamentlichen Wortschatzes, Zürich ³1983, 38, eine Referenz, die vor allem in Einleitungen regelmäßig angeführt wird (vgl. die in Anm. 135 Genannten); vgl. jedoch METZGER, Reconsideration (s. Anm. 135); KENNY, Study (s. Anm. 135), 5–9.13–16.

[139] BEYER, Syntax (s. Anm. 135), 232, gibt für das Verhältnis von Gräzismen gegenüber Semitismen in den Pastoralbriefen eine Zahl von 1100% an; die höchste Zahl bei Paulus liege bei 300% (Phil). Allerdings sind auch hier die Pastoralbriefe als Einheit herangezogen, wobei in Beyers Übersicht gut sichtbar wird, dass der Prozentsatz *in höchstem Maße* durch den 1Tim verursacht ist.

[140] Vgl. die zahlreichen Abschnitte im hymnischen Stil, die – wie auch bei Paulus selbst – von anderen geprägte Vorstellungen eintragen. Interessant ist in diesem Zusammenhang, dass die Pastoralbriefe an keiner Stelle auf Stücke zurückgreifen, die auch Paulus schon verwendet hätte oder gar auf Zitate aus den Briefen des Apostels selbst.

[141] Ein eindeutig übernommener Begriff ist z.B. in 1Tim 6,20, wie aus dem Text selbst hervorgeht, derjenige der γνῶσις, den der Verfasser betont, sie werde fälschlicherweise – d.h. von anderen – so genannt. Allerdings ist davon auszugehen, dass in vielen Fällen die Identifikation der Herkunft auffälliger Begriffe nicht sicher bestimmbar ist und daher notwendig strittig bleiben muss – einschließlich eventueller Schlussfolgerungen, die aus einem Urteil in die eine oder andere Richtung gezogen werden könnten. Vgl. ferner auch die Äußerung zur Bedeutung der Schrift in 2Tim 3,16, die im Zusammenhang konkreter Auseinandersetzungen zu verstehen ist; vgl. dazu G. HÄFNER, „Nützlich zur Belehrung" (2Tim 3,16). Die Rolle der Schrift in den Pastoralbriefen im Rahmen der Paulusrezeption, HBS 25, Freiburg i. Brsg. u.a. 1998, bes. 279; J. HERZER, „Von Gottes Geist durchweht" – Die Inspiration der Schrift nach 2Tim 3,16 und bei Philo von Alexandrien, in: R. Deines / K.-W. Niebuhr (Hg.), Philo und das Neue Testament. Wechselseitige Wahrnehmungen, WUNT 172, Tübingen 2004, 223–240.

[142] Vgl. etwa C. K. BARRETT, Titus (1969), in: ders., Essays on Paul, Philadelphia 1982, 118–131, gegenüber der These, Gal 2,3–8 sei eine Interpolation aus der Feder des

Untersuchung von Percy N. Harrison[143] wird deutlich, dass die Verhältnisbestimmung zum paulinischen Sprachgebrauch anders ausfällt, wenn man die Pastoralbriefe je einzeln bestimmt bzw. das Kriterium der Hapaxlegomena nur auf das *Corpus Paulinum* beschränkt. Dann ergeben sich bei 309 Wörtern der Pastoralbriefe, die nicht in den anderen Briefen des *Corpus Paulinum* vorkommen, für den 1Tim mit Abstand die meisten (127), für 2Tim hingegen nur 81, für Tit noch 45 innerhalb des Corpus Paulinum. Ordnet man die Briefe jeweils zu zweit, ergeben sich für 1Tim und 2Tim 17, für 1Tim und Tit 20, sowie für 2Tim und Tit nur 7.[144]

Eine weitere ausführliche Untersuchung hat Anthony Kenny 1986 vorgelegt.[145] Obwohl er versucht, den positiven Beitrag der stylometrischen Analyse zum Verstehen der neutestamentlichen Traditionen unter Beweis zu stellen, ist sich Kenny der Grenzen und Unsicherheiten des Verfahrens bewusst: „The most serious limitation of the statistical study of literary texts concerns the difficulty of applying stylometric methods to short passages. This affects the confidence of conclusions both about short works (such as the Epistle to Titus) or about short passages alleged to be interpolations (such as the final chapter of Romans). The difficulty is not merely the general difficulty, in statistical studies, of drawing conclusions about large populations from small samples: there is also a peculiar problem inherent in the literary subject-matter."[146] Darüber hinaus stelle sich das bereits erwähnte Problem, die Verwendung von Zitaten für oder gegen

---

Titus vor allem wegen der Hapaxlegomena: „The *hapax legomena* are required in the description of circumstances which Paul did not have to describe elsewhere" (122). Das gilt *cum grano salis* generell für den Umgang mit statistischen Argumenten hinsichtlich von Hapaxlegomena. Als solche sind sie – selbst in einer relativ ungewöhnlichen Konzentration – kein *sicheres* Indiz zur Bestimmung von Texten.

[143] P. N. HARRISON, The Problem of the Pastoral Epistles, Oxford 1921, der aus seinen Beobachtungen eine Fragmententheorie entwickelt; vgl. die Kritik bei MICHAELIS, Wortstatistik (s. Anm. 135), gegenüber der Zustimmung etwa in der Rezension von E. LOHMEYER, in: ThBl 1 (1922), 208f.

[144] Zahlen nach HARRISON, a.a.O. 137–139; vgl. dagegen MICHAELIS, Wortstatistik (s. Anm. 135), mit dem Grundtenor: „Grundlage aller statistischen und graphischen Arbeit nach Verhältniszahlen ist die, daß die richtigen Größen in Beziehung zueinander gesetzt werden" (74), sowie GRAYSTON / HERDAN, Linguistics (s. Anm. 135), 4–8. Ausgehend von einer Kritik an der Argumentation Harrisons versucht BAUM, Semantic Variation (s. Anm. 137), die sprachlichen und stilistischen Unterschiede der Pastoralbriefe zu den anderen Paulusbriefen dadurch zu erklären, dass die Pastoralbriefe eine größere Affinität zu geschriebener Sprache hätten (der Autor also mehr Zeit zur Abfassung gehabt habe), während die anderen Paulusbriefe eher den Charakter der Mündlichkeit aufwiesen.

[145] KENNY, Study (s. Anm. 135).
[146] A.a.O. 118.

den Stil eines Autors in Anschlag zu bringen, denn Zitate werden entweder stilistisch angepasst oder wörtlich übernommen und mit eigenen Worten ergänzt, so dass Kenny vorschlägt, wörtliche Zitate bei der Auswertung statistischer Ergebnisse nicht zu berücksichtigen.[147] Von weit reichenden Konsequenzen jedoch suspendiert Kenny den Statistiker ausdrücklich: „What is to be said of the authorship of the Epistles is in the end a matter for the Scripture scholar, not the stylometrist. But on the basis of the evidence in this chapter for my part I see no reason to reject the hypothesis that twelve of the Pauline Epistles are the work of a single, unusually versatile author."[148]

Eine erneute Analyse hat Kenneth J. Neumann 1990 vorgenommen.[149] Seine Darstellung ist oft kaum durchschaubar, Voraussetzungen und Ergebnisse sind nur schwer nachvollziehbar. Interessant ist jedoch im Blick auf die Pastoralbriefe, dass für Kenny 1Tim und 2Tim stilistisch Paulus zugewiesen werden können und Tit von den statistischen Mittelwerten zu stark abweicht und deshalb „unter Verdacht" steht. Für Neumann hingegen ist klar, dass aufgrund der von ihm definierten Maßstäbe 1Tim und 2Tim (und damit aus seiner Sicht die Pastoralbriefe insgesamt) einen nichtpaulinischen Stil aufweisen.[150] Zum Tit macht Neumann keine abschließende Aussage;[151] Eph, Kol und 2Thess seien unter stilistischen Gesichtspunkten Paulus zuzuweisen,[152] wobei Neumann es letztlich offen lässt, ob nicht

---

[147] A.a.O. 119f. Der Tit bildet für Kenny offenbar eine Ausnahme (vgl. a.a.O. 98.118), da dessen Kürze und die im Verhältnis dazu hohen Anteile traditionellen Gutes für eine statistische Auswertung sowie zuverlässige Aussagen über die Autorschaft große Probleme bereiten.

[148] A.a.O. 100. Demgegenüber kommen A. Q. MORTON / J. MCLEMAN, Paul, the Man and the Myth. A Study in the Authorship of Greek Prose, New York 1966, 94, zu dem Ergebnis, am Corpus Paulinum hätten neben Paulus als Verfasser der vier Hauptbriefe noch sechs weitere Personen mitgeschrieben.

[149] NEUMANN, Authenticity (s. Anm. 135).

[150] A.a.O. 213; vgl. GRAYSTON / HERDAN, Linguistics (s. Anm. 135), 15. Die Aussage Neumanns bezieht OBERLINNER, 1Timotheus (s. Anm. 79), XXXVII Anm. 36, ebenfalls auf die Pastoralbriefe insgesamt, mit jedoch maßgeblicher Bezugnahme auf BEYER, Syntax (s. Anm. 135), 229–232.293–295.299.

[151] Vgl. NEUMANN, Authenticity (s. Anm. 135), 213f. Der Philemonbrief wird aufgrund seiner Kürze von der statistischen Analyse ausgenommen; als anerkanntermaßen authentisches Basismaterial werden Röm, 1Kor, 2Kor und Gal sowie 1Thess und Phil zugrunde gelegt (vgl. 124). Zum Tit findet sich kein Hinweis – in der Auswertung und in den Tabellen ist nur von 1 und 2Tim die Rede (vgl. auch 131).

[152] A.a.O. 213; vgl. 215: „On the basis of the most effective indices discovered, the disputed letters, especially Ephesians, are found to be closest to the Pauline writing style ... Of course, the use of *hapax legomena* so often cited has been shown to be among the least effective indices."

auch ein anderer Autor im paulinischen Stil hätte schreiben können.[153] Dann aber ist umso fraglicher, was die statistische Methode überhaupt zur Frage der Autorschaft *zuverlässig* beitragen kann, zumal immer offen bleibt, wie Unterschiede erklärt werden bzw. mit welchen Differenzen unter bestimmten Umständen bei einem Autor zu rechnen ist.[154] Immerhin stellt auch Neumann fest, dass zwischen 1Tim und 2Tim unbestreitbar stilistische Unterschiede bestehen, was nicht zuletzt auf das unterschiedliche Genre zurückzuführen sei.[155]

Diese kurzen Referate genügen, um den Wert statistischer und stylometrischer Analysen deutlich zu relativieren, wenn nicht generell zu bezweifeln, so dass nach wie vor Jerôme Murphy-O'Connor zuzustimmen ist: „An important implication ... is that the argument from style, which has been used to determine the authenticity and inauthenticity of certain letters, can no longer be considered valid."[156] Selbst Norbert Brox, der die Untersuchungen von Harrison und Grayston / Herdan positiv aufnimmt,[157] weist die Kritik an den stylometrischen Analysen zwar als überzogen zurück, mahnt aber dennoch zur Vorsicht gegen eine Überschätzung dieses Befundes. Wichtiger seien die „begrifflichen Verschiebungen", in denen

---

[153] A.a.O. 218f.: „... skilled at imitating Pauline language and thought."

[154] Für eine positive Heranziehung von Arbeiten zu Stylometrik muss man sich bewusst machen, dass sie aufgrund der zugrunde gelegten und als in sich geschlossenes System anzusehenden statistischen Methode nur insgesamt rezipiert und nicht beliebig selektiv „benutzt" werden dürfen, um eine bestimmte Auffassung zu einer bestimmten Schrift zu untermauern. Wer sich z.B. auf Neumann beruft, um den statistischen Nachweis gegen die Autorschaft der Pastoralbriefe aufzunehmen, muss dessen Ergebnisse für Eph, Kol und 2Thess ebenso ernst nehmen und diese als echte Paulusbriefe ansehen, denn deren Analyse beruht auf denselben methodischen Grundsätzen wie diejenige der Pastoralbriefe. Und umgekehrt: Wer diesen Schritt nicht vollziehen will, stellt gleichzeitig die methodischen Voraussetzungen für die Analyse der Pastoralbriefe infrage – und damit wäre das ganze Verfahren *ad absurdum* geführt.

[155] NEUMANN, Authenticity (s. Anm. 135), 200f. Aus rein statistischen Gründen müsste man – so Neumann – Ignatius als Autor der Pastoralbriefe annehmen.

[156] J. MURPHY-O'CONNOR, Paul the Letter-Writer. His World, His Options, His Skills, Collegeville 1995, 34. Vgl. a.a.O. 35, zu den Studien von Kenny und Neumann: „Both studies highlight their own lack of precision and, somewhat surprisingly in view of the current consensus, conclude that Ephesians, Colossians, and 2 Thessalonians have as much in common with Romans, Galatians, and 1 and Second Corinthians as these latter have with each other. There is doubt that a single mind lies behind most of the Pauline corpus. But the differences, even between letters universally accepted as authentic, are far from being negligible, and demand an explanation. Of the possible explanations a variety of secretaries and coauthers is the simplest (Prior 1989, 49; Richards 1991, 186)." Vgl. auch die kritischen Überlegungen bei W. C. MOUNCE, Pastoral Epistles, WBC 46, Nashville 2000, XCIX–CXVIII. Zur Kritik an Kenny und Neumann vgl. auch LEDGER, Exploration (s. Anm. 135), 85.

[157] BROX, Pastoralbriefe (s. Anm. 137), 46f.

sich „eine inhaltlich-theologische Verschiedenheit gegenüber Paulus" abzeichne.[158]

Im Ergebnis ist daher festzuhalten: Die vielfältigen statistischen Versuche, Sprache und Stil der Pastoralbriefe mit computergestützten Methoden zu analysieren, zu vergleichen und daraus Schussfolgerungen zu ziehen, müssen – jedenfalls nach dem gegenwärtigen Stand – als gescheitert gelten. Aus den vorliegenden, zum großen Teil widersprüchlichen Daten lassen sich keine zuverlässigen Konzequenzen hinsichtlich der Verfasserschaft ziehen bzw. anderweitige Annahmen in Verfasserfragen unterstützen.[159] Problematisch ist vor allem die hypothetische Voraussetzung der einheitlichen Komposition der Pastoralbriefe bzw. ihr Zusammenschluss als eine einheitlich zu behandelnde Gruppe, was die statistischen Ergebnisse im Sinne einer Voraussetzung beeinflusst, die eine darauf aufbauende Argumentation zirkulär werden lässt. Darüber hinaus stellt sich das Problem, welche Texte bzw. Textabschnitte überhaupt sinnvoll verglichen werden können, was u.a. von Genretypen, vergleichbaren Themen, vorauszusetzenden Situationen, Adressaten, Gegnerprofilen – und nicht zuletzt von der Beteiligung anderer an der Abfassung abhängt. Der einzige sichere Ertrag statistischer Erhebungen ist daher die Tatsache, dass eine je separate Betrachtung der Pastoralbriefe nicht nur stylometrisch, sondern auch bereits in der einfachen Wortstatistik zu signifikant unterschiedlichen Ergebnissen führt, die ebenfalls die Zusammenordnung der Pastoralbriefe als Korpus problematisch erscheinen lässt.

4. Fazit

Nach den forschungsgeschichtlichen, methodischen und inhaltlichen Überlegungen ergibt sich notwendig das Fazit, dass das etablierte Paradigma der Interpretation der Pastoralbriefe als ein einheitlich komponiertes,

---

[158] A.a.O. 47.

[159] Vgl. bereits F. TORM, Über die Sprache in den Pastoralbriefen, ZNW 18 (1917–1918), 225–243, dessen Beobachtungen zum Vorkommen bestimmter Begriffe in zusammengehörenden Briefgruppen (die beiden Thessalonicherbriefe, die vier Hauptbriefe Röm, Gal, 1 und 2Kor, die Gefangenschaftsbriefe Phil, Kol, Eph, Phlm sowie die Past) zwar auch Fragen hinsichtlich möglicher Überschneidungen aufwerfen, aber dennoch aufschlussreich sind und im Blick auf die unterschiedliche Bewertung der Pastoralbriefe größere Differenzierungen zulassen als reine Wortstatistik – und dies ausdrücklich gegen Holtzmanns Zuordnungen, der bei der Erwähnung des Fehlens bestimmter Begriffe nicht beachtet, dass solche auch in den anerkannten Paulinen nicht durchgängig vorhanden sind; vgl. ferner MICHAELIS, Wortstatistik (s. Anm. 135), 69–76; ROBINSON, Formula (s. Anm. 135), 282–288; METZGER, Reconsideration (s. Anm. 135), 94.

pseudonymes Briefkorpus dringend der Revision bedarf, anstatt immer neue und immer stärker divergierende Interpretationsversuche zu unternehmen, deren intersubjektive Plausibilität immer schwerer zu vermitteln ist. Nur nebenbei gesagt ist diese Konstellation im Blick auf die Pastoralbriefe auch deshalb verwunderlich, weil es bereits in vielen Bereichen der neutestamentlichen Forschung zur Revision solcher idealistischen forschungsgeschichtlichen Paradigmen des 19. Jh. gekommen ist, die unsere Sicht etwa auf das Judentum (Stichwort: Vielfalt des hellenistisch beeinflussten Judentums), auf die Jesusbewegung und die Jesusüberlieferung (Stichwort: „Third Quest") oder auch auf Paulus (Stichwort: „New Perspective") *grundlegend* verändert haben. Der entscheidende Schritt in die richtige Richtung zu dieser Revision wäre es, die Frage nach einer pseudepigraphischen Abfassung der Pastoralbriefe vor allem im Blick auf ihre konkrete literarische Gestalt differenzierter zu behandeln, als es bisher in der Forschung geschehen ist. Insbesondere sind die Briefsammlungen und die Merkmale pseudepigraphischer Schreiben innerhalb solcher Briefsammlungen stärker in den Blick zu nehmen, wenn die Charakteristika der drei Briefe erörtert werden. Einzelne Versuche dazu sind bereits unternommen worden, aber hier ist noch viel Arbeit zu leisten.[160]

Vor allem ist stets methodische Vorsicht geboten: Man darf nicht erwarten, dass alle Spannungen in der Frage nach der pseudepigraphischen Abfassung neutestamentlicher Schriften aufzulösen sind. Das eingangs zitierte Diktum Adolf von Harnacks gilt nach wie vor. Selbst in anerkanntermaßen echten Paulusbriefen gibt es zahlreiche umstrittene Passagen, Be-

---

[160] Vgl. – um nur zwei Studien zu nennen – die beiden sehr divergenten Ansätze von W. A. RICHARDS, Difference and Distance in Post-Pauline Christianity. An Epistolary Analysis of the Pastorals, Studies in Biblical Literature 44, New York 2002, und R. FUCHS, Unerwartete Unterschiede. Müssen wir unsere Ansichten über „die" Pastoralbriefe revidieren?, Wuppertal 2003. – KLAUCK, Briefliteratur (s. Anm. 18), 304f., hat hierzu einen wichtigen Anstoß gegeben, der bisher nicht substantiell aufgenommen wurde: „Der Grad an Pseudepigraphie und ihre Realisierungsweise fällt bei den einzelnen neutestamentlichen Schriften, die davon betroffen sind, unterschiedlich aus ... Differenzieren muss man auch hinsichtlich einer anderen Frage, inwieweit nämlich die Fiktion für die Adressaten durchschaubar war und inwieweit sie für bare Münze genommen wurde. Eine vom Autor eingeplante Transparenz der Pseudepigraphie für die Adressaten ist bei den Pastoralbriefen eher denkbar als beim Kol oder Eph, beim 2Petr eher als beim 1Petr. ... Vielleicht hat der Verfasser, sagen wir der Pastoralbriefe, mit verschiedenen Gruppen unter seinen Adressaten gerechnet, mit solchen, die über das gleiche Bildungsniveau wie er verfügten und die Pseudepigraphie durchschauten, und mit solchen, die sich mit der ausgeborgten Verfasserangabe ohne Rückfrage zufrieden gaben und die man mit den Feinheiten der Brieferstellung besser nicht behelligte. Daß dies für unser Empfinden etwas Anrüchiges an sich hat, sei gar nicht geleugnet. Aber ... man (wird) auch unter Einsatz aller apologetischer Kunst der urchristlichen Pseudepigraphie nicht alles Anstößige nehmen können ..."

griffe und Vorstellungen, die nicht ohne Schwierigkeit zu dem passen, was man sonst von Paulus weiß oder meint, als „typisch paulinisch" ansehen zu müssen. Ähnliches gilt auch hinsichtlich des Problems einer plausiblen historischen Darstellung der Geschichte der paulinischen Mission und Literatur und ihrer Nachgeschichte sowie darin das schwierige Verhältnis der paulinischen Briefe – einschließlich der Pastoralbriefe! – zur Apostelgeschichte.[161] Allzu spannungsfreie Konstruktionen stehen dabei immer im Verdacht, zu viel selbst aufzufüllen, wo Informationslücken offenkundig sind oder bestimmte Angaben in eine nicht aufzulösende Spannung treten.[162] Im Blick auf das Verhältnis der Pastoralbriefe untereinander muss auch ernst genommen werden, dass die Briefe unterschiedliche Adressaten benennen und darüber hinaus unterschiedliche Situationen voraussetzen – auch und erst recht unter pseudepigraphischen Vorzeichen. Wie dies allerdings als pseudepigraphische Fiktion rezeptionstheoretisch funktionieren sollte, ist nach wie vor unklar und bisher nicht plausibel gemacht worden. Beide Adressaten stehen zudem in einem unterschiedlichen Verhältnis zu Paulus, das unter pseudepigraphischer Voraussetzung sowohl dem Autor als auch den (realen) Adressaten vor Augen steht, und dies ist umso mehr ein Problem, wenn man in den fiktiven Adressaten die realen Autoren sieht, wobei damit die Unterscheidung zwischen fiktiv und real zu verschwimmen beginnt. Die Frage nach den unterschiedlichen Entstehungsbedingungen hinsichtlich der vorausgesetzten Adressaten sowie Einzelheiten im Detail können daher auch unter pseudepigraphischen Vorzeichen nicht einfach ignoriert oder zu geläufigen Stilmitteln erklärt werden, die womöglich noch – um die negativen Implikationen des Begriffes Fälschung zu vermeiden – mit einem tieferen theologischen Sinn zu belegen sind.[163]

Wie gezeigt, haben andere inzwischen sehr viel klarer die Konsequenzen aus den unabweislichen Beobachtungen gezogen: Unter den gegebenen Umständen müsste man die Pastoralbriefe „geplante und raffinierte Fälschungen" nennen.[164] Dahinter sollte man nicht zurück, dahinter kann man nicht zurück, wenn man die Pastoralbriefe insgesamt als pseudepigraphi-

---

[161] Vgl. dazu R. RIESNER, Once More. Luke-Acts and the Pastoral Epistles, in: S.-W. Son (Hg.), History and Exegesis (FS Ellis), New York/London 2006, 239–258.

[162] Vgl. etwa die Rekonstruktionen bei J. VAN BRUGGEN, Die geschichtliche Einordnung der Pastoralbriefe, Wuppertal 1981, sowie im Anschluss daran FUCHS, Unterschiede (s. Anm. 160).

[163] Vgl. etwa die Interpretationen von „Mantel und Schriften" (2Tim 4,13) bei BROX, Notizen (s. Anm. 7), passim, oder P. TRUMMER, „Mantel und Schriften" (2 Tim 4,13). Zur Interpretation einer persönlichen Notiz in den Pastoralbriefen, BZ 18 (1974), 193–207.

[164] FRENSCHKOWSKI, Pseudepigraphie (s. Anm. 6), 262.

sches Briefkorpus beurteilen will. Doch gibt es hinreichende, an dieser Stelle nicht mehr darzulegende Gründe, dies nicht mehr vorauszusetzen und auf diese Weise Problemlösungen und Interpretationsperspektiven zu entwickeln, die jenseits falscher und aporetischer Alternativen liegen.

5. Perspektiven für die Arbeit an den Pastoralbriefen – zusammenfassende Thesen

Um in der Beurteilung der Pastoralbriefe angesichts der nach wie vor kontroversen Diskussion weiterzukommen, war es notwendig, die Entstehung des forschungsgeschichtlich begründeten Interpretationsparadigmas nachzuzeichnen, um die daraus resultierenden Probleme aufzuzeigen und mögliche Perspektiven zu benennen. Diese sollen im Folgenden thesenartig zusammengefasst werden. Auf dieser Grundlage gilt es, eine Neuinterpretation der Texte vorzunehmen, die hier nicht mehr zu leisten ist und an anderen Stellen zum Teil bereits vorgelegt wurde.[165]

1. Die nach wie vor die Forschung prägende Alternative zwischen Echtheit und Unechtheit der Pastoralbriefe ist zu einfach. Die unsachgemäße Einseitigkeit in der pauschalen Betrachtung führt auf *beiden* Seiten in Aporien, die nicht aufgelöst werden können. Es sind daher *hinreichende* Differenzierungen nötig, die eine angemessene Verhältnisbestimmung der drei Briefe untereinander wie zu anderen Schriften des *Corpus paulinum* ermöglichen.

2. Die Hypothese eines bewusst komponierten, dreiteiligen *Corpus pastorale* hat sich als nicht tragfähig erwiesen und muss aufgegeben werden. Auch unter pseudepigraphischer Perspektive sind die Pastoralbriefe als einzelne Schreiben anzusehen und erst unter dieser Voraussetzung sind eine sachgemäße Verhältnisbestimmung sowie eine Verortung innerhalb der Paulusbriefsammlung und der paulinischen Traditionsgeschichte möglich.[166]

3. Die aus literarhistorischen Gründen notwendige Unterscheidung zwischen Fiktion und Fälschung muss konsequent durchgehalten und damit die Frage der Täuschungs*absicht* ernst genommen werden. Jede Fälschung beinhaltet notwendig eine Fiktion, aber nicht jede Fiktion ist auch Fälschung. Die Begriffe Fiktion und Fälschung liegen daher inhaltlich auf unterschiedlichen Ebenen und dürfen nicht vermischt werden, wie das oft und vor allem bei dem Versuch geschieht, die selbstverständliche und ge-

---

[165] S.o. Anm. 103.
[166] Nicht zuletzt deshalb, weil auch eine pseudepigraphische Fiktion genau das bei den Rezipienten voraussetzt.

nerelle Legitimität von Pseudepigraphie vorauszusetzen. Diese Vermischung ist eine entscheidende Ursache für allzu spekulative Erklärungen der Pseudepigraphie der Pastoralbriefe, die an den Texten selbst und deren Vergleich mit antiken Briefkonventionen nicht verifizierbar sind. Fiktion ist dabei als überwiegend literarisch bezogener Begriff, Fälschung als ein Begriff mit ideologischen und damit in gewisser Weise moralischen Hintergründen auf die zu untersuchenden Briefe anzuwenden. Bei der Beurteilung einer *Fälschung* darf die „moralische" Frage nicht als irrelevant erklärt werden. Die Behauptung, mit moralischen Kategorien dürfe im Blick auf das Neue Testament nicht gearbeitet werden, ist unangemessen, weil sie nicht dem Befund der Beurteilung von Pseudepigraphie in der Antike entspricht.

4. Bei der Beschreibung und Begründung einer *Fiktion* ist die Anwendung geschichtstheoretischer Erkenntnisse konsequenter durchzuführen, insbesondere im Blick auf das Problem von geschichtlicher Fiktion durch den pseudepigraphischen Autor auf der einen und der Fiktionalität moderner (Re-)Konstruktionen auf der anderen Seite.[167]

5. Entscheidend ist dabei eine differenzierte Wahrnehmung verschiedener Formen von legitimer und illegitimer Pseudepigraphie. Der begründbare Sachverhalt, dass eine sogenannte Schulpseudepigraphie nicht nur einen anderen Charakter hat als die Fälschung, sondern auch in literarischer Hinsicht anderen Gestaltungskriterien unterliegt, kann zu einer differenzierten Beurteilung der Pastoralbriefe und ihrer konkreten literarischen Gestaltung beitragen.

6. Die Verhältnisbestimmung von Schulpseudepigraphie und Fälschung beruht auf der Unterscheidung literarischer und intentionaler Merkmale. Als Merkmale pseudepigraphischer Schreiben, die in einem positiven Sinne – d.h. ohne Fälschungsabsicht – zu beurteilen sind, können gelten: 1) Vorhandene Schreiben gleicher Art sind Ausgangspunkt für die Anknüpfung einer akzeptierten pseudepigraphischen Fiktion in einem Schulkontext.[168] 2) Der Stil der Vorlage bzw. des als Pseudonym verwendeten Autors wird nachgeahmt.[169] 3) Bekannte Positionen und Äußerungen der Schulautorität werden auf eine neue Situation bezogen und in einem neuen Kontext verortet. 4) *Bekanntes* Material an persönlichen Notizen bzw. *unkonkreter Alltäglichkeiten* wird *zurückhaltend* und der literarischen Absicht dienend eingesetzt. 5) Die Pseudonymität beruht auf einem offenen Konsens und es ist somit keine Voraussetzung für die Akzeptanz der

---

[167] Vgl. z.B. K. Backhaus / G. Häfner (Hg.), Historiographie und fiktionales Erzählen. Zur Konstruktivität in Geschichtstheorie und Exegese, BThSt 86, Neukirchen 2007.

[168] Vgl. SPEYER, Fälschung (s. Anm. 22), 83f.136f.

[169] Vgl. a.a.O. 82.85.

Schrift, dass sie unerkannt bleibt.[170] Die Akzeptanz einer solchen gewissermaßen „offenen" Pseudonymität innerhalb eines engeren Traditionszusammenhanges bei der Entstehung einer Schrift wird im Übrigen nicht dadurch infrage gestellt, dass eine solche Schrift im Verlauf der Überlieferung aus diesem Entstehungszusammenhang heraustritt und (irrtümlich) für eine authentische, nicht-pseudonyme Schrift *gehalten* wird, weil der ursprüngliche Kontext nicht mehr bekannt oder nicht mehr von Bedeutung ist.

7. Daraus ergibt sich im Blick auf die Pastoralbriefe folgende These: In dieses Muster akzeptierter und damit als legitim zu verstehender (Schul-) Pseudepigraphie passt aufgrund seiner spezifischen Merkmale nur der Erste Timotheusbrief, der darin dem Epheserbrief vergleichbar ist. In anderem Maße als 2Tim und Tit setzt der 1Tim eine von einem Bischofsamt (ἐπισκοπή, 3,1) geführte Gemeindestruktur bereits *als gegeben* voraus und interpretiert vor diesem Hintergrund verschiedene Topoi paulinischer Überlieferung, die in der Tradition relativ offen geblieben sind, so z.B. die Rolle der Frau in der Gemeinde (1Tim 2,9–15) oder auch das Verständnis der Gemeinde als οἶκος θεοῦ (3,15).[171] Anlass und Ziel ist dabei einerseits die Konsolidierung der Gemeinde nach innen als „Haus Gottes", in dem die Wahrheit sicher bewahrt wird (3,15f.), andererseits zugleich auch die Abgrenzung gegenüber sich herausbildenden gnostischen Gruppen (vgl. 6,20).[172] Der Autor greift literarisch das bereits mit 2Tim und Tit vorhan-

---

[170] Vgl. a.a.O. 82. Entscheidend ist bei derartigen persönlichen Notizen, dass es sich um bekanntes bzw. unspezifisches Material handelt, das die offene Fiktion auch akzeptabel macht. Der im Zusammenhang mit den Pastoralbriefen als Illustration für die Selbstverständlichkeit erfundener persönlicher Notizen als pseudepigraphisches Stilmittel gern zitierte Satz Speyers: „Je genauer die Angaben sind, desto falscher sind sie" (ebd.) bezieht sich *nicht* auf erfundene, sondern auf *bekannte* persönliche Daten („gesicherte geschichtliche Tatsachen"); er ist daher z.B. bei BROX, Verfasserangaben (s. Anm. 7), 61 Anm. 19, gegen den ursprünglichen Sinn bei Speyer zitiert; ebenso bei WOLTER, Paulustradition (s. Anm. 115), 17. Insbesondere die Sokratikerbriefe legen nahe, dass erfundene Details in der Regel Bekanntes verstärken. Vgl. zu Recht LOOKS, Rezeption (s. Anm. 64), 32: „... erfundene Bemerkungen (bergen) die Gefahr, daß die Fälschung erkannt wird. Somit würde sich die vom Verfasser beabsichtigte Wirkung – nämlich den Brief als Echt [sic] erscheinen zu lassen – kontraproduktiv auswirken. Wenn die Pastoralbriefe noch vor 100 datiert werden, dann ist davon auszugehen, daß noch eine größere Zahl von Menschen lebte, die den Apostel persönlich kannten. Sie hätten aufgrund ihrer eigenen Erlebnisse die Angaben der Pastoralbriefe überprüfen und gegebenenfalls als falsch erweisen können." Freilich mit der Schlussfolgerung: „Wenn man die Briefe weit nach 100 ansetzt, ergibt sich dieses Problem nicht mehr" (ebd.).

[171] Vgl. dazu HERZER, Rearranging the ‚House of God' (s. Anm. 103), passim.

[172] Vgl. dazu ders., Juden – Christen – Gnostiker (s. Anm. 71), 157–162; sowie ausführlicher in ders., Was ist falsch an der „fälschlich so genannten Gnosis" (1Tim 6,20)?

dene Muster des Mitarbeiterbriefes auf, transformiert dieses aber ebenfalls, indem er es nicht in der auffälligen Weise mit Personalhinweisen und persönlichen Notizen gestaltet, wie es für den 2Tim und den Tit charakteristisch ist, und kann deshalb unter allen diesen Voraussetzungen im Sinne eines Schulpseudepigraphons verstanden werden, bei dem die Pseudonymität gruppenintern auf einem anerkannten Konsens beruht. Eine Täuschungsabsicht und damit eine Fälschung kann aufgrund der literarischen Merkmale in diesem Fall ausgeschlossen werden. Es würde sich beim 1Tim aber auch nicht um eine literarische Fiktion im eigentlichen Sinn handeln, etwa wie bei Briefromanen, da das gruppeninterne Interesse deutlich erkennbar ist und damit das Element der Paulusfiktion deutlich relativiert wird. Das Pseudonym dient hier gewissermaßen als „identity marker" der eigenen Tradition.

8. Versteht man 2Tim und Tit ebenfalls unter pseudepigraphischen Vorzeichen, dann wären diese im Unterschied zum 1Tim aufgrund ihrer besonderen, mit Täuschungsabsicht zu verbindenden literarischen Merkmale als Fälschungen einzustufen. Allerdings lässt sich unter der Voraussetzung einer differenzierten Wahrnehmung nicht nur der Unterschied zum 1Tim in der literarischen Eigenart feststellen. Es lässt sich auf dieser Basis auch eine Neubewertung sprachlicher, inhaltlicher und historischer Aspekte vornehmen, so dass auch die Diskussion um die Echtheit des 2Tim und des Tit im Unterschied zum 1Tim auf eine neue Basis gestellt würde, insbesondere wegen der erwähnten Tendenz des 1Tim der Fortschreibung und Verallgemeinerung wichtiger Aspekte, die im Tit bzw. im 2Tim allenfalls ansatzweise erkennbar sind. Der 2Tim und der Tit können so als Teil der Paulusüberlieferung angesehen werden, die der 1Tim bereits voraussetzt; dieser ist daher deutlich davon abzusetzen und gehört sehr wahrscheinlich in die Zeit der Auseinandersetzungen mit der aufkommenden Gnosis in der späten ersten Hälfte des 2. Jh.[173] Mit dieser Unterscheidung verschiedener Autoren in verschiedenen Zeiten würden viele Aporien gelöst, die sowohl unter der Voraussetzung der Echtheit aller drei Briefe als auch der pseudepigraphischen Abfassung eines *Corpus pastorale* erst entstehen. Rückt man den 1Tim von den beiden anderen ab, wie dies aus literarischen und inhaltlichen Gründen naheliegend ist, dann gibt es jedoch hinreichende Gründe, die paulinische Verfasserschaft des Tit und des 2Tim historisch wie inhaltlich neu zu bedenken, ohne auf die üblichen Hilfskonstruktionen wie etwa die sog. Fragmententheorie zurückgreifen zu müssen. Dies wäre

---

Zur Paulusrezeption des 1. Timotheusbriefes im Kontext seiner Gegnerpolemik (Vortrag auf der SNTS-Tagung in Lund 2008; in Vorbereitung zum Druck).

[173] S. Anm. 172; für den 1Tim kann daher tatsächlich Baurs Einschätzung im Blick auf die Gnosis gelten (s.o. 504f.); im literarischen Verbund mit 2Tim und Tit ist dies nicht mehr plausibel.

im Einzelnen weiter durchzuführen; die hier vorgelegten Überlegungen sollten vor allem dazu dienen, die Möglichkeit einer solchen Differenzierung und der daraus folgenden Neubewertung jenseits der bekannten ‚Fronten' plausibel und diskursfähig zu machen.

9. Die Bedeutung oder gar Dignität der Pastoralbriefe ergibt sich jedoch weder aus der Tatsache, dass sie Teil des Kanons sind, noch daraus, dass sie Paulus zugeschrieben wurden oder er sie selbst geschrieben hat. Ihre Kanonizität würde, wenn sie alle drei pseudepigraphisch sind, auf einem Irrtum beruhen, der durch „raffinierte Täuschung" verursacht und durch die neuzeitliche Kritik aufgedeckt worden wäre. Das aber kann kein Grund sein, unter Absehung der Konventionen antiker Pseudepigraphie eine pseudepigraphische Fälschung nachträglich schön zu reden und für legitim zu erklären und den Briefen eine theologische Bedeutung beizumessen, die sie *de facto* nicht haben. Das heißt, wenn die Pastoralbriefe unecht sind, dann hätte Holtzmann durchaus Recht, wenn er sie theologisch als marginal beurteilt, weil sie an das ‚große Genie' eines Paulus des Römerbriefes nicht heranreichen. Aber dadurch wäre auch nicht viel verloren, es sei denn, man meinte, darauf angewiesen zu sein, eine kirchliche Hierarchie, die Ordination von Amtsträgern oder eine apostolische Sukzession unbedingt aus dem Neuen Testament begründen zu müssen. Wenn man sie hingegen für echt hielte, würde sich an ihrer Marginalität allerdings wenig ändern; auch dann blieben sie in ihrem *theologischen* Gewicht weit hinter anderen Schriften nicht nur des Paulus selbst, sondern auch anderer „Schulschriften" der nach- oder nebenpaulinischen Tradition wie etwa dem Epheserbrief oder dem Ersten Petrusbrief zurück.

Zum Schluss soll noch einmal Adolf von Harnack zu Wort kommen, um das eingangs zitierte Diktum über die Pastoralbriefe in seinen Kontext zu stellen:

„Das Rätsel, das über diesen Briefen schwebt, hat noch niemand wirklich gelöst und ist auch mit unseren geschichtlichen Hilfsmitteln unlösbar. Sie sind der Sammlung hinzugefügt worden, als noch Zeitgenossen des Paulus am Leben waren. Nicht nur das spricht für ihre Echtheit – doch ist es kein durchschlagendes Argument –, sondern auch zahlreiche geschichtliche Einzelheiten in den Briefen, die sich dagegen sträuben, als Fälschungen beurteilt zu werden, sowie einige persönliche Ergüsse und lehrhafte Stellen, größtenteils in II. Tim. Aber andererseits kann alles das, was den eigentlichen Charakter der Briefe darstellt ..., in sachlicher und noch mehr in stilistischer Hinsicht nicht vom Apostel herrühren. Ohne einen kritischen Gewaltstreich kann man daher weder die Echtheit noch die Unechtheit dieser Briefe, so wie sie vorliegen, behaupten. Es bleibt also nichts übrig, als sie für pseudopaulinische Schriftstücke zu halten, in welche paulinisches Gut eingearbeitet ist, am meisten in II. Tim., der umgekehrt auch ein interpolierter Paulusbrief sein kann. Aber mit dieser Erkenntnis ist leider noch wenig gewonnen, da eine einfache Ausscheidung des paulinischen Guts nicht gelingen will und da uns alle Mittel fehlen, positiv die Entstehung dieser Briefe zu begreifen. Sie würden eine Hauptquelle für den Ausgang des Lebens des Apostels und für die Geschichte der paulinischen Gemeinden um das J. 100 sein, wenn nicht alles in ihnen so abgerissen und deshalb so dunkel wäre, daß man beim Versuch einer geschichtlichen Verwertung in große Verlegenheit gesetzt wird."[174]

Vielleicht lässt sich mit Hilfe methodisch geschärfter und präziser als bisher gebrauchter „geschichtlicher Hilfsmittel" in dem oben beschriebenen Sinne doch weiterkommen, als von Harnack dies für möglich hielt.

---

[174] VON HARNACK, Briefsammlung (s. Anm. 4), 14f.

Hebrews as a Guide to Reading Romans*

by

CLARE K. ROTHSCHILD

1. Introduction

In her 2001 publication, *Ancient Epistolary Fictions: The Letter in Greek Literature*, Patricia Rosenmeyer argues that occasionally final letters serve as guides for letter collections.[1] Subsequently, in a 2004 publication, *Fiktive Selbstauslegung des Paulus: Intertextuelle Studien zur Intention und Rezeption der Pastoralbriefe*, Annette Merz interprets the Pastoral Letters as letter guides, as if by Paul, to the Pauline corpus.[2] Moreover, in a 2008 article entitled, "Corrective Composition, Corrective Exegesis: The Teaching on Prayer in 1 Tim 2,1–15," Margaret M. Mitchell supports Merz's view, arguing that First Timothy's teaching on prayer offers a specific example of guiding interpretations of the corpus Paulinum. Mitchell, however, boosts the argument by demonstrating that late antique interpreters, including Athenagoras, Origen and John Chrysostom, recognized the connection and therefore used First Timothy as a hermeneutical lens for interpreting Paul.[3] The present essay attempts to build on these proposals with a

---

* I wish to thank R. Matthew Calhoun and Alec J. Lucas for generous criticism in the development of the thesis. I also wish to thank Trevor Thompson who, in a casual discussion of my work, first mentioned the possibility of Hebrews as a reading guide for Romans.

[1] P. A. Rosenmeyer, *Ancient Epistolary Fictions: The Letter in Greek Literature* (Cambridge/New York: Cambridge University Press, 2001), 215–17.

[2] A. Merz, *Die fiktive Selbstauslegung des Paulus: Intertextuelle Studien zur Intention und Rezeption der Pastoralbriefe* (Göttingen: Vandenhoeck & Ruprecht / Freiburg [CH]: Academic Press, 2004); *eadem*, "The Fictitious Self-Exposition of Paul," in *Intertextuality of the Epistles: Explorations of Theory and Practice* (eds. D. R. McDonald, S. E. Porter and T. L. Brodie; Sheffield: Sheffield Phoenix Press, 2006), 113–32.

[3] M. M. Mitchell, "Corrective Composition, Corrective Exegesis: The Teaching on Prayer in 1 Tim 2,1–15," in *1 Timothy Reconsidered* (ed. K. P. Donfried; Leuven: Peeters, 2008), 41–62 (57–62). Mitchell writes, "Building on Merz's conclusions about 1 Tim 2, 1–8, I would like to turn my attention to the first half of the chapter, 1 Tim 2, 1–8. Are there fictional self-references to Pauline passages in 1 Tim 2, 1–8, also, and, if so, what elements in Paul's own teaching on prayer did this author think required correction (both emendation and emphatic underscoring) for his present context?" (48).

related thesis about Hebrews. Namely, this essay argues that one of the original purposes for Hebrews was to serve as a reading guide or instructional appendix, as if by Paul, for Romans.[4] At least four observations commend this theory. First, Hebrews cites many of the same passages from the Jewish scriptures decisive to Paul's argument in Romans, in particular Hab 2:4, a seminal piece of Romans's 'thesis' statement (Rom 1:17). The new contexts of these recitations suggest that one intention of Hebrews was to clarify and develop Paul's interpretations of them. Second, Heb 13:20–25 borrows important elements of the postscript of Romans, indicating deliberate alignment with Romans at the place in the text where authorial ἦθος is traditionally emphasized and final impressions are made.[5] Third, outside of the postscript, Hebrews imitates the language of Romans in ways that imply continuity with Paul's letter while avoiding its slavish imitation. Fourth and most importantly, as arguably its primary purpose of composition, Hebrews illustrates, explains and develops the ἐφάπαξ death of Jesus, a theme that can only derive from Rom 6:10. Of interest to this thesis is how media supports the interpretation. That is, Hebrews's placement *after* Romans in P[46] and *with* (perhaps) Romans in P[13] suggests that it was understood, if not intended, as an appendix to Romans.[6]

2. Letters as Guides to Letter Collections

In her important volume *Ancient Epistolary Fictions*, Patricia Rosenmeyer discusses the organization and order of pseudonymous letter collections. "No one, I suspect," she writes, "would agree with the seventeenth-century editor of Themistocles' letters, who places all the letters alphabetically in

---

[4] Elsewhere I have argued that Hebrews demonstrates literary reliance on diverse parts of an early Pauline corpus and was in fact written deliberately to amplify such a corpus. In this short paper, however, I focus not on literary reliance but Hebrews's specific goal of elucidating Romans. See C. K. Rothschild, *Hebrews as Pseudepigraphon: The History and Significance of the Pauline Attribution of Hebrews* (WUNT 235; Tübingen: Mohr Siebeck, 2009).

[5] Aristotle, *Rhet.* 1.2; 2.1.1–7, 12–17; Quintilian, *Inst.* 6.2.8–9; Demetrius, *Eloc.* 226. Cf. προσωποποιία: Demetrius, *Eloc.* 265–266. In *Rhet. Her.* 4.66 the technique is treated as an aspect of the ἐπίλογος. Cf. Theon of Alexandria, *Progymnasmata* ii, p. 117, 30–32; Cicero, *De or.* 85; and Rutilius Lupus 2.6.

[6] P[13], dated to the third or fourth century, contains nearly all of Hebrews: Heb 2:14–5:5, 10:8–22, 10:29–11:13 and 11:28–12:17. It is an opisthograph. NT passages are recorded on the back of a manuscript of Livy. It is clear from the evidence that the full-length scroll on which it was written could (and probably would) have contained slightly more than twice the material found in Hebrews. With some important similarities to P[46], experts believe P[13] may have contained *only* Romans and Hebrews in that order.

accordance with the names of the addressees—using the Latin alphabet."[7] Rather, Rosenmeyer postulates, *chronology* seems to dictate order for some collections, whereas *addressee* or *subject matter* provides the link for others.[8] Furthermore, it is not uncommon, according to Rosenmeyer, for such collections to trickle out information slowly over the course of the letters. She writes: "Frequently the structure is that of gradual revelation of information that is explained fully by a longer explanatory letter at the end."[9] As Rosenmeyer points out, complications may be caused by collections that begin *in medias res*. In such a case the collection requires context for understanding.[10] Context may also be demanded when letters allude to prior interactions or correspondence outside of the collection. Multiple editors or narrators of a collection may compound this difficulty. Sometimes narratives or introductions provide the missing context. In their absence, however, an additional letter could fill this role.

Hebrews is not a pseudonymous letter added to a pseudonymous letter collection. It is, rather, a pseudonymous letter added to a genuine or mixed (i.e., part genuine and part pseudonymous) collection.[11] Nevertheless, Rosenmeyer's observations concerning pseudonymous letter collections may be applied to early letter collections of the apostle Paul that included Hebrews. Specifically, the nature of pseudonymous letter collections may help us to understand Hebrews through a better appreciation of its role in an early *corpus Paulinum*. Insofar as placement in letter collections is not random, but reveals views about the content and function of the individual texts, collectors of the earliest Pauline letter collections represent among the earliest interpreters of, for example, Hebrews. The greeting in Heb 13:24 ἀπὸ τῆς Ἰταλίας may have been construed as an initial link between the addressees of Romans and Hebrews. Furthermore, P[46] begins *in medias res* with Romans and as such demands context. Thus, on the basis of Rosenmeyer's observations alone we might postulate that Hebrews was added to this collection as an explanatory letter providing some of the missing context. One thinks particularly of Paul's exposition of the significance of Jesus' death as sacrifice in Rom 3:25. Once Rom 1–3 (summarized in Rom 3:9–20) indicts humanity for sin, Paul offers as solution Jesus' death:

---

[7] *Ancient Epistolary Fictions* (see n. 1), 215.

[8] As we will see below, both addressee (i.e., congregation[s] in Rome) and subject matter, in addition to authorship, might have compelled association of Hebrews with Romans.

[9] *Ancient Epistolary Fictions* (see n. 1), 215. As Rosenmeyer acknowledges her hypothesis presumes sequential reading. The book's format as a scroll encourages this assumption.

[10] Ibid., 216.

[11] See full argument in my book, *Hebrews as Pseudepigraphon* (see n. 4).

δικαιούμενοι δωρεὰν τῇ αὐτοῦ χάριτι διὰ τῆς ἀπολυτρώσεως τῆς ἐν Χριστῷ Ἰησοῦ ὃν προέθετο ὁ θεὸς ἱλαστήριον διὰ [τῆς] πίστεως ἐν τῷ αὐτοῦ αἵματι (Rom 3:24–25). However, the summary statement in v. 25 leaves open whether Paul envisages ἱλαστήριον as a general or a particular Jewish view of the expiation of sins. Background on the Jewish sacrificial system might not eliminate all ambiguity, but would certainly heighten appreciation of Paul's claim. It is also possible that Paul's summary assumes an interpretation that a later author might wish to modify. Such a goal would also be achievable by means of an appendix letter.

Furthermore, Rom 3:25 specifies that Jesus' sacrifice of atonement is only effective 'through faith in his [Jesus'] blood': ἱλαστήριον διὰ [τῆς] πίστεως ἐν τῷ αὐτοῦ αἵματι. An elaboration of the nature and requirements of such a 'faith,' as for example can be found in Heb 11, would have commended a particular view of Paul's appeal to faith. In conclusion, Rosenmeyer's proposal concerning logical connections between letters in ancient pseudonymous collections suggests that early collections of Paul's letters too may imply relationships between the texts. The hypothesis is now tested through a comparative analysis. The following four objects are compared: (1) scriptural correspondences in Romans and Hebrews; (2) common postscript elements in Romans and Hebrews; (3) echoes of Romans in Heb 13; and (4) echoes of Romans in Heb 1–12.

3. Textual Analysis

3.1 Scriptural Correspondences between Hebrews and Romans and their Possible Meaning

Eight of seventeen citations of the Jewish scriptures shared by Hebrews and Paul's letters merely draw from the same text and chapter (i.e., chapter in Hebrews matches a chapter cited in Paul's letters, but the verses cited in the two texts do not match). In three of the eight occurrences (Deut 17, 29, and 32), the chapter is not cited elsewhere in the NT (i.e., the correspondence is exclusive in the NT). In the remaining two occurrences, the chapter match is exclusive to Hebrews, Paul and one other NT text: 2 Sam 9 is also cited in Acts (e.g., 2:30) and Isa 8 is also cited in First Peter (3:14–15 [Isa 8:12–13], 2:8 [Isa 8:14]). This evidence is of moderate interest. Chapters are not a relic of the earliest phase of textual production of the Hebrew scriptures and were not in place in the first century.[12] Chapters

---

[12] Although this interpretation aims at statistical precision such a goal is unrealizable. Results are valued only for their accurate *general* impression of Hebrews's reliance on Paul's undisputed corpus.

held in common by Hebrews and the Pauline letter corpus, not appearing elsewhere in the NT, indicate shared interest in the same materials, but require investigation on a case-by-case basis to determine any alleged proximity of the traditions. Borrowing a phrase from Richard Hays's appraisal of Paul's use of scripture, these passages may or may not reflect the same "cave of resonant signification."[13]

However, in the other nine (of seventeen) citations shared by both Hebrews and the undisputed Pauline corpus, chapter and verse match identically. In seven of the nine instances in which the identical verse is cited by both Hebrews and Paul (excluding [1] Ps 110:1 which is cited in the following NT passages: Matt 22:44; Mark 12:36; 14:62; 16:19; Luke 20:42–43; 22:69; Acts 2:34–35; 1 Cor 15:25; Eph 1:20; Col 3:1; Heb 1:3, 13; 8:1; 10:12–13; 12:2; and [2] Ps 8:6 which is also cited by Eph 1:22), the passage is not cited elsewhere in the NT (asterisks below indicate these passages). Interestingly six of these seven citations are found in Romans.

1. Gen 2	1 Cor 15:45 (Gen 2:7); 1 Cor 6:16 (Gen 2:24); Heb 4:4 (Gen 2:2)
2. Gen 15:5*	*Rom 4:18*; Heb 11:12
3. Gen 21:12*	*Rom 9:7*; Heb 11:18 (cf. Gal 4:30)
4. Gen 22	Gal 3:8, 16 (Gen 22:18); Heb 6:13–14 (Gen 22:16–17); Heb 11:12 (Gen 22:17)
5. Deut 17	1 Cor 5:13 (Deut 17:7); Heb 10:28 (Deut 17:6)
6. Deut 29	*Rom 11:8* (Deut 29:4); Heb 12:15 (Deut 29:18)
7. Deut 32	1 Cor 10:20 (Deut 32:17); *Rom 10:19*; 1 Cor 10:22 (Deut 32:21); Heb 10:30 (Deut 32:36)
8. Deut 32:35*	*Rom 12:19*; Heb 10:30a
9. Deut 32:43*	*Rom 15:10*; Heb 1:6
10. 2 Sam 7:14*	2 Cor 6:18 (2 Sam 7:8, 14); Heb 1:5 (2 Sam 7:14)
11. Ps 8:6	1 Cor 15:27 (Ps 8:6); Heb 2:6–8 (Ps 8:4–6)
12. Ps 110:1	1 Cor 15:25 (Ps 110:1); Heb 1:3, 13; 8:1; 10:12–13; 12:2
13. Prov 3	2 Cor 8:21 (Prov 3:4); Heb 12:5–6 (Prov 3:11–12)
14. Isa 8	*Rom 9:33* (Isa 8:14); Heb 2:13 (Isa 8:17–18)
15. Isa 53	*Rom 10:16* (Isa 53:1); Heb 9:28 (Isa 53:12)
16. Jer 31:33–34*	*Rom 11:27* (Jer 31:33–34); Heb 8:8–12 (Jer 31:31–34); Heb 10:16–17 (Jer 31:33–34)
17. Hab 2:4*	*Rom 1:17*, Gal 3:11 (Hab 2:4); Heb 10:37–38 (Hab 2:3–4)

In contrast, the degree of correspondence between scriptural citations in other NT texts and Paul's undisputed letters is much lower than Hebrews. Of course the likelihood of a higher proportion of correspondences is increased by the relatively higher concentration of scriptural allusions in Hebrews than, for example, the Pastorals. However, the relatively short

---

[13] See J. Hollander, *The Figure of Echo: A Mode of Allusion in Milton and After* (Berkeley, Calif.: University of California Press, 1981), 65–6; cited by Richard B. Hays in *Echoes of Scripture in Paul* (New Haven, Conn./London: Yale University Press, 1989), 21.

length of Hebrews (as compared with, for example, Acts) decreases the likelihood of an inflated frequency of correspondences—effectively canceling the exception. What is more, such correspondences drop off so precipitously from Hebrews that, even granting the full force of the exceptions, some connection seems undeniable. For example, the next highest number of exact (viz., chapter and verse) citations shared between a NT text and the undisputed Pauline letters is Acts with six (out of an estimated thirty-nine total citations). However, in this instance all six citations derive from Genesis and fit compactly into only two verses in both Acts and Galatians.[14] In contrast, correspondences between Hebrews and Paul's undisputed letters are distributed throughout Hebrews.

3.2 Exact Correspondences

If some connection between the scriptural citations in Romans and Hebrews is undeniable it remains to discover the precise nature of the exact correspondences. In some cases the scriptural correspondences reveal Hebrews recontextualizing Paul's interpretations, often with specific objections in mind. Five instances are salient.

3.2.1 Genesis 15:5

Gen 15:5 is God's revelation to Abraham that his descendants will be as numerous as the stars in the heaven: "He brought him outside and said, 'Look toward heaven and count the stars, if you are able to count them.' Then he said to him, 'So shall your descendants be.'" Gen 15:6 narrates: "He [Abraham] believed the Lord; and the Lord reckoned it to him as righteousness." The latter passage, in particular, plays an important role in Paul's arguments in Galatians (e.g., 3:6) and Romans (e.g., 4:3, 9, 22). In Rom 4:18, Paul cites Gen 15:5–6, arguing that Abraham is evidence that "a person is justified by faith apart from works of the law" (Rom 3:28). The defense is an integral part of Paul's larger argument summarized by Hab 2:4 as stated in Rom 1:16–17 that ὁ δὲ δίκαιος ἐκ πίστεως ζήσεται. Paul argues that because the law came after God reckoned Abraham as righteous, legal requirements of all kinds—in particular, circumcision—will be superfluous in the judgment (e.g., Gal 3:6–29, Rom 1:17, 4:1–25). Paul does not, however, treat the possible objection that Abraham, although regarded by God as righteous, *did not live*, but eventually died (Gen 25:7–11).

---

[14] (1) Acts 3:25 and Gal 3:8 cite Gen 12:3; (2) Acts 7:5 and Gal 3:16 cite Gen 17:8; (3) Acts 3:25 and Gal 3:8 cite Gen 18:18; (4) Acts 3:25 and Gal 3:8, 16 cite Gen 22:18; (5) Acts 3:25 and Gal 3:8, 16 cite Gen 26:3–4; (6) Acts 3:25 and Gal 3:8 cite Gen 28:13–14. These NT authors are the only two to cite Gen 12, 17 or 18.

In Heb 11:12, Gen 15:5 is quoted in the catalogue of heroes: "Therefore from one person, and this one as good as dead, descendants were born, 'as many as the stars of heaven and as the innumerable grains of sand by the seashore.'" In the next verse (v. 13), however, the author follows up with the surprising conclusion that: "all of these [descendants] died in faith without having received the promises." It is possible here that the author is dealing with an objection to Paul's claim that the righteous did not 'live,' but died.[15] Moreover, the author emphasizes that Abraham was not anomalous in righteousness leading to death. Rather, numerous Israelites were faithful and thus reckoned as righteous both prior to and after the law, yet none of these notable faithful "lived," rather "all died in faith without having received the promises" (Heb 11:13). In short, to Paul's argument that "the righteous will live by faith," the author of Hebrews counters (having himself cited Hab 2:4 in his argument at Heb 10:37–38; see next paragraph) that the righteous, reckoned as such on the basis of faith, do not "live" without first dying, redefining 'life' as eternal existence *following* death and exaltation.[16]

This meaning is clear in Hebrews's treatment of Hab 2:4 in 10:37–38, a passage in which believers are invited to accept salvation, defined not in terms of a pre-death extension of earthly life, a post-death earthly life, a pre-, post-, or extra-death bodily resurrection[17] or an extra-death translation[18] (all possible interpretations of Paul's argument in, for example, 1 Cor 15:35–58, cf. 1 Thess 4:15),[19] but in terms of a metaphysical existence post-dating physical death. A possible summary paraphrase of Heb 10:32–39 reads: In the early days after your enlightenment you willfully accepted persecution. You must continue to do so. Those who shrink back

---

[15] Paul lays the foundation for this interpretation in Rom 2, esp. 2:7. "Life" in Paul's undisputed letters is the reward for survivors of the divine trial. This is the crux of Hebrews's correction of Paul. In Romans, ζωή and ζῆν have an eschatological focus, invariably referring to living beyond the acquittal obtained from Christ (σωτηρία, δικαιοῦσθαι). Hebrews clarifies this question. The author either misunderstands—or understands and sees the possibility of misunderstanding—so steps forward to clarify ζωή.

[16] Hebrews stresses the inevitability of death. The heroes of ch. 11's catalogue maintain their fidelity in extreme hardship, facing the threat of death. The author of Hebrews implies parallel threats faced by his readers, exhorting the same kind of πίστις. The author, thus, reappropriates Paul's πίστις and σωτηρία (that is, its reward) for new circumstances that, he argues, bear much in common with circumstances faced by Israelites of old. The idea originates with Paul who, however, only applied it to Abraham (e.g., esp. Gal 3 and Rom 4) in Gen 15, thus without direct application to a situation of persecution.

[17] Paul's position on bodily resurrection is unclear. Cf. e.g., 1 Cor 15:12–19, 35–37; 2 Cor 4:16–5:10; Phil 1:21–25; 3:21; 1 Thess 4:14.

[18] As the author makes clear, even Enoch, who "did not experience death" (v. 5), died (v. 13).

[19] Contrast 2 Cor 5:1–5, Phil 1:20–23.

will be lost. Those who have faith, that is, who accept persecution unto death, *will* be saved. Faith in this instance is the ability to see not *life per se*, but its qualified form, after-*life* as the final goal. In Heb 11:1–3, emphasizing physical death as necessary prerequisite, faith is defined as the same hope held by Israel's now dead heroes. Death in Hebrews is, thus, the necessary catalyst for transition from the shadow-like (8:5) to the cloud-like existence (12:1).[20] In 11:35, Hebrews refers to *this* transition as a "better resurrection."[21]

Thus, Hebrews and Paul not only cite Gen 15:5 exclusively in the NT, but Hebrews's appropriation of this passage appears to have a dialogical relationship with the argument in which Paul first brought this proof-text to bear. Heb 11:12 functions as another admonition to endure persecution whether 'real' or perceived (cf. Heb 10:32–34, 11:27, 12:2, 13:13). The message, succinctly put, is: the righteous die; salvation (i.e., "life") of the righteous is obtained after death.[22] Although in the context of pseudo-Pauline authorship of Hebrews, the passage is perhaps a prediction of Paul's own death, it may also genuinely exhort readers and/or listeners to submit to unjust suffering.

3.2.2 Genesis 21:12

In Gen 21:12, disconcerted by Sarah's demand that Hagar and Ishmael be sent away, Abraham is told by God to obey Sarah ("do as she tells you") because it is through Isaac that his descendants will be brought forth. In Rom 9:7 (in line with arguments in Gal 3–4 and Rom 4), Paul appropriates this passage to support and explain inclusion of the Gentiles in God's election of Israel.[23] Paul appropriates Gen 21:12 as a principle: "child of God" status relies on promise as opposed to physical descent.[24]

---

[20] Deaths listed in Heb 11:32–38 make this point; in particular, the rhetorical climax, "They were stoned to death, they were sawn in two, they were killed by the sword; they went about in skins of sheep and goats, destitute, persecuted, tormented—of whom the world was not worthy!" The "cloud" reference for these witnesses in Heb 12:1 signifies their current liminal agency and existence.

[21] This "resurrection" emphasizes a specific reading of the one offered by Paul.

[22] ἄθλησις = death; Heb 10:32.

[23] J. A. Fitzmyer, *Romans* (AB 33; New York: Doubleday, 1993), 560–61.

[24] Rom 9:6–8: "It is not as though the word of God had failed. For not all Israelites truly belong to Israel, and not all of Abraham's children are his true descendants; but 'It is through Isaac that descendants shall be named for you.' This means that it is not the children of the flesh who are the children of God, but the children of the promise are counted as descendants" (NRSV). As we can see from this passage, Paul and Hebrews make opposite points, reflecting differences in what they are doing with the sacrifice of Isaac. Paul is driving a wedge into the usual ways that the promise of Isaac is understood, i.e., as conferring the status of both σπέρμα Ἀβραάμ and τέκνα τοῦ θεοῦ upon the

Heb 11:18 adopts Gen 21:12 to nuance Paul's point. Hebrews argues that, having been promised by God that descendants would come through Isaac, Abraham nevertheless demonstrates willingness to sacrifice Isaac, rendering him faithful in the eyes of the Lord. However, Hebrews notes that *God cancels the sacrifice* (Gen 22:11–13)[25] and its termination brings about resumption of the previous order, namely, "child" status through physical descent. The principle that the author of Hebrews derives from God's withdrawal of his command to sacrifice Isaac nevertheless takes Paul's interpretation into account. Hebrews proffers that "child of God" status relies on promise *as well as* physical descent. To be sure both Paul and Hebrews agree that Abraham's willingness to forgo God's promise demonstrates faith. However, according to Hebrews, having demonstrated faith, God returns Isaac to Abraham, guaranteeing the original promise of physical descendants through this son:

> By faith Isaac invoked blessings for the future on Jacob and Esau. By faith Jacob, when dying, blessed each of the sons of Joseph, and "he bowed in worship over the top of his staff."[26]

Tying this interpretation to the one of Gen 15:5, the natural result of physical descent, for even the most faithful, is physical death (11:13). Promises of exaltation with Christ are in Hebrews only accomplishable after all necessary physical phases reach their completion.[27]

3.2.3 Deuteronomy 32:35

The citation of Deut 32:35 in Heb 10:30a is identical to that in Rom 12:19 over and against both the LXX and the MT.[28] Attridge attributes this

---

Israelites. The overall goal of Paul's presentation is a demonstration of God's absolute sovereignty when confronted with questions regarding theodicy (9:6). This goal is absent from Heb 11:17–19 the objective of which is Abraham's radical reliance on God to make good on his promises, even when asked to slay the fruit of the promise. Hebrews's goal is not to correct Rom 9:7, but to reapply it. In sum, Hebrews is drawing Paul back into line with an older Jewish perspective probably because Paul's arguments have lost their urgency. Cf. message of John the Baptist (Matt 3:9/Luke 3:8), also arguing that "child of God" status must be based on something other (or more) than physical descent.

[25] According to Hebrews, Abraham knew that God would postpone the sacrifice: "He considered the fact that God is able even to raise someone from the dead" (Heb 11:19).

[26] Following LXX: Gen 47:31.

[27] The genealogy of the faithful in Heb 11 stresses physical descent as a primary component of the promise.

[28] The wording of Deut 32:35 "Mine is judgment; I shall repay (ἐμοὶ ἐκδίκησις, ἐγὼ ἀνταποδώσω)" differs from both the MT and LXX, but is attested in Targums (*Tg. Onq*; *Tg. Pal.*) and in Rom 12:19 where some MSS add "says the Lord" (Harold W. Attridge, *The Epistle to the Hebrews: A Commentary on the Epistle to the Hebrews* [Hermeneia; Philadelphia: Fortress Press, 2001], 295). Although Attridge points to the similarity with

shared reading to "a corruption within the Hebrew textual tradition that served as the basis for the Greek version used by Hebrews."[29] Kenneth J. Thomas, however, admits another possibility: "The author of Hebrews possibly borrowed this form of the text from Romans."[30] Noting that the original context of the citation does not influence the appropriation of the passage, Attridge concludes simply that Paul's use "differs."[31] It is nevertheless still possible that Hebrews builds on Paul's published opinion of this passage. A closer examination supports this option.

In an application somewhat closer to the original context of the passage (in Deuteronomy), in Rom 12:19 Paul warns his addressees not to take revenge against enemies, assuring them rather that God will do so.[32] In contrast, Heb 10:30a warns readers and/or listeners that God will take revenge against *them* if they are not careful! This interpretation fits comfortably within Hebrews's program of clarifying, on Paul's behalf, shortcomings of Pauline theology. This clarification concerns the possibility of second repentance, a point on which Paul was, (intentionally perhaps) vague (cf. esp. 1 Cor 5:5–7, 11:30–32, 2 Cor 7:10, also: Rom 8:10, 2 Cor 5:17). As elsewhere, ambiguity in Paul's letters[33] provokes Hebrews to explain.[34] Requiring second forgiveness, according to Hebrews, is impossible without exposing the Son of God to outrage (Heb 10:29) and bringing judgment upon oneself.[35] Second forgiveness turns friends of God into enemies against whom God must eventually exact punishment. Although, in Heb 6:4, apostasy is the circumstance for which second repentance is viewed as untenable (cf. Matt 12:32, Mark 3:29, Luke 12:10), Heb 10:26 may suggest that other such willful sins are also implied.[36] Thinking of only apostasy,

---

Romans on this point, in his extended discussion of the use of scripture in Hebrews, emphasizing reliance on a Greek text of the OT, he is silent on connections to Paul (ibid., 23–5).

[29] Ibid., 295–96.

[30] "The Old Testament Citations in Hebrews," *NTS* 11 (1964–65): 303–25 (315). Cf. P. Katz, "The Quotations from Deuteronomy in Hebrews," *ZNW* 49 (1958): 213–23 (221).

[31] Attridge, *Hebrews* (see n. 28), 296.

[32] So also ibid., 296.

[33] Perhaps in the wake of Paul's death and ensuing dispersal of followers (e.g., 2 Tim 1:15 and 4:9–16).

[34] Cf. Acts 8:22.

[35] Moving beyond the elementary teaching of repentance (Heb 6:2) may imply this impossibility.

[36] Heb 10:26–27: "For if we willfully persist in sin after having received the knowledge of the truth, there no longer remains a sacrifice for sin, but a fearful prospect of judgment, and a fury of fire that will consume the adversaries."

desertion in the wake of Paul's death may have elicited from Hebrews a fine-tuning, as if by Paul, of Paul's message.[37]

3.2.4 Jeremiah 31:33–34

In the reprise of Jer 31:33 in Heb 10:16 (first cited in Heb 8:10), instead of a covenant formed "with the house of Israel" (τῷ οἴκῳ Ἰσραήλ) the text abbreviates: "a covenant that I will make with them (πρὸς αὐτούς)." Harold Attridge attributes this replacement to a "more universal scope" of the new covenant in Hebrews.[38] Kenneth J. Thomas mentions the inclusion of Gentile Christians, in particular Hebrews's author and audience.[39] Neither Attridge nor Thomas acknowledges the possibility of a more universal, Gentile-inclusive approach vis-à-vis Romans. However, the LXX version of Isa 59:21 (which refers to Jer 31:33)[40] used by Paul in Rom 11:27 also possesses the abbreviated formulation "with them" (καὶ αὕτη αὐτοῖς ἡ παρ' ἐμοῦ διαθήκη).[41] This observation suggests either that Hebrews's citation of Jer 31:33–34 also admitted the influence of Isa 59:20–21 (LXX) although Hebrews betrays no other direct knowledge of this passage or that conflation of the two passages in Romans[42] is reflected in Hebrews. Such a minor modification is subtle enough to suggest that the author of Hebrews worked from a written copy of Romans. It also commends the hypothesis that the universal version of the new covenant in Hebrews derives from Romans.

---

[37] Cf. 2 Tim 1:15; 4:10, 16.

[38] Attridge, *Hebrews* (see n. 28), 281.

[39] Thomas, "The Old Testament Citations in Hebrews" (see n. 30), 311. Thomas writes: "By the use of πρὸς αὐτούς, the author is including his readers and himself under the designation 'the house of Israel.' The change may have been necessitated by the inclusion of Gentile Christians among those to whom the epistle was written. This would give a broader application to the phrase 'house of Israel.' At least it may be said, the change was made to make a direct connection between ἡμῖν in verse 15 and the citation" (311).

[40] B. Sommer, *A Prophet Reads Scripture: Allusion in Isaiah 40–66* (Stanford, Calif.: Stanford University Press, 1998), 49–50; Fitzmyer, *Romans* (see n. 23), 625.

[41] Fitzmyer, ibid., 625. One may wish to compare the entire phrase in Heb 10:16: αὕτη ἡ διαθήκη ἣν διαθήσομαι πρὸς αὐτούς.

[42] Fitzmyer attests Paul's combination of Isaiah and Jeremiah in this passage in Romans: "Paul quotes Isa 59:21a according to the LXX, which is close to the MT. To it he adds Isa 27:9 ... changing the object to the pl. ... The first part of the Isaian quotation seems to refer to Jer 31:33. ... The 'covenant' [of Rom 11:27] is undoubtedly a reference to the 'new covenant' of Jer 31:31" (*Romans* [see n. 23], 625). It is possible that Paul was aware of the derivation of Isa 59:21a in Jeremiah.

3.2.5 Habakkuk 2:4

Hab 2:4 is arguably the most important biblical citation in Paul's undisputed letters, occurring first in Gal 3:11 and then in the thesis statement of Romans in Rom 1:17.[43] That the passage is also cited in Heb 10:37–38, yet nowhere else in the NT, is striking.[44] Furthermore, its appearance in Hebrews is problematic. As Attridge observes, the passage seems to possess no intra-Hebrews "polemical or apologetic" point.[45] Overlooked, perhaps, is the citation's possible polemic or apology vis-à-vis Paul's use of the passage in Romans.[46] For Paul, faith is the apprehension of a favorable relationship between human beings and God through Christ with special regard to apocalyptic judgment and cosmic restoration (e.g., Rom 1:17, cf. 3:3).[47] In contrast, faith in Hebrews is a principle guiding the relationship between the seen and the unseen (Heb 11:1). That faith for Paul is applied to a cosmic restoration is the crux. Hebrews seems to regard cosmic restoration in a historical sense as an argument susceptible to invalidation. Alternatively, it subscribes to a Platonic or platonic-like view of the cosmos (e.g., Heb 8:5)—one impervious to the vicissitudes of history. It, thus, diverts faith's focus to the restoration of relationship between human beings and God recognizable before death if realizable only after it.

3.3 Inexact Scriptural Correspondences

One inexact (chapter only) but exclusive (only in Romans and Hebrews) scriptural citation supports the view of Hebrews as a reading guide to Romans.

3.3.1 Genesis 22

Both Paul (Gal 3:8, 16) and Hebrews (6:13–14, 11:12) cite Gen 22. Such references are not exclusive in the NT: Jas 2:21 cites Gen 22:9, and Acts

---

[43] E.g., Robert Jewett who writes, "That this passage contains the theme or thesis of Romans is almost universally accepted among commentators" (*Romans* [Hermeneia; Minneapolis: Fortress Press, 2007], 135).

[44] Paul's citation of the passage varies slightly from the Greek text. The version in Hebrews is also slightly different from the LXX. In both cases the variant is μου. Hab 2:4 (LXX) = ὁ δὲ δίκαιος ἐκ πίστεώς μου ζήσεται; Rom 1:17 = ὁ δὲ δίκαιος ἐκ πίστεως ζήσεται; Heb 10:38: ὁ δὲ δίκαιός μου ἐκ πίστεως ζήσεται. See J. A. Fitzmyer, "Habakkuk 2:3–4 and the New Testament," in *To Advance the Gospel: New Testament Studies* (2d ed.; Grand Rapids, Mich.: Eerdmans, 2004), 236–48.

[45] *Hebrews* (see n. 28), 304.

[46] Attridge writes, "Hebrews's use of Hab 2:4 is also distinct from the prominent use of the verse in Paul" (ibid., 303).

[47] Fitzmyer, *Romans* (see n. 23), 254–55.

3:25 cites Gen 22:18. However, whereas Jas 2:21 cites Gen 22 on the *sacrifice* of Isaac, the citations in Paul, Hebrews and Acts refer to God's *promise* to Abraham of offspring through Isaac (Gen 15:5).[48] Moreover, Heb 11:12 suggests literary reliance on Paul's argument.[49] Heb 11:12 discusses how descendants of Abraham emerged from "one as good as dead" (διὸ καὶ ἀφ' ἑνὸς ἐγεννήθησαν, καὶ ταῦτα νενεκρωμένου). In Rom 4:19 "one as good as dead" is an epithet for Abraham (τὸ ἑαυτοῦ σῶμα [ἤδη] νενεκρωμένον) (cf. Gen 17:1–21). Apart from Hebrews, this epithet is otherwise unattested. At this point in his argument (Rom 4:18), Paul is citing the second (Gen 15:5) rather than the first (Gen 13:16) statement of God's promise to Abraham. His point is that death has no effect on the faithful.[50] In Hebrews, however, the meaning is reversed such that the faithful experience death as the only and necessary vehicle to after-life— an existence eminently superior to (if postdating) life on earth.[51] Death, for Hebrews, has no *ultimate* effect on the faithful but it is necessary nonetheless. Harold Attridge agrees that Hebrews's hyperbolic description of the old man Abraham as "as good as dead" (καὶ ταῦτα νενεκρωμένου) recalls Paul's discussion of Isaac's birth in Rom 4:19.[52] Although Attridge offers that both passages probably depend on a traditional description, no evidence supports such a contention.[53] Recalling that Heb 11:12 and Rom 4:18 are the only two references to Gen 15:5 within the NT, it is again possible, that Hebrews develops Romans on the topic of eternal life. Followers trusting Paul *unto death* inherit the promise of eternality now (purportedly) known by Jesus and perhaps Paul. The clarification is plain: resurrection never implies an avoidance of death.[54]

---

[48] For Heb 11:12, if it were not for the presence of "stars" (τὰ ἄστρα τοῦ οὐρανοῦ) and "sand" (ἡ ἄμμος ἡ παρὰ τὸ χεῖλος), the context of Abraham's childlessness and absence of any reference to the sacrifice of Isaac might suggest that the author cited not the repetition of the promise in Gen 22, but its initial declaration in Gen 15. Cf. Heb 11:8 and Gen 15:7ff.

[49] James too implies a post-Pauline literary context. In Jas 2:21–22, the author discusses the aptness of works for salvation: "Was not our ancestor Abraham justified by works when he offered his son Isaac on the altar? You see that faith was active along with his works, and faith was brought to completion by the works." See M. Jackson-McCabe, *Logos and Law in the Letter of James: The Law of Nature, The Law of Moses, and The Law of Freedom* (NovTSup 100; Leiden: Brill, 2001), 243–52.

[50] Cf. 1 Cor 15:54–55.

[51] E.g., Heb 12:4. Cf. Attridge who characterizes such a belief as distinctive of Hebrews (*Hebrews* [see n. 28], 326).

[52] Col 3:5 is the only other NT occurrence of the verb νεκροῦν. See ibid., 326.

[53] Attridge writes, "Both passages probably depend upon a traditional description of the event" (ibid., 326).

[54] The immediacy of the *parousia* for Paul is the primary difference; cf. 1–2 Thess.

In sum, Romans (esp. 9–11) initiates a discussion of how Paul's εὐαγγέλιον fulfills God's promises in the scriptures, a question answered preliminarily by the opening lines of Hebrews: "Long ago God spoke to our ancestors in many and various ways by the prophets, but in these last days he has spoken to us by a Son,"[55] but spelled out in the body of Hebrews in exegetical interactions on the specific scriptural texts Romans brings forward. Of roughly twenty-nine occasions on which Hebrews cites the Jewish scriptures seventeen are also cited by Paul.[56] More than half of the time, the identical passage is used. Most of these identical citations are found in the NT in Paul and Hebrews exclusively. Six out of seven of the citations come from Romans. The cumulative effect of so many allusions to identical passages cited in Romans suggests that Hebrews aims to guide readers in their study of this important Pauline letter.[57]

3.4 Common Postscript Elements

Common elements in the postscripts of both Romans and Hebrews likewise commend a deliberate connection between these two texts. The following list summarizes ten important points of contact.

1. The phrase ὁ δὲ θεὸς τῆς εἰρήνης ("God of peace"; Heb 13:20) is a regular feature of Pauline epistolary benedictions. It appears twice in Romans (Rom 15:33, 16:20, cf. 2 Cor 13:11, Phil 4:9, 1 Thess 5:23). It is also pervasive in the prescripts of both undisputed and disputed letters of Paul. A version of it occurs in Rom 1:7 (cf. also 1 Cor 1:3, 2 Cor 1:2, Gal 1:3, Eph 1:2, Phil 1:2, Col 1:2, 2 Thess 1:2, 1 Tim 1:2, 2 Tim 1:2, Titus 1:4, Phlm 3).[58]

2. Similarly, the phrase ἐκ νεκρῶν (Heb 13:20) is a frequent element in the Pauline corpus (Rom 1:4, 4:24, 8:11, Gal 1:1, Eph 1:20, Col 2:12). While the general affirmation that God raised Jesus from the dead can be identified in many quarters of early Christianity, this prepositional phrase is a hallmark of Paul's. As in Hebrews (ὁ ἀναγαγὼν ἐκ νεκρῶν), it oc-

---

[55] Esp. Rom 9:6: "It is not as though the word of God had failed."

[56] Thomas, "The Old Testament Citations in Hebrews" (see n. 30), 303. Enumerating the citations of the Jewish scriptures in Hebrews is not an exact science. In addition to explicit citations, Hebrews frequently alludes to biblical motifs and phrases.

[57] See J. A. Kelhoffer, *Miracle and Mission: The Authentication of Missionaries and Their Message in the Longer Ending of Mark* (WUNT II/112; Tübingen: Mohr Siebeck, 2000), 137.

[58] Franz Delitzsch describes ὁ δὲ θεὸς τῆς εἰρήνης as "one of Paul's favourite designations for God" (*Commentary on the Epistle to the Hebrews*, [trans. T. L. Kingbury; 2 vols.; Edinburgh: Clark, 1868], 2:402).

curs with the verb ἀνάγειν in Rom 10:7 (ἐκ νεκρῶν ἀναγαγεῖν).[59] However, in neither Paul's undisputed letters nor Hebrews is this phrase typical. The verb ἀναγεῖν occurs nowhere else in either. In the NT this verb refers to resurrection in only these two occurrences. Thus the phrase likely does *not* point with, for example, William L. Lane to "common early Christian tradition,"[60] but to literary reliance by the author of Hebrews on Romans, even if Paul knew it from pre-Pauline tradition.

Furthermore, ἐκ νεκρῶν[61] is the only direct reference to Jesus' resurrection in Hebrews and appears with prominence in this passage.[62] Although integral to Paul's theology, resurrection *per se* is foreign to the argument of Hebrews—one aspect of its radicalism vis-à-vis Paul's letters and other early Christian writings.[63] Rewriting Isa 63:11,[64] the phrase may reflect Paulinization of the claim that God "raises from the ground Moses, a shepherd of the sheep" (ὁ ἀναβιβάσας ἐκ τῆς γῆς τὸν ποιμένα τῶν προβάτων).[65] Use of ἀνάγειν over ἐγείρειν may represent a compromise, at the point in the treatise most fixed on Paul's authorship (i.e., the postscript), between the author's preference for exaltation and Paul's, for resurrection.

Also, Heb 13:20–21 exemplifies artful integration of the author's predilection for LXX citations with Paul's resurrection theology. William Lane argues that, because Paul never weaves LXX passages into his doxologies or homiletical benedictions, Heb 13:20–21 is "clearly independent of Paul."[66] Of course, pseudepigraphy is not slavish copying, but creative composition geared to make its own point as if that of another; and Rom 11:33–36 and 15:9–13 successfully unseat Lane's claim.

---

[59] NB: contrast in Rom 10:6–7 between κατάγειν and ἀνάγειν, explaining Paul's peculiar use of the latter.

[60] *Hebrews 9–13* (WBC 47B; Dallas, Tex.: Word, 1991), 562.

[61] Forty-four times in the NT with greatest percentage in Romans and First Peter.

[62] E.g., A. J. M. Wedderburn comments: "Only in 13.20 is Jesus' resurrection explicitly mentioned" ("'Letter' to the Hebrews and its Thirteenth Chapter," *NTS* [2004]: 390–405 [398]). However, cf. Heb 7:16, 24 and 11:35 where the idea might be implied. In Heb 6:1, teaching about resurrection is rejected or, at least, moved beyond. See R. Jewett, "The Form and Function of the Homiletic Benediction," *AThR* 51 (1969): 18–34 (28).

[63] Although Jesus' enthronement logically depends on his resurrection.

[64] Use of ἀνάγειν meaning "to lead" or "to bring up," from the realm of the dead may suggest the writer's knowledge of the pattern in Psalms (e.g., Ps 29:4 [LXX], 70:20 [LXX], 85:13 [LXX]).

[65] Attridge refers to the allusion as "faint at best" (*Hebrews* [see n. 28], 406). Contrast Lane, *Hebrews 9–13* (see n. 60), 560–61; cf. C. R. Koester, *Hebrews: A New Translation with Introduction and Commentary* (AB 36; New York: Doubleday, 2001), 573.

[66] *Hebrews 9–13* (see n. 60), 562. Claim also made by C. R. Williams, "A Word-Study of Hebrews 13," *JBL* (1911): 129–36 [135].

3. Although references to a "covenant" in the gospels and Acts are few (twice in the Synoptic gospels—Matt 26:28/Mark 14:24/Luke 22:20, Luke 1:72, twice in Acts—3:25, 7:8), ἡ διαθήκη occurs often in Paul's letters with two examples in Romans (Rom 9:4; 11:27;[67] 2 Cor 3:6, 14; Gal 3:15, 17; 4:24; Eph 2:12).[68]

4. The expression, "our Lord Jesus (τὸν κύριον ἡμῶν Ἰησοῦν)," a classic Pauline idiom, occurs only in the postscript in Hebrews.[69] Many Pauline passages record the entire phrase: "the grace of our Lord Jesus Christ" (Rom 16:20, 2 Cor 13:13, Gal 6:18, Phil 4:23, 1 Thess 5:28, cf. Eph 6:24, 2 Thess 3:18). As in Hebrews, however, 1 Cor 16:23 utilizes the abbreviated form.[70]

5. The main verb of the benediction, καταρτίσαι occurs thirteen times in the NT: four times in the Synoptics (Mark 1:19/Matt 4:21 [of the repairing of nets], Matt 21:16 [citing Ps 8:3 LXX], Luke 6:40), five in the undisputed letters of Paul (Rom 9:22, 1 Cor 1:10, 2 Cor 13:11 [cf. 13:9],

---

[67] Citation of Jer 31:33–34.

[68] Cf. "eternal covenant" in Isa 55:3, 61:8, Jer 32(39):40, Ezek 16:60, 37:26. Although not all occurrences are identical, in Paul's letters covenant often has a future orientation (not however in 9:4). Hebrews adopts this view. Regarding God's covenant, the starting premise in Hebrews is that Christ establishes a second, new and better one: "For, if that first covenant had been faultless, there would have been no need to look for a second one" (8:7); and, "He abolishes the first in order to establish the second" (10:9). Like these passages, Heb 7:22 clarifies a future orientation of the new covenant: "accordingly Jesus has also become the guarantee of a better covenant." The quotation from Jeremiah in Heb 8:8–10 too emphasizes manifestation in the future: "The days are surely coming (ἔρχονται), says the Lord, when I will establish a new covenant with the house of Israel and with the house of Judah ... This is the covenant that I will make (διαθήσομαι) with the house of Israel ..." (cf. Heb 9:15–17, 20; 10:16). Heb 10:29, furthermore, points to future punishment of those spurning Christ and Heb 13:20 pronounces a final benediction of wish, expressing the hope that God will complete them in Christ to do his will.

Moreover, the reverse principle is also true. Namely, the first or old covenant, obsolete since Jesus' death, has almost disappeared: "And what is obsolete and growing old will soon disappear" (8:13b). Recurring *a fortiori* arguments in Hebrews emphasize this principle (e.g., 1:4, 3:3, 7:22, 8:6).

Yet statements about Christ as mediator imply he is already installed in his position (Heb 12:24). Thus the author suggests that his own time is the last days of the Jewish covenant. Jesus is enthroned in heaven as the old covenant disappears and the new covenant awaits full instantiation. No explanation is offered for why Christ does not intervene to hasten the old covenant to its end. In Hebrews, this future orientation is a relic of Paul's day.

[69] Cf. Heb 1:10, 2:3, 7:14 and 12:14.

[70] Attridge, *Hebrews* (see n. 28), 407 n. 33. Here, as Attridge points out, there are some discrepancies in the MS(S). As Wedderburn notes, κύριος ... Ἰησοῦς has its nearest parallels in Rom 16:20; 1 Cor 5:4; 2 Cor 1:14; 1 Thess 2:19; 3:11; 2 Thess 1:8, 12 ("'Letter' to the Hebrews and its Thirteenth Chapter" [see n. 62], 390 n. 25).

Gal 6:1, 1 Thess 3:10, cf. Eph 4:12), three in Hebrews (10:5, 11:3, 13:21) and one in the postscript of First Peter (1 Pet 5:10).[71] Paul's undisputed letters and Hebrews, thus, exhibit a preponderance (eight of thirteen) of NT occurrences. The aorist optative καταρτίσαι is the only optative in Hebrews and expresses wish. Of thirty-eight NT optatives, sixteen are found in similar circumstances of prayer-wishes or blessings.[72] The optative mood of the verb is a feature of Pauline benedictions (cf. 1 Thess 5:23 [ἁγιάσαι], 2 Thess 3:16, Phil 4:19, cf. 1 Pet 5:10). More significant, however, is that, although this Greek word occurs elsewhere in Hebrews, nowhere does it possess the present meaning "to perfect."[73] To convey this meaning Heb 1–12 prefers τελειόω.[74] The verb does, however, possess this meaning twice in Paul (1 Cor 1:10, 2 Cor 13:11), possibly suggesting a concerted effort in the postscript to qualify concepts on Pauline terms. The further idea in this verse (Heb 13:21) that God "works among" believers to accomplish his will may strike us as too general to establish any literary connection. Yet it finds an important Pauline parallel in Phil 2:13: θεὸς γάρ ἐστιν ὁ ἐνεργῶν ἐν ὑμῖν καὶ τὸ θέλειν καὶ τὸ ἐνεργεῖν ὑπὲρ τῆς εὐδοκίας.[75]

6. Heb 13:21 is unusual for its reference to ἐν παντὶ ἀγαθῷ. This abstract concept of goodness arises nowhere else in Hebrews. The idea is, however, present in Paul's letters, particularly reminiscent of Rom 2:10: εἰρήνη παντὶ τῷ ἐργαζομένῳ τὸ ἀγαθόν.[76] That the perfection of believers is ultimately accomplished by God, points to an interpretation of "every good" not as "good deed," but as the God-given goodness prerequisite to all ethical action. God's calling believers to ethical action and equipping them for this work is a Pauline theme found in 1 Thess 5:23–24 and elsewhere (cf. Rom 12:1–2, Gal 5:22–26, also, 2 Thess 2:17).[77]

---

[71] Paul J. Achtemeier judiciously summarizes First Peter's literary reliance on the Pauline tradition in *1 Peter* (Hermeneia; Minneapolis: Fortress Press, 1996), 15–9. Achtemeier rejects (much like Attridge on Hebrews) literary dependence as, at best, difficult to demonstrate. An important difference between First Peter and Hebrews, however, is the latter's widespread and longstanding Pauline attribution. Such an attribution begs the question, even if one ultimately decides it is meaningless.

[72] Jewett suggests that the concentration of optatives in prayer units represents influence by LXX ("Form and Function of the Homiletic Benediction" [see n. 62], 23–4). With H. Smyth, however, the usage reflects regular syntax: §1814.

[73] Heb 10:5 = "to prepare" and Heb 11:3 = "to create."

[74] E. D. Jones, "Authorship of Hebrews xiii," *ExpTim* 46 (1934–35): 562–67 (565).

[75] F. F. Bruce includes this parallel in his commentary with the explanatory remark: "as Paul would put it" (*Epistle to the Hebrews* [rev. ed.; Grand Rapids, Mich.: Eerdmans, 1990], 389).

[76] E.g., Rom 3:8; 7:13, 18, 19; 8:28; 9:11; 13:3, 4; 2 Cor 5:10; Gal 6:6, 10; 1 Thess 5:15; Phlm 6.

[77] Cf. Rom 15:3, 13 and 2 Cor 1:3–4. Lane, *Hebrews 9–13* (see n. 60), 564.

7. The benediction concludes with mention of how "what is pleasing to God" (τὸ εὐάρεστον) is the result of the addressees's performance of the divine will through Jesus Christ.[78] While the reference to "Jesus Christ," also occurring in Heb 10:10 and 13:8, *may* derive from Paul, the word, τὸ εὐάρεστον, apart from this passage, appears *only* in the Pauline and deutero-Pauline letters, including three instances toward the end of Romans (Rom 12:1, 2; 14:18; 2 Cor 5:9; Eph 5:10; Phil 4:18; Col 3:20; Titus 2:9).

8. Furthermore, the concluding expression, ᾧ ἡ δόξα εἰς τοὺς αἰῶνας [τῶν αἰώνων], ἀμήν, closely resembles Rom 16:27: ᾧ ἡ δόξα εἰς τοὺς αἰῶνας, ἀμήν (cf. Rom 11:36, αὐτῷ ἡ δόξα εἰς τοὺς αἰῶνας, ἀμήν).[79] This doxology suggests literary reliance on Rom 16, even bearing in mind the question of the latter's originality to that letter.[80]

9. Heb 13:22–25 comprises the second half of the postscript.[81] The section begins with the verb παρακαλεῖν found in similar circumstances in Rom 15:30, 16:17, 1 Cor 16:15, 1 Thess 5:14, 2 Thess 3:12, and 1 Pet 5:1.[82] In v. 22 the author refers, as in Heb 3:1 and 10:19, to the addressees as ἀδελφοί, an expression scattered over the NT as a reference to believers, but occurring in both prescripts (Gal 1:2, Phil 1:14) and postscripts by Paul (Rom 16:14, 1 Thess 5:26, 1 Cor 16:20, and Phil 4:21).

10. Details of travel plans in epistolographical postscripts occur with regularity in the NT, for example, in Rom 15:22–29, Phlm 21–22, 2 John 12, and 3 John 13. The plans in Heb 13:23 resemble those in Rom 15:25–28 by their explanation of circumstances surrounding *a departure to visit the addressees*. In Romans, Paul will travel first to Jerusalem to turn over the collection. In Hebrews, the author will travel with Timothy, if Timothy arrives before too long.[83] In Rom 16:21, Timothy, Paul's co-worker, extends his greeting to the addressees through Paul.

---

[78] Cf. *1 Clem.* 21.1, 35.5, 60.2, 61.2.

[79] Interestingly the phrase "through Jesus Christ," immediately preceding the doxological conclusion in Hebrews, may also be found immediately before its parallel in Rom 16:27: διὰ Ἰησοῦ Χριστοῦ, ᾧ ἡ δόξα εἰς τοὺς αἰῶνας, ἀμήν.

[80] Many scholars view Rom 16:25–27 as a gloss. See Jewett, *Romans* (see n. 43), 998–1002.

[81] Wedderburn refers to the "Pauline flavour of 13.22–25" ("'Letter' to the Hebrews and its Thirteenth Chapter" [see n. 62], 395 n. 20).

[82] Imitative of Heb 13:19: περισσοτέρως δὲ παρακαλῶ τοῦτο ποιῆσαι, ἵνα τάχιον ἀποκατασταθῶ ὑμῖν, linking the postscript to the ending of the homily. Cf. Phlm 22.

[83] The attributive perfect passive participle ἀπολελυμένον (without the article) most likely means "has been released from prison," suggesting Timothy's release from an otherwise unknown imprisonment. It may, however, simply connote a dismissal unrelated to imprisonment. See BDAG 117. It may also suggest mere "departure." Cf. M. Zerwick and M. Grosvenor, *A Grammatical Analysis of the Greek New Testament* (Rome: Biblical Institute, 1981), 689; P. Ellingworth, *The Epistle to the Hebrews* (NIGTC; Grand Rapids, Mich.: Eerdmans / Carlisle: Paternoster, 1993), 734. Paul does not mention imprisonment

11. Not only is the two-part structure of Heb 13:24 standard to Pauline letters (2 Cor 13:12a, 12b; Phil 4:21, 22; 2 Tim 4:19, 21),[84] but the imperative verb ἀσπάσασθε is prevalent in Pauline postscripts (Rom 16:3–16, 1 Cor 16:20, 2 Cor 13:12, Phil 4:21, 1 Thess 5:26, 2 Tim 4:19, 1 Pet 5:14, cf. 3 John 15). While the formula "all the [fill in the blank] greet you" is clearly Pauline (e.g., Rom 16:16, 2 Cor 13:12, and Phil 4:22 [cf. 1 Cor 16:20]), its subject in Hebrews "those from Italy" (οἱ ἀπὸ τῆς Ἰταλίας) is notoriously ambiguous.[85] One possibility is that Aquila and Priscilla are implied. They are the only people in the NT referred to as "from Italy" (see Acts 18:2). They are the Jews expelled from Rome by the Edict of Claudius (Acts 18:2) who evidently worked together with Paul as tentmakers in Corinth.[86] The phrase could conceivably represent their greeting back to the congregation in Rome. Other possible implications include that the author is with *other* Roman Christians writing to Rome or sends greetings from Rome elsewhere in the Empire. All options associate Hebrews and Romans.

12. The final extension of grace (χάρις) in Heb 13:25 reflects perhaps the most regular convention of Pauline and deutero-Pauline postscripts (cf. Rom 16:20, 2 Cor 13:13, Gal 6:18, Eph 6:24, Phil 4:23, Col 4:18, 1 Thess 5:28, 2 Thess 3:18, 1 Tim 6:21, Titus 3:15, Phlm 25).

While true that Hebrews lacks Paul's 'holy kiss' (ἐν φιλήματι ἁγίῳ) in Rom 16:16a (cf. 1 Cor 16:20b, 2 Cor 13:12a, 1 Thess 5:26, 1 Pet 5:14a), close imitation of Paul's letters (Romans in particular) in Hebrews's postscript suggests that Hebrews sought to be understood in relation to this Pauline letter.

3.5 Echoes of Romans in Hebrews 13

Building on the work of C. R. Williams,[87] Edmund D. Jones took numerous correspondences between Heb 13 and Paul's letters to indicate that the last chapter of Hebrews was the conclusion to an authentic Pauline letter,

---

of Timothy although it is sometimes inferred from 2 Tim 4:9, 11, 13, and 21. Timothy is mentioned in connection with Paul's imprisonment in Phil 2:19–23.

[84] As Attridge points out, in the following texts the order is reversed: Col 4:10–14, 15–18; Titus 3:15, 15b; 1 Pet 5:13, 14; 3 John 15a, 15b; Ignatius, *Smyrn.* 12.1, 2. Also, Rom 16:21–23 lacks this two-part structure (Attridge, *Hebrews* [see n. 28], 409 nn. 73 and 74).

[85] For a discussion of textual evidence for the addressees, see ibid., 12–3.

[86] Hugh Montefiore notes the possibility of Paul's relationship with Aquila and Priscilla, but is thinking of an actual historical connection (*The Epistle to the Hebrews* [BNTC; London: Black, 1964], 254).

[87] "A Word-Study of Hebrews 13" (see n. 66), 129–36.

even speculating that it completed the lost 'severe letter' by Paul to the Corinthians. Although I reject Jones's ultimate conclusion, some of the evidence he marshals is summoned here for its usefulness in demonstrating literary resonance in Heb 13 of Romans. Jones lists,[88] for example: κοίτη (Heb 13:4) is used in the same sense in Romans twice; βρῶμα (Heb 13:9) occurs three times in Romans (Rom 14:15 [2x], 20);[89] περιπατεῖν (Heb 13:9) is used metaphorically, as in Hebrews, about thirty times in the *corpus Paulinum*, including three times in Romans (Rom 6:4, 8:4, 13:13); χεῖλος (Heb 13:15) occurs in the same sense as Hebrews once in Romans; κοινωνία (Heb 13:16) occurs once in Romans (15:26); and στενάζειν (Heb 13:17) occurs in the same sense once in Romans (8:23).[90]

Jones's evidence provides a foundation on which to build. In addition to the above-mentioned parallels, Heb 13 begins with an exhortation to "brotherly love" (φιλαδελφία) in v. 1. Although Attridge describes this affection as "common in early Christian paraenesis," his enumeration of parallels to the passage suggests greatest frequency and probable origination point in Paul's letters (e.g., Rom 12:10, 1 Thess 4:9).[91] Occurrences of this word in Hebrews, First and Second Peter and *First Clement* (1 Pet 1:22, 2 Pet 1:7, *1 Clem*. 47.5, 48.1) postdate Paul's letters.[92] Furthermore, Heb 13:2 exhorts the virtue of hospitality (φιλοξενία). This exhortation

---

[88] Jones does not supply verses, his point being that the quantities (omitted by Williams) are of primary importance. In most cases the verses are easy to deduce from a concordance ("The Authorship of Hebrews xiii" [see n. 74], 562–67).

[89] Jones lists three occurrences but does not specify which ones. The word occurs more than three times in Second Corinthians. The meaning of each occurrence is disputed.

[90] I have excluded from Jones's list parallels with deutero-Pauline letters. However, I include them here for the sake of completion: ἀφιλάργυρος in Heb 13:5 occurs in 1 Tim 3:3; περιφέρεσθαι in 13:9 occurs in a metaphorical sense also in Eph 4:14 (contrast 2 Cor 4:10); and ἀγρυπνέω in Heb 13:17 occurs in Eph 6:18 (cf. ἀγρυπνία in 2 Cor 6:5, 11:27).

[91] Attridge enumerates the following parallels: Rom 12:10, 1 Thess 4:9, 1 Pet 1:22, 2 Pet 1:7, *1 Clem*. 1.2, Herm. *Mand*. 8.10 (*Hebrews* [see n. 28], 385 n. 18).

[92] Scholarship has fluctuated on whether First Peter relied on Paul. During the first half of the twentieth century scholars such as Ora Delmar Foster (*The Literary Relations of the "First Epistle of Peter"* [Transactions of the Connecticut Academy of the Arts and Sciences; New Haven, Conn.: Yale University Press, 1913]) and Albert E. Barnett (*Paul Becomes a Literary Influence* [Chicago: University of Chicago Press, 1941], 52) favored reliance. Since then, however, the pendulum has swung the other way. See, e.g., Paul Achtemeier, *1 Peter* (see n. 71), 15–9; J. Herzer, *Petrus oder Paulus? Studien über das Verhältnis des ersten Petrusbriefes zur paulinischen Tradition* (WUNT 103; Tübingen: Mohr Siebeck, 1998). The opposite proposal, namely that Paul relied on First Peter has also been made. See B. Weiss, *Der Petrinische Lehrbegriff* (Berlin: Schultze, 1855), 406–25.

possesses a warrant from scripture based on the many biblical heroes surprised by divine messengers (e.g., Abraham/Sarah, Lot, Gideon et al.). While parallels to the motif in early Christian literature are widespread,[93] the one to Rom 12:13 is most compelling on account of its position immediately after an exhortation to brotherly love (v. 12) as in Hebrews. φιλοξενία is at issue in both of these texts. Other New Testament passages reflecting essentially the same advice do not utilize this particular expression.[94]

Occasionally the advice in Heb 13:3 to "remember prisoners as though you were in prison with them (ὡς συνδεδεμένοι)" is interpreted in terms of Paul's image of the body of Christ (e.g., Rom 12:4–5, 1 Cor 6:15, 12:12–27).[95] Attridge rightly rejects this interpretation rather favoring the notion of empathizing with victims attested in Philo (*Spec.* 3,161).[96] Given, however, correspondence between the exhortations to φιλαδελφία and φιλοξενία in Heb 13:1, 2 and Rom 12:10, 13 respectively, it is interesting to note that Paul's image of the body of Christ also occurs in Rom 12 (vv. 4–8). Furthermore, solidarity in persecution is also a Pauline sentiment expressed in 1 Cor 12:26 and 2 Cor 11:29. It is possible, thus, that the exhortation in Hebrews melds the two ideas as if reading Romans informed by First Corinthians. The purpose might be to enhance the trustworthiness of the speaker and bolster the authority of the exhortations by evoking Paul's ἦθος as prisoner.

The subjects of Heb 13:4–5, purity in marriage and unmercenary conduct, are widespread in ancient moral discourse and as such difficult to trace to any single Graeco-Roman, Jewish or early Christian tradition or group of traditions.[97] Moreover, key words in this passage, such as ἀφιλάργυρος and ἀρκούμενοι, are attested only in deutero-Pauline literature (esp. 1 Tim 3:3 and 1 Tim 6:8 respectively). However, the syntax of the exhortations in vv. 4–5, as Attridge points out, is paralleled in Rom

---

[93] E.g., Baucis and Philemon (Ovid, *Metam.* 8.620–720). For additional examples, see Attridge, *Hebrews* (see n. 28), 386 n. 23.

[94] Matt 25:35, 1 Pet 4:9, 1 Tim 5:10, 3 John 5 (see Attridge, ibid., 386 n. 23). 1 Tim 3:2 and Titus 1:8 use φιλόξενος as a qualification of a bishop. This word is, however, common in later literature; see Herm. *Sim.* 9.27.2, *Mand.* 8.10, *1 Clem.* 1.2, 10.7, 11.1, 12.1. Cf. Lucian, *Peregr.* 16.12.

[95] So Calvin, Bleek and Buchanan. See Attridge, *Hebrews* (see n. 28), 387 n. 40. Rom 12:4–5: "For as in one body we have many members, and not all the members have the same function, so we, who are many, are one body in Christ, and individually we are members one of another" (NRSV).

[96] *Hebrews* (see n. 28), 386–87.

[97] However, specific Pauline parallels occur in 1 Thess 4:3–7 and 1 Cor 5:10.

12:9: "where the nominal sentence is followed by a participle with imperatival force."[98] Attridge refers to the passage as representative of early Christian paranesis offering Romans as sole example in a supporting note.[99]

The exhortation in Heb 13:6 to be "courageous" utilizes the verb, θαρρεῖν, an expression that occurs elsewhere in the NT only in Second Corinthians (i.e., 5:6, 8; 7:16; 10:1, 2). The psalm in this verse (Ps 118:6) does not appear in the undisputed Pauline letters, although the compositional strategy of incorporating a psalm at this stage in a letter is mirrored in Rom 15:3 (Ps 69:9), Rom 15:9 (Ps 18:49) and Rom 15:11 (Ps 117:1).

"Jesus Christ" is described in v. 8 with the predicate "the same" (ὁ αὐτός), a word used by Paul in a key passage in 1 Cor 12:4–6. In that context the modifier possesses the meaning eternally "undivided" and "indivisible."[100] However, the idea that Jesus is eternal (εἰς τοὺς αἰῶνας) is a recurring theme in Romans (1:25, 9:5, 11:36, 16:27) also appearing in 2 Cor 11:31 and Phil 4:20.[101] Whether Hebrews echoes Paul's idea is impossible to prove. With other clear links to Paul's letters in this section, however, the possibility should not be ignored.

The next warning to avoid strange teachings is correctly referred to by Attridge as "quite conventional in Christian literature."[102] However, the specific phrase "it is good," also occurring in the gospels of Mark and Matthew,[103] is found in five places in Paul's letters (i.e., Rom 14:21; 1 Cor 7:1, 8, 26; and Gal 4:18). Furthermore, the promise of "strengthening" by food is made by Paul in 1 Cor 1:6 and 2 Cor 1:21 (cf. Col 2:7); and, strengthening of heart appears in 1 Thess 3:13 (cf. 2 Thess 2:17). Like ideas can be traced in Philo, but the insufficiency of food juxtaposed with the sufficiency of Christ in Heb 13:9, looks suspiciously Pauline (e.g., Rom 14:17, 1 Cor 8:8, cf. Eph 5:18 and Ignatius, *Trall.* 2.3).[104]

---

[98] *Hebrews* (see n. 28), 387 n. 44.

[99] See ibid., 387 n. 44.

[100] See M. M. Mitchell, *Paul and the Rhetoric of Reconciliation* (Louisville, Ky.: Westminster John Knox, 1991), 268.

[101] Cf. Heb 13:21.

[102] Attridge, *Hebrews* (see n. 28), 393.

[103] Mark 7:27; 9:43, 45, 47; cf. Matt 15:26; 18:8–9.

[104] Ignatius's use of Paul is a related question. William R. Schoedel writes, "Certain usage by Ignatius of Paul can be established only for First Corinthians (see on *Eph.* 16.1, 18.1, *Rom.* 5.1, 9.2, *Phld.* 3.3). But Ignatius knew that Paul was the author of more than one letter (cf. *Eph.* 12.2), and it is possible that we should be more generous" (*Ignatius of Antioch* [Philadelphia: Fortress Press, 1985], 9). Cf. "Paul seems to have exercised the profoundest formulative influence on Ignatius, not least because Ignatius found in the apostle a model for understanding his own sense of rejection" (ibid., 10).

NT parallels for the important term θυσιαστήριον are identified in Rom 11:3, 1 Cor 9:13 (twice) and 10:18. The phrase, "sacrifice of praise to God, that is, the fruit of lips that confess his name"—together with the next two verses (vv. 15–16) in which praise and good deeds characterize sacrifices God considers pleasing—echoes Paul particularly in Rom 12:1–2, 10:9–10, Phil 2:17 and 4:18 (cf. 1 Pet 2:5).[105]

The last two verses of Heb 13 urge submission to leaders who, the author warns, control individual destinies (v. 17). In light of other evidence the purpose of this text seems to be to hone Paul's advice in Rom 13:1–7 to submit to leaders for new ecclesiastical contexts. In vv. 18–19, the author requests prayer, although adding that his conscience is clear, a combination of two contradictory yet characteristic Pauline claims (e.g., "conscience": Rom 2:15; 9:1; 13:5; 1 Cor 8:7, 10, 12; 10:25, 27, 28, 29; 2 Cor 1:12; 4:2; 5:11; and "pray": προσεύχεσθε περὶ ἡμῶν [1 Thess 5:25 = identical to Heb 13:18a]; cf. Rom 15:30). An otherwise unattested link between obedience to authorities (Heb 13:7 and Rom 13:1–7) and conscience (Heb 13:18 and Rom 13:5) further commends a relationship between these two texts.[106] In Romans, addressees are commanded to obey political leaders out of fear of punishment and with respect to their own consciences. In Hebrews, addressees are commanded to obey church leaders out of fear of recourse in the final judgment (when the leaders will play an instrumental role in their ultimate vindication). The author's conscience, we are told, is clear.

3.6 Echoes of Romans in Hebrews 1–12

In addition to numerous echoes of Romans in Hebrews's citation of the Jewish scriptures, postscript and chapter on moral discourse (Heb 13), Heb 1–12 also imitates, explains and develops Romans on at least five important issues. They are: (1) Jesus' sonship (υἱός); (2) the σκληρ- root; (3) Jesus as mercy seat (ἱλαστήριον); (4) Jesus' once-for-all death (ἐφάπαξ); and (5) the nature of πίστις.

3.6.1 Jesus' Sonship

First, both Romans and Hebrews ring forth in their opening verses with claims about Jesus as υἱός.[107] In Rom 1:3 Jesus descends from the seed of

---

[105] These passages are absent from Attridge's treatment of the passage (*Hebrews* [see n. 28], 400–1).

[106] First Peter contains both ideas, but they are not linked: 1 Pet 5:5 (obey leadership) and 1 Pet 3:16, 21 (conscience).

[107] To my knowledge, no commentary on Romans or Hebrews correlates the openings of these two texts.

David (περὶ τοῦ υἱοῦ αὐτοῦ τοῦ γενομένου ἐκ σπέρματος Δαυὶδ κατὰ σάρκα) and in vv. 4 (τοῦ ὁρισθέντος υἱοῦ θεοῦ) and 9 (ἐν τῷ εὐαγγελίῳ τοῦ υἱοῦ αὐτοῦ) he is God's son.[108] Some interpreters understand Rom 1:3–4 as a citation from an otherwise unknown confession. Whether that claim can be sustained or not, the passage does seem to reflect a view that Jesus as Son of David is installed in the office of Son of God by his resurrection (cf. Acts 13:33, also, 2 Cor 8:9 and Phil 2:6–11).

Likewise, the opening of Hebrews, as in a confession, exalts Jesus as God's eternal Son. Heb 1:2 states the premise: "But in these last days he has spoken to us by a *Son* whom he appointed heir of all things, through whom he also created the worlds" (ἐπ' ἐσχάτου τῶν ἡμερῶν τούτων ἐλάλησεν ἡμῖν ἐν υἱῷ, ὃν ἔθηκεν κληρονόμον πάντων, δι' οὗ καὶ ἐποίησεν τοὺς αἰῶνας). V. 5 develops this main contention with declarative premises from the Jewish scriptures, such as, "You are my Son; today I have begotten you" (Ps 2:7); "I will be his Father, and he will be my Son" (2 Sam 7:14) and "Let all God's angels worship him" (Deut 32:43 LXX). Jesus' sonship is, furthermore, reiterated in v. 8: "But to the *Son* (πρὸς δὲ τὸν υἱόν) he says, "Your throne, O God, is forever and ever, and the righteous scepter is the scepter of your kingdom" (cf. also 3:6). The theme of Jesus' sonship is not particular to these two sections of the NT, but is nevertheless not developed at length elsewhere. As the opening theme it gives these two texts an impression of continuity.

3.6.2 The σκληρ- Root

Second, the σκληρ- root is relatively rare in the NT.[109] Moreover, Rom 9:18; Heb 3:8, 13, 15 and 4:7 and Acts 19:9 share the verb σκληρύνειν exclusively in the NT. These two observations could imply a connection between the occurrences. However, a closer look at Romans and Hebrews demonstrates that by its use of σκληρύνειν Hebrews offers a reading strategy for Romans.

In Rom 9:18 God performs acts of hardening on whomever he chooses: ἄρα οὖν ὃν θέλει ἐλεεῖ, ὃν δὲ θέλει σκληρύνει (comparison is made in v. 17 with Pharaoh in Exod 4:21; 7:3; 9:12; 10:1, 20, 27; 11:10; 14:4 and

---

[108] Furthermore, Rom 8 pursues the topics of sonship, adoption, children and family. Cf. πρωτότοκος in Rom 8:29 and Heb 1:6, 11:28 and 12:23.

[109] Examples include: σκληροκαρδία—Matt 19:8/Mark 10:5, Mark 16:14; σκληρός—Matt 25:24, John 6:60, Acts 26:14, Jas 3:4, Jude 15; σκληρότης—Rom 2:5; σκληροτράχηλοι—Acts 7:51; (as above) σκληρύνειν—Acts 19:9; Rom 9:18; Heb 3:8, 13, 15; 4:7. Cf. the equally rare rough semantic equivalent: πωροῦν (esp. Rom 11:7) and πώρωσις (esp. Rom 11:25).

8).¹¹⁰ In contrast, Rom 2:5 (using the adjective σκληροτής) and Heb 3:8, 15 and 4:7 (using the verb σκληρύνειν) depict human beings as responsible for their obduracy. Heb 3:13 offers a twist on the theme of human culpability utilizing a passive form of the verb. Sin not God is the subject: ἵνα μὴ σκληρυνθῇ τις ἐξ ὑμῶν ἀπάτῃ τῆς ἁμαρτίας ("so that none of you may be hardened by the deceitfulness of sin").¹¹¹ Thus, two initial similarities between Romans and Hebrews are (1) Rom 2:5 and Heb 3:8, 15 and 4:7 share a somewhat rare early Christian interest in the σκληρ- root; and (2) both deploy σκληρ- actively blaming humans for their stubbornness. The next section examines these two sections of text in greater detail.

Human obduracy is an important part of Paul's argument in Rom 1–3. Having just indicted pagans for idolatry (Rom 1:18–32), Paul uses the adjective σκληρότης in 2:5 as part of a parallel indictment against Jews: "But by your hard and impenitent heart (κατὰ δὲ τὴν σκληρότητά σου καὶ ἀμετανόητον καρδίαν) you are storing up wrath for yourself on the day of wrath when God's righteous judgment will be revealed."¹¹² A new thesis by Alec J. Lucas, evidence for which includes but is not limited to σκληροτράχηλος in Exod 33:3, 5, σκληρότητα in Deut 9:27¹¹³ and σκληροκαρδίαν in Deut 10:16,¹¹⁴ claims that Rom 2 draws upon the calf rebellion for its indictment of idolatry (pagan idolatry: Rom 1:22–23)¹¹⁵

---

¹¹⁰ Elsewhere, however, Pharaoh hardens his own heart: Exod 7:22, 8:15, 9:35, 13:15.

¹¹¹ Technically speaking, in the phrase ἀπάτῃ τῆς ἁμαρτίας, ἀπάτη is a dative of means with ἁμαρτία as a subjective genitive. Thus, sin is not 'subject,' but causative agent.

¹¹² The parallel is not strict. Rom 1:18–32 and 2:1–11 are not bifurcated into the categories of "Gentile" and "Jew" respectively. Paul has not even introduced these concepts into his main argument yet (although they are present in his thesis in 1:16–17). Rather the passage works abstractly by furnishing an account of the origin of religion in which he explains why all human beings have defective 'minds' (moral reasoning) and 'hearts' (the part of the human being that worships God) and building upon this point by condemning anyone who either anticipates divine judgment or encroaches upon God's sovereign right to judge, since all share in the blame and the consequences that result from a primordial ancestor's grievous error. My thanks to R. Matthew Calhoun for this nuanced approach to Rom 1–2.

¹¹³ μὴ ἐπιβλέψῃς ἐπὶ τὴν σκληρότητα τοῦ λαοῦ τούτου καὶ τὰ ἀσεβήματα καὶ τὰ ἁμαρτήματα αὐτῶν.

¹¹⁴ καὶ περιτεμεῖσθε τὴν σκληροκαρδίαν ὑμῶν καὶ τὸν τράχηλον ὑμῶν οὐ σκληρυνεῖτε ἔτι.

¹¹⁵ According to Lucas, although parallel pagan guilt for idolatry is the subject and purpose of Rom 1:18–32, Paul takes it more or less for granted. In Rom 1:23 he indicts a Jewish interlocutor by evoking Ps 106(105 LXX):20 concerning Israel's idolatrous (i.e., theriolatrous) incident with the golden calf. The evocations of Deut 9:1–10:22 in Rom 2:5–11 underscore this point.

against the Jews (cf. Deut 9:1–10:22, Ps 106[105]:19–23).[116] The calf rebellion is, of course, a paradigmatic example of Jewish idolatry.

---

[116] Lucas does not simply argue that Paul references the calf rebellion in Romans. Rather he claims that Paul counters the construction of Jewish identity reflected in Wis 11–19 (similar to, if not reliant on, Ps 105[104 LXX]) with Ps 106(105 LXX), esp. its account of the golden calf incident in vv. 19–23. See A. J. Lucas, "Evocations of the Characteristic Calf Rebellion: Romans 2:5–11 and LXX Deuteronomy 9:1–10:22." Lucas delivered this paper at the Midwest Society of Biblical Literature Meeting at Olivet Nazarene University in Bourbonnais, Ill. on Saturday, February 14, 2009, where I heard it. The paper, which won the Midwest SBL Graduate Student Paper Prize for 2009, is a part of Lucas's Loyola University of Chicago PhD Dissertation under Thomas Tobin the tentative title of which is "An Intertextual Debate concerning the Calf? Jewish Identity in Romans 1:18–2:11 and Wisdom of Solomon 11–19." The abstract for this award-winning paper is: "Building upon an earlier study in which I argued that Paul's allusion in Rom 1:23 to the golden calf incident as recounted in Ps 106(LXX 105):19–23 serves as the foundation for indicting the Jewish interlocutor in Rom 2:1–4 and commends the construal of Jewish identity in Ps 106(105) over and against Wis 11–19, this paper argues that Rom 2:5–11 continues to evoke the golden calf, this time as recounted in LXX Deut 9:1–10:22 and that this version may have been evoked to counter the implicit interpretation of Exod 32–34's version in Wis 15:1–6." Lucas has also written a presently unpublished paper entitled: "Romans 1:18–2:4; Wisdom of Solomon 11–19; and Psalm 106(LXX 105): A Three-Way Metaleptic Interplay?" part of which informs the discussion in my essay. This paper is the 'earlier study' referred to in his abstract (cited above). This paper won the Midwest SBL Graduate Student Paper Prize for 2008 and was presented at Olivet Nazarene University, Bourbonnais, Ill. on Saturday, February 16, 2008.

Concerning σκληροτράχηλος Lucas clarifies the argument: "LXX Deut 9:13 does not just identify Israel as σκληροτράχηλος but places particular emphasis on this fact: καὶ εἶπεν κύριος πρός με Λελάληκα πρὸς σὲ ἅπαξ καὶ δὶς λέγων Ἑώρακα τὸν λαὸν τοῦτον, καὶ ἰδοὺ λαὸς σκληροτράχηλός ἐστιν. Regarding this verse, J. W. Wevers notes: "LXX has inserted between 'and the Lord said to me' and the direct speech marker the words λελάληκα πρὸς σὲ ἅπαξ καὶ δὶς, the source of which is unknown ... If one examines the parallel account in Exod, one notes that the characterization of Israel as λαὸς σκληροτράχηλος occurs twice in Exod 33 (vv. 3, 5) as well as once in Moses' intercessory prayer on behalf of the people in 34:9. It is actually the case in the golden calf episode that God spoke not just once but twice accusing the people of being stiff-necked ... This strikes me as convincing proof that the Deut translator made use of the Exod account" (*Notes on the Greek Text of Deuteronomy* [SBLSCS 39; Atlanta: Scholars Press, 1995], 164; cited in Lucas, "Evocations of the Characteristic Calf Rebellion," 18 n. 18).

Furthermore, Lucas demonstrates Paul's familiarity with Deuteronomy in a footnote: "Significantly, in Rom 10:6a Paul imports the phrase μὴ εἴπῃς ἐν τῇ καρδίᾳ σου from Deut 9:4 to introduce his exegesis of Deut 30:12–14 which follows in Rom 10:6bff. While the phrase μὴ εἴπῃς ἐν τῇ καρδίᾳ σου also occurs in Deut 8:17, as J. R. Wagner notes, Deut 9:4 is most likely the 'source of Paul's quotation due to the (metaleptically suppressed) catchword "righteousness" (δικαιοσύνη) in [Deut] 9:4–6,' but absent from Deut 8:17 as well as its surrounding co-text." See J. R. Wagner, *Heralds of the Good News: Isaiah and Paul in Concert in the Letter to the Romans* (Boston/Leiden: Brill, 2003), 161–62 (Lucas, ibid., 18 n. 17).

Lucas further argues that Paul's indictment against the Jews for idolatry also alludes to the Kadesh Barnea rebellion in Numbers 14, since this egregious episode in Israelite history is referred to in both Ps 106(105 LXX):24–27 and Deut 9:23 (texts that seem to inform Rom 2). Hardness of heart, according to Rom 2:5, nullifies God's promise of deliverance (i.e., μὴ ἐπιβλέψῃς ἐπὶ τὴν σκληρότητα τοῦ λαοῦ τούτου καὶ τὰ ἀσεβήματα καὶ τὰ ἁμαρτήματα αὐτῶν ... καὶ παρὰ τὸ μισῆσαι αὐτοὺς ἐξήγαγεν αὐτοὺς ἀποκτεῖναι ἐν τῇ ἐρήμῳ [Deut 9:27–28]; cf. Num 14:28–35). Lucas claims that Paul adjudicates his view of both the calf and the Kadesh Barnea rebellion through their interpretations in Psalm 106 (and Deut 9:1–10:22) where the emphasis, as in Rom 2:5, is on human culpability for sin and apostasy.[117]

On the other hand, Hebrews does not allude to the calf rebellion in its warnings against obduracy. Rather, references in Heb 3–4 to the stubbornness of the Jews rely on Ps 94:8 (LXX): μὴ σκληρύνητε τὰς καρδίας ὑμῶν ὡς ἐν τῷ παραπικρασμῷ / κατὰ τὴν ἡμέραν τοῦ πειρασμοῦ ἐν τῇ ἐρήμῳ. Hebrews echoes the warning from this psalm three times (3:8, 15; 4:7). The psalm itself (95[94 LXX]) probably alludes to both the Meribah/Massah (Ps 95[94]:8, Exod 17:1–7) *and* the Kadesh Barnea (Ps 95[94]:10–11; Num 14:26–35) incidents. However, because Hebrews frames its response to the psalm's warnings in terms of Num 14 (Heb 3:16–19), the refrain probably intends to recollect primarily the Kadesh Barnea incident. Kadesh Barnea, after all, signifies not just another example of Israelite obduracy, but *the* incident prompting final punishment for all wilderness noncompliance.[118]

The relationship between Romans and Hebrews on the issue of obduracy can now be summarized. Four similarities are salient: (1) both texts exploit the σκληρ- root to issue warnings concerning the final judgment; (2) both texts emphasize human culpability for σκληρότης ('hardness' or 'stubbornness'); (3) the Kadesh Barnea incident offers the background for

---

Finally, Lucas explains the link between the golden calf incident in Ps 106(105 LXX):19–23 and Deut 9–10 in Romans: "It is important to recognize that there is an exegetical rationale in the transition from the account of the golden calf incident in Ps 106(LXX 105):19–23 to the account in Deut 9–10. While the mention of Χωρηβ and the phrase ἠλλάξαντο τὴν δόξαν αὐτῶν in Ps 106(LXX 105):19–20 recalls Exod 33:5–6, and thus the account in Exod 32–34, the statement εἶπεν τοῦ ἐξολεθρεῦσαι αὐτούς evokes Deut 9:1–10:11 where the verb ἐξολεθρεύω occurs 10x (Deut 9:3, 4, 5, 8, 14, 19, 20, 25, 26; 10:10) and is central to the comparison between Gentile inhabitants of the Land and Israel, as the discussion which follows will make clear" (Lucas, ibid., 12–3).

[117] Lucas argues that Paul does so in reaction to Wis 11–19 which instead uses Ps 105 (with its decided de-emphasis of human culpability) as the lens by which it views Jewish history.

[118] I wish to express gratitude to Lucas for emphasizing this point to me.

punishment in the judgment about which both texts warn; and (4) the texts utilize psalms as lenses by which to view events of the wilderness generation.[119] The primary difference between the two texts is one of context. Hebrews highlights obduracy resulting from apostasy as opposed to idolatry.[120] Although it is possible that Hebrews constructs its warnings against obduracy independent of the influence of Romans, multiple convergences of the two *approaches* suggest that while independence is possible it is not probable. Rather it is more likely that Hebrews's position is deliberately imitative of Romans with the goal of instructing readers on how to apply Paul's message to a post-Pauline context of real or perceived persecution.

Nevertheless, the point of this section should not be overstated. Some question remains as to the centrality of the narratives of the calf rebellion and the Kadesh Barnea incidents in Paul's argument in Rom 1:18–2:11. The imagery of "hardness of heart" and "hardening" in this section evokes these incidents to be sure, however they remain at the periphery as mere allusive precedents. Moreover, they represent the sort of indictment (cf. Wis 11–19) that Paul wishes to counter. One must be careful not to overstate intertextual cross-references and the degree to which Paul is *exegeting*, rather than merely applying, merging or evoking the texts to which he refers. Hebrews picks up the warning from Ps 95 and applies it in a manner similar to Paul's warning in Rom 2:5. However, Hebrews is much more explicitly exegeting its *Urtext* than Paul. In its exegesis of the scriptures one might say Hebrews is more like Wisdom than Romans. Furthermore, Hebrews applies the warning against hardening as exhortation. It neither *indicts* its audience for a systemic or primordial 'hardness of heart,' nor *explains* a temporary 'hardening' of Israelites until the fullness of the Gentiles have 'come in' (Rom 9–11). Hebrews simply urges its readers (more than once) not to harden their hearts. If Hebrews is correcting Romans on this point, the author is appropriating an important theme delivered synecdochically by Paul and amplifying it with further literature from the LXX to enhance it suitability for a different purpose. In sum, it seems that the type of approach Paul sought to counter in Romans through peripheral references to precedents for the behavior of his contemporaries and kinsmen, Hebrews viewed as a drawback to the letter's full appreciation and understanding. Hebrews thus returns Jewish precedents to the fore adapting them to a post-Pauline context.

---

[119] I wish to express gratitude to Lucas for this point.
[120] Except when idolatry is construed as a form of apostasy.

3.6.3 Jesus as Mercy Seat

Third, Hebrews offers a possible context for understanding Paul's solution to the pan-indictment of humanity by sin in Rom 1–3. Having indicted all humanity in Rom 1:18–3:20, Paul proffers a solution in (esp.) 3:24–25. In Christ, Paul claims, the relationship of human beings to God is rectified. Specifically Christ as propitiation or mercy seat (ἱλαστήριον: Lev 16:13–15) resolves humanity's indictment for sin.[121] The meaning of this passage, in particular the single word ἱλαστήριον (without article), is crucial. The only and decisive remedy against eternal damnation rides on Jesus as "mercy seat" yet Paul refers to it only generally and without explanation.[122]

Interpreters have spent much time and effort attempting to explain Paul's use of ἱλαστήριον in Rom 3:25. Its role as either location or means of expiation has been debated. The possible effects of forgiveness, expiation, propitiation, atonement, reconciliation and/or redemption have each been explored. Late antique writers, including John Chrysostom, also debated the meaning of this passage, with no consensus.[123] Most recently Robert Jewett favors "mercy seat" as "a new institutional vehicle for atonement,"[124] "overcoming human enmity against God and restoring humans to righteousness 'in him,' that is, in the new community of faith."[125]

Other than Rom 3:25, ἱλαστήριον occurs only in Heb 9:5 in the NT.[126] The passage in Hebrews cites Lev 16:13–15 (LXX):

Now even the first covenant had regulations for worship and an earthly sanctuary. For a tent was constructed, the first one, in which were the lampstand, the table, and the bread of the Presence; this is called the Holy Place. Behind the second curtain was a tent called the Holy of Holies. In it stood the golden altar of incense and the ark of the covenant overlaid on all sides with gold, in which there were a golden urn holding the manna, and Aaron's rod that budded, and the tablets of the covenant; above it were the cherubim of glory overshadowing the mercy seat. Of these things we cannot speak now in detail.

Subsequently, vv. 6–10 explain the ritual duties of the sanctuary specifying regulations for the Day of Atonement. In its immediate context in Hebrews these passages (Heb 9:1–10) develop the theme stated in 8:13 of the new covenant. However, in the larger context of Heb 8:1–10:18 the passage constitutes an exegetical homily on Jesus' sacrificial act. The entire section

---

[121] Ex 25:17: כפרת.

[122] The ambiguity is probably deliberate. Paul is referring to a concept of atonement of which he knows but otherwise makes little use.

[123] *hom. Rom.* 7 (NPNF 1,11:378); cf. Theodoret, *Interpretation of the Letter to the Romans* (PG 82 ad loc).

[124] Jewett, *Romans* (see n. 43), 287.

[125] Ibid., 286.

[126] Attridge, *Hebrews* (see n. 28), 238 n. 100.

might be understood as an interpretation of Paul's general reference to Jesus as mercy seat. According to Hebrews, Jesus is not 'mercy seat' *per se*; rather he is high priest (9:11) sprinkling his own blood as a means of purification from sin (Heb 9:21–22). *That is, as both priest and sacrifice, Jesus embodies the 'place of propitiation.'* According to Hebrews, Jesus is "mercy seat" insofar as the expression serves as synecdoche for purification of the altar, the temple and its sacrifices overall. Thus, Jesus' death satisfies long-held demands of the entire Jewish sacrificial system. On its own it is difficult to prove that Hebrews's homily on Jesus' sacrificial act in 8:1–10:18 is *necessarily* a response to Rom 3:25. The uniqueness of ἱλαστήριον in early Christian literature is telling but not definitive. However, as one aspect of a cumulative argument featuring both the *criticality and ambiguity* of Paul's summative solution to the *condicio humana* in Romans, the connection seems valid. Without Romans, the lengthy discussion of ritual atonement in Hebrews is almost anomalous in early Christian literature.

3.6.4 Jesus' Once-for-all Death

Fourth, Hebrews's central theme, the once-for-all death of Jesus, also most likely derives from Romans.[127] Heb 7:26–27 constitutes the first announcement of an important theme of the writing: "For it was indeed fitting for us to have such a high priest, holy, blameless, undefiled, separated from the sinners and higher than the heavens, who does not have daily need, like the high priests, to offer sacrifices, first on behalf of their own sins then on behalf of the sins of the people. For this he did *once and for all* when he offered himself (τοῦτο γὰρ ἐποίησεν ἐφάπαξ ἑαυτὸν ἀνενέγκας)." Furthermore, Christ's once and for all sacrifice is reiterated using the adverb ἐφάπαξ in both Heb 9:12 and 10:10. The adverb occurs elsewhere in the NT only in Rom 6:10 and 1 Cor 15:6.[128] In 1 Cor 15:6 ἐφάπαξ refers

---

[127] James W. Thompson refers to the "pervasiveness of this theme in Hebrews and its *relative absence* elsewhere in the New Testament" ("*EPHAPAX*: The One and the Many in Hebrews," *NTS* 53 [2007]: 566–81 [567, emphasis added]).

[128] The adverb occurs in the abbreviated form ἅπαξ in Heb 6:4; 9:7, 26, 27, 28; 10:2; cf. 12:26, 27. The abbreviated form is found in the NT in 2 Cor 11:25; Phil 4:16; 1 Thess 2:18; 1 Pet 3:18 and Jude 3, 5. Attridge refers to ἐφάπαξ as "a traditional part of affirmations about Christ's death," citing Rom 6:10 and 1 Pet 3:18 (*Hebrews* [see n. 28], 214 n. 121). As noted (see n. 127), J. Thompson refers to the "pervasiveness of this theme in Hebrews." However, Thompson references only BDAG for occurrences (567 n. 4). See also *TDNT* 1:381–84. A similar idea is expressed in 2 Cor 5:14 and 1 Tim 2:5–6. Latin equivalent: *semetipsum*. In terms of orthography, BDF notes possibility of the word's division (§12.3). See LSJ for addition of ἐπί to lend superiority, authority, motive, force or intensity to a verb (623); no mention is made of adverbs. BDF considers the possibility of a parallel between ἐφ' ἅπαξ and ἐπί + τρίς (§12.3) = "and one-third more" (LSJ 623).

to Jesus' appearance: "Then he appeared to more than five hundred brothers at one time (ἐφάπαξ), most of whom are still alive although some have died."[129] In the maxim in Rom 6:10, however, ἐφάπαξ refers not to an appearance of Jesus but, as in Hebrews, to Jesus' death: "The death he died, he died to sin, once and for all; but the life he lives, he lives to God (ὃ γὰρ ἀπέθανεν, τῇ ἁμαρτίᾳ ἀπέθανεν ἐφάπαξ ὃ δὲ ζῇ, ζῇ τῷ θεῷ)." As in Romans, Heb 7:27, 9:12 and 10:10[130] place the adverb after the word with which it is connected rather than before it.[131]

Although Heb 9:26–28 uses only the abbreviated form ἅπαξ, closeness of these verses to Rom 6:10 is also apparent:

[26] ἐπεὶ ἔδει αὐτὸν πολλάκις παθεῖν ἀπὸ καταβολῆς κόσμου· νυνὶ δὲ *ἅπαξ* ἐπὶ συντελείᾳ τῶν αἰώνων εἰς ἀθέτησιν [τῆς] ἁμαρτίας διὰ τῆς θυσίας αὐτοῦ πεφανέρωται. [27] καὶ καθ᾽ ὅσον ἀπόκειται τοῖς ἀνθρώποις *ἅπαξ* ἀποθανεῖν, μετὰ δὲ τοῦτο κρίσις, [28] οὕτως καὶ ὁ Χριστὸς *ἅπαξ* προσενεχθεὶς εἰς τὸ πολλῶν ἀνενεγκεῖν ἁμαρτίας ἐκ δευτέρου χωρὶς ἁμαρτίας ὀφθήσεται τοῖς αὐτὸν ἀπεκδεχομένοις εἰς σωτηρίαν. (Heb 9:26–28)

ὃ γὰρ ἀπέθανεν, τῇ ἁμαρτίᾳ ἀπέθανεν ἐφάπαξ ὃ δὲ ζῇ, ζῇ τῷ θεῷ. (Rom 6:10)[132]

The usage of ἐφάπαξ in this passage might initially strike us as conventional. As many commentators acknowledge, it gains force from its comparison with καθ᾽ ἡμέραν.[133] That First Peter picks up a closely related idea (using ἅπαξ not ἐφάπαξ) causes some interpreters (as in so many cases in Hebrews) to conclude that Paul's letters, Hebrews, First Peter and Paul shared access to stock tradition (cf. related idea in 2 Cor 5:14 and 1 Tim 2:5–6).[134] However, of one hundred and ninety-six hits *Thesaurus Linguae Graecae* produces in a search for ἐφάπαξ, only two occurrences

---

[129] ἔπειτα ὤφθη ἐπάνω πεντακοσίοις ἀδελφοῖς ἐφάπαξ, ἐξ ὧν οἱ πλείονες μένουσιν ἕως ἄρτι, τινὲς δὲ ἐκοιμήθησαν.

[130] ἐφάπαξ in Heb 10:10 has special emphasis as the last word in the sentence.

[131] Although used in the same sense as ἐφάπαξ, ἅπαξ in Heb 6:4; 9:26, 27, 28; 10:2; 12:26, 27 (cf. 9:7) occurs before the verb. See B. F. Westcott, *The Epistle to the Hebrews* (London: Macmillan, 1892; repr. Grand Rapids, Mich.: Eerdmans, 1980), 197.

[132] Christ's appearance once in 1 Cor 15:6: ἔπειτα ὤφθη ἐπάνω πεντακοσίοις ἀδελφοῖς ἐφάπαξ, ἐξ ὧν οἱ πλείονες μένουσιν ἕως ἄρτι, τινὲς δὲ ἐκοιμήθησαν may imply that readers of Hebrews were intended to hear its echo as well.

[133] E.g., W. L. Lane, *Hebrews 1–8* (WBC 47A; Dallas, Tex.: Word, 1991), 193.

[134] Only Attridge explicitly states this point (*Hebrews* [see n. 28], 214 n. 121), the others simply note the comparison: Koester, *Hebrews* (see n. 65), 368; Ellingworth, *The Epistle to the Hebrews* (see n. 83), 394–96; Lane, ibid., 193; Westcott, *The Epistle to the Hebrews* (see n. 131), 197 (cf. 148); F. W. Farrar, *The Epistle of Paul the Apostle to the Hebrews, with Notes and Introduction* (London: Cambridge University Press, 1888), 104. 1 Pet 3:18: ὅτι καὶ Χριστὸς ἅπαξ περὶ ἁμαρτιῶν ἔπαθεν, δίκαιος ὑπὲρ ἀδίκων, ἵνα ὑμᾶς προσαγάγῃ τῷ θεῷ. Paul Achtemeier notes Rom 6:10 in a footnote (*1 Peter* [see n. 71], 247 n. 80).

predate Paul's letters: (1) the Athenian poet, Eupolis's (ca. 446–411 BCE) Comicorum Atticorum fragmenta (TKock 175)[135] and (2) Aristophanes of Byzantium's (ca. 257–185/180 BCE,[136] successor to Eratosthenes as head of the Library of Alexandria) *Aristophanis historiae animalium epitome subjunctis Aeliani Timothei aliorumque eclogis*, a work based on the Περὶ Ζῴων studies by Aristotle, Theophrastus and the Paradoxographers.[137] Numerous subsequent occurrences in late antique writings (excluding Dio [ca. 155 or 163/164 to after 229] who also uses this word)[138] cite or allude to the NT.[139] The likelihood, therefore, that the tradition of Jesus' ἐφάπαξ death in Hebrews originated in Romans is very high.[140]

---

[135] This fragment possesses only the single word ἐφάπαξ. Cf. 174: λευκὴ ἡμέρα and 176: περίστατοι.

[136] Aristophanes of Byzantium 2.439.3: πτητικῶν ζῳοτόκον. τίκτει γὰρ σκυμνία, καὶ ταῦτα θηλάζει ἅμα πετομένη, ὑπὸ τὰς μασχάλας αὐτὰ ἔχουσα. τίκτει δὲ δύο ἐφάπαξ καὶ τρία· λέγεται δὲ καὶ τετριχῶσθαι μικροῖς καὶ δυσθεωρήτοις τριχιδίοις.

[137] *OCD*: 165. ἐφάπαξ is stronger form of ἅπαξ (cf. Heb 6:4); ἐπί + ἅπαξ. However, LSJ and BDAG note only *Eupolis* 175, Romans and First Corinthians. G. Stählin in *TDNT* treats only NT texts. Cf. also *TLNT* 1:139–42. J. Fitzmyer does not mention occurrences (*Romans* [see n. 23], 438). R. Jewett argues that Stählin's view of ἐφάπαξ as a "technical term for the definitiveness and therefore the uniqueness or singularity of the death of Christ and the redemption thereby accomplished" in Rom 6:10 is unwarranted. Jewett thinks that the term only acquires its technical sense in Hebrews. With C. Spicq, Jewett understands ἐφάπαξ as a simple synonym of ἅπαξ, offering only parallel use of the word in Pseudo-Lucian *Encom. Demosth.* 18.6 (*Romans* [see n. 43], 407 esp. n. 182). Also, G. Abbott-Smith, *A Manual Greek Lexicon of the New Testament* has only Eupolis, Romans, First Corinthians and Hebrews. BAG (1957) uses an asterisk at the end of the entry to denote that its references for both the first meaning: "at once, at one time," 1 Cor 15:6, P.Lond. 483,88; 1708,242; P.Flor. 158,10 and the second meaning: "once for all" Eupolis; Rom 6:10, Heb 7:27, 9:12, 10:10 represent all of the passages in which the word occurs (p. xxvii). E. Hatch and H. A. Redpath, *A Concordance to the Septuagint and the Other Greek Versions of the Old Testament (Including the Apocryphal Books)* has no entry for ἐφάπαξ, although ἅπαξ is attested in the LXX, e.g., Gen 18:32, Exod 30:10, Lev 16:34 and Num 16:21. *A Patristic Greek Lexicon* (20th ed.; ed. G. W. H. Lampe, 2007) also has no entry (see explanation vis-à-vis LSJ on p. vii).

[138] Dio Cassius, *Hist. Rom.* 66.17.15.5; 69.2.3; S211.4; S246. Robert Jewett notes these parallels (*Romans* [see n. 43], 407 n. 181).

[139] Eusebius, *Hist. eccl.* 1.12.4 cites 1 Cor 15:6; Origen: 11 occurrences; Basil of Caesarea: 7 occurrences; John Chrysostom: 13 occurrences; John of Damascus: 7 occurrences; Photius: 10 occurrences; Theodoret: 7 occurrences; Cyril of Alexandria: 13 occurrences.

[140] Albert Edward Barnett came to the same conclusion: "ἐφάπαξ is used in the New Testament in Rom 6:10, 1 Cor 15:6 and Heb 7:27, 9:12, 10:10. Its meaning in Hebrews is in exact agreement with its use in Romans, denoting something that is final in the sense of not being repeated. Its application in 10:10 to the sacrifice of Christ makes dependence on Romans particularly probable" ("The Use of the Letters of Paul in Pre-Catholic Christian Literature" [PhD diss., University of Chicago, 1932], 100). Barnett rates the

Even more significant than correspondence of the word ἐφάπαξ in Hebrews and Romans is prominence of the theme it signifies in Hebrews. Montefiore refers to the "once for all" theme signified by ἐφάπαξ and ἅπαξ in Hebrews as one of the "key concepts of the Epistle."[141] Westcott refers to ἅπαξ as "characteristic of the Epistle."[142] Recently, James W. Thompson devoted an entire article to this concept in Hebrews.[143] Thompson not only refers to "once-for-all" as a "consistent feature of the argument of Hebrews"[144] but further underscores its importance as follows:

> The importance of this focus on the 'once for all' quality of the Christ event is evident in the fact that the term [ἅπαξ or ἐφάπαξ] is used more in Hebrews than in all other New Testament books combined ... This contrast between the one and the many is a distinctive feature of Hebrews.[145]

Absence of prior occurrences of the word ἐφάπαξ before Romans *with* prominence of the theme it signifies in Hebrews suggest that a primary motivation for the composition of Hebrews was to explain and develop the enthymeme in Rom 6:10.[146]

3.6.5 The Nature of πίστις

Finally, the concept of πίστις is largely taken for granted by Paul in Rom 3. Yet it is expounded at length in Hebrews. If we accept Harold Attridge's structure of Hebrews dividing the text into five parts: (1) "Christ is exalted" (1:5–2:18); (2) Christ is *faithful* (3:1–5:10); (3) "difficult discourse," Christ's role as high priest and his sacrificial act (5:11–10:25); (4) "exhortation to *faithful* endurance" (10:26–12:13); and (5) "concluding exhortations" (12:14–13:21), then we observe that both the second and fourth sections, (that is, the two outer sections into which the homily on Christ's role as high priest and sacrificial act are intercalated) treat faith.[147] To an even greater extent than Paul's claim that Christ is ἱλαστήριον in Rom 3:25, the meaning of πίστις in Romans is a source of debate. Of particular importance for the present argument is its occurrence in the phrase διὰ πίστεως in Rom 3:25. As Robert Jewett explains:

---

comparison with a "B" = "high degree of probability" on scale for evaluating literary reliance of pre-Catholic Christian literature on Paul's epistles (2–3).

[141] *Epistle to the Hebrews* (see n. 86), 131.
[142] Ibid., 148.
[143] "*EPHAPAX*: The One and the Many in Hebrews" (see n. 127), 566–81.
[144] Ibid., 566.
[145] Ibid., 567.
[146] In Romans, Paul extends the application of the enthymeme to believers. See Jewett, *Romans* (see n. 43), 407.
[147] Attridge, *Hebrews* (see n. 28), 19.

Paul's view of the effectiveness of the blood of Christ is visible in his addition of διὰ πίστεως ("through faith"), an expression that is "singular in the New Testament" because nowhere else do we find faith "in the blood" or even followed by the preposition ἐν ("in") itself. There are distant parallels elsewhere to an association between faith and atonement or blood, but none that fully clarifies this verse.[148]

Accepting what he refers to as "strange wording" as Paul's redactional insertion into a prior confessional statement, Jewett understands the phrase as emphasizing "that access to this new institution of atonement through the blood of Christ was available to everyone through faith."[149] Whether Jewett represents Paul's original intention or not, many late antique Pauline interpreters struggled with the meaning of this passage. The first such interpreter may have written Hebrews. Once again, it seems that criticality coupled with ambiguity in Romans demanded context. Interestingly, Hebrews's exegetical homily on Christ's sacrificial act (5:11–10:25)—the heart of this text—concludes with a passage offering a few important similarities to Rom 3:25. Not only is the phrase ἐν τῷ αἵματι Ἰησοῦ (Heb 10:19) parallel to ἐν τῷ αὐτοῦ αἵματι (Rom 3:25), but as in Romans, Hebrews claims with this expression that *faith* makes available such an atonement through Jesus' blood. Specifically, v. 19 states: "since we have boldness (παρρησία) to enter the sanctuary by the blood of Jesus." Although the phrase is deliberately enigmatic insofar as it utilizes a metaphor of entering the sanctuary to describe salvation, the meaning of παρρησία is clarified by comparison to its next occurrence in the text. It is not so much, as one might expect, empowerment to approach God,[150] but 'faith' as in v. 35 (word creates an *inclusio* with v. 35):[151] "Do not, therefore, abandon that confidence (παρρησία) of yours; it brings a great reward (μισθαποδοσία)." Subsequently Hebrews clarifies that only πίστις brings reward: "And without faith it is impossible to please God, for whoever would approach him must believe that he exists and that he rewards (μισθαποδότης γίνεται) those who seek him" (11:6, cf. also 11:24–26). These passages imply that commentators are correct to interpret παρρησία in v. 19 as synonymous with πίστις. Although he takes synonymity to be overstatement, Harold Attridge agrees that the three virtues are congruent: "The series of paraenetic remarks that conclude the chapter feature three

---

[148] Jewett, *Romans* (see n. 43), 287–88.
[149] Both citations ibid., 288.
[150] So Attridge, *Hebrews* (see n. 28), 285.
[151] So ibid., 284 n. 13.

closely related items, 'boldness' (παρρησία), 'endurance' (ὑπομονή) and 'faith' (πίστις)."[152]

The symmetry of the period further helps to clarify the meaning of its individual parts.

[19] Therefore, my friends,

    A. *since* we have *confidence/boldness* (παρρησία)[153]

        a. *in* the *blood* of Jesus,

            i.[20] [that is] in the *new and living way that he opened for us through the curtain (that is, through his flesh),*

        to enter the sanctuary

[SACRIFICE]

    B. [21]and *since* we have *a great priest over the house of God,*

[SACRIFICER]

I. [22]*let us approach*

    1. with a true heart in an abundance of faith,
    2. [namely] with our hearts sprinkled clean from an evil conscience [BLOOD]
    3. and our bodies washed with pure water. [WATER]

II. [23]*Let us hold fast* to the confession of our hope without wavering, for he who has promised is faithful.

III. [24]*And let us consider* how to provoke one another to love and good deeds,

    1. [25] not neglecting to meet together, as is the habit of some,
    2. but encouraging one another, and all the more as you see the Day approaching.

This schematic representation of the complex Greek period extending from Heb 10:19–22 shows that *boldness* or *confidence in blood* equals the abundance of faith necessary to 'enter the sanctuary,' that is, to persist unto the point ('day') of salvation.

Hence, Heb 10:19 is closely related to Rom 3:24, arguably more closely related than any other NT passage. The only difference between the two texts is that in Hebrews, atonement is construed metaphorically as "confidence to enter the sanctuary" and insists it is available, not to everyone through faith, but to everyone who sustains faith. Anyone willfully persisting in sin after having received knowledge of the truth is, according to Hebrews (10:26–31), excluded from the full assurance of faith. Hebrews,

---

[152] Erich Gräßer sees the three expressions even more closely related than Attridge (E. Gräßer, *Der Glaube im Hebräerbrief* [Marburger Theologische Studien 2; Marburg: Elwert, 1965], 42; Attridge, *Hebrews* [see n. 28], 300 and 300 n. 47).

[153] παρρησία has both a subjective and objective aspect. See H. Schlier, "παρρησία," *TDNT* 5:871–76. Cf. Heb 3:6; 4:16; 10:19, 35.

thus, seems to reflect an interpretation of Rom 3 for a context of apostasy perhaps the result of persecution.

Of final interest is the well-known problem in Rom 3:26 of whether to read ἐκ πίστεως Ἰησοῦ as subjective or objective genitive. Concerning this problem, Carl R. Holladay draws a comparison with Hebrews:

> The understanding of Jesus' faith in Hebrews is a more fully developed understanding of what many scholars now understand Pauline 'faith of Christ' to mean—the absolute fidelity of Christ to the will of God and its fully exemplary character for other believers.[154]

Thomas H. Olbricht rightly picks up on the potential problem suggested by Holladay's statement of "whether Paul ever refers to the faith of Jesus, or only to faith in Jesus."[155] I wish to reply to Olbricht that, for Hebrews, the issue is not whether Paul ever refers to the faith of or in Jesus, but whether the author of Hebrews might have read Paul (specifically Rom 3:26) in one of these ways. In the end I agree with Holladay completely that Hebrews develops the distinctly Pauline "faith of Christ."

4. Conclusion

This essay attempts to add Hebrews to a growing list of early Christian writings understood as guides to early Pauline letter collections. Hebrews, although probably informed by other letters of Paul as well as by Acts, offered to readers of an early *corpus Paulinum* context, clarification and/or development of key ideas in Romans. Its author regarded several areas of Romans as requiring elaboration and/or correction and thus furnishes a tool designed to impact its interpretation. Hebrews signals its aim of expounding Romans not only in its use of vocabulary, stylistic features and scriptural citations distinctive to that letter but by imitating exegetical maneuvers in Romans including topical links brought forward by Paul from the same texts, for example "faith" in the Abraham cycle, "life" and "salvation" in Hab 2:4 and Christ as "mercy seat." Moreover, Hebrews offers a dramatic expansion of the exquisitely terse, memorable enthymeme in Rom 6:10 that puts forth the once-for-all sacrifice of Jesus. Additionally, it provides context for Paul's solution to the pan-indictment of humanity for sin through a sophisticated exposition of the Jewish cultic system, showing how Jesus' death satisfies an ultimate interpretation of its long-held de-

---

[154] *A Critical Introduction to the New Testament: Interpreting the Message and Meaning of Jesus Christ* (Nashville: Abingdon, 2005), 463.

[155] "The Faith [Faithfulness] of Jesus in Hebrews," in *Renewing Tradition: Studies in Texts and Contexts in Honor of James W. Thompson* (eds. M. H. Hamilton, T. H. Olbricht and J. Peterson; Eugene, Oreg.: Pickwick Publications, 2007), 116–32 (116).

mands. The horizon of both books is related: (1) "son"—Rom 1, Heb 1–3; (2) Jesus as propitiation/"mercy seat"—Rom 2, Heb 7–10; (3) ἐφάπαξ sacrifice—Rom 6, Heb 7, 9, 10; (4) faith—Rom 3:25–26 *et al*, Heb 11 *et al*;[156] (5) moral exhortation—Rom 12–15, Heb 13; (6) postscript—Rom 15, 16, Heb 13:20–25. Although influenced by Pauline theology, both the development of and new context for interpreting Romans represent the views of an otherwise unknown second-century author. "Paul as prisoner" offered an ideal scenario for extending his letter collection.

Of course this is not the only aim of Hebrews. Even as a guide to reading Romans, Hebrews presents ideas lying outside the purview of Romans. Naturally also many ideas in Romans do not occur in Hebrews.[157] Nevertheless, sufficient evidence supports the claim that one overarching purpose of Hebrews was to guide early readers of Romans; and, Hebrews offers a guide for modern readers of Romans too—those wishing to learn ways in which Paul's letter was first read.

---

[156] Heb 4:2; 6:12; 10:22, 39; 12:2; 13:7.

[157] Paul's expression εὐαγγέλιον (e.g., Rom 1:1, 9, 16; 2:16; 10:16; 11:28; 15:16, 19, 25, 29; εὐαγγελίζειν: Rom 1:15, 10:15, 15:20), for example, never arises in Hebrews. Cf. εὐαγγελίζειν: Heb 4:2, 6.

„Jakobus, der Gerechte"

Erwägungen zur Verfasserfiktion des Jakobusbriefes

von

MATTHIAS KONRADT

Es besteht ein breiter Konsens, dass für die Identifikation der in der *superscriptio* in Jak 1,1 genannten Person von den im Neuen Testament genannten Personen mit Namen Jakobus nur der Bruder Jesu[1] in Frage kommt.[2] Dass der Jakobusbrief aber tatsächlich vom Bruder Jesu stammt, wird in der kritischen Forschung zumeist verneint.[3] Stimmen, die den Brief

---

[1] Zum Herrenbruder s. vor allem die monographischen Studien von W. PRATSCHER, Der Herrenbruder Jakobus und die Jakobustradition, FRLANT 139, Göttingen 1987, und J. PAINTER, Just James. The Brother of Jesus in History and Tradition, Studies on Personalities of the New Testament, Columbia ²1998, ferner den Sammelband B. Chilton / C. A. Evans (Hg.), James the Just and Christian Origins, NT.S 98, Leiden 1999. Für eine Skizze meiner eigenen Sicht s. M. KONRADT, Der Jakobusbrief als Brief des Jakobus. Erwägungen zum historischen Kontext des Jakobusbriefes im Lichte der traditionsgeschichtlichen Beziehungen zum 1 Petr und zum Hintergrund der Autorfiktion, in: P. von Gemünden / M. Konradt / G. Theißen (Hg.), Der Jakobusbrief. Beiträge zur Rehabilitierung der „strohernen Epistel", Beiträge zum Verstehen der Bibel 3, Münster 2003, 16–53 (30–39). – Für Hilfe danke ich Esther Schläpfer.

[2] Siehe exemplarisch M. DIBELIUS, Der Brief des Jakobus, mit Ergänzungen von H. Greeven, mit einem Literaturverzeichnis und Nachtrag hg. v. F. Hahn, KEK 15, Göttingen ¹²[⁶]1984, 24: „Es hat ... nach unsern Quellen im Urchristentum nur *einen* Mann von Ansehn [sic] gegeben, an den bei einer solcher [sic] Einführung des Namens, wie sie in unserm Präskript vorliegt, gedacht werden kann; das ist *Jakobus, der Bruder Jesu.*"

[3] Siehe z.B. J. H. ROPES, A Critical and Exegetical Commentary on the Epistle of St. James, ICC, Edinburgh 1916 (Nachdruck 1991), 48–51; DIBELIUS, a.a.O. 23–35; S. LAWS, A Commentary on the Epistle of James, BNTC, London 1980, 40f.; F. SCHNIDER, Der Jakobusbrief, RNT, Regensburg 1987, 16f.; H. FRANKEMÖLLE, Der Brief des Jakobus. Kapitel 1, ÖTBK 17/1, Gütersloh u.a. 1994, 45–54; M. KLEIN, „Ein vollkommenes Werk". Vollkommenheit, Gesetz und Gericht als theologische Themen des Jakobusbriefes, BWANT 139, Stuttgart u.a. 1995, 206f.; M. TSUJI, Glaube zwischen Vollkommenheit und Verweltlichung. Eine Untersuchung zur literarischen Gestalt und zur inhaltlichen Kohärenz des Jakobusbriefes, WUNT II/93, Tübingen 1997, 38–44; H.-J. KLAUCK, Die antike Briefliteratur und das Neue Testament. Ein Lehr- und Arbeitsbuch, UTB 2022, Paderborn u.a. 1998, 254f.; C. BURCHARD, Der Jakobusbrief, HNT 15/I, Tübingen 2000,

für echt halten, sind gleichwohl bis in die gegenwärtige Forschung hinein keineswegs verstummt.[4] Ich werde im Folgenden in einem ersten Schritt die Argumente, die gegen die Autorschaft des Herrenbruders vorgetragen wurden, kritisch sichten. Die Indizien sprechen m.E. in der Summe dafür, dass es sich beim Jak um ein Pseudepigraphon handelt, auch wenn einzuräumen ist, dass das eine oder andere der traditionell für die Pseudepigraphiethese vorgebrachten Argumente zumindest für sich genommen nicht zwingend ist, sondern eher eine Wahrscheinlichkeitstendenz anzeigt. Wer Pseudepigraphie vertritt, kann bei der Bestreitung der Echtheit aber nicht stehen bleiben. Vielmehr ist in einem zweiten Schritt plausibel zu machen, warum der tatsächliche Autor den Brief ausgerechnet unter die Autorität des Jakobus gestellt hat.[5]

1. Der Jak als Pseudepigraphon

1.1 Überblickt man die Argumente, die gegen die Abfassung des Jak durch den Herrenbruder geltend gemacht wurden, ist, wie angedeutet, gegenüber Vertretern der Echtheit zu konzedieren, dass keineswegs alle vorgebrachten Indizien in gleicher Weise zu überzeugen vermögen. So lässt sich die Beobachtung, dass im Jak „typische Probleme der 2.–3. Generation ... sichtbar [werden]: Nachlassen der Spannkraft und der Tätigkeit des Glaubens, Welt-Zugewandtheit, Wohlstand und Prestigedenken, soziale

---

3–6; W. POPKES, Der Brief des Jakobus, ThHK 14, Leipzig 2001, 64–69; I. BROER, Einleitung in das Neue Testament, Bd. II: Die Briefliteratur, die Offenbarung des Johannes und die Bildung des Kanons, NEB.AT Erg. 2/II, Würzburg 2001, 598–602; U. SCHNELLE, Einleitung in das Neue Testament, Göttingen [4]2002, 430–434; D. R. NIENHUIS, Not by Paul Alone. The Formation of the Catholic Epistle Collection and the Christian Canon, Waco 2007, bes. 110–118.

[4] Siehe F. MUSSNER, Der Jakobusbrief, HThK.NT XIII/1, Freiburg i. Brsg. u.a. [5]1987, 1–8; M. HENGEL, Der Jakobusbrief als antipaulinische Polemik, in: G. F. Hawthorne / O. Betz (Hg.), Tradition and Interpretation in the New Testament (FS Ellis), Grand Rapids u.a. 1987, 248–278; J. B. ADAMSON, James. The Man and His Message, Grand Rapids 1989, 3–52; L. T. JOHNSON, The Letter of James. A New Translation with Introduction and Commentary, AncB 37A, New York u.a. 1995, bes. 118–121; D. J. MOO, The Letter of James, The Pillar New Testament Commentary, Grand Rapids u.a. 2000, 9–22; siehe ferner auch P. J. HARTIN, James, Sacra Pagina Series 14, Collegeville 2003, 24f. K.-W. NIEBUHR, Der Jakobusbrief im Licht frühjüdischer Diasporabriefe, NTS 44 (1998), 420–443, hält die Verfasserfrage für „weiterhin offen" (431).

[5] Vgl. G. THEISSEN, Die pseudepigraphe Intention des Jakobusbriefes. Ein Beitrag zu seinen Einleitungsfragen, in: von Gemünden / Konradt / Theißen, Jakobusbrief (s. Anm. 1), 54–82 (54): „Bei der Erforschung neutestamentlicher Pseudepigraphie kann man zwei Fragen unterscheiden: die Echtheitsfrage, die klärt, *ob* Pseudepigraphie vorliegt, und die Interpretationsfrage, die erklärt, *warum* ein pseudepigrapher Name gewählt wurde."

Unterschiede, Gruppenegoismus"[6], schwerlich als ein tragfähiges Indiz geltend machen. Denn der Befund, dass solche Probleme für die zweite bis dritte Generation des entstehenden Christentums typisch gewesen sein mögen, besagt nicht, dass sie exklusiv erst zu dieser Zeit vorkamen, so dass zumindest kein zwingendes Ausschlusskriterium für eine frühere Ansetzung gegeben ist.[7]

1.2 Im Jak fehlen Beschneidung, Sabbat und Reinheitsgebote, also klassische jüdische Identitätsmerkmale. Dagegen wird dem Herrenbruder aufgrund von Gal 2,1–14; Apg 15 zugeschrieben, er habe „im frühen Urchristentum für die Ritualgebote wie Beschneidung, Speisegebote, Sabbatheiligung und die Abgrenzung vom Götzendienst"[8] gestritten, was gegen die Abfassung des Briefes durch Jakobus spreche.[9] Ein zwingendes Argument ist aber auch hier nicht gegeben,[10] denn für sichere Rückschlüsse aus den Leerstellen des Briefes ist dieser zu kurz. Zu bedenken ist ferner die offene Adresse, die Heidenchristen einschließen dürfte (vgl. unten 1.5).[11] Die Beschneidung hat Jakobus nach Gal 2,1–10; Apg 15 von ihnen nicht verlangt, und im Blick auf Speisefragen hat Jakobus nicht mehr erwartet als das im Apostedekret (Apg 15,20.29) Geforderte.[12] Christoph Burchard hat daher mit Recht geltend gemacht, dass man „gerade vom Herrenbruder nicht zu erwarten [braucht], daß er anders als Jak auf Beschneidung, Speisegebote, Sabbat u.a. drängte, wenn er an Heidenchristen schrieb".[13]

---

[6] POPKES, Brief (s. Anm. 3), 43.

[7] Treffend K.-W. NIEBUHR, „A New Perspective on James"? Neuere Forschungen zum Jakobusbrief, ThLZ 129 (2004), 1019–1044: „Es wäre ... unschwer möglich, all die aufgezählten Probleme auch mit Stellen z.B. aus dem 1. Thessalonicherbrief oder den Korintherbriefen des Paulus zu belegen" (1024).

[8] THEISSEN, Intention (s. Anm. 5), 55.

[9] Siehe z.B. DIBELIUS, Brief (s. Anm. 2), 31f.; PRATSCHER, Herrenbruder (s. Anm. 1), 211f.; FRANKEMÖLLE, Brief (s. Anm. 3), 53f.; TSUJI, Glaube (s. Anm. 3), 42; BROER, Einleitung (s. Anm. 3), 602; THEISSEN, ebd.; NIENHUIS, Paul (s. Anm. 3), 111f. Für eine kritische Zurückweisung dieses Arguments s. MOO, Letter (s. Anm. 4), 15–18.

[10] THEISSEN, ebd., wertet das Argument hingegen als eines von zwei „ausschlaggebende[n]" Argumenten für Pseudepigraphie.

[11] Für Heidenchristen im Adressatenkreis s. C. BURCHARD, Nächstenliebegebot, Dekalog und Gesetz in Jak 2,8–11, in: E. Blum / C. Macholz / E. W. Stegemann (Hg.), Die Hebräische Bibel und ihre zweifache Nachgeschichte (FS Rendtorff), Neukirchen-Vluyn 1990, 517–533 (531); KLEIN, Werk (s. Anm. 3), 206f.; M. KONRADT, Christliche Existenz nach dem Jakobusbrief. Eine Studie zu seiner soteriologischen und ethischen Konzeption, StUNT 22, Göttingen 1998, 332f.

[12] Zu ihrem Zusammenhang mit Jakobus s. unter 1.5.

[13] BURCHARD, Jakobusbrief (s. Anm. 3), 4.

1.3 Großes Gewicht ist im Rahmen der Pseudepigraphiethese häufig dem Argument beigemessen worden, dass dem Galiläer Jakobus das rhetorisch gepflegte Griechisch des Briefes nicht zuzutrauen sei.[14] Vertreter der Echtheitsthese haben dagegen die weite Verbreitung der griechischen Sprache in Palästina im 1. Jh. n. Chr.[15] ins Feld geführt.[16] Unumstritten ist diese nicht.[17] Zu bedenken ist ferner, dass auch dann, wenn man von einer weiten Verbreitung griechischer Sprache ausgeht, es gleichwohl fraglich bleibt, dass einem galiläischen Handwerkersohn das rhetorische und sprachliche Niveau des Jak zuzutrauen sei. Man kann darauf zwar wiederum entgegnen, dass hinter Jakobus, wenn der Brief in seine letzten Lebensjahre fällt, mehrere Jahrzehnte lagen, in denen er eine leitende Funktion in der Jerusalemer Gemeinde innehatte und er einen bilingualen Bildungsschub erlebt haben mag. Aber auch in diesem Fall bleibt es mehr als fraglich, ob dies das literarische Niveau des Briefes adäquat zu erklären vermag. Oder anders: Es liegt wesentlich näher, im Verfasser einen Muttersprachler zu sehen.[18]

---

[14] Siehe z.B. DIBELIUS, Brief (s. Anm. 2), 31; PRATSCHER, Herrenbruder (s. Anm. 1), 210f.; SCHNIDER, Jakobusbrief (s. Anm. 3), 16; FRANKEMÖLLE, Brief des Jakobus (s. Anm. 3), 52f.; THEISSEN, Intention (s. Anm. 5), 55; TSUJI, Glaube (s. Anm. 3), 41f.; BROER, Einleitung (s. Anm. 3), 601; NIENHUIS, Paul (s. Anm. 3), 110f.

[15] Zur Verbreitung der griechischen Sprache s. J. N. SEVENSTER, Do You Know Greek? How Much Greek Could the First Jewish Christians Have Known?, NT.S 19, Leiden 1968; M. HENGEL, Judentum und Hellenismus. Studien zu ihrer Begegnung unter besonderer Berücksichtigung Palästinas bis zur Mitte des 2. Jh.s v. Chr., WUNT 10, Tübingen ³1988, 108–114; ders. (unter Mitarbeit v. C. Markschies), The ‚Hellenization' of Judaea in the First Century after Christ, London u.a. 1989, 7–18.

[16] Siehe vor allem HENGEL, Polemik (s. Anm. 4), 251; JOHNSON, Letter (s. Anm. 4), 116–118; T. C. PENNER, The Epistle of James and Eschatology. Re-reading an Ancient Christian Letter, JSNT.S 121, Sheffield 1996, 35–47; MOO, Letter (s. Anm. 4), 14f.; HARTIN, James (s. Anm. 4), 22–24. Das Sprachargument wird zuweilen aber auch von Vertretern der Pseudepigraphiethese als nicht stichhaltig bewertet. Siehe z.B. SCHNELLE, Einleitung (s. Anm. 3), 431, oder LAWS, Commentary (s. Anm. 3), 40: „It is certainly no longer possible to assert with complete confidence that James of Jerusalem could not have written the good Greek of the epistle, since the wide currency of that language in Palestine is increasingly appreciated."

[17] Siehe L. H. FELDMAN, Jew and Gentile in the Ancient World. Attitudes and Interactions from Alexander to Justinian, Princeton 1993, 19: „Josephus's admission (*Against Apion* 1.50) that he needed assistants in composing the version in Greek of the *Jewish War* illustrates that few attained the competence in the language necessary for reading and understanding Greek literature."

[18] Ebenso z.B. DIBELIUS, Brief (s. Anm. 2), 31 („Unser Autor schreibt Griechisch als seine Muttersprache"); PRATSCHER, Herrenbruder (s. Anm. 1), 211; TSUJI, Glaube (s. Anm. 3), 42; NIENHUIS, Paul (s. Anm. 3), 110.

Andere haben vorgebracht, dass Jakobus sich eines Sekretärs[19] oder Übersetzers[20] bedient haben könnte. Hinweise darauf gibt es im Brief freilich nicht. Der Jak zeigt keine Spuren eines Übersetzungsgriechisch. Zudem sprechen die im Jak rezipierten Traditionen dezidiert gegen die These einer Übersetzung. Insbesondere im Falle von Jak 1,2f. (vgl. 1Petr 1,6f.; Röm 5,3–5)[21] lässt sich nicht bestreiten, dass die vom Verfasser rezipierte Tradition in griechischer Sprache umlief, denn Jak 1,2f. berührt sich mit 1Petr 1,6f. nicht nur in der Verwendung von πειρασμοὶ ποικίλοι, sondern auch in der Wendung τὸ δοκίμιον ὑμῶν τῆς πίστεως, die in der gesamten antiken Literatur nur an den genannten beiden Stellen begegnet. Liefen im Brief rezipierte Traditionen in griechischer Sprachgestalt um, liegt es zugleich aber überhaupt näher, an ein Entstehungsgebiet zu denken, in dem Griechisch selbstverständlich Verkehrssprache war. Dem sprachlichen Befund ist also zumal dann, wenn man den Verweis auf das gepflegte Griechisch des Briefes um die Sprachgestalt der rezipierten Tradition erweitert, durchaus ein Hinweis auf die Abfassung des Briefes in der griechischsprachigen Diaspora zu entnehmen.

1.4 Das Gedankengut des Jak ist stark hellenistisch geprägt. So steht die jak ἐπιθυμία-Konzeption, nach der die ἐπιθυμία als *der* Quellgrund menschlicher Sünden erscheint (Jak 1,14f.),[22] traditionsgeschichtlich im Zusammenhang einer von hellenistischer Philosophie beeinflussten Entwicklung im hellenistischen Judentum,[23] wie exemplarisch die Darstellung

---

[19] Siehe z.B. HENGEL, Hellenization (s. Anm. 15), 17; HARTIN, James (s. Anm. 4), 24. MUSSNER, Jakobusbrief (s. Anm. 4), 8, rechnet mit der Möglichkeit, dass „das sprachliche und stilistische Kleid des Briefes von einem griechisch sprechenden Mitarbeiter" stammt, will diese Annahme aber von der Sekretärsthese unterschieden wissen. Kritisch zur Plausibilität der Sekretärshypothese z.B. SEVENSTER, Greek (s. Anm. 15), 10–14.

[20] Nach NIEBUHR, Diasporabriefe (s. Anm. 4), 431, bleibt „die Möglichkeit, daß ein für die Gemeinden in der Diaspora bestimmtes Schreiben des Herrnbruders in Jerusalem *übersetzt* worden ist, ... durchaus plausibel".

[21] Zur Analyse der Tradition s. KONRADT, Existenz (s. Anm. 11), 101–109.

[22] Zur Interpretation von Jak 1,14f. s. a.a.O. 85–92.

[23] Man kann hier zwar auch auf eine Affinität zwischen der jak ἐπιθυμία-Konzeption und der rabbinischen Lehre vom bösen Trieb verweisen, doch lässt sich diese nicht aus jener oder aus einer Vorform der rabbinischen יצר-Lehre ableiten (s. dazu KONRADT, a.a.O. 90–92; anders z.B. J. MARCUS, The Evil Inclination in the Epistle of James, CBQ 44 [1982], 606–621; P. H. DAVIDS, Themes in the Epistle of James that are Judaistic in Character, Diss. masch., Manchester 1974, 1–93). Insbesondere ist hier zu bedenken, dass ἐπιθυμία in der Septuaginta einschließlich Jesus Sirach nie als Übersetzung von יצר begegnet.

der ἐπιθυμία als „Quelle aller Übel" im Rahmen der Interpretation des zehnten Dekaloggebots[24] in Philo spec. IV 84[25] zeigt.[26]

In 1,25; 2,12 bezeichnet der Verfasser das Gesetz als „Gesetz der Freiheit". Thematisch geht es hier darum, dass das Gesetz dem, der es annimmt und sich in dieses vertieft, Freiheit von der Begierde samt ihren Folgeerscheinungen Sünde und Tod vermittelt (1,14f.).[27] Die mit der Wendung „Gesetz der Freiheit" auf den Punkt gebrachte positive Allianz von Gesetz und Freiheit verweist wieder auf hellenistischen, hier speziell stoischen Einfluss,[28] der über das hellenistische Judentum vermittelt ist, wie Philos Freiheitsschrift *Quod omnis probus liber sit* eindrücklich illustriert, wo es programmatisch heißt: ὅσοι ... μετὰ νόμου ζῶσιν, ἐλεύθεροι (prob. 45,

---

[24] Philo zitiert dieses in decal. 142 ohne Objekt! Vgl. Philo her. 173, sowie ferner 4Makk 2,6 und Röm 7,7; 13,9.

[25] Auch außerhalb der Auslegung des zehnten Gebots (decal. 142–153.173; spec. IV 79–131) ist die Begierde bei Philo in Bezug auf die gottwidrige Verhaltensweise von elementarer Bedeutung (s. nur post. 26f.; ebr. 223; spec. I 206), wobei er verschiedentlich auf die stoische Lehre von den vier Hauptaffekten ἐπιθυμία, ἡδονή, λύπη und φόβος (vgl. exemplarisch das Referat über die stoische Lehre von den πάθη bei Cicero, Tusculanae Disputationes 4,10–32) rekurriert (Philo LA III 113.250; det. 110; conf. 90; migr. 219; her. 269f.; congr. 172; mut. 72; Abr. 236.238; Jos. 79; Mos. II 139; decal. 142–145; spec. II 30; praem. 71; prob. 18 und öfter) oder die platonische Lehre von den drei Seelenteilen (λογικόν, θυμικόν, ἐπιθυμητικόν, s. exemplarisch Plato Tim. 69C–70A) aufnimmt (Philo LA I 70ff.; III 115ff.; conf. 21; migr. 67; spec. IV 92; virt. 13 und öfter).

[26] Zu beachten ist allerdings, dass die Begierde neben Philo noch in anderen frühjüdischen Schriften als Quellgrund der Sünde erscheint. ApkMos 19,3 erweitert Gen 3 unter anderem um das Motiv, dass die Schlange die Frucht, bevor sie sie Eva gab, mit „dem Gift ihrer Bosheit, das ist: der Begierde" kontaminierte und kommentiert dies mit den Worten: ἐπιθυμία γάρ ἐστι κεφαλὴ πάσης ἁμαρτίας. Nach ApkAbr 24,8 hält die Begierde „in ihrer Hand das Haupt jeder Gesetzlosigkeit". Nun geht der erhaltene slawische Text der ApkAbr auf eine griechische Vorlage zurück. In 24,8 dürfte in der griechischen Fassung ἐπιθυμία gestanden haben (s. dazu R. RUBINKIEWICZ, Apocalypse of Abraham, in: J. H. Charlesworth [Hg.], The Old Testament Pseudepigrapha, Bd. 1: Apocalyptic Literature and Testaments, New York u.a. 1983, 681–705 [701 Anm. h]). Die griechische Fassung wiederum dürfte auf einem hebräischen Original fußen (vgl. B. PHILONENKO-SAYAR / M. PHILONENKO, Die Apokalypse Abrahams, JSHRZ V/5, Gütersloh 1982, 417), so dass palästinische Herkunft naheliegt. Hebräisches Original und palästinische Herkunft sind auch für die ApkMos möglich (zurückhaltend zur Frage eines hebräischen Originals äußern sich O. MERK / M. MEISER, Das Leben Adams und Evas, JSHRZ II/5, Gütersloh 1998, 768). Hinreichend sichere Indizien für palästinische Parallelen zu Jak 1,14f. sind damit jedoch nicht gegeben, da man über den Wortlaut einer (etwaigen) hebräischen Vorlage für die genannten Texte nur spekulieren kann und die Rede von der ἐπιθυμία in den griechischen Fassungen auf hellenistischen Kultureinfluss am Ort der Übersetzung zurückgehen *kann*.

[27] Zu dieser Interpretation vgl. KONRADT, Existenz (s. Anm. 11), 92–99.

[28] Zu den einschlägigen Texten s. a.a.O. 94.

vgl. 62, ferner auch conf. 94).[29] Die Beispiele für die hellenistische Prägung des Jak ließen sich fortsetzen, etwa im Blick auf das Gottesbild des Jak, das Gott als den wesenhaft und unveränderlich Guten, der nicht zum Bösen versucht, zu verstehen lehrt (Jak 1,13.17).[30] Inwiefern man dem starken hellenistischen Kolorit des Jak Gewicht für die Herkunft des Briefes beimisst, hängt von der Einschätzung ab, wie stark die hellenistischen Einflüsse auf das Judentum Palästinas im 1. Jh. n. Chr. waren. Auch wenn man diese in einem erheblichen Umfang zu konzedieren bereit ist[31] und an einzelnen Punkten eine zeitgenössische Rezeption von im Jak begegnenden hellenistisch geprägten Motiven im Judentum Palästinas nachweisbar sein sollte,[32] ist allerdings wiederum zuzuspitzen, dass es nicht nur allgemein um die Frage des hellenistischen Kultureinflusses in Palästina im 1. Jh. n. Chr. geht, sondern spezieller darum, dem Herrenbruder Jakobus eine massive hellenistische Prägung zuzuschreiben. Es ist zu betonen: Ein sicheres Indiz ist hier nicht zu gewinnen, zumal aufgrund der Quellenlage nur sehr fragmentarische Kenntnisse über den Herrenbruder Jakobus zu gewinnen sind. Mit aller Vorsicht kann man das *starke* hellenistische Gepräge des Jak aber immerhin als ein Tendenzargument geltend machen: Dieses wird in einem diasporajüdischen Kontext leichter verständlich als bei der Annahme der Abfassung des Briefes durch den Bruder Jesu.

---

[29] Hinzuweisen ist aber auch auf ein Wort von Rabbi Jehoschua ben Levi in mAv 6,2, der in Ex 32,16: „und die Tafeln waren ein Werk Gottes, und die Schrift war Gottesschrift, eingegraben (חרות) auf die Tafeln" statt „*charut*" „*cherut*" gelesen haben möchte und damit begründet, dass es keinen Freien gebe „außer dem, der sich mit der Tora beschäftigt". Rabbi Jehoschua ben Levi gehört zur ersten Generation der Amoräer in *Palästina*. Geht das zitierte Diktum tatsächlich auf ihn zurück (zur Problematik s. K. MÜLLER, Zur Datierung rabbinischer Aussagen, in: H. Merklein [Hg.], Neues Testament und Ethik [FS Schnackenburg], Freiburg i. Brsg. u.a. 1989, 551–587), wäre die im Jak vorliegende Allianz von Gesetz und Freiheit auch für das palästinische Judentum belegt, wenn auch erst über ein Jahrhundert später (zur Möglichkeit, dass die Auslegung von Ex 32,16 älter ist, s. KONRADT, Existenz [s. Anm. 11], 94). Immerhin wird deutlich, dass Jakobus' Rede vom Gesetz der Freiheit zwar auf einen hellenistischen Kontext verweist, aber für sich genommen eine palästinische Herkunft des Briefes nicht zwingend ausschließt.

[30] Vgl. exemplarisch Sen.ep. 95,49: „Was ist für die Götter die Ursache, Wohltaten zu erweisen? Ihr Wesen. Es irrt, wenn einer meint, sie wollten nicht schaden: sie *können* es nicht. Weder können sie Unrecht erleiden noch tun …" (Übers. nach L. Annaeus Seneca, Philosophische Schriften. Lateinisch-deutsch, hg. v. Manfred Rosenbach, Bd. 4: Ad Lucilium Epistulae Morales LXX–CXXIV [CXXV], übers., eingel. u. m. Anm. vers. v. M. Rosenbach, Sonderausgabe, Darmstadt 1995, 493).

[31] Siehe auf der einen Seite vor allem HENGEL, Judentum (s. Anm. 15), während auf der anderen Seite FELDMAN, Jew (s. Anm. 17), 3–44, die Hellenisierung Palästinas zurückhaltender beurteilt.

[32] Siehe dazu oben Anm. 26 und Anm. 29.

1.5 Ein starkes Indiz für Pseudepigraphie ist m.E. dem Präskript zu entnehmen. Die Adressierung an die „zwölf Stämme" liest sich nämlich als ein schriftgelehrtes Namensspiel: „Zwölf Stämme" lässt an den Patriarchen Jakob denken (vgl. Gen 29f.; 35,16–26[33]), d.h. der Verfasser „spielt" mit einer assoziativen Verknüpfung des Namens Ἰάκωβος mit dem Stammvater Israels.[34] Eine solche Anspielung ist kaum dem Herrenbruder selbst zuzuweisen, zumal sie sich, wenn sie vom Herrenbruder stammte, hart mit dem im Brief prominenten Demutsmotiv (s. Jak 4,6–10) reiben würde.

Es kommt hinzu, dass der Jak eine rein binnenkirchliche Kommunikation ist, was entschieden dafür spricht, dass mit den „zwölf Stämmen" in der *adscriptio* nicht allgemein das jüdische Volk gemeint ist.[35] Sind aber Christen adressiert, kann man die übertragene Rede von den „zwölf Stämmen" nicht apriori auf Judenchristen begrenzen. Bereits Ropes hat treffend notiert: „No kind of early, or of ingenious, dating can bring us to a time when a writer addressing Jewish *Christians* in distinction from unbelieving Jews would have addressed them as ‚the twelve tribes,' if by the *term* he meant ‚the Jews'; and if the term is here used for ‚the People of God,' then the limitation to *Jewish* Christians is not contained in it."[36] Kurzum: Mit den „zwölf Stämmen in der Diaspora" in der *adscriptio* ist, wie die überwiegende Mehrheit der Ausleger zu Recht annimmt, metaphorisch die Gruppe der Christusgläubigen bezeichnet.[37] Das hier zutage tretende kirchliche Israelbewusstsein steht dabei nicht isoliert im Brief da. Vielmehr ist auch die Rede von der ἀπαρχή in Jak 1,18b als Übertragung von Israelselbstverständnis (vgl. Philo spec. IV 180) auf die Kirche zu lesen.[38] Abraham, „unser Vater" (2,21), ist nun Vater der Christen,[39] zu denen im Adressatenkreis des Briefes kaum allein Judenchristen zählen.[40]

Mit der ekklesiologischen Position des Herrenbruders dürfte die im Jak begegnende Übertragung von Israelbewusstsein auf die Kirche, ohne dass Israel noch im Blick zu sein scheint, schwerlich in Deckung zu bringen

---

[33] Siehe ferner Sir 44,23; 2Bar 78,4; 1Clem 31,4.
[34] Vgl. FRANKEMÖLLE, Brief (s. Anm. 3), 123–125.
[35] Anders z.B. J. B. ADAMSON, The Epistle of James, NIC, Grand Rapids ²1993, 49–51.
[36] ROPES, Commentary (s. Anm. 3), 127.
[37] Vgl. für viele BURCHARD, Jakobusbrief (s. Anm. 3), 50.
[38] Zur Deutung s. KONRADT, Existenz (s. Anm. 11), 59–66. – Wird man nach Jak 1,18 (erst) durch die Konversion zum christlichen Glauben zum Eigentum Gottes, ist damit die Sonderstellung Israels faktisch ausgeblendet.
[39] Vgl. BURCHARD, Jakobusbrief (s. Anm. 3), 126f.
[40] Siehe oben Anm. 11.

sein. Die offenbar schon in den frühen judäischen Gemeinden[41] erfolgte Verwendung von קהל / ἐκκλησία – genauer: von קהל אל / ἐκκλησία τοῦ θεοῦ (s. 1Kor 15,9; Gal 1,13; 1Thess 2,14) – als Selbstbezeichnung spiegelt nämlich keineswegs ein Selbstverständnis der Gemeinde als neues, eschatologisches Israel. Vielmehr kommt darin zum Ausdruck, dass die Jerusalemer Gemeinde „sich als das von Gott erwählte Aufgebot [wusste], das von ihm dazu bestimmt war, Mitte und Kristallisationspunkt des nun von ihm zu berufenden endzeitlichen Israel zu werden".[42]

Im Blick auf den Herrenbruder ist in diesem Zusammenhang ferner auf die Klauseln des Apostedekrets (Apg 15,20.29) hinzuweisen. Lukas verbindet sie mit Jakobus und dürfte damit den historischen Sachverhalt zutreffend abbilden,[43] nur gehören die Klauseln nicht, wie Lukas dies darstellt, in den Zusammenhang des Apostetreffens in Jerusalem, sondern sie waren, wie häufig und m.E. mit Recht angenommen wird, die Lösung des antiochenischen Zwischenfalls.[44] Die Forderungen der Enthaltung von

---

[41] Siehe dazu L. SCHENKE, Die Urgemeinde. Geschichtliche und theologische Entwicklung, Stuttgart u.a. 1990, 87; J. ROLOFF, Die Kirche im Neuen Testament, GNT 10, Göttingen 1993, 83–85.

[42] J. ROLOFF, Art. ἐκκλησία, EWNT I ²1992, 998–1011 (1001). Vgl. K. BERGER, Volksversammlung und Gemeinde Gottes. Zu den Anfängen der christlichen Verwendung von „ekklesia", ZThK 73 (1976), 167–207 (198): „Die Auffassung ist ohne Zweifel zunächst, daß durch Jesus der qahal bzw. die Ekklesia Gottes begründet ist, und zwar *in* Israel." Siehe auch a.a.O. 199: „Israel und seine Erwählung stehen jedenfalls nicht angesichts des Begriffes ‚Ekklesia Gottes' zur Debatte oder konkurrieren dieser gar."

[43] In diesem Sinn auch J. ROLOFF, Die Apostelgeschichte, NTD 5, Göttingen u.a. 18[2]1988, 227; M. HENGEL, Jakobus der Herrenbruder – der erste „Papst"?, in: E. Gräßer / O. Merk (Hg.), Glaube und Eschatologie (FS Kümmel), Tübingen 1985, 71–104 (94); A. WEISER, Das „Apostelkonzil" (Apg 15,1–35). Ereignis, Überlieferung, lukanische Deutung, BZ NF 28 (1984), 143–167 (152); L. WEHR, Petrus und Paulus – Kontrahenten und Partner. Die beiden Apostel im Spiegel des Neuen Testaments, der Apostolischen Väter und früher Zeugnisse ihrer Verehrung, NTA NF 30, Münster 1996, 174 („Lukas hätte von sich aus zweifellos Petrus oder einem anderen der Zwölf die Rolle des Initiators überlassen"); J. WEHNERT, Die Reinheit des „christlichen Gottesvolkes" aus Juden und Heiden. Studien zum historischen und theologischen Hintergrund des sogenannten Apostedekrets, FRLANT 173, Göttingen 1997, 66f.68–70 („Bei aller gebotenen Vorsicht darf ... angenommen werden, daß in der von Lukas benutzten Überlieferung die Formulierung der Enthaltungsvorschriften mit der Person des Jakobus verknüpft war" [67]); s. auch C. C. HILL, Hellenists and Hebrews. Reappraising Division within the Earliest Church, Minneapolis 1992, 144f.

[44] Siehe dazu z.B. HENGEL, a.a.O. 94f.; A. STROBEL, Das Apostedekret als Folge des antiochenischen Streites. Überlegungen zum Verhältnis von Wahrheit und Einheit im Gespräch der Kirchen, in: P.-G. Müller / W. Stenger (Hg.), Kontinuität und Einheit (FS Mußner), Freiburg i. Brsg. u.a. 1981, 81–104 (86); R. PESCH, Das Jerusalemer Abkommen und die Lösung des Antiochenischen Konflikts. Ein Versuch über Gal 2, Apg 10,1–11,18; Apg 11,27–30; 12,25 und Apg 15,1–41, in: Müller / Stenger, a.a.O. 105–122 (106f.); WEISER, a.a.O. 152; T. HOLTZ, Der antiochenische Zwischenfall (Galater 2.11–

Götzendienst, von Blut und Ersticktem und von Unzucht bilden eine Minimalanforderung an Heidenchristen, die sich an den Regelungen für *Gerim* im Lande Israel (vgl. Lev 17f.) orientieren.[45] Diese Lösung für das Problem der Tischgemeinschaft von Juden- und Heidenchristen nimmt die im Rahmen des Jerusalemer Apostelfreffens ausgesprochene Akzeptanz der beschneidungsfreien Völkermission nicht zurück. Heidenchristen bleiben als „Heiden" akzeptiert, aber zugleich wird Judenchristen die Bewahrung ihrer jüdischen Identität ermöglicht.[46] Von Bedeutung ist hier nun das ekklesiologische Verständnis, das sich in den Jakobusklauseln ausspricht: Die Heidenchristen erscheinen in der Rolle von Gästen im Bund Gottes mit Israel.

Zieht man zusammen, so zeigt sich eine doppelte Differenz in der Ekklesiologie des Jak gegenüber dem, was als Position des Jakobus zu erkennen ist: Die christusgläubigen Gemeinden werden als Israel angesprochen, nicht mehr „nur" als Kristallisationspunkt des eschatologischen Israels, und Heidenchristen sind nicht Gäste am Bund Gottes mit Israel, sondern in dieses Israel integriert.[47]

---

14), NTS 32 (1986), 344–361 (354f.); J. BECKER, Paulus. Der Apostel der Völker, Tübingen ³1998, 103. Dagegen sehen z.B. D. R. CATCHPOLE, Paul, James and the Apostolic Decree, NTS 23 (1977), 428–444 (442), und WEHNERT, a.a.O. 129, die Forderungen des Apsosteldekrets als Auslöser des antiochenischen Streites. Sie seien „Teil der in Gal 2,12 erwähnten Jakobus-Botschaft" (ebd.). Zur Kritik an dieser Position s. W. KRAUS, Zwischen Jerusalem und Antiochia. Die ‚Hellenisten', Paulus und die Aufnahme der Heiden in das endzeitliche Gottesvolk, SBS 179, Stuttgart 1999, 151f.

[45] Siehe dazu ROLOFF, Apostelgeschichte (s. Anm. 43), 227; HOLTZ, a.a.O. 355; A. WECHSLER, Geschichtsbild und Apostelstreit. Eine forschungsgeschichtliche und exegetische Studie über den antiochenischen Zwischenfall (Gal 2,11–14), BZNW 62, Berlin u.a. 1991, 361; K. MÜLLER, Tora für die Völker. Die noachidischen Gebote und Ansätze zu ihrer Rezeption im Christentum, SKI 15, Berlin 1994, 157–163; WEHR, Petrus (s. Anm. 43), 168.173; C. HEIL, Die Ablehnung der Speisegebote durch Paulus. Zur Frage nach der Stellung des Apostels zum Gesetz, BBB 96, Weinheim 1994, 151f.; WEHNERT, Reinheit (s. Anm. 43), 209–245; KRAUS, a.a.O. 146–149. Anders aber z.B. A. J. M. WEDDERBURN, The ‚Apostolic Decree'. Tradition and Redaction, NT 35 (1993), 362–389.

[46] Vgl. HOLTZ, Zwischenfall (s. Anm. 44), 355. – Auch dazu hatte schließlich der Apostelkonvent sein Ja gesprochen, während für Paulus die Akzeptanz der beschneidungsfreien Heidenmission bedeutete, dass den Heiden auch sonst *nichts* auferlegt war.

[47] NIEBUHR, Perspective (s. Anm. 7), 1030, hat meine Inanspruchnahme von Jak 1,1 als Argument für Pseudepigraphie (s. KONRADT, Jakobusbrief [s. Anm. 1], 52) als „eine bemerkenswerte Pirouette" zurückgewiesen, doch beruht dies auf dem Missverständnis, dass er die offene Deutung von 1,1 auf die Gruppe der Christusgläubigen als Konsequenz der Pseudepigraphie hinstellt (s. a.a.O. 1029, wo Niebuhr im Anschluss an den Verweis auf die Annahme von Pseudepigraphie fortfährt: „Die Adresse an ‚die zwölf Stämme in der Diaspora' [1,1] muss *folglich* metaphorisch auf die ganze Christenheit gedeutet werden" [Hervorhebung von mir]). Das dargelegte Verständnis von Jak 1,1b beruht aber

Eine enge Parallele findet dies in der Übertragung von Würdeprädikaten Israels auf die Kirche im ebenfalls pseudepigraphen 1Petr (s. 1Petr 2,9), zu dem der Jak insgesamt sehr enge Berührungspunkte aufweist.[48] Auch im – zumindest vorrangig an Heidenchristen gerichteten – 1Petr scheint dabei Israel selbst schon nicht mehr im Blick zu sein.[49] Die Berührungen zwischen Jak und 1Petr an dieser Stelle werden noch dadurch unterstrichen, dass die „zwölf Stämme" in Jak 1,1 ἐν τῇ διασπορᾷ lokalisiert werden und das Präskript des 1Petr die Adressaten als ἐκλεκτοὶ παρεπίδημοι διασπορᾶς anspricht. Die Fremdlingsexistenz der Christen in der Welt ist ein ekklesiologisches Grundmotiv des 1 Petr,[50] das neben παρεπίδημος (1,1; 2,11) durch πάροικος/παροικία verbalisiert wird (1,17; 2,11), aber zugleich in διασπορά zumindest anklingt. Ganz ähnlich verweist ἐν τῇ διασπορᾷ in Jak 1,1 nicht in erster Linie auf die Zerstreuung auch der christlichen Gemeinde, sondern besagt, „daß sie in der Welt getrennt von der Welt leben müssen (s. 1,27)".[51] In ἐν τῇ διασπορᾷ klingt damit auch im Jak ein wesentlicher Zug des ekklesiologischen Programms an (vgl. noch 1,18b; 4,4).[52] Der im NT nur in Jak 1,1; 1Petr 1,1 mit Bezug auf die christlichen Gemeinden begegnende Gebrauch von διασπορά[53] ist offenbar dem die beiden Schriften verbindenden Traditionsreservoir zuzuweisen, ja „Diasporaexistenz" und Israelbewusstsein gehören als ekklesiologische Eckpfeiler zum gemeinsamen Traditionsfundament von Jak und 1Petr.

Die *adscriptio* ist also im Ganzen metaphorisch konnotiert bzw. in ihrem Sinngehalt erst dann hinreichend erfasst, wenn sie auf zwei Ebenen gelesen wird. Im Sinne der Verfasserfiktion ist hier zunächst gesagt, dass sich der Leiter der Jerusalemer Gemeinde an die Christusgläubigen außerhalb Palästinas richtet. Zugleich aber wird – und dies ist im Blick auf das

---

keineswegs auf der vorgängigen Annahme von Pseudepigraphie, sondern besteht unabhängig davon.

[48] Siehe dazu KONRADT, Jakobusbrief (s. Anm. 1), 19–30.

[49] Treffend ROLOFF, Kirche (s. Anm. 41), 275: „Weder wird dabei ein heilsgeschichtlicher Zusammenhang der Kirche mit Israel vorausgesetzt, noch wird das Recht dieser Übertragung reflektiert."

[50] Grundlegend dazu R. FELDMEIER, Die Christen als Fremde. Die Metapher der Fremde in der antiken Welt, im Urchristentum und im 1. Petrusbrief, WUNT 64, Tübingen 1992. Siehe auch ROLOFF, Kirche (s. Anm. 41), 268–273.

[51] BURCHARD, Jakobusbrief (s. Anm. 3), 50. Siehe dazu ferner KONRADT, Existenz (s. Anm. 11), 64–66. – Zur in der neueren Forschung verschiedentlich vorgebrachten Einstellung des Jak in die Tradition der jüdischen Diasporabriefe (s. dazu TSUJI, Glaube [s. Anm. 3], 18–37; NIEBUHR, Diasporabrief [s. Anm. 4]; D. J. VERSEPUT, Genre and Story. The Community Setting of the Epistle of James, CBQ 62 [2000], 96–110 [99–104]) s. KONRADT, Jakobusbrief (s. Anm. 1), 50f. Anm. 172.

[52] Siehe dazu KONRADT, Existenz (s. Anm. 11), 59–66.

[53] Ansonsten überhaupt nur noch Joh 7,35.

Gesamtverständnis des Briefes der wichtigere Aspekt – eine ekklesiologische Ortsbestimmung vorgenommen: Christen sind in der Welt Fremde, sie leben in Distanz zur Welt oder sollen dies nach dem Verfasser zumindest. Mit der theologischen Ortsbestimmung ἐν τῇ διασπορᾷ wird der soziale Erfahrungshorizont des Diasporajudentums aufgerufen, als Minderheit der steten Gefährdung ausgesetzt zu sein, im paganen gesellschaftlichen Umfeld die eigene Glaubensidentität aufzuweichen oder gar zu verlieren. Mit dem Erfahrungsraum des Diasporajudentums ist zugleich der Ort angegeben, in dem der Jak entstanden ist.

Festzuhalten ist also: Das jak Präskript bietet ein geistreiches schriftgelehrtes Wortspiel, mit dem sich primär eine theologische Ortsbestimmung verbindet. Dass dabei „zwölf Stämme" als Israelbezeichnung benutzt wird, hat damit zu tun, dass der Verfassername „Jakobus" an den Erzvater Jakob denken lässt.[54] Dass hier der Herrenbruder selbst schreibt, ist aus den genannten Gründen m.E. mehr als unwahrscheinlich.

1.6 Die Pseudepigraphiethese lässt sich durch die traditionsgeschichtlichen Beziehungen des Jak weiter erhärten.

a) Auf die Berührungspunkte mit dem 1Petr ist bereits hingewiesen worden. Sie sind an mehreren Stellen so eng und heben sich in ihrer Ausprägung derart signifikant von verwandten Aussagen ab, dass es nicht möglich ist, sie suffizient durch einen allgemein gehaltenen Verweis auf das weite Meer paränetischer Traditionen zu erklären. Instruktiv ist insbesondere Jak 1,18.21/1Petr 1,22–2,2, weil sich zu den einzelnen Gliedern auch im Corpus Paulinum Parallelen finden, Jak und 1Petr diesen gegenüber aber einen eigenen Traditionszweig repräsentieren: Die Interpretation der Konversion als (Wieder-)Geburt begegnet auch andernorts (z.B. Tit 3,5), aber nur im Jak und 1Petr erscheint das Wort als Wirkmittel der „Geburt"; das zweigliedrige paränetische Schema in Jak 1,21; 1Petr 2,1f. hat Parallelen in Röm 13,12.14; Eph 4,22–24; Kol 3,8–10, aber nur im Jak und 1Petr steht dem Ablegen des Alten im positiven Glied die Annahme des Wortes gegenüber, und nur im Jak und 1Petr sind „Geburtsaussage" und paränetisches Schema miteinander verbunden.[55] Jak und 1Petr repräsentieren hier ein und denselben Traditionsstrang, der deutlich vom paulinisch-deuteropaulinischen Traditionsbereich unterscheidbar, mit diesem aber an der Wurzel verbunden ist.

In einem früheren Beitrag habe ich plausibel zu machen versucht, dass diese gemeinsame Wurzel als antiochenisches Traditionsfundament identifiziert und die Verzweigung der Traditionsstränge mit dem Resultat des

---

[54] Treffend BURCHARD, Jakobusbrief (s. Anm. 3), 49: „Die Adresse ... steht hier wohl, weil der Absender Jakobus heißt."

[55] Ausführlicher dazu KONRADT, Jakobusbrief (s. Anm. 1), 23–28.

antiochenischen Zwischenfalls in Beziehung gesetzt werden kann.[56] Das Zusammenwachsen ursprünglich selbständiger Traditionsstücke wie in Jak 1,18.21 par. 1Petr 1,22–2,2 repräsentiert eine Traditionsfortbildung *nach* dem Zwischenfall, deren Trägerkreis das antiochenische Christentum (samt Umfeld) war, in dem Petrus und auch Jakobus als gewichtige Autoritäten galten. Aber auch dann, wenn man angesichts dessen, dass die erhaltenen Quellen nur einen fragmentarischen Einblick in die Entwicklung des frühen Christentums gewähren, gegenüber Versuchen, identifizierbare traditionsgeschichtliche Verzweigungen mit bekannten Daten der frühchristlichen Geschichte zu vernetzen, methodisch zurückhaltend ist,[57] bleibt festzuhalten, dass das im Jak vorliegende traditionsgeschichtliche Entwicklungsstadium mit seiner Nähe zum 1Petr es wahrscheinlich macht, dass der Jak auch zeitlich ins Umfeld des 1Petr gehört. Anders gesagt: Die engen Übereinstimmungen mit dem 1Petr erklären sich zwangloser bei nicht allzu großem zeitlichen Abstand.

b) Als wichtiges Indiz für Pseudepigraphie wird in traditionsgeschichtlicher Hinsicht häufig das Verhältnis zur pln Tradition angeführt. Basis dieses Arguments ist die These, dass Jak 2,14–26 auf eine Paulus missverstehende bzw. verkürzende Rezeption der Rechtfertigungsaussagen des Völkerapostels reagiere,[58] so dass das Verhältnis zur pln Tradition in die nachpaulinische Zeit weise.[59] Die Frage des Verhältnisses des Jak zu Paulus ist freilich in der gegenwärtigen Forschung umstritten. Auf der einen Seite ist verschiedentlich vertreten worden, dass der Verfasser sich nicht

---

[56] A.a.O. bes. 30–42.

[57] Dass die Gefahr besteht, dass das wenige Bekannte eine Sogwirkung ausübt, ist nicht von der Hand zu weisen.

[58] So u.a. G. EICHHOLZ, Jakobus und Paulus. Ein Beitrag zum Problem des Kanons, TEH NF 39, München 1953; E. LOHSE, Glaube und Werke. Zur Theologie des Jakobusbriefes, ZNW 48 (1957), 1–22 (6f.); LAWS, Commentary (s. Anm. 3), 128–132; W. POPKES, Adressaten, Situation und Form des Jakobusbriefes, SBS 125/126, Stuttgart 1986, 116.186; F. HAHN, Theologie des Neuen Testaments, Bd. I: Die Vielfalt des Neuen Testaments. Theologiegeschichte des Urchristentums, Tübingen 2002, 403.

[59] PRATSCHER, Herrenbruder (s. Anm. 1), 212, wertet den „nachpaulinische[n] Charakter von 2,14ff" (im Original kursiv) als das „wichtigste Argument". Siehe ferner z.B. DIBELIUS, Brief (s. Anm. 2), 31; SCHNIDER, Jakobusbrief (s. Anm. 3), 16; POPKES, Brief (s. Anm. 3), 67. – In der neueren Forschung ist zuweilen postuliert worden, dass sich der Brief nicht nur in 2,14–26, sondern auch in anderen Passagen kritisch auf durch (verzerrte) paulinische Theologumena genährte Überzeugungen der Adressaten beziehe. Siehe dazu vor allem TSUJI, Glaube (s. Anm. 3), 133–199, und POPKES, Brief (s. Anm. 3), 59. – Vgl. dazu M. KONRADT, Der Jakobusbrief im frühchristlichen Kontext. Überlegungen zum traditionsgeschichtlichen Verhältnis des Jakobusbriefes zur Jesusüberlieferung, zur paulinischen Tradition und zum 1 Petr, in: J. Schlosser (Hg.), The Catholic Epistles and the Tradition, BEThL 176, Leuven 2004, 171–212 (175f.).

bloß mit einem „Parolen-Paulinismus"[60], sondern auf der Grundlage der Kenntnis von Paulusbriefen, allem voran dem Röm, direkt mit Paulus selbst auseinandersetze.[61] Liest man den Jak als Auseinandersetzung mit Paulus, ist jedoch der Herrenbruder als Verfasser keineswegs ausgeschlossen. So deutet Martin Hengel[62] den seines Erachtens zwischen 58 und 62 entstandenen Brief[63] als subtile polemische Auseinandersetzung mit Paulus, die dem Zweck diene, „die durch den Kapitalprozeß gegen ihren Heros und Gründer verunsicherten, überwiegend heidenchristlichen Missionsgemeinden der griechischsprechenden Diaspora auf die Gefahren einer – gewiß mißverstandenen – paulinischen Theologie, die nach Meinung der Gegner des Paulus zu einer libertinistischen Gesetzlosigkeit, zu einem Glauben ohne Werke führen konnte, hinzuweisen und zugleich gewisse fragwürdige Züge im Verhalten des verehrten Lehrers bloßzustellen".[64] Auch wenn man der Gesamtthese von Hengel nicht zu folgen vermag, bleibt dennoch festzuhalten: Falls Jak 2,14–26 auf Paulus' Rechtfertigungsaussagen bzw. ihre Rezeption reagiert, muss dies nicht gegen den Herrenbruder sprechen,[65] denn zum einen gab es schon früh Missverständnisse (vgl. Röm 3,8), zum anderen hat Jakobus zwar auf dem Apostelkonvent der beschneidungsfreien Völkermission zugestimmt (Gal 2,1–10; Apg 15), doch kann sich seine Einschätzung des „Völkerapostels" zwischen Apostelkonvent und letztem Jerusalembesuch von Paulus (Apg 21,18–26)

---

[60] POPKES, Brief (s. Anm. 3), 59.

[61] So z.B. A. LINDEMANN, Paulus im ältesten Christentum. Das Bild des Apostels und die Rezeption der paulinischen Theologie in der frühchristlichen Literatur bis Marcion, BHTh 58, Tübingen 1979, 243–252; G. LÜDEMANN, Paulus, der Heidenapostel, Bd. II: Antipaulinismus im frühen Christentum, FRLANT 130, Göttingen 1983, bes. 198; M. SATO, Wozu wurde der Jakobusbrief geschrieben? Eine mutmaßliche Rekonstruktion, AJBI 17 (1991), 55–76 (67f.); TSUJI, Glaube (s. Anm. 3), 189–193; F. AVEMARIE, Die Werke des Gesetzes im Spiegel des Jakobusbriefes. A Very Old Perspective on Paul, ZThK 98 (2001), 282–309 (289–294), sowie extensiv K. SYREENI, James and the Pauline Legacy. Power Play in Corinth, in: I. Dunderberg / C. Tuckett / K. Syreeni (Hg.), Fair Play. Diversity and Conflicts in Early Christianity (FS Räisänen), NT.S 103, Leiden u.a. 2002, 397–437 (kritisch zu Syreeni KONRADT, Kontext [Anm. 59], 173–175). – NIENHUIS, Paul (s. Anm. 3), 113–117, wertet Abhängigkeit von paulinischen Briefen als gewichtiges Argument gegen die Echtheit des Briefes.

[62] HENGEL, Polemik (s. Anm. 4).

[63] A.a.O. 259.

[64] Ebd. – Die Polemik ist dabei nach Hengel so subtil, dass nur Eingeweihte, d.h. „nur ... von dem Streit Betroffene" (253) hinter der „lockere[n], weisheitlich-rhetorisch stilisierte[n] Mahnrede" (265) die eigentliche Intention des Schreibens entziffern können.

[65] Siehe dazu MUSSNER, Jakobusbrief (s. Anm. 4), 18f., der den Jak in den zeitlichen Zusammenhang der Auseinandersetzungen um Paulus' Äußerungen im Gal und Röm einstellt und den Brief um 60 n. Chr. datiert.

oder auch danach noch aufgrund der weiteren Entwicklungen verändert haben.

Auf der anderen Seite haben sich in der jüngeren Forschung die Stimmen gemehrt, die eine (polemische) Bezugnahme des Jak auf Paulus oder auf zu Parolen verkommene Paulinismen überhaupt bestreiten.[66] Ich selbst habe mich in früheren Veröffentlichungen ebenfalls in diesem Sinne geäußert.[67] Die Selbstverständlichkeit etwa, mit der der Verfasser das Abrahambeispiel in 2,21 in Form einer rhetorischen, das Einverständnis des Adressaten voraussetzenden Frage als Erkenntnisgrund vorbringt, spricht deutlich dagegen, dass er hier *seine* Interpretation gegen eine differierende, auf Paulus zurückgehende Inanspruchnahme Abrahams in Stellung bringt. Beim Rekurs auf Abraham in Jak 2,21–23 handelt es sich entweder um die Ausformulierung frühjüdischer Abrahamtraditionen[68] – die verbalen Berührungen mit Paulus müssten dann durch das gemeinsame Traditionsfundament erklärt werden. Oder aber – so man Letzteres, da die Übereinstimmungen als zu signifikant erscheinen, für eine nicht hinreichende Erklärung erachtet – der Verfasser nimmt eine frühchristliche Fortschreibung des angeführten jüdischen Abrahambildes auf, deren sprachliche Gestalt sich der judenchristlichen Replik auf die entsprechenden paulinischen Aussagen im Gal (und Röm) verdankt,[69] die sich in der Weitertradierung aber längst von diesem Konflikt gelöst hat und jedenfalls in der Kommunikationssituation des Jak nicht mit einem paulinisch inspirierten Abrahambild konkurriert, sondern vom Verfasser als selbstverständliche, gemeinsame Ausgangsbasis verwendet werden kann.[70]

---

[66] Siehe E. BAASLAND, Der Jakobusbrief als neutestamentliche Weisheitsschrift, StTh 36 (1982), 119–139 ([127–]133); P. H. DAVIDS, The Epistle of James. A Commentary on the Greek Text, NITGC, Grand Rapids 1982, 21.128; R. HEILIGENTHAL, Werke als Zeichen. Untersuchungen zur Bedeutung der menschlichen Taten im Frühjudentum, Neuen Testament und Frühchristentum, WUNT II/9, Tübingen 1983, 49–52; K. BERGER, Theologiegeschichte des Urchristentums. Theologie des Neuen Testaments, Tübingen u.a. ²1995, 188f.; W. BINDEMANN, Weisheit versus Weisheit. Der Jakobusbrief als innerkirchlicher Diskurs, ZNW 86 (1995), 189–217 (210); JOHNSON, Letter (s. Anm. 4), 58–64.249f.; PENNER, Epistle (s. Anm. 16), 47–74; K. HAACKER, Justification, salut et foi. Étude sur les rapports entre Paul, Jacques et Pierre, ETR 73 (1998), 177–188 (180–182).

[67] Siehe dazu KONRADT, Existenz (s. Anm. 11), 210–213.241–246, und insbesondere ders., Kontext (s. Anm. 59), 172–190.

[68] Dazu ders., Kontext (s. Anm. 59), 181f.

[69] Siehe dazu a.a.O. 183–186.

[70] Diese zweite Option trifft sich an einem wesentlichen Punkt mit der Position von Burchard, der sich ebenfalls gegen die These einer antipaulinischen Stoßrichtung von Jak 2,14–26 wendet (pointiert BURCHARD, Jakobusbrief [s. Anm. 3], 126: „Man verdirbt sich die Auslegung, wenn man Jak durchlaufend von Paulus weg oder auf ihn zu interpretiert"), aber erwägt, dass der Passus „Paulus' sprachliche Vorarbeit voraussetzt" (ebd.). Burchard geht aber davon aus, dass der Verfasser des Jak selbst die Wendungen als pau-

Weist Letzteres in die richtige Richtung, wäre ein weiteres Indiz gegeben, dass der Herrenbruder, dem man eine Kenntnis der Rechtfertigungsaussagen des Paulus kaum wird absprechen können, nicht der Verfasser sein kann. Der Jak repräsentiert ein unpaulinisches Christentum und gehört in einen nachpaulinischen Kontext.

1.7 Fasst man zusammen, so ergeben Indizien aus verschiedenen Bereichen eine deutliche Tendenz: Das sprachliche Niveau, das eher auf einen Muttersprachler weist, welcher Jakobus nicht war, auch wenn er Griechisch als Zweitsprache gelernt haben wird, das starke hellenistische Gepräge des Briefes, das sich außerhalb Palästinas zumindest graduell besser verstehen lässt als im Falle einer Abfassung durch Jakobus, und die traditionsgeschichtliche Verortung des Briefes, die in die nachpaulinische Zeit weist, legen – zumal in ihrem kumulativen Gewicht – die Annahme von Pseudepigraphie nahe. Es kommt ferner das mit einer Schriftassoziation „spielende" Präskript hinzu, das kaum Jakobus selbst zuzuweisen ist und dessen ekklesiologischer Standpunkt im Blick auf das Verhältnis von Kirche und Israel schwerlich mit dem des Herrenbruders in Deckung zu bringen ist. Kurzum: Trotz einer bei einzelnen Indizien ausdifferenzierten Argumentationslage, die ein weniger eindeutiges Bild zeichnet, als vielfach postuliert wurde, ist die von der Mehrheit vertretene Pseudepigraphiethese nach wie vor die deutlich plausiblere Option.[71]

Ist der Jak also ein Pseudepigraphon, bleibt die Frage zu beantworten, warum ein anderer ihn unter die Autorität des Jerusalemer Gemeindeleiters gestellt hat.

2. Erwägungen zur Verfasserfiktion

2.1 Die Wahl des Verfassernamens wäre suffizient erklärt, wenn im Jak ein Schülerkreis das Erbe des Lehrers zu sichern suchte, wenn also zwischen dem Brief und der Unterweisung des Herrenbruders insofern ein enger materialer Zusammenhang bestünde, als im Jak Stoffe aufgenommen

---

linische kannte, während auch bei der im Voranstehenden vorgetragenen zweiten Option die „paulinische" Diktion auf Tradition zurückgeführt wird.

[71] Nur ergänzend ist noch auf das Argument der späten kanonischen Anerkennung und des frühen Zweifels an der Echtheit des Briefes (vgl. die Notiz von Eus.h.e. 2,23,24f.: „Von Jakobus soll der erste der sogenannten Katholischen Briefe verfasst sein. Doch ist zu bemerken, dass er für unecht gehalten wird.") hinzuweisen, das verschiedentlich für die Pseudepigraphiethese in Anspruch genommen wurde (s. z.B. SCHNIDER, Jakobusbrief [s. Anm. 3], 16f.; SCHNELLE, Einleitung [s. Anm. 3], 432f.).

und/oder fortgeschrieben wären, die auf den Jerusalemer Gemeindeleiter zurückgehen.[72] Eine solche Entstehungstheorie lässt sich aber nicht nur nicht positiv erweisen, sie hat auch deutliche Indizien gegen sich.[73]

Fällt die Option einer engeren materialen Beziehung zwischen dem Jak und Unterweisungsgut des Herrenbruders aus, kann man erwägen, die Verfasserfiktion damit zu erklären, dass der Brief einem christusgläubigen Kreis entstammt, in dem der Herrenbruder als *die* Autorität galt, so dass geradezu von einem jakobeischen Christentum geredet werden kann.[74] Zwingend ist die Annahme eines solchen Entstehungskontexts zur Erklärung der Verfasserzuschreibung jedoch keineswegs. Es genügt ohne weiteres die Annahme, dass Jakobus im Entstehungskreis als *eine* Autorität positiv gewürdigt wurde, sofern sich *inhaltliche* Gründe benennen lassen, die eine Zuschreibung an Jakobus nahelegten. Umgekehrt formuliert: Die Wahl des Jakobus musste für den tatsächlichen Verfasser um so näher liegen, wenn dieser der Meinung sein konnte, ganz im Sinne des Jerusalemer Apostels zu schreiben, wenn es, anders gesagt, Berührungen seines Anliegens mit dem gab, was ihm vom Herrenbruder bekannt war. Eine solche Affinität ist im Übrigen ebenso im Blick auf die Plausibilität der Verfasserzuschreibung im Adressatenkreis zu bedenken.

Damit ist – abseits der negativ zu beantwortenden Frage nach der Aufnahme von Unterweisungsgut des Herrenbruders im Brief – also die Frage nach dem Bild des tatsächlichen Verfassers vom Herrenbruder aufgeworfen, das die Autorfiktion möglicherweise mit motiviert hat. Es geht darum zu eruieren, inwiefern der Herrenbruder dem tatsächlichen Verfasser aufgrund seines Bildes von jenem als geeignete Autorität für den Inhalt des Briefes erschienen sein mag. Ist davon auszugehen, dass der Brief zwi-

---

[72] So hat P. H. DAVIDS, Palestinian Traditions in the Epistle of James, in: Chilton / Evans, James the Just (s. Anm. 1), 33–57, postuliert, „that the Epistle of James is either a product of James himself or, more likely, a Diaspora letter preserving his sayings for the church at large shortly after his martyrdom" (55, ähnlich HARTIN, James [s. Anm. 4], 25). B. R. HALSON, The Epistle of James. ‚Christian Wisdom?', StEv IV (= TU 102), Berlin 1968, 308–314 (312f.), sieht im Jakobusbrief eine Sammlung katechetischen Materials, die auf eine mit dem Herrenbruder Jakobus eng verbundene Katechetenschule zurückgehe. Und nach R. P. MARTIN, James, WBC 48, Waco 1988, lxxvi, siedelten Schüler des Jakobus im Gefolge des Römisch-Jüdischen Kriegs nach Antiochien über und brachten auf diesem Weg Unterweisungsgut des Herrenbruders in die syrische Metropole, das dort zusammengestellt und überarbeitet wurde, „to meet the pastoral needs of some community in the Syrian province" (PAINTER, James [s. Anm. 1], 264).

[73] Siehe dazu KONRADT, Jakobusbrief (s. Anm. 1), 42–45.

[74] Dass es solche Kreise gegeben hat, ist durch die hinter EvThom 12 stehende Tradition oder EvHebr 7 sowie eine Reihe weiterer frühchristlicher Zeugnisse (s. die Aufarbeitung bei PRATSCHER, Herrenbruder [s. Anm. 1], 102ff.; PAINTER, James [s. Anm. 1], 105ff.) sicher.

schen 70 und 80/85 n. Chr. abgefasst wurde,[75] so dass zwischen Jakobus' Tod und der Abfassung des Briefes nicht mehr als ca. 10 bis 20 Jahre liegen, wäre dabei in sachlicher Hinsicht mit Kontinuitätslinien zwischen dem „historischen Jakobus" und dem Jakobusbild, das im Jak Pate steht, zu rechnen.

2.2 Fragt man so, ist grundlegend auf die Konvergenz zwischen der starken ethischen Ausrichtung des Briefes und der bereits durch das EvThom 12 bezeugten Würdigung des Herrenbruders als eines „Gerechten" zu verweisen.[76] Der entscheidende Grund, warum der Brief gerade unter die Autorität des Jakobus gestellt wurde, dürfte, kurz gesagt, Jakobus' Nachwirkung als ethisches Vorbild gewesen sein, die sich recht bald in seinem Beinamen „der Gerechte" verdichtete und ihn für ein ethisches „Korrekturschreiben"[77] wie den Jak als passende Autorität erscheinen ließ.[78] Freilich ist hier nicht stehen zu bleiben. Vielmehr lässt sich dieser fundamentale Aspekt durch weitere Konvergenzpunkte profilieren.

Pseudo-Jakobus bezeichnet in 1,25 den ἔμφυτος λόγος nach seiner imperativischen Seite als νόμος.[79] Die den Jak im Ganzen kennzeichnende uneingeschränkt positive Rede vom Gesetz harmoniert damit, dass die Treue zur Tora offenkundig ein wesentliches Charakteristikum des Herrenbruders bildete,[80] das auch im lukanischen Jakobusbild, wie es in Apg

---

[75] Ist der Jak ein Pseudepigraphon, ist mit dem Tod des Herrenbruders im Jahre 62 n. Chr. der *terminus post quem* gegeben. Für den *terminus ad quem* kann man darauf verweisen, dass der Verfasser des Jud den Jak offenbar kennt (Jud 1). Weiter helfen vor allem die Affinitäten zum Mt, wenn es richtig ist, dass diese nicht auf literarischer Kenntnis beruhen (s. dazu KONRADT, Kontext [s. Anm. 59], 205–207). Da nämlich das Mt sehr schnell Verbreitung fand (s. dazu U. LUZ, Das Evangelium nach Matthäus, Teilbd. 1: Mt 1–7, EKK I/1, Düsseldorf u.a. ⁵2002, 103f.; W.-D. KÖHLER, Die Rezeption des Matthäusevangeliums in der Zeit vor Irenäus, WUNT II/24, Tübingen 1987), kann man den Jak, je nach Datierung des Mt, kaum später als etwa 80/85 n. Chr. ansetzen. Der Jak dürfte daher zwischen 70 und 80/85 n. Chr. geschrieben sein.

[76] Siehe ferner EvHebr 7; Hegesipp bei Eus.h.e. 2,23,4.7.12.15.16; 4,22,4 u.ö. – Vgl. HENGEL, Jakobus (s. Anm. 43), 79–81; PAINTER, James (s. Anm. 1), 125.157.162f.169. 185.

[77] So die treffende Bezeichnung von POPKES, Adressaten (s. Anm. 58), 209.

[78] Ähnlich bereits DIBELIUS, Brief (s. Anm. 2), 34f.: Der Autor „war sich bewußt, dem Gesetz der Freiheit zu dienen und einem Ideal praktischen Christentums nachzustreben ... Für ein solches Schriftstück schien ihm ... Jak der ‚Gerechte', der Gesetzeseiferer, der rechte literarische Schutzpatron zu sein."

[79] Zum Verhältnis von λόγος und νόμος im Jak s. KONRADT, Existenz (s. Anm. 11), 67–74.

[80] Zur Toratreue des Jakobus vgl. BURCHARD, Jakobusbrief (s. Anm. 3), 3; HENGEL, Jakobus (s. Anm. 43), 80; PRATSCHER, Herrenbruder (s. Anm. 1), 101.

15,13–21 sichtbar wird, zutage tritt (s. v.a. 15,21[81]). Zugleich weist die Rede vom „Gesetz *der Freiheit*", wie gesehen, auf einen hellenistisch geprägten Kontext. Was sich über den Inhalt des „Gesetzes der Freiheit" im Jak ausmachen lässt, nämlich die deutliche Konzentration auf den Bereich der Sozialethik,[82] fügt sich hier nahtlos ein. Kurzum: Auch wenn das Gesetzesverständnis des Jak schwerlich mit dem des Herrenbruders identisch ist, sondern eher von einer Transformation auszugehen ist, die auf ein anderes kirchliches Milieu verweist, so besteht doch in jedem Fall darin sachliche Kontinuität, dass das Tun des Gesetzes als wesentliches Strukturelement christlichen Glaubens erscheint. Christsein ohne ποιεῖν νόμον ist für Pseudo-Jakobus wie für den Herrenbruder ein Selbstwiderspruch.

Dieser Konvergenzpunkt lässt sich in materialethischer Hinsicht profilieren. Pseudo-Jakobus sieht seine „Brüder und Schwestern" ethisch vor allem durch das mit gemeinschaftsschädigendem Verhalten einhergehende Streben nach Reichtum und Sozialprestige gefährdet (4,1–4[83]). Um sie hier zur „Wahrheit" zurückzuführen (5,19), übt er scharfe Kritik an den Reichen und verweist auf deren schreckliches Ende (1,10f.; 2,6f.; 4,13–5,6). Von Christenmenschen erwartet er nicht völligen Besitzverzicht, wohl aber Barmherzigkeit gegenüber Armen, die mit einem respektvollen Umgang mit ihnen beginnt (2,1–5) – Ansehen der Person, in dem sich die Orientierung am „weltlichen" Status- und Wertesystem äußert, verletzt das Gebot der Nächstenliebe[84] – und sich in konkreter Hilfeleistung fortsetzt (1,27; 2,15f.).

Blickt man auf den sozialen Kontext des Herrenbruders, so weisen Gal 2,10 und Röm 15,26 darauf hin, dass die (meisten) judäischen Christen

---

[81] In Apg 15 schließt sich an Jakobus' Vorschlag, den Heidenchristen lediglich die Meidung der Befleckung durch Götzen, von Unzucht, Ersticktem und Blut aufzuerlegen (Apg 15,20), als Begründung der Verweis an, dass Mose seit ältesten Zeiten in jeder Stadt seine Verkündiger habe, da er an jedem Sabbat in den Synagogen verlesen werde (15,21). Zu verstehen ist diese Begründung, bezieht man sie direkt auf V.20, offenbar so, dass das „Dekret" deshalb nötig ist, „weil die Juden seit Urzeiten an das im Synagogengottesdienst verlesene Gesetz gebunden sind und ihnen nicht ohne weiteres zugemutet werden kann, sich davon zu lösen" (ROLOFF, Apostelgeschichte [s. Anm. 43], 233).

[82] Dazu KONRADT, Existenz (s. Anm. 11), 176–206; K.-W. NIEBUHR, Tora ohne Tempel. Paulus und der Jakobusbrief im Zusammenhang frühjüdischer Torarezeption für die Diaspora, in: B. Ego / A. Lange / P. Pilhofer (Hg.), Gemeinde ohne Tempel. Zur Substituierung und Transformation des Jerusalemer Tempels und seines Kultes im Alten Testament, antiken Judentum und frühen Christentum, WUNT 118, Tübingen 1999, 427–460 (452–455).

[83] Zu dieser Deutung KONRADT, a.a.O. 125–135.

[84] Zur Deutung des Liebesgebotes im Jakobusbrief s. BURCHARD, Nächstenliebegebot (s. Anm. 11); KONRADT, a.a.O. 184–194, sowie G. THEISSEN, Nächstenliebe und Egalität. Jak 2,1–13 als Höhepunkt urchristlicher Ethik, in: von Gemünden / Konradt / Theißen, Jakobusbrief (s. Anm. 1), 120–142.

wirtschaftlich in bescheidenen Verhältnissen gelebt haben.[85] Was die besitzethische Orientierung der Jerusalemer betrifft, bietet Lukas zwar in Apg 2,42–47; 4,32–35 eine idealisierte Darstellung,[86] die mit ἅπαντα κοινά (Apg 2,44; 4,32) einen Topos hellenistischer Freundschaftsethik aufnimmt („Besitz der Freunde ist gemeinsam"[87]) und ihn auf die Gemeinschaft der *Glaubenden* anwendet, doch besagt dies keineswegs, dass es sich um eine reine literarische Fiktion handelt. Lukas dürfte vielmehr Notizen darüber, „wie in der Urgemeinde das soziale Gefälle durch tätige Liebe vor allem der Besitzenden ausgeglichen wurde"[88], verallgemeinert[89] und durch die Aufnahme des besagten Topos hellenistisch koloriert haben.[90] In der Urgemeinde dürfte also ein Besitzethos in Geltung gestanden haben, das an sozialem Ausgleich orientiert war und das „Hängen am Besitz" – im Gefolge der reichtumskritischen Motive der Verkündigung Jesu – verwarf. Vor diesem Hintergrund ist es eine plausible Annahme, dass Jakobus, der Leiter der Jerusalemer Gemeinde, die im Jak vertretene Absage an den „Mammon" glaubhaft verkörperte und dies zum Bild gehörte, das man vom Herrenbruder hatte. Pseudo-Jakobus konnte also auch in seinem Anliegen, den Reichtum als zentrales Gefährdungsmoment christlicher Existenz einzuschärfen, mit sachlichem Recht die Autorität des Herrenbruders in Anspruch nehmen.

Cum grano salis lässt sich schließlich auch auf das im Brief zutage tretende Israelbewusstsein verweisen, das nicht nur, wie dargelegt wurde, in seiner am jüdischen Volk vorbeigehenden Ausrichtung ein Indiz für Pseudepigraphie liefert, sondern sich zugleich auch als Transformation und Fortschreibung des israelbezogenen Selbstverständnisses der Jerusalemer Ur-

---

[85] Vgl. E. W. STEGEMANN / W. STEGEMANN, Urchristliche Sozialgeschichte. Die Anfänge im Judentum und die Christusgemeinden in der mediterranen Welt, Stuttgart u.a. 1995, 193f.; PAINTER, James (s. Anm. 1), 249.

[86] Schon in Apg 6,1–6 wird eine Spannung zwischen verschiedenen Kreisen der Urgemeinde deutlich, in der es um die Witwenversorgung geht.

[87] Siehe exemplarisch Arist.e.N. 1159b, frühjüdisch Philo Abr. 235.

[88] SCHENKE, Urgemeinde (s. Anm. 41), 91.

[89] Auch Apg 6,1–6 belegt ja, dass es in der Urgemeinde eine Armenversorgung gegeben hat.

[90] Eine erwägenswerte alternative historische Rekonstruktion hat G. Theißen vorgelegt (Urchristlicher Liebeskommunismus. Zum ‚Sitz im Leben' des Topos ἅπαντα κοινά in Apg 2,44 und 4,32, in: T. Fornberg / D. Hellholm [Hg.], Texts and Contexts. Biblical Texts in their Textual and Situational Contexts [FS Hartman], Oslo u.a. 1995, 689–712). Er führt den Freundschaftstopos nicht auf Lukas selbst, sondern auf eine von ihm rezipierte Tradition zurück (698–703), deren Ausgangspunkt „eine Reformidee der Jerusalemer Urgemeinde selbst", genauer: der „Hellenisten" gewesen sein könnte (707, vgl. 709). Als konkreter Entstehungskontext der Idee einer Gütergemeinschaft kommt nach Theißen der in Apg 6,1–6 bezeugte Konflikt um die Witwenversorgung in Frage, den die „Hellenisten" durch den Topos „allen Gläubigen ist alles gemeinsam" zu lösen suchten (707).

gemeinde in einem sozialen Kontext verstehen lässt, in dem der enge Bezug auf das nicht-christusgläubige Israel keine vorrangige Bedeutung (mehr) hatte. Noch eine weitere Linie mag hier gezogen werden. Die „Jakobusklauseln" (Apg 15,20.29) lassen das Anliegen zutage treten, die Grenze zwischen dem Gottesvolk und den Völkern nicht zu verwischen.[91] Auch der Jak ist um eine klare Grenzziehung bemüht, nämlich zwischen christlicher Gemeinde und „Welt". Christen haben sich „von der *Welt unbefleckt* zu halten" (Jak 1,27). Auch hier ist es ohne weiteres möglich, die Mahnungen des Jak als Transformation eines theologischen Anliegens des Herrenbruders zu lesen.

2.3 Überblickt man die voranstehenden Überlegungen, ist festzuhalten, dass die Verfasserzuschreibung grundlegend durch Jakobus' Nachwirkung als ethisches Vorbild motiviert sein dürfte, die sich in seinem Beinamen „der Gerechte" verdichtete und ihn für einen Brief wie den Jak in seinem Charakter als ethisches Korrekturschreiben als passende Autorität erscheinen ließ. Darüber hinaus sind aber – auch wenn es keine Anhaltspunkte dafür gibt, dass spezifisches Unterweisungsgut des Herrenbruders in den Brief Eingang gefunden hat – weitere Bezüge namhaft zu machen: Der selbstverständliche Rekurs auf das Gesetz, die besitzethische Orientierung bzw. das sozialdiakonische Engagement sowie auch – allerdings mit einem erheblichen Transformationsgrad – der Bezug auf Israel im ekklesialen Selbstverständnis geben Positionen von Pseudo-Jakobus zu erkennen, die am „historischen Jakobus" Anhalt haben. Vor diesem Hintergrund betrachtet ist die Autorfiktion schwerlich bloß am „Ruhm" der Jerusalemer Autorität orientiert,[92] sondern auch durch ein bestimmtes Jakobusbild motiviert, in dem theologische Standpunkte des Herrenbruders nachwirken. Mit einem Wort: Pseudo-Jakobus schreibt mit der Überzeugung, Positionen des Herrenbruders zu vertreten. Insofern kann man den Jak tatsächlich als ein theologisches Vermächtnis des Herrenbruders Jakobus lesen, freilich eben als ein Vermächtnis, das Standpunkte nur spiegelt und in transformierter Gestalt bietet, das lediglich ein Jakobusbild reflektiert, nicht aber Jakobustraditionen zitiert.[93]

---

[91] Vgl. WEHNERT, Reinheit (s. Anm. 43), 239–255.

[92] Anders die Tendenz bei PRATSCHER, Herrenbruder (s. Anm. 1), 221: Im Jak liege „eine *sekundäre Herrenbrudertradition* vor, die sich primär nicht an dessen Vorstellungen, sondern an *dessen Ruhm orientiert*".

[93] Einen anderen Vorschlag, die pseudepigraphe Intention des Jak zu entschlüsseln, hat THEISSEN, Intention (s. Anm. 5), vorgebracht: Jakobus werde „im Jakobusbrief als Symbol des Judenchristentums in Anspruch genommen, um das Judenchristentum gegen Missverständnisse zu verteidigen. Der Brief ... verteidigt sich (Ende des 1. Jh. n. Chr.) gegen das Bild, das die Konflikte der ersten Generation hinterlassen haben – also gegen das Bild eines ritualistischen, konfliktsüchtigen, engherzigen Judenchristentums, dem es

Ist dies richtig, geht der die frühchristliche Pseudepigraphie wesentlich motivierende Gedanke der Orientierung an den apostolischen Anfängen[94] hier nicht darin auf, dass ein Unbekannter sich der Autorität des Herrenbruders bedient hat, um seinen eigenen Ansichten und Belangen Nachdruck zu verschaffen.[95] Der Brief lässt vielmehr erwarten, dass sich sein Autor zugleich auch *unter* die Autorität des Herrenbruders gestellt sah. Oder anders: Es erscheint plausibel, dass der Autor davon ausging, Anliegen des Herrenbruders zu artikulieren. Anzufügen ist, dass sich die Etablierung der Verfasserfiktion auf das Präskript beschränkt. Im weiteren Brief wird – anders als etwa in 2Petr 1,16–18 – nie explizit auf den vermeintlichen Verfasser verwiesen.

Festzuhalten ist ferner, dass es, wie angeführt, keineswegs zwingend ist, dass der Jak einem spezifisch jakobeischen Zirkel entstammt. Es genügt die Annahme, dass der Jak in einem kirchlichen Milieu entstanden ist, das Jakobus als *eine* bedeutsame frühchristliche Persönlichkeit in Ehren hielt. Will man den Briefautor lokalisieren, bildet Syrien bzw. Antiochien samt Ausstrahlungsgebiet die plausibelste Option. Zum einen weist der Jak enge traditionsgeschichtliche Bezüge zum Mt auf, die auf lokale Nähe hindeuten.[96] Zum anderen ist für diesen Raum durch den Apostelkonvent und den

---

an höherer theologischer Weisheit fehlt und das die Einheit der Kirche unnötig aufs Spiel setzt. Diesem ... Bild, für das der Paulinismus verantwortlich ist, setzt der Jakobusbrief das Konzept eines ethischen Christentums entgegen, dem es um den Frieden in der Gemeinde und eine konsequente Verwirklichung des Glaubens geht" (58). Theißen interpretiert dazu das Fehlen ritueller Gebote als bewusste Auslassung, um das Bild eines Jakobus, der „in Fragen ritueller Gebote ‚hart' geblieben war", zu korrigieren (63). Ähnlich führt die im Jak vorliegende, „gemessen an den spekulativen ‚Weisheitstheologien' der paulinischen Schule" (66) schlichte Form einer praxisorientierten Weisheit zu der These, dass der Autor „die einfache ‚Weisheit' des Judenchristentums (d.h. des Jakobus) verteidigen" (ebd.) wolle. Beweisbar ist eine solche Frontstellung nicht. Insgesamt birgt der Ansatz von Theißen m.E. das Problem, dass die Missverständnisse oder Problemlagen, auf die der Brief eine Antwort sein soll, nicht durch klare Hinweise aus dem Brief selbst abzuleiten sind, sondern auf einer in hohem Maße spekulativen Form des „mirror reading" basieren (zur methodischen Problematik s. die Überlegungen von J. M. G. BARCLAY, Mirror-Reading a Polemical Letter. Galatians as a Test Case, JSNT 31 [1987], 73–93 [74–86]). NIEBUHR, Perspective (s. Anm. 7), 1030, hat zudem zu Recht darauf hingewiesen, dass es für die von Theißen vorausgesetzte „Bewertung des Judenchristentums keinerlei Belege" gibt.

[94] Siehe exemplarisch F. LAUB, Falsche Verfasserangaben in neutestamentlichen Schriften. Aspekte der gegenwärtigen Diskussion um die neutestamentliche Pseudepigraphie, TThZ 89 (1982), 228–242 (231f.); SCHNELLE, Einleitung (s. Anm. 3), 327f.

[95] Zu diesem grundlegenden Motiv antiker Pseudepigraphie vgl. N. BROX, Falsche Verfasserangaben. Zur Erklärung der frühchristlichen Pseudepigraphie, SBS 79, Stuttgart 1975, 52–54.105f.

[96] Zur Nähe zum Mt vgl. oben Anm. 75.

antiochenischen Zwischenfall (Gal 2,11–14) belegt, dass Jakobus dort als Autorität galt.[97]

---

[97] Zu Syrien als Ort der Abfassung vgl. z.B. M. H. SHEPHERD, The Epistle of James and the Gospel of Matthew, JBL 75 (1956), 40–51 (49–51); K. KÜRZDÖRFER, Der Charakter des Jakobusbriefes. Eine Auseinandersetzung mit den Thesen von A. Meyer und M. Dibelius, Diss. masch., Tübingen 1966, 128–130; A. F. ZIMMERMANN, Die urchristlichen Lehrer. Studien zum Tradentenkreis der διδάσκαλοι im frühen Urchristentum, WUNT II/2, Tübingen ²1988, 194–196; PRATSCHER, Herrenbruder (s. Anm. 1), 219 Anm. 51; BURCHARD, Jakobusbrief (s. Anm. 3), 7 (zu den gehandelten Alternativen ebd.).

The Politics of Pseudepigraphy and the Letter of James

by

MATT JACKSON-MCCABE

The retrojection of cultural innovation into a revered past is a widespread, cross-cultural phenomenon. It is particularly well documented in the realm of religion, where the tendency to appeal to "hoary tradition" is especially characteristic.[1] Among its common manifestations in literate cultures is the misattribution of texts to venerated figures of tradition. Such pseudepigraphic texts can serve a variety of purposes, and the rationale for their creation no doubt varies widely by individual circumstances. But the common denominator, particularly for texts composed within religious groups, would seem to be an interest in investing a work that might otherwise appear to be simply the result of ordinary human creativity with an air of special legitimacy, authority, or, in a word, sacrality.[2]

The various ancient groups who venerated Jesus of Nazareth provide a multitude of examples of this phenomenon. In a setting where legitimacy was closely correlated with the category 'apostolic,' one finds numerous instances of texts wrongly ascribed to this or that apostle.[3] Sometimes this seems to have occurred more or less innocently, in the form of subsequent attributions of originally anonymous texts to heroes of the apostolic era; such is apparently the case with the so-called Johannine literature and in what some editions of the Bible still refer to as Paul's letter to the Hebrews.[4] But in other cases it is plain that we are dealing less with interpre-

---

[1] J. R. Lewis and O. Hammer, eds., *The Invention of Sacred Tradition* (Cambridge: Cambridge University Press, 2007), 1. I owe special thanks to Chris Mount for invaluable comments on earlier drafts of the present essay.

[2] Ibid., 4–7. For a wider theoretical context within which such appeals to authority in religious settings can be understood see B. Lincoln, "On the Relation of Religion and Culture," in *Holy Terrors: Thinking about Religion after September 11* (ed. idem; Chicago: University of Chicago Press, 2003), 51–61, and further, in the same volume, "The Study of Religion in the Current Political Moment," 1–18 (5–8).

[3] E. Thomassen, "'Forgery' in the New Testament," in *Invention of Sacred Tradition* (see n. 1), 141–57; cf. E. E. Ellis, "Pseudonymity and Canonicity of New Testament Documents," in *History and Interpretation in New Testament Perspective* (ed. idem; BibInt 54; Leiden: Brill, 2001), 17–29.

[4] Recent attempts to link Hebrews to Apollos represent a modern analogue—and one that is all the more potentially effective insofar as it is not complicated by the existence

tive wishful thinking than with deliberate attempts to present recent compositions as older, apostolic ones. Concern about the latter practice was registered within the movement itself already in antiquity, and its occurrence is acknowledged on all hands by contemporary scholars. The question is thus not whether followers of Jesus produced pseudepigraphic texts, but which (if any) of the extant texts attributed to figures of the apostolic era are genuine compositions of their ostensible authors.

There are in fact only seven texts—commonly referred to, accordingly, as the 'undoubted letters of Paul'—that a consensus of scholars would accept as such.[5] The ascribed authorship of many others is universally rejected, while still others, as the present volume well illustrates, are subjects of varying degrees of controversy. To bring this discussion round to the central subject of this essay: of the various ancient texts ascribed to the James Paul calls "brother of the Lord" (Gal 1:19), the gospel (*Protevangelium of James*), the two *Apocalypses*, and the two extra-canonical letters (*Apocryphon of James, Letter of James to Quadratus*) are universally regarded as pseudepigraphic in modern scholarship; the authorship of the canonical Letter of James, on the other hand, is among the most hotly contested.

The debate about the Letter of James has changed little over the last two centuries of critical scholarship. The issues are well documented and relatively easily summarized, and they will be dealt with below.[6] My central concern in this essay, however, is less to simply walk yet again over this well-trod ground than to reflect more generally on the cultural location and purpose of the debate itself. I take as my starting point the sobering as-

---

of other extant writings by the figure. So, e.g., B. Witherington III, *Letters and Homilies for Jewish Christians: A Socio-Rhetorical Commentary on Hebrews, James and Jude* (Downers Grove, Ill.: IVP Academic; Nottingham: Apollos, 2007), 22–4, citing for support L. T. Johnson, *Hebrews* (NTL; Louisville, Ky.: Westminster John Knox, 2006)—a work Witherington predicts will "become the standard for pastors and seminary students" (70).

[5] It is a somewhat ironic quirk of history that these come from one whose status as 'apostle' was a matter of dispute in his own day (e.g., 1 Cor 9:2). The early debate about Paul's apostleship is interesting here insofar as it indicates that the inextricable link between apostolicity and institutional authority that would come to be so important to the phenomenon of Christian pseudepigraphy was being forged already in the group's first generation. That is, just as in later ecclesiastical usage, so already at this time the term 'apostolic' seems to serve as much to signal a link to the mythic source of primal authority as to refer to a specific group of people.

[6] One can consult virtually any critical commentary or critical introduction to the New Testament for a treatment of the main issues. Wesley Wachob boils the arguments on both sides down to a single (admittedly long) sentence each in *The Voice of Jesus in the Social Rhetoric of James* (Cambridge: Cambridge University Press, 2000), 28–9.

sessment of critical scholarship on the matter offered by Luke Timothy Johnson in his very helpful sketch of the reception history of the Letter of James:

> By the end of the nineteenth century, the battles within the historical-critical approach had reached a stalemate. Using the same methods and identical evidence, scholars came to diametrically opposed conclusions [about the dating and authorship of the Letter of James]. No one convinced anyone else. Criticism was less a matter of incremental progress than of proclaiming allegiance.[7]

Nor, he observes, did a hundred years of subsequent scholarship do much to advance the discussion:

> As in the nineteenth century, the debate concerning James' place in early Christianity has [in the twentieth century] largely consisted in 'talking past each other,' which continues with little new evidence or insight. The growth of the more radical position [i.e., the view that the letter is pseudonymous] owes as much to the politics and fashion of scholarship as it does to argumentation.[8]

If this is true with respect to the position that the letter is pseudepigraphic, the continued affirmation of its authenticity itself surely owes no less to the politics of New Testament scholarship—a point that is ironically underscored by Johnson's repetitious use of the highly charged term "radical" to effectively marginalize the position he sides against.[9] In any event, these observations raise very important questions about the politics underlying the detection of pseudepigraphy and even the nature and purpose of biblical scholarship itself. In what cultural context or contexts are debates about New Testament pseudepigraphy being played out? To whom or what are scholars effectively "proclaiming allegiance" when making pronounce-

---

[7] L. T. Johnson, *The Letter of James: A New Translation with Introduction and Commentary* (AB 37A; New York: Doubleday, 1995), 151.

[8] Ibid., 155–56.

[9] Johnson approaches the matter less in terms of authorship *per se* than one of date and provenance. Nonetheless, his conclusion that it is "a very early writing from a Palestinian Jewish Christian source" effectively excludes the possibility that the work is pseudepigraphic, whether written by James the brother of Jesus or not: "These arguments do not prove that James of Jerusalem, 'the Brother of the Lord,' wrote the letter. Such proof is unavailable, for the simple reason that, even if early, the document could still have been penned by some other 'James' ..." (ibid., 121). In any event, his repeated framing of the debate in terms of "conservative" versus "radical" positions (e.g., 148, 150, 155) is striking, particularly given the fact that both positions are already plain in antiquity, and that the latter has been if anything the majority opinion over much of the history of critical scholarship (cf. W. Pratscher, *Der Herrenbruder Jakobus und die Jakobustradition* [Göttingen: Vandenhoeck & Ruprecht, 1987], 209). In framing the matter this way, then, Johnson effectively aligns himself with (is "proclaiming allegiance" to?) medieval Christian tradition as normative center.

ments about the authorship of the Letter of James—and to what end? And if the formulation of scholarly positions is as much a function of "proclaiming allegiance" as of rational argumentation from empirical evidence, what does that say about the nature, purpose, and even integrity of the study of biblical literature as an academic field? The scholarly debate about the authorship of James presents an interesting opportunity to consider these fundamental questions.

1. The Politics of Pseudepigraphy

As noted at the outset of this essay, the possibility that deliberate forgeries may be found in a collection of sacred texts is not particularly remarkable from the point of view of the comparative study of religion. The simple fact of the matter is that misinformation and even outright deception sometimes come into play when humans compose texts and contend for authority. The task of the historian of religion who turns her attention to this issue is to understand religious pseudepigraphy, whether in general or in specific cases, precisely as an instance of this wider social construction of tradition and authority. And the first question that must be addressed when interpreting a particular work in this context is obviously whether or not it is in fact pseudepigraphic.

This project is in nature and purpose fundamentally different from that which occurs when a given religious group is confronted with the possibility of pseudepigraphic compositions within their own revered collection of scriptures. If the historian of religion is methodologically constrained to understand sacrality and its concomitant authority as social constructions (whatever their correlation with 'actual reality')[10], these are immediately present and profoundly formative realities in their own right within a religious group. There is thus much more at stake in the detection of pseudepigraphy in this context than simply 'getting it right' in an academic sense. The admission of false attributions—or, to put the matter more sharply, deliberate forgery—in the texts that one's group considers sacred may have profound ramifications for the construction of authority within

---

[10] I follow the programmatic account of the history of religions approach by B. Lincoln, "Theses on Method," in *The Insider/Outsider Problem in the Study of Religion* (ed. R. T. McCutcheon; London/New York: Cassell, 1999), 395–98: "To practice history of religions in a fashion consistent with the discipline's claim of title is to insist on discussing the temporal, contextual, situated, interested, human, and material dimensions of those discourses, practices, and institutions that characteristically represent themselves as eternal, transcendent, spiritual, and divine" (395).

that group, and thus for the social and cultural institutions that constitute its very identity. Understandably, then, interpreters who belong to a given religious group are often more reticent to acknowledge the existence of pseudepigrapha within their own scriptures than historians of religion might be.

The contemporary example of the Church of Scientology is quite instructive in this respect. It is the official and fundamental claim of Scientology to be "based exclusively upon L. Ron Hubbard's research, writings and recorded lectures—all of which constitute the Scriptures of the religion."[11] By Scientologists' own count, this canon amounts to over a half million pages of writing—on top of the more than one hundred films attributed to Hubbard, as well as the recordings and transcripts of almost three thousand lectures.[12] Insofar as Hubbard himself—or better, Hubbard as enshrined in the canon—is purportedly the sole basis for the determination of what is and is not acceptable within the religion and, more generally, to the construction of a notion of the religion's 'purity,' the claim of his actual and unadulterated authorship of all this material is crucial to the group's institutions and identity.[13] Within the group, then, the veracity of the claim is all but beyond question; and it is forcefully reasserted when those outside the group, "for simple rational reasons," find this to be an impossibly large and wide-ranging body of work for a single human being to have produced.[14]

While Scientology's various detractors might highlight this fact with the intention of undermining the religion's credibility, for the historian of religion it is neither surprising nor particularly damning.[15] From the point of view of the religion itself, however, it all amounts to the same thing: a challenge to the construction of authority around which group identity and institutions have been built, and one that therefore demands a response. Part of the group's strategy in this respect has been an attempt to add an air of scholarly legitimacy to what would otherwise be understood as a baldly dogmatic claim by appealing to the methods of critical scholarship in the

---

[11] Cited from www.scientology.org/world/worldeng/corp/des4.htm, an official website of the group, by M. Rothstein, "Scientology, Scripture, and Sacred Tradition," in *The Invention of Sacred Tradition* (see n. 1), 18–37 (21).

[12] Ibid., 21–2.

[13] Ibid., esp. 23–6.

[14] For a discussion of the metrics see ibid., 22–3 (23).

[15] As Rothstein puts it: "To the historian of religions, who understands that religious texts are produced and altered in complicated cultural processes, the fact that Scientology does the very same thing is not particularly alarming. Creating myths about sacred texts—and distancing oneself from simple historical facts—is typical in many religious contexts, so why not suspect the same in Scientology?" (ibid., 18).

service of its apologetics. The scriptural canon, it is said, has been subjected to a rigorous textual criticism, "word by word," in order to ensure "that the authenticity of each work was verified."[16] Insofar as such work is (explicitly or implicitly) informed by the *a priori* religious commitments of the group, however, it can only be seen as apologetics in a scholarly mode—simply a perpetuation of pseudepigraphy by other means. Another interesting datum for a history-of-religions study of pseudepigraphy to be sure, but not itself an example of such an investigation.

The general dynamic is not altogether different in the case of Christianity and its canon. A substantial body of Christians similarly rejects out of hand the notion of biblical pseudepigraphy, though sometimes with at least a veneer of academic argumentation.[17] On the other hand, the simple fact that many self-described Christians concede the pseudepigraphic character of some New Testament works shows that the situation presented by Christianity is much more complex in this respect. Nor is this particularly surprising given that Christianity has roughly 1,900 more years of history behind it, and encompasses a much wider array of institutional and theological variations. Particularly consequential in this connection is the fact that the academic study of religion itself developed within a predominantly Christian culture, not a Scientological one. In particular, the critical study of the New Testament began as, and in very large measure remains today, the province of Christianity itself, an expression of Christianity's own intellectual culture.[18] Thus while it is true that some contemporary Christians flatly dismiss the findings of critical scholarship regarding canonical pseudepigraphy, it is also true that in most cases those very findings were pioneered internally, by other Christian theologians, and sometimes for no less pious reasons. Quite differently than with Scientology, then, *the academy is itself one of the arenas in which Christian apologetics play out.*

In this setting, the ecclesiastical projects of canon maintenance and authority negotiation involve a more complex array of strategies. One might, for example, play genuine works off against pseudepigraphic ones to great

---

[16] www.scientology.org/p_jpg/world/worldeng/corp/rtc2.htm, cited by Rothstein, ibid., 25. This move can be understood in light of Rothstein's more general observation regarding Scientology's characteristic "strategy of defense and counter-strike" to deal with the myriad charges of its detractors, including "call[ing] upon the scholarly community in order to obtain objective assessments" (18).

[17] Cf. D. G. Meade, *Pseudonymity and Canon: An Investigation into the Relationship of Authorship and Authority in Jewish and Earliest Christian Tradition* (Grand Rapids, Mich.: Eerdmans, 1987), 3 with n. 6.

[18] One need only consider the number of standard publishing outlets for biblical scholarship that have Christian affiliations, or the number of academic series produced explicitly with pastoral or seminary audiences in mind.

effect.[19] More subtly, studies of canonical pseudepigraphy may be driven by a second-order anxiety to interpret the phenomenon in a way that preserves at least the *moral* authority of the relevant texts.[20] To the extent that this is the case, pseudepigraphy is being processed ecclesiastically as much as studied critically, with such scholarship itself becoming yet another interesting datum for a history-of-religions study of the phenomenon.

It is interesting to observe in this connection that of all the ancient works ascribed to James the brother of Jesus, the only one whose authenticity is ardently defended among modern scholars happens also to be the only one considered sacred scripture by Christians. Nor is this an isolated phenomenon. In point of fact, while few if any of the ostensibly apostolic works outside the canon have ever been considered anything but pseudepigraphic over the history of scholarship, one need not look far to find scholarly publications supporting the genuinely apostolic character of most if not all those included in the New Testament.[21] To be sure, in some cases this correlation simply reflects the nature of the evidence in the individual texts themselves; no doubt the so-called 'undoubted letters of Paul' generally present much more compelling cases for authenticity than, say, Paul's purported correspondence with Seneca. On the other hand, the broad correlation between canonical status and intensity of scholarly debate regarding authenticity is precisely what one might predict given the historical and sociological relationship between the academic study of Christianity and Christianity itself.

Whether the evidence for or against the Letter of James's authorship by the brother of Jesus is as compelling as in, say, the case of Galatians or of

---

[19] One thinks, for example, of the importance that the distinction between doubted and undoubted letters of Paul has had for feminist theology and for its reconstruction of Christian origins.

[20] An anxiety about the moral implications of the phenomenon is a driving force in a number of major studies of New Testament pseudepigraphy. See esp. Meade, *Pseudonymity and Canon* (see n. 17), 1–12, which surveys the scholarly attempts to deal with "the ever present tension between the concept of canon and the discovery of pseudonymity in the NT" (1) before offering its own attempt to resolve the tension. See further Ellis, "Pseudonymity and Canonicity" (see n. 3), which analyzes the scholarly preoccupation, particularly after Baur, with the patently ecclesiastical question of whether pseudepigraphic works should remain in the canon. With respect to the Letter of James in particular, Ellis notes F. H. Kern's early view that its pseudonymity posed no ethical problem (20, citing "Der Charakter und Ursprung des Briefs Jakobi," *Tübinger Zeitschrift für Theologie* [1835]); cf. further in this respect M. Dibelius, *James: A Commentary on the Epistle of James* (11th ed.; rev. H. Greeven; trans. M. Williams; Hermeneia; Philadelphia: Fortress Press, 1988), 19–20.

[21] Ellis ("Pseudonymity and Canon" [see n. 3], 19 n. 16), for example, points out that the first edition of the Roman Catholic *Jerome Biblical Commentary* "identified only II Peter as a pseudepigraphon."

Paul's correspondence with Seneca is of course debatable. If nearly two hundred years of critical scholarship on the matter has taught us anything, it is that. But it is equally certain that this very scholarship represents a complex tangle of what are in fact two fundamentally different projects: a history-of-religions project that seeks to explain the letter's composition in relation to a historical account of early Jesus veneration; and an ecclesiastical project that seeks to clarify the letter's authority in relation to the primal, sacred (i.e., apostolic) authority of Christianity itself. It is not altogether surprising then, to see a vigorous debate regarding the authenticity of a canonical work that some Christians have found to be *theologically* problematic; to find scholarship on the letter that is "less a matter of incremental progress than of proclaiming allegiance."[22] In any event, if there is to be any progress made toward an explanation of the Letter of James from the perspective of the history of religion, we must no doubt begin by disembedding this project from the ecclesiastical one.

2. Christian Debates on the Apostolic Authorship of James

Evidence for Christian rejection of the authenticity of the Letter of James appears virtually as early as evidence for the letter itself. The first indisputable references to the letter appear in the third-century writings of Origen. For his part, the Alexandrian clearly considered it to be the work of an apostle and thus authoritative scripture,[23] though his reference to it as ἡ φερομένη Ἰακώβου ἐπιστολή may well signal his awareness that this position was not entirely non-controversial.[24] In fact, the letter is strikingly absent from the list of works "accepted in the catholic church" according to the Muratorian Canon[25]—an omission, though, that may signal that it

---

[22] Johnson, *Letter of James* (see n. 7), 151.

[23] For evidence see J. H. Ropes, *A Critical and Exegetical Commentary on the Epistle of St. James* (ICC; Edinburgh: T&T Clark, 1991), 92–3. Ropes's suggestion that Origen may however have "believed the epistle to have been written by some other Apostle James" than the brother of Jesus overlooks the explicit description of the author as "James, the brother of the Lord" in Origen's commentary on Romans (*Origen: Commentary on the Epistle to the Romans Books 1–5* [trans. T. P. Scheck; FC; Washington, D.C.: Catholic University of America Press, 2001], 280 [4.8.2 = PG 14:989]).

[24] That is, "the letter bearing [the title] 'of James.'" The Greek text is cited from Ropes, ibid., 92. Cf. the translation of R. E. Heine, *Origen: Commentary on the Gospel According to John Books 13–32* (FC; Washington, D.C.: The Catholic University Press of America, 1993), 202 (19, 152): "the epistle that is in circulation as the work of James."

[25] I follow the translation in H. Y. Gamble, *The New Testament Canon: Its Making and Meaning* (Philadelphia: Fortress Press, 1985), 93–5.

was not yet known to the second- or third-century compiler of this canon rather than an explicit rejection of it. At any rate, the picture becomes much clearer in the fourth century. Like Origen, Eusebius treats the Letter of James as "apostolic" and "scriptural" in practice.[26] However, with phrases reminiscent of Origen's he elsewhere concedes quite explicitly that the authenticity of the letter "said to be of James" is denied by some, and thus includes it in a category of "disputed writings."[27] Decades later Jerome would acknowledge plainly that some considered the Letter of James to have been a pseudonymous work that only gradually came to be considered authoritative.[28]

The arguments raised against the letter's authenticity in antiquity cannot be reconstructed with any depth. While dutifully acknowledging the debate, both Eusebius and Jerome consider the letter to be authoritative, and neither seems particularly interested in laying out the case made against it in detail. If Eusebius' comments on the detection of "heretical" pseudepigrapha can serve as any sort of guide, one might expect the arguments to have run in one or more of three directions: (i) the extent to which it was used by one's favored prior authorities (i.e., what Eusebius calls "the succession of the orthodox"); (ii) the character of its discourse in relation to some assumed construction of "apostolic ethos" (τὸ ἦθος τὸ ἀποστολικόν); and (iii) the nature of its theology in relation to an assumed construction of "true orthodoxy" (ἡ ἀληθὴς ὀρθοδοξία).[29] It must immediately be pointed out, however, that Eusebius's whole presentation implies that he had no reason to believe that the third of these, at least, had been any kind of an issue in the case of our letter. The disputes with which he is above all concerned when discussing the Letter of James seem not to be inter-sectarian, but those taking place within his own group, i.e., the one he

---

[26] Johnson, *Letter of James* (see n. 7), 127.

[27] See *Hist. eccl.* 2.23.24–25, referring to Ἰάκωβον, οὗ ἡ πρώτη τῶν ὀνομαζομένων καθολικῶν ἐπιστολῶν εἶναι λέγεται; and *Hist. eccl.* 3.25.3, which calls the letter ἡ λεγομένη Ἰακώβου [ἐπιστολή] in this connection.

[28] *Vir. ill.* 2: "[James] wrote a single epistle, which is reckoned among the seven Catholic Epistles, and even this is claimed by some to have been published by someone else under his name, and gradually as time went on to have gained authority" [*unam tantum scripsit epistolam, quae de septem Catholicis est, quae et ipsa ab alio quodam sub nomine ejus edita asseritur, licet paulatim tempore procedente obtinuerit auctoritatem*] (*Saint Jerome: On Illustrious Men* [trans. T. P. Halton; FC; Washington, D.C.: Catholic University of America Press, 1999], 7 [= PL 23:639]).

[29] *Hist. eccl.* 3.25.6–7: "To none of these [pseudepigrapha composed by 'heretics'] has any who belonged to the succession of the orthodox ever thought it right to refer in his writings. Moreover, the type of phraseology differs from apostolic style (τὸ ἦθος τὸ ἀποστολικόν), and the opinion and tendency of their contents is widely dissonant from true orthodoxy and clearly shows that they are the forgeries of heretics."

equated with "true orthodoxy."[30] On the other hand, Eusebius is quite explicit elsewhere that the first of these factors was a major issue in the case of the Letter of James: "its authenticity is denied," he says, "since few of the ancients quote it" (*Hist. eccl.* 2.23.25). The extent to which "apostolic ethos" was also an issue is less clear.[31]

Whether an actual composition of James or not, the letter did indeed, as Jerome's report says, come to be generally *considered* authentic only gradually. And if the lack of precedent for its authoritative usage was a major factor in its rejection, it was precisely the increase in such usage that would ultimately become definitive for its acceptance. Eusebius counters those who would point out that the letter does not figure importantly into earlier ecclesiastical writings by asserting that "nevertheless we know that [it has] been used publicly with the rest in most churches."[32] And as the list of ecclesiastical authorities who acknowledged the letter's apostolic status gradually increased, the earlier absence of such became a moot point; challenges to its authenticity on any grounds would increasingly imply a challenge to the acknowledged authorities of the Church. A critical mass of such authorities was apparently reached by the end of the fourth century, at least among Greek and Latin writers.[33] With the inclusion of the letter in

---

[30] In Eusebius's taxonomy of early Christian literature the *prima divisio* is orthodox/heterodox, with "recognized," "disputed," and even "spurious" serving as varieties of the former. He draws a distinction, first, "between those writings which, *according to the tradition of the Church*, are true, genuine and recognized, and those which differ from them in that they are not canonical but disputed, yet nevertheless are known *to most of the writers of the Church*" (*Hist. eccl.* 3.25.6). Both of these, however, are to be distinguished from "writings which are put forward *by heretics* under the name of the apostles," to which "orthodox" writers never refer—and which thus are to be "reckoned not even among spurious books but shunned as altogether wicked and impious."

[31] It is possible that Jerome's use of *edita* in the passage quoted above (see n. 28) implies that the position in question was that some genuine teaching of James had been compiled and "edited" by a later hand. If that is the case, the position presumably would have arisen out of a concern that the style of the letter seemed somehow incongruous with James, even if its teaching did not. The theory of such an editor would thus serve to concede an argument from "apostolic ethos" while still safeguarding the all-important claim of apostolicity. For modern examples of this position see below.

[32] *Hist. eccl.* 2.23.25. It is doubtful that this argument can be taken as straightforward evidence for the letter's popular usage beyond Eusebius' own time and place. If, on the other hand, it were taken as such, the letter's omission from the Muratorian Canon would begin to look more like conscious rejection than ignorance of the text's existence.

[33] Johnson's explanation of the "dramatic appearance of James by way of canonical lists and extensive citation in the last two decades of the fourth century" in terms of institutional loyalty is very much to the point (*Letter of James* [see n. 7], 136). The Syrian church, where the letter continued to be disputed, is a different story, see Ropes, *Epistle of St. James* (see n. 23), 96–100.

the New Testament canon, the question of its apostolicity was for all practical purposes settled.

Christian debate regarding the authorship of the Letter of James, however, found new life—and took a decidedly different turn—during the Protestant Reformation. The critical spirit that characterized the Renaissance had already led Christian intellectuals like Erasmus to re-raise old doubts about the letter—albeit without entirely abandoning allegiance to the orthodox consensus concerning its authoritative status.[34] For Martin Luther, however, allegiance to established ecclesiastical tradition was scarcely a decisive consideration. What is more, when Luther devoted his entire preface to the letter to explaining why he did "not regard [the Letter of James] as the writing of an apostle,"[35] the central issue, perhaps for the first time in the letter's reception history, became something approaching Eusebius' third consideration: concern regarding its coherence with an assumed understanding of Christian truth.

> In the first place it is flatly against St. Paul and all the rest of Scripture in ascribing justification to works ... This fault, therefore, proves that this epistle is not the work of any apostle.[36]

Indeed, as Luther goes on to develop a second point along the lines of the criterion of apostolic ethos, the argument again turns entirely on the content of James's teaching:

> In the second place its purpose is to teach Christians, but in all this long teaching it does not once mention the Passion, the resurrection, or the Spirit of Christ ... Now it is the office of a true apostle to preach of the Passion and resurrection and office of Christ, and to lay the foundation for faith in him ... All the genuine sacred books agree on this ... And that is the true test by which to judge all books, when we see whether or not they inculcate Christ ... But this James does nothing more than drive to the law and to its works.[37]

It is particularly important to observe that Luther's primary concern in developing these arguments is not the letter's authorship *per se* so much as its apostolicity. His thesis, that is, is stated and re-stated not in terms of the

---

[34] Johnson, *Letter of James* (see n. 7), 140–41, who points out that what Erasmus did however dispute was that Jas 5:14–16 provided scriptural support for the rite of extreme unction.

[35] "Preface to the Epistles of St. James and St. Jude," in *Luther's Works* (ed. E. T. Bachman; Philadelphia: Muhlenberg, 1967), 35:395–97 (396). In what would become the classic Protestant move, Luther sought to leapfrog ecclesiastical authority by rooting his position in an *earlier* (cf. 'original') Christian tradition, opening his preface to the letter cleverly, if perhaps somewhat disingenuously, by insisting on his own high regard for it despite the fact that it was, he says, "rejected by the ancients" (395)!

[36] Ibid., 35:396.

[37] Ibid., 35:396–97.

letter's authorship by *James*, but its authorship by "*an apostle*" or indeed "*any apostle*." To be sure, Luther does finally get around to arguing against the likelihood of its authorship by James in particular, citing more historical arguments like the nature of its composition and its apparent (to Luther) reliance on 1 Peter.[38] But as he himself makes plain, this is all quite secondary to his core point about apostolicity:

> Whatever does not teach Christ is not yet apostolic, even though St. Peter or St. Paul does the teaching. Again, whatever preaches Christ would be apostolic, even if Judas, Annas, Pilate, and Herod were doing it.[39]

Implicit in this argument is an acknowledgment of the logical distinction between two concepts that had (and have) long been conflated in the Christian discourse of apostolicity: authorship and authority.[40] Clearly the latter is Luther's real concern, and the reason he questioned the letter's authorship in the first place. The underlying purpose of the argument emerges unmistakably as he concludes the *Preface*:

> [The author of the letter] tries to accomplish by harping on the law what the apostles accomplish by stimulating people to love. *Therefore, I will not have him in my Bible to be numbered among the true chief books*, though I would not prevent anyone from including or extolling him as he pleases, for there are otherwise many good sayings in him. One man is no man in worldly things. How then should this single man alone avail against Paul and all the rest of Scripture?[41]

In short, Luther's argument was less about the human authorship of a text from the Christian past than the sacred authority of a scripture in the Christian present—a point scarcely lost on those Christian intellectuals, Catholic and Protestant, who reacted with pointed reassertions of the letter's authority.[42] To argue about the historical question of James's authorship in this ecclesiastical setting is simply to negotiate group authority by other means.

Nonetheless, it was precisely on the terrain of historical argumentation that Christian debate about the status of the letter of James vis-à-vis sacred authority and Christian truth would be increasingly carried out in subsequent centuries. If the Reformers' distinction between ecclesiastical tradi-

---

[38] Ibid., 35:397.

[39] Ibid., 35:396–97.

[40] A conflation apparently read into Luther by Johnson when he says that "apostolic authorship ... for Luther determined [the letter's] authority" (*Letter of James* [see n. 7], 141).

[41] Cf. *Luther's Works* (see n. 35), 35:397 with n. 53 (emphasis added). This conclusion is softened somewhat in editions published after 1530, when the first clause in the second sentence was changed to read simply, "Therefore I cannot include him among the chief books," and the elaboration of the proverbial *Einer ist keiner* was dropped entirely.

[42] For a brief sketch see Johnson, *Letter of James* (see n. 7), 141–43.

tion and Christian truth became the driving force behind a Protestant intellectual quest to recover the 'original,' 'genuine' gospel of Jesus and the apostles, the critical humanism of the Enlightenment furnished the tools with which subsequent layers of Catholic doctrine could be peeled back to reveal that supposed 'original Christianity.' The eventual result was what we now recognize as the historical-critical study of the New Testament.[43] Luther's preoccupation with the *logical* relationship of our letter's teaching to Paul's—is the former's position on faith, works, and the law consistent with the latter's, and indeed with "all the rest of Scripture"?—was now reframed as an *historical* question: Does the Letter of James presuppose, and perhaps even react against, Paul's teaching on faith, works, and the law? More fundamentally, the logical distinction between apostolic authorship and Christian authority implicitly acknowledged by Luther was itself given a historical twist, particularly in the influential work of F. C. Baur.

Baur's liberal Protestantism manifested itself in the notion that the 'original Christianity' of Jesus—and, what is more, its "superiority above all that more or less resembled it in the ancient world"—consisted in a certain "inner disposition," a universal "spirituality" that utterly transcended any "outward act" or religious doctrine.[44] He also argued, however, that this was understood neither by Peter and the original apostles nor by James the brother of Jesus, who propagated instead a misunderstanding of Jesus' teaching that amounted to merely "a new and stronger form of the old [Jewish] Messianic expectations," not true Christianity.[45] It was only with the apostle Paul, in a manner that even the avowedly humanistic Baur could only describe as a "miracle,"[46] that true Christianity was kept alive.[47] Catholicism, on the other hand, was to be explained as the result of

---

[43] Seen in this light, the fact that Roman Catholics were comparatively slow to embrace critical biblical scholarship is less than surprising.

[44] F. C. Baur, *The Church History of the First Three Centuries* (3d ed.; trans. A. Menzies; 2 vols.; London: Williams & Norgate, 1878), 1:9–37 (9, 29).

[45] Ibid., 1:43.

[46] Albeit a "miracle" that can be couched in quasi-historical terms as "a spiritual process"; see ibid., 1:47–8. Cf. in this respect Baur's appeal to the "miracle of the resurrection" of Jesus, though with the caveat that this may have been either "an outward objective miracle" or "a subjective psychological" one (1:42). Compare to both of these passages Baur's otherwise cogent remarks on the methodological problem that appealing to miracle poses for those engaged in the academic study of history (1:1–2).

[47] "Had no new development [i.e., Paul's conversion] taken place, the only difference between the believing disciples and their unbelieving countrymen would have been that to the former the Messiah would have been one who had come already, and to the latter one who was still to come. The Christian faith would have become the faith of a mere Jewish sect, in whose keeping the whole future of Christianity would have been imperilled" (ibid., 1:43).

the combination of the 'true' gospel of Jesus and Paul with the 'misunderstood' version propagated by James and the apostles.

With this reconstruction, Baur effectively severed the long-standing Christian correlation of 'apostolicity' with 'truth' and 'authority'—and with a force that had not been seen since the days of Marcion. Christian interpreters were confronted with the startling proposition that the Letter of James, if an authentic work of the brother of Jesus, would be substantially less than a true and authoritative expression of Christianity; that if, on the other hand, it actually agreed with Paul's 'true' gospel it could not be genuinely apostolic. In fact, despite what he took to be the letter's "distinctly anti-pauline" treatment of justification, Baur concluded from its concepts of "implanted *logos*" (1:21) and "law of freedom" (1:25, 2:12) that it also embraced at least to some extent "the Pauline idea of making the law an inward thing." Such a combination, he argued, could only be understood in the context of the post-apostolic reconciliation of the Pauline gospel with so-called "Jewish Christianity."[48] While thus agreeing with Luther that the letter was not written by James, Baur argued that this was so precisely insofar as it *agreed with Paul* in some measure. Baur's ambivalence about the validity of the letter's witness to 'Christian truth' in any case approached that of Luther himself.[49]

From Eusebius to Luther, the issue driving the Christian debate regarding the apostolic authorship of the Letter of James was less its composition history than its authoritative status for Christians in the present; less the authenticity of its authorial ascription than the authenticity of its witness to 'Christian truth.' After Luther, though, this negotiation of group authority became increasingly bound up in historical-critical analysis of the letter's authorship. If by the end of the nineteenth century interpretation had increasingly become the property of the academy, however, the scholarly interpreters themselves remained nonetheless in large measure church-

---

[48] Ibid., 1:128–29; the points are developed with more depth in an appendix to Baur's *Paul the Apostle of Jesus Christ: His Life and Works, His Epistles and Teachings* (repr. 2 vols. in one; Peabody, Mass.: Hendrickson, 2003), 297–313.

[49] "What is this but going back to a position which Paul had already overcome? The absolute standpoint of Christian consciousness which Paul took up in his doctrine of faith is degraded again to that of Judaeo-Christianity, at which a value is ascribed to works, which from their very nature they cannot possibly have" (ibid., 304). Note in this connection that despite his historical orientation, Baur remained, like Luther, particularly preoccupied by the *logical* relationship of James's soteriology to Paul's. To be sure, he is aware of "other ways" in which "the Epistle betrays the circumstances of a later age" (*Church History* [see n. 44], 1:130); but the fact that he does not spell them out indicate that they are peripheral to his argument. See further on this general distinction below.

men.⁵⁰ The tangle of ecclesiastical apologetics and historical analysis evident in the work of Baur has continued, sometimes in more subtle and sometimes more obvious forms, and in arguments both for and against the letter's authorship by James.⁵¹ Indeed, even where such apologetics are not explicitly invoked, one suspects that ecclesiastical concerns—to make a point about the 'original gospel'; to ensure the apostolic authority of the canon; to ensure at any rate its moral integrity—are not infrequently the unseen thumb on the scale when the evidence for the authorship of the Letter of James is weighed. Seen in this context, the curious mix of historical argumentation and simple "proclaiming allegiance" that Johnson has observed in scholarship on our letter is less than surprising.

3. Historical Analysis of the Authorship of James

If Christian debate regarding the authorship of the Letter of James has been generated largely as a secondary function of ecclesiastical disputes about the authority of tradition, the nature of the 'true gospel,' and the integrity of the scriptural canon, it has nonetheless brought to the surface a series of historical considerations that can be critically analyzed as such by the historian of religion. Two such issues were raised by Luther himself, albeit apparently as afterthoughts and merely suggestive ones at that. The first concerns the manner of the letter's composition.

Besides, [the author of the letter] throws things together so chaotically that it seems to me he must have been some good, pious man, who took a few sayings from the disciples of the apostles and thus tossed them off on paper.⁵²

---

[50] Cf. Johnson, *Letter of James* (see n. 7), 151: "The scholars [at the close of the nineteenth century] were almost all churchmen, but interpretation increasingly became the property of the academy."

[51] For a recent and particularly heavy-handed example, see Witherington, *Letters and Homilies* (see n. 4), 395–401. While conceding that he "cannot a priori rule out the possibility of a pseudonymous document in the canon" since the practice is attested in antiquity (and "even," he allows, "in Jewish and Christian contexts"!), he opens his treatment of the issue by declaring that "one must decide whether such a deception comports with the idea of conveying Christian truth" (396). Cf. in this respect the two principle arguments against James's pseudonymity identified and addressed by Dibelius, *James* (see n. 20), 19: first, that "the text nowhere tries to prove that its author was the well-known James"; and second, "the refusal to believe such a Christian teacher capable of a deliberative fraud." Dibelius, who concludes that the work is pseudonymous, proceeds to argue for "the complete *innocence of this pseudonymity*" (20 [emphasis original]).

[52] *Luther's Works* [see n. 35], 35:397. For a much more negative appraisal of the author's motive and relation to apostolic teaching by Luther, see 54:424: "I maintain that some Jew wrote it who probably heard about Christian people but never encountered any. Since he heard that Christians place great weight on faith in Christ, he thought 'Wait a

This line of argument found full flower in the commentary of Martin Dibelius, which presented a running argument that the text was not a real letter at all, but a random collection of sayings and short treatises compiled by a Christian of the "second generation" "at the earliest."[53] But while Dibelius's treatment of the letter proved to be the most influential of the 20th century, scholarship in recent decades has shown that it is untenable. It is now clear that the letter is no mere collection, being both in structure and in thought much more coherent than Dibelius's (and Luther's) reading allows.[54]

A different sort of argument from composition is also frequently invoked to support the letter's authenticity. The fact that the letter neither magnifies the authority of its author, nor makes reference to specific historical situations of James, nor mentions other individuals in his orbit, it is said, indicates that it was not engaged in the sort of "fictional elaboration" frequently found in pseudepigraphic works.[55] But the letter's failure to situate its author in personal relationships or situations may simply be a function of its wide-open address "to the twelve tribes in the Diaspora" (1:1) rather than to some particular, localized community. And if the letter assumes that its open-ended audience will recognize the identity and authority of its author merely by identifying him as "James, slave of God and of the Lord Jesus Christ," this is at least as understandable, if not more so, in the post-apostolic era.[56]

The other historical line of argument initiated by Luther concerns the literary relationship of our letter to other early Christian works.

> Moreover he [sc. the author of the letter] cites the sayings of St. Peter [several references to 1 Peter follow] ... [and] also the saying of St. Paul in Galatians [citing 5:17, cf. Jas 4:5] ... And yet, in point of time, St. James was put to death by Herod in Jerusalem, before St. Peter. So it seems that [this author] came long after St. Peter and St. Paul.[57]

---

moment! I'll oppose them and urge works alone.'" This view is expressed immediately following a suggestion that "We ... throw the Epistle of James out of this school."

[53] Dibelius, *James* (see n. 20), 21.

[54] For convenient summaries see M. E. Taylor, "Recent Scholarship on the Structure of James," *Currents in Biblical Research* 3 (2004): 86–115; M. Konradt, "Theologie in der 'strohernen Epistel': Ein Literaturbericht zu neueren Ansätzen in der Exegese des Jakobusbriefes," *VF* 44 (1999): 54–78.

[55] Cf. Johnson, *Letter of James* (see n. 7), 118. Dibelius took this instead as an indication of the "complete *innocence of this pseudonymity*"; that the letter's ascription to James "cannot be regarded as a fraudulent attempt to deceive" (*James* [see n. 20], 20 [emphasis original]).

[56] Contrast P. Hartin, *James* (SP 14; Collegeville, Minn.: Liturgical Press, 2003), 24. Indeed, even modern interpreters have no trouble agreeing on which James is intended by the address; see below n. 58.

[57] *Luther's Works* (see n. 35), 35:397.

The reference to the death of the apostle James as reported in Acts 12 is irrelevant if, as is overwhelmingly probable, the James in question in our letter is to be taken with reference to the brother of Jesus, not the brother of John.[58] Nor are the specific instances of dependence cited by Luther particularly compelling. The Greek texts of Jas 4:5 and Gal 5:17 have little in common, and the similarities between 1 Peter and James, while certainly striking, could be explained equally well, if not better, in terms of their reliance on a common ancient discourse[59] or the reliance of 1 Peter—itself now widely acknowledged to be pseudonymous—on our letter.[60] By the same token, subsequent attempts to shore up support for the authenticity of the Letter of James by establishing that it was known by one or more second-century works are scarcely more decisive, particularly for the question of authorship.[61] Nor is its oft-discussed relation to the synoptic tradition.[62]

More potentially fruitful for anchoring the letter historically is the question of its knowledge of Pauline teaching. The issues that have garnered the most attention in this respect are its mockery of the notion that "faith apart from works" (ἡ πίστις χωρὶς τῶν ἔργων) is soteriologically efficacious (2:14–26, esp. vv. 18, 20, 26; cf. Rom 3:28; Gal 2:15–16); its interpretation in this connection of Abraham and especially of Gen 15:6 (2:20–

---

[58] On this point, at least, virtually all contemporary scholars agree. See, e.g., Dibelius, *James* (see n. 20), 11–2 for the basic argument.

[59] So, e.g., Ropes, *Epistle of St. James* (see n. 23), 22–3; Dibelius, *James* (see n. 20), 30–1; M. E. Boismard, "Une liturgie baptismale dans la Prima Petri: II – Son Influence sur l'Épître de Jacques," *RB* 64 (1957), 161–83; F. Mußner, *Der Jakobusbrief* (3d ed.; HTKNT 13/1; Freiburg i. Brsg.: Herder, 1975), 33–5; cf. W. Popkes, *Der Brief des Jakobus* (THKNT 14; Leipzig: Ev. Verlagsanstalt, 2001), 39–40, and Johnson, *Letter of James* (see n. 7), 54–5.

[60] So, e.g., J. Mayor, *The Epistle of St. James* (3d ed.; repr. Grand Rapids, Mich.: Zondervan, 1954), cii–cviii.

[61] Perhaps the most extreme example is provided by Mayor, who seeks to support the letter's authenticity with arguments that it was used, among others, by Clement, Ignatius, Polycarp, *Didache*, *Epistle of Barnabas*, *Shepherd of Hermas*, and Justin Martyr (*Epistle of James* [see n. 60], lxvi–lxxxiv). More recently—and rather more modestly—Johnson has argued that use of the Letter of James by *Shepherd of Hermas* is "virtually certain"; that its use by *1 Clement* is a "strong probability"; and that there is "some possibility" that it was used also by *Sentences of Sextus* and the *Teachings of Silvanus* (*Letter of James* [see n. 7], 79).

[62] While the text seems in some way related to the synoptic tradition, it does not show direct dependence on any one or another of the gospels. This is sometimes interpreted as evidence for the author's special closeness to Jesus (e.g., Hartin, *James* [see n. 56], 22, 81–8)—indeed the closeness of a brother. However, one might also compare in this respect *Didache*, a text frequently dated to the post-70 CE era. Making this still more unlikely in the case of our letter is the Hellenistic twist it gives to some, at least, of these sayings (see below).

24, cf. Rom 4, Gal 3:6–9); and its repeated association of the law with "freedom" (1:25, 2:12, contrast Gal 4:21–5:1 and 2:4).[63] Given the resonance of these items with both Luther's critique of the letter and Baur's reconstruction of Christian origins, it is here above all that ostensibly historical argumentation seems frequently to become little more than a vehicle for ecclesiastical apologetics—and on both sides of the debate.[64] One must in any case take great care to distinguish clearly several logically distinct issues that too often run together in the scholarly literature. First, the letter's knowledge of Pauline teaching and the historical relationship between the brother of Jesus and the apostle Paul are not the same issue. Much as in the case of the relationship of our letter to *Hermas* or *1 Clement*, one can investigate the relationship of two sets of discourse quite apart from any particular reconstruction of the social relationship of their ostensible authors. Second, one must be careful to distinguish the issue of the *historical* relationship between our letter and Paul's teaching from the *logical* relationship of their respective soteriologies. Despite the frequent conflation in the scholarly literature, the question of whether the letter *actually* contradicts Paul's teaching on faith and works is different from the question of whether it *intends* to do so. The former issue, naturally, may be of utmost concern to Christians who are concerned with matters of canonical and/or apostolic harmony, or who find actual soteriological realities expressed in these works. But it is rather beside the point if we are simply

---

[63] Less discussed, but also important, is its treatment of Lev 19:18 in Jas 2:8–11, on which see M. Jackson-McCabe, *Logos and Law in the Letter of James: The Law of Nature, the Law of Moses, and the Law of Freedom* (NovTSup 100; Leiden: Brill, 2001), 165–76, 248–49.

[64] Johnson chalks up scholarship's "constant, if not obsessive, attention" to our letter's relation to Paul at least in part to "the theological preoccupations that have dominated a purportedly 'scientific' study of the Bible" (*Letter of James* [see n. 7], 156). And if it is easy to see how pious anxieties for the unity of the canon and/or the apostolic era might lead to a denial that our letter had any knowledge of (let alone intention to dispute) Paul's teaching, defenders of the latter position find the opposing view to be equally ideologically driven. Thus recently Hartin: "Those scholars who see [Jas 2:14–26] as an attack on Paul's understanding of 'justification through faith alone' are influenced by an ideological perception that wishes to see everything in the New Testament as related to Paul and his thought" (*James* [see n. 56], 22). Johnson's commentary manifests a similar (and similarly Catholic) sensitivity to such a "Lutheran" reading of history in general and of James in particular; see, e.g., his observation regarding "the historical and theological bias still very influential in NT scholarship, which sees Paul not only as the first of our extant Christian witnesses but also as the most important" (*Letter of James* [see n. 7], 111). Like Hartin, Johnson rejects the idea that the Letter of James reacts to Pauline teaching (120).

interested to determine whether one has some knowledge—however fairly portrayed—of the other.[65]

On the face of it, the same three logical possibilities for explaining the relationship between the Letter of James and 1 Peter obtain here as well. The view that Paul relies on the Letter of James, however, finds little support.[66] In practice, the argument is really between those who think that the Letter of James reacts to Pauline teaching (the majority position) and those who would argue that the two are simply drawing on a common ancient discourse (the position of the minority, albeit a growing one particularly in English-language scholarship). The issues are complex; but in this case, at least, the majority opinion happens also to be the one best supported by the evidence. Whether "actually contradicting" Paul or not, it is overwhelmingly probable that our letter reacts in some way to formulations that were peculiarly Pauline.[67]

Even granting this, however, does not settle the question of the letter's authorship. One need not subscribe to any particular reconstruction of the relationship of the brother of Jesus to the apostle Paul to conclude that the historical interaction of the two, particularly in situations that apparently gave rise to the Pauline notions in question in the first place (cf. Gal 1:18–2:14), could well have resulted in the former having some knowledge of the distinctive ideas of the latter. In fact it seems rather clear that—however deep it ran and however long it lasted—there was at least at some point some manner of tension between the two men on precisely these questions of Torah observance and Jew-Gentile relations within the group (esp. Gal 2:11–14). To be sure, if the Letter of James could be shown to be drawing on Paul's letters,[68] that would be a strong indication that it was

---

[65] To frame the matter in terms of logical contradiction is to overlook the possibility of polemical caricature. Those Paul refers to in Rom 3:8, for example, clearly had both some knowledge of his teaching and some intention to make a mockery of it. This is obvious regardless of whether their own position on ethics (whatever it may have been) represented an actual, logical contradiction of what can be reconstructed of his.

[66] Mayor, not surprisingly (see above n. 61!), is a notable exception. He concludes not only that Paul knew our letter, but that he indeed "writes with constant reference" to it (*Epistle of St. James* [see n. 60], xci–cii). The argument has for good reason found little or no traction in subsequent scholarship—though note the passing comment of Johnson, *Letter of James* (see n. 7), 110.

[67] Johnson's attempt to overturn this view is thoroughly flawed; see Jackson-McCabe, *Logos and Law* (see n. 63), 243–52.

[68] So, e.g., M. Tsuji, *Glaube zwischen Vollkommenheit und Verweltlichung: Eine Untersuchung zur literarischen Gestalt und zur inhaltlichen Kohärenz des Jakobusbriefes* (WUNT II/93; Tübingen: Mohr Siebeck, 1997), 187–99; M. M. Mitchell, "The Letter of James as a Document of Paulinism?" in *Reading James with New Eyes: Methodological Reassessments of the Letter of James* (eds. R. L. Webb and J. S. Kloppenborg; Library of New Testament Studies 342; London/New York: T&T Clark, 2007), 75–98.

written well after the death of James in 62 CE. But one must also reckon with the possibility that the letter interacts with orally transmitted theologoumena rather than actual texts.[69] The most we can conclude from this, then, is that the letter could have been composed no earlier than what would have been the last several years of its ostensible author's life.

More important than the question of the letter's knowledge of Pauline ideas, then, is the coherence of its teaching with what is otherwise known about the teaching of James the brother of Jesus. This seemingly straightforward question is itself quite complicated, however, and not least by the fact that our evidence for him is regrettably slim. All the other ancient texts attributed to him (or, in the case of the Pseudo-Clementine *Epistula Petri*, written to him) are universally recognized to be pseudepigraphic. Third-person reports about him are often brief, sometimes legendary, and always informed by the rhetorical and theological purposes of their tradents.[70] In short, the evidence yields little for purposes of comparison with our letter, let alone with any depth, about what exactly Jesus veneration entailed as far as Jesus' brother James was concerned. And for reasons that should by now be obvious, reconstruction of the messianic thought and praxis of a leading figure of the apostolic era—particularly in relation to Paul—will be no less loaded from an ecclesiastical point of view than the interpretation of a text bearing his name; indeed, apologetic creativity will only have freer reign where the evidence is as spotty as it is in the case of the brother of Jesus. In short, arguments along this line, too, have the potential to involve a particularly knotty tangle of ecclesiastical apologetic and historical analysis, and must be appraised with great care.

If anything seems reasonably clear from the various sources about the brother of Jesus, it is that he assumed that Torah observance was important, at least on the part of Jews.[71] The significance of the theme in the Letter of James (esp. 1:22–25, 2:1–13, 4:11–12) is therefore striking. However, if this might on the face of it seem to lend credence to the letter's authenticity, some interpreters have concluded precisely the opposite. In-

---

[69] E.g., "salvation by faith apart from works"; "Abraham was justified by faith"; "the law is a yoke of slavery." Determination of the relative strength of this possibility as compared to the possibility that the letter knows Pauline texts would require a much more detailed analysis of the arguments of Tsuji and Mitchell (see previous note) than is possible within the constraints of this essay.

[70] For recent survey and analysis see Pratscher, *Der Herrenbruder Jakobus* (see n. 9); J. Painter, *Just James: The Brother of Jesus in History and Tradition* (Columbia: University of South Carolina Press, 1997); P. Hartin, *James of Jerusalem: Heir to Jesus of Nazareth* (Interfaces; Collegeville, Minn.: Liturgical Press, 2004).

[71] See esp. Gal 2:12, noting how the association of James with concern for Torah observance recurs in Acts 21:18–25 (cf. Acts 15) and the *Epistula Petri*; cf. also Eusebius, *Hist. eccl.* 2.23.4–19.

deed, much like Baur, Dibelius considered the letter's stance on the law to be "the decisive argument *against* James as the author."[72] The letter's definition of "pure religion" as "to care for orphans and widows in their distress and to keep oneself unstained by the world" (Jas 1:27), he argued, could not have been written by a "ritualist" like James, particularly not in the time after Paul, and especially when coupled by the letter's silence on matters like diet and circumcision. Nor, he said, are the repeated references to the "law of freedom" conceivable as the words of a "strict legalist."[73] In fact, the very phrase "law of freedom" was for Dibelius "a clear indication that in his ritual and moral injunctions the author does not have the Mosaic Law in mind at all."[74]

But the view that James's "law of freedom" is a new Christian law rather than the Torah, though quite common over the history of interpretation, is very problematic.[75] Moreover, while it does seem likely that the brother of Jesus affirmed both the importance of Torah observance and the significance of the distinction between Jew and Gentile even among those who venerated Jesus,[76] it is by no means clear that he shared Paul's preoccupation with so-called "ritual law," even after the conflict in Antioch. Nor is it obvious that he was characterized by a "strict legalism."[77] In short, if there is little in our scant evidence for James to demonstrate clearly that he, like our letter, combined a basic (and for first-century Jews, scarcely unusual) conviction regarding the importance of Jewish Torah observance with a special concern for socio-economic matters, neither is there any good reason to exclude it out of hand.[78] The significance of the letter's approach to Torah observance, therefore, is inconclusive for the matter of authorship.[79]

---

[72] Dibelius, *James* (see n. 20), 17 (emphasis added).

[73] Ibid., 18: *"Jas 1:25 and 2:12 were obviously not written by a Christian who was a strict legalist; Jas 1:27 was surely not written by a Christian ritualist"* (emphasis original).

[74] Ibid., 18.

[75] For full discussion of the issues see Jackson-McCabe, *Logos and Law* (see n. 63), 154–85.

[76] This is the most straightforward way to read Gal 2:7–14.

[77] Unless we interpret the arrival of "men from James" in Antioch (Gal 2:11–14) as signaling James's shift to a position of formal exclusion of non-observant Gentiles from the group, what little evidence there is suggests that he was consistent in *not* requiring Torah observance for Gentiles. That is, the tension in Antioch seems to have arisen over a disagreement as to how *Jewish* members should handle group meals, not whether non-observant Gentiles could belong, at least in some manner, to the group.

[78] Paul claims that James, Cephas, and John made only one request concerning Paul's mission to non-Jews, namely that he "remember the poor" (Gal 2:10).

[79] Much the same could be said regarding its messianism, on which see M. Jackson-McCabe, "The Messiah Jesus in the Mythic World of James," *JBL* 122 (2003): 701–30.

If all the issues considered to this point seem to leave both the possibility of authenticity and the possibility of pseudonymity reasonably open,[80] it is through consideration of the Hellenistic character of the letter that the former begins to look much more remote. The quality of the letter's Greek has long been noted, and also long raised as an argument against its authenticity.[81] Defenders of its authenticity have argued that it is not out of the question for a first-century Palestinian to have developed the kind of fluency in Greek found in this letter.[82] Of course, the real question for the historian is not simply whether it is *possible* that *Jews* in this time and place could have gained such proficiency, but whether it is *probable* that *the brother of Jesus in particular* actually did. Richard Bauckham's defense on this point is representative—and telling.

> [I]t is not possible to know what degree of competence in Greek the historical James could have acquired in his native Galilee ... But James lived for some thirty years in the cosmopolitan city of Jerusalem, where, Hengel estimates, some 10–20 per cent of the population were Jews whose vernacular or mother tongue was Greek ... James had every opportunity and very good reasons for acquiring good proficiency in Greek ... Finally, in the composition of his letter he could easily have had the assistance of a more Hellenized Jew than himself, a native Greek speaker with a good Greek education ...[83]

If the point about James's decades in a Jerusalem populated in part by Greek speakers is meant to establish a reasonable possibility that he may have learned Greek, the recourse to a hypothetical assistant is a tacit ac-

---

The letter's expectation of an avenger messiah to destroy the wicked and restore Israel's twelve tribes makes sense in the historical James's setting; but the present state of the evidence for James simply does not allow us to reconstruct his own thinking on the subject.

[80] The variety of other issues periodically raised as supporting arguments in the debate—e.g., whether it shows a familiarity with Palestinian climate; whether it assumes a 'delay of the *parousia*'; the nature of the institutional hierarchy it assumes; its sectarian character—are equally inconclusive.

[81] The skill and even relative polish of the letter's Greek (e.g., Ropes, *Epistle of St. James* [see n. 23], 24–7; Mayor, *Epistle of St. James* [see n. 60], ccvi–cclix) is generally acknowledged. Dibelius (*James* [see n. 20], 56–7) finds this raised as an argument against the letter's authenticity as early as 1826 in W. M. L. de Wette's *Lehrbuch der historisch-kritischen Einleitung in die kanonischen Bücher des Neuen Testaments* (Berlin: Reimer, 1826). Interestingly, sensitivity to the issue of the historical James's language is already apparent in the so-called *Apocryphon of James*, which takes pains to highlight its ostensible author's supposed *Hebrew* composition (1.15).

[82] Most extensively, J. N. Sevenster, *Do You Know Greek? How Much Greek Could the First Jewish Christians Have Known?* (NovTSup 19; Leiden: Brill, 1968).

[83] R. J. Bauckham, *James: Wisdom of James, Disciple of Jesus the Sage* (New Testament Readings; London/New York: Routledge, 1999), 23–4, citing M. Hengel, *The 'Hellenization' of Judaea in the First Century after Christ* (trans. J. Bowden; London: SCM Press / Philadelphia: Trinity Press International, 1989), 10.

knowledgment that there is on the face of it a basic improbability in an artisan-class Galilean villager acquiring the sort of literary skill represented by the Letter of James.[84] This concession is even clearer on the part of those who would separate James from this hypothetical assistant still further by positing a later, more independent redaction of earlier James material.[85]

In any case, we must be clear that the issue is not simply a work that shows a relatively high proficiency in Greek grammar, vocabulary, and style, but one that is more generally at home in literate, Hellenistic culture. Recent studies have highlighted the fact that the letter reflects the conventions of Hellenistic rhetorical culture.[86] It is also familiar with commonplaces of Greco-Roman moralistic literature, such as controlling horses with bits, and ships with rudders.[87] Most importantly, the Hellenistic character of the work cannot be reduced to matters of arrangement and illustration. The theological and ethical discourse of the letter is itself shot through with Hellenistic concepts and ideas—an interweaving of Jewish, Christian and Greco-Roman discourse that is not separable into dualities of substance and form, composition and redaction.[88] For example, it is not as though the author simply uses typically Hellenistic imagery to elaborate a point about controlling speech; the whole notion that controlling the tongue is key to mastery of the body underlying all of Jas 3:1–12 finds analogies only in the ancient philosophical literature.[89] In fact, a Hellenistic distinction between *logos* and desire is fundamental to the letter in general, and even to its understanding of the Torah in particular; its correlation

---

[84] Such a hypothetical assistant appears also in Witherington, *Letters and Homilies* (see n. 4), 400.

[85] E.g., P. Davids, *The Epistle of James: A Commentary on the Greek Text* (NIGTC; Grand Rapids, Mich.: Eerdmans, 1982), 22; R. Martin, *James* (WBC 48; Waco, Tex.: Word, 1988), lxix–lxxvii; Hartin, *James* (see n. 56), 24–5; cf. Wachob, *Voice of Jesus* (see n. 6), 29–30.

[86] E.g., D. F. Watson, "James 2 in Light of Greco-Roman Schemes of Argumentation," *NTS* 39 (1993): 94–121; idem, "The Rhetoric of James 3:1–12 and a Classical Pattern of Argumentation," *NovT* 35 (1993): 48–64; L. Thurén, "Risky Rhetoric in James," *NovT* 37 (1995): 262–84; idem, "The General New Testament Writings," in *Handbook of Classical Rhetoric in the Hellenistic Period 330 B.C. – A.D. 400* (ed. S. E. Porter; Leiden: Brill, 1997), 587–607 (592–96).

[87] Jas 3:3–4; see, e.g., the discussions of Dibelius, *James* (see n. 20), 185–90; Johnson, *Letter of James* (see n. 7), 257–58 and, more generally, 27–9.

[88] See Jackson-McCabe, "The Messiah Jesus" (see n. 79) and, more extensively, *Logos and Law* (see n. 63), esp. 193–239.

[89] Idem, *Logos and Law* (see n. 63), 224–30. Compare in this connection the analysis of Jas 3:13–4:10 vis-à-vis Greco-Roman moralistic discourse on envy in L. T. Johnson, "James 3:13–4:10 and the *Topos* ΠΕΡΙ ΦΘΟΝΟΥ," *NovT* 25 (1983): 327–47.

of "the law of freedom" with "the implanted *logos*" (1:21–25) is more in the vein of Cicero, *4 Maccabees*, and Justin Martyr than of Jesus on virtually any recent reconstruction of the latter.[90] Indeed, as John Kloppenborg has recently shown, the Hellenistic character of the letter's thought comes through even in its much-discussed iteration of the Jesus tradition itself.[91]

Of course, it is not impossible that the brother of Jesus may have somehow found the inclination, the financial resources, and the leisure time to pursue and thoroughly absorb a cosmopolitan Hellenistic education in the final decades of his life, and to re-think his understanding of the meaning and implications of Jesus veneration light of it. But where the context is not apologetic, the question is not merely possibility, but relative likelihood. And on balance, this does not seem nearly so likely as the possibility that someone who did have such an education wrote a letter in the name of a revered figure of the apostolic era whose reputation for Jewish piety seemed to mirror his own concerns; a figure whose authority he wished to co-opt. Others in the group surely did.

Similarly, one cannot deny at least the possibility that James himself recruited someone with such a Hellenistic education and sensibility to help him compose the letter; or that such a person later, after James's death, took it upon himself to redact James's own teaching into the form of a letter "to the twelve tribes." But given how thoroughly Hellenistic discourse pervades the very warp and woof of the letter's fabric, it is not at all clear why we should consider this to be especially probable. One would in any case be left to wonder how much of the historical James would really remain here at all—not to mention how we might be able to distinguish his voice from that of the actual writer.

In any event, when arguments turn from determining probabilities to defending possibilities, one must ask whether the real purpose of such argumentation has become something other than the historical reconstruction of early Jesus veneration; whether the underlying motivation is less an academic curiosity about the letter's composition than an ecclesiastical con-

---

[90] On *logos* and desire in James, see Jackson-McCabe, ibid., 193–239; and on the Hellenistic context of James's correlation of law and "implanted *logos*" in particular, 29–154.

[91] J. S. Kloppenborg, "Stoic Psychagogy and James 1:2–15" (a paper presented at the annual meeting of the SBL, Boston, Mass., November 2008). He concludes: "in paraphrasing and re-presenting sayings of Jesus, the author of the letter reveals an array of interests in psychagogy and care of the soul which we know to have also characterized Stoicism of the early Roman period. This had a demonstrable effect on such works of Hellenistic Judaism as 4 Maccabees, the *Testaments of the Twelve Patriarchs*, Philo, and the *Testament of Job*." My thanks to Professor Kloppenborg for sharing a copy of this essay with me.

cern to ensure its apostolic authority, even if at some remove, for contemporary Christians.[92] As one recent advocate of the hypothesis has put it:

> Such a view would ... resolve the concerns of those who feel that James of Jerusalem would not have had the education necessary to be able to compose the quality of Greek that this letter demonstrates. *This would still uphold the authority and voice of James of Jerusalem behind the letter* ... [T]he best reading of the evidence points to James of Jerusalem as *the authority behind* this circular or encyclical letter ...[93]

But if the "best reading" is to maintain the letter's genuinely apostolic authority even while conceding the improbability of its actual composition by James, one must ask: The "best reading" for whom, and for what purpose? Even if one must of course acknowledge that such a reconstruction is not impossible, one also wonders whether the hypothesis itself simply represents another interesting datum for the study of pseudepigraphy in the history of religions.

---

[92] Cf. the reflection on this hypothesis in D. Hutchinson Edgar, *Has God Not Chosen the Poor? The Social Setting of the Epistle of James* (JSNTSup 206; Sheffield: Sheffield Academic Press, 2001), 21: the "basic assumption appears to be the desirability of maintaining the insubstantial link between the epistle and the figure of James. To do this, an even more insubstantial transmission and compilation process is proposed."

[93] Hartin, *James* (see n. 56), 24–5 (emphasis added).

Die Stimme des Apostels erheben

Pragmatische Leistungen der Autorenfiktion in den Petrusbriefen

von

KARL MATTHIAS SCHMIDT

1. Einleitung

Im Korpus der Katholischen Briefe finden sich zwei Texte, die in der *superscriptio* den Namen des Apostels Petrus tragen. In der neutestamentlichen Forschung besteht ein weit reichender Konsens darüber, dass es sich bei diesen Texten um Pseudepigraphen handelt. Petrus war weder der Verfasser des einen noch des anderen Schreibens.[1] Das bedeutet jedoch nicht, dass die Texte als Fälschungen verstanden werden *müssen*. Dieser kleine Beitrag versucht zu zeigen, dass die beiden Briefe auch als Fiktion und nicht nur unter der Voraussetzung einer Täuschung ihren Zweck erfüllen konnten.[2]

---

[1] Zur Frage der Verfasserschaft und den gemeinhin vorgebrachten Argumenten und Erwiderungen vgl. etwa N. BROX, Der Erste Petrusbrief, EKK XXI, Zürich u.a. ⁴1993, 43–47; J. H. ELLIOTT, 1 Peter. A New Translation with Introduction and Commentary, AncB 37B, New York u.a. 2000, 118–130, und R. FELDMEIER, Der erste Brief des Petrus, ThHK 15/1, Leipzig 2005, 23–26; bzw. A. VÖGTLE, Der Judasbrief. Der 2. Petrusbrief, EKK XXII, Solothurn u.a. 1994, 122–125, und H. PAULSEN, Der Zweite Petrusbrief und der Judasbrief, KEK 12/2, Göttingen 1992, 93–95. Zuletzt legt sich die Pseudepigraphie des Ersten Petrusbriefes wegen intertextueller Beziehungen und der daraus resultierenden Datierung nahe. Jens Herzer hat auf die Berührungen des Schreibens mit der Apostelgeschichte verwiesen, während Rainer Metzner die Kenntnis des Matthäusevangeliums wahrscheinlich gemacht hat; vgl. J. HERZER, Petrus oder Paulus? Studien über das Verhältnis des Ersten Petrusbriefes zur paulinischen Tradition, WUNT 103, Tübingen 1998, 62–73.164f.177–181.192–195.262–264, und R. METZNER, Die Rezeption des Matthäusevangeliums im 1. Petrusbrief. Studien zum traditionsgeschichtlichen und theologischen Einfluß des 1. Evangeliums auf den 1. Petrusbrief, WUNT II/74, Tübingen 1995, bes. 7–68. Von daher ist mit einer Abfassung des Textes nicht vor der Jahrhundertwende zu rechnen. Das Argument der späten Entstehung gewinnt im Fall des Zweiten Petrusbriefes noch an Bedeutung.

[2] „Fiktion" meint hier im Gegensatz zu „Täuschung", dass der reale Autor den Text derart konzipierte, dass dieser *nicht* dem in der *superscriptio* angegebenen Verfasser zuzuschreiben war. Zur Diskussion über das Phänomen der Pseudepigraphie im Neuen

Dazu soll zunächst die Absenderangabe des Briefes unter Rückgriff auf einen fraglos fiktiven Brief Ovids erzähltheoretisch eingeordnet werden.[3] In einem zweiten Schritt ist unter Verweis auf das rhetorische Stilmittel der Prosopopoiie zu zeigen, dass die Verfasserfiktion dem Ziel, die Leserinnen und Leser zu einer bestimmten Haltung zu bewegen, nicht entgegenstand. Nach diesen Vorarbeiten werden die beiden Petrusbriefe im Hinblick auf die narrativen Ebenen ansatzweise als fiktionale Literatur analysiert, bevor abschließend anstelle einer Zusammenfassung eine hypothetische Lektüresituation skizziert wird, in der die Texte in den Gemeinden verankert gewesen sein könnten.

2. Autor und Erzähler des fiktiven Briefs

„Ich würde gerne mehr schreiben, aber meine Hand erschlafft unter dem Gewicht der Kette und allein schon die Angst raubt mir die Kräfte."[4] So endet der Brief Hypermestras an Lynceus. Kein antiker Leser hätte diesen Brief für ein echtes Schreiben der Danaide gehalten. Der Text gehört zu

---

Testament vgl. M. JANSSEN, Unter falschem Namen. Eine kritische Forschungsbilanz frühchristlicher Pseudepigraphie, ARGU 14, Frankfurt a.M. u.a. 2003. Seitdem wurde die Diskussion vor allem im Bereich der Pastoralbriefe, insbesondere im Zusammenhang mit der These, die drei Briefe seien als einheitlich konzipiertes *Corpus Pastorale* verfasst worden, fortgeführt; vgl. für die Diskussion im deutschsprachigen Raum etwa J. HERZER, Abschied vom Konsens? Die Pseudepigraphie der Pastoralbriefe als Herausforderung an die neutestamentliche Wissenschaft, ThLZ 129 (2004), 1267–1282; ders., „Das Geheimnis der Frömmigkeit" (1Tim 3,16). Sprache und Stil der Pastoralbriefe im Kontext hellenistisch-römischer Popularphilosophie – eine methodische Problemanzeige, ThQ 187 (2007), 309–329; G. HÄFNER, Das Corpus Pastorale als literarisches Konstrukt, ThQ 187 (2007), 258–273; A. MERZ, Die fiktive Selbstauslegung des Paulus. Intertextuelle Studien zur Intention und Rezeption der Pastoralbriefe, NTOA 52, Göttingen/Freiburg (CH) 2004, 195–387; dies., Amore Pauli. Das Corpus Pastorale und das Ringen um die Interpretationshoheit bezüglich des paulinischen Erbes, ThQ 187 (2007), 274–294.

[3] Mit der Wahl eines römischen Kunstbriefes als Vergleichstext wird eine hellenistisch-römische Perspektive für den literaturtheoretischen Vergleich gewählt. Die Bedeutung der jüdisch-hellenistischen Tradition für die Pseudepigraphie wird damit nicht geleugnet. Da sich die beiden Petrusbriefe zumindest auch an griechische Leserinnen und Leser wandten, scheint es mit Blick auf die Rezipientinnen und Rezipienten jedoch gerechtfertigt, die Texte auch im griechisch-römischen Umfeld zu verankern.

[4] Ovid, Heroides 14,131f.: „Scribere plura libet, sed pondere lapsa catenae | est manus, et vires substrahit ipse timor." Text und Übersetzung hier und im Folgenden: P. Ovidius Naso, Heroides – Briefe der Heroinen. Lateinisch-deutsch. Übers. u. hg. v. D. Hoffmann / C. Schliebitz / H. Stocker, Reclam Universal-Bibliothek 1359, Stuttgart 2000. Leicht zugänglicher Text mit deutscher Übersetzung auch bei P. Ovidius Naso, Liebesbriefe. Heroides – Epistulae. Lateinisch-deutsch. Hg. u. übers. v. B. W. Häuptli, Sammlung Tusculum, Zürich 1995.

einer Reihe elegischer Briefe, die von Ovid verfasst und von Beginn an als Sammelwerk ediert wurden.[5] Wenngleich die Heroides der Gattung nach Briefe sind, lässt sich die Rolle der Absenderin gut mit Kategorien der Erzähltheorie beschreiben, wie sie etwa von Gérard Genette bereitgestellt wurden.[6]

Hypermestra erzählt ihre Leidensgeschichte, eine Geschichte, in der sie selbst vorkommt; sie ist somit eine homodiegetische Erzählerin und kann – da sie selbst die Heldin, die Heroin, der von ihr erzählten Geschichte ist – mit Genette als autodiegetische Erzählerin bezeichnet werden.[7] Nachdem sich Danaos mit seinen fünfzig Töchtern vergeblich gegen seinen Bruder Aegyptus und dessen fünfzig Söhne zur Wehr gesetzt hatte und der verhasste Bund mit dem Bruder unausweichlich schien, empfahl der Vater den sich gegen die Ehe sträubenden Töchtern, ihre Bräutigame in der Hochzeitsnacht zu ermorden. Hypermestra führte als einzige den Plan nicht aus, sondern verhalf Lynceus zur Flucht und wurde daraufhin vom Vater eingesperrt.[8]

Diese Geschichte wird von Hypermestra im Rahmen eines Rückblicks erzählt, der am Abend vor der Hochzeitsnacht einsetzt und bis zur Inhaftierung im Kerker voranschreitet (Ovid, Heroides 14,21–84). Die Danaide schildert zuletzt die Situation, in der sie sich befindet, als sie den Brief schreibt. Sie ist nicht nur Erzählfigur, sondern auch Erzählerin. Das Abfassen des Briefes fungiert als extradiegetischer Erzählakt,[9] der selbst thema-

---

[5] Zur Kommentierung des Hypermestra-Briefes vgl. J. REESON, Ovid Heroides 11, 13 and 14. A Commentary, Mn.S 221, Leiden u.a. 2001, 210–314. Zu den Heroides insgesamt vgl. etwa H. Casanova-Robin (Hg.), Amor Scribendi. Lectures des Héroïdes d'Ovide, Grenoble 2007; J. FARRELL, Reading and Writing the Heroides, HSCP 98 (1998), 307–338; L. FULKERSON, The Ovidian Heroine as Author. Reading, Writing, and Community in the Heroides, Cambridge u.a. 2005; J.-C. JOLIVET, Allusion et fiction épistolaire dans les Héroïdes. Recherches sur l'intertextualité ovidienne, CEFR 289, Paris u.a. 2001; E. SPENTZOU, Readers and Writers in Ovid's Heroides. Transgressions of Genre and Gender, Oxford 2003; F. SPOTH, Ovids Heroides als Elegien, Zet. 89, München 1992, bes. 189–198.

[6] Vgl. G. GENETTE, Die Erzählung, UTB 8083, München ²1998. Zu den Möglichkeiten und Grenzen der modernen Narratologie in Anwendung auf antike Texte vgl. T. A. SCHMITZ, Moderne Literaturtheorie und antike Texte. Eine Einführung, Darmstadt 2002, bes. 55–75.

[7] Vgl. GENETTE, a.a.O. 175f.

[8] Impulse für Ovids Hypermestra-Brief dürfte vor allem Hor.carm. 3,11,22–52 geliefert haben. Zum Mythos vgl. Apollodor, Bibliotheca 2,11–22 und Aischylos, Prometheus Vinctus 853–869; außerdem Ov.met. 4,462f.; 10,43f.; Pausanias, Descriptio Graeciae 2,21,2; 2,24,2; 3,12,2; Pindar, Nemeische Oden 10,6; Pythische Oden 9,112–116. Von den Bearbeitungen der Tragiker sind nur Aischylos' Hiketiden erhalten geblieben.

[9] Die „Abfassung ... ist ein (literarischer) Akt, der auf einer ersten Ebene vollzogen wird, die wir extradiegetisch nennen wollen", GENETTE, Erzählung (s. Anm. 6), 163. Die

tisiert wird, so etwa im oben zitierten Schlussakt, der auf die von der Fessel beschwerte Hand der Schreiberin verweist.[10]

Ovid bietet mit seiner Sammlung der ersten fünfzehn Briefe keinen Briefroman, der es erlaubt, das gleiche Ereignis aus dem jeweiligen Gesichtspunkt verschiedener Autoren zu betrachten.[11] Vielmehr blicken die Leserinnen und Leser jeweils aus einer Perspektive auf das Geschehen. Der Dichter arbeitet mit einer internen Fokalisierung, er beschreibt die Ereignisse aus der Perspektive der Heldin.[12] Lynceus reagiert nicht auf das Schreiben – im Gegensatz zu den Heroinnen in den Briefpaaren (Ovid, Heroides 16–21), die in einer Zweitauflage der Heroides beigefügt wurden[13] und gewissermaßen Mini-Briefromane bilden. Die Erzählung umfasst nur dieses eine Schreiben. Der Brief ist aber auch hier „gleichzeitig Medium der Erzählung und Element der Handlung"[14], denn Hypermestra erzählt im Brief ihre Geschichte bis zu dem Punkt, an dem sich die Geschichte in ihrem Briefschreiben fortsetzt. Die Zeit der Narration changiert zwischen der gleichzeitigen Narration, dem Erzählen während des Briefschreibens, und der späteren Narration, dem Erzählen der vergangenen Ereignisse.[15]

Dabei begnügt sich Hypermestra nicht mit dem Rückblick auf die Hochzeitsnacht, in den ein Monolog und zwei kurze Appelle an den Cousin eingelassen sind (Ovid, Heroides 14,53–66.73f.77), sondern schaut noch weiter zurück. An die erste Retrospektive schließt sich zunächst die in V.23 vorbereitete Geschichte von Io an, die von Argos nach Ägypten floh (V.85–108). Damit leitet Hypermestra zum zweiten, sehr kurzen, Rückblick über, in dem sie erzählt, wie der Vater gegen seinen Bruder Krieg führte und schließlich in die andere Richtung, nach Argos, floh (V.111–114). Nach einer kurzen Beschreibung des Status quo (V.115–118)

Ereignisse, die in dieser ersten Erzählung erzählt werden, nennt Genette entsprechend „intradiegetisch" (ebd.).

[10] Die Briefsituation schafft insbesondere für die Kommunikationsfunktion des Erzählens Raum. Hypermestra wendet sich direkt an den Adressaten ihrer Erzählung. Zu den verschiedenen Erzählfunktionen vgl. GENETTE, a.a.O. 83–186.

[11] Trotz der Beziehungen, die zwischen den Briefen bestehen, sind die Texte im Hinblick auf die Abfassungsfiktion als singuläre Schreiben anzusehen; vgl. dagegen FULKERSON, Heroine (s. Anm. 5), 67–86.

[12] Der Fokus beschreibt die Perspektive, aus der eine Geschichte erzählt wird. Intern ist die Fokalisierung, wenn aus der Perspektive einer Erzählfigur erzählt wird. Im Fall des Briefromans spricht Genette von einer multiplen internen Fokalisierung. Zur Fokalisierung vgl. GENETTE, Erzählung (s. Anm. 6), 132–138.

[13] Zu den Briefpaaren vgl. etwa C. M. HINTERMEIER, Die Briefpaare in Ovids Heroides. Tradition und Innovation, Palingenesia 41, Stuttgart 1993, Exkurs zu Entstehungsgeschichte und Datierung a.a.O. 190–195, und V. RIMELL, Ovid's Lovers. Desire, Difference and the Poetic Imagination, Cambridge u.a. 2006, 156–204.

[14] GENETTE, Erzählung (s. Anm. 6), 155.

[15] Vgl. a.a.O. 153–162.

schließt sich sodann ein Ausblick auf die Zukunft an, der als Alternativen zur bevorstehenden Strafe jedoch nur die Befreiung oder Tötung durch den Vetter vorsieht (V.119–130). Die Geschichte dieser früheren Narration bleibt hypothetisch. Die antiken Leserinnen und Leser wussten, dass die Ereignisse einen anderen Verlauf nahmen, weil der Vater Hypermestra schließlich aus der Haft entließ und Lynceus zur Frau gab. Im Rahmen der Brieffiktion berührt die Zeit der Narration das Phänomen der Erzählordnung. So lassen sich die Rückblicke als Analepsen verstehen; sie ergänzen die Geschichte bis zur Zeitspanne des Erzählaktes, in dem sich Narration und Geschichte überlagern.[16] Das Schreiben verknüpft aber auch die jüngste Vergangenheit mit der nahen Zukunft. Der Akt der Narration rückt zwischen das Vergehen, den Widerstand gegen den Vater, und das zu erwartende Gericht.[17]

Die Brieffiktion ermöglicht eine Modifikation der Erzählperspektive. Der Brief verknüpft „ständig ... eine Art inneren Monolog mit einem nachträglichen Bericht. Der Erzähler ist hier, und zwar zugleich, *noch* der Held und *schon* ein anderer: Die Ereignisse des Tages sind schon vergangen, und der *point of view* kann sich seitdem verändert haben; die Gefühle und Ansichten am Abend oder am folgenden Tag jedoch gehören völlig zur Gegenwart."[18] Hypermestra bleibt sich und ihrer Entscheidung, sich dem Geheiß des Vaters zu widersetzen, treu.[19] Gleichwohl macht Ovid deutlich, dass sich die Leserinnen und Leser zwei Heldinnen gegenüber sehen, die sich in unterschiedlichen Situationen befinden. Denn während die Hypermestra der intradiegetischen Erzählung den Dolch zur Hand nimmt, die sie im Angesicht des Verbrechens jedoch sinken lässt, sodass diese frei von Blut bleibt (V.5.8.43–50.56–60.76), umfasst die Hand der extradiegetischen Hypermestra den Griffel, erstarrt aber in Erinnerung an das Blutbad,

---

[16] Zu den Analepsen vgl. a.a.O. 32–45. Streng genommen handelt es sich um eine externe Analepse, weil der Erzählstrang der knappen Erzählung „Hypermestra sitzt im Kerker und schreibt einen Brief an Lynceus" erst in dem Moment beginnt, als die Heldin zur Feder greift. Fasst man trotz der verschiedenen Erzählebenen die vorausgesetzte Hypermestra-Geschichte als Erzählrahmen auf, ist die Analepse gleichwohl kompletiv, sie ergänzt, was sich bis zum Zeitpunkt der Briefabfassung zugetragen hat.

[17] Besonders deutlich wird die Korrelation von Vergehen und erwarteter Strafe in der Einleitung, wo die Hochzeitsfackel und das nicht verwendete Mordinstrument aus der Hochzeitsnacht als Folterutensilien beschrieben werden. Hypermestra fürchtet Feuer und Tod zu leiden, weil sie dieses Schicksal ihrem Cousin nicht zufügen wollte (Ovid, Heroides 14,9–12). Der Brief scheint so am Wendepunkt geschrieben zu sein.

[18] GENETTE, Erzählung (s. Anm. 6), 155.

[19] „Die ist nicht wirklich fromm, die ihre Frömmigkeit bereut", Ovid, Heroides 14,14: „non est, quam piget esse, pia." Hypermestra unterstreicht, dass sie ihre missliche Lage ungerechterweise ihrer *pietas* verdankt, an der sie bis zum Tod festhalten will (vgl. V.49.84.129 und V.4.26.64.123).

bevor sie schließlich unter der Last der Ketten erlahmt (V.17–20.131f.).[20] Durch das Schreiben wird das Vergangene gegenwärtig, in der Narration wird das Erzählte erneut präsent. Diese Überlappung der Erzählebenen zeigt sich auch beim Blick auf den Adressaten des Briefes. Denn Lynceus ist seinerseits nicht nur Briefpartner, sondern auch eine Figur der intradiegetischen Erzählung, innerhalb derer er aber als Gegenüber der Briefkommunikation (vgl. V.47), als „Du", angesprochen wird (V.41f.48.68.72.75–80).

Es besteht also eine Differenz zwischen der Hypermestra, die neben ihrem Vetter saß, und der Hypermestra, die allein im Kerker sitzt. Die Erzählerin ist ebenso wenig wie der Adressat mit sich in ihrer Rolle als Erzählfigur identisch, obwohl es sich um die gleiche mythische Person handelt, die eine Figur im Kontinuum der gleichen, allerdings auf verschiedenen Erzählebenen verhandelten, Geschichte ist, weswegen sich die Perspektive als interne feste Fokalisierung umreißen lässt. Denn der Perspektivenwechsel vollzieht sich nicht zwischen verschiedenen Erzählfiguren, sondern innerhalb der gleichen, sich entwickelnden Erzählfigur. Von daher kann man von Fokusvarianten sprechen. Dabei überschneiden sich im Fall des Briefes auch die Erzählinstanzen, weil die Heldin im Verlauf der Ereignisse schließlich zur Erzählerin wird.[21]

3. Prosopopoiien in Briefform

Was trägt der kurze Ausflug in die Erzähltheorie am Beispiel eines Heroidenbriefes für die Analyse der neutestamentlichen Petrusbriefe bei? Zunächst ist zu konzedieren, dass die Unterschiede zwischen den Heroides und den Petrusbriefen unverkennbar sind. Ovid entwirft das Porträt von mythischen Gestalten aus einer längst vergangenen Zeit. Die Petrusbriefe stammen dagegen vorgeblich von einer realen Person aus der jüngeren Geschichte der Gemeinden. Der Dichter wollte in erster Linie seine Leserinnen und Leser unterhalten, die neutestamentlichen Texte reagierten dagegen auf eine kritische Situation, in denen sie den christlichen Gemeinden Orientierung bieten wollten. Während Lynceus als Adressat des fiktiven Briefes kein reales Pendant in der Leserschaft hatte, sprachen die Petrusbriefe indirekt in die Situation ihrer Leserinnen und Leser hinein. Konnten die Petrusbriefe angesichts dieser Unterschiede ihren pragmatischen Zweck, die Gemeinde zu ermuntern und zu ermahnen, erfüllen, wenn sie als Fiktion verstanden wurden?

---

[20] Vgl. auch SPOTH, Heroides (s. Anm. 5), 193–195.
[21] Vgl. GENETTE, Erzählung (s. Anm. 6), 155f.243f.

Es gibt auch Gemeinsamkeiten. Ovid lässt mit seinen Briefen gewissermaßen Tote auferstehen und verleiht ihnen Stimme. Das gilt auch für die Petrusbriefe, wenn man sie nach der Jahrhundertwende datiert.[22] Dabei konnten sich die Briefautoren eine Technik zunutze machen, die in der Rhetorik angewendet wurde. Das Stilmittel der Prosopopoiie sah vor, dass der Redner während seiner Rede gleichsam eine andere Figur reden ließ, indem er einer existierenden oder fiktiven Person seine Worte in den Mund legte, einen Toten aus dem Hades hinauf rief, oder gar einen Gegenstand zum Leben erweckte.[23] Ein klassisches Beispiel bietet Ciceros *Pro M. Caelio oratio*. Nacheinander inszeniert Cicero zunächst den verstorbenen Appius Claudius Caecus, dann den noch lebendigen Bruder der Angeklagten, Publius Clodius Pulcher, auf seiner Rednerbühne, um seinen Argumenten mehr Gewicht zu verleihen. Das klang für die Zuhörinnen und Zuhörer dann wie folgt:

---

[22] Unsicher ist, welche literarischen Vorlagen den Autoren der Petrusbriefe bei der Abfassung fiktiver Briefe zur Verfügung standen. Ovid glaubte, mit den Heroides eine neue literarische Gattung geschaffen zu haben (vgl. Ovid, Ars amatoria 3,345f.), dazu etwa SPOTH, Heroides (s. Anm. 5), 22–34.215–231. Nichtsdestotrotz wird immer wieder Properz, Carmina 4,3 als mögliches Vorbild für die Heroides gehandelt. C. WALDE, Literatur als Experiment? Zur Erzähltechnik in Ovids Heroides, AuA 46 (2000), 124–138 (129f.135f.), stellt diese Verbindung in Frage und verweist stattdessen auf Properz, Carmina 4,7; vgl. auch etwa SPOTH, a.a.O. 190. Cynthia erscheint nach ihrem Tode Properz im Traum und beansprucht ihre eigene Dichtung für sich (V.77f.). Sie erzählt, wie sie in der Unterwelt mit den Heroinnen, unter anderem mit Hypermestra, als Beispiel der Treue im Gegensatz zur Ehebrecherin (V.53.57f.) in elysischen Gefilden zusammensitzt. Dort erzählen sie sich ihre altbekannten Geschichten (V.63–69). In der Tat gewinnt Ovids Briefsammlung ihren Reiz – auch wenn darin allein kaum die Neuheit begründet lag – zu einem großen Teil aus den Möglichkeiten der Intertextualität, die Properz' Arethusa-Brief vermissen lässt. Ovid dachte jedenfalls kaum an die Gattung des fiktiven Briefes an sich, als er seine Innovation feierte. In Ansätzen zeigt sich das Spiel mit den literarischen Vorgaben allerdings auch in den Petrusbriefen. Die Autoren der Petrusbriefe konnten dabei aber durchaus auf Beispiele außerhalb der Heroides zurückgreifen. Erwähnt seien nur die pseudepigraphischen Kynikerbriefe (Text mit deutscher Übersetzung bei E. MÜSELER, Die Kynikerbriefe. Mit Beiträgen und dem Anhang „Das Briefcorpus Ω" von M. Sicherl, 2 Bd., SGKA.M 6–7, Paderborn u.a. 1994). Fraglich bleibt, ob der Autor des Ersten Petrusbriefes bereits christliche Beispiele fiktiver Briefe vor Augen hatte. Das hängt zum einen von den Hypothesen zur Intertextualität ab, zum anderen davon, ob die als Pseudepigraphen identifizierten Texte als Fiktion oder als Täuschung einzustufen sind. Im Fall des Jakobus- und des Judasbriefes ist schon der Nachweis, dass der Text ein Pseudepigraph ist, dadurch erschwert, dass keine eindeutige Inanspruchnahme einer christlichen Autorität vorliegt.

[23] Zur in der Antike divergierenden Terminologie vgl. Quintilian, Institutio oratoria 9,2,31f., sowie H. LAUSBERG, Handbuch der literarischen Rhetorik. Eine Grundlegung der Literaturwissenschaft, Stuttgart [4]2008, §§ 820–829.1131f.

Wenn Du es aber lieber hast, daß ich mich mehr als Weltmann gebe, dann will ich folgendermaßen mit dir reden. Ich lasse den strengen und fast bäurisch groben alten Herrn abtreten und zitiere einen aus deiner Generation hierher, am liebsten deinen jüngeren Bruder ... Nimm also an, er rede so mit dir: „Was machst du für einen Wirbel, Schwester – was regest du dich so auf?"[24]

Quintilian hebt die pragmatische Leistung des Stilmittels für die Erregung von Mitleid hervor und weist der Prosopopoiie damit einen außerhalb der Unterhaltung liegenden Zweck zu.

(25) Für solche Stellen sind die Prosopopoiien besonders nützlich, das heißt erfundene Reden fremder Personen, wie sie der Anwalt den Prozessierenden in den Mund legt. Schon die nackten Tatsachen vermögen zu rühren. Wenn wir aber die beteiligten Personen selbst reden lassen, wird auch aus den Personen noch eine Gefühlswirkung gewonnen. (26) Denn der Richter hat nicht den Eindruck, Menschen über fremdes Unglück weinen zu hören, sondern Empfindung und Stimme der Armen selbst in sein Ohr aufzunehmen ...; und wie es noch mitleiderregender wäre, wenn sie selbst es vortrügen, so ist es doch schon um einen gewissen Grad mächtiger in seiner rührenden Wirkung, wenn es gleichsam aus ihrem eigenen Mund kommt – wie ja auch bei den Schauspielern auf der Bühne dasselbe Wort und derselbe Vortrag, unter der Maske gesprochen, mehr Kraft zur Erregung der Gefühle entfaltet.[25]

Die Anwendung der Prosopopoiie war freilich nicht auf anwesende Prozessbeteiligte begrenzt, ihre Wirkungen reduzierten sich nicht auf das Erregen von Mitleid, wie das Beispiel aus der Rede Ciceros zeigt, und der Sache nach war sie auch nicht auf die Gattung der Rede oder gar der Gerichtsrede beschränkt.

Der Brief eignete sich als Realisierung der Prosopopoiie schon deswegen besonders gut, weil eine seiner Aufgaben darin bestand, im Rahmen der brieflichen *Parusia* die Trennung der Briefpartner zu überwinden.[26] Im

---

[24] Cic. Pro M. Caelio oratio 36 (15): „Sin autem urbanius me agere mavis, sic agam tecum. Removebo illum senem durum ac paene agrestem; ex his igitur tuis sumam aliquem ac potissimum minimum fratrem qui est in isto genere urbanissimus ... Eum putato tecum loqui: ‚Quid tumultuaris, soror? quid insanis?'" Text und Übersetzung: M. Tullius Cicero, Pro M. Caelio oratio – Rede für M. Caelius. Mit einem Anhang ausgewählter Briefe des Caelius an Cicero. Lateinisch-Deutsch. Übers. u. hg. v. M. Giebel, Reclam Universal-Bibliothek 1237, Stuttgart 1994.

[25] Quintilian, Institutio oratoria 6,1,25f.: „His praecipue locis utiles sunt prosopopoeiae, id est fictae alienarum personarum orationes, † quales litigatore dicit patronum, nudae tantum res movent: at cum ipsos loqui fingimus, ex personis quoque trahitur adfectus. 26 non enim audire iudex videtur aliena mala deflentis, sed sensum ac vocem auribus accipere miserorum ...: quantoque essent miserabiliora, si ea dicerent ipsi, tanto sunt quadam portione ad afficiendum potentiora, cum velut ipsorum ore dicuntur, ut scaenicis actoribus eadem vox eademque pronuntiatio plus ad movendos adfectus sub persona valet." Text und Übersetzung: M. Fabius Quintilianus, Ausbildung des Redners. Zwölf Bücher. Hg. u. übers. v. H. Rahn, 2 Bd., TzF 2–3, Darmstadt ²1988.

[26] Zur brieflichen *Parusia* vgl. H. KOSKENNIEMI, Studien zur Idee und Phraseologie des griechischen Briefes bis 400 n. Chr., STAT 102/2, Helsinki 1956, 38–42.

Brief wurde der abwesende Briefpartner gleichsam gegenwärtig. Es bot sich daher an, Hypermestra im Rahmen eines Briefes zum Leben zu erwecken, wie Cicero den verstorbenen Appius Claudius Caecus aus der Unterwelt herauf rief. Von daher können die Heroides als Prosopopoiien in Briefform verstanden werden. Da sich fiktionale Briefe auch zu anderen Zwecken als dem der Unterhaltung einsetzen ließen und nicht weniger als Redeeinlagen eine pragmatische Wirkung entfalten konnten, um die Leserinnen und Leser in die eine oder andere Richtung zu bewegen, ist nicht grundsätzlich auszuschließen, dass auch der Apostel Petrus durch ein fiktives Schreiben im Rahmen einer brieflichen Prosopopoiie vergegenwärtigt wurde.

Nach Pseudo-Demetrius, De elocutione 227 war es die vornehmliche Aufgabe des Briefes, der als Spiegel der Seele gelten durfte, das Ethos des Briefschreibers zum Ausdruck zu bringen. Auch für die Prosopopoiie spielte das Ethos eine wichtige Rolle und zwar das Ethos der kreierten Figur. Sollte die Inszenierung glaubwürdig sein, musste die Darstellung des Charakters zur Person passen (vgl. Quintilian, Institutio oratoria 9,2,29f.). Wollte man das Ethos des Apostels Petrus in Erinnerung rufen und den Leserinnen und Lesern vor Augen stellen, um sie durch sein hervorragendes Beispiel zu ermuntern, bot sich daher die Prosopopoiie und insbesondere die Prosopopoiie in Briefform als literarische Form an. Die realen Autoren der Petrusbriefe verwiesen nicht auf ihr eigenes Ethos, sondern auf das des Petrus und machten sich so ein geliehenes Ethos zu Nutze, um die Gemeinde zum Glaubenszeugnis zu bewegen. Sie konnten Petrus im Rahmen einer brieflichen Prosopopoiie gewissermaßen von den Toten herauf rufen, um ihn zur Gemeinde in seinem – mutmaßlichen – Sinne sprechen zu lassen.

4. Fiktionale Verfasserangaben in den Petrusbriefen?

Nicht alle im Zusammenhang mit dem Hypermestra-Brief gemachten Beobachtungen lassen sich auf die Petrusbriefe übertragen. Aber es kann hilfreich sein, sich von den kanonischen Texten zunächst zu entfernen, um dadurch einen anderen Blickwinkel auf sie zu gewinnen. Im Gegensatz zu Ovid, der die Texte seiner griechischsprachigen Briefschreiberinnen in lateinischer Sprache abfasste und schon so eine Distanz zwischen der angeblichen Absenderin und dem Text schuf, sind die beiden realen Autoren der Petrusbriefe mindestens den heutigen Rezipientinnen und Rezipienten nicht bekannt. Für beide Schreiben gilt aber, sofern man sie für Pseudepigraphen hält, dass der reale Autor gerade nicht Petrus ist. Hingegen kann Petrus jeweils als „Erzähler" gelten wie Hypermestra im vierzehnten

Heroidenbrief. Der Apostel schreibt Briefe an die Gemeinden und „erzählt" damit selbst nicht nur – sehr fragmentarisch – die Geschichte der intradiegetischen Erzählfiguren, nämlich seine eigene Geschichte und die der Gemeindemitglieder, sondern auch die Geschichte der extradiegetischen Briefabfassung.

Die Ungewissheit über die Identität der tatsächlichen Autoren wirft allerdings die Frage auf, ob die Verfasser der Petrusbriefe ihre Leserinnen und Leser täuschen wollten, indem sie suggerierten, dass die Briefe tatsächlich vom Apostel Petrus stammten, oder ob es sich bei den Texten um fiktionale Briefe ähnlich den Heroides handelt, die gar nicht für sich in Anspruch nehmen, vom Apostel selbst verfasst zu sein. Auch die Unterscheidung von Fiktion und Täuschung lässt sich narratologisch beschreiben. Denn während im Fall der Täuschung der implizite Autor Petrus ist, ist er im Fall der Fiktion nicht Petrus. Entsprechend war Petrus im einen Fall ein zuverlässiger Erzähler, im anderen Fall ein unzuverlässiger, dem man in der Frage der Verfasserschaft keinen Glauben schenken sollte.[27] Bei einer intendierten Täuschung sollten die Leserinnen und Leser Petrus für den Autor halten, den Text also so verstehen, als sei er von Petrus geschrieben worden, bei einer intendierten Fiktion sollten sie den Autor ausdrücklich nicht für Petrus halten, sondern erkennen, dass Petrus nur als fiktiver Erzähler fungiert. Die hier vorgenommene Unterscheidung orien-

---

[27] Die Begriffe *implied author* und *unreliable narrator* hat Wayne C. Booth geprägt; vgl. W. C. BOOTH, The Rhetoric of Fiction, Chicago u.a. 1983 (Erstausgabe 1961). GENETTE, Erzählung (s. Anm. 6), 284–295, hält den impliziten Autor für eine weitestgehend überflüssige Instanz. Das mag damit zusammenhängen, dass Genette den impliziten Leser mit dem extradiegetischen Adressaten identifiziert und folglich mit einer unnötigen Verdoppelung der Instanzen rechnet. Doch Lynceus ist zwar extradiegetischer Adressat, aber nicht der implizite Leser des vierzehnten Heroidenbriefes. Man kann dagegen fragen, ob es sinnvoll ist, zwischen implizitem Autor und implizitem Leser zu unterscheiden, da beide Instanzen zuletzt nur das Ergebnis der Textanalyse repräsentieren. Mit dem Verweis auf den impliziten Autor wird der Akzent allerdings stärker auf die Rezeption gelegt, handelt es sich doch um den Autor, dessen Stimme man aus dem Text rekonstruiert. Umgekehrt repräsentiert der implizite Leser als Konstrukt jenes Textverständnis, das der reale Autor im Text verankerte. Abgesehen davon, dass man Genettes Vorbehalte nicht teilen muss, ist die Instanz des impliziten Autors zumindest äußerst hilfreich zur Unterscheidung von Fiktion und Täuschung des pseudepigraphischen Briefes. C. ROSE, Theologie als Erzählung im Markusevangelium. Eine narratologisch-rezeptionsästhetische Untersuchung zu Mk 1,1–15, WUNT II/236, Tübingen 2007, 55, unterscheidet in einer Randnotiz seiner narrativen Analyse im Kontext der Pseudepigraphie zwar den empirischen und den impliziten Autor, verwendet „implizit" aber „in einem etwas anderen Gebrauch. Nicht der in der Erzählstrategie codierte Autor ist jetzt gemeint, sondern derjenige, als der sich der empirische Autor verstanden wissen will. Es wäre dann angemessener, von einem ‚empirischen Autor 2' zu sprechen." Aber gerade, weil der Autor – im Fall der Täuschung – als Apostel verstanden werden will, ist der implizite Autor „der in der Erzählstrategie codierte Autor".

tiert sich also an der mutmaßlichen Autorenintention. Im einen Fall gab der Autor eine Entsprechung von Erzähler und Autor vor, im anderen Fall wurde gerade die Differenz von Autor und Erzähler für die Darstellung nutzbar gemacht.

4.1 Der Leidenszeuge spricht

Die Frage, ob die beiden Petrusbriefe besser als Fiktion oder als Täuschung zu verstehen sind, kann nur für jeden der beiden Texte getrennt beantwortet werden. Der Erste Petrusbrief[28] bietet keine offensichtlichen Hinweise darauf, wie er rezipiert werden will, wer als impliziter Autor zu gelten hat. Informationen aus sekundären Quellen fehlen; und selbst wenn der Text erst zu Beginn des 2. Jh. entstand, ist nicht auszuschließen, dass er als angeblich echter, zwischenzeitlich verschollener Brief in die Lesegemeinde eingeführt wurde. Wenn sich Gemeindemitglieder am guten Griechisch des Apostels störten oder andere biographische Argumente Zweifel aufkommen ließen, werden sie den Brief nicht zwangsläufig als Fiktion rezipiert, sondern gegebenenfalls als vermeintliche Fälschung enttarnt haben. Mangels äußerer Anhaltspunkte kann nur der Text selbst darüber Auskunft geben, ob er als Fiktion oder als Täuschung verstanden werden will. Denn wenn eine Ebene des Textes unverstanden bleibt, sofern der Text nicht als Fiktion rezipiert wird, ist eine Täuschung auszuschließen. Umgekehrt ist von einer Täuschung auszugehen, wenn sich einzelne Aspekte ihrer Wirksamkeit nur entfalteten, wenn der Brief als echtes Schreiben eingestuft wurde.

Das deutlichste Indiz dafür, dass der Erste Petrusbrief als fiktionale Literatur gedacht sein könnte, findet sich in 1Petr 5,1. Denn der Vers stellt Petrus vermutlich als Märtyrer vor. Wenn vom μάρτυς τῶν τοῦ Χριστοῦ παθημάτων die Rede ist, ist damit nicht gemeint, dass Petrus Augenzeuge der Passion war, sondern dass er selbst zum Teilhaber an den Leiden Christi geworden ist und sein Bekenntnis mit dem eigenen Leib bezeugt hat. Das macht 1Petr 4,13 deutlich, wo in Entsprechung zu 1Petr 5,1 davon die Rede ist, dass die Adressaten, die an den Leiden Christi teilhaben (κοινωνεῖτε τοῖς τοῦ Χριστοῦ παθήμασιν), bei der Offenbarung seiner Herrlichkeit (ἐν τῇ ἀποκαλύψει τῆς δόξης αὐτοῦ, vgl. 1Petr 5,1: δόξης κοινωνός, vgl. auch 1Petr 5,10) jubeln werden. Im Gegensatz zu 1Petr 4,13 ist in 1Petr 5,1 kein finales Verhältnis ausgesagt, Petrus ist bereits Teilhaber an der Herrlichkeit Christi. Zwar wird dieser Lohn für die Lei-

---

[28] Forschungsüberblicke bei A. CASURELLA, Bibliography of Literature on First Peter, NTTS 23, Leiden u.a. 1996; E. COTHENET, La Première de Pierre. Bilan de 35 ans de recherches, ANRW II 25.5 (1988), 3685–3712, und J. H. ELLIOTT, The Rehabilitation of an Exegetical Step-Child. 1 Peter in Recent Research, JBL 95 (1976), 243–254.

den auch hier mit τῆς μελλούσης ἀποκαλύπτεσθαι als zukünftiges, noch ausstehendes Heil qualifiziert und auch 1Petr 1,7 und 1Petr 5,14 binden die Herrlichkeit an die Offenbarung. Dennoch hat Petrus bereits Anteil an der kommenden Herrlichkeit.

Der enge Zusammenhang von Leiden und Herrlichkeit (vgl. auch 1Petr 4,14) setzt allerdings nicht notwendig den Tod voraus. Auch für die Leiden der Gemeindemitglieder, die nicht zwangsläufig alle das Martyrium erwartet, wird die Herrlichkeit in Aussicht gestellt. In 1Petr 1,11 sind aber augenscheinlich die Todesleiden Jesu und die ihn nach dem Tod erwartende Herrlichkeit angesprochen (τὰ εἰς Χριστὸν παθήματα καὶ τὰς μετὰ ταῦτα δόξας). Verstärkt wird der Nachhall dieser Entsprechung durch 1Petr 1,21, wo von der Herrlichkeit Jesu nach der Auferstehung die Rede ist. Vor diesem Hintergrund zeichnet sich der Tod des Apostels zumindest am Horizont ab.

Versteht man das Zugleich von bereits erlangter Teilhabe und Erwartung der kommenden Herrlichkeit in 1Petr 5,1 als Hinweis auf Petrus' Martyrium, statt es auf ein nicht näher bestimmtes Leidenspensum des Apostels zurückzuführen, spiegelt der Vers zwei unterschiedliche Instanzen wider. Denn im Rahmen der Erzählung hat der den Brief abfassende Petrus das Martyrium natürlich noch nicht erlitten. Der implizite Autor, d.h. der Text, erinnert außerhalb der Erzählung aber offenbar an Petrus' Sterben als Glaubenszeuge.[29]

Das legt sich zumindest nahe, wenn man die Vita des Apostels berücksichtigt. Anders als Hypermestra blickt Petrus nicht zurück, er erinnert nicht an den Moment seiner Versuchung im Hof des Hohepriesters, als er Jesus verleugnete und so dem Kreuz aus dem Weg ging. Damals konnte er nicht als Zeuge für die Leiden des Christus gelten – weder im forensischen noch im existentiellen Sinn. Aber auch wenn Petrus seine unrühmliche Vergangenheit im Dunkeln lässt, ist sie als Kontext des Briefes doch laut vernehmbar. Angesichts der Verleugnung reichten die Leiden des Apostels, die er im Rahmen von Verfolgungen, wie sie Apg 5,40f. schildert, erlitten haben mag, kaum aus, um ihn als Zeugen für Christi Leiden auszu-

---

[29] In übertragenem Sinn könnte man davon sprechen, dass sich der implizite Autor „zu Wort meldet". Da er selbst jedoch keine Stimme hat, spricht erzähltheoretisch betrachtet Petrus von seinem eigenen Tod. Dadurch liegt gewissermaßen eine externe Fokalisierung zumindest aber eine Fokusvariante vor, weil von außen auf das Lebensende des Petrus geblickt wird. Es geht jedenfalls nicht um die Leiden des realen Autors, so etwa BROX, Petrusbrief (s. Anm. 1), 228f. Denn für die Annahme, dass der reale Autor in 1Petr 5,1 spricht, gibt es keine Hinweise im Text. Vgl. auch W. MARXSEN, Der Mitälteste und Zeuge der Leiden Christi. Eine martyrologische Begründung des „Romprimats" im 1. Petrus-Brief?, in: C. Andresen / G. Klein (Hg.), Theologia Crucis – Signum Crucis (FS Dinkler), Tübingen 1979, 377–393, der 1Petr 5,1 daher losgelöst vom brieflichen Rahmen interpretiert.

weisen, der 1Petr 1,11 zufolge Todesleiden erlitten hatte. Erst aufgrund seines Martyriums konnte er als Vorbild und Zeuge für die Lesegemeinde fungieren, die sich ihrerseits in letzter Konsequenz mit dem Tod konfrontiert sah (vgl. 1Petr 3,17f.; 4,1).

Das gilt insbesondere dann, wenn man eine Situation voraussetzt, wie sie Plinius der Jüngere in seinem Brief an Trajan (ep. 10,96) schildert.[30] Plinius war zwischen 111 und 113 Legat der Provinz *Bithynia et Pontus*. Während seiner Amtszeit führte er Prozesse gegen Christen durch. Man wird zögern, den Ersten Petrusbrief erst nach 111 n. Chr. zu datieren und als direkte Reaktion auf die Maßnahmen des römischen Statthalters zu verstehen, wenngleich die Versuchung angesichts der *adscriptio* und der frappierenden Berührungen zwischen den beiden Texten groß ist.[31] Wenn Plinius in seinem Brief an den Kaiser hervorhebt, dass er selbst keine Erfahrungen im Zusammenhang mit dem speziellen Kasus hat, weil er Christenprozessen noch nie beiwohnte (ep. 10,96,1), ist damit angedeutet, dass es schon vor ihm Christenprozesse gab; und es ist nicht ausgeschlossen, dass es auch in Kleinasien vor Plinius zu Gerichtsverhandlungen kam, in denen sich Christen für ihren Glauben verantworten mussten. Setzt man eine gewisse Tradition der römischen Rechtssprechung voraus, kann der Pliniusbrief daher mit Einschränkungen als Zeugnis für die Rechtsverfahren dienen, unter denen die Leserinnen und Leser des Ersten Petrusbriefes zu leiden hatten. Denn der Erste Petrusbrief diente als Ratgeber dafür, wie man sich gegenüber Staat und Gesellschaft bei Anfeindungen wegen des christlichen Glaubens verhalten sollte.

Plinius beschreibt seinen Umgang mit den Beschuldigten in den Prozessen sehr genau: „Ich habe sie gefragt, ob sie Christen seien. Die Geständigen fragte ich unter Androhung der Todesstrafe ein zweites und ein drittes Mal. Diejenigen, die hartnäckig darauf beharrten, ließ ich zur Hinrichtung abführen."[32] Der Statthalter eröffnete den Angeklagten die Möglichkeit,

---

[30] Vgl. dazu etwa R. FREUDENBERGER, Das Verhalten der römischen Behörden gegen die Christen im 2. Jahrhundert. Dargestellt am Brief des Plinius an Trajan und den Reskripten Trajans und Hadrians, MBPF 52, München 1969; J. MOLTHAGEN, Der römische Staat und die Christen im zweiten und dritten Jahrhundert, Hyp. 28, Göttingen 1970, 13–20; A. REICHERT, Durchdachte Konfusion. Plinius, Trajan und das Christentum, ZNW 93 (2002), 227–250, und K. THRAEDE, Noch einmal: Plinius d. J. und die Christen, ZNW 95 (2004), 102–128.

[31] So thematisiert 1Petr 4,14–16 mit der Differenzierung zwischen der Schmähung aufgrund des Namens Christi und der Leiden aufgrund von Verbrechen genau die Unterscheidung von Straftatbeständen, die Plinius in ep. 10,96,2 vornimmt.

[32] Ep. 10,96,3: „Interrogavi ipsos an essent Christiani. Confitentes iterum ac tertio interrogavi supplicium minatus; perseverantes duci iussi." Text und Übersetzung hier und im Folgenden: C. Plinius Secundus, d. Ä., Sämtliche Briefe. Lateinisch-Deutsch. Übers. u. hg. v. H. Philips / M. Giebel, Stuttgart 1998.

sich vom Christentum zu distanzieren. „Da gab es nun welche, die leugneten, Christen zu sein oder jemals gewesen zu sein. ... Außerdem lästerten sie Christus, und zu all dem lassen sich, so heißt es, wahre Christen nicht zwingen."[33] Diese Einschätzung ist insbesondere mit Blick auf die Evangelientradition von Interesse. Echte Christen ließen sich nicht zwingen, den Namen Christi zu leugnen. Doch im Markusevangelium tut Petrus genau das: Er leugnet und flucht.[34] Setzt man voraus, dass der Evangelist mit seiner Darstellung der Verleugnungsszene auch auf die römische Rechtspraxis anspielte, ergibt sich, dass ähnliche Praktiken wie die von Plinius geschilderten schon lange vor dessen Entsendung nach *Bithynia et Pontus* angewandt wurden.

Es ist nicht ohne weiteres vorauszusetzen, dass die Leserinnen und Leser des Ersten Petrusbriefes das Markusevangelium kannten, doch die Szene ist in den entscheidenden Punkten weitgehend unverändert in das Matthäusevangelium eingeflossen, das zumindest der Autor des Textes kannte[35] und mit ihm vermutlich auch dessen Leserinnen und Leser. Trotz seines zuvor abgelegten vollmundigen Bekenntnisses leugnet Petrus und flucht angesichts der sich abzeichnenden Todesgefahr (vgl. Mt 26,34f.69–75). Nach dem Zeugnis der Evangelien bekannte sich Petrus nicht etwa trotz zweimaliger Nachfrage unter Todesdrohung zu Jesus, sondern leugnete gleich dreimal, zu ihm zu gehören, noch bevor er direkt mit dem Tod bedroht wurde. 1Petr 4,16 fordert dagegen, Gott unter dem Namen Χριστιανός trotz der Diffamierung durch die Umwelt zu verherrlichen.

Vor dem Hintergrund der Passionsgeschichte erwies sich Petrus damit als äußerst ungeeigneter Zeuge für die Leiden Christi. Wie konnte gerade der Apostel, der Jesus dreimal verleugnet hatte, dazu auffordern, sich gegenüber jedem und jederzeit wegen der eigenen Hoffnung zu verantworten (vgl. 1Petr 3,15)? „Der traut sich was", durften jene sagen, die das Schrei-

---

[33] Ep. 10,96,5: „Qui negabant esse se Christianos aut fuisse ..., praeterea male dicerent Christo, quorum nihil cogi posse dicuntur qui sunt re vera Christiani."

[34] Mk 14,70f.: ὁ δὲ πάλιν ἠρνεῖτο. καὶ μετὰ μικρὸν πάλιν οἱ παρεστῶτες ἔλεγον τῷ Πέτρῳ· ἀληθῶς ἐξ αὐτῶν εἶ, καὶ γὰρ Γαλιλαῖος εἶ. ὁ δὲ ἤρξατο ἀναθεματίζειν καὶ ὀμνύναι ὅτι οὐκ οἶδα τὸν ἄνθρωπον τοῦτον ὃν λέγετε. (Er leugnete aber wieder. Wenig später sagten die Dabeistehenden wieder zu Petrus: „Wahrlich, du bist einer von ihnen, denn du bist auch ein Galiläer. Er aber begann zu fluchen und zu schwören: „Ich kenne diesen Menschen nicht, von dem ihr sprecht.") So wie Markus die Verleugnungsszene schildert, „entspricht sie in den wesentlichen Punkten einer Nostrifizierung, wie sie römischem Rechtsempfinden zu eigen ist: *Leugnung*, Christ zu sein, und *Verfluchung* des Gruppenidols. Beides sind die entscheidenden Punkte in der Verleugnungsgeschichte", M. EBNER, Du hast eine zweite Chance! Das Markusevangelium als Hoffnungsgeschichte, in: O. Fuchs / M. Widl (Hg.), Ein Haus der Hoffnung (FS Zerfaß), Düsseldorf 1999, 31–40 (37).

[35] Vgl. METZNER, Rezeption (s. Anm. 1), 7–68.

ben für einen echten Brief des Apostels hielten, „läuft selbst vor der Gefahr davon und gibt nun gute Ratschläge." Natürlich wussten die Leserinnen und Leser, dass Petrus am Ende seines Lebens treu zu Christus gestanden hatte und der Gefahr nicht mehr ausgewichen war. Deshalb konnte der Text auch als Täuschung funktionieren, wenn er für einen echten Brief gehalten wurde. In diesem Fall fügten die Leserinnen und Leser dem Text aber etwas aus ihrem Informationsschatz hinzu.

Das Martyrium des Apostels war bekannt, es gehörte im Fall der Täuschung aber nicht zur „Stimme" des impliziten Autors. Deshalb wirkte der Text als Fiktion überzeugender. Der implizite Autor war glaubwürdiger als Nicht-Petrus denn als Petrus, weil er als Nicht-Petrus das Martyrium des Apostels bereits implizierte, das notwendig außerhalb des Textes blieb, wenn Petrus als impliziter Autor verstanden wurde. Mit anderen Worten: Die Aufforderung, jederzeit Rechenschaft über den Glauben abzulegen, war überzeugender, wenn sie mit Verweis auf einen Märtyrer erging oder eben „von einem Märtyrer" erging, wo ein anderer im Namen des Apostels zur Standhaftigkeit aufrief. Es liegt in der Natur der Sache, dass der Märtyrer selbst nicht mehr dazu in der Lage war, deswegen konnte nur in der Fiktion auf Petrus als Märtyrer zurückgegriffen werden.

Das Ethos des Märtyrers, das der Text voraussetzt, ließ sich nur im Rahmen der Fiktion für die Argumentation des Briefes nutzbar machen. Hielt man den Text für einen echten Brief, war für das Ethos des Apostels seine Verleugnung prägend. Das im Brief skizzierte Ethos passte deshalb nur bedingt zur Person. Umgekehrt gilt, dass sich das vom Brief vorausgesetzte Ethos erst vom Martyrium und damit von der Fiktion her entfaltete. Hielt man den ersten Brief für echt, war seine paränetische Leistung trotz der Autorität des Apostels geringer als bei der Fiktion. Denn trotz seines Martyriums musste Petrus im Moment der Abfassung, in dem er den Brief verantwortet hätte, eher als unglaubwürdiger Zeuge gelten.

Die Leistung der Fiktion kommt auch zum Tragen, wenn man die Unterscheidung von Adressatinnen und Lesern berücksichtigt. Denn die realen Leser Kleinasiens, für die der Brief vermutlich bestimmt war, waren ja nicht mit den extradiegetischen Adressatinnen des Briefes identisch, Letztere hatten einen Brief von Petrus erhalten, Erstere nicht. Versteht man den Text als Fiktion, haben die fiktiven Adressatinnen einen Brief von Petrus erhalten, die damaligen realen Leser dagegen außerhalb der Erzählsituation einen fiktiven Brief. Petrus hat ihnen keinen Brief geschrieben, der Brief ist aber für sie als intendierte Leser bestimmt. Hielten die damaligen Leserinnen den Brief dagegen für echt, mussten auch sie davon ausgehen, dass der längst verstorbene Petrus ihnen keinen Brief geschrieben hatte, sondern der Gemeinde zwei Generationen zuvor. In diesem Fall war der Brief aber auch nicht für sie bestimmt, er passte nur zufällig zu ihrer Situation. Die

Kommunikationssituation war also eine andere. Nur im Fall der Fiktion korrespondierte der Text direkt mit der Situation der intendierten Leserinnen und Leser, wo der implizite Leser den intendierten entsprach.

4.2 Der Offenbarungszeuge spricht

Die Kommunikationssituation des Zweiten Petrusbriefes[36] ist insofern noch etwas komplexer, als die Rolle der früheren Narration und damit die fiktive Zukunft eine größere Rolle spielt. In diesem Fall werden die intendierten Leserinnen und Leser des Textes nämlich von Petrus im Rahmen der „Erzählung" selbst angesprochen, wenn auch indirekt. Wie im Hypermestra-Brief liegt auch im Zweiten Petrusbrief partiell eine frühere Narration vor. Petrus blickt in die Zukunft und erzählt, was sich in kommenden Tagen ereignen wird. Ähnlich wie Hypermestra scheint er am Lebensende angekommen zu sein. Der Brief berührt die Gattung des literarischen Testaments.[37] Der Apostel schildert die Zukunft der Gemeinde seiner Gegenwart, die Zukunft der Gemeinde der fiktiven Abfassungszeit; das war jedoch die Gegenwart der intendierten Leserinnen und Leser zur realen Abfassungszeit des Textes, sofern diese eine Kontinuität der Gemeindegeschichte voraussetzten. Umgekehrt war die Gegenwart der fiktiven Abfassungssituation ihre eigene Vergangenheit, mit dem Brief blickten sie scheinbar in die eigene Gemeindegeschichte zurück. Über dieses Zeitschema wird die historische Figur Petrus mit der realen Welt der Gegenwart verknüpft.

Doch auch im Zweiten Petrusbrief erweist sich zumindest an zwei Stellen die Rezeption des Textes als fiktionales Schreiben wirkungsvoller denn als echtes. Denn in 2Petr 1,12 enthält der Text eine *captatio benevolentiae*, die sich im Rahmen der Erzählsituation nicht an die intendierten Leserinnen in der ersten Hälfte des zweiten Jahrhunderts,[38] sondern an die fiktiven, extradiegetischen Adressaten, die Zeitgenossen des Petrus, richtet. Denn nur sie erhalten von dem Apostel einen Brief, in dem er ihnen zugesteht, dass sie in der Wahrheit gestärkt sind. Wurde der Text als fiktionales Schreiben verfasst, war der implizite Leser Nicht-Petrus-Rezipient, das bedeutet, dass die intendierten Leserinnen und Leser den Text als nicht von Petrus verfasst erkennen und sich folglich selbst direkt vom Text angesprochen fühlen sollten. In 2Petr 3,1 wird entsprechend die lautere Gesin-

---

[36] Forschungsüberblicke bei R. J. BAUCKHAM, 2 Peter. An Account of Research, ANRW II 25.5 (1988), 3713–3752; M. J. GILMOUR, 2 Peter in Recent Research. A Bibliography, JETS 42 (1999), 673–678, und P. MÜLLER, Der 2. Petrusbrief, ThR 66 (2001), 310–337.

[37] Vgl. dazu etwa R. J. BAUCKHAM, Jude, 2 Peter, WBC 50, Dallas 1983, 131–134.159–162.

[38] Zur Datierungsdiskussion vgl. MÜLLER, 2. Petrusbrief (s. Anm. 36), 332f.

nung der Adressaten gelobt. Die intendierten Leserinnen durften sich zwar als spätere Generation, die in einer kontinuierlichen Gemeindetradition stand, indirekt angesprochen fühlen, aber eben nicht direkt, wenn sie den Brief im Rahmen einer Täuschung als echt einstuften. Sie profitierten allenfalls mittelbar von den Lorbeeren der früheren Generation, denn sie selbst hatten keinen Brief von Petrus erhalten.

Es ist nicht auszuschließen, dass genau das vom realen Autor intendiert war. Vielleicht wollte er durch das Lob der früheren Generationen die Gemeinde zur Treue im Glauben anspornen. Es gibt aber eine Beobachtung, die es unwahrscheinlich erscheinen lässt, dass der Text als Täuschung geplant war. Denn da die *salutatio* in 2Petr 1,2 mit χάρις ὑμῖν καὶ εἰρήνη πληθυνθείη trotz Jud 2 (ἔλεος ὑμῖν καὶ εἰρήνη καὶ ἀγάπη πληθυνθείη) offenbar 1Petr 1,2 wörtlich aufnimmt,[39] dürfte sich 2Petr 3,1 auf den Ersten Petrusbrief beziehen und die Kenntnis dieses Textes bei seinen Leserinnen und Lesern voraussetzen.[40] Stilistisch unterscheidet sich der Zweite Petrusbrief jedoch deutlich vom Vorgänger.[41] Der Text lässt kaum ein Bemühen erkennen, eine sprachliche, theologische oder thematische Nähe zum Ersten Petrusbrief zu suggerieren. Der Autor machte offenbar gar nicht den Versuch, den Brief als echten Brief des Apostels Petrus auszugeben, ganz unabhängig davon, ob der Erste Petrusbrief der Gemeinde als echter Brief oder als Fiktion galt. Indem sich der Autor mit 2Petr 3,1 zum Ersten Petrusbrief bekennt und ihn somit seinem eigenen Erzähler als Produkt zuschreibt, macht er deutlich, dass er gerade nicht Petrus als Autor verstanden wissen will. 2Petr 3,1 weist Petrus daher vor dem Hintergrund des Ersten Petrusbriefes geradezu als *unreliable narrator* aus.

Dem scheint 2Petr 1,16–18 zu widersprechen, denn in diesem Abschnitt rekurriert der Text ausdrücklich auf die Autorität des Offenbarungszeugen Petrus, eine Autorität, die der reale Autor nicht für sich in Anspruch nehmen konnte.[42] Das bedeutet aber nicht, dass eine Täuschung vorliegt, denn

---

[39] Vgl. auch die Hervorhebung der acht bei der Sintflut geretteten Menschen in 2Petr 2,5, die sich als Adaption von 1Petr 3,20 verstehen lässt.

[40] Die Kenntnis des Ersten Petrusbriefes bedeutet nicht, dass man mit einer petrinischen Schule zu rechnen hat, der sich auch der Judasbrief verdanken würde, so zuletzt wieder P. CHATELION COUNET, Pseudepigraphy and the Petrine School. Spirit and Tradition in 1 and 2 Peter and Jude, HTS 62 (2006), 403–424.

[41] Zum Stil des Zweiten Petrusbriefes vgl. T. J. KRAUS, Sprache, Stil und historischer Ort des zweiten Petrusbriefes, WUNT II/136, Tübingen 2001.

[42] So urteilt E. E. Ellis über die Petrusbriefe: „Given the unique authority of the apostle in the church, theses letters display, if they are pseudepigrapha, clear and sufficient evidence of a deceptive intention", E. E. ELLIS, Pseudonymity and Canonicity of New Testament Documents, in: ders., History and Interpretation in New Testament Perspective, Biblical Interpretation Series 54, Leiden u.a. 2001, 17–29 (28). Zu den Problemen, welche die behauptete Augenzeugenschaft des Erzählers verursacht, vgl. H. J. RIEDL, Der

der reale Autor musste die Autorität des Apostels gar nicht für sich selbst in Anspruch nehmen, um sie ins Spiel zu bringen.

Anders als der Erste Petrusbrief kennt der Zweite Petrusbrief nicht nur den Erzähler Petrus, der in gleichzeitiger Narration sein Briefschreiben reflektiert, er schildert in späterer Narration in Ansätzen auch die Geschichte der Erzählfigur Petrus. Dabei verhält sich der Briefschreiber in Kontinuität zu seinem früheren Ich. Petrus steht zu seiner Vergangenheit, wobei er allerdings nur den großen Moment der Offenbarung in den Blick nimmt. Wie Hypermestra blickt er zurück auf einen zentralen Moment seiner Vita: Er hörte auf dem Berg die Stimme Gottes. Der Text erinnert so an die Glaubwürdigkeit des Apostels, er „erzählt" Petrus' Geschichte und übernimmt dabei wie die Prosopopoiie in der Rhetorik die pragmatische Funktion, die Leserinnen und Leser zu bewegen. Der reale Autor erinnerte in Form einer brieflichen Prosopopoiie an die Offenbarung, die Petrus zuteil geworden war, und führte dessen Autorität so als Argument ein. Der Text realisiert damit die Funktion, die sein Erzähler für sich in Anspruch nimmt; er will an Petrus erinnern, wie Petrus durch den fiktiven konservierten Brief selbst in der Zukunft erinnern will (2Petr 1,12.13.15; 3,1.2).[43]

Indem Petrus in der fiktiven Gegenwart die Parusie verteidigt und das Gericht für die künftige Zeit der Spötter ankündigt, richtet er die Naherwartung für die Zeit der intendierten Leserinnen und Leser, die aller Wahrscheinlichkeit mit solchen Spöttern zu kämpfen hatten, wieder auf. Wie Hypermestras Brief steht auch sein Schreiben zwischen der fiktionalen Vergangenheit, die mit dem Rückblick auf die Offenbarung gleichsam in Form einer Analepse eingeholt wird, und der Zukunft, in der – wie in der Vergangenheit offenbart – Christus als Herrscher kommen wird. Der Petrus des Zweiten Petrusbriefes ist somit gewissermaßen ein homodiegetischer Erzähler, wenn auch kein autodiegetischer. Auch Petrus bleibt sich treu, aber er hat sich zumindest insofern gegenüber dem intradiegetischen Petrus vom Berg der Offenbarung verändert, als er dem Tode nahe steht und die schriftliche Erinnerung der Gemeinde durch einen Brief deshalb für notwendig erachtet. Dieser Brief ist wiederum Medium der Erzählung und Element der Handlung, mit dem großen Unterschied, dass das in der

---

Zweite Petrusbrief und das theologische Problem neutestamentlicher Pseudepigraphie, RSTh 64, Frankfurt a.M. u.a. 2005, 216–224.

[43] Das impliziert jedoch nicht etwa „den *objektiven* Tatbestand, daß der Verfasser einer solchen Schrift – sofern er durch Erinnerung die apostolische Verkündigung interpretierend weitergibt und dadurch neu präsent macht – gleichsam nur als Werkzeug fungiert, durch den der eigentliche Verkündiger redet", J. ZMIJEWSKI, Apostolische Paradosis und Pseudepigraphie im Neuen Testament. „Durch Erinnerung wachhalten" (2Petr 1,13; 3,1), in: ders., Das Neue Testament – Quelle christlicher Theologie und Glaubenspraxis. Aufsätze zum Neuen Testament und seiner Auslegung, Stuttgart 1986, 185–196 (194); vgl. auch RIEDL, a.a.O. 231–241.

Zukunftsvision beschriebene Auftreten der Spötter nicht nur Teil der von Petrus erzählten Geschichte seiner fiktiven Adressatengemeinde, sondern auch die reale Situation der als Leserinnen intendierten Gemeindemitglieder der Abfassungszeit war. Der Brief sollte nicht nur Element der erzählten Handlung sein, sondern auch Element der Gemeinderealität.

5. Briefe aus den Gemeinden?

Die Petrusbriefe sind keine narrativen Texte im engeren Sinn, sie erzählen keine mythischen Geschichten. Das aus den Heroides Ovids entnommene Beispiel des Hypermestra-Briefes wirft gleichwohl ein anderes Licht auf das Pseudonym des Apostels Petrus in den kanonischen Petrusbriefen. Denn die Texte lassen sich offenbar *auch* als briefliche Prosopopoiien respektive als fiktionale Briefe verstehen.

Die Äußerungen einer mittels Prosopopoiie im Rahmen einer Rede vorgestellten Figur werden allerdings von den Ausführungen des Redners gerahmt, der die Fiktion einführt, ähnlich wie bei den Heroides der Buchtitel, die Sammlung und der Autorenname Ovids eine Rahmung schaffen, die die Fiktion transparent machen. Weder der Erste noch der Zweite Petrusbrief sind im Rahmen einer Briefsammlung oder unter dem Namen ihres tatsächlichen Autors überliefert worden.

Die Tatsache, dass die Fiktion anders als im Hypermestra-Brief nicht von einer realen Autorenangabe umgriffen wird, steht der Interpretation der Petrusbriefe als fiktive Schreiben jedoch nicht grundsätzlich entgegen. Wie der Brief in die Gemeinde eingeführt wurde, ist nämlich nicht überliefert. Es ist denkbar, dass die realen Autoren der Schreiben und mit ihnen die Texte selbst der Gemeinde entstammten, für welche die Briefe bestimmt waren. Durch Mimik und Betonung sowie den Kontext des Vortrages konnte eine Täuschungsabsicht ausgeschlossen und die Fiktionalität der Briefsituation markiert werden. Im Akt der Narration wurde der Vortragende gleichsam zum Erzähler einer Rahmengeschichte, in welche die Geschichte von Petrus, der einen Brief abfasste, eingebettet war.

Ungeachtet der ernsthaften Anliegen der Texte lässt sich die Vortragssituation mit einer Büttenrede vergleichen: Trotz einer entsprechenden Kostümierung und Selbstvorstellung glaubt im Rahmen von Fastnachtsfeierlichkeiten niemand, einen Till Eulenspiegel vor sich zu haben. Das Stilmittel der Prosopopoiie zeigt, dass auch ernsthafte Anliegen, selbst Fragen von Leben und Tod, unter der Maskerade verhandelt werden konnten. Es ist nicht unmöglich, dass die Autoren der Petrusbriefe ihre Texte in den Gemeinden als Fiktion deklarierten oder durch ihren Habitus die spielerische Komponente der Autorenfiktion transparent machten.

Einen situativen Rahmen muss man nicht nur postulieren, wenn man die Texte im Kontext der fiktionalen Literatur verankern will, sondern auch wenn man davon ausgeht, dass sie als echte Schreiben des Apostels Petrus ausgegeben wurden. Den Gemeinden musste ja plausibel gemacht werden, warum plötzlich alte Briefe in ihren Reihen auftauchten. Im Fall der Täuschung musste sich der Autor überlegen, was der Apostel Brauchbares zur vorgegebenen Gemeindesituation gesagt haben könnte. Die Fiktion erlaubte ihm, die Leserinnen und Leser in diese Überlegung einzubeziehen. Leider liegen uns keine Informationen darüber vor, wie die Schreiben in die Gemeinden eingeführt wurden, daher sind wir auf die Briefe selbst angewiesen. Da eindeutige Hinweise im Text fehlen, bleibt mindestens im Fall des Ersten Petrusbriefes unsicher, ob der Text als Fiktion oder Täuschung geplant war. Der Vergleich mit den *Heroides* Ovids zeigt aber, dass die Texte als fiktive Briefe ihren pragmatischen Zweck mindestens ebenso gut erfüllen konnten.

Apostle, Co-Elder, and Witness of Suffering

Author Construction and Peter Image in First Peter

by

Lutz Doering

1. Introduction

In an article on the pseudepigraphal frame of First Peter published in 1975, the late Norbert Brox claimed that First Peter belongs "to those examples of ancient Christian pseudepigraphy, in which there is no patent connection between the fictive name of the author and the writing that comes under it—in terms of contents, disposition or historical setting—that would render the choice of name *a posteriori* at least somewhat plausible."[1] Key to Brox is the assumption that the choice of a certain apostle as fictive author tends not to relate to the specific theology of this apostle. To the contrary, Brox claims, the name is often chosen for merely formal authorisation, as a badge of truth, while the letter does not refer to individual characteristics of the apostle. Indeed, one might speak of a "de-individualization of the apostles."[2] For the author of the letter, "Peter" thus means "apostolic authority (as for other writers other names do)."[3] To be sure, Brox briefly acknowledges the view that 1 Pet 5:1 presents a specific Peter image, to allow for application in terms of paraenesis and engagement with a specific situation.[4] But he is quick to leave this passage again, and ties the pseudepigraphal fiction only to the epistolary framework of the letter in

---

[1] N. Brox, "Zur pseudepigraphischen Rahmung des ersten Petrusbriefes," *BZ* 19 (1975): 78–96 (78): First Peter belongs "zu den Beispielen altkirchlicher Pseudepigraphie, in denen zwischen dem fiktiven Autornamen und der mit ihm bedachten Schrift nach deren Inhalt, Charakter oder historischen Umständen kein erkennbarer Konnex besteht, welcher die Namenwahl für die historische Rückfrage ... nachträglich wenigstens relativ einleuchtend macht." Translations from German in the present contribution are mine. On the question of *whether* First Peter is a pseudepigraphon, see below, n. 9.

[2] Brox, ibid., 92: "Entindividualisierung der Apostel."

[3] Idem, "Tendenz und Pseudepigraphie im ersten Petrusbrief," *Kairos* 20 (1978): 110–20 (118).

[4] Idem, "Rahmung" (see n. 1), 81.

1:1; 5:12, 13. This, I will suggest in this paper, is a reductionist approach to the author fiction in First Peter that should be reconsidered.

For Brox, there is one single element that explains the choice in favour of Peter, and that is the connection with Rome, referred to as "Babylon" in 5:13: "In Rom war das die 'natürliche Wahl', Petrus war der 'natürliche Kandidat' für die Verfasserschaft eines Briefes aus Rom."[5] Brox, however, briefly adds two reservations: First, due to the state of the sources we cannot be quite sure of how widespread the Peter-Rome tradition was in the last quarter of the first century. Second, the lack of a Petrine author fiction in *First Clement* is difficult for the claim that Petrine authorship was somehow "natural" for Rome.[6] To these reservations one could add that in early texts linking Peter with Rome, Paul is mentioned as well (*1 Clem.* 5.4–7; Ignatius, *Rom.* 4.3). Although it is possible to infer Peter's leading position from the fact that these texts mention Peter first, this is far from certain; Andreas Lindemann, for one, has argued for *Achtergewicht* (stress on the final unit) in *1 Clem.* 5.4–7, thus an emphasis on Paul not Peter.[7] Be this as it may, I do not think "Rome" alone sufficiently explains why "Peter" was chosen as the name of the letter writer. Brox's approach suffers from his decision to require for a substantial connection with "Peter," apart from the link with Rome, either original documents of Peter's theology or the theology of a Petrine "school"—the former we do not have, and the latter, according to Brox, cannot be substantiated from the sources.[8] The factor neglected is the one he briefly mentions but does not pursue further: the quest of the *Peter image* (*Petrusbild*) that the letter offers its addressees. The present paper will therefore ask for the contribution of the Peter image for the author construction in First Peter.[9] I shall proceed in three steps. First, I

---

[5] N. Brox, "Tendenz" (see n. 3), 115. Cf. already idem, "Rahmung" (see n. 1), 95–6.

[6] Idem, "Tendenz" (see n. 3), 116.

[7] A. Lindemann, *Paulus im ältesten Christentum: Das Bild des Apostels und die Rezeption der paulinischen Theologie in der frühchristlichen Literatur bis Marcion* (BHT 58; Tübingen: Mohr Siebeck, 1979), 75–6.

[8] Cf. Brox, "Tendenz" (see n. 3), 114. Critical on the assumption of a Petrine "circle" or "school" also D. G. Horrell, "The Product of a Petrine Circle? A Reassessment of the Origin and Character of 1 Peter," *JSNT* 86 (2002): 29–60. Cf. further below, n. 109. Horrell largely follows Brox in his answer to the question, "Why Peter?" (ibid., 52–4), but adds that Paul and his legacy may have been controversial in the areas to which First Peter is addressed.

[9] For the purpose of this article I assume that First Peter is a pseudepigraphon. However, it should be noted that no single argument can be considered compelling and that my judgment is informed by the cumulative weight of arguments. The main reasons to doubt the letter's orthonymity are the likely post-70 CE use of "Babylon" (1 Pet 5:13) with reference to Rome (discussed below, section 3.2), the spread of Christianity throughout the northern regions of Asia Minor, the tensions with non-Christian population in these areas, the absence of concern for the relation between Jewish and Gentile

shall analyse the Peter image materially developed in First Peter. Second, I shall look at the relations in which Peter is being presented (Silvanus, Mark, and "Babylon"). And third, I shall discuss the epistolary form and the letter type of First Peter, as well as the apostle image evoked by it.

2. The Peter Image Materially Developed in First Peter

In contrast to Rainer Metzner I do not postulate methodologically that First Peter develops its Peter image in direct dependence on one specific New Testament text (for Metzner: the Gospel of Matthew).[10] Because of links with several early Christian texts and/or traditions[11] the analysis must be kept more open. In doing so, I work on the assumption that the individual and concrete "Peter image" resonated, on the author as well as presumably on the reader end, with a wider stock of "knowledge" about Peter that I call "Peter tradition."[12]

Christians, and perhaps the elegant Greek (contrast Acts 4:13 ἀγράμματος) and consistent use of the Septuagint. Cf. the recent circumspect discussion by R. Feldmeier, *The First Letter of Peter: A Commentary on the Greek Text* (trans. P. H. Davids; Waco, Tex.: Baylor University Press, 2008), 32–40; German: *Der erste Brief des Petrus* (THK 15/1; Leipzig: Ev. Verlagsanstalt, 2005), 23–7. More consideration of orthonymity and at least maintenance of a link with Peter's ministry are allowed by J. D. G. Dunn, *Beginning from Jerusalem* (Christianity in the Making 2; Grand Rapids, Mich.: Eerdmans, 2009), 1148–57. Despite the different link between the real and the explicit author (on this below), several of the following observations on author construction would also be relevant if orthonymity were assumed (the question would then be "How," not "Why Peter?"). See also below, n. 75.

[10] Cf. R. Metzner, *Die Rezeption des Matthäusevangeliums im 1. Petrusbrief: Studien zum traditionsgeschichtlichen und theologischen Einfluß des 1. Evangeliums auf den 1. Petrusbrief* (WUNT II/74; Tübingen: Mohr Siebeck, 1995), especially 107–42 ("Das Petrusbild").

[11] Cf. D. G. Horrell, *1 Peter* (NTG; London: T&T Clark, 2008), 41: "richly intertextual" (cf. 35–42).

[12] I.e., tradition about Peter, not "Petrine theology," though specific viewpoints for which Peter stood could well be reflected in it. My use of "Peter image" thus differs from that of C. Grappe, *Images de Pierre aux deux premiers siècles* (EHPhR 75; Paris: Presses Universitaires de France, 1995), who looks at "axes" (cf. 32–3) of related or antagonistic image-components in a range of texts across five phases of the history of early Christianity up to the 2d century. Grappe's image-components rather represent elaborations on what I refer to as the stock of knowledge about Peter. Recently, M. Bockmuehl has pointed to the importance of living memory for "knowledge" about Peter up to the second century: idem, "Peter's Death in Rome? Back to Front and Upside Down," *SJT* 60 (2007): 1–23.

In what follows I shall adopt a *theoretical model of author and reader* that can be easily applied to the situation of epistolary communication and distinguishes between the following factors:[13]

(1) the real author—the real readers;
(2) the abstract/implied author—the abstract/implied readers;
(3) the explicit author (addressor, narrator)—the explicit reader (addressee, narratee).

The "real author" and the "real readers" of a letter are outside the text. The "implied author" is the abstract authorial consciousness throughout the text, whereas the "implied reader" is the textually encoded norm of the adequate act of reception. The implied author creates the "explicit author," i.e., the "addressor" mentioned in the letter prescript, who as "narrator" is the voice used to tell the "story" or contents of the letter. The equivalent is the "explicit reader," i.e., the "addressee" mentioned in the letter prescript, to whom as "narratee" the "story" is told. Author and reader can also become part of

(4) the world of the text, i.e., the letter contents; they do so by becoming characters in the text.

Materially, the following elements of the Peter image in First Peter can be distinguished: The addressor is presented as "apostle," as "co-elder" (probably implying the "shepherd" image), as "witness of suffering," and as "partner in the glory that is to be revealed,"[14] each element carrying strong rhetorical appeal.

2.1 "Apostle"

At the very beginning of the letter we find, within the prescript (1 Pet 1:1a), the mention of the explicit author (addressor), consisting of the *superscriptio* Πέτρος and the *intitulatio* ἀπόστολος Ἰησοῦ Χριστοῦ. The latter, with the use of the title "apostle," corresponds to the majority of letters in the Pauline corpus (Romans, First and Second Corinthians, Galatians, Ephesians, Colossians, and the Pastorals) but gives a different order in the genitive: "of Jesus Christ" rather than "of Christ Jesus." For the choice of the title "apostle" some commentators claim influence of the Pauline letter prescript, which, as will be shown further below, in my view cannot be questioned for the word order in the *salutatio*. However, for the

---

[13] Cf. H. Link, *Rezeptionsforschung: Eine Einführung in Methoden und Probleme* (2d ed.; Stuttgart et al.: Kohlhammer, 1980), 25–9. I have added the terms "addressor" and "addressee" as epistolary forms of the explicit author and reader, respectively, and "narratee," in line with narrative-critical terminology; cf. M. A. Powell, *What is Narrative Criticism?* (Minneapolis: Augsburg, 1990), 27. For another model cf. K. M. Schmidt, *Mahnung und Erinnerung im Maskenspiel: Epistolographie, Rhetorik und Narrativik der pseudepigraphen Petrusbriefe* (HBS 38; Freiburg i. Brsg. et al.: Herder, 2003), 171–75, whose levels 1 and 3–5 correspond to our levels 1–4.

[14] Cf. the brief discussion in D. G. Meade, *Pseudonymity and Canon: An Investigation into the Relationship of Authorship and Authority in Jewish and Earliest Christian Tradition* (WUNT 39; Tübingen: Mohr Siebeck, 1986), 175–77. Cf. also Schmidt, ibid., 186–91 ("Die Vita des Petrus").

title "apostle" such dependence is questionable. Peter was known as apostle in early Christianity without any reservation. This applies also (and perforce) when one is inclined to reckon with an initial openness of the title, from which subsequently different developments took off.[15] *Peter fulfils any criteria.*

A few sidelights must suffice here. According to synoptic tradition, he was the first one called (Mark 1:16–20 par. Matt 4:18–22) and holds the first place in the list of Twelve (Mark 3:16–19 parr., Matt 10:2 with emphatic πρῶτος, Luke 6:13–14 with reference to the Twelve, "whom he also named apostles"). He functions as protagonist and spokesperson of the disciples (e.g., Mark 8:29, 10:28, 11:21), of the inner group of three (together with the sons of Zebedee, Mark 5:37; 9:2, 5; 14:33, 37) and of four (joined by Andrew, Mark 1:29, 13:3). Further, Cephas, i.e., Peter, according to Paul, is the recipient of the protophany of the resurrected Christ (1 Cor 15:5, cf. Luke 24:34). Even where other traditions about the resurrection are used, Peter's role is emphasised (Mark 16:7, εἴπατε τοῖς μαθηταῖς αὐτοῦ καὶ τῷ Πέτρῳ). And even in John, where Peter is not the first one called, he has a leading role (he is mentioned in first position in John 20:2–10 and carries out a careful inspection of the tomb). Finally, Peter's post-Easter position as foundational apostolic figure must be mentioned; suffice it to point to the "rock" saying Matt 16:18, the saying about turning back and strengthening the brothers Luke 22:31–32, and the leading role of Peter in Acts 1–12. John 21—in delicate positioning vis-à-vis the Beloved Disciple—assigns precedence in mission to Peter (v. 1–14 catch of fish, though it is the Beloved Disciple who "recognizes" the "Lord," v. 7) and emphasizes his leading position in the church (v. 15–17, although this is delimited by the special mission of the Beloved Disciple, v. 20–23). In Gal 1:17 Paul probably thinks particularly of Peter regarding "those who were already apostles before me." In Gal 1:18–19 he highlights him as the single one of "the apostles" whom he visited in Jerusalem. And in 1 Cor 9:5 he mentions him separately (οἱ λοιποὶ ἀπόστολοι καὶ οἱ ἀδελφοὶ τοῦ κυρίου καὶ Κηφᾶς), certainly not in contrast to the group of "the other apostles," but with special emphasis.

As this brief overview shows, Peter is the apostle *par excellence*, across the various strands of New Testament tradition. Insofar as the divine authorisation of the addressor in the *intitulatio* is a conventional option (cf. Ep. Jer. inscriptio, *4 Bar.* 6.14, Jas 1:1, but not 1 Thess 1:1), the specification "[apostle] *of Jesus Christ*" need not depend on Pauline usage, especially since here the inverse order "of Christ Jesus" is the rule. Thus, one might be able to cautiously state with Jens Herzer that the presentation of the addressor as apostle of Jesus Christ in the succinct brevity of expression could hardly have been different.[16] Against this backdrop, the *pecu-*

---

[15] For such a view cf. J. Frey, "Paulus und die Apostel: Zur Entwicklung des paulinischen Apostelbegriffs und zum Verhältnis des Heidenapostels zu seinen 'Kollegen,'" in *Biographie und Persönlichkeit des Paulus* (eds. E.-M. Becker and P. Pilhofer; WUNT 187; Tübingen: Mohr Siebeck 2005), 192–227.

[16] Cf. J. Herzer, *Petrus oder Paulus? Studien über das Verhältnis des Ersten Petrusbriefes zur paulinischen Tradition* (WUNT 103; Tübingen: Mohr Siebeck, 1998), 36.

liarities of the *intitulatio* in First Peter carry more weight. In contrast to Paul, who typically argues for his apostolate in the prescript[17] and even included the title "apostle" in the prescript (lacking in First Thessalonians) only after it became necessary for him to defend his apostolic authority,[18] Peter's apostolate *does not need any further corroboration*. This suggests that the *intitulatio* in First Peter is not "used almost formulaically"[19] in the first place; rather, it reflects the undisputed quality of the Petrine apostolate that is based on both the earthly Jesus' calling and Peter's vision of the resurrected Christ. Among the apostolic figures, only Peter would properly be able to write in the style of 1 Pet 1:1.[20]

The name "Peter," here used in absolute form, is the Greek translation of the sobriquet-turned-proper name *Kepha'*, by which Simon was known to speakers of Greek probably soon after Easter and certainly by the time First Peter was written. Against the views of O. Knoch, R. Pesch and R. Metzner, "Peter" is not a "title," "official name" (*Amtsname*) or "functional name" (*Funktionsname*).[21] In contrast, if we are to look for an "official" designation, we will find it in the title "apostle." In contrast, "Peter" is one of the apostle's Greek *proper name*.

A renewed investigation of the Aramaic references for *kepha'*, of which only some examples can be reported here due to space restrictions, suggests against Peter Lampe's

---

[17] Paul's respective praxis is continued in the Deutero-Pauline tradition. Cf. the formulations with διά in 1 Cor 1:1, 2 Cor 1:1, Gal 1:1 (also ἀπό), Col 1:1, Eph 1:1, with κατά 1 Tim 1:1, Titus 1:1, with κατά and διά 2 Tim 1:1, and with mention of the purpose Rom 1:1.

[18] Cf. T. Holtz, *Der erste Brief an die Thessalonicher* (3d ed.; EKKNT 13; Zürich/Düsseldorf: Benzinger / Neukirchen-Vluyn: Neukirchener Verlag, 1998), 38; cf. Frey, "Paulus und die Apostel" (see n. 15), 199: The lack of the title in 1 Thess 1:1 should not be attributed to mention of co-senders; see 1 Cor 1:1, 2 Cor 1:1, Col 1:1 for the title despite mention of co-senders.

[19] Thus L. Goppelt, *A Commentary on 1 Peter* (trans. J. E. Alsup; Grand Rapids, Mich.: Eerdmans, 1993), 63; German: *Der Erste Petrusbrief* (8th ed. [1st ed. of this revision]; KEK 12/1; Göttingen: Vandenhoeck & Ruprecht, 1978), 77.

[20] Already 2 Pet 1:1 waters this aspect down ("*servant and* apostle of Jesus Christ"), probably echoing Jud 1; but its presentation of the explicit author follows another line with the reference to "Symeon" (thus not P[72] B et al.), which adds both an archaic note (thus most commentators) and "a Semitic air"; thus C. K. Barrett on the name in Acts 15:14: idem, *The Acts of the Apostles* (2 vols.; ICC; Edinburgh: T&T Clark, 1994–98), 2:723.

[21] See O. Knoch, *Der erste und zweite Petrusbrief. Der Judasbrief* (RNT; Regensburg: Pustet, 1990), 13: "Titel"; R. Pesch, *Simon-Petrus: Geschichte und geschichtliche Bedeutung des ersten Jüngers Jesu Christi* (Päpste und Papsttum 15; Stuttgart: Hiersemann, 1980), 33–4 ("'Amtsname,'" "Amts-Eigenname"); Metzner, *Rezeption* (see n. 10), 109: "Funktionsnamen."

early and influential essay[22] that the varieties of Aramaic most relevant to the time and place of Jesus and Peter, i.e., those attested by Aramaic texts from Qumran, Targum Onqelos and Jonathan, and the Palestinian Targumim, do use *kepha'* with the meaning "rock" or "piece of rock," hence also "rocks" (German *Gestein*);[23] in contrast, there is no conclusive evidence in these texts for the meaning favoured by Lampe, namely (individual) "stone," and no evidence at all for the special meaning assumed by Pesch, "precious stone."[24] Consequently, *Kepha'* is most likely one of the nicknames or sobriquets widely attested for the Second Temple period.[25] A good context for the conferral of this nickname is the presence of at least one bearer of the name "Simon" among the disciples, Simon ὁ Καναναῖος (Mark 3:18, Matt 10:4) or (καλούμενος) ζηλωτής (Luke 6:15, Acts 1:13), one of the Twelve; apart from this, one of Jesus' brothers was also called Simon (Mark 6:3, Matt 13:55). Whether the sobriquet *Kepha'* refers to physical properties ("the hulk"),[26] a quality of character (sturdiness?), or perhaps expectations connected with the name bearer must remain open. New Testament and Jewish examples also show that the nickname could function as a proper name (similar to a Roman *supernomen*) already in

---

[22] P. Lampe, "Das Spiel mit dem Petrusnamen – Matt. xvi. 18," *NTS* 25 (1979): 227–45.

[23] Cf. for the evidence from Qumran, J. A. Fitzmyer, "Aramaic *Kephā'* and Peter's Name in the New Testament," in *To Advance the Gospel: New Testament Studies* (2d ed.; ed. idem; Grand Rapids, Mich.: Eerdmans, 1998), 112–24 (115). Four out of five references clearly attest to the meaning "rock, crag" (11QtgJob 32.1 [on Job 39:1]; 33.9 [on Job 39:28]; 4QEn^c ar 4 iii 19 [= *1 En.* 89.29]; 4QEn^c ar frg. 4 3 [= *1 En.* 89.32]); only for one (4QEn^a ar 1 ii 8 [= *1 En.* 4]) the meaning "stones" would be possible though not likely: the reference is to blazing hot rocky soil. In the Targumim we find not only *selaʿ* (e.g., *Tg. Neof.*, *Tg. Onq.*, and *Tg. Ps.-J. Num* 20:8, 10, 11) but occasionally also *ṣur* (e.g., *Tg. Neof. Deut* 8:15, cf. Deut 32:13, *Tg. Jonathan Isa* 8:14) rendered with *kepha'*. For a good survey of theories on the situation and development of Aramaic see W. F. Smelik, *The Targum of Judges* (OTS 36; Leiden: Brill, 1995), 1–23.

[24] Pesch, *Simon-Petrus* (see n. 21), 29–34. The expression "precious stones" (as a feminine plural) is attested in *Tg. Prov* 3:15, 8:11, 20:15, 31:10. This is, however, a peculiar text with certain connections to the Peshitta; cf. J. F. Healey, *The Targum of Proverbs* (ArBib 15; Edinburgh: T&T Clark, 1991), 7–10. In Jewish Babylonian Aramaic, (*masculine*) *kephe* is used as shorthand for "(precious) stones" or, perhaps more precisely, "ear/nose rings"; cf. M. Sokoloff, *A Dictionary of Jewish Babylonian Aramaic of the Talmudic and Geonic Periods* (Ramat Gan: Bar Ilan University Press, 2002), 578. This suggests a semantic shift not yet detectable in the earlier Palestinian sources.

[25] For Jewish names in Second Temple Palestine see T. Ilan, *Lexicon of Jewish Names in Late Antiquity, Part I: Palestine 330 BCE – 200 CE* (TSAJ 91; Tübingen: Mohr Siebeck, 2002); for nicknames in particular: R. Hachlili, "Names and Nicknames of Jews in Second Temple Times," in *Eretz Israel* 17 (A. J. Brawer Memorial Volume; Jerusalem: Israel Exploration Society, 1984), 188–211 (in Hebrew); eadem, "Hebrew Names, Personal Names, Family Names, and Nicknames of Jews in the Second Temple Period," in *Families and Family Relations as Represented in Judaisms and Early Christianities: Texts and Fictions* (eds. J. W. van Henten and A. Brenner; Leiden: Deo, 2000), 83–115. For double names in the Greco-Roman world cf. G. H. R Horsley, "Names, Double," *ABD* 4:1011–17. On *Kepha'* as "punning nickname," see ibid., 1015.

[26] Thus K. Beyer, *Die Aramäischen Texte vom Toten Meer I* (Göttingen: Vandenhoeck & Ruprecht, 1984), 608: "der Mann wie ein Fels, der Hüne."

life. According to Acts 4:36, Joseph was called Barnabas by the apostles, and the individuals bearing the rabbinic mock-patronyms Ben Nanas, Ben Azzai, or Ben Zoma were thus known during their lifetime.[27] *Kepha'* might well have been translated into Greek *after* it had become a proper name.[28] It is likely that in early stages of the mission to the Gentiles it was deemed insufficient to simply transcribe the name and fit a Greek ending (Κηφᾶς). The translation preferred πέτρος, which tends to mean "stone," to πέτρα, the normal word for "rock," presumably because Greek male names ending in *-a* are rare and confusion with place names—such as the Nabataean capital—should be avoided. In addition, πέτρος is sparsely attested for "rock" as well.[29]

In short, since "Peter" is one of the disciple's *proper names* there is no need for additional mention of "Simon"; thus, we have no reason to assume that the explicit author does *not* establish his identity with the first among the disciples.[30] On the contrary, the self-designation of the addressor as "Peter, apostle of Jesus Christ" allows for *the full range* of associations connected to the figure thus described.

2.2 "Co-Elder"

This becomes immediately clear in the next passage in which a renominalisation of the addressor occurs, i.e., in 1 Pet 5:1. Here we do not see the title "apostle" but instead a qualification that at first sight comes as a surprise: ὁ συμπρεσβύτερος, "the co-elder." This expression in 1 Pet 5:1 thus brings the addressor, who in 1:1 has been introduced as "Peter, apostle of Jesus Christ," in line with the "elders" or "presbyters"[31] explicitly addressed in this verse. In this, First Peter follows a route different from the Pauline letters, in which the addressor attaches individual "co-workers" *to*

---

[27] Cf. J. Naveh, "Nameless People," *IEJ* 40 (1990): 108–23 (116); Ilan, *Lexicon* (see n. 25), 46; M. Öhler, *Barnabas: Die historische Person und ihre Rezeption in der Apostelgeschichte* (WUNT 156; Tübingen: Mohr Siebeck, 2003), 142–51.

[28] This is denied by Lampe, "Spiel" (see n. 22), 230: Proper names would be merely transcribed. But there are exceptions, cf. Acts 9:36 Ταβιθά—Δορκάς.

[29] Cf. here C. C. Caragounis, *Peter and the Rock* (BZNW 58; Berlin: De Gruyter, 1990), 9–16. Cf. M. Hengel, *Der unterschätzte Petrus: Zwei Studien* (Tübingen: Mohr Siebeck, 2006), 35–7, who considers that the "Hellenists" might have been responsible for the translation.

[30] Contra Metzner, *Rezeption* (see n. 10), 108: "keine unmittelbare Identität zum Jesusjünger Simon bzw. Simeon." Metzner believes that First Peter is dependent on Matthew for the alleged reduction to the apostolic function (ibid., 108–10).

[31] According to what 1 Pet 5:2–4 says about the activities of the πρεσβύτεροι, these are not merely elderly people contrasted with younger ones (see v. 5 νεώτεροι) but have a leading function in the local communities, but this is likely to correspond to higher age. Cf. Goppelt, *I Peter* (see n. 19), 340 (German: 321); E. Bosetti, *Il Pastore: Cristo e la chiesa nella prima lettera di Pietro* (SRivBib 21; Bologna: Edizioni Dehoniane, 1990), 187–88; R. A. Campbell, *The Elders: Seniority within Earliest Christianity* (Edinburgh: T&T Clark, 1994), 206–7.

himself as συνεργοί or σύνδουλοι.³² In contrast, a speech act more similar to 1 Pet 5:1 can be found at Rev 19:10, 22:9, where an angel tells the seer: "I am your co-servant" (σύνδουλός σού εἰμι). We will not be mistaken in viewing in 1 Pet 5:1 generally an expression of social solidarity,³³ and we can compare this with other formulations built on συν-, of which the real author is apparently fond. Thus, in the exhortation of husbands he emphasises that the women are "co-heirs" of the grace of life (συγκληρονόμοις χάριτος ζωῆς, 3:7), and according to 5:13 the "co-elect in Babylon" (ἡ ἐν Βαβυλῶνι συνεκλεκτή) sends greetings, for which the designation of the addressees as "elect" (ἐκλεκτοῖς παρεπιδήμοις, 1:1; γένος ἐκλεκτόν, 2:9) should be compared.³⁴ It is therefore possible that the real author has formed the term συμπρεσβύτερος in analogy to these other terms. Nevertheless, the typical assertion in commentaries and lexica that there is no other early evidence for the term³⁵ is in need of revision. The term συμπρεσβύτερος is attested in a papyrus from Oxyrhynchus dated to the third year of the reign of Titus (80/81 CE) and published in 1976, but so far overlooked by New Testament scholars.³⁶

The text is a declaration to an official, a certain Hermophilus, by three village πρεσβύτεροι relating to a case of bribery. They are introduced with their names and the specification "the elders, with others ([τῶ]ν σὺν ἄλλο[ις πρ]εσβυτέρων), of the village of Peenno in the middle toparchy" (lines 5–7). The document is a follow-up on a petition made to the *strategos* "by us and the co-elders" (ὑπὸ τε ἡμῶν καὶ τῶν συμπρεσ[β]υτέρων, lines 8–9) in which they complained against a superintendent of the dykes who had taken bribes from fifty-one men for exempting them from the annual dyke duty; in the present document the elders affirm that they have already given the names of some of those involved but are unable to procure further names.

---

³² Cf. συνεργός Rom 16:3; 9:21; 2 Cor 8:23; Phil 2:25; 4:3; 1 Thess 3:2; Phlm 1, 24; Col 4:11; σύνδουλος Col 1:7; 4:7. Cf. also Ignatius, *Eph.* 2.1; *Magn.* 2.1; *Phld.* 4.1; *Smyrn.* 12.2.

³³ With B. L. Campbell, *Honor, Shame, and the Rhetoric of 1 Peter* (SBLDS 160; Atlanta: Scholars Press, 1998), 219; also P. H. Davids, *The First Epistle of Peter* (NIC; Grand Rapids, Mich.: Eerdmans, 1990), 176.

³⁴ For further συν- composites cf. 1 Pet 1:14; 3:7–8; 4:4, 12.

³⁵ E.g., in BDAG 959, and recent commentaries, such as P. J. Achtemeier, *1 Peter: A Commentary on First Peter* (Hermeneia; Minneapolis: Fortress Press, 1996), 323; J. H. Elliott, *1 Peter: A New Translation with Introduction and Commentary* (AB 37B; New York et al.: Doubleday, 2000), 816–17; Feldmeier, *First Letter of Peter* (see n. 9), 232 with n. 5 (German: 155 with n. 577).

³⁶ A. K. Bowman, ed., P.Coll. Youtie 1.21 = P.Oxy. 45.3264, line 9, in *Collectanea Papyrologica: Texts Published in Honor of H. C. Youtie, Part One: Number 1–65* (ed. A. E. Hanson; PTA 19; Bonn: Habelt, 1976), 197–201; repr.: *The Oxyrhynchus Papyri, vol. XLV* (eds. A. K. Bowman et al.; Graeco-Roman Memoirs 63; London: Egypt Exploration Society, 1977), 145. Cf. the entry in LSJ Supplement, 284.

Even if the occurrence of the term in First Peter is a case of analogous use rather than direct dependence on the Egyptian usage, in which πρεσ-βύτερος is the title of village elders functioning as extension of the *nome* administration,[37] this papyrus shows that the coinage συμπρεσβύτερος is not an unconventional way of expressing the belonging of individuals to a group whose members are πρεσβύτεροι. This belonging is also underlined by the use of separate σύν in the phrase [τῶ]ν σὺν ἄλλο[ις πρ]εσβυτέρων, where the emphasis is on further members of the group. The term thus clearly expresses membership of a group defined by its status and function.

At any rate, it is evident that no *explicit* reference to apostolic authority is being made in 1 Pet 5:1 (more on this below). The self-designation of the addresser as συμπρεσβύτερος probably involves more than a mere gesture of modesty,[38] although the aspect of *captatio benevolentiae* vis-à-vis the specific addressees of this passage plays a role in terms of rhetoric.[39] It is thus possible that the elders, with whom the addresser associates himself, should, as it were, also profit from the splendour of the apostle.[40] But the central point is not the apostolic legitimisation of the office of presbyter[41] or, more specifically, the continuity between the office of apostle and presbyter,[42] but rather the addresser's special *responsibility and qualification as "co-elder" for their exhortation*.[43] I therefore deem it highly unlikely that the addresser here drops out of the fiction and discloses the real author's identity as an early Christian church leader or teacher, as has been suggested by Brox in his commentary, with some emi-

---

[37] Cf. Campbell, *Elders* (see n. 31), 75–6; A. Tomsin, "Étude sur les πρεσβύτεροι des villages de la χώρα égyptienne," in *Académie Royale de Belgique. Bulletin de la classe des lettres et des sciences morales et politiques* 5/38 (Brussels: Hayez, 1952), 95–130, 467–532; on 1st century Roman Egypt: 468–79.

[38] Thus, however, H. Windisch, *Die katholischen Briefe* (3d rev. ed. by H. Preisker; HNT 15; Tübingen: Mohr Siebeck, 1951), 78–9; R. Knopf, *Die Briefe Petri und Judä* (7th ed. [1st ed. of this revision]; KEK 12; Göttingen: Vandenhoeck & Ruprecht, 1912), 188; J. N. D. Kelly, *The Epistles of Peter and of Jude* (BNTC 17; London: Black, 1969), 198.

[39] Cf. R. E. Brown, K. P. Donfried and J. Reumann, eds., *Peter in the New Testament: A Collaborative Assessment by Protestant and Roman Catholic Scholars* (Minneapolis: Augsburg / New York et al.: Paulist Press, 1973), 152: "a polite strategem of benevolence."

[40] So K. Schelkle, *Die Petrusbriefe. Der Judasbrief* (HTK 13/2; Freiburg i. Brsg. et al.: Herder, 1961), 128.

[41] Thus, however, Goppelt, *1 Peter* (see n. 19), 340–41 (German: 322); cf. Achtemeier, *1 Peter* (see n. 35), 323: "the term clearly implies that apostolic authority is involved in the functioning of the elder."

[42] Thus Bosetti, *Il Pastore* (see n. 31), 200–1; M. E. Boring, *1 Peter* (ANTC; Nashville: Abingdon, 1999), 165–66.

[43] With Elliott, *1 Peter* (see n. 35), 816.

nent predecessors and notable successors.[44] That the *rhetorical function* is key to the self-characterisation of the addressor as ὁ συμπρεσβύτερος is further supported by the observation that what the "co-elder" does in 5:1 and what the addressor states in 5:12 as one aim of the letter is both expressed by forms of one and the same word, παρακαλῶ(ν) "exhort(ing)."[45] This choice of words suggests a *careful construction of authorial consciousness*, in other words: a *consistent* implied author. Text-pragmatically speaking, it is not to be expected at all that the addressor would step outside the author fiction or construction in 5:1.

For the connectivity of the apostolic addressor to the "elders" it may be considered whether the designation of early Christian authorities as πρεσβύτεροι does not play a role here. As is well known, it is debated whether Papias (*apud* Eusebius, *Hist. eccl.* 3.39.3–4) reserves the plural πρεσβύτεροι for those reporting the words of the Lord's disciples or uses it for the disciples proper as well. By any count, the syntax remains ambiguous, and Eusebius (*Hist. eccl.* 3.39.7) took the πρεσβύτεροι for the apostles. Consequently, Martin Hengel considers the debate about the syntax "futile" because Papias seems to deliberately avoid a fundamental distinction here.[46] Moreover, Richard Bauckham has suggested that the

---

[44] Cf. Brox, *Der erste Petrusbrief* (4th ed.; EKKNT 21; Zürich: Benzinger / Neukirchen-Vluyn: Neukirchener Verlag, 1993), 228. Cf. already A. Harnack, *Geschichte der altchristlichen Literatur bis Eusebius II/1* (Leipzig, 1897): this is written by an authoritative personality (451), a renowned "Lehrer und Confessor" (452, 455). More cautious Feldmeier, *First Letter of Peter* (see n. 9), 232 (German: 155): "Possibly the real author here falls out of his fiction of being the apostle and speaks as that which he is, as a Christian presbyter." Cf. P. Stuhlmacher, *Biblische Theologie des Neuen Testaments II* (Göttingen: Vandenhoeck & Ruprecht, 1999), 79: The author uses the term "co-presbyter" because he is a leader of the (Roman?) church. Cf. also Campbell, *Elders* (see n. 31), 207. According to W. Marxsen, "Der Mitälteste und Zeuge der Leiden Christi: Eine martyrologische Begründung des 'Romprimats' im 1. Petrus-Brief?" in *Theologia crucis, signum crucis: FS E. Dinkler* (eds. C. Andresen and G. Klein; Tübingen: Mohr Siebeck, 1979), 377–93, we hear here the author of the added (thus Marxsen) passage 4:12–5:11.

[45] Similarly Schmidt, *Mahnung* (see n. 13), 186 n. 72. Schmidt, however, considers the possibility that the author has stylised Peter as elder because he was one himself. "Doch die Erzählposition wird nicht aufgegeben." However, if we are able to establish a *rhetorical* reason for stylising the explicit author as "co-elder," as I believe we are, we need not ask whether the real author was a presbyter or not, nor will our interpretation of the text be helped by answering this question.

[46] M. Hengel, *Die johanneische Frage: Ein Lösungsversuch, mit einem Beitrag zur Apokalypse von J. Frey* (WUNT 67; Tübingen: Mohr Siebeck, 1993), 105: "Bei einem unbefangenen Lesen wird man die aufgezählten Jünger durchaus zu den 'Alten' rechnen dürfen ..." Cf. also D. G. Deeks, "Papias Revisited (Part I)," *ET* 88 (1977): 296–301 (297): "The most natural interpretation of the clauses ... is that 'presbyter' and 'disciple of the Lord' are synonymous." Different, however, R. J. Bauckham, *Jesus and the Eyewitnesses: The Gospels as Eyewitness Testimony* (Grand Rapids, Mich.: Eerdmans,

"elders" of the Jerusalem community according to Acts were not an office introduced later but formed a group that comprised also members of the former Twelve.[47] Such an assumption would explain the responsibility of the "elders," abruptly mentioned in Acts 11:30, for receipt of the Antiochene collection, as well as their sole presence with James in Acts 21:18. Significantly, it would allow an *epexegetical* interpretation of καί in the expression οἱ ἀπόστολοι καὶ οἱ πρεσβύτεροι (Acts 15:2, 4, 6, 22f.; 16:4); in fact, Campbell has strongly argued that πρεσβύτερος, outside Egypt, was rather a vague title of honour than of an office *sensu stricto* and that it "would naturally have been applied" to any remaining disciples of Jesus whom Luke calls "the apostles."[48]

Thus, the traditio-historical connections between ἀπόστολος and πρεσβύτερος seem to be closer than at times allowed for in scholarship. That the perspective of communication established in 1:1 ("apostle of Jesus Christ") must not be forgotten is in my view also confirmed by the fact that the "co-elder" actually *exhorts* the (other) elders. This implies—the συν- rhetoric notwithstanding—an appropriate authority. This ambivalence regarding solidarity and authority is perhaps also expressed by the determined form "*the* co-elder." The apostolic letter writer does not become "*a* co-elder," as many commentators translate, but retains an element of prominence and authority by presenting himself as "*the* co-elder."[49] What we find, therefore, is indeed a *mixture of authority and collegiality* in the Peter image developed in First Peter.[50]

2.3 Shepherding

In 1 Pet 5:2 the narrator gives as the first topic of exhortation, directed to the elders, "Shepherd God's flock that it is in you(r charge), watching over it" (ποιμάνατε τὸ ἐν ὑμῖν ποίμνιον τοῦ θεοῦ ἐπισκοποῦντες). What is immediately striking is the use of ποιμαίνειν and ποίμνιον, which differs from the Pauline corpus where the motif of "flock" lacks ecclesiogical sig-

---

2006), 15–6; U. H. J. Körtner (and M. Leutzsch), *Papiasfragmente. Hirt des Hermas* (Schriften des Urchristentums 3; Darmstadt: Wiss. Buchgesellschaft, 1998), 37.

[47] Cf. R. J. Bauckham, *Jude and the Relatives of Jesus in the Early Church* (Edinburgh: T&T Clark, 1990), 74–5.

[48] Campbell, *Elders* (see n. 31), 67–79, 162–63 (quotation: 163).

[49] Cf. Elliott, *1 Peter* (see n. 35), 817; *pace* his weak text-critical argument for the reading ὡς ibid., 816 n. 645. K. H. Jobes, *1 Peter* (ECNT; Grand Rapids, Mich.: Baker Academic, 2005), 300, takes the article + συν- as "your fellow-."

[50] Here with Metzner, *Rezeption* (see n. 10), 112–15 (though with too one-sided derivation from Matthew).

nificance.[51] The best parallel to 1 Pet 5:2 is found in Paul's farewell speech to the elders of Ephesus at Miletus (Acts 20), which also shows that the root ἐπισκοπ- is closely connected to this motif. On account of the overlaps in the semantic field employed[52] it is likely that either 1 Pet 5:1–4 and Acts 20:17, 28–29 go back to common tradition or First Peter is familiar with Acts.[53] For the application of the motif in First Peter we need to keep the connection with both 5:4 and 2:25 in view: Superior to the elders shepherding the flock locally (ἐν ὑμῖν; cf. 5:3, τῶν κλήρων) is the chief-shepherd (ἀρχιποίμην) Christ (5:4), who in 2:25 is referred to as "shepherd and overseer of your souls" (τὸν ποιμένα καὶ ἐπίσκοπον τῶν ψυχῶν ὑμῶν).

Which role, if any, does the addresser play in this structure? Our discussion so far suggests that the "co-elder," rhetorically joined to the "elders" whom he is exhorting to "shepherd" God's flock locally, should himself also have "pastoral" responsibility.[54] Reading the passage from the perspective of the letter opening, the letter thus indirectly constructs the *image of Peter as shepherd* that also appears in John 21:15–17, but due to the post-Easter standing of Peter was perhaps more widespread in early Christian tradition.[55] It is implied that the apostolic "co-elder," writing to the addressees in Asia Minor from "Babylon" (more on this below), is responsible for more than the local community (contrast ἐν ὑμῖν). However the role of "chief-shepherd" is explicitly reserved for Christ, and a precise positioning of Peter in the structure is avoided, not least through the merely indirect reference of his own "shepherding" via the self-designation of "co-elder."[56]

---

[51] Herzer, *Petrus* (see n. 16), 190; cf. ibid., n. 150 on 1 Cor 9:7 and Eph 4:11. On the difference vis-à-vis the Pastorals, see ibid., 176–77, 193.

[52] Cf. 1 Pet 5:2, ποιμάνατε τὸ ἐν ὑμῖν ποίμνιον τοῦ θεοῦ ἐπισκοποῦντες ... with Acts 20:28, ... τῷ ποιμνίῳ, ἐν ᾧ ὑμᾶς ... ἔθετο ἐπισκόπους ποιμαίνειν τὴν ἐκκλησίαν τοῦ θεοῦ ... In the New Testament ποίμνιον is only attested in Luke 12:32, Acts 20:28–29, 1 Pet 5:2–3. Cf. Elliott, *1 Peter* (see n. 35), 822–24. For the likelihood that ἐπισκοποῦντες in 1 Pet 5:2 (attested by P[72] ℵ[2] A 81 1739 etc. but lacking in ℵ* B sa etc.) is original, cf. ibid. 824 n. 665 and Herzer, ibid., 190–91 n. 151.

[53] The former is assumed by Goppelt, *I Peter* (see n. 19), 343 (German: 324); the latter is considered by Herzer, ibid., 180–81, 192–93; Schmidt, *Mahnung* (see n. 13), 189–90. See further below, section 4.2.

[54] Cf. Bosetti, *Il Pastore* (see n. 31), 179, 204.

[55] Cf. Brown et al., *Peter* (see n. 39), 144, 152–54, 163–64; Meade, *Pseudonymity* (see n. 14), 176–77; C. Grappe, *Images* (see n. 12), 116–18; Elliott, *1 Peter* (see n. 35), 823.

[56] That it is Paul, not Peter, who is associated with the exhortation of elders to shepherd the flock in Acts 20 does not at all diminish the value of 1 Pet 5:1–2 for our hypothesis of the construction of a Peter image in this letter, since it remains to be noted that "Paul" in Acts 20, contrary to "Peter" in 1 Pet 5:1, does not count himself amongst the

One of the qualifications the addressor makes about "shepherding" is that the elders should carry it out "not as those who lord it over the assigned ones (μηδ' ὡς κατακυριεύοντες τῶν κλήρων) but as those who become examples to the flock" (1 Pet 5:3). The emphasis on humility is continued in the exhortation of the νεώτεροι in v. 5a and of "all" in v. 5b; it matches the designation of the apostolic addressor as "co-elder," who thereby becomes a practical example[57] and is thus particularly apt to reach the addressees with his exhortation. At the same time he points to the example of Christ. This becomes immediately clear in the next self-stylisation, which reaches beyond the circle of elders and is open for reception by all addressees.

2.4 "Witness of the sufferings of Christ"

Any attempt to interpret this phrase in relation to Peter's *eyewitness testimony* of Jesus' Passion[58] meets "the historical difficulty that Peter, according to the witness of all the gospels, was precisely not present at the Passion."[59] Where he was present in the wider context of the Passion he is known in the gospels to have *failed*[60]—hardly a facet to which the letter wishes to appeal here. Thus, we are left with two further interpretations, the second one of which can be subdivided into two options: (a) The phrase could be understood in terms of *verbal testimony (Wortzeugnis)*, which falls within normal New Testament usage.[61] Here, particularly the proclamation of Christ's cross would be in view.[62] However, it needs to be asked what pragmatic aim the mere *reference* to Peter's proclamation would serve. In addition, since the next element of self-designation refers to Peter's participation in glory, it is likely that the suffering mentioned

---

elders and is therefore not even indirectly construed as a "shepherd." For the unimportance of the motif of "shepherding the flock" in Paul's letters see above.

[57] Cf. Brown et al., *Peter* (see n. 39), 153.

[58] E.g., E. G. Selwyn, *The First Epistle of St. Peter: The Greek Text with Introduction, Notes and Essays* (2d ed.; London: Macmillan, 1947), 228.

[59] Feldmeier, *First Letter of Peter* (see n. 9), 233 (German: 155).

[60] Sleeping in Gethsemane: Mark 14:32–43 parr.; fleeing with the other disciples: Mark 14:43–52 par.; denial: Mark 14:53–72 parr.; John 18:15–27. Whether a reference such as Luke 22:28 (cf. J. B. Green, *1 Peter* [Two Horizons New Testament Commentary; Grand Rapids, Mich.: Eerdmans, 2007], 165) would counterbalance this reputation is debatable.

[61] Cf. N. Brox, *Zeuge und Märtyrer: Untersuchungen zur frühchristlichen Zeugnis-Terminologie* (SANT 5; München: Kösel, 1961), 38; overview in H. Strathmann, "μάρτυς κτλ.," *TWNT* 4:477–520 (492–500).

[62] Thus D. H. Schmidt, "The Peter Writings: Their Redactors and their Relationships" (PhD diss.; North-Western University [Evanston, Ill.], 1972), 69; J. R. Michaels, *1 Peter* (WBC 49; Waco, Tex.: Word, 1988), 281.

here is equally Peter's. Some scholars have suggested a verbal testimony whose consequence is the suffering of the witness,[63] but this is hardly a straightforward understanding of the expression in question. Paul Achtemeier[64] addresses the problem by assuming an objective genitive for τὰ τοῦ Χριστοῦ παθήματα, "the sufferings *for Christ's sake*." However, comparison with 1 Pet 4:13 renders this unlikely. Here, τοῖς τοῦ Χριστοῦ παθήμασιν is paired with ἀποκαλύψει τῆς δόξης αὐτοῦ, both of which need to be taken as subjective genitives: "*Christ's* sufferings" and "the revelation of *his* glory." The connections between 4:13 and 5:1 are obvious and need to be taken into account for the interpretation of the latter passage.

(b) It is therefore more convincing to interpret the witness in 5:1 as involving *practical testimony* (*Tatzeugnis*). The addressor establishes a correlation between the addressees and himself. As they "are partners (κοινωνεῖτε) in the sufferings of Christ" (1 Pet 4:13), Peter, in turn, is a practical "witness" (μάρτυς) of these sufferings (5:1). The sufferings experienced are thus understood as an actualisation of Christ's suffering. This use goes beyond normal New Testament usage of μάρτυς, but there are other instances in the New Testament in which testimony occurs through gestures or actions.[65] The pragmatic aim of the reference would again be to *portray the addressor as apt to deal with the situation of the addressees*, this time their general situation of suffering.[66] This is not merely a "generic"[67] reference to suffering but contributes a text-pragmatically relevant element to the *Peter image* in First Peter.

What should we imagine this practical testimony to be? Some scholars assert (b.1) that the reference is to *persecution* but not to martyrdom in the technical sense.[68] New Testament texts that reflect a temporary suffering of Peter are Acts 5:18, 40–41 ("the apostles") or 12:3–11. Apart from this, Jesus' saying about the cost of discipleship (Mark 8:34–37 parr.) also refers to suffering, with death as the ultimate perspective, and it could have

---

[63] Cf. Kelly, *Epistles* (see n. 38), 198–99; Davids, *First Epistle of Peter* (see n. 33), 177. Cf. Elliott, *1 Peter* (see n. 35), 819–20.

[64] Achtemeier, *1 Peter* (see n. 35), 324 with n. 47, who does not rule out a genitive of origin either ("suffering whose origin for his followers is Christ").

[65] Cf. Brox, *Zeuge* (see n. 61), 39. Cf. Mark 1:44 parr., Mark 6:11 par. Luke 9:5, Acts 14:3, Heb 2:4, 12:1.

[66] Cf. Brown et al., *Peter* (see n. 39), 153.

[67] Thus D. P. Senior, *1 Peter* (and D. J. Harrington, *Jude and 2 Peter*) (SP 15; Collegeville, Minn.: Liturgical Press, 2003), 4.

[68] Cf. already Strathmann, "μάρτυς κτλ." (see n. 61), 498–99; then Brox, *Zeuge* (see n. 61), 39; idem, *Der erste Petrusbrief* (see n. 44), 229–30; T. Baumeister, *Die Anfänge der Theologie des Martyriums* (MBTh 45; Münster: Aschendorff, 1980), 209 (but see n. 70).

easily been associated with the apostles as Jesus' first disciples.[69] Other scholars, however, allow (b.2) for a reference to *Peter's martyrdom*.[70]

In my view, the two options should not be distinguished too sharply. *1 Clem.* 5.4 states about Peter that he "endured not one or two but many labours (πλείονας ... πόνους)" and that he "thus having born witness (καὶ οὕτω μαρτυρήσας) went (ἐπορεύθη) to the due place of glory." To be sure, μαρτυρήσας here does not refer to the martyrdom proper but rather to the practical testimony of suffering;[71] however, this is closely related to Peter's death (cf. "went"). It might be argued that First Peter, which shares with *1 Clem.* 5.4 the connection of "witness" and "glory," draws for its Peter image on a similar tradition in which persecution and death are closely related. If the letter is pseudonymous, Peter's death will probably have been known to the readers, as further reflected—limiting myself to references up to the middle of the second century—in John 21:18–19, *Ascen. Isa.* 4.2–3, *Apoc. Pet.* 14 (Ethiopic and "Rainer Fragment")[72], and Ignatius, *Rom.* 4.3.[73]

That the addressor is "still alive"—writing!—is not an objection. The letter may be seen as a testament,[74] for which one could also point to the farewell exhortation discussed above, and the introduction of the pseudepigraphon could have happened in such a way that it was claimed that the letter resurfaced after the death of Peter.[75] The relative vagueness of Pe-

---

[69] James, son of Zebedee, was known to have been killed under Agrippa I (Acts 12:2), in the context of the action against Peter (Acts 12:3–11), which is in turn reflected in Mark 10:38–40.

[70] Cf. already Knopf, *Briefe* (see n. 38), 13, 188 (as an alternative); cautiously Pesch, *Simon-Petrus* (see n. 21), 118 (referring to communalities with *1 Clem.* 5.4), 151 (1 Pet 5:1 imagines Peter "wohl im Blick auf sein Martyrium, aber doch fiktiv als noch lebender Apostel"); further, e.g., Grappe, *Images* (see n. 12), 52; J. Gnilka, *Petrus und Rom: Das Petrusbild in den ersten zwei Jahrhunderten* (Freiburg i. Brsg. et al.: Herder, 2002), 111, 182, 187, 191; Feldmeier, *First Letter of Peter* (see n. 9), 233 (German: 156); cf. Hengel, *Petrus* (see n. 29), 8 with n. 10 (and see below n. 74). See also Baumeister, *Anfänge* (see n. 68), 209 n. 62 (as alternative).

[71] With Brox, *Zeuge* (see n. 61), 200; H. E. Lona, *Der erste Clemensbrief* (KAV 2; Göttingen: Vandenhoeck & Ruprecht, 1998), 160. For the view that martyrdom is directly referred to by οὕτω μαρτυρήσας cf. Bockmuehl, "Peter's Death" (see n. 12), 16 with n. 50.

[72] P.Vindob. G 39756. Cf. T. J. Kraus and T. Nicklas, eds., *Das Petrusevangelium und die Petrusapokalypse: Die griechischen Fragmente mit deutscher und englischer Übersetzung* (GCS N.S. 11; Berlin: De Gryuter, 2004), 121–30.

[73] For further evidence up to ca. 200 cf. R. J. Bauckham, "The Martyrdom of Peter in Early Christian Literature," *ANRW* II 26.1:539–95; Bockmuehl, "Peter's Death" (see n. 12), 17 n. 56.

[74] Cf. Hengel, *Petrus* (see n. 29), 160.

[75] In terms of the classification proposed by R. J. Bauckham, "Pseudo-Apostolic Letters," *JBL* 107 (1988): 469–94, this could move First Peter to type "AP5," the pseudepi-

ter's respective statement would fit such a scenario, since it would be conceivable in both an "ante-" and a "post-mortem" situation of Peter, with an increase of meaning toward martyrdom after his death. Alternatively, it may be considered that the author fiction here presents itself as transparent, at least to a certain type of readers, who would have viewed the letter as a fictional commemoration of Peter.[76] The question whether the addressor is still alive when readers are supposed to read the letter has also an impact on the next and final qualification of the addressor.

2.5 "Partner in the glory that is to be revealed"

Christ's sufferings are closely connected to future glory. 1 Pet 1:11 affirms this for Christ himself, but in a manner that it is transparent for the current situation of the addressees.[77] Similarly, 1 Pet 4:13, as we have seen, links the rejoicing of the addressees as "being partners (κοινωνεῖτε) in the sufferings of Christ" with the joy "in the revelation of his glory" (ἐν τῇ ἀποκαλύψει τῆς δόξης αὐτοῦ). Again, the addressor himself belongs into this structure of correspondences, in which the addressees are called to follow the example of Christ (2:21), whose sufferings are inseparably joined to the following "glory" (1:11). Peter is not only "witness of the sufferings of Christ," but "also the partner in the glory that is to be revealed" (ὁ καὶ τῆς μελλούσης ἀποκαλύπτεσθαι δόξης κοινωνός, 5:1).[78] And again (cf. shepherding), the text avoids assigning to the addressor a *clearly defined* position in this structure. On the one hand, *Christ himself* is the example, and Peter in this respect belongs clearly on the side of the addressees. On the other hand, however, Peter attests to the connection between suffering and glory through the *reference to his own example* and rhetoric underlining this example.

There might be a further detail that fits well a reading of First Peter as a pseudepigraphon, looking back at the death of the real Peter. Whereas the addressees are presently partners (present tense κοινωνεῖτε) in the sufferings of Christ (1 Pet 4:13), the addressor is a witness of these sufferings, but partner (κοινωνός) of the "glory that is to be revealed" (5:1). This seems to imply that "Peter" has already *arrived* at the glory that is however yet to be revealed to all.[79] Thus, the text does not just suggest a necessary

---

graphal testamentary letter; since Bauckham does not see this element, he classifies First Peter as authentic (490).

[76] Thus K. M. Schmidt, *Mahnung* (see n. 13), 186–87.

[77] Cf. Feldmeier, *First Letter of Peter* (see n. 9), 94 (German: 62–3).

[78] Note again the article, which here, however, is needed to give the genitive the correct referent.

[79] Cf. Bosetti, *Il Pastore* (see n. 31), 197–98. Cf. also Knopf, *Briefe* (see n. 38), 189; Windisch, *Briefe* (see n. 38), 79; F. W. Beare, *The First Epistle of Peter* (3d ed.; Oxford:

link between suffering and glory but also presents "Peter" as someone who by his own example attests to the validity of this link.

3. Peter in Company: Silvanus, Mark, and "Babylon"

3.1 The Connection with Silvanus

At the beginning of the letter closing the narrator states (1 Pet 5:12):

"Through Silvanus, the faithful brother as I reckon, I have written to you briefly (διὰ Σιλουανοῦ ὑμῖν τοῦ πιστοῦ ἀδελφοῦ, ὡς λογίζομαι, δι' ὀλίγων ἔγραψα), exhorting and fully witnessing (παρακαλῶν καὶ ἐπιμαρτυρῶν) that this is the true grace of God. Stand fast in it!"

The narrator here provides, on the one hand, a résumé of the letter body[80] and, on the other hand, introduces a named character, Silvanus, in a specific function with respect to the letter. What does διὰ Σιλουανοῦ ... ἔγραψα mean? A number of scholars have suggested that "through Silvanus" refers to the true author of the letter; Silvanus would have composed the letter but "the thoughts behind it are those of Simon Peter."[81] Sometimes the more technical role of amanuensis is proposed.[82] Against

---

Blackwell, 1970), 198. This is contested by Goppelt, *1 Peter* (see n. 19), 342 with n. 14 (German: 323 with n. 14) on the grounds that the glory for Peter, too, must be hidden until the parousia (referring to 1 Pet 4:13; 1:11, 21; 3:22). But apart from the linguistic argument one should not ignore the similar (though not identical) correlation of μαρτυρ- and δόξα in 1 Pet 5:1 and *1 Clem.* 5.4 discussed above. Elliott, *1 Peter* (see n. 35), 820–21, rightly criticises the suggestion made, e.g., by Selwyn, *First Epistle of St. Peter* (see n. 58), 228–29, that the expression under discussion refers to the Transfiguration, but he does not address the question how "Peter" in particular is said to be *already* a "partner" in the glory to be revealed; similarly Achtemeier, *1 Peter* (see n. 35), 324. The use of κοινωνός does not support the suggestion made in Brown et al., *Peter* (see n. 39), 153, that the reference is to the protophany before Peter.

[80] The participle παρακαλῶν links with the use of the verb in 1 Pet 2:11, 5:1 and "aptly characterizes the hortatory thrust of the letter as a whole," Elliott, *1 Peter* (see n. 35), 877; ἐπιμαρτυρῶν (an intensified form of μαρτυρῶν; cf. συνεπιμαρτυροῦντος, Heb 2:4) refers back to 1 Pet 5:1, the presentation of the addresser as μάρτυς of the sufferings of Christ. The "true grace" is "Gnade als Hoffnung im Leiden" (cf. 2:19–20), to which the letter in all its parts points (cf. "*this* is the true grace"), Brox, *Der erste Petrusbrief* (see n. 44), 244–46 (246). The reference to the "brevity" of the letter is probably a conventional expression of respect for the addressees but may also refer to the density of issues, Elliott, ibid., 876.

[81] Davids, *First Epistle of Peter* (see n. 33), 198. Cf., e.g., Kelly, *Epistles* (see n. 38) 214–16; E. Best, *1 Peter* (NCeB; London: Oliphants, 1971), 176–77; Goppelt, *1 Peter* (see n. 19), 369–71 (German: 347–49).

[82] Cf. P. Wendland, *Die urchristlichen Literaturformen* (2d & 3d ed.; HNT 1/3; Tübingen: Mohr Siebeck, 1912), 367: "Petrus diktiert wie Paulus." On the role of "secre-

this, other scholars have argued that the phrase γράφειν διὰ δεῖνος refers to the despatch of the letter; Silvanus would then have been mentioned as the (real or fictive) *letter-carrier*.[83] In favour of this interpretation, one can refer to close linguistic parallels in the letters of Ignatius and Polycarp.[84] In addition, S. R. Llewelyn and E. Randolph Richards have pointed to a number of non-Christian documentary papyri that attest forms of γράφειν διὰ δεῖνος denoting the letter-carrier.[85] While some of their examples are from the end of the second century or later, further pieces of earlier evidence can be added, so that four or five clear examples dating from the late 1st to early 2d century CE can now be secured.[86] Scepticism whether this was an

---

tary" in ancient letter writing cf. E. R. Richards, *The Secretary in the Letters of Paul* (WUNT II/42; Tübingen: Mohr Siebeck, 1991).

[83] E.g., real: Michaels, *1 Peter* (see n. 62), 306–7; Elliott, *1 Peter* (see n. 35), 872–74; Jobes, *1 Peter* (see n. 49), 320–21; possibly real: Achtemeier, *1 Peter* (see n. 35), 349–52; fictive: Brox, "Rahmung" (see n. 1), 87–9; idem, *Der erste Petrusbrief* (see n. 44), 242–43; Boring, *1 Peter* (see n. 42), 179–80.

[84] Ignatius, *Rom.* 10.1, *Phld.* 11.2, *Smyrn.* 12.1, *Pol.* 14.1. Cf. Brox, "Rahmung" (see n. 1), 87: "An der Bedeutung des διά (per) an allen vier Stellen gibt es keinen Zweifel, es kennzeichnet den (die) Überbringer des Briefes."

[85] Cf. S. R. Llewelyn, "The Conveyance of Letters," *NDIEC* 7 (1994): 1–57 (54 n. 19), who mentions (date/century in parentheses) CPR 6.80 (II), P.Mich. 15.751 (II), P.Ant. 2.94 (VI), and P.Oxy. 42.3067 (III) (as well as P.Wisc. 2.69 and P.Mich. 8.501, which are however no exact parallels), and E. R. Richards, "Silvanus Was Not Peter's Secretary: Theological Bias in Interpreting διὰ Σιλουανοῦ ... ἔγραψα in 1 Peter 5:12," *JETS* 43 (2000): 417–32, who refers to P.Fay. 123 (ca. 100 CE [?]), BGU 1.33 (II/III), P.Oxy. 6.937 (III), and P.Mich. 8.466 (107 CE) (which he considers grammatically too different to be used: ibid., 424 n. 36, but see the following note).

[86] P.Leid. Inst. 31, lines 4–13 (Ptolemais [?], I/II): "Dius also called ... us [= name], who brings you this letter, is a friend of mine. So help (?) him in order that (?) he may buy - - -. Write me back through him (γράψις [= γράψεις] μοι διὰ τοῦ αὐτοῦ, lines 12–3) on any other matter you need in Ptolemais" (ET: *Papyri, Ostraca, Parchments and Waxed Tablets in the Leiden Papyrological Institute [P. L. Bat. 25]* [eds. F. A. J. Hoogendijk and P. van Minnen; PLB 25; Leiden: Brill, 1991], 148–49); also SB 20.14278, lines 3–4 (Alexandria [?], I): "Please do not neglect to write me, through anyone you may find (δι' οὗ ἂν εὕρῃς γράψαι)" (ET: J. Long, ed., "Confidential Business: P. Col. Inv. 316," *BASPap* 24 [1987]: 9–15), may refer to a letter-carrier; the availability of a carrier is a topos in documentary letters, cf. P. M. Head, "Named Letter-Carriers among the Oxyrhynchus Papyri," *JSNT* 31 (2009): 279–99 (284). By the palaeographic dating, this would be the oldest example known thus far. In O. Claud. 2.290, lines 3–4 (Mons Claudianus [Upper Egypt], ca. 140 CE), a letter-carrier is explicitly mentioned: "I did not give a *stater* to the *tabellarius*, but I had written to you through him (ἀλλ' ἔγραψά σοι δι' αὐτοῦ)" (and cf. lines 6–7; ed.: *Mons Claudianus: Ostraca graeca et latina, vol. II* [eds. J. Bingen et al.; DFIFAO 32; Cairo: Inst. Français d'Archéologie Orientale du Caire, 1997], 128–29). Other early specimens are two of those mentioned by Richards, P.Fay. 123, lines 4–5 (= *CPJ* 2:431; Euhemeria [Fayûm], ca. 100 CE [?]): "I wrote to you yesterday too by your servant Mardon (σοι ἔγραψα διὰ Μάρδωνος τοῦ σοῦ)," where

established idiom during the time First Peter was written[87] is thus hardly warranted. What characterises the idiom is that each case involves an addressor who "writes through" = "sends" (*active* voice), as well as one or more carriers to deliver the letter, be it a previous or future one or, like in 1 Pet 5:12, the present letter.[88]

This bears also on the assessment of a passage sometimes invoked for the argument that the phrase refers to Silvanus as author.[89] This passage is a statement by Dionysius of Corinth (ca. 170, *apud* Eusebius, *Hist. eccl.* 4.23.11) that refers to *First Clement* as τὴν προτέραν [sc. ἐπιστολήν] ἡμῖν διὰ Κλήμεντος γραφεῖσαν, thus clearly to Clement as author. However, apart from the slightly later date, the use of the *passive* participle, implying *Clement* as the logical subject of the phrase, renders this example less relevant than the ones previously discussed.[90] In addition, the *recommendation* (cf. 1 Pet 5:12 "the faithful brother as I reckon") of the letter-carrier is a frequent topos in the documentary letters,[91] the Pauline corpus,[92] and the passages from the letters of Ignatius and Polycarp mentioned above, whereas it would be unusual with respect to the secretary or author. Further objections against the interpretation of Silvanus as named letter-carrier do not stand scrutiny either. The expression δι' ὀλίγων "briefly" (sc. I have written) does not present a problem because, as Richards has convincingly argued, "The carrier idea does not come from the

---

the returning servant is named as bearer of the letter; and P.Mich. 8.466, lines 4–8 (Karanis [Fayûm], 107 CE): "I have very often written to you through Saturninus (μου γρ[άψαντος διὰ] Σατουρνίνου) the *signifer*, likewise through Julianus the son of Longinus (and through Dius)" (ET: *Michigan Papyri, vol. VIII: Papyri and Ostraca from Karanis, Second Series* [eds. H. C. Youtie and J. G. Winter; UMS.H 50; Ann Arbor, Mich.: University of Michigan Press, 1951], 9–16), where the addressor later (lines 12–3) mentions Longinus as the bearer of the present letter, thus here identifies the carriers, not the scribes, of previous letters. *Pace* Richards I see no reason why this example should be discounted. I hope to be able to discuss further evidence in a separate publication.

[87] As voiced by Herzer, *Petrus* (see n. 16), 65–6 with nn. 189, 190.

[88] The four specimens from Ignatius and Polycarp come under the last rubric. An example from the papyri is P.Oxy. 42.3067, lines 3–5 (III): "Since I am about to send for my sister, by force, I write to you through those whom I have sent off for this purpose (διὰ τῶν εἰς τοῦτο ὑπ' ἐμοῦ διαπεμφθέντων γράφω)" (my translation).

[89] E.g., by Kelly, *Epistles* (see n. 38), 215; Davids, *First Epistle of Peter* (see n. 33), 198; Goppelt, *I Peter* (see n. 19), 369; mentioned also by Brox, *Der erste Petrusbrief* (see n. 44), 242.

[90] Cf. also Michaels, *1 Peter* (see n. 62), 306–7.

[91] Cf. Head, "Letter-Carriers" (see n. 86), 285–87.

[92] See Rom 16:1–2, 1 Cor 4:17, 16:10–11, 2 Cor 8:17–18, Eph 6:21–22, Phil 2:25–30, Col 4:7–9. Cf. E. R. Richards, *Paul and First-Century Letter Writing: Secretaries, Composition and Collection* (Downers Grove, Ill.: InterVarsity, 2004), 77, 188–89, 208–9; Elliott, *1 Peter* (see n. 35), 875.

meaning of γράφω. γράφω means 'to write' and not 'to send.' The carrier idea is idiomatic and comes from the διά construction."[93] Several scholars have argued that the task of despatch would be unachievable for a single courier and that 1 Pet 5:12 therefore cannot refer to the letter-carrier.[94] However, it is conceivable that the carrier would have reached only the main centres en route,[95] where copies would have been taken and sent to the *Hinterland*,[96] or even only the initial port (in Pontus?), whereupon his "personal greetings from Peter would ... have been conveyed by word of mouth from congregation to congregation."[97] If the reference were an element of the pseudepigraphic apparatus, it would suffice that this were merely *imaginable*, while the mention of Silvanus would be meant, above all, to establish a credible link between the addresser and the addressees (not the real readers) and, as will become clear further below, to create a "Petrine" context for the addresser.

In sum, according to 1 Pet 5:12 the apostolic addresser avails himself of the help of Silvanus as a named letter-carrier. This means, however, that he appears in a familiar role. According to Acts 15:22–23, the Jerusalem church chooses Judas called Barsabbas and *Silas*[98] to send them with Paul

---

[93] Richards, "Silvanus Was Not" (see n. 85), 429; against the objection by, e.g., Kelly, *Epistles* (see n. 38), 215. Herzer, *Petrus* (see n. 16), 65–8, interprets the passage in light of his view of Acts 15:22–23 (see below, n. 100) as referring to both the bearer and the writer; cf. earlier Selwyn, *First Epistle of St. Peter* (see n. 58), 241: "both as draftsman and as bearer of the Epistle." But *if* we are to assume *idiomatic* usage here ("send") this will be expected to *exclude* concomitant literal usage.

[94] Cf. Beare, *First Epistle of Peter* (see n. 79), 209; Goppelt, *1 Peter* (see n. 19), 369 (German: 347); T. Seland, *Strangers in the Light: Philonic Perspectives on Christian Identity in 1 Peter* (BIS 76; Leiden: Brill, 2005), 22–37. Seland, writing after, and referring to, Richards, "Silvanus Was Not" (see n. 85), simply ignores the latter's examples from the papyri in discussion of the linguistic evidence (24–8).

[95] Some have suggested that 1 Pet 1:1 might give the areas of the addressees' residence in the imagined order of despatch; cf. C. J. Hemer, "The Address of 1 Peter," *ET* 89 (1978): 239–43; Achtemeier, *1 Peter* (see n. 35), 85–6 with n. 88 (mentioning further supporters, but remaining sceptical). For a ("royal," to be sure) travel route through some of the areas mentioned in 1 Pet 1:1 cf. Josephus, *Ant.* 16.23.

[96] On despatch to multiple destinations, cf. briefly Richards, *Letter Writing* (see n. 92), 199–200; also ibid., 189–99 on despatch times.

[97] Thus Michaels, *1 Peter* (see n. 62), 307.

[98] It is widely agreed that the two names designate the same bearer: Σιλᾶς is a Greek form of the Aramaic name שילא/שאילא (Ilan, *Lexicon* [see n. 25], 414), *Silvanus* a Latin names. R. J. Bauckham has suggested that Silvanus was the *cognomen* of this person (a Roman citizen according to Acts 16:37), that the sound-equivalence of the Latin and Aramaic names was important, and that he may have borne both names from birth; cf. idem, "Paul and Other Jews with Latin Name in the New Testament," in *Paul, Luke and the Graeco-Roman World: FS A. J. M. Wedderburn* (eds. A. Christophersen et al.; JSNTSup 217; London: Sheffield Academic Press, 2002), 202–20 (204, 210, 218–19).

and Barnabas to Antioch, "writing through their hand" (γράψαντες διὰ χειρὸς αὐτῶν). This phrase does not *fully* match the diction discussed above, but Barsabbas and Silas's task is clearly to *deliver* the letter with the Apostolic Decree and, fulfilling one possible function of carriers,[99] interpret it (cf. vv. 25, 27). The phrase therefore most likely refers to despatch too and not to scribal activity.[100] At least to the readers of Acts the envoys are recommended as "leading men" (ἄνδρας ἡγουμένους, v. 22) of the Jerusalem church. Thus, Silas in Acts 15 is involved in the delivery of a letter that is closely connected to Peter and James, and he does so *before* he becomes the travel companion of Paul (Acts 15:40). It may be this feature that triggered his role in First Peter.

Alternatively, one could consider that Silas, after his association with Paul,[101] came closer to Peter again during his later life, perhaps on the basis of their common Palestinian Jewish background.[102] This, however, remains conjectural; and the further assumption that Silas-Silvanus became a member of a specifically "Petrine group" in Rome responsible for First Peter rests on the double hypothesis that such a group existed and that First Peter was in fact written in Rome, both sides of which are open to debate.[103] While the connection of the *historical* Silvanus with First Peter remains unclear, his previous association with the Jerusalem church and the despatch of the letter with the Apostolic Decree seems to have been known, through knowledge either of Acts or of its traditions.[104] Historical or fictive—even if his main task is not to *reconcile* "Peter" and "Paul," Silas-Silvanus can be regarded as a *bridge* between the two. It may be considered whether the capability to accommodate a figure who was then known to be, or have been, associated with Paul's mission does not reflect an *integrative* aspect of the Peter image of First Peter that can be related to the perception of Peter as "foundational" in various early Christian texts.[105]

---

[99] Cf., e.g., the summary in Head, "Letter-Carriers" (see n. 86), 287–88.

[100] Both despatch and involvement in writing has been argued by Herzer, *Petrus* (see n. 16), 65–8. One of his reasons is that Acts 15:22–23 distinguish between "sending" (πέμψαι) and "writing" (γράψαντες διὰ χειρὸς αὐτῶν), so that the latter cannot mean the same as the former; but this overlooks that πέμψαι relates to the *"chosen men,"* whereas the second expression may well refer to sending the *letter*. For a similar example from the documentary papyri see above, n. 88. For the anacolouthon ἔδοξε ... πέμψαι ... γράψαντες cf. BDR §468.2 n. 3.

[101] 1 Thess 1:1, 2 Thess 1:1, 2 Cor 1:19, Acts 15:40–18:5.

[102] Thus Feldmeier, *First Letter of Peter* (see n. 9), 253–54 (shorter in German: 169).

[103] See below, section 3.2 with n. 109.

[104] Cf. Brox, "Rahmung" (see n. 1), 89–90 ("ältere Tradition," in 1 Pet "eine[.] andere[.] Überlieferungslinie als Apg 15"); Herzer, *Petrus* (see n. 16), 67, 70 (probably knowledge of Acts). See below, section 4.2.

[105] Cf. Matt 16:18, Luke 22:31–32, John 21:15–17, and the aspects discussed above,

Thus, we can say that Silvanus as letter-carrier *contributes to the Peter image in First Peter.*

3.2 The Connection with "Babylon" and Mark

The list of greetings in 1 Pet 5:13 connects the addressor with Babylon and Mark: "The co-elect in Babylon sends you greetings, also my son Mark" (ἀσπάζεται ὑμᾶς ἡ ἐν Βαβυλῶνι συνεκλεκτὴ καὶ Μᾶρκος ὁ υἱός μου). "The co-elect [fem.] in Babylon"[106] is most likely a personification of the Christian *community* in the city designated by this name.[107] Most interpreters take "Babylon" as a reference to Rome. An important role in the history of research is occupied by an article by Claus-Hunno Hunzinger from 1965, in which he argued that this designation of Rome requires a post-70 date of the relevant sources, and consequently a date of First Peter after Peter's death in the mid-60s, since such a usage presupposes the historical analogy of the Temple destructions by the Romans and the Babylonians, respectively.[108] This has re-enforced the widely held view that Rome was

---

section 2.1. Cf. also below, (at) n. 154. For Peter's foundational role cf. also Hengel, *Petrus* (see n. 29), 21–58.

[106] Attempts to see here an anonymous woman, be it Peter's wife (thus already J. A. Bengel, *Gnomon Novi Testamenti. In quo ex nativa verborum vi simplicitas, profunditas, concinnitas, salubritas sensuum coelestium indicatur* [8th ed. by P. Steudel; Stuttgart, 1891], 990), be it an unknown female Christian (thus M. Karrer, "Petrus im paulinischen Gemeindekreis," *ZNW* 80 [1989]: 210–31 [226]) have proven unsuccessful; cf. Elliott, *1 Peter* (see n. 35), 881: "the anonymity of this person would be inconsistent with the explicit naming of Silvanus and Mark." J. K. Applegate, "The Co-Elect Woman of 1 Peter," *NTS* 38 (1992): 587–604, has suggested that the reference, in contrast, is to a well-known woman, whose name did not have to be mentioned and who as a church leader in Asia Minor was to authorise the *Haustafel* vis-à-vis her female colleagues. But this is a huge bill, and the expression would seem to me far too cryptic to fit it.

[107] The most convincing grammatical explanation of συνεκλεκτή is to take it as substantival; cf. Goppelt, *I Peter* (see n. 19), 373 n. 28 (German: 351 n. 28). Alternative suggestions are an elliptic statement, with mental supplementation of either ἀδελφότης (thus Elliott, *1 Peter* [see n. 35], 882) or διασπορά (thus T. W. Martin, *Metaphor and Composition in 1 Peter* (SBLDS 131; Atlanta: Scholars Press, 1992], 145–46); but the former does not denote the individual community elsewhere in First Peter (cf. 2:17, 5:9), and "Diaspora" in 1 Pet 1:1, Jas 1:1 is *the "area" in which* the Christians reside, rather than the individual Christian community residing *in a given place* (and thus the immediate *subject* of greeting, thus 1 Pet 5:13). That the expression denotes a community or church is further held by, e.g., Windisch, *Briefe* (see n. 38), 82; Selwyn, *First Epistle of St. Peter* (see n. 58), 243; Kelly, *Epistles* (see n. 38), 217–18; Best, *1 Peter* (see n. 81), 177–78; Brox, *Der erste Petrusbrief* (see n. 44), 247; Achtemeier, *1 Peter* (see n. 35), 353; Davids, *First Epistle of Peter* (see n. 33), 201.

[108] C.-H. Hunzinger, "Babylon als Deckname für Rom und die Datierung des 1. Petrusbriefes," in *Gottes Wort und Gottes Land: FS H.-W. Hertzberg* (ed. H. Graf Reventlow; Göttingen: Vandenhoeck & Ruprecht, 1965), 67–77.

the *real* place of origin of First Peter.[109] Hunzinger, to be sure, did not draw this conclusion but suggested that the evidence "weist ... viel eher in den östlichen Raum," because it is here that the cryptogram "Babylon" for Rome was attested first.[110] Occasionally, traditions First Peter shares with *First Clement* (and *Hermas*) are invoked for an origin in Rome,[111] but shared traditions need not imply shared residence of authors, at least not extended residence; our letter has also close links with traditions in the

---

[109] E.g., Schelkle, *Petrusbriefe* (see n. 40), 11; Kelly, *Epistles* (see n. 38), 33–4 (both of them cautiously); R. E. Brown (and J. P. Meier), *Antioch and Rome: New Testament Cradles of Catholic Christianity* (London: Chapman, 1983), 130–33; (H. Balz and) W. Schrage, *Die "Katholischen" Briefe: Die Briefe des Jakobus, Petrus, Johannes und Judas* (14th ed. [4th ed. of this revision]; NTD 10; Göttingen: Vandenhoeck & Ruprecht, 1993), 63–4; Feldmeier, *First Letter of Peter* (see n. 9), 40–2 (German: 27–8; combining Roman origin with a symbolic interpretation of "Babylon," see below).—A *Petrine "group"* or *"circle"* in Rome that produced First Peter is assumed, e.g., by Best, *1 Peter* (see n. 81), 59–65; Goppelt, *1 Peter* (see n. 19), 48–53 (German: 64–70); Elliott, *1 Peter* (see n. 35), 127–34 (thus already idem, "Peter, Silvanus and Mark in I Peter and Acts: Sociological-Exegetical Perspectives on a Petrine Group in Rome," in *Wort in der Zeit: FS K. H. Rengstorf* [eds. W. Haubeck and M. Bachmann; Leiden: Brill, 1980], 250–67); Achtemeier, *1 Peter* (see n. 35), 41–2; Boring, *1 Peter* (see n. 42), 38; Senior, *1 Peter* (see n. 67), 5–7. Arguments for a *more developed Petrine "school"* come from M. L. Soards, "1Peter, 2Peter, and Jude as Evidence for a Petrine School," *ANRW* II 25.5:3827–49, and O. B. Knoch, "Gab es eine Petrusschule in Rom? Überlegungen zu einer bedeutsamen Frage," *SNTU.A* 16 (1991): 105–26. J. Prasad, *Foundations of the Christian Way of Life According to 1 Peter 1, 13–25: An Exegetico-Theological Study* (AnBib 146; Rome: Ed. Pontificio Istituto Biblico, 2000), 36–46, dismisses their arguments and prefers to speak of a Petrine group instead. Horrell, "Petrine Circle?" (see n. 8), 29–60, is critical of all hypotheses of "Petrine circles" but nevertheless in favour of Rome as place of origin; he mentions, but does not engage, alternative views of the letter's origin (ibid., 31 n. 8; more cautiously: idem, *1 Peter* [see n. 11], 23–5).—Already Eusebius (*Hist. eccl.* 2.15.2) states "they say" (φασίν) that the letter was written in Rome, referred to "figuratively" (τροπικώτερον) as Babylon, with quotation of 1 Pet 5:13. The statement follows a reference to Papias but is probably not part of it; cf. Körtner, *Papiasfragmente* (see n. 46), 93–4 (who considers the Papias passage secondarily developed from *Hist. eccl.* 3.39.15).

[110] Hunzinger, "Babylon" (see n. 108), 77; similarly Lindemann, *Paulus* (see n. 7), 253; Herzer, *Petrus* (see n. 16), 263–64. Cf. *Sib.* 5.143: "From Babylon will flee the fearful and shameless lord" (φεύξεται ἐκ Βαβυλῶνος ἄναξ φοβερὸς καὶ ἀναιδής, on Nero's flight from Rome); 159–60: a star falling from heaven "will burn the deep see, and Babylon itself, and the land of Italy" (φλέξει πόντον βαθὺν αὐτήν τε Βαβυλῶνα Ἰταλίης γαῖάν θ')—both passages with mention of the Temple destruction in the literary context; further Rev 14:8; 16:19; 17:5; 18:2, 10, 21; *4 Ezra*; *2 Bar*. Note that Hunzinger, ibid., 73–4, does not yet consider "Babylon" in the two latter works a "code name" and reserves the analogy between Rome and Babylon for their *general setting*.

[111] E.g., Bosetti, *Il Pastore* (see n. 31), 287–91; Boring, *1 Peter* (see n. 42), 38; Horrell, "Petrine Circle?" (see n. 8), 50–2. Elliott, *1 Peter* (see n. 35), 134, speaks of "a common reservoir of tradition in Rome."

Letter of James and may have known the gospel of Matthew and Acts, or at least their traditions. All of this does not rule out Rome as the real place of origin, but it does not conclusively speak in favour of Rome either.

Questionable in my view is particularly the assumption that with "Babylon" the author makes a *veiled reference to the real place of origin* of the letter. Why would he have done so? In contrast to Revelation, First Peter does not directly draw a negative picture of "Rome" so that the reference to the alleged place of origin would have had to be suppressed.[112] I therefore prefer the view that the cryptogram—a term used in a neutral sense here—is *not a code name but rather a qualifying cipher*.[113] "Babylon" is a cipher for the capital of an empire ultimately responsible for the trials and sufferings mentioned in the letter.[114] However, in view of the specific data about the areas in which the explicit addressees reside (1 Pet 1:1) it seems unlikely that the reference to the place of origin is entirely fictive, leaving the addressor (and the community with which he stays) literally in utopia.[115] If "Babylon," with the above-mentioned sources, indeed refers to Rome, then it is most probably related to the *Peter-Rome tradition*, which is sparsely but nevertheless clearly attested for the first and early second century.[116] Thus, "Babylon" as reference to Rome does indeed play a role, but it does so as part of the *Peter image* of First Peter as the *purported* place of despatch, which does not necessarily imply that it is also the *historical* origin of the letter.

It should be noted that the reference to "Diaspora" and "Babylon" in the letter opening and closing, as well as the qualification of the addressees and the greeting church as "elect" (ἐκλεκτοῖς παρεπιδήμοις διασπορᾶς κτλ., 1 Pet 1:1; ἡ ἐν Βαβυλῶνι συνεκλεκτή, 5:13), create a twofold *inclusio* around the letter. We find here that the situation from which the ad-

---

[112] This is also observed by Elliott, *1 Peter* (see n. 35), 132–33.

[113] The other two real places called "Babylon" in antiquity, namely a location at the Egyptian Trajan's Canal (cf. Ptolemaeus, *Geographica* 4.5.54; Strabo, *Geogr.* 17.1.30), today belonging to Old Cairo, and the well-known city in Mesopotamia, are hardly intended in First Peter since we know of no early traditions connecting Peter or Christians with them.

[114] Cf. Kelly, *Epistles* (see n. 38), 219; Brox, *Der erste Petrusbrief* (see n. 44), 41–3; Martin, *Metaphor* (see n. 107), 146 n. 44; Herzer, *Petrus* (see n. 16), 264–65. Cf. also Feldmeier, *First Letter of Peter* (see n. 9), 40–2 (German: 27–8), who combines this with assumption of Rome as historical place of origin.

[115] I see this danger in Kelly, *Epistles* (see n. 38), 219; Jobes, *1 Peter* (see n. 49), 323; but also Herzer, *Petrus* (see n. 16), 265. Where should readers *imagine* Peter, and "Babylon," to be?

[116] *1 Clem.* 5.4, *Ascen. Isa.* 4.2–3, Ignatius, *Rom.* 4.3. See further below on Papias. Contra the recent denial of Peter's death in Rome by M. D. Goulder, "Did Peter Ever Go to Rome?" *SJT* 57 (2004): 377–96; cf. Bockmuehl, "Peter's Death" (see n. 12), *passim*.

dressor writes to the addressees *is presented as correlated to their own*. We will take this up in section 4 below on the letter type.

Before doing so, we need to look at the second name. "Mark" is most probably *John Mark* of Acts 12–13, 15.[117] It is now more clearly grasped than previously that Mark is not misplaced in the Peter tradition.[118] According to the account in Acts, his connection with Paul is *ambivalent*. After Barnabas and Paul had taken him on the first missionary journey (Acts 12:25), he separated from them in Pamphylia and returned to Jerusalem (13:13); therefore, Paul later refused to accept him back as a travel companion, whereupon Paul and Barnabas split and the latter travelled with Mark while Paul chose Silas (15:37–40). In contrast, it is in relation to *Peter* that John Mark is first mentioned in Acts. After his liberation from prison, Peter came to the house of Mary, mother of John Mark (Acts 12:12). The sonship mentioned in 1 Pet 5:13, probably implying that Mark was converted by Peter and followed him,[119] might allude to some early connection between Peter and the family of the Greco-Palestinian Mark. In addition, the language of fictive kinship employed in the letter closing (see also ἀδελφός for Silvanus, 5:12),[120] together with mention of the "co-elect" (sc. community), serves to highlight a "network" of individuals and communities with mutual concern for each other, into which the letter integrates the addressees in their location of "Diaspora" (1:1) for the time of their "being foreigners" (τὸν τῆς παροικίας ὑμῶν χρόνον, 1:17).[121] Instead of being out of place, Mark in 1 Pet 5:13 thus recalls one episode of the *vita Petri* as narrated in Acts. Again, it has been suggested that the historical Mark was for some time Peter's collaborator, which seems reflected in the Papias fragment discussed below.[122] But the additional conjecture that he was a leading member of a "Petrine circle" in Rome af-

---

[117] The pairing of Mark with Silvanus in 1 Pet 5:12–13, the mention of Mark alongside Silas in the wider context in Acts (see below), some link of both with Peter in both documents, and the respective connection of Silvanus/Silas with letter despatch, would in my view require too much coincidence for the assumption of different Marks.

[118] Cf. Brox, "Rahmung" (see n. 1), 90; idem, *Der erste Petrusbrief* (see n. 44), 246–48; Karrer, "Petrus" (see n. 106), 223; Herzer, *Petrus* (see n. 16), 71–3. But see the caveat by C. C. Black, *Mark: Images of an Apostolic Interpreter* (Columbia, S.C.: University of South Carolina Press, 1994), 64–6, who sees Mark (and Silvanus) mediated into an amalgamative Petrine Christianity via Pauline tradition. See further below, (at) n. 123.

[119] Cf., e.g., Brox, *Der erste Petrusbrief* (see n. 44), 248. Cf. similar notions in the Pauline corpus, e.g., 1 Cor 4:15; Phlm 10; 1 Tim 1:2, 18; 2 Tim 1:2; 2:1; Titus 1:4.

[120] Cf. also the reference to the ἀδελφότης in the whole world within the final paraenesis, 1 Pet 5:9.

[121] Cf. Black, *Mark* (see n. 118), 62.

[122] Cf. Feldmeier, *First Letter of Peter* (see n. 9), 255 (German: 170–71).

ter Peter's death not only faces the problem of the existence of such a circle (see above) but also needs to account for the fact that Mark is mentioned by Paul as one of his "co-workers" during later stages of his mission and apparently *remembered* as such in the Deutero-Pauline tradition.[123]

As is well known, there is an additional link between Peter and Mark in *Papias's testimony about Mark*. According to Eusebius's excerpt (*Hist. eccl.* 3.39.15), Papias cites the "Elder"[124] to have said that Mark "became Peter's interpreter (ἑρμηνευτής) and wrote accurately all that he remembered, not, indeed in order, of the things said or done by the Lord." He adds that Mark "had not heard the Lord, nor had he followed (παρηκολούθησεν) him, but later on, as I said, (followed) Peter"; it is unclear whether Papias continues to quote here or adds his own interpretation.[125] Shortly thereafter (*Hist. eccl.* 3.39.17), Eusebius attests that Papias used "testimonies" (μαρτυρίαι) from First John and First Peter. Thus, the excerpt from Papias in *Hist. eccl.* 3.39.15 does *not* link Peter or Mark with Rome, and Eusebius's reference to Papias's use of "testimonies" from First Peter is too hazy to allow for the assumption that Papias would have made the inference to Rome from 1 Pet 5:13.[126] We should beware of circular argumentation at this point, for example by filling in later Patristic evidence for a Roman origin of the gospel of Mark[127] or modern exegetical

---

[123] See Phlm 24, Col 4:10, 2 Tim 4:11. Cf. Horrell, "Petrine Circle?" (see n. 8), 48–50; Black, *Mark* (see n. 118), 50–60, 66–7.

[124] Probably John the Elder, cf. Eusebius, *Hist. eccl.* 3.39.4, 14.

[125] Cf. Black, *Mark* (see n. 118), 83, 90. According to Bauckham, *Eyewitnesses* (see n. 46), 204–5, Papias offers a paraphrase throughout the entire passage of what he remembered the "Elder" to have said. The translation follows K. Lake, *Eusebius: The Ecclesiastical History* (2 vols.; LCL; Cambridge, Mass. et al.: Harvard University Press, 1926), 1:297 (except for the parentheses around "followed").

[126] The reference to 1 Pet 5:13 and the letter's origin in Rome (*Hist. eccl.* 2.15.2) does not seem to be Papias's own words but Eusebius'; see above n. 109 (end).

[127] It is debated whether Irenaeus's statement (*Haer.* 3.1.1 = Eusebius, *Hist. eccl.* 5.8.3) that, after the death of Peter and Paul in Rome, Mark, ὁ μαθητὴς καὶ ἑρμηνευτὴς Πέτρου, "transmitted to us" (ἡμῖν παραδέδωκεν) in writing what Peter had preached, points to a Roman origin of the gospel of Mark. It has been suggested that he depends here on local Roman tradition, and that ἡμῖν referred to the Roman church; thus C.-J. Thornton, *Der Zeuge des Zeugen: Lukas als Historiker der Paulusreisen* (WUNT 56; Tübingen: Mohr Siebeck, 1991), 22: "scheint eine römische Gemeindetradition zu sein, die Irenäus etwa bei einem Besuch in Rom kennengelernt haben konnte"; cf. ibid., 10–22. Others consider that Irenaeus, who knows the work of Papias (cf. *Haer.* 5.33.4), and probably depends on it for his information on Mark, "drew these conclusions himself" and "seems to assume" Roman origin of the gospel; thus A. Yarbro Collins, *Mark: A Commentary* (Hermeneia; Minneapolis: Fortress Press, 2007), 7. Still others, however, take ἡμῖν to be generic and conclude that "… on closer inspection it is clear that Irenaeus speaks only of the timing of Mark's composition, not of its place of origin"; so Black, *Mark* (see n. 118), 100. Although Irenaeus quotes from First Peter (cf. *Haer.* 4.9.2,

hypotheses that it was composed in Rome. Conversely, the link in First Peter is hardly due to knowledge of a Roman origin of the gospel; rather, there are *two links culminating in Peter*: between Peter and Rome, on account of the end of Peter's life in the capital, and between Peter and Mark, probably referring to a tradition (or the account in Acts) about some contact between Peter and (John) Mark's family prior to the temporary missionary travel with Paul and perhaps the general association of (John) Mark with the Jerusalem church.

Is Papias's testimony of a link between Peter and Mark *independent* from 1 Pet 5:13? This is heavily debated. Some scholars have suggested that Papias, who used testimonies from First Peter, may have construed his statement about Mark the "interpreter" of Peter from this particular passage.[128] Against this it can be argued, first, that 1 Pet 5:13 does not say anything about a specific role of Mark beyond his being Peter's "son" and transmitting greetings; while the designation "son" could be related to Papias's παρηκολούθησεν, there is no hint of Mark being shaped as Peter's "interpreter" in First Peter. Thus, it would be difficult to derive the details about his activity in Papias's fragment from this passage. Second, it can be asked with Clifton Black, "had Papias drawn such an unwarranted inference from 1 Peter 5:13, why would he not have ascribed that tradition to Peter himself, an esteemed apostle and the supposed author of the letter"?[129] On the other hand, even scholars doubting the reliability of Papias's testimony assume that the gospel had already been ascribed to (one) Mark, which would have precluded direct ascription to Peter; thus, the link with Peter taken from 1 Pet 5:13 was as close as one could get to Petrine authority.[130] In this case, however, it would remain difficult that Papias is *more specific* than this passage about the relation between Peter

---

4.16.5, 5.7.2), we have no evidence how he might have understood 1 Pet 5:13. The Anti-Marcionite Prologue to Mark, a text difficult to date but most likely not earlier than Irenaeus, says that Mark, Peter's *interpres*, wrote his gospel after Peter's death "in the regions of Italy" (*in Italiae partibus*); cf. J. Regul, *Die antimarcionitischen Evangelienprologe* (VL 6; Freiburg i. Brsg.: Herder, 1969), 97–9. Black, *Mark* (see n. 118), 109–10, wonders whether this indeterminacy reflects the lack of a precise location in Irenaeus, on whom the prologue seems to depend. The *clear and explicit* connection of the gospel with Rome is attested from Clement of Alexandria onward; see his *Hypotyposes*, *apud* Eusebius, *Hist. eccl.* 6.14.6 (cf. 2.15.1–2). For a discussion of the sources from the 3d and 4th century cf. Black, *Mark* (see n. 118), 114–91.

[128] E.g., K. Niederwimmer, "Johannes Markus und die Frage nach dem Verfasser des zweiten Evangeliums," *ZNW* 58 (1967): 172–88 (186); Regul, ibid., 96–7.

[129] Black, *Mark* (see n. 118), 87–8.

[130] Cf. P. Vielhauer, *Geschichte der urchristlichen Literatur: Einleitung in das Neue Testament, die Apokryphen und die Apostolischen Väter* (Berlin: De Gruyter, 1975), 260–61; recently J. Marcus, *Mark 1–8: A New Translation with Introduction and Commentary* (AB 27; New York et al.: Doubleday, 1999), 22–4 (23).

and Mark.[131] It also needs to be recalled that Papias is rather *critical* of Mark's work, which "makes it more likely that he inherited the tradition of the apostolic authority of Mark and had to come to terms with it, rather than that he invented it."[132] Although questions of historical context, textual interpretation and transmission by Eusebius remain, Papias seems to have had a tradition about Mark as the "interpreter" of Peter that cannot be directly derived from 1 Pet 5:13.[133] Whether the two traditions are truly independent[134] or go back to a common ancestor[135] is difficult to say. All in all, then, Mark proves to be "good company" for Peter in 1 Pet 5:13. As in the case of Silas-Silvanus,[136] it is possible that the fact that Mark was also known as attached to Paul contributes an integrative element to the Peter image in First Peter.

4. Letter Type and Evoked Peter Image

4.1 First Peter as Early Christian Diaspora Letter

First Peter can text-pragmatically be viewed as an early Christian Diaspora letter.[137] Such letters are influenced by early Jewish Diaspora letters, which are directed by an authorised addressor to addressees who live either in the Diaspora or at the fringes of the land of Israel. An important feature of

---

[131] It is unlikely that Papias's statement is a reaction against the claim the Gnostic leader Basilides was taught by Glaucias, the ἑρμηνευτής of Peter (Clemens Alex., *Strom.* 7.106): The inverse scenario is more probable, perhaps in an Alexandrian setting, in which followers of Basilides reacted to the legend of Mark as the founder of the Alexandrian church; cf. W. A. Löhr, *Basilides und seine Schule: Eine Studie zur Theologie- und Kirchengeschichte des zweiten Jahrhunderts* (WUNT 83; Tübingen: Mohr Siebeck, 1996), 21–2.

[132] Yarbro Collins, *Mark* (see n. 127), 4.

[133] Cf. also Justin, *Dial.* 106.3, where ἐν τοῖς ἀπομνημονεύμασιν αὐτοῦ (sc. Peter's) seems to refer to the gospel of Mark; cf. C.-J. Thornton, "Justin und das Markusevangelium," *ZNW* 84 (1993): 93–110. More reserved is Black, *Mark* (see n. 118), 94–6.

[134] This seems to be suggested by Black, ibid., 88: "... toward the end of the first century, more than one tradition, trickling to more than one region of primitive Christianity (Rome [1 Peter]/Asia Minor [the Elder John/Papias]), associated the figures of Peter and Mark."

[135] Cf. Hengel, Petrus (see n. 29), 75: 1 Pet 5:13 and Papias "weisen beide unabhängig voneinander auf dieselbe ältere, zuverlässige Überlieferung zurück."

[136] See above, at n. 105.

[137] See in greater detail L. Doering, "First Peter as Early Christian Diaspora Letter," in *The Catholic Epistles and Apostolic Tradition* (eds. K.-W. Niebuhr and R. Wall; Waco, Tex.: Baylor University Press, forthcoming, 2009). In order to avoid reduplication, the following will focus on aspects relevant for the author construction in First Peter.

such letters is their *quasi-official character*: In terms of genre, their closest analogy is not the private but the official, diplomatic letter. In contrast to these letters, however, directed to the inhabitants of a city, a province or the Empire, such Jewish letters are addressed to a specific group, the Jewish inhabitants of a town or region, probably locally organised according to the model of the Greco-Roman voluntary associations (θίασοι, *collegia* etc.).[138]

Amongst the *Jewish Diaspora letters*,[139] two main types can be distinguished: One type is linked to the prophet Jeremiah, partly also to his companion Baruch, and is to be found in Jeremiah's letter in Jer 29:1–23 (36 LXX); the Letter of Jeremiah LXX; *Targum Jonathan* on Jer 10:11; a piece of writing mentioned in 4QApocryphon of Jeremiah C^d (4Q389 frg. 1), allegedly sent by Jeremiah from Egypt to Babylon, where the exiles read it (the important word קראו was originally misread here); the book of Baruch, after public reading secondarily sent from Babylonia; then Baruch's letter in *2 Bar.* 78–86 (87); and the exchange of letters between Baruch in Jerusalem and Jeremiah in Babylon in *4 Bar.* 6–7. The other type is issued by Jewish communities or their representatives, deals mainly with halakhah and calendar issues, and is attested from the Passover Papyrus from Elephantine through the introductory letters to Second Maccabees (2 Macc 1:1–10a, 1:10b–2:18) up to Rabbinic letters, such as those by Rn. Gamaliel (*t. Sanh.* 2:6 and parallels). The Jeremiah-Baruch letters, apart perhaps from a nucleus in Jer 29, are pseudonymous. They involve communication between the Exiles in "Babylon" and Jews elsewhere that becomes transparent for the situation of Jews in the Greco-Roman period. However, contrary to previous opinion, it has emerged that such letters do not have to be sent (or purportedly sent) from Jerusalem. Other locations of the authoritative letter writer may be Babylon (*4 Bar.* 7; Baruch LXX)

---

[138] Cf. P. Richardson, "Early Synagogues as Collegia in the Diaspora and Palestine," in *Voluntary Associations in the Greco-Roman World* (eds. J. S. Kloppenborg and S. G. Wilson; London: Routledge, 1996), 90–109; W. Ameling, "Die jüdischen Gemeinden im antiken Kleinasien," in *Jüdische Gemeinden und Organisationsformen von der Antike bis zur Gegenwart* (eds. R. Jütte and A. P. Kustermann; Aschkenas Beiheft 3; Wien et al.: Böhlau, 1996), 29–55 (34–7); J. M. G. Barclay, "Money and Meetings: Group Formation among Diaspora Jews and Early Christians," in *Vereine, Synagogen und Gemeinden im kaiserzeitlichen Kleinasien* (eds. A. Gutsfeld and D.-A. Koch; STAC 25; Tübingen: Mohr Siebeck, 2006), 113–27.

[139] Cf. I. Taatz, *Frühjüdische Briefe: Die paulinischen Briefe im Rahmen der offiziellen religiösen Briefe des Frühjudentums* (NTOA 16; Freiburg [CH]: Universitätsverlag; Göttingen: Vandenhoeck & Ruprecht, 1991); M. F. Whitters, *The Epistle of Second Baruch: A Study in Form and Message* (JSPSup 42; London: Sheffield Academic Press, 2003), 86–101, and texts discussed under 1.1–2.6 in Doering, "First Peter" (see n. 137).

or Egypt (4QApocrJer C^d).[140] Thus, these letters are more concerned with the unity of the people than with the authoritative role of Jerusalem.

Amongst the letters in the New Testament, James and First Peter adopt the *Diaspora motif* and develop it in different directions consistent with the overall emphasis of the respective letter. James is addressed "to the twelve tribes in the Diaspora" (Jas 1:1), thus viewing "all Israel" in the Dispersion and subject to various trials.[141] Its real addressees are probably Christians particularly in the field of vision of the Jerusalem community.[142] First Peter, in contrast, develops the Diaspora motif towards the addressees' existence as "elect foreigners" (ἐκλεκτοῖς παρεπιδήμοις, 1:1) and "outsiders and foreigners" (ὡς παροίκους καὶ παρεπιδήμους, 2:11).[143] It addresses

---

[140] Cf. L. Doering, "Jeremiah and the 'Diaspora Letters' in Ancient Judaism: Epistolary Communication with the Golah as Medium for Dealing with the Present," in *Reading the Present in the Qumran Library: The Perception of the Contemporary by Means of Scriptural Interpretation* (eds. K. De Troyer and A. Lange; SBLSymS 30; Atlanta: SBL, 2005), 43–72; idem, "Jeremia in Babylonien und Ägypten: Mündliche und schriftliche Toraparänese für Exil und Diaspora nach *4QApocryphon of Jeremiah C*," in *Frühjudentum und Neues Testament im Horizont Biblischer Theologie: Mit einem Anhang zum Corpus Judaeo-Hellenisticum Novi Testamenti* (eds. W. Kraus and K.-W. Niebuhr, collaboration of L. Doering; WUNT 162; Tübingen: Mohr Siebeck, 2003), 50–79.

[141] On James as Diaspora letter cf. K.-W. Niebuhr, "Der Jakobusbrief im Licht frühjüdischer Diasporabriefe," *NTS* 44 (1998): 420–43; further M. Tsuji, *Glaube zwischen Vollkommenheit und Verweltlichung: Eine Untersuchung zur literarischen Gestalt und zur inhaltlichen Kohärenz des Jakobusbriefes* (WUNT II/93; Tübingen: Mohr Siebeck, 1997), 18–27; R. J. Bauckham, *James: Wisdom of James, Disciple of Jesus the Sage* (New Testament Readings; London: Routledge, 1999), 11–28; D. Verseput, "Genre and Story: The Community Setting of the Epistle of James," *CBQ* 62 (2000): 96–110. Some caution is expressed by W. Popkes, *Der Jakobusbrief* (THK 14; Leipzig: Ev. Verlagsanstalt, 2001), 61–4 ("[n]ur im allgemeinen Sinn" a Diaspora letter [63]).

[142] Syria is considered, e.g., by M. Konradt, *Christliche Existenz nach dem Jakobusbrief: Eine Studie zu seiner soteriologischen und ethischen Konzeption* (SUNT 22; Göttingen: Vandenhoeck & Ruprecht, 1998), 333–36; C. Burchard, *Der Jakobusbrief* (HNT 15/1; Göttingen: Vandenhoeck & Ruprecht, 2000), 6 (literature). Note that both authors question the anti-Pauline thrust of Jas 2:14–26 (Konradt, ibid., 241–46; Burchard, ibid., 125–26). Authors reckoning with such a thrust assume areas of Pauline influence; cf., e.g., M. Klein, *"Ein vollkommenes Werk": Vollkommenheit, Gesetz und Gericht als theologische Themen des Jakobusbriefes* (BWANT 139; Stuttgart et al.: Kohlhammer, 1995), 185–206, 207. It is debated whether the real addressees of James should be seen as Jewish Christians or not. Niebuhr, ibid., 423, suggests "diejenigen, die sich als Glieder der Jesusbewegung dem biblischen Gottesvolk zurechnen" and considers the differentiation between Jewish and Gentile Christianity too rigid to be useful for assessment of James. Konradt, ibid., 332–33: presumably predominantly Gentile Christians, with prior contact to Diaspora Judaism.

[143] On the issue of foreignness in First Peter cf. R. Feldmeier, *Die Christen als Fremde: Die Metapher der Fremde in der antiken Welt, im Urchristentum und im 1. Petrusbrief* (WUNT 64; Tübingen: Mohr Siebeck, 1992).

predominantly[144] Gentile Christians[145] with Israel epithets and is not sent from Jerusalem but from "Babylon," which as we have seen may refer to Rome but qualifies it as the place responsible for Exile and Dispersion and thus evokes the setting of the Exilic-Diasporic "Babylon" of the Diaspora letters of the Jeremiah-Baruch type. Consideration of the letter form and type thus strengthens the interpretation of the "Babylon" reference suggested above (section 3.2).

Apart from First Peter and James, also the letter containing the Apostolic Decree Acts 15:23–29 and, outside the New Testament, probably *First Clement* (with characterisation of the addressor and addressee communities as παροικοῦσα "sojourning, staying as foreigners") can be regarded as early Christian Diaspora letters. Influence of this tradition can also be traced in Jude and Second Peter, as well as in the *Letter of Polycarp* and the *Martyrdom of Polycarp*.[146] Like First Peter, all of these texts—except for Acts 15 and James—display variations of an *epistolary salutation* in their prescript that eventually goes back to royal encyclicals in the versions of the book of Daniel[147] and is similarly employed in Aramaic in the Gamaliel letters. This salutation that in the Jewish references consists of the phrase "may your peace be abundant" (שלמכון ישגא; εἰρήνη ὑμῖν πληθυνθείη) appears in First and Second Peter as well as in *First Clement* in a form in which the verb πληθυνθείη follows the phrase χάρις ὑμῖν καὶ εἰρήνη.[148] This phrase, however, is the short form of salutation in the Pauline letters, as attested in 1 Thess 1:1. This allows for a twofold conclusion: First, in contrast to the considerations regarding the *superscriptio* (presentation of the addressor) I deem it likely here that First Peter as the presumably oldest of the three letters picks up the phrase from

---

[144] Not necessarily exclusively. The possibility of an ethnically mixed audience, perhaps with Gentile predominance, is advocated, e.g., by Elliott, *1 Peter* (see n. 35), 95–7. A "vast preponderance" of Gentile readers is assumed by Achtemeier, *1 Peter* (see n. 35), 50–1 (51). I wonder whether one can neatly recognise the "Israelite origin of some" by, inter alia, "concepts, terms, and images drawn from Israel's Scripture and tradition" (Elliott, ibid., 95). Also former sympathisers with Judaism may be assumed (thus also Elliott, ibid., 96), who could have mediated Jewish concepts, as well as initial evangelisers in the addressees' areas (cf. 1 Pet 1:12); cf. also Achtemeier, ibid., 51.

[145] With, e.g., Kelly, *Epistles* (see n. 38), 4; Best, *1 Peter* (see n. 81), 19–20; Brox, *Der erste Petrusbrief* (see n. 44), 25; Goppelt, *1 Peter* (see n. 19), 6–7 (German: 30); Boring, *1 Peter* (see n. 42), 43; Feldmeier, *First Letter of Peter* (see n. 9), 42–3 (German: 29). *Pace* Dunn, *Beginning from Jerusalem* (see n. 9), 1158–60.

[146] Cf. Tsuji, *Glaube* (see n. 141), 28–9, 32–6, and texts discussed under 3.2–3.4 in Doering, "First Peter" (see n. 137).

[147] Dan 3:98 [4:1] θ', 6:25 [26] θ', 4:24 [37] c LXX, cf. 3:31, 6:26 MT (Aramaic).

[148] In *1 Clem.* inscriptio with intervening theological and christological expansions; in Jude it follows ἔλεος ὑμῖν καὶ εἰρήνη καὶ ἀγάπη; cf. for ἔλεος also Pol. *Phil.* and *Mart. Pol.* inscriptio.

Pauline tradition; it is unlikely in my view that the author would have reinvented it independently, with the preference for χάρις to ἔλεος and the peculiar position of ὑμῖν, but it cannot be regarded as the default common Christian greeting either.[149] Second, and this immediately *delimits* the Pauline influence, First Peter and the other letters by virtue of the addition of the verb πληθυνθείη add an *un-Pauline* tone and, beyond Paul, seek *to connect with the tradition of encyclical letters* as attested in Daniel and Jewish literature.

4.2 Peter and James in Acts 15 and Peter's Authorial Image in First Peter

It is in my view not by chance that the two apostolic figures who are each represented in the New Testament with a Diaspora letter, are also significantly involved in the *third* Diaspora letter in the New Testament, containing the so-called Apostolic Decree, in Acts 15:23–29, already mentioned above. Writing *quasi-official encyclical letters* is connected with the *images* of Peter and James in all three of these New Testament texts. Generally, the sparseness and indirectness of the connection with Paul in the Lucan account of the decree is notable, as a synchronic reading shows: Whereas Peter (Acts 15:7–11) and James (15:13–21) have ample opportunity to speak, there is only a brief note about Barnabas and Paul's (in this order, thus also 15:25) account of the "signs and wonders" that God had worked through them amongst the Gentiles (15:12). James virtually skips over their testimony and goes back to what "Symeon"[150] had expounded (15:14); he then suggests that a letter be written (15:20) that therefore can be largely seen as "collusion" between the two main apostolic figures of the Jerusalem church. The decree is then not given to Paul and Barnabas to take with them to Antioch, but as discussed above (section 3.1), the assembly resolves to send along with them Judas Barsabbas and Silas to despatch the letter; the phrases "leading men among the brothers" (15:22), as well as "their hand" through which the apostles and elders "write," i.e., send (15:23), refer to Judas and Silas alone. Consequently, Acts 15:32 focuses solely on the Jerusalemites as prophetic interpreters of the Decree. And it is only after Paul had chosen Silas as travel companion that he "went through Syria and Cilicia, strengthening the churches" (15:41), which is often related to the promulgation of the Decree in these remaining

---

[149] Herzer, *Petrus* (see n. 16), 32–3, suggests participation in early Christian tradition, but the evidence of, e.g., Jude 2 or 2 John 3 points to a more peculiar origin of the "grace to you and peace" wish. For the Pauline origin of preference for grace in the salutation cf. J. M. Lieu, "'Grace to You and Peace': The Apostolic Greeting," *BJRL* 68 (1985/86): 161–78.

[150] On the form of the name see above, n. 20.

addressee regions.[151] On the whole, Paul in these contexts plays a subordinate role. Crucial for the realisation of the Decree are Peter and James, whereas Judas Barsabbas and Silas are significantly involved in its despatch and interpretation. As we have seen, this can be compared to the function of Silvanus in 1 Pet 5:12.

Further details of the portrayal of Peter in Acts 15 (or the traditions it reflects, see below) may provide clues to the addressor construction in First Peter.[152] In Acts 15:7–11, with recourse to Acts 10–11, Peter is portrayed as the initiator of the Gentile mission, and in v. 11 he champions with Paulinising[153] soteriology that "we believe that through the grace of the Lord Jesus we will be saved, just as they [sc. the Gentiles] will." This can be related to the responsibility of Peter for the predominantly Gentile Christian addressees in First Peter. It is well possible that this aspect of the Peter image in First Peter relates to some knowledge of what the historical Peter stood for, particularly in the context of the incident at Antioch, where he apparently struggled to keep the balance between unconditional table-fellowship with Gentile Christians and the affirmation of a historical notion of the "people of God."[154] To be sure, this aspect would have undergone a significant shift and transformation in its realisation in First Peter, where the emphasis is on the addressees' "becoming the people of God" through rebirth (cf. 1 Pet 2:1–10), with the consequence that the previous "Israel existence" of any Jewish Christian addressees, as well as of Jews outside the Christian community, would have *de facto* been ignored.[155] But similar shifts can for example also be observed for the James image in the Letter of James[156] and may be due to the lessening importance of the

---

[151] Cf. only Barrett, *Acts* (see n. 20), 2:758.

[152] The perspective taken here is thus not "to regard the *theology* of 1 Peter as reflected in Acts 15," an approach rightly criticised by Black, *Mark* (see n. 118), 65 (emphasis added).

[153] Cf. Barrett, *Acts* (see n. 20), 2:719: "superficially Pauline"; R. Pervo, *Acts: A Commentary* (Hermeneia; Minneapolis: Fortress Press, 2009), 374.

[154] Cf., with respect to Gal 2:11–21, C. Böttrich, *Petrus: Fischer, Fels und Funktionär* (Biblische Gestalten 2; Leipzig: Ev. Verlagsanstalt, 2001), 207. Cf. already J. D. G. Dunn, *Unity and Diversity in the New Testament: An Inquiry into the Character of Earliest Christianity* (2d ed.; London: SCM, 1990), 385: "... *Peter was probably in fact and effect the bridge-man who did more than any other to hold together the diversity of first-century Christianity.* ... Peter, as shown particularly by the Antioch episode in Gal. 2, had both a care to hold firm to his Jewish heritage which Paul lacked, and an openness to the demands of developing Christianity which James lacked" (emphasis original).

[155] Cf. Karrer, "Petrus" (see n. 106), 225: "Damit ist eine eigenständige Lösung der paulinischen Spannung des Petrusbildes zwischen Israel-Apostolat und Ethne-Öffnung entworfen: Zwischen Heiden und Juden gibt es keinen Heilsunterschied. Vor- und außerchristlich sind sie allesamt Nicht-Gottes-Volk."

[156] Cf. M. Konradt, "The Historical Context of the Letter of James in Light of its

connection with Judaism. Compared with Peter, the focus of James's activity in Acts 15 is orientation to the Torah, as expressed in the abstentions suggested and, with modifications, formulated in the Decree (Acts 15:20, 29; cf. 21:25), and this corresponds to the James image in the Letter of James.[157]

Moreover, when we compare the alleged or implicit *addressor-addressee relation* in First Peter and James as two Diaspora Letters, we can see the different specifics of the respective addressor construction: Whereas James writes "to the Twelve Tribes in the Diaspora," thus at least implicitly from the point of view of Jerusalem, Peter writes his letter allegedly from "Babylon" to Christians under pressure in the "Diaspora" of regions in Asia Minor that largely do not belong to Pauline areas of mission,[158] or, as some have suggested, are areas in which Paul's figure was controversial.[159] With respect to the direction of communication, First Peter is, as it were, a letter "from the Exile/Diaspora to the Diaspora." This fits well the tradition about an apostle who—after a short imprisonment under Agrippa I—went to "another place" (Acts 12:17),[160] travelled apparently in his ministry (cf. 1 Cor 9:5, Gal 2:11–15), and at the end of his life stays in Rome, to which "Babylon" probably alludes.

Traditio-Historical Relations with First Peter," in *The Catholic Epistles* (see n. 137), at n. 175 of the manuscript, on James: "The church is no longer the core of the eschatological Israel that has to be gathered ...; it has simply become Israel, apparently without taking non-Christian Israel into its field of vision anymore."

[157] Cf. in particular Konradt, ibid., *passim*. "Torah" remains the point of orientation although, as Konradt argues, in James the notion of Torah has undergone significant transformations (cf. earlier idem, *Existenz* [see n. 142], 325); cf. Niebuhr, "Jakobusbrief" (see n. 141), *passim*, who speaks of "Torah paraenesis." This point of reference would remain even if we were to accept the argument by R. Deines that the Decree, instead of implying a "halakhic" obligation of Gentile Christians in line with the regulations of Lev 17–18, requires them to respect Jewish taboos in the Diaspora; cf. idem, "Das Aposteldekret – Halacha für Heidenchristen oder christliche Rücksichtnahme auf jüdische Tabus?" in *Jewish Identity in the Graeco-Roman World* (eds. J. Frey, D. R. Schwartz and S. Gripentrog; AJAC 71; Leiden: Brill, 2007), 323–95.

[158] With the exception of Asia and perhaps Galatia these areas comprise significant areas outside the Pauline sphere of influence: Pontus, Bithynia, and Cappadocia; the only "Pauline" connection with Pontus is Aquila, if he hailed indeed from there (Acts 18:2; cf. 18:18, 26; Rom 16:3; 1 Cor 16:19; 2 Tim 4:19). There is no room here to address the vexed question of whether these are provinces or regions, and I hope to be able to clarify my point of view on this elsewhere.

[159] Cf. Horrell, "Petrine Circle?" (see n. 8), 53–4, referring to Acts 16:7, 2 Tim 1:15, cf. 2 Pet 3:16.

[160] Cf. J. A. Fitzmyer, *The Acts of the Apostles: A New Translation with Introduction and Commentary* (AB 31; New York et al.: Doubleday, 1998), 489–90 (literature): "left Jerusalem for security" (489).

The connection between the Peter image in First Peter and Acts 15, as well as Acts 12:12 (see above, section 3.1), might suggest that the (real) author of First Peter knew Acts. Recently, a few scholars, with more or less determination, have drawn this conclusion.[161] The discussion cannot be taken up here in detail. The problem is compounded by scholarly unanimity about the sources used in Acts and growing disagreement about the dating of Acts. A date for Acts of ca. 115, as suggested by Richard Pervo,[162] is probably too late for the author of First Peter to have known the final form of the work. On the other hand, although Acts 15 in its present form is a Lucan composition, it makes use of sources and/or traditions. Some scholars assign various parts of Acts 15 to different sources or traditions.[163] The observations above have suggested that the author of First Peter knew about a connection between (at least) Peter, the Decree, and its despatch by Barsabbas and Silas. Thus, he had likely access to either Acts or the traditions Luke used in Acts 15:6–35 (40) and 12:12. Something similar can be said regarding 1 Pet 5:1–4 and Acts 20:17, 28–29.[164]

5. Conclusion

We have started with the suggestion that Brox's connection of the (presumable) pseudonym to Rome as the purported origin of the letter reflects a reductionist approach to the author fiction and addressor construction in First Peter. Considering the image of the apostle materially developed in the letter, implied by the relations in which he is portrayed, and evoked by the epistolary form and letter type of First Peter, we have arrived at a more nuanced and yet more specific addressor construction that nevertheless incorporates some of the ideas advocated by Brox: The letter presents an

---

[161] With less determination, Herzer, *Petrus* (see n. 16), 67 ("wahrscheinlich"), 73 ("Indiz für die Kenntnis der Apg"), 165 ("kann nicht festgestellt werden"), 180–81 ("setzt entweder die lukanische Redaktion voraus oder zumindest die gleiche Überlieferung, wie sie auch die lukanische Redaktion verwendet" [181]), 262–63, 267–68. With more determination Schmidt, *Mahnung* (see n. 13), 187–91.

[162] Cf. Pervo, *Acts* (see n. 153), 5–7. Contrast Barrett, *Acts* (see n. 20), 2:xlii: late 80s to early 90s.

[163] E.g., Fitzmyer, *Acts* (see n. 160), 544, who distinguishes two Antiochene sources, one for Acts 15:3–12 and one for 15:13–33. A. Weiser, *Die Apostelgeschichte: Kapitel 13–28* (ÖTK 5/2; Gütersloh: Gütersloher Verlagshaus / Würzburg: Echter, 1985), 371–77, distinguishes traditions about the Jerusalem agreement from those about the conflict in Antioch, including the Decree, but assigns the mention of Silas to Lucan redaction. Barrett, ibid., 2:740–41, remains vague about a traditional connection between Decree and setting.

[164] See above, nn. 53, 104. Cf. also at nn. 47, 48.

addressor who, authorised as the apostle κατ' ἐξοχήν, writes, like James, in the tradition of "quasi-official" Jewish Diaspora letters (not to be subjected to a requirement of individuality derived from the private letter tradition), to predominantly Gentile Christians but with an ecclesiology informed by the notion of the "elect people," i.e., "Israel." Unlike (presumably) James, the addressor is not writing from Jerusalem but from "Babylon," which both refers to Rome as the place of Peter's martyrdom and is a cipher for the situation of suffering and dispersion the addressor shares with the addressees. With rhetorical appeal to the elders amongst the addressees, he presents himself as the co-elder, showing both collegiality and authority; potentially to all addressees he offers himself as an experienced example of suffering, perhaps even alluding at his martyrdom, and vouches the subsequent glory as a (present?) participant in it. His own mode of solidarity exemplifies what he preaches; he refers to the example of Christ and makes room for Christ by his own example. Finally, the addressor is connected to Jewish Christian figures that play a role in the *vita Petri* according to Acts (or its traditions) but are also known to have been associated for some time with Paul. The letter shows some influence of Pauline tradition but limits this strongly. It is directed to areas that are largely not Pauline territory of mission and/or in which Paul may not have been an undisputed figure.

In sum, the image of Peter developed in the letter is in several aspects significantly shaped towards "reaching" the predominantly Gentile Christian addressees in their situation of "dispersion" and suffering, including their intra-communal relations. It refers to a foundational, "integrative" apostle of uncontested authority in the areas explicitly addressed. "Peter" stands (similar to "James") for a different type of letter writing, not uninfluenced by Paul but distinct[165] in its connection with the Jewish encyclical letter tradition. The historical ramifications of this Peter image are yet to be spelt out in full.

---

[165] As has been argued, with different emphases and results, particularly by Elliott, *1 Peter* (see n. 35), 37–40 (and *passim*), and Herzer, *Petrus* (see n. 16), *passim*. Horrell, "Petrine Circle?" (see n. 8), may be right in criticising some overstatement in Herzer's analysis (e.g., ibid., 33) but tends to make too little of the distinctive features of First Peter he notes (ibid., 38–42) vis-à-vis the Pauline letter tradition; note his formulation, First Peter is "both Pauline ... and non-Pauline" (42)—but this means it is distinct, and I would add, presents itself as distinct, from the Pauline letter tradition.

Autorfiktion und Gegnerbild
im Judasbrief und im Zweiten Petrusbrief

von

JÖRG FREY

1. Von der Autorfiktion zur Gegnerfiktion

Die Diskussion um Pseudepigraphie im Neuen Testament soll mit dem vorliegenden Band auf eine differenziertere Basis gestellt werden. Bewegte sich die historisch-kritische Diskussion seit ihren Anfängen bei Johann David Michaelis oder Friedrich Daniel Ernst Schleiermacher[1] bis ins späte 20. Jh. oft nur um die Alternative von ‚echt' oder ‚unecht', pseudonym oder orthonym, so erscheint diese inzwischen unbefriedigend und unfruchtbar.

Denn das Phänomen pseudonymer Abfassung als solches ist mittlerweile in weiten Kreisen der akademischen Bibelwissenschaft weithin akzeptiert,[2] wenngleich dessen Erklärung und Bewertung im Einzelnen strittig sind[3] und ein differenzierteres Gefüge von Kategorien erfordern. Im

---

[1] S. zur Forschungsgeschichte den schönen Überblick von M. JANSSEN, Unter falschem Namen. Eine kritische Forschungsbilanz frühchristlicher Pseudepigraphie, ARGU 14, Frankfurt a.M. u.a. 2003. S. a.a.O. 251–268, auch hilfreiche Ansätze zur Differenzierung der Diskussion.

[2] Dies gilt, sofern man von populären, eher konservativen Einführungen und Auslegungen und von einem unbelehrbaren, seine ‚Ergebnisse' dogmatisch präjudizierenden Fundamentalismus absieht. S. wesentliche Meilensteine der Diskussion bei M. HENGEL, Anonymität, Pseudepigraphie und „Literarische Fälschung" in der jüdisch-hellenistischen Literatur (1972), wieder abgedruckt mit Literaturergänzungen von J. Frey in: M. HENGEL, Judaica et Hellenistica. Kleine Schriften I. Unter Mitarbeit von R. Deines, J. Frey, C. Markschies, A. M. Schwemer mit einem Anhang von H. Bloedhorn, WUNT 90, Tübingen 1996, 196–251; N. Brox (Hg.), Pseudepigraphie in der heidnischen und jüdisch-christlichen Antike, WdF 484, Darmstadt 1977; D. G. MEADE, Pseudonymity and Canon. An Investigation into the Relationship of Authorship and Authority in Jewish and Earliest Christian Tradition, WUNT 39, Tübingen 1986. S. zum Ganzen den Forschungsbericht von JANSSEN, a.a.O., außerdem H. J. RIEDL, Anamnese und Apostolizität. Der Zweite Petrusbrief und das theologische Problem neutestamentlicher Pseudepigraphie, RStTh 64, Frankfurt a.M. 2005, 13–142.

[3] S. etwa die Beiträge von A. D. BAUM, Pseudepigraphie und literarische Fälschung im frühen Christentum. Mit ausgewählten Quellentexten samt deutscher Übersetzung,

Blick auf einzelne Briefe wie z.B. 2Petr ist mittlerweile ein Konsens erreicht, der nur selten hinterfragt wird und kaum mehr zu erschüttern ist, während die Diskussion um andere Texte wie etwa Jak, Kol oder 2Thess nach wie vor nicht abgeschlossen ist.

Tiefgreifende Unterschiede bestehen z.B. in der Durchführung der pseudonymen Autorfiktion und der Dichte der sie stützenden Textelemente. So liegen Welten zwischen den sehr ‚locker' dem Apostel Paulus zugeschriebenen Kol oder Eph und der detailliert durchgeführten Fiktionalität der Past oder – im Corpus der ‚Katholischen Briefe' – zwischen der gleichfalls eher ‚schwach' konzipierten Autorfiktion des 1Petr und der sehr massiven fiktionalen Autorisierung des 2Petr. Sachlich ist daher über die bloße Frage nach der Glaubwürdigkeit der Verfasserangaben hinaus nach der konkreten Durchführung und der sachlichen und kommunikativen Funktion der pseudonymen Konstruktion zu fragen. Dabei ist zu bedenken, dass die fiktionale Konstruktion über den Autor hinaus auch die Adressaten und die literarisch repräsentierte Situation, mithin auch die Gegner und die strittigen Sachverhalte, einbezieht.

Dieser Aspekt ist in der Forschung häufig vernachlässigt worden. Es ist zwar weithin klar, dass Timotheus und Titus als *Adressaten* der Pastoralbriefe fiktionale Gestalten sind, auch wenn Paulus in seinen Briefen von beiden Personen spricht. Es ist auch deutlich, dass der deuteropaulinische Eph keineswegs zwingend nach Ephesus adressiert sein muss und 2Thess nicht an dieselbe Gemeinde, an die Paulus 1Thess geschrieben hat.

Schon weniger selbstverständlich ist die Einsicht, dass die in den Briefen skizzierte *Situation* – auch in orthonymen Texten – eine Konstruktion darstellt, die natürlich tendenziös ist und auch fiktionale Elemente enthalten kann.

So kann man nicht voraussetzen, dass Paulus im Galaterbrief die strittige Frage der Beschneidungsforderung seiner Gegner ‚objektiv' darstellt. Vielmehr ist die Darlegung von der höchst selektiven und tendenziösen biographischen Skizze in Gal 1,12–2,21, die die göttliche Autorität und Unabhängigkeit seines Evangeliums und dann die Anerkennung desselben durch die Jerusalemer zeigen will, über die Beschreibung der alternativen Option als ‚anderes Evangelium' (Gal 1,8) und Rückfall in neue Sklaverei (Gal 5,1) bis hin zur Diskreditierung der Gegner als unlauter und leidensscheu (Gal 5,11f.; 6,12f.) eine rhetorisch wirkungsvolle, aber sehr einseitige Konstruktion, aus der sich die tatsächliche Argumentation der Gegner nur noch mit Mühe und ihr wahres Bild noch viel weniger sicher erheben lässt.

WUNT II/138, Tübingen 2001, und M. FRENSCHKOWSKI, Pseudepigraphie und Paulusschule. Gedanken zur Verfasserschaft der Deuteropaulinen, insbesondere der Pastoralbriefe, in: F. W. Horn (Hg.), Das Ende des Paulus. Historische, theologische und literaturgeschichtliche Aspekte, BZNW 106, Berlin/New York 2001, 239–272.

Da ein Brief nur eine Seite eines Diskurses repräsentiert und die andere Seite uns meist nicht mehr zugänglich ist, steht die historische Rekonstruktion insbesondere der *Gegner* und der von ihnen vertretenen Positionen vor großen Problemen, wenn man nicht annehmen will, dass die ‚Gegner' eines Autors all das ablehnten, was dieser vertritt, und all das vertraten, was dieser kritisiert. Noch komplexer werden die kommunikativen Strukturen, wenn zwischen den adressierten Gemeindegliedern und den bekämpften Gegnern zu differenzieren ist oder gar – wie im 1Kor – innerhalb der Adressatengemeinde mit einem differenzierten Gefüge von Gruppen zu rechnen ist.

Auch in der Auslegung der pseudonymen Briefe wurde in der Forschung oft zu ausschließlich die Autorfiktion (etwa das Paulusbild des Eph oder der Past) beachtet, während der gleichfalls fiktionale Charakter der dargestellten Gegner und der literarisch repräsentierten Gemeindesituation weniger wahrgenommen wurden. Deshalb wurden diese Bilder noch allzu gutgläubig als Abbildung der tatsächlichen Verhältnisse angesehen.

Für die religions- oder theologiegeschichtliche Einordnung eines Briefes ist die Rekonstruktion der Situation und des Gegnerprofils in der Tat unverzichtbar – nur wird diese methodisch viel schwieriger, wenn die Verweise auf Gegner oder die Vorwürfe gegen sie ebenfalls zweifelhaft werden. Dies gilt besonders dort, wo – wie im Fall des Jud und des 2Petr – eine schroffe Polemik vorliegt, die alles andere als eine ‚tatsachentreue' Beschreibung der Lehre oder des Verhaltens der Gegner bieten dürfte. Inwiefern hier zwischen Fiktion und Wirklichkeit noch zu unterscheiden ist, sei dahingestellt, doch ist zunächst das methodische Problem zu erkennen. Erst eine differenzierte Beschreibung der jeweils vorliegenden Konstruktion von Autor, Gegnern und Situation ermöglicht ein präzises Urteil über die Art, die Funktion und die Implikationen der vorliegenden literarischen Gestaltung.

Jud und 2Petr bilden dafür ein außerordentlich interessantes Studienobjekt. Dass es sich im Falle beider Briefe um Pseudepigrapha handelt, kann ich mit weiten Teilen der neueren kritischen Forschung hier ohne detaillierte Begründung voraussetzen.[4] Doch weisen beide Schriften trotz ihrer literarischen Verwandtschaft große Unterschiede auf hinsichtlich der Wahl des Pseudonyms, aber auch hinsichtlich der Art und Dichte der Durchführung der jeweiligen Autorfiktion. Während 2Petr als ‚Testament' des Apostels und Augenzeugen vielleicht – neben den Past – die kühnste Form einer ‚literarischen Fälschung' im Neuen Testament bildet, erscheint die Wahl des Pseudonyms und die Durchführung der Autorfiktion im Jud eher

---

[4] Zur detaillierten Begründung verweise ich auf meinen 2010 in der Reihe ThHK erscheinenden Kommentar: J. FREY, Der Judasbrief. Der zweite Petrusbrief, ThHK 16/2, Leipzig 2010. Im Folgenden kann ich mich daher auf knappe Hinweise und sehr selektive Literaturangaben beschränken.

„schüchtern".[5] Die Differenzen der jeweiligen Autorfiktion und die Probleme der ebenfalls differierenden Bilder der Situation und der bekämpften Gegner sollen im Folgenden erörtert werden, um die Funktion und die Implikationen der vorliegenden pseudonymen Legitimationsstrategien präziser zu erfassen.

2. Autorfiktion und Gegnerbild im Judasbrief

Der Jud ist einer der rätselhaftesten Texte des Neuen Testaments. Das kurze Schreiben bietet immense textliche und interpretatorische Probleme. Gravierende Fragen stellen sich auch hinsichtlich seiner Verfasserangabe, wenn man diese als ein Pseudonym einzuschätzen hat: In diesem Falle stellt sich nämlich sofort die Frage, warum der tatsächliche Autor im Vergleich zu den anderen neutestamentlichen Pseudonymen wie Paulus, Petrus, Jakobus oder Matthäus eine eher randständige, relativ unbedeutende Figur zur Autorisierung seines Schreibens gewählt hat: den ‚Herrenbruder' Judas. Und warum führt er diese nicht als ἀδελφὸς τοῦ κυρίου oder ἀδελφὸς (τοῦ) Ἰησοῦ, sondern ‚bescheidener' als ἀδελφὸς ... Ἰακώβου ein? Was bedeutet die Wahl dieses Pseudonyms für die Zuordnung des Schreibens zu einem spezifischen Milieu und zu theologischen Diskursen im frühen Christentum, und welche Tragweite hat die Form und Durchführung der pseudonymen Konstruktion für die Interpretation des Schreibens?

2.1 Die Wahl des Pseudonyms: Der Herrenbruder
Judas als ‚zweiter Jakobus'

Die Frage, welcher Judas in der nachträglichen Überschrift ΙΟΥΔΑ und in der *superscriptio* Ἰούδας Ἰησοῦ Χριστοῦ δοῦλος, ἀδελφὸς δὲ Ἰακώβου gemeint ist, erscheint heute relativ unproblematisch. Da eine Näherbestimmung des genannten Jakobus fehlt, muss dieser eine den Adressaten bekannte Gestalt gewesen sein, wenn sie die Einführung des fiktiven Autors verstehen sollten. Da aber im frühen Christentum nur ein einziges Brüderpaar mit den Namen Judas und Jakobus bekannt ist und der Herrenbruder Jakobus ‚der Gerechte' (Eus.h.e. 2,23,4 u.ö.) als Leiter der Jerusalemer Gemeinde und schließlich durch sein Martyrium (Eus.h.e. 2,23; Flav.Jos.Ant. 20,200f.) breiteste Bekanntheit erlangte, kann nur die-

---

[5] So die Charakterisierung bei P. VIELHAUER, Geschichte der urchristlichen Literatur, Berlin 1975, 593.

ser gemeint sein. Damit ist Judas der in Mk 6,3 unter den Brüdern Jesu an dritter, in Mt 13,55 an vierter Stelle erwähnte ‚Herrenbruder'.[6]

Von diesem Judas erfahren wir im NT nichts Näheres. Paulus erwähnt in 1Kor 9,5 eine Missionstätigkeit der Brüder Jesu, ohne Judas eigens zu nennen. Jakobus, der zur Zeit der Abfassung des 1Kor die Leitungsfunktion in der Jerusalemer Urgemeinde innehatte, kann dabei nicht in erster Linie im Blick sein. Dies spricht indirekt für eine missionarische Wirksamkeit der anderen Herrenbrüder, von der aber wenig bekannt ist. Julius Africanus berichtet über das Wirken der ‚Herrenverwandten' (δεσπόσυνοι) in Palästina (Eus.h.e. 1,7,14).[7] Die erste konkretere Nachricht über Judas stammt von dem judenchristlichen Autor Hegesipp (um 180 n. Chr.), der eine Episode aus der letzten Phase der Regierung Domitians berichtet (bei Eus.h.e. 3,20,1–6; vgl. 3,25,5f.), derzufolge zwei Großneffen Jesu, Enkel des Judas, als Davididen denunziert und aus Galiläa nach Rom vor den Kaiser geführt worden seien. Dieser habe sie nach dem Verhör als ‚gemeine Leute' freigelassen, sie aber hätten als Herrenverwandte und Bekenner bis in die Zeit Trajans gelebt. So problematisch diese Episode im Einzelnen sein mag, bietet sie doch einen Hinweis auf die Bedeutung des Herrenbruders Judas, der aber – wenn seine Enkel im Zentrum der Episode stehen – zur fraglichen Zeit bereits nicht mehr gelebt haben dürfte. Explizit begegnet die Identifikation des Autors mit dem Herrenbruder zum ersten Mal bei Origenes (comm. in Matt. 10,17), doch dürfte sie bereits für die ersten Leser des Schreibens erkennbar gewesen sein.[8]

Bis in die Anfänge der neuzeitlichen Exegese wurde der Autor des Schreibens allerdings anders bestimmt: Wohl schon seit Tertullian, der den Autor als „Apostel" bezeichnet (De cultu feminarum 1,3), sah man in dem genannten Judas einen Jünger Jesu und Apostel aus dem Zwölferkreis. Dazu identifizierte man den Autor mit dem in den Apostellisten Lk 6,14–16 und Apg 1,13 aufgeführten Ἰούδας Ἰακώβου.[9] Dieser begegnet in den bei-

---

[6] Andere in der Forschung vorgeschlagene Identifikationen sind hier nicht zu erwähnen. S. dazu meinen in Anm. 4 genannten Kommentar.

[7] Dazu R. J. BAUCKHAM, Jude and the Relatives of Jesus in the Early Church, Edinburgh 1990, 61ff.

[8] Dies ist vor allem dann anzunehmen, wenn Jud 1 bereits den Jakobusbrief als bekannt voraussetzt, was durch die auffällige Wortstellung Ἰησοῦ Χριστοῦ δοῦλος nahegelegt wird. Auf dem Hintergrund von Jak 1,1 wird die Nennung des Absenders in Jud 1 eindeutig. S. dazu bereits J. FREY, Der Judasbrief zwischen Judentum und Hellenismus, in: W. Kraus / K.-W. Niebuhr (Hg., unter Mitwirkung von L. Doering), Frühjudentum und Neues Testament. Mit einem Anhang zum Corpus Judaeo-Hellenisticum Novi Testamenti, WUNT 162, Tübingen 2003, 180–210.

[9] Dabei wurde der Genitiv dann statt der normalen und nächstliegenden Auflösung „Sohn des Jakobus" im (zwar belegten, aber sehr unüblichen) Sinn „Bruder des Jakobus" verstanden.

den genannten Apostellisten an der Stelle des Thaddäus aus Mt 10,3 und Mk 3,18. Im Versuch, diese Listen zu harmonisieren, sah man seit Origenes (praefatio in Romanos) in diesem „Judas Thaddäus" eine einzige Person, die dann mit dem Bruder (bzw. in späterer Sicht dem Cousin) Jesu namens Judas identifiziert wurde. Da gleichzeitig auch der Zwölferjünger Jakobus, Sohn des Alphäus (Mk 3,18par), mit dem gleichnamigen Bruder (bzw. Cousin) Jesu identifiziert wurde, konnte auch der Judas aus dem Zwölferkreis als „Bruder des Jakobus" gelten.[10] Diese Tradition schlägt sich in Erweiterungen der Überschrift des Judasbriefs in der handschriftlichen Tradition nieder, in denen das Schreiben gelegentlich als „Brief des heiligen Apostels Judas" o.ä. überschrieben wird.[11] Diese Konstruktion der ‚Apostolizität' – nicht die Zuschreibung an den Herrenbruder – ist bei Martin Luther und den Humanisten vorausgesetzt und z.T. kritisiert; sie wurde im Tridentinum dogmatisch festgeschrieben und erst relativ spät von der Kritik angegriffen. In der Einleitungswissenschaft wurde sie (verbunden mit der Annahme der ‚Echtheit') erst 1836 von K. A. Credner im Sinne des Bezugs auf den Herrenbruder korrigiert.[12]

Diese alte Sicht der ‚Apostolizität' spielt heute jedoch keine Rolle mehr. Wenn von ‚Echtheit' oder Authentizität die Rede ist, so ist die Abfassung durch den ‚Herrenbruder' Judas gemeint, der in der *superscriptio* bezeichnet sein soll.

Die tatsächliche Zuschreibung des Textes an einen palästinischen Judenchristen und eine relativ frühe Datierung hat zuletzt Richard Bauckham mit großer Gelehrsamkeit zu stützen versucht,[13] und einige, v.a. evangelikale, Kommentatoren sind ihm darin gefolgt,[14] doch konnte er die Gründe, die für eine nachapostolische Situierung (vgl. V.17f.) und gegen den galiläischen Herrenbruder sprechen,[15] nicht wirklich entkräften. Die Mehrheit

---

[10] Für die Westkirche wurde diese Identifikation ebenso wie die Annahme der Herrenvetternschaft und Apostolizität des Judas durch Hieronymus zur Anerkennung geführt. Vgl. dazu T. ZAHN, Brüder und Vettern Jesu, Forschungen zur Geschichte des christlichen Kanons VI, Leipzig 1900, 225–364 (322ff.; zur Kritik der Judas-These a.a.O. 344ff.).

[11] So Cod. L und abweichend 049 sowie zahlreiche Minuskeln. S. die Zusammenstellung zur Inscriptio bei T. WASSERMAN, The Epistle of Jude. Its Text and Transmission, CB.NT 43, Stockholm 2006, 132f.

[12] K. A. CREDNER, Einleitung in das Neue Testament, Halle 1836, 612. Wesentliche Anregungen gab dazu Johann Gottfried Herder in seiner Schrift ‚Über die Briefe zweener Brüder Jesu' von 1775. Zu dieser Schrift s. J. FREY, Herder und die Evangelien, in: M. Keßler / V. Leppin (Hg.), Johann Gottfried Herder. Aspekte seines Lebenswerks, AKG 92, Berlin/New York 2005, 47–91 (59–61).

[13] R. J. BAUCKHAM, Jude. 2 Peter, WBC 50, Waco 1983; ders., Jude and the Relatives (s. Anm. 7).

[14] S. zuletzt die Kommentare von T. R. SCHREINER, 1, 2 Peter, Jude, The New American Commentary, Nashville 2003, und P. H. DAVIDS, The Letters of 2 Peter and Jude, The Pillar New Testament Commentary, Grand Rapids/Cambridge 2006.

[15] Hier ist v.a. auf das hohe sprachliche und auch rhetorische Niveau zu verweisen; dazu – paradoxerweise in Verbindung mit einer Annahme der ‚Echtheit' – J. D. CHARLES, Literary Artifice in the Epistle of Jude, ZNW 82 (1991), 106–124; ders., Literary Strategy in the Epistle of Jude, Scranton u.a. 1993.

der kritischen Kommentatoren ist daher nach wie vor von der pseudonymen Ausgestaltung des Schreibens und einer Ansetzung nicht vor Ende des 1. Jh. überzeugt.[16]

Auffällig ist jedoch die Einführung des fiktiven Autors: Dessen Verhältnis zu Jesus wird mit der Wendung Ἰησοῦ Χριστοῦ δοῦλος bezeichnet, während der Status als ‚Herrenbruder' nur in Relation zum ‚Herrenbruder' Jakobus durch ἀδελφὸς δὲ Ἰακώβου markiert wird. Aber auch die Wendung Ἰησοῦ Χριστοῦ δοῦλος verbindet Judas mit Jakobus, insofern die Wortstellung hier exakt der *superscriptio* des Jakobusbriefs entspricht.[17]

Grundlegend sind daher die Bezüge zum Jakobusbrief:[18] Die Rede von den Irrlehrern als ψυχικοί Jud 19 erinnert an Jak 3,15, wo die Weisheit anderer Lehrer als ψυχική gekennzeichnet wird; Jud 22f. knüpft an den Schluss der Paränese Jak 5,19f. an, und Jud 21 erinnert zumindest an Jak 2,12ff. Beiden Schreiben fehlt ein formeller Briefschluss, beide sind paränetisch ausgerichtet und operieren mit *exempla* aus der biblischen Tradition. Beide zeigen eine intensive Kenntnis jüdischer Traditionen und Interpretationstechniken, beide sind zugleich in relativ guter Koine verfasst. Beide benutzen vielfältige Stilmittel und ein reiches Vokabular mit relativ dichten Übereinstimmungen.[19]

Diese Entsprechungen ließen sich evtl. aus einer gemeinsamen jüdischen bzw. judenchristlichen ‚Matrix' erklären, doch sind die Anklänge am Anfang und am Ende sowie das Fehlen eines brieflichen Schlusses bemerkenswert und legen eine bewusste Anknüpfung an den Jak bzw. die durch ihn repräsentierte Tradition nahe. Damit verweist auch die Einführung des Autors als „Bruder des Jakobus" nicht allein (bzw. nur noch indirekt) auf die Person, sondern zugleich oder gar primär auf den diesem Jakobus zugeschriebenen Brief. Der Autor präsentiert sich als Bruder des aus seinem Brief bekannten Jakobus.

Die Tatsache, dass sich der Autor nur als „Bruder des Jakobus" und nicht als „Bruder des Herrn" einführt, hat vielfältige Überlegungen ausgelöst. Unter Voraussetzung der Orthonymie konnte diese Einführung als ein

---

[16] S. auch die Einleitungen, zuletzt U. SCHNELLE, Einleitung in das Neue Testament, UTB 1830, Göttingen ⁶2007, 452–460; M. GIELEN, Der Judasbrief, in: M. Ebner / S. Schreiber (Hg.), Einleitung in das Neue Testament, Stuttgart 2008, 552–558.

[17] Jak 1,1: Ἰάκωβος θεοῦ καὶ κυρίου Ἰησοῦ Χριστοῦ δοῦλος. Im Unterschied dazu nennt sich Paulus in seinen Präskripten δοῦλος Χριστοῦ Ἰησοῦ (Röm 1,1; vgl. Phil 1,1).

[18] Dazu CHARLES, Literary Strategy (s. Anm. 15), 74–77.

[19] Charles hat im Vokabular abgesehen von Präpositionen, Pronomina, Partikeln und εἶναι bei insgesamt 227 Vokabeln 93 Entsprechungen mit dem Vokabular des Jak festgestellt, davon begegnen 27 Lexeme in beiden Schreiben mehr als zweimal. „Aside from Jude – 2 Peter and Colossians – Ephesians comparisons, the verbal correspondence in James and Jude, considering the brevity of the latter, is unmatched anywhere else in the NT" (a.a.O. 77).

besonderer Ausdruck von Demut oder Bescheidenheit gelten[20] – ein Aspekt, der dann umgekehrt wieder als Argument für die Authentizität gewertet wurde.[21] Andere Autoren vermuteten, dass die Berufung auf die leibliche Verwandtschaft mit Jesus als anstößig angesehen und deshalb vermieden worden wäre.[22] Doch scheint dies zu unhistorisch gedacht, in Anbetracht der späteren Tradition über die ‚Herrenverwandten' im palästinischen Judenchristentum, die sich durchaus auf das gegebene Verwandtschaftsverhältnis bezogen und daraus ihre Autorität ableiteten. Die Zuschreibung des Jud an den ‚Bruder des Jakobus' ist nur im Sinne der Anknüpfung an die Jakobustradition bzw. den Jak zu erklären. Ein Ausdruck der Demut liegt darin nicht vor, vielmehr wird durch die Epitheta „Jesu Christi Knecht und Bruder des Jakobus" eine spezifische Autorität beansprucht: die Autorität eines christlichen Verkündigers, zugleich aber eine Autorität, die sich aus der Verbindung mit der Kerngestalt der palästinischen Urgemeinde herleitet. Der Autor nimmt insofern eine ‚abgeleitete' Autorität in Anspruch.

Eine solche Legitimationsstruktur ist freilich nur dann plausibel, wenn der hier gemeinte Judas den Adressaten(gemeinden) *nicht* persönlich bekannt war. Nichts deutet auf bestehende oder frühere Beziehungen zu Judas oder einer von ihm ausgehenden Mission hin. Bestünden solche Beziehungen, dann hätte der reale Autor, auch wenn er kein Schüler oder ‚Nachlassverwalter' des Judas wäre, wohl in irgendeiner Form an sie angeknüpft. Doch wird die Autorität des Judas als einer Gestalt der Zeit des Anfangs allein über den bekannteren Jakobus vermittelt. Dieser Bezug legitimiert Judas „gewissermaßen als einen zweiten Jakobus, als eine ebenfalls maßgebliche Gestalt des Anfangs".[23] Die Wahl des Pseudonyms und seine Zuordnung ist daher gleichermaßen ein Zeichen der Wirkung des

---

[20] S. etwa G. WOHLENBERG, Der erste und zweite Petrusbrief. Der Judasbrief, KNT 15, Leipzig 1915, 279: „aus Bescheidenheit"; s. bereits Clemens von Alexandrien, adumbrationes in ep. Iudae: *Judas frater filiorum Joseph exstans valde religiosus, et cum sciret propinquitatem domini, non tamen dicit se ipsum fratrem eius esse ...* (zit. n. WOHLENBERG, ebd.).

[21] So etwa bei BAUCKHAM, Jude. 2 Peter (s. Anm. 13), 14: „The description of Jud as ‚brother of James' only (v 1) is much more easily explicable on the hypothesis of authenticity than on that of pseudepigraphy."

[22] So Wolfgang Schrage in: H. BALZ / W. SCHRAGE, Die katholischen Briefe, NTD 10, Göttingen [11]1973, 227. Theologisch grundsätzlicher meinte W. GRUNDMANN, Der Brief des Judas und der zweite Petrusbrief, ThHK 15, Berlin 1974, 24, dass „die Herrenstellung des Christus Jesus" Judas „allen verwandtschaftlichen Beziehungen entnommen" hätte. Abwegig ist die Annahme von H. KOESTER, ΓΝΩΜΑΙ ΔΙΑΦΟΡΑΙ, ZThK 65 (1968), 160–203 (181), dass damit die wahre Identität des Autors verschleiert werden solle.

[23] So A. VÖGTLE, Der Judasbrief. Der 2. Petrusbrief, EKK XXII, Solothurn u.a. 1994, 17.

Jakobus bzw. des Jakobusbriefs wie auch ein Indiz dafür, dass sich der reale Autor der ‚nachapostolischen' Situation, in der er schrieb, bewusst war.[24]

Zugleich erklärt sich das Fehlen konkreter Autor-Adressaten-Beziehungen und das völlige Zurücktreten der Person des Judas nach V.1 nur, wenn man – wie hier vorausgesetzt – das Schreiben als ein pseudonym konstruiertes versteht.

2.2 Die brüchige Durchführung der Autorfiktion

Nach V.1 tritt der pseudonyme Autor Judas nicht mehr hervor. Nach seiner Einführung in der *superscriptio* fehlt jeder weitere explizite Bezug auf ihn, die ‚Familie Jesu' oder den palästinisch-judenchristlichen ‚Standpunkt' des Autors. Die Adressaten werden nicht mit einer Mission der Herrenbrüder in Verbindung gebracht, und der Briefschluss enthält keine persönlichen Grüße, sondern eine Doxologie (V.24f.). Die starke Verwendung jüdischer Traditionen, v.a. des Henochbuches, wurde zwar oft als Argument für eine palästinisch-jüdische Perspektive angeführt, doch können diese Traditionen – zumal in griechischer Sprache – ebenso gut in Kleinasien und in anderen Regionen der Diaspora rezipiert worden sein, wie z.B. die vermutlich griechische Abfassung des 2Hen zeigt. Auch die Verwendung des Terminus δεσπότης als Gottes- oder Christusprädikat (V.4) bietet keine Brücke zur Bezeichnung der ‚Herrenverwandten' als δεσποσύνοι, der die Autorschaft des Judas stützen könnte.

In der Anrede an die Adressaten in V.3.5.12.17.20–23 erscheint der Verfasser als eine autoritative Gestalt, die über den „ein für allemal" gegebenen Glauben (V.3) Bescheid weiß und aus der damit gegebenen Autorität zu mahnen vermag (V.4). Doch spricht ‚Judas' – im Unterschied zum fiktiven Autor des 2Petr – die Situation seiner Adressaten aus der Perspektive eines Zeitgenossen an. Die Irrlehrer, die als Anlass der Abfassung genannt werden (V.4), haben sich schon in die Gemeinde(n) der Adressaten eingeschlichen. Ihr sündhaftes Tun wird als gegenwärtig beschrieben (V.8.11), und ihre Präsenz bei den Gemeindemählern (V.12) wird vorausgesetzt. Diese Zeitgenossenschaft und Kenntnis der Situation der Adressaten wird durch die *superscriptio* für den fiktiven Autor Judas reklamiert, ohne dass die Spannung, die zu der Einführung des Herrenbruders als einer Autorität der Anfangszeit besteht, reflektiert würde.

Diese Spannung zeigt sich an einer Stelle, an der das Schreiben fast aus der gewählten Fiktion herausgleitet: ‚Judas' ermahnt seine Adressaten in V.17, sich der Worte zu „erinnern", „die im voraus von den Aposteln unse-

---

[24] Dies zeigt sich ja auch in Aussagen wie Jud 3, Jud 20 und besonders Jud 17. S. dazu F. HAHN, Randbemerkungen zum Judasbrief, ThZ 37 (1981), 209–218 (209f.).

res Herrn Jesus Christus gesprochen wurden". Die Apostel bzw. zumindest ihre Prophetie sind offenbar eine Größe der Vergangenheit. Die Weissagung des Auftretens von „Spöttern" „am Ende der Zeit" (V.18) soll aber auf die gegenwärtig wirksamen, bereits aufgetretenen Gegner bezogen werden. Die Stellung des ‚Judas', der ja als Zeitgenosse sprach, zu den Aposteln, die ja ihrerseits Zeitgenossen des Jakobus waren, bleibt unklar. Nichts lässt erkennen, dass ‚Judas' in seinem Rückblick auf ‚die Apostel' bzw. ihre Weissagung als alter Mann oder in Todesnähe (wie ‚Petrus' in 2Petr 1,14f.), evtl. gar als ein Übriggebliebener der ersten Generation (vgl. Joh 21,22f.) gilt. Die Zeitstruktur des Schreibens ist also ‚brüchig', und der Autor lässt mit dieser brüchigen Zeitstruktur einen ‚nachapostolischen' Standpunkt erkennen; er ‚verrät' sich zumindest implizit als Angehöriger der dritten Generation des Christentums.

Autoren, die Jud als authentisches Schreiben des Herrenbruders einer relativ frühen Zeit der Kirche zuordnen wollen, haben Mühe, dieser Konsequenz zu entgehen. So wird z.B. recht ‚sophistisch' argumentiert, die Formulierung besage lediglich, dass die Instruktion der Apostel in der Vergangenheit liege, während sie selbst zur Zeit der Abfassung des Schreibens noch am Leben sein könnten, oder gar, dass die Wendung ἔλεγον ὑμῖν (V.18) darauf hindeute, dass die ursprünglichen Adressaten der Unterweisung noch am Leben und unter den Adressaten des Briefes seien. Im Übrigen weise die Formulierung nicht auf ein Kollektiv der (zwölf?) Apostel, vielmehr seien hier nur die Apostel gemeint, die die Kirche(n) gründeten, an die Judas schreibt.[25] Freilich lässt die Formulierung nicht erkennen, dass spezifische Personen aus dem Zwölferkreis oder aus einem weiteren Kreis gemeindegründender Missionare im Blick wären.[26] Vielmehr vermittelt die gebrauchte Formulierung gerade keine konkrete Vorstellung von einzelnen Personen der apostolischen Zeit mehr, sondern führt ‚die Apostel unseres Herrn Jesus Christus' als ein einheitliches Kollektiv an. Diese Rede von ‚den Aposteln' unterscheidet sich insofern nicht nur von der paulinischen Verwendung des Terminus ἀπόστολος, sondern auch von der lukanischen Rede von den ‚Zwölf' als Augenzeugen und Garanten der ursprünglichen Überlieferung, sie besitzt hingegen enge Parallelen in Eph 2,20; 3,5; 1Clem 42,1ff. oder bei Ignatius (Trall 2,2; 3,1; Magn 6,1), d.h. in Schriften der dritten oder gar vierten christlichen Generation, in denen das Bild der Apostel fast aller geschichtlichen Konkretionen enthoben und im Rückblick verklärt ist und so zu einer unangefochtenen Norm des Anfangs werden kann. Jud hat in seinem Apostelbild und im Rückbezug auf das von ‚den Aposteln' Vorhergesagte ebenso wie in der Rede von dem „ein für allemal" überlieferten Glauben Teil an dem Ringen um die ‚Apostolizität' des Glaubens in nachapostolischer Zeit.[27]

---

[25] So etwa die Argumentation bei BAUCKHAM, Jude. 2 Peter (s. Anm. 13), 103f.

[26] Historisch scheinen die Zwölf in Jerusalem recht bald an Bedeutung verloren zu haben, wo dann die Leitungsfunktion bekanntlich an den Herrenbruder Jakobus übergeht. Insofern kann man auch zwischen den Herrenbrüdern und den Mitgliedern des Zwölferkreises kein völlig spannungsfreies Verhältnis voraussetzen.

[27] S. dazu J. FREY, Apostelbegriff, Apostelamt und Apostolizität. Neutestamentliche Perspektiven zur Frage nach der ‚Apostolizität' der Kirche, in: T. Schneider / G. Wenz (Hg.), Das kirchliche Amt in apostolischer Nachfolge, I: Grundlagen und Grundfragen

Die Autorfiktion im Jud ist also relativ unbetont und nicht konsequent durchgehalten. Offenbar entspringt die Autorität, die der reale Autor in Anspruch nimmt, um in der gegebenen Situation vor den ‚Spöttern' zu warnen, in erster Linie der Schrift und den in ihr gegebenen Beipielen sowie – als deren Klimax – der Prophetie Henochs[28] und der damit in Einklang befindlichen Ankündigung der Apostel. Die als Pseudonym gewählte Gestalt des Herrenbruders Judas bietet dagegen nur eine relativ schwache Autorisation, und sie wird somit auch nur ‚schüchtern' zur Legitimation des Schreibens genützt – ihr primärer ‚Zweck' scheint eher in der Zuordnung zu der durch ‚Jakobus' bzw. den Jak markierten Tradition zu liegen.

2.3 Die Gemeindesituation und das polemisch angereicherte Gegnerbild

Die Näherbestimmung der damit verbundenen Anliegen und der theologiegeschichtlichen Stellung des Autors bereitet jedoch große Schwierigkeiten, ebenso die Einordnung der Gegner, die nur mit großer Vorsicht und beträchtlichen Unsicherheiten vorgenommen werden kann.

Methodisch kommt es darauf an zu erkennen, dass in einem so polemischen Schreiben auch das Bild der Gegner Bestandteil der fiktionalen Gestaltung ist und nicht als exakte Beschreibung des realen Wirkens der bekämpften Personen fungieren kann. Zwischen den literarisch dargestellten Gegnern und ihrem realen Pendant in der Welt der Adressaten ist grundsätzlich zu unterscheiden[29] – ungeachtet der Frage, ob sich das Bild der realen Gegner historisch noch rekonstruieren lässt.

Rhetorisch ist zu beobachten, dass der gesamte Brief in einer klaren Entgegensetzung die ‚berufenen' (V.1) und ‚geliebten' (V.17.20) Adressaten (V.17.20: ὑμεῖς, vgl. V.2.3) und die nirgendwo direkt angesprochenen noch überhaupt ‚namentlich' genannten (V.4: τινες ἄνθρωποι, V.8.10.12.16.19: οὗτοι) Gegner schroff voneinander scheidet. Während die einen von Gott geliebt sind und bis zum Ende bewahrt werden (V.1.24), steht über den anderen das eschatologische Verdammungsurteil

---

(DiKi 12), Freiburg i. Brsg./Göttingen 2004, 91–188 (174–176); s. dort 99ff. zu 1Clem und Ign; 166ff. zu Eph.

[28] Die in Jud 14f. zitierte Gerichtsankündigung aus 1Hen 1,3c–9 bietet eine Zusammenfassung alttestamentlicher Theophanietexte wie Dtn 33,1–3, Jer 25,31 und Mi 1,3f.; s. dazu G. W. E. NICKELSBURG, 1 Enoch 1. A Commentary on the Book of 1 Enoch, Chapters 1–36; 81–108, hg. v. K. Baltzer, Minneapolis 2001, 143.

[29] S. dazu A. DU TOIT, Vilification in Early Christian Epistolography, Bib 75 (1994), 403–412 (404): „The depiction of opponents ... is a construct of the author. We should therefore differentiate between the ‚encoded opponents' and their real-life counterparts." Der Versuch von F. WISSE, The Epistle of Jude in the History of Heresiology, in: M. Krause (Hg.), Essays on the Nag Hammadi Texts (FS Böhlig), Leiden 1972, 133–143, den Bezug auf konkrete Gegner ganz in Abrede zu stellen, geht m.E. allerdings zu weit.

schon fest (V.4), wie es der Autor dann aus den biblischen Beispielen (V.5–7.11) und insbesondere der Prophetie Henochs (V.14f.) belegt. Auch im Schlussteil rät V.22f.[30] nur zu einer ‚seelsorgerlichen' Bemühung um die Gefährdeten, nicht aber zu einer Beschäftigung mit den Irrlehrern selbst, deren Verderben ja schon feststeht.

Die historische Rekonstruktion der *Situation* kann bei der relativ beiläufigen, aber hinreichend konkreten Aussage über die Gemeindemähler (ἀγάπαι) in V.12 ansetzen.[31] Wenn man diese ernst nehmen darf, ist von der Präsenz der Gegner in Veranstaltungen der Gemeinde (V.4)[32] und bei diesen Mählern auszugehen – eine faktische Trennung ist also noch nicht erfolgt. Man wird von hier aus weiter annehmen müssen, dass auch die hier bekämpften und rhetorisch von den Adressaten ‚himmelweit' geschiedenen Gegner sich selbst noch als Gemeindeglieder und ihr eigenes Denken als einen legitimen Entwurf christlicher Existenz verstanden haben dürften. Mit der pauschalen Etikettierung als „Gottlose" (V.4.15; vgl. V.18)[33] und „Spötter" (V.18) dürften sie selbst nicht einverstanden gewesen sein.

Zwischen dem Selbstverständnis der Gegner und der schroff polemischen Aburteilung durch den Autor ist also mit einer tief greifenden Diskrepanz zu rechnen. Das Problem verschärft sich dadurch, dass die Polemik in diesem Schreiben so scharf ist und für eine Argumentation oder überhaupt eine Sinnesänderung der Gegner keinerlei Raum lässt. Vielmehr werden diese ‚gewissen Leute' (V.4), die für die Adressaten offenbar erkennbar sein sollen, in einer fast den ganzen Brief beherrschenden polemi-

---

[30] Die textlichen Probleme dieser Passage sind für die hier erörterte Frage nicht relevant.

[31] Dabei ist unwesentlich, ob es sich bei den mit ἀγάπαι bezeichneten Mählern um ‚eucharistische' Mähler oder um den ersten Beleg der später so genannten nicht-eucharistischen Agapen handelt – der Sprachgebrauch des kurzen Jud erlaubt hier kaum eine Entscheidung. Wesentlich ist aber, dass der Autor die Teilnahme der Irrlehrer für eine ‚Schamlosigkeit' hält (d.h., sie gehören nach seinem Urteil nicht mehr dazu) und zugleich für eine Gefährdung der Gemeinde.

[32] Die Formulierung suggeriert, dass sich die Gegner den Gemeinden von außen angeschlossen haben. Doch darf man daraus nicht gleich auf Wanderprediger schließen. Der Terminus παρεισέδυσαν („sie haben sich eingeschlichen") könnte auch ein polemischer Topos sein. Die Aussage insinuiert Heimlichkeit und Unrechtmäßigkeit; sie fungiert dazu, die Gegner von den Adressaten zu distanzieren. Vgl. dazu WISSE, Epistle (s. Anm. 29), 143.

[33] Der Terminus ἀσεβεῖς bzw. davon abgeleitete Verbalformen haben im Jud leitmotivische Funktion. Sie dienen zur durchgehenden Etikettierung der bekämpften Gegner und begegnen in besonderer Dichte in dem Zitat aus 1Hen 1,9 in V.15, wo zweimal das Nomen und einmal das Verbum verwendet wird und am Ende klimaktisch den Gegnern das Etikett „Gottlose" angeheftet wird. Von hier aus wird das Nomen schon in V.4 programmatisch verwendet, außerdem klingt es in einem Derivat in V.18 nach.

schen Komposition als paradigmatische Gottlose und Sünder präsentiert, über die das eschatologische Verdammungsurteil unabänderlich feststeht. Dabei verwendet der Autor in hohem Maße polemische Stereotypen,[34] so dass Grund zum Zweifel besteht, ob der so bezeichnete Sachverhalt im Denken und Wirken der Gegner tatsächlich Anhalt hat oder nur dem fiktionalen Gegnerbild des Autors zugehört.

Auch V.22f. dürfte insoweit auswertbar sein, dass die Gegner in den Gemeinden der Adressaten Einfluss und Anhänger gewonnen und manche Gemeindeglieder ‚infiziert' haben. Durch die massive Diskreditierung der Gegner will der Autor seine Adressaten veranlassen, sich von diesen Leuten im Denken und Lebenswandel zu distanzieren – und wohl auch eine Trennung in der Gemeinde herbeiführen.

Der Vorwurf in V.19, die Gegner verursachten Spaltungen, ist hingegen ein polemischer Angriff, dessen realer Grund im Brief so nicht zu erkennen ist. Wenn der Autor seinerseits die Adressaten zur Distanzierung bewegen will, dann ist der Sachverhalt eher umgekehrt, dass der Autor selbst – subjektiv wohl begründet – eine ‚Spaltung' herbeiführt und dazu rhetorisch alle Mittel aufbietet. Dies zeigt, wie wenig die polemischen Aussagen zur Rekonstruktion der tatsächlichen Streitigkeiten auswertbar sind.

Auch ist klar, dass der Autor selbst sich auf der Seite des ‚einmal überlieferten Glaubens' (V.3) sieht, während die Gegner davon abweichen. Ein von dieser Perspektive unabhängiger, ‚neutraler' Blick auf die Situation ist nicht zu gewinnen. Hier liegt das methodische Problem.

Eine Reihe von Aussagen erscheinen sehr deutlich als polemische Topoi. Hierzu gehört die Etikettierung als „Gottlose" (V.4.15f.), Lästerer (V.8.10) und „Spötter" (V.18), Verleugner des einen Gebieters und des Herrn Jesus Christus (V.4), die die „Herrenmacht" verwerfen (V.8). Mit der abschließenden Denunziation der Gegner als (bloße) „Psychiker", „die den Geist nicht haben" (V.19), wird ihnen nicht nur ein (elitärer?) Geistbesitz, sondern das Christsein überhaupt abgesprochen (was dann auch ihre Teilnahme an den Gemeindemählern illegitim erscheinen lässt).

Ein polemischer Topos ist sehr wahrscheinlich auch die *moralische Disqualifizierung* der Gegner: Sie leben nach ihren gottlosen Begierden (V.16.18), verkehren Gottes Gnade in Ausschweifung (V.4), bringen Schändliches hervor (V.13), beflecken das Fleisch (V.8) und führen auch andere zur Befleckung (V.23).

Topisch sind auch Vorwürfe, die sich auf die *Worte der Gegner* oder ihr Wirken in der Gemeinde beziehen: Sie reden überheblich (V.16) und murren bzw. widersprechen Gott (V.16; vgl. V.11); sie handeln zu ihrem Vorteil (V.12.16) und damit unlauter und bringen nicht die zu erwartende Frucht (V.12), sondern liefern als ‚Klippen' (σπιλάδες) andere der Gefahr des Schiffbruchs aus (V.12).

---

[34] Zu der Liste der polemischen Stereotypen s. DU TOIT, Vilification (s. Anm. 29), der folgende Bereiche nennt: „1. Hypocrisy and falseness … 2. Obscure, shadowy characters … 3. Sorcery … 4. Inflated self-esteem … 5. Moral depravity … 6. A perversive influence … 7. Associated with dubious historical characters … 8. Prone to judgment … 9. Ludicrous characters" (405–410).

Fast alle dieser Vorwürfe besitzen Parallelen in anderen Texten, die abweichende Gruppen polemisch angreifen, könnten also zumindest in gewissem Maße polemische Hülsen sein, die zur Disqualifikation der Gegner verwandt werden, ohne der Lehre oder dem Lebenswandel der Gegner tatsächlich zu entsprechen.[35]

Ein individuelles Profil der Gegner zeigt sich am ehesten dort, wo Aussagen nicht in die polemischen Stereotypen passen. Schwer einzuordnen ist hier der Vorwurf in V.8, die Gegner seien „Träumer". Besonders auffällig und relativ eigentümlich ist ebenfalls in V.8 die Aussage, die Gegner lästerten die δόξαι, d.h. Engelmächte, so dass manches dafür spricht, dass wir hier dem Profil der Gegner am nächsten kommen. Die theologiegeschichtliche Einordnung der Gegner ist auf diesem Hintergrund jedoch äußerst schwierig. Viele der älteren Einordnungsversuche leiden gerade an der ungenügenden Berücksichtigung des Sachverhalts, dass im Gegnerbild des Jud massiv mit polemischen Topoi gearbeitet wird und dass gerade die ‚moralischen' Vorwürfe dazu gehören:

Die lange geläufige Einordnung der Gegner als *Gnostiker*,[36] oft inhaltlich mit dem Gedanken des Libertinismus und der Annahme verbotener sexueller Praktiken verbunden,[37] wurde in der Forschung mit Recht weithin aufgegeben,[38] zumal auch der Vorwurf

---

[35] Vgl. auch H. PAULSEN, Der Zweite Petrusbrief und der Judasbrief, KEK 17/2, Göttingen 1992, 46; W. BROSEND, The Letter of Jude. A Rhetoric of Excess or an Excess of Rhetoric?, Interpr. 60 (2006), 292–305 (302f.). Zu Kriterien der Unterscheidung zwischen Topik und konkret begründeten Vorwürfen s. auch schon K. BERGER, Die impliziten Gegner. Zur Methode des Erschließens von ‚Gegnern' in neutestamentlichen Texten, in: D. Lührmann (Hg.), Kirche (FS Bornkamm), Tübingen 1980, 373–400 (380).

[36] R. HEILIGENTHAL, Zwischen Henoch und Paulus. Studien zum theologiegeschichtlichen Ort des Judasbriefes, TANZ 6, Tübingen 1992, 133, spricht von einem „Forschungsstereotyp". Die These reicht letztlich bis zu den Kirchenvätern zurück (vgl. K. H. SCHELKLE, Der Judasbrief bei den Kirchenvätern, in: ders., Wort und Schrift, Düsseldorf 1966, 300–308 [302]) und wird dann in der kritischen Auslegung des 19. Jh. aufgenommen. S. zur älteren Forschung F. MAIER, Der Judasbrief. Seine Echtheit, Abfassungszeit und Leser. Ein Beitrag zur Einleitung in die Katholischen Briefe, Freiburg i. Brsg. 1906, 9 Anm. 2; außerdem die Monographie von H. WERDERMANN, Die Irrlehrer des Judas- und des 2. Petrusbriefes, BFChTh 17/6, Gütersloh 1913.

[37] Hier treibt die Phantasie der Ausleger gelegentlich besondere Blüten. Unter den z.T. sehr detaillierten Vorstellungen finden sich „Orgien …, in denen es zu unzüchtigen Handlungen kam" (WERDERMANN, a.a.O. 83), „sexuelle Ausschreitungen nach Art der Sodomiter" (H. WINDISCH / H. PREISKER, Die katholischen Briefe, HNT 15, Tübingen ³1951, 41) und „homosexuelle Ausschweifungen …, bei denen die Irrlehrer ihre ekstatischen Offenbarungen erhalten" (VIELHAUER, Geschichte [s. Anm. 5], 591f.).

[38] Ganz abgesehen davon, dass gnostische Systembildungen erst deutlich im 2. Jh. belegt sind, gibt es im Text des Jud keine spezifischen Hinweise auf einen gnostischen Hintergrund der Gegner. Aus V.19 lässt sich keine gnostische Stufenlehre entnehmen, aus V.18 keine Leugnung der Parusie und aus V.12 keine gnostische Sakramentenlehre. „Murrende, die mit ihrem Schicksal hadern" (V.16), brauchen dies nicht aufgrund gnosti-

des Antinomismus bzw. Libertinismus – wenn er denn auf die realen Gegner appliziert werden kann – nicht einfach auf ein gnostisches Milieu weist.[39] Eine Einordnung der Gegner als *Libertinisten* und *Antinomisten*[40] ist nur dann möglich, wenn man den Vorwurf der Verkehrung der Gnade in Ausschweifung (ἀσέλγεια) in V.4 als wenigstens prinzipiell zutreffend ansehen kann. Dann könnten die Gegner eine evtl. visionär (V.8) oder pneumatisch (V.19) begründete, aber im Sinne des Autors falsch verstandene, vielleicht sogar auf Paulus rückbezogene Freiheitslehre vertreten haben.[41] Allerdings besteht in dieser Interpretation die Gefahr, dass gerade die moralischen Anschuldigungen zum Schlüssel der Rekonstruktion der Gegner werden, obwohl diese am stärksten von polemischen Stereotypen geprägt sein dürften.

Unterscheidet man methodisch zwischen topischen und stärker spezifischen Vorwürfen, dann dürfte der Konfliktpunkt zwischen dem Autor und seinen Gegnern am ehesten hier in V.8–10, d.h. im Streit um die Position und Würde der Engel zu lokalisieren sein, zumal sich hier auch umgekehrt ein besonderes theologisches Anliegen des Autors in seiner Rezeption der Henochtradition (V.6.14f.) und anderer angelologischer Traditionen (V.9) erkennen lässt.

Nach der Analyse von Roman Heiligenthal sind die Gegner popularphilosophisch geprägte, aber zugleich in der Wirkungsgeschichte der paulinischen Theologie stehende Skeptiker,[42] die die Realität der Engelmächte leugneten (V.8), welche der Autor selbst mit großer Vehemenz vertritt. Gerhard Sellin sieht in ihnen wandernde Lehrer, „die pneumatisch bewirkte Ekstasen erleben, bei denen sie über die Engel erhöht werden und wahrscheinlich in historischer Kontinuität zur Theologie des Kol und des Eph Engel und kosmische Mächte verachten. Sie sind unter Berufung auf Paulus Antinomisten und betonen ausschließlich χάρις und Pneuma."[43] Deutlicher greifbar ist nach Peter Müller „einzig der Vorwurf, dass die Gegner κυριότητα δὲ ἀθετοῦσιν δόξας δὲ βλασφημοῦσιν (V.8). Sie handeln vermessen, indem sie Herrschaften und himmlische Mächte verachten, von denen sie freilich nach dem polemischen Urteil des Autors gar nichts verstehen

---

scher Weltverneinung tun, und die Verachtung von Engelwesen ist ebenfalls nicht typisch gnostisch.

[39] Im Gegensatz zu den polemischen Aussagen der Kirchenväter haben nicht zuletzt die Nag-Hammadi-Texte gezeigt, dass die ethische Konsequenz gnostischen Denkens häufiger asketisch und nur gelegentlich auch libertinistisch war. Vgl. G. SELLIN, Die Häretiker des Judasbriefes, ZNW 77 (1986), 206–225 (207 Anm. 5).

[40] So in neuerer Zeit insbesondere die Kommentare von BAUCKHAM, Jude. 2 Peter (s. Anm. 13), 11, SCHREINER, 1, 2 Peter, Jude (s. Anm. 14), 413f., und DAVIDS, The Letters of 2 Peter and Jude (s. Anm. 14), 22.

[41] R. J. BAUCKHAM, The Letter of Jude. An Account of Research, ANRW II 25.5 (1988), 3791–3826 (3811), spricht von „charismatics who, on the basis of their understanding of grace, rejected all moral constraint and authority".

[42] „Für sie war die paulinische Erlösungslehre eine Möglichkeit, ihre skeptizistische Grundhaltung zu überwinden und gleichzeitig wesentliche Grundüberzeugungen und Lebensformen beibehalten zu können. ... Gemeindepraktisch verteidigen sie einen Lebensstil, der sich eher in die pagane Gesellschaft einfügt, als sich von ihr abzugrenzen" (HEILIGENTHAL, Zwischen Henoch und Paulus [s. Anm. 36], 149f.).

[43] SELLIN, Häretiker (s. Anm. 39), 224.

(V.10). Denn faktisch verleugnen sie damit nach der Auffassung des Jud zugleich ‚den alleinigen Herrscher und Herrn Jesus Christus' (V.4) sowie den alleinigen Gott und Retter (V.25)."[44] Nur an diesem einen Punkt der Verehrung himmlischer Mächte erscheint es möglich, „die typisierende Polemik zu durchdringen".[45] Denn offenbar wollte der Autor die gegnerischen Positionen gar nicht detailliert beschreiben, sondern nur „das Grundübel ihrer Gottlosigkeit ... in mehreren Anläufen" herausstellen, andererseits muss er „in der Verachtung und Verleugnung der himmlischen Mächte durch die Gegner offenbar ein besonderes Merkmal ihrer Gottlosigkeit" gesehen haben.[46]

Diese Interpretation hat den Vorzug, dass sie den Kern des Streits dort lokalisiert, wo vermutlich auch das theologische Anliegen des Autors liegt: Der Rekurs auf die Tradition des Henochbuchs, das für den Autor ‚kanonischen'[47] Rang einnimmt und die einzige in diesem Schreiben (als prophetisch) zitierte Schrift ist, belegt den Rang der Angelologie im Denken des Autors zu Genüge. Auch die Aufnahme der Wächterepisode in V.6 und der Rückgriff auf ein Exempel aus der Welt der Engel in V.9 zeigen, dass in der Angelologie ein für den Autor entscheidender Punkt liegt.[48] Der vom Autor präzise konstruierte Zusammenhang[49] der Sünde der Wächterengel, die „ihren eigenen Wohnsitz verlassen haben" (V.6), und der Sodomiten, die „fremdem Fleisch nachliefen" (V.7), liegt wohl darin, dass beide die schöpfungsgemäße Grenze zwischen Engeln und Menschen überschritten und darin ‚frevelhaft' und strafwürdig gehandelt haben.[50] Hingegen wird in V.9 das vorbildhafte Handeln Michaels zitiert, der sich gemäß der hier aufgenommen jüdischen Tradition gegenüber einem anderen Engelwesen, nämlich dem Satan, nicht zu einer herabwürdigenden, ‚blasphemischen'

---

[44] P. MÜLLER, Der Judasbrief, ThR 63 (1998), 267–289 (284).
[45] Ebd.
[46] Ebd. Ebenso PAULSEN, Der Zweite Petrusbrief und der Judasbrief (s. Anm. 35), 49: Der Mangel der Gegner „liegt deshalb kaum im ethischen Bereich, wie der Jud suggerieren möchte, sondern in der tiefen Skepsis gegenüber dem Rang der Engel, der für den Vf. zweifelsfrei ist".
[47] Freilich ist die Rede von einem ‚Kanon' für das gesamte Urchristentum noch ein Anachronismus, wie insbesondere das zeitgenössische Schrifttum von Qumran zeigt. Einen ‚Kanon' im Sinne einer fest abgegrenzten Liste verbindlicher oder als inspiriert angesehener Texte gab es im Judentum des Zweiten Tempels noch nicht, und die Diskussionen gingen auch in der rabbinischen Tradition über die häufig mit dem Lehrhaus von ‚Jabne' verbundenen Diskussionen hinaus weiter. Im frühen Christentum ist ein fixiertes und v.a. abgrenzendes ‚Kanon'-Konzept erst im 4. Jh. erkennbar. S. zu den Problemen J. FREY, Qumran und der biblische Kanon. Eine thematische Einführung, in: M. Becker / ders. (Hg.), Qumran und der biblische Kanon, BThS 92, Neukirchen-Vluyn 2009 (im Druck).
[48] PAULSEN, Der Zweite Petrusbrief und der Judasbrief (s. Anm. 35), 47f.
[49] V.7: τὸν ὅμοιον τρόπον τούτοις.
[50] Dieser Punkt wird interessanterweise in der Rezeption in 2Petr 2,4.6 preisgegeben.

Aussage hinreißen ließ.⁵¹ Daraus geht hervor, welche Dignität himmlische Wesen in der Sicht des Autors genießen. Engel haben für ihn eine protologische und eschatologische Bedeutung, sie sind Teil des irdischen und himmlischen Weltgeschehens und zugleich Garanten der Ordnung der Welt. Sie verbal herabzusetzen oder gar ihre Bedeutung zu leugnen, kommt einer frevelhaften Grenzverletzung gleich, wie sie nach V.6 in der Verbindung der Wächterengel mit Menschentöchtern oder in V.7 mit dem Vergehen der Sodomiten an den sie besuchenden Engeln vorlag.⁵² Mit der Verweigerung der Anerkennung der Engelmächte liegt in der Sicht des Autors eine „Überschreitung des den Menschen zugemessenen Platzes"⁵³ und damit eben ein Akt der Gottlosigkeit vor.

Andere Fragen lassen sich nur noch bruchstückhaft klären: Ob diese ‚Verachtung' der Engelmächte auf einen ursprünglich paganen Skeptizismus oder auf visionär-pneumatische Erfahrungen zurückging und ob sich mit ihr – möglicherweise unter Berufung auf Paulus⁵⁴ – antinomistische oder libertinistische Züge verbanden, lässt sich nicht mehr klar erkennen.

Für eine Lokalisation des Konflikts um die Anerkennung von Engelmächten im Rahmen der Wirkungsgeschichte paulinischer Theologie sprechen einige Gründe: In den paulinischen Gemeinden konnte die Gabe der Glossolalie als Begabung mit „Engelssprachen" gedeutet werden (1Kor 13,1), was zeigt, dass in der pneumatischen Praxis auch der Grund für ein neues Selbstbewusstsein liegen konnte, in dem die so Begabten selbst in die Sphäre der Engel oder gar über sie erhoben erscheinen. Dem entsprechend werden auch nach Paulus „Herrschaften, Mächte und Gewalten" als inferiore Mächte am Ende Christus unterworfen sein (1Kor 15,24), und nach 1Kor 6,3 sollen die Glaubenden sogar selbst über die Engel zu Gericht sitzen.⁵⁵ Soteriologisch kommt diesen Mächten keinerlei heilsmittlerische

---

[51] Auch dieser Punkt ist in der Rezeption der Passage in 2Petr 2,11 völlig verundeutlicht.

[52] Es ist hingegen kaum anzunehmen, dass die Gegner den sexuellen Verkehr mit Engelmächten propagierten, wie K. M. SCHMIDT, Mahnung und Erinnerung im Maskenspiel. Epistolographie, Rhetorik und Narrativik der pseudepigraphen Petrusbriefe, HBS 38, Freiburg i. Brsg. u.a. 2003, 317f., behauptet. Damit werden die polemischen Stereotypen (‚sexuelles Fehlverhalten') in letztlich unkritischer Weise in die Rekonstruktion der Gegner einbezogen.

[53] PAULSEN, Der Zweite Petrusbrief und der Judasbrief (s. Anm. 35), 65.

[54] SELLIN, Häretiker (s. Anm. 39), 209f., verweist auf V.4 und auf Vorwürfe, die schon Paulus entgegengehalten wurden (Röm 3,8). Auch in der deuteropaulinischen Tradition ist die χάρις stark betont (Eph 2,7–9) – was im Rückschluss aus V.4 für die Gegner vermutet werden könnte.

[55] H. ROOSE, Eschatologische Mitherrschaft. Entwicklungslinien einer urchristlichen Erwartung, NTOA 54, Göttingen/Freiburg (CH) 2004, 264, folgert gerade aus der Beiläu-

Funktion mehr zu, so dass sie von Christus und Gott nicht mehr trennen können (Röm 8,38): Sie haben weder negativ noch positiv eine Relevanz für die Glaubenden und verdienen daher weder furchtsame Scheu noch dienstbare Verehrung. In den Deuteropaulinen verstärken sich die Tendenzen zur christologischen Depotenzierung der Mächte und Gewalten: Diese sind Teil der von Christus beherrschten Schöpfung (Kol 1,16; 2,10; Eph 1,21), ja sie sind durch Christi Triumph ihrer Macht entkleidet (Kol 2,15). Daher ist jede ‚Verehrung' von Engeln überflüssig und verfehlt (Kol 2,18). Es ist daher durchaus denkbar, dass eine Haltung, wie sie der Autor des Kol zur Sprache bringt, dem Verfasser des Jud als Leugnung der kosmologischen und eschatologischen Bedeutung der Engel und der durch sie repräsentierten Ordnung erscheinen.[56] Daraus konnten sich für den Autor des Jud, der die Henochtradition und ihre Angelologie hochschätzte, weitergehende Vorwürfe nahelegen: Wer die göttliche Weltordnung leugnet, wird in seiner Vermessenheit auch Gottes und Christi Herrschaft (V.4) verleugnen und letztlich alle moralischen Maßstäbe vergessen. Dass sich auch in dem Vorwurf der Verkehrung der Gnade ein „Streit um das Paulus-Erbe"[57] spiegeln könnte, ist insofern eine plausible Hypothese.[58]

2.4 Zur Funktion der fiktionalen Strukturen

Von hier aus lässt sich noch einmal die *Funktion der Autorfiktion* des Jud reflektieren. Mit der Inanspruchnahme des Judas als „Bruder des Jakobus" und mit dem gleichzeitigen Anklang an den Jak schließt sich der Jud an eine spezifische Linie frühchristlicher Überlieferung an, in der – aus unterschiedlichen Gründen – eine kritische Auseinandersetzung mit der paulinischen bzw. sich auf Paulus berufenden Traditionslinie vorlag. Immerhin bietet der Jak in besonders deutlicher Form eine Auseinandersetzung mit antinomistischen Tendenzen, wie sie sich aus einem bestimmten Blickwinkel sicher bereits bei Paulus vermuten ließen und in der nachpaulinischen Tradition in verstärktem Maße auftraten. Indem sich der Jud an dieses Schreiben bzw. seinen Autor ‚anhängt', reiht er sich in die durch Jakobus bzw. den Jakobusbrief begründete Tradition ein und macht sich die schon im Jak geäußerte Kritik an einigen Tendenzen der nachpaulinischen Tradi-

---

figkeit dieser Aussage, dass diese Vorstellung bei den Adressaten wohl vertraut war. Sie ist innerhalb der paulinischen Theologie singulär (vgl. später ActPaul 2,6).

[56] Vgl. SELLIN, Häretiker (s. Anm. 39), 221f.: „Die kolossische Philosophie hat natürlich kaum mehr etwas mit dem orthodoxen Verfasser des Judasbriefes zu tun. Wohl aber könnte es Verbindungslinien geben zwischen dem Verfasser des Kolosserbriefes, der gegen die Engel-Verehrer polemisiert, und den Häretikern des Judasbriefes."

[57] A.a.O. 211.

[58] Dies gilt, auch wenn man in Jud 4 nicht (wie SELLIN, ebd.) mit einem expliziten Rückbezug auf Röm 3,8 rechnen kann.

tion zu Eigen. Der Autor verortet sich somit in einer Linie der gegenüber Paulus bzw. den durch ihn ausgelösten Tendenzen kritischen Sichtweisen – und es ist interessant, dass 2Petr in einer anderen Situation ebenfalls diese Linie weiterführt und dabei sogar Paulus und seine Briefe eigens erwähnt (2Petr 3,15f.).

Doch ist das Leitinteresse des Jud nicht der Kampf gegen einen Antinomismus – so sehr dieses Motiv in V.4 mit anklingt. Vielmehr scheint sich der Autor vor allem an der Bestreitung der Würde himmlischer Gewalten zu stören, die ihm – im Lichte der Henochtradition und anderer jüdischer, aber auch in griechischer Sprache vorliegender Überlieferungen – als eine Respektlosigkeit auch gegenüber der Macht des Kyrios und der Herrschaft Gottes selbst erscheinen musste. Möglicherweise verband er mit der Respektlosigkeit gegenüber himmlischen Mächten auch die Befürchtung, dass, wer so denkt, auch alle anderen von Gott gesetzten Ordnungen preisgeben müsse. Dies würde einige der polemischen Stereotypen erklären.

Die konkrete *Situation* der Adressatengemeinde(n) kommt in dem Schreiben am Rande und indirekt zur Sprache (V.4.12.22f.). Sie hat im fiktionalen und argumentativen Gesamtgefüge des Schreibens keine tragende Funktion. Sie musste nicht besprochen werden. Es ist vielmehr anzunehmen, dass die Adressaten nach der Einschätzung des realen Autors hinreichend in der Lage waren, die Anliegen des Schreibens zu verstehen und aufzunehmen. Die wenigen indirekten Hinweise zur Situation dürften daher auch für die Rekonstruktion der tatsächlichen Situation verwertbar sein. Allerdings bleiben viele Details, die heutige Interpreten gerne wüssten – angefangen von der Lokalisation der Adressaten –, in dem knappen Schreiben unklar.

Von größerer Bedeutung im fiktionalen Gefüge ist das *Bild der Gegner*. Dabei ist m.E. damit zu rechnen, dass es diese Gegner tatächlich gab – sonst wäre das Schreiben in der Tat wenig sinnvoll. Die ‚Gottlosen' sind also keine bloße Fiktion, die Frage ist jedoch, wie ‚gottlos' sie waren bzw. wie viele der ihnen angehängten Vorwürfe wirklich einen Anhalt an ihrem Denken und ihrem Lebenswandel hatten. Ein Kernpunkt der Auseinandersetzung lässt sich, wie oben gezeigt, aus dem Schreiben rekonstruieren, aber der Realgrund der anderen Vorwürfe – z.B. der ‚murrenden' Unzufriedenheit, der stolzen Reden, der Schmeichelei um des eigenen Vorteils willen oder des Lebens „nach ihren Begierden" (V.16) – muss zumindest offen bleiben. Eigennutz ist ein häufiger Vorwurf, mit dem konkurrierende Lehrer diskreditiert werden, ‚Murren' und Überheblichkeit sind topische Attribute derer, die sich gegen Gott und seine Ordnungen auflehnen, und moralische Vergehen lassen sich solchen Gegnern nur allzu leicht anhängen. Die Basis einiger dieser Vorwürfe hat der Autor in den rezipierten biblischen Paradigmen von Kain, Bileam, Korach (V.11) oder auch den

Sodomiten (V.7) gefunden. Den eigentlichen Legitimationsgrund seiner Gerichtsankündigung an die ‚Gottlosen' scheint er jedoch aus dem Henochzitat V.14f. zu entnehmen, in dem den Gottlosen für ihre gottlosen Werke und ihre harten Worte (!) das Gericht des kommenden Herrn prophetisch angesagt wird. Hier zeigt sich für den Autor der wahre Charakter der Gegner, der dann in den applizierenden οὗτοι-Passagen nur noch expliziert werden muss.

Die Legitimation der Aussagen des Jud erfolgt insofern primär aus den Schriften (unter Einschluss der Henochüberlieferung), in denen das Gericht über die ‚Gottlosen' festgeschrieben und in Exempeln vorgeführt ist. Die Aussagen der Schriften werden dabei durch die den Aposteln zugeschriebene Prophetie über die Spötter „zur letzten Zeit" (V.18) bestätigt. Dass diese letzte Zeit angebrochen ist und das Gericht mithin bevorsteht, ergibt sich dann für die ‚apokalyptische' Zeitauffassung des Autors aus dem Auftreten der Gegner in der Gemeinde.

Für all diese – mehr oder weniger zugkräftigen – Begründungen ist das Pseudonym des Judas unbedeutend. Die Wahl dieses Pseudonyms dient insofern nicht oder nur sehr wenig der Legitimation des Schreibens und seines Inhalts, sondern primär der Zuordnung zu einer Traditionslinie, die durch die Gestalt des Jakobus markiert und durch den Jakobusbrief repräsentiert ist und verschiedenartigen Entwicklungen in der paulinisch-deuteropaulinischen Tradition kritisch gegenübertritt.

3. Die kühne Konstruktion eines ‚Testamentum Petri' im Zweiten Petrusbrief

Im bemerkenswerten Gegensatz zum Jud steht die pseudonyme Legitimationsstruktur im 2Petr, dessen Autor ja nach einem breiten Konsens der Forschung den Jud als Quelle benutzt hat.[59] Dass es sich bei diesem Brief um ein relativ spätes Pseudepigraphon handelt, gilt in der neueren kritischen Forschung weithin als sicher.[60]

---

[59] Dazu der jüngste, überzeugende Aufweis bei WASSERMAN, The Epistle of Jude (s. Anm. 11), 73–98.

[60] S. neben den Einleitungen und Kommentaren den Forschungsbericht bei RIEDL, Anamnese (s. Anm. 2). Die pseudonyme Abfassung des 2Petr haben selbst so konservative Exegeten wie Theodor Zahn und Richard Bauckham zugestanden (s. BAUCKHAM, Jude. 2 Peter [s. Anm. 13], 158f.). Gelegentliche Gegenstimmen aus dem ultrakonservativen evangelikalen Lager (s. etwa D. J. MOO, 2 Peter, Jude, NIVAC, Grand Rapids 1996, 24; SCHREINER, 1, 2 Peter, Jude [s. Anm. 14], 276) sind wissenschaftlich kaum ernst zu nehmen. Die gelegentlich favorisierte Lösung, die Frage – in einer gewissen

3.1 Die Wahl des Pseudonyms: Der Apostel und Augenzeuge

Dass sich der Apostel Petrus als Zentralgestalt des vorösterlichen Jüngerkreises Jesu wie auch der frühesten nachösterlichen Gemeinde in Jerusalem als Pseudonym für spätere Schriften eignete, ist kaum verwunderlich, zumal Petrus selbst nichts Schriftliches hinterlassen hat, das den fiktionalen ‚Spielraum' hätte einengen können. Eher erstaunlich ist, dass die Zuschreibung eines breiten Schrifttums an Petrus erst relativ spät erfolgte. Sieht man einmal von dem kaum sicher datierbaren, aber doch wohl noch im 1. Jh. anzusetzenden 1Petr ab, so begegnen pseudo-petrinische Schriften wie das Petrusevangelium, die Petrusapokalypse, die Petrusakten, das Kerygma Petri u.a. erst im 2. Jh. in größerer Zahl.[61] Die ‚Karriere' des Petrus als Autor beginnt also spät, verläuft dann allerdings umso steiler.

Freilich bestehen zwischen den einzelnen pseudo-petrinischen Schriften große Unterschiede hinsichtlich der je vorliegenden pseudonymen Konstruktion, der literarischen Form und auch der theologischen Ausrichtung und Intention, so dass sich aus der gemeinsamen Zuschreibung an Petrus kein gemeinsames Milieu oder gar eine petrinische ‚Schule' konstruieren lässt.[62]

Wie keine andere Gestalt der christlichen Urzeit bot sich Petrus als Zeuge und Gewährsmann der christlichen Verkündigung an, war er doch sowohl Zeuge des Erdenwirkens Jesu und – im hervorgehobenen Kreis der drei Jünger (Mk 9,2parr.) – auch seiner Verklärung als auch Adressat der ersten Erscheinung des Auferweckten (1Kor 15,5), ‚Säule' der Jerusalemer Urgemeinde (Gal 2,9), reisender Missionar (1Kor 9,5), ‚Fels' der Kirche (Mt 16,18) und schließlich Märtyrer (1Clem 5,4). Seine Personalautorität war im ganzen Urchristentum unstrittig[63] und wurde auch von Paulus – bei

---

Selbstbescheidung – offen zu lassen (so M. J. GILMOUR, Reflections on the Authorship of 2 Peter, Evangelical Quarterly 73 [2001], 291–309), führt nicht weiter.

[61] Hinzu kommen noch einige Petrus-Schriften aus Nag Hammadi, sowie dann zahlreiche spätere Petrus-Apokrypha. S. zu den Petrus-Apokryphen SCHMIDT, Mahnung (s. Anm. 52), 410–418; ausführlich K. BERGER, Unfehlbare Offenbarung. Petrus in der gnostischen und apokalyptischen Offenbarungsliteratur, in: P.-G. Müller / W. Stenger (Hg.), Kontinuität und Einheit (FS Mußner), Freiburg i. Brsg. u.a. 1981, 261–326.

[62] Anders M. L. SOARDS, 1 Peter, 2 Peter and Jude as Evidence for a Petrine School. With addenda by V. Oliver Ward, ANRW II 25.5 (1988), 3827–3849; vgl. P. CHATELION COUNET, Pseudepigraphy and the Petrine School. Spirit and Tradition in 1 and 2 Peter and Jude, HTS 62 (2006), 403–424.

[63] Der Bericht des Paulus über den antiochenischen Zwischenfall Gal 2,11ff. macht dies deutlich. Das Verhalten des Petrus führt letztlich die Veränderung in der Missions- und Mahlpraxis des Barnabas und der antiochenischen Gemeinde herbei, die Paulus seiner einstigen Stützpunktgemeinde entfremdet. Gegenüber der Personalautorität des Petrus führte Paulus einen relativ vergeblichen Kampf, s. dazu J. FREY, Paulus und die Apostel. Zur Entwicklung des paulinischen Apostelbegriffs und zum Verhältnis des Hei-

allen Spannungen – respektiert. Dabei war Petrus durch seine Augenzeugenschaft im Erdenwirken Jesu dem Völkerapostel stets einen entscheidenden Schritt voraus, woraus dann nur zu leicht eine Infragestellung der Autorität des Paulus und der Authentizität seiner Botschaft entstehen konnte.[64]

Die Wahl des Pseudonyms im 2Petr ist daher weniger verwunderlich als im Falle des Jud. Petrus legte sich als Gewährsmann nahe angesichts seiner unbestrittenen kirchlichen Autorität. Als erstberufener Jünger (Mk 1,16) und erster Osterzeuge (1Kor 15,5), dessen Zeugnis nicht zuletzt hinter der Überlieferung der synoptischen Evangelien gesehen wurde,[65] konnte er als Garant der ursprünglichen Wahrheit fungieren. Besser als Paulus konnte er als Zeuge der Verklärung für die Wahrheit der göttlichen Herrlichkeit Christi und seines Kommens angeführt werden. Grund der Wahl des Pseudonyms war daher wohl weder die Herkunft des Verfassers aus einer petrinischen ‚Schule'[66] noch die Berufung der ‚Gegner' auf Petrus, speziell ‚petrinische' Verkündigungsthemen[67] oder gar den 1Petr. Wenn sich diese möglicherweise gar auf Paulus oder dessen Briefe beriefen, hätte dem auch ein ‚Testament des Paulus' entgegengesetzt werden können, freilich ist damit zu rechnen, dass ein solches angesichts einer schon vorliegenden Sammlung der Paulusbriefe (und vielleicht sogar schon der Existenz des 2Tim[68]) nicht mehr leicht in Umlauf zu bringen war.

---

denapostels zu seinen „Kollegen", in: E.-M. Becker / P. Pilhofer (Hg.), Biographie und Theologie des Paulus, WUNT 187, Tübingen 2005, 192–227. Zur Bedeutung der Petrusgestalt s. M. HENGEL, Der unterschätzte Petrus. Zwei Studien, Tübingen 2006.

[64] Die Argumentation des Paulus im Galaterbrief und auch im 2. Korintherbrief lässt erkennen, dass die Gegner des Paulus diesen Punkt sehr wohl argumentativ zu nutzen wussten.

[65] S. die Markus-Notiz des Papias (bei Eus.h.e. 3,39,15), die – unabhängig von ihrem historischen Wert – den Ruf des Petrus als Garanten der Jesusüberlieferung belegt. Die Tatsache, dass ein so selbstbewusster Autor wie Matthäus das Mk aufgenommen hat, bestätigt dessen frühe Autorität, und auch im Johannesevangelium wird Petrus in seiner Rolle als Sprecher des Jüngerkreises und „Felsenmann" (Joh 1,42) akzeptiert, auch wenn er wie alle vorösterlichen Jünger dem Jüngermissverständnis unterliegt und insofern dem „idealen" Nachfolger, dem „Lieblingsjünger" untergeordnet wird.

[66] Nichts weist positiv auf ein „Mitglied des Petruskreises der Gemeinde Roms", wie VÖGTLE, Der Judasbrief. Der 2. Petrusbrief (s. Anm. 23), 125, für plausibel hält und BAUCKHAM, Jude. 2 Peter (s. Anm. 13), 146f.158–162, nachdrücklich behauptet. Wenn man das Schreiben aufgrund seiner Abhängigkeit von 1Petr, Mt und Jud (der seinerseits von Jak abhängt), nicht mehr ins 1. Jh. datieren darf, ist auch ein solcher ‚Petruskreis' kaum nachweisbar.

[67] Die häufig hier genannte Frage der Einheit von Juden- und Heidenchristen oder die Frage nach der heidenchristlichen Rücksichtnahme auf Judenchristen spielt im 2Petr keine Rolle.

[68] Dies hält VÖGTLE, Der Judasbrief. Der 2. Petrusbrief (s. Anm. 23), 126, immerhin für möglich.

Allerdings scheint dem Verfasser auch die Schwierigkeit bewusst gewesen zu sein, gut zwei Generationen nach dem Märtyrertod des Petrus ein Schreiben in dessen Namen glaubhaft zu machen, so dass er – obwohl er 1Petr kennt – sich nicht an diesen anlehnt, sondern das Risiko eingeht, ein auch stilistisch ganz andersartiges Schreiben zu verfassen. Dabei wählt er eine sehr viel dichtere und massivere pseudonyme Legitimationsstruktur und unternimmt zur Stütze seines Sachanliegens (bzw. *vor* der eigentlichen Diskussion der Streitpunkte) eine im NT beispiellose polemische Diskreditierung seiner Gegner.[69]

3.2 Die dichte Durchführung der pseudonymen Legitimationsstruktur

Die Pseudepigraphie im Zweiten Petrusbrief ist wesentlich massiver als etwa im 1Petr oder auch im Jud, und sie ist im Vergleich zum Jud auch deutlich dichter und konsequenter durchgeführt. Dabei kommen zahlreiche Attribute der Petrusgestalt zur Geltung: der Name mit Beinamen und die Apostelwürde, die Augenzeugenschaft und der vertraute Umgang mit Jesus und nicht zuletzt die Beziehung zu ‚unserem lieben Bruder Paulus' (2Petr 3,15f.). Auch der Tod des Petrus – wenngleich nicht explizit als Martyrium – ist aufgenommen. Die Augenzeugenschaft ist schließlich konzentriert auf den Aspekt der göttlichen Herrlichkeit Christi (in der Verklärungs-Episode), die für die Argumentation im Blick auf „die Macht und das Kommen unseres Herrn Jesus Christus" (2Petr 1,16) wesentlich ist.[70]

3.2.1 Die massive Beanspruchung der petrinischen Autorität

Schon im Eingang ist der autoritativ-apostolische Anspruch stark hervorgehoben durch die feierliche Nennung des Namens in der hebraisierenden Form Συμεὼν Πέτρος (2Petr 1,1).[71] Damit unterscheidet sich die Einführung des fiktiven Autors vom 1Petr, der in 2Petr 3,1 sehr wahrscheinlich vorausgesetzt wird.[72] Offenbar bemüht sich der Autor hier – anders als z.B.

---

[69] S. dazu die ausführliche Diskussion in J. FREY, Disparagement as Argument. The Polemical Use of Moral Language in Second Peter, in: J. van der Watt / R. Zimmermann (Hg.), Moral Language in the New Testament, WUNT II, Tübingen 2010 (im Druck).

[70] Auffälligerweise fehlt auch die Osterzeugenschaft. Dazu SCHMIDT, Mahnung (s. Anm. 52), 312: „Die Auferstehung rückt Jesus ... näher an das Kreuz und seine Niedrigkeit heran, die in 2Petr nicht thematisiert wird."

[71] Sie begegnet bezeichnenderweise nur noch einmal im NT, in Apg 15,14, im Munde des Herrenbruders Jakobus, daneben für andere Personen in Lk 2,25.35; 3,30; Apg 13,1 und Apk 7,7; sie ist jedoch gebräuchlich in der LXX (v.a. für den Stammvater Simeon) und in den Patriarchentestamenten, hingegen dominiert Σίμων in 1/2Makk sowie in den Evangelien und der Apg, ebenso in den Schriften des 2. Jh.

[72] 1Petr 1,1 bietet nur Πέτρος ἀπόστολος.

der Autor des 2Thess[73] – nicht um einen Anklang oder gar eine stilistische Imitation.[74] Er leitet seine Autorität nicht von dem ‚literarischen' Petrus des 1Petr ab, sondern bietet eine unmittelbare, sehr kräftige Inanspruchnahme der Petrusgestalt.

Auffällig ist, dass die hebraisierende Transkription Συμεών hier nicht mit dem aramäischen Beinamen Κηφᾶς[75], sondern mit dessen griechischer Übersetzung Πέτρος verbunden ist. Die Kombination zeigt, dass die archaisierende Form absichtsvoll gesetzt ist und „die Legitimität des Vf.s hervorheben"[76] bzw. die petrinische Verfasserschaft glaubhaft machen soll. Über den faktischen Autor sagt die Namensform hingegen kaum mehr aus, als dass er mit der LXX (und natürlich der älteren Petrustradition) vertraut ist.[77]

Mit der Erweiterung „Diener und Apostel Jesu Christi"[78] formuliert der Verfasser die apostolische Autorität, unter die er sein Schreiben stellen möchte und die im Folgenden durch die Hinweise auf die Augenzeugenschaft des fiktiven Autors (V.16–18) aufgenommen wird. Dabei spricht ‚Petrus' nicht nur für sich selbst, sondern für die Gesamtheit der Apostel, wie schon die pluralische Rede von einem „dem unseren gleichwertigen Glauben" (2Petr 1,1), wie auch dann der ‚apostolische' Plural in 2Petr 1,16.18 zeigen.

Zu Beginn des Briefcorpus (2Petr 1,12) kommt die Person des Apostels erneut ins Spiel, doch zunächst im Singular, in dem ‚Petrus' als herausgehobener Zeuge und ‚Amtsträger' die Adressaten „wachhalten" und „erinnern" (2Petr 1,13) will, solange er lebt (vgl. 2Petr 3,17). In Aufnahme des Motivs, dass Jesus seinem Apostel den Tod angesagt hat (Joh 13,36f.; 21,18; vgl. ActPetr 35), kommt hier nicht nur das besonders vertraute Verhältnis zu Jesus zur Geltung. Vielmehr wird somit zugleich literarisch eine

---

[73] 2Thess 1,1f. bietet einen weitgehenden wörtlichen Anklang an 1Thess 1,1.

[74] Die stilistische Differenz zwischen 1Petr und 2Petr hat dann auch später sehr wesentlich zur Wahrnehmung der Authentizitätsprobleme beigetragen (so schon Hier. vir.ill 1), wobei dann gelegentlich 2Petr (aufgrund seiner kräftigeren Autorisierung) als authentisch aufgefasst wurde, während man für 1Petr eine Abfassung durch den ‚Sekretär' Silvanus (1Petr 5,12) annehmen konnte.

[75] Dieser begegnet nur bei Paulus in Gal und 1Kor sowie in Joh 1,42 (wo der Beiname eigens übersetzt wird).

[76] So PAULSEN, Der Zweite Petrusbrief und der Judasbrief (s. Anm. 35), 104. S. auch T. FORNBERG, An Early Church in a Pluralistic Society. A Study of 2 Peter, CB.NT 9, Lund 1977, 9f.

[77] Dass die Form auf einen judenchristlichen Autor aus dem Umkreis des Petrus in Rom verweise, wie BAUCKHAM (Jude. 2 Peter [s. Anm. 13], 167) vermutet, lässt sich nicht begründen.

[78] Hier könnte der Verfasser Wendungen aus Jud 1 „Jesu Christi Knecht" und 1Petr 1,1 „Apostel Jesu Christi" kombiniert haben, doch lässt sich die Formulierung auch ohne Annahme einer solchen Anlehnung verstehen, denn beide Attribute finden sich bereits bei Paulus in Röm 1,1 (vgl. Tit 1,1).

,Abschiedsszene' konstruiert,[79] die den Worten des dem Tode entgegensehenden Apostels zusätzliches Gewicht verleiht. 2Petr 1,15 bringt das Bemühen (des fiktiven Autors) zum Ausdruck, dass seine Adressaten dies auch nach seinem Tode noch im Gedächtnis halten können (vgl. auch 3,17). Damit beschreibt der faktische Autor indirekt die Konzeption, nach der die apostolische Präsenz im vorliegenden Schreiben auch über den Tod des Apostels hinaus – und d.h. bleibend – gegeben sein soll. Das Schreiben soll also ein ‚Testament des Petrus' sein und als solches die Stimme des Apostels als des Garanten für die ursprüngliche Wahrheit des Glaubens auch nach dessen Tod bleibend präsent halten.

Zur sachlichen Verstärkung (und in Vorbereitung des späteren Sacharguments) wird nun die Augenzeugenschaft des Petrus hervorgehoben, und zwar spezifisch als Augenzeugenschaft der Verklärung Jesu.[80] In dieser synoptischen Szene (Mt 17,1–8parr.) ist – zumindest für die drei ausgewählten Jünger – die μεγαλότης und δόξα Christi in besonderem Maße erschlossen, was im Blick auf die Argumentation des Schreibens hinsichtlich der Parusieverheißung (2Petr 3,2ff.) bzw. – wie es hier heißt – seiner δύναμις und παρουσία (2Petr 2,16) von Bedeutung ist. Die so reklamierte Augen- und Ohrenzeugenschaft des fiktiven Autors wird dem Gedanken entgegengesetzt, dass „wir" (d.h. wohl die Apostel und die ihnen Folgenden) bloß erfundenen Geschichten (σεσοφισμένοις μύθοις) gefolgt sein könnten. Ganz gleich, ob darin schon ein Vorwurf der erst später eingeführten Gegner anklingt oder nicht, wird zunächst die Augenzeugenschaft des ‚Petrus' (und seiner Mitzeugen) nachdrücklich betont. Sie beruht nicht auf bloßer Fiktion, sondern auf tatsächlichem Sehen und Hören der apostolischen Zeugen. Darin liegt freilich ein besonders kühnes Argument, wenn man bedenkt, dass der Autor selbst den Anspruch der Augenzeugenschaft fiktional konstruiert.

---

[79] Es ist hier nicht erforderlich, an die zahlreichen jüdischen Abschiedsreden und literarischen Testamente zu erinnern, deren Reihe einerseits mit dem Dtn, andererseits in Qumran mit den aramäischen Visionen Amrams beginnt und die insbesondere in den Testamenten der zwölf Patriarchen eine einheitliche literarische Form gefunden haben. Im Neuen Testament sind die johanneischen Abschiedsreden (Joh 13,31–16,33; mit der einleitenden Mahlszene 13,1–30 und dem abschließenden Abschiedsgebet 17,1–24), die Abschiedsrede des Paulus in Milet (Apg 20,18–35) und der Zweite Timotheusbrief weitere Beispiele. Alle diese literarischen Abschiedsreden gehören ins weitere Feld der Pseudepigraphie, dabei ist interessant, dass sich die frühjüdischen Reden auf Gestalten einer fernen Epoche (Patriarchen, Mose, Esra) berufen, während die frühchristlichen Abschiedsreden Jesus und die Apostel, d.h. Gestalten der unmittelbaren Vergangenheit aufnehmen.

[80] Diese wird auch in ApkPetr 15f. (äth; bzw. 1–20 im Akhmim-Text) aufgenommen. Das Verhältnis zwischen 2Petr und ApkPetr ist hier nicht zu erörtern.

Im gesamten polemischen (2Petr 2,1–22) und argumentativen (2Petr 3,1–13) Mittelteil des Corpus tritt die Person des Petrus sonst nicht hervor, außer an der Nahtstelle zwischen beiden, wo der Autor darauf hinweist, dass der vorliegende Brief schon der zweite an die Adressaten sei (2Petr 3,1). Damit kann nur auf 1Petr verwiesen sein. Inhaltliche Bedeutung hat der Hinweis nicht; er dient v.a. der Stütze der pseudonymen Autorfiktion, die ja in den ausgedehnten polemischen Passagen aus dem Blick kommen könnte. So wird die Autorität des ‚Petrus' erneut in Erinnerung gerufen, bevor der Autor zum sachlichen Kernargument hinsichtlich der Parusieerwartung kommt.

Nach diesem argumentativen Teil tritt ‚Petrus' wieder im Corpus-Abschluss (2Petr 3,14–16) auf, in dem er seine Mahnung noch einmal auf die Adressaten hin wendet. Dabei wird in einer im NT einzigartigen Weise auf Paulus zurückgegriffen, der den Adressaten in „allen Briefen" letztlich nichts anderes geschrieben habe, als was auch ‚Petrus' seinen Lesern in Erinnerung rufen will.[81] Das Verhältnis von Paulus und Petrus erscheint dabei durchaus harmonisch, von einem Streit, wie er in Gal 2,11–21 belegt ist, ist nichts mehr zu erkennen,[82] vielmehr wird ein ‚brüderliches' Verhältnis beider und die ‚Harmonie' ihres Zeugnisses vorausgesetzt, wobei im vorliegenden Schreiben natürlich ‚Petrus' die Interpretationsinstanz für die paulinischen Briefe bildet, während diese wohl von den Gegnern und den von ihnen beeinflussten „Ungefestigten" missverstanden und „verdreht" werden.

Insgesamt (und explizit in 2Petr 1,14f.) zeichnet der Text „das Bild eines gealterten Apostels, der sich am Ende seines Lebens um die Gemeinde sorgt. Schon bald kann er sie nicht mehr persönlich ermahnen, dabei lauern in der Zukunft Gefahren."[83] Das hier gezeichnete Bild des Petrus differiert deutlich von dem des 1Petr, auf den in 2Petr 3,1 immerhin verwiesen wird.[84] Hier ist Petrus nicht „Zeuge der Leiden Christi" (1Petr 5,1), sondern Zeuge seiner Macht und Herrlichkeit, nicht „Mitältester" (1Petr 5,1), sondern der entscheidende Zeuge der Wahrheit und Lehrautorität auch für die Interpretation anderer frühchristlicher Schriften. Als solcher schreibt er den Brief, um auch die Gemeinden nach seinem Tode (2Petr 1,15) vor den

---

[81] Der vergleichende Anschluss in 2Petr 3,15 bleibt sachlich etwas unklar. Grundsätzlich geht es aber um die Betonung der Übereinstimmung „aller" Briefe des Paulus mit dem Zeugnis des „Petrus" – sofern man mit den Paulusbriefen nicht unangemessen umgeht. D.h. „Petrus" wird zum Maßstab der Auslegung des Paulus. Auch hier zeigt sich also ein Diskurs um das ‚Erbe' des Paulus.

[82] Dieser ist im Licht des Martyriums beider schon in 1Clem 5,1–5 zugunsten der gemeinsamen Zeugenschaft in Vergessenheit geraten.

[83] So die Beschreibung bei SCHMIDT, Mahnung (s. Anm. 52), 312.

[84] S. die Darstellung des Petrusbildes des 1Petr a.a.O. 177–191.

gefährlichen Irrlehrern zu warnen. Die fiktive Abfassungssituation ist damit wesentlich klarer markiert als z.B. im 1Petr oder auch in Jak und Jud.[85]

Die Inanspruchnahme der petrinischen Autorität ist dabei fokussiert auf die Abwehr von Irrlehrern, deren Lehre in 2Petr 3,3f. explizit zitiert und dann widerlegt wird. Die Themen, um die es hier geht – die Erwartung der Parusie und mit ihr die Frage der Verlässlichkeit der eschatologischen Weissagung und letztlich die Verlässlichkeit und Treue Gottes selbst –, schwingen jedoch schon von Beginn des Schreibens an mit und werden insbesondere im Abschnitt über die Augenzeugenschaft der Verklärung (2Petr 1,16) und über die Auslegung des prophetischen Wortes (2Petr 1,19f.), aber auch in weiteren Nuancen der Formulierung von Kap. 1 und 2 argumentativ vorbereitet.

3.2.2 Die zeitliche Struktur des Textes

Zur Durchführung der pseudonymen Struktur gehört auch die Zeitstruktur des Textes, die hier konsequenter als im Jud durchgehalten ist.[86] Der fiktive Autor Petrus schreibt natürlich an seine Zeitgenossen, denen, wie 2Petr 1,3f. betont, alles zum Heil Notwendige gegeben ist, die also die Wahrheit wissen und ‚eigentlich' keine Erinnerung benötigen (2Petr 1,12f.). Erinnerung muss aber möglich sein in der Zeit nach dem Tod des Petrus, dem gilt das Bemühen des fiktiven (2Petr 1,15) und noch mehr des realen Autors. Die fiktiven Adressaten wissen alles „im Voraus" (2Petr 3,17), und wenn es dann heißt, sie sollen sich „bewahren", um den Irrlehrern nicht zu verfallen, liegt hier eine implizite Anrede der späteren, faktischen Adressaten vor.

Aus der Perspektive des fiktiven Autors liegen die Irrlehrer, die in der Endzeit auftreten sollen (2Petr 3,3), natürlich in der Zukunft. Dementsprechend ist das Schreiben zur konsequenten Aufrechterhaltung der Autorfiktion an entscheidenden Stellen deutlich anders ausgestaltet als Jud – was v.a. dort auffällt, wo 2Petr auf Jud als Vorlage zurückgreift.

Obwohl das Schreiben faktisch wohl durch die Wirkung der gegnerischen Lehre veranlasst ist (2Petr 3,3f.), wird der Anlass aus der Perspektive des ‚Petrus' anders formuliert: Grund der schriftstellerischen Tätigkeit ist nicht das Eingedrungensein irgendwelcher Menschen (τίνες ἄνθρωποι, Jud 4), sondern die vorausschauende Sorge des alten Petrus, der den Adressaten auch für die Zukunft noch das Wahrheitszeugnis bereitstellen will und daher vor seinem baldigen Tod noch zur Feder greift (2Petr 1,14f.), damit sich die Gemeinden – wenn die Situation eintritt – „erinnern" (2Petr 3,1; s. auch 3,17).

Die Einführung der Irrlehrer und die Polemik gegen sie erfolgt daher konsequent im Modus der Weissagung (2Petr 1,1–3): Wie es in biblischer Zeit ‚Falschpropheten' gab, die dem wahren, göttlich inspirierten ‚prophetischen Wort' (2Petr 1,19–21) gegenüber-

---
[85] S. dazu a.a.O. 314.
[86] S. o. zu Jud 17.

stehen, so wird es auch „bei euch", d.h. in der Zukunft der (fiktiven) Adressaten, „Falschlehrer" geben (2Petr 2,1: καὶ ἐν ὑμῖν ἔσονται ψευδοδιδάσκαλοι)[87], die der wahren Lehre entgegenstehen. ‚Petrus' sagt voraus, dass diese verderblichen Lehren einführen und Gefolgschaft haben werden. Die Verben in 2Petr 1–3 sind daher ins Futur gesetzt,[88] bevor die Darstellung dann ab V.4 über die biblischen Exempel (2Petr 2,4–9) zu einer allgemeinen Polemik gegen diese ‚typischen' Irrlehrer ins Präsens übergleitet.[89]

In Anlehnung an Jud 17f., aber charakteristischer Modifikation bietet 2Petr 3,1–3 dann einen Neueinsatz, der nun wieder im futurischen Modus das Auftreten der „Spötter" thematisiert, die „am Ende der Tage" kommen sollen (2Petr 3,3: ἐλεύσονται ἐπ' ἐσχάτων τῶν ἡμερῶν). Der fiktive Autor erinnert zunächst an sein früheres Schreiben (2Petr 3,1) und expliziert die Intention seines Schreibens: Die Leser – zunächst die fiktiven Adressaten zur Zeit des alten Petrus, aber mit ihnen auch die späteren Leser – sollen um das endzeitliche Auftreten der Irrlehrer wissen. Doch ist dies dann nicht als Weissagung „der Apostel", sondern davon abgesetzt und als Lehraussage des hier sprechenden Apostels ‚Petrus' formuliert (2Petr 3,3). Dazu wird zuvor in der Nennung des Gegenstands der Erinnerung die textliche Vorlage aus Jud 17 unter fast völliger Beibehaltung ihres Wortbestandes[90] durch kleine, aber geschickte Hinzufügungen präzise verändert. Erinnern sollen sich die Adressaten des 2Petr nicht (wie in Jud) an die Weissagung der Apostel, sondern an „die vorhergesagten Worte der heiligen Propheten *und* das von euren Aposteln (gesprochene) Gebot des Herrn und Retters." Durch die Hinzufügung der Worte τῶν ἁγίων προφητῶν (als Ergänzung zu „der vorhergesagten Worte") und καὶ ... ἐντολῆς (als Ergänzung zu τῶν ἀποστόλων τοῦ κυρίου) gilt nun die Erinnerung den Weissagungen der *Propheten* und dem von den Aposteln gegebenen *Gebot*. Die Weissagung wird den Propheten (vor ‚Petrus'), d.h. den alttestamentlichen Schriftpropheten zugeordnet, das Gebot den (von Petrus selbst unterschiedenen, anderen) Aposteln, d.h. den Gründungsaposteln der Adressatengemeinden. Die im Jud so unglückliche Zeitstruktur einer Erinnerung an die Weissagung der Apostel wird so vermieden, gemäß der vorliegenden Verfasserfiktion: ‚Petrus' kann nicht an die früheren Worte der Apostel erinnern, sondern nur an die Propheten und – wie die anderen Apostel – an das Gebot des Herrn.[91]

Die zeitliche Fiktion der Verfasserschaft des Petrus ist insofern durchgehalten. Die in 2,10–22 sowie in 3,5–13 erfolgenden lehrmäßig-präsenti-

---

[87] Der Terminus begegnet sonst nicht vor Just.dial. 82,1. Vgl. noch ψευδοδιδασκαλία in Polyk 7,2. Die Gegner werden als ‚Lehrer' eingeführt, nicht als Propheten.

[88] 2Petr 2,1: παρεισάξουσιν αἱρέσεις ἀπωλείας, 2Petr 2,2: καὶ πολλοὶ ἐξακολουθήσουσιν ... ἡ ὁδὸς βλασφημηθήσεται, 2Petr 3,3: πλαστοῖς λόγοις ὑμᾶς ἐμπορεύσονται.

[89] Ab V.10 sind die Irrlehrer präsentisch allgemein charakterisiert. Darin zeigt sich der Einfluss der Vorlage des Jud. S. dazu WINDISCH / PREISKER, Die katholischen Briefe (s. Anm. 37), 92.

[90] Mit nur einer kleinen Umstellung werden die Worte τῶν ῥημάτων τῶν προειρημένων ὑπὸ τῶν ἀποστόλων τοῦ κυρίου (Jud 17) übernommen – hier zeigt sich das Geschick der Textadaption durch den Autor des 2Petr.

[91] Dabei ist die sprachliche Konstruktion elliptisch und etwas unklar, insofern mit „Gebot" (ἐντολή) zwei Genitive verbunden sind: τῶν ἀποστόλων und τοῦ κυρίου καὶ σωτῆρος.

schen Darlegungen über die Irrlehrer bzw. die Eschatologie stören hier nicht. Die fiktionalen Adressaten des alten ‚Petrus' sind seine Zeitgenossen, mit denen sich die später, nach dem Tod des Petrus, lesenden faktischen Adressaten, die nun ihrerseits auf den autoritativen Zeugen zurückblicken können, verbinden.

3.3 Die Adressatensituation und das Gegnerbild

Mit der Zeitstruktur gehört auch die in dem Schreiben zur Darstellung gebrachte Situation und natürlich das Bild der Gegner zum fiktionalen Gesamtgefüge. Dies stellt hier ebenso wie im Jud die historische Rekonstruktion vor erhebliche Schwierigkeiten.

3.3.1 Die Situation der fiktiven und der faktischen Adressaten

Die Gemeindesituation ist in der Spannung der zwei zeitlichen Ebenen – des fiktiv an seine Zeitgenossen schreibenden Petrus und der nach dem Tod des Petrus das Schreiben empfangenden realen Adressaten – zu beschreiben.

Direkt spricht der fiktive Autor ‚Petrus' (im ‚Ich'-Stil oder auch im Plural) Zeitgenossen an, mit denen er sich in einem ‚gleichwertigen' Glauben verbunden sieht (2Petr 1,1) und die (wie ‚Petrus' selbst) alles zu „Leben und Frömmigkeit" Notwendige empfangen haben und zum ewigen Heil bestimmt sind (2Petr 1,3f.11). Auf eine Lokalisation dieser Adressaten wird (anders als in 1Petr 1,1) verzichtet. Nähere Konturen kommen nicht in den Blick; die fiktiven Adressaten sind auch nicht als eine von Petrus gegründete oder mit ihm spezifisch verbundene Gemeinde vorzustellen. Im Blick auf die Vermittlung des Gebots Christi spricht ‚Petrus' vielmehr von anderen Aposteln, d.h. es wird eine Gemeindegründung durch andere vorausgesetzt. Petrus spricht in ‚allgemeinkirchlicher' Verantwortung alle ‚rechtgläubigen' Zeitgenossen an, um ihnen jetzt und für die Zeit nach seinem Tod ‚Erinnerung' zu bieten.

Diese nur wenig konkretisierte Ebene der fiktiven Adressaten ist offen für die Rezeption durch die intendierten Leser, die ihre eigene Situation in dem Schreiben wiederfinden und sich angesprochen sehen sollen.

Die kommunikative Struktur ist durchaus vergleichbar der in den Evangelien – besonders bewusst bei Johannes – praktizierten Verschmelzung der Horizonte der Zeit Jesu und der Adressaten, in der Jesu Anrede an seine Jünger (z.B. in den Abschiedsreden Joh 13–17) sachlich für die Probleme der Jüngergemeinde in nachösterlicher Zeit offen ist und etwa die Probleme der späteren ‚Abwesenheit' und ‚Unsichtbarkeit' Jesu (Joh 16,16ff.), der Gegnerschaft und Verfolgung (Joh 15,18ff.; 16,2f.) oder auch das Phänomen des Wirkens des Heiligen Geistes (Joh 14,16f.26; 15,26; 16,7–15) in der vorösterlichen Situation des Abschieds anspricht.

Es gibt im 2Petr kaum Textelemente, die die Rezeption durch spätere Adressaten etwa aufgrund ihrer raum-zeitlichen Konkretheit behindern oder die Wahrnehmung einer Distanz begründen könnten. So fehlt nicht nur jede Angabe über den Ort der Adressatengemeinde, sondern auch jede konkretere Beschreibung einer Beziehung der Adressaten zu ‚Petrus' oder einer von ihm ausgehenden Mission, jeder Hinweis auf eine nähere persönliche Kenntnis der Gemeindesituation oder einzelner Personen, ganz zu schweigen von persönlichen Notizen, Grußaufträgen etc., die z.B. in den paulinischen Briefen deren Situationsbezug markieren und auch späteren Lesern immer vor Augen halten, dass die Briefe zunächst anderen galten. Hingegen ist 2Petr von so persönlichen Notizen, auch im Briefschluss, ganz frei und damit völlig offen für die Rezeption durch spätere heidenchristliche Leser. An solche Leser nach dem in 2Petr 1,15 erwähnten Tod des Petrus ist der Text faktisch adressiert.

Die Situation der tatsächlichen Adressaten lässt sich aus den textlichen Daten nur mit Vorbehalten rekonstruieren, zumal sie mit dem Gegnerbild eng zusammenhängt und hier Wahrheit, Übertreibung und bloße Fiktion schwer zu trennen sind.[92]

Denkbar wäre, dass der Brief gar nicht an einen lokal oder regional begrenzten Adressatenkreis gerichtet ist. Die unspezifische Adresse und die Person des Petrus könnten auf eine von vornherein gesamtkirchliche, ‚katholische' Ausrichtung hindeuten. Andererseits wäre dann die spezifische Ausrichtung auf das in 2Petr 3,3–13 diskutierte Problem der Parusieerwartung doch verwunderlich. Man müsste entweder voraussetzen, dass dieses Problem zur Zeit der Abfassung ein ‚gesamtkirchliches' wäre – oder eben doch damit rechnen, dass der reale Autor eine spezifischere Situation im Blick hatte, was dann auch einen realen, lokal oder regional begrenzten Kreis von Adressaten bzw. Adressatengemeinden impliziert.

Wenn sich die realen Adressaten in der im Brief anklingenden Situation wiederfinden und die Gegner, von denen es sich zu distanzieren galt, erkennen sollten, ist anzunehmen, dass einige der z.T. nur beiläufig erwähnten oder besonders spezifischen Hinweise die Situation zutreffend beschreiben:

– Die fiktiven (und faktischen) Adressaten werden als *Heidenchristen* gezeichnet,[93] die sich von Irrtum und Befleckung (d.h. dem heidnischen Leben) abgewandt (2Petr 2,18.20) und Reinigung von ihren Sünden empfangen haben (2Petr 1,9). Diese Christen leben eine unbestimmte Zeit nach dem Tod des Petrus und sollen nach 2Petr 1,15 in dem Schreiben sein Vermächtnis erkennen. Sie kennen wohl schon eine Sammlung der Briefe des Paulus (deren Umfang unklar bleibt), um deren Deutung gestritten wird.

---

[92] S. dazu ausführlich FREY, Disparagement as Argument (s. Anm. 69).

[93] Der Sachverhalt, dass Petrus früh noch als Verkündiger des Evangeliums für die ‚Beschneidung' bezeichnet werden konnte (Gal 2,7), ist längst nicht mehr im Blickfeld.

– Anzunehmen ist auch, dass die Adressaten die bekämpften „Falschlehrer" identifizieren konnten. Dabei ist weniger an die stark stereotypisiert dargestellten Details des Lebenswandels dieser Gegner zu denken,[94] als vielmehr an ihre sehr präzise angeführte, sogar zitierte Ansicht hinsichtlich der Erwartung der Parusie. Ob es sich dabei um ein wirkliches Zitat oder nur um ein Referat handelt, ist nicht entscheidend, aber wenn die Argumentation des Schreibens wirken sollte, dann dürfte der Autor die Argumente der Gegner hier „in der Substanz zutreffend wiedergeben."[95]

– Die gegnerischen Lehrer scheinen innerhalb der Gemeinde aufzutreten (2Petr 2,1) und somit zu ihr zu gehören. D.h., auch hier ist eine Trennung noch nicht erfolgt.[96] In einer evtl. bedeutungsvollen Ergänzung der Vorlage des Jud wird angekündigt, dass die Gegner viele Nachfolger haben werden (2Petr 2,2), später heißt es, sie verführen die ungefestigten Seelen (2Petr 2,14), wobei in einer längeren Erweiterung der Vorlage v.a. der Rückfall von neuen, frisch aus dem Heidentum konvertierten Gemeindegliedern hervorgehoben wird (2Petr 2,19–22). Diese über Jud hinausgehenden Zusätze sind kaum nur als fiktionale Elemente zu deuten. Es lässt sich zumindest festhalten, dass die Gegner einigen Erfolg hatten und als Gefahr für die Gemeinden erscheinen konnten.

– Interessant ist andererseits, dass der im Jud konkrete Hinweis auf gemeindliche Mähler (Jud 12) in der Rezeption durch den Autor des 2Petr getilgt wird. 2Petr 2,13 erwähnt hingegen, dass die Gegner „mit euch [sc. den Adressaten] schmausen" (συνευωχούμενοι ὑμῖν). Von hier aus kann man vermuten, dass die Adressaten mit den Falschlehrern gute Verbindungen pflegten und evtl. Einladungen zum Essen in privatem Rahmen annahmen.[97]

– Im Zusammenhang damit lässt sich vielleicht sogar folgern, dass die Adressaten selbst von der gegnerischen Argumentation beeindruckt waren. So betont der Autor, dass der Herr die Frommen aus der Versuchung zu retten vermag (2Petr 2,9), und ermahnt ganz am Ende noch einmal zur

---

[94] S. unten im nächsten Abschnitt und ausführlich FREY, Disparagement as Argument (s. Anm. 69).
[95] So mit Recht VÖGTLE, Der Judasbrief. Der 2. Petrusbrief (s. Anm. 23), 118, der zu Recht festhält: „Daß er hinsichtlich des offenbar heikelsten Streitpunktes den Gegnern Behauptungen unterstellt, die diese gar nicht aussprachen, ist kaum vorstellbar; damit hätte er sein ohnehin schwieriges Unternehmen ja völlig diskreditiert" (118).
[96] Anders VÖGTLE, a.a.O. 128, der aus dem Fehlen von Verhaltensregeln zum Umgang mit den Gegnern (vgl. Jud 22f.) schließen will, „daß diese im allgemeinen wenigstens auf dem Weg der Trennung von den Gemeinden waren".
[97] 2Petr 2,13 bringt in diesem Zusammenhang den Begriff der ἡδονή. Für die Beteiligten war offenbar das eine Lust, worin der Autor eine Gefahr sieht – sowohl hinsichtlich unangemessener Schwelgerei als auch der Gefährdung durch das Gedankengut der Gegner.

Standfestigkeit gegenüber der Position der Gegner (2Petr 3,17). Sahen die Adressaten sich in der ‚Versuchung' – oder sah der Autor sie so stark gefährdet, was die von ihm gewählten drastischen Mittel der Autorisierung und Polemik begründen konnte? Auffällig ist zudem, dass anders als in Jud 22f. hier keine Aufforderung zur ‚seelsorgerlichen' Bemühung um verunsicherte Mitchristen begegnet. Im 2Petr geht es nur (noch) um die Standfestigkeit; dabei bleibt der Appell im Vergleich zum stärker gemeindeorientierten Jud allgemeiner und ‚individueller'.

3.3.2 Das diffamierende Gegnerbild

Die Situation der Adressatengemeinde kommt jedoch nur implizit und am Rande zur Sprache. Die genannten Aspekte sind lediglich ein Baustein in der Bekämpfung der gegnerischen Lehrer, die das primäre Ziel des realen Autors ist, wie die Schlussmahnung (2Petr 3,17) deutlich macht.

Zur Auseinandersetzung mit ihnen wird in Kapitel 3 der offenbar zentrale Streitpunkt aufgenommen und ausführlich widerlegt (2Petr 3,1–13), doch werden sie zuvor in einem längeren Abschnitt – weithin in Adaption der Polemik des Jud – in einer analogielos scharfen Polemik diskreditiert (2Petr 2,1–22). Die Gegner werden nicht nur mit dem gesamten Arsenal der Vorwürfe unmoralischer Lebensführung, hochtrabender Reden und unlauteren Vorgehens bekämpft, ihnen wird darüber hinaus ein ‚animalisches' Wesen zugeschrieben, kraft dessen sie letztlich zu nichts anderem als dem Verderben bestimmt sind. Zwei polemische Sprichwörter bilden den Abschluss (2Petr 2,22): „Ein Hund kehrt zu seinem eigenen Gespei zurück." Und: „Eine Sau hat gebadet, um sich wieder in ihrem eigenen Dreck zu suhlen."

Angesichts dieser im NT beispiellosen Polemik stellt sich noch mehr als im Falle des Judasbriefs die Frage, in welchem Maße hier Stereotypen zur Geltung kommen, die das tatsächliche Profil der Gegner überlagern, und ob dieses Profil hinter der Konstruktion des Gegnerbildes überhaupt noch zu erkennen ist. Jedenfalls führt hier kein Weg an der Erkenntnis vorbei, dass dieses Bild der Gegner eine fiktionale Konstruktion darstellt, die in ihrer Intention zu verstehen und in mehrfacher Hinsicht – historisch wie ethisch – kritisch zu interpretieren ist.[98]

Während der Autor den sachlichen Streitpunkt erst in Kapitel 3 erkennen lässt, werden die Gegner selbst erstmals in 2Petr 2,1 eingeführt.[99]

---

[98] S. zum Folgenden ausführlicher FREY, Disparagement as Argument (s. Anm. 69).

[99] Einige Wendungen zuvor könnten schon auf die Auseinandersetzung bezogen sein, so der Hinweis, dass die Adressaten „nicht untätig oder unfruchtbar" hinsichtlich der christlichen Tugenden sein sollen (2Petr 1,8) und dass diejenigen, die diese Tugenden

Schon die Einführung der Gegner erfolgt in einem klaren eschatologischen Gegensatz: Wie die Lügenpropheten der biblischen Zeit (vgl. Dtn 18,20) der wahren, von Gott autorisierten Prophetie entgegenstanden, so stehen die kommenden und für den faktischen Autor und seine Adressaten gegenwärtigen Lügenlehrer (ψευδοδιδάσκαλοι) der wahren apostolischen Lehre entgegen. Von der ersten Erwähnung der Gegner an wird deutlich gemacht, dass das endgerichtliche Urteil über sie bereits feststeht und ihr Verderben (ebenso wie die Parusie) keineswegs ausbleibt, sondern „unabänderlich andrängend"[100] am Werk ist.

Die einführende Passage trägt eine Fülle weiterer Aspekte zur gründlichen Diskreditierung der Gegner bei: Diese führen verderbliche Lehrmeinungen (αἱρέσεις ἀπωλείας) ein, und zwar heimlich und ‚von außen' (παρεισάξουσιν), womit zugleich ein Aspekt von Unlauterkeit mitschwingt.[101] Sie agieren mit „erdichteten Worten" (πλαστοῖς λόγοις),[102] um Anhänger zu gewinnen, wobei ihnen zugleich „Habgier" unterstellt wird. Noch schärfer ist der Vorwurf der Verleugnung Christi, wobei ausdrücklich auf das vormalige Zugehörigkeitsverhältnis zum ‚Herrscher' (δεσπότης), „der sie erkauft hat" (vgl. 2Petr 1,9; 2,20–22), hingewiesen wird. Die Gegner sind also Apostaten, die durch ihr Wirken und die Anhängerschaft, die sie gewinnen, zur Diskreditierung des „Weges der Wahrheit", d.h. des apostolischen Glaubens und der damit verbundenen Lebensführung beitragen.

Die folgende Reihe biblischer Exempel basiert zwar auf Jud 5–7, adaptiert die Vorlage aber sehr eigenständig und mit spezifischen Ergänzungen, die auf ein eigenständiges Argumentationsinteresse hindeuten. Von den drei Paradigmen des Gerichts (Wüstengeneration, Wächterengel, Sodomiten) werden nur die beiden letzten übernommen, stattdes-

---

nicht hervorbringen, die erfahrene Vergebung der Sünden vergessen hätten (2Petr 1,9), weiter die Beteuerung, dass die Glaubenden „nicht ausgeklügelten Mythen" gefolgt seien (2Petr 2,16), sowie schließlich die Aussage über die Interpretation des „prophetischen Wortes" (2Petr 1,19–21).

[100] H. FRANKEMÖLLE, 1. Petrusbrief. 2. Petrusbrief. Judasbrief, NEB.NT 18/20, Würzburg 1987, 104.

[101] Hier ist die Formulierung von Jud 4, dass die dort bekämpften Gegner von außen in die Gemeinde eingedrungen seien (παρεισέδυσαν), in charakteristischer Weise abgewandelt und auf die Lehrmeinungen bezogen. Der Aspekt des ‚Fremden' ist dabei ebenso enthalten wie der Aspekt der Heimlichkeit oder gar Heimtücke (s. dazu T. J. KRAUS, Sprache, Stil und historischer Ort des Zweiten Petrusbriefes, WUNT II/136, Tübingen 2001, 297f.). In diesem Sinne wird der Terminus in der späteren christlichen Literatur mehrfach auf Häretiker bezogen (vgl. Hegesipp bei Eus.h.e. 4,22,5; Hipp.haer 5,17,10; 7,29,8). Ein ähnlicher Gebrauch von Bildungen mit παρεισ- liegt schon bei Paulus in Gal 2,4 vor: παρεισάκτοι ψευδαδελφοί.

[102] Nach BAUCKHAM, Jude. 2 Peter (s. Anm. 13), 243, ist dies „a classical expression ... for deceitful speech". Die erdichteten Worte stehen den „ausgeklügelten Mythen" in 2Petr 1,16 gegenüber.

sen werden zwei Paradigmen der Rettung (Noah und Lot) hinzugefügt. D.h. es geht dem Autor nicht nur (wie im Jud) um den Aufweis der Gerichtsverfallenheit der Gegner, sondern um den Beleg der Macht Gottes, die Frommen aus der Versuchung zu retten, „die Ungerechten aber für den Tag das Gericht zur Bestrafung aufzubewahren" (2Petr 2,9).[103] Dabei werden die für das Profil der im Jud bekämpften Gegner charakteristischen Aspekte ausgelassen oder verschleiert: Von den Engeln wird in 2Petr 2,4 nur allgemein ein „Sündigen" (ἁμαρτάνειν) erwähnt, nicht das Detail, dass sie ihre himmlische Wohnstatt verließen oder die gottgesetzte Grenze zwischen Engeln und Menschen überschritten; von den Sodomiten wird nicht mehr gesagt, dass sie „in ähnlicher Weise" wie die Wächterengel „fremdem Fleisch" hinterherliefen (Jud 7), also eine vergleichbare Grenzüberschreitung praktizierten. Vielmehr ist diese Formulierung hier verschoben und auf die dem Gericht verfallenen Ungerechten bezogen, die – wie es verallgemeinert heißt – „dem Fleisch hinterherlaufen", und zwar in Gier nach Beschmutzung und Verachtung der Macht des Herrn (2Petr 2,10a).

In 2Petr 2,4–10a kommen damit wesentliche neue Aspekte zum Gegnerbild hinzu: Mit dem (aus Jud übernommenen) Terminus „Gottlose" (ἀσεβεῖς) werden diese den Gerechten schroff entgegengesetzt; den Gottlosen wird zudem ein „ausschweifender Lebenswandel" (2Petr 2,7: ἐν ἀσελγείᾳ ἀναστροφή) angelastet, dessen bloßer Anblick die Frommen „quält" und „bedrängt" (2Petr 2,7f.). Mit dem ‚Sündenbegriff'[104] ἐπιθυμία (2Petr 2,10a), der allgemeinen Rede vom „Fleisch" und dem Aspekt der „Beschmutzung" wird den Gegnern ein massiver moralisch-sexueller Vorwurf gemacht. Dies zeigt besonders der Vergleich mit Jud. Aus der dort formulierten Anklage, die spezifisch auf die als ‚frevelhafte' Grenzüberschreitung geltende Herabwürdigung von Engelmächten[105] bezogen war, wird hier ein allgemeiner Vorwurf sexuellen Fehlverhaltens, das als Verachtung der Herrenmacht Christi, fehlgeleitete ‚Nachfolge' des ‚Fleisches' und eschatologisch relevante ‚Befleckung' angesehen wird.

In der zweiten Hälfte von 2Petr 2 steigert sich die Schärfe und Dichte der Polemik noch weiter zu einer dichten und im Neuen Testament analogielosen Tirade, die den Gegnern neben dem zutiefst amoralischen Lebenswandel ein hochtrabendes Wesen und eine animalische Natur ‚anhängt'.

---

[103] Von der thematischen Erörterung aus 2Petr 3 ausgehend, ist denkbar, dass die Gegner tatsächlich die Lehre, dass Gott eschatologisch zu retten und zu richten vermag, in Zweifel gezogen haben. In diesem Fall würde 2Petr 2,9 diese Skepsis aufnehmen und mit biblischen Beispielen widerlegen.

[104] Vgl. z.B. im Dekalog in Ex 20,17 LXX und Dtn 5,21 LXX.

[105] Nicht, wie SCHMIDT, Mahnung (s. Anm. 52), 316–318, erwägt, auf sexuellen Verkehr mit Engeln, selbst wenn dieser nur ‚erträumt' sein sollte (vgl. Jud 8). Eine solche Annahme führt eher dazu, die Gegner als abseitige Charaktere zu werten und in ihrer theologischen Position nicht ernst zu nehmen – was letztlich ein Erfolg der Diskreditierungs-Strategie des Autors wäre.

Die Passage beginnt mit einem entrüsteten Ausruf „Selbstgefällige Freche!" (τολμηταὶ αὐθάδεις),[106] die nun über die schon bekannten Vorwürfe der Verleugnung des Herrn (V.1) und der Verachtung der Herrenmacht (V.10a) hinaus das *Wesen* der Gegner als frech und respektlos charakterisiert.

Die Aussage, dass diese Leute nicht einmal die δόξαι fürchten, sondern sie ‚lästern' (βλασφημοῦντες), ist ein knappes Relikt des im Jud spezifischer ausgeführten Vorwurfs der Lästerung der Engel, der hier nur noch blass nachklingt[107] und allgemein die Respektlosigkeit der Gegner illustriert.

Mit V.12–14 beginnt eine längere Sequenz von Beschimpfungen, die v.a. auf die „geistige und moralische Verkommenheit"[108] der Gegner zielen. Ein Großteil der Formulierungen ist aus Jud 10.12 übernommen, wobei z.T. die rhetorische Intensität gesteigert wird.[109] Insbesondere wendet der Autor nun das, was im Jud über das Verhalten der Gegner gesagt wurde, in eine Beschreibung ihres Wesens:[110] Sie sind „wie unvernünftige Tiere (nur) als Naturwesen geboren" (d.h. wesenhaft ohne Geist und Vernunft), mit der bloßen Bestimmung, gefangen und getötet zu werden.

Die Natur der Gegner wird also mit der von Tieren verglichen, denen der Autor keine bleibende Bestimmung zuschreibt. Zielpunkt der Darstellung ist insofern das Verderben, dem die Irrlehrer entgegengehen. Doch werden sie darüber hinaus mit der Einordnung als vernunftlose ‚Naturwesen' aufs Äußerste herabgewürdigt, und es ist nicht ohne Bedeutung, dass dies in einem literarischen Prozess, nämlich der Rezeption und Modifikation der Vorlage des Judasbriefes, geschieht.

---

[106] τολμηταί ist ein ntl. *hapax legomenon*, das Verb ist allerdings in Jud 9 gebraucht; αὐθάδεις begegnet auch in Tit 1,7; beide Termini zusammen in 1Clem 30,8. Dieser Ausruf ist vom Autor geschickt in die Vorlage aus Jud 8 eingefügt, so dass sie die dort vorliegende Doppelaussage κυριότητα δὲ ἀθετοῦσιν δόξας δὲ βλασφημοῦσιν aufspaltet. Damit wird κυριότητος καταφρονοῦντας (V.10a) zum Abschluss der vorigen Passage, während δόξας οὐ τρέμουσιν βλασφημοῦντες (V.10b) nun zum nächsten, mit τολμηταὶ αὐθάδεις beginnenden Abschnitt gehört.

[107] Dieses Spezifikum der Polemik des Jud, das wohl mit dem spezifischen Profil der dort bekämpften Gegner zu tun hat, ist für den Autor des 2Petr nicht mehr von Bedeutung.

[108] So VÖGTLE, Der Judasbrief. Der 2. Petrusbrief (s. Anm. 23), 201.

[109] Das οὗτοι in V.12 ist wörtlich von Jud 10 übernommen, doch hat es im 2Petr nicht die strukturierende Funktion wie in Jud (vgl. Jud 8.10.12.16.19).

[110] In beiden Schriften liegt ein Vergleich vor (s. die Vergleichspartikel ὡς in Jud 10 und 2Petr 2,12), doch ist die Wendung ὡς τὰ ἄλογα ζῷα in Jud 10 adverbial, auf das „naturhafte" Verstehen bezogen, in 2Petr 2,12 ist ὡς ἄλογα ζῷα hingegen attributiv auf die Existenz, das Geborensein als Naturwesen bezogen. Ihr ‚animalisches' Wesen impliziert dabei ihre Bestimmung zur Gefangenschaft und zum Verderben.

Es folgt ein Stakkato von Anklagen,[111] das interessanterweise nicht auf den im vorherigen Vers beherrschenden Vorwurf der Unverständigkeit zurückgreift, sondern wie aus einem bereitliegenden ‚Waffenarsenal' andere, z.T. stereotype, Vorwürfe hinzufügt: Allgemein und ohne nähere Erläuterung wird gesagt, dass die Irrlehrer „den Lohn der Ungerechtigkeit erleiden" (2Petr 2,13).[112] Dann wird ihnen ein lustorientierter, schwelgerischer Lebensstil und – in Verbindung damit – betrügerisches Verhalten[113] vorgeworfen. Dazwischen eingefügt ist eine Charakterisierung der Gegner als „Schmutz- und Schandflecken", die der Autor ebenfalls durch eine leichte Veränderung seiner Vorlage aus dem Jud gewonnen hat[114] und die den Gedanken an moralische Verfehlungen weiter intensiviert. Drei weitere Anschuldigungen bringen die Habitualität des sündhaften Verhaltens zur Sprache: Sie haben „Augen voll [Begierde] nach einer Ehebrecherin", sie „sind unaufhörlich auf Sünde aus" und besitzen „ein in Habgier geübtes Herz" (2Petr 2,14). All diese Anklagen verstärken die schon zuvor geäußerten unter Verstärkung des Aspekts der Dauerhaftigkeit und Wesenhaftigkeit: Die Sünde ist das Wesen der Gegner. Der Abschluss der Passage erfolgt daher wirkungsvoll (und dem Beginn V.10b korrespondierend) mit einem Ausruf: κατάρας τέκνα, „Kinder des Fluchs!" Diese Verfluchung ist der Gipfel der Reihe vielfältiger, nur wenig zusammenhängender Anklagen.

In V.15f. nimmt der Autor eines der drei in Jud 11 vorgegebenen biblischen Paradigmen auf, Bileam, der in der hellenistisch-jüdischen Tradition, z.B. bei Philo, als „Gottloser" gilt (migr. 113),[115] der die von Gott gegebene Prophetie fälschte (mut. 203), trotz seiner Visionen als erdenverhaftetes Wesen den Engel Gottes nicht sah (Deus 181; vgl. Num 22,31) und letztlich zugrunde ging (mut. 203; Deus 183; vgl. Num 31,8). Wie bei Philo (Mos. I 295–301) erscheint Bileam auch im Liber Antiquitatum Biblicarum (LAB 18,13)

---

[111] Syntaktisch ist dieses bewirkt durch eine Reihung von rein nominalen Ausdrücken und Partizipien.

[112] Dabei verwendet der Verfasser ein wirkungsvolles Wortspiel: ἀδικούμενοι μισθὸν ἀδικίας.

[113] Das Wort ἀπάται (2Petr 2,13) entsteht durch bloße Vertauschung zweier Buchstaben aus ἀγάπαι (Jud 12). Die nun erreichte Aussage, dass die Gegner „in Betrügereien schwelgen, wenn sie mit euch schmausen", ist schwer zu deuten. An gemeindliche Mähler scheint hier (anders als im Jud) nicht mehr gedacht zu sein. Der Vorwurf geht wohl dahin, dass der Kontakt mit den Adressaten beim gemeinsamen Essen den Gegnern auch die Gelegenheit verschaffte, ihre Tischgenossen von ihren Ansichten zu überzeugen oder zu ihrer Lebensweise zu verleiten (vgl. 2Petr 2,2).

[114] Auf die textkritischen Fragen kann hier nicht eingegangen werden. Das m.E. in Jud ursprüngliche metaphorische σπιλάδες „Klippen" ist im 2Petr in σπίλοι „Schmutzflecken" verändert.

[115] Bemerkenswerterweise ist das Bileambild bei Josephus (Ant. 4,102–158) positiver; s. dazu L. H. FELDMAN, Studies in Josephus' Rewritten Bible, JSJ.S 58, Leiden 1998, 110–136.

als Verführer zum Götzendienst, und auch in Apk 2,14 wird er als Prototyp der Verführer zu Unzucht und Götzendienst gebraucht. Der auch in der rabbinischen Tradition belegte[116] Vorwurf der Gewinnsucht des Bileam war schon in Jud 11 zentral aufgenommen und wird hier, zusammen mit dem Motiv der Unverständigkeit und dem Tiervergleich, noch verbreitet. Die Erwähnung des stummen Esels kompromittiert die Gegner weiter: Während sie Erkenntnis beanspruchen, sind sie selbst nicht nur gänzlich unverständig (als ‚Naturwesen', s. V.12), sondern stehen selbst hinter einem Esel zurück (V.16).

Nach diesem biblischen Beispiel bietet der Autor noch einmal eine Serie von Vorwürfen, die dann in den beiden Sprichworten in V.22 zu ihrem Höhepunkt gelangt. Zunächst werden die komplizierten Metaphern aus Jud 12 wirkungsvoll vereinfacht: Die Gegner sind „wasserlose Quellen" und „vom Sturm getriebene Nebelschwaden", d.h. trügerisch, ohne Substanz und vergänglich. Dass sie dem Verderben entgegengehen, kommt in der Wendung zum Ausdruck, die in Jud 13 noch auf wandernde Sterne und die gefallenen Engel der Henochtradition bezogen und nur metaphorisch auf die Gegner übertragen ist[117]: Den Gegnern ist „die dunkelste Finsternis aufbewahrt".

Weitere Beschuldigungen sind ohne Rückgriff auf die Judas-Vorlage formuliert und wiederholen und verstärken frühere Vorwürfe. Erneut werden die Gegner verbaler und sexueller Sünden beschuldigt: Sie reden „hochtrabende Worte der Nichtigkeit" und ködern andere „in den Begierden des Fleisches mit Ausschweifungen", und zwar besonders solche, die erst kurz dem Irrtum entflohen und auf den „Weg der Wahrheit" (V.2) gekommen sind. Da ein solcher Rückfall nach Überzeugung des Autors[118] die Lage der Betreffenden noch prekärer werden lässt als vor ihrer Bekehrung (2Petr 2,21), wird dies durch die beiden abschließend gebotenen Sprichworte vom Hund und vom Schwein drastisch expliziert. Dabei ist der hier dargestellte Sachverhalt weniger auf die von den Gegnern ‚Geköderten' als vielmehr auf diese selbst zu beziehen, die selbst aus der Gemeinde kommen und sich zu einer verderblichen Lehre und einer verderblichen Le-

---

[116] Vgl. bSanh 106a; NumR 22,5; Sifre Num 157: Dort wird die knappe Notiz, dass er bei den Midianiterkönigen war, als diese von den Israeliten erschlagen wurden (Num 31,8), dahingehend erklärt, dass er seinen Lohn für den durch seine Verführung verursachten Tod von 24000 Israeliten hätte abholen wollen.

[117] In 1Hen 18,13–16 und 21,3–6 sind die Wächterengel (vgl. Jud 6) selbst als wandernde Sterne dargestellt, die Gott ungehorsam waren (vgl. auch Theophilus, ad Autolycum 2,15: Die Planeten sind „ein Bild ... jener, die von Gott abgefallen sind und sein Gesetz und seine Gebote verlassen haben".). Dies wird in Jud 13 metaphorisch auf die dort bekämpften Gegner bezogen. 2Petr 2,17 streicht in der Aufnahme von Jud 13 die Worte ἀστέρες πλανῆται weg und bezieht den Nachsatz somit direkt auf die hier bekämpften Gegner.

[118] Vgl. schon Mt 12,45/Lk 11,26; s. auch die Position des Hebr zur sogenannten zweiten Buße (Hebr 6,4–6; 10,26–31).

benshaltung gewendet haben, also ‚Apostaten' geworden sind (2Petr 2,1; vgl. 1,9).

Das Bild der gegnerischen Lehrer ist in diesem Kapitel – vor jeder sachlichen Auseinandersetzung und unabhängig von dieser – durch eine Fülle von Aspekten bestimmt, die diese von vornherein moralisch und eschatologisch disqualifizieren:[119]

a) Sie sind *lügnerische* Lehrer (V.1). Ihre selbstfabrizierten Worte (V.3) und leeren Versprechungen (V.18) stehen der göttlich inspirierten Prophetie entgegen. Sie *verleugnen den Herrn* und seine Herrschaft, sind also Apostaten (V.1) und unrettbar dem Gericht geweiht (V.1.3f.6.9f.12.17.20). Wie sie selbst dem Verderben entgegen gehen (V.12), bringen auch ihre Lehren *Verderben* (V.1).

b) Ihre Agitation wird als *unlauter* diskreditiert: Sie führen ihre Lehrmeinungen heimlich ein (V.1), gewinnen Anhänger durch Betrug und leere Worte (V.3.13.19), sind habgierig (V.13.15) und versuchen, die Adressaten zu ihrem eigenen Vorteil zu ‚kaufen' (V.3) und ködern (V.14), insbesondere Instabile oder frisch Konvertierte (V.14.19), wobei die Versprechung von ‚Freiheit' (V.19) und die eigenen Ausschweifungen (V.2.18) offenbar attraktiv wirken.

c) Insbesondere wird den Gegnern ein *unmoralischer Lebensstil* vorgeworfen. Ihr Lebenswandel ist *ausschweifend* (V.2.7.18) und *lustorientiert* (V.13).[120] Mit ἐπιθυμία (V.10) wird ein traditionell auf Sünde bezogener Terminus verwendet und insbesondere auf das ‚Fleisch' bezogen (V.18). ‚Fleisches'-Nachfolge (V.10) steht der Christus-Nachfolge entgegen. Noch konkreter wird den Gegnern ein ehebrecherisches Wesen (V.14.18) zugeschrieben.

d) Vermutlich besonders mit dem sexuellen Fehlverhalten verbindet sich der Aspekt der Unreinheit oder Befleckung (V.10.13.20), der in den Sprichworten V.22 wiederkehrt.

e) Allgemein wird den Gegnern vorgeworfen, dass sie die Herrenmacht (V.10) – und präziser den Herrn selbst (V.3) – verachten. Damit verbindet sich allgemein der Vorwurf von Frechheit und Respektlosigkeit (V.10), selbst gegenüber himmlischen Mächten, ja von Apostasie.

f) Damit verbunden ist der Verwurf, dass die Gegner völlig unverständig sind. Generell wird gesagt, dass sie von dem, was sie verlästern, nichts erkennen (V.12; vgl. V.17).

---

[119] S. die ausführlichere Zusammenfassung und Auswertung in FREY, Disparagement as Argument (s. Anm. 69).

[120] Die Verwendung von ἡδονή V.13 lässt dabei erkennen, dass das, was für die Gegner (und vielleicht für die Adressaten auch) eine Freude war, dem Autor verwerflich erscheint.

g) Allgemeiner wird ihnen ‚Ungerechtigkeit' (ἀδικία) vorgeworfen (V.13), noch stärker ist der Vorwurf, dass sie unablässig sündigen (V.14). Überhaupt zielt die Diskreditierung auf das *Wesen* der Gegner: Sünde, Habgier und Ehebruch sind habituell (V.14).

h) Letztlich werden die Gegner nicht als menschliche Wesen gewürdigt, sondern wesenhaft wie unvernünftige Tiere (V.12) angesehen. Sie sind bloß ‚natürliche' Wesen ohne Verstand und Geist, deren Bestimmung nicht die Unvergänglichkeit, sondern das Verderben ist.

i) In einer Spitzenaussage werden die Gegner sogar als ‚Kinder des Fluchs' verflucht (V.14).

3.3.3 Die Frage nach dem tatsächlichen Gegnerprofil

Lässt sich hinter diesem massiv polemischen Bild überhaupt noch nach dem ‚wahren' Profil der gegnerischen Lehrer fragen? Die Beurteilung der fiktionalen Gesamtkonstruktion hängt nicht zuletzt an der Frage, was von den Vorwürfen des Autors zutrifft und in welchem Maße er seine Gegner in einer auch ethisch fragwürdigen Weise zu ‚vernichten' sucht.

An der Einsicht führt m.E. kein Weg vorbei, dass das literarische Bild der Irrlehrer in 2Petr 2 eine Konstruktion ist, von der die realen Gegner, die der Autor mit seinem pseudonymen Schreiben bekämpfen will, zu unterscheiden sind.[121] Und manches spricht dafür, dass die Darstellung mehr über die Sichtweisen des Autors als über die tatsächliche Natur und Lebensführung seiner Gegner verrät.[122] Es wäre allzu bequem, auf einer rein literarischen Ebene zu verharren, aber die Frage nach der außertextlichen Referenz des gezeichneten Bildes bzw. seiner Teile lässt sich nicht ausklammern. Die historische Frage nach dem tatsächlichen Profil der Gegner und nach der Entstehungssituation des Schreibens ist auch um der theologischen Wahrheit willen zu stellen, wenn man die fiktionale Konstruktion im Ganzen angemessen beurteilen will. Drei Kriterien könnten helfen, im Gegnerbild zu differenzieren:

a) Zunächst sind zahlreiche Einzelaspekte aus dem Judasbrief übernommen. Eine solche Übernahme beweist nicht zwingend, dass der Sachgehalt auf die Gegner des Zweiten Petrusbriefes nicht auch zuträfe, zumindest in der Vorstellung des Autors. Weiter führen kann die Frage, inwiefern die einzelnen Aspekte sich mit dem sachlichen Hauptstreitpunkt, wie er in 2Petr 3,3ff. ausgeführt wird, verbinden oder ob sie mit diesem relativ unverbunden sind.

---

[121] S. den o. Anm. 29 zitierten Grundsatz von DU TOIT, Vilification (s. Anm. 29), 404.
[122] So M. R. DESJARDINS, The Portrayal of the Dissidents in 2 Peter and Jude. Does It Tell Us More about the ‚Godly' and the ‚Ungodly'?, JSNT 30 (1987), 89–102.

b) Andere Vorwürfe erwecken angesichts zahlreicher Parallelen in anderen polemischen Texten des NT, der Apostolischen Väter und altkirchlichen Häresiologen, aber auch der frühjüdischen oder paganen Polemik den Verdacht, Standardvorwürfe gegen religiöse oder philosophische Konkurrenten zu sein.[123]

c) In der Rezeption der Judas-Vorlage lässt sich erkennen, dass der Autor des Zweiten Petrusbriefs bestimmte, für das Profil der Gegner des Judasbriefs charakteristische Züge tilgt oder verwischt. So werden z.B. die Hinweise auf die Engel (Jud 8–10) insgesamt verkürzt, der Vorwurf der ‚Lästerung' der δόξαι verwischt und die spezfische Charakterisierung der Sünde der Wächterengel und der Sodomiten (Jud 6f.) als einer Überschreitung der Grenze von Engeln und Menschen getilgt. Dies mag mit einem verminderten Interesse des Autors des 2Petr an angelologischen Sachverhalten zusammenhängen, zeigt aber auch, dass dieser das literarische Bild seiner Gegner nicht unabhängig von dem realen Profil derselben zeichnen konnte, wenn die Darstellung denn bei den Adressaten ‚wirken' sollte. Insofern lässt sich nach Zügen im Gegnerbild suchen, die weder aus Jud übernommen noch topisch sind, sondern eher situationsspezifisch erscheinen und damit für die historische Rekonstruktion des tatsächlichen Profils der bekämpften Gegner bzw. der tatsächlichen Situation Anhaltspunkte geben.[124]

Das letztgenannte Kriterium führt zu der Einsicht, dass sich die Gegner im 2Petr offenbar deutlich von den im Jud bekämpften unterschieden. Obwohl der Autor die Polemik seiner Vorlage gut aufnehmen konnte, hat er dies nur unter Weglassung und Verallgemeinerung einiger Aspekte sowie der Hinzufügung neuer Themen – insbesondere des Themas der Parusie in Kapitel 3 – getan. Den vielfältigen Versuchen der Forschung, beide Gegnergruppen im engen theologischen oder religionsgeschichtlichen Zusammenhang zu sehen, ist daher zu widersprechen.[125] So wenig sich der Autor des 2Petr für die Henochtradition und die Stellung der Engel interessiert,[126] so wenig lässt sich das Problem der Leugnung

---

[123] S. die o. Anm. 34 zitierte Liste von Topoi aus DU TOIT, Vilification (s. Anm. 29), 405–410.

[124] S. besonders J. H. NEYREY, The Form and Background of the Polemic in 2 Peter, JBL 99 (1980), 407–431.

[125] Die Tendenz, beide Briefe z.B. gegen Gnostiker gerichtet zu sehen, geht schon auf die Alte Kirche zurück. Für die neuzeitliche Forschung grundlegend war WERDERMANN, Irrlehrer (s. Anm. 36).

[126] Die verkürzte Rezeption von Jud 8–10 in 2Petr 2,10f., insbesondere der Satz, dass „selbst Engel, die doch größer an Kraft und Macht sind, gegen sie kein lästerndes Urteil beim Herrn vorbringen" (2Petr 2,11), ist ohne eine Kenntnis des Jud bzw. der dort zugrunde liegenden Traditionen aus der Himmelfahrt Moses kaum verständlich. Undeutlich bleibt, welche Engel ein solches Urteil nicht zu sprechen wagen und wer hier das Gegenüber ist. Dass es ursprünglich um eine Szene mit Michael und dem Satan ging, ist völlig verwischt.

der Parusie bereits in die Situation des Jud eintragen.[127] Gemeinsam sind den beiden Schreiben v.a. die topischen und stereotypen Vorwürfe – der Apostasie, verbalen Überheblichkeit, sexuellen Vergehen oder Unlauterkeit –, die auf alle ‚Häretiker' anwendbar, aber für das Profil der jeweiligen Gegner gerade *nicht* signifikant sind.

Der entscheidende Punkt der Auseinandersetzung dürfte in der Tat die Frage sein, die dann in 2Petr 3,4 thematisiert wird: Ganz gleich, ob es sich hier um wörtliche Zitate der Gegner oder nur Zusammenfassungen ihrer Argumentation handelt, wird man diesem Vers den primären Streitpunkt entnehmen können: Die Spötter verweisen auf das Ausbleiben der Parusie und auf den seit der Zeit der ‚Väter' (d.h. wohl der apostolischen Urzeit des Christusglaubens) unveränderten Fortbestand der Welt. 2Petr 3,9 fügt einen Aspekt hinzu: „Einige" reden von der „Verzögerung" oder der Langsamkeit der Verheißung der Parusie (τινες βραδύτητα ἡγοῦνται).

Zwei weitere Formulierungen könnten in dieselbe Richtung weisen: Bereits in 2Petr 2,3b wird betont, dass das Gericht über die Irrlehrer nicht untätig ist (οὐκ ἀργεῖ) und ihr Verderben nicht „schläft" (οὐ νυστάζει). Auch dies könnte Aussagen der Gegner spiegeln, dass das mit der Parusie erwartete Gericht ‚schlafe' und daher nicht drohend zu erwarten sei, oder dass evtl. sogar Gott selbst im Blick auf diese Welt ‚untätig' und daher die Weissagung eines endzeitlichen Gerichts ein ‚bloßer Mythos' (2Petr 1,16), d.h. eine unglaubhafte Erfindung sei. Die Aussagen in 2,4–8 zielen darauf, die Macht Gottes, die Frommen zu retten und die Gottlosen auf den Gerichtstag hin aufzubewahren (2,9), biblisch zu begründen.[128] Auch 2Petr 1,19–21 dürfte das eigentliche Sachthema bereits präludieren, wenn ‚Petrus' die Zuverlässigkeit des prophetischen Wortes begründet und dessen ‚eigenmächtige' Auslegung zurückweist. Auch dies dürfte auf die ‚eigenen' Ansichten der Gegner hinsichtlich der eschatologischen Erwartung zielen.

Es ist anzunehmen, dass die Gegner mit ihrem Hinweis auf den schon länger eingetretenen Tod der ersten Zeugengeneration und auf das bisherige Nichteintreten der Parusie durchaus Gehör fanden (2Petr 2,2), so dass sie für den Autor als eine Gefährdung der Gemeinden und des überlieferten Glaubens erscheinen und die Abfassung des Schreibens mit seiner scharfen Polemik und seiner kühnen Autorfiktion veranlassen konnten. Wie erwähnt, könnten die Adressaten mit den Gegnern auch bei Einladungen in privatem Rahmen zusammengetroffen sein, was durchaus den Verdacht wecken konnte, dass es dabei allzu schwelgerisch oder moralisch laszlv zuging.

Die Frage nach der religions- und theologiegeschichtlichen Verortung dieser Gegner kann hier nicht näher erörtert werden. Doch wenn der Hinweis auf den Gedanken der ‚Freiheit' (ἐλευθερία) – ungeachtet der Frage, wo-

---

[127] Gegen VÖGTLE, Der Judasbrief. Der 2. Petrusbrief (s. Anm. 23), 95–98.
[128] NEYREY, Form and Background (s. Anm. 124), 415f.

von Befreiung erstrebt wurde[129] – ein Stichwort der Gegner aufgreift (2Petr 2,19),[130] dann lässt sich verstehen, warum der Autor so stark mit ethisch-moralischen Anschuldigungen arbeitet. Andererseits besteht auch in diesem Fall kein Recht, all diese Vorwürfe von Ausschweifung, Ehebruch, Habgier und Befleckung etc. als zutreffende Beschreibung des Lebenswandels der Gegner zu werten. Die einflussreiche und für manche, v.a. angelsächsische, Interpreten charakteristische ‚harmonisierende' Aussage, dass die Gegner „combined scepticism with the parousia with moral libertinism",[131] ist deutlich zu unkritisch.

3.3.4 Die Notwendigkeit einer kritischen Interpretation

Vielmehr sind nach den o.g. Kriterien an einer Reihe von Punkten des gezeichneten Gegnerbildes deutliche Zweifel angebracht:

– *Respektlosigkeit* gegenüber Christus oder überhaupt Autoritäten wird schon in Jud 4.8.18 den dortigen Gegnern vorgeworfen und begegnet häufig als Anklage gegen konkurrierende Lehrer oder Leute, die traditionelle Werte in Frage stellen. Was in Jud 8 spezifisch auf die Herabsetzung von Engelmächten bezogen ist, wird in 2Petr 2,10 ohne einen konkreten Bezug aufgenommen. Freilich konnte die Skepsis gegen die Parusieerwartung ebenso als eine unangemessen arrogante, eigenmächtige Stellung gegenüber der Prophetie (2Petr 3,3; vgl. 1,20f.) oder gar der Herrlichkeit Christi selbst (2Petr 1,16f.) erscheinen, die ‚Petrus' bezeugt.

– Als *Apostaten* erscheinen die Gegner in 2Petr 2,1 (vgl. 1,9; 2,22) wie in Jud 4. Doch zeigt sowohl die in Jud 12 erkennbare Gemeindesituation als auch die in 2Petr 2,13 zu vermutende Situation, in der zwischen den Gegnern und den Adressaten offenbar noch keine Trennung erfolgt ist, dass sich die Gegner selbst als Christen verstanden und ihre Position evtl. sogar durch den Hinweis auf Paulus und seine Briefe begründeten (2Petr 3,15).

– Der Vorwurf der *Unverständigkeit* in geistlichen Dingen wird in Jud 10 auf die Frage der Engel bezogen, in 2Petr 2,12 hingegen verallgemeinert, wobei sich ein Bezug auf die Parusie bzw. Herrlichkeit Christi nahelegt. Freilich ist ein solcher Vorwurf letztlich nur Spiegel eines Streits um theologische Positionen und letztlich ein wenig zugkräftiges Argument.

---

[129] S. etwa FORNBERG, Early Church (s. Anm. 76), 106: „exemption from moral standards", ähnlich neuerdings T. SCOTT CAULLEY, „They Promise Them Freedom". Once again, the ψευδοδιδάσκαλοι in 2 Peter, ZNW 99 (2008), 128–138 (138): „freedom from doctrinal ‚tyranny' and accompanying moral constraints", etwas anders NEYREY, a.a.O. 419f.: Freiheit von ‚trouble' und der Furcht vor dem künftigen Gericht.

[130] So NEYREY, ebd.

[131] R. J. BAUCKHAM, 2 Peter. An Account of Research, ANRW II 25.5 (1988), 3713–3752 (3724).

– Der daraus abgeleitete Vorwurf eines *„animalischen'* Wesens ist in 2Petr 2,12 deutlich gegenüber dem Vergleich in Jud 10 gesteigert. Hier liegt offenkundig eine rhetorisch wirksame, aber zugleich recht problematische polemische Verzerrung vor, die allein auf literarischem Weg (durch Textveränderung) zustande kommt.

– *Eigennutz* bzw. der Verdacht der *unlauteren Motive* ist ebenfalls ein sehr häufiger Vorwurf gegenüber konkurrierenden Lehrern, der mit großer Wahrscheinlichkeit als topisch anzusehen ist. Im Judasbrief findet er sich in Jud 11 (zu Bileam) und Jud 16; im Bileam-Exempel von 2Petr 2,15f. ist der Aspekt ausgebaut, doch begegnet darüber hinaus der Vorwurf der Habsucht (2Petr 2,14) und betrügerischen Verhaltens (2Petr 2,13), wobei der ‚ökonomische' Aspekt des ‚Köderns' (2Petr 2,18) oder ‚Kaufens' (2Petr 2,3: ἐμπορεύσονται) von Anhängern gegenüber dem Jud noch verstärkt ist. Hier liegt mit hoher Wahrscheinlichkeit ein Element vor, das die Gegner in den Augen der Adressaten diskreditieren sollte.

– Ein besonders häufig gegen ‚Häretiker' gerichteter Topos ist auch der *moralische* Vorwurf der *Ausschweifung* (ἀσέλγεια, Jud 4; 2Petr 2,2.7), im Sinne von Schwelgerei (Jud 12; 2Petr 2,13), aber insbesondere auch *sexuellen Fehlverhaltens* bzw. Ehebruch (2Petr 2,10.14.18). Dieser Vorwurf, dass die Gegner ‚hinter dem Fleisch herlaufen', ist in 2Petr 2,10 aus der Verallgemeinerung der in Jud 7 beschriebenen ‚speziellen' Sünden der Sodomiten gebildet, die Rede von den ‚eigenen Begierden' in Jud 16 erweitert er zu ‚Begierden des Fleisches' (2Petr 2,18), und auch der Vorwurf des ehebrecherischen Wesens in der Reihe der Vorwürfe von 2Petr 2,14 könnte ein Topos der Ketzerpolemik sein.

– Mit dem Vorwurf sexuellen Fehlverhaltens verbunden ist schließlich auch der Aspekt der *Befleckung* bzw. *Schmutzigkeit*, der sich schon in Jud 8.13 und dann auch in 2Petr 2,10.22 findet. Dieser Aspekt dürfte eher für das Denken des Autors Aufschluss bieten (vgl. 2Petr 3,14).

Eine exakte und methodisch kontrollierbare Beschreibung des wahren Profils der Gegner ist kaum mehr möglich, doch ist die Annahme unvermeidlich, dass wesentliche Punkte des vom Autor gezeichneten Gegnerbildes weit über das hinausgehen, was historisch plausibel ist. Die polemischen Übertreibungen und Verzerrungen betreffen insbesondere die diffamierende Charakterisierung des Wesens der Gegner als ‚animalisch' und bloß ‚naturhaft', worin ihre Humanität und wohl auch die *ratio* ihrer Argumentation zu Unrecht ignoriert wird. Dies betrifft weiter die Anklagen hinsichtlich der Habitualität und Wesenhaftigkeit des sündigen Verhaltens und die ‚Aufladung' der konkreten Vorwürfe durch das Motiv der Unreinheit und Befleckung, aber vermutlich auch manche Detailvorwürfe hinsichtlich des unmoralischen Verhaltens der Gegner, die eher im Denken des Autors und seiner polemischen Intention begründet sein könnten als im tatsächlichen Lebenswandel der konkurrierenden Lehrer.[132]

Zwar lässt sich dieser nicht mehr im Einzelnen erheben, doch ist damit zu rechnen, dass in der Vorstellung des Autors Leute, die die Parusie und das letzte Gericht leugneten, zu jeder Form amoralischen Verhaltens bereit sein mochten. Die Annahme liegt nahe, dass die Verurteilung der Gegner durch den Autor zumindest in einigen Punkten ungerechtfertigt ist und in der bloßen Absicht erfolgte, diese für die Adressaten möglichst nachhaltig zu diskreditieren, ja sie letztlich literarisch zu ‚vernichten'. Ob der Zweck der Verteidigung des überlieferten Glaubens oder – in der Perspektive des Autors – der Rettung der Adressaten vor dem eschatologischen Verderben solche Mittel ‚heiligt', sei dahingestellt. Der Autor des 2Petr hätte diese Frage in seinem dualistisch geprägten eschatologischen Denken, in dem zwischen ‚wahrer Lehre' und ‚lügnerischer Lehre' bzw. ‚Rettung' und ‚Verderben' keine ‚Zwischentöne' Platz haben, vermutlich bejaht.

Es ist jedoch eine Frage der Wahrheit – auch der theologischen Wahrheit –, ein solches Vorgehen in der Auslegung nicht zu verschleiern oder gar zu beschönigen, sondern als ein dem Evangelium schwerlich angemessenes, zumindest aus heutiger Sicht ethisch inakzeptables Vorgehen zu benennen. Einerseits waren die Konventionen antiker Polemik überall rau,[133] und es ist fragwürdig, antike Kommunikation nach Kriterien heutiger Diskursethik zu beurteilen. Andererseits ist es im Blick auf die Wirkung kanonischer Texte geboten, die Fortwirkung einer derartigen Rhetorik und ihre Applikation in gegenwärtigen theologischen Diskursen zu unterbinden. Gegenüber der polemischen Rhetorik des 2Petr (und auch schon des Jud) ist – ebenso wie z.B. im Falle antijüdischer Polemik im NT – historische Aufklärung und ethischer Widerspruch geboten. Im Übrigen könnte die ‚argumentative' Technik in 2Petr 2 darauf hindeuten, dass der Autor die Erfolgsaussichten seiner sachlichen Argumentation in 2Petr 3,3–13

---

[132] So auch J. H. NEYREY, 2 Peter, Jude, AncB 37C, New York 1993, 192, der meint, die moralischen Vorwürfe seien „less actual statements of what the author's opponents did or said than projections of what their errors lead to". Umgekehrt, aber m.E. verfehlt, argumentiert DAVIDS, The Letters of 2 Peter and Jude (s. Anm. 14), 223, wenn er festhalten will, dass „the main charges against the false teachers are ethical". Damit unterschätzt er das eschatologische Argument in Kapitel 3 und übernimmt – viel zu unkritisch – die moralischen Stereotypen als zutreffend.

[133] Dies zeigt z.B. L. T. JOHNSON, The New Testament's Anti-Jewish Slander and the Conventions of Ancient Polemic, JBL 103 (1989), 419–441. Zur Polemik der Kirchenväter s. C. COLPE, Formen der Intoleranz. Altkirchliche Autoren und ihre antipagane Polemik, in: R. Kampling / B. Schlegelberger (Hg.), Wahrnehmung des Fremden. Christentum und andere Religionen, Schriften der Diözesanakademie Berlin 12, Berlin 1996, 87–123.

nicht besonders gut eingeschätzt haben dürfte – und deshalb zu einer derart ‚vorbereitenden' Polemik Zuflucht nahm.

3.4 Zur Funktion der fiktionalen Strukturen

Wie lässt sich nun das Ensemble von Verfasser- und Autorfiktion einschätzen?

Was die Verfasserfiktion anbetrifft, so muss ein Zusatzproblem bedacht werden, das die Forschung immer wieder beschäftigt hat:[134] Das Schreiben in apostolischer Autorität nimmt ja über mehr als ein Drittel seiner Länge ein anderes Schreiben zur Vorlage, das ebenfalls pseudonym, wenngleich nicht unter dem Namen eines Apostels und in einem ganz anderen ‚Grad' pseudonymer Autorschaft, gestaltet ist. Mit seiner Übernahme der Polemik des Judasbriefes in 2Petr 2,1–3,3 könnte der Zweite Petrusbrief in diesem Teil fast als ein „Plagiat" erscheinen,[135] allerdings würde diese Klassifizierung die Eigenständigkeit der Rezeption und argumentativen Ausgestaltung im 2Petr unterschätzen. Diese ist in der Spärlichkeit der exakten Zitate,[136] den bedachten Umformulierungen, der Auslassung wesentlicher Abschnitte (z.B. eines Teils der biblischen Exempel und des Henochzitats) und der Hinzufügung anderer (z.B. von Noah und Lot, aber auch des Abschnitts 2Petr 2,18–22) stärker zu beachten und verdeutlicht auch das differierende Argumentationsinteresse.

Dennoch stellt sich die Frage, wie ein Autor, der zu einer so massiven pseudonymen Legitimation greift, ein anderes, weniger stark autorisiertes Schreiben so intensiv als Vorlage benutzen konnte. Seitens der Rezipienten setzt dies voraus, dass diese Jud wohl nicht kannten – sonst hätte dies die Rezeption des Schreibens noch mehr erschwert. Seitens des Autors ist zumindest anzunehmen, dass er mit dem Jud sachlich in wesentlichen Punkten übereinstimmte und die dort vorliegende Gegnerpolemik – vielleicht deshalb, weil sie bereits relativ stark topisch war – für seine eigenen Zwecke als brauchbar ansah. Obwohl er sich in einer anderen Situation andersartigen Gegnern ausgesetzt sah als der Autor des Jud, hat der Autor des

---

[134] Nicht selten erschien es vorstellbar, dass Judas einen Brief des Petrus benutzt hätte, aber nicht umgekehrt. Dies hat gelegentlich dazu geführt, dass man den 2Petr doch als authentisch ansehen oder das Verhältnis beider Schreiben umkehren wollte. So urteilte z.B. Martin Luther, dem in der älteren Auslegung Hugo Grotius, Johann Albrecht Bengel, Johann Salomo Semler und Johann David Michaelis folgten. S. dazu T. ZAHN, Einleitung in das Neue Testament II, Leipzig ²1900, 104.

[135] So JANSSEN, Unter falschem Namen (s. Anm. 1), 254. Die andere dort genannte Möglichkeit, ‚Zitat', erscheint weniger passend, da im 2Petr nur an wenigen Stellen ein ‚Zitat' von mindestens 3 Worten erfolgt.

[136] Die längste ununterbrochene wörtliche Entsprechung besteht zwischen Jud 13 und 2Petr 2,17 und umfasst genau fünf Worte.

2Petr der Auffassung, dass in der Endzeit gottlose ‚Spötter' aufkommen sollen (Jud 17f.), zugestimmt und diese ‚Spötter' in den Bestreitern der Parusiehoffnung, die ihm vor Augen standen, wiedergefunden. Zustimmen konnte er auch dem Aufweis der Gerichtsverfallenheit dieser ‚Gottlosen' aus der Schrift, auch wenn er die Auswertung der biblischen Exempla anders zuspitzte und das Zitat aus Henoch wegließ.[137] Schließlich konnte sich der Autor ebenfalls in den Chor derer einreihen, die der paulinisch-deuteropaulinischen Überlieferung – aus unterschiedlichen Gründen – kritisch gegenübertraten. Das theologische Gepräge des Autors des 2Petr differiert freilich von dem des Jud ebenso wie die jeweiligen Gegner ein im Detail sehr verschiedenes Gepräge haben.[138]

Die fiktionalen Züge im Gegnerbild des 2Petr dienen im Wesentlichen der Diskreditierung der gegnerischen Lehrer, denen nicht nur zahlreiche moralische Verfehlungen vorgehalten werden, sondern eine generelle Verderbtheit ihres Wesens, was ihr tatsächliches Erscheinungsbild bis zur Grenze der Unkenntlichkeit verzerren dürfte.

Festeren Boden betreten wir erst in 2Petr 3,3f., wo die These der Gegner zitiert und – mit eschatologisch durchaus interessanten Überlegungen – zurückgewiesen wird.

Allerdings ist das Profil der Gegner auch aufgrund dieser Argumentation nicht sicher zu bestimmen. Dies gilt auch für die neuere, sehr ansprechende These, die die Gegner in die Nähe einer epikureischen Auffassung rückt, dass Gott nicht in den Weltlauf eingreife.[139] Letztlich bleibt unklärbar, ob die Gegner selbst eine derart geprägte Auffassung hatten oder ob der Autor sie selbst durch bestimmte Formulierungen in eine ‚epikureische Ecke'

---

[137] Dies sollte aber nicht mit einem gegenüber Jud schon ausgeprägteren ‚Kanonbewusstsein' begründet werden, vielmehr ist hier (wie auch bei der Kürzung des angelologischen Exempels aus Jud 9) das geringere Interesse des Autors und vermutlich auch seiner Adressaten an angelologischen Sachverhalten eine hinreichende Begründung. Die kirchliche Zurückweisung des Henochbuches erfolgte erst wesentlich später. Das Buch wird vermutlich in 1Clem 19f., in der ApkPetr und bei Irenäus rezipiert (s. NICKELSBURG, 1 Enoch 1 [s. Anm. 28], 87f.) und etwa gleichzeitig mit 2Petr in Barn 4,3 und 16,5 (als „Schrift") zitiert, ebenso dann bei Clemens, Origenes und Tertullian. Die Zurückweisung erfolgte erst, als das Buch den entwickelteren christologischen Auffassungen nicht mehr entsprach und in den Verdacht der ‚Fälschung' kam.

[138] Hingegen gibt es keine positiven Indizien dafür, dass der Autor „mit seiner Neuinterpretation des Jud diesen Text begrenzt ersetzen" wollte (PAULSEN, Der Judasbrief. Der zweite Petrusbrief [s. Anm. 35], 99). Wir wissen zu wenig über die ‚kirchliche Geltung' des Jud zur Zeit der Abfassung des 2Petr.

[139] K. BERGER, Streit um Gottes Vorsehung. Zur Position der Gegner im 2. Petrusbrief, in: J. W. van Henten u.a. (Hg.), Tradition and Re-Interpretation in Jewish and Early Christian Literature (FS Lebram), StPB 36, Leiden 1986, 121–135; NEYREY, Form and Background (s. Anm. 124); s. dazu auch J. FREY, Judgment on the Ungodly and the Parousia of Christ. Eschatology in Jude and 2 Peter, in: J. van der Watt (Hg.), Eschatology in the New Testament, WUNT II, Tübingen 2010 (im Druck).

rückt[140] – zumal ‚Epikureer' ebenfalls ein beliebter polemischer Topos war, von der paganen philosophischen Diskussion bis hin zu den Rabbinen.

Die massive Gegnerpolemik und die gleichfalls sehr kühne Autorfiktion spiegeln womöglich auch die Schwierigkeit, vor die sich der Autor in seinem Versuch, die gegnerischen Lehrer zu bekämpfen und die Adressaten ihrem Einfluss zu entwinden, gestellt sah. Die Wahl des fiktiven Autors Petrus als apostolische Autorität und Augenzeugen der Herrlichkeit Christi und die massive Betonung der tatsächlichen Augenzeugenschaft im Gegensatz zu ‚bloßen' Geschichten (μῦθοι) dient in diesem Text sehr eindeutig dem Zweck der Autorisation im Streit mit den konkurrierenden Lehrern bzw. im Werben um die ‚Gefolgschaft' und Standfestigkeit (2Petr 3,17) der Adressaten.

Die pseudonyme Struktur ist daher recht konsequent durchgeführt. Sie hat auch in ihrer Zeitstruktur keine ‚entlarvenden' Brüche,[141] vielmehr zeigt gerade der Hinweis auf den früheren Brief des Autors ‚Petrus' an die Adressaten (2Petr 3,1), der keine unmittelbare sachliche Funktion hat, dass der Autor um ‚Beglaubigung' seiner Autorfiktion bemüht ist. Die Autorisierung des 2Petr durch den Apostel ist daher nicht im Sinne einer bloßen Einreihung in eine frühchristliche Tradition zu verstehen, vielmehr will der Autor wohl tatsächlich glaubhaft machen, dass das Schreiben von dem Apostel Petrus stammt und sein Wahrheitszeugnis durch dessen Augenzeugenschaft beglaubigt ist. Es geht nicht einfach nur darum, „die Figur des Petrus mit einer bestimmten Vorstellung des Christentums zu verbinden",[142] und die beschwichtigende Aussage, es ginge nur um „an assertion of authoritative tradition, not literary origin",[143] ist angesichts von 2Petr 1,12–15 fraglich. Die These von Richard Bauckham schließlich, der behauptet, hier liege „an entirely *transparent* fiction" vor,[144] gleicht an Kühn-

---

[140] So BERGER, a.a.O. 132: „Er verteidigt sein genuin jüdisches ‚Weltbild' mit Hilfe von Vorstellungen, die sich aus der anti-epikureischen Tradition anboten."

[141] Dass die Gegnerpolemik in 2,4–22 und auch die Auseinandersetzung in 3,3–13 in eine präsentisch-allgemeine Charakterisierung der Gegner übergleitet und darin die Fiktion zeitweise vergessen macht, bedeutet noch keinen ‚Bruch' in der Fiktion, erst recht keinen Bruch, der die Verfasserfiktion für jedermann offenlegen und damit vom Verdacht der ‚Täuschungsabsicht' freisprechen könnte. Die These von BAUCKHAM, Jude. 2 Peter (s. Anm. 13), 134f., dass der Autor mit dieser Gestaltung bewusst die Konventionen eines literarischen Testaments aufbreche, ist daher sehr fragwürdig, desgleichen seine Folgerung: „such deliberate breaches of the fiction of Petrine authorship are possible only if the fiction was a transparent one" (135).

[142] Diese m.E. völlig realitätsfremde Sichtweise äußert F. VOUGA, Der Brief als Form apostolischer Autorität, in: K. Berger (Hg.), Studien und Texte zur Formgeschichte, TANZ 7, Tübingen/Basel 1997, 7–58 (55).

[143] So MEADE, Pseudonymity and Canon (s. Anm. 2), 190.

[144] BAUCKHAM, Jude. 2 Peter (s. Anm. 13), 134f.; zustimmend aufgenommen bei

heit fast der Fiktion des 2Petr und zielt erkennbar bemüht auf die ‚Rettung' des Schreibens vor dem Verdikt ‚Fälschung', die mit der für den Kanon geltenden Wahrheitsvermutung nicht mehr vereinbar wäre. Doch wenn die Fiktion so leicht entschlüsselbar wäre, dann müsste man eine solche Einsicht – mit welchen Konsequenzen auch immer – schon bei den altkirchlichen Rezipienten des 2Petr und auch anderer neutestamentlicher Pseudepigrapha vermuten.

Zwar könnte der Hinweis, dass die Erinnerung für die Zeit nach dem Tod des Petrus schriftlich verfügbar sein soll (2Petr 1,15; vgl. 3,1f.17), für literarisch gebildete Leser erkennen lassen, dass hier ein literarisches Testament vorliegt,[145] doch gibt die ansonsten sehr massive Beanspruchung der Autorität des Augenzeugen in Verbindung mit der noch massiveren Gegnerpolemik in Kap. 2 keinen positiven Anhalt dafür, dass der Autor seinen Lesern ein solches Signal hätte geben wollen oder dass diese in der Lage sein sollten, die Fiktionalität zu erkennen und positiv zu goutieren.

Davon ist in der Interpretationsgeschichte des Schreibens jedoch nichts zu erkennen. Umgekehrt lässt die verzögerte Rezeption des Schreibens, das erst bei Origenes (Homiliae in librum Jesu Nave 7,1; bei Eus.h.e. 6,25,8), d.h. fast hundert Jahre nach seiner Entstehung anerkennend erwähnt wird, eher vermuten, dass das ‚Testament des Petrus' nicht überall bereitwillig aufgenommen wurde, als es – wohl gut zwei Generationen nach dem Tod des Petrus – plötzlich auftauchte.[146] Zwar wurde das Schreiben aufbewahrt und weitergegeben, d.h. eine gewisse Rezeption ist vorauszusetzen, doch ist als Basis einer solchen Rezeption wohl eher anzunehmen, dass die Ad-

---

VÖGTLE, Der Judasbrief. Der 2. Petrusbrief (s. Anm. 23), 129f., der immerhin hinzufügt, dass die pseudonyme Struktur in der Verwendung des testamentarischen Genus (nur) „führenden Lehrerpersönlichkeiten mancher Gemeinden bekannt sein konnte". Die Diskussion des Themas bei RIEDL, Anamnese (s. Anm. 2), 23–29, bleibt leider etwas diffus; klarer ist die Kritik bei JANSSEN, Unter falschem Namen (s. Anm. 1), 182–185; vgl. auch H.-J. KLAUCK, Die antike Briefliteratur und das Neue Testament. Ein Lehr- und Arbeitsbuch, UTB 2022, Paderborn u.a. 1998, 304, der gegen die ‚Durchschaubarkeitsthese' mit Recht einwendet, „ob sich die unbekannten Verfasser durch Annoncierung des Kunstgriffs, dessen sie sich bedienen, nicht selbst die Autoritätsbasis unter den Füßen wegziehen, die sie vorher zu schaffen versuchten". Für 2Petr urteilt P. MÜLLER, Der 2. Petrusbrief, ThR 66 (2001), 310–337 (335), daher m.E. zutreffend: „Angesichts des Grundthemas der Zuverlässigkeit (Gottes, des prophetischen Wortes, der apostolischen Überlieferung, der Parusieerwartung) überzeugt diese Auffassung ... nicht."

[145] Bauckhams Voraussetzung fester Konventionen für die Gattung des literarischen Testaments, die dann bewusst und mit der Funktion eines Signals für die Leser ‚durchbrochen' werden könnten, ist kaum zutreffend. ‚Abschiedsreden' und ‚literarische Testamente' hatten sowohl im antiken Judentum als auch darüber hinaus eine große Variabilität und konnten mit zahlreichen anderen literarischen Gestaltungsformen verbunden werden.

[146] So die Vermutung von VÖGTLE, Der Judasbrief. Der 2. Petrusbrief (s. Anm. 23), 129.

ressaten oder ein Teil von ihnen den Anspruch des Schreibens – sachlich, aber auch hinsichtlich der auktorialen ‚Beglaubigung' – akzeptierten.

4. Schlussbemerkungen zum sachlichen und methodischen Ertrag

Vergleicht man die beiden literarisch zusammenhängenden Schreiben, so zeigen sich hinsichtlich der jeweiligen pseudonymen Legitimationsstruktur tief greifende Unterschiede:

Während Jud eine relativ unbedeutende Person als fiktiven Autor heranzieht und diese Fiktion sehr bald wieder in den Hintergrund treten lässt und an einer Stelle sogar durchbricht, wird im 2Petr die – neben Jesus – höchste Autorität des frühesten Christentums in Anspruch genommen und die Autorfiktion relativ dicht und letztlich bruchlos durchgeführt.

Die Autoriät des Jud ist weniger in dem fiktiven Autor begründet als vielmehr in der Linie, die durch Jakobus und den Jak markiert ist; sie ist eine abgeleitete Autorität, die auf der Ebene des Verfassers ‚schwach' sein kann, weil sie ihre Stärke aus der Schrift (unter Einschluss von Henoch) und dem Einklang von Schriftaussage und ‚apostolischer' Überlieferung bezieht. Die Wahl des Judas als fiktivem Autor spiegelt die Zuordnung zu einer bestimmten frühchristlichen Traditionslinie.

Hingegen ist die Autorität des 2Petr bzw. ihre Wirkung im Streit mit den Gegnern primär in der Augenzeugenschaft und Autorität des gewählten apostolischen Gewährsmanns begründet, dessen Vermächtnis den Glaubenden auch nach seinem Tod verfügbar sein soll. Dabei wird die Zuschreibung an Petrus durch zahlreiche Darstellungsmittel gestützt, was nahelegt, dass die Fiktion auch als solche wirken wollte und nicht etwa nur konstruiert war, um von den Adressaten dechiffriert zu werden. Dies hätte seine Wirkung auf die Adressaten vermutlich deutlich reduziert. Ein literarisches Milieu, in dem eine künstlerische oder gar ‚spielerische' Freude an literarischen Fiktionen bestanden hätte, ist im frühen Christentum noch kaum vorstellbar; vielmehr würde eine solche Technik dem eschatologischen Ernst und ‚Wahrheitspathos' eines Schreibens wie 2Petr nicht entsprechen und seinen sachlichen Anspruch korrumpieren.[147]

Autorfiktion und Gegnerfiktion sind in ihrer Wirkung unterschiedlich eng verbunden. Während im Jud die Gegnerpolemik insbesondere mit den biblischen Exempeln verbunden ist, ohne auf die Person des Herrenbruders

---

[147] Zwischen 2Petr und z.B. Lukians ‚Lügenfreund' besteht hier ein ‚garstiger Graben'. S. zum Problem – und zum Einfluss des ‚subkulturellen' Charakters des frühen Christentums – den Beitrag von Marco Frenschkowski in diesem Band.

Judas zu rekurrieren, ist die Gegnerpolemik im 2Petr wesentlich stärker mit der vorgängigen Autorfiktion bzw. mit der durch den fiktiven Autor repräsentierten Autorität des grundlegenden Wahrheitszeugen verbunden. Vermutlich konnte der reale Autor des 2Petr zur Bekämpfung der gegnerischen Auffassungen und angesichts der von ihm wahrgenommenen Bedrohung der Adressatengemeinden nur die Möglichkeit einer derart massiven (und entsprechend ‚gewagten‘) Autorisation sehen.

Methodologisch ist deutlich, dass die fiktionalen Elemente von Autor, Situation und Gegnern in pseudonymen Briefen in ihrem Zusammenhang zu analysieren sind. Dabei muss für jede dieser Größen mit der Möglichkeit einer rein fiktionalen Gestaltung gerechnet werden, andererseits ist auf die Frage nach der außertextlichen Referenz und damit auf eine ‚historische‘ Auswertung nicht zu verzichten, da erst die präzisere historische Einschätzung von Situation und Gegnern die Funktion der pseudonymen Verfasserkonstruktion zu bestimmen erlaubt. Umgekehrt erlaubt erst der Gedanke, dass auch das literarisch repräsentierte Gegnerbild – ebenso wie das Autorbild – in zahlreichen Details fiktional sein könnte, eine Scheidung zwischen bloßen polemischen Topoi und verwertbaren Hinweisen zur tatsächlichen Intention der Gegner und damit deren präzisere Einordnung in theologie- oder religionsgeschichtliche Diskurse.

Erst aufgrund einer möglichst sorgfältigen und differenzierten Klärung und Einordnung der pseudonymen Strukturen von Autor *und* Gegnern kann dann auch nach ihrer leitenden Intention, ihrem argumentativen Wert und ihrer ethischen und kanontheologischen Legitimität gefragt werden. Das Beispiel von Jud und 2Petr zeigt, mit welchen Unterschieden hier innerhalb der neutestamentlichen Briefliteratur zu rechnen ist.

Pseudepigraphie und Gemeinde in den Johannesbriefen

von

JUTTA LEONHARDT-BALZER

1. Einleitung

Pseudepigraphie ist grundsätzlich die Abfassung einer Schrift unter einem anderen Namen. Hier ist nicht der Ort, die Bandbreite antiker Pseudepigraphie oder allgemein die Motive für ein solches Vorgehen zu erörtern.[1] In dem hier gegebenen Rahmen ist es nur möglich, den individuellen Kontext der johanneischen Briefe zu untersuchen. Hierbei stellt sich jedoch eine weitere, grundsätzliche Problematik in der Frage, ob es sich bei den johanneischen Briefen überhaupt um Pseudepigraphie handelt.

Die johanneischen Briefe werden von allen uns erhaltenen Manuskripten dem Autor Johannes zugeschrieben[2] und so dem des Johannesevangeliums zugeordnet. Keiner der Textzeugen lässt sich zwar früher als auf das 3. Jh. n. Chr. datieren,[3] doch Euseb erkennt schon bei Papias (Eus.h.e. 3,39,1–7.17) in der ersten Hälfte des 2. Jh., relativ bald nach ihrer Abfassung (um 100 n. Chr.)[4], die Verbindung von Evangelium und Briefen mit dem Namen ‚Johannes‘. Diese Identifizierung ist jedoch nicht so eindeutig, wie es scheinen mag, denn Papias selbst unterscheidet zwischen dem Apostel Johannes, zu dem er nie Kontakt hatte, und dem Presbyter des gleichen Namens, von dem er gelernt hat (wobei es unklar ist, ob eine per-

---

[1] Die Breite der neutestamentlichen Pseudepigraphie zeigt der vorliegende Band; zur antiken Pseudepigraphie im hellenistischen Judentum s. M. HENGEL, Anonymität, Pseudepigraphie und „Literarische Fälschung" in der jüdisch-hellenistischen Literatur, in: ders., Judaica et Hellenistica. Kleine Schriften I. Unter Mitarbeit von R. Deines, J. Frey, C. Markschies, A. M. Schwemer mit einem Anhang von H. Bloedhorn, WUNT 90, Tübingen 1996, 196–291.

[2] Vgl. J. LIEU, I, II, & III John. A Commentary, NTLi, Louisville 2008, 1f.

[3] Vgl. H.-J. KLAUCK, Der erste Johannesbrief, EKK XXIII/1, Zürich/Neukirchen-Vluyn 1991, 13–16; ders., Der zweite und dritte Johannesbrief, EKK XXIII/2, Zürich/Neukirchen-Vluyn 1992, 9–14.

[4] Vgl. ders., Die Johannesbriefe, EdF 276, Darmstadt 1991, 163–166. Als Abfassungsort hat Ephesus noch immer die größte Wahrscheinlichkeit.

sönliche Begegnung stattgefunden hat; Eus.h.e. 3,39,1–7). Dass diese Unklarheit nicht allein bei Papias bestand, zeigt sich darin, dass Euseb aus dieser Unterscheidung des Papias die Existenz zweier Johannesgräber in Ephesus herleitet.[5] Somit lassen sich Evangelium und Briefe durch die Verbindung mit dem Namen Johannes schon seit der Antike nicht eindeutig einem bestimmten Autor zuordnen, und die moderne exegetische Untersuchung von Evangelium und Briefen hat darüber hinaus Zweifel daran aufkommen lassen, dass sie alle einem einzigen Autor zuzuschreiben sind.[6] Dennoch lassen sie sich aufgrund der linguistischen und theologischen Übereinstimmungen zwischen diesen Texten in einem einzigen Trägerkreis verorten.[7] Dass dieser Trägerkreis einen ungewöhnlich engen Zusammenhalt gehabt haben muss, zeigt sich gerade darin, dass die Schriften, die aus ihm hervorgegangen sind, seit den frühesten Zeugen nie mit einem anderen Namen als mit dem des Johannes verbunden worden sind[8] – wer auch immer damit gemeint war.

Dennoch geben sich weder das Evangelium noch die Briefe ausdrücklich als Werke eines ‚Johannes' aus, sondern vermeiden die Nennung des Namens ihres Autors. Daher sind sie nicht im strengen Sinn Pseudepigraphie und werden auch in der Regel in Untersuchungen zur neutestamentlichen Pseudepigraphie nicht behandelt.[9] Es ist versucht worden, ihre Anonymität nicht nur als negative Schlussfolgerung, sondern als positiven hermeneutischen Ansatz zu sehen, der seine Autorität nicht aus einem Namen, sondern aus der Wahrheit der Botschaft bezieht.[10] Auf diese Weise

---

[5] Eine Übersicht über die patristische Bezeugung der Brieftitel findet sich bei LIEU, I, II, & III John (s. Anm. 2), 2f.; eine detaillierte Diskussion der Bezüge auf die johanneischen Schriften im 2. Jh. n. Chr. gibt M. HENGEL, Die johanneische Frage. Ein Lösungsversuch, mit einem Beitrag zur Apokalypse von J. Frey, WUNT 67, Tübingen 1993, 9–95, s. auch R. E. BROWN, The Epistles of John, AncB 30, New York 1982, Paperback 2006, 5–13; KLAUCK, Die Johannesbriefe (s. Anm. 4), 17–35.

[6] Vgl. z.B. LIEU, a.a.O. 17f.; einen Überblick über die verschiedenen Argumente gibt BROWN, a.a.O. 14–30.

[7] Vgl. KLAUCK, Die Johannesbriefe (s. Anm. 4), 89–126. Eine genauere Untersuchung der johanneischen Sprache findet sich im Vergleich mit der Johannesapokalypse bei J. FREY, Erwägungen zum Verhältnis der Johannesapokalypse zu den übrigen Schriften im Corpus Johanneum, Appendix zu HENGEL, Die johanneische Frage (s. Anm. 5), 326–429.

[8] HENGEL, a.a.O. 97–107; LIEU, I, II, & III John (s. Anm. 2), 3.

[9] Ein repräsentatives Beispiel ist hier immer noch D. G. MEADE, Pseudonymity and Canon. An Investigation into the Relationship of Authorship and Authority in Jewish and Earliest Christian Tradition, WUNT 39, Tübingen 1986. Hier werden die johanneischen Traditionen nur unter dem Aspekt der „Vergegenwärtigung" der Jesustraditionen behandelt (110–114, zu den Briefen bes. 114); vgl. J. D. G. DUNN, The Problem of Pseudonymity, in: ders., The Living Word, London 1987, 80.

[10] So M. WOLTER, Die anonymen Schriften des Neuen Testaments. Annäherungsver-

gehen die verschiedenen Autoren in der gemeinsamen Deutung der johanneischen Gruppe auf. Dennoch belegt die frühe und konsistente Zuordnung der Schriften, dass sie nicht nur in einen einheitlichen historischen Kontext hinein gelesen wurden, sondern dass die Leser auch keinen Zweifel daran hatten, wer sie durch die Briefe ansprach.[11] So wird von modernen Exegeten bis heute die Schlussfolgerung vertreten, dass alle drei Briefe von derselben Gründergestalt der johanneischen Gemeinde geschrieben worden sind.[12] Jedoch könnte derselbe Effekt der Zuschreibung zu einem einzigen Autor durch geschickte Pseudepigraphie erzielt worden sein, und so bleibt die Aufgabe, die Briefe nach ihrem Autor/ihren Autoren zu befragen.

Da die externe Bezeugung keine eindeutigen Hinweise auf der Suche nach dem Verfasser oder den Verfassern gibt, ist zu fragen, inwiefern die Briefe über interne Andeutungen Autorität aus der Identifizierung mit einer bestimmten Persönlichkeit beziehen (hierbei kann der Vergleich mit dem Johannesevangelium in dem gegebenen Rahmen nicht durchgeführt werden). In jedem Fall ist diese Autorität zunächst eine gemeindeinterne, da sie nicht aus der Verbindung mit einem identifizierbaren Namen, sondern aus dem Inhalt der Schriften und – wo vorhanden – dem Titel des Autors herrührt. Es ist anzunehmen, dass der Schritt von der gemeindeinternen Autorität zu der Verwendung in der Gesamtkirche mit der Zuschreibung zu dem Namen Johannes verbunden ist.

Über die zeitliche Abfolge der drei Schriften ist viel spekuliert worden.[13] Auch in den Theorien über ihre gegenseitige Abhängigkeit ist in der Forschung jede denkbare Kombination vertreten worden.[14] Um Zirkelschlüsse zu vermeiden, werden hier die drei Briefe in der traditionellen

---

suche an ein literarisches Phänomen, ZNW 79 (1988), 1–16; vgl. auch LIEU, I, II, & III John (s. Anm. 2), 9.

[11] HENGEL, Die johanneische Frage (s. Anm. 5), 107.

[12] So BROWN, Epistles (s. Anm. 5), 86–109.679, der ihn unbenannt lässt, oder HENGEL, a.a.O. 109–119, der „das autoritative Schulhaupt" (111) mit „dem Alten Johannes" identifiziert.

[13] Einen Überblick über die Diskussion gibt J. C. THOMAS, The Order of the Composition of the Johannine Epistles, NT 37 (1995), 68–75 (67–70). Er schließt daraus, dass der 3. Johannesbrief nicht auf Irrlehrer verweist, da dieser vor dem Ausbruch des Konflikts geschrieben worden sei (71). Jedoch ist dieser Schluss nicht zwingend, da das Thema des 3. Johannesbriefs nichts mit Irrlehre zu tun hat. Auch seine Vorstellung, dass sich der 2. Brief an „a particular community" richtet (72), berücksichtigt nicht die Offenheit der Anrede der „erwählten Herrin". Die These des 2. Briefes als Notmaßnahme bis zur Abfassung einer geregelten Antwort auf die Irrlehrer – dem 1. Brief – (72–74) wird der Tatsache nicht gerecht, dass der 1. Brief eben keine konkreten Ratschläge zum Umgang mit den Irrlehrern gibt, sondern nur wie Irrlehre zu vermeiden ist.

[14] Vgl. BROWN, Epistles (s. Anm. 5), 30–35.

Reihenfolge behandelt, die auf der Länge der Texte basiert. Sie werden der Reihe nach auf Verfasser und Adressaten, wie sie im Text begegnen, befragt und dann miteinander verglichen. Anhand dieser internen Daten erfolgen dann Schlussfolgerungen zu ihrer Verfasserschaft und der Versuch, die drei Briefe einander zuzuordnen. Da es bei der Kürze des zweiten und dritten Briefes statistisch nicht möglich ist, aufgrund von Unterschieden im Wortgebrauch auf Pseudepigraphie zu schließen,[15] soll so weder der linguistische noch der theologische Ansatz der Briefe allein, sondern das in ihnen dargestellte Verhältnis von Autor und Lesern darüber Aufschluss geben, ob hier Pseudepigraphie vorliegt. Ausgehend von diesem Befund entsteht dann ein Bild von dem Umgang mit der Pseudepigraphie innerhalb der johanneischen Gemeinde.

2. Der 1. Johannesbrief

2.1 Der Verfasser im Text

Streng genommen ist es weder möglich, den 1. Johannesbrief einen Brief zu nennen, da er keinen Absender, keinen Empfänger und keinen Briefschluss hat,[16] noch eine pseudepigraphe Schrift, da er sich nirgends einem bestimmten Autor zuordnet. Dieser Sachverhalt hat dazu geführt, dass er formal unterschiedlich bestimmt worden ist, so z.B. als an mehrere Gemeinden gerichteter Traktat, Aufsatz, Manifest, Diatribe, Homilie oder Predigt,[17] wobei die genaue Definition des jeweiligen Genres oft vermieden wird.[18] Bei fehlendem Briefrahmen entspräche zunächst am ehesten die Form der Predigt, da die Gattung der Predigt keinen Absender benötigt, solange der Sprecher den Hörern gegenüber steht. Dennoch ist der Erste Johannesbrief kein mündliches Zeugnis, sondern verweist selbst wieder-

---

[15] KLAUCK, Der zweite und dritte Johannesbrief (s. Anm. 3), 17–19.

[16] Vgl. eine kurze Zusammenfassung von Argumenten für und gegen die Einordnung als Brief bei R. B. EDWARDS, The Johannine Epistles, Sheffield 1996, 34f.; ausführlicher BROWN, Epistles (s. Anm. 5), 86–92; KLAUCK, Die Johannesbriefe (s. Anm. 4), 68–74. Die Annahme, es seien verschiedene Anfänge oder Schlüsse je nach Gemeinde hinzugefügt worden, lässt sich textlich nicht belegen und widerspricht dem formellen Anfang, und die Theorie, 1Joh sei an die Kirche im Allgemeinen gerichtet, scheitert sowohl an der fehlenden Anrede als auch an der Tatsache, dass sich 1Joh auf ein konkretes Gemeindeproblem bezieht – die jüdisch-gnostische Irrlehre, die aus der Gemeinde hervorgegangen ist.

[17] Vgl. P. PERKINS, The Johannine Epistles, NTMes 21, Wilmington 1979, XVIf.3; H.-J. KLAUCK, Zur rhetorischen Analyse der Johannesbriefe, ZNW 81 (1990), 205–224 (209).

[18] EDWARDS, The Johannine Epistles (s. Anm. 16), 35.

holt auf seine schriftliche Abfassung (zuerst in 1Joh 1,4).[19] Er ist auch kein allgemeiner Traktat, denn er nimmt auf eine konkrete Situation Bezug und spricht seine Leser direkt an, wenn er die Notwendigkeit des rechten Bekenntnisses und Verhaltens im Blick auf die, die von der Gemeinde ausgegangen sind, hervorhebt. Insofern ist er in jedem Fall ein Beispiel einer „Gesprächsform mit Abwesenden", wie der antike Brief definiert wird.[20] Lässt er sich jedoch bei allen Widersprüchen als Brief definieren, ergibt sich die Notwendigkeit, entweder anzunehmen, dass ein Briefrahmen gänzlich weggefallen ist (wofür es keinerlei textliche Hinweise gibt), oder dass die schriftlich abgefasste Predigt mit einer schriftlichen oder mündlichen Erläuterung versehen worden ist: Entweder ist sie von ihrem Überbringer eingeführt worden oder besaß ein Begleitschreiben.[21]

Betrachtet man den Text selbst, so zeigt der sich zwar als anonym, aber nicht als charakterlos. Auch wenn sich der Verfasser nicht namentlich vorstellt, stellt er sich von Anfang an in eine konkrete Tradition: die der johanneischen Gemeinde. Der Anfang ist dem Anfang des Johannesevangeliums sehr ähnlich,[22] und die Betonung des Zeugnisses, das durch Augen, Ohr, Tastsinn und Mund vermittelt worden ist (1Joh 1,1–5), verwurzelt den gesamten Brief in dem Objekt der Verkündigung, im Zeugnis „vom Wort des Lebens" (περὶ τοῦ λόγου τῆς ζωῆς, 1,1). So findet sich die im Johannesevangelium erst am Schluss erfolgende Berufung auf Augenzeugenschaft (Joh 21,24) im Brief gleich am Anfang. Im Evangelium wird auf den Lieblingsjünger als Zeugen verwiesen, im Brief sieht sich der Autor selbst in dieser Rolle (1Joh 1,1–3). Unabhängig davon, ob der Brief oder die jeweiligen Teile des Evangeliums älter sind, zeigt diese Parallele, dass es sich hier um Grundlagen der johanneischen Gemeindelehre handelt, auf die der Verfasser des 1. Johannesbriefes zurückgreift. Jedoch geht es bei diesem Rückgriff nicht darum, eine eventuelle Identität mit dem Verfasser des Johannesevangeliums zu implizieren,[23] sondern den Brief fest im Kontext der Gesamtverkündigung der Gemeinde zu verankern. Diese Absicht zeigt sich auch darin, dass der Autor von sich in der 1. Ps. pl. schreibt: Sein Zeugnis ist nicht sein eigenes, privates, sondern repräsentiert die wahre christliche Verkündigung.[24] Das „wir" betont hier weder die Autorität des

---

[19] Vgl. z.B. KLAUCK, Zur rhetorischen Analyse der Johannesbriefe (s. Anm. 17), 205–224 (209); LIEU, I, II, & III John (s. Anm. 2), 5.

[20] Zitat von R. HAHN, Morphologie der antiken Literatur, Darmstadt 1969, 109, bei WOLTER, Die anonymen Schriften des Neuen Testaments (s. Anm. 10), 5.

[21] Vgl. HENGEL, Die johanneische Frage (s. Anm. 5), 154. In jedem Fall ist das Endergebnis das einer schriftlichen Mitteilung an eine Gemeinde, und daher wird auch hier der Name „Brief" weiter benutzt.

[22] Vgl. PERKINS, The Johannine Epistles (s. Anm. 17), 8–10.

[23] Vgl. WOLTER, Die anonymen Schriften des Neuen Testaments (s. Anm. 10), 7f.

[24] So auch LIEU, I, II, & III John (s. Anm. 2), 38f.

Verfassers noch beschreibt es einen Autorenkreis, sondern steht zunächst für die Traditionsträger der johanneischen Gemeinde.[25] Jedoch schafft es keine Grenze zwischen diesen Zeugen und den Lesern, denn durch die inklusive Ausdrucksweise wird unmittelbar nach dem ersten Verweis auf die Augenzeugenschaft der Unterschied zwischen Leser und Autor verwischt, es geht nicht um das Hervorheben historischer Augenzeugen, sondern um das Erkennen der Wahrheit Christi, vermittelt durch das Zeugnis des Autors.[26] Autor und Leser gehen beide in der in 1,3 heraufbeschworenen Gemeinschaft untereinander und mit Christus und dem Vater auf. Nimmt man die Augenzeugenschaft im übertragenen Sinn als Erkennen der Wahrheit des „Wortes des Lebens", dann muss der Autor nicht selbst Zeitgenosse Jesu gewesen sein. In diesem Fall träten von Anfang an die Leser, wenn das Zeugnis bei ihnen Glauben findet, in dieselbe Zeugenrolle wie der Autor. Die Betonung der Sinnlichkeit der Wahrnehmung des Zeugnisses stellt jedoch auch einen deutlichen Gegensatz zu dem „Geschichtsverlust" der Gegner dar[27] und führt das Zeugnis der Gemeinde letztlich auf die ersten Augenzeugen zurück.

So steht der erste Brief gänzlich in der Autorität der Gemeindeverkündigung. Der Autor selbst erscheint nur an wenigen Stellen als Individuum: so in 1Joh 2,1 nach der Anrede der Leser als τεκνία μου, im Diminutiv: „meine Kindchen", ταῦτα γράφω ὑμῖν, „dies schreibe ich euch".[28] Schon im nächsten Satz fällt er jedoch wieder in das inklusive „wir" zurück. Unmittelbar nach der nächsten Anrede der Leser in 2,7f. ist er wieder Einzelperson: οὐκ ἐντολὴν καινὴν γράφω ὑμῖν ... πάλιν ἐντολὴν καινὴν γράφω ὑμῖν, „ich schreibe euch kein neues Gebot ... wiederum schreibe ich euch ein neues Gebot". Im Anschluss daran tritt der Autor in 2,12–14 persönlich mit Ratschlägen und Weisungen an bestimmte Gruppen in der Gemeinde heran („Ich schreibe euch"/„Ich habe euch geschrieben", 2,12–14). Nach der nächsten Anrede der Gemeinde in seinen Erörterungen zur letzten Stunde kehrt der Autor in 2,18 dann zur 1. Ps. pl. zurück. Im weiteren Brief verweist der Autor nur an wenigen Stellen auf sich selbst. Er erscheint dann als Verfasser von schriftlichen Ermahnungen und Lehren, und das immer dann, wenn er seine Lehren präzisiert: so in 2,21, in einem Ver-

---

[25] Vgl. BROWN, Epistles (s. Anm. 5), 158–161.

[26] In diesem Zusammenhang ist Joh 20,29–31 ein Beleg dafür, dass innerhalb der johanneischen Gemeinde der Gedanke der reellen Augenzeugenschaft für das Sehen des Glaubens geöffnet wurde, gegen BROWN, a.a.O. 159f.

[27] Vgl. KLAUCK, Der erste Johannesbrief (s. Anm. 3), 76f.

[28] Im gesamten 1Joh gibt es zwölf Verbformen in der 1. Ps. sg., elf davon von dem Verb „schreiben", während sich in dem bedeutend kürzeren 3Joh elf Verbformen in der 1. Ps. sg. von zehn verschiedenen Verben finden; vgl. LIEU, I, II, & III John (s. Anm. 2), 14.

weis darauf, dass die Leser schon in der Wahrheit sind, in 2,26 auf die Verführer der Gemeinde und zum Schluss in 5,13 auf das ewige Leben der Leser.

Somit bezieht sich der Verfasser grundsätzlich in seine Lehren mit ein, er geht in der Gemeinschaft mit der Gemeinde auf. Als Individuum tritt er nur als Autor des Textes und Autor bestimmter Weisungen hervor. Dennoch erzeugt die Tatsache, dass er diese Weisungen gibt und dass er der Träger der Lehre ist, ein deutliches Autoritätsgefälle – in der Wahrnehmung des Autors.[29] Die Art des Verhältnisses zwischen Verfasser und Lesern lässt sich in der Anrede der Leser genauer bestimmen.

2.2 Die Empfänger im Text

Die Empfänger werden nicht konkreter beschrieben als der Autor. Auch hier wird selbstverständlich vorausgesetzt, dass sie bekannt sind.

Wie schon dargelegt, überwiegt im 1. Johannesbrief bei den Verbformen die 1. Ps. pl. Dennoch wandelt sich der mit „wir" bezeichnete Personenkreis im Laufe des Briefes. So beschreibt in 1,1–4 das „wir" die Gemeinschaft der Zeugen gegenüber dem „ihr" (1Joh 1,3) der Leser,[30] während nach der Betonung der κοινωνία (1,3) in diesem Abschnitt, in die die Leser eingehen sollen, ab 1,5 das kommunikative „wir" überwiegt, das Autor und Leser zu einer Gemeinschaft zusammenfasst. Die Wahl der inklusiven Perspektive betont grundsätzlich die Gemeinschaft mit den Lesern gegenüber denen, die sich von der Gemeinde getrennt haben.[31] Die Leser werden nur in der 2. Ps. pl. angeredet, wenn sie dem Verfasser unumgänglich als Gegenüber begegnen, wenn der Verfasser konkrete Ratschläge gibt (so in 2,15, die Welt nicht zu lieben) oder sie auf etwas hingewiesen werden, das sie empfangen haben (so in 2,18 im Verweis auf die ihnen bekannte Erwartung des Antichristen, in 2,20.27 auf die ihnen widerfahrene Salbung und in 2,24.26f; 3,11 auf die von ihnen gehörte Botschaft). Nur in diesen von der Notwendigkeit diktierten Fällen weicht der Verfasser von der inklusiven Sprache der 1. Ps. pl. ab, in der er seine Lehren formuliert. Auf der Suche nach Informationen über die Adressaten ist

---

[29] Vgl. P. TREBILCO, What Shall We Call Each Other? Part Two: The Issue of Self-Designation in the Johannine Letters and Revelation, TynB 54 (2003), 51–73 (51f.).

[30] Vgl. KLAUCK, Der erste Johannesbrief (s. Anm. 3), 73–78.240f.

[31] LIEU, I, II, & III John (s. Anm. 2), 15. Ein Überblick über die Einzelheiten der Gegnerdiskussion findet sich z.B. bei J. BEUTLER, Krise und Untergang der johanneischen Gemeinde. Das Zeugnis der Johannesbriefe, in: ders., Studien zu den johanneischen Schriften, SBAB 25, Stuttgart 1998, 141–162, Nachdruck des Beitrags in: J.-S. Sevrin (Hg.), The New Testament in Early Christianity. La réception des écrits néotestamentaires dans le christianisme primitif, BEThL 86, Leuven 1989, 85–104 (152–162).

es somit nötig, auf die Abschnitte mit Mahnungen und Weisungen zurückzugreifen.

Zu Beginn werden die Leser nicht explizit angeredet. Die erste Anrede erfolgt in 1Joh 2,1: τεκνία μου, „meine Kindchen". Sie setzt die Leser und den Autor unmittelbar in ein persönliches Verhältnis zueinander. Dieses Verhältnis zwingt den Verfasser, wie oben beschrieben, zum ersten Mal die 1. Ps. sg. zu gebrauchen und den Lesern als Einzelperson zu begegnen, die den Lesern schreibt, um sie durch Erkenntnis Christi vor Sünde zu schützen (2,1–6). Diese erste direkte Anrede der Gemeinde ist die einzige im ganzen Brief, in der den τεκνία das Pronomen μου hinzugefügt wird. Die Vater-Sohn-Metaphorik charakterisiert im weisheitlichen Kontext häufig das Lehrer-Schüler-Verhältnis in der Anrede „mein Sohn" (Sir 2,1; 3,1.17 etc.). Derselbe Rahmen findet sich am Anfang der Abschiedsreden des Johannesevangeliums. So erscheint die Anrede τεκνία in den johanneischen Schriften außerhalb des ersten Briefes allein hier in Joh 13,33f. im Munde Jesu, nachdem Judas den Raum verlassen hat und nur die echten Jünger geblieben sind.[32] Jesus gibt den Jüngern Anweisungen für die Zeit nach seinem Weggang. Dabei spiegeln die Abschiedsreden eher die Situation der nachösterlichen Gemeinde als die der Jünger wider. Die Anrede τεκνία charakterisiert somit die Lehrsituation innerhalb der johanneischen Gemeinde. Entsprechend ist sie auch die häufigste Anrede im 1. Johannesbrief.

Der erste Abschnitt mit Weisungen an die Gemeinde (1Joh 2,7–17) beginnt mit der Anrede ἀγαπητοί, „ihr Lieben" (2,7), die sich gut in den Zusammenhang des Gebots der Bruderliebe einfügt.[33] Die Aufforderungen an die einzelnen Gruppen in der Gemeinde werden zunächst zusammenfassend mit der Anrede τεκνία, „Kindchen", (2,12) eingeleitet und dann aufgegliedert durch die getrennte Anrede der πατέρες, „Väter", νεανίσκοι, „junge Männer", und παιδία, „Kinder".[34] Auf diese Weise erscheint die Gemeinde in Altersschichten strukturiert und wiederum dem Lehrer, der sie alle als seine Kinder anredet, unterstellt. Frauen scheint der Lehrer nicht direkt anzureden.[35] Dieser Sachverhalt und die Unterteilung in „Vä-

---

[32] Vgl. PERKINS, The Johannine Epistles (s. Anm. 17), 20. LIEU, a.a.O. 60f., bezweifelt im Blick auf den Wechsel der Anrede, dass die Wortwahl ein weisheitliches Lehrer-Schüler-Verhältnis ausdrücken soll. Die Häufigkeit der Anrede und das unten beschriebene Muster bestärken jedoch das so beschriebene Autoritätsgefälle.

[33] KLAUCK, Der erste Johannesbrief (s. Anm. 3), 121.

[34] Selbst eine Deutung der Passage als Anrede der Gemeindemitglieder im übertragenen Sinn als Väter, junge Männer und Kinder im Glauben (vgl. KLAUCK, a.a.O. 132–135) setzt das übliche antike Autoritätsgefälle nach Alter voraus. Diese Deutung berücksichtigt jedoch nicht den Unterschied zwischen der ersten Anrede τεκνία, die sich auf alle Gemeindemitglieder unter dem Aspekt des Glaubens bezieht, und den Einzelgruppen.

[35] Verschiedene Versuche, die Altersgruppen als eine oder zwei verschiedene Grup-

ter", „junge Männer" und „Kinder" und nicht in „Väter" und „Söhne" zeigt, dass es hier nicht um eine familiäre Beschreibung der Gemeinde geht. Die Altersstrukturen bezeichnen jedoch auch keine Amtshierarchie, sondern die in der Antike übliche Unterscheidung der Autorität nach Alter.[36]

Der folgende Teil des Briefes zeigt einen strukturierten Gebrauch der Anreden an die Gemeinde: Auch wenn die Anreden variiert werden, so wird für Handlungsaufforderungen ausschließlich die Anrede τεκνία gebraucht: In dem Hinweis auf die letzte Stunde in 2,18 werden die Leser als παιδία, „Kindchen", angesprochen, in der Aufforderung zum Bleiben in Christus in 2,28 mit dem Synonym τεκνία. Im Zusammenhang der Ausführungen zu der Gemeinde als „Kinder Gottes", τέκνα θεοῦ (1Joh 3,1–10, bes. 1f.10), drückt der Autor im deskriptiven Teil die Beziehung zu den Lesern zunächst mit der Anrede ἀγαπητοί, „ihr Lieben", aus (3,2), während er die Ermahnung erneut mit τεκνία einleitet (3,7). Ähnliches lässt sich in 3,11–18 beobachten: Die Erläuterung zu dem Hass der Welt wird durch die (im johanneischen Schrifttum einmalige) Anrede „Brüder", ἀδελφοί, eingeleitet (3,13), die auf dem vorausgehenden Abschnitt zur Kindschaft Gottes aufbaut und aus dem Kontext mit Kains Brudermord (3,13) resultiert,[37] während der abschließende Ruf zur gegenseitigen Liebe mit der Anrede τεκνία (3,18) beginnt und die Beschreibung der Zuversicht vor Gott in 3,21 wiederum mit ἀγαπητοί eingeführt wird. Es ist zwar möglich, dass die Einmaligkeit der Anrede „Brüder" daran liegt, dass die Gemeindemitglieder untereinander diesen Begriff gebrauchten, während der Verfasser sie hauptsächlich als seine „Kindchen" sieht. Diese Deutung ließe sich aus den Erörterungen zum Bruderhass (1Joh 2,9–11) und zur Bruderliebe (1Joh 3,13–17) herleiten.[38] Wahrscheinlicher ist es jedoch aufgrund der Einmaligkeit der Anrede „Brüder" in den johanneischen Schriften, dass die übliche Anrede unter den johanneischen Christen ἀγαπητέ war.

Die Untersuchung von 1Joh 2,18–3,18 hat ein Muster aufgedeckt, in dem der Autor jedes Mal, wenn er die Gemeinde zu konkreten Handlungen auffordert, den Ausdruck τεκνία wählt, der ein eindeutiges, aber liebevolles Autoritätsgefälle beinhaltet, während er in der Beschreibung des Zustandes der Christen im Allgemeinen und der Gemeinde im Besonderen häufiger Begriffe wie ἀγαπητοί oder ἀδελφοί gebraucht, die eine gleichberechtigte Stellung der Leser mit ihm implizieren. Auch der letzte Satz

---

pen (πατέρες und νεανίσκοι) innerhalb einer Gesamtgruppe zu deuten, finden sich bei BROWN, Epistles (s. Anm. 5), 297–300.

[36] Vgl. LIEU, I, II, & III John (s. Anm. 2), 86f.
[37] Vgl. BROWN, Epistles (s. Anm. 5), 444.
[38] So TREBILCO, What Shall We Call Each Other? Part Two (s. Anm. 29), 53f.

des Textes, die Ermahnung, sich vor den Götzen zu hüten, beginnt mit der Anrede τεκνία und fällt somit in dasselbe Muster.

Nur in 1Joh 4, im Kontext der Definition der Gemeinde nach außen (Pseudopropheten und Antichrist) und nach innen (gegenseitige Liebe), kehrt sich der Wortgebrauch um: In der Mahnung zur Prüfung der Geister in 4,1 und zur gegenseitigen Liebe in 4,7.11 erscheint die Anrede „ihr Lieben", ἀγαπητοί, während in der Beschreibung der Gemeinde als „aus Gott", ἐκ τοῦ θεοῦ, die Anrede τεκνία gebraucht wird (4,4). Dieser Wortgebrauch ist theologisch bedingt: ἀγαπητοί in 4,7.11 spricht die Gemeinde als in Gottes und der gegenseitigen Liebe ruhend an,[39] und in der Anrede τεκνία, verbunden mit der Aussage „ihr seid aus Gott", ὑμεῖς ἐκ τοῦ θεοῦ ἐστε, in 4,4, wird der in 3,1–10 erörterte Gedanke der Gotteskindschaft heraufbeschworen. Die Abweichungen von dem beschriebenen Muster haben somit einen inhaltlichen Grund. Auch wenn das beschriebene Muster somit nicht statisch ist, sondern an den jeweiligen Kontext angepasst werden kann, drückt es eine Grundhaltung aus. Diese Grundhaltung entspricht dem Befund für den Gebrauch der 1. Ps. pl.: Der Verfasser stellt sich in seinen theologischen Ausführungen in die liebevolle Gemeinschaft mit den Adressaten, während er sie in seinen Weisungen als der weisheitliche und väterliche Lehrer anredet. Bei den Anreden im 1. Johannesbrief handelt es sich somit nicht um einen willkürlichen Wechsel von Synonymen, sondern um den bewussten Gebrauch von Begriffen, durch die der Verfasser sich in konkret die Beziehung zu den Lesern setzt, die zu seiner jeweiligen Aussage passt.[40]

Die angesprochenen Leser sind die Christen, die dem „Geist der Wahrheit" (4,6) folgen. Unterteilungen in verschiedene Gemeinden gibt es nicht, sondern die Leser sind alle Kinder des einen Gottes, Geschwister in der gegenseitigen Liebe. Sie stammen von der wahren Lehre ab, vermittelt durch den Verfasser, der sie seine geliebten Kinder nennt.

2.3 Die Funktion der Selbstbezeichnung und der Anrede im 1. Johannesbrief

Somit begegnet der Autor der Gemeinde auf zwei Ebenen: auf der einen als Mitglied der Gemeinde der Kinder Gottes, die sich durch gegenseitige Liebe und Bruderschaft definiert. Die zweite Ebene zeigt ihn als den Weisheitslehrer, der seine Leser als seine „Kindchen" betrachtet, die seiner Weisung bedürfen. Diese Anrede beschreibt ein Autoritätsgefälle, von dem seine Mahnungen ausgehen. Dieses Autoritätsgefälle zeigt sich auch darin, dass der Verfasser der Autor des Textes ist und die Gemeinde die Leser

---

[39] Vgl. a.a.O. 52f.
[40] Gegen z.B. BROWN, Epistles (s. Anm. 5), 18.

sind, die ihr Verhalten – der Erwartung nach – an ihm ausrichten. Seine Autorität wurzelt gänzlich in der Wahrheit dessen, was er vermittelt, und in der Tatsache, dass er diese Wahrheit vermittelt.

Dass das genannte Autoritätsgefälle nicht unbedingt von der Gemeinde auch so gesehen werden muss, ist eine Tatsache, die durch die im Dritten Johannesbrief genannten Konflikte deutlich wird. Jedoch ist die andere Tatsache, dass der Autor im Ersten Johannesbrief sich nicht erst identifizieren muss, Ausdruck dafür, dass er zum Zeitpunkt der Abfassung seine Autorität bei den Lesern nicht in Frage gestellt sieht.

3. Der 2. Johannesbrief

3.1 Der Verfasser im Text

Der Zweite Johannesbrief ist formal eindeutig ein Brief. Er beginnt mit dem Absender, ὁ πρεσβύτερος, der an einen Adressaten schreibt und diesem „Gnade, Barmherzigkeit und Friede" wünscht (2Joh 1–3). Auch der Schluss ist ein klassischer Briefschluss, in dem der Verfasser sein Kommen ankündigt und Grüße schickt (V.12f.).[41]

Im Gegensatz zum ersten Brief beginnt der zweite den Hauptteil sofort mit der 1. Ps. sg. und einem sehr persönlichen Gefühl, „ich bin froh", ἐχάρην (V.4), das dann in eine direkte Bitte zur gegenseitigen Liebe mündet, eingeleitet durch „ich bitte dich", ἐρωτῶ σε (V.5). Dass der Verfasser sich mit dem des 1. Johannesbriefs identifiziert, zeigt sich in der stellenweise fast wörtlichen Anspielung auf den ersten Brief.[42] Er betont: „nicht als schriebe ich dir ein neues Gebot", οὐχ ὡς ἐντολὴν καινὴν γράφων σοι (V.5), was fast wörtlich 1Joh 2,7f. oder 3,11 entspricht.[43] Auch der Inhalt des Gebots „lasst uns einander lieben", ἀγαπῶμεν ἀλλήλους, in 2Joh 5 findet sich wörtlich in 1Joh 4,7 und fasst die dort folgenden Ausführungen zusammen (1Joh 4,7–21). Die Verbindung der Liebe mit dem Gebot Gottes in 2Joh 6 entspricht 1Joh 2,3–6. Nur in diesen Parallelen zum ersten Brief in 2Joh 5f. findet sich das kommunikative „wir", das im ersten Brief die inklusive Grundstimmung in der Lehre schafft. Im übrigen zweiten Brief herrscht die 1. Ps. sg. vor. Die Übereinstimmungen zwischen den

---

[41] Vgl. z.B. KLAUCK, Zur rhetorischen Analyse der Johannesbriefe (s. Anm. 17), 216f. (mit einer Liste von Arbeiten zum Briefformular); ders., Der zweite und dritte Johannesbrief (s. Anm. 3), 14–17; PERKINS, The Johannine Epistles (s. Anm. 17), 73f.; EDWARDS, The Johannine Epistles (s. Anm. 16), 22–29; LIEU, I, II, & III John (s. Anm. 2), 246f.; BROWN, a.a.O. 647. Der 3. Johannesbrief entspricht dem Formular noch deutlicher als der zweite.

[42] Dass die Abhängigkeit nicht umgekehrt ist, zeigt u.a. LIEU, a.a.O. 238–264.

[43] Vgl. EDWARDS, The Johannine Epistles (s. Anm. 16), 30.

beiden Briefen setzen sich jedoch fort. In 2Joh 7 werden die „vielen Irrlehrer" (πολλοὶ πλάνοι) beschrieben, in diesem Kontext wird für sie auch der Begriff ἀντίχριστος gebraucht, die „hervorgegangen sind", ἐξῆλθον, und „die leugnen, dass Jesus Christus im Fleisch gekommen ist" (οἱ μὴ ὁμολογοῦντες Ἰησοῦν Χριστὸν ἐρχόμενον ἐν σαρκί). Ähnliches findet sich in der Warnung vor den falschen Geistern in 1Joh 4,1, insbesondere dem „Geist des Frevels" (πνεῦμα τῆς πλάνης) in 4,6, oder dem „des Antichristen" (τὸ τοῦ ἀντιχρίστου) in 4,3. Die Bemerkung zu den Irrlehrern in 2Joh 7 entspricht auch den „vielen Antichristen" (ἀντίχριστοι πολλοί, 1Joh 2,18), die aus der Gemeinde „hervorgegangen" sind, ἐξῆλθαν (1Joh 2,19). Auch die Leugnung Christi bei den Gegnern erscheint in 1Joh 2,22f. als Leugnung dessen, dass „Jesus der Christus, der Sohn des Vater" ist, und wird in 1Joh 4,2f. im Gegensatz zu dem Geist beschrieben, „der bekennt, dass Jesus Christus im Fleisch gekommen ist", ὃ ὁμολογεῖ Ἰησοῦν Χριστὸν ἐν σαρκὶ ἐληλυθότα als der Geist, ὃ μὴ ὁμολογεῖ τὸν Ἰησοῦν.[44] Im 2. Johannesbrief steht diese Kurzfassung der Lehre des 1. Johannesbriefs in Verbindung mit der Mahnung, dass die Gemeinde ihren Lohn nicht verspielen soll (2Joh 8). Impliziert ist, dass dies erfolgt, wenn sie die Lehre des Presbyters nicht annimmt. Es folgt die Aufforderung, die falschen Lehrer weder ins Haus zu lassen noch sie zu grüßen, sondern sich von ihnen fern zu halten, um nicht beeinflusst zu werden (2Joh 9–11).

Der Verfasser beendet seinen Brief mit dem Hinweis, dass er noch viel zu schreiben hätte, jedoch lieber persönlich mit der Gemeinde reden möchte (2Joh 12).

Die wörtlichen Übereinstimmungen zwischen dem Ersten und dem Zweiten Johannesbrief werfen die Frage nach der literarischen Abhängigkeit der beiden auf. Beide beziehen sich auf das identische Problem der Irrlehrer, die aus der Gemeinde hervorgegangen sind und die den inkarnierten Christus leugnen, und beide rufen innerhalb der Gemeinde zur Bruderliebe auf. Da der Zweite Johannesbrief jedoch diese Lehren gezielt zur Begründung des Abbruchs jedes Kontakts mit den Irrlehrern verwendet, scheint es sich bei ihm um die Anwendung der im ersten Brief entwickelten Lehren auf das konkrete Leben der Gemeinde zu handeln. Es ist weniger plausibel anzunehmen, dass ein kurzer praktischer Brief in einen theoretischen Traktat erweitert wurde, ohne dessen Aufruf zum Kontaktabbruch aufzunehmen, als dass eine theoretische Abhandlung durch einen kurzen Brief auf eine Gemeindesituation angewendet wurde. Die wörtlichen Übereinstimmungen zwischen den beiden Briefen sind also zusammenfassende Zitate des ersten im zweiten, die den Gesamtzusammenhang

---

[44] Eine Übersicht der verschiedenen Theorien zu den Gegnern findet sich bei BROWN, Epistles (s. Anm. 5), 45–86.

des ersten Briefes mit sich ziehen. Es ist zwar möglich, dass sich der Presbyter im zweiten Brief in seiner Wortwahl auf allgemein verständliche johanneische Lehren bezieht, jedoch im Blick auf die Existenz dieser Lehren in schriftlicher Form im 1. Johannesbrief ist es wahrscheinlicher, dass er sich auf diesen beruft.[45] Somit übernimmt der Presbyter die Lehren des 1. Johannesbriefes; und im Blick auf die identischen Lehren, die betonte Schriftlichkeit des 1. Johannesbriefes und den im zweiten Brief angekündigten Besuch lässt sich fragen, ob der Erste Johannesbrief nicht dem Zweiten beigelegt wurde. Dieser Sachverhalt würde das Fehlen der Anrede im 1. Johannesbrief erklären und die inhaltliche und sprachliche Übereinstimmung der beiden in denselben Gesamtkontext stellen. In diesem Zusammenhang ist die Bezeugung durch Irenäus von Bedeutung, der den Ersten und den Zweiten Johannesbrief nicht nur demselben Verfasser zuschreibt, sondern sie als ein und denselben Brief bezeichnet (haer. 3,16,8).[46] Das unterstützt die Schlussfolgerung, dass der Zweite Johannesbrief ein Begleitbrief für den ersten war und dementsprechend mit ihm zusammen überliefert wurde.[47]

Auch wenn der 2. Johannesbrief ohne Zweifel der Briefform zuzuordnen ist, sind aufgrund der oben beschriebenen Eigenarten Zweifel an seiner Authentizität aufgekommen: Der Verfasser nennt weder sich noch seine Adressaten beim Namen, Formulierungen aus dem ersten Brief werden übernommen, und der Briefschluss ist mit dem des 3Joh (3Joh 13) fast identisch.[48] So ist immer wieder die These aufgestellt worden, dass es sich bei dem 2Joh um einen fiktiven, von dem ersten und dritten abhängigen Brief handelt.[49] Inhaltlich unterscheidet sich jedoch der zweite Brief von dem ersten allein durch die explizite Briefform mit der Erwähnung des Presbyters und der „Herrin" mit ihren „Kindern" und durch die Aufforderung zur Verweigerung der Gastfreundschaft für die Irrlehrer, also in der konkreten Anrede einer Gruppe durch einen Einzelnen mit einer direkten Handlungsaufforderung. Bei der Annahme eines fiktiven Briefes wird der gesamte Brief sinnlos. So ist es plausibler, anzunehmen, dass hier eine konkrete Gestalt an eine bestimmte Gruppe herantritt. Die Leser müssen sich durch die Metapher der Herrin mit ihren Kindern angesprochen gefühlt haben, und das Fehlen eines Namens oder eines Verweises auf einen

---

[45] Vgl. LIEU, I, II, & III John (s. Anm. 2), 250f.; KLAUCK, Der zweite und dritte Johannesbrief (s. Anm. 3), 48f.52.58f.
[46] Vgl. KLAUCK, Die Johannesbriefe (s. Anm. 4), 27f.
[47] Vgl. PERKINS, The Johannine Epistles (s. Anm. 17), 75–77. Perkins nimmt an, dass der Verfasser der beiden Briefe identisch ist.
[48] Vgl. LIEU, I, II, & III John (s. Anm. 2), 241.
[49] Z.B. schon R. BULTMANN, Die drei Johannesbriefe, KEK 14, Göttingen [8]1976, 10.103–105.

Ort in Verbindung mit der Bezeichnung ‚Presbyter' verweist auf die einmalige Identität des Autors, die innerhalb der johanneischen Gemeinden bekannt gewesen sein muss.

Die Übereinstimmung des Schlusses des 2. und 3. Briefes lässt sich auch ohne die Annahme eines fiktiven Briefes erklären. Entweder handelt es sich um eine variable Schlussformel des Presbyters, dann wären die beiden Briefe unterschiedliche Ausdrücke desselben Autors an verschiedene Adressaten. Da die Formulierung in 2Joh 12 komplizierter ist als in 3Joh 13, ist jedoch auch gefolgert worden, dass der zweite Brief sekundär ist.[50] Die umständlichere Formulierung könnte jedoch auch an dem Unterschied zwischen der Anrede einer Einzelperson und einer Gemeinde liegen. In jedem Fall zeigt die Übereinstimmung, dass die in 2Joh 12 angekündigte Begegnung nicht so wörtlich zu nehmen ist, wie es auf Anhieb scheint. So ist nicht die Ankündigung des Besuches, sondern die Bitte um die Wahrung der schon im 1. Johannesbrief dargelegten Lehre das Hauptanliegen des Briefes.[51] Wenn es sich bei der Besuchsankündigung um eine Nachahmung des dritten Briefs handeln sollte, hieße das erstens, dass der an eine Privatperson adressierte dritte Brief schon so weit verbreitet war, dass sich der Autor des zweiten Briefes durch Imitation des Stils mit dem Presbyter identifizieren konnte, und zweitens, dass ‚Presbyter' ein so bekannter Titel war, dass es empfehlenswert war, sich seiner Autorität zu bedienen. Wahrscheinlicher ist im Blick auf die Häufigkeit von Besuchsankündigungen in antiken Privatbriefen[52] die Existenz einer leicht variierbaren johanneischen Schlussformel, zu der die Besuchsankündigung und der Verweis auf das persönliche Gespräch (ohne „Feder und Tinte" oder „Tinte und Papier") gehört. Die Existenz einer solchen Formel sagt nichts über die ‚Echtheit' des zweiten Briefes aus.

Insgesamt zeigt die Darstellung des 2. Johannesbriefs, dass der Autor sich gänzlich hinter die Aussage und den Autor des ersten stellt. Während jedoch die Autorität des ersten Autors ganz aus der Wahrheit seines Zeugnisses und dessen Übereinstimmung mit der johanneischen Tradition entsprang und so ein Autoritätsgefälle gegenüber den Lesern schuf, leitet sich die Autorität des Presbyters nicht mehr ungeteilt aus seiner Lehre her, sondern wurzelt zum einen in seinem Titel „Presbyter" und zum anderen in der Anerkennung der Wahrheit seiner Lehre durch die „Kinder" der Ge-

---

[50] EDWARDS, The Johannine Epistles (s. Anm. 16), 31f., D. MOODY SMITH, First, Second, and Third John, Interpretation, Louisville 1991, 148f.

[51] Vgl. auch BROWN, Epistles (s. Anm. 5), 694f., der die Besuchsankündigung auf den Abschluss des Hauptteils und Übergang zum Schluss bezieht.

[52] Vgl. KLAUCK, Zur rhetorischen Analyse der Johannesbriefe (s. Anm. 17), 217; D. F. WATSON, A Rhetorical Analysis of 2 John According to Greco-Roman Convention, NTS 35 (1989), 104–130 (129).

meinde (2Joh 4). Man könnte hervorheben, dass selbst die Wahrheit seiner Lehre hier nicht auf seiner eigenen Zeugenschaft, sondern darauf beruht, dass er die Lehren des ersten Briefs zusammenfassend zitiert. Doch stellt sich auch der erste Brief von Anfang an, wie oben dargestellt, durch Zitate bestimmter Traditionen in den johanneischen Gesamtzusammenhang. Insofern ist der Gebrauch von Zitaten allein kein Zeichen sekundärer Mittel der Autoritätsvermittlung im zweiten Brief. Ein deutlicherer Hinweis auf sekundäre Mittel ist die Anwendung des Titels Presbyter, der grundsätzlich schon im Judentum eine Amtsbezeichnung ist.[53] Auf den johanneischen Gebrauch des Presbytertitels muss nach der Gesamtuntersuchung des zweiten und dritten Briefes noch näher eingegangen werden, wenn mehr Informationen vorliegen, wieweit der Titel ein ähnliches Lehrer-Schüler Verhältnis beschreibt, wie das im ersten Brief vorhandene. In diesem Kontext genügt es, darauf hinzuweisen, dass über ihn ein ähnliches Autoritätsgefälle geschaffen wird wie im ersten Brief, wodurch der Eindruck erweckt wird, dass es sich um denselben Verfasser handelt. Jedoch ist die Autorität im zweiten Brief deutlich von der Akzeptanz der Leser abhängig, und so tritt der Autor stärker als Individuum hervor. Auch lässt sich hier ein deutlicher Unterschied zum ersten Brief in der Anrede der Leser erkennen.

3.2 Die Empfänger im Text

Der Brief des Presbyters wird adressiert an „die auserwählte Herrin und ihre Kinder" (ἐκλεκτῇ κυρίᾳ καὶ τοῖς τέκνοις αὐτῆς, 2Joh 1). Der Wechsel im Gesamtbrief zwischen der „Herrin", der 2. Ps. pl. in 6.8.10 und 12 und der 2. Ps. sg. im Schlussgruß (V.13) wie auch der Gruß *der Kinder* ihrer Schwester (und nicht der Schwester selbst) legen es nahe, auf die Personifizierung einer Gemeinde zu schließen.[54] Es ist zwar möglich, dass die

---

[53] KLAUCK, Die Johannesbriefe (s. Anm. 4), 117–121; ders., Der zweite und dritte Johannesbrief (s. Anm. 3), 30.

[54] BROWN, Epistles (s. Anm. 5), 652–655. Brown listet auch fünf weitere Deutungen auf: 1. Die Herrin Electa (nach Clemens von Alexandrien, der hier an eine Frau in Babylonien denkt), doch fehlt hier in der Anrede der Artikel. 2. Die edle Kyria (nach Athanasius), hier wäre der 2. Brief nur auf die Hausherrin einer Gemeinde beschränkt. 3. Die liebe Herrin, auch hier wäre die Adressatin eine Einzelperson, die einer Hausgemeinde vorsteht. 4. Eine auserwählte Herrin, d.h. die Kirche im Allgemeinen, doch der Gruß der Schwester ergibt hier dann keinen Sinn. 5. Eine auserwählte Herrin, d.h. eine johanneische Gemeinde als Adressatin eines Rundbriefes. Die individuellen Deutungen in 1–3 sind zwar theoretisch möglich, scheinen aber im Blick auf den Gruß *der Kinder der auserwählten* Schwester eher unwahrscheinlich. Hier müsste man den Tod der Schwester annehmen, was ins Reich der Spekulation führt. Auch erklärt die Annahme einer Einzelperson die 2. Ps. sg. als Anrede im Gruß nicht, denn so sind die Kinder der „Herrin" bei dem Gruß ausgeschlossen. Vgl. auch KLAUCK, Die Johannesbriefe (s. Anm. 4), 155–158; ders., Der zweite und dritte Johannesbrief (s. Anm. 3), 33–38.

„Herrin" eine reale Person ist,[55] in deren Haushalt sich die Gemeinde trifft, wie etwa in Kol 4,15, aber im Blick auf die „erwählte Schwester" im Schlussgruß (13) müsste man für die johanneischen Gemeinden dann eine häufig von Frauen geleitete Organisationsstruktur annehmen. Dies lässt sich nicht nur nirgends in der johanneischen Literatur belegen,[56] es widerspricht auch der Unterweisung in 1Joh 2,12–14, die ausschließlich die männlichen Formen in den Anreden gebraucht. Somit tritt hier dem Presbyter die Adressatengemeinde als Herrin gegenüber, deren Kinder die einzelnen Mitglieder sind. Die Bezeichnung „Herrin" ist zwar ungewöhnlich, da sich keine Parallelen im antiken Griechisch finden, aber die Personifizierung einer Gemeinde oder der Kirche als Frau ist geläufig genug, um als Hintergrund zu dienen (2Kor 11,2; 1Petr 5,13; Herm 1,1–2,4),[57] basierend auf der biblischen Personifizierung Jerusalems als Mutter mit ihren Kindern (Jes 54,1–6; 62,4; Ez 16; Bar 4,10–16).[58] Im Gegensatz zu dem 1. Johannesbrief ist die Gemeinde eindeutig den einzelnen „Kindern" als „Herrin" in der Autorität übergeordnet, und die einzelnen Mitglieder sind die Kinder der Gemeinde und nicht die des Presbyters. So freut sich in 2Joh 4 der Presbyter, „dass ich unter deinen Kindern solche gefunden habe, die in der Wahrheit wandeln" (ὅτι εὕρηκα ἐκ τῶν τέκνων σου περιπατοῦντας ἐν ἀληθείᾳ). Auch redet der Presbyter die Gemeindemitglieder nicht direkt an, sondern wendet sich auch in seinem Verweis auf das Liebesgebot an die Gemeinde (2Joh 5): „und nun bitte ich dich, Herrin, ... dass wir einander lieben" (καὶ νῦν ἐρωτῶ σε, κυρία, ... ἵνα ἀγαπῶμεν ἀλλήλους). Die anschließende Aufforderung, sich danach zu richten, gebraucht wieder die 2. Ps. pl. (ἵνα ἐν αὐτῇ περιπατῆτε, 2Joh 6). Hier ist nichts von der im 1. Johannesbrief vorhandenen Anrede der Gemeinde als „ihr Lieben", „Brüder", „meine Kindchen" zu finden. Die Gemeinde erscheint auch nicht nach Altersstrukturen aufgegliedert, denn sie ist lediglich das abstrakte Symbol, während ihre Kinder die eigentlichen Gemeindemitglieder sind.

Die Metapher beschreibt die Situation eines Haushaltes: In diesem Rahmen gibt es nur die Gemeinde als Hausherrin und die ihr angehörenden Kinder, die von dem „Presbyter" in ihrem Verhalten Weisung erhalten.[59] So erwägt J. Lieu unter Verweis auf Celsus (Or.Cels. 3,55) die Möglichkeit, dass die weibliche Personifizierung der Gemeinde auch auf die antike Vorstellung anspielt, dass sich Frauen und Kinder ohne Anleitung durch vertrauenswürdige Männer leicht von Scharlatanen irreführen lassen. Je-

---

[55] Vgl. EDWARDS, The Johannine Epistles (s. Anm. 16), 26–29.
[56] So trotz ihrer vorhergehenden Interpretation der „Herrin" als Person auch EDWARDS, a.a.O. 91f.
[57] Vgl. a.a.O. 26–29.
[58] LIEU, I, II, & III John (s. Anm. 2), 244.
[59] A.a.O. 259f.

doch widerspricht diese Deutung der ehrenvollen Anrede „Herrin" und dem insgesamt respektvollen Umgang des Presbyters, auch wenn in der weiblichen Personifizierung gegenüber dem Titel Presbyter, der in jedem Fall eine männliche Respektsperson bezeichnet, ein Autoritätsgefälle enthalten ist.

Die Folgerung, dass die Gemeinde eine Hauskirche ist, wird durch die Aufforderung in 2Joh 9–11 unterstützt, den Irrlehrer nicht ins Haus zu lassen: „nehmt ihn nicht ins Haus und bietet ihm keinen Willkommensgruß" (μὴ λαμβάνετε αὐτὸν εἰς οἰκίαν καὶ χαίρειν αὐτῷ μὴ λέγετε). Die beiden Satzteile beziehen sich nicht auf zwei verschiedene Aktionen, sondern verweisen auf die Einladung ins eigene Heim.[60] Hierbei geht es in diesem Brief, adressiert an die „Herrin", nicht nur um allgemeine Gastfreundschaft, sondern um die Aufnahme in das Haus, in dem die Gemeinde sich versammelt.[61] Wer die Irrlehrer in dieses Haus lässt und sie willkommen heißt, unterstützt das, was sie in der Versammlung verbreiten und ist nach 2Joh 11 mitverantwortlich für das Unheil, das ihre Lehre in der Gemeinde anrichtet: „Denn wer ihn willkommen heißt, hat Anteil an seinen bösen Werken" (ὁ λέγων γὰρ αὐτῷ χαίρειν κοινωνεῖ τοῖς ἔργοις αὐτοῦ τοῖς πονηροῖς).

Dass die Gemeinde als Hauskirche keine Einzelerscheinung ist, zeigt der Abschlussgruß: „Es grüßen dich die Kinder deiner Schwester, der auserwählten" (ἀσπάζεταί σε τὰ τέκνα τῆς ἀδελφῆς σου τῆς ἐκλεκτῆς).[62] Hier hat selbst die Gemeinde, von der aus der Presbyter schreibt, keine grundsätzlich andere Stellung als die, die den Brief erhält. Sie wird genauso als „auserwählt" beschrieben wie die angeredete Gemeinde und beide werden einander als „Schwestern" zugeordnet. Die Geschwistermetapher wird somit nicht mehr auf die einzelnen Christen angewendet, sondern auf die Hausgemeinden. Beide Gemeinden sind gleichberechtigte Teile der johanneischen Gesamtgruppe.

Die Anrede einer unbenannten Gemeinde ohne Hinweis auf eine Einzelperson, die ihr vorsteht, oder einen Ort unterstützt die Schlussfolgerung, dass die „Herrin" eine Chiffre ist, die es erlaubt, den 2Joh als Rundbrief an mehrere betroffene Gemeinden zu schicken, um den beigelegten 1Joh innerhalb der johanneischen Gemeinden zu verbreiten. Dabei weist die Ankündigung des Besuchs in 2Joh 12, selbst wenn sie Teil einer Abschiedsformel ist, darauf hin, dass die Gemeinden wohl nicht übermäßig weit von-

---

[60] Vgl. MOODY SMITH, First, Second, and Third John (s. Anm. 50), 145.
[61] Vgl. KLAUCK, Der zweite und dritte Johannesbrief (s. Anm. 3), 65f.; BROWN, Epistles (s. Anm. 5), 676, obwohl beide den Gruß als allgemeinen Gruß bei der Begegnung (Brown) oder im Zusammenhang des Gottesdienstes (Klauck) sehen.
[62] Vgl. PERKINS, The Johannine Epistles (s. Anm. 17), 76f.

einander entfernt waren.[63] Auch wenn ein Paulus große Distanzen überwinden kann, um zu ‚seinen' Gemeinden zu gelangen, spricht gerade die Tatsache, dass der Presbyter an Hausgemeinden und nicht an Städte oder Regionen schreibt, dafür, dass sich die einzelnen Häuser in derselben Gegend, wenn nicht sogar in derselben Stadt, befanden. Das weist wiederum darauf hin, dass es regelmäßige Besuche des Presbyters oder seiner Gesandten in den verschiedenen Gemeinden geben konnte.

3.3 Die Funktion der Selbstbezeichnung und der Anrede im 2. Johannesbrief

So entsteht das Bild einer Reihe von nicht zu weit voneinander entfernten Gemeinden, für die sich der Presbyter verantwortlich sieht. Sie werden von ihm grundsätzlich als Hauskirchen beschrieben. Wie er zu ihren ‚Kindern' steht, wird nicht deutlich, da er sie nicht direkt anredet. In jedem Fall ist seine Autorität in seinem Titel des ‚Presbyters', des Ältesten, begründet und nicht in der Metapher des Eltern-Kind-Verhältnisses, das der Weisheitslehrer im 1. Johannesbrief für die Anrede der Leser gebraucht. Es ist möglich, dass dieser Unterschied aus der unterschiedlichen Ausrichtung der beiden Texte resultiert, wo sich der zweite Brief an die Einzelgemeinden richtet und der erste an die johanneische Gesamtgemeinde. Doch bleibt das Verhältnis zwischen Autor und Leser im zweiten Brief deutlich abstrakter.

Es ist auch möglich, dass der 2. Johannesbrief, der ja den Irrlehrern das Haus verbieten möchte, deswegen nur die Hausherrin anredet. Dennoch wird das Verhältnis zwischen den „Kindern" der Gemeinde und dem Presbyter durch die Distanz definiert, die im 2. Johannesbrief durch die Personifizierung der Hauskirche als „Herrin" erzeugt wird. Dieses Verhältnis ist von grundsätzlich anderer Art als die väterliche Nähe, die durch die Anrede „meine Kinder" im 1. Johannesbrief entsteht. Im 2. Johannesbrief hat die Gemeindestruktur eine solche Bedeutung, dass die Mitglieder nur durch sie angesprochen werden können. Im ersten gibt es keine „Herrin" der Kinder Gottes. Eine Entwicklung der Gemeindestruktur vom ersten zum zweiten Brief ist unwahrscheinlich, denn im Blick auf die andauernden Konflikte mit den Irrlehrern über dieselben Bekenntnisse lässt sich kein großer zeitlicher Abstand zwischen den beiden Briefen belegen.[64]

Ein so deutlicher Perspektivenunterschied ist daher nur durch die Annahme entweder zweier verschiedener Verfasser oder zweier verschiedener Verhältnisse zu den Adressaten plausibel zu machen. Entweder ist hier

---

[63] Vgl. LIEU, I, II, & III John (s. Anm. 2), 262f.
[64] Vgl. BEUTLER, Krise und Untergang der johanneischen Gemeinde (s. Anm. 31), 149–151.

eine vorliegende Predigt eines Gemeindevaters von dem ‚Presbyter' übernommen und an eine konkrete Gemeinde weitergeleitet worden, oder der ‚Presbyter' hat seine Anrede im 2. Brief gänzlich auf die Gemeindestruktur ausgerichtet, um deren Hausrecht zu betonen und sie zu disziplinarischen Maßnahmen aufzufordern. Beide Theorien erklären, weshalb außer der konkreten Briefform und dem Aufruf zum Hausverweis kein inhaltlicher Unterschied zwischen dem ersten und dem zweiten Brief erkennbar ist.[65] Jedoch wäre ein solcher Wechsel in der Anrede bei einem einzigen Verfasser ein dramatisches Zeichen für die Bedeutung, die der Hausverweis für ihn hat. Auch gibt es einen Unterschied im Autoritätsbewusstsein der beiden Briefe: Während der Verfasser im ersten Brief selbstverständlich seine Autorität aus seiner Lehrvermittlung bezieht, basiert sie im zweiten auf dem Titel ‚Presbyteros', doch auch dies ließe sich eventuell durch Probleme mit der Anerkennung seiner Autorität erklären.

Der Presbyter weist sich selbst keine besondere Funktion in seiner ‚Heimatgemeinde' zu. Demgegenüber nimmt er für sich die Autorität in Anspruch, die Lehre auch in anderen Gemeinden verpflichtend festzulegen und sogar vorzuschreiben, wen die einzelnen Gemeinden in ihre Versammlungen lassen dürfen. Diese Autorität liegt nicht in seiner Person oder in einer engen Beziehung zu den Adressaten begründet, sondern in seinem Titel. Der ‚Presbyter' hat gewissermaßen die ‚Kanzelhoheit' in den Gemeinden. Wenn der Presbyter als Basis dieser Lehre die Predigt des Weisheitslehrers übernimmt, zeigt das, dass sein Amt in der Weitergabe dieser Traditionen begründet ist.

So gibt es zwei Möglichkeiten: Entweder der Autor des 2. Briefes ist mit dem des ersten identisch oder er übernimmt dessen Lehre. Wenn er dessen Lehre übernimmt, entsteht die Frage, ob er auch dessen Titel übernommen hat oder ob er den Titel ‚Presbyter' hatte und der Weisheitslehrer unabhängig von ihm bekannt war. In jedem Fall erstreckt sich die Autorität des Presbyters über alle Gemeinden, die seine Lehre akzeptieren. Dass diese Autorität nicht unangefochten ist, zeigt der 3. Johannesbrief.

---

[65] Zur Identität der Aussage zwischen 1Joh und 2Joh und der daraus folgenden Notwendigkeit der Annahme eines realen Briefes für 2Joh, z.B. MOODY SMITH, First, Second, and Third John (s. Anm. 50), 146f. Vertreterin der gegensätzlichen Meinung, dass der 2. Johannesbrief kein „echter" Brief sei, ist z.B. LIEU, I, II, & III John (s. Anm. 2), 5.239f.

4. Der 3. Johannesbrief

4.1 Der Verfasser im Text

Im 3. Johannesbrief findet sich erneut eine klare Briefstruktur.[66] Der Verfasser stellt sich wieder als ὁ πρεσβύτερος vor (3Joh 1), jedoch ist der Gesamtcharakter deutlich persönlicher als im 2Joh. Der Brief ist wieder hauptsächlich in der 1. Ps. sg. geschrieben. Die 1. Ps. pl. kommt nur im Verweis auf die Bürgschaft des Presbyters, die er „unser Zeugnis", ἡ μαρτυρία ἡμῶν, nennt (3Joh 12), vor. Somit beruft sich der Verfasser darauf, dass die Bürgschaft nicht nur seine eigene ist. An dieser Stelle, wo es um die Garantie für die Glaubhaftigkeit des Wanderpredigers Demetrius geht,[67] gebrauchet er dieselbe inklusive Sprache, die sich im Zeugnis des 1. Johannesbriefs findet. Die einzige andere Stelle, an der der Verfasser die 3. Ps. pl. verwendet, ist in V.8, wo er schreibt: „wir sind verpflichtet" (ἡμεῖς ὀφείλομεν), die Wanderprediger zu beherbergen, „damit wir Mitarbeiter der Wahrheit werden" (ἵνα συνεργοὶ γινώμεθα τῇ ἀληθείᾳ), und im darauf folgenden Vers, in dem er erwähnt, dass Diotrephes „uns" (ἡμᾶς) nicht aufnimmt (V.9). So bleibt die inklusive Sprache konsequent auf die Aufnahme fremder Brüder beschränkt. In diesem Kontext stellt der Verfasser einerseits die Verpflichtung zur Gastfreundschaft für alle dar (und schließt sich über das kommunikative „wir" in den Empfängerkreis ein). Andererseits macht die inklusive Sprache in der Bürgschaft deutlich, dass der Verfasser nicht allein steht mit seiner Garantie für den Gast. Schließlich zeigt der Verfasser, dass die Verweigerung der Gastfreundschaft für einen seiner Gesandten die Verweigerung der Gastfreundschaft für ihn selbst und alle, die hinter ihm stehen, bedeutet.

Doch bleibt die inklusive Sprache auf diese drei Verse beschränkt. Im 3. Johannesbrief geht es grundsätzlich um den Verfasser selbst, der hier nicht nur Tradent von Lehren und Weisungen ist, sondern auch persönlich gefordert wird. Er beginnt mit seiner Freude darüber, dass er bei dem Empfänger Anhänger seiner Lehre gefunden hat (3Joh 2–4). Er lobt das Verhalten des Empfängers (3Joh 5) und berichtet von der Ablehnung, die sein voriger Brief bei der Gemeinde gefunden hat und die eine Zurechtweisung in einem persönlichen Besuch nötig macht (3Joh 9f.). Hier – im Gegensatz zu 2Joh 12 und 3Joh 13 – findet sich der Hinweis auf den Besuch nicht erst im Schluss, sondern ist Teil des Hauptteils und daher Teil der Mitteilung.

---

[66] Vgl. LIEU, a.a.O. 265.

[67] Über Demetrius sind Einzelheiten unbekannt, jedoch ist es unwahrscheinlich, dass er aus dem Umfeld des Gaius oder Diotrephes stammt, da er sonst dem Gaius bekannt sein müsste. Vgl. KLAUCK, Der zweite und dritte Johannesbrief (s. Anm. 3), 118–120.

Im Schlussteil wird die Besuchsabsicht der Formel nach lediglich noch einmal wiederholt.

Der 3. Johannesbrief zeigt den Verfasser in einem Kampf um seine Autorität. Er sieht seine Prediger angegriffen und wendet sich an eine Einzelperson, die zu ihm hält. So unterscheidet er sich grundsätzlich in der Betonung des Verfassers von dem Ersten Johannesbrief mit dessen überlegener Autorität. In der Ansprache des Adressaten unterscheidet er sich auch von dem 2. Johannesbrief.[68]

4.2 Der Empfänger und sein Umfeld im Text

Der 3. Johannesbrief wendet sich nicht an ‚die Gemeinde' im Sinn der johanneischen Gesamtgemeinde wie der 1. Johannesbrief, er wendet sich auch nicht an die ‚Herrin' als Hausgemeinde. Er richtet sich an eine namentlich genannte Einzelperson: Gaius (3Joh 1), einen Mann, der offensichtlich einem Haushalt vorsteht, da er Gäste empfangen kann.[69] Da der Name Gaius häufig vorkommt, ist es unmöglich, die Person genauer zu bestimmen.[70] Er wird „der Liebe" (τῷ ἀγαπητῷ) genannt. Diese Anrede, die im 1. Johannesbrief diejenigen auszeichnet, die die Worte des Weisheitslehrers hören, weist im johanneischen Kontext von Anfang an darauf hin, dass der so angesprochene Adressat Mitglied der johanneischen Gemeinde ist. Sie ist keine Anspielung darauf, dass der Adressat dem Presbyter persönlich bekannt sei oder gar ein enges persönliches Verhältnis zwischen den beiden bestehe.[71] Die Anrede kommt im 1. Johannesbrief im Zusammenhang der Darstellung der johanneischen Lehre den Einzelchristen der Gemeinde zu. Auch im dritten Brief wird die Annahme der Lehre betont (3Joh 3f.), denn der Presbyter hat erfahren, dass Gaius „in der Wahrheit wandel[t]" (ἐν ἀληθείᾳ περιπατεῖς, 3Joh 3). Die Brüder haben sogar von der „Wahrheit" des Gaius berichtet (μαρτυρούντων σου τῇ ἀληθείᾳ, 3). Entsprechend hält es der Presbyter nicht für nötig, den Gaius inhaltlich über die Wahrheit aufzuklären. Gaius ist der Inhalt der Lehre schon bekannt und er verhält sich entsprechend. So wird Gaius auch im

---

[68] Der Gebrauch des Begriffs φίλοι für die Mitgrüßenden und die Mitgegrüßten im 3. Johannesbrief sagt zwar nichts über das Verhältnis von Absender und Empfänger aus, er stellt jedoch eine weitere Eigenart des 3. Briefs dar, da der Begriff in den beiden anderen Briefen nicht vorkommt. Jedoch findet sich hier johanneische Sprache wieder, insofern im Johannesevangelium die Menschen um Jesus (der Täufer und die Jünger) mit diesem Begriff beschrieben werden (Joh 3,29; 11,11; 15,13–15).

[69] LIEU, I, II, & III John (s. Anm. 2), 266f.

[70] Allein im Umfeld des Paulus gibt es den Gastgeber des Paulus in Korinth (1Kor 1,14 und Röm 16,23), einen Gaius aus Mazedonien (Apg 19,29) und einen aus Derbe (Apg 20,4).

[71] Gegen HENGEL, Die johanneische Frage (s. Anm. 5), 126.

Fortlauf des Briefes konsistent als „Lieber", ἀγαπητέ, angesprochen (3Joh 2.5.11). Somit findet sich eine wichtige Anredeform des Ersten Johannesbriefs wieder, hier nicht im Plural, sondern bezogen auf eine Einzelperson. Wenn man das oben beschriebene Muster des ersten Briefes zugrunde legt, dann ist jedoch zumindest der Gebrauch von „Lieber" in der Aufforderung in 3Joh 11 auffallend, da Aufforderungen im 1. Johannesbrief in der Regel durch τεκνία eingeleitet werden, doch lässt es die Kürze des dritten Briefes nicht zu, aufgrund der einen Abweichung einen wesentlichen Unterschied im Wortgebrauch zu behaupten.

Vom 1Joh abweichend ist jedoch der Gebrauch von τεκνία. Die im Ersten Johannesbrief so häufige Anrede fehlt im dritten Brief gänzlich. Das verwandte τέκνα kommt zwar einmal vor, aber nicht in einer Anrede und in einem von dem ersten Brief unterschiedenen Kontext: Der Verfasser erwähnt seine Freude darüber, dass „meine Kinder in der Wahrheit wandeln" (τὰ ἐμὰ τέκνα ἐν τῇ ἀληθείᾳ περιπατοῦντα, 3Joh 4). Im 1Joh wird demgegenüber τέκνον nur für die Kinder Gottes gebraucht. Auch hier erlaubt der eine Vers für sich keine Verallgemeinerung.

Auch der Gebrauch einer weiteren Anrede des 1. Johannesbriefs, „Brüder", unterscheidet sich deutlich von dem im 3Joh.[72] Der Verfasser erwähnt, dass die Nachricht von Gaius' Verhalten ihm übermittelt wurde, „als die Brüder kamen" (ἐρχομένων ἀδελφῶν, V.3). Dass es sich um Gesandte des Presbyters handelt und nicht um Christen im Allgemeinen, zeigt sich in 3Joh 5–8: Der Presbyter lobt Gaius: „du handelst treu in dem, was du an den Brüdern getan hast, und das noch an fremden" (πιστὸν ποιεῖς ὃ ἐὰν ἐργάσῃ εἰς τοὺς ἀδελφοὺς καὶ τοῦτο ξένους, V.5).[73] Der Verfasser erhofft sich, dass Gaius sie auch weiterhin unterstützt, da sie im Dienst Gottes ausgezogen sind und „von den Heiden" (ἀπὸ τῶν ἐθνικῶν, V.7) nichts annehmen. Gaius wird nirgends als ‚Bruder' angeredet. Die genannten „Brüder" sind auch keine Mitglieder der Ortsgemeinde, sondern Wanderprediger, die auf die Unterstützung der jeweiligen Gemeinde vor Ort angewiesen und mit einem Empfehlungsschreiben des Presbyters ausgestattet sind, die aber nicht überall aufgenommen werden (V.10).[74] Bei aller Kürze des Briefes erscheint der Begriff doch häufig und konsistent genug (3 Mal gegenüber den 15 Vorkommen im 1. Brief), dass ein inhaltlicher

---

[72] Weitere Beispiele des gemeinsamen Sprachgebrauchs finden sich bei EDWARDS, The Johannine Epistles (s. Anm. 16), 24.

[73] Gegen TREBILCO, What Shall We Call Each Other? Part Two (s. Anm. 29), 54f., der hier einen weiteren Hinweis auf eine christliche Eigenbezeichnung sieht.

[74] Dass es sich bei dem erwähnten ersten Brief des Presbyters um den 2. Johannesbrief handelt, ist gänzlich unwahrscheinlich, da es im 3. Brief nicht um Irrlehre geht. Vgl. z.B. KLAUCK, Der zweite und dritte Johannesbrief (s. Anm. 3), 99f.

Unterschied zum ersten Brief festgestellt werden muss: Im dritten Brief wird der Bruderbegriff nur den einer Ortsgemeinde nicht zugehörenden Wanderpredigern zugewiesen. In diesem Zusammenhang ist die Arbeit P. Trebilcos aufschlussreich, der eine Vermeidung der Anrede „Bruder" in den Pastoralbriefen feststellt und darauf zurückführt, dass die Gemeinde zunehmend als Haushalt dargestellt wurde, innerhalb dessen es gerade nicht nur gleichberechtigte Brüder, sondern auf verschiedenen Ebenen den *pater familias* mit seiner Familie und den Sklaven gab.[75] Die Darstellung der Gemeinde als Haushalt findet sich in gleicher Weise insbesondere im 2. und 3. Johannesbrief, die beide die Mitglieder der Ortsgemeinden nicht als Brüder ansprechen. Im ersten Brief gibt es zwar keine Darstellung der Gemeinde als Haushalt, die in ihm implizit beanspruchte Autorität ähnelt jedoch der eines Familienoberhauptes und die Vermeidung der Anrede „Bruder" lässt sich auch beobachten.

So lassen sich bei aller Kürze des dritten Briefes in allen Anreden des ersten Briefes bis auf ἀγαπητοί Unterschiede zum Gebrauch im dritten Brief belegen. Auch wenn die Häufigkeit der Vorkommen Schlüsse für je einen einzelnen Begriff nicht zulassen, akkumuliert sich ein konsistenter Befund, demzufolge außer ἀγαπητέ keine Anrede in gleicher Weise angewendet wird.

Der Unterschied zwischen dem 1Joh und dem 3Joh zeigt sich nicht nur in dem Gebrauch der Anreden des 1Joh, sondern auch in der Einführung eines abstrakten Begriffs für die Einzelgemeinde, der im gesamten johanneischen Korpus sonst nicht vorkommt:[76] Der Presbyter erwähnt, dass die Missionare die Hilfe des Gaius „vor der Gemeinde" (ἐνώπιον ἐκκλησίας) bezeugt haben (3Joh 6), was sich auf die Heimatgemeinde des Presbyters bezieht. Auch beschreibt er, dass er, der Presbyter, einen Brief „an die Gemeinde" (τῇ ἐκκλησίᾳ) geschrieben hat, zu der sein Gegner Diotrephes und dem Anschein nach auch Gaius[77] gehören (3Joh 9), der aber auf taube Ohren gestoßen ist. Der Anrede an die „erwählte Herrin" (ἐκλεκτῇ κυρίᾳ) des 2. Johannesbriefes entspricht so die Rede von der „Gemeinschaft der Erwählten", der ἐκκλησία, im 3. Johannesbrief. Die Begriffe „Erwählte" für die Christen und *Ekklesia* für die Gemeinde finden sich in gleicher Weise auch in den Pastoralbriefen: Die ‚Erwählten' werden in 2Tim 2,10;

---

[75] P. TREBILCO, What Shall We Call Each Other? Part One: The Issue of Self-Designation in the Pastoral Epistles, TynB 53 (2002), 239–258 (249–253).

[76] LIEU, I, II, & III John (s. Anm. 2), 274.

[77] BROWN, Epistles (s. Anm. 5), 702, ist sich nicht sicher, ob Gaius der Gemeinde des Diotrephes angehört, jedoch erklärt sich der unbestimmte Bezug auf den ersten Brief des Presbyters eher dadurch, dass Gaius an den Vorfällen direkt beteiligt war, als dass er einer anderen Gemeinde angehört.

Tit 1,1 erwähnt, und in 1Tim 3,5 wird die Leitung der *Ekklesia* direkt mit der eines Haushalts verglichen.[78]

Wenn der 2. Johannesbrief eine Hausgemeinde anspricht, und sich zwischen dem 2. und dem 3. Brief (welchen auch immer man als älter ansehen möchte) nicht zu viel an den Strukturen geändert hat, dann ist anzunehmen, dass der im 3. Brief im Zusammenhang der angeschriebenen Gemeinde erwähnte Diotrephes, „der der erste bei ihnen sein möchte" (ὁ φιλοπρωτεύων αὐτῶν, 3Joh 9),[79] auch einer Hausgemeinde vorsteht. Es gibt nichts in diesem oder einem anderen johanneischen Brief, das darauf hinweist, dass Diotrephes ein Anwärter auf ein sich entwickelndes monarchisches Bischofsamt sei oder dass er die aus dem 1. und 2. Brief bekannten Irrlehrer vertrete.[80] Im Gegensatz dazu beschreibt der Text sein Verhalten mit Begriffen, die konkret auf die Verweigerung von Gastfreundschaft hinweisen:[81] „er nimmt [uns/die Brüder] nicht auf" (οὐκ ἐπιδέχεται ..., V.9.10), „er hindert die, die es tun wollen und wirft sie aus der Gemeinde" (τοὺς βουλομένους κωλύει καὶ ἐκ τῆς ἐκκλησίας ἐκβάλλει, V.10). Auch wird der Gemeinde, die zu Diotrephes gehört, nirgends der Status einer christlichen Gemeinde abgesprochen, was der Fall sein müsste, wenn sie ein Haus der Irrlehre wäre.

Somit geht es hier, im Gegensatz zum zweiten Brief, hauptsächlich um Gastfreundschaft.[82] Es spricht alles dafür, dass Diotrephes der Hausherr des Hauses ist, in dem sich die Gemeinde trifft,[83] dass er sich deshalb das Recht vorbehält, über die Aufnahme von Fremden zu entscheiden und sich weigert, die durch das genannte Begleitschreiben empfohlenen Missionare aufzunehmen. Dass er auch andere daran hindert, das zu tun, und die, die sich daran nicht halten, sogar „aus der Gemeinde hinauswirft", zeugt zwar von äußerst feindseligem Verhalten dem Presbyter und allen seinen Angehörigen gegenüber, hat aber nichts mit bischöflicher Amtsausübung oder gar Exkommunikation zu tun. Sein Verhalten ist die Ausübung des Hausrechts, es schafft jedoch eine Reihe von Problemen für den Presbyter, die er in dem Brief angeht: Da er auf die Gastfreundschaft des Diotrephes

---

[78] Vgl. TREBILCO, What Shall We Call Each Other? Part One (s. Anm. 75), 256.

[79] Auch über die Identität des Diotrephes lässt sich nur spekulieren. Einen Überblick über die Forschung gibt KLAUCK, Der zweite und dritte Johannesbrief (s. Anm. 3), 106–110.

[80] Zu den verschiedenen Ansätzen vgl. BROWN, Epistles (s. Anm. 5), 106–108.732–739; BEUTLER, Krise und Untergang der johanneischen Gemeinde (s. Anm. 31), 143–147. Eine vorsichtige Diskussion des Konflikts mit Diotrephes im Kontext der Theorie des Frühkatholizismus findet sich bei C. CLIFTON BLACK II, The Johannine Epistles and the Question of Early Catholicism, NT 28 (1986), 131–158 (143–145).

[81] Vgl. EDWARDS, The Johannine Epistles (s. Anm. 16), 24f.

[82] Vgl. PERKINS, The Johannine Epistles (s. Anm. 17), 94–98.

[83] Vgl. KLAUCK, Der zweite und dritte Johannesbrief (s. Anm. 3), 104f.

nicht mehr bauen kann, schreibt er den Brief an Gaius, der offensichtlich die Brüder aufgenommen und dafür die Konsequenzen getragen hat,[84] und der auf diese Weise zu weiterer Unterstützung aufgefordert wird und einen persönlichen Empfehlungsbrief für den Missionar Demetrius erhält[85] – wahrscheinlich von Demetrius selbst überbracht (3Joh 11f.).[86] Andererseits kündigt der Presbyter einen persönlichen Besuch an, in dem er Diotrephes an seine Verantwortung erinnern (3Joh 10) und so wieder die Einheit der Gemeinde herstellen will.

Es ist nicht anzunehmen, dass Gaius eine Hauskirche leitet,[87] der Gebrauch von *Ekklesia* für die Gemeinde des Diotrephes und die Ankündigung des Versuchs des Presbyters, Diotrephes zur Einsicht zu bringen, deuten auch nicht auf die Absicht hin, Gaius zum Leiter einer neuen Hauskirche zu machen.[88] Der Brief ist vielmehr ganz konkret das Empfehlungsschreiben für Demetrius, für den sich der Presbyter bei Gaius im Blick auf dessen frühere Aufnahme der von Diotrephes des Hauses verwiesenen Missionare Gastfreundschaft erhofft.[89]

So entsteht auch hier ein Bild von Einzelgemeinden, die den im 2. Johannesbrief angesprochenen Hausgemeinden entsprechen. In ihnen haben die Hausherren eine besonders verantwortliche Stellung, sie können Gemeindemitglieder oder Fremde einladen oder des Hauses verweisen. Der Presbyter ist in dieser Lage auf das Wohlwollen des Hausherrn angewiesen. Hier stellt sich die Lage im Vergleich zu der im 2. Johannesbrief umgekehrt dar: Hat dort der Presbyter versucht zu verhindern, dass fremde Lehrer in die Gemeinde eindringen, muss er hier zur Kenntnis nehmen, dass seine eigenen Gesandten abgewiesen werden. Ob Diotrephes auf die im zweiten Brief erfolgte Mahnung zur Vorsicht mit Wanderpredigern überreagiert hat, lässt sich nicht entscheiden, da die beiden Briefe sich zeitlich einander nicht zuordnen lassen. Im Blick auf die im 3Joh entwickelte Form der Beschreibung einzelner Gemeinden als *Ekklesia* ist es unwahrscheinlich, dass er älter als der 1Joh ist oder gar ein ‚Gründungsdokument' der johanneischen Gemeinde darstellt.[90]

---

[84] Gegen KLAUCK, a.a.O. 120f., der annimmt, Gaius sei kein Mitglied der Gemeinde des Diotrephes gewesen. Diese Möglichkeit lässt sich zwar nicht ausschließen, aber der Verweis auf „die Gemeinde" impliziert doch, dass es nicht noch eine weitere gibt, der Gaius dann angehört.

[85] Antike Beispiele für Empfehlungsbriefe gibt KLAUCK, a.a.O. 114–116.

[86] Vgl. EDWARDS, The Johannine Epistles (s. Anm. 16), 23.

[87] Gegen A. J. MALHERBE, The Inhospitality of Diotrephes, in: J. Jervell / W. A. Meeks (Hg.), God's Christ and His People (FS Dahl), Oslo 1977, 222–232.

[88] So BROWN, Epistles (s. Anm. 5), 730–732.

[89] Vgl. P. PERKINS, Koinonia in 1 John 1:3–7. The Social Context of Division in the Johannine Letters, CBQ 45 (1983), 631–641 (631f.).

[90] Gegen LIEU, I, II, & III John (s. Anm. 2), 284.

4.3 Die Funktion der Selbstbezeichnung und der Anrede im 3. Johannesbrief

So passt sich die Selbstbezeichnung und die Anrede des Adressaten im 3. Johannesbrief der konkreten Problematik an. Der Presbyter beruft sich zwar auf Amt und Würde, muss jedoch Gaius auch persönlich ansprechen, da die Autorität seines Amtes im Umfeld des Gaius von dem Leiter der Ortsgemeinde nicht akzeptiert wird. So ist er darauf angewiesen, den einzelnen Gaius, der wahrscheinlich von Diotrephes aus der Gemeinde ausgeschlossen wurde, der in jedem Fall jedoch durch seine Unterstützung der Brüder mit einer einflussreichen Persönlichkeit in Konflikt geraten ist, als seinen lieben Mitchristen, als Empfänger seiner Lehre und geistliches Kind anzusprechen. So greift er auf die persönlichere johanneische Anredeform ἀγαπητέ, bekannt aus dem 1. Johannesbrief, zurück. Der Presbyter geht jedoch nicht, wie der Verfasser im 1. Johannesbrief, in seiner Lehre auf, sondern er tritt als Gegenüber deutlicher hervor. Er würdigt das Verhalten des Gaius und kritisiert das des Diotrephes. Gleichzeitig fällt es auf, dass er gerade an der Stelle, an der er für den Gesandten Demetrius bürgt, in die 1. Ps. pl. verfällt, durch die er sein Zeugnis in das der Kirche einfügt.

Der 3. Johannesbrief zitiert im Gegensatz zum zweiten den ersten nicht wörtlich, er zitiert überhaupt keine johanneischen Lehren, sondern er gebraucht viele Begriffe, die im ersten Brief als Anrede dienen, jedoch in deutlich unterschiedener Weise. Aufgrund dieses Unterschieds ist es unwahrscheinlich, jedoch nicht ausgeschlossen, dass der dritte Brief von demselben Autor geschrieben ist wie der erste. Mit dem zweiten Brief ergeben sich bis auf den Titel ‚Presbyter' und die Schlussformel keine Übereinstimmungen in Selbstbeschreibung und Anreden, außer dass in beiden die Autorität des Verfassers mit dem Titel verbunden ist. Gerade darin liegt jedoch auch ein deutlicher Unterschied, da der Presbyter den Gaius im dritten Brief gleichzeitig auch persönlich anspricht, während der zweite unpersönlicher bleibt.

5. Die johanneische Gemeinde

5.1 Die johanneischen „Briefe" als Ausdruck eines einzigen Trägerkreises

So zeigen sich die drei Briefe eindeutig demselben Trägerkreis zugehörig: Sie alle gehen für den Autor von einer ähnlichen Autorität aus, jedoch zeigen sie grundsätzliche Unterschiede in den Verweisen auf die Beziehung von Autor und Adressaten. Dieser Unterschied lässt sich auf zwei Arten erklären: Die erste Möglichkeit ist, dass es sich um denselben Verfasser, aber um unterschiedliche Kontexte handelt: Der erste Brief wäre demnach ursprünglich nur an die Wanderprediger gerichtet, die der Presbyter „Brüder" nennt,[91] der zweite wäre der unpersönliche Begleitbrief für den ersten an die Hauskirchen und der dritte ein persönliches Empfehlungsschreiben. Jeder der drei Briefe wäre dann Ausdruck eines unterschiedlichen Verhältnisses zu den Adressaten: So entspräche nur der erste dem johanneischen Grundverständnis der Gemeinde als definiert durch gegenseitige Geschwisterliebe, da der zweite selbst in der Mahnung zur Liebe nicht die Beziehung zu den einzelnen Gemeindemitgliedern sucht, sondern diese nur an die Gemeinde richtet. Nach dieser Deutung müsste der zweite Brief als ein drastischer Versuch angesehen werden, sich in das Recht der Hausherrn einzumischen, darüber zu entscheiden, wen sie auf ihren Grund und Boden lassen. Jedoch erwähnt er nirgends den „Hausherrn". Seine weibliche Personifikation der Gemeinde als „Herrin" gegenüber seinem eigenen Titel „der Alte" würde demnach andeuten, dass er als der ältere Mann das Recht hat, der schwachen Frau und ihren Kindern zu sagen, was sie zu glauben und zu tun hätten.[92] Jedoch wird diese Deutung von dem traditionsgeschichtlichen Hintergrund der Personifikation der Kirche als Frau, der immer nur ehrenvoll ist, widerlegt. Auch würde sie heißen, dass die Haltung des Presbyters zu seinen Mitchristen grundlegend verschieden war, je nachdem ob jemand zu seinem „Missionskreis" gehörte oder einer Hauskirche vorstand, und dass er den Kontakt zu „einfachen" Mitgliedern der Hauskirchen nicht suchte, es sei denn – wie im Fall des Gaius – er bräuchte sie für die Unterbringung seiner Gesandten. Somit wäre der Autor zwar derselbe, aber seine Beziehung zu den johanneischen Christen grundsätzlich verschieden. Diese Unterscheidung würde dem Grundsatz der gegenseitigen Liebe widersprechen, die so grundlegend für die johanneische Lehre nicht nur im ersten Brief, sondern auch im Evangelium ist. Auch erfordert diese Theorie eine lange Reihe von Annahmen zu Entwicklung des Autors und Kontextes der Briefe.

Demgegenüber erfordert die Annahme dreier verschiedener Autoren nur diese eine Hypothese zur Erklärung der Unterschiede in den Anreden. Demnach wendet sich jeder Autor auf seine Weise an die johanneischen Adressaten: an die Gesamtgemeinde im ersten, an die Hauskirchen im zweiten und an eine Einzelperson im dritten Brief. Bei der Annahme dreier Autoren mit drei verschiedenen Stilen muss die Beziehung nicht umdefi-

---

[91] Wenn der Gebrauch des Bruderbegriffs im ersten und dritten Brief durch denselben Autor erfolgt, dann müssen die angeredeten „Brüder" im ersten Brief die Wanderprediger sein, oder es ist ein deutlicher Bedeutungswandel im Lauf des Lebens des Autors eingetreten, was lediglich ein weiterer Notbehelf zur Unterstützung der Grundtheorie eines einzelnen Autors ist.

[92] S. oben 3.2, und LIEU, I, II, & III John (s. Anm. 2), 259f., unter Verweis auf Celsus (Or.Cels. 3,55).

niert werden, um den Unterschieden in der Anrede gerecht zu werden. Die Beziehung ist dann in allen drei Fällen gleichermaßen durch die im ersten Brief festgelegten Säulen von Bekenntnis und Bruderliebe definiert. Nach Ockhams Prinzip ist diese Deutung vorzuziehen, solange es keine weiteren Belege für das Gegenteil gibt. Somit besteht hier der Definition nach ein Fall von Pseudepigraphie. Auffallend ist dabei, dass beide „echten" Briefe, sich je auf ihre Weise der Terminologie des ersten, anonymen Briefs bedienen und ihr erst einen Titel geben, dass sich also die Pseudepigraphie zunächst auf den Inhalt der Lehre und die Autorität des Lehrers bezieht.

Die feste Autorität des ersten Briefes lässt zwar den Gedanken an die Irrlehrer, die aus der Gemeinde hervorgegangen sind, zu, aber sie erheben eher ein theologisches Problem der Wahrheit der Verkündigung als dass sie als konkrete Personen erscheinen, mit denen man auf irgendeine Weise umgehen muss.[93] Die Gemeinde definiert sich durch ihr Bekenntnis zu Christus und ihre gegenseitige Liebe. Diese beiden Eckpfeiler wendet der zweite Brief konkret in der Anrede einer Hausgemeinde an, indem er versucht, sie dazu zu bewegen, Vertreter einer anderen Lehre nicht in die Gemeinde zu lassen. Die entgegengesetzte Situation findet sich im dritten Brief, wo die Gesandten des Presbyters selbst der Hausgemeinde verwiesen werden und die Autorität der Lehre abgelehnt wird. So zeigt sich der Erste Johannesbrief als eine Grundlagenschrift, in der die Eckpfeiler der johanneischen Gemeinde festgelegt werden, und die beiden anderen Briefe sind der Versuch, diese Lehre in der konkreten Situation verschiedener Gemeinden anzuwenden.

Dabei kommt der erste Brief ohne Titel aus, während die beiden anderen die Autorität nicht nur an die Wahrheit, sondern an den Presbytertitel binden. Bei dem Presbyter scheint es sich, bei allen Problemen, eine johanneische Gemeindestruktur zu rekonstruieren, doch um die Bezeichnung für einen (Amts-)Titel zu handeln und nicht nur die Ehrenbezeichnung eines ehrwürdigen Ältesten.[94] Aufgrund der Identifizierung der johanneischen Schriften mit einem einzigen Autor ist es möglich, dass der Titel ‚der Presbyter' (mit dem bestimmten Artikel) nur eine einzige Person innerhalb des johanneischen Kreises bezeichnet hat. Im Blick auf die Unterschiede der einzelnen Briefe könnte es sich auch um ein immer wieder mit einer Einzelperson besetztes Amt in der johanneischen Gemeinde handeln. Jedoch erklärt das nicht, weshalb so kurz nach ihrer Abfassung alle drei Briefe unter dem Namen Johannes überliefert wurden. Selbst in diesem Fall jedoch handelt es sich bei ‚dem Presbyter' nicht nur um einen Namen, sondern um ein Amt, da die Autorität in dem Titel enthalten ist, die an-

---

[93] Vgl. dies., „Authority to Become Children of God". A Study of 1 John, NT 23 (1981), 210–228 (216).

[94] Gegen PERKINS, The Johannine Epistles (s. Anm. 17), 82.

scheinend im 2Joh gebraucht wurde, um die Lehre des ersten in den Einzelgemeinden zu verbreiten.[95] Seine Autorität beruht zwar auf der Anerkennung der örtlichen Gemeinde, ist jedoch nicht auf eine einzige Gemeinde beschränkt; daher lässt er sich nicht mit den Ältesten in Apg 14,23; 20,28 oder 1Tim 5,17 identifizieren.[96] Der johanneische Presbyter ist zwar wie die in 1Tim 5,17 erwähnten für die Lehre verantwortlich und scheint auch wie in der Apostelgeschichte gewisse gemeindeleitende Aufgaben zu haben, jedoch ist sein Einfluss innerhalb der johanneischen Gemeinde kein lokaler, sondern ein überregionaler.[97] So finden sich eher mit dem Presbyter Johannes bei Irenäus Übereinstimmungen (haer. 4,26,2.4.5; 27,1; 28,1; 30,1; 31,1; 32,1–33,1), der auch überregionalen Einfluss zu haben scheint und die Verantwortung für die Überlieferung der Tradition trägt. Doch hat der Presbyter, den Irenäus beschrieb, keine kirchliche Autorität.[98] Der johanneische Presbyter dagegen ist in der Lage, drastisch in die Führung der Einzelgemeinden einzugreifen und scheint so die Einheit der johanneischen Gemeinden zu gewährleisten. Umso bedrohlicher ist es, wenn einzelne Hausgemeinden seine Autorität missachten.

So dienen alle drei Briefe der Untermauerung derselben johanneischen Lehre. Während der erste Brief die johanneische Lehre als von zwei Säulen, Bekenntnis und Bruderliebe, getragen darstellt, behandelt der zweite Brief die Bedrohung der ersten Säule der johanneischen Lehre, des wahren Bekenntnisses, während der dritte die Bedrohung der zweiten Säule behandelt, der Bruderliebe: Die Weigerung des Diotrephes, die Prediger des Presbyters aufzunehmen, gefährdet den Zusammenhalt der johanneischen Gemeinde, die sich so eindeutig auf die gegenseitige Liebe und Gemein-

---

[95] Brown beschreibt den johanneischen Presbyter zusammenfassend als jemanden, der über die Tradition entscheiden, der Anweisungen betreffs der Irrlehrer geben kann und die Ortsgemeinden informiert. Der Begriff selbst bezeichnet im griechischen und jüdischen Kontext ein Amt. Brown beschreibt fünf mögliche Deutungen: 1. ein Ehrenname für eine Würdenperson, doch wäre es unwahrscheinlich, dass dies eine Selbstbezeichnung wäre. 2. Ein Mitglied eines Gremiums (,Presbyterium') seiner Heimatgemeinde, doch müsste er den Titel dann mit dem seiner Gemeinde konkretisieren. 3. Einer der Apostel, der durch den Titel genauer bezeichnet wird, doch gibt es darauf keine Hinweise. 4. Ein Begleiter Jesu, der kein Apostel war, doch eine solche Person dürfte weniger Probleme mit Autorität haben als es der 2. und 3. Brief belegen, auch gibt es keine externen Hinweise auf eine solche Person. 5. Ein Schüler eines Jüngers, nach Irenäus (haer. 4,27,1). Vgl. BROWN, Epistles (s. Anm. 5), 647–651. S. auch KLAUCK, Die Johannesbriefe (s. Anm. 4), 117–121; ders., Der zweite und dritte Johannesbrief (s. Anm. 3), 30–33.
[96] Vgl. MOODY SMITH, First, Second, and Third John (s. Anm. 50), 159f.; LIEU, I, II, & III John (s. Anm. 2), 242.
[97] Vgl. HENGEL, Die johanneische Frage (s. Anm. 5), 108f.
[98] Vgl. LIEU, I, II, & III John (s. Anm. 2), 242f.; dies., The Second and Third Epistles of John, SNTW, Edinburgh 1986, 55–63; auch HENGEL, a.a.O. 103–108.

schaft beruft.[99] In diesem Zusammenhang muss jedoch das Phänomen der johanneischen Pseudepigraphie berücksichtigt werden.

5.2 Die Funktion der Pseudepigraphie in den johanneischen Briefen

Auch bei der Annahme, dass die drei Briefe von verschiedenen Autoren stammen, gibt es zwei Möglichkeiten: entweder sind der Weisheitslehrer des 1. Briefes und der Presbyter zwei verschiedene Personen, die ursprünglich nie miteinander identifiziert werden sollten, oder die Autoren des zweiten und dritten Briefes statten sich mit der Autorität des Presbyters aus, indem sie in seinem Namen schreiben. Die äußere Bezeugung des Namens Johannes unterstützt jedoch die Theorie, dass der 2. und 3. Brief absichtlich mit dem Autor des ersten identifiziert werden sollten. Auch die innere Bezeugung belegt, dass absichtlich der Eindruck eines einzigen Autors, des Presbyters, erweckt werden sollte, denn der zweite Brief zitiert bewusst den ersten und identifiziert sich mit dem Autor. So ergibt sich die Schlussfolgerung, dass innerhalb der johanneischen Gemeinden mehrere Schriften im Namen des Presbyters verfasst wurden, während die eine Schrift, auf die sie sich berufen und die mit seiner originalen Autorität spricht, anonym bleibt.

Auffallend ist dabei, dass gerade die beiden Briefe, die als Pseudepigraphen beschrieben werden müssen, nicht nur den Presbyter benennen, sondern die Möglichkeit eines persönlichen Besuchs andeuten. Für sich genommen könnte die Besuchsankündigung literarisches Mittel zur Verstärkung des Eindrucks der Pseudepigraphie sein. Doch stellt der 3. Johannesbrief eindeutig eine konkrete persönliche Kommunikation dar. Ein Empfehlungsschreiben zu verfassen, nachdem der Absender verstorben ist, ist sinnlos. Nimmt man daher an, dass hier die Autorität des lebenden Presbyters für einen Empfehlungsbrief eines Wanderpredigers in Anspruch genommen wird, so erscheint der 3. Johannesbrief als Brief eines Mitarbeiters, der den Gaius im Namen des Presbyters um Hilfe bittet. Auch für den 1. und 2. Brief ist eine ähnliche Situation anzunehmen, denn im Blick auf das andauernde Problem derer, „die von uns ausgegangen sind", ist ihre Abfassung nicht weit voneinander anzusetzen.[100] Wenn der 2. Johan-

---

[99] Vgl. PERKINS, Koinonia in 1 John 1:3–7 (s. Anm. 99).

[100] Es sei denn, man betone den jüdischen Charakter der Gegner im 1. Brief anhand von 1Joh 2,22 und 4,2 (vgl. WOLTER, Die anonymen Schriften des Neuen Testaments [s. Anm. 10], 8f.) und behaupte, dass eine solche Deutung in 2Joh 7 ausgeschlossen ist (vgl. G. STRECKER, Die Anfänge der johanneischen Schule, NTS 32 [1986], 31–47). Eine solche Schlussfolgerung ist jedoch im Blick auf den parallelen Wortlaut von 1Joh 4,2 und 2Joh 7 nicht haltbar (vgl. BEUTLER, Krise und Untergang der johanneischen Gemeinde [s. Anm. 31], 149f.). Der zweite Brief fasst lediglich die Kernpunkte des ersten zusammen. Eine neue Front wird nicht aufgebaut.

nesbrief ein Begleitschreiben des ersten war, dann erscheint er so als das Schreiben eines Vertrauten des Presbyters, der seine Lehren zitiert, um sie an die verschiedenen Gemeinden weiterzuleiten, und sie im Namen des „Alten" zu entsprechendem Handeln auffordert.

So sind, streng genommen, alle drei Briefe anonym, da auch der zweite und der dritte Brief nur den Titel und keinen Namen gebrauchen.[101] Schon der Autor des ersten Briefes, der Weisheitslehrer und eigentliche Presbyter, leitet seine Autorität nicht aus sich selbst, sondern aus der Wahrheit seines Zeugnisses ab. Der zweite und dritte Brief stellen sich dann in die Tradition des ersten Briefes, sie implizieren gemeinsame Autorschaft, indem sie Sprache und Titel des Presbyters gebrauchen. Die Autorität des jeweiligen Autors hängt an der Zugehörigkeit der Lehre zu dem Gesamttraditionskreis. Solange ein Autor die Wahrheit der Tradition verteidigt und vertritt, spricht er im Namen des Presbyters. In dieser Hinsicht sind die johanneischen Schriften in ähnlicher Weise Pseudepigraphie, wie die Schriften, die sich in die Autorität eines Mose, Jesaja oder Henoch stellen, oder die Traditionen, die mit dem Namen eines bestimmten rabbinischen Lehrers verbunden sind.[102] Das Ungewöhnliche ist jedoch, dass der hier dargelegte Befund nahelegt, dass sie wahrscheinlich schon zu Lebzeiten des Presbyters und in seinem engen Umfeld geschrieben worden sind. Dies drückt die enge Verbundenheit des Umfeldes des Presbyters aus und belegt, dass innerhalb der johanneischen Gemeinde die Wahrheit des Zeugnisses über die Autorschaft entscheidet und nicht die Person, die sie niederschreibt.

---

[101] Vgl. LIEU, I, II, & III John (s. Anm. 2), 1.

[102] Zu den biblischen Texten s. HENGEL, Anonymität (s. Anm. 1), 199; DUNN, The Problem of Pseudonymity (s. Anm. 9), 65–85 (67–78). Zu den Pseudepigrapha im Namen des Mose in Qumran s. M. J. BERNSTEIN, Pseudepigraphy in the Qumran Scrolls. Categories and Functions, in: E. G. Chazon / M. E. Stone (Hg.), Pseudepigraphic Perspectives. The Apocrypha and Pseudepigrapha in Light of the Dead Sea Scrolls. Proceedings of the International Symposium of the Orion Center for the Study of the Dead Sea Scrolls and Associated Literature, 12–14 January 1997, StTDJ 31, Leiden 1999, 1–26 (19–22.25f.). Zum rabbinischen Umgang mit Pseudepigraphie s. M. BREGMAN, Pseudepigraphy in Rabbinic Literature, in: Chazon / Stone, a.a.O. 27–41.

Was ist „schlechte" Pseudepigraphie?

Mittel, Wirkung und Intention von Pseudepigraphie in den Epistolae Senecae ad Paulum et Pauli ad Senecam

von

STEFAN KRAUTER

Das Urteil der modernen Forschung über die Epistolae Senecae ad Paulum et Pauli ad Senecam[1] ist vernichtend: Der Briefwechsel gebe sich durch grobe Anachronismen und Fehler als Fälschung zu erkennen, verzerre senecanische Philosophie und paulinische Theologie zu abstrusen Banalitäten, sei sprachlich und stilistisch auf unterstem Niveau und streckenweise vollkommen inhaltsleer.[2] Dagegen zu argumentieren – wie es manche der wenigen Verfechter der Authentizität des Werkes in beinahe komischer Weise tun[3] – ist kaum erfolgversprechend. Es kann nur darum gehen, dieses negative Urteil zu differenzieren und zu versachlichen. Wann und warum also ist ein pseudepigraphisches Werk „schlechte" Pseudepigraphie?

Dass ein pseudepigraphisches Werk als ein solches erkannt werden kann, ist an sich noch kein Grund für ein negatives Urteil – selbst wenn die „Entlarvung" als „Fälschung" sehr leicht ist. Auch die Pastoralbriefe sind

---

[1] Textausgabe: C. W. BARLOW, Epistolae Senecae ad Paulum et Pauli ad Senecam <quae vocantur>, Papers and Monographs of the American Academy in Rome 10, Rom 1938 (Text auch in PLS I,673–678). Vgl. daneben: P. BERRY, Correspondence Between Paul and Seneca A.D. 61–65, ANETS 12, Lewiston u.a. 1999; L. BOCCIOLINI PALAGI, Il carteggio apocrifo di Seneca e San Paolo. Introduzione, testo, commento, Academia Toscana di Scienze e Lettere, Studi XLVI, Florenz 1978; Anonimo, Epistolario tra Seneca e San Paolo, Saggio introduttivo, traduzione, note e apparati di M. Natali, Testi a fronte, Mailand 1995; Der apokryphe Briefwechsel zwischen Seneca und Paulus. Zusammen mit dem Brief des Mordechai an Alexander und dem Brief des Annaeus Seneca über Hochmut und Götterbilder, eingel., übers. u. m. interpret. Essays vers. v. A. FÜRST u.a., SAPERE XI, Tübingen 2006.

[2] Vgl. für viele andere das außerordentlich scharfe Urteil bei A. FÜRST, Pseudepigraphie und Apostolizität im apokryphen Briefwechsel zwischen Seneca und Paulus, JAC 41 (1998), 77–117.

[3] Hinweise bei H.-J. KLAUCK, Die apokryphe Bibel. Ein anderer Zugang zum frühen Christentum, Tria Corda 4, Tübingen 2008, 201f.

deutlich als nachpaulinisch erkennbar, und doch möchte man sie nicht wie den Seneca-Paulus-Briefwechsel als „miserables Machwerk"[4] bezeichnen. Dass ein einem Autor zugeschriebenes Werk inhaltlich von den Positionen in den authentischen Werken dieses Autors abweicht, rechtfertigt ebenfalls nicht automatisch seine negative Bewertung. Der Epheserbrief ist nicht einfach theologisch „falsch", sondern eben eine in ihrem eigenen Recht zu würdigende Rezeption und Weiterentwicklung der paulinischen Theologie. Dass ein pseudepigraphisches Werk stilistisch ungenügend und sein theologischer Gehalt eher dürftig ist, mag zwar zu Kritik berechtigen, nicht aber zu einem völligen Unwerturteil – zumal diese Schwächen ja nicht notwendig mit seinem Charakter als Pseudepigraphie zusammenhängen. Auch authentische Werke können schlecht geschrieben oder inhaltsarm sein.

Was man allerdings überprüfen kann, ist, ob der anonyme Autor sein eigenes Ziel erreicht: ob also die von ihm eingesetzten Mittel der Pseudepigraphie (samt ihrer Wirkung, der durch sie erzeugten Autorfiktion) zu der Intention, die er mit seinem Werk verfolgt, beitragen oder sie unterlaufen.

Dies soll im Folgenden in drei Schritten geschehen: Erstens werden die verschiedenen Mittel der Pseudepigraphie im Briefwechsel zwischen Seneca und Paulus dargestellt, und zwar recht ausführlich. Die „großen" Fragen nach Aussage, Zweck, Wirkung und gar moralischer bzw. theologischer Bewertung pseudepigraphischer Texte (zumal kanonischer) stellen nämlich meistens die schlichte, aber doch grundlegende Frage in den Schatten, wie Pseudepigraphie „funktioniert", d.h. wie bestimmte Signale in pseudepigraphischen Texten zu deren Autorfiktion beitragen[5] – und darum wird diese oft recht kursorisch abgehandelt.[6] Gerade ein so „langweiliger" Text wie der Briefwechsel zwischen Seneca und Paulus erlaubt und erzwingt hier ein genaueres Hinsehen, sozusagen einen unverstellten

---

[4] FÜRST, Pseudepigraphie (s. Anm. 2), 96.

[5] E. REINMUTH, Zur neutestamentlichen Paulus-Pseudepigraphie, in: N. Walter / ders. / P. Lampe, Die Briefe an die Philipper, Thessalonicher und an Philemon, NTD 8/2, Göttingen 1998, 190–202 (193f.).

[6] Vgl. z.B. N. BROX, Falsche Verfasserangaben. Zur Erklärung der frühchristlichen Pseudepigraphie, SBS 79, Stuttgart 1975, 57, der pauschal auf Namen, fingierte Zeit-, Orts-, Umstands-, Situations-, Personenangaben und Versuche der Stilgebung verweist. Problematisch ist die Darstellung von „Mitteln der Echtheitsbeglaubigung" bei W. SPEYER, Die literarische Fälschung im heidnischen und christlichen Altertum. Ein Versuch ihrer Deutung, HAW I/2, München 1971, 44–84. Dort werden sehr verschiedene Dinge vermischt: Textsignale, die eine bestimmte Autorfiktion erzeugen, Textsignale, die Authentizität und/oder inhaltliche Glaubwürdigkeit des Textes vermitteln sollen, sowie außerhalb des Textes liegende Mittel der Echtheitsbeglaubigung wie Siegel, Begleittexte etc.

Blick auf das grundlegende Handwerkszeug in der Werkstatt eines literarischen Fälschers.

Zweitens wird (deutlich knapper) untersucht, welche Autorfiktion mit diesen pseudepigraphischen Mitteln beim Leser erzeugt wird: Welches Bild von Paulus und Seneca entsteht bei der Lektüre des Textes und wie lässt es sich in die uns aus anderen Quellen bekannten Bilder dieser beiden Personen einordnen?

Drittens schließlich wird danach gefragt, welche Intention der anonyme Autor des Briefwechsels mit seinem Werk verfolgte und wie sich die angewandten Mittel zu diesem Zweck des pseudepigraphischen Briefwechsels verhalten. Auf dieser Grundlage ist dann eine Präzisierung der Bewertung der Epistolae Senecae ad Paulum et Pauli ad Senecam als „schlechte" Pseudepigraphie möglich.

Bei allen drei Schritten dienen weitere Paulus bzw. Seneca zugeschrieben Werke als Vergleich, um das spezifische Vorgehen des Autors des Seneca-Paulus-Briefwechsels zu profilieren.

1. Mittel der Pseudepigraphie

Der anonyme Autor des Briefwechsels zwischen Paulus und Seneca wendet verschiedene, teilweise sehr einfache, aber dennoch untersuchenswerte Methoden an, um die von ihm gewünschte Autorfiktion zu erzeugen. Im Folgenden wird (ohne Anspruch auf Vollständigkeit oder zwingende Systematisierung) ein Überblick über sie gegeben.

1.1 Namen

1.1.1 Autor und Adressat

Sowohl Paulus als auch Seneca werden vielfach als Autor bzw. Empfänger der Briefe namentlich genannt.[7] Dass ein pseudepigraphischer Text – wie ja das Wort selbst oder noch deutlicher der verwandte Begriff „pseudonym" schon sagen – den Namen dessen nennt, dem er zugeschrieben werden soll, und ein pseudepigraphischer Brief darüber hinaus auch den Namen eines fiktiven Adressaten, scheint banal, ist es aber nicht. Gewiss ist die schlichte Nennung des gefälschten Namens (bzw. der gefälschten Na-

---

[7] In der Superscriptio (*incipiunt epistolae Senecae ad Paulum et Pauli ad Senecam*), dann regelmäßig in den Briefpräskripten (*Seneca Paulo salutem*; bzw. *Senecae Paulus salutem*; mit Gentilnamen in Brief 2 und 4 als Adressat: *Annaeo Senecae*; in 7 als Absender: *Annaeus Seneca*), außerhalb der Präskripte in einem Anfangsgruß in 11 und 12 (*Paule*), in einem Schlussgruß in 3, 9 und 12 (*Paule*) bzw. 14 (*Seneca*), im Text in 1 als Anrede (*Paule*) und 12 als Selbsterwähnung (*Seneca*).

men) in Superscriptio oder Subscriptio (bei Briefen darüber hinaus in Präskript und ggf. Korpus) wohl die elementarste Technik der Pseudepigraphie. Notwendig ist sie jedoch nicht. Der Hebräerbrief etwa, der sich in Hebr 13,18–25 durch ein dichtes Netz von Anspielungen – insbesondere durch den Namen eines Dritten: Timotheus – als Paulusbrief gibt, nennt Autor und Adressaten an keiner Stelle namentlich. 2Thess 3,17 setzt hingegen mit der Fiktion eines eigenhändigen namentlichen Grußes dieses Mittel sehr nachdrücklich ein. Der Epheserbrief nennt zwar Paulus in Eph 1,1 als Autor, laut P^{46}, $\aleph^*$, B^* aber keine Adressaten.

Die besondere Dichte der Namensnennungen, d.h. die fast penetrante Verwendung dieses pseudepigraphischen Mittels in den Paulus-Seneca-Briefen ist gewiss in erster Linie den Gattungskonventionen geschuldet, die eben in den Briefpräskripten die Namensnennung verlangen. Daneben kann man aber erwägen, ob sie ihren Grund auch darin hat, dass andere – raffiniertere – Mittel der Pseudepigraphie dem Autor offensichtlich nur begrenzt zur Verfügung standen. So ist Brief 2 bis auf die eine Anspielung auf den Status des Seneca als Erzieher des Kaisers (*magister tanti principis*)[8] ganz unspezifisch. In Brief 4 ist die Namensnennung im Präskript sogar das einzige pseudepigraphische Mittel;[9] das Briefkorpus, eine Ansammlung von antiken Brieftopoi, könnte von jeder beliebigen Person an jede beliebige Person geschrieben sein. Ein weiteres Beispiel dafür ist der Brief des Annaeus Seneca über Hochmut und Götterbilder.[10] Auch hier ist der Name in der Superscriptio – wenn man nicht einige sehr schwache Anklänge an Senecaschriften im Text als solche werten will[11] – das einzige Mittel zur Erzeugung der Autorfiktion.

In der Verwendung der Namen in den Briefcorpora lässt sich ein auffälliges Ungleichgewicht feststellen: Seneca redet Paulus sechsmal namentlich an, umgekehrt ist dies nur einmal der Fall. Das ist kaum Zufall, passt es doch zum Befund bei den übrigen Anreden. Seneca redet Paulus dreimal als *frater* an (Brief 1, 7, 11)[12] und fünfmal mit *carissime* (Brief 3, 9, 11,

---

[8] Die beiden anderen Epitheta *censor* und *sophista*, vermutlich auf die seit der Spätantike durch das ganze Mittelalter gegebene Verwechslung zwischen Seneca maior rhetor und Seneca minor philosophus zurückzuführen (vgl. FÜRST, Der apokryphe Briefwechsel [s. Anm. 1], 40f.; BOCCIOLINI PALAGI, Carteggio [s. Anm. 1], 98–100; NATALI, Epistolario [s. Anm. 1], 34), sind nicht ganz so spezifisch; sie würden auch auf andere rhetorisch und philosophisch tätige Personen passen.

[9] Vgl. dazu BROX, Verfasserangaben (s. Anm. 6), 58.

[10] In: FÜRST, Der apokryphe Briefwechsel (s. Anm. 1), 176–197. A. Fürst zeigt dort im Anschluss an R. Jakobi gegen den Erstherausgeber B. Bischoff, dass es sich nicht um einen fiktiven Brief des jüdischen Hohenpriesters Hannas an Seneca handelt (176–180).

[11] Vgl. a.a.O. 187 Anm. 39; 195 Anm. 73 u. 76.

[12] Das ist keine spezifisch christliche Anrede; vgl. K. H. SCHELKLE, Art. Bruder, RAC II (1954), 631–641 (632); gegen z.B. BOCCIOLINI PALAGI, Carteggio (s. Anm. 1), 90f.

12); Paulus hingegen redet Seneca in Brief 10 als *devotissime magister* an und nur in seinem[13] letzten Brief 14 mit *carissime*. Schon durch die (namentlichen) Anreden konstruiert der Autor also ein doppeltes Beziehungsgefälle: Einerseits handelt es sich um soziale Deixis; die Sprache spiegelt das gesellschaftliche Gefälle zwischen dem Senator Seneca und dem einfachen römischen Bürger Paulus – ein wichtiges Thema des Werkes insgesamt.[14] Andererseits ist dies ein erster Hinweis darauf, dass der Briefwechsel sozusagen ein „Handlungsgefälle" hat: Die Freundschaft wird zu Paulus' letztem, Seneca am weitesten vereinnahmenden Brief hin tendenziell enger.

1.1.2 Weitere Personen

Der anonyme Autor nennt auch einige weitere Namen, die die gewünschte Autorfiktion unterstützen sollen. An erster Stelle sind dabei zwei Personen zu nennen, die als Begleiter oder sogar Freunde von Paulus und Seneca vorgestellt werden und daher neben ihrer Nennung im Briefkorpus (Brief 1) auch in zwei Präskripten als Mitadressaten aufgeführt werden (Brief 6 und 7): Lucilius und Theophilus.

Damit wird nicht die Form der Briefe des Paulus bzw. des Seneca nachgeahmt.[15] Die Epistulae morales sind alle stereotyp mit *Seneca Lucilio suo salutem* überschrieben; die Briefe des Paulus kennen zwar Mitabsender[16] – und einige der Deuteropaulinen ahmen dies nach[17] –, aber mit Ausnahme von Phlm 2 (Apphia und Archippos) keine Mitadressaten.

Es geht also vielmehr darum, den Namen einer Person fallen zu lassen, die vom Leser mit dem zugeschriebenen Autor in Verbindung gebracht wird; ein Textsignal zu setzen, das an das Vorwissen des impliziten Lesers über den fiktiven Autor anknüpft. Im Falle Senecas ist dies eben der aus den Epistulae morales bekannte Lucilius. Ironischerweise ist damit der Autor wohl selbst einer literarischen Fiktion aufgesessen. Erklärungsbedürftig ist hingegen die Erwähnung des Theophilus: Im Neuen Testament

---

[13] Die Reihenfolge der Briefe 10–14 ist unklar und umstritten, weil die Folge der Datumsangaben und die inhaltliche Abfolge nicht zur Deckung gebracht werden können (vgl. FÜRST, Der apokryphe Briefwechsel [s. Anm. 1], 22). Brief 14 ist nicht unbedingt der letzte Brief des Briefwechsels, aber auf jeden Fall Paulus' letzter Brief im Briefwechsel.

[14] S. dazu u. 1.4.

[15] Zu den bemerkenswerten stilistischen Unterschieden zwischen den Präskripten und Grußformeln im Briefwechsel und in den echten Paulinen vgl. BOCCIOLINI PALAGI, Carteggio (s. Anm. 1), 91.103.

[16] 1Kor 1,1: Sosthenes; 2Kor 1,1: Timotheus; Phil 1,1: Timotheus; 1Thess 1,1: Silvanus, Timotheus; Phlm 1: Timotheus.

[17] Kol 1,1: Timotheus; 2Thess 1,1: Silvanus, Timotheus.

hat Theophilus als Widmungsträger des lukanischen Doppelwerkes (Lk 1,3; Apg 1,1) mit Paulus nichts zu tun. Eventuell steht 3Kor 1,1 im Hintergrund. Dort ist er einer der Presbyter in Korinth, die an Paulus schreiben. Oder es liegt eine Verwechslung mit dem aus den Paulinen bekannten und in den Deuteropaulinen gerne zu Zwecken der Pseudepigraphie eingesetzten Timotheus vor.[18]

Die Nennung der Namen von Personen, die mit dem fiktiven Autor in Verbindung gebracht werden, ist ein verbreitetes Mittel der Pseudepigraphie. Sehr zurückhaltend nutzt es der Epheserbrief mit dem aus Apg 20,4 bekannten und aus Kol 4,7 übernommenen Tychikus in Eph 6,21; ebenfalls nur einmal, doch – wie oben schon erwähnt – mit wesentlich stärkerer Signalwirkung der Hebräerbrief mit dem wohl prominentesten Paulusmitarbeiter Timotheus in Hebr 13,23; massiv der Kolosserbrief mit Epaphras (aus Phlm 23 bekannt) in Kol 1,7 und seinem Postskript Kol 4,7–17, in dem sich immerhin elf namentlich genannte, ebenfalls v.a. aus dem Philemonbrief bekannte Personen finden. Der 2. Thessalonicherbrief hingegen nutzt dieses Mittel – vom nach 1Thess 1,1 formulierten Präskript abgesehen – gar nicht. Eine gewisse Sonderrolle nehmen die Pastoralbriefe ein, da in ihnen die prominenten Paulusbegleiter Timotheus und Titus als Adressaten erscheinen. Daneben finden sich in 2Tim 4,10–15.19f. und wesentlich knapper in Tit 3,12f., nicht hingegen im 1. Timotheusbrief, Listen von Grüßen bzw. kurzen Notizen mit (teilweise) bekannten Namen.

Im Briefwechsel zwischen Seneca und Paulus sind die beiden Möglichkeiten verwirklicht, entweder nur einen Namen zu nennen (Brief 6 und 7; vgl. z.B. Kol 4,14) oder ihm einen minimalen narrativen Kontext beizufügen, der die Beziehung zum fiktiven Autor in Erinnerung ruft (Brief 1: Lucilius philosophiert mit Seneca im Garten des Sallust; vgl. z.B. Kol 1,7; 4,7–13.17; Eph 6,21).

1.2 Historische Anspielungen

Die mit Namen verbundenen minimalen narrativen Kontexte gehen schon in Richtung eines zweiten, deutlich elaborierteren pseudepigraphischen Mittels, der Anspielung auf mit dem fiktiven Autor (bzw. Adressaten) verbundene Begebenheiten. Grob lassen sich zwei Gruppen solcher Anspielungen unterscheiden: solche auf die gegenwärtigen persönlichen Umstände bzw. die vorangegangene Biographie und solche auf zeitgeschichtliche historische Ereignisse.

Die Technik der Anknüpfung an das Vorwissen der intendierten Leser über den fiktiven Autor/Adressaten kann dabei unterschiedlich sein: Hin-

---

[18] Vgl. FÜRST, Der apokryphe Briefwechsel (s. Anm. 1), 47; BARLOW, Epistolae (s. Anm. 1), 86.

weise auf dessen vergangene Biographie sind oft von der Art, dass sie direkt einen bekannten Sachverhalt nennen; Hinweise auf die gegenwärtigen Umstände setzen zuweilen eher darauf, dass sie mit dem Vorwissen in einen plausiblen Zusammenhang zu bringen sind; Hinweise auf historische Ereignisse arbeiten oft indirekt, indem sie nur auf das Erkennen der zeitlichen Gleichzeitigkeit abzielen.

1.2.1 Biographische Anspielungen und Hinweise auf persönliche Umstände

Auf die zurückliegende Biographie des Paulus wird eher wenig angespielt: Nach Brief 7 hat er keine griechisch-römische Schulbildung,[19] nach Brief 12 ist er römischer Bürger, beides Dinge, die man aufgrund der Lektüre der Apostelgeschichte wissen kann (Apg 22,3; 16,37f.; 22,25–29; 23,27). Auf die Bekehrung des Paulus wird in Brief 5 hingewiesen: *quod a ritu et secta veteri recesseris et aliorsum converteris.*[20]

Sehr im Ungefähren bleiben die persönlichen Umstände des Paulus zur Zeit des Briefwechsels: Nach Brief 3 könnte er am Kaiserhof zugegen sein, ist also wohl in Rom; nach Brief 2 kann er Briefboten schicken;[21] laut Brief 5 und 8 wird er von der Kaiserin angefeindet, weil er sich vom Judentum abgekehrt hat; Brief 3 und 6 suggerieren eine undeutliche Bedrohungslage. Die mangelnde Konkretion wird mit dem Argument kaschiert, dass Briefe eventuell abgefangen werden könnten und man sich daher über manches nicht schriftlich äußern könne (Brief 2 und 6).

Die Darstellung passt grob zu dem, was man aus verschiedenen Quellen über die letzten Jahre des Paulus in Rom wissen oder erschließen kann: Die Vorausdeutungen in der Apostelgeschichte über das Schicksal des Paulus in Rom, 1Clem 5,4 und die Darstellung in den Acta Pauli bilden einen Rahmen, innerhalb dessen ein Briefkontakt zwischen Paulus und Seneca immerhin möglich wäre. Phil 1,13 und 4,22 geben, wenn man als Abfassungsort des Philipperbriefes Rom ansieht, sogar einen noch etwas konkreteren Anhalt, Kontakte des Paulus zum Kaiserhof zu vermuten. Die Begegnung des Paulus mit Senecas Bruder Gallio in Korinth (Apg 18,12–17) mag als Anstoß gedient haben, dabei speziell an Seneca zu denken.

---

[19] Daraus und aus dem Vergleich mit Vatienus zu schließen, Paulus werde im Briefwechsel durchgehend als ungebildeter Bauer dargestellt (NATALI, Epistolario [s. Anm. 1], 30–32), ist eine Überinterpretation.

[20] Oder: *alios rursum converteris* (vgl. den Apparat bei BARLOW, Epistolae [s. Anm. 1], 127, und BOCCIOLINI PALAGI, Carteggio [s. Anm. 1], 116), was ein Hinweis auf die Missionstätigkeit des Paulus wäre.

[21] Beides sind freilich nicht nur Informationen über die Situation des Paulus, sondern auch Brieftopoi (παρουσία, ἀφορμή); vgl. BOCCIOLINI PALAGI, Carteggio (s. Anm. 1), 94f.107; KLAUCK, Apokryphe Bibel (s. Anm. 3), 212f.

Ausdrücklich erwähnt wird ein Briefwechsel zwischen Seneca und Paulus erst in der Passio Sancti Pauli Apostoli 1.[22] Diese stammt frühestens aus dem 5. Jh. und ist schon als Rezeption des apokryphen Briefwechsels anzusehen.[23]

Etwas mehr erfährt man über die Situation des Seneca: Er ist Philosoph (Brief 1), er ist Senator (Brief 10), er liest dem Kaiser eigene philosophische Werke vor (Brief 3) und er liest ihm aus den Paulusbriefen vor (Brief 7). Die Bezeichnung als *magister tanti principis* (Brief 2) ist wohl darauf zu beziehen – oder auf seine frühere Rolle als Prinzenerzieher. Dann wäre sie der einzige Hinweis auf die Biographie Senecas; ansonsten erfährt man über diese nichts.

Auffälligerweise findet sich in den Briefen keine Vorausdeutung auf die wohl prominenteste Gemeinsamkeit in den Biographien von Paulus und Seneca: beider „Märtyrertod" unter dem „Tyrannen" Nero.[24] Was Seneca angeht, wird darauf nirgends auch nur andeutungsweise eingegangen.[25] Was Paulus angeht, bleibt es bei den oben erwähnten Hinweisen auf die Feindschaft der Kaiserin. Dass der Kaiser ihn töten lassen würde, kann man allenfalls erahnen.[26]

Ein Vergleich mit den Deuteropaulinen profiliert auch hier wieder das Vorgehen des anonymen Autors. In den sogenannten Gefangenschaftsbriefen Eph, Kol und 2Tim spielt ein Hinweis auf die persönlichen Umstände des fiktiven Autors Paulus eine zentrale Rolle, nämlich derjenige auf seine Gefangenschaft einschließlich seines bevorstehenden Todes (Eph 3,1.13; 4,1; 6,20; Kol 1,24; 4,18; 2Tim 4,6–8). Man wird ihn nicht nur als pseudepigraphisches Mittel zur Erzeugung einer bestimmten Autorfiktion, sondern darüber hinaus als hermeneutischen Schlüssel dieser Briefe zu verstehen haben, die die apostolische Botschaft im nachapostolischen Zeitalter weitergeben wollen.

Ansonsten verraten die Deuteropaulinen unterschiedlich viel über „Paulus": Der Epheserbrief ist äußerst zurückhaltend; in Eph 6,21f. dient der angekündigte mündliche Bericht des Tychikus sozusagen als „Leerstelle". Eine Antwort auf Fragen nach dem Wo und Wie des Paulus wird

---

[22] Acta Apostolorum Apocrypha, Pars Prior: Acta Petri, Acta Pauli, Acta Petri et Pauli, Acta Pauli et Theclae, Acta Thaddaei, hg. v. R. A. Lipsius, Leipzig 1891 (Nachdruck Darmstadt 1959), 24,6.

[23] Vgl. dazu KLAUCK, Apokryphe Bibel (s. Anm. 3), 199–206; daneben auch NATALI, Epistolario (s. Anm. 1), 41–48.

[24] Vgl. z.B. Hier.vir.ill. 12: *hic [sc. Seneca] ante biennium quam Petrus et Paulus martyrio coronarentur a Nerone interfectus est*; FÜRST, Der apokryphe Briefwechsel (s. Anm. 1), 4.

[25] Doch s.u. 1.2.2.

[26] Nero erscheint meist ausgesprochen positiv (s. dazu u.); in Brief 11, wo es anders ist, wird kein Bezug zu Paulus hergestellt.

dadurch verweigert. Die Pastoralbriefe sind hier sehr viel auskunftsfreudiger (und phantasievoller), v.a. 2Tim 4,9–21 (vgl. auch 1Tim 1,18–20; Tit 3,12f.).

Auch Hinweise auf die frühere Biographie des Paulus dienen in den Deuteropaulinen nicht nur der Autorfiktion, sondern haben (Ansätze in den echten Paulusbriefen aufgreifend) eine theologische Bedeutung: So reflektiert Eph 3,1–10 anhand des Paulus über den Heilsplan Gottes und die Rolle der Apostel in ihm und 1Tim 1,12–17 nimmt die Bekehrung des Paulus als Beispielfall für die Rechtfertigung des Sünders. Etwas Ähnliches kann man im Briefwechsel zwischen Seneca und Paulus feststellen: Die Bekehrung des Paulus, in Brief 5 als Abkehr von den Bräuchen (*ritus*) seiner alten Religion beschrieben, ist das Modell für die in Brief 14 angestrebte Konversion des Seneca, die in der Vermeidung sowohl des heidnischen als auch des jüdischen Kultes (*observatio*) besteht.[27]

Über die fiktiven Adressaten geben die Deuteropaulinen sehr unterschiedlich viele Informationen: der Epheserbrief überhaupt keine, Kol 2,4.8.16 eher solche, die auf die intendierten Leser zu beziehen sind, die Pastoralbriefe hingegen durchaus viele und detaillierte – bis hin zum empfindlichen Magen des Timotheus (1Tim 5,23) und den lügnerischen Kretern in Tit 1,12.

1.2.2 Hinweise auf zeitgeschichtliche Ereignisse

Historische Hinweise im Sinne von Hinweisen auf Ereignisse, die dem fiktiven Autor/Adressaten zeitgeschichtlich sind, finden sich im Briefwechsel zwischen Seneca und Paulus in verschiedener Form. An erster Stelle sind die Datumsangaben am Ende von Brief 10–14 zu nennen: 27. Juni 58, 28. März 64, 23. März 59, 6. Juli 58, 1. August 58. Diese sind chronologisch ungeordnet – wie ja auch diese Briefe inhaltlich kaum in eine sinnvolle Reihenfolge zu bringen sind – und an einer Stelle fehlerhaft überliefert.[28] Mit der Mehrheitsmeinung der Paulusforschung, dass dieser erst 60 n. Chr. nach Rom gekommen sei, lassen sie sich nicht vereinbaren, aber immerhin weisen sie grob auf den Zeitraum hin, der für den Romaufenthalt des Paulus plausibel ist.

---

[27] Falls in Brief 5 *alios rursum converteris* zu lesen ist (s.o. Anm. 20), wäre die Parallele sogar noch deutlicher; denn auch Seneca soll nach seiner Abwendung von den heidnischen und jüdischen Riten zum Verkünder Christi werden.

[28] In Brief 10 muss es *Nerone III et Messalla consulibus* statt *Nerone IIII et Messalla consulibus* heißen (in anderen Datumsangaben finden sich kleinere Abschreibefehler); vgl. BARLOW, Epistolae (s. Anm. 1), 83; BOCCIOLINI PALAGI, Carteggio (s. Anm. 1), 45–47.

Enger mit dem Inhalt der Briefe verknüpft sind die Hinweise auf die Kaiserin Poppaea (Brief 5, 8: *domina*;[29] Brief 8: *regina*; nie namentlich)[30] und den Kaiser Nero (Brief 2: *princeps*; Brief 3, 8, 9: *Caesar*; Brief 7: *Augustus*; Brief 14: *rex temporalis*; namentlich nur in der Datumsangabe von Brief 10). Die Kaiserin erscheint, wie schon angedeutet, als Feindin des Paulus aufgrund ihrer – aus Flav.Jos.Ant. 20,195 und Flav.Jos.vita 16 (vgl. auch Tacitus, Annales 16,6,2) bekannten – Zuneigung zum Judentum. Nero hingegen erscheint in diesen Briefen eher positiv: jedenfalls allgemein politisch (Brief 2: *tantus princeps*; Brief 8: *Caesar noster*), tendenziell auch gegenüber Paulus und dem Christentum (Brief 8f.).

Das steht in einem recht harten Kontrast zu seiner Rolle in der dritten, in einem eigenen Brief breit ausgeführten historischen Anspielung: der auf den Brand Roms. Daraus literarkritische Schlüsse zu ziehen und diesen Brief als spätere Hinzufügung zu werten,[31] gibt es allerdings keine guten Gründe.[32] Eher liegt es nahe, dass der Autor hier Tacitus, Annales 15,44 aufnimmt und in Briefform umsetzt,[33] wobei er die Wertungen des Tacitus hinsichtlich Neros unbesehen übernimmt: Er hat den Brand befohlen (Tacitus, Annales 15,44,2, in Brief 11 nur angedeutet,[34] weil im Rahmen der brieflichen Fiktion eine offene Nennung zu gefährlich wäre), er schiebt die Christen bzw. Juden und Christen als Schuldige vor, er befriedigt mit ihrer Bestrafung sein perverses Vergnügen an Grausamkeit (Tacitus, Annales 15,44,5). Hinsichtlich der Bewertung der Christen weicht der anonyme Autor freilich in charakteristischer Weise von seiner Vorlage ab: Hält diese sie für auf jeden Fall strafwürdig, so hält er als Christ sie natürlich für tatsächlich unschuldig. Ob die Angaben über den Brand, die nicht aus

---

[29] Zum textkritischen Problem in Brief 5 (*dominae* oder *domini*) vgl. BOCCIOLINI PALAGI, a.a.O. 114f.

[30] Ihre Erwähnung macht die chronologische Verwirrung noch größer, denn sie führt dazu, dass man die miteinander zusammenhängenden Briefe 5–9 in die Jahre 62 bis 65 datieren muss, also nach den datierten Briefen 10 und 12–14; vgl. dazu auch KLAUCK, Apokryphe Bibel (s. Anm. 3), 215.

[31] BOCCIOLINI PALAGI, Carteggio (s. Anm. 1), 43f. Vgl. auch NATALI, Epistolario (s. Anm. 1), 35; die zweite von ihr vorgeschlagene Erklärung für den Wechsel im Nerobild, es solle eine Entwicklung zwischen seiner frühen Herrschaft (dem glücklichen Quinquennium Neronis) und seiner Spätzeit als Tyrann angedeutet werden, scheitert daran, dass auch Brief 5–9 in die Zeit nach 62 n. Chr. fallen (s. Anm. 30).

[32] Vgl. FÜRST, Der apokryphe Briefwechsel (s. Anm. 1), 9. Schon generell sind derartige Widersprüche kein gutes Argument: Warum sollten Autoren immer kohärent sein, Redaktoren hingegen nie?

[33] BARLOW, Epistolae (s. Anm. 1), 83.

[34] Dies in einem sehr ungeschickt formulierten Satz, weil zwei Gedanken vermischt werden: dass es in Rom oft brennt (was tatsächlich zutrifft, aber nicht hierher passt) und dass Nero am Brand schuldig ist; vgl. FÜRST, Der apokryphe Briefwechsel (s. Anm. 1), 55.

Tacitus stammen, aus einer anderen Quelle gewonnen[35] oder freie Erfindung sind,[36] lässt sich nicht sagen.

Auffällig ist, dass Paulus nicht in einen *direkten* Zusammenhang mit dem Brand gebracht wird. Er scheint von den Maßnahmen gegen Christen und Juden persönlich nicht betroffen zu sein. Auf keinen Fall wird ein Zusammenhang mit seinem Tod hergestellt.[37] Bei Seneca ist das etwas anders. Auch er ist zwar nur Beobachter.[38] Doch er wird mit Hilfe des Hinweises auf die Folgen des Brandes positiv gezeichnet, weil er für die unschuldig Bestraften Partei ergreift. Zudem erhält er Gelegenheit, „stoischen" Gleichmut angesichts der Katastrophe zu demonstrieren. Vor allem aber transportiert er mit seinem Brief eine christliche Wertung der Ereignisse: Der Brand Roms war der Vorwand für die erste Christenverfolgung;[39] Nero zeigt sich dadurch als der Antichrist.[40]

1.3 Literarische Anspielungen

Ein wichtiges Mittel der Pseudepigraphie, das dem Hinweis auf die Biographie des fiktiven Autors verwandt ist, ist der Hinweis auf bereits existierende, bekannte (echte oder auch zugeschriebene) literarische Werke. Der Autor des Briefwechsels nutzt es insbesondere für Paulus: In Brief 1 werden ein Thessalonicherbrief oder ein Korintherbrief,[41] in Brief 7 der Galaterbrief sowie die beiden Korintherbriefe erwähnt. Anachronistisch wird dabei das Vorhandensein eines „Corpus Paulinum" als Briefsammlung vorausgesetzt.[42]

---

[35] BARLOW, Epistolae (s. Anm. 1), 83.

[36] FÜRST, Der apokryphe Briefwechsel (s. Anm. 1), 57.

[37] Dies spricht dagegen, dass der Brief und damit der Brand mit Bedacht gegen die Angabe bei Tacitus, Annales 15,41,2 (19. Juli 64) auf den 28. März 64 und damit vor das traditionelle Datum des Paulusmartyriums (29. Juni – allerdings 67) datiert sei; gegen FÜRST, Der apokryphe Briefwechsel (s. Anm. 1), 57f.; NATALI, Epistolario (s. Anm. 1), 33.

[38] Unwahrscheinlich ist, dass die plötzliche negative Zeichnung Neros als blutrünstigen Tyrannen auf seinen eigenen Tod hinweisen soll.

[39] Anachronistisch gibt der Brief Hinweise, dass weitere folgten: *quod de innocentia vestra subinde supplicium sumatur; ... putans a vobis effici quicquid in urbe contrarium fit.*

[40] Dies wird in der theologischen Deutung am Ende des Briefes deutlich: *tempori suo destinatus est, et ut optimus quisque unum pro multis datum est caput, ita et hic devotus pro omnibus igni cremabitur.* Vgl. dazu FÜRST, Der apokryphe Briefwechsel (s. Anm. 1), 56f.; KLAUCK, Apokryphe Bibel (s. Anm. 3), 221f.

[41] Zu *caput provinciae* (Provinzhauptstadt) vgl. BOCCIOLINI PALAGI, Carteggio (s. Anm. 1), 85f.

[42] A.a.O. 83.

Die paulinischen Briefe werden inhaltlich charakterisiert als Anleitung zum moralischen Leben – ob das nun das besondere Interesse des fiktiven Briefschreibers Seneca als eines Moralphilosophen spiegeln soll oder die Wahrnehmung der Paulusbriefe durch den anonymen Autor des Briefwechsels ist, kann offenbleiben. Besonderer Wert wird auf die Beschreibung der Wirkung gelegt, die die Paulusbriefe trotz ihrer stilistischen Mängel (Brief 13; s. dazu u.) haben: Sie erbauen (*reficere*; Brief 1) und bewegen (*movere*; Brief 7); sie sind inspiriert (Brief 1);[43] sie erwecken den Wunsch, mit ihrem Autor in Kontakt zu kommen (Brief 1, der dadurch als Auftakt des Briefwechsels dient).[44]

Auf Senecas Werke wird weniger explizit hingewiesen. Lucilius, in Brief 1 der Begleiter des Seneca beim Gang durch einen Garten, den topischen Ort für philosophische Gespräche, lässt natürlich an die Epistulae morales denken.[45] In Brief 3 erscheint Seneca allgemein als Schriftsteller.[46] Die Bezeichnung als *sophista*/Redelehrer in Brief 2 – neben der als *censor*/Sittenlehrer – und die Erwähnung des (seines?) Werkes „De verborum copia"[47] in Brief 9 deuten wohl beide auf eine Verwechslung mit seinem Vater Seneca rhetor hin.[48] Der alphabetische Tyrannenkatalog in Brief 11 könnte aus einem Nachschlagewerk zu Senecas Schriften stammen, denn die Genannten werden in diesen an verschiedenen Stellen erwähnt.[49]

In den anderen Paulus zugeschriebenen Briefen sind explizite Hinweise auf seine bekannten früheren Briefe (von der Sammlung der Paulusbriefe zu schweigen[50]) eher selten. Am deutlichsten ist der Laodizenerbrief, der sich in Laod 20 sozusagen ausdrücklich als „Füllung" der „Lücke" im Corpus Paulinum nach Kol 1,16 zu erkennen gibt. Ob sich 2Thess 2,2 auf einen konkreten Brief bezieht, ist umstritten; die sehr offene Formulierung μήτε διὰ πνεύματος μήτε διὰ λόγου μήτε δι' ἐπιστολῆς ὡς δι' ἡμῶν spricht eher dagegen. Jedenfalls wäre dies kein positiver Bezug.

1.4 Stilimitation

Der Briefwechsel zwischen Paulus und Seneca ist selbst für spätantike Verhältnisse in stilistisch schlechtem Latein verfasst.[51] Viele Sätze sind so

---

[43] A.a.O. 88f.
[44] A.a.O. 77f.; KLAUCK, Apokryphe Bibel (s. Anm. 3), 212.
[45] Dazu kommt wenig später das Stichwort *vita moralis*; vgl. KLAUCK, a.a.O. 210.
[46] BOCCIOLINI PALAGI, Carteggio (s. Anm. 1), 105, zeigt, dass es um Werke Senecas, nicht des Paulus geht.
[47] Vgl. FÜRST, Der apokryphe Briefwechsel (s. Anm. 1), 50f.
[48] S. dazu o. Anm. 8.
[49] BOCCIOLINI PALAGI, Carteggio (s. Anm. 1), 166.
[50] Diese wird nur in 2Petr 3,16f. erwähnt.
[51] Ausführlich zur Sprache des Werkes BARLOW, Epistolae (s. Anm. 1), 70–79.

umständlich formuliert, dass sie trotz ihres schlichten Inhaltes kaum zu verstehen sind. Der Abstand zu Senecas glänzend prägnanter Rhetorik und auch zu Paulus' zwar unkonventionellem, aber doch eindrucksvollem Griechisch (bzw. in Übersetzung: Latein) könnte kaum größer sein.

Dennoch kann man an einigen Stellen immerhin ein leises Echo von Senecas bzw. Paulus' Stil erahnen,[52] z.B. das Polyptoton *omnes omnia viderent* in Brief 11 (Sen.dial 9,17,2); als paulinisches Pendant das *cum omnibus omnia esse* in Brief 10 (1Kor 9,22; 10,33); in Brief 11 die durchaus passenden Vergilanspielungen *finem malis imponat* (Verg.Aen 4,639; Sen.ep. 61,1) und *optimus quisque unum pro multis datum est caput* (Verg.Aen 5,815),[53] ebenda die Sentenz *quibus quicquid libuit licuit* (Seneca, Troades 336), schließlich die paulinisch klingende Wendung *et hoc scias volo* in Brief 1 (vgl. Kol 2,1; Phil 1,12; 2Kor 1,8; 1Thess 4,13) – freilich einem Brief Senecas![54]

Die nächstliegende Erklärung für diesen mageren Befund ist gewiss das fehlende Können des Autors, freilich ist es nicht die einzige. Auch andere pseudepigraphische Schriften versuchen oft erstaunlich wenig, den Stil der echten Werke des angeblichen Autors nachzuahmen. In Fälschungen literarischer Werke steht dieser Aspekt zwar im Mittelpunkt, z.B. bei den beiden unter Senecas Namen überlieferten Dramen Hercules Oetaeus und Octavia. Aufgrund der für die gesamte antike Literatur zentralen Ideen der *imitatio* und *aemulatio* ist das nicht verwunderlich.[55] In den Paulus zugeschriebenen Briefen hingegen ist der Befund unterschiedlich: Während der 2. Thessalonicherbrief sich sprachlich sehr eng an den 1. Thessalonicherbrief anlehnt und der Laodizenerbrief als Sammlung von Pauluszitaten sogar das Extrem fast wörtlicher Übereinstimmung bietet, weicht etwa der Epheserbrief mit seiner liturgisch-meditativen Sprache vom üblichen Stil des Paulus stark ab, ebenso der Hebräerbrief mit seinem sehr gepflegten Griechisch.

Spielt also direkte Stilimitation als Mittel der Pseudepigraphie im Briefwechsel eine sehr geringe Rolle, so taucht das Thema Stil in zwei verschiedenen Zusammenhängen sozusagen auf einer „Metaebene" auf.

Dies sind erstens die Briefe Senecas, in denen er über den Stil der bekannten echten Paulusbriefe urteilt und entsprechende Ratschläge erteilt (Brief 7, 9 und ausführlich 13). Der paulinische Stil wird dort – durchaus

---

[52] Vgl. dazu insgesamt FÜRST, Pseudepigraphie (s. Anm. 2), 81–84.

[53] Der Satz ist grammatikalisch nicht korrekt: *optimus quisque* ist wohl als Subjekt zu verstehen, *caput* als Objekt, *datum est* als aktivisches [!] Prädikat.

[54] BOCCIOLINI PALAGI, Carteggio (s. Anm. 1), 83; vgl. auch BARLOW, Epistolae (s. Anm. 1), 84–86.

[55] Zur Centotechnik literarischer Nachahmung in der Antike vgl. BOCCIOLINI PALAGI, Carteggio (s. Anm. 1), 52.92.

zutreffend – als schwierig (*aenigmatice*, Brief 13) charakterisiert. Paulus wird aufgefordert, dem erhabenen, göttlich inspirierten Inhalt seiner Briefe entsprechend eine bessere Sprache zu pflegen – allerdings nicht über dem stilistischen Schmuck die Sache zu vernachlässigen. Als Urteil eines rhetorisch gebildeten Nichtchristen über die paulinischen Briefe mag dies plausibel sein und somit zu einer stimmigen Autorfiktion beitragen, ein Anachronismus unterläuft dem anonymen Autor jedoch, wenn er Seneca Paulus das Ideal der *latinitas* aus dem Rhetorikunterricht der Spätantike empfehlen lässt.[56] Auffälligerweise äußert sich Paulus in seinen Antwortbriefen nicht zu diesem Thema.[57]

Ebenfalls ein Anachronismus ist der zweite Fall von Reflexion über den Schreibstil. In dem Briefwechsel schreibt, den Gepflogenheiten ab dem 2. Jh. n. Chr. entsprechend,[58] Paulus im Briefpräskript jeweils *Senecae Paulus salutem*, setzt also als sozial niedriger stehende Person seinen Namen an die zweite Stelle.[59] Gegenüber den echten Paulusbriefen und den Deuteropaulinen (einschließlich Laod und 3Kor), deren erstes Wort ohne Ausnahme Παῦλος ist,[60] ist das eine deutliche Abweichung. Darüber wird in Brief 10 offen nachgedacht: Paulus erklärt dort, schon die von ihm verwendete Form des Präskripts sei ein schwerer Fehler, denn in einem Brief an einen Senator müsse er eigentlich seinen eigenen Namen ganz an den Schluss setzen. Diese Ansicht – nicht nur anachronistisch, sondern auch mit demjenigen, was man über Paulus aus seinen Briefen (und den ihm zugeschriebenen Briefen) wissen kann, kaum vereinbar – wird sogar theologisch begründet. Der Brief verweist auf 1Kor 9,22; 10,33 als paulinische Maxime „allen alles zu werden", was hier dahingehend verstanden wird, sich auch den Regeln der Höflichkeit im Umgang mit einem Senator anzupassen.[61]

---

[56] FÜRST, Der apokryphe Briefwechsel (s. Anm. 1), 61; KLAUCK, Apokryphe Bibel (s. Anm. 3), 219.

[57] Außer vielleicht indirekt in Brief 14, wo er andeutet, dass Seneca, wenn er konvertierte, seine rhetorischen Fähigkeiten (*persuasio*, *insinuatio*) für die Verkündigung einsetzen könnte.

[58] FÜRST, Der apokryphe Briefwechsel (s. Anm. 1), 39.

[59] Dies ganz passend zu den übrigen Signalen sozialer Deixis; s.o. 1.1.1.

[60] Das liegt nicht nur daran, dass in dieser Zeit die Reihenfolge Adressant – Adressat – Gruß die übliche ist (aber nicht die einzige; vgl. J. L. WHITE, New Testament Epistolary Literature in the Framework of Ancient Epistolography, ANRW II 25.2 [1984], 1730–1756 [1734]), sondern bringt auch das apostolische Selbstbewusstsein des Paulus zum Ausdruck, insbesondere da, wo die Adressantenangabe erweitert ist.

[61] Die Deutung gesellschaftlich üblicher Höflichkeitsbezeugungen als christliche Demut ist in der Entstehungszeit des Werkes nicht ungewöhnlich; vgl. BOCCIOLINI PALAGI, Carteggio (s. Anm. 1), 93f. Ob man freilich so weit gehen sollte, in der Namensreihenfolge ein Signal für die Religion der beiden fiktiven Briefschreiber zu sehen, ist doch zweifelhaft.

Textkritisch unsicher ist das Präskript des letzten Paulusbriefes innerhalb des Briefwechsels (Brief 14). Falls *Paulus Senecae salutem* zu lesen ist,[62] würde Paulus der freundschaftlichen Aufforderung Senecas in Brief 12 folgen, und dies wäre ein weiteres Anzeichen dafür, dass die Beziehung zwischen beiden im Laufe der Korrespondenz enger wird.[63]

1.5 Gedankenwelt

Nur wenige Stellen im Briefwechsel sind Reminiszenzen an die Gedankenwelt von Paulus und Seneca.

Die größte Dichte an senecanischen Gedanken findet sich in Brief 11. Der angesichts der Bestrafung von unschuldigen Christen und Juden für die Brandkatastrophe gegebene Rat *feramus aequo animo et utamur foro quod sors concessit, donec invicta felicitas finem malis imponat* ist immerhin eine recht grobe Zusammenfassung von Senecas stoischer Lehre.[64]

Am „paulinischsten" – oder jedenfalls: am „theologischsten" – ist Brief 14 mit seiner Aufnahme vom Bild der Saat des göttlichen Wortes (Mk 4,13–20; Mt 13,18–23; Lk 8,11–15; 1Petr 1,23) und des neuen/inneren Menschen (Röm 6,6; 2Kor 4,16; Kol 3,9f.; Eph 4,22–24).

2. Mittel der Pseudepigraphie und Autorfiktion

Mit den verschiedenen Mitteln der Pseudepigraphie, die der Autor des Briefwechsels anwendet, knüpft er an ein bestimmtes Vorwissen des Lesers über die beiden fiktiven Autoren an und erzeugt so ein Bild von ihnen. Bei beiden ist dies ein eher undeutliches Bild. Über weite Strecken ist das Werk sogar so unspezifisch, ja eine bloße Reihung von Brieftopoi, dass man überhaupt keine Anknüpfungspunkte für ihre Identifizierung als Paulus und Seneca hat. Einige Punkte lassen sich allerdings herausarbeiten.

Seneca erscheint als Moralphilosoph und Rhetor am Hofe Neros. Dieses – durch die Verwechslung von Seneca maior und Seneca minor als spätantik erkennbare[65] – Bild bekommt noch einen spezifisch christlichen Einschlag: Seneca stimmt mit den christlichen Moralvorstellungen überein (Brief 1 und 7), er ergreift für die Christen Partei (Brief 11), er verhält sich im Gegensatz zum Rest des Kaiserhofes moralisch einwandfrei (Brief 11),

---

[62] So BARLOW, Epistolae (s. Anm. 1), 137; dagegen: BOCCIOLINI PALAGI, Carteggio (s. Anm. 1), 188; FÜRST, Der apokryphe Briefwechsel (s. Anm. 1), 61.
[63] S. dazu o. 1.1.1.
[64] FÜRST, Der apokryphe Briefwechsel (s. Anm. 1), 53f.
[65] S.o. Anm. 8.

er ist *beinahe* ein Christ (Brief 14; s. dazu u.).[66] Damit unterscheidet das Senecabild des Briefwechsels sich charakteristisch von demjenigen der nichtchristlichen Spätantike. Dort war seine Philosophie aufgrund der Dominanz des Neuplatonismus bedeutungslos und seine Rolle als Erzieher und Berater Neros wurde zumindest ambivalent (so bereits Tacitus, Annales 13,11), wenn nicht ausgesprochen negativ (Cassius Dio 61,10,1–6) gesehen, während er sich bei den Theologen des lateinischen Westens einer großen Wertschätzung erfreute (vgl. Tert.an. 20,1 sowie zahlreiche Stellen bei Lact.inst.).[67]

Paulus erscheint als Briefschreiber, dessen göttlich inspirierte Worte trotz ihrer sprachlichen Mängel Bewunderung und Erstaunen hervorrufen.[68] Kernpunkte seiner Botschaft sind eine Anweisung zum ethischen Leben (Brief 1, 7) und die Trennung von jüdischen und heidnischen Gebräuchen (Brief 5, 14). Die beinahe magische Anziehungskraft seiner Worte ist auch in den apokryphen Apostelakten ein wichtiges Motiv. Der dort und teilweise schon in der Apostelgeschichte (Apg 28,3–10) prominente Zug des Wundertäters spielt jedoch keine Rolle. Ein wichtiger Aspekt des Paulusbildes der Apostelgeschichte, dass Paulus auserwählt ist, die christliche Botschaft „vor Heiden und vor Könige" (Apg 9,15) und nach Rom (Apg 23,11) zu bringen, hat auch für den Briefwechsel große Bedeutung – wenn auch in eigentümlich gebrochener Form: Er zeigt Paulus im Kontakt mit dem Kaiserhof, doch eben nicht wirklich als Zeugen Jesu Christi vor diesem Forum. Er schreckt vielmehr davor zurück, wartet auf eine günstigere Gelegenheit (Brief 6), rechnet schon im Voraus mit Erfolglosigkeit (Brief 8) und gibt schließlich seine Aufgabe sozusagen an Seneca weiter (Brief 14): Wenn dieser Christ wird – was aber nirgends ausdrücklich festgestellt wird[69] –, dann hat er die besseren rhetorischen und gesellschaftlichen Möglichkeiten, die christliche Botschaft an den Kaiserhof zu bringen. An dem voraussichtlichen Misserfolg wird freilich auch dies nichts ändern.

---

[66] NATALI, Epistolario (s. Anm. 1), 33f.

[67] Ausführliche Darstellung bei W. TRILLITZSCH, Seneca im literarischen Urteil der Antike. Darstellung und Sammlung der Zeugnisse, Amsterdam 1971, Bd. 1, 120–185; Sammlung der Testimonien a.a.O. Bd. 2, 362–384.

[68] NATALI, Epistolario (s. Anm. 1), 30f.

[69] Vgl. dazu (und zur Entwicklung der Legende, dass Seneca tatsächlich konvertiert sei) A. MOMIGLIANO, Note sulla leggenda del christianesimo di Seneca, in: ders., [Primo] Contributo alla storia degli studi classici, Storia e letteratura 47, Rom 1955, 13–32.

3. Mittel der Pseudepigraphie und Intention des Werkes

3.1 Die Intention des Werkes

Über die Intention, die der anonyme Autor des Seneca-Paulus-Briefwechsels mit der Abfassung seines Werkes verfolgte, wurde in der Forschung viel gerätselt. Dass er eine bestimmte Rezeption und Fortentwicklung paulinischer Theologie oder senecanischer Philosophie unter dem Namen der beiden berühmten Zeitgenossen verbreiten wollte, scheidet aus. Ebenso, dass er *irgendeine* Lehre oder Botschaft vermitteln wollte – ist der Text doch ganz generell theologisch und philosophisch vollkommen inhaltsleer.[70] Weit verbreitet ist die Ansicht, er wolle mit Hilfe des berühmten Philosophen Seneca gebildeten nichtchristlichen Lesern die Briefe des Paulus empfehlen.[71] Dies scheitert an der im vorangehenden Abschnitt erwähnten Tatsache, dass Seneca außerhalb des lateinischen Christentums in der Spätantike unbekannt bzw. unbeliebt war. Dass der Autor umgekehrt an Bildung interessierten christlichen Lesern die Werke des Seneca ans Herz legen wollte,[72] kann man den Briefen nicht entnehmen. Dass er die Notwendigkeit eines rhetorisch und philosophisch niveauvollen Christentums aufzeigen wolle,[73] hat zwar einen Anhaltspunkt an einigen Briefen (s.o. 1.4), vermag jedoch als Erklärung für das gesamte Werk nicht zu überzeugen.

Beinahe ist man geneigt, der Ansicht C. W. Barlows, des Herausgebers der maßgeblichen kritischen Textausgabe des Briefwechsels, zu folgen, das Werk habe überhaupt keine Intention, sondern sei eine bloße Stilübung, wie sie in den antiken Rhetorikschulen üblich waren.[74] Dem anonymen Autor ging es jedoch – wie A. Fürst methodisch sorgfältig unter aufwendiger Heranziehung von Vergleichsmaterial aus spätantiken Briefwechseln gezeigt hat – durchaus um etwas: eben darum, *dass* Paulus und Seneca angeblich freundschaftliche Briefe gewechselt hätten.[75] Damit verfolgte er das Ziel, die erwähnte allgemeine Hochschätzung Senecas in der

---

[70] Vgl. FÜRST, Der apokryphe Briefwechsel (s. Anm. 1), 11.

[71] So z.B. T. ZAHN, Geschichte des neutestamentlichen Kanons, Bd. 2/2, Erlangen/Leipzig 1892, 621; A. VON HARNACK, Geschichte der altchristlichen Literatur bis Eusebius, Bd. 1/2, Leipzig 1893, 765.

[72] So z.B. F. X. KRAUS, Der Briefwechsel Pauli mit Seneca. Ein Beitrag zur Apokryphen-Litteratur, ThQ 49 (1867), 603–624 (608).

[73] BOCCIOLINI PALAGI, Carteggio (s. Anm 1), 49–57; NATALI, Epistolario (s. Anm. 1), 35–40.

[74] BARLOW, Epistolae (s. Anm. 1), 91f. [PLS I 673].

[75] FÜRST, Der apokryphe Briefwechsel (s. Anm. 1), 11.

lateinischen christlichen Antike zu „personalisieren" und damit als „apostolisch" zu sanktionieren.[76]

3.2 Das Verhältnis von Mitteln, Wirkung und Intention des Werkes

Pseudepigraphische Werke wollen in ihrer Gegenwart in ihrem Umfeld etwas erreichen, doch dies in Gestalt eines Werkes aus einem anderen Umfeld, oft aus der Vergangenheit. Der fiktive Autor und der implizite Autor, die fiktiven Adressaten (wenn es sich um Briefe handelt) und die impliziten, intendierten Leser sind also nie ganz deckungsgleich.[77] Diese grundlegende Spannung ist Voraussetzung für das Funktionieren pseudepigraphischer Texte – und zugleich für die Möglichkeit der Aufdeckung der Pseudepigraphie. Brüche in der Autor- bzw. Adressatenfiktion sind also dann nicht einfach „Fehler", die dem „Fälscher" unterlaufen sind und die helfen, ihn zu „entlarven", wenn sie für das Erreichen der kommunikativen Intention des Werkes notwendig sind. Dann erlauben sie auch kein negatives Urteil über die Pseudepigraphie. Denn sonst wäre „gute" Pseudepigraphie nur das vollkommene Imitat – um den Preis der Wirkungslosigkeit.

Wie ist unter diesen Voraussetzungen der Briefwechsel zwischen Seneca und Paulus zu bewerten? Inwieweit sind die gegen ihn getroffenen sehr scharfen Urteile der Forschung angemessen?

Zunächst ist festzustellen, dass sich der anonyme Autor mit seiner Intention, nachzuweisen, *dass* Paulus und Seneca freundschaftlich kommunizierten, und dadurch dem positiven Senecabild der lateinischen christlichen Antike eine apostolische Grundlage zu geben, unter dem Gesichtspunkt der Pseudepigraphie eine sehr *schwierige* Aufgabe gestellt hat. Mit der apostolischen Autorität des Paulus einen Brief zu theologischen Problemen in den Gemeinden des 2. Jh. n. Chr. zu schreiben, mag inhaltlich fordernder sein, gegenüber Brüchen in der pseudepigraphischen Autorfiktion ist ein solches Unternehmen jedoch deutlich „unempfindlicher". Die beinahe vollständige Einschränkung des Zweckes der Pseudepigraphie auf ein bloßes „Dass" macht sie hingegen äußerst sensibel gegenüber Brüchen und Anachronismen. Dieser Anforderung zeigt sich der Autor des Briefwechsels in mehrerer Hinsicht nicht gewachsen. Dies sei an einigen Punkten aufgezeigt.

Besondere Kritik zog der Briefwechsel immer wieder wegen seines dürftigen theologischen und philosophischen Gehalts auf sich. Der Grund dafür ist wohl, dass der Titel des Werkes entsprechende Erwartungen weckt. Über Paulus und Seneca – bzw. frühes Christentum und Stoa – gibt

---

[76] Ders., Pseudepigraphie (s. Anm. 2), 114–117.
[77] Vgl. REINMUTH, Paulus-Pseudepigraphie (s. Anm. 5), 194.

es ja in der Tat einiges Interessante zu sagen. Nur wird es eben in diesem Briefwechsel nicht gesagt und daher wirkt er auf viele Leser frustrierend.

Dies zu kritisieren ist in einer Hinsicht nicht gerechtfertigt, sondern ein schlichtes Missverständnis der Intention des Werkes: Es will ja gar nicht Erkenntnisse über Berührungen zwischen senecanischer Philosophie und paulinischer Theologie mittels der Fiktion einer Korrespondenz zwischen beiden vermitteln, sondern hat eben nur das Ziel, eine freundschaftliche Beziehung zwischen ihnen zu fingieren.

In anderer Hinsicht ist die Kritik allerdings berechtigt. Gedanken aus der senecanischen Philosophie und der paulinischen Theologie werden im Briefwechsel ja zumindest gelegentlich aufgenommen. Gegenüber ihrer Form in den authentischen Werken ist dabei stets eine recht große Abweichung zu konstatieren. Man kann diese als „Banalisierung" bewerten. Doch um dieses inhaltliche Urteil, nach welchem Maßstab und in welchem Kontext es auch immer getroffen werden mag, geht es hier nicht. Die Frage ist vielmehr, ob diese Modifikationen vom kommunikativen Zweck des pseudepigraphischen Textes her gerechtfertigt sind – wie etwa die von Paulus abweichenden Positionen der Deuteropaulinen als Fortentwicklung von dessen Theologie unter den Bedingungen der nachapostolischen Zeit gedeutet werden können (ob man sie dann sachlich als Verflachung, Verfälschung o.ä. ansieht, ist eine andere Frage). Das Problem an den Anspielungen des Briefwechsels auf Gedanken des Paulus oder des Seneca ist, dass sie *nur* Mittel der Pseudepigraphie sind. Mit ihnen wird keine inhaltliche Aussage für den intendierten Leser gemacht, sondern sie sind nur als Signale eingesetzt, die ihn dazu bewegen sollen, Paulus bzw. Seneca als Autoren des ihm vorliegenden Textes anzunehmen. In diesem Fall aber sind Abweichungen tatsächlich „Fehler" – und solche starken Abweichungen, wie sie im Briefwechsel vorkommen, grobe Fehler.

Ein zweiter, oft weniger beachteter Punkt, sind die historischen Anspielungen im Briefwechsel: Die expliziten Datierungen der Briefe 10–14 und die indirekte Datierung der Briefe 5–9 durch die Erwähnung Poppaeas als Kaiserin ergeben schon in sich keinen stimmigen chronologischen Rahmen für die Korrespondenz (s.o. 1.2.2),[78] mit der Ordnung der Briefe aufgrund inhaltlicher Bezugnahmen lassen sie sich vollends nicht in Einklang bringen. Da die historischen Anspielungen als Mittel der Pseudepi-

---

[78] Gegen den Versuch, eine „Geschichte" der Beziehung zwischen Seneca und Paulus aus den Briefen zusammenzustellen bei z.B. NATALI, Epistolario (s. Anm. 1), 29. Selbst wenn man die Lücke zwischen 59 und 64 n. Chr. innerhalb der datierten Briefe mit Hilfe der Tradition erklärt, Paulus sei nach seinem ersten Romaufenthalt noch einmal freigekommen, habe seine geplante Spanienmission verwirklicht und sei dann nach Rom zurückgekehrt (33), bleibt immer noch die Verwirrung durch die Briefe, die auf Poppaea hinweisen.

graphie im Briefwechsel keinen anderen Zweck haben als den, die Briefe zu Zeiten von Paulus und Seneca geschrieben erscheinen zu lassen, gibt es für diese Unstimmigkeit keine andere Erklärung als die Unfähigkeit des Autors. Das ist also etwas anderes, als wenn die deuteropaulinischen Gefangenschaftsbriefe eine Situation im Leben des Paulus voraussetzen, die man nicht in dessen rekonstruierter Biographie unterbringen kann. Dieser chronologische „Fehler" hat sozusagen durchaus seinen Sinn, nämlich den Apostel in die nachapostolische Zeit hinein sprechen zu lassen, ihn als Abwesenden fiktiv per Brief anwesend sein zu lassen.

Differenziert sind die sprachlichen und stilistischen Abweichungen des Briefwechsels von den authentischen Werken der beiden fiktiven Autoren zu bewerten. Einige davon sind durch das Ziel, eine Freundschaft zwischen Seneca und Paulus zu fingieren, und die Wahl eines Textes der Gattung „freundschaftliche briefliche Korrespondenz" als Medium zur Erreichung dieses Zieles gedeckt. Der anonyme Autor will ja gar nicht eine weitere *epistula moralis* schreiben und auch keinen weiteren Paulusbrief. Eine Korrespondenz, die aufgrund der Gattungskonvention nicht viel mehr sein kann als eine Sammlung von „Grußbilletts", als Stilimitat der hochliterarischen Senecabriefe oder auch der Paulusbriefe zu verfassen, wäre eher unpassend.

Das bedeutet freilich nicht, dass dem Autor nicht Stilbrüche unterliefen, die wirkliche Fehler sind. Seneca spätantikes Latein schreiben zu lassen und Paulus zu empfehlen, auf *latinitas* zu achten, ist ein harter, durch nichts gerechtfertigter Bruch in der Autorfiktion. Dasselbe gilt für die anachronistische Verwendung des spätantiken Briefformulars. Doch hängt diese wenigstens mit einem für den Autor offensichtlich wichtigen inhaltlichen Aspekt zusammen, nämlich Paulus als höflichen, seiner sozialen Stellung bewussten Menschen zu zeichnen – etwas, was bis zu einem gewissen Grade auch schon die Apostelgeschichte tut.

Man kann darüber hinaus fragen, ob überhaupt die Wahl der speziellen Gattung glücklich war. Gewiss, ein Briefwechsel ist *per se* geeignet, zwei Menschen, die sich historisch hätten begegnen können, es aber nicht sind, nun in einem fiktiven Raum zusammenzubringen.[79] Und sicher ist, wenn man diese beiden in ein fiktives Freundschaftsverhältnis bringen will, die Wahl der Untergattung „Freundschaftsbrief" naheliegend. Dennoch ist zu überlegen, ob die Kombination gerade dieser auf eine eng begrenzte Topik festgelegten Gattung mit der Aufgabe, sehr „authentische" Pseudepigraphie mit einer dichten, stimmigen Autorfiktion zu schreiben, nicht von vornherein zum Scheitern verurteilt ist.

---

[79] KLAUCK, Apokryphe Bibel (s. Anm. 3), 228.

Ein letzter Punkt, der Beachtung verdient, ist das charakteristische Bild der beiden fiktiven Autoren Paulus und Seneca, das der Briefwechsel beim Leser evoziert. Das Paulusbild bleibt eher blass. Das Senecabild ist sehr klar das der lateinischen christlichen Antike. Als solches ist es innerhalb der Fiktion des Briefwechsels anachronistisch. In Bezug auf die Intention des Werkes hingegen ist es stimmig: Gerade dieses Senecabild – diese Mischung aus Seneca maior und minor, die für die Christen *saepe noster* ist – soll ja in die apostolische Zeit zurückprojiziert und dadurch legitimiert werden. Gerade das, dass aus dem Werk derjenige Seneca spricht, den die Zeit des Autors kennt, und nicht der authentische, ist wohl ausschlaggebend für seinen großen Erfolg über Jahrhunderte hinweg – und dies, obwohl es sich in vielerlei Hinsicht tatsächlich an ihrem selbstgesteckten Maßstab gemessen um „schlechte" Pseudepigraphie handelt.

Nachwort

Reconceptualizing the Phenomenon of Ancient Pseudepigraphy

An Epilogue

by

DAVID E. AUNE

1. Introduction

The enormous and complex bibliography on Israelite-Jewish, Greco-Roman and early Christian pseudepigraphy has now been augmented by the twenty-seven additional entries in this volume.[1] The purpose of this collection of essays is not simply to add to the number of existing studies, but rather to review the current state of the study of ancient pseudepigrapha and in so doing to rethink and reconceptualize what has become the customary way of understanding ancient pseudepigraphy and in particular the critical paradigms that have become attached to New Testament pseudepigrapha.

Though the focus of this book is on the pseudonymous letters of the New Testament (sixteen essays), with one or more substantive discussions of each of the epistolary pseudepigraphs in the New Testament, the two primary ancient contexts are also treated: the early Jewish and Greco-Roman contexts (three and six essays respectively). The importance of these two ancient cultural contexts lies in the presumption that early Christian pseudepigraphic activity was modeled on existing Jewish and Greco-Roman practice.

This collection of essays had its beginning in a two-day conference in München in 2007 at which ten papers were given. Expanding this base into a larger and more comprehensive collection seemed appropriate to the conveners, so more invitations were issued to colleagues representing a wider spectrum of expertise and the result is the rather large volume you have in your hand. Generally speaking, each essay examines either a par-

---

[1] Jörg Frey, Jens Herzer, Martina Janßen and Clare K. Rothschild (eds.), *Pseudepigraphie und Verfasserfiktion in frühchristlichen Briefen – Pseudepigraphy and Author Fiction in Early Christian Letters* (WUNT; Tübingen: Mohr Siebeck, 2009).

ticular text or cluster of related texts, typically by reviewing and critiquing earlier research on the general phenomenon of pseudepigraphy in the ancient world as well as the more important studies that pertain specifically to the text or group of texts under consideration. The contributors reflect on just how pseudonymity functions in the particular text or group of texts under examination, often challenging received opinion. While it cannot be claimed that previous attempts to deal with the phenomenon of pseudepigraphy have treated it as a homogenous phenomenon, the tendency to do so has often been a tempting option in the history of research. Though pseudonymous authorship was widely practiced in the literary cultures of early Judaism, Greco-Roman civilization and early Christianity, there is little consensus among scholars about how this practice was understood. Writing under the name of another in the ancient world occurred in a variety of different contexts, in many different genres and for a variety of motivations, making it clear that pseudonymity cannot be considered a monolithic literary phenomenon.

In order to stimulate progress in research, a number of the essays have sought to call into question some of the cherished paradigms in scholarship on New Testament epistolary pseudepigrapha. For example, in his contribution to this volume,[2] Jens Herzer sketches the 19th century origins of what he labels the "idealistic paradigm" that became the dominant modern critical consensus view of the Pastoral Letters (i.e., the Pastorals were written by a single author), a view he thinks is badly in need of revision (see below *9.1.5 The Pastoral Letters*). This is one instance in which the received wisdom of the past may require rethinking and reconceptualizing in light of new methods and approaches. While earlier critical scholarship was frequently occupied with demonstrating through linguistic, structural and thematic arguments that certain New Testament letters were in fact pseudepigraphic, those battles are largely over and can now be considered the basis for more complex systematic approaches to understanding pseudepigrapha.

Jörg Frey, one of the editors of this volume, is another contributor who maintains that the current antithetical distinctions between "genuine" and "counterfeit," between "orthonymity" and "pseudonymity" and between "fact" and "fiction" have become both static and problematic categories.[3] In the same vein, Nicole Frank also speaks of the "one-dimensional discussion" about "genuine" and "counterfeit" and "legitimate" and "illegitimate" pseudepigraphy and recommends that the focus rather be on the

---

[2] Jens Herzer, "Fiktion oder Täuschung? Zur Diskussion über die Pseudepigraphie der Pastoralbriefe" (*in hoc voluminis*).

[3] Jörg Frey, "Autorfiktion und Gegnerbild im Judasbrief und im Zweiten Petrusbrief" (*in hoc voluminis*).

more comprehensive literary methods and strategies of pseudepigraphy.[4] These calls for greater complexity in understanding pseudepigrapha are supported by another observation made by Frey that even orthonymic texts contain fictional constructions by actual authors, as in Paul's highly selective and tendentious autobiographical narrative in Gal 1:12–2:21. New Testament letters written in situations of theological conflict present only one side of the situation obscured still further by the ancient penchant to use slander as a default weapon against one's opponents. Letters such as Galatians, then, reveal only one side of a disputed issue and the author is able to misrepresent an opponent's position for his own advantage. In such cases, the distinction between "fact" and "fiction" is not only not very helpful, it is misleading.

1.1 Pseudepigraphy in the New Testament

For students of the New Testament and early Christian literature, pseudepigraphy is a centrally important literary and historical issue, reflected in the fact that in the view of critical scholars there are just eight writings in the New Testament that are orthonymous: the seven authentic letters of Paul (Romans, 1–2 Corinthians, Galatians, Philippians, 1 Thessalonians, Philemon) and the Apocalypse of John. Several writings were originally anonymous, but have become secondarily pseudonymous (the four Gospels, 1 John), two works are anonymous (Hebrews, Acts of the Apostles). 2–3 John claim to have been written by "the elder," though it is far from certain that they were written by the same individual. According to Jackson-McCabe (*in hoc voluminis*), the question is not whether or not the followers of Jesus produced pseudepigraphic works, but rather which of the extant Christian texts are written under the names of their actual authors. Writing under the name of another in the ancient world occurred in a variety of different contexts, in many different genres and for a variety of motivations, making it clear that pseudonymity is scarcely a monolithic literary phenomenon. Further pseudonymity is inherently deceptive, since authors who use pseudonyms say one thing but mean another. Yet the modern practice of labeling certain texts, including New Testament texts, as "pseudonymous" (a term that because of the pseudo- prefix places emphasis on the deceptive character of this authorship category), situates such works in a unified category based only on a single criterion: the work is thought to have been attributed to someone other than the actual author for deceptive purposes. Authors who attribute their writing to someone other

---

[4] Nicole Frank, "Der Kolosserbrief und die 'Philosophia': Pseudepigraphie als Spiegel frühchristlicher Auseinandersetzungen um die Auslegung des paulinischen Erbes" (*in hoc voluminis*).

than themselves are in effect saying one thing, but meaning another. This is a basic definition of metaphor, yet no one would consider metaphor as an inherently deceptive practice. Despite many attempts to finds ways to ethically neutralize the practice, the notion of deception is intrinsic to pseudepigraphy.

1.2 Recent Interest in Pseudepigraphy

There have been two spurts of scholarly interest in ancient pseudepigraphy since World War II. The first occurred during the 1960's and 1970's and is reflected in monographs and comprehensive essays focusing on the general phenomenon of ancient pseudepigraphy produced by Josef Sint (1960),[5] the September 1966 conference on ancient pseudepigraphical texts sponsored by the Fondation Hardt,[6] Wolfgang Speyer (1971),[7] Martin Hengel (1972),[8] and Norbert Brox (1975 and 1977).[9] These were accompanied, in the 1970's and 1980's by several monographs focusing on particular texts or problems, such as the Pastorals (Peter Trummer, 1978;[10] Lewis R. Donelson, 1986;[11] Michael Wolter, 1988[12]), 2 Thessalonians (Wolfgang

---

[5] J. A. Sint, *Pseudonymität im Altertum: Ihre Formen und ihre Gründe* (Commentationes Aenipontanae 15; Innsbruck: Universitätsverlag Wagner, 1960). The author, who does not discuss New Testament pseudepigrapha at all, repeatedly claims that ancient religious pseudepigrapha was not written with the intent to deceive, perhaps with an eye on the theological problem of canonical pseudepigrapha.

[6] *Pseudepigrapha I: Pseudopythagorica – Lettres de Platon, Littérature pseudépigraphique juive* (K. von Fritz, ed., Entretiens sur l'antiquité classique 18; Vandœuvres-Genève: Fondation Hardt, 1972). This collection contains eight essays, including M. Hengel, "Anonymität, Pseudepigraphie und 'Literarische Fälschung' in der jüdisch-hellenistischen Literatur," (229–308), republished in idem, *Judaica et Hellenistica: Kleine Schriften I* (WUNT 90; Tübingen: Mohr Siebeck, 1996), 196–251, and W. Speyer, "Fälschung, pseudepigraphische freie Erfindung und 'echte religiöse Pseudepigraphie'" (331–66).

[7] W. Speyer, *Die literarische Fälschung im heidnischen und christlichen Altertum: Ein Versuch ihrer Deutung* (Handbuch der Altertumswissenschaft I/2; München: Beck, 1971).

[8] See n. 6.

[9] N. Brox, *Falsche Verfasserangaben: Zur Erklärung der frühchristlichen Pseudepigraphie* (SBS 79; Stuttgart: KBW Verlag, 1975), followed in 1977 by a collection of essays from the previous century of scholarship on pseudepigraphy: N. Brox (ed.), *Pseudepigraphie in der heidnischen und jüdisch-christlichen Antike* (Wege der Forschung 484; Darmstadt: Wissenschaftliche Buchgesellschaft, 1977).

[10] P. Trummer, *Die Paulustradition der Pastoralbriefe* (BET 8; Frankfurt a.M./Bern: Peter Lang, 1978).

[11] L. R. Donelson, *Pseudepigraphy and Ethical Argument in the Pastoral Epistles* (HUT 22; Tübingen: Mohr Siebeck, 1986). A 1984 University of Chicago dissertation directed by Hans Dieter Betz.

[12] M. Wolter, *Die Pastoralbriefe als Paulustradition* (FRLANT 146; Göttingen: Vandenhoeck & Ruprecht, 1988).

Trilling, 1980[13]), Colossians (Walter Bujard, 1973;[14] Mark Kiley, 1986[15]), pseudonymity and canon (David G. Meade, 1982[16]).

The second period of interest, which began just after the turn of the 21st century and is still going strong (this volume is the most recent instance of this interest) is associated with monographs on Greek pseudepigraphal letters by Patricia A. Rosenmeyer (2001),[17] on the phenomenon of early Christian pseudepigraphy by Armin D. Baum (2001),[18] Terry L. Wilder (2001)[19] and Martina Janßen (2003),[20] with other monographs focusing on specific pseudepigraphic texts, such as the Pastorals (Annette Merz, 2004[21]) and 2 Peter (Hermann Josef Riedl, 2005[22]).

---

[13] W. Trilling, *Der zweite Brief an die Thessalonicher* (Zürich: Benziger Verlag / Neukirchen-Vluyn: Neukirchener Verlag, 1980).

[14] W. Bujard, *Stilanalytische Untersuchungen zum Kolosserbrief als Beitrag zur Methodik von Sprachvergleichen* (StUNT 11; Göttingen: Vandenhoeck & Ruprecht, 1973).

[15] M. Kiley, *Colossians as Pseudepigraphy* (Sheffield: JSOT, 1986). A 1983 Harvard University dissertation directed by George MacRae.

[16] D. G. Meade, *Pseudonymity and Canon: An Investigation into the Relationship of Authorship and Authority in Jewish and Early Christian Tradition* (WUNT 39; Tübingen: Mohr Siebeck, 1986). A dissertation written under J. D. G. Dunn at the University of Nottingham in 1984.

[17] P. A. Rosenmeyer, *Ancient Epistolary Fictions: The Letter in Greek Literature* (Cambridge/New York: Cambridge University Press, 2001).

[18] A. D. Baum, *Pseudepigraphie und literarische Fälschung im frühen Christentum: Mit ausgewählten Quellentexten samt deutscher Übersetzung* (WUNT II/138; Tübingen: Mohr Siebeck, 2001).

[19] T. L. Wilder, *Pseudonymity, the New Testament and Deception: An Inquiry into Intention and Reception* (Lanham: University Press of America, 2004). 1998 dissertation at the University of Aberdeen.

[20] M. Janßen, *Unter falschem Namen: Eine kritische Forschungsbilanz frühchristlicher Pseudepigraphie* (ARGU 14; Frankfurt a.M.: Peter Lang, 2003).

[21] A. Merz, *Die fiktive Selbstauslegung des Paulus: Intertextuelle Studien zur Intention und Rezeption der Pastoralbriefe* (NTOA 52; Göttingen/Freiburg [CH]: Vandenhoeck & Ruprecht, 2004).

[22] H. J. Riedl, *Anamnese und Apostolizität: Der Zweite Petrusbrief und das theologische Problem neutestamentlicher Pseudepigraphie* (RStTh 64; Frankfurt a.M.: Peter Lang, 2005). A Regensburg dissertation completed in 2003.

2. The Complexity of Pseudepigraphy

"Die Ursachen der Pseudepigraphie sind vielfältig."[23] If recent research on pseudepigraphy has made anything at all clear, it is the fact of the variety and complexity of the phenomenon. Jens Herzer rightly maintains that even within the New Testament there are different kinds of pseudepigraphy and cites the essential monographs of Josef A. Sint and particularly Wolfgang Speyer as basic for such a discussion.[24] Following Speyer the first important step is to use the term "pseudepigraphy" in a neutral sense so that various literary forms of pseudepigraphy can be distinguished without being preoccupied by ethical or theological issues (terms like "Verfasserfiktion" and "allonymity" are examples of value-free labels). Such distinctions could include determining whether:[25] (1) works that are partly authentic, but have been amplified by material added by one or more persons other than the original author, (2) works written by the author to whom they are attributed, but containing some ideas that originated with the named author, (3) works that are more generally influenced by earlier works of the authors to whom they are attributed, (4) a writing belongs to a recognized type of "school pseudepigraphy" in which no deception is intended and pseudonyms are used within a restricted social context based on an open consensus (when the social context changes, "open" pseudepigraphy may no longer function in the same way it comes to function as forgery),[26] (5) the writing is a literary work, i.e., a transparent literary fiction attributed to a fictional author who uses the first-person singular as the narrative voice, (6) originally anonymous works that are later attributed to the actual author or to a pseudonymous author, (7) the document is written with the intent of deceiving the addressees through indications of authenticity (e.g., a forged signature, personal information, etc.) apart from which it would not be accepted.

---

[23] M. Frenschkowski, "Pseudepigraphie und Paulusschule: Gedanken zur Verfasserschaft der Deuteropaulinen, insbesondere der Pastoralbriefe," in *Das Ende des Paulus: Historische, theologische und literaturwissenschaftliche Aspekte* (ed. F. W. Horn; BZNW 106; Berlin/New York: Walter de Gruyter, 2001), 251.

[24] Sint, *Pseudonymität im Altertum* (see n. 5); Speyer, *Die literarische Fälschung* (see n. 7).

[25] Some of these categories are based on suggestions made by James H. Charlesworth, "Pseudepigraphy," *Encyclopedia of Early Christianity* (2 vols.; 2nd ed.; New York/London: Garland Publishers, 1997), 2:961–64.

[26] At this point Herzer cites Speyer, *Die literarische Fälschung* (see n. 7), 24, 33.

3. Pseudepigraphy and New Testament Canon

The presence of pseudepigrapha in the New Testament canon is an historical as well as (for some) a theological problem. In his comprehensive discussion of the presence of pseudonymous works in the NT canon, Harry Gamble reminds us that just eight documents in the NT are written under the names of their actual authors: the seven genuine letters of Paul and the Apocalypse of John.[27] Gamble argues that the earliest collection of Pauline letters was a "seven churches" edition (symbolizing universal applicability) consisting of ten letters universally received and recognized as authentically Pauline (perhaps as early as the end of the first century). Yet even this earliest collection contains some pseudonymous letters: Ephesians (indispensable for the view that Paul wrote to *seven* churches) as well as Colossians and 2 Thessalonians. The Pastorals, however, written to individuals, could have no place in a "seven churches" edition, were absent from the three early forms of the *Corpus Paulinum* (the "seven churches" edition, Marcion's collection, ca. 140 CE, and the collection reflected in P^{46}, ca. 200 CE). Gamble emphasizes the existence of a single collection from the beginning, without seriously considering the likely possibility of the growth of a number of smaller collections that would explain different arrangements in the collection of ten and then thirteen Pauline letters.[28] If the earliest collection of Pauline letters was made by Paul himself and consisted of Romans, 1–2 Corinthians and Galatians (as Trobisch proposes), it is obvious that no pseudepigrapha would have been present.

The four Gospels, all written anonymously, were attributed to disciples or apostles of Jesus (Matthew and John) or disciples of Peter and Paul (Mark and Luke) in their superscriptions (though when this occurred is debated) and thus, they are examples of the phenomenon of *secondary pseudonymity*. A collection of the fourfold Gospel, first mentioned by Irenaeus (ca. 180 CE), was probably made no earlier than the middle of the second century. The fact that the Gospels are not generally cited by name before ca. 150 CE (Papias mentioned Mark and Matthew ca. 130 CE; Theophilus mentions John ca. 170) suggests that authorship attributions had little significance for most of the second century. Gamble argues that ascriptions of authorship could not have been the decisive factor in the canonical standing of the four Gospels.

---

[27] Harry Y. Gamble, "Pseudonymity and the New Testament Canon" (*in hoc voluminis*).

[28] See D. Trobisch, *Die Entstehung der Paulusbriefsammlung: Studien zu den Anfängen christlicher Publizistik* (NTOA 10; Göttingen/Freiburg [CH]: Vandenhoeck & Ruprecht, 1989); D. C. Parker, *An Introduction to the New Testament Manuscripts and Their Texts* (Cambridge: Cambridge University Press, 2008), 249–56.

The collection of seven Catholic Epistles, in contrast to the collection of the Pauline letters and the Gospels, did not come into being before the late third or early fourth centuries. Four of these letters are pseudonymous (James, 1–2 Peter, Jude), while three are anonymous (1–2–3 John; though see the essay by Jutta Leonhardt-Balzer *in hoc voluminis*) and the authenticity of all but 1 John and 1 Peter was widely doubted well into the fourth century. Despite this, the Catholic Epistles appear on several fourth century canonical lists and issues of theological utility and apostolic witness superseded questions of authenticity.

In the history of the NT canon, confidence in apostolic authorship was consistent with regard to the Pauline letters, slower to develop with regard to the Gospels and weak for several centuries for the Catholic Epistles. Many documents claiming apostolic authorship (e.g., the *Didache*, the *Gospel of Peter*, the *Gospel of Thomas*, the *Apocalypse of Peter*) failed to gain canonical status, indicating that authorship alone was not the *sine qua non* of canonicity. Since the relationship between authorship and authority varied considerably, two questions arise: (1) How invested were the early Christian communities in authorship issues? (2) To what extent were they capable of adjudicating such issues? The "apostolic age" was regarded as the normative period for revelation and authoritative teaching and the passing of that period produced three ways of appropriating and perpetuating the authority of the apostles and their teaching which became informally operative during the second century: (1) apostolic tradition (teaching), (2) apostolic succession (office) and (3) apostolic writings (authoritative scriptures). Documents attributed to apostles were rejected primarily because of the perception of heterodox content rather than the recognition of pseudonymous authorship, though both criteria were often applied in tandem. Eusebius (*Hist. eccl.* 3.25) puts the criterion of apostolic authorship into prominence, opposing pseudonymous apostolic writings and insisting on orthodox content: the "acknowledged" writings are those whose authorship is undoubtedly authentic; the "disputed" writings are those whose authorial authenticity is doubtful, while the authorship of the heretical writings is false (there are twenty-two "acknowledged" writings). Gamble draws four conclusions about the significance of pseudonymity for the history of the NT canon: (1) For most of the second century, claims of authorship remained undisputed. (2) The proliferation of Christian literature, much of it pseudonymous, provoked discussion about which documents should be regarded as authoritative. (3) In discussions about authorship and authority, the authorship issue never stood alone. (4) The widespread and customary use of each text became an important consideration, particularly in the third and fourth centuries (when a long history of usage could be established). On the other hand, the church had misgivings about pseudonymous writings and rejected those that it suspected were pseudonymous. In light of the many factors contributing to canonical status it is not surprising that many pseudonymous writings and misattributed anonymous writings found their way into the canon. Apostolicity was not limited to direct authorship by an apostle, yet no document secured authority or canonical status by presumed authorship by an apostle alone.

Finally, Gamble moves from historical issues to the theological problem of canonical pseudepigrapha. Pseudepigrapha are intrinsically deceptive and therein lies the problem for canonical literature. Modern Christians of conservative, moderate and liberal theological orientations regard the possible presence of pseudepigraphal writings in markedly different ways: (1) From a conservative Protestant perspective, pseudonymity is a deceptive literary device that is at odds with the theological view of Scripture as inspired and true and rooted in the witness of the apostles; pseudonymity is inconsistent with canonicity. (2) Moderately conservative Protestant and Catholic scholars have tried to understand pseudonymity in less theologically problematic ways, often by emphasizing authority over authorship. (3) Liberal Protestant and Catholic scholars regard pseudonymity as a widespread ancient literary practice.

4. Social and Cultural Contexts of Pseudepigraphy

Since the essays on the Jewish and Greco-Roman contexts of pseudepigraphy are not comprehensive introductions to those two social and cultural settings I have chosen to discuss the contributions of those essays in various sections throughout this essay. In this subsection I will comment on the contributions of Eibert Tigchelaar on pseudepigraphy in the Dead Sea Scrolls, Wolfgang Speyer on divine and human authorship in antiquity and Marco Frenschkowski on fictional discourse in antiquity and Christianity.

4.1 The Dead Sea Scrolls

Since the publication of nearly all the texts and fragments of texts collectively known as the Dead Sea Scrolls, our knowledge of late second temple Jewish literature has increased enormously. Many of these hitherto unknown texts are pseudepigraphic and Eibert Tigchelaar has contributed a discussion of the forms of pseudepigraphy found in this corpus of texts.[29] A striking feature of the texts from Qumran is that a contemporary figure is never named as the actual author of a text. A major problem is to define

---

[29] Eibert Tigchelaar, "Forms of Pseudepigraphy in the Dead Sea Scrolls" (*in hoc voluminis*).

just what is meant by pseudepigraphic texts and Tigchelaar proposes two main categories of texts that might qualify as pseudepigraphic: (1) extensions of scripture by interpretive rewriting, in which the literary form and narrative voice of their models is adopted (examples: *Jubilees*, the *Temple Scroll*, the *Genesis Apocryphon*, the *Words of Moses* [1Q22], the *Apocryphon of Joshua, Pseudo-Ezekiel*) and (2) expanding scriptures by ascribing traditions to "biblical" figures (examples include figures like Enoch and Daniel; texts include the *Aramaic Levi Document* [4Q440–41], *the Testament of Kohat* [4Q442], the *Visions of Amram* [4Q543–48], the *Aramaic New Jerusalem* texts).

In the case of rewritten scripture, both *Jubilees* and the *Temple Scroll* were written to supplement the Pentateuch and are not typical pseudepigrapha, since they are not attributed to Moses but to God: the *Temple Scroll* is authorized by rephrasing third-person discourse in Deuteronomy to the first-person of God; *Jubilees* is authorized by being angelic revelation and ultimately as the text of the heavenly tablets.

Many of those works expanding the scriptures are written in the first person and in Aramaic, and since they engage figures like Enoch and Daniel, they are characterized as "apocalyptic pseudepigraphy." Here the strategy of pseudepigraphy is used for authorizing apocalyptic prophecy by placing it in the mouth of an ancient figure using the device of *ex eventu* prophecy, though this does not entirely explain the pseudepigraphy of the Enochic writings where *ex eventu* prophecy is missing.

Tigchelaar notes that there are some observable relationships between the genre or content of the pseudepigraphal texts and the figure to whom they are attributed. Texts attributed to Moses typically deal with the law; heavenly journeys are ascribed to Enoch. Social correspondences between the biblical figures and the real authors of the texts are also probable. The authors of the Enochic literature could have been scribes who, like Enoch, had encyclopedic interests. Tigchelaar briefly discusses the work of Hindy Najman, who focuses on what she calls "Mosaic discourse,"[30] which calls attention to the relationship between new texts and their previous texts and traditions as well as to persons to whom those earlier texts are attributed. Najman proposes a new understanding of pseudepigraphy. Composing a text under the pseudonym of a famous ancient Israelite is not done for the purpose of authorizing a text by deception. Rather, a pseudonym is a metaphorical device involving the entire text and which acknowledges the authority of texts and traditions that derive from those ancient figures or "founders," with whom the actual author both emulates and identifies.

---

[30] H. Najman, *Seconding Sinai: The Development of Mosaic Discourse in Second Temple Judaism* (JSJSup 77; Leiden: Brill, 2003), 41–69.

Finally, Tigchelaar notes that if pseudepigraphy is defined as an author ascribing his texts falsely to another instead of himself, then the term should not be used for Hebrew or Aramaic literature, since authors almost never name themselves as authors of their own works.

4.2 Divine and Human Authorship in Antiquity

Wolfgang Speyer, who has made a number of critically important contributions to the study of pseudepigraphy in antiquity, provides a précis of his previous work in his essay on divine and human authorship in antiquity.[31]

For the oldest stages of intellectual creativity among the Greeks, the gods were the source of speaking and writing; the opening lines of the *Iliad*, for example, presents the entire epic as originating, not with a human author, but with the Muse. The poet-singer-prophet of ancient Greece did not regard himself as the creator of his poem or literary work, but rather considered himself as a spokesperson for the divinity, whether the Muse, Apollo, Hermes or Dionysos. In Greece, divine speech was particularly connected with the various oracle shrines, of which the most famous was the oracle at Delphi where Apollo spoke through his priestess addressing issues relating to the spiritual and moral life of the Greeks. The oldest form of authorship in Greece was therefore divine authorship. Just as all human arts and skills originated with the gods and heroes, so did all forms of speech and writing. Specific examples include legendary ancient lawgivers who had contact with the gods, including Hammurabi, who received the law from the sun god Shamash or king Numa who received the law code from the spring nymph Egeria of Aricia, or Moses who received material in the books of Exodus and Deuteronomy written on tablets by the finger of God.

Turning to pseudepigraphy in the Bible, Speyer reminds us how frequently "the word of the Lord" is uttered by prophets speaking in the name of Yahweh. He also mentions the distinction between authentic revelatory messages and the reworking of those messages in forms that depart from the phraseology of the original. Similarly, in the four Gospels sayings are placed in the mouth of Jesus by the evangelists or by traditions that he did not originally utter. Luke composed speeches appropriate for the context in which they were given and placed them in the mouth of both apostles and their followers in the tradition of Greek historiography. All of these biblical examples of attributing sayings and speeches to God, Jesus or the apostles are types of pseudepigraphy, though lacking the intent to deceive.

---

[31] Wolfgang Speyer, "Göttliche und menschliche Verfasserschaft im Altertum" (*in hoc voluminis*).

In these and other instances, according to Speyer, "fictive truth can sometimes possess a higher truth content than historical truth which is often simplistic."

4.3 Types of Fictional Discourse in Antiquity

Marco Frenschkowski asks a series of penetrating questions about the contexts of pseudepigraphy in antiquity.[32] He is particularly interested in the cultural milieu in which pseudepigraphs were written and read and whether or not pseudepigraphs were recognized for what they were through a kind of tacit agreement ("eine stillschweigende Übereinkunft"). Were pseudepigraphs (when recognized as such) considered as forgeries or simply as a harmless stylistic device? How were pseudepigraphs distributed and how did they reach the Christian book market? Frenschkowski's purpose is to consider both Greco-Roman and early Christian fictional discourse with the intention of disclosing conceptual and ideational links between them.

In a major section of his study, Frenschkowski asks whether early Christians were conscious of the fact that a significant part of their literature was written under pseudonyms. In most cases, it appears that they did not recognize pseudepigraphy, which on the face of it is rather remarkable. Even the pseudepigraphal correspondence between Paul and Seneca was recognized by Erasmus, though not by earlier Christian scholars such as Augustine and Jerome. Educated Christians of the fourth century were remarkably uncritical and the author's citation of parts of the conversation between the Manichean Faustus and Augustine is revealing. While Faustus claims that there are pseudepigrapha in the New Testament, Augustine replies that Faustus cannot prove any of his claims. Of course, Faustus was right and Augustine was wrong. Frenschkowski also briefly discusses Salvian of Marseilles (400–480 CE), who used the pseudonym "Timotheus" in a work criticizing wealth. In a letter to Salonius, Salvian defends himself and maintains that his motivation was to honor God and that the name of the author is only a metaphor, not a forgery. This is a fine line and Salvian polemicizes elsewhere against the heretical proclivity to produce pseudepigraphal literature (cf. 2 Thessalonians, a forgery in which the author polemicizes against forgers: 2 Thess 2:2). Not all early Christian scholars were naïve: Tertullian was upset by a forgery in the name of Paul perpetrated by a "false brother" and Eusebius did not consider forged writings as canonical. What passed for "Echtheitskritik" in the early church is essentially pre-critical—it is directed against the "other" and the "heretical."

---

[32] Marco Frenschkowski, "Erkannte Pseudepigraphie? Ein Essay über Fiktionalität, Antike und Christentum" (*in hoc voluminis*).

Frenschkowski returns to an important question: to what extent was pseudepigraphy recognizable among the educated of antiquity? It is well known, he maintains, that among philosophical schools of the Hellenistic period pseudepigrapha were produced in the name of a master. This is touched on in Iamblichus, *De vita Pythagorica* 29.157:[33]

> If, then, it be agreed that some writings now circulated are by Pythagoras, but others were composed on the basis of his lectures, and on this account the authors did not give their own names, but attributed them to Pythagoras as his work, it is clear from all these treatises that Pythagoras was sufficiently experienced in all wisdom.

This is one way of defusing the problem of pseudepigrapha, but Frenschkowski rightly observes the wide social and cultural gap between the educated adherents of the philosophical schools and the subculture inhabited by early Christians. Porphyry, a Neoplatonist, practiced a surprisingly penetrating form of *Echtheitskritik* when he unmasked a Greco-Iranian apocalypse written under the name of Zoroaster as a fraud. He was also the first to argue that the book of Daniel was actually written during the time of Antiochus IV.

Frenschkowski then turns to several early Christian examples, the Pastoral Letters, Jude and 2 Peter to formulate several ideas on "frühchristliche und antike Fiktionalitätsdiskurse." The complex of personal notices in the Pastorals suggests a high literary level approaching the world of the ancient novel. Following Herzer (who is skeptical of the relevance of the *Briefroman* for understanding the genre of the Pastorals generally), he maintains that each of the three Pastorals has a different theological profile; some have even suggested that they were written by three different authors. In comparing 2 Thessalonians, the Pastoral Letters and Ephesians, it becomes obvious that a different type of pseudepigraphy is involved, which is not only divergent theologically, but also with regard to their literary character and *Autorenfiktion*.

These considerations suggest the need to formulate a typology of pseudepigraphical forms, long a desideratum of scholarship, based in part on the type of author fiction. Frenschkowski proposes a typology of pseudepigraphy based on the category of *"gestus"* in terms of three degrees of proximity: near deixis, intermediate deixis and far deixis. Using pseudonyms from the distant or mythical past (Enoch, Abraham, Moses, Orpheus, Musaeus, Linus) belongs to the *gestus* of far deixis, whereas names from the non-mythical past (Ezra, Baruch, Jeremiah) belongs to the category of middle deixis. A *gestus* of near deixis appeals to authorities of the recent

---

[33] J. Dillon and J. Hershbell, *Iamblichus* On the Pythagorean Way of Life: *Text, Translation and Note* (Texts and Translations 29; Greco-Roman Religions Series 11; Atlanta: Scholars Press, 1991), 173.

past and thus, early Christianity produced pseudepigraphy exclusively in the *gestus* of near deixis (Paul, James, Peter), while Hellenistic Judaism used the *gestus* of far deixis (Moses, Enoch, Noah, Solomon). Only in the post-canonical period did Christians begin to use the *gestus* of far deixis and middle deixis (the *Testaments of the Twelve Patriarchs*, the *Christian Sibylline oracles*, additions to *4 Ezra*, the *Ascension of Isaiah*, etc.). The reason early Christianity used the gestus of near deixis is because the recent past, not the distant past, is the period of revelation. Pseudepigraphy, according to Frenschkowski, is a special form of fictionalization in which the text as a whole contains both fictional and nonfictional properties. Yet fictional discourse in early Christianity, in comparison with antiquity in general, developed a marked reduction of fictional discourse, since Christians lived in a world in which truth and falsehood as well as orthodoxy and heresy were clearly distinguished and in which subtle variations between the antithetic realities were lost.

5. Degrees of Systematic Fictional Elaboration in Pseudepigraphic Letters

In most cases, more is involved in crafting a pseudepigraphal letter than simply selecting what the real author considered an appropriate *nom de plume*. It is essential that epistolary pseudepigraphy be regarded as a pseudepigraphic system, ranging from the simple to the complex (here using the terms "pseudepigraphy" and "pseudepigraphic" in a neutral sense). In his essay in this volume, Jörg Frey speaks of "das fiktionale Gefüge," of which the fictive author, addressees and situation are important elements and part of an overall pseudepigraphal structure. Marco Frenschkowski prefers the more general term "frühchristliche und antike Fiktionalitätsdiskurse," while Martin Hüneburg uses the phrase "Ausbau der Verfasserfiktion," referring to all the fictional elements that are part of the real author's systemic pseudepigraphic strategy.

There is a continuum from relatively simply to relatively complex types of pseudepigraphical discourse. Among the simplest examples of pseudepigraphic letters in the New Testament are the letters of James and Jude, in which the pseudonym is found only in the *superscriptio* and not elaborated in terms of fictional addressees, the mention of people known to the author or to the recipients, references to past or present relationships between the author and the addressees, and so forth. Examples of more systemically complex epistolary pseudepigrapha are 2 Peter and the Pastoral Letters. The explication of pseudepigraphic communication systems, though often neglected, is a pressing issue in the case of *canonical* pseudepigraphal letters, primarily because close reading and detailed textual interpretation are required for writing commentaries on such letters, where the commentator must try to understand the systemic complexity of each element of the fictional *mise-en-scène*.

Authors with pseudepigraphic intentions typically had available to them a palette of options (some less and some more). They grapple with the primary problem, namely to present the fiction as a reality or more likely, to frame their actual rhetorical purpose with a fictional author, fictional recipients and fictional circumstances, each element capable of elaboration to the degree thought necessary by the real author.

In his analysis of the *Epistolae Senecae ad Paulum et Pauli ad Senecam*, Stefan Krauter uses this relatively uninteresting collection of fourth century pseudepigraphical letters as a springboard for examining the systemic features of pseudepigraphal letters.[34] With regard to the convention of naming people with whom the fictive author has a relationship, the Seneca-Paul correspondence mentions Lucilius and Theophilus, the first a recipient of letters written by the historical Seneca, while the latter has no explicit relationship to Paul in the New Testament, but is mentioned only in the dedications of Luke and Acts. The mention of associates of the fictive author is a widespread convention in pseudepigraphal letters, examples in the New Testament include the mention of Tychicus (a figure mentioned in Acts 20:4) in Col 4:7 and Eph 6:21 and the mention of Timothy, the most prominent of Paul's coworkers in Heb 13:23 (an otherwise anonymous letter).

In Matt Jackson-McCabe's discussion of the letter of James,[35] he mentions one feature used in support of the letter's authenticity: the authority of James is not amplified in the epistolary *superscriptio* (Jas 1:1a: "James the slave of God and of the Lord Jesus Christ"), nor is reference made to specific historical situations, nor are individuals mentioned who might be associated with the author, all as part of a fictional elaboration.[36] For Jackson-McCabe, however, the letter's failure to situate the author in situations and personal relationships may be the result of its open *adscriptio* (Jas 1:1b: "to the twelve tribes in the diaspora"). Yet the *adscriptio* can be construed to function as part of the letter's fictional elaboration, since James,

---

[34] Stefan Krauter, "Was ist 'schlechte' Pseudepigraphie? Mittel, Wirkung und Intention von Pseudepigraphie in den Epistolae Senecae ad Paulum et Pauli ad Senecam" (*in hoc voluminis*).

[35] Matt Jackson-McCabe, "The Politics of Pseudepigraphy and the Letter of James" (*in hoc voluminis*).

[36] For this position, Jackson-McCabe cites L. T. Johnson, *The Letter of James: A New Translation with Introduction and Commentary* (AB 37A; New York: Doubleday, 1995), 118.

like 1 Peter, Jude and the *Martyrdom of Polycarp*, can be seen as an early Christian diaspora letter, analogous to the Christian diaspora letter quoted in Acts 15:25–29, for which James is presented as having primary responsibility in formulating (Acts 15:15–21, 21:25).[37] Thus the association of James with the Diaspora letter in Acts makes the adscription in Jas 1:1b part of the modest pseudepigraphic strategy.

Trevor Thompson's discussion of the problem of interpreting pseudepigraphic texts such as 2 Thessalonians reveals the inconsistencies among scholars who have written commentaries on 2 Thessalonians as a pseudepigraphal letter, yet read the details of the text as if they are windows on the real world of the past.[38] In an article referred to by Thompson, Margaret Mitchell refers to 2 Thessalonians in a salutary way as a "double pseudepigraphon," which seems both a logical and necessary move.[39] Yet Thompson cites some who maintain that, despite being pseudonymous, the letter was actually written to the Thessalonians, while others maintain that it was written to a real congregation other than the Thessalonians.

The critical question here is the extent to which the use of a pseudonym in the writing of an early Christian letter signals a systemic pseudepigraphal strategy, including not only a pseudonymous author, but pseudonymous recipients as well as fictional rhetorical situations. Thompson is quite right to call our attention to inconsistencies in the interpretation of pseudepigraphal letters (his focus is exclusively on 2 Thessalonians) by regarding some features of the letter as fictional and others as real with no clear criteria regarding how to tell the difference. It needs to be pointed out that pseudepigraphal letters are in a class by themselves, because unlike pseudepigraphal gospels, acts and apocalypses, a pseudepigraphal letter involves a sender, a receiver and a rhetorical situation, all of which are essential ingredients in a fictional epistolary system, though it seems likely that the purpose of such pseudepigraphal letters would be primarily evident in the rhetorical situation, which could reflect reality.

Lutz Doering also shows how systemic pseudepigraphical features can be more complex than some have recognized in his essay on 1 Peter.[40] In this article he questions the reductionist view of Norbert Brox that 1 Peter

---

[37] See Lutz Doering, "Apostle, Co-Elder, and Witness of Suffering: Author Construction and Peter Image in First Peter" (*in hoc voluminis*) under 4.1, "First Peter as Early Christian Diaspora Letter" and 4.2, "Peter and James in Acts 15 and Peter's Authorial Image in First Peter." Doering also proposes regarding *1 Clement* as a Christian diaspora letter. However, Doering wrongly categorizes Pol. *Phil.* as Christian diaspora letter.

[38] Trevor Thompson, "As if Genuine: Interpreting the Pseudepigraphic Second Thessalonians" (*in hoc voluminis*).

[39] M. M. Mitchell, "Thessalonicherbriefe," *RGG*[4] 8:360–61.

[40] Lutz Doering, "Apostle, Co-Elder, and Witness of Suffering: Author Construction and Peter Image in First Peter" (*in hoc voluminis*).

belonged to those examples of early Christian pseudepigrapha "in which there is no patent connection between the fictive name of the author and the writing that comes under it—in terms of contents, disposition or historical setting ... that would render the choice of name *a posteriori* at least somewhat plausible."[41] For Brox, the use of the name "Peter" in 1 Peter is analogous to the use of the names of other apostles in pseudepigraphic writings, where they are "de-individualized" and used as generic representations of "apostolic authority." In a convincing essay, Doering explores the image of Peter in 1 Peter associated with the phrases (1) "Peter apostle of Jesus Christ" (1:1), (2) "co-elder" (5:1), (3) "shepherding" (5:2), (4) "witness of the sufferings of Christ" (5:1) and then turns to an analysis of the associations of Peter with Silvanus, Mark and "Babylon." Finally, he links the genre of 1 Peter (an early Christian diaspora letter) with the same genre used by Peter and James in Acts 15. Doering has produced a model essay for showing the complexity of associations linked to the name of a prominent apostle.

One problematic feature of pseudepigraphal letters is reconstructing just how they could have been put into circulation without anyone being the wiser. For letters there is no counterpart, to my knowledge, to the story of the finding of the *Apocalypse of Paul* in 388 CE in a marble box (also containing Paul's shoes) hidden in the foundation of a home once owned by Paul, through a dream repeated twice to the present occupant (*Apoc. Paul* 1–2).

6. The Theological and Ethical Problem of Canonical Pseudepigrapha

The title of this volume uses two expressions "pseudepigraphy" and "author fiction" with the assumption that they represent two different ways of understanding the phenomenon of people writing under the names of those other than themselves. Both terms are useful, for "Pseudepigraphie" emphasizes the deceptive nature of the practice, while "Verfasserfiktion" is an ethically neutral term for the same phenomenon. The use of both terms in the title emphasize two ways of looking at the same phenomenon as ethically laden or ethically neutral. Viewing New Testament letters which are written under *noms de plume* (to use an ethical neutral phrase), raised no ethically questions, while viewing the same letters under the category of "pseudepigraphy" does. Certainly the theological and ethical problem of

---

[41] Doering's translation of the thesis of Norbert Brox, "Zur pseudepigraphischen Rahmung des ersten Petrusbriefes," *BZ* 19 (1975): 78–96 (78).

pseudepigraphal letters in the New Testament has dominated research on the subject throughout the twentieth and twenty-first centuries.

Since the terms "pseudepigraphy" and "pseudonymity" are compound nouns beginning with a transliterated form of the Greek word ψεῦδος meaning "lie, falsehood," they have an implicitly pejorative sense. The inherently deceptive character of literature characterized as "pseudepigraphy" ethically and theologically problematizes the presence of such texts in the NT canon. Some have sought to neutralize the implications of the term "pseudepigraphy" by proposing more neutral terms. Marshall has suggested "allonymity" and "allepigraphy" as terms for writing in the name of another person without the intent to deceive.[42]

The central issues in the two upsurges of interest in the phenomenon of ancient pseudepigraphy briefly discussed above (1.2), are the theological and ethical problems of canonical pseudepigrapha. In her brief survey of scholarship on Pauline pseudepigrapha, Eve-Marie Becker maintains that since the 19th century, the relationship between literary forgery with the truth of the New Testament texts (*pia fraus*) as an ethical-moral question has been a debated issue. She calls attention to Wolfgang Speyer's distinction between "Pseudepigraphie" and "literarischer Fälschung," and his insistence that *Fälschung* is a particular form of *Pseudepigraphie*, the former is the species, while the latter is the genus (i.e., not all pseudepigraphy is intentionally deceptive).[43] At this point I would call attention to an essay of Speyer in which he deals with "Fälschung, pseudepigraphische freie Erfindung und 'echte religiöse Pseudepigraphie.'"[44]

Various scholars have called attention to the phenomenon of "*Schultradition*," particularly in philosophical schools such as the Pythagoreans, as one context for the production of pseudepigrapha in which the use of the name of the founder or teacher was a transparent fiction used by students to transmit school tradition in written form. The debated issue of a Pauline school appears as an attractive way of accounting for the origin for Pauline pseudepigrapha that avoids the issue of literary forgery. Karl Matthias Schmidt (*in hoc voluminis*) for example argues that both 1 and 2 Peter are intentionally written as *Fiktion* rather than *Täuschung*. Though he does not spell out the theological or ethical implications of these two understandings of fictionality, it seems clear that they are lurking in the background.

---

[42] I. H. Marshall, *A Critical and Exegetical Commentary on the Pastoral Epistles* (ICC; Edinburgh: T&T Clark, 1999), 84.

[43] Eve-Marie Becker, "Von Paulus zu 'Paulus.' Paulinische Pseudepigraphie-Forschung als literaturgeschichtliche Aufgabe" (*in hoc voluminis*) cites Speyer, *Die literarische Fälschung* (see n. 7), 13.

[44] W. Speyer, "Fälschung, pseudepigraphische freie Erfindung und 'echte religiöse Pseudepigraphie,'" (see n. 6), 331–66.

In the methodological part of his essay on the Pastoral Letters, Jens Herzer broaches the problem of whether it is legitimate to distinguish between theological legitimate literary fiction on the one hand and deception on the other.

7. Selecting Noms de Plume

As already mentioned, the reason while Jewish pseudepigrapha are routinely ascribed to famous figures in the Hebrew Bible and early Christian pseudepigrapha are typically ascribed to apostles is that in both bodies of literature the function of the pseudonym chosen is often a means for conferring authority, legitimacy and antiquity to the pseudepigraphal work. Nevertheless the specific rational for choosing a particular pseudonym is often far from clear. As mentioned above, Frenschkowski (in this volume) proposes a typology for the use of pseudonyms based on temporal proximity using three categories, which I will simply abstract as (1) early, (2) intermediate and (3) late. Early names like Adam, Enoch, Abraham and Moses and intermediate names like Ezra, Baruch and Jeremiah were used as pseudonyms in Jewish pseudepigrapha, late names such as Jesus, Peter, Paul and John were exclusively used in early Christian pseudepigrapha, though later intermediate names were also used such as Isaiah (as in the *Ascension of Isaiah*) and Ezra (the Christian additions to *4 Ezra*). The reason for the early Christian preference for late names is apparently based on the recent occurrence of divine revelation.

Karina Martin Hogan, who deals with the choice of pseudonyms in Jewish apocalypses,[45] asks how the authors of Jewish apocalypses might be linked to the particular pseudonyms they used. In the case of Jewish apocalypses, pseudonymity seems to have been the only authorial option and the function of whatever *nom de plume* was chosen seems to have been motivated by what Hindy Najman has designated as an "authority-conferring strategy."[46] Hogan maintains that in Judaism, pseudepigraphy must have been recognized as conventional in the circles of those who produced apocalypses. Her project focuses on the periodization of history in six Jewish historical apocalypses, i.e., apocalypses containing *ex eventu* prophecy (and therefore with a deterministic emphasis), which require pseudepigraphy: (1) the Animal Vision (*1 En.* 85–90), (2) the Apocalypse of Weeks (*1 En.* 93.1–10, 91.11–17), (3) Daniel 7–12, (4) *Testament of*

---

[45] Karina Martin Hogan, "Pseudepigraphy and the Periodization of History in Jewish Apocalypses" (*in hoc voluminis*).

[46] Martin Hogan credits this phrase to H. Najman, "Interpretation as Primordial Writing: *Jubilees* and is Authority Conferring Strategies," *JSJ* 30 (1999): 379–410.

Moses, (5) *4 Ezra* and (6) *2 Baruch*. In these apocalypses, she identifies three critical breaking-points in biblical history that apocalyptic seers regard as paradigmatic for the events they are experiencing: the Flood and the Babylonian Exile (symbolizing judgment), framed by the Exodus (symbolizing salvation). Apocalyptic seers understood the crisis of historical discontinuity in their own time as analogous return, which they understand to constitute a historical breaking-point. Hogan argues that the choice of particular pseudonyms was related to actual historical locations of real authors who understood their roles to be that of providing continuity and the preservation of tradition (particularly written tradition) between historically discontinuous periods. The symbolic "bridge" figures which Hogan discusses include Enoch and Noah (apocalyptic writings originated with Enoch, but were transmitted by the actual "bridge" figure Noah, linked to the Flood), Moses (linked to the Exodus) and Daniel, Ezra and Baruch (linked to the Babylonian Exile).

8. Introducing Letter Collections

8.1 The Letter of Mithridates

The essay on the *Letter of Mithridates* by Robert Matthew Calhoun provides an important entré into the role of pseudepigraphal letters in introducing letter collections, which can themselves be pseudepigraphal.[47] The *Letter of Mithridates* is a secondary cover letter to the collection of Greek pseudepigraphal letters attributed to Marcus Junius Brutus, which were regarded in antiquity as examples of exemplary epistolary style. Calhoun has prepared both a translation of and succinct commentary on the *Letter of Mithridates*,[48] which begins "Mithridates to [my] cousin the King Mithridates, greetings." It is not obvious whether the letter is actually pseudepigraphal or the extent to which the pseudonyms are transparent to the reader (if they are in fact pseudonyms). The content of the *Letter of Mithridates* suggests that the collection of the letters of Brutus existed and was circulated before the *Letter* was prefixed to a second edition. The purpose of the author was to augment the letters of Brutus by furnishing appropriate replies and he indicates this purpose in the introductory letter. In order to draft replies to the letters of Brutus, "Mithridates" claims to have consulted the appropriate histories so that his replies will have the

---

[47] Robert Matthew Calhoun, "The *Letter* of Mithridates: A Neglected Item of Ancient Epistolary Theory" (*in hoc voluminis*).

[48] Calhoun is in part dependent on L. Torraca, *Marco Giunio Bruta: Epistole Greche* (Collana di Studi Greci 31; Naples: Liberia Scientifica Editrice, 1959).

appearance of verisimilitude. The second edition of the letters of Brutus, with both replies and the introductory letter can be dated between 40 CE and 200 CE (Calhoun prefers the latter). The *Letter of Mithridates* suggests that it was written as a rhetorical-epistolary exercise in *prosopopoiia*. The *Letter of Mithridates* is striking because it is the only letter from antiquity in which an author openly acknowledges his pseudepigraphal authorship and is analogous to Thucydides's statement about his composition of speeches appropriate for their historical context. Despite the cultural difference between the second edition of the letters of Brutus and New Testament pseudepigraphal letters, Calhoun draws several analogies that the reader will want to consider.

8.2 The Letter to the Hebrews

In Clare Rothschild's essay in this volume on "Hebrews as a Guide to Reading Romans," she builds on the work of Patricia Rosenmeyer who argues that some Greek letter collections have a longer explanatory letter at the end of a collection of letters by the same author.[49] Rothschild also refers to the monograph of Annette Metz, who proposes that the Pastoral Letters serve as guides, pretending to be from Paul, to the *Corpus Paulinum*.[50] She might also have mentioned the view of Edgar J. Goodspeed, who proposed that Ephesians was a pseudonymous letter designed to head a collection of the Pauline letters and introduce major themes of the Pauline letters. Analogously, Rothschild claims that Hebrews is a pseudonymous letter added to collections of Pauline letters as an explanatory letter that provided some of the missing context of the *Corpus Paulinum*. In the body of the essay, however, the author is not concerned with Hebrews as a guide to the *Corpus Paulinum* so much as a guide for contextualizing, clarifying, elaborating and correcting some of the key ideas in Romans. She attempts to do this by demonstrating some interesting links between Hebrews and the Romans: both use five of the same OT passages; both share elements in their epistolary postscripts; echoes of Romans are identified in Hebrews, especially Heb 13. Unfortunately, these ostensible links between Hebrews and Romans have many explanations and the proposal that Hebrews was written as a guide to reading Romans is not the obvious option. Not discussed are the reasons for regarding Hebrews as pseudonymous (neither author nor addressees are named, though the dense network of allusions and the specific mention in Heb 13:18–25 of Timothy, the most prominent of Paul's coworkers, may intentionally suggest Pauline authorship, though secondary pseudonymity is found in those

---

[49] Rosenmeyer, *Ancient Epistolary Fictions* (see n. 17), 215.
[50] Merz, *Die fiktive Selbstauslegung des Paulus* (see n. 21).

Greek manuscripts in which Hebrews is explicitly attributed to Paul).[51] There is also the problem of dating Hebrews, which according to Rothschild's thesis must have been produced after the Pauline letters existed as some kind of collection.

9. New Testament Epistolary Pseudepigrapha

9.1 Pauline Pseudepigrapha

9.1.1 Introduction

Eve-Marie Becker focuses on the research on the Pauline pseudepigrapha in the context of the history of literature. Her essay serves as an introduction to the general problems and issues involved in the study of the Pauline pseudepigrapha.[52] Toward the end of a helpful *Forschungsbericht*, Becker touches on recent proposals that maintain that a Pauline school is responsible for the production of some or all of the Pauline pseudepigrapha. She is critical of aspects of this proposal and revises it by emphasizing instead the more demonstrable effects of the transmission and revision of the authentic Pauline letters toward the end of the first century. This process in its initial stages involved Paul himself and was then supplemented by others including a circle of tradents and copyists.[53] Becker distinguishes between (1) a "Tradentenkreis der Paulusbriefe," (2) a group of theologically motivated writers of pseudepigraphal Pauline letters, made up in part by Pauline coworkers such as Timothy and Titus who functioned as co-senders of Pauline letters (e.g., 2 Cor 1:1), and then a broader independent group that could be designated the "Pauline school." Becker rejects a simplistic conception of the intention of Pauline pseudepigrapha as primarily literary imitation for the purpose of emphasizing Pauline authority and rightly argues that each writing must be individually analyzed in order to discover its original purpose. Referring to Martin Hengel's emphasis on the dominance of anonymity and pseudonymity in early Jewish literature, Becker argues that Paul's use of his name in his letters stands out as unusual. The problem here is that despite the widespread use of anonymity and pseudonymity in Judaism and the widespread use of orthonymity and

---

[51] The discussion of this issue is the subject of her recent monograph, *Hebrews as Pseudepigraphon: The History and Significance of the Pauline Attribution of Hebrews* (WUNT 235; Tübingen: Mohr Siebeck, 2009).

[52] Eve-Marie Becker, "Von Paulus zu 'Paulus': Paulinische Pseudepigraphie-Forschung als literaturgeschichtliche Aufgabe" (*in hoc voluminis*).

[53] Becker refers to her earlier study, *Schreiben und Verstehen: Paulinische Briefhermeneutik im Zweiten Korintherbrief* (NET 4; Tübingen/Basel: Francke, 2002), 56ff.

pseudonymity in Roman Hellenism, it is precisely in the writing of letters that orthonymity became necessary, both in the east and in the west.

Becker turns to 2 Thessalonians as a special case among the Pauline pseudepigrapha. She calls attention to two striking features of 2 Thessalonians: (1) 2 Thessalonians reproduces the identical *superscriptio* found in 1 Thessalonians and includes an "apostolic autograph" (2 Thess 3:17), with no counterpart in 1 Thessalonians. (2) 2 Thess 2:2 and 2:15 function as key passages for understanding the literary and theological relationship between 2 Thessalonians and 1 Thessalonians. While 2 Thess 2:2 refers to a false interpretation of 1 Thessalonians, 2 Thess 2:15 constitutes a correct rereading of 1 Thessalonians. According to Becker, from the perspective of the author of 2 Thessalonians (this is a very important point), there are three types of Pauline teaching and Pauline letters: (1) correct Pauline teaching (e.g., 1 Thessalonians) in the form of orthonymic letters, (2) substantially correct Pauline teaching (e.g., 2 Thessalonians), letters in pseudepigraphal form (cf. 2 Thess 3:17), and (3) false Pauline teaching (e.g., the lost letter referred to in 2 Thess 2:2). 2 Thessalonians should then be understood as a substantially correct continuation of 1 Thessalonians and should be accepted as being *substantially authentic theologically*, which of course is not the same as *literary authenticity*. Using this model, Becker thinks that she has found a way out of the antithetical categories "'richtige' oder 'verfälschende' paulinische Lehre," which have typically been correlated with literary authenticity or pseudepigraphy. The questions remain, however, whether an author's good intentions in using a pseudonym (*pia fraus*) are an adequate theological and ethical basis on which to base a theory of theologically correct pseudepigrapha. Becker's essay is itself part of the new trend in research in pseudepigraphy in that she tries to correct older simplistic models and replace them with a more nuanced and systemic approach to the Pauline pseudepigrapha. Like several other contributors, she is vitally interested in the problem of pseudepigraphy and theological truth.

9.1.2 The Second Letter to the Thessalonians

The essay by Edgar Krentz on 2 Thessalonians as a pseudepigraphon was written in 1983, but not published until it appeared in this volume[54] and for that reason it is introduced by Trevor Thompson, who situates the genesis of the essay in the context of American biblical scholarship 25 years ago. The essay by Krentz is essentially a *Forschungsbericht* in which he traces the historical development of the recognition of 2 Thessalonians as a

---

[54] Edgar Krentz, "A Stone that Will Not Fit: The Non-Pauline Authorship of Second Thessalonians" (*in hoc voluminis*).

Pauline pseudepigraphon. Krentz's article was very helpful for American New Testament scholars, who were slowly coming to terms with the pseudepigraphal character of 2 Thessalonians in the 1970's and 1980's. Krentz covers the evidence in three categories: (1) the linguistic data, (2) the argument from structure (where he relies heavily on an important 1903 monograph by William Wrede),[55] (3) the argument from theological content and (4) characteristics that support a later date (the formal tone, the stress on authority which is more typical of a later period and the distinctive reference to "Paul's" signing the letter with his own hand, "this is the mark in every letter of mine; it is the way I write" [3:17]). The fact that Krentz's essay was written more than twenty-five years ago is revealed by a lack of concern with the pseudepigraphal strategy and structure of 2 Thessalonians (apart from his discussion of 2 Thess 3:17). He deals with the purpose and situation of 2 Thessalonians in just a half page. Since New Testament scholars now assume the pseudepigraphical character of 2 Thessalonians, other important aspects of understanding the pseudepigraphal phenomenon can now be given their rightful place on the research agenda.

9.1.3 The Letter to the Colossians

In her discussion of Colossians as a pseudepigraphal letter, Nicole Frank focuses on the interaction between what she calls "die pseudopaulinischen Briefkonstitutions-Koordinaten" consisting of author—addressees—opponents, regarding all three as fictional constructs. The claim of apostolic authority gives Colossians a legitimate teaching function in issues of early Christian community practice. The letter is addressed to "the faithful brethren in Colossae," but also occasionally mentions the neighboring Laodicea (2:1; 4:13, 16) and in the thanksgiving is expanded "to you just as in the whole world" (Col 1:6). The polemic against the opponents (Col 2:8, 16–23) emphasizes the exclusive relationship of the believer to Christ as head of "the body of Christ," within which the members of this body participate in the present reality of salvation through the reality of the resurrection of Christ.

9.1.4 The Letter to the Ephesians

Martin Hüneburg contributes an essay on Ephesians as a correction of Colossians.[56] Hüneburg assumes, rather than argues, that both Ephesians and Colossians are pseudepigrapha, that the author of Ephesians was heavily

---

[55] W. Wrede, *Die Echtheit des zweiten Thessalonicherbriefs* (TU 24; Leipzig: J. C. Hinrichs, 1905).

[56] Martin Hüneburg, "Paulus versus Paulus: Der Epheserbrief als Korrektur des Kolosserbriefes" (*in hoc voluminis*).

dependent on Colossians and that he probably regarded Colossians as an authentic Pauline letter. In itself, Ephesians is a puzzling pseudepigraphon, since it lacks any controversy and therefore reflects no polemic against opponents, even though such a polemic is an important part of the pseudepigraphal strategy of Colossians. Further, Ephesians exhibits no clear purpose. The few bits of *Verfasserfiktion* used by the unknown Paulinist include the mention of the author's imprisonment twice (3:1, 4:1) and the mention of Tychicus (6:21–22) is verbally identical with the author's Vorlage in Col 4:7–8, where Tychicus is also mentioned (Tychicus is associated with Paul in Acts 20:4 as well as in 2 Tim 4:12, Titus 3:12 and in the *subscriptiones* of both Colossians and Ephesians).

Hüneburg focuses on whether in fact a purpose can be discerned for the writing of Ephesians by exploring the reception of Colossians by the author of Ephesians. He first summarizes the various types of evidence for the massive use of Colossians in Ephesians and also for the fact that Ephesians alludes to all the accepted Pauline letters. One of the more striking features of the reworking of Colossians in Ephesians emphasized by Hüneburg is the unusual insertion of a eulogy or *berakah* in Eph 1:3–14, inserted before the typical Pauline thanksgiving in Col 1:3–8, expanded in Eph 1:15–23, where the author clearly departs from Colossians. The author of Ephesians also expanded the paranetic section of Colossians and introduced a clearer structure. Hüneburg goes on to discuss several ways in which the author of Ephesians introduced corrections to the theology of Colossians, a text that he regarded as Pauline.

9.1.5 *The Pastoral Letters*

Jens Herzer, in an essay focusing on the pseudepigraphal problems posed by the Pastoral Letters, provides a historical review of the development of the idealistic paradigm that became the modern consensus view on the Pastoral Letters as a corpus of three pseudepigraphal letters that constitute a related corpus produced by a single author for the purpose of protecting and passing on tradition in a post-apostolic period. This idealistic paradigm that evolved during the 19th century, which began with Schleiermacher, was developed by Baur and reached its final form in the work of Heinrich Julius Holtzmann, continued to be dominant during the 20th and into the 21st century. Even with the revival of interest in pseudepigraphical studies in the 1960's and 1970's, the 19th century paradigm remained unquestioned. For Herzer, three assumptions widely represented in contemporary discussion are not completely satisfactory: (1) the view that the pseudepigraphic composition of the three Pastoral Letters is unproblematic and legitimate, (2) the assumption that the Pastorals arose as illegitimate deception, (3) the view that the Pastoral Letters are authentically Pauline.

Currently, there is no material agreement among scholars on three crucial issues: (1) the original purpose behind the composition of the Pastoral Letters, (2) the reason why the author chose the particular literary form, (3) the profile of the addressees and their situation. For Herzer, one of the greatest problems in the current interpretation of the Pastoral Letters is the assumption of the conscious composition of the threefold *Corpus Pastorale* by a single author, a hypothesis that was not demonstrated by Holtzmann so much as assumed and which continues to dominate the interpretation of the Pastoral Letters. It must be made plausible why there are three letters to two addressees and why the three writings are so very different. For Herzer, the Pastoral Letters cannot be meaningfully interpreted as a letter corpus and therefore he proposes that this interpretive assumption must be abandoned. On the basis of literary, linguistic and content criteria, each letter must be analyzed individually. A generic distinction must be made between individual literary letters and collections of literary letters. 1 Timothy and Titus are often identified with the so-called *mandata principis* (though how this related to the issue of pseudepigraphy is debated).

Herzer rejects Richard Pervo's proposal that the Pastoral Letters conform to the genre of an epistolary novel, calling attention to the absence of a continuing narrative from the Pastoral Letters as a decisive flaw in the proposal.[57] Herzer's rejection of the Pastoral Letters as a *Briefroman* is also a necessary consequence of the fact that he rejected their unity.

At this point it is important to call attention to Katharina Luchner's carefully argued essay on "Pseudepigraphie und antike Briefromane" (*in hoc voluminis*). She approaches the subject of the supposed genre of the epistolary novel by beginning with the work of the British classicist Richard Bentley, who published his famous "Dissertation upon the Epistles of Phalaris, Themistocles, Socrates, Euripides etc." in 1697, in which he proved that these letter collections were forgeries perpetrated by pedants. Since Bentley, it has been widely assumed that such letter collections, typically attributed to famous men of antiquity, are pseudepigraphal works. Luchner then turns to the issue of how one should read collections of letters of "famous men," whether as simply arbitrary "Briefsammlungen" consisting of a random set of letters that are inherently interesting because they were supposedly written by famous people, or as "Briefromane," i.e., pseudepigraphic letters intentionally assembled in a novelistic fashion. These pseudepigraphal letter collections are available in Hercher's *Epis-*

---

[57] R. I. Pervo, "Romancing an Oft-Neglected Stone: The Pastoral Epistles and the Epistolary Novel," *The Journal of Higher Criticism* 1 (1994): 25–47.

tolographi Graeci,⁵⁸ including fourteen collections of "letters of famous men" that are very probably pseudonymous and seven collections that are a mixture of orthonymous and pseudonymous letters. Luchner traces the history of research on the "antike Briefroman" genre from Immisch (1913), through Dornseiff (1934, 1939) including Dornseiff's proposal that the thirteen letters of Plato form a "Buch Briefe" (a sequence of letters with the author, Plato, as hero), culminating in the work of Holzberg (1994) and Rosenmeyer (2002).⁵⁹ Luchner observes that the supposition of a unified intention behind a collection of letters considered an epistolary novel actually preceded the systematic examination of the available texts. Based on the work of Dornseiff and particularly Holzberg, Luchner proposes four characteristic features for the epistolary novel: (1) the character of the hero, (2) the establishment of narrative continuity, (3) dramatic disclosure, and (4) the presence of particular themes, e.g., the letter writer and the ruler, the letter writer and his friends and enemies, the value of money, and so forth. Using these criteria, she then analyzes the letter collections ascribed to Plato and Chion to determine whether or not the features of the epistolary novel are actually present in the text or in the mind of the critic. She carefully concludes that the application of the term "novel" to these collections of letters is problematic.

Returning to Herzer's essay on the Pastoral Letters, he considers the possibility that the genre of the "Schulpseudepigraphon" might be helpful to explain the differences within the tree Pastoral Letters. A "Schulpseudepigraphon" can be written in the name of the head or founder of the school and yet is not meant to deceive and in fact the identity of the real author cannot remain undiscovered for the writing to be acceptable. As he clearly distinguishes between 1 Timothy on the one hand and 2 Timothy and Titus on the other in terms of the characteristics of the "literarische Stilmittel," Herzer maintains that only 1 Timothy shows the characteristics of a "Schulpseudepigraphon," mainly because it is largely lacking the extensive personal material which on the other side is specifically present in 2 Timothy and Titus. Thus, 2 Timothy and Titus should either be received as deceptive forgeries or, he argues, the issue of their authenticity could be

---

⁵⁸ R. Hercher, *Epistolographi Graeci* (Bibliotheca scriptorium Graecorum; Paris: A. Firmin Didot, 1873; reprinted Amsterdam, 1965).

⁵⁹ Luchner refers to the following works: O. Immisch, "Der erste platonische Brief," *Philologus* 72 (1913); F. Dornseiff, "Platons Buch 'Briefe,'" *Hermes* 69 (1934): 223–26, and idem, *Echtheitsfragen antik-griechischer Literatur* (Berlin: de Gruyter, 1939); N. Holzberg (ed.), *Der griechische Briefroman: Gattungstypologie und Textanalyse*, Classica Monacensia 8 (Tübingen: Gunter Narr, 1994); Rosenmeyer, *Ancient Epistolary Fictions* (see n. 17).

reconsidered, if they are not as closely bound to 1 Timothy as usually assumed in scholarship.

9.2 The Catholic Letters

9.2.1 The Letter of James

Those who argue for or against pseudepigraphical authorship of the Letter of James agree that the James to whom the letter is attributed in Jas 1:1 must be the brother of Jesus, who according to Wilhelm Pratscher is "one of the most significant personalities of early Christianity."[60] In Matthias Konradt's discussion of the Letter of James, he first reviews the conventional arguments of those (like himself) who hold that James is a pseudepigraphon and then discusses the possible reasons why the unknown author chose to write precisely in the name of James the Just. He discounts the proposals that the letter was written by a member of a school of James that preserved and propagated his teaching of the leader of the Jerusalem church or that the author was a member of a Christian wing who regarded James as a paramount authority. Rather, the unknown author was someone who regarded James as an important early Christian authority whose image was consistent with the type of teaching contained in the Letter of James including the positive attitude expressed toward the law. In the *Gos. Thom.* 12 (cf. Eusebius, *Hist. eccl.* 2.23.4), James is already called "the Just," an epithet that fits well with the image of James as a teacher of wisdom.

9.2.2 The First Letter of Peter

1 and 2 Peter are the focus of a comparative study by Karl Matthias Schmidt, who emphasizes the distinction between *Fiktion* and *Täuschung*; he considers the Petrine letters as examples of the former rather than the latter.[61] By "fiction" he means that the real author of the text composes it in such a way that it is not understood as ascribed to the author named in the *superscriptio*. By contrasting "Fiktion" with "Täuschung," Schmidt approaches one of the central problems of canonical pseudepigraphy for New Testament scholars, though he does not treat it so much as a theological problem than as neutral literary alternatives. Using the categories of Gérard Genette, Schmidt uses Ovid's *Heroides*, a collection of verse letters written in two series. The first series (letters 1–15) consists of letters written by famous women, while the second series (letters 16–21), consists of

---

[60] W. Pratscher, *Der Herrenbruder Jakobus und die Jakobustradition* (FRLANT 139; Göttingen: Vandenhoeck & Ruprecht, 1987), 10.

[61] Karl Matthias Schmidt, "Die Stimme des Apostels erheben: Pragmatische Leistungen der Autorenfiktion in den Petrusbriefen" (*in hoc voluminis*).

three letters by three male lovers and the replies by their respective women. Schmidt categorizes the stylistic device of this collection of letters as *prosopopoiia* (i.e., fictitious speeches by other persons; Quintillian 6.1.25: *fictae alienarum personarum orationes*), in which an author adopts the persona of a real or fictitious person, usually of the past. However, *prosopopoiia* is primarily a rhetorical exercise,[62] and Ovid regards the *Heroides* as a new literary genre that he himself has created (*Ars amatoria* 3.345). For Schmidt, the Petrine letters are analogous to Ovid's *Heroides*, since he argues that both are transparent fictions rather than attempts to deceptively write a letter in the name of someone other than the real author. According to Schmidt, if 1–2 Peter are forgeries, Peter is presented as the real author, but if they are fiction, Peter is not presented as the real author. Whether they are *Fiktion* or *Täuschung* can only be answered by looking at the two works separately. The clearest evidence that 1 Peter is fictional is found in 1 Pet 5:1, where the author refers to himself as μάρτυς τῶν τοῦ Χριστοῦ παθημάτων. If 1 Peter is a forgery, then the real Peter has not yet died when the letter was written and the fact that he denied Christ three times would have been uppermost in the minds of the readers. However, if 1 Pet 5:1 is read as referring to the historical martyrdom of Peter (overshadowing his denial of Christ), then 1 Peter is a fiction, since otherwise it could not have been written after Peter's execution nearly two generations earlier. When it comes to 2 Peter, Schmidt emphasizes the fact that the author makes no attempt to emulate the linguistic, theological or thematic features of 1 Peter and is therefore not attempting to pass off 2 Peter as an authentic letter of Peter, a feature underscored by the reference in 2 Pet 3:1 by the fictive author to the first letter which he wrote to his audience. Schmidt uses more similar arguments to maintain that 2 Peter like 1 Peter is *Fiktion* rather than *Täuschung*. His arguments are clever as well as innovative and presuppose original audiences capable of making subtle inferences. However, Schmidt's view of the intentional linguistic, theological and thematic disjunction between 2 Peter and 1 Peter is in tension with a central feature of *prosopopoiia*, namely *imitatio*.

---

[62] The Progymnasmata (books of rhetorical exercises) typically have a section devoted to *prosopopoiia* or *ethopoiia*, e.g., Aelius Theon, *Progymn.* 9; Hermogenes, *Progymn.* 9; Aphthonius, *Progymn.* 11; Nikolaus, *Progymn.* 10.

9.2.3 The Letter of Jude

Jörg Frey's essay on the Letters of Jude and 2 Peter,[63] mentioned above in the introduction, focuses on the systemic pseudepigraphal features of these two closely related letters. The *superscriptio* of the Letter of Jude, written at the end of the first century CE, is the only place in the letter where the name "Jude" appears: "Jude, servant of Jesus Christ and brother of James" (the fictive author is not much emphasized in this short work). Though sometimes identified as the apostle Jude, the brother of James (Acts 1:13; cf. Tertullian, *De cultu feminarum* 1.3), critical scholars agree that the pseudonym is intended to refer to that Jude who, along with James, were the brothers of Jesus (first so identified by Origen). The fact that Jude is a minor figure in early Christian history, together with the fact that the *subscriptiones* of Jude and James are identical, suggests that the intention of the real author is to link his pseudepigraphon to Jacobite tradition rather than simply to the obscure figure "Jude."[64] The *adscriptio* is very general ("To those who are called, beloved in God the Father and kept for Jesus Christ"), indicating that "Jude" is unknown to the addressees, supporting the view that the letter is a pseudepigraphon. The author addresses his audience as an authoritative figure and describes their situation as a contemporary and probably was a third-generation Christian. The apostles, however, are authoritative figures of the past (v. 17).

A major problem is that of reconstructing the profile of the real opponents of the actual author, whose constructed literary image of the opponents functions as part of the fictional structure of the letter, using many of the traditional *topoi* for slandering enemies. The old hypothesis that the opponents were Gnostics has been abandoned. The point of conflict between the author and his opponents is the focus in vv. 8–10. The author appeals to *1 Enoch* (which he regards as authoritative). Angelology is very important for the author; angels have protological and eschatological significance, are part of the earthly and heavenly order and guarantee the order of the world. This angelology can be linked to a development of the conception of angelic powers alluded to in the Pauline letters (1 Cor 6:3, 13:1, 15:24). There appears to be an argument between the tradition represented by the author and Pauline tradition with regard to antinomian ten-

---

[63] Jörg Frey, "Autorfiktion und Gegnerbild im Judasbrief und im Zweiten Petrusbrief" (*in hoc voluminis*). The features discussed in this essay are treated in greater detail in Frey's commentary, which is in press: *Der Judasbrief. Der zweite Petrusbrief*, ThHK 16/2 (Leipzig: Evangelische Verlagsanstalt, 2010, forthcoming).

[64] On the subject of Jacobite tradition, see Pratscher, *Der Herrenbruder Jakobus* (see n. 60). However, what Pratscher means by "Jakobustradition" has nothing to do with a "school of James," but simply means all of the evidence, historical and legendary, about James in the early church.

dencies (v. 4), though an even more important interest of the author is the conflict. However, the concrete situation of the community or communities addressed finds only marginal expression in the fictional structure of the letter.

9.2.4 The Second Letter of Peter

In the same essay in which he focused on the fictive features of the Letter of Jude, Frey analyzes the constituent elements of 2 Peter under the generic category "*testamentum Petri*." Critical scholars generally agree that 2 Peter is literarily dependent on Jude. "Peter," in contrast to the obscure "Jude," is a major figure in the Gospels as the first apostle to be called (Mark 1:16) and the first witness of the resurrection (1 Cor 15:5) and a central authority among the apostles in the early post-Easter period. It is therefore surprising that Peter's name was not fictively used earlier and more frequently than it was. Peter left no literary heritage himself and 1 Peter, written before the end of the first century CE, is the first (and strikingly moderate) Petrine pseudepigraphon until 2 Peter and then the *Gospel of Peter* (like 2 Peter, before ca. 150 CE), followed by the *Kerygmata Petrou*, the *Acts of Peter*, the *Apocalypse of Peter* and three Coptic Petrine pseudepigrapha from Nag Hammadi: the *Apocalypse of Peter*, the *Letter of Peter to Philip* and the *Acts of Peter*. Despite these fictive appeals to the name of Peter, Frey is no doubt correct that there is no convincing evidence for the existence of a "Petrine school."[65]

The author of 2 Peter pulls out all the stops in elaborating a "denser and more massive pseudonymous legitimation structure" (Frey). Although the actual author knew 1 Peter (3:1: "This is now the second letter that I have written to you"), unlike the author of 2 Thessalonians who stylistically and structurally imitated 1 Thessalonians, the actual author of 2 Peter exhibits no literary dependence on 1 Peter nor did he choose to imitate the Greek style of that letter. The author emphasizes Peter, together with the other apostles and therefore using the apostolic plural "we," as an eyewitness of the transfiguration of Jesus (2 Pet 1:17–18). The author also refers harmoniously to "our beloved brother Paul," sliding over the historical tensions between the two figures, and even mentions a collection of Pauline letters (2 Pet 3:15–16). "Peter" also refers to his imminent death "as our Lord

---

[65] Nevertheless there are those who argue for a Petrine school behind 1–2 Peter and Jude: M. L. Soards, "1 Peter, 2 Peter, and Jude as Evidence for a Petrine School" (with addenda [on a Petrine Community] by V. Oliver Ward), *ANRW* II 25.5:3827–49, and P. Chatelion Counet, "Pseudepigraphy and the Petrine School: Spirit and Tradition in 1 and 2 Peter and Jude," *Hervormde Teologiese Studies* 62 (2006): 403–24. Frey refers to both Anton Vögtle and Richard Bauckham as two scholars who speak positively about a Petrine circle in Rome.

Jesus Christ showed me," alluding to John 13:36–37, 21:18, constructed as a "departure scene." As a *"testamentum Petri,"* 2 Peter functions as the postmortem voice of the apostle.

The fictive addressees would have been contemporaries with Peter at a time just prior to his death; the real addressees, some time after the death of Peter, are intended to regard the literary presentation of Peter as an authoritative apostolic witness. Since the depiction of the opponents is a fictional construct, the problem of historical reconstruction is fraught with difficulties. Frey proposes the existence of a tension between the two temporal planes that divide the fictive contemporaries addressed by Pseudo-Peter and the real addresses intended by the real author.

The focal intention of the text lies in the warnings against false teachers who are expected to arrive in the end time (2 Pet 3:3); n.b. that in Jude they were present.

9.3 The Johannine Letters

The special case of the Johannine letters, which avoid using the name(s) of their author(s) and so appear to be anonymous rather than pseudonymous, is discussed in a carefully argued and provocative essay by Jutta Leonhardt-Balzer.[66] 1 John lacks all the formal features of a letter including the *superscriptio, adscriptio* and an epistolary ending; it is anonymous rather than pseudonymous. 2 and 3 John, on the other hand are relatively short letters, complete with *superscriptiones, adscriptiones* and epistolary endings. The author of 2 John identifies himself as "the elder" and his recipients as "the elect lady and her children" (2 John 1). The concluding greeting, "the children of your elect sister greet you" (2 John 13), makes it clear that the *adscriptio* is a metaphor for a house church and the church from which the author writes is given the metaphor "your elect sister." 3 John, like 2 John, is a real letter, complete with *superscriptio, adscriptio* and epistolary conclusion. As in the case of 2 John, 3 John is ascribed to "the elder," but the letter is directed to an individual named Gaius, doubtless the head of a household. The genre of 1 John has been a matter of debate, but it generally fits the parameters of a sermon or homily. Since 2 John contains allusions to 1 John and deals with a similar problem, it was probably written shortly after 1 John and appears to have been written as a circular letter for the purpose of introducing 1 John.

Leonhardt-Balzer argues that the authors of 2 John and 3 John (two different people) appropriate the authority of "the elder" and write in his name, fostering the impression of a single author for the entire corpus. The

---

[66] Jutta Leonhardt-Balzer, "Pseudepigraphie und Gemeinde in den Johannesbriefen" (*in hoc voluminis*).

author of 2 John consciously cites 1 John and identifies himself with the author of that work. 2 and 3 John are therefore pseudepigrapha, which not only use the name of "the elder" but also enhance their letters with the announcement of an impending visit (2 John 12, 3 John 13–14), a well-worn epistolary device for strengthening the impression of a concrete personal communication. 1 John and 2 John assume a similar situation (e.g., the problem of "those who have gone out from us"), and 2 John was probably written shortly after 1 John and functioned as a circular letter that served to introduce the anonymous 1 John. The author of 1 John, a teacher of wisdom and the primary "elder," derived the author fiction not from himself but from the truth of his testimony. 2 and 3 John stand in the tradition of 1 John by implying common authorship by using the language and title of "the elder." The Johannine letters are therefore pseudepigrapha (like the works attributed to Moses, Isaiah or Enoch), the primary difference being that 2 and 3 John were written during the lifetime of "the elder." One lingering problem lies in the fact that identifying the author of 1 John as "the elder" finds no explicit textual support, though that does not nullify the argument.

10. Concluding Observations

After commenting on the many contributions to this volume, at this point it is appropriate to make a series of concluding observations. These observations are far from complete. A careful reading of each of the contributions in this volume is necessary for the reader to appreciate fully the overall contribution of this collection of essays.

1. While the meaning of "pseudepigraphy" might seem clear enough (the prefix ψεῦδος means "lie, falsehood"), the application of the term to Jewish, Greco-Roman and Christian literature of antiquity is both complex and problematic. Wolfgang Speyer calls for the neutral use of "pseudepigraphy" so that ethical and theological issues do not dominate the discussion when different forms of pseudepigrapha are being considered. Speyer is quite right, for though the term "pseudepigraphy" has an ancient origin,[67] it is now widely used to describe all types of ancient fictional authorship for which the ancients had no consistent vocabulary. While pseud-

---

[67] The term ψευδεπίγραφος appears as early as the second century BCE, but thereafter occurs only rarely (Polybius 23.5.5; Dionysius of Halicarnassus, *Dem.* 57; Plutarch, *Frat. amor.* 479e (where it is used as a synonym of ψευδώνυμος); Serapion of Antioch (late 2nd century CE), used the phrase τὰ ψευδεπίγραφα for writings falsely attributed to the apostles, particularly the Gospel of Peter (Eusebius, *Hist. eccl.* 6.12.3); *Canones Apostolorum* 60 (4th century CE).

epigraphy (and cognates) has a negative meaning, alternatives such as "Verfasserfiktion," "Autorfiktion," "*nom de plume*" and "allonymity" do not; in the case of *Verfasserfiktion* and its synonym *Autorfiktion*, fiction and nonfiction are simply two basic categories for discourse, while in the case of *nom de plume* and allonymity, both are ethically neutral synonyms of "pseudonym."

2. The rarity of orthonymity in the Hebrew and Aramaic literature of antiquity (a fact emphasized by both Perdue and Tigchelaar) means that anonymity and fictional authorship or pseudonymity were the two basic literary options, both of which shared a social value: community traditions and community history are the primary considerations in textual attribution. Literary culture in the Greco-Roman world, on the other hand, placed a greater value on orthonymity, which took two primary antithetical forms, orthonymity and allonymity or pseudonymity. While a Jewish author had a choice between anonymity and allonymity, for a Hellenistic author the choice was between orthonymity and allonymity or pseudonymity. Thus while deception is certainly a universal human social vice, the literary culture of the Greco-Roman world made forgery with an obvious intent to deceive a clearer option. There are many examples from Hellenistic literature of those who forged documents with malevolent intentions. According to Diogenes Laertius 10.3, Diotimus the Stoic, who was hostile toward Epicurus, wrote fifty letters he falsely ascribed to Epicurus in order to slander him. Diogenes also mentions another unnamed opponent of Epicurus who also wrote letters under the name of Chrysippus for the same purpose. On the other hand, *noms de plume* or *allonyms* could be used by writers to protect themselves from a hostile public. In Aristophanes, *Vespae* 1015–1025 the poet provides an autobiographical reflection on the fact the public disliked his work only when his real name was attached to his poetry:

Hence, people, lend me your ear, if you love frank speaking. The poet has a reproach to make against his audience; he says you have ill-treated him in return for the many services he has rendered you. At first he kept himself in the background and lent help secretly to other poets, and like the prophetic Genius, who hid himself in the belly of Eurycles, slipped within the spirit of another and whispered to him many a comic hit. Later he ran the risks of the theatre on his own account, with his face uncovered, and dared to guide his Muse unaided. Though over laden with success and honors more than any of your poets, indeed despite all his glory, he does not yet believe he has attained his goal; his heart is not swollen with pride and he does not seek to seduce the young folk in the wrestling school.

On the other hand, all known Jewish apocalypses are written under the names of famous Israelites of the past, suggesting that allonymity or pseudepigraphy was a generic feature of apocalypses. There are no examples of Jewish apocalypses written for malevolent reasons as in the case of the pseudepigraphal letters of slander directed against Epicurus mentioned above. Eibert Tigchelaar mentions the work of Hindy Najman, who proposes that writing under such names as "Moses" is not a deceptive way of authorizing a text, but a means of acknowledging the texts and traditions associated with such ancient "founder" figures as Moses.

3. Detailed arguments demonstrating the pseudonymous character of six Pauline letters and four Catholic letters are now part of the received tradition of critical New Testament scholarship. The task that lies ahead is even more complex, since it involves the continued exploration of the fictional elements, i.e., the fictional author, the fictional recipients and a fictional rhetorical situation, each of which not only needs to be considered individually but also has to be recognized as structural features of a fictional communication situation. Each of the three elements constitutes a fictional "image" within each letter that has associations external to each letter that together help us to understand how the letter might have been understood as authentic by Christians in the late first and early second centuries (and beyond). Lutz Doering has contributed an essay to this volume that provides an excellent model for how the image of the person chosen as the fictional author can be unpacked. Similarly, Jörg Frey has provided a detailed discussion of image of the opponents in Jude and 2 Peter and has faced the difficult problem of separating historical from fictional elements in the *Gegnerbild* of those letters. This type of detailed examination of the pseudonymous image is particularly important for authors of commentaries on pseudonymous letters, since every aspect of the entire fictional construct needs careful exposition.

4. One aspect of the complexity of pseudepigraphy in antiquity is the problematic use of common antithetical models that reflect modern ethical values: "genuine"/"counterfeit," "pseudonym"/"orthonym," "fact"/"fiction." In reality, these are concepts at opposite ends of a continuum consisting of subtle gradations. There is a danger that using such simplistic and superficial categories will lull the critic into thinking that he or she has an adequate grasp of various problems surrounding fictional letters when such is not the case.

5. The extent to which fictional authorship and anonymity pervades the developing early Christian literary culture is striking. In just eight of the twenty-seven works in the New Testament does the actual author write under his own name.[68] The reasons for the popularity of pseudonymity or allonymity remain difficult to understand. This phenomenon undergoes a transformation during the first few centuries of the Common Era. Or-

---

[68] The eight orthonymous works are made up of the seven authentic Pauline letters (Romans, 1–2 Corinthians, Galatians, Philippians, 1 Thessalonians, Philemon) and the Apocalypse of John.

thonymity and fictional authorship appear to be favored by the two basic social strata within the church from the last first- through the fourth-century and beyond, namely the educated minority and the unlettered majority. Christians with some education typically use orthonymity in their writings (e.g., Ignatius, the Apologists, Polycarp, Justin, Irenaeus), while representatives of more popular forms of Christianity seem to use *noms de plume* or pseudepigraphy almost by default (e.g., the authors of the *Didache*, the apocryphal gospels and acts, including the *Gospel of Thomas*, the *Gospel of Peter*, the *Acts of Paul*). It is difficult for scholars in the twenty-first century to understand the cultural values and conceptions surrounding the issue of authorship for Christians in the ancient church. The literary culture in which various fictional types of writings, including pseudepigraphy, arose was strikingly different from that of the modern world and many of the simplistic understandings of authorship arise from the fact that the "individual" in the modern West differs striking from conceptions of the person in antiquity. Social science criticism has great deal to teach us about how we retroject the values and assumptions of the modern world into the ancient world.

Autorenverzeichnis

DAVID E. AUNE, PhD, Professor of New Testament, University of Notre Dame, Ind. (USA)

EVE-MARIE BECKER, Dr. theol. habil., Professor of New Testament, Department of Biblical Studies, Faculty of Theology, University of Aarhus (Denmark)

ROBERT MATTHEW CALHOUN, University of Chicago, Ill. (USA)

LUTZ DOERING, Dr. theol., Reader in New Testament and Ancient Judaism, Department of Theology and Religion, Durham University (United Kingdom)

MICHAELA ENGELMANN, Dipl. theol., Wissenschaftliche Mitarbeiterin, Institut für Neutestamentliche Wissenschaft, Theologische Fakultät der Universität Leipzig

NICOLE FRANK, Dr. theol., 2005–2009 Department of Theology, Utrecht University (Netherlands), z. Zt. Tübingen

MARCO FRENSCHKOWSKI, Dr. theol. habil., Privatdozent für Neues Testament, Evangelisch-theologische Fakultät, Johannes Gutenberg-Universität Mainz

JÖRG FREY, Dr. theol. habil., Professor für Neues Testament, Evangelisch-theologische Fakultät, Ludwig-Maximilians-Universität München

HARRY Y. GAMBLE, PhD, Professor of Religious Studies, University of Virginia, Charlottesville, Va. (USA)

TIMO GLASER, Dr. theol., Bibliotheksreferendar/Fachreferat Theologie, Universitätsbibliothek der Philipps-Universität Marburg

JENS HERZER, Dr. theol. habil., Professor für Neues Testament, Institut für Neutestamentliche Wissenschaft, Theologische Fakultät der Universität Leipzig

KARINA MARTIN HOGAN, PhD, Assistant Professor of Theology (Biblical), Fordham University, New York, N.Y. (USA)

MARTIN HÜNEBURG, Dr. theol., Wissenschaftlicher Mitarbeiter, Institut für Neutestamentliche Wissenschaft, Theologische Fakultät der Universität Leipzig

MATT JACKSON-MCCABE, PhD, Associate Professor and Chair of the Department of Religious Studies, Cleveland State University, Cleveland, Ohio (USA)

MARTINA JANSSEN, Dr. theol., Pastorin und Lehrbeauftragte an der Technischen Universität Braunschweig

MATTHIAS KONRADT, Dr. theol. habil., Professor für Neues Testament, Theologische Fakultät der Ruprecht-Karls-Universität Heidelberg

STEFAN KRAUTER, Dr. theol., Pfarrer z.A. und wissenschaftlicher Mitarbeiter, Institut für antikes Judentum und hellenistische Religionsgeschichte, Evangelisch-theologische Fakultät der Eberhard Karls Universität Tübingen

EDGAR KRENTZ, PhD, Professor em., Lutheran School of Theology, Chicago, Ill. (USA)

JUTTA LEONHARDT-BALZER, PhD, Lecturer in New Testament, King's College, University of Aberdeen (United Kingdom)

KATHARINA LUCHNER, M.A., Dr. phil., Institut für Griechische und Lateinische Philologie, Ludwig-Maximilians-Universität München

LEO G. PERDUE, PhD, Professor of Hebrew Bible, Brite Divinity School, Forth Worth, Tex. (USA)

CLARE K. ROTHSCHILD, PhD, Assistant Professor for Scripture Studies, Lewis University of Romeoville, Ill. (USA)

KARL MATTHIAS SCHMIDT, Dr. theol., Departement für Biblische Studien, Universität Freiburg (Schweiz)

WOLFGANG SPEYER, Dr. phil., Professor em. für Klassische Philologie, Fachbereich Altertumswissenschaften, Kultur- und Gesellschaftswissenschaftliche Fakultät der Universität Salzburg (Österreich)

TREVOR THOMPSON, Instructor of New Testament, Abilene Christian University, Abilene, Tex. (USA)

EIBERT J. C. TIGCHELAAR, PhD, Research Professor of Religion, Katholieke Universiteit Leuven (Belgium)

Stellenregister

Seitenzahlen sind *kursiv* gesetzt, wenn eine Textstelle nur in den Anmerkungen erscheint.

1. Bibel

1.1 Altes Testament (einschließlich Apokryphen)

Die Anordnung der biblischen Bücher folgt der Septuaginta.

Genesis		28,13f.	*542*
(ganze Schrift)	94, 542	29f.	582
Gen 1–Ex 12	76	35,16–26	582
1	76	47,31^{LXX}	545
2	*541*		
2,2	*541*	*Exodus*	
2,7	*541*	(ganze Schrift)	110
2,20–24	615f.	4,21	560
2,24	*541*	7,3	560
3	*580*	7,22	*561*
5,22	94	8,15	*561*
5,24	94	9,12	560
12	*542*	9,35	*561*
12,3	*542*	10,1	560
13,16	549	10,20	560
15	*543, 549*	10,27	560
15,5f.	*542*	11,10	560
15,5	541–545, 549	12	76
15,6	542, 615	13,15	*561*
15,7ff.	*549*	14,4	560
17,1–21	*549*	14,8	561
17,8	*542*	17,1–7	563
18,8	*542*	20,12	392, 405
18,32^{LXX}	*568*	20,17^{LXX}	*716*
21,12	541, 544f.	24,18	*81*
22	541, 548f.	25,17	*565*
22,9	548	30,10^{LXX}	*568*
22,11–13	545	32,16	*581*
22,16f.	541	33,3	*561*
22,17	541	33,5	*561*
22,18	541, *542*, 549	34,28	*81*
25,7–11	*542*		
26,3f.	*542*		

Leviticus			*Josua*	
16,13–15^{LXX}	565		(ganze Schrift)	91, 93
16,29	*423*		14,6–10	76
16,31	*423*		24,29	76
16,34^{LXX}	*568*			
17f.	584, *679*		*Ruth*	
19,18	*616*		(ganze Schrift)	86
Numeri			*2. Samuel*	
14	563		7	57
14,26–35	563		7,8	541
14,28–35	563		7,14	541, 560
14,30	76		9	540
16,21^{LXX}	*568*		21,12–15	*110*
22,31	718			
31,8	718f.		*1. Könige*	
			3,1–15	56f.
Deuteronomium			5,21	394
(ganze Schrift)	40, 79, 92, 98, 110,			
	181, 546, *562, 707*		*2. Könige*	
5,15	405		22f.	40
5,16	392			
5,21^{LXX}	*716*		*1. Chronik*	
7,6	396		(ganze Schrift)	86
9–10	563		23,31	*419*
9,1–10,22	*561f.*, 563			
9,23	563		*2. Chronik*	
9,27f.	563		(ganze Schrift)	86, *394*
9,27	561		2,11f.	*394*
10,16	561		8,13	*419*
14,2	396		26,22	41
17	540f.		35,25	41
17,6	541			
17,7	541		*Esra*	
18,20	715		(ganze Schrift)	86
29	540f.		7,6	81
29,4	541		8,21	*423*
29,18	541			
31–34	77		*Nehemia*	
32	77, 540f.		8	81
32,8^{LXX}	66			
32,13	*651*		*Judith*	
32,17	541		8,6	*419*
32,21	541			
32,35	541, 545		*Tobit*	
32,36	541		(ganze Schrift)	86f., 89, 94,
32,43	541			96, 99
32,43^{LXX}	560		1,21f.	39
33,1–3	693		2,10f.	39
			2,19	39

Stellenregister

Tobit (Fortsetzung)
14,10   39

1. Makkabäer
(ganze Schrift)   705

2. Makkabäer
(ganze Schrift)   674, *705*
1,1–10a   674
1,10b–2,18   674
2,13–15   42

4. Makkabäer
(ganze Schrift)   622
2,6   *580*
5,22–24   *415*
9,23   49
13,9   49

Psalmen
(ganze Schrift)   40f., *551*
2,7   560
4,4   392
8,3[LXX]   552
8,4–6   541
8,6   541
8,7   392
18,49   558
29,4[LXX]   *551*
33[LXX]   219
34[LXX]   219
35,13   *423*
64   41
68,19   392
69,9   558
70,20[LXX]   *551*
82   *66*
85,13[LXX]   *551*
89   57
94,8[LXX]   563
95   564
95(94)   563
95(94),8   563
95(94),10f.   563
105(104)   *562*
106   563
106(105)   *562*
106(105),20   *561*
106(105),24–27   563
110,1   541

117,1   558
118,6   558
145–148   41

Sprüche
(ganze Schrift)   41, 49, *201*
1–9   91, 93
1,1   41, 49
2,1   *299*
3   541
3,4   541
3,11f.   541
3,14f.   56
8,10f.   56
10,2   41
16,16   56
25,1   41
25,1[LXX]   201

Prediger
(ganze Schrift)   41, 49, 86, *218*
1,1   49
1,2   50
2,7–9   41
12,9–14   50

Hohes Lied
(ganze Schrift)   41, 86
1,1   41
5,1   201

Hiob
(ganze Schrift)   49
33,23   *70*
39,1   *651*
39,28   *651*

Sapientia Salomonis
(ganze Schrift)   17, 27, *46*, 49f., 52, 58, 162, 198, 200f., 349
1,1   53, 57
1,4   57
1,7–11   57
1,13f.   57
1,15   57
2   *55*
2,1–3,19   54
2,1–3,9   54
2,1–20   55

Sapientia Salomonis (Fortsetzung)
2,21–24	55
3,1–9	55
3,4	57
3,10–13	57
4,3–5	53
4,7–19	57
5,9–12	53
5,13	53
5,15–23	57
5,17–23	55, *392*, 405
5,18–23	57
6,1f.	52
6,1	53
6,12–16	54
6,12	55
7–9	53f., 56f.
7,1–9,18	56
7,1–22	54
7,1a	56
7,5f.	56
7,9f.	53
7,22–8,1	55
7,22b–8,1	54f.
8,2–9,18	54
8,8c	53
8,12	53
8,20	56
9,5	56
9,7	56
10,1–11,1	54
11–19	*562f.*, 564
11,1–14	55
11,15–12,2	55, 57
12,3–18	55
12,19–27	54
15,18–16,1	*55*
16–18	55
16,1–4	*55*
16,5–14	*55*
16,15–29	*55*
17,1–18,4	*55*
17,18f.	53
18,5–25	*55*
19,1–12	*55*
19,22	55, 57f.

Jesus Sirach
(ganze Schrift)	86, 212, *579*
2,1	740
3,1	740
3,17	740
44,23	*582*
50,27	40

Prolog Jesus Sirach
5	*299*

Hosea
(ganze Schrift)	41
2,13^{LXX}	54
9,5^{LXX}	54

Amos
(ganze Schrift)	41
5,21^{LXX}	54

Micha
(ganze Schrift)	41
1,3f.	*693*

Habakuk
2,3f.	541
2,4	538, 541–543, 548, 572
2,4^{LXX}	*548*

Zephanja
(ganze Schrift)	41

Haggai
(ganze Schrift)	41

Sacharja
(ganze Schrift)	41
1–6	94
5,1–4	*110*
8,16	392
11	66

Maleachi
(ganze Schrift)	41

Jesaja
(ganze Schrift) 40f.
1,13 *419*
8 540f.
8,12f. 540
8,14 540f.
8,17f. 541
52,7 *399*
53 541
53,1 541
53,12 541
54,1–6 748
55,3 *552*
57,19 *392, 399*
58,3 *423*
58,5 *423*
59,16f. 405
59,17 *55, 392*
59,20f.^{LXX} 547
59,21^{LXX} 547
59,21a *547*
61,8 *552*
62,4 748
63,11 551

Jeremia
(ganze Schrift) 41, 181, *547, 552*
8,8 181
25,31 *693*
29 674
29(36),1–23 674
31,31–34 541
31,33f. 541, 547, *552*
31,33 547
32(39),40 *552*
43,6f. 78

Baruch
(ganze Schrift) 63, 78, 674
1,1 78
4,10–16 748

Klagelieder
(ganze Schrift) 41, 91

Epistula Jeremiae
(ganze Schrift) 101, 649, 674

Ezechiel
(ganze Schrift) 41, 91
2,9 *110*
14,14 41, 49
16 748
16,60 *552*
34 *66*
37,26 *552*
40–48 94
45,17 *419*
46,11^{LXX} 54

Susanna
(ganze Schrift) 354

Daniel
(ganze Schrift) 61, 68f., 74, 79f., 88f., 211, 474, 676f.
1–6 68, 96
1,8 80
1,17 80
2 66, 68
2,25 79
3,17ff. 49
3,31 *676*
3,98$^{Theod.}$ *676*
4 96
4,34^{LXX} *676*
5,2 68
5,13 79
6,1 68
6,11 80
6,14 79
6,25$^{Theod.}$ *676*
6,26 *676*
6,29 68
7–12 41, 65–69, 72, 80
7 66, 68f., 79, 96
7,25 68
8 68
8,14 68
8,26 80
9 66, 68, *70*, 80
9,2 80
9,17 80
9,26f. 68
9,27 69, 80
10–12 68
10,1 68
11 68, 80

1.2 Neues Testament

Daniel (Fortsetzung)			
11,2	80	11,40	80
11,3–20	80	12,4	80f.
11,21–45	80	12,7	68
11,25–27	68	12,9	80
11,33	80	12,11	69

Matthäus		1,44	*659*
(ganze Schrift)	198, *221*, 343, *436*, 443, 558, *592*, 596, *625*, 638, *647*, *652*, *656*, 669, *704*	3,16–19	649
		3,18	651, 688
		3,29	546
		4,13–20	779
3,9	*545*	5,37	649
4,18–22	649	6,3	651, 687
4,21	552	6,11	*659*
5,9	*305*	7,27	*558*
10,2	649	8,29	649
10,3	688	8,34–37	*659*
10,4	651	9,2	649, *703*
12,32	546	9,5	649
12,45	*719*	9,43	*558*
13,18–23	779	9,45	*558*
13,55	651, 687	9,47	*558*
15,26	*558*	10,5	*560*
16,18	649, *666*, 703	10,28	649
17,1–8	707	10,38–40	*660*
18,8f.	*558*	11,21	649
19,8	*560*	12,36	541
21,16	552	13	438
22,15–22	*124*	13,3	649
22,21	*124*	14,24	552
22,44	541	14,32–43	*658*
24	438	14,33	649
25,24	*560*	14,37	649
25,35	*557*	14,43–52	*658*
26,28	552	14,53–72	*658*
26,34f.	638	14,62	541
26,69–75	638	14,70f.	*638*
		16,7	649
Markus		16,14	*560*
(ganze Schrift)	196, 198, *324*, 340, 343, 443, 558, 638, *704*	16,19	541
1,16–20	649	Lukas	
1,16	704	(ganze Schrift)	196, 198, 340, 342f., 443
1,19	552		
1,29	649	1,1–4	*307*, 342

Stellenregister 835

Lukas (Fortsetzung)	
1,2	*302*
1,3	*329*, 770
1,72	552
2,25	*705*
2,35	*705*
3,8	545
3,30	*705*
6,13f.	649
6,14–16	687
6,15	651
6,40	552
8,11–15	779
9,5	*659*
11,26	*719*
12,10	546
12,32	*657*
20,42f.	541
21	438
22,20	552
22,28	*658*
22,31f.	649, *666*
22,69	541
24,34	649

Johannes	
(ganze Schrift)	198, 341–343, 443, *471*, 649, *704*, 733–735, 737, 740, *753*
1,42	*704*, 706
3,29	*753*
6,60	*560*
7,35	*585*
11,11	*753*
13–17	711
13,1–30	*707*
13,31–16,33	*707*
13,33f.	740
13,36f.	706
14,16f.	711
14,26	711
15,13–15	*753*
15,18ff.	711
15,26	711
16,2f.	711
16,7–15	711
16,16ff.	711
17,1–24	*707*
18,15–27	*658*
20,2–10	649
20,29–31	*738*
21	342, 649
21,1–14	649
21,7	649
21,15–17	649, 657, *666*
21,18f.	660
21,18	706
21,20–23	649
21,20	342
21,22f.	692
21,24	342, 737

Apostelgeschichte	
(ganze Schrift)	198, 290, 292, *303*, 323, 333f., 341, 345, 350, 443, 530, 542, 549, 552, 572, *625*, 656f., 666, 669f., 672, 680f., *705*, 761, 771, 780, 784
1–12	649
1,1	770
1,3	155
1,13	651, 687
2,30	540
2,34f.	541
2,42–47	594
2,44	594
3,25	*542*, 549, 552
4,13	*647*
4,32–35	594
4,32	594
4,36	652
5,18	659
5,40f.	636, 659
6,1–6	*594*
7,5	*542*
7,8	552
7,51	*560*
8	*329*
8,22	546
9,15	780
9,36	*652*
10f.	678
11,30	656
12f.	670
12	615
12,2	*660*
12,3–11	659, *660*
12,12	*328*, 670, 680

836 Stellenregister

Apostelgeschichte (Fortsetzung)
12,17	679
12,25	*328*, 670
13,1	705
13,33	560
14,3	*659*
14,23	761
15	577, 588, *593*, *618*, 666, 670, 676–680
15,2	656
15,3–12	*680*
15,4	656
15,6–35	680
15,6	656
15,7–11	677f.
15,11	678
15,13–33	*680*
15,13–21	593
15,14	*650, 705*
15,20	577, 583, *593*, 595, 679
15,21	593
15,22–32	*150*
15,22f.	656, 665, *666*
15,22	666
15,23–29	676f.
15,25	666
15,27	666
15,29	577, 583, 595, 679
15,30	*304*
15,32	677
15,37–39	*328*
15,40–18,5	666
15,40	666, 680
16,4	656
16,7	679
16,37f.	771
16,37	*665*
17,34	194
18,2	555, *679*
18,12–17	771
18,18	679
18,26	679
19f.	292
19,9	560
19,29	753
20	657
20,4	753, 770
20,17	657, 680
20,18–35	707
20,28f.	657, 680

20,28	*657*, 761
21,18–26	588
21,18–25	*618*
21,18	656
21,25	679
22,3	771
22,25–29	771
23,11	780
23,26–30	*321*
23,27	771
26,14	*560*
27	*292*
27,2	*328*
28,3–10	780

Römerbrief
(ganze Schrift)	22, 198, *392*, *403*, 420, 453, 509, 524, *526*, *528*, 588f.
1–3	*539, 561, 565*
1f.	*561*
1	573
1,1	*323, 381, 573, 650, 689, 706*
1,3f.	*329*, 560
1,3	559
1,4	550
1,7	*325, 335*, 550
1,8	*325*, 474
1,9	*325, 573*
1,15	*335, 573*
1,16f.	*542, 561*
1,16	*573*
1,17	538, 541f., 548
1,18–3,20	565
1,18–2,11	564
1,18–32	561
1,22f.	561
1,23	445, *561*
2	*543*, 561, 563, 573
2,1–11	*561*
2,5–11	*561*
2,5	445, *560*, 561, *563f.*
2,7	*543*
2,10	553
2,15	559
2,16	*573*
2,25–29	*328*
2,28f.	*401*
3	569, 572

Römerbrief (Fortsetzung)		9,1	559
3,3	548	9,4f.	401
3,7	445	9,4	552
3,8	*553*, 588, 617, *699f.*	9,6–8	*544*
3,9–20	539	9,6	*550*
3,21	*402*	9,7	541, 544, *545*
3,23	445	9,11	*553*
3,24f.	540, 565	9,17	560
3,24	571	9,18	560
3,25f.	573	9,21	*653*
3,25	539f., 565f., 569f.	9,22	552
3,26	572	9,33	541
3,28	542, 615	10,6f.	*551*
3,31	*401*	10,7	551
4	*543*, 544, 616	10,9f.	559
4,1–25	542	10,15	*573*
4,13ff.	*375*	10,16	541, *573*
4,18	541f., 549	10,19	541
4,19	549	11,3	559
4,20	445	11,7	*560*
4,24f.	428	11,8	541
4,24	550	11,12	*328*
5,2	445	11,25	*328*, 560
5,3–5	579	11,27	541, 547, 552
5,15	*328*	11,28	*573*
6	*328*, *398*, *428*, *429*, *430*, 573	11,29	445
		11,33–36	551
6,2–8	428	11,36	454, 554
6,4	*328*, 428f., 445, 556	12–15	*573*
6,6	779	12,1f.	553, 559
6,8	*328*, 429, *430*	12,1	403, 554
6,10	538, 566–569, 572	12,2	554
6,11	*398*	12,4–8	557
7,2	*401*	12,4f.	557
7,6	*401*	12,9	558
7,7	*580*	12,10	556f.
7,13	451, *553*	12,12	557
7,18	*553*	12,13	557
7,19	*553*	12,16	*423*
8	*560*	12,19	541, 545f.
8,4	*328*, 468, 556	13,1–7	559
8,9–11	428	13,3	*553*
8,10	546	13,4	*553*
8,11	550	13,5	559
8,23	556	13,9	*580*
8,28	*553*	13,10	*328*
8,29	396, *560*	13,11f.	*465*
8,38	700	13,12	586
9–11	564	13,13	*328*, 556
9	*402*	13,14	586

Römerbrief (Fortsetzung)

14f.	421
14	420f., 432
14,3	*417*, 420f.
14,4f.	420
14,6	421
14,10–12	465
14,13	420f.
14,15	556
14,17	444, 558
14,18	554
14,19	421
14,20	420, 556
14,21	558
15	573
15,2	421, 451
15,3	*553*, 558
15,9–13	551
15,9	558
15,10	541
15,11	558
15,13	*328*
15,16	*573*
15,19	*573*
15,20	*573*
15,22–29	554
15,25–28	554
15,25	573
15,26	*323*, 556, 593
15,29	*328*, 573
15,30	554, 559
15,31	451
15,33	466, 550
16	554, 573
16,1f.	*664*
16,3–16	555
16,3	*653, 679*
16,14	*346*, 554
16,16	555
16,16a	555
16,17–20	*425*
16,17	554
16,18	425
16,20	466, 550, 552, 555
16,21–23	*555*
16,21	554
16,22	*150*
16,23	*753*
16,25–27	*425*, 554
16,27	554

1. Korintherbrief

1–2	*328*
1,1	*150*, *325*, 381, *650*, *769*
1,2	*335*
1,3	550
1,4	*325*
1,6	558
1,7	444
1,9	466
1,10	552f.
1,14	*753*
1,16	*329*
1,26	445
1,27	*396*
2,4	*474*
3,3	*328*
3,6–11	422
3,9–15	*328*
3,18	*417*
3,21	*417*
4,5	444
4,15	*670*
4,16	49
4,17	*664*
4,20	444
5,5–7	546
5,9–11	*477*
5,9	329, *339*, 480
5,10	*557*
5,13	541
6,3	699
6,9f.	463
6,9	444
6,10	444
6,14	428
6,15	557
6,16	541
7	432
7,1	329, 423f., 558
7,8	558
7,17	*328*
7,20	445
7,26	558
7,29	*465*
7,31	*465*
8	432
8,1–13	421
8,7	559
8,8	558
8,10	559

1. Korintherbrief (Fortsetzung)

8,12	559
9,1	381
9,2	*600*
9,3–12	*477*
9,5	649, 679, 687, 703
9,7	*657*
9,13	451, 559
9,22	777f.
9,24	*417*
10	432
10,13b	466
10,18	559
10,20	541
10,22	541
10,23–11,1	421
10,23f.	422
10,24	*417*
10,25	559
10,27	559
10,28	559
10,29	559
10,31	445
10,33	777f.
11,1	49, *474*
11,2–16	*328*
11,30–32	546
12	427
12,4–6	558
12,12–27	426, 557
12,20f.	427
12,26	557
13,1	699
13,4	450
13,7	450
14,6	445
14,20	445
14,33	466
14,34f.	*177*
15	*329*, 430
15,1	422
15,5	649, 703f.
15,6	566, *567f.*
15,8	381
15,9	583
15,12–22	428
15,12–19	*543*
15,20–28	464, 467
15,21–28	464
15,23–52	474
15,24	*429*, 444, 699
15,25	541
15,27	541
15,35–58	543
15,35–37	*543*
15,45	541
15,50	444, 463
15,54f.	*549*
15,58	*328*
16	292
16,10f.	*664*
16,15	554
16,19	*679*
16,20	554f.
16,21	*150*, 380, 384, 469
16,22	*465*
16,23	552

2. Korintherbrief

1,1	*150*, *325*, 374, 381, 650, 769
1,2	550
1,3ff.	394
1,3–10	394
1,3f.	*553*
1,3	*325*
1,8	777
1,12	559
1,18	466
1,19	*666*
1,21	558
1,22	*395*
3,6	552
3,14	552
3,18	445
4,2	559
4,4	445
4,6	445
4,10	*556*
4,14	428
4,16–5,10	*543*
4,16	779
5,1–5	*543*
5,9	554
5,10	465, *553*
5,11	559
5,14	*566*, 567
5,17	546
6,5	*556*
6,18	541

2. Korintherbrief (Fortsetzung)

7,2	*474*
7,6	*423*
7,10	546
8,9	560
8,17f.	*664*
8,21	541
8,23	*653*
10–13	382
10	386
10,1	*423*
10,8	*422*
11	468
11,2	748
11,12	451
11,13	382
11,25	*566*
11,27	*556*
11,29	557
11,31	558
12	380
12,1	445
12,2–4	155
12,7	445
12,19	*422*
13,9	552
13,10	*422*
13,11	466, *477*, 550, 552f.
13,12	555
13,12a	555
13,12b	555
13,13	552, 555

Galaterbrief

1–2	*323*
1f.	380
1,1	381, 550, *650*
1,2	*150*, 554
1,3	550
1,4	464
1,6	*300*, 445
1,8	684
1,9	422
1,11	454
1,12–2,21	684
1,12	445, 454
1,13	583
1,15	445
1,16	381
1,17	649
1,18–2,14	617
1,18f.	649
1,19	600
2,1–14	577
2,1–10	577, 588
2,2	445
2,3–8	*524*
2,4	*715*
2,7–14	*619*
2,7	*712*
2,9	345, 703
2,10	*323*, 593, *619*
2,11ff.	*703*
2,11–21	*678*, 708
2,11–15	679
2,11–14	597, 617, *619*
2,12	*618*
2,14	468
2,15f.	615
3–4	544
3	*402, 543*
3,6ff.	*375*
3,6–29	542
3,6–9	616
3,8	541, *542*, 548
3,11	541, 548
3,14	451
3,15	552
3,16	541, *542*, 548
3,17	552
4,3	*328*, 407
4,4	*328*
4,9	*328*, 407
4,18	558
4,21–5,1	616
4,24	552
4,30	541
5,1	684
5,11f.	684
5,13	445
5,16	*328*
5,17	615
5,21	444, 463
5,22–26	553
5,25	468
6,1	553
6,6	*553*
6,10	*553*
6,11	*150*, 380, 384, 469
6,12f.	684

Stellenregister

Galaterbrief (Fortsetzung)		3,6	402f.
6,17	*417*	3,8	389
6,18	552, 555	3,10	405
		3,13	772
Epheserbrief		3,17	399
1–3	391	3,19	399
1,1	*325, 335, 389, 400,*	4,1–6,9	404
	650, 768	4,1–16	*404*
1,2	550	4,1–6	404
1,3–14	394f.	4,1	389, 403f., 772
1,3	*325*	4,3	404
1,4	396, *400, 403*	4,4	404
1,7	396f., *403*	4,7–16	404
1,10	397	4,8	392
1,11	396, 404	4,11	*657*
1,13f.	*395, 403*	4,12	553
1,13	395, *403*	4,13	404
1,15–23	394	4,14	*556*
1,16	*325*	4,16	*404*
1,20	541, 550	4,17–24	*404*
1,21	405, 700	4,17	*403f.*, 405
1,22	392, 541	4,18	*403*
2,1ff.	398	4,21f.	399
2,1–10	*398*, 399	4,22–24	586, 779
2,1–3	401	4,22	*403*
2,1	397, *398, 403*	4,24	*403*
2,2	398, 405	4,25–32	*404*
2,3	*403*	4,25f.	392
2,5f.	397, 402	4,30	*403*
2,5	*398*	5,1f.	404
2,6f.	398	5,1	49
2,7–9	699	5,3–14	*404*
2,8–10	*398*	5,6	399
2,8	398	5,8	*403*
2,10	398, *403*, 404	5,10	554
2,11ff.	396	5,15–20	*404*
2,11–22	*389*, 399	5,18	558
2,11f.	399	5,21–6,9	*328, 404*
2,12	401, *403*, 552	5,31	392
2,14	399f.	6,2f.	392
2,15	402, *403*	6,2	405
2,16	400	6,10–20	*392*, 405
2,17	*392*, 400	6,10–17	*389*
2,18	400	6,18	*556*
2,19	*400*, 402	6,20f.	389
2,20	*408*, 692	6,20	772
3,1–10	*408*, 773	6,21f.	391, *664*, 772
3,1	*328*, 389, 403, *404*, 772	6,21	215, 770
3,3f.	408	6,24	552, 555
3,5	692		

Philipperbrief
(ganze Schrift)   198, 443, 453, *524,*
                  526, 528
1,1   *150, 323, 325,* 381,
                  689, 769
1,2   550
1,3f.   *325*
1,3   *325*
1,4   *325*
1,9f.   451
1,12–18   327
1,12   777
1,13   771
1,14   554
1,18   446
1,20–23   *543*
1,21–26   327
1,21–25   *543*
1,27   446
2,3   *423*
2,6–11   560
2,13   553
2,17   559
2,19–30   327
2,19–23   *555*
2,25–30   *664*
2,25   *653*
3   468
3,3   *401*
3,14   *417*
3,17   49
3,21   *543*
4,3   *653*
4,5   465
4,9   422, 466, 550
4,12   *423*
4,15f.   469
4,16   566
4,18   554, 559
4,19   553
4,20   558
4,21   327, 554f.
4,22   555, 771
4,23   552, 555

Kolosserbrief
1,1   151, *325,* 650, *769*
1,2   412, 550
1,3   *325*
1,6   413

1,7f.   *329*
1,7   *653,* 770
1,9   *325*
1,14   396
1,15–20   *388,* 397, 426f.
1,16   700, 776
1,18   *417,* 426f.
1,20–23   *388*
1,20   396
1,22   396
1,23   397, 406
1,24f.   *328*
1,24   772
1,26f.   403
2   412, 420f.
2,1   *408,* 412f., 777
2,4   773
2,6–23   397
2,6–13   *328*
2,6f.   399, 422, 427
2,6   *328*
2,7   *328,* 397, 558
2,8–3,4   391
2,8ff.   382
2,8   *328,* 399, 407, 411,
                  414, *415,* 417–419,
                  428, 773
2,9f.   399
2,9   *328*
2,10   *328, 429,* 700
2,11–13   *328*
2,11   *401*
2,12–14   426
2,12   397, 428f., 431, 550
2,13   397
2,14   402, 430
2,15   *429,* 700
2,16–23   411f., 414–416, 418,
                  420, 423–426, 431
2,16   *416,* 417, *418,* 420, 773
2,18   *416,* 417, *418f.,* 700
2,19f.   426
2,19   *417,* 421, 426–428
2,20–23   423
2,20   404, 407, 425f.,
                  428, 430
2,21ff.   423
2,22f.   *418*
2,23   *419, 423,* 424f.
3,1–4   404

Stellenregister 843

Kolosserbrief (Fortsetzung)		2,12	444, 459, *466*
3,1	404, 541	2,13	422, 459, *466*, *483*
3,2	406	2,14–16	474
3,5	406, *549*	2,14f.	459
3,8–10	586	2,14	459, 583
3,9f.	779	2,18	*566*
3,12–15	404	2,19	459, 552
3,12	*423*	3,2	445, 460, *653*
3,20	554	3,4	460, *483*
4,7–17	770	3,6	460
4,7–9	328, *664*	3,8	445, 460
4,7f.	391, 407	3,10	552f.
4,7	215, *653*, 770	3,11–4,2	458
4,10–14	*555*	3,11–13	*474*
4,10	328, *671*	3,11	444, 459f.
4,11	*653*	3,12	459f.
4,13	*408*, 412	3,13	445, 459f., 558
4,14	770	4f.	384
4,15–18	*555*	4,1f.	458, 460
4,15	748	4,1	422, 458–461
4,16	155, 329, 334, *339*, *408*, 412	4,1–12	458
		4,2	458, 460
4,18	151, 555, 772	4,3–7	*557*
		4,3–9	458
1. Thessalonicherbrief		4,5f.	459
1,1	*150*, *325*, 381, 383, 457, 459, 649f., *666*, 676, *706*, *769*, 770	4,7–10	449
		4,7	445, 460
		4,9	556
1,2–8	458	4,10–12	458, 461
1,2–4	448	4,13–5,11	457
1,2f.	459	4,13–18	438
1,2	*325*, 444, 460	4,13	777
1,3	459f., 463	4,14–18	474
1,4	460, 466	4,14–17	428
1,5	*474*	4,14f.	460
1,6f.	448, 460	4,14	*543*
1,6	49, *377*, 459, *474*, *479*	4,15	438, 465, *543*
1,7f.	448, 459	4,16	459
1,8	*474*	4,17	460
1,9f.	465	5,1–11	449, 464
1,15	467	5,1f.	464
1,17	459	5,3	465
2,1–6	458	5,9	460
2,1	460	5,11	422
2,2	*466*	5,12	460
2,5	*474*	5,13f.	461
2,6–12	*474*	5,14	460f., 554
2,7–3,10	458	5,15	451, *553*
2,9	454, 460f., 468, *485*	5,16–22	449
2,12f.	460	5,19f.	451

1. Thessalonicherbrief (Fortsetzung)

5,21	468
5,23f.	553
5,23	459, 461, 466, *474*, 550, 553
5,24	458, 460, 466
5,25	460, *474*, 559
5,26	554f.
5,27	380
5,28	461, 552, 555

2. Thessalonicherbrief

1,1f.	457, 459, 463, 706
1,1	151, *325*, 383, 439, 444, *666*, 769
1,2	550
1,3–12	437, 449, 458
1,3	*325*, 446, 457, 459, 463, *474*, 482
1,4–6	444
1,4	439, 457–459, 473, 479, 485f.
1,5	444, 459, 463
1,6–10	444, 457
1,6	449
1,7–10	438
1,7	444, 459, *475*
1,8	*438*, 451, 459, *475*, *552*
1,10	451, 459, *474*, 481f.
1,11	*325*, 445, 451, 459f., 463
1,12	466, *552*
2	382, 475
2,1–12	439f., 464, 472, 475
2,1–3	181
2,1f.	384
2,1	460
2,2–9	457
2,2	158, *182*, 202, *383f.*, 385, 407, 474f., 478, 480f., *484*, 776
2,3–12	475, *477*
2,3–9	474
2,3	482
2,3b	*482*
2,4	464
2,5	436, 460, 473, 476f., 482f.
2,7	444, 475
2,8	465, *475*
2,9	452, 475
2,10	*474*
2,11	475
2,13f.	460, *483*
2,13	459, 466, *482*
2,14f.	483
2,14	445, 483
2,15–3,5	458
2,15	384, 445, 460, 474, 484
2,16	459f.
2,17	445, 455, 460, 553, 558
3	478
3,1–3	458
3,1f.	*474*, 486f.
3,1	459f.
3,2	488
3,2b	449
3,3	460, 466
3,4	460
3,5	444, 460, *474*
3,6–12	458, *474*
3,6–10	484
3,6f.	458, 460
3,6	484
3,7–13	488
3,7–9	477, 485
3,7	49, *377*, 468, 477
3,8	460f., *485*
3,9	49, *377*, 460, 469
3,10–12	458, 461
3,10	460, *483*, 485
3,11	487
3,12	554
3,14	*477*
3,15	439, 461
3,16	459, 461, 466, *474*, 477, 553
3,17	151, 380, 384, 449, 469, 768
3,17b	*478*
3,18	461, 552, 555

1. Timotheusbrief

1,1–3	292
1,1	*325, 650*
1,2	299, *325*, 550, *670*
1,3ff.	382
1,3	279, 290
1,12–17	*311*, 773
1,12	*325*

Stellenregister

1. Timotheusbrief (Fortsetzung)

1,18–20	773
1,18	*670*
1,20	278
2,1f.	293
2,5f.	*566*, 567
2,7	*311*
2,9–15	533
2,11	*365*
3,2	557
3,3	*556*, 557
3,5	756
3,14f.	292, *311*
4,1–5	*503*
4,8	424f.
4,13	292, 444
5,3–16	*503*
5,10	557
5,17	761
5,23	773
6,3ff.	382
6,8	557
6,12f.	213
6,20f.	291
6,20	213, 382, 505, *524*
6,21	555

2. Timotheusbrief

1	291
1,1	*325, 650*
1,2	299, *325*, 550, *670*
1,3–7	*311*
1,3	*325*
1,4	*290*
1,5	*276*
1,6	*290*
1,8	*329*
1,12	291
1,13	*290*
1,14	291
1,15	*290, 546f., 679*
1,16–18	*276*
1,16f.	*276*
1,18	*290*
2,1	*670*
2,10	755
2,14ff.	382
2,16–18	*276*
2,17f.	278
2,18	213
3,10f.	*311*
3,11f.	293
3,16	*524*
4,6–18	*311*
4,6–8	291, 772
4,9–21	773
4,9–20	293
4,9–16	546
4,9	555
4,10–15	770
4,10	290, *547*
4,11	555, *671*
4,12	278
4,13	326, 530, 555
4,14f.	278
4,16–18	291
4,16	547
4,19–21	*329*
4,19f.	278, 770
4,19	276, 555, *679*
4,21	278, *329*, 555

Titusbrief

1,1	325, 382, *650, 706*, 756
1,4	299, *325*, 550, *670*
1,5	279, 290
1,7	*717*
1,8	557
1,10ff.	382
1,12	773
2,9	554
3,1f.	293
3,5	586
3,12–14	*329*
3,12f.	278, 770, 773
3,12	278
3,15	555

Philemonbrief

(ganze Schrift)	198, *202*, 328, 334–336, 381, 388, *392*, *526*, 528, 770
1	*150*, 327, 381, *653*, 769
2	*336*, 769
3	550
4	*325*
6	*553*
9	327
10	*670*
11	*150*

846 Stellenregister

Philemonbrief (Fortsetzung)		8,1	541
21f.	380, 554	8,5	548
22	*554*	8,8–12	541
23f.	*328*	8,8–10	*552*
23	*336*, 770	8,10	547
24	*653, 671*	8,13	565
25	555	9	573
		9,1–10	565
Hebräerbrief		9,5	565
1–12	540, 553, 559	9,7	*566f.*
1–3	*573*	9,12	566f., *568*
1,2	541	9,15–17	*552*
1,3	541	9,20	*552*
1,5	541, 560	9,21f.	566
1,6	541, *560*	9,26–28	567
1,8	560	9,26	*566f.*
1,10	*552*	9,27	*566f.*
1,13	541	9,28	541, *566f.*
2,3	*552*	10	573
2,4	*659, 662*	10,2	*566f.*
2,6–8	541	10,5	553
2,13	541	10,8–22	*538*
2,14–5,5	*538*	10,10	554, 566f., *568*
3f.	563	10,12f.	541
3,1	554	10,16f.	541
3,6	*571*	10,16	547, *552*
3,8	560f.	10,19–22	571
3,13	560f.	10,19	554, *570f.*
3,15	560f.	10,22	*573*
3,16–19	563	10,26–31	571, *719*
4,2	*573*	10,26f.	*546*
4,4	541	10,26	546
4,6	*573*	10,28	541
4,7	560f.	10,29–11,13	*538*
4,16	*571*	10,29	546, *552*
6,1	*551*	10,30	541
6,2	*546*	10,30a	541, 545f.
6,4–6	*719*	10,32–39	543
6,4	546, *566–568*	10,32–34	544
6,12	*573*	10,32	*554*
6,13f.	541	10,35	*570, 571*
7–10	573	10,37f.	541, *543*, 548
7	573	10,38	*548*
7,14	*552*	10,39	*573*
7,16	*551*	11	540, *545*, 573
7,22	*552*	11,1–3	544
7,24	*551*	11,1	548
7,26f.	566	11,3	*553*
7,27	567, *568*	11,4ff.	49
8,1–10,18	565	11,4	*346*

Stellenregister 847

Hebräerbrief (Fortsetzung)

11,5	*543*
11,6	570
11,8	*549*
11,12	541, 543f., 549
11,13	543
11,17–19	*545*
11,18	541, 545
11,19	*545*
11,27	544
11,28–12,17	*538*
11,28	*560*
11,32–38	544
11,35	*551*
12,1f.	49
12,1	*544, 659*
12,2f.	49
12,2	541, 544, *573*
12,4	*549*
12,5f.	541
12,14	*552*
12,15	541
12,23	*560*
12,24	*552*
12,26	*566f.*
12,27	*566f.*
13	540, 555f., 559, 573
13,1	*556f.*
13,2	*556f.*
13,3	557
13,4f.	557
13,4	556
13,5	*556*
13,6	558
13,7	559, *573*
13,8	554, 558
13,9	556, 558
13,13	544
13,15	556
13,16	556
13,17	556, 559
13,18–25	768
13,18	559
13,18a	559
13,19	*554*
13,20–25	538, 573
13,20f.	551
13,20	550, *552*
13,21	553, *558*
13,22–25	554
13,22	554
13,23	*327*, 554, 770
13,24	539, 555
13,25	555

Jakobusbrief

1,1	575, *584*, *585*, 649, 667, 675, *687*, *689*
1,1b	*584*
1,2f.	579
1,5f.	*324*
1,7	*324*
1,9	*324*
1,11	*324*
1,13	581
1,14f.	579f.
1,16	*324*
1,17	581
1,18	*582*, 586f.
1,18b	582, 585
1,21	586f.
1,27	595, 619
2,1–7	*323*
2,8–11	*616*
2,12ff.	689
2,14ff.	*375*
2,14–26	587f., *589, 675*
2,14	*324*
2,15–17	*324*
2,17	*324*
2,18f.	*324*
2,18	322
2,19	*324*
2,21–23	589
2,21f.	*549*
2,21	548f.
3,1–12	621
3,3f.	*621*
3,4	*560*
3,13–4,10	*621*
3,15	689
4,4	585
4,5	615
4,6–10	582
5,14–16	*609*
5,19f.	689

1. Petrusbrief

1,1	585, 650, *665*, 667, 669, *705f.*, 711

1. Petrusbrief (Fortsetzung)

1,1a	648
1,2	641
1,3	*394*
1,6f.	579
1,7	636
1,11	636f., 661, *662*
1,12	*676*
1,14	*653*
1,17	585
1,21	636, *662*
1,22–2,2	586f.
1,22	556
1,23	779
2,1–10	678
2,1f.	586
2,5	559
2,9	585
2,11	585, *662*
3,7f.	*653*
3,15	638
3,16	*559*
3,17f.	637
3,18	*566f.*
3,20	*641*
3,21	*559*
3,22	*662*
4,1	637
4,4	*653*
4,9	*557*
4,12	*653*
4,13	635, 659, 661, *662*
4,14–16	*637*
4,14	636
4,16	638
5,1–4	657, 680
5,1f.	*657*
5,1	554, 635f., 645, 652–654, 659, *660*, 661, *662*, 708
5,2–4	652
5,2f.	*657*
5,2	656f.
5,3	658
5,5	*559*, 652
5,5a	658
5,5b	658
5,9	670
5,10	553, 635
5,11	*662*
5,12f.	670
5,12	150, 662, 664f., 678, 706
5,13	*555*, *646*, 667, *668*, 670–673, 748
5,14	555, 636
5,14a	555

2. Petrusbrief

1–3	710
1,1–3	709
1,1	*650*, 705f., 711
1,2	641
1,3f.	709, 711
1,7	556
1,8	*714*
1,9	712, 715, 720, 724
1,11	711
1,12–15	729
1,12f.	709
1,12	640, 642, 706
1,13	642, 706
1,14f.	692, 708f.
1,15	642, 707–709, 712, 730
1,16–18	596, 641, 706
1,16f.	724
1,16	705f., 709, *715*, 723
1,18	706
1,19–21	709, *715*, 723
1,19f.	709
1,20f.	724
2	382, 716, 721, 726
2,1–3,3	727
2,1–22	708, 714
2,1	710, 713f., 717, 720, 724
2,2	*710*, 713, *718*, 719f., 723, 725
2,3f.	720
2,3	720, 725
2,3b	723
2,4–10a	716
2,4–9	710
2,4	698, 710, 716
2,5	*641*
2,6	698, 720
2,7f.	716
2,7	720, 725
2,9f.	720
2,9	713, 716

Stellenregister

2. Petrusbrief (Fortsetzung)		1,1–5	737
2,10f.	*722*	1,1–3	737
2,10	*710*, 720, 724f.	1,1	737
2,10a	716f.	1,3	739
2,10b	717f.	1,4	737
2,11	*699, 722*	2,1	738, 740
2,12–14	717	2,3–6	743
2,12	*717*, 719–721, 724f.	2,7–17	740
2,13	713, 718, 720f., 724f.	2,7f.	743
2,14	713, 718, 720f., 725	2,9–11	741
2,15f.	718, 725	2,12–14	748
2,15	720	2,18–3,18	741
2,16	707, *715*, 719	2,18	744
2,17	*719*, 720, *727*	2,19	744
2,18–22	727	2,22f.	744
2,18	712, 720, 725	2,22	*762*
2,19–22	713	3,1–10	741
2,19	720, 724	3,1f.	741
2,20–22	715	3,10	741
2,20	712, 720	3,11	743
2,21	719	3,13–17	741
2,22	714, 719f., 724f.	4	382, 742
3	*716*	4,1	744
3,1–13	708, 714	4,2f.	744
3,1–3	710	4,2	*762*
3,1f.	730	4,7–21	743
3,1	216, 640–642, 705, 708–710, 729	4,7	743
3,2ff.	707	2. Johannesbrief	
3,2	642	(ganze Schrift)	333, 343f., 350, 743–746, 749f., *751*, 752f., *754*, 755–757, 761–763
3,3ff.	721		
3,3–13	712, 726f.		
3,3f.	709, 728	1–3	743
3,3	709f., 724	1	747
3,4	723	3	677
3,9	723	4	743, 747f.
3,14–16	708	5f.	743
3,14	725	5	743, 748
3,15f.	216, *375*, 701, 705	6	743, 747f.
3,15	385, *708*, 724	7ff.	382
3,16f.	*776*	7	744, *762*
3,16	*679*	8	744, 747
3,17	706f., 709, 714, 729f.	9–11	744, 749
		10	747
1. Johannesbrief		11	749
(ganze Schrift)	*218*, 333, 343–345, 350, 353, 355, 443, 671, 736, 738–740, 742–746, 748–750, 751–755, 757f., 760	12f.	743
		12	554, 744, 746f., 749, 752
		13	747f.

3. Johannesbrief

(ganze Schrift)	23, 333, 343f., 350, 443, *735, 738*, 743, 745, 751–755, 757f., 762
1	752f.
2–4	752
2	754
3f.	753
3	753f.
4	754
5–8	754
5	*557,* 752, 754
6	755
7	754
8	752
9f.	752
9	752, 755f.
10	754, 756f.
11f.	757
11	754
12	752
13	554, 745f., 752
15	555
15a	*555*
15b	*555*

Judasbrief

1	158, 216, *592, 650, 687,* 691, 693, *706*
2	*641, 677,* 693
3ff.	382
3	*566,* 691, 693, 695
4	691, 693–695, 697, 699–701, 709, *715,* 724f.
5–7	694, 715
5	*566,* 691
6f.	722
6	697–699, *719*
7	698f., 702, 716, 725
8–10	697, 722
8	691, 693, 695–697, *716f.,* 724f.
9	697f., *717,* 728
10	693, 695, 717, 724f.
11	691, 694f., 701, 718f., 725
12	691, 693–695, *696,* 701, 713, 717, *718,* 719, 724f.
13	695, 719, 725, *727*
14f.	*693,* 694, 697, 702
15f.	695
15	*560,* 694
16	693, 695, *696,* 701, *717,* 725
17f.	688, 710, 728
17	691, 693, *709,* 710
18	692, 694f., *696,* 702, 724
19	689, 693, 695, *696,* 697, *717*
20–23	691
20	*691,* 693
21	689
22f.	689, 694f., 701, *713,* 714
23	695
24f.	691
24	693

Johannesapokalypse

(ganze Schrift)	129, 198, *324,* 438f., 443, 475, 669, *734*
1,9	*379*
2f.	198, *375*
2,14	719
2,20	470
6,10f.	464
7,7	*705*
7,14	464
11,18	464
13,1–8	69
13,2	464, *475*
13,4	464
13,6	464
13,8	464
13,12	464
13,13	*475*
13,14	464, *475*
13,15	464
14,8	*668*
16,13	464
16,19	*668*
17,5	475, *668*
17,7	*475*
17,18	464

Johannesapokalypse (Fortsetzung)		19,14	464
18,2	668	19,15	475
18,10	668	19,18	475
18,21	668	19,20	464, 475
19,10	653	20,10	464
19,12	464, 475	22,9	653

2. Altorientalische Literatur

*Prophezeihungen eines
ägyptischen Weisen*
(ganzes Werk)   37

Babylonische Theodizee
(ganzes Werk)   38

*Die Geschichte und die Sprüche des
weisen Achiqar*
(ganzes Werk)   35, 99

*Dumizi und Enkidu: Der Disput
zwischen dem Hirten-Gott
und dem Bauern-Gott*
(ganzes Werk)   29

Geburtslegende des Sargon
(ganzes Werk)   30

Gedicht des leidenden Gerechten
(ganzes Werk)   38

Gesetzeskodex des Hammurapi
(ganzes Werk)   29

Gesetzeskodex des Lipit-Ishtar
(ganzes Werk)   29

Gilgameschepos
(ganzes Werk)   30

Katalog von Texten und Autoren
(ganzes Werk)   38

Klage des Khakheperre-sonbe
(ganzes Werk)   37

Legende des Naram Sin
(ganzes Werk)   30

Lehre Amenemhets
(ganzes Werk)   32

Lehre des Amenemope
(ganzes Werk)   34

Lehre des Amennakhte
(ganzes Werk)   37

Lehre des Anchscheschonqi
(ganzes Werk)   45

Lehre des Any
(ganzes Werk)   34

Lehre des Kheti, des Sohnes von Duauf
(ganzes Werk)   36f.

Lehre des Pordjel
(ganzes Werk)   37

Lehre des Prinzen Hordedef
(ganzes Werk)   36

Lehre des Ptahhotep
(ganzes Werk)   31

Lehre des Schuruppak
(ganzes Werk)   38

Lehre eines Mannes für seinen Sohn
(ganzes Werk)   36

Lehre für Kagemni
(ganzes Werk)   36

Lehre für Merikare
(ganzes Werk)   32

Lied des Era
(ganzes Werk) 30

Lob des gelehrten Schreibers
(ganzes Werk) 36

Rede des Sisobek
(ganzes Werk) 37

Schamasch-Hymnus
(ganzes Werk) 38

3. Frühjüdische Literatur

3.1 Philo von Alexandrien

De Abrahamo
235	*594*
236	*580*
238	*580*

De confusione linguarum
21	*580*
63	*49*
90	*580*
94	*581*

De congressu eruditionis gratia
74–76	*45*
172	*580*

De decalogo
111	*49*
142–145	*580*
142–153	*580*
142	*580*
173	*580*

De ebrietate
223	*580*

De Josepho
79	*580*

De migratione Abrahami
67	*580*
113	*718*
149	*49*
219	*580*

De mutatione nominum
72	*580*

203	*718*
223	*415*

De opificio mundi
128	*45*

De posteritate Caini
26f.	*580*

De praemiis et poenis
71	*580*

De providentia
2,44–46	*45*

De sacrificiis Abelis et Caini
68	*49*
123	*49*

De specialibus legibus
I,206	*580*
II,30	*580*
II,62	*45, 50*
II,63f.	*45*
II,230	*45*
III,161	*557*
IV,73	*49*
IV,79–131	*580*
IV,84	*580*
IV,92	*580*
IV,180	*582*

De virtutibus
13	*580*
168	*49*

Stellenregister

De vita contemplativa		III,250	*580*
25	41		
26	*415*	*Quis rerum divinarum heres sit*	
		173	*580*
De vita Mosis		269f.	*580*
I,158	49		
I,295–301	*718*	*Quod deterius potiori insidiari soleat*	
II,16	50	110	*580*
II,139	*580*		
II,216	45	*Quod Deus sit immutabilis*	
		183	*718*
Legum allegoriae			
I,48	49	*Quod omnis probus liber sit*	
I,70ff.	*580*	18	*580*
III,113	*580*	45	*580*
III,115ff.	*580*	62	*581*

3.2 Flavius Josephus

Antiquitates Judaicae		18,23	*415*
4,102–158	*718*	20,195	*774*
4,303	*77*	20,200f.	*686*
4,313f.	*77*		
5,98	49	*Bellum Judaicum*	
8,53	*394*	1,529	*202*
8,143–149	*201*		
8,315	49	*Contra Apionem*	
10,276	69	1,8	41
12,203	49	1,109–120	*201*
16,23	*665*		
17,97	49	*Vita*	
18,11	*415*	16	*774*

3.3 Jüdisch-hellenistische Literatur

Apokalypse des Abraham		210	49
(ganzes Werk)	*72, 83*	256	*415*
24,8	*580*	280	49
		281	49
Apokalypse des Mose			
19,3	*580*	*Ascensio Iesaiae*	
		4,2f.	660, *669*
Aristeasbrief			
(ganzes Werk)	42, 117f., *269*	*2. Baruch*	
139	*401*	(ganzes Werk)	65, 71–73, *83*, 668
142	*401*	1,1	78
188	49	3,1–9	78

2. Baruch (Fortsetzung)

4,1–6	78
4,5	76
5,1	78
10,2f.	78
10,5	78
13	82
13,3	78
13,5–11	78
19,1–3	79
25,1	78
28,2	72, 73
31–34	78
32,4	78
35,1	78
36f.	73
39f.	73
39	74
39,5–8	69
40	74
43,2	78
44–46	78
44,2	78
46,7	78
48,30	78
53	73
55–74	73
56–74	73
56,5–16	73
57	73
58	73
59	73
59,3–11	76
59,4	79
60	73
61	73
62	73
64f.	73
66	73
67	73
68	73
68,7	74
70f.	73
70	74
72–74	73f.
76,2	78
76,3–5	79
77	78
77,12	79
77,17	79
77,19	79
78–87	*78*, 79
78–86 (87)	674
78,1	79
78,4	*582*
78,5	*78*
84,1–7	79
84,1	*78*
84,4f.	*77*
84,9	79, 81
85,6	79

4. Baruch

6f.	674
6,14	649
7	674

4. Esra

(ganzes Werk)	65, 73f., *83*, 98, 226
3	71
3,1	71, 81
3,10	72
3,20–22	72
3,29	81
4,23	81
6,26	82
7,28	82
10,45	72
11f.	71
11,39f.	71
12,11	69, 71
12,37f.	81
13,39–50	*72*
14	42, 81
14,1–8	81
14,5f.	76
14,9	81
14,11f.	72
14,21	81
14,22	81
14,42–44	*81*
14,45	81
14,47	81
14,49	72
14,50	81f.

1. Henoch

(ganzes Werk)	65, 75, *83*, 89f., 220
1,3c–9	*693*
1,9	*694*

1. Henoch (Fortsetzung)

1,12	69
4	*651*
6–11	65
12,4	75
18,13–16	*719*
21,3–6	*719*
65–67	75
68,1	75
72–82	75
81,1–82,4	75
81,6	75
82,1	*81*
83,10	75
85–90	65
85,3–89,8	65
86,1	65
88,1	65
88,3	65
89,1	65, 75
89,9–90,27	65
89,9	65
89,10f.	65
89,12	65
89,16–18	65
89,26	65
89,28–58	66
89,29	*651*
89,32	*651*
89,36	66, 75
89,55–58	66
89,59–90,27	66
90,20–27	66
90,28–38	65f.
91,1–17	66
92–105	66
92,1	75
93,1–10	66
93,3–17	67
93,4	75
104,9–105,2	76
104,11f.	75
104,11	*81*
106f.	76
107,3	76

2. Henoch

(ganzes Werk)	75
23	76
23,6	75
33	76
33,8f.	*75*
35	76
35,2	*75*
36–68	76
40,2–13	*75*
47,1f.	*75*
47,2	76
48,6f.	*75*
64,5	*75*
66,8	*75*
68,2	*75*, 76
69–72	76
73	76

Joseph und Aseneth

8,9	397

Jubiläenbuch

(ganzes Werk)	76, 83, *87*, 89–93, 98
2,19f.	397
6,22	92
7,38f.	76
10,13f.	75
15,32	66
21,10	75

Liber Antiquitatum Biblicarum

18,13	718
19,2–7	77

Sibyllinische Orakel

(ganzes Werk)	226
5,143	668

Testament des Abraham

4,3	49
4,5	49

Testament des Mose

(ganzes Werk)	65, 69, 71
1,5	77
1,14	77
1,17	77, 81
1,18	77
2	70
3	70
3,11–13	77, 81
3,12	77
4	70

Testament des Mose (Fortsetzung)
4,1	77
4,7	77
5,2	70
5,3–6	70
6	70
8	70
9,6f.	70
10,11	77
11,1	77
11,17	77

Testamente der zwölf Patriarchen
(ganzes Werk) 89, 95

Testament Levi
(ganzes Werk) 95

Testament Juda
(ganzes Werk) 95

Testament Joseph
3,1   49

Testament Benjamin
(ganzes Werk) 95
4,1   49

3.4 Qumran

Aramäisches Levi-Dokument
(ganzes Werk) 90, 95
10,10 (Greenfield) 75

1Q21
(ganzes Werk) 95

1Q22
(ganzes Werk) 91, 96

1Q29
(ganzes Werk) 96

1QapGen^{ar}
(Genesis-Apokryphon)
V,29   75
XIX,1–22   94
XXI,23–XXII,34 94

1QpHab
VII,3–5   88

2Q21
(ganzes Werk) 96

4Q88
(ganzes Werk) 96

4Q179
(ganzes Werk) 91

4Q184
(ganzes Werk) 91

4Q204
(ganzes Werk) 101

4Q212
(ganzes Werk) 101

4Q213
(ganzes Werk) 95

4Q214
(ganzes Werk) 95

4Q215 (Naphtali-Testament)
(ganzes Werk) 90, 96

4Q242 (Gebet des Nabonid)
(ganzes Werk) 96

4Q342
(ganzes Werk) 101

4Q343
(ganzes Werk) 101

4Q365 (4QRP^C)
(ganzes Werk) 92

4Q368
(ganzes Werk) 91

4Q375
(ganzes Werk) *96*

4Q376
(ganzes Werk) *96*

4Q377
(ganzes Werk) *91*

4Q378 (Apokryphon des Josua)
(ganzes Werk) *93*

4Q383
I,2 *96*

4Q389
Frgm. 1 *674*
I,6 *101*

4Q404
(ganzes Werk) *96*

4Q465
(ganzes Werk) *101*

4Q525
(ganzes Werk) *91, 93*
I,1 *93*

4Q529
(ganzes Werk) *99*

4Q537
(ganzes Werk) *95*

4Q538
(ganzes Werk) *95*

4Q539
(ganzes Werk) *95*

4Q540
(ganzes Werk) *95*

4Q541
(ganzes Werk) *95*

4Q542
(ganzes Werk) *95*

4Q543
(ganzes Werk) *95*

4Q544
(ganzes Werk) *95*

4Q545
(ganzes Werk) *95*
IV,18 *95*

4Q546
(ganzes Werk) *95*

4Q547
(ganzes Werk) *95*

4Q548
(ganzes Werk) *95*

4Q549
(ganzes Werk) *95*

4QDivreHaMeorot
(ganzes Werk) *96*

4QMMT
(ganzes Werk) *101*

5Q16
(ganzes Werk) *91*

7Q2
(ganzes Werk) *101*

7Q4
(ganzes Werk) *101*

7Q8
(ganzes Werk) *101*

7Q11–14
(ganzes Werk) *101*

11Q5 (11QPs^a)
(ganzes Werk) *96*
XXVII,2–11 *40*

11Q10 (11QtgJob)
32,1 *651*
33,9 *651*

11Q11
(ganzes Werk) *96*

11Q19 (Tempelrolle)
(ganzes Werk) *76, 88, 90–92, 98f.*

CD
(ganzes Werk) *97*

3.5 Rabbinisches Schrifttum

Midraschim

Numeri Rabba
22,5   *719*

Sifre Numeri
157   *719*

Mischna
Avot
1,1   *42*
6,2   *581*

Tosefta
Sanhedrin
2,6   *674*

Babylonischer Talmud

Baba Batra
14b–15a   *41*

Sanhedrin
106a   *719*

Targumim

Jonathan
Jes 8,14   *651*
Jer 10,11   *674*

Neofiti
(ganzes Werk) *651*
Dtn 8,15   *651*

Onqelos
(ganzes Werk) *651*

Pseudo-Jonathan
Num 20,8   *651*
Num 20,10   *651*
Num 20,11   *651*

Targum Proverbia
3,15   *651*
8,11   *651*
20,15   *651*
31,10   *651*

4. Griechische und römische Literatur

Achilleus Tatios
Leukippe und Kleitophon
(ganzes Werk) *264*

(Claudius) Aelianus

Epistulae
(ganzes Werk) *239*

Varia historia
13,22   *143*

Aelius Aristides
Ars rhetorica
2,21   *300*
2,36   *300*

Aelius Donatus
Commentum Terenti
Praefatio ad Terentium
(ganzes Werk) *177*

Vita Terenti
7   *169*

Stellenregister

Aischines

Epistulae
(ganzes Werk) 242, 246, *270*
1,1   283
2,1   275f.
2,2   275
4,2f.   *275*
4,4f.   *275*
6   *293*
7,2   275
8   *293*
10   275
12,1   *283*
12,6f.   *284*
12,14–16   283

Orationes
3,66   *284*
3,215   *284*

Aischylos
Frgm. 294   *178*

Hiketiden
(ganzes Werk) *627*

Prometheus Vinctus
853–869   *627*

Alcman
Frgm. 29   *105*

Pseudo-Alexander der Große
Epistulae
(ganzes Werk) *160*, 247, *518*

Alexander Numenius (Rhetor)
De figuris
2,1   *300*
2,17   *300*

Alkiphron
Epistulae
(ganzes Werk) *145*, *239*

Anacharsis
Epistulae
(ganzes Werk) *242*

Andocides
De mysteriis
47   *314*

Anthologia Palatina
7,75   *143*

Antigonos von Karystos
Frgm.   *248*

Aphthonius von Antiochien
Progymnasmata
2   *300*
2,117,30–32 *538*

Apollodor von Athen
Bibliotheca
2,11–22   *627*

Apollonios von Tyana
Epistulae
(ganzes Werk) *243*

Apuleius von Madaura

Apologia
10   *140*
87,2–5   157
87,2   168

Asinus Aureus / Metamorphoses
(ganzes Werk) *265*
11,23   *416*

Aristainetos
Epistulae
(ganzes Werk) *239*

Aristophanes

Batrachoi
76–82   287
83–85   288
787–793   287

Hippeis / Equites
502f.   144
541   144

Nephelai / Nubes
533ff.   *148*
530f.   143f.

Sphekes / Vespae
1018–1022   142

Aristophanis historiae animalium
epitome subiunctis Aeliani Timothei
aliorumque eclogis
(ganzes Werk)   568
2,439,3   568

Aristoteles

Ethica Nicomachea
1159b   594

Epistulae
(ganzes Werk)   243

Poetica
1451a   167
1454b   303f.
1460a 7–8   146

Politica
1311b 30–34   285

Rhetorica
(ganzes Werk)   47
1355b–1358a
(1,2)   538
1366b (1,9,11)   301
1377b (2,1,1–7)   538
1377b–1378a
(2,1,12–17)   538
1393a–1394a
(2,20)   46, 54
1409b (3,9)   448
1409b (3,9,7)   300

Aristoxenos
Frgm.   248

Arrianus von Nikomedien
Anabasis
2,14,4   302

Artemidor
Onirocriticon
2,45   143

Athanaeus
Deipnosophistai
8,347e   143
9,62   305
14,40   302

Brutus
Epistulae
1   308
25   308f.
69   308

Cassius Dio
Historia Romana
54,9,3   315
61,10,1–6   780
66,17,15,5   568
69,2,3   568
69,11,2   144
S211,4   568
S246   568

Censorinus
De die natali
21,1   106

Chion von Herakleia
Epistulae
(ganzes Werk)   240, *242*, 246f., 257–
                 262, *266*, *270*, 289,
                 518–520
1–17   257–262
1–4   259
1   258, 260
1,44,2–4   258
2,46,6f.   258
3   260, 281
3,46,9f.   258
3,50,20f.   259
4   260
4,54,2f.   259
5–13   259
5   261
5,54,8f.   259
7   280
8   258, 280f.
9   257
13   260
13,1   *278*
14–17   260

Chion von Herakleia (Fortsetzung)
15	280
15,1	*281*
15,3	274, *281*
16	257f., 280f.
16,1	*281*
16,4–7	281
16,5	*281*
17	257
17,78,11f.	260

Cicero

Brutus
11,42	*178, 494*
13,51	*283*

Cato maior de senectute
1,3	164, 166

De finibus
1,3,7	*169*
5,13	*166*

De inventione
1,27	166f.

De legibus
2,11,27	*113*

De re publica
2,28	168

Epistulae ad Atticum
1,13,1	*139*
1,13,2	138
1,18,2	*139*
1,19,11	*139*
2,19,5	139
2,20,3	139
2,20,5	*139*
3,12,2	*138, 142*
3,15,8	149
4,1,1	*139*
4,18(15),3	*139*
5,8,3	*149*
6,6(7),1	*139*, 140
10,9(8),1	*138*
10,12(11),1	*139*
10,13(12),3	*139*
11,2,4	150
11,3,3	149
11,6(5),3	150
11,9(8),2	*149*
11,13(12),4	*149*
11,14(13),5	*149*
11,17(16),1	139
13,(17)16,1	168
13,24(12),3f.	*168*
13,26(14,2+15),1f.	*149, 168*
13,27(16),1f.	*149*
13,28(17+18),2	*149*
13,29(19),3–6	*168*
13,29(19),3f.	*149*, 165, 168
13,30(21),4–7	142
13,39(44),3	*168*
13,43,3	*149*
15,5(3),2	*149*
15,6(5),4	*139*
16,6,4	165
16,11,1	*141*

Epistulae ad familiares
3,11,5	139
7,32,2	*164*
8,1,1	150
9,8,1	*166, 168*

Epistulae ad Quintum fratrem
3,5,2	165

Laelius de amicitia
1,4	164f., 168
1,5	165, 169

Orationes Philippicae
(ganzes Werk)	*177*

Orator
8,25	*283*
85	*538*

Partitiones oratoriae
31f.	*300*

Pro Marco Caelio oratio
(ganzes Werk)	631
36 (15)	632

Tusculanae Disputationes
1,26	*113*
4,10–32	*580*

Columella
1,7	208
7,5,17	207
11,3,64	208

Comicorum Atticorum fragmenta
174	568
175	568
176	568

Corpus Hermeticum
(ganzes Werk) 135

David (Philosophus)
In Porphyrii isagoge commentarium
1	*163*, 203

Demetrius Phalereus

De elocutione
7	*300, 320*
8f.	*300*
10–18	*448*
19–21	*448*
137	*300*
223	*267, 319*
224	*317f.*
225	*319*
227	133, *267*, 300, 633
228	*330*
230	*310, 319*
232	*318*
233	*319*
234	*319*
241–243	*300*
265f.	*538*
266	*538*

Typoi epistolikoi
1	*318*

Demokrit
Frgm. 39	47
Frgm. 79	47

Demosthenes

Epistulae
(ganzes Werk) 243

Orationes
18,51f.	*284*
39	*275*
40	*275*

Diogenes Laërtios
1,72	*153*
2,6,57	144
2,11	*303*
2,42	*153*
2,60	*160*
3,61	*251*
5,92f.	134
5,93f.	*129*
6,15	*301*
7,59	*300*
7,93	*301*
8,54	160
9,13	208
10,3	*156*, 197

Diogenes der Kyniker
Epistulae
(ganzes Werk) 242

Dion Chrysostomos
Epistulae
(ganzes Werk) 243

Orationes
18	45
21,12	154
53,10	146

Dionysius von Halikarnass

De compositione verborum
4,30	*303*

De imitatione
(ganzes Werk) 47

De Isaeo
3	*300*
18	*307*

De Isokrate
20	*301*

De Lysia
1	*301*
4	*300*
11	*301*
12	*307*

De Thukydide
1,8	48
22f.	*300*

Demosthenes
57   *234*
58   *300*

Epistula ad Pompeium Geminum
3   *300*
6   *48*

Dorotheus von Sidon
Pentateuch   209f.

Epiktet
Diatribai
(ganzes Werk)   *161*
3,23,30   *300*

Eupolis
Baptai
415   *148*

Euripides
Epistulae
(ganzes Werk)   *242*, 246, *270*, *285–288*
1,2   278
2,2   277
3–5   285
3   278
5   288
5,1   286
5,2   289
5,5f. 286

Helena
940f.   48

Galen von Pergamon

De libris propriis
praef.   *141*, 205f.

In Hippocratis de natura hominis commentarium
2 pr.   *152*, 207
1,44   *152*
15,105   *238*
15,109   *238*

Gellius
Noctes Atticae
2,3   153
10,12   172

10,12,1–8   208
10,12,1   172
10,12,4   172
10,12,6   172
10,12,8f.   172
10,12,8   163

Heliodor
Aithiopika   265

Heraclitus Ephesius
Epistulae
(ganzes Werk)   *242*

Hermippos von Smyrna
Frgm. 42   248
Frgm. 43   248
Frgm. 84   248

Herodot
2,145,4   *108*

Hesiod
Theogonia
22f.   377
52–62   *109*

Hippokrates
Epistulae
(ganzes Werk)   *242*, *244f.*, 246, *270*
1   299
13   299

Historia Augusta
(ganzes Werk)   135

Antonius Pius
11,3   *149*

Gordian
10,6ff.   *157*

Hadrian
1,1   *144*
3,3   *144*
3,5   *144*
7,2   *144*
16,1   145

Septimus Severus
1,6   *144*

Verus
2,8 149

Homer
Ilias
1,1 *108*
2,484–493 *109*
6,167–170 *280*

Odyssee
13,102–112 *114*
108f. *178*

Pseudo-Homer
Hymni Homerici
Ad Apollinem
166–178 *108*

Horaz
Ars poetica
1,26,10–12 *48f.*
1,32 *49*
3,30,13f. *49*
128–135 *176*

Carmina
2,12 *140*
3,11,22–52 *627*
3,30,1–6 *141*

Epistulae
1,19 *176*
1,19,32f. *49*
2,1,20–27 *153*
2,1,50 *169*
2,1,156f. *169*

Isokrates
Epistulae
(ganzes Werk) *243*, 246

In sophistas
6f. *47*
16–18 *47*

Panegyrikos
1 *300*

Iuvenal
Satiren
41 *169*

Jamblichos von Chalkis
De mysteriis
(ganzes Werk) 210
1 131

De vita Pythagorica
25 162
29,157f. 203
104 160
158 159
198 160, 162f., 177
258–260 156f.

Julian Apostata
Epistulae
(ganzes Werk) 239

Krates
Epistulae
(ganzes Werk) 242

Libanius
Epistulae
(ganzes Werk) 239

Pseudo-Libanius
De forma epistulari
2 273

Characteres Epistolici
11 *318*
47 *317*
50 318
58 *318*

Livius
1,21,3 *110*

Pseudo-Longinus
De sublimitate
6 *132*
13,2 *143*
14,2 *173*

Longos von Lesbos
Daphnis und Chloe
(ganzes Werk) 264

Lukian von Samosata

Aletheis historiai
2,35 *274*

De Dea Syria
(ganzes Werk) 204

De historia conscribenda
58 132

De morte Peregrini
16,12 *557*

Demosthenous encomium
18,6 *568*

Epistulae
(ganzes Werk) *239*

Nigrinus
11 *143*

Philopseudes
1 *178*

Pseudo-Logistes
30 154

Lydus
De ostendis
157,18 208

Lysias
Epistulae
(ganzes Werk) *242*

Marcus Aurelius
Meditationes
6,38 427
7,9 427

(Marcus Valerius) Martialis
Epigrammata
2,20 147
10,3 *142*
11,3,5 141
12,(47)46 148

Martianus Capella
2,134–146 *143*

Mithridates
Epistula
(ganzes Werk) 136, 298–307, 310, 316–322, 326, 330

Olympiodorus
Prolegomena
(ganzes Werk) 203

Ovid

Amores
2,18,19–26 131
2,18,27–34 136

Ars amatoria
3,339ff. 131
3,345f. *631*

Epistulae ex Ponto
(ganzes Werk) 293
3,9,51 *273*
4,16,13–17 136

Heroides
(ganzes Werk) *145*
14 633f.
14,4 *629*
14,5 629
14,8 629
14,14 *629*
14,17–20 630
14,21–84 627
14,23 628
14,26 *629*
14,41f. 630
14,43–50 629
14,47 630
14,48 630
14,49 *629*
14,53–66 628
14,56–60 629
14,64 *629*
14,68 630
14,72 630
14,73f. 628
14,75–80 630
14,76 629
14,77 628
14,84 *629*
14,85–108 628
14,111–114 628

Heroides (Fortsetzung)
14,115–118	628
14,119–130	629
14,123	*629*
14,129	*629*
14,131f.	630
16–21	628

Metamorphoses
4,462f.	*627*
8,620–720	*557*
10,43f.	*627*

Tristia
(ganzes Werk)	293
1,1,1–4	*141*
1,1,62	*141*
1,1,63	*141*
2,427	*140*
4,10,128	141

Pausanias
Descriptio Graeciae
2,21,2	*627*
2,24,2	*627*
3,12,2	*627*

Phaedrus
1 prol 1f.	170
1 prol 1	*171*
2 prol 8–12	*170*
2 prol 9	171
2 epil 12	*171*
3 prol 1	*171*
3 prol 29	171
3 prol 38f.	170
4 prol 7f.	171
4 prol 10–14	170
4,7	170, *171*
4,22	170f.
4,22,7–9	171
5 prol 1–9	171
5 prol 1	171
5 prol 10	*171*

Phalaris
Epistulae
(ganzes Werk)	237, *242*, 247

Philagyrius
Vita
1,1	*170*

Philostratos
De epistulis
(ganzes Werk)	309
9–11	*317*
14–19	*300*
15f.	*317*

Epistulae
(ganzes Werk)	*239*

Vita Apollonii
7,35	*157*

Vitae sophistarum
1,8 (509)	*284*
2,24,1	133, 149

Pindar
Nemeische Oden
10,6	*627*

Pythische Oden
9,112–116	*627*

Plato
Epistulae
(ganzes Werk)	*243*, 245f., 250–256, 258, 262, 264, *270*, 372, 518
1	*251f.*
2	*238*, 253
3	*251–253*
4	*251–253*
5	*251f.*
6	*238*, *251f.*
7	*238–240, 250, 251–255*
7 (341ab)	*160*
8	*251–253*
9	*251f.*
10	*251f.*
11	251
12	*251–253*
13	*238, 252f.*
13 (361a1–6)	252

Ion
534ab	*143*

Parmenides
128d   *160*

Phaidon
60d   *153*

Philebos
16c   *113*

Politeia (De re publica)
376e–392c   *359*
382c   *494*
389b   *494*
414c–e   *359*
459d   *359*
459v   *494*

Politikos
382f.   *178*

Sophistes
252c   *143*

Timaios
31b–32b   *427*
44d   *427*
69c–70a   *580*
69c   *427*

Plato, Komiker
Peisandros
Frgm. 99   *148*

Plinius der Ältere
Naturalis historia
7,30   *141*
13,12   *153*
21,62   *208*
24,159   *203*
24,160–166   *208*
24,160   *172, 208*
26,18f.   *208*
27,141   *208*
28,112   *172*

Plinius der Jüngere
Epistulae
(ganzes Werk)   *272*
1,1   *273*
1,16,6   *145*
1,16,8f.   *153*
2,10,2   *141*
8,19,2   *141*

9,11,2   *141*
10,96,1   *637*
10,96,3   *637*
10,96,5   *638*

Plutarch

Brutus
2,5–8   *308f.*

Coniugalia praecepta
138a–146a   *145*

Consolatio ad uxorem
609ab   *146*

Crassus
33   *315*

De animae procreatione
1016f–1017a   *427*

De Gloria Atheniensium
345e   *144*

De se ipsum laudando
539a–547Ende   *145*

Vita Numae
4,2,62a   *110*

Phocion
5,2f.   *300*

Pseudo-Plutarch
Vitae decem oratorum
(ganzes Werk)   *284*

Pollux
Onomastikon
3,28   *314*

Porphyrius

De antro nympharum
(ganzes Werk)   *114*

Vita Plotini
81   *210*
82   *210*

Propertius
Carmina
4,3   *631*
4,7   *631*

Elegie
4,1,64 *169*

Pseudopythagorica
(ganzes Werk) 177, *242*

Frauenbriefe *146*

Lysis-Brief 240

Ptolemaeus
Geographica
4,5,54 *669*

Quintilian
Institutio oratoria
praef. *141*
2,15,2 48
4,2,31–33 *300*
4,2,31 *268*
6,1,25f. *632*
6,1,25 132
6,2,8f. *538*
8,3,70 167
9,2,29f. *167*, 633
10,2 47
10,2,12 *173*
10,3,1 *164*
12,10,18f. *283*

Quintus Ennius
Annales
2 Frgm. 1,113 *110*

Rhetorica ad Alexandrum
1420a (2–3) 312
1438a *300*

Rhetorica ad Herennium
1,8,14 *300*
4,66 *538*

Rutilius Lupus
2,6 *538*

Satyros von Kallatis
Frgm. *248*

Seneca
Dialogi
9,17,2 777

Epistulae
33,4 161
40,1 *300*
61,1 777
90,5 *113*
95,49 *581*

Troades
336 777

Sokratiker
Epistulae
(ganzes Werk) *242, 246, 266, 270, 289, 518–520*

Strabo
Geographica
17,1,30 *669*

Sueton
De grammaticis
7 161

Divus Augustus
51 138
55 138

Domitianus
20 149, *152*

Vespasian
8,5 *152*

Tacitus
Annales
13,11 780
14,26 *315*
14,27,1 413
15,44 774
15,44,2 774
15,44,5 774
16,6,2 774

Dialogus de oratoribus
(ganzes Werk) *52*

Terenz

Adelphoe
(ganzes Werk)   *177*
Prolog   *148*

Heautontimorumenos
(ganzes Werk)   *148*

Themistokles
Epistulae
(ganzes Werk)   237, *242*, 246, *270*

Pseudo-Theokritos
Sphragis
(ganzes Werk)   *129*

Theon (Rhetor)
Progymnasmata
2,117,30–32   *538*
4   *300*
8   132, *320*

Theophylaktos Simokates
Epistulae
(ganzes Werk)   *239*

Thukydides
1,21,1–4   *303*

Vergil

Aeneis
4,639   777
5,815   777

Bucolica
2. Ekloge   *140*

Vita Aeschinis
(ganzes Werk)   *284*

Vita Donatiana
9   *140*

Vita Focae
28–34   *143*
29–33   *141*

Vitruv
De architectura
7 praef. 3   *151*, 207

Xenophon

Anabasis
(ganzes Werk)   144
4,7,24   281
6,2   *281*
7,1   281

Epistulae
(ganzes Werk)   *243*, 247

Hellenica
3,1,2   144

Memorabilia
1,1,1   *300*
1,2,3   48
2,3,12   287
4,2,14–18   *494*
6,3   48

5. Apostolische Väter

Barnabasbrief
(ganzes Werk)   346, 350
4,3   728
5,3   463
16,5   *728*

Brief des Polykarp
(ganzes Werk)   676
7,2   710

1. Clemensbrief
(ganzes Werk)   200, *323*, 338, 346, 375, 616, 676
1,2   *556f.*
5,1–5   *708*
5,4–7   646
5,4   660, *662*, *669*, 703, 771
10,7   *557*
11,1   *557*
12,1   *557*

1. Clemensbrief (Fortsetzung)
19f.	*728*
21,1	*554*
30,8	*717*
31,4	*582*
35,5	*554*
38,4	*463*
41,4	*463*
47,5	*556*
48,1	*556*
50,2	*463*
60,2	*554*
61,2	*554*

Didache
(ganzes Werk) 346, 350, 354

Hirt des Hermas
(ganzes Werk) 346, 350, 616
1,1–2,4 *748*

Mandata
8,10 *556f.*

Similitudes
9,27,2 *557*

Ignatius

Briefe *267*

Brief an die Epheser
2,1	*653*
4,3	*669*
20,1	*463*

Brief an die Magnesier
1,2	*463*
2,1	*653*
6,1	*692*

Brief an die Philadelphier
4,1	*653*
11,2	*663*

Brief an Polykarp
14,1 *663*

Brief an die Römer
4,3	646, 660
10,1	*663*

Brief an die Smyrnäer
12,1	*555, 663*
12,2	*555, 653*

Brief an die Traller
2,2	*692*
2,3	*558*
3,1	*692*

6. Nag Hammadi-Texte und gnostische Literatur

BG 1
Mariaevangelium
17ff. *158*

CT 1
Epistula Petri
(ganzes Werk) 228

CT 2
1. Jakobus-Apokalypse
(ganzes Werk) 228

CT 3
Judasevangelium
(ganzes Werk) 228

NHC I,2
Jakobus-Apokryphon
(ganzes Werk) 600

NHC II,2
Thomasevangelium
(ganzes Werk)	346
12	*591*, 592
51	213

NHC V,2
Paulus-Apokalypse
(ganzes Werk) 339

NHC V,3
1. Jakobus-Apokalypse
(ganzes Werk)   600

NHC V,4
2. Jakobus-Apokalypse
(ganzes Werk)   600

NHC VII,3
Petrus-Apokalypse
(ganzes Werk)   346, 350, 353, *728*
14   660
15f.   *707*
73,18ff.   *158*

Pistis Sophia
36   *158*

7. Antikes Christentum

Aineias von Gaza
Epistulae
(ganzes Werk)   *239*

Ambrosius
De Abrahamo
(ganzes Werk)   *197*

Anabatikon Paulou
(ganzes Werk)   183, 201

Alexandrinerbrief
(ganzes Werk)   198, 339

Brief des Jakobus an Quadratus
(ganzes Werk)   600

Constitutiones Apostolicae
6,3,16   351

Athanasius
Epistulae
39   202

Athenagoras
Supplicatio
37,1   *337*

Augustinus von Hippo

Contra Faustum Manichaeum
11,1   189
32,1   189
32,2   189
32,8   189
32,16   189

32,21f.   192

De civitate dei
15,23   183, 212
18,18   230
18,38   154, 212

De consensu evangelistarum
1,10,15f.   *172*
1,10,16   174

De fide et operibus
14,21   *137*

De doctrina christiana
2,8,13   *212*

Epistulae
153   354
153,14   188

Expositio ad Galatas
12f.   *129*

Opus imperfectum contra Iulianum
4,123   200

Retractationes
2,20   *234*

Berliner Koptisches Buch (P 20915)
(ganzes Werk)   220

Canon Muratori
(ganzes Werk)   *50*, 195, 197, 199
Z. 61–63   *337*
Z. 63–65   *383*
Z. 63f.   *339*
Z. 64–67   *349*
Z. 69–72   *349*

Canon Muratori (Fortsetzung)
Z. 69f.   162
Z. 73–80   349

Cassiodorus
Institutiones divinarum et saecularium litterarum
1,1,5   200

Clemens von Alexandrien
Paidagogos
1,37,3   *224*
3,8,44ff.   *344*
3,63,1   *224*
3,79,3–81,3   *224*
97,2   *224*

Stromateis
1,1,1   *346*
1,15,69,4   *208*
1,85,4   *346*
1,181,1   *346*
2,3,5   *346*
2,11   *344*
2,15,66   *343*
3,90,1   *224*
4,108,1   *224*
5   *439*
6,106,2   *224*
6,107,2   *225*
7,9   *359*
7,106   *673*

Codex Theodosianus
1,4,3   228

Cyprian

Ad Fortunatum
9   *212*

Ad Quirinum testimoniorum libri tres
2,1   *212*
3,6   *212*
3,12   *212*
3,35   *212*
3,51   *212*
3,53   *212*
3,95f.   *212*
3,109   *212*
3,131   *212*

De opere et eleemosynis
5   *212*

Epistulae
3,2   *212*
9,2   197

Cyrill von Jerusalem
Catechetica 4,36

Decretum Gelasianum
(ganzes Werk) 199, 217

Dionysius Bar Salibi
In Apokalypsin
1   *342*

Dionysius von Antiochia
Epistulae
(ganzes Werk) *239*

Epiphanius von Salamis
Liber de haeresibus (Panarion)
38,2,5   201
38,25   183
42,9,4   *339*
42,12,3   *339*
51,4,5–12,6   *342*

Epistolae Senecae ad Paulum
et Pauli ad Senecam
(ganzes Werk) 187, 339, *373*, 374,
               518, 520
1   *187*, 768–770, 772,
               775–777, 779f.
2   767, 768, 771f.,
               774, 776
2,6   *139*
3   767, 768, 771f.,
               774, 776
4   767, 768
5–9   774, 783
5   771, *773f.*, 780
6   769–771, 780
7   767, 768–772, 774–
               777, 779f.
8   771, 774, 780
9   767, 768, 774, 776f.
10–14   773, 783
10–12   *774*

Epistolae Senecae ... (Fortsetzung)
10	769, 772–774, 777f.
11	767, 768, 774, 776f., 779
12	767, 769, 771, 779
13	776–778
14	*187*, 769, 774, 779f.

Eugippius
Vita Severini
36,2	202

Eusebius von Caesarea

Chronicon
1,17,1–13	*201*

Historia ecclesiastica
1,7,14	687
1,12,4	*568*
1,13,5	*273*
1,13,6–22	*175*
2,2,1–6	354
2,15,1f.	*672*
2,15,2	*668, 671*
2,23	686
2,23,4–9	*618*
2,23,4	*592*, 686
2,23,7	*592*
2,23,12	*592*
2,23,15	*592*
2,23,16	*592*
2,23,24f.	*590, 607*
2,23,25	343, 608
3,3,1	220
3,3,5	350
3,3,6	*346*
3,19,1–20,6	218
3,20,1–6	687
3,24,7–13	*342*
3,25	349
3,25,1f.	350
3,25,3–5	350
3,25,3	344, *607*
3,25,4–7	*195*
3,25,5f.	687
3,25,6f.	*607*
3,25,6	350f., *608*
3,25,7	350f.
3,28,1f.	353
3,39,1–7	734
3,39,3f.	655
3,39,4	*671*
3,39,7	655
3,39,14	*671*
3,39,15f.	340
3,39,15	*668*, 671
3,39,17	671
4,22,4	*592*
4,22,5	*715*
4,23,11	664
4,23,12	196
5,1	439
5,8,3	*671*
6,12,2–6	*177*, 202, 347
6,14,1	353
6,14,2–4	147, 338
6,14,2f.	353
6,14,6	*672*
6,14,7	342
6,20,3	353
6,25	338
6,25,8	343, 730
6,25,10	344
6,25,11–14	353
7,24f.	345
7,25	353
7,25,1–27 (14)	129
7,25,2f.	*172*
7,25,11	344

Gennadius
De viris illustribus
68	*192*

Gregor von Nazianz
Epistulae
51	*317*
51,5	*318*

Hebräerevangelium
(ganzes Werk)	350
Frgm. 7	*591f.*

Hieronymus

Commentarii in Danielem
2,48	211
9,21	211
12,1	211

Commentariorum in Epistulam
ad Titum liber
PL 26,555   *503*

Contra Rufinum
2,24   *158*

De viris illustribus
1   *220*
2   *607*
4   *130*, 218
10   *346*
12   *188*, 354

Epistulae
22,35,8   *169*
58,5   *169*

In Philemonem prologus
(ganzes Werk)   *202*

Prologus in libros Salomonis
(ganzes Werk)   *200*

Hilarius von Poitiers
Tractatus super Psalmos
140,5   *212*

Hippolytus
Refutatio omnium haeresium
5,17,10   *715*
7,29,8   *715*

Irenaeus von Lyon
Adversus haereses
1 praef   *337*
1,31,1   228
2,14,7   *337*
3,1,1   *304*, 341, *671*
3,1,7   341
3,3,4   *337*
3,4   *50*
3,7,2   439
3,11,8   340
3,11,9   *342*
3,12,1–15   345
3,14,1   *337*, 341
3,16,5–8   *343*
3,16,8   *745*
4,9,2   *671*
4,16,5   *672*
4,20,2   *346*

4,26,2   761
4,26,4   761
4,26,5   761
5,7,2   *672*
5,33,4   *671*
7,5   *50*
27,1   761
28,1   761
30,1   761
31,1–33,1   761
31,1   761

Isidor von Sevilla
Etymologiarum libri viginti
6,2,30   200

Julius Africanus
Epistula ad Origenem
(ganzes Werk)   212

Kestoi
Frgm. 5 (Vieillefond) 212

Julius Firmicius Maternus (Astrologus)
Matheseos libri VII
2,29,2   210

Julius Victor
Ars rhetorica
27   *300*

Justin
Apologia
1,35   354
1,48   354
1,61,4   *341*

Dialogus cum Tryphone Judaeo
71   *181*
82,1   *710*
106,3   *673*
110   439

Johannes Chrysostomos
Epistulae
(ganzes Werk)   *267*, 293

3. Korintherbrief
(ganzes Werk)   218, 329, 339, *348*, 778
1,10–15   *329*

Lactantius
Divinae institutiones
(ganzes Werk) 780
1,22,2 *110*

Laodicenerbrief
(ganzes Werk) *155*, 187, 198, 329, 339, 776, 778

Legenda aurea
142 *217*
212 *217*

Martyrium des Polykarp
(ganzes Werk) 676

Melito von Sardes
Passahomilie
(ganzes Werk) 219

Narratio des Pseudo-Nilos
(ganzes Werk) *230*

Nestorius
Liber Heracleides
(ganzes Werk) *147*

Oden Salomos
11 219

Origenes
Commentarii in evangelium Joannis
13–32 *606*
19,23,152 *343*
20,10,66 *343*

Commentarium in evangelium Matthaei
3 *305*
10,17 *687*
17,30,9f. *344*

Commentarii in Romanos
1–5 *606*
10,31 *346*

Contra Celsum
(ganzes Werk) *359*
3,55 748, *759*

De principiis
praef. 8 *353*

Epistula ad Africanum
(ganzes Werk) 212

Fragmenta ex commentaries in epistulam I ad Corinthios
33,14 *302*

Homiliae in librum Jesu Nave
7,1 *730*

Orosius
Historiae adversum Paganos
7,7,11 413

39. Osterfestbrief des Athanasius
(ganzes Werk) 199

Passio Sancti Pauli Apostoli
1 772

Paulinus von Nola
Vita Ambrosii
43 202

Paulusakten
(ganzes Werk) 289, *346, 348*, 354

Phileasapologie
(ganzes Werk) 219

Photius
Bibliotheca
61,20a,22–26,264 *284*

Epistula
207,10–16 309

Polykarp von Smyrna
Brief an die Philipper
11,3 439
11,4 439

Prokopios von Gaza
Epistulae
(ganzes Werk) *239*

Protevangelium des Jakobus
(ganzes Werk) 218, 600

Pseudoclementinen
(ganzes Werk) 230

Homiliae
5,9f. 140

Epistula Petri
2,4–7 193

Rufinus von Aquileia
Vorrede zu Origenes' Peri Archon
1 praef. 4–6 194

Salvian von Marseille

De gubernatione Dei
5,2 193

Epistulae
9 193, *321*
9,5 174
9,14–17 *172*
9,17–20 179
9,17 146
9,18 179

Timothei ad Ecclesiam libri quattuor
(ganzes Werk) 127, 131, 192, 348

Suda
B 481 208
B 482 208
B 561 310
Φ 43 *310*

Sulpicius Severus
Vita Martini
20,159f. 146

Synesius von Cyrene
Epistulae
(ganzes Werk) 239

Tatian
Oratio ad Graecos
17,1 *208*, 223

Tertullian

Adversus Marcionem
1,1f. 196
4,5,3f. *115*, 161

4,5,4 196
5,11 *339*
5,17 *339*
5,21 *337*, *503*

Apologeticum
5 354
31 337

De anima
2 337
16 337
20,1 187, *521*, 780

De baptismo
17 348
17,4f. *177*
17,5 162f., 195

De corona
8 337
10 337
15 337

De cultu feminarum
1,3 130, 687
1,3,1–3 212, 344
1,3,3 218, 220

De idolatria
11 337

De oratione
16 346

De pudicitia
10 346
20 338

De resurrectione mortuorum
24 439

Scorpiace
7,1 *212*

Theophilos von Antiochia
Ad Autolycum
2,15 *719*
2,22 342
3,22 *201*

Visio Zosimi
(ganzes Werk) 230

8. Papyri

Corpus Papyrorum Raineri			Papyrus Oxyrhynchos	
6,80	*663*		6,937	*663*
			9,1176	*287*
Papyrus Antinopolis			39,10	*287*
2,94	*663*		39,15	*287*
			39,17–19	*287*
Papyrus Berlin			39,17	*288*
3022, col. 311	30		39,18	*288*
3024, col. 154f.	30		42,3067	*663f.*
			45,3264,9	*653*
Papyrus Florenz			115 (Trostbrief	
158,10	*568*		der Eirene)	*277*
			744	*276*
Papyrus London				
483,88	*568*		*Papyrus Prisse*	
1708,242	*568*		2,9	*30*
			19,9	*30*
Papyrus Michigan				
8,466	*663f.*		*Papyrus Wisconsin*	
8,501	*663*		2,69	*663*
15,751	*663*			

9. Koran

Sure 2,140   *227*   Sure 3,65–70   *227*

Autorenregister

Abbott-Smith, G. 568
Abegg Jr., M. 86
Achelis, T. O. 296
Achtemeier, P. J. 492, 553, 556, 567, 653f., 659, 662f., 665, 667f., 676
Adamson, J. B. 576, 582
Adler, A. 208, 310
Adler, W. 27, 212
Agersnap, S. 429
Aland, B. 13, 178, 218, 374, 386
Aland, K. 8–10, 174, 183, 357, 369, 374, 415, 443, 449, 453, 495
Albrecht, M. von 140
Alexander, L. C. A. 307
Alexander, P. H. 295
Ameling, W. 674
Andresen, C. 201, 523, 636, 655
Applegate, J. K. 667
Armstrong, A. 199
Arndt, C. 132f., 246, 271, 279, 281f.
Arnold, C. E. 407
Attridge, H. W. 545–549, 551–553, 555–559, 565–567, 569–571
Auffahrth, C. 109
Auger, D. 285f.
Aune, D. E. 184, 307
Auwers, J.-M. 197
Avemarie, F. 588

Baasland, E. 589
Babbitt, F. C. 144
Bachmann, E. T. 609f.
Bachmann, M. 668
Backhaus, K. 14, 166, 532
Bailey, J. A. 442, 456f., 463, 465f., 468f.
Baltensweiler, H. 204
Baltzer, K. 693
Balz, H. R. 12, 183, 360, 369, 382, 425, 495, 668, 690
Bappert, W. 128
Barclay, J. M. G. 45, 417, 596, 674
Bardy, G. 7, 125, 128, 155, 158, 366

Barlow, C. W. 133, 765, 770f., 773–777, 779, 781
Barnett, A. E. 514, 556, 568f.
Barr, G. K. 523
Barr, J. 62
Barrett, C. K. 524, 650, 678, 680
Barrett, D. P. 210
Barth, M. 392, 400
Barthes, R. 29
Barton, J. 471
Bassler, J. M. 484
Bauckham, R. J. 12, 134, 183, 204, 215, 217, 322f., 620, 640, 655–657, 660, 665, 671, 675, 687f., 690, 692, 697, 702, 704, 706, 715, 724, 729f.
Bauer, B. 509
Bauer, K. 508, 510
Bauer, T. 30
Bauer, W. 185, 368, 493
Baum, A. D. 10, 15, 27f., 135, 152, 159, 163, 177, 183, 192, 195, 201–203, 206f., 212, 222, 349f., 357, 362, 365, 371, 387, 498, 524f., 683f.
Baumbach, M. 230
Baumeister, T. 659f.
Baumgarten, M. 505
Baur, F. C. 364f., 473–481, 488f., 502–511, 534, 605, 611f., 619
Bautz, F. W. 364
Beale, G. K. 69, 435
Beare, F. W. 661, 665
Beatrice, P. F. 7, 183, 493
Becker, E.-M. 374–376, 379f., 382–384, 386, 480, 649, 704
Becker, J. 413, 584
Becker, M. 86, 698
Beetham, C. A. 392
Behm, J. 440
Bengel, J. A. 667
Bentley, R. 4, 236–238, 240, 268, 278, 287, 299
Benz, E. 120f.
Berenson McLean, J. 393, 396, 408

Bergant, D. 471
Berger, K. 137, 366, 412, 515f., 583, 589, 696, 703, 728f.
Berkovitz, P. 470
Bernabé, A. 114, 226
Bernstein, M. J. 87, 92, 99f., 763
Berry, P. 765
Beschorner, A. 233, 270
Best, E. 388, 398, 440, 457, 462, 465, 472, 483, 662, 667f., 676
Bethge, H.-G. 213, 228
Betz, H. D. 54, 107, 299, 318, 436
Betz, O. 576
Beutler, J. 739, 750, 756, 762
Beyer, K. 523f., 651
Bietenhard, H. 382
Bilgri, A. 428
Billault, A. 257, 261
Bindemann, W. 589
Bingen, J. 663
Birt, T. 128, 154, 162
Birus, H. 175
Black, D. A. 184, 356f.
Black II, C. Clifton 670–673, 678, 756
Blanck, H. 374
Blanke, H. 427
Blass, F. 240f., 365
Blenkinsopp, J. 64
Bloedhorn, H. 6, 183, 269, 496, 733
Bludau, A. 181, 193f.
Blum, E. 577
Blum, R. 127f., 142, 144, 148, 152
Blümer, W. 7, 183, 493
Boccaccini, G. 97
Bocciolini Palagi, L. 765, 768f., 771, 773–779, 781
Bockmuehl, M. 647, 660, 669
Bodnár, I. 208
Böhme, R. 114
Boismard, M. E. 615
Bolognesi, G. 132
Boman, T. 62
Bompaire, J. 205
Booth, W. C. 634
Boring, M. E. 441, 654, 663, 668, 676
Borleffs, W. P. J. 195
Bornemann, W. 434, 439, 443, 449, 452, 455, 457
Bornkamm, G. 268, 373, 415f.
Börschel, R. 13

Borza, E. N. 285
Bosetti, E. 652, 654, 657, 661, 668
Böttrich, C. 678
Bousset, W. 159f., 440
Boustan, R. 75
Bovon, F. 340
Bowersock, G. W. 231
Bowie, A. 265
Bowman, A. K. 653
Brankaer, J. 228
Braun, H. 444, 465f., 472
Bredow, I. von 314
Bregman, M. 763
Breitenbach, H. R. 144
Brenner, A. 651
Brisson, L. 250, 252, 255
Brodersen, K. 134, 166
Brodie, T. L. 537
Broer, I. 523, 576–578
Brooke, G. J. 89
Brooks, J. A. 353
Brosend, W. 696
Brown, R. E. 471, 654, 657–659, 662, 668, 734–736, 738, 741–744, 746f., 749, 755–757, 761
Brox, N. 3, 5–10, 16, 62, 125–128, 130, 135, 146, 153, 177, 183f., 192f., 289f., 347, 356, 359, 366, 368–371, 376, 381, 387, 490–492, 495, 498–500, 521, 524, 527f., 530, 533, 596, 625, 636, 645f., 654f., 658–660, 662–664, 666f., 669f., 676, 680, 683, 766, 768
Bruce, F. F. 435, 442, 553
Brucker, R. 510
Brückner, W. 121
Brunner, H. 37
Bryder, P. 228
Bryskog, S. 472
Büchner, K. 168
Bujard, W. 388, 411
Bultmann, R. 448, 450, 508, 745
Bungarten, J. J. 132
Burchard, C. 575–577, 582, 585f., 589f., 592f., 597, 675
Burgess, T. C. 55
Burk, K. 257
Burkard, G. 37
Burke, T. J. 480
Burkert, W. 159, 202, 208

Burlingame, A. E. 237
Burnet, R. 434
Butler, H. E. 141
Buzón, R. 234

Cadbury, H. J. 303
Calhoun, R. M. 136, 300, 320
Campbell, R. A. 652–656
Campenhausen, H. von 197, 201
Campos, J. 197f.
Cancik, H. 295
Candlish, J. S. 5, 357, 366
Canfora, L. 151
Caragounis, C. C. 652
Carson, D. A. 183
Carter, D. A. 27f.
Casanova-Robin, H. 627
Casey, P. M. 210
Casson, L. 374
Casurella, A. 635
Cataudella, Q. 257
Catchpole, D. R. 584
Caulley, T. Scott 724
Cerfaux, L. 56
Cerri, G. 244
Chantry, M. 288
Charles, J. D. 688f.
Charles, R. H. 70, 86
Charlesworth, J. H. 87, 579
Chatelion Counet, P. 641, 703
Chazon, E. G. 62, 87, 763
Chilton, B. D. 64, 575, 591
Christophersen, A. 307, 665
Cichorius, C. 296, 299, 310, 314f.
Cizek, A. N. 131f., 166f.
Clabeaux, J. J. 336
Clark, D. L. 45
Clarke, K. D. 61, 356
Clements, R. A. 87
Coggins, R. J. 71
Cole, T. 45f.
Collins, A. Yarbro 671, 673
Collins, J. J. 43, 50, 61–63, 68–71, 80, 86, 88, 95, 97, 289
Collins, R. F. 434, 438, 482
Colpe, C. 120, 726
Comfort, P. W. 219
Connor, W. R. 303
Conzelmann, H. 373, 523
Costa, C. D. N. 241, 257, 300, 321

Cothenet, E. 635
Cousland, J. R. C. 436
Coutts, J. 388
Credner, K. A. 688
Cremer, F. W. 131
Cribiore, R. 42, 44, 46, 234
Crosby, H. L. 146
Cross, F. M. 85
Crouch, J. E. 328
Cunliff, R. J. 314

Dahl, N. A. 197, 335–337, 394
Danneberg, L. 230
Dassmann, E. 10, 183, 289
Davids, P. H. 183, 324, 579, 589, 591, 621, 653, 659, 662, 664, 667, 688, 697, 726
Davies, P. R. 29, 40
De Jong, A. 214, 514
De Jong, I. J. F. 265
De Jonge, H. J. 197
De Jonge, M. 86
De Lange, N. 212
De Oliveira, A. 428
De Roton, M. 121
De Troyer, K. 39, 101, 675
De Wette, W. M. L. 620
Deeks, D. G. 655
Deines, R. 6, 183, 269, 496, 524, 679, 733
Deininger, J. 296, 315
Deißmann, G. A. 235, 277, 366f.
Delcor, M. 94
Delitzsch, F. 550
Delling, G. 463
DeMaris, R. E. 415
Derrida, J. 282
DeSilva, D. A. 492
Desjardins, M. R. 721
Dettenhofer, M. D. 380
Dibelius, M. 303, 324, 416, 440, 575, 577f., 587, 592, 605, 613–615, 619–621
Diels, H. 116, 207
Dihle, A. 128f., 154, 174, 303
Dimant, D. 87, 90, 95–97, 100f.
Dinzelbacher, P. 121
DiTommaso, L. 63f., 71
Dobschütz, E. von 217, 383, 440, 444, 449, 455

Dochhorn, J. 230
Dockery, D. S. 184, 356f.
Doeker, A. 130
Doenges, N. A. 270
Doering, L. 101, 673–676
Donelson, L. R. 61, 311, 321, 352, 359, 368, 500, 521
Donfried, K. P. 436f., 537, 654
Döpp, S. 133, 169–171
Doran, R. 43
Dornseiff, F. 238, 245–248, 254, 256, 367–369
Dörrie, H. 105
Doty, W. G. 269, 272, 282
Du Toit, A. 693, 695, 721f.
Dübner, F. 149
Duff, J. 356
Dunderberg, I. 588
Dunn, J. D. G. 183, 415, 430, 647, 676, 678, 734, 763
Düring, I. 240, 257f., 270, 278, 280
Dürrbach, F. 144
Dyce, A. 237
Dziatzko, K. 148

Easterling, P. E. 303
Easton, S. 134, 162
Ebenbauer, P. 130
Ebner, M. 182, 638, 689
Eckstein, H.-J. 429
Eddelbüttel, A. 510
Edelstein, L. 250
Edgar, D. Hutchinson 623
Edwards, R. B. 736, 743, 746, 748, 754, 756f.
Ego, B. 593
Ehrman, B. 344
Eichholz, G. 587
Eichhorn, J. G. 365, 504, 506
Eisenhut, W. 140
Ellingworth, P. 554
Elliott, J. H. 625, 653f., 656f., 659, 662–664, 667–669, 676, 681
Elliott, J. K. 329, 480
Ellis, E. E. 130, 183, 357, 500, 508, 515, 599, 605, 641
Epp, E. J. 337
Erlemann, K. 13
Erler, M. 248
Ernst, M. 437

Esler, P. F. 471, 479
Evans, C. A. 27, 183, 575, 591
Evanson, E. 4

Falconer, W. A. 164
Falk, D. K. 87, 89f.
Falter, O. 174
Faltner, M. 164, 166
Farkasfalvy, D. 355
Farrar, F. W. 567
Farrell, J. 627
Fascher, E. 492
Faust, E. 389
Fee, G. D. 435
Feeney, D. C. 167
Feine, P. 440
Feldman, L. H. 578, 581, 718
Feldmeier, R. 585, 625, 647, 653, 655, 658, 660f., 666, 668, 670, 675f.
Ferguson, E. 197f.
Fiore, B. 521f.
Fischer, G. 181
Fischer, K. M. 11, 129, 389, 398, 400, 491
Fitzgerald, J. T. 328
Fitzmyer, J. A. 544, 547f., 568, 651, 679f.
Flint, P. 86, 89f.
Fontenrose, J. 109
Foraboschi, D. 313
Forderer, M. 163
Fornberg, T. 594, 706, 724
Forster, E. S. 372
Foster, B. R. 29f., 39
Foster, O. D. 556
Frame, J. E. 440, 443, 445f., 472, 482–484
Francis, F. O. 416f., 419
Frank, K. S. 10, 183
Frank, N. 397
Frankemölle, H. 398, 575, 577f., 582, 715
Fraser P. M. 116, 152, 207, 313
Frede, H.-J. 335f.
Freedman, D. N. 471
Freese, J. H. 46
Frenschkowski, M. 9, 133, 153, 162, 178, 182f., 185, 194–197, 210, 220, 227, 230, 361, 367, 371, 373, 376,

387, 490–492, 497, 501f., 519, 521f., 530, 684, 731
Freudenberger, R. 637
Freund, S. 231
Frey, J. 6, 86, 175, 183, 269, 379, 382, 496, 649f., 679, 685, 687f., 692f., 698, 703–705, 712–714, 720, 728, 733f.
Frickenschmidt, D. 146f.
Friedman, R. E. 68
Frisk, H. 314
Fritz, K. von 6, 10, 62, 113f., 183f., 250, 369, 496
Fuchs, E. 126, 166, 529f.
Fuchs, O. 638
Fuhrmann, M. 140, 167, 169, 377
Fulkerson, L. 627f.
Fuller, R. H. 441
Furley, D. J. 372
Furnish, V. P. 435, 479f., 487
Fürst, A. 133, 178, 187–189, 224f., 369, 373f., 518, 520f., 765f., 768–770, 772, 774–779, 781f.
Fusillo, M. 235

Gaines, R. N. 300
Gaiser, K. 253
Gall, D. 177
Gamble, H. Y. 336, 353, 374, 376, 606
Gammie, J. G. 53, 328
García Martínez, F. 87f., 91
Gaudard, F. 228
Gauger, J.-D. 234
Gaventa, B. R. 435, 471
Gavrilov, A. 285
Gebauer, R. 364
Geerlings, W. 133
Geldart, W. M. 142
Gemeinhardt, P. 224
Gemünden, P. von 13, 575f., 593
Genette, G. 627–630, 634
Gerhards, A. 130
Gerlitz, P. 183, 495
Gese, H. 390, 392f.
Giblin, C. H. 485–487
Gibson, R. K. 235, 239
Giebel, M. 632, 637, 689
Gilbert, M. 53, 55
Gill, C. 167, 178
Gilmour, M. J. 640, 703

Glaser, T. 125, 132f., 269f., 275, 283, 289, 519
Gnilka, J. 392, 428, 660
Goehring, J. E. 218
Goldstein, J. A. 70, 284
Goodman, M. 71
Goodspeed, E. J. 137, 479
Goold, G. P. 141
Goppelt, L. 650, 652, 654, 657, 662, 664f., 667f., 676
Görgemanns, H. 105, 132, 135, 194
Gößwein, H.-U. 132, 278, 285
Götte, J. 140
Goulder, M. D. 433, 436, 669
Gow, A. S. F. 129
Graf, F. 203
Grafton, A. 10, 126
Grant, F. C. 322
Grant, R. M. 338, 353
Grappe, C. 647, 657, 660
Gräßer, E. 571, 583
Grayston, K. 444, 523, 525–527
Green, G. L. 435
Green, J. B. 492, 658
Green, W. S. 64
Greenfield, J. 95
Greeven, H. 303
Gregory, A. 341
Gregory, C. R. 447
Gripentrog, S. 679
Grosvenor, M. 554
Grundmann, W. 690
Gryson, R. 200
Gudeman, A. 128, 134, 138, 141f., 144, 153, 155f., 159, 295
Gunther, J. J. 130
Günther, M. 293
Guthrie, D. 357, 441
Gutsfeld, A. 674

Haacker, K. 589
Haag, E. 405
Haase, F. 130
Habinek, T. 44, 52
Hachlili, R. 651
Haefner, A. E. 127, 321
Häfner, G. 14, 133, 166, 289, 291, 524, 532, 626
Hagen, H. 128, 152–154, 156
Hagen, H.-M. 131

Hahn, F. 463, 575, 587, 691
Hahn, J. 13
Hahn, R. 737
Hahneman, G. M. 197f., 200f., 339
Haines-Eitzen, K. 219
Hainz, J. 130
Hall, F. W. 142
Halson, B. R. 591
Hamburger, K. 272
Hamilton, M. H. 572
Hammer, C. 295, 300
Hammer, O. 29, 599
Hammer-Jensen, I. 208
Hammerstaedt, J. 140
Hanson, A. E. 653
Harlow, D. C. 86
Harnack, A. von 137, 182, 215, 489–491, 503, 512, 529, 535f., 655, 781
Harrington, D. J. 77
Harris, H. A. 44
Harris, W. V. 42
Harrison, P. N. 524f., 527
Hartenstein, J. 129f., 176
Hartin, P. J. 323, 576, 578f., 591, 614–616, 618, 621, 623
Hatch, E. 568
Hatch, W. H. P. 338
Haubeck, W. 668
Haug, W. 231
Häuptli, B. W. 626
Havener, I. 471, 483
Hawthorne, G. F. 576
Hays, R. B. 541
Head, P. M. 663f., 666
Healey, J. F. 651
Heath, M. 47
Heckel, T. 341
Heckel, U. 492
Hegermann, H. 12, 134
Heil, C. 193, 584
Heiligenthal, R. 215f., 589, 696f.
Heimgartner, M. 184
Heine, R. E. 342
Heinemann, M. 131
Heininger, B. 373, 386
Helck, W. 32
Hellholm, D. 594
Hemer, C. J. 665
Hengel, M. 6, 8, 51, 113f., 183, 269, 340f., 369, 378f., 496, 576, 578f.,

581, 583, 588, 592, 620, 652, 655, 660, 667, 673, 683, 704, 733–735, 737, 753, 761, 763
Henne, P. 198
Hennecke, E. 130, 155
Hercher, R. 160, 239, 242f., 295
Herdan, G. 444, 523, 525–527
Hermann, S. 32
Herzer, J. 16, 125, 214, 290, 371, 373, 489, 502, 505, 514, 524, 533f., 556, 625f., 649, 657, 664–666, 668–670, 677, 680f.
Hicks, R. D. 156
Hilhorst, A. 95, 436, 475
Hill, C. C. 583
Hill, C. E. 197, 341
Hillmer, M. R. 341
Hilton, M. L. 523
Hintermeier, C. M. 628
Hinz, V. 233, 237
Hirzel, R. 148, 161, 164, 166
Hochadel, O. 15, 176
Hock, R. F. 43
Hodkinson, O. 270, 282
Höeg, C. 144
Hoehner, H. 388
Hoesen, H. B. von 313
Hoffmann, D. 626
Hogan, K. Martin 71f.
Hoheisel, K. 109
Holladay, C. R. 572
Holladay, W. L. 181
Holland, G. S. 434, 438
Hollander, J. 541
Hollmann, G. 440, 465, 472
Holmes, D. I. 523
Holmes, M. W. 435
Hölter, A. 183
Holtz, G. 494
Holtz, T. 463, 583f., 650
Holtzmann, H. J. 134, 185, 373, 383, 434, 439f., 445, 449, 457, 464, 466, 472, 502, 510–512, 514
Holzberg, N. 12, 133, 140f., 166, 233–235, 242, 246–250, 252, 254–257, 259–262, 264–266, 269–271, 282, 291, 372, 519
Hömke, N. 230
Hoogendijk, F. A. J. 663
Hoppe, R. 395, 403–405, 428, 430

Horbury, W. 197f., 200f.
Horn, C. K. 183f.
Horn, F. W. 9, 133, 182, 361, 367, 379, 387, 490, 684
Hornschuh, M. 130, 245
Horrell, D. G. 646f., 668, 671, 679, 681
Horsley, G. H. R. 651
Hose, M. 126, 132, 144, 159, 161, 267
Hotze, G. 438
Houldon, J. L. 514
Hourani, G. F. 210
Houtman, A. 214, 514
Howald, E. 372
Howe, H. M. 257
Hübner, H. 177, 394, 397f., 400, 403, 420
Hübner, R. 267
Hübner, W. 109
Huffman, C. A. 238, 256
Hunger, H. 29, 184
Hunzinger, C.-H. 667f.
Hurd, J. C. 433f., 445
Hurtado, L. 220

Ilan, T. 651
Immisch, O. 245
Irmscher, J. 6, 194
Isnardi Parente, M. 250, 252

Jachmann, G. 154
Jackson, D. R. 97
Jackson-McCabe, M. 323, 549, 616f., 619, 621f.
Jacobson, T. 39
Jacoby, F. 156
Jaeger, W. 105
Janßen, M. 4, 6, 11, 126f., 130, 155, 174f., 178, 184, 195, 204, 356, 387, 411, 492–495, 497, 626, 683, 727, 730
Japhet, S. 64
Jauß, H. R. 236
Jenkins, C. 302
Jervell, J. 757
Jewett, R. K. 434f., 472, 548, 551, 553f., 565, 568–570
Jindo, J. Y. 64
Jobes, K. H. 656, 663, 669
Johnson, A. C. 313
Johnson, E. E. 435, 471

Johnson, L. T. 322, 324, 504, 517f., 576, 578, 589, 600f., 606–610, 613–617, 621, 726
Johnson, P. F. 523
Jolivet, J.-C. 627
Jones, E. D. 553, 555f.
Jones, P. R. 218
Jones, W. H. S. 156
Jordan, H. 10
Jost, F. 279
Jouan, F. 285f.
Jouanna, J. 245
Jülicher, A. 492
Jütte, R. 674

Kaestli, J.-D. 197
Kah, D. 42, 45
Kaibel, G. 142
Kaiser, U. U. 213
Kalin, E. 349f.
Kambylis, A. 143
Kampling, R. 726
Kannengiesser, C. 218
Karpp, H. 194
Karrer, M. 667, 670, 678
Karris, R. J. 471
Käsemann, E. 504
Kasser, R. 218, 228
Kasten, H. 139, 145, 150
Katz, P. 546
Kayser, C. L. 309
Kelhoffer, J. A. 550
Kelly, J. N. D. 654, 659, 662, 664f., 667–669, 676
Kennedy, G. A. 44f., 47, 306
Kennel, N. M. 42
Kenny, A. 390, 523–527
Kenyon, F. G. 337
Kern, F. H. 472, 475, 605
Kern, O. 448
Kertelge, K. 137, 337, 393, 398, 441, 500
Keßler, M. 688
Ketts, P. 107
Kiley, M. 321, 360, 377
Kim, S. 435
Kindstrand, J. F. 275, 283
Kinzig, W. 502
Kirchgessner, B. 428
Klampfl, T. 193

Klassen, W. 335
Klauck, H.-J. 12, 56, 132–134, 136f.,
  222f., 242f., 289, 296, 304, 377,
  414, 476, 493, 515, 521f., 529, 575,
  730, 733f., 736–740, 743, 745–747,
  749, 752, 754, 756f., 761, 765,
  771f., 774–776, 778, 784
Klein, G. 130, 373, 523, 636, 655
Klein, M. 575, 577, 675
Klein, U. 230
Klijn, A. F. J. 383
Kloocke, K. 270
Kloppenborg, J. S. 323, 617, 622, 674
Knab, R. 240, 250
Knibb, M. 71
Knoch, O. B. 650, 668
Knopf, R. 654, 660f.
Knowles, M. P. 81
Knox, B. M. W. 285, 303
Koch, D.-A. 374, 674
Koch, T. 148
Kocher, U. 15, 176
Koechly, A. 209
Koester, C. R. 551, 567
Koester, H. 324, 328, 341, 434f., 441f.,
  444, 470, 690
Köhler, B. 155
Köhler, W.-D. 492
Kolarchik, M. 50
Konradt, M. 13, 575–577, 579–582,
  584–589, 591–593, 614, 675, 678f.
Konstan, D. 257, 261
Köpf, U. 364f., 504, 508
Korenjak, M. 264, 289
Körte, A. 148
Körtner, U. H. J. 656, 668
Koskenniemi, H. 380, 632
Köster, B. 183
Köster, H. 130, 158
Köstlin, K. R. 4f.
Kottsieper, I. 39
Kovacs, D. 285, 287
Kowalski, B. 130
Kraft, R. A. 95
Krämer, T. 232
Kranz, W. 116, 207
Kraus, F. X. 781
Kraus, T. J. 198, 215, 219f., 641, 660
Kraus, W. 584, 675, 684
Krause, M. 693

Krauter, S. 133, 519
Kreinrath, J. 512
Krentz, E. 158, 433–438, 471, 484,
  486f.
Krodel, G. 433f., 441, 450, 452, 465–
  467, 469, 486
Kroh, P. 136
Kroll, W. 208f.
Krötke, H. 505
Krüger, G. 106
Kuch, H. 270f., 282
Kuhn, T. K. 267
Kuhn, T. S. 503
Kümmel, W. G. 184, 364, 441, 523
Kürzdörfer, K. 597
Kustermann, A. P. 674
Kytzler, B. 369

LaBonnardière, A.-M. 200
Lagarrigue, G. 146, 192, 321
Lake, K. 671
Lambert, W. G. 29, 37–39
Lampe, G. W. H. 568
Lampe, P. 14, 360, 511, 651f., 766
Lane, W. L. 551, 553, 567
Lange, A. 39, 89f., 101, 593, 675
Längin, H. 250
Lanham, R. A. 43
Laourdas, B. 309
Lapidge, M. 427
Larcher, C. 46, 53, 201
Lardet, P. 158
Larson, E. 101
Latte, K. 280
Laub, F. 184, 596
Lausberg, H. 132, 167, 631
Lawlor, H. J. 212
Laws, S. 575, 578, 587
Layton, B. 213
Lea, T. D. 184, 357
Ledger, G. 523, 527
Lee, T. R. 54
Leeman, A. D. 167
Légasse, S. 434, 486
Lehnert, V. A. 375
Leidl, C. G. 134
Lejeune, M. 217
Lenzo Marchese, G. 31
Leppä, O. 413f.
Leppin, V. 502, 688

Lesky, A. 128
Leutzsch, M. 656
Levine, J. M. 237
Lewis, C. S. 231
Lewis, J. R. 29, 599
Licht, J. 70f.
Lichtheim, M. 32–35, 37, 299
Lied, L. I. 78
Lietzmann, H. 130, 376
Lieu, J. M. 374, 677, 733–735, 737–741, 743, 745, 748, 750–753, 755, 757, 759–761, 763
Lightfoot, J. B. 427
Lightfoot, J. L. 204f.
Lincoln, A. T. 392–395, 402
Lincoln, B. 599, 602
Lindblom, J. 120
Lindemann, A. 182, 375, 392–394, 413, 416, 427f., 430, 442, 470, 472, 588, 646, 668
Lindsay, W. M. 200
Link, H. 648
Link, S. M. 230
Linke, B. 167
Lips, H. von 194, 213, 514
Lipschitz, O. 64
Lipsius, R. A. 474
Llewelyn, S. R. 663
Lohmeyer, E. 525
Löhr, W. A. 673
Lohse, E. 328, 413, 416, 441, 587
Lona, H. E. 660
Long, J. 663
Looks, C. 503, 533
Loprieno, A. 33
Lucas, A. J. 561–563
Luchner, K. 132, 519
Ludolph, M. 272
Ludwig, H. 430
Ludwig, H.-W. 270
Lüdemann, G. 137, 155, 158, 176, 588
Lührmann, D. 345, 696
Luther, W. 126
Lux, R. 14
Luz, U. 14, 166, 289, 403, 413, 417, 423, 592

MacDonald, D. R. 289
MacDonald, M. Y. 400, 416, 420
MacDowell, D. 142

Macholz, C. 577
Mack, B. 54
MacLaren, M. 144
Macleod, C. W. 49
Magie, D. 145
Mahaffy, J. P. 313
Maier, F. 696
Maier, J. 378
Maisch, I. 414, 419, 428
Malherbe, A. J. 132, 234, 295, 309, 435f., 469, 472, 483, 495, 516f., 757
Malosse, P.-L. 257
Maman, A. 95
Mann, G. 271f., 293
Manson, T. W. 436
Marcus, J. 579, 672
Markschies, C. 6, 183, 197f., 269, 376, 496, 578, 733
Marrou, H. I. 43
Marshall, I. H. 10, 125f., 134, 325f., 442, 462
Martin, J. 105
Martin, R. P. 183, 591, 621
Martin, T. W. 415, 418, 667, 669
Martinet, H. 138
Martini, C. M. 219
Martyn, J. L. 471
Marxsen, W. 441, 636, 655
Masson, C. 434, 472
Matthews, E. 313
Maurer, M. 380
Mayer, W. 267
Mayor, J. 615, 617, 620
Mayordomo, M. 424
Mays, J. L. 479
McCutcheon, R. T. 602
McDonald, D. R. 537
McDonald, L. M. 27, 61, 86, 337, 376
McGing, B. 282
McKinnish Bridges, L. 435, 471, 483, 486
McLean, B. H. 437
McLeman, J. 526
McNeile, A. H. 440f.
Meade, D. G. 5, 8, 61f., 134, 137, 176, 184, 358f., 361, 376, 378, 604f., 648, 657, 683, 729, 734
Mealand, D. L. 523
Meeks, W. A. 416, 757
Meinhold, P. 508

Meiser, M. 580
Meister, K. 302f.
Mellmann, K. 230
Mendelson, A. 43
Menken, M. J. J. 434, 438,
    479, 482–487
Merk, O. 364, 366, 377, 383,
    512, 580, 583
Merkel, H. 137, 391
Merkel, R. F. 5, 495
Merkelbach, R. 132
Merkle, S. 233
Merklein, H. 391, 393, 402f.,
    405, 425, 581
Merz, A. 13, 15, 178, 268, 371, 489f.,
    537, 626
Metzger, B. M. 28, 61, 184, 295f., 356,
    492, 523f., 528
Metzger, S. 230
Metzner, R. 625, 638, 647,
    650, 652, 656
Meurer, S. 415
Mewaldt, J. 207, 238
Meyer, A. 5, 130, 368, 495
Meyer, E. 156
Meyer, M. W. 228
Meyer, R. D. 167f.
Michaelis, D. 683
Michaelis, W. 48, 441, 523, 525, 528
Michaels, J. R. 658, 663–665
Michaelson, S. 523
Mignogna, E. 284
Mihailov, G. 313
Milik, J. T. 85, 87, 94f.
Millar, F. 71, 211
Miller, S. G. 43
Milligan, G. 439, 443, 462, 472
Misset-van de Weg, M. 214, 514
Mitchell, M. M. 304, 308, 323, 471,
    480, 517f., 537, 617f.
Mitsis, P. 257, 261
Mitton, C. 388, 390–392
Modrzejewski, J. M. 58
Moffatt, J. 130, 440, 449, 455, 464,
    467, 469
Moles, J. 296, 308
Molthagen, J. 637
Momigliano, A. 68, 188, 780
Montefiore, H. 555, 569
Moo, D. J. 576, 578, 702

Moore, A. L. 440
Moore-Blunt, J. 250f.
Morello, R. 229, 235
Moreschini, C. 371
Morgan, J. R. 167, 265, 272
Morgan, T. 46
Morgenthaler, R. 524
Moritz, T. 392
Morris, J. 117
Morris, L. 435, 440
Morrison, A. D. 229, 235, 239
Morrow, G. R. 250
Morthley, R. 108
Morton, A. Q. 523, 526
Mossman, J. 282, 296
Mounce, W. C. 527
Mowinckel, S. 105
Moxon, I. S. 296
Muddiman, J. 471
Muhlack, U. 502f.
Müller, C. G. 193
Müller, C. W. 127, 152f., 159, 161f.,
    166f., 238f.
Müller, K. 581, 584
Müller, P. 10, 129, 640, 697f., 730
Müller, P.-G. 391, 434, 487, 583, 703
Müller, W. G. 133, 267, 282
Mumprecht, V. 157
Murphy-O'Connor, J. 290, 527
Murray, O. 117
Murrmann-Kahl, M. 506
Müseler, E. 226, 631
Mußner, F. 576, 579, 588, 615
Mynors, R. A. B. 200

Nails, D. 251
Najman, H. 8, 62, 76, 83,
    91f., 97f., 100
Naschert, G. 234
Natali, M. 765, 768, 771f.,
    774f., 780, 783
Nau, F. 147
Naveh, J. 652
Neil, W. 440
Nestle, W. 108
Neuhausen, K. A. 164–168
Neumann, K. J. 523, 526f.
Neusner, J. 64, 69
Newman, J. H. 83
Newsom, C. A. 471

Neyrey, J. H. 722–724, 726, 728
Nicholl, C. R. 436
Nickel, R. 242
Nickelsburg, G. W. E. 64–67, 69–71, 73, 76f., 94f., 97, 693, 728
Nicklas, T. 196, 198, 219f., 660
Niebuhr, B. G. 509
Niebuhr, K.-W. 524, 576f., 579, 584f., 593, 596, 673, 675, 679, 687
Niedermeier, L. 171
Niederwimmer, K. 672
Nienhuis, D. R. 137, 221, 345, 350, 361, 576–578, 588
Nietzsche, F. 507
Nilsson, M. P. 43
Noethlichs, K. L. 13
Norden, E. 369, 394, 448
Norelli, E. 371
Novak, K. 508
Novotný, F. 250
Nünlist, R. 265
Nussbaum, M. C. 257

O'Sullivan, J. 348
Obbink, D. 209
Oberg, E. 170f.
Oberlinner, L. 178, 506, 524, 526
Ochel, W. 390
Oeming, M. 64
Oepke, A. 440
Oertelt, F. 275
Ogilvie, R. M. 188
Ohlig, K.-H. 10, 135, 355
Olbricht, T. H. 572
Olshausen, E. 315f.
Osten-Sacken, P. von der 466
Owen, A. S. 141

Packer, J. 357
Paige, T. 357
Painter, J. 575, 591f., 594, 618
Pape, W. 314
Parry, D. W. 95
Parsons, E. A. 116
Parsons, P. J. 371f.
Paschke, F. 194
Pasquali, G. P. 250
Patillon, M. 132, 300
Patsch, H. 3f.
Paul, S. M. 86

Paulsen, H. 625, 696, 698f., 706, 728
Pélékidis, C. 43
Penner, T. C. 578, 589
Pépin, J. 109
Percy, E. 417, 419, 430
Perdelwitz, R. 130
Perdue, L. G. 39, 51, 53, 63, 328
Perkins, P. 479, 736f., 740, 743, 745, 749, 756f., 760, 762
Pervo, R. I. 133, 214, 289f., 519f., 678, 680
Pesch, C. 120
Pesch, R. 583, 650f., 660
Peter, H. 126, 178
Petersen, N. R. 269
Peterson, J. 572
Pfeiffer, R. 116
Pfligersdorffer, G. 113
Philips, H. 637
Philonenko, M. 580
Philonenko-Sayar, B. 580
Pickard-Cambridge, A. 142, 148
Picone, M. 166
Pietersma, A. 219
Pilhofer, P. 227, 379, 382, 593, 649, 704
Pink, K. 155
Pinkster, H. 167
Pitts, A. W. 51
Plümacher, E. 106, 117
Pokorný, P. 11, 184, 357, 360, 366, 390, 398, 411, 414, 430, 492, 494f.
Popkes, E. E. 175
Popkes, W. 576f., 587f., 592, 675
Porter, S. E. 27, 44, 51, 183, 303, 357, 383, 537, 621
Powell, M. A. 648
Prasad, J. 668
Pratscher, W. 575, 577f., 587, 591f., 595, 597, 601, 615, 618
Preisigke, F. 277, 313
Preisker, H. 654, 696, 710
Price, S. R. F. 56
Priest, J. 71
Prior, J. 341
Pritchard, J. B. 37
Puech, É. 93, 95
Puelma, M. 109

Qimron, E. 93

Autorenregister

Quinn, J. D. 289, 292

Rad, G. von 63
Rahn, H. 164, 632
Ranke, L. von 511
Rantzow, S. 390, 393
Ratschow, C. R. 105
Raupp, W. 364
Rawson, E. 296, 306
Redpath, H. A. 568
Reed, A. Y. 75
Reeson, J. 627
Regul, J. 672
Rehm, B. 194
Reichert, A. 637
Reiff, A. 161f., 170f.
Reinhardt, K. 110
Reinmuth, E. 14, 134, 360, 496f., 509f., 766, 782
Reitzenstein, R. 429
Repschinski, B. 130
Reumann, J. 654
Reuter, R. 390, 392
Reventlow, H. Graf 504, 507f., 510f., 667
Reynolds, L. D. 161
Richard, E. J. 435, 471, 479, 483, 487
Richards, E. R. 148, 150, 318, 326, 663–665
Richards, K. H. 437
Richards, W. A. 214, 529
Richardson, P. 674
Riedel, V. 170
Riedl, H. J. 11, 15, 184, 360, 382, 641f., 683, 702, 730
Riepl, W. 139
Riesner, R. 530
Rigaux, B. 364f., 434, 439, 445, 449, 451f.
Riggenbach, E. 147
Riginos, A. Swift 255f.
Rimell, V. 282, 628
Ringe, S. H. 471
Rist, J. M. 184, 253
Robbins, G. A. 349f.
Robert, L. 44
Robinson, H. W. 62
Robinson, J. M. 219f., 442
Robinson, T. A. 523, 528
Roetzel, C. 400

Rogerson, J. W. 62
Roh, T. 384
Rolfe, J. C. 161, 172
Roloff, J. 137, 524, 583–585, 593
Römer, C. 518, 520
Ronning, C. 13, 386
Roose, H. 393, 426f., 699
Ropes, J. H. 324, 575, 582, 606, 608, 615, 620
Rose, C. 634
Rose, H. J. 371f.
Rose, V. 300
Rosenbach, M. 581
Rosenbaum, H. U. 183
Rosenberger, V. 109
Rosenmeyer, P. A. 12, 132, 229, 241, 245–247, 257–259, 266, 271f., 274, 279–291, 537–539
Rothe, R. 505
Rothschild, C. K. V, 22, 147, 327, 538f.
Rothstein, M. 603f.
Röwekamp, G. 133, 155, 176
Rowland, C. 62f., 419
Royality, R. M. 417
Rubinkiewicz, R. 580
Rühl, F. 136, 296, 299, 310
Rüsen-Weinhold, U. 375
Runia, D. T. 200
Rupprecht, K. 109
Rusam, D. 428
Russell, D. A. 306
Russell, D. S. 10, 54, 62
Ruwet, J. 353

Sampley, J. P. 43, 54
Sanders, E. P. 328
Sanders, J. A. 27, 61, 86, 337, 376
Sato, M. 588
Scarpat, G. 187
Schäfer, R. 522
Schaff, A. 32
Schalit, A. 202
Schelkle, K. H. 11, 150, 654, 668, 696, 768
Schenk, W. 178, 414
Schenke, H.-M. 129, 213, 218
Schenke, L. 583, 594
Schickert, K. 8, 128, 141f., 148, 174, 176

Schiffman, L. H. 91f.
Schirren, T. 244
Schlegelberger, B. 726
Schleiermacher, F. D. E. 3, 364, 489, 502f., 505, 522, 683
Schleyer, D. 195
Schliebitz, C. 626
Schlier, H. 571
Schlosser, J. 587
Schmeling, G. 233, 270
Schmeller, T. 134, 373
Schmid, J. 393
Schmid, U. 182, 336, 503
Schmid, W. 108, 142
Schmidt, D. 437, 482
Schmidt, D. H. 658
Schmidt, J. E. C. 364, 439, 441, 472, 503
Schmidt, K. M. 13, 132, 134, 148, 648, 655, 657, 661, 680, 699, 703, 705, 708f., 716
Schmidt, L. 126
Schmidt, M. 130
Schmitz, T. A. 627
Schnabel, E. J. 357
Schneemelcher, W. 130, 155, 201, 383, 518
Schneider, H. 295
Schneider, J. 132, 148
Schneider, T. 692f.
Schnelle, U. 11, 150, 173, 182, 185, 213, 414, 429, 431, 434, 491–493, 497, 514, 524, 576, 578, 590, 596, 689
Schnider, F. 575, 578, 587, 590
Schoedel, W. R. 558
Scholder, K. 364, 504f., 508f., 512
Schöllgen, G. 184
Scholtissek, K. 428, 438
Scholz, P. 42, 45
Scholz, S. 386
Schorn, S. 248
Schottky, M. 315
Schottroff, W. 107
Schrage, W. 668, 690
Schreiber, S. 182, 689
Schreiner, T. R. 688, 697, 702
Schröter, J. 175, 373, 510
Schubart, W. 141, 153
Schubert, C. 134, 166, 395

Schürer, E. 71, 114, 117–119, 201, 378
Schütte, H.-W. 505
Schuster, M. 169
Schwartz, D. R. 679
Schwebel, H. 275
Schwemer, A. M. 6, 183, 213, 269, 496, 733
Schweitzer, A. 504
Schweizer, E. 415, 425, 428
Schwietering, S. 146
Schwindt, R. 389
Scullion, S. 285
Seland, T. 665
Selle, J. 161
Sellin, G. 400, 402–404, 430, 697, 699f.
Selwyn, E. G. 658, 662, 665, 667
Semler, J. S. 364, 366
Sengebusch, M. 314
Senior, D. P. 659, 668
Sevenster, J. N. 578f., 620
Sevrin, J.-S. 739
Shepherd, M. H. 597
Showerman, G. 136
Siller, H. P. 429
Simpson, W. K. 31, 33, 37
Singer, F. N. 206
Sinko, T. 144
Sint, J. A. 5f., 11, 132, 135, 153, 159f., 184, 369–372, 498
Skeat, T. C. 341
Smart, J. D. 296
Smelik, W. F. 651
Smith, A. 482–487
Smith, D. Moody 746, 749, 751, 761
Smith, R. E. 296, 299, 302, 304, 308–310, 313, 318f.
Smyly, J. G. 313
Smyth, H. 553
Snell, B. 314
Snyder, G. F. 335
Soards, M. L. 668, 703
Sokoloff, M. 651
Sommer, B. 547
Son, S.-W. 530
Sophocles, E. A. 314
Spengel, L. 295, 300
Spentzou, E. 627
Speyer, W. 5–7, 10, 27, 62, 105–107, 110–120, 123, 126–128, 131f., 134f.,

138, 142, 144–148, 152–154, 156, 159f., 172, 174f., 184, 197, 201–203, 207, 211, 231, 297, 299, 314, 353, 356, 359, 366, 369f., 373, 376–378, 381, 494–499, 501, 515, 519–521, 532f., 766
Spicq, C. 568
Spoth, F. 627, 630f.
Städele, A. 145, 240
Stählin, G. 568
Stamps, D. L. 366
Standaert, B. 418
Standhartinger, A. 13, 133, 148, 152, 160, 178, 269, 275, 415, 420, 495, 497, 500f., 521
Stanton, G. N. 341
Starcky, J. 95
Stärk, E. 177
Steckel, H. 208
Stegemann, E. W. 267, 577, 594
Stegemann, V. 209
Stegemann, W. 594
Stemberger, G. 367
Stemberger, M. 167, 184
Stemplinger, E. 154, 237f.
Stendahl, K. 335
Stenger, J. 108, 246, 257–260
Stenger, W. 8, 272, 391, 583, 703
Sterling, G. E. 43
Stern, M. 211
Stettner, W. 142
Steudel, P. 667
Sticherl, M. 131
Stirewalt, M. L. 132, 138, 234, 243, 295, 304
Stocker, H. 626
Stone, M. E. 53, 61f., 71f., 75, 81, 87, 95, 763
Stoneman, R. 272
Stowers, S. K. 55, 132, 234
Strachotta, A. 4
Strasburger, G. 144
Strathmann, H. 658f.
Streck, M. 30, 38
Strecker, G. 162, 185, 493, 762
Strelka, J. P. 279
Strobel, A. 583
Strohmaier, G. 205
Stübe, R. 176
Stuckenbruck, L. T. 86

Stuhlmacher, P. 366, 430, 655
Suchla, B. R. 194
Suerbaum, W. 142
Sullivan, R. D. 315
Sumney, J. L. 425
Sunckel, J. 130
Sundberg, A. C. 197f.
Sykutris, J. 132f., 234, 271
Syme, R. 10, 152
Synge, F. C. 388
Syreeni, K. 588
Szlezák, T. A. 240, 250, 253

Taatz, I. 674
Talbert, C. H. 289
Taylor, M. E. 614
Tcherikover, V. 45
Testuz, M. 193, 219, 329
Teufel, W. S. 136, 140
Theißen, G. 13, 134, 137, 162, 185f., 202f., 215, 221–223, 368, 371, 386, 501, 575–578, 593–596
Theobald, M. 395, 425
Thomas, J. C. 735
Thomas, K. J. 546f., 550
Thomassen, E. 599
Thompson, J. W. 566, 569
Thompson, M. M. 492
Thompson, T. 158, 325, 496
Thornton, C.-J. 671, 673
Thraede, K. 108, 110f., 120, 377, 380, 637
Thrall, M. E. 382
Thurén, L. 621
Thurston, B. 434f., 471, 484–487
Thurston, R. W. 436
Thyen, H. 107, 120–122
Tieleman, T. 427
Tigchelaar, E. 86, 91, 93, 95f.
Tilly, M. 196
Toman, R. 507
Tomsin, A. 654
Tonsriau, J. 56
Too, Y. L. 47
Torm, F. 5, 184, 366, 368, 494, 528
Torraca, L. 295–301, 303–306, 308, 310, 314
Tov, E. 87, 89, 95
Towner, P. H. 366
Townsend, J. 469

Trampedach, J. 250f., 257
Trapp, E. 314
Trapp, M. 235, 241, 247, 257, 267, 270–273, 277, 282, 292
Trebilco, P. 739, 741f., 754–756
Tregelles, S. P. 200f.
Trilling, W. 182, 433f., 439, 441f., 445f., 449f., 452–456, 463, 466, 468f., 472
Trillitzsch, W. 187, 780
Trobisch, D. 376, 515
Troeltsch, E. 507f.
Tromp, J. 70
Trummer, P. 16, 137, 178, 337, 500, 514, 518, 530
Tsuji, M. 575, 577f., 585, 587f., 617f., 675f.
Tuckett, C. 588

Uhland, L. 511f.
Ullmann, M. 209
Ulrich, E. 86

Van Bruggen, J. 530
Van der Toorn, K. 28, 40
Van der Waerden, B. L. 160, 177
Van der Watt, J. 705, 728
Van Henten, J. W. 651
Van Kooten, G. 389–393, 415, 427, 436, 475
Van Minnen, P. 663
VanderKam, J. 89f., 212
Vawter, B. 467
Vegge, T. 132, 373, 523
Verheyden, J. 197f.
Verhoef, E. 61
Vermès, G. 69, 71, 114, 201, 378
Verseput, D. J. 585, 675
Vielhauer, P. 383, 421f., 672, 686, 696
Vögtle, A. 12, 134, 203f., 215, 625, 690, 704, 713, 717, 723, 730
Vogt-Spira, G. 169, 177
Volkmann, R. 131, 448
Vollenweider, S. 385f., 424
Vollmer, F. 136
Volten, A. 32
Vouga, F. 137, 412, 729

Wachob, W. 600, 621
Wachsmuth, C. 208
Wacker, W. C. 292
Wagner, G. 429
Wagner, J. R. 562
Walde, C. 631
Wall, R. 673
Walter, N. 6, 14, 360, 463, 766
Wanamaker, C. A. 435f.
Wander, B. 117
Wartenberg, G. 502
Wasserman, T. 218–221, 688, 702
Waszink, J. H. 208
Watson, D. F. 54, 621, 746
Weatherly, J. A. 435
Webb, R. L. 323, 617
Weber, R. 200
Wechsler, A. 584
Wedderburn, A. J. M. 429, 551f., 554, 584
Weder, H. 366
Wehnert, J. 583f., 595
Wehr, L. 583f.
Weidlich, T. 208
Weima, J. A. D. 383
Weinreich, O. 157
Weiser, A. 276, 517, 583, 680
Weiss, B. 556
Weiß, J. 322, 447–452
Weissenberg, H. von 101
Welles, C. B. 303f.
Wellmann, M. 208
Welte, M. 183
Wendel, C. 116, 118
Wendland, P. 448, 450, 470, 662
Wenz, G. 692f.
Werdermann, H. 696, 722
Werman, C. 75
West, D. 46
Westcott, B. F. 567, 569
Westerink, L. G. 309
Wevers, J. W. 562
Wheeler, A. L. 141
White, J. L. 234f., 295, 778
Whiteley, D. E. H. 440, 465
Whitters, M. F. 73, 78f., 674
Wilamowitz-Moellendorff, U. von 146
Widl, M. 638
Widmann, H. 128, 138, 141, 152f.
Wikenhauser, A. 441
Wilckens, U. 430
Wilder, T. L. 134f., 184, 356

Wilhelm, W. 145
Wilkins, M. J. 357
Williams, C. R. 551, 555f.
Williams, C. S. C. 441
Williams, D. J. 435
Wills, L. M. 63
Wilson, N. G. 54
Wilson, R. 413
Wilson, S. G. 674
Windisch, H. 654, 661, 667, 696, 710
Winiarczyk, M. 108
Winkler, J. J. 265
Winston, D. 50f., 55f., 58
Winter, J. G. 664
Wischmeyer, O. 366, 373, 375, 378f., 386
Wischmeyer, W. 386
Wiseman, T. P. 167, 178
Wisse, F. 693f.
Witherington III, B. 435, 600, 613, 621
Wlosok, A. 56
Wohlenberg, G. 440, 690
Wolter, M. 13, 158, 175, 184, 337, 347, 360f., 379, 403, 411, 413–415, 417–419, 428, 430, 491f., 498, 517f., 533, 734f., 737, 762
Woodmann, A. J. 296
Woodmann, T. 46
Wooten, C. W. 306
Worthington, I. 43

Wrede, W. 365, 383, 434, 440, 442, 445, 454, 457–459, 461–463, 466, 470, 472
Wright, J. E. 78
Wright III, B. G. 63
Wurst, G. 228
Wyrick, J. 29, 40

Youtie, H. C. 664

Zahn, M. M. 92
Zahn, T. 147, 197, 199–201, 221, 335, 468, 688, 702, 727, 781
Zeller, D. 429
Zeller, E. G. 473
Zembathy, J. S. 178
Zerwick, M. 554
Ziegler, J. 50
Ziegler, K. 308
Zimmerli, W. 121
Zimmermann, A. F. 597
Zimmermann, R. 13, 15, 126, 150f., 166, 176, 184, 366f., 375, 492f., 501, 521, 705
Zingerle, A. 212
Zmijewski, J. 11, 360, 642
Zoepfl, F. 218
Zucchelli, B. 257
Zycha, J. 190

Sach- und Personenregister

Abraham 49, 65, 67, 72f., 83, 100, 111, 120, 227, 542–549, 582, 589, 615f.
– cycle 572
Abschrift 373f.
– nichtautorisiert 195, 205f.
Absender 626f., 633
– Co-sender 374, 381
– Mitabsender 769
Achill 108
Acts of Paul and Thecla 339
Adam 72f., 111, 119
Adressat / addressor 628, 630, 634f., 639–641, 684
– faktisch 711
– Mitadressaten 769
~enfiktion 413f., 711
~engemeinde 643
~ensituation 711–714
adscriptio 324f., 407, 582, 585, 637
Ägypten 110
Aischines 160, 242, 246, 275f., 285, 290, 293
~brief 274f. (s.a. Briefroman)
Alexandria 42–59, 117f., 159, 568, 673
Alter Orient 110
Altersbeweis 227
Altes Testament 110, 115, 117, 119–123
Anachronismus 765, 782
Angaben, persönliche 387–389, 499, 771–773 (s.a. Notiz, persönliche)
Angelologie 700
Anonymität / anonymity 36, 111f., 115, 118, 311, 497f.
Anspielung
– biographisch 771–773
– historisch 770–775, 783f.
– literarisch 775f.
– stilistisch 776–779
Antinomismus 697, 701
Antiochenischer Zwischenfall 583–587, 596f., 703
apocrypha 85–98

Apokalypse / apocalypse 113, 333–335, 345, 350, 353
– of Peter 350, 353
– Sendschreiben 375
– of weeks 65–67
Apollon 107, 109
Apologetik 113, 118
Apostel 599–602, 648–652
– als Autorität / as authority 118, 123, 190f., 222f., 340–342, 347, 358–361, 468–470, 492, 512, 622f., 645–654, 673, 691f.
– Pseudoapostel 381f.
~dekret 583f., 595
~konvent 584, 588f., 596f.
Apostelgeschichte / Acts of the Apostles 333f., 340f., 345–350, 354, 386, 625, 761, 771, 780
Apostolic Constitution 351
Apostolizität / apostolicity 354f., 374, 381–383, 600, 608–610, 612, 688, 692
argument, statistical (s. Wortstatistik)
Aristeasbrief 42, 49, 117f., 269
Aristophanes 142–144, 174, 286–288, 567f.
Askese 419f., 423–425
Athanasius 199, 202, 344, 747
Atomisten 106, 108
attribution of authorship
– in Early Jewish Tradition 41f.
Augenzeuge 703–705, 738
Authentizität 363–366, 380–384
authority (s. Autorität)
Autobiographie 380
Autodiegese 269, 271, 290, 292
Autograph 380
Autor / author
– actual 473, 477–488
– ascribed 473–488 (s.a. attribution of authorship)
– Doppelpersönlichkeit des 476, 480f.
– implizit 782

~enfiktion 215, 414, 422, 643, 684, 691–693, 731f., 782
~enpersönlichkeit 377–379
~enzuschreibung (s. ascribed author) Autorität / authority 375, 492, 599–613, 622f.

Babylon 37–39, 68, 79f., 90, 96, 646f., 667–681
~isches Exil 65–82, 101
Bakis 107, 226
Barnabasbrief 344, 346, 350
Baruch 57, 63, 65, 76–83, 226, 674
~apokalypse 496
2. Baruch 71–79, 674
Bearbeitung, redaktionelle 118, 136f., 233, 254, 256, 265f., 373–376, 379
Begierde 579
benediction 550–554
Bentley, Richard 4, 236–241, 263, 268, 278, 287, 295f., 310
Besitzethos 594
Bewusstseinsgeschichte 105–107
Bibliothek / library 38, 42, 116–118, 129, 151f., 154, 567f.
Bileam 718
Bildung
~sabstand 223
~skultur 117, 189, 203–212, 222–224, 517, 781
~sniveau 529, 578
~swesen 187f.
Biographie 135, 144f., 147, 248, 256, 267, 283–293, 380, 770f., 775
Bodmer Papyri 218–220, 329
Brief (s.a. letter)
– Freundschaftsbrief 517, 784
– als Gattungsbegriff 234
– Gefangenschaftsbriefe 528, 772, 784
– katholisch 333f., 343–346
~eingangseulogie 394
~formular 382, 784
~präskript 778
~rezeption 380
~roman 132f., 234–236, 268–271, 518–520, 628
~roman des Aischines 283–285, 287, 292
~roman des Euripides 285–290, 292
~romancharakter 247–266

~sammlung 515
~theorie 516–518

canon (s. Kanon)
captatio benevolentiae 640, 654
Chester Beatty Papyrus 337, 538f.
Chion 242, 246f., 274, 278f., 289, 519
~brief 242, 246f., 257–262, 274, 278, 280f., 519f.
Christentum, als subkulturelles Phänomen 223–229
Christians, gentile 646f., 652, 675–681
christology 438, 445, 466f.
Chrysostomos
– Johannes 267, 293
– Dion 146, 154, 243
Cicero 138–142, 149–151, 164–169, 283, 631–633
cipher 669, 681
Claudius 44, 52
~edikt 555
Clemens von Alexandrien 218, 338, 341–359, 672
code name 668f.
Codex
– Alexandrinus 346
– Claromontanus 346f.
– Crosby-Schøyen 218
– Sinaiticus 346
– Tchacos 228
– Vaticanus 346
colloquia 44
Conflation 391, 393 (s.a. Epheserbrief / Kolosserbrief)
Corpus
– Dionysiacum 194
– der Katholischen Briefe 221
– pastorale 133, 514, 518, 531, 534, 626 (s.a. Pastoralbriefe)
– Paulinum 334–339, 361, 537–572, 648, 656, 664, 775
covenant 547, 552, 565
Cyrill von Jerusalem 351

Daniel 41, 65, 67–69, 83, 97
~buch 41, 62f., 67–70, 79f., 211f.
data, linguistic 442–455
Day of Atonement 565f.
Dead Sea Scrolls 85–101
deception (s. Fälschung)

dedication 40, 307, 316, 319f.
Deixis 225–227, 769, 778
– Ferndeixis 225–227 (s.a. Zeitalter, myth-historisches)
– mittlere 225–227
– Nahdeixis 225f.
Demokrit 115, 128, 172, 208
– Pseudodemokritea 172, 207–209, 223
Diaspora 117, 585, 673–681
~judentum 586
Diatessaron 341
Diatribe 448, 454
Didache 344–346, 350, 353f., 615
Dionysius
– von Alexandrien 344f., 353
– von Halicarnassus 48, 300–303, 318f.
Dionysos 109
dolus malus 370, 378

Echtheitsbeglaubigung 6, 14, 118, 499, 766
Echtheitskritik 363, 365, 509
– altkirchlich 187–192, 194–202, 208, 211, 217f.
– antik 116, 151–154
Egeria 110
Eigentum, geistiges 7f., 11, 128f., 149, 159–161, 228, 359, 367, 499
Ekklesia 402, 406, 613, 616, 585, 622f., 757 (s.a. Gemeinde)
Ekklesiologie 399, 401f., 405, 584f.
Ekstase 111, 697
encomion 33
Engel 699, 716 (s.a. Angelologie)
Epheserbrief 387–409
– im Verhältnis zum Kol 391, 396f., 402f., 406 (s.a. Kolosserrezeption)
Epicharmos 116
Epikur 156, 197
– Epikureer 106, 160f., 728f.
epistle (s. Brief / letter)
Erfinder, erster 109f.
Erfindung 112, 114, 121, 123
Eratosthenes 108
Eschatologie / eschatology 439f., 445, 464, 467, 709
Esra / Ezra 42, 63, 65, 69–83, 226
Ethopoiie 131f., 167, 234, 248
Ethos 132f., 160, 399, 404, 633, 639
– apostolic 607–609

Eucharistie 394f.
Eulogie 394f.
Eupolis 567f.
Euripides 108, 277f., 290 (s.a. Briefroman)
Eusebius 195, 199, 273, 338–355, 413, 607–609, 671–673, 733f.
Eva (s. Adam)
exhortation 51

faith 542–548, 569–572
Fälschung / forgery 28, 113f., 118f., 121, 123, 181f., 193, 489–491, 494, 497, 531, 625
– zu Lebzeiten der Betroffenen 196f.
– literarisch 112, 115, 370f.
Fatima 121
figures
– bridge 74–82
– rhetorical 324
Fiktion 500, 531, 625–644
– literarisch 109, 489–491
– pseudepigraphisch 497
– transparent 729f.
Fiktionalität
– reduziert 231
~sdiskurs 229–232
forgery (s. Fälschung)
Freiheit 723
Fremdbestimmung 105f., 112
Frühjudentum 111, 113, 115, 118f.
fullness of expression 453
Fundamentalismus 683
Funktion 727–731
– der Autorfiktion 700
– kommunikativ 684

Galen 152–154, 205–207
Gastfreundschaft 749, 756
Gegenfälschung 123, 521
Gegner 685, 694, 696f., 713
~bild 693–701, 711–721
~fiktion 731f.
~profil 721–724
Gemeinde (s.a. Ekklesia)
– als Leib Christi 423–428, 431
~korrespondenz 383
~situation 693–700
Genre 85, 89, 94–101

Geschichtsschreibung 106, 117, 123
 (s.a. Historismus)
Gesetz 592, 595 (s.a. law)
– der Freiheit 580, 593 (s.a.
 Jakobusbrief)
~geber 107, 110
Gestaltung, pseudepigraphische 388,
 408
Gnosis 201f., 224f., 227f., 504f., 696f.
Gospel
– collection of 340
– of Peter 342f., 346–348
– of Thomas 342f., 346
– traditions of authorship 341–350
Gott
~esbild 581
~esfürchtige 117
~eskindschaft 741f.
Gymnasia 43f., 46, 53

Habakkuk 548
Hammurapi 110
Handbuch / handbook 43f., 156, 312,
 319, 517
Handlungskontinuum 281f.
hapax legomena 442–444, 453
Hebräerbrief 215, 333, 338f., 346–353
Hegel, Georg Wilhelm Friedrich 504,
 506–508
Hegesipp 687
Heilige, das 112
Hellenismus 116–119, 581
Henoch / Enoch 64, 75f., 93f., 97f.
~tradition 697–702
Hermas, Hirt des 344–350
Hermeneutik 366
Hermes 109
Herodot 106, 108, 116
~imitation 204f.
Heroides 626–634, 643f.
Herrenverwandte 687, 690f. (s.a.
 Jakobus / Judas)
Herrin 745–759
Hesiod 108, 115
Hieronymus 158, 188, 202, 211f., 503
Himmelsstimme 120
Hippokrates 115, 242
historiography, apocalyptic 63f., 82f.,
 303

Historismus 506–511 (s.a.
 Geschichtsschreibung)
history 303
– deuteronomistic 40
Hochschätzung des Alten 113f., 119
Homer 107–111, 114f., 146
~imitation 143
Homonymität 127–130, 162f.

Ich-bin-Rede, der ägyptischen und
 mesopotamischen Götter 107
Ich-Bin-Worte
– Jahwes 120
– Jesu 121f.
Ich-Erzähler 279, 290, 293
Ich-Erzählung 271–273, 282–286
Idealismus 506, 509
Identitätsmerkmal 577
Ignatius 558
~brief 267, 663f.
Imitation 42, 44, 46–49, 53, 57f., 127,
 143, 161, 173, 176, 204f., 272f., 296,
 310, 318f., 324–326, 392, 404, 456,
 477, 538, 555, 705f., 746, 776–779
impersonation 46
Inkorporation 376
Inspiration 10f., 62, 111f., 120, 122,
 126, 142f., 174, 495
~slehre 11, 364
Intention 766, 781f.
Irenäus 337–346, 355, 672, 745
Irrlehrer 382, 735, 743f., 749f., 760
Isis 110, 429
Israel 110f., 119f., 405, 582–585, 594,
 673–681
~thematik 396, 399f.
~tradition 407

Jahwe 111
Jakobus / James
– der „Herrenbruder" 575, 600, 605–
 616, 620, 622, 656–681, 686f.
~brief 575, 631, 689
Jesus (Christus) 117, 648f.
– als Autorität 118f.
– Familie Jesu 217 (s.a.
 Herrenverwandte / Jakobus / Judas)
– literarisch 122, 175f., 273
– aus Nazareth 119–123, 438, 558–560,
 565–569, 689f.

~worte 121
Johannes
– der Apostel 733f.
– der Evangelist 121f.
– der Täufer 119, 122
~gemeinde 758–763
1. Johannesbrief 733, 736–743, 760, 762
2. Johannesbrief 733, 743–751, 760, 762
3. Johannesbrief 733–758, 760, 762
Jubilees 76
Judas 218, 686
~brief 130, 158, 215–222, 631, 641, 685–702, 731f.
Justin der Märtyrer 341, 439, 622

Kanon / Canon 4–20, 85–89, 122f., 125, 134–136, 187, 192, 195, 202f., 212, 219–224, 245f., 490, 535, 590, 603–605, 698, 729f., 732
– Muratori 50, 125, 162, 195–201, 235–249, 335–354, 439, 606–608
– New Testament 333–362
~bewusstsein 4, 8f., 728
~ical pseudepigrapha 356–362
~isierungsgeschichte 376
~ization 9, 17, 19, 85, 88, 135–137, 176
~kriterium 10, 135, 183
~kritik 364f.
~liste 199, 228
Kirche (s. Ekklesia / Gemeinde)
Kolosserbrief 387–409
– kolossische Philosophie 389, 391, 404, 406
– Neufassung im Eph 402f.
– (Neu)kontextualisierung 390–396, 402f.
– Transformation 391, 396
~rezeption 391f., 406
Kompilation 373f. (s.a. Zusammenstellung)
Kontext
– weisheitlich 740
~ualisierung 403
Konversion 586
Kopist 374

Laodizenerbrief 334–339, 349

law 542f., 609f., 619 (s.a. Gesetz)
Lehrer-Schüler-Verhältnis 224f., 740, 747
Leser, intendierter 782 (s.a. reader)
letter (s.a. Brief)
– carrier 662–667
– collection, pseudonymous 538f.
– composition 613f.
– didactic 319f.
– diplomatic 303f., 319f.
– fictional 321
– friendly 319f.
Libertinisten 697
library (s. Bibliothek)
Lieblingsjünger 737
Linos 107, 114
Literarkritik 363
– ancient literary criticism 353f.
Literatur / literature
– cuneiform 29f.
– egyptian 30–36
– gnostisch 201f., 224f., 227f.
– instructional 299
Lukas 116f., 123, 338, 340f., 583, 594
Lukian 132, 143, 154, 204, 239
Lukrez 106
Luther, Martin 609–614
Lykurgos 110

Mahl 713
mandata principis 517f.
Manichäismus 189–192, 228
Markion 182, 221, 334–340, 503
Markus 662–673
~evangelium 638
Matthäusevangelium 625, 638
Menes 110
Menschen, göttliche 107, 114
Meribah / Massah 563
Messias 119
Michaelis, Johann David 683
mimesis 17, 27–59, 143, 377 (s.a. Nachahmung)
Minos von Kreta 110
Mission 118, 123
Mnemosyne 108f.
Mose 40f., 65, 76f., 91f., 110f., 115, 120
– Testament des 69–71
Musaios 107f., 114

Muse 107–109, 111, 143, 174
Mystifikation 112
Mythos 108, 174, 723

Nachahmung 17, 170, 176, 185, 272f., 370f., 375f., 378, 746 (s.a. mimesis)
Naherwartung 642
Name, als Pseudepigraphiemittel 767–769
narrator 648, 656, 662
Nebo 110
Neukontextualisierung 391, 396f.
Noah 64–67, 75f., 111, 120
Notiz, persönliche 6, 500, 520, 522, 532 (s.a. Angaben, persönliche)
Numa 110

obduracy 560–564
Offenbarung 111, 113f., 118–122, 155, 174f., 211, 227, 280, 402, 640–643
~sliteratur 378, 381
~sübermittlung 111
Oikodome 421f., 427
Orakel von Delphi 109
Origenes / Origen 194, 212, 225, 305, 338–359, 606, 687f., 730
ornamentation 53
Orpheus 107f., 114f.
Orphica 113, 225
Orthonymität 112, 118, 272, 368, 376–381
Osterfestbriefe 199
Ovid 135f., 140f., 273, 289, 293, 626–631, 633, 643f.

P^{13} 538f.
P^{46} 538 (s.a. Chester Beatty Papyrus)
Paideia 42f., 45f.
Palästina 117
Papias 340–342, 655f., 668–673, 733f.
Parallele / parallelism 390, 447–454, 462f.
Paränese 391, 399, 403–405
Parusie 632, 723
– apostolisch 380f.
Pastoralbriefe 213–215, 278f., 289–294, 337, 352–360, 489–536
Paulus 118, 276, 289–293, 363–386, 387–409, 587, 646–652, 705, 708 (s.a. Schrift)
– als (pseudepigraphischer) Autor 115–117
– Paulinisierung 393
– Paulus und Seneca 133, 187, 339, 354, 765–785
~briefsammlung 376, 383
~gegner 381f.
~imitation 392
~mitarbeiter 373f., 770
~rezeption 385, 390
~schule 127, 163, 216, 371–374, 386, 388, 390, 409, 501, 522f.
Pentateuch, des Dorotheus von Sidon 209
periodization of history 64
Petrus / Peter 645–681, 703, 706, 708 (s.a. Schrift)
– Petrine circle 668–671
~akten 703
~apokalypse 158, 200, 703
~apokryphon 703
~evangelium 202, 703
~schule 646, 668
1. Petrusbrief 585, 625f., 630–644
2. Petrusbrief 215–222, 625f., 630–644, 685, 702–732
Phalarisbriefe 233–249
Philo 45, 117f., 200, 349, 557f., 580f., 718f.
Philosophenschule 161, 185, 225, 373, 415, 522
pia fraus 202, 359, 366f., 494
Plagiat / plagiarism 46, 142, 148, 151f., 159f., 211, 727
Plato 106, 143, 148, 234, 238, 245, 250
– Neuplatonismus 113, 126f., 129, 153, 159, 161, 194, 203, 210–212, 780
~briefe 250–256
Plausibilisierungsstrategie 154, 387f., 515f.
Polemik / polemic 50, 158, 342, 415, 439f., 548, 588, 685, 694, 709f., 714, 716f., 722f., 725f.
– gegen Gegner 415, 417–432, 729–732
– Übertreibung 725
– Verzerrung 725
Polybios 106
postscript 550–555
praise 46
Präskript / prescript 299f., 767f.

Prätext 405
Presbyter 733, 743–761
propaganda, political 32
Propheten, alttestamentliche 115, 119f.
Prophetie 693f., 702, 715, 718, 720, 724
propriety 321
– ex eventu 64
Prosopopoiie 14, 18, 131–134, 626, 630–633, 642f.
proverb 307f.
Pseudepigraphie / pseudepigraphy
– als Auftrag 147–151
– Durchschaubarkeit der 187–222
– Gestus der 225–228
– im Alten Testament 40–42
– imitativ 501
– offen 131–135
– paulinisch 337–339, 361, 387f.
– religiös 111, 113, 495
– als zeitlich befristetes Phänomen 185f.
~forschung 363–371
~milieu 184, 186, 222, 234
~mittel 766–785
Pseudepigraphon 234, 310, 471–473, 480, 488
Pseudoapostel (s. Apostel)
Pseudoclementinen 193, 209, 230, 235, 618 (s.a. Clemens von Alexandrien)
Pseudonymität / pseudonymity 112, 311, 497f.
– in the Old Testament 40–42
Ptolemaios II. Philadelphos 117
Public Domain 206f.
publication 304, 316
Pythagoras 156, 159–163, 177
– Pseudopythagorica 145f., 159–163, 177, 203, 359
– Pythagoreer 113, 145, 159–163, 177, 251

Qumran 86–101, 651, 698, 707, 763

reader 33, 190, 254, 256, 310f., 325, 356, 359f., 473, 477f., 648
rebellion
– calf 561–564
– Kadesh Barnea 563f.

Reden
– Abschiedsrede 707
– Jesus 123
– Paulus 123
Reichtum 593f.
Religionswissenschaft 367f.
resurrection 543f., 549, 551, 560
Rezeption 393, 396, 730
Rhetorik / rhetoric 45–57, 131–134, 166f., 173, 234, 267f., 283, 300, 317, 320, 324f., 372, 406f., 437, 447–455, 621, 631, 642, 654–657, 776–781
– graeco-roman 27–59
~schule 44, 46, 117, 778, 781
Rom 73, 117f., 147, 152, 169, 187, 205, 276, 555, 646, 666–681, 771
Roman 234–236, 263–266, 270f. (s.a. Briefroman)
– Detektivroman 282

salutatio 641
Salvian von Marseille 126f., 131, 146, 192–194, 321, 348
Schleiermacher, Friedrich Daniel Ernst 3f., 15, 364, 489, 502f., 505, 522, 683
Schöpfung 413
Schrift / scripture
– pseudo-demokritisch 207–209, 223
– pseudo-paulinisch 20, 115, 162, 177, 367, 382, 390, 424, 431, 523, 535
– pseudo-petrinisch 703
– rewritten 90–93, 98
~lehre 366
~lichkeit 108
Schule / school 42–46, 50, 57–59, 360 (s.a. Paulusschule / Petrusschule)
– Sabbath 45
– Schulgründer 112
– Schulpseudepigraphie 21, 159–163, 174, 177, 498f., 501, 521–523, 532
– Schultradition 160, 371f., 392, 521f.
~hypothesis 360
scripture (s. Schrift)
Sekretärswesen / secretary 147–151, 304, 316, 318f., 326, 579, 662–667
Selbstbestimmung 105, 107, 112
Seneca 161f., 187–189, 765–785 (s.a. Paulus und Seneca)
sentence length 448 (s.a. Stil)

Septuaginta 41, 117f.
Seschat 110
Silvanus–Silas 150, 436, 455, 481f., 662–680, 706
Sitz im Leben 471–481, 488
Skeptiker 106
Sokrates 153, 242f., 246f., 253, 261, 518f., 521
Sophisten 43, 45f., 108, 236–238, 264f., 295f., 572f.
Soubirous, Bernadette 120f.
Speisegebot 418, 420–422
stage, literary 481
statements, antithetical 464
Stereotyp 516, 714, 718, 726, 769
– polemisch 23, 695, 697, 701
Stil / style
– epistolary 300
– imitation 132, 156, 776–779, 784
– periodic 448
– pseudepigraphisch 389f., 521
– virtues of 300
Stoicism 50
Strategie, literarische 382
Stylometrie 523–528
Subskription, autographe 387f.
Sumerian King List 39
superscriptio 626
Synoptiker 118, 122

Tatian 208, 223, 338, 341, 503
Täuschung 492, 494, 500, 521, 625, 631, 634f., 641, 644
~sabsicht 499, 501, 521, 531, 643
Tendenzkritik 504f., 509
Tertullian 162f., 177, 194–197, 212f., 220, 337–348, 354, 439, 503, 521, 687, 728
Testament
– literarisch 640, 707, 729f.
– des Mose 69–71
– des Petrus 702–731
text, parabiblical 87–96, 100
2. Thessalonicherbrief 181f.
Thot 110
Thukydides 106, 108
Timotheus / Timothy 127, 131, 146, 179, 192–194, 276, 290, 292, 554f., 684, 770, 773
– Apokryphen 194

Tischgemeinschaft 584
Tora 117, 119f., 617f.
Tradition / tradition
– cuneiform wisdom 37–39
– synoptic 615
~sliteratur 227–229
~ssicherung 382, 491, 495, 502
Transformation 396
~sregel 391

Uhland, Johann Ludwig 511f.
Urchristentum 115
Urheberrecht 7f., 128, 159, 161, 376
Urheberschaft 114, 119f., 141, 145, 164, 377
– geistig 7, 493

Verfasser
~angabe als Metapher 193
~fiktion 388, 394 (s.a. Fiktion)
~zuschreibung 17–23, 126–128, 146, 244f., 412, 590–596, 684–691, 702–705, 731f., 736–739
Vergegenwärtigung 360
Vision
– animal 65–67
– neuzeitlich 120f.
voice 87, 92–96, 99
Vorbild, ethisches 592, 595
Vorwurf
– stereotyp 723
– topisch 723

Weisheit
– Salomos 199–201
~slehrer 742
Weissagungsbeweis 119
Wirkungswille 163–173
Wissenssoziologie 512
Wortstatistik 462, 523–528

Zalmoxis 110
Zarathustra 110
Zeitalter
– geschichtlich 106, 112f.
– myth-historisch 106–108, 110f. (s.a. Ferndeixis)
Zeitstruktur 692, 709
Zusammenstellung 219, 221, 228, 516 (s.a. Kompilation)

Register griechischer Begriffe

ἀγαπητός 740–742, 753–755
ἀπολογία 55
ἀποστροφή 54f.
γυμνασία 43
διαίρεσις 54f.
διασπορά 585
δίπτυχος 54f.
ἐγκώμιον 46, 53–55
ἐκκλησία 583, 755
ἐπιδεικτικός 53–55
ἐπιθυμία 579
ἐπισκοπή 533
ἑρμήνευμα 44
εὐλογία 54f.
ἡδονή 713
ἠθοποιΐα 46, 54

κατηγορία 55
λόγος προτρεπτικός 54f., 58
μίμησις 42, 44, 46
μῦθος 707
οἶκος θεοῦ 533
παιδεία 42–43, 45
πανηγυρικός 53–55
περιαυτολογία 54
πρεσβύτερος 743, 752
προγύμνασμα 43
προσωποποιΐα 54f., 56
προτρεπτικός 53
σύγκρισις 54f.
συνεκδοχή 54f., 566
τεκνία 740–742

Wissenschaftliche Untersuchungen zum Neuen Testament
Alphabetische Übersicht der ersten und zweiten Reihe

Ådna, Jostein: Jesu Stellung zum Tempel. 2000. *Bd. II/119.*
Ådna, Jostein (Hrsg.): The Formation of the Early Church. 2005. *Bd. 183.*
– und *Hans Kvalbein* (Hrsg.): The Mission of the Early Church to Jews and Gentiles. 2000. *Bd. 127.*
Aland, Barbara: Was ist Gnosis? 2009. *Bd. 239.*
Alexeev, Anatoly A., Christos Karakolis und *Ulrich Luz* (Hrsg.): Einheit der Kirche im Neuen Testament. Dritte europäische orthodox-westliche Exegetenkonferenz in Sankt Petersburg, 24.–31. August 2005. 2008. *Band 218.*
Alkier, Stefan: Wunder und Wirklichkeit in den Briefen des Apostels Paulus. 2001. *Bd. 134.*
Allen, David M.: Deuteronomy and Exhortation in Hebrews. 2008. *Bd. II/238.*
Anderson, Paul N.: The Christology of the Fourth Gospel. 1996. *Bd. II/78.*
Appold, Mark L.: The Oneness Motif in the Fourth Gospel. 1976. *Bd. II/1.*
Arnold, Clinton E.: The Colossian Syncretism. 1995. *Bd. II/77.*
Ascough, Richard S.: Paul's Macedonian Associations. 2003. *Bd. II/161.*
Asiedu-Peprah, Martin: Johannine Sabbath Conflicts As Juridical Controversy. 2001. *Bd. II/132.*
Attridge, Harold W.: siehe *Zangenberg, Jürgen.*
Aune, David E.: Apocalypticism, Prophecy and Magic in Early Christianity. 2006. *Bd. 199.*
Avemarie, Friedrich: Die Tauferzählungen der Apostelgeschichte. 2002. *Bd. 139.*
Avemarie, Friedrich und *Hermann Lichtenberger* (Hrsg.): Auferstehung – Ressurection. 2001. *Bd. 135.*
– Bund und Tora. 1996. *Bd. 92.*
Baarlink, Heinrich: Verkündigtes Heil. 2004. *Bd. 168.*
Bachmann, Michael: Sünder oder Übertreter. 1992. *Bd. 59.*
Bachmann, Michael (Hrsg.): Lutherische und Neue Paulusperspektive. 2005. *Bd. 182.*
Back, Frances: Verwandlung durch Offenbarung bei Paulus. 2002. *Bd. II/153.*
Backhaus, Knut: Der sprechende Gott. 2009. *Bd. 240.*
Baker, William R.: Personal Speech-Ethics in the Epistle of James. 1995. *Bd. II/68.*

Bakke, Odd Magne: 'Concord and Peace'. 2001. *Bd. II/143.*
Balch, David L.: Roman Domestic Art and Early House Churches. 2008. *Bd. 228.*
Baldwin, Matthew C.: Whose *Acts of Peter*? 2005. *Bd. II/196.*
Balla, Peter: Challenges to New Testament Theology. 1997. *Bd. II/95.*
– The Child-Parent Relationship in the New Testament and its Environment. 2003. *Bd. 155.*
Bammel, Ernst: Judaica. Bd. I 1986. *Bd. 37.*
– Bd. II 1997. *Bd. 91.*
Barrier, Jeremy W.: The Acts of Paul and Thecla. 2009. *Bd. II/270.*
Barton, Stephen C.: siehe *Stuckenbruck, Loren T.*
Bash, Anthony: Ambassadors for Christ. 1997. *Bd. II/92.*
Bauckham, Richard: The Jewish World around the New Testament. Collected Essays Volume I. 2008. *Bd. 233.*
Bauernfeind, Otto: Kommentar und Studien zur Apostelgeschichte. 1980. *Bd. 22.*
Baum, Armin Daniel: Pseudepigraphie und literarische Fälschung im frühen Christentum. 2001. *Bd. II/138.*
Bayer, Hans Friedrich: Jesus' Predictions of Vindication and Resurrection. 1986. *Bd. II/20.*
Becker, Eve-Marie: Das Markus-Evangelium im Rahmen antiker Historiographie. 2006. *Bd. 194.*
Becker, Eve-Marie und *Peter Pilhofer* (Hrsg.): Biographie und Persönlichkeit des Paulus. 2005. *Bd. 187.*
Becker, Michael: Wunder und Wundertäter im frührabbinischen Judentum. 2002. *Bd. II/144.*
Becker, Michael und *Markus Öhler* (Hrsg.): Apokalyptik als Herausforderung neutestamentlicher Theologie. 2006. *Bd. II/214.*
Bell, Richard H.: Deliver Us from Evil. 2007. *Bd. 216.*
– The Irrevocable Call of God. 2005. *Bd. 184.*
– No One Seeks for God. 1998. *Bd. 106.*
– Provoked to Jealousy. 1994. *Bd. II/63.*
Bennema, Cornelis: The Power of Saving Wisdom. 2002. *Bd. II/148.*
Bergman, Jan: siehe *Kieffer, René*

Bergmeier, Roland: Das Gesetz im Römerbrief und andere Studien zum Neuen Testament. 2000. *Bd. 121.*
Bernett, Monika: Der Kaiserkult in Judäa unter den Herodiern und Römern. 2007. *Bd. 203.*
Betz, Otto: Jesus, der Messias Israels. 1987. *Bd. 42.*
- Jesus, der Herr der Kirche. 1990. *Bd. 52.*
Beyschlag, Karlmann: Simon Magus und die christliche Gnosis. 1974. *Bd. 16.*
Bieringer, Reimund: siehe *Koester, Craig.*
Bittner, Wolfgang J.: Jesu Zeichen im Johannesevangelium. 1987. *Bd. II/26.*
Bjerkelund, Carl J.: Tauta Egeneto. 1987. *Bd. 40.*
Blackburn, Barry Lee: Theios Aner and the Markan Miracle Traditions. 1991. *Bd. II/40.*
Blanton IV, Thomas R.: Constructing a New Covenant. 2007. *Bd. II/233.*
Bock, Darrell L.: Blasphemy and Exaltation in Judaism and the Final Examination of Jesus. 1998. *Bd. II/106.*
Bockmuehl, Markus N.A.: Revelation and Mystery in Ancient Judaism and Pauline Christianity. 1990. *Bd. II/36.*
Bøe, Sverre: Gog and Magog. 2001. *Bd. II/135.*
Böhlig, Alexander: Gnosis und Synkretismus. Teil 1 1989. *Bd. 47* – Teil 2 1989. *Bd. 48.*
Böhm, Martina: Samarien und die Samaritai bei Lukas. 1999. *Bd. II/111.*
Böttrich, Christfried: Weltweisheit – Menschheitsethik – Urkult. 1992. *Bd. II/50.*
- */ Herzer, Jens* (Hrsg.): Josephus und das Neue Testament. 2007. *Bd. 209.*
Bolyki, János: Jesu Tischgemeinschaften. 1997. *Bd. II/96.*
Bosman, Philip: Conscience in Philo and Paul. 2003. *Bd. II/166.*
Bovon, François: New Testament and Christian Apocrypha. 2009. *Bd. 237.*
- Studies in Early Christianity. 2003. *Bd. 161.*
Brändl, Martin: Der Agon bei Paulus. 2006. *Bd. II/222.*
Breytenbach, Cilliers: siehe *Frey, Jörg.*
Brocke, Christoph vom: Thessaloniki – Stadt des Kassander und Gemeinde des Paulus. 2001. *Bd. II/125.*
Brunson, Andrew: Psalm 118 in the Gospel of John. 2003. *Bd. II/158.*
Büchli, Jörg: Der Poimandres – ein paganisiertes Evangelium. 1987. *Bd. II/27.*
Bühner, Jan A.: Der Gesandte und sein Weg im 4. Evangelium. 1977. *Bd. II/2.*
Burchard, Christoph: Untersuchungen zu Joseph und Aseneth. 1965. *Bd. 8.*
- Studien zur Theologie, Sprache und Umwelt des Neuen Testaments. Hrsg. von D. Sänger. 1998. *Bd. 107.*

Burnett, Richard: Karl Barth's Theological Exegesis. 2001. *Bd. II/145.*
Byron, John: Slavery Metaphors in Early Judaism and Pauline Christianity. 2003. *Bd. II/162.*
Byrskog, Samuel: Story as History – History as Story. 2000. *Bd. 123.*
Cancik, Hubert (Hrsg.): Markus-Philologie. 1984. *Bd. 33.*
Capes, David B.: Old Testament Yaweh Texts in Paul's Christology. 1992. *Bd. II/47.*
Caragounis, Chrys C.: The Development of Greek and the New Testament. 2004. *Bd. 167.*
- The Son of Man. 1986. *Bd. 38.*
- siehe *Fridrichsen, Anton.*
Carleton Paget, James: The Epistle of Barnabas. 1994. *Bd. II/64.*
Carson, D.A., Peter T. O'Brien und *Mark Seifrid* (Hrsg.): Justification and Variegated Nomism.
   Bd. 1: The Complexities of Second Temple Judaism. 2001. *Bd. II/140.*
   Bd. 2: The Paradoxes of Paul. 2004. *Bd. II/181.*
Chae, Young Sam: Jesus as the Eschatological Davidic Shepherd. 2006. *Bd. II/216.*
Chapman, David W.: Ancient Jewish and Christian Perceptions of Crucifixion. 2008. *Bd. II/244.*
Chester, Andrew: Messiah and Exaltation. 2007. *Bd. 207.*
Chibici-Revneanu, Nicole: Die Herrlichkeit des Verherrlichten. 2007. *Bd. II/231.*
Ciampa, Roy E.: The Presence and Function of Scripture in Galatians 1 and 2. 1998. *Bd. II/102.*
Classen, Carl Joachim: Rhetorical Criticism of the New Testament. 2000. *Bd. 128.*
Colpe, Carsten: Griechen – Byzantiner – Semiten – Muslime. 2008. *Bd. 221.*
- Iranier – Aramäer – Hebräer – Hellenen. 2003. *Bd. 154.*
Coppins, Wayne: The Interpretation of Freedom in the Letters of Paul. 2009. *Bd. II/261.*
Crump, David: Jesus the Intercessor. 1992. *Bd. II/49.*
Dahl, Nils Alstrup: Studies in Ephesians. 2000. *Bd. 131.*
Daise, Michael A.: Feasts in John. 2007. *Bd. II/229.*
Deines, Roland: Die Gerechtigkeit der Tora im Reich des Messias. 2004. *Bd. 177.*
- Jüdische Steingefäße und pharisäische Frömmigkeit. 1993. *Bd. II/52.*
- Die Pharisäer. 1997. *Bd. 101.*

Deines, Roland und *Karl-Wilhelm Niebuhr* (Hrsg.): Philo und das Neue Testament. 2004. *Bd. 172.*

Dennis, John A.: Jesus' Death and the Gathering of True Israel. 2006. *Bd. 217.*

Dettwiler, Andreas und *Jean Zumstein* (Hrsg.): Kreuzestheologie im Neuen Testament. 2002. *Bd. 151.*

Dickson, John P.: Mission-Commitment in Ancient Judaism and in the Pauline Communities. 2003. *Bd. II/159.*

Dietzfelbinger, Christian: Der Abschied des Kommenden. 1997. *Bd. 95.*

Dimitrov, Ivan Z., James D.G. Dunn, Ulrich Luz und *Karl-Wilhelm Niebuhr* (Hrsg.): Das Alte Testament als christliche Bibel in orthodoxer und westlicher Sicht. 2004. *Bd. 174.*

Dobbeler, Axel von: Glaube als Teilhabe. 1987. *Bd. II/22.*

Docherty, Susan E.: The Use of the Old Testament in Hebrews. 2009. *Bd. II/260.*

Downs, David J.: The Offering of the Gentiles. 2008. *Bd. II/248.*

Dryden, J. de Waal: Theology and Ethics in 1 Peter. 2006. *Bd. II/209.*

Dübbers, Michael: Christologie und Existenz im Kolosserbrief. 2005. *Bd. II/191.*

Dunn, James D.G.: The New Perspective on Paul. 2005. *Bd. 185.*

Dunn , James D.G. (Hrsg.): Jews and Christians. 1992. *Bd. 66.*

– Paul and the Mosaic Law. 1996. *Bd. 89.*
– siehe *Dimitrov, Ivan Z.*

Dunn, James D.G., Hans Klein, Ulrich Luz und *Vasile Mihoc* (Hrsg.): Auslegung der Bibel in orthodoxer und westlicher Perspektive. 2000. *Bd. 130.*

Ebel, Eva: Die Attraktivität früher christlicher Gemeinden. 2004. *Bd. II/178.*

Ebertz, Michael N.: Das Charisma des Gekreuzigten. 1987. *Bd. 45.*

Eckstein, Hans-Joachim: Der Begriff Syneidesis bei Paulus. 1983. *Bd. II/10.*

– Verheißung und Gesetz. 1996. *Bd. 86.*

Ego, Beate: Im Himmel wie auf Erden. 1989. *Bd. II/34.*

Ego, Beate, Armin Lange und *Peter Pilhofer* (Hrsg.): Gemeinde ohne Tempel – Community without Temple. 1999. *Bd. 118.*

– und *Helmut Merkel* (Hrsg.): Religiöses Lernen in der biblischen, frühjüdischen und frühchristlichen Überlieferung. 2005. *Bd. 180.*

Eisen, Ute E.: siehe *Paulsen, Henning.*

Elledge, C.D.: Life after Death in Early Judaism. 2006. *Bd. II/208.*

Ellis, E. Earle: Prophecy and Hermeneutic in Early Christianity. 1978. *Bd. 18.*

– The Old Testament in Early Christianity. 1991. *Bd. 54.*

Elmer, Ian J.: Paul, Jerusalem and the Judaisers. 2009. *Bd. II/258.*

Endo, Masanobu: Creation and Christology. 2002. *Bd. 149.*

Ennulat, Andreas: Die 'Minor Agreements'. 1994. *Bd. II/62.*

Ensor, Peter W.: Jesus and His 'Works'. 1996. *Bd. II/85.*

Eskola, Timo: Messiah and the Throne. 2001. *Bd. II/142.*

– Theodicy and Predestination in Pauline Soteriology. 1998. *Bd. II/100.*

Fatehi, Mehrdad: The Spirit's Relation to the Risen Lord in Paul. 2000. *Bd. II/128.*

Feldmeier, Reinhard: Die Krisis des Gottessohnes. 1987. *Bd. II/21.*

– Die Christen als Fremde. 1992. *Bd. 64.*

Feldmeier, Reinhard und *Ulrich Heckel* (Hrsg.): Die Heiden. 1994. *Bd. 70.*

Fletcher-Louis, Crispin H.T.: Luke-Acts: Angels, Christology and Soteriology. 1997. *Bd. II/94.*

Förster, Niclas: Marcus Magus. 1999. *Bd. 114.*

Forbes, Christopher Brian: Prophecy and Inspired Speech in Early Christianity and its Hellenistic Environment. 1995. *Bd. II/75.*

Fornberg, Tord: siehe *Fridrichsen, Anton.*

Fossum, Jarl E.: The Name of God and the Angel of the Lord. 1985. *Bd. 36.*

Foster, Paul: Community, Law and Mission in Matthew's Gospel. *Bd. II/177.*

Fotopoulos, John: Food Offered to Idols in Roman Corinth. 2003. *Bd. II/151.*

Frenschkowski, Marco: Offenbarung und Epiphanie. Bd. 1 1995. *Bd. II/79* – Bd. 2 1997. *Bd. II/80.*

Frey, Jörg: Eugen Drewermann und die biblische Exegese. 1995. *Bd. II/71.*

– Die johanneische Eschatologie. Bd. I. 1997. *Bd. 96.* – Bd. II. 1998. *Bd. 110.*
– Bd. III. 2000. *Bd. 117.*

Frey, Jörg und *Cilliers Breytenbach* (Hrsg.): Aufgabe und Durchführung einer Theologie des Neuen Testaments. 2007. *Bd. 205.*

– *Jens Herzer, Martina Janßen* und *Clare K. Rothschild* (Hrsg.): Pseudepigraphie und Verfasserfiktion in frühchristlichen Briefen. 2009. *Bd. 246.*

– und *Udo Schnelle* (Hrsg.): Kontexte des Johannesevangeliums. 2004. *Bd. 175.*

– und *Jens Schröter* (Hrsg.): Deutungen des Todes Jesu im Neuen Testament. 2005. *Bd. 181.*

–, *Jan G. van der Watt,* und *Ruben Zimmermann* (Hrsg.): Imagery in the Gospel of John. 2006. *Bd. 200.*

Freyne, Sean: Galilee and Gospel. 2000. Bd. 125.
Fridrichsen, Anton: Exegetical Writings. Hrsg. von C.C. Caragounis und T. Fornberg. 1994. Bd. 76.
Gadenz, Pablo T.: Called from the Jews and from the Gentiles. 2009. Bd. II/267.
Gäbel, Georg: Die Kulttheologie des Hebräerbriefes. 2006. Bd. II/212.
Gäckle, Volker: Die Starken und die Schwachen in Korinth und in Rom. 2005. Bd. 200.
Garlington, Don B.: 'The Obedience of Faith'. 1991. Bd. II/38.
– Faith, Obedience, and Perseverance. 1994. Bd. 79.
Garnet, Paul: Salvation and Atonement in the Qumran Scrolls. 1977. Bd. II/3.
Gemünden, Petra von (Hrsg.): siehe *Weissenrieder, Annette.*
Gese, Michael: Das Vermächtnis des Apostels. 1997. Bd. II/99.
Gheorghita, Radu: The Role of the Septuagint in Hebrews. 2003. Bd. II/160.
Gordley, Matthew E.: The Colossian Hymn in Context. 2007. Bd. II/228.
Gräbe, Petrus J.: The Power of God in Paul's Letters. 2000, ²2008. Bd. II/123.
Gräßer, Erich: Der Alte Bund im Neuen. 1985. Bd. 35.
– Forschungen zur Apostelgeschichte. 2001. Bd. 137.
Grappe, Christian (Hrsg.): Le Repas de Dieu – Das Mahl Gottes. 2004. Bd. 169.
Gray, Timothy C.: The Temple in the Gospel of Mark. 2008. Bd. II/242.
Green, Joel B.: The Death of Jesus. 1988. Bd. II/33.
Gregg, Brian Han: The Historical Jesus and the Final Judgment Sayings in Q. 2005. Bd. II/207.
Gregory, Andrew: The Reception of Luke and Acts in the Period before Irenaeus. 2003. Bd. II/169.
Grindheim, Sigurd: The Crux of Election. 2005. Bd. II/202.
Gundry, Robert H.: The Old is Better. 2005. Bd. 178.
Gundry Volf, Judith M.: Paul and Perseverance. 1990. Bd. II/37.
Häußer, Detlef: Christusbekenntnis und Jesusüberlieferung bei Paulus. 2006. Bd. 210.
Hafemann, Scott J.: Suffering and the Spirit. 1986. Bd. II/19.
– Paul, Moses, and the History of Israel. 1995. Bd. 81.
Hahn, Ferdinand: Studien zum Neuen Testament.
 Bd. I: Grundsatzfragen, Jesusforschung, Evangelien. 2006. Bd. 191.
 Bd. II: Bekenntnisbildung und Theologie in urchristlicher Zeit. 2006. Bd. 192.
Hahn, Johannes (Hrsg.): Zerstörungen des Jerusalemer Tempels. 2002. Bd. 147.
Hamid-Khani, Saeed: Relevation and Concealment of Christ. 2000. Bd. II/120.
Hannah, Darrel D.: Michael and Christ. 1999. Bd. II/109.
Hardin, Justin K.: Galatians and the Imperial Cult? 2007. Bd. II /237.
Harrison; James R.: Paul's Language of Grace in Its Graeco-Roman Context. 2003. Bd. II/172.
Hartman, Lars: Text-Centered New Testament Studies. Hrsg. von D. Hellholm. 1997. Bd. 102.
Hartog, Paul: Polycarp and the New Testament. 2001. Bd. II/134.
Heckel, Theo K.: Der Innere Mensch. 1993. Bd. II/53.
– Vom Evangelium des Markus zum viergestaltigen Evangelium. 1999. Bd. 120.
Heckel, Ulrich: Kraft in Schwachheit. 1993. Bd. II/56.
– Der Segen im Neuen Testament. 2002. Bd. 150.
– siehe *Feldmeier, Reinhard.*
– siehe *Hengel, Martin.*
Heiligenthal, Roman: Werke als Zeichen. 1983. Bd. II/9.
Heliso, Desta: Pistis and the Righteous One. 2007. Vol. II/235.
Hellholm, D.: siehe *Hartman, Lars.*
Hemer, Colin J.: The Book of Acts in the Setting of Hellenistic History. 1989. Bd. 49.
Hengel, Martin: Jesus und die Evangelien. Kleine Schriften V. 2007. Bd. 211.
– Die johanneische Frage. 1993. Bd. 67.
– Judaica et Hellenistica. Kleine Schriften I. 1996. Bd. 90.
– Judaica, Hellenistica et Christiana. Kleine Schriften II. 1999. Bd. 109.
– Judentum und Hellenismus. 1969, ³1988. Bd. 10.
– Paulus und Jakobus. Kleine Schriften III. 2002. Bd. 141.
– Studien zur Christologie. Kleine Schriften IV. 2006. Bd. 201.
– Studien zum Urchristentum. Kleine Schriften VI. 2008. Bd. 234.
– und *Anna Maria Schwemer:* Paulus zwischen Damaskus und Antiochien. 1998. Bd. 108.
– Der messianische Anspruch Jesu und die Anfänge der Christologie. 2001. Bd. 138.

- Die vier Evangelien und das eine Evangelium von Jesus Christus. 2008. *Bd. 224.*
- Hengel, Martin und *Ulrich Heckel* (Hrsg.): Paulus und das antike Judentum. 1991. *Bd. 58.*
- und *Hermut Löhr* (Hrsg.): Schriftauslegung im antiken Judentum und im Urchristentum. 1994. *Bd. 73.*
- und *Anna Maria Schwemer* (Hrsg.): Königsherrschaft Gottes und himmlischer Kult. 1991. *Bd. 55.*
- Die Septuaginta. 1994. *Bd. 72.*
- –, *Siegfried Mittmann* und *Anna Maria Schwemer* (Hrsg.): La Cité de Dieu / Die Stadt Gottes. 2000. *Bd. 129.*

Hentschel, Anni: Diakonia im Neuen Testament. 2007. *Bd. 226.*

Hernández Jr., Juan: Scribal Habits and Theological Influence in the Apocalypse. 2006. *Bd. II/218.*

Herrenbrück, Fritz: Jesus und die Zöllner. 1990. *Bd. II/41.*

Herzer, Jens: Paulus oder Petrus? 1998. *Bd. 103.*
- siehe *Böttrich, Christfried.*
- siehe *Frey, Jörg.*

Hill, Charles E.: From the Lost Teaching of Polycarp. 2005. *Bd. 186.*

Hoegen-Rohls, Christina: Der nachösterliche Johannes. 1996. *Bd. II/84.*

Hoffmann, Matthias Reinhard: The Destroyer and the Lamb. 2005. *Bd. II/203.*

Hofius, Otfried: Katapausis. 1970. *Bd. 11.*
- Der Vorhang vor dem Thron Gottes. 1972. *Bd. 14.*
- Der Christushymnus Philipper 2,6–11. 1976, ²1991. *Bd. 17.*
- Paulusstudien. 1989, ²1994. *Bd. 51.*
- Neutestamentliche Studien. 2000. *Bd. 132.*
- Paulusstudien II. 2002. *Bd. 143.*
- Exegetische Studien. 2008. *Bd. 223.*
- und *Hans-Christian Kammler:* Johannesstudien. 1996. *Bd. 88.*

Holloway, Paul A.: Coping with Prejudice. 2009. *Bd. 244.*

Holmberg, Bengt (Hrsg.): Exploring Early Christian Identity. 2008. *Bd. 226.*
- und *Mikael Winninge* (Hrsg.): Identity Formation in the New Testament. 2008. *Bd. 227.*

Holtz, Traugott: Geschichte und Theologie des Urchristentums. 1991. *Bd. 57.*

Hommel, Hildebrecht: Sebasmata.
  Bd. 1 1983. *Bd. 31.*
  Bd. 2 1984. *Bd. 32.*

Horbury, William: Herodian Judaism and New Testament Study. 2006. *Bd. 193.*

Horn, Friedrich Wilhelm und *Ruben Zimmermann* (Hrsg): Jenseits von Indikativ und Imperativ. Bd. 1. 2009. *Bd. 238.*

Horst, Pieter W. van der: Jews and Christians in Their Graeco-Roman Context. 2006. *Bd. 196.*

Hvalvik, Reidar: The Struggle for Scripture and Covenant. 1996. *Bd. II/82.*

Janßen Martina: siehe *Frey, Jörg.*

Jauhiainen, Marko: The Use of Zechariah in Revelation. 2005. *Bd. II/199.*

Jensen, Morten H.: Herod Antipas in Galilee. 2006. *Bd. II/215.*

Johns, Loren L.: The Lamb Christology of the Apocalypse of John. 2003. *Bd. II/167.*

Jossa, Giorgio: Jews or Christians? 2006. *Bd. 202.*

Joubert, Stephan: Paul as Benefactor. 2000. *Bd. II/124.*

Judge, E. A.: The First Christians in the Roman World. 2008. *Bd. 229.*

Jungbauer, Harry: „Ehre Vater und Mutter". 2002. *Bd. II/146.*

Kähler, Christoph: Jesu Gleichnisse als Poesie und Therapie. 1995. *Bd. 78.*

Kamlah, Ehrhard: Die Form der katalogischen Paränese im Neuen Testament. 1964. *Bd. 7.*

Kammler, Hans-Christian: Christologie und Eschatologie. 2000. *Bd. 126.*
- Kreuz und Weisheit. 2003. *Bd. 159.*
- siehe *Hofius, Otfried.*

Karakolis, Christos: siehe *Alexeev, Anatoly A.*

Karrer, Martin und *Wolfgang Kraus* (Hrsg.): Die Septuaginta – Texte, Kontexte, Lebenswelten. 2008. *Band 219.*

Kelhoffer, James A.: The Diet of John the Baptist. 2005. *Bd. 176.*
- Miracle and Mission. 1999. *Bd. II/112.*

Kelley, Nicole: Knowledge and Religious Authority in the Pseudo-Clementines. 2006. *Bd. II/213.*

Kennedy, Joel: The Recapitulation of Israel. 2008. *Bd. II/257.*

Kieffer, René und *Jan Bergman* (Hrsg.): La Main de Dieu / Die Hand Gottes. 1997. *Bd. 94.*

Kierspel, Lars: The Jews and the World in the Fourth Gospel. 2006. *Bd. 220.*

Kim, Seyoon: The Origin of Paul's Gospel. 1981, ²1984. *Bd. II/4.*
- Paul and the New Perspective. 2002. *Bd. 140.*
- "The 'Son of Man'" as the Son of God. 1983. *Bd. 30.*

Klauck, Hans-Josef: Religion und Gesellschaft im frühen Christentum. 2003. *Bd. 152.*

Klein, Hans: siehe *Dunn, James D.G.*

Kleinknecht, Karl Th.: Der leidende Gerechtfertigte. 1984, ²1988. *Bd. II/13.*
Klinghardt, Matthias: Gesetz und Volk Gottes. 1988. *Bd. II/32.*
Kloppenborg, John S.: The Tenants in the Vineyard. 2006. *Bd. 195.*
Koch, Michael: Drachenkampf und Sonnenfrau. 2004. *Bd. II/184.*
Koch, Stefan: Rechtliche Regelung von Konflikten im frühen Christentum. 2004. *Bd. II/174.*
Köhler, Wolf-Dietrich: Rezeption des Matthäusevangeliums in der Zeit vor Irenäus. 1987. *Bd. II/24.*
Köhn, Andreas: Der Neutestamentler Ernst Lohmeyer. 2004. *Bd. II/180.*
Koester, Craig und *Reimund Bieringer* (Hrsg.): The Resurrection of Jesus in the Gospel of John. 2008. *Bd. 222.*
Konradt, Matthias: Israel, Kirche und die Völker im Matthäusevangelium. 2007. *Bd. 215.*
Kooten, George H. van: Cosmic Christology in Paul and the Pauline School. 2003. *Bd. II/171.*
– Paul's Anthropology in Context. 2008. *Bd. 232.*
Korn, Manfred: Die Geschichte Jesu in veränderter Zeit. 1993. *Bd. II/51.*
Koskenniemi, Erkki: Apollonios von Tyana in der neutestamentlichen Exegese. 1994. *Bd. II/61.*
– The Old Testament Miracle-Workers in Early Judaism. 2005. *Bd. II/206.*
Kraus, Thomas J.: Sprache, Stil und historischer Ort des zweiten Petrusbriefes. 2001. *Bd. II/136.*
Kraus, Wolfgang: Das Volk Gottes. 1996. *Bd. 85.*
– siehe *Karrer, Martin.*
– siehe *Walter, Nikolaus.*
– und *Karl-Wilhelm Niebuhr* (Hrsg.): Frühjudentum und Neues Testament im Horizont Biblischer Theologie. 2003. *Bd. 162.*
Krauter, Stefan: Studien zu Röm 13,1–7. 2009. *Bd. 243.*
Kreplin, Matthias: Das Selbstverständnis Jesu. 2001. *Bd. II/141.*
Kuhn, Karl G.: Achtzehngebet und Vaterunser und der Reim. 1950. *Bd. 1.*
Kvalbein, Hans: siehe *Ådna, Jostein.*
Kwon, Yon-Gyong: Eschatology in Galatians. 2004. *Bd. II/183.*
Laansma, Jon: I Will Give You Rest. 1997. *Bd. II/98.*
Labahn, Michael: Offenbarung in Zeichen und Wort. 2000. *Bd. II/117.*
Lambers-Petry, Doris: siehe *Tomson, Peter J.*
Lange, Armin: siehe *Ego, Beate.*

Lampe, Peter: Die stadtrömischen Christen in den ersten beiden Jahrhunderten. 1987, ²1989. *Bd. II/18.*
Landmesser, Christof: Wahrheit als Grundbegriff neutestamentlicher Wissenschaft. 1999. *Bd. 113.*
– Jüngerberufung und Zuwendung zu Gott. 2000. *Bd. 133.*
Lau, Andrew: Manifest in Flesh. 1996. *Bd. II/86.*
Lawrence, Louise: An Ethnography of the Gospel of Matthew. 2003. *Bd. II/165.*
Lee, Aquila H.I.: From Messiah to Preexistent Son. 2005. *Bd. II/192.*
Lee, Pilchan: The New Jerusalem in the Book of Relevation. 2000. *Bd. II/129.*
Lee, Simon S.: Jesus' Transfiguration and the Believers' Transformation. 2009. *Bd. II/265.*
Lichtenberger, Hermann: Das Ich Adams und das Ich der Menschheit. 2004. *Bd. 164.*
– siehe *Avemarie, Friedrich.*
Lierman, John: The New Testament Moses. 2004. *Bd. II/173.*
– (Hrsg.): Challenging Perspectives on the Gospel of John. 2006. *Bd. II/219.*
Lieu, Samuel N.C.: Manichaeism in the Later Roman Empire and Medieval China. ²1992. *Bd. 63.*
Lindemann, Andreas: Die Evangelien und die Apostelgeschichte. 2009. *Bd. 241.*
Lindgård, Fredrik: Paul's Line of Thought in 2 Corinthians 4:16-5:10. 2004. *Bd. II/189.*
Loader, William R.G.: Jesus' Attitude Towards the Law. 1997. *Bd. II/97.*
Löhr, Gebhard: Verherrlichung Gottes durch Philosophie. 1997. *Bd. 97.*
Löhr, Hermut: Studien zum frühchristlichen und frühjüdischen Gebet. 2003. *Bd. 160.*
– siehe *Hengel, Martin.*
Löhr, Winrich Alfried: Basilides und seine Schule. 1995. *Bd. 83.*
Lorenzen, Stefanie: Das paulinische Eikon-Konzept. 2008. *Bd. II/250.*
Luomanen, Petri: Entering the Kingdom of Heaven. 1998. *Bd. II/101.*
Luz, Ulrich: siehe *Alexeev, Anatoly A.*
– siehe *Dunn, James D.G.*
Mackay, Ian D.: John's Raltionship with Mark. 2004. *Bd. II/182.*
Mackie, Scott D.: Eschatology and Exhortation in the Epistle to the Hebrews. 2006. *Bd. II/223.*
Magda, Ksenija: Paul's Territoriality and Mission Strategy. 2009. *Bd. II/266.*
Maier, Gerhard: Mensch und freier Wille. 1971. *Bd. 12.*
– Die Johannesoffenbarung und die Kirche. 1981. *Bd. 25.*

Markschies, Christoph: Valentinus Gnosticus? 1992. Bd. 65.
Marshall, Jonathan: Jesus, Patrons, and Benefactors. 2009. Bd. II/259.
Marshall, Peter: Enmity in Corinth: Social Conventions in Paul's Relations with the Corinthians. 1987. Bd. II/23.
Martin, Dale B.: siehe *Zangenberg, Jürgen.*
Mayer, Annemarie: Sprache der Einheit im Epheserbrief und in der Ökumene. 2002. Bd. II/150.
Mayordomo, Moisés: Argumentiert Paulus logisch? 2005. Bd. 188.
McDonough, Sean M.: YHWH at Patmos: Rev. 1:4 in its Hellenistic and Early Jewish Setting. 1999. Bd. II/107.
McDowell, Markus: Prayers of Jewish Women. 2006. Bd. II/211.
McGlynn, Moyna: Divine Judgement and Divine Benevolence in the Book of Wisdom. 2001. Bd. II/139.
Meade, David G.: Pseudonymity and Canon. 1986. Bd. 39.
Meadors, Edward P.: Jesus the Messianic Herald of Salvation. 1995. Bd. II/72.
Meißner, Stefan: Die Heimholung des Ketzers. 1996. Bd. II/87.
Mell, Ulrich: Die „anderen" Winzer. 1994. Bd. 77.
– siehe *Sänger, Dieter.*
Mengel, Berthold: Studien zum Philipperbrief. 1982. Bd. II/8.
Merkel, Helmut: Die Widersprüche zwischen den Evangelien. 1971. Bd. 13.
– siehe *Ego, Beate.*
Merklein, Helmut: Studien zu Jesus und Paulus. Bd. 1 1987. Bd. 43. – Bd. 2 1998. Bd. 105.
Metzdorf, Christina: Die Tempelaktion Jesu. 2003. Bd. II/168.
Metzler, Karin: Der griechische Begriff des Verzeihens. 1991. Bd. II/44.
Metzner, Rainer: Die Rezeption des Matthäusevangeliums im 1. Petrusbrief. 1995. Bd. II/74.
– Das Verständnis der Sünde im Johannesevangelium. 2000. Bd. 122.
Mihoc, Vasile: siehe *Dunn, James D.G..*
Mineshige, Kiyoshi: Besitzverzicht und Almosen bei Lukas. 2003. Bd. II/163.
Mittmann, Siegfried: siehe *Hengel, Martin.*
Mittmann-Richert, Ulrike: Magnifikat und Benediktus. *1996. Bd. II/90.*
– Der Sühnetod des Gottesknechts. 2008. Bd. 220.
Miura, Yuzuru: David in Luke-Acts. 2007. Bd. II/232.
Mournet, Terence C.: Oral Tradition and Literary Dependency. 2005. Bd. II/195.

Mußner, Franz: Jesus von Nazareth im Umfeld Israels und der Urkirche. Hrsg. von M. Theobald. 1998. Bd. 111.
Mutschler, Bernhard: Das Corpus Johanneum bei Irenäus von Lyon. 2005. Bd. 189.
Nguyen, V. Henry T.: Christian Identity in Corinth. 2008. Bd. II/243.
Niebuhr, Karl-Wilhelm: Gesetz und Paränese. 1987. Bd. II/28.
– Heidenapostel aus Israel. 1992. Bd. 62.
– siehe *Deines, Roland*
– siehe *Dimitrov, Ivan Z.*
– siehe *Kraus, Wolfgang*
Nielsen, Anders E.: "Until it is Fullfilled". 2000. Bd. II/126.
Nielsen, Jesper Tang: Die kognitive Dimension des Kreuzes. 2009. Bd. II/263.
Nissen, Andreas: Gott und der Nächste im antiken Judentum. 1974. Bd. 15.
Noack, Christian: Gottesbewußtsein. 2000. Bd. II/116.
Noormann, Rolf: Irenäus als Paulusinterpret. 1994. Bd. II/66.
Novakovic, Lidija: Messiah, the Healer of the Sick. 2003. Bd. II/170.
Obermann, Andreas: Die christologische Erfüllung der Schrift im Johannesevangelium. 1996. Bd. II/83.
Öhler, Markus: Barnabas. 2003. Bd. 156.
– siehe *Becker, Michael.*
Okure, Teresa: The Johannine Approach to Mission. 1988. Bd. II/31.
Onuki, Takashi: Heil und Erlösung. 2004. Bd. 165.
Oropeza, B. J.: Paul and Apostasy. 2000. Bd. II/115.
Ostmeyer, Karl-Heinrich: Kommunikation mit Gott und Christus. 2006. Bd. 197.
– Taufe und Typos. 2000. Bd. II/118.
Paulsen, Henning: Studien zur Literatur und Geschichte des frühen Christentums. Hrsg. von Ute E. Eisen. 1997. Bd. 99.
Pao, David W.: Acts and the Isaianic New Exodus. 2000. Bd. II/130.
Park, Eung Chun: The Mission Discourse in Matthew's Interpretation. 1995. Bd. II/81.
Park, Joseph S.: Conceptions of Afterlife in Jewish Insriptions. 2000. Bd. II/121.
Pate, C. Marvin: The Reverse of the Curse. 2000. Bd. II/114.
Pearce, Sarah J.K.: The Land of the Body. 2007. Bd. 208.
Peres, Imre: Griechische Grabinschriften und neutestamentliche Eschatologie. 2003. Bd. 157.
Perry, Peter S.: The Rhetoric of Digressions. 2009. Bd. II/268.

Philip, Finny: The Origins of Pauline Pneumatology. 2005. *Bd. II/194.*
Philonenko, Marc (Hrsg.): Le Trône de Dieu. 1993. *Bd. 69.*
Pilhofer, Peter: Presbyteron Kreitton. 1990. *Bd. II/39.*
- Philippi. Bd. 1 1995. *Bd. 87.* - Bd. 2 2000. *Bd. 119.*
- Die frühen Christen und ihre Welt. 2002. *Bd. 145.*
- siehe *Becker, Eve-Marie.*
- siehe *Ego, Beate.*
Pitre, Brant: Jesus, the Tribulation, and the End of the Exile. 2005. *Bd. II/204.*
Plümacher, Eckhard: Geschichte und Geschichten. 2004. *Bd. 170.*
Pöhlmann, Wolfgang: Der Verlorene Sohn und das Haus. 1993. *Bd. 68.*
Pokorný, Petr und *Josef B. Souček:* Bibelauslegung als Theologie. 1997. *Bd. 100.*
Pokorný, Petr und *Jan Roskovec* (Hrsg.): Philosophical Hermeneutics and Biblical Exegesis. 2002. *Bd. 153.*
Popkes, Enno Edzard: Das Menschenbild des Thomasevangeliums. 2007. *Band 206.*
- Die Theologie der Liebe Gottes in den johanneischen Schriften. 2005. *Bd. II/197.*
Porter, Stanley E.: The Paul of Acts. 1999. *Bd. 115.*
Prieur, Alexander: Die Verkündigung der Gottesherrschaft. 1996. *Bd. II/89.*
Probst, Hermann: Paulus und der Brief. 1991. *Bd. II/45.*
Räisänen, Heikki: Paul and the Law. 1983, [2]1987. *Bd. 29.*
Rehkopf, Friedrich: Die lukanische Sonderquelle. 1959. *Bd. 5.*
Rein, Matthias: Die Heilung des Blindgeborenen (Joh 9). 1995. *Bd. II/73.*
Reinmuth, Eckart: Pseudo-Philo und Lukas. 1994. *Bd. 74.*
Reiser, Marius: Bibelkritik und Auslegung der Heiligen Schrift. 2007. *Bd. 217.*
- Syntax und Stil des Markusevangeliums. 1984. *Bd. II/11.*
Reynolds, Benjamin E.: The Apocalyptic Son of Man in the Gospel of John. 2008. *Bd. II/249.*
Rhodes, James N.: The Epistle of Barnabas and the Deuteronomic Tradition. 2004. *Bd. II/188.*
Richards, E. Randolph: The Secretary in the Letters of Paul. 1991. *Bd. II/42.*
Riesner, Rainer: Jesus als Lehrer. 1981, [3]1988. *Bd. II/7.*
- Die Frühzeit des Apostels Paulus. 1994. *Bd. 71.*
Rissi, Mathias: Die Theologie des Hebräerbriefs. 1987. *Bd. 41.*

Röcker, Fritz W.: Belial und Katechon. 2009. *Bd. II/262.*
Röhser, Günter: Metaphorik und Personifikation der Sünde. 1987. *Bd. II/25.*
Rose, Christian: Theologie als Erzählung im Markusevangelium. 2007. *Bd. II/236.*
- Die Wolke der Zeugen. 1994. *Bd. II/60.*
Roskovec, Jan: siehe *Pokorný, Petr.*
Rothschild, Clare K.: Baptist Traditions and Q. 2005. *Bd. 190.*
- Hebrews as Pseudepigraphon. 2009. *Band 235.*
- Luke Acts and the Rhetoric of History. 2004. *Bd. II/175.*
- siehe *Frey, Jörg.*
Rüegger, Hans-Ulrich: Verstehen, was Markus erzählt. 2002. *Bd. II/155.*
Rüger, Hans Peter: Die Weisheitsschrift aus der Kairoer Geniza. 1991. *Bd. 53.*
Sänger, Dieter: Antikes Judentum und die Mysterien. 1980. *Bd. II/5.*
- Die Verkündigung des Gekreuzigten und Israel. 1994. *Bd. 75.*
- siehe *Burchard, Christoph.*
- und *Ulrich Mell* (Hrsg.): Paulus und Johannes. 2006. *Bd. 198.*
Salier, Willis Hedley: The Rhetorical Impact of the Se-meia in the Gospel of John. 2004. *Bd. II/186.*
Salzmann, Jorg Christian: Lehren und Ermahnen. 1994. *Bd. II/59.*
Sandnes, Karl Olav: Paul – One of the Prophets? 1991. *Bd. II/43.*
Sato, Migaku: Q und Prophetie. 1988. *Bd. II/29.*
Schäfer, Ruth: Paulus bis zum Apostelkonzil. 2004. *Bd. II/179.*
Schaper, Joachim: Eschatology in the Greek Psalter. 1995. *Bd. II/76.*
Schimanowski, Gottfried: Die himmlische Liturgie in der Apokalypse des Johannes. 2002. *Bd. II/154.*
- Weisheit und Messias. 1985. *Bd. II/17.*
Schlichting, Günter: Ein jüdisches Leben Jesu. 1982. *Bd. 24.*
Schließer, Benjamin: Abraham's Faith in Romans 4. 2007. *Band II/224.*
Schnabel, Eckhard J.: Law and Wisdom from Ben Sira to Paul. 1985. *Bd. II/16.*
Schnelle, Udo: siehe *Frey, Jörg.*
Schröter, Jens: Von Jesus zum Neuen Testament. 2007. *Band 204.*
- siehe *Frey, Jörg.*
Schutter, William L.: Hermeneutic and Composition in I Peter. 1989. *Bd. II/30.*
Schwartz, Daniel R.: Studies in the Jewish Background of Christianity. 1992. *Bd. 60.*
Schwemer, Anna Maria: siehe *Hengel, Martin*

Schwindt, Rainer: Das Weltbild des Epheserbriefes. 2002. *Bd. 148.*
Scott, Ian W.: Implicit Epistemology in the Letters of Paul. 2005. *Bd. II/205.*
Scott, James M.: Adoption as Sons of God. 1992. *Bd. II/48.*
– Paul and the Nations. 1995. *Bd. 84.*
Shi, Wenhua: Paul's Message of the Cross as Body Language. 2008. *Bd. II/254.*
Shum, Shiu-Lun: Paul's Use of Isaiah in Romans. 2002. *Bd. II/156.*
Siegert, Folker: Drei hellenistisch-jüdische Predigten. Teil I 1980. *Bd. 20* – Teil II 1992. *Bd. 61.*
– Nag-Hammadi-Register. 1982. *Bd. 26.*
– Argumentation bei Paulus. 1985. *Bd. 34.*
– Philon von Alexandrien. 1988. *Bd. 46.*
Simon, Marcel: Le christianisme antique et son contexte religieux I/II. 1981. *Bd. 23.*
Smit, Peter-Ben: Fellowship and Food in the Kingdom. 2008. *Bd. II/234.*
Snodgrass, Klyne: The Parable of the Wicked Tenants. 1983. *Bd. 27.*
Söding, Thomas: Das Wort vom Kreuz. 1997. *Bd. 93.*
– siehe *Thüsing, Wilhelm.*
Sommer, Urs: Die Passionsgeschichte des Markusevangeliums. 1993. *Bd. II/58.*
Sorensen, Eric: Possession and Exorcism in the New Testament and Early Christianity. 2002. *Band II/157.*
Souček, Josef B.: siehe *Pokorný, Petr.*
Southall, David J.: Rediscovering Righteousness in Romans. 2008. *Bd. 240.*
Spangenberg, Volker: Herrlichkeit des Neuen Bundes. 1993. *Bd. II/55.*
Spanje, T.E. van: Inconsistency in Paul? 1999. *Bd. II/110.*
Speyer, Wolfgang: Frühes Christentum im antiken Strahlungsfeld. Bd. I: 1989. *Bd. 50.*
– Bd. II: 1999. *Bd. 116.*
– Bd. III: 2007. *Bd. 213.*
Spittler, Janet E.: Animals in the Apocryphal Acts of the Apostles. 2008. *Bd. II/247.*
Sprinkle, Preston: Law and Life. 2008. *Bd. II/241.*
Stadelmann, Helge: Ben Sira als Schriftgelehrter. 1980. *Bd. II/6.*
Stein, Hans Joachim: Frühchristliche Mahlfeiern. 2008. *Bd. II/255.*
Stenschke, Christoph W.: Luke's Portrait of Gentiles Prior to Their Coming to Faith. *Bd. II/108.*
Sterck-Degueldre, Jean-Pierre: Eine Frau namens Lydia. 2004. *Bd. II/176.*
Stettler, Christian: Der Kolosserhymnus. 2000. *Bd. II/131.*

Stettler, Hanna: Die Christologie der Pastoralbriefe. 1998. *Bd. II/105.*
Stökl Ben Ezra, Daniel: The Impact of Yom Kippur on Early Christianity. 2003. *Bd. 163.*
Strobel, August: Die Stunde der Wahrheit. 1980. *Bd. 21.*
Stroumsa, Guy G.: Barbarian Philosophy. 1999. *Bd. 112.*
Stuckenbruck, Loren T.: Angel Veneration and Christology. 1995. *Bd. II/70.*
–, *Stephen C. Barton* und *Benjamin G. Wold* (Hrsg.): Memory in the Bible and Antiquity. 2007. *Vol. 212.*
Stuhlmacher, Peter (Hrsg.): Das Evangelium und die Evangelien. 1983. *Bd. 28.*
– Biblische Theologie und Evangelium. 2002. *Bd. 146.*
Sung, Chong-Hyon: Vergebung der Sünden. 1993. *Bd. II/57.*
Svendsen, Stefan N.: Allegory Transformed. 2009. *Bd. II/269*
Tajra, Harry W.: The Trial of St. Paul. 1989. *Bd. II/35.*
– The Martyrdom of St.Paul. 1994. *Bd. II/67.*
Tellbe, Mikael: Christ-Believers in Ephesus. 2009. *Bd. 242.*
Theißen, Gerd: Studien zur Soziologie des Urchristentums. 1979, ³1989. *Bd. 19.*
Theobald, Michael: Studien zum Römerbrief. 2001. *Bd. 136.*
Theobald, Michael: siehe *Mußner, Franz.*
Thornton, Claus-Jürgen: Der Zeuge des Zeugen. 1991. *Bd. 56.*
Thüsing, Wilhelm: Studien zur neutestamentlichen Theologie. Hrsg. von Thomas Söding. 1995. *Bd. 82.*
Thurén, Lauri: Derhethorizing Paul. 2000. *Bd. 124.*
Thyen, Hartwig: Studien zum Corpus Iohanneum. 2007. *Bd. 214.*
Tibbs, Clint: Religious Experience of the Pneuma. 2007. *Bd. II/230.*
Toit, David S. du: Theios Anthropos. 1997. *Bd. II/91.*
Tomson, Peter J. und *Doris Lambers-Petry* (Hrsg.): The Image of the Judaeo-Christians in Ancient Jewish and Christian Literature. 2003. *Bd. 158.*
Tolmie, D. Francois: Persuading the Galatians. 2005. *Bd. II/190.*
Toney, Carl N.: Paul's Inclusive Ethic. 2008. *Bd. II/252.*
Trebilco, Paul: The Early Christians in Ephesus from Paul to Ignatius. 2004. *Bd. 166.*
Treloar, Geoffrey R.: Lightfoot the Historian. 1998. *Bd. II/103.*
Tsuji, Manabu: Glaube zwischen Vollkommenheit und Verweltlichung. 1997. *Bd. II/93*

Twelftree, Graham H.: Jesus the Exorcist. 1993. Bd. II/54.
Ulrichs, Karl Friedrich: Christusglaube. 2007. Bd. II/227.
Urban, Christina: Das Menschenbild nach dem Johannesevangelium. 2001. Bd. II/137.
Vahrenhorst, Martin: Kultische Sprache in den Paulusbriefen. 2008. Bd. 230.
Vegge, Ivar: 2 Corinthians – a Letter about Reconciliation. 2008. Bd. II/239.
Visotzky, Burton L.: Fathers of the World. 1995. Bd. 80.
Vollenweider, Samuel: Horizonte neutestamentlicher Christologie. 2002. Bd. 144.
Vos, Johan S.: Die Kunst der Argumentation bei Paulus. 2002. Bd. 149.
Waaler, Erik: The Shema and The First Commandment in First Corinthians. 2008. Bd. II/253.
Wagener, Ulrike: Die Ordnung des „Hauses Gottes". 1994. Bd. II/65.
Wahlen, Clinton: Jesus and the Impurity of Spirits in the Synoptic Gospels. 2004. Bd. II/185.
Walker, Donald D.: Paul's Offer of Leniency (2 Cor 10:1). 2002. Bd. II/152.
Walter, Nikolaus: Praeparatio Evangelica. Hrsg. von Wolfgang Kraus und Florian Wilk. 1997. Bd. 98.
Wander, Bernd: Gottesfürchtige und Sympathisanten. 1998. Bd. 104.
Wasserman, Emma: The Death of the Soul in Romans 7. 2008. Bd. 256.
Waters, Guy: The End of Deuteronomy in the Epistles of Paul. 2006. Bd. 221.
Watt, Jan G. van der: siehe *Frey, Jörg.*
Watts, Rikki: Isaiah's New Exodus and Mark. 1997. Bd. II/88.
Wedderburn, A.J.M.: Baptism and Resurrection. 1987. Bd. 44.
Wegner, Uwe: Der Hauptmann von Kafarnaum. 1985. Bd. II/14.
Weiß, Hans-Friedrich: Frühes Christentum und Gnosis. 2008. Bd. 225.
Weissenrieder, Annette: Images of Illness in the Gospel of Luke. 2003. Bd. II/164.
–, *Friederike Wendt* und *Petra von Gemünden* (Hrsg.): Picturing the New Testament. 2005. Bd. II/193.
Welck, Christian: Erzählte ‚Zeichen'. 1994. Bd. II/69.
Wendt, Friederike (Hrsg.): siehe *Weissenrieder, Annette.*

Wiarda, Timothy: Peter in the Gospels. 2000. Bd. II/127.
Wifstrand, Albert: Epochs and Styles. 2005. Bd. 179.
Wilk, Florian: siehe *Walter, Nikolaus.*
Williams, Catrin H.: I am He. 2000. Bd. II/113.
Winninge, Mikael: siehe *Holmberg, Bengt.*
Wilson, Todd A.: The Curse of the Law and the Crisis in Galatia. 2007. Bd. II/225.
Wilson, Walter T.: Love without Pretense. 1991. Bd. II/46.
Winn, Adam: The Purpose of Mark's Gospel. 2008. Bd. II/245.
Wischmeyer, Oda: Von Ben Sira zu Paulus. 2004. Bd. 173.
Wisdom, Jeffrey: Blessing for the Nations and the Curse of the Law. 2001. Bd. II/133.
Witmer, Stephen E.: Divine Instruction in Early Christianity. 2008. Bd. II/246.
Wold, Benjamin G.: Women, Men, and Angels. 2005. Bd. II/2001.
– siehe *Stuckenbruck, Loren T.*
Wolter, Michael: Theologie und Ethos im frühen Christentum. 2009. Band 236.
Wright, Archie T.: The Origin of Evil Spirits. 2005. Bd. II/198.
Wucherpfennig, Ansgar: Heracleon Philologus. 2002. Bd. 142.
Yates, John W.: The Spirit and Creation in Paul. 2008. Vol. II/251.
Yeung, Maureen: Faith in Jesus and Paul. 2002. Bd. II/147.
Zangenberg, Jürgen, Harold W. Attridge und *Dale B. Martin* (Hrsg.): Religion, Ethnicity and Identity in Ancient Galilee. 2007. Bd. 210.
Zimmermann, Alfred E.: Die urchristlichen Lehrer. 1984, ²1988. Bd. II/12.
Zimmermann, Johannes: Messianische Texte aus Qumran. 1998. Bd. II/104.
Zimmermann, Ruben: Christologie der Bilder im Johannesevangelium. 2004. Bd. 171.
– Geschlechtermetaphorik und Gottesverhältnis. 2001. Bd. II/122.
– (Hrsg.): Hermeneutik der Gleichnisse Jesu. 2008. Bd. 231.
– siehe *Frey, Jörg.*
– siehe *Horn, Friedrich Wilhelm.*
Zugmann, Michael: „Hellenisten" in der Apostelgeschichte. 2009. Bd. II/264.
Zumstein, Jean: siehe *Dettwiler, Andreas*
Zwiep, Arie W.: Judas and the Choice of Matthias. 2004. Bd. II/187.

Einen Gesamtkatalog erhalten Sie gerne vom Verlag
Mohr Siebeck – Postfach 2040 – D–72010 Tübingen
Neueste Informationen im Internet unter www.mohr.de